"With his newly published *Truth Is a Synthesis: Catholic Dogmatic Theology*, Fr. Gagliardi has made a significant contribution in the area of theological formation. This text should prove of valuable assistance to both student and teacher alike, as a comprehensive, detailed, and faithful overview of Catholic teaching found in Sacred Scripture, Tradition, papal teaching, and scholarship through the centuries to the present day. This work in English should enjoy a receptive and expanded audience."

MOST. REV. GLEN PROVOST
Bishop of Lake Charles

"This book is long because it is patient. It is as lucid as it is long. It is in itself a fulsome theological education, accessibly organized. Teachers and students, clergy and laity—anyone with an enquiring mind who seeks knowledge, insight, and coherence in the things that matter most—will not only enjoy reading it but will return to it regularly. It will be one of the first books to which I point my own students."

DOUGLAS FARROW
McGill University

"With this volume, Fr. Gagliardi presents us with a compelling and comprehensive synthesis of Catholic dogmatic theology. His thoroughly researched and accessibly written work offers to students—and to other interested readers—a crystal clear account of the cohesive and harmonious structure of Catholic theology. This book is an invaluable *vademecum* for all those wishing to understand, probe, and appreciate Catholicism's precise formulation of divine Revelation."

THOMAS G. GUARINO
Seton Hall University

"Fr. Gagliardi has gifted us with a timely and much-needed book. In clear and incisive writing he sets forth the Catholic theological Tradition as a rich organic unity that does not countenance either the reductionism or the relativism so prevalent today. Trinitarian Christocentrism provides the focus and logic of his work and is the source of its unity and the measure of its catholicity. Gagliardi's work presents a salutary challenge to all serious students of theology whether in seminaries and universities or in pulpit and pews."

ROBERT IMBELLI
Boston College

"*Truth Is a Synthesis* is a very welcome contribution to the New Evangelization, and especially to the formation of priests and other pastoral ministers, as Fr. Gagliardi skillfully takes his readers beyond the fragmentation that too often characterizes theological reflection and education today."

GEORGE WEIGEL
Ethics and Public Policy Center

TRUTH IS A SYNTHESIS

TRUTH IS A SYNTHESIS

CATHOLIC DOGMATIC THEOLOGY

MAURO GAGLIARDI

INTRODUCTION BY
CARDINAL GERHARD L. MÜLLER

EMMAUS
ACADEMIC

Steubenville, Ohio
www.emmausacademic.com

EMMAUS
ACADEMIC

Steubenville, Ohio
www.emmausacademic.com
A Division of The St. Paul Center for Biblical Theology
Editor-in-Chief: Scott Hahn
1468 Parkview Circle
Steubenville, Ohio 43952

© 2020 Mauro Gagliardi
All rights reserved. 2020
Printed in the United States of America

Translated from the original Italian edition, *La verità è sintetica: Teologia dogmatica cattolica* (Edizioni Cantagalli, 2017).

Library of Congress Cataloging-in-Publication Data
Names: Gagliardi, Mauro, 1975- author.
Title: Truth is a synthesis : Catholic dogmatic theology / Mauro Gagliardi ; introduction by Cardinal Gerhard L. Müller.
Other titles: Verità è sintetica. English
Description: Steubenville, Ohio : Emmaus Academic, 2020. | Includes bibliographical references and index. | Summary: "A comprehensive presentation of all treatises of Fundamental and Dogmatic Theology aiming also at retrieving the unity of Theology. The volume presents a comprehensive, organic view of the Catholic faith, also spotlighting the different views about Christian Dogmatics on the part of Protestant and Orthodox. More than a "synthesis of Dogmatic theology", the book presents Dogmatic theology according to the theological concept of "synthesis""-- Provided by publisher.
Identifiers: LCCN 2020021678 (print) | LCCN 2020021679 (ebook) | ISBN 9781645850441 (hardcover) | ISBN 9781645850458 (paperback) | ISBN 9781645850465 (ebook)
Subjects: LCSH: Catholic Church--Doctrines. | Theology, Doctrinal.
Classification: LCC BX1751.3 .G3413 2020 (print) | LCC BX1751.3 (ebook) |

DDC 230/.2--dc23
LC record available at https://lccn.loc.gov/2020021678
LC ebook record available at https://lccn.loc.gov/2020021679

Scripture texts in this work are taken from the *New American Bible, revised edition* © 2010, 1991, 1986, 1970 Confraternity of Christian Doctrine, Washington, D.C. and are used by permission of the copyright owner. All Rights Reserved. No part of the New American Bible may be reproduced in any form without permission in writing from the copyright owner.

Excerpts from the Catechism of the Catholic Church, second edition, copyright (c) 2000, Libreria Editrice Vaticana—United States Conference of Catholic Bishops, Washington, D.C. Noted as "CCC" in the text.

Nihil Obstat: Rev. James M. Dunfee
Censor Librorum
September 19, 2019

Imprimatur: Jeffrey M. Monforton
Bishop of Steubenville
September 19, 2019

The nihil obstat and imprimatur are declarations that work is considered to be free from doctrinal or moral error. It is not implied that those who have granted the same agree with the content, opinions, or statements expressed.

Cover design and layout by Emily Demary
Cover image: *Adoration of the Trinity* (1511) by Albrecht Dürer, Kunsthistorisches Museum, Vienna, Austria

For my students and auditors.

We have seen and testify that the Father sent His Son as Savior of the world. Whoever acknowledges that Jesus is the Son of God, God remains in him and he in God.

1 John 4:14–15

Primum quod est necessarium christiano, est fides, sine qua nullus dicitur fidelis christianus—The first thing that is necessary for a Christian is faith, without which nobody can be called a faithful Christian.

Saint Thomas Aquinas,
Collationes in Symbolum Apostolorum, "Prooemium" (our translation)

What seems to me especially to prove the strength and power of truth is the fact that when from the beginning of the nascent Church the heretics together with the Catholics were busy writing books, and when Irenaeus wrote, Valentine also wrote; when Athanasius wrote, Arius wrote; when Basil wrote, Eunomius wrote; when Jerome wrote, Jovinian wrote; when Augustine wrote, Pelagius wrote; when Cyril wrote, Nestorius wrote, and there were other similar cases; nevertheless, all the works of the heretics perished, and also their name and memory would also have perished, unless they had been preserved in the books of Catholics, which remain to this day. And why is this? Because the monuments of heretics are the homes of lies, which immediately disappear and perish, but the books of Catholics are the seats of truth, 'and the truth of the Lord endures for ever' (Ps 116:2)

Saint Robert Bellarmine,
Explanatio in Psalmum 90: Sermo 5.2
(in *Sermons of Saint Robert Cardinal Bellarmine, S.J.*, Part III, trans. Kenneth Baker [Saddle River, NJ: Keep the Faith, Inc., 2018], 254 [with our corrections])

The Logos becomes flesh: we have grown so accustomed to these words that God's colossal synthesis of seemingly unbridgeable divisions, which required a gradual intellectual penetration on the part of the Fathers, no longer strikes us as very astonishing. Here lay, and still lies, the specifically Christian novelty that appeared unreasonable and unthinkable to the Greek mind. What this passage says does not derive from a particular culture, such as the Semitic or the Greek, as is thoughtlessly asserted over and over again today. This statement is opposed to all the forms of culture known to us. It was just as unthinkable for the Jews as it was (although for altogether different reasons) for the Greeks or the Indians or even, for that matter, for the modern mind, which looks upon a synthesis of the phenomenal and the noumenal world as completely unreal and contests it with all the self-awareness of modern rationality. What is said here is "new" because it comes from God and could be brought about only by God himself. It is something altogether new and foreign to every history and to all cultures; we can enter into it in faith and only in faith, and when we do so, it opens up to us wholly new horizons of thought and life.

JOSEPH RATZINGER,
"*Et incarnatus est de Spiritu Sancto ex Maria Virgine...*"
(in Joseph Ratzinger and Hans Urs von Balthasar,
Mary: The Church at the Source,
trans. Adrian Walker [San Francisco: Ignatius Press, 2005], 90).

TABLE OF CONTENTS

Foreword to the English Edition	xv
Preface	xix
Abbreviations	xxiii
Niceno-Constantinopolitan Creed	xxv
Credo of the People of God	xxvii
Introduction by Cardinal Gerhard L. Müller	1
1. The "Synthetic" Principle	13
2. Revelation, Faith, Theology	115
3. The Creator	201
4. The Redeemer	261
5. The Sanctifier	343
6. The Trinity	399
7. The Mother of God	481
8. The Church	541
9. The Sacraments in General and the Liturgy	617
10. The Sacraments in Particular	673
11. The Eucharist	769

12. THE LAST THINGS	865
EPILOGUE	941
BIBLICAL INDEX	943
INDEX OF NAMES	961
INDEX OF MAGISTERIAL DOCUMENTS	975
GENERAL INDEX	1001

Foreword to the English Edition

The Italian edition of this work of dogmatic theology was published at the end of April 2017. The first edition sold out in about two weeks, and the Italian publisher immediately made the reprint available. A second, revised reprint was subsequently published in February 2018 and a third reprint at the beginning of 2019. At the moment of writing, a fourth reprint is under preparation. For a book in the Italian language of this size—which deals with a theme that is not very popular—this success was unexpected. The book had in fact attracted attention both on the part of students of theology and also among other readers. Moreover, some prominent figures of the Catholic world took notice of it, encouraging me to also prepare editions in other languages.

Accepting their invitation, I have decided to begin with an English edition. The most obvious motivation for this choice is that for several decades English has been the language most used in international relations, and this not only for commerce, politics, and travel, but also for the cultural and academic world. Theology is no exception.

The potential public of readers of theology in English is larger today than that of other linguistic groups. Scholars of the English language, especially Americans, have long since gained a very important place in the international scene of biblical and theological studies—and deservedly so. This translation allows overseas colleagues to become aware of a work of Italian theology and, at the same time, it can ensure that the work is known within their context.

At any rate, the privileged recipients of this work are not the scholars, but rather the students. This is a book written mainly for those who are at the beginning of their theological studies. The volume is also tailored to those who would like to approach dogmatic theology without taking an academic course. Various people who have a strong personal devotion to theological themes have expressed to me their satisfaction for, in addition to the content, the accessible language in which the work is written. However, it is also a useful book for priests, to brush up on their knowledge and also for the preparation of catechesis and homilies so that they may have solid content.

As the reader will notice, this book also proposes to represent an antidote to the excessive modern fragmentation of theology. Specialization in particular sectors is necessary, but a dispersal that does not return to unity hurts the cause of evangelization. This treatise therefore aims to show the unity of theology by bringing out at least the unity of dogmatic theology. Other books could then be written to show that this unity is found, and must be preserved and maintained, in other branches of theological science as well.

The unitary principle is the classical one of *et-et* (both-and), for which we refer the reader to Chapter One to find a description.

***

I would also like to take this opportunity to thank some people, without whose moral support and active help this English translation would not exist. Out of respect for their role, I will not mention the Cardinals and Bishops who have encouraged the publication of this book in other languages. In my soul, I address feelings of sincere gratitude to them.

Among my colleagues, I would like to thank Matthew Levering (University of St. Mary of the Lake), Reinhard Huetter (Catholic University of America), and Fr. Robert Imbelli (Emeritus, Boston College) for their moral support. Matthew Levering, in particular, worked to help make this volume known in the United States even before the present publication in English. George Weigel (Ethics & Public Policy Center) and Fr. Thomas Joseph White, O.P. (Angelicum) discretely but actively attended to the project of procuring a translation of this book, from its beginning through publication. Much advice and many contacts have been provided to me by Anthony Valle (Ave Maria University), who I thank in a special way for his great help, without which this English edition would not have come into existence. This is also true for the generous support offered by Colin Moran and Sean Fieler, as well as The Institute on Religion and Public Life, and in particular R.R. Reno, editor of the journal *First Things*, and Victor Chong. All of these persons believed in the good that this volume can do for the Church and, consequently, also for the society of our time.

I would now like to express my gratitude to Scott Hahn (Franciscan Uni-

Foreword to the English Edition

versity of Steubenville), who has encouraged the publication of this English version of the treatise at the prestigious Emmaus Academic publishing house. I also thank Chris Erickson, Senior Editor of Emmaus Road Publishing/Emmaus Academic for his diligent collaboration throughout the whole editorial preparation phase, and Daniel Seseske, a copyeditor for Emmaus, for his important help in improving the English text. Michael Hahn (Mount St. Mary's Seminary, Emmitsburg) read the entire manuscript more than once and made apt and intelligent observations. I am very grateful for his courtesy and his priceless commitment, and of course, the reader knows that none of the flaws of this book should be attributed to him, but only to the author. Finally, a strong thank you goes to Tom and Kira Howes (TYT Translation Services) for doing the demanding work of translating the whole book and for the patience with which they have assisted me in the long process of revising the English text.

Preparing the English translation of this book has allowed me to make or strengthen the friendships with the aforementioned colleagues. I am truly grateful to all of them, and I trust that in the future our friendship and collaboration will continue to grow and to produce good fruits for the path of the Church and for theology in the twenty-first century.

New York. February 22, 2019.
Feast of the Chair of Saint Peter, Apostle
Fr. Mauro Gagliardi

Preface

I began writing this book in 2010, and I completed it only after great difficulty, resuming work each time that it was interrupted—sometimes for long periods—by other research projects or publications. In order to write it, I studied and consulted a great deal of sources. To some extent, all of the studies that I have carried out, both at the philosophical and theological levels from 1993 until today, converge in this book as if flowing into a single basin. Naturally, there is much more that remains in the background—not cited or made explicit—than is expressed; yet in some way, often very indirectly, it is all equally present.

This volume was composed with the readers of the work in mind: people who are not experts in theological science, who are going to study Catholic dogmatic theology for the first time. Therefore, I ask my fellow theologians who read this work to keep in mind its purpose and literary genre. This work neither attempts to treat all the questions, nor to analyze in minute detail what it treats.[1] In fact, I thought to offer not a "dogmatic synthesis," but rather "dogmatics as synthesis," particularly adapted to the students of the first cycle of the theological Faculties and Institutes. Many of these students are pre-

---

[1] "And now I will, in the Lord's name, set about my purpose, which is to write down as a trusty narrator, rather than as presuming to pose as an author, what our forefathers have handed down and entrusted to us; observing this rule, however, in what I write, namely, not by any means to touch upon every point, but only the points that are necessary; and not even to do that in a polished and precise style, but in easy and plain language, so that most of the points may seem to be intimated rather than set forth at length." (Saint Vincent of Lerins [d. ca. 450] *Commonitorium* 1.3, in *Commonitory of St. Vincent of Lerins*, trans. T. Herbert Bindley [New York: E.S. Gorham, 1914], 21).

paring for priestly ministry—and this is another motive that has guided the redaction of the present text. However, this book is also suitable for all those who want to acquire a basic formation in dogmatic subjects, even if they are not enrolled in curricular theological courses.

The thinkers who have reflected on the current historical era, defined by some as "post-modernity," identify the transition from synthesis to fragmentation as one of the era's most important distinguishing characteristics. Modernity had rebelled against the medieval synthesis, replacing it with a new one based on different criteria. Post-modernity exalts the greatness of the subjective at the expense of the objective, the part at the expense of the whole, the particular at the expense of the universal, and the relative at the expense of the absolute. Not even Catholic theology has been completely preserved from the influence of this Zeitgeist. This is the temporal context in which the present work is situated, and its assumed starting point is that there is need of a new synthesis, which, as such, retrieves the treasure of the great Tradition; and, insofar as it is new, it is not limited to only repeating what was already said in the classic, "great past," but it does so while taking into account—in our case, while leaving it only in the background—what has happened and what has been said in the meantime.

This book always revolves around the principle of *et-et* (both/and). This principle consists of two aspects: (1) The truths of the faith are generally structured on a fundamental bipolarity of elements; (2) the two elements are in a hierarchical order. Confusion and error regarding faith and morals almost always derive from the negation or simple reduction of one or both of these aspects. There can be an error that derives from the temptation to eliminate the fundamental bipolarity of the truths of Catholic faith and morals. But the error can also arise from inverting the hierarchical order between the elements. For example, this currently happens in the moral sphere, in which error often does not arise from denying the inevitable intertwining of the objective norm with the existential circumstances of the moral act, but rather from the inversion of the hierarchical order, through which greater weight is given to the second aspect than to the first. Each time we find ourselves confronted with an error concerning faith and morals, this happens either because the *et-et* is denied, or because its intrinsic order is subverted.

If it is permissible to hope that this book reaches a wide audience, it is not so that its author can acquire fame, but rather so that it can contribute—alongside and together with better works than this—to the renewal in the heart of the Church of the love for the truth and, consequently, toward a time of new strengthening of theology, and at the same time a true ecclesial renewal. Fifty years after Vatican II, we still recognize the need for "fresh air." And if this work—with all its limitations, which are well-known to the writer—is able to be a tessera that contributes to the formation and growth of a new spirit in the Church, then there is sure reason to be satisfied.

Rome. September 21, 2016.
Feast of Saint Matthew, Apostle and Evangelist
Fr. Mauro Gagliardi

ABBREVIATIONS

A. Books of the Bible

Acts	Acts	2 Kgs	2 Kings
Am	Amos	Lam	Lamentations
Bar	Baruch	Lev	Leviticus
1 Chron	1 Chronicles	Luke	Luke
2 Chron	2 Chronicles	1 Macc	1 Maccabees
Col	Colossians	2 Macc	2 Maccabees
1 Cor	1 Corinthians	Mal	Malachi
2 Cor	2 Corinthians	Mark	Mark
Dan	Daniel	Matt	Matthew
Deut	Deuteronomy	Mic	Micah
Eccles	Ecclesiastes	Nah	Nahum
Eph	Ephesians	Neh	Nehemiah
Est	Esther	Num	Numbers
Ex	Exodus	Obad	Obadiah
Ezek	Ezekiel	1 Pet	1 Peter
Ezra	Ezra	2 Pet	2 Peter
Gal	Galatians	Philem	Philemon
Gen	Genesis	Phil	Philippians
Hab	Habakkuk	Prov	Proverbs
Hag	Haggai	Ps	Psalms
Heb	Hebrews	Rev	Revelation
Hos	Hosea	Rom	Romans
Isa	Isaiah	Ruth	Ruth
James	James	1 Sam	1 Samuel
Jdt	Judith	2 Sam	2 Samuel
Jer	Jeremiah	Sir	Sirach
Job	Job	Song	Song of Songs
Joel	Joel	1 Thess	1 Thessalonians
John	John	2 Thess	2 Thessalonians
1 John	1 John	1 Tim	1 Timothy
2 John	2 John	2 Tim	2 Timothy
3 John	3 John	Titus	Titus
Jonah	Jonah	Tob	Tobit
Josh	Joshua	Wis	Wisdom
Jude	Jude	Zech	Zechariah
Judg	Judges	Zeph	Zephaniah
1 Kgs	1 Kings		

B. OTHERS

ANF	*Ante-Nicene Fathers*
CCC	*Catechism of the Catholic Church*
DS	H. Denzinger – A. Schönmetzer, *Enchiridion Symbolorum* [P. Hünermann, ed.]
FCNT	*Fathers of the Church: A New Translation*
NABRE	*New American Bible, Revised Edition*
NPNF	*Nicene and Post-Nicene Fathers*
ST	Saint Thomas Aquinas, *Summa Theologiae*

NICENO-CONSTANTINOPOLITAN CREED

Recited in the Eucharistic Celebration for Sundays and Solemnities

I believe in one God,
the Father almighty,
Maker of heaven and earth,
of all things visible and invisible.

I believe in one Lord Jesus Christ,
the Only Begotten Son of God,
born of the Father before all ages.
God from God, Light from Light,
true God from true God,
begotten, not made, consubstantial with the Father;
through Him all things were made.
For us men and for our salvation
He came down from heaven,
and by the Holy Spirit was incarnate of the Virgin Mary,
and became man.

For our sake He was crucified under Pontius Pilate,
He suffered death and was buried,
and rose again on the third day
in accordance with the Scriptures.
He ascended into heaven
and is seated at the right hand of the Father.
He will come again in glory
to judge the living and the dead
and His kingdom will have no end.

I believe in the Holy Spirit, the Lord, the Giver of life,
Who proceeds from the Father and the Son,
Who with the Father and the Son is adored and glorified,
Who has spoken through the prophets.

I believe in one, holy, catholic and apostolic Church.
I confess one Baptism for the forgiveness of sins
and I look forward to the resurrection of the dead
and the life of the world to come.
Amen.

CREDO OF THE PEOPLE OF GOD

Issued by Saint Paul VI on June 30, 1968

We believe in one only God, Father, Son and Holy Spirit, Creator of things visible such as this world in which our transient life passes, of things invisible such as the pure spirits which are also called angels, and Creator in each man of his spiritual and immortal soul.

We believe that this only God is absolutely one in His infinitely holy essence as also in all His perfections, in His omnipotence, His infinite knowledge, His providence, His will and His love. He is He who is, as He revealed to Moses (see Ex 3:14); and He is love, as the apostle John teaches us (1 John 4:8): so that these two names, being and love, express ineffably the same divine reality of Him who has wished to make Himself known to us, and Who, "dwelling in light inaccessible" (1 Tim 6:16) is in Himself above every name, above every thing and above every created intellect. God alone can give us right and full knowledge of this reality by revealing Himself as Father, Son and Holy Spirit, in Whose eternal life we are by grace called to share, here below in the obscurity of faith and after death in eternal light. The mutual bonds which eternally constitute the Three Persons, Who are Each one and the same divine being, are the blessed inmost life of God thrice holy, infinitely beyond all that we can conceive in human measure. We give thanks, however, to the divine goodness that very many believers can testify with us before men to the unity of God, even though they know not the mystery of the most holy Trinity.

We believe then in the Father who eternally begets the Son; in the Son, the Word of God, who is eternally begotten; in the Holy Spirit, the uncreated Person who proceeds from the Father and the Son as their eternal Love. Thus in the Three Divine Persons, *coaeternae sibi et coaequales*, the life and beatitude of God perfectly one superabound and are consummated in the supreme excellence and glory proper to uncreated Being, and always "there should be venerated unity in the Trinity and Trinity in the unity."

We believe in our Lord Jesus Christ, who is the Son of God. He is the Eternal Word, born of the Father before time began, and one in substance with the Father, *homoousios to Patri*, and through Him all things were made. He was incarnate of the Virgin Mary by the power of the Holy Spirit, and was made man: equal therefore to the Father according to His divinity, and inferior to the Father according to His humanity; and Himself one, not by some impossible confusion of His natures, but by the unity of His Person.

He dwelt among us, full of grace and truth. He proclaimed and established the kingdom of God and made us know in Himself the Father. He gave us His new commandment to love one another as He loved us. He taught us the way of the beatitudes of the Gospel: poverty in spirit, meekness, suffering borne with patience, thirst after justice, mercy, purity of heart, will for peace, persecution suffered for justice sake. Under Pontius Pilate He suffered—the Lamb of God bearing on Himself the sins of the world—and He died for us on the cross, saving us by His redeeming blood. He was buried, and, of His own power, rose on the third day, raising us by His resurrection to that sharing in the divine life which is the life of grace. He ascended to heaven, and He will come again, this time in glory, to judge the living and the dead: each according to his merits—those who have responded to the love and piety of God going to eternal life, those who have refused them to the end going to the fire that is not extinguished.

And His kingdom will have no end.

We believe in the Holy Spirit, who is Lord and Giver of life, who is adored and glorified together with the Father and the Son. He spoke to us by the prophets; He was sent by Christ after His resurrection and His ascension to the Father; He illuminates, vivifies, protects and guides the Church; He purifies the Church's members if they do not shun His grace. His action, which penetrates to the inmost of the soul, enables man to respond to the call of Jesus: "Be perfect as your Heavenly Father is perfect" (Matt 5:48).

We believe that Mary is the Mother, who remained ever a Virgin, of the Incarnate Word, our God and Savior Jesus Christ, and that by reason of this singular election, She was, in consideration of the merits of Her Son, redeemed in a more eminent manner, preserved from all stain of original sin and filled with the gift of grace more than all other creatures.

Joined by a close and indissoluble bond to the Mysteries of the Incarnation and Redemption, the Blessed Virgin, the Immaculate, was at the end of Her earthly life raised body and soul to heavenly glory and likened to Her risen Son in anticipation of the future lot of all the just; and we believe that the Blessed Mother of God, the New Eve, Mother of the Church, continues in heaven Her maternal role with regard to Christ's members, cooperating with the birth and growth of divine life in the souls of the redeemed.

We believe that in Adam all have sinned, which means that the original offense committed by him caused human nature, common to all men, to fall to a state in which it bears the consequences of that offense, and which is not the state in which it was at first in our first parents—established as they were in holiness and justice, and in which man knew neither evil nor death. It is human nature so fallen, stripped of the grace that clothed it, injured in its own natural powers and subjected to the dominion of death, that is transmitted to all men, and it is in this sense that every man is born in sin. We therefore hold, with the Council of Trent, that original sin is transmitted with human nature, "not by imitation, but by propagation" and that it is thus "proper to everyone."

We believe that our Lord Jesus Christ, by the sacrifice of the cross redeemed us from original sin and all the personal sins committed by each one of us, so that, in accordance with the word of the apostle, "where sin abounded, grace did more abound" (Rom 5:20).

We believe in one Baptism instituted by our Lord Jesus Christ for the remission of sins. Baptism should be administered even to little children who have not yet been able to be guilty of any personal sin, in order that, though born deprived of supernatural grace, they may be reborn "of water and the Holy Spirit" to the divine life in Christ Jesus.

We believe in one, holy, catholic, and apostolic Church, built by Jesus Christ on that rock which is Peter. She is the Mystical Body of Christ; at the same time a visible society instituted with hierarchical organs, and a spiritual community; the Church on earth, the pilgrim People of God here below, and the Church filled with heavenly blessings; the germ and the first fruits of the kingdom of God, through which the work and the sufferings of redemption are continued throughout human history, and which looks for its perfect accomplishment beyond time in glory. In the course of time, the Lord Jesus forms His Church by means of the Sacraments emanating from His plenitude. By these she makes her members participants in the mystery of the death and resurrection of Christ, in the grace of the Holy Spirit who gives her life and movement. She is therefore holy, though she has sinners in her bosom, because she herself has no other life but that of grace: it is by living by her life that her members are sanctified; it is by removing themselves from her life that they fall into sins and disorders that prevent the radiation of her sanctity. This is why she suffers and does penance for these offenses, of which she has the power to heal her children through the blood of Christ and the gift of the Holy Spirit.

Heiress of the divine promises and daughter of Abraham according to the Spirit, through that Israel whose Scriptures she lovingly guards, and whose patriarchs and prophets she venerates; founded upon the apostles and handing on from century to century their ever-living word and their powers as shepherds in the successor of Peter and the bishops in communion with him; perpetually assisted by the Holy Spirit, she has the charge of guarding, teaching, explaining and spreading the Truth which God revealed in a then veiled manner by the prophets, and fully by the Lord Jesus. We believe all that is contained in the Word of God written or handed down, and that the Church proposes for belief as divinely revealed, whether by a solemn judgment or by the ordinary and universal Magisterium. We believe in the infallibility enjoyed by the successor of Peter when he teaches *ex cathedra* as shepherd and teacher of all the faithful, and which is assured also to the episcopal body when it exercises with him the supreme Magisterium.

We believe that the Church founded by Jesus Christ and for which He prayed is indefectibly one in faith, worship and the bond of hierarchical communion. In the bosom of this Church, the rich variety of liturgical rites and the legitimate diversity of theological and spiritual heritages and special disciplines, far from injuring her unity, make it more manifest.

Recognizing also the existence, outside the organism of the Church of Christ, of numerous elements of truth and sanctification which belong to her as her own and tend to Catholic unity, and believing in the action of the Holy Spirit who stirs up in the heart of the disciples of Christ love of this unity, we entertain the hope that the Christians who are not yet in the full communion of the one only Church will one day be reunited in one flock with one only Shepherd.

We believe that the Church is necessary for salvation, because Christ, who is the sole Mediator and Way of salvation, renders Himself present for us in His Body which is the Church. But the divine design of salvation embraces all men; and those who without fault on their part do not know the Gospel of Christ and His Church, but seek God sincerely, and under the influence of grace endeavor to do His will as recognized through the promptings of their conscience, they, in a number known only to God, can obtain salvation.

We believe that the Mass, celebrated by the priest representing the Person of Christ by virtue of the power received through the Sacrament of Orders, and offered by him in the name of Christ and the members of His Mystical Body, is the Sacrifice of Calvary rendered sacramentally present on our altars. We believe that as the bread and wine consecrated by the Lord at the Last Supper were changed into His body and His blood which were to be offered for us on the cross, likewise the bread and wine consecrated by the priest are changed into the body and blood of Christ enthroned gloriously in heaven, and we believe that the mysterious presence of the Lord, under what continues to appear to our senses as before, is a true, real and substantial presence.

Christ cannot be thus present in this Sacrament except by the change into His body of the reality itself of the bread and the change into His blood of the reality itself of the wine, leaving unchanged only the properties of the bread and wine which our senses perceive. This mysterious change is very appropriately called by the Church *transubstantiation*. Every theological explanation which seeks some understanding of this mystery must, in order to be in accord with Catholic faith, maintain that in the reality itself, independently of our mind, the bread and wine have ceased to exist after the consecration, so that it is the adorable body and blood of the Lord Jesus that from then on are really

Credo of the People of God

before us under the sacramental species of bread and wine, as the Lord willed it, in order to give Himself to us as food and to associate us with the unity of His Mystical Body.

The unique and indivisible existence of the Lord glorious in heaven is not multiplied, but is rendered present by the Sacrament in the many places on earth where Mass is celebrated. And this existence remains present, after the Sacrifice, in the Blessed Sacrament which is, in the tabernacle, the living heart of each of our churches. And it is our very sweet duty to honor and adore in the blessed Host which our eyes see, the Incarnate Word whom they cannot see, and who, without leaving heaven, is made present before us.

We confess that the Kingdom of God begun here below in the Church of Christ is not of this world whose form is passing, and that its proper growth cannot be confounded with the progress of civilization, of science or of human technology, but that it consists in an ever more profound knowledge of the unfathomable riches of Christ, an ever stronger hope in eternal blessings, an ever more ardent response to the love of God, and an ever more generous bestowal of grace and holiness among men. But it is this same love which induces the Church to concern herself constantly about the true temporal welfare of men. Without ceasing to recall to her children that they have not here a lasting dwelling, she also urges them to contribute, each according to his vocation and his means, to the welfare of their earthly city, to promote justice, peace and brotherhood among men, to give their aid freely to their brothers, especially to the poorest and most unfortunate. The deep solicitude of the Church, the Spouse of Christ, for the needs of men, for their joys and hopes, their griefs and efforts, is therefore nothing other than her great desire to be present to them, in order to illuminate them with the light of Christ and to gather them all in Him, their only Savior. This solicitude can never mean that the Church conform herself to the things of this world, or that she lessen the ardor of her expectation of her Lord and of the eternal kingdom.

We believe in the life eternal. We believe that the souls of all those who die in the grace of Christ whether they must still be purified in Purgatory, or whether from the moment they leave their bodies Jesus takes them to Paradise as He did for the good thief are the People of God in the eternity beyond death, which will be finally conquered on the day of the resurrection when these souls will be reunited with their bodies.

We believe that the multitude of those gathered around Jesus and Mary in Paradise forms the Church of heaven where in eternal beatitude they see God as He is, and where they also, in different degrees, are associated with the holy angels in the divine rule exercised by Christ in glory, interceding for us and helping our weakness by their brotherly care.

We believe in the communion of all the faithful of Christ, those who are pilgrims on earth, the dead who are attaining their purification, and the blessed in heaven, all together forming one Church; and we believe that in this communion the merciful love of God and His saints is ever listening to our prayers, as Jesus told us: "Ask and you will receive" (Luke 10:9–10; John 16:24). Thus it is with faith and in hope that we look forward to the resurrection of the dead, and the life of the world to come.

Blessed be God Thrice Holy. Amen.

Introduction: On the Work of Mauro Gagliardi*

Cardinal Gerhard L. Müller
Prefect Emeritus of the Congregation for the Doctrine of the Faith

In primis I would like to express my gratitude for having had the honor of being able to present this great work by a young theology professor to an audience of scholars. In almost one thousand pages, this book offers an overview of the essential questions of Catholic doctrine. One might think that it is the umpteenth manual in a long series of similar works that form, for university students, a solid foundation for taking dogmatics exams and, for the theologians who deal with science and pastoral care, support to refresh their overview of the *Mysterium Fidei*. I shall focus later on the particular attributes that distinguish this work from other similar ones.

As an anticipation of my general impression, allow me to say that I have a deep admiration for the enormous theological and spiritual contribution of Mauro Gagliardi. With a deep love for the Holy Trinity and the Church as well as an astonishing knowledge of systematic theology, this author manages to present the individual topics in a logical and comprehensive way. The Holy

---

* This is the text of the presentation to the public of the Italian edition of this work: *La Verità è sintetica. Teologia dogmatica cattolica*, Cantagalli, Siena 2017, 941 pp. The presentation took place on December 13, 2007 in the "Benedetto XVI – Joseph Ratzinger" Hall of the Pontificio Collegio Teutonico di Santa Maria in Campo Santo (Vatican City). The Italian version of this speech has been published in *Rivista teologica di Lugano* 23 (2018), 481–491, while the German version is found in *Forum Katholische Theologie* 34 (2018), 146–156.

Scriptures, the Fathers of the Church, and the great ecclesiastical Doctors of the Middle Ages and the Modern era represent their foundation. The reader is accompanied in the exploration of the inexhaustible legacy that has accumulated over the thirty-five hundred year-long history of biblical Revelation and the evolution of thought, starting from ancient philosophy.

However, neither an ideological system conceived by the author nor a materialistic ideology are imposed on the reader. The author develops his thought with respect for the ever-expanding mystery of the truth and charity of God. His approach is not that of some old or new "Gnostics" who, based on a superior speculative knowledge, seek to manipulate the reader and make him uncritically accept the contents. The reader is encouraged to, step by step, let himself be illuminated by the splendor of the truth and to let his heart be warmed by divine charity. The author fraternally joins the believer and continues the Church's path of "a stranger in a foreign land [...] amid the persecutions of the world and the consolations of God" (*Lumen gentium*, 8). As a matter of fact, the disciples are like students who approach the faith through the Word of God, enlightened by the Holy Spirit, in order to recognize and freely accept the truth of God.

"Every scribe who has been instructed in the kingdom of heaven is like the head of a household who brings from his storeroom both the new and the old" (Matt 13:52); however, he must not forget that there is only one Guide and all of us are and remain disciples of Christ (see Matt 23:10). "Theology is at the service of the faith and the Church," states Gagliardi in the first pages of the book (p. 27). We all, however, need mystagogy and catechesis, and this is even more true for the human mediator, the priest and doctor of the faith. Saint Bernard of Clairvaux, referring to the arrogance and ostentation of intellectual autonomy, which does not need the Church as a mediator between human beings and God, pointed out: "*Qui se sibi magistrum constituit, stulto se discipulum subdit*" (Ep. 87, 7): "Whoever makes himself his own teacher makes himself a madman's student." Theology does not remain an intellectual artifice for its own sake if it is nourished by a deep spirituality and put in the service of the ecclesiastical message of supernatural salvation and the divine vocation of all people. Whoever recognizes the inner unity of life and faith, which is reflected in the unity of systematic and practical disciplines in the theological field, is also immune to the influence of heartless "desk-bound theology" and meaningless actionistical pastoral work, that is, "sell-off theology."

Professor Gagliardi's book is in every way a *magnum opus*, both from the qualitative and the quantitative standpoint.

As is well known, I am certainly not one of those people who is afraid of

Introduction: On the Work of Mauro Gagliardi

lengthy books—not as a reader, even less as an author. There are always those who harbor an anti-intellectual resentment, who consider it useless to write books, simply because they lack the talent to do so. And then there is the arrogance of the scholars who do not want to use their talent to serve a just cause, but prefer to flaunt it for the sake of their own vanity. Let us ignore these human weaknesses and turn to the various particular manifestations of the Spirit that have been given to us for the common good (see 1Cor 12:7) and from which the body of Christ builds itself (see Eph 4:16). Let's consider the profession of the Catholic theologian in a positive light and follow the imperative of the Apostle Paul: "If ministry, in ministering; if one is a teacher, in teaching" (Rom 12:7). Nonetheless, it is still legitimate to ask whether there are already enough books in this world. Would it not be better to dedicate one's time and energy to practical pursuits that aim to solve the great challenges of our time? Have we not reached the era of practicality? Is it possible that the era of great ideas is over? Let us not forget, moreover, that Jesus and the Apostles did not consider writing books to be their mission, and that all human beings receive the faith that is necessary for salvation by listening to the Word, and they will be blessed if they follow the path of Christ, in love, to the end. Reaching salvation does not require the reading of any theology book. However, this does not apply to those who teach the faith, because they have a sacred duty to study theology so as not to sin in the salvific mission toward the flock that has been entrusted to them.

Is it right—as we often hear it said these days—to lose one's faith in the study of dogmatics, an unnecessarily complicated discipline, or to lose one's ethical principles studying moral theology? Is it right to waste time studying canon law?

Jesus did not write any books. However, He was able to read the Holy Scriptures, and at only twelve years of age He was capable of interacting with the teachers, not without provoking their amazement, listening attentively to their words and asking them questions. "And all who heard him were astounded at his understanding and his answers" (Luke 2:47). He is therefore the *Logos* that was and is with God. Everything was made in Him and through Him, and in this we recognize Him as God. We recognize the wisdom and the life in their entirety through the Word who is made flesh (see John 1:14). The many individual writings and the "words of eternal life" (John 6:68) that Jesus, as a man, knew to spread in the vocabulary, in the syntax and grammar of human language and in the articulation of the human spirit in the plurality of its ideas and concepts that follow in succession in space and time, are inherent in the uncreated Word that He represents in His divine nature, and they spring from it.

Truth Is a Synthesis

The truth of God is inexhaustible to us. This statement refers to the divine mystery not only in the period prior to the Revelation, in which we recognize God in His power and eternal divinity through the work of the creation and in His presence as Creator of the world, without comprehending His essence. Even after the Revelation and its presence in the Word made flesh and in the Holy Spirit, we are not capable of understanding God as an object of our natural and empirical experience (that is, we are unable to empirically prove or refute His mysterious existence). He remains a mystery—certainly not obscure, but in the abundance of His light. It is only through the humanity of Jesus and of its presence in the Church and in the Sacraments that we can participate in God's truth and life in Jesus Christ.

To be able to defend (apo-logia) the *Logos* for our hope (see 1 Peter 3:15), it is also necessary to reflect on the faith. We do not have a positivist view of Revelation. The Word of God was not dictated in Heaven in Hebrew or Arabic to an angel who in turn entrusted it to a chosen prophet to be mechanically repeated. God comes to meet us in the life and words of His Son, Jesus, who is the Word made flesh. If the Word of God took on human form in Jesus, His fruition in the Church's community of faith must have its own history: the history of dogma, that is, of definitive knowledge. According to this perspective, new elements do not emerge in history. We instead acknowledge the character of unsurpassed novelty, the *Verbum incarnatum*, understood by us ever more deeply in His entirety and His richness; and therefore, He is recommunicated in the course of ecclesiastic and dogmatic history.

Christ has trusted the testimony of His salvific work to the Apostles. It is for this very reason that the Apostle Paul thanks the Thessalonians who have received his words of preaching, not as human words, but as the Word of God, who works through the words of a man (see 1 Thess 2:13). Faith in the divine *Logos* is already *per se* an act of the intellect. We cannot at all diminish it by considering it blind trust. Having faith means daring to sacrifice ourselves, but this is not the same as a reckless leap in the dark.

Considering that faith is an act of participation in the mutual recognition of the Father and the Son in the Holy Spirit, it is always knowledge. That is why the faith of the Church follows rational structures, and why the teaching of the Church can be imparted in a dialogical way, because it is logical in itself. If we refute fideism, we must not fall into the opposite extreme, that is, the attempt to rationally reduce faith to the created mind's capacity for understanding, or even to use only what we are rationally and scientifically able to accept or reject as a yardstick. Faith does not need to account for itself before the tribunal of human reason, which is *per se* fallible, but only before the tribunal of divine and infallible reason, to which the infallibility of the

Introduction: On the Work of Mauro Gagliardi

Church with her doctrine of faith and her teachings participates. Truth is reason, and reason is truth. Every act of faith toward the truth of God is an act of participation in the reason of God. The natural *lumen* of human reason transcends itself in the *lumen fidei*, if the reason allows itself to be illuminated by the Holy Spirit. On the basis of the inner unity of faith and reason, the necessity of a rational reflection on faith emerges. Faith is not made to derive from reason, much less to be reduced to it. Catholic theology, however, being a function of the Church and her message, conceives its epistemological principle as *fides quaerens intellectum* (Saint Anselm of Canterbury).

One might wonder why the spiritual and conceptual interpretation of the Catholic faith cannot be considered completed once and for all. Would it not be enough to limit ourselves to publishing and re-publishing critical editions of the works of the Fathers of the Church? Or else, after having reached the apex of the synthesis of faith and reason in the *Summa theologiae* of Thomas Aquinas, the most illustrious intellectual that Catholic theology has known since Saint Augustine, who would think himself to be capable of adding something new? Who would think himself to be capable of surpassing Newman's theory of the development of doctrine?

It is true that we all continue to be disciples of Saint Thomas, and we cannot allow ourselves to take a step back from his level of reflection. However, it is also true that it is important not to continue to mechanically repeat the intellectual contributions of our predecessors, but rather to make these contributions our own in the sphere of an intellectual process that communicates with the human and natural sciences, and to update them in creative ways. We will never be able to re-elaborate and set in writing what Jesus accomplished and what He has always meant to us in the past and will continue to mean today and in the future, given that "the whole world would [not] contain the books that would be written," as John the Evangelist states of the *Logos* who is God and who has taken on our flesh. Theology is the discipline of the *Verbum incarnatum*. The activity of writing theological works, and the contents of faith and reason expressed in them, will not end until the Lord appears to us in all His glory and we can admire Him face to face through the *lumen gloriae*. Only then will we be able to recognize, in all its fullness, the reasonableness of Revelation as the substance of what we have understood in faith and hope, when as pilgrims we were in no condition to see the goal of faith (Heb 11:1).

Professor Gagliardi does not propose a summary of dogmatics or a new *Summa theologiae dogmaticae*. The salient characteristic of his work is, rather, that of knowing how to represent the main topics of the Credo in its individual articles, based on the internal synthesis of Revelation, and making them comprehensible in the fulfillment of their salvific history. We cannot take as our starting point (as in German idealism) an objective or absolute idea of the mind, not even if we wanted to conceive of it as a dialectic moment of the self-construction of the absolute spirit to then arrange all the phenomena of natural and intellectual history into specific categories. Instead, we recognize in faith the presence of God's reason which surrounds us, and which will always remain the greatest mystery. However, we begin to understand just how we have been known. Faith in the mysteries of divine revelation and grace compels us in a dynamic movement of the whole human being, body and soul, heart and mind, with all our efforts, which aims at unity with God in truth and charity. The difference between God and His creatures is not eliminated, but the separation between them is overcome, to arrive at a communion in knowledge and charity. In the *theologia viatorum*, in the state of faith, hope, and charity, "we see indistinctly, as in a mirror, but then [*lumen gloriae*] face to face. At present I know partially; then I shall know fully, as I am fully known" (1 Cor 13:12).

Catholic theology differs from idealistic or rationalistic metaphysics by virtue of its character of creatural humility. Catholic theology bows before the mystery of God and does not propose to define it or impose a regulatory ideology of reason, nor to subject the Word of God to a postulate of moral reason, much less to "re-fit" God into a projection of our own religious sentiments. The faith is based on the very message of God, which is real and historical, and is firmly based in the Incarnation of the *Logos*, the Son of the Father, and His related salvific episodes of suffering, death, Resurrection, and the outpouring of the Holy Spirit and the Second Coming of Christ at the end of time.

It is from here that the completely logical structure of this work emerges. After having developed the "synthetic principle" of Revelation in the hypostatic union in Chapter 1; and after having discussed the relation between Revelation, faith, and theology in Chapter 2, Professor Gagliardi associates the whole salvific history of biblical testimony with God the Creator, with the Son the Redeemer, and the Holy Spirit as Sanctifier. The culmination of Revelation in the history of salvation consists in knowledge of the Holy Trinity: A single divine nature in three divine Persons—the Father, the Son, and the Holy Spirit. The different emphases associated with Trinitarian theology are well-known. We can begin with the unity of God in His essence as true God, to then represent the Trinity of three Persons that, in their relational subsistence, do not undermine or triple the unity and unicity of the divine Being and His essence. We can also start from the monarchy of the Father and the Trinity of Persons, to then go on to the unitary nature of the one God who holds them together.

Introduction: On the Work of Mauro Gagliardi

Within the framework of the current interreligious and philosophical debate, we can ascertain that the divine Trinity can neither be speculatively derived from, for example, the immanent logic of the concept of charity, nor (in comparison with Islam) can it be compelled in a speculative way. Without positive Revelation, we cannot overcome the modalist approach, and it is not even possible to avoid the misunderstanding of tritheism. However, the argument of Old Testament scholars that the Old Testament does not know the Revelation of the Trinity is not entirely true. Of course, before the definitive self-revelation of God in the Person of the Logos who took on our flesh, and the eschatological outpouring of the Spirit by the Father and the Son, there can be no proof of the Trinity of God as a mystery of salvation either on the basis of faith or from the conceptual standpoint. However, a divine nature is not revealed in the ancient covenant, but the Person of the Father, who possesses the divine nature in a complete and exclusive way. God's existence as a Person does not emerge from the relation of God with creation and with human beings, otherwise God could not reveal Himself in the Word and Spirit and enter into a personal relationship with us. If it were not so, the personification of God would start from us. Or God's existence as a Person would be a mere projection, and this would correspond to the nullification of the concept of God. The human being would only be dealing with himself. God would just be a phantasm reflecting the self-referentiality of His creatures. Since, however, God as Person is in relation with Himself, in the process of self-revelation and through the Incarnation, one can recognize the relational subsistence of the Son and therefore the subsistence of the Spirit of the Father and of the Son, precisely because they are revealed. In this way, the mystery of the Trinity is not opposed to the unicity of the divine nature and the existence of a single God. Trinitarian monotheism, in light of the effective self-revelation of God, proves to be unsurpassedly more sensible than unitary monotheism.

In the following six chapters, the author consequently goes from the mystery of God, who became man, to Mary, the Mother of the eternal Son of God, who has taken on human form thanks to Her. The consideration of the Church as Virgin and Mother follows from this. The hierarchical-apostolic constitution of the Church does not, as Luther said, contradict the equality of all Christians in relation to God on the basis of the common priesthood of the faithful. After presenting the general theology of the Sacraments and the Liturgy as adoration and glorification of God and not only as the transmission of the grace of redemption, the following chapter is entirely dedicated to the Eucharist. Professor Gagliardi rightly evaluates the key importance of the Holy Mass as a Sacrifice and Sacrament for Christians and the whole Church, so much so that it cannot be treated only as the third Sacrament of initiation. Chapter 12 follows with the representation of the last things, eschatology *stricto sensu*, in which God is revealed as the beginning and end of all creation, and the human being substantially defines his ultimate relationship with God in heaven or hell. Although everything depends on grace and predestination, God has given human beings intellect and freedom, so that they must achieve salvation "with fear and trembling." Here too it emerges that faith and reason, predestination and freedom, and grace and good works, are indivisible. If because of the *Logos'* assumption of human nature in Christ, two natures, two energies, two wills are all one and act together, then the primacy of God can never correspond to the elimination of creatures. Contrary to pantheism and panentheism, the human being's own reality and activity must be sustained. And contrary to the Lutheran doctrine of the unfree will, it must be emphasized that the human being, even after the original fall, has not completely lost the ability to accomplish natural good and to recognize the existence of God as Creator of the world and Judge of good and evil. It is precisely through the grace of Christ that the human being is made fit to do good in a natural way and made worthy of the supernatural, and of knowing God in His Revelation of truth and salvation. At the base of various erroneous conclusions in anthropology, there is an erroneous concept, of a monophysite or Nestorian variety, of the hypostatic union.

At the end of this rapid review of the very rich contents of this work, which is characterized by an innate intellectual clarity and by an admirable completeness, we can ask ourselves what the ordering principle is, that is, the overall design of the whole. This is described extensively in Chapter 1 (pp. 25–116.

According to everything that has been said so far, this is not a principle that is applied from outside like form to prime matter. It is, rather, the reality of Revelation that determines theological thinking. Being precedes being-thought. The order of *auditus fidei* and *intellectus fidei* is not reversable. In human reason, the project in the architect's mind precedes the execution *in realitate*. Divine reason carries out its plan of salvation in creation, in the history of salvation, and in the justification of the sinner.

"In this book we intend to present a theology that is understood as a recognition of the 'synthesis', which is the union of aspects that have, between them, an objective hierarchical order; a union not fused extrinsically, but one which constitutes reality and is learned from it" (p. 33).

"The supreme synthesis that has been ruptured is thus, before any other, that between God and man in Jesus Christ, the cause and model of every other synthetic composition of the faith" (p. 34; see 44).

Introduction: On the Work of Mauro Gagliardi

Aside from the Trinity, which is conceived in another way because of the absolute transcendence of God that eludes any type of categorization (p. 439), a certain dipolarity emerges in all the mysteries of the faith. The Catholic *et-et* principle is opposed to the Protestant *aut-aut* principle which excludes the other member of the relation of unity. The difference does not consist in the dogmaticity of Catholicism in questions of faith compared to a more liberal view of the classical Protestantism of the Reformation. Luther, in the treatise "*De servo arbitrio*" of 1525, had markedly emphasized the dogmatic principle of Christianity in contrast with the "liberal" view of Erasmus: "*Tolle assertiones – et Christianismum tulisti.*"

In Luther, however, a unilateral interpretation that does not do justice to the complexity of Revelation follows from the dogmatic principle. From the principles of the *solus*, nothing but an apparent radicalism follows, which, even though it seems interesting at first, unfortunately misses the essence of Christianity upon closer inspection. Of course, there is only one Mediator (*solus Christus*). This applies to the denial on the part of non-Christians, but not to the principle of its application in the Church of Christ. Indeed, Christ as Head of the Church is never separated from the Body. The principle of justification by faith alone (*sola fide*) is indisputably valid in comparison with the opinion that, in addition to Christ, there may be other paths that lead to God. However, it does not apply with respect to the principle that communion with Christ and our neighbor are fulfilled in good works, and this is of primary importance for our relationship with God. Of course, the Holy Scriptures as the Word of God are the reference point for faith and theology (*sola Scriptura*). However, Christianity is not a textbook religion. The humanity of Christ is the Word of God made flesh. The oral and written Tradition of the Apostles, as well as the continuation of the tradition within the Church, show the presence of Christ who speaks to us today and acts for our salvation in the Sacraments.

God's creatures are a composition. The human person, in his being, is constituted by being here (*Da-sein*) and by being as he is (*So-sein*), body and soul, personality and sociality. There is no faith without reason, and dedication to Christ in faith also requires dedication to Him in works. The common priesthood of the faithful requires sacramental priesthood, "to equip the holy ones for the work of ministry, for building up the body of Christ" (Eph 4:12). In the First Letter of Peter, which speaks of the regal priesthood of the whole Church (1 Peter 2:9), reference is also made to the shepherds who, in the name of Christ as supreme Shepherd, are responsible for the Church of God (1 Peter 5:2–4).

The unity of a composite whole is always achieved through a guiding principle that reunifies the composition. The soul is the form of the body, and it gives human beings their concrete existence. Christ, Head of the Church, is the source of all grace, which is still communicated through the Church, His body. This is how Christ is shown to be one and total, in the unity of Head and body.

It is also how Christ proves to be the synthetic Principle in all the truths of the faith, a fact that does not, however, invalidate the realities that are linked to His humanity, the Church, and the Sacraments, but instead gives them their efficacy. That is how the various articles of the faith do not disintegrate. The dogmas are not like a mechanical sum of disconnected truths and phrases, but they are linked according to the law of *analogia fidei* in a *nexus mysteriorum* and are intertwined according to the hierarchy of truths, in an organic and logically ordered way.

We must not commit the error of exchanging this aspect with the Lutheran principle of *simul iustus et peccator*, which is only the consequence of the interpretation of grace as a favor of God (*favor Dei*) toward the sinner. According to this doctrine, the justified sinner is declared legitimate but not legitimized, thus going from a state of sin that separates him from God to the salvific state of grace. Unlike the synthetic principle of the *et-et* of Catholicism, the Protestant principle of *simul iustus et peccator* is in opposition to the principle of non-contradiction. The same object cannot simultaneously have one attribute and, at the same time and in the same respect, have the opposite attribute. It goes without saying that Catholic theology cannot dispense with the non-contradiction principle by accepting Hegel's dialectical thought. The inclination of Mauro Gagliardi is therefore inspired by the great thinkers of the Catholic Tradition. In his thought, the strength and serenity of Saint Thomas Aquinas and his synthetic intellect are perceived in all its breadth and depth. The author does not have a detailed discussion with contemporary theology, although it is well-known to him, and he always keeps it in mind and responds to it. He prefers to limit himself to the authors of the Tradition and to the official documents of the Magisterium. The bibliographical references show how comfortable Professor Gagliardi feels with the Holy Scriptures, all Catholic theology, and the magisterial tradition.

Regarding the revolutionary *pathos* of the Lutheran principles of the *solus*, Catholic theology may seem less radical and at times more open to compromises. It does not exclude *a priori* any relation with philosophy and non-Christian ethics. It accepts and recognizes elements of good and truth even in the pagan criticism of the other religions, elements that come from God and refer to His truth and goodness. The Church does not move forward untouched by the vicissitudes of history, as pure as if it were a community of

Introduction: On the Work of Mauro Gagliardi

Platonic ideas, in the world infected by sin and evil. The Church needs an ongoing internal renewal, benefitting from the presence of Christ. However, in the attempt to overcome sin, even within herself, she cannot eliminate the corporeal, the visible, and the concrete, which can indeed give rise to sin, but are never the reason for it.

The grave failure of the German Bishops and the Church of Rome with the selling of indulgences, which unleashed the Protestant Reformation and led to the removal of millions of Catholics from the Church, cannot justify the abolition of the indulgence as a prayer of intercession for overcoming the penalty of sins or even questioning the existence of the primacy of Rome and the sacramental office of the bishops. Church reform is always necessary. However, we cannot "throw the baby out with the bathwater." We can even express our concerns towards the ecclesiastical policy of a pontiff, or towards a ruinous event, as in the case of the Fifth Lateran Council, which took place shortly before Luther published his theses against the abuses within the Church. Such criticisms contribute to the improvement of the Church's life. However, we cannot reject the Church *in toto*, in her institutions, and in the form that has been handed down to us.

After having reviewed the enormous legacy of the history of theology and dogmas and having taken flight with theological thought, the author manages to make a soft and precise landing, like an expert pilot would be able to do.

Theology always begins with the simplicity of faith and brings all Christians together in the faith of the simplest ones: children. After all, are we not all—from Paul to John, from Origen to Augustine and from Thomas Aquinas to John Henry Newman, from Joseph Ratzinger to Hans Urs von Balthasar, from Saint Teresa of Avila to Mother Teresa—nothing other (that is to say, nothing less) than children of God, who through Christ in the Holy Spirit can turn to God as Abba, Father?

Professor Gagliardi's brilliant work concludes precisely with the Word of the Lord, as he collects all theology in the spirit of a filial faith:

"Unless you turn and become like children, you will not enter the kingdom of heaven. Whoever humbles himself like this child is the greatest in the kingdom of heaven" (Matt 18:3–4).

1

The "Synthetic" Principle

1. A Glance at the Faith, Preaching, and Theology of Today

1.1. After the Council

Saint Paul VI, who with great joy had reopened the Second Vatican Council, and had happily led it to its conclusion, was forced to recognize in the years that followed that not everything went as he had hoped. Some of his expressions in this regard are very well known, and for that reason it is not necessary to repeat them here. John Paul II also noted this in his different texts and interventions, as did Benedict XVI on certain occasions.

On the fiftieth anniversary of the famous *Moonlight Speech* that Saint John XXIII gave at the beginning of Vatican II (October 11, 1962), Benedict XVI, from the window of the Apostolic Palace, said the following:

> Fifty years ago on this day I too was in this square, gazing towards this window where the good Pope, Blessed Pope John looked out and spoke unforgettable words to us, words that were full of poetry and goodness, words that came from his heart.
>
> We were happy—I would say—and full of enthusiasm. The great Ecumenical Council had begun; we were sure that a new spring of the Church was in sight, a new Pentecost with a new, strong presence of the freeing grace of the Gospel.

The "Synthetic" Principle

We are also happy today, we hold joy in our hearts but I would say it is perhaps a more measured joy, a humble joy. In these 50 years we have learned and experienced that original sin exists and that it can be evermore expressed as personal sins which can become structures of sin. We have seen that in the field of the Lord there are always tares. We have seen that even in Peter's net there were bad fish. We have seen that human frailty is present in the Church, that the barque of the Church is ever sailing against the wind in storms that threaten the ship, and at times we have thought: "the Lord is asleep and has forgotten us."[1]

Naturally, in the second part of his greeting, the Pope also recalled the undeniable positive fruits that exist in the life of the Church today. We cannot help but be grateful for all the good that came about after the Council, and that can be found today, because, as Benedict XVI said at the conclusion of the same blessing, this has happened and happens because the Lord "does not forget us."

And yet it is undeniable that the Church has experienced great difficulty for several decades now: the drastic decline in vocations (although the total number has always grown, it is still in constant decline when compared to both the general and ecclesial demographic rate of growth); the cooling of faith, penance, and prayer; the decrease in devotion; a broader than ever interpretation of certain fundamental virtues, as can be noted in broad sectors of consecrated life; and so on. But behind all of this and much else, the *true problem* lies in the background: the weakening of a unitary and solid vision with respect to the faith.

It is certain that "at the evening of life, we shall be judged on our love,"[2]

---

[1] Benedict XVI, *Benediction Bestowed upon Participants in the Candlelight Procession Organized by the Italian Catholic Action*, October 11, 2012. All Papal documents that are available in English, unless stated otherwise, are taken from the Vatican website: www.vatican.va. This also applies to citations from the *Catechism of the Catholic Church* and the 1983 *Code of Canon Law*. Biblical citations are taken from *The New American Bible, Revised Edition* (NABRE), as it appears on *usccb.org*. If a document also features a Denzinger citation (DS) then, unless otherwise noted, it will be taken from Heinrich Denzinger, *Enchiridion Symbolorum: Compendium of Creeds, Definitions, and Declarations on Matters of Faith and Morals*, ed. Peter Hünermann (eds. Robert Fastiggi and Anne Englund Nash for the English edition), 43rd ed. (San Francisco: Ignatius Press, 2012). In certain places, for the Denzinger text and the Vatican website documents, improvements have been made to the translation if parts are not sufficient.

[2] Saint John of the Cross, *Dichos* 64, cited in the *Catechism of the Catholic Church* CCC §1022.

A Glance at the Faith, Preaching, and Theology of Today

as is evident from Matthew 25. But it is also true that love is lived by putting the truth into practice. It is the lack of truth, or perhaps better, the disinterest in it, that characterizes vast areas of the Church today. Doctrine is considered a secondary element in Christian life. Only charity is taken as important in these contexts.

Therefore, it is useful to recall the Gospel passage in which a young man approaches Jesus and asks him what he must do to attain eternal life. The Master responds to him, "You know the commandments" (Mark 10:19); in other words, if he wants to live in love, then he must *know* the truth. Only such knowledge will be able to guide him in a life of charity that will eventually obtain for him eternal life. But today, are we sure that all Catholics know the commandments? There are indications that lead us to think the answer is no. In fact, it has been proven that even some priests—who hear Confessions—when questioned about this, are not capable of repeating the Ten Commandments from memory!

Now, in our time, perhaps theology can lend a hand, one full of charity, to the Church for which it is the handmaiden, encouraging the baptized to rediscover the beauty and importance of the truth: a truth that can also be called "sound doctrine." Yes, we need the courage to say it: we have an extreme, urgent need of orthodoxy in the faith! And thus we need a serious, solid, and believing theology.

Holy Father Francis, on more than one occasion, has offered the invitation of exercising *"parrhesia,"* namely, clarity in speech directed toward fraternal edification. Catholic theology today must absolutely listen to this call of the Pope and carry out this *parrhesia* in a mode that is proper to it, that is, in a doctrinal mode.

Few times in history was theology so far from the life of the Church as it is today. It is too often reduced to what Pope Francis has defined as a *"teología de escritorio"* (*"desk-bound theology"*):

> The Church, in her commitment to evangelization, appreciates and encourages the charism of theologians and their scholarly efforts to advance dialogue with the world of cultures and sciences. I call on theologians to carry out this service as part of the Church's saving mission. In doing so, however, they must always remember that the Church and theology exist to evangelize, and not be content with a desk-bound theology.[3]

---

[3] Francis, *Evangelii Gaudium* (2013), §133.

The "Synthetic" Principle

Theology is at the service of the faith and the Church. As a science of faith and of divine revelation, it must offer instruments and contents for the preservation and sharing of both. It is not always easy for a pastor to find in the bookshop recent texts of exegesis and theology that offer him good inspiration for homilies and catechesis. And this is something that does not happen when reading the Fathers, the Doctors, or the *probati auctores*—even the more recent ones. The poor quality of some homilies and catechesis of today may perhaps depend on the laziness of those who do not prepare well, or at all. However, this is not the only cause. Many priests and catechists are conscientious and properly prepared: the problem in this case are the texts with which such willing people prepare. Sometimes these are the aforementioned specialized books, which are not very enlightening, even if they offer much scholarship and speculation. More often, they read catechetical or pastoral aids, and these aids represent a popular translation of the theological currents that are in vogue. And even from these, although even less so than the specialized books, one can hope for a positive inspiration for evangelization. Theology is often sufficiently folded in on itself, self-satisfied, or—to say it again along with Pope Francis—narcissistic.[4] In short, it is anything but a handmaiden that serves the faith and the Church.

The recent *Homiletic Directory* seeks to fix this, connecting liturgical preaching to various themes taught by the *Catechism of the Catholic Church*, as if to remind us of the need to preach the Gospel in the doctrinal forms in which it has come to be expressed by the Church, and not according to personal, imaginative, or fashionable ideas.[5] Pope Francis also calls attention to the urgency of the problem, to the point of having dedicated a healthy section of his Apostolic Exhortation *Evangelii Gaudium* precisely to the theme of homilies and catechesis.

On the other hand, a good number of more sensible priests have been aware of the problem for a long time. Some complain of not finding "nourishment" in many of the recent publications. Certainly, this can also happen because of a misunderstanding about what is to be expected from a book of theology. Beyond these cases, however, different priests who love to study and read—who therefore know what they should expect to find in the books they

---

[4] "And the theologian who does not pray and who does not worship God ends up sunk in the most disgusting narcissism. And this is an ecclesiastical illness. The narcissism of theologians, of thinkers, is disgusting" (Francis, *Address to the Community of the Pontifical Gregorian University, Together with Members of the Pontifical Biblical Institute and the Pontifical Oriental Institute*, April 10, 2014).

[5] Congregation for Divine Worship and the Discipline of the Sacraments, *Homiletic Directory*, June 29, 2014, Appendix 1.

read—complain of the problem we are now addressing: to find something that nourishes the soul and is useful for preaching and catechesis, they feel compelled to return to publications from at least fifty years ago. Not that this is bad, of course, but why should it be impossible to write books *today* that are theologically solid and at the same time directed toward evangelization, in the most meaningful sense of the expression?

1.2. Fideism and Pragmatism

If what we have just mentioned is not done, one runs the risk of endorsing two possible erroneous opinions. The first is fideism, which is recognized in the *credo quia absurdum* of Tertullian.[6] We could express the second with the formula *credo quia practicum*. In the first case, the rejection of theology is more theoretical: theology neither knows God, nor makes Him known; thus, it is an impossible science. In the second case, theology is rejected in favor of a pastoral approach: what the theologians write in the books will perhaps also be true, but it serves no purpose: thus, theology is useless.

Concerning the first of these two erroneous attitudes, Benedict XVI expressed the following:

> The Catholic Tradition, from the outset, rejected what is called "fideism," which is the desire to believe against reason. *Credo quia absurdum* (I believe because it is absurd) is not a formula that interprets the Catholic faith. Indeed God is not absurd, if anything he is a mystery. The mystery, in its turn, is not irrational but is a superabundance of sense, of meaning, of truth. If, looking at the mystery, reason sees darkness, it is not because there is no light in the mystery, but rather because there is too much of it. Just as when humans raise their eyes to look at the sun, they are blinded; but who would say that the sun is not bright or, indeed, the fount of light? Faith permits us to look at the "sun," God, because it is the acceptance of his revelation in history and, so to speak, the true reception of God's mystery, recognizing the great miracle. God came close to man, he offered himself so that man might know him, stooping to the creatural limitations of human reason.[7]

---

[6] Tertullian of Carthage (d. 220), *De carne Christi* 5.4. The text is cited in Chapter Two, note 147

[7] Benedict XVI, *General Audience*, November 21, 2012.

The "Synthetic" Principle

As for the second risk, it derives from a very common attitude: the pragmatism in the pastoral life of the Church. Because of this, only that which produces an immediate effect is considered useful, and even preaching and catechesis are often no longer "gratuitous," but rather "directed" to one problem or particular purpose. Now, it is correct to say that the truth always entails practical consequences, as is also the case with falsehoods. But this does not imply the uselessness of preaching or explaining the gospel truth in a "gratuitous" manner, that is, for its own sake. The Word should be preached for love of the Word, not for the demands of *praxis*. Certainly, action (*praxis*) always arises from the truth, but this happens in the right way only when the practical implication is not sought, or at least is not sought first. The faith needs to be preached for the faith—for the enjoyment and the need to make the divine Truth known—not to resolve a particular problem in each case. When preaching and catechesis are always directed toward particular ends to be resolved, perhaps in a hurried or carefree manner, a "prostitution" of the Word occurs.[8] But the Gospel cannot be subjected to this sort of commercial activity. It goes without saying that someone who thought in such a pragmatic way, and arranged his pastoral activity accordingly, would find theology useless.

These two risks are due to mistaken mentalities that do not depend on theology. However, a certain way of doing theology can encourage these risks and even justify them. Much of the current theological literature actually has this effect. For this reason, it will be considered unfounded or useless, and moreover it will remain "desk-bound theology." By contrast, writing to future priests, Benedict XVI had recommended precisely to take care of the "gratuitousness" of the study of theology, the only mode of intellectually preparing a practical ministry that is truly fruitful:

> Above all, your time in the seminary is also a time of study. . . . Certainly, the subjects which you are studying can often seem far removed from the practice of the Christian life and the pastoral min-

---

[8] As strong as the expression may appear, it was pronounced by Benedict XVI: "In this context, a beautiful phrase from the First Letter of St. Peter springs to my mind. It is from verse 22 of the first chapter. The Latin goes like this: '*Castificantes animas nostras in oboedentia veritatis.*' Obedience to the truth must 'purify' our souls and thus guide us to upright speech and upright action. In other words, speaking in the hope of being applauded, governed by what people want to hear out of obedience to the dictatorship of current opinion, is considered to be a sort of prostitution: of words and of the soul" (*Eucharistic Concelebration with the Members of the International Theological Commission*, October, 6, 2006).

A Glance at the Faith, Preaching, and Theology of Today

istry. Yet it is completely mistaken to start questioning their practical value by asking: Will this be helpful to me in the future? Will it be practically or pastorally useful? The point is not simply to learn evidently useful things, but to understand and appreciate the internal structure of the faith as a whole, so that it can become a response to people's questions, which on the surface change from one generation to another yet ultimately remain the same. For this reason it is important to move beyond the changing questions of the moment in order to grasp the real questions, and so to understand how the answers are real answers.[9]

Looking only at Italy, the national episcopal conference has admitted that there is a clear educational emergency. The Pastoral Directions of the Italian Episcopate for the present decade (2010–2020) are structured around the theme of education.[10] The Church in Italy has taken note that even in its own territory—and not only contemporary western society as a whole—it is often no longer educated. An educational emergency means, translated into simpler terms: we need teachers! Everyone knows the expression of Paul VI: "Modern man listens more willingly to witnesses than to teachers, and if he does listen to teachers, it is because they are witnesses."[11] If it is true that the task of teaching and the witness of a good life go together, it is also true that the indiscriminate repetition, for forty years now, of this very popular statement has provoked—even if unintentionally—a situation in which everyone wants to be, or at least to seek out, witnesses, and no one is a teacher or listens to teachers. The educational emergency is thus: We need teachers!

Behold our task in theology today: the recovery of the *munus docendi* ("teaching function") in the Church, at all levels. This is not to say that the Church as a whole has lost it—clearly she has not! But the implementation of such a *munus* has been reduced in certain aspects, so to speak, even if at the material level there has instead been a multiplication of the number of texts and the quantity of documents of various types. But here we are referring to the *munus docendi* as the preaching—done with total *parrhesia*—of the "scandal" of the Gospel. In other words, we need the spirit of Saint Paul to enter the Church once again. We need shepherds who, at all levels of the sacred hierarchy, do not tire of letting everyone know, in opportune and inop-

---

[9] Benedict XVI, *Letter to Seminarians*, October 18, 2010, §5.
[10] Italian Episcopal Conference, *Educare alla vita buona del Vangelo*, October 4, 2010.
[11] Saint Paul VI, *Address to the Members of the "Consilium de Laicis,"* October 2, 1974) in *AAS* 66 (1974): 568; restated in *Evangelii Nuntiandi* (1975), §41.

····19

portune times (see 2 Tim 4:2), that we *truly* believe a number of things that for the wise of this world are foolishness. We profess *with firm faith and without doubt* that God is one and triune. We believe that God *truly* became incarnate of a Virgin. We *firmly* believe that this God-Man shed his blood in expiation for our sins. We believe *without hesitation* in original sin and its consequences. We believe that Christ has *truly* risen from the tomb with his physical body and that there will also be a resurrection of the flesh for us at the end of time. We believe *without any shadow of a doubt and without any watering down of the faith* that in the validly consecrated Eucharist there is the "true, real, and substantial" presence of the Body, Blood, Soul, and Divinity of Our Lord Jesus Christ, and so on.

Is the theology of today capable of expressing itself with this *parrhesia*? Or should it hide behind circumlocutions, bombastic but at the same time devoid of meaning? Do theologians and pastors always announce with frankness the *content* of our faith? In the rite of Baptism it is stated: "This is our faith. This is the faith of the Church. We are proud to profess it, in Christ Jesus our Lord." Do the books of today's theologians always correspond to this spirit? Are today's theology and pastoral service proud of the Catholic faith? Or, deep down, are they ashamed of it? Are the Incarnation, Passion, Death, and Resurrection of Jesus, or the dogma of the Holy Trinity and other dogmas, at the center of what we proclaim, or do we think that "there's much more" to be concerned about? Can there be anything more important than God and His truth? And yet, often the impression given is that the faith is marginal and the other stuff is essential. But precisely the opposite is true! In fact, Christ sent the Apostles to evangelize in the name of the Trinity and to baptize and guide all people (see Matt 28:19–20). The other stuff is, if anything, secondary, or at least consequential. In prioritizing what is secondary, the parameters have been reversed.

1.3. *"Synthetic" Theology*

What has caused this reversal? Even if we are not proposing a complete analysis of this, limiting ourselves to the area of theology, we recognize that theology bears some responsibility for such a change. Many problems of theology—and, relatedly, of preaching and catechesis—are today a result of the tendency to emphasize one aspect, while forgetting its corresponding "synthetical." The meaning of this word will emerge in the following pages. For now, we shall focus only on noting that many sectors of contemporary theology have committed what we could define as an "error of emphasis." With this expression we want to indicate that in recent times theological

A Glance at the Faith, Preaching, and Theology of Today

discourse has not always developed by writing mistaken words (though there have been plenty of examples of this as well); it was enough to simply point them in the wrong direction. It would be like writing a word correctly from the orthographic standpoint, but pronouncing it incorrectly by putting the accent in the wrong place.

Contemporary theology often sought to become an antithesis to the preceding eras and, to accomplish this, it was not satisfied to delve deeper into what had already been obtained in order to deepen the understanding of faith. Instead, it has sought to subvert paradigms. This methodological change has been accompanied by a change in content, in which the emphases of the past are replaced with new ones. In appearance, most of the time, the discourse remains the same, but the mode of pronouncing it (the direction it takes) is radically different. This is why, even if the listener or reader remains perplexed by the new direction, it is difficult to clearly point out the error of the proposed exposition. To put it in simpler and clearer terms, a significant number of people advance doubts concerning the positions of various recent theologians, but few feel they can point out with certainty where the error lies—or its precise nature—when it occurs in a given instance. However, the various errors or omissions often derive from a fundamental one, which is what we called above the "error of accent": if secondary aspects are emphasized as if they were principal (and vice versa), the essential and primary elements will be interpreted as if they were accessories or optional. Based on this way of proceeding, then, the main element often ends up being eliminated altogether, having been forgotten as a result of being relegated to a secondary position. The whole process occurs in a hushed, almost painless way.

Today, who would write clearly that the consecrated Host is *not* the Body of Christ? Probably no one. But it is sufficient to develop a Eucharistic theology in which this point is not fundamental and others—even if they are important aspects—are privileged instead, such as a privileged attention for the suffering body of the poor, in which there is the "presence" of Jesus; or else the love for creation, given that the Eucharistic bread and wine come from creation, and so on. It is enough to give primacy to what is secondary so that what is primary might in fact disappear from the horizon. In this way the Church is truly transformed into that NGO (non-governmental organization) that Pope Francis has criticized since the day after his election.[12]

---

[12] "We can walk as much as we want, we can build many things, but if we do not profess Jesus Christ, things go wrong. We may become a charitable NGO, but not the Church, the Bride of the Lord. When we are not walking, we stop moving. When we are not building on the stones, what happens? The same thing that happens to children on the

The "Synthetic" Principle

Giving primacy to what is secondary and derivative, and vice versa, by hiding what is more important in the shadows, the Church is transformed into a service agency in which it is said, with respect to the truth of the faith to be announced: "There are more important things to worry about."

In this book we intend to present a theology that is understood as a recognition of the "synthesis," which is the union of aspects that have, between them, an objective hierarchical order; a union not fused extrinsically, but one which constitutes reality and is learned from it. There are certain elements that are more important than others; despite this fact, *both are necessary*. The entire faith, as will be seen, is structured in this way. The Tradition of Catholic thought has translated this vision with the two Latin conjugations *et-et* (both/and), which is contrasted with the other model of western Christianity, the Protestant one, which instead focuses on an *aut-aut* (either/or). In the Catholic vision, to choose one aspect and exalt it to the point of denying its corresponding *synthetical* aspect is heresy in the etymological sense of the term—from the Greek *airesis*, meaning "choice." In this sense, while sharing the invitation of the Second Vatican Council to be respectful in addressing our separated Christian brothers and sisters, the heretical character of, above all, Protestantism needs to be recognized honestly. Without desire to personally offend any Protestant brother or sister—with whom we share both the fundamental elements of the faith and Baptism, and with whom we are united by the charity of Christ—we must also practice evangelical *parrhesia* in saying that the fundamental model of *aut-aut*, precisely by forcing a choice between the two aspects, is a "heretical" model that does not allow for a complete understanding of the content of revelation, as we shall show in what follows.

In recent times, however, even large sectors of Catholic theology have allowed themselves to be conditioned more or less consciously by this model. It should be said with conviction, and not for a mere *captatio benevolentiae*, that recent theology has also produced notable and, probably, lasting fruits. For example, it has brought greater balance to certain ways of presenting doctrine, which also run the risk of being unilateral. Thus, in moral theology, there has been a certain emphasis on the intention of the subject alongside the act carried out; in sacramental and liturgical theology, there is an emphasis on grace and the interior participation of believers with respect to the celebration of the

---

beach when they build sandcastles: everything is swept away, there is no solidity. When we do not profess Jesus Christ, the saying of Léon Bloy comes to mind: 'Anyone who does not pray to the Lord prays to the devil.' When we do not profess Jesus Christ, we profess the worldliness of the devil, a demonic worldliness" (Francis, *Homily for the "Missa pro Ecclesia" with the Cardinal Electors*, March 14, 2013).

A Glance at the Faith, Preaching, and Theology of Today

ritual; in ecclesiology there has been a better recovery of the mystical element alongside the institutional aspect, etc. But in attempting such a rebalancing, it has often taken us to the other extreme. In the present context, it has produced a spiritualistic reading of the Christian faith that in its ultimate outcome, probably unforeseen and unintended, denies the Incarnation of the Word.[13]

The supreme synthesis that has been ruptured is thus, before any other, that between God and man in Jesus Christ, the cause and model of every other synthetic composition of the faith. By detaching the Word from the flesh, Jesus is left as a Palestinian man of the first century, an "apocalyptic prophet" that lived in the Second Temple period. Holy Scripture, then, is no longer the "matter" permeated by the invisible presence of the Holy Spirit that has inspired it, but remains only a human book, to be read and interpreted like all other ancient books of the Middle and Near East. Exegesis becomes only historical-critical, researching the literal sense of the Bible, while the other senses of Scripture are completely forgotten. The synthesis between Spirit and matter is reduced: the writing remains a merely human product, and the Word of God does not resound in it.

And because the Spirit is so impalpable, theology will concentrate on the material dimension of reality: it becomes a theology of this world, of terrestrial realities, of politics, of social liberation, of feminism. "God is up there in Heaven, far away. Let us concern ourselves with the earth!" "If theology is to be significant"—this is the *slogan* for the battle—"then it needs to put its focus on man and the world."

It can be said that with the synthesis between Heaven and earth broken, theology becomes deist: God exists and has created the world, but He is far from here and is not interested in us (the *deus otiosus* of the pagan myths returns). We must take care of it ourselves. The responsibility of theology—and also that of the shepherd of souls, or rather, in the language that is approved of today, the *leader* of men—is not in speaking of what is "spiritual" and invisible, but in working for a better world. It is not concerned with becoming divinized but rather humanized. Behold the Christianity of the NGO, proposed with great elegance and annotated in the margins with great scholarship, by scholars of great culture and enviable intelligence, who are putting themselves in the service of a mistaken cause.

The *et-et* saves us from all of this. It recalls that both spiritualism and materialism are erroneous attitudes, because Spirit and matter should always

---

[13] This is, among other things, the recurring temptation—in every age—of Gnosticism, which separates matter and spirit and, in fact, denies the Incarnation. In this regard, see the upcoming citation of Saint Irenaeus of Lyon (d. ca. 202), *Adversus haereses* 3.11.3.

The "Synthetic" Principle

be kept together, as in Christ. Moreover, it recalls that the Spirit comes first and then the material. There is the primacy of the divine over the human, a hierarchy of value. This does not imply in any way that the second member of the pair is optional. The material side is not optional, and neither are the world and humanity! But in the Catholic vision they are valued in the right way only if they remain in the second place, with God in the first. Is it possible to propose such a theology today? Not only is it possible, but it is necessary and urgent to do so.

A "synthetic" theology is capable of noting the connection between different aspects that appear to contradict one another, but in fact *together* form the reality of things and, thus, the truth of things; ontological and epistemological truth, or rather, the true being of things as they are and as they are known by us. Yes, because we must not forget that faith is not only obscurity; it is also knowledge and vision.[14] Faith is the obedient response to the Revelation of God. God teaches, and the human being accepts this teaching, trusting Him who imparts it. Thus, the human being learns, and knows to repeat what he or she has learned. Faith is not only mystery, but also knowledge, and we must say that faith is also a series of notions that we know!formuła[15] It is not *only* this (*aut-aut*), but it is *also* this (*et-et*). Thus, radical apophaticism has no part in the right interpretation of the faith, or else there is a tendency to think, at a basic level, that we cannot know or express anything about God at all. If this were so, why would God have revealed Himself? Are the words of Scripture meaningless? Or should we concede the argument to Modernism, for which the doctrines of the faith are nothing more than derivative and secondary formulations that attempt to translate previous and fundamental spiritual experiences? But this means, again, to separate the letter of Scripture from the divine Spirit. Scripture, from this point of view, would remain a "human, all too human" product of an author or community that transcribes its own, culturally determined ideas of some experience of the divine, which in other traditions can be expressed through other concepts. Is this all worthy of the God of Truth? Is it worthy of the intelligence that God has given to humanity? Is it not instead a miserable and unfair vision of both God and His creature?

If one cultivates radical apophaticism—which deep down is a form

---

[14] See the second chapter of Pope Francis's encyclical *Lumen Fidei* (2013). And Saint Paul could affirm "*scio cui credidi*" ("I know Him in Whom I have believed" [2 Tim 1:12]).

[15] Even Martin Luther writes against Erasmus of Rotterdam in the *De servo arbitrio*: "*Tolle assertiones et Christianismum tulisti*" ("Eliminate assertions [notions of faith] and you have eliminated Christianity itself," in Martin Luther, *Lateinisch-Deutsche Studienausgabe*, ed. Michael Beyer, volume 1: *Der Mensch vor Gott* [Leipzig: Evangelische Verlagsanstalt, 2007], 229 [our translation]).

A Glance at the Faith, Preaching, and Theology of Today

of theological relativism—one will end up developing within theology the Cartesian method of systematic doubt. Each affirmation of faith—even the dogmas—will be unceasingly subjected not only to necessary reflection and development but also to verification and even dispute. It will be acceptable to put everything into doubt, even the articles of the Creed; or at least it will be acceptable to propose new "interpretations" of them, even interpretations that radically change the content. How does this harmonize with one particular characteristic of the faith, certainty? Mind you, a certainty that is not human but divine. One believes not by trusting in oneself, but rather by trusting in God. It is based on the authority of God that one believes. Thus, the faith is not only a knowledge, but it is a certain knowledge. Can doubting the truth of the faith in such a way be part of theological method? Yet there is no shortage of books and pastoral aids that do this. Is it any wonder that so many priests do not find them truly helpful in the work of evangelization?

Finally, to conclude this quick glance at the situation of faith, preaching, and the theology of our time, we can allude to the great problem of the fragmentation of knowledge. Theology, along with other sciences, has known in the modern and contemporary eras widespread specialization, which has also produced various fruits. What has often been lacking in this process, however, has been the capacity of reuniting the disparate fragments. Scholars are specialized to increasingly limited and restricted areas, which is in itself good; nonetheless, the small segments must eventually be brought together into a whole figure (if one wishes, in the "polyhedron" of which Pope Francis sometimes speaks[16]). Theology, in accord with the synthetic nature proper to the faith, must also represent a synthesis, not in the sense that it absolutely must be brief, but that it must maintain the organic unity of its own expression, an organic unity that—at least according to our proposal—is based on that fundamental characteristic expressed by the bipolarity of *et-et* (both/and).

With this, we do not want to open a discussion about the suitability and modalities of a "systematic" theology: this term, in fact, can be utilized in very different ways, according to the philosophical framework of reference. Certainly, a systematic in the Hegelian sense of the term is not exactly what we desire for Catholic theology! More than a system, we are speaking about something organic. In the faith there is a fundamental *nexus mysteriorum*, called also a *analogia fidei* (we shall speak about this again at the end of the chapter): the fact that all the mysteries of the faith are connected to one another and gathered around a central nucleus, like the petals of a corolla

---

[16] See Francis, *Evangelii Gaudium*, §236. The image was taken up in different discourses, above all as applied to the theme of globalization.

The "Synthetic" Principle

form a single flower while being connected to the receptacle, or like the rays of the sun. Pope Francis also spoke of the *analogia fidei* from the standpoint, privileged by him, of the pastoral proclamation of the faith. Moreover, the Pontiff recalled that the varied relationship of the individual truths with the center of faith ("hierarchy of truths") does not actually imply that there are optional dogmas, but rather that all the truths should be maintained and presented in an organic and non-disassociated way:[17]

> All revealed truths derive from the same divine source and are to be believed with the same faith, yet some of them are more important for giving direct expression to the heart of the Gospel. In this basic core, what shines forth is the beauty of the saving love of God made manifest in Jesus Christ who died and rose from the dead. In this sense, the Second Vatican Council explained, "in Catholic doctrine there exists an order or a 'hierarchy' of truths, since they vary in their relation to the foundation of the Christian faith." This holds true as much for the dogmas of faith as for the whole corpus of the Church's teaching, including her moral teaching [. . .].
>
> Just as the organic unity existing among the virtues means that no one of them can be excluded from the Christian ideal, so no truth may be denied. The integrity of the Gospel message must not be deformed. What is more, each truth is better understood when related to the harmonious totality of the Christian message; in this context all of the truths are important and illumine one another.[18]

The synthesis of which we speak is therefore not put forward by us in a speculative way, but rather it is constitutive of the faith itself. It is the co-presence and unity of the various elements of the faith (dogmatic and moral), which are gathered together "hierarchically," or rather "with order" around the center, who is Jesus Christ—He who is *Unus de Trinitate*. Christ is the

---

[17] Saint Thomas Aquinas, treating faith at the beginning of the II-II of the *Summa Theologiae*, recalls that the Christian doctrines are called "articles" of faith precisely because they form together a connected and structured organism, an 'articulation' (see *ST* II-II, q. 1, a. 6).

[18] Francis, *Evangelii Gaudium*, §36 and §39. The *General Catechetical Directory*, published April 11, 1971, by the Sacred Congregation for the Clergy, already recalled that "in the message of salvation there is a certain hierarchy of truths, which the Church has always recognized when it composed creeds or summaries of the truths of faith. This hierarchy does not mean that some truths pertain to faith itself less than others, but rather that some truths are based on others as of a higher priority, and are illumined by them" (§43).

synthetic principle of the faith and is thus the same for theology as well. Having established these points, we can now move forward to shine light on the synthetic hinge of our discourse: Jesus.

2. Jesus Christ: "Synthetic" Principle of the Faith and of Theology

It is the New Testament, above all, that teaches us who Jesus Christ is. And here as well, at least to begin, we can go looking for a "synthetic" definition of Him. In this case, "synthetic" will be taken, for the moment, in its common usage as a brief definition.[19] We also note that we do not seek immediately to know what He has done for us, but rather who He is. The first question regards being, not action, because *"agere sequitur esse"* ("action follows from being").[20] Let us also emphasize that we are seeking a definition, not a description. The Gospels, on the other hand, never provide a physical description or psychological profile of Christ. But even if they did, what interests us here is first to understand who Jesus is, and that this is to be said with as few words as possible.

Now, the concise New Testament definition of Jesus that seems to us to be the best of all of them is the one provided by John in his Gospel or, rather, what can be derived from what he attests: "And the Word became flesh" (John 1:14). It is true that this phrase indicates an action, a work. But here the accent does not fall on the dynamic, but rather on what results from it: Jesus is the incarnate Word, He is God-Word (see John 1:1), having become a true human being like us.

Saint John's definition manifests itself as a synthesis not only in the common sense of the term, but also in the theological sense of a principle, center, and foundation. In Jesus, as the New Testament tells us, we have the actualization of a synthesis between God and humanity. God and humanity stand together in a single Subject. Two apparently irreducible realities now coexist indissolubly, while remaining distinct. In the Old Testament we have

---

[19] Translator's note: Here the author is referring to the common usage of *"sintetico"* in Italian, which is often used to mean summary, concise, or brief. This is in contrast to the way it has been used up to this point in the text, where it has been used in a technical sense that is common in philosophical and theological writings to refer to the result of a synthesis that brings together more than one truth or aspects of the truth, sometimes even when these different aspects seemed at first to be opposed to one another.

[20] Saint Thomas Aquinas, *Summa contra gentiles* III, ch. 69, no. 20. See *Scriptum super Sententiis*, III, d. 2, q. 1.

The "Synthetic" Principle

the God of the covenant who comes to meet His beloved and chosen people, but despite this, the limit between God and humanity remains clearly marked: "God is in heaven and you are on earth" (Eccl 5:1). Then the New Testament cuts down that distance and says the divine Word became flesh; God is no longer simply in Heaven but has descended to the earth, in human form. Other passages of the New Testament, which speak of the resurrection and ascension of Christ, allow us to complete the sketch and add that humanity is no longer only on the earth, it is also in Heaven. Thus, Jesus is the great synthetic Principle who unites Heaven and earth, God and humanity, Spirit[21] and matter.[22]

It is necessary to begin with Christ, and constantly refer back to this nucleus of the faith, preaching, and theology. The faith is called "Christian"; we the believers are called "Christians," having chosen this name since the Apostolic era (see Acts 11:26). There are certain tendencies in recent theology that would like to center the discourse less on Christ and more on God. Jesus is presented as the One who is sent by God (Messiah), as the greatest prophet of God. Theologians use titles like "eschatological prophet" or "apocalyptic prophet" for Jesus. They often emphasize, in recent exegesis and theology, that the core of Jesus' announcement is the kingdom of God, a phrase of which they underline the last two words: *of God*. Even for Jesus, then, the center would not be Himself but rather God. Consequently, we would also be pushed to concentrate less on Jesus, and more on the "God of Jesus Christ." It would also be said of Jesus that He was the "Revealer of the Father," that is, that He has revealed the merciful face of God, and so on.

Of course, in all of these affirmations there is something, and even much, that is true. The problem is the lack of the second part of the equation, and thus they remain isolated and without the reciprocal "synthetic" element. For example, when it is said that Jesus is the Revealer of the Father, it is not often added that, by revealing the mystery of the Father, Jesus has also revealed at the same time His own mystery as Son.[23] On the other hand, this observation would also make good sense given that "Father" is a relational term that indicates a relationship between two Persons: One who generates and One

---

[21] Here this is intended as synonymous with God, not as the name of the Third Person of the Trinity.

[22] From a standpoint of social doctrine and pastoral activity, Pope Francis writes in *Evangelii Gaudium*, §229: "Christ has made all things one in himself: heaven and earth, God and man, time and eternity, flesh and spirit, person and society."

[23] Unless one wants to reduce the paternity of God to the relation He has with us, His adopted children. But this kind of reductionism would draw the New Testament completely to the Old Testament—which already speaks in a metaphorical sense of God's paternity in relation to the elect (see Chapter Six)—denying the novelty of the New Testament revelation.

Jesus Christ: "Synthetic" Principle of the Faith and of Theology

who is generated by Him. Among human beings, no one is called father or mother without at least one child.[24] Thus, when Jesus reveals the face of God as Father, it is unmistakable that He is also revealing the face of God the Son. This is why in the second century, Saint Irenaeus writes: "And through the Word Himself who had been made visible and palpable was the Father shown forth, although all did not equally believe in Him; but all saw the Father in the Son: for the Father is the invisible of the Son, but the Son the visible of the Father."[25]

Faith and theology, if they are truly Christian, can neither prescind from nor relativize the centrality of Jesus Christ: they must be Christocentric. However, this Christocentrism, if well understood, will always be a Trinitarian Christocentrism. Jesus, in fact, is true man, but not only a man. He is not only a Jew who lived between Galilee and Judea in the first century. As John the Evangelist has taught us, Jesus is above all the Word, who is God. As will be seen in its place, Christian theology has introduced the technical term "Persons" to refer to the Three in God: Father, Son, and Holy Spirit. Theology has moreover introduced the term "Trinity" (see Chapter Six). In theological terms, Jesus is the second Person of the Holy Trinity, the Son who has taken on flesh. The centrality of Christ is therefore always the centrality of the Trinity as well, the centrality of God as He is known and adored by those who have accepted in faith the revelation of Jesus. Saint Thomas Aquinas has expressed the Christ-Trinity bond through one of his many striking phrases when he writes: "*In Christo continetur implicite Trinitas*" ("the Trinity is implicitly contained in Christ").[26] The need to choose between a faith and theology that is either Theocentric or Christocentric is, in reality, a false dilemma. The *et-et* (both/and) is also present here because Trinity and Jesus Christ are two sides of the same coin: "It is not possible to explicitly believe in the mystery

---

[24] "When you hear the name Father, you understand the Father of the Son, whose Son is the image of the aforementioned substance (Heb 1:3; Col 1:15). In fact, just as no one is called lord if he does not have a possession or servant over which he has dominion, and just as no one is called master if he does not have a disciple, so also a father in no way can be defined as such if he does not have a son [or daughter]. Thus, with the same name in which God is defined Father it is shown that the Son must likewise subsist with the Father as well" (Origen of Alexandria [d. 254], *Explanatio Symboli* 4 [our translation]). See also Saint Athanasius of Alexandria (d. 373), *Oratio I contra Arianos*: "The word Father reveals the Son." The theme will be developed by the Cappadocian Fathers (see Chapter Six).

[25] Saint Irenaeus of Lyon, *Adversus haereses* 4.6.6, in *ANF*, vol. 1, trans. James Donaldson and Alexander Roberts (Peabody, MA: Hendrickson Publishers, Inc., 1994), 469.

[26] Saint Thomas Aquinas, *Super Matthaeum*, lec. 28.

The "Synthetic" Principle

of Christ without faith in the Trinity, because the mystery of Christ implies the assumption of flesh on the part of the Son of God, the renewal of the world through grace, and the conception of Christ through the work of the Holy Spirit."[27]

2.1. The Particular Importance of the Second Council of Constantinople

From the dogmatic point of view, the face of Jesus Christ was sketched by the Church above all on the occasions of the ecumenical councils of the first millennium. Those who have no familiarity with the Christological dogmas defined there will have to stop reading here and pass to Chapter Four, dedicated to Jesus Christ, in order to have a better idea of it[28]—then return to read what is presented here. An ontological understanding of Jesus emerges from the Christological dogmas; that is to say, the believing reflection and the profession of faith are driven to investigate the being of Christ, His essential and personal makeup.

The Christological dogmas can be summarized in the formula "Jesus Christ is one Person in two natures." Reference is typically made to the fourth Council, that of Chalcedon, as a particularly noticeable moment in the development of the Christological dogma. At Chalcedon it is said with definitive clarity that Jesus is one alone, but there are two natures in Him, which are neither divided or separated, nor confused or mixed with each other; that is, the divine nature and the human nature. It is obviously correct to recall that Chalcedon teaches this, as it is also true that this Council concludes the series of the first four councils that—exceptions aside—are unanimously received by all Christians, and which Saint Gregory the Great (d. 604) said to venerate on par with the four books of the Gospels.[29] Thus, it is not incorrect to say that the orthodox Christological expression coincides with the Chalcedonian faith.

Consequently, generally speaking, the two or three councils that followed Chalcedon, which also defined Christological dogmas, are considered as applications to particular aspects of the doctrine of Chalcedon. This will be recognized without any issues for the Third Council of Constantinople (dedicated to the two operations and the two wills of Christ) and for the Second

---

[27] *ST* II-II, q. 2, a. 8.

[28] In particular, the doctrine of the councils is briefly presented in section 1.3, which has the title "The Person and Natures of Christ."

[29] For the citation of Pope Saint Gregory, see Chapter Four, footnote no. 25.

Jesus Christ: "Synthetic" Principle of the Faith and of Theology

Nicene Council, which discussed the iconographic representation of Christ and its traditional doctrinal foundations. This interpretation, however, is not completely correct when applied to the Council immediately following that of Chalcedon, namely, the Second Council of Constantinople. This Council is often undervalued because of the interweaving of entangled historical elements, which have even led to doubts concerning its ecumenical character. For this reason, it is generally considered not to be of the same importance as Chalcedon, and it tends to be placed among the series of Councils that apply what was said in the Council of Chalcedon. In response to this view, we must say that—at the level of both historical and doctrinal causes—if Chalcedon was able to have great effect on the faith of the Church, this is due precisely to the authentic interpretation of its decrees and the new light shed on it by the Second Council of Constantinople. Thus, if we want to place at the center of our discussion the figure of Christ as He is sketched by ecclesial dogma, and if we want to base this on Chalcedonian Christocentrism, we need the Second Council of Constantinople. The truth is, when we speak of the "Christ of Chalcedon," we really mean the Christ of Chalcedon according to the interpretation of Chalcedon given by the Fathers reunited in the Second Council of Constantinople.

It is well known to specialists that the roughly one hundred years that passed between the Council of Chalcedon (AD 451) and the Second Council of Constantinople (AD 553) were characterized by bitter doctrinal disputes, which dealt precisely with the correct interpretation of the first of these two Councils. There were those who, despite the clear affirmation of the two natures in Christ, accused the followers of Chalcedon of over-emphasizing their unity in Christ (an accusation of "Cyrillism"; that is, following and radicalizing the Christology of Saint Cyril of Alexandria [d. 444]); others, by contrast, despite the affirmation of that Council that Jesus Christ is "one and the same," accused it of having revived the heresy of Nestorius (d. 451), already condemned by the Council of Ephesus (AD 431). Such a heresy consisted in an excessive emphasis on the duality of nature in Christ, which led to speaking even of two "persons," or two "sons" in Him. This brief historical synthesis confirms what was said: Chalcedon, in itself, is enough for the correct faith, but its reception was not automatic. Many suspicions weighed down the Council after its celebration and, as often happens, while some sought to pull the Council to their side, others instead accused it of heresy.

In the situation of doctrinal conflict, which also implied a social conflict, the emperor Zeno intervened with a decree entitled *Henotikon* (AD 482), which sought to find a compromise between the two main parties of the dispute. But as was to be expected the text, precisely due to its character of being

The "Synthetic" Principle

a compromise, did not convince either side. Therefore, after several decades the emperor Justinian I, determined to find a solution, set off from afar, both, on one hand, seeking (to no avail) to get the different sides to dialogue with one another, and, on the other hand, to promote a theological interpretation of Chalcedon that modern scholars have called "Neochalcedonism." To put it simply, the Neochalcedonian interpretation interprets the Council of Chalcedon not as an element of rupture, but rather in continuity with the preceding Ecumenical Council, the one held at Ephesus, in which the standpoint of Saint Cyril clearly prevailed over that of Nestorius. Neochalcedonism, applying what we today call a "hermeneutic of reform, of renewal in ... continuity"[30] (or more briefly "hermeneutic of continuity"), managed to reach the goal that had been sought in vain through the path of compromise or dialogue between the different sides. Thus, Neochalcedonism reads the dogma of Chalcedon in continuity with the Cyrillian theology defined at Ephesus, and not in opposition to it. Cyrillian theology, canonized at Ephesus, emphasizes the unity in Christ, without denying the duality of nature. On the other hand, Chalcedon emphasizes the duality of nature (human and divine) without denying the fundamental unity in Jesus. This concerns emphases, but the emphases are important! Both Councils represent the *et-et*, but which of the two members of this bipolarity is hierarchically the primary one? The unity of the Person or the duality of nature? In Cyril, the unity; at Chalcedon it is the duality. It is here that Neochalcedonism intervenes, placing the emphasis back on unity, while maintaining very clearly the duality of nature as a second element that is in no way optional or nonessential. The Second Council of Constantinople thus magnificently represents the principle of *et-et*: two elements together, of which one is first and the other second, without the latter becoming optional on account of being second.

We owe the concept of *enhypostasia* to Neochalcedonism, which holds that in Jesus Christ there is a true human nature but—in contrast to all other human beings—a personality (*hypostasis* or *substantia* in the sense of *subsistens*, not of *essentia*), or individual human subsistence, does not correspond to this nature. The unique *hypostasis* or person of Jesus Christ is the Person of the Word, or Son—the Second Person of the Holy Trinity. The *Logos* (Word) is the unique person of Christ and the human nature of Jesus is personalized by this Person and in this Person.[31] Thus, there is no need that Jesus, while being true man, be

---

[30] Benedict XVI, *Address to the Roman Curia Offering Them His Christmas Greetings*, December 22, 2005.

[31] Thus, the great theologian Leontius of Jerusalem, who came shortly after, interpreted the Second Council of Constantinople in *Adversus Nestorianos* 1.29: "The flesh was not trans-

Jesus Christ: "Synthetic" Principle of the Faith and of Theology

a human person. He is, however, a person—a divine Person. The Incarnation, thus, is explained as the assumption of a true human nature on the part of the Word, and this means that this assumed human nature, precisely because it is assumed by a divine Person, does not need a human subject. In Christ there is only one Subject, only one Person, while there are also two natures. One will say that this was already clearly defined at Chalcedon, and this is true. The point is that Chalcedon limited itself to defining the terms of the dogma: Christ is "one and the same, to be recognized in two natures," which are united to one another but not confused. Thus, the Chalcedonian explanation, while affirming all the essential terms of the question, places more focus on defining the reciprocal relationship between the two natures than in explaining in what way Christ continues to be one and the same. It is said there and, in itself, is enough. But it was not enough for those who debated for a long while after the Council. This is why there was a need for Neochalcedonism and the Council into which it flowed, the Second Council of Constantinople.

The great contribution of Neochalcedonism and the Second Council of Constantinople was, to put it briefly, that of defining the synthetic character of the union of the two natures in Christ. And here it was not us who chose the word "synthetic"; the Council itself did so.[32] The Church had already defined that the two natures in Christ occur "according to the *Hypostasis*," namely, in the unity of the divine Subject (the Person of the Word). At this point it can be clarified that the formula "according to the *Hypostasis*," should be explained thus: the Word, assuming to Himself the human nature and uniting it to the divine nature that He has always possessed as God (see John 1:1), has carried out a wondrous "composition" or "synthesis" of the two natures in His unique Person. The natures of Christ are together, without confusion or mixing, without separation or division, in a marvelous synthesis. Behold the primordial *et-et*, explained and defined by this ecumenical Council. The *et-et* as a non-confusion of elements that are together in an inseparable way, with a hierarchical relationship of a first and a second. This *et-et*, as we describe and develop it here, is found first and foremost in Jesus Christ, in the heart of the mystery of the Incarnation, which is the principle, center, and foundation of the Christian faith.

It should also be noted attentively that the same Second Council of Con-

---

formed first and then assumed by the *Logos*, [...] but from the beginning of its existence it was 'personalized' in the *Hypostasis* of the *Logos*, in Christ" (our translation).

[32] Second Council of Constantinople, *Anathematismi de Tribus Capitulis*, can. 4 (DS 424–425), in which excommunication follows for those who do not profess that the union of natures in Christ happened "by way of synthesis [it can also be translated "by composition"; in Greek, *kata synthesin*], that is, according to the *Hypostasis*." This expression is used twice in the text of the same set of anathemas.

The "Synthetic" Principle

stantinople, along with the union of elements, also emphasizes their difference in value. One of the criticisms of the Chalcedonian treatment consisted, in fact, in the accusation that the Council had placed the human nature on the same level as the divine. The Second Council of Constantinople also clarifies this point, recalling that, while the human nature in Christ is not optional, it certainly has less value than His divine nature, given that it is the nature of things that humanity has infinitely less value than God. Moreover, the profile of the *et-et* is confirmed again because, while saying that the human nature is of less value than the divine, in no way does the Second Council of Constantinople affirm that the mystery of the Incarnation could be dissolved without damage. The human nature is decisive in the mystery of Christ and is in no way optional. This is not denied by the fact that the divine nature has a privileged position in the hierarchical scale, which must always be present among the two elements of a synthesis.

In conclusion, if for around fifteen hundred years the Council of Chalcedon has represented the orthodox Christological faith, this is due to the fact that we interpret it in light of the Council that followed it, which had the merit of applying the hermeneutic of continuity and of having allowed the emergence of the primordial synthesis that is verified in Christ, and which is the basis of all we refer to as *et-et* in the structuring of the realities and doctrines of the Christian faith. It is for this reason that the fundamental option of the Protestants (*aut-aut*) is condemned to failure. The *et-et*, in fact, is not simply the referential principle of Catholic thought; it is the constitutive principle of the primordial mystery of the faith, Jesus Christ. For this reason, we are convinced that the true and complete vision and interpretation of the Christian faith is the Catholic one, even if in Protestant faith many elements of truth and grace remain. The *aut-aut*, however, insofar as it is a principle that contradicts the very ontology of Christ, will never be able to serve as a basic principle for a theological-doctrinal expression that adequately enters into the mystery of Christ and, more generally, into the faith that He has given us.

3. The Missing Synthesis: The Orthodox and the Protestants

We must carefully distinguish between the Orthodox and Protestants, these two large groupings of our Christian brothers who we do not find in full communion with the Catholic Church. Although among believers in Christ there is a common set of beliefs, made up of dogmas that are, so to speak, most crucial concerning the Trinity and the Incarnation of the Word, along

The Missing Synthesis: The Orthodox and the Protestants

with others, such as the "necessity" (see the chapters on the Sacraments) of Baptism for salvation, it is also true that there is no commonality between the professions of faith of the disciples of Christ concerning other doctrines. This gap is more accentuated between Catholics and Protestants[33] than between Catholics and the Orthodox. We shall now proceed to a brief exposition of the different doctrinal visions, which have also clearly originated from different pastoral and spiritual practices in their respective communities.

3.1. *The Orthodox*

In regard to the Orthodox, it is well known that the division of the Churches is especially stressed concerning two doctrinal points: the *Filioque*, and the primacy of the jurisdiction of the Bishop of Rome. For the Catholic doctrine in this regard, one can see the chapters dedicated to Trinitarian theology and ecclesiology. It is established that at the base of the division with the Orthodox there is a good dose of extra-theological reasons as well, which we need not evoke here, whose responsibility can be distributed between various actors of the era in which such divisions occurred, first under the patriarch Photios (venerated as a saint by the Orthodox) and, centuries later, in 1054, definitively consummated by Michael I Cerularius.

On account of this schism with the East, the Orthodox—although they know and respect our name "Catholic Church"—also make use of the term "catholic" for themselves, speaking for example of an Orthodox Catholic Church. This is because they decline to understand the adjective "catholic" as a name, which beyond such a use also indicates one of the essential marks of the Church in the Creed. If "Catholic" indicates one of the denominations of Christianity, namely the Roman Church, then this word refers only to those who are in the community of Christians that are linked to the See of Rome. But for the Orthodox, "catholic"—in the sense of the Creed—refers to those who are in the true Church, and they are convinced of being the true Church of Christ (a claim that, from their standpoint, makes sense).

Moreover, since 1054, the Orthodox have not accepted the saints can-

---

[33] Here we are content to use the term in a general way, including under this term both the communities that derive from the modern reform movements of Luther, Zwingli, and Calvin, and the various other forms of Protestantism that have arisen recently, as well as the Anglican Communion, even if it has a different historical origin. The criterion for such a wide use of the term is that of a valid Eucharist. Only the Orthodox have preserved the valid celebration of the Holy Sacrifice; thus one can distinguish on one side the Orthodox Christians, and on the other all the Christians that do not have a valid Eucharist.

The "Synthetic" Principle

onized by the Church of Rome in their calendar, while we share with them many of those canonized prior to that, or also those whose fame of sanctity precedes that time. The Roman Catholic Church, on the other hand, has allowed—particularly for the Eastern Catholic Churches—the veneration of the saints canonized by the Orthodox since the schism. We must honestly acknowledge that the denial of the saints canonized by Rome after 1054 is not a simple question of obstinacy, but rather the liturgical implication of the primacy of the true ecclesial community, which is rooted in the faith. Since, for the Orthodox, we Catholics have not kept the apostolic faith pure and thus are not in full communion with them, they cannot accept having a liturgical celebration in common either. Celebratory communion is reached as a goal of a full communion of faith[34] and, under this aspect, it is possible not only to understand their attitude, but even to agree with it in principle, even if not in its application.

Additionally, with respect to the theme of the saints, there is the Orthodox practice of "decanonization," which the Catholic Church does not acknowledge. For Catholics, the canonization of a saint (at least when the formal procedure perfected by Benedict XIV [d. 1758][35] is followed) is an infallible act,[36] and is thus also irreformable. On the other hand, the Orthodox know the practice of decanonization, for which it is possible that a saint recognized by them becomes downgraded at a later time.

In general, it can be observed that the Orthodox Church has denied all of the development—not only doctrinal but also theological and disciplinary—that has come since 1054. It is a Church almost "frozen" in the doctrine and practices of the first millennium. We shall now sketch this "freezing" through a concise—though certainly not exhaustive—exposition divided according to subject matter.

---

[34] Some Orthodox Churches even rebaptize Catholics that convert to them. This also motivates the different practice concerning "intercommunion." In cases of necessity, the Catholic Church permits its own faithful to receive Eucharistic Communion from Orthodox ministers (see *Codex Iuris Canonici*, can. 844 §2), while for Orthodox faithful there is an absolute ban on receiving Communion from a minister of another Christian denomination. The principle is the same: Eucharistic Communion implies belonging to the (Orthodox) Church and its faith. Thus, the Orthodox baptized can in no case receive Eucharistic Communion from non-Orthodox ministers.

[35] See his *De Servorum Dei beatificatione et Beatorum canonizatione*, published in 1750.

[36] Not all theologians agree on the doctrinal infallibility of canonizations, even by referencing recent controversial cases. Without examining the question here, it can be said that the canonizations are infallible if the procedure provided for ascertaining the holiness of the subject is *truly* observed.

The Missing Synthesis: The Orthodox and the Protestants

3.1.1. Ecumenical Councils

The Orthodox only recognize the ecumenical councils convened in the first millennium. There are eight of them. The first seven recognized councils coincide with those also recognized by the Catholics, while there is a discrepancy with respect to the eighth. For the Catholic Church, the eighth ecumenical Council (the final council of the first millennium) is the Fourth Council of Constantinople, held from 869–870. By contrast, the Orthodox recognize as the eighth Council the Synod held at Constantinople from 879–880, which rehabilitated Photios, reversing the previous judgment. Significantly, all of the councils that were held in the second millennium and retained as ecumenical by the Catholics have taken place in the West, while the first eight were in the East (at Nicaea, Constantinople, Ephesus, and Chalcedon). After the Great Schism of 1054, the first ecumenical council recognized by Catholics, but not by the Orthodox, is the First Lateran Council (1123), after which three others followed (1139, 1179, 1215), for a total of four Lateran councils in a row. Then there were two at Lyon (1245 and 1274); one in Vienne (1311–1312); one in Constance (1414–1418); an itinerant council in Basel, Ferrara, Florence, and Rome (1431–1445); the Fifth Lateran Council (1512–1517); the long Council of Trent (1545–1563); and, finally, two Vatican Councils (1869–1870 and 1962–1965). Consequently, a significant difference also arises regarding the basic criterion according to which the ecumenical character of a council is established. For Catholics, the ultimate criterion (even if it is not the only one) is the ratification (confirmation or at least acceptance) of the council, as being ecumenical, on the part of the Pope.[37] Obviously, the Orthodox cannot agree with this, because it would imply a primacy of jurisdiction of the Bishop of Rome over all of the Church and all of the episcopal college. Thus, they affirm that the criterion of ecumenicity consists in the fact that there was an imperial convocation, and there was the presence of all five major patriarchs (Rome, Constantinople, Alexandria, Antioch, and Jerusalem). For the Orthodox, these two elements are found in all the ecumenical councils of the first millennium, but not in those of the second millennium.[38]

---

[37] Second Vatican Council, *Lumen Gentium* (1964), §22: "A council is never ecumenical unless it is confirmed or at least accepted as such by the successor of Peter; and it is prerogative of the Roman Pontiff to convoke these councils, to preside over them and to confirm them." See also *Codex Iuris Canonici*, canons 338 and 341.

[38] At least in the case of the Second Council of Constantinople, however, it could be objected that the presence of the Pope was not free but imposed by the emperor—something that casts doubt on the deliberate presence of the Roman See at this Council. Nonetheless, even for Catholics it is ecumenical, because it was approved by future popes.

The "Synthetic" Principle

This also implies another aspect; namely, that the Orthodox Church does not accept, at least with the same judgment of the Catholic Church, the principle of the "development of doctrine." In fact, one of the reasons why the councils of the second millennium are rejected is that they represent, in the view of the Orthodox, undue developments of doctrine in contrast to the pure and simple preservation of the patristic Tradition. The "freezing" to which we have alluded also regards theological reflection, which by its nature flows into—after the appropriate filters—the magisterial teaching. Having concluded the patristic era with Saint Bede the Venerable (d. 735) or—according to others—Saint Bernard of Clairvaux (d. 1153), a new approach for study and thought was created in the West—the Scholastic approach—which, while remaining faithful to the patrimony of the Fathers, led to different and important innovations that also prepared for the doctrinal development of the Catholic Magisterium. By contrast, in the eastern environment, the end of the patristic era (conventionally coinciding with the work of Saint John Damascene [d. 749]) never gave rise to an eastern Scholastic period, but rather the so-called Neopatristic era, which—it can be said—lasts even into the present day, and has also generated figures of great importance for Christian thought. For the Orthodox, it is even difficult to accept the idea that the era of the Fathers is "concluded." In some way it always remains open, because the Tradition of the Fathers must always be preserved. The task of Orthodox theology is, therefore, above all to preserve the Tradition of the Fathers. For Catholic theologians, there is a focus on an incessant deepening, and the search for new categories and new expressive methods for speaking the faith of all times.

3.1.2. Sacramental and Liturgical Aspects[39]

The divergences concerning the sacramental and liturgical aspects are less evident today after the post-conciliar liturgical reform carried out by Catholics, which has reintegrated and placed greater value on different aspects dear to the eastern Tradition (e.g., concelebration; we shall not make reference here to the problem of liturgical abuses within the Catholic Church, nor to other newer liturgical norms that represent a stumbling block for many Orthodox Christians). There remain, despite this, different points of view and different practices, of which we mention only certain examples without any pretense of being exhaustive.

---

[39] It should be noted that, while for Catholics "liturgy" indicates the whole of divine worship officiated by the Church, for the Orthodox the term exclusively indicates the Eucharistic celebration. The arguments presented here have the Latin use of the word in mind.

The Missing Synthesis: The Orthodox and the Protestants

1. Sacramental Character

The Orthodox do not accept that three Sacraments (Baptism, Confirmation, and Holy Orders) impress a 'character' onto the one who receives them (see our chapters on the Sacraments, in which we explain this teaching). For the Orthodox, this doctrine was defined by the Council of Trent based on scholastic theological reflection and, they say, it would have been unknown to the Fathers. For this reason (and because of certain additional theological considerations), they deny it. Moreover, concerning Baptism, they do not accept the doctrinal development according to which—as the western Church says—in case of necessity even a non-baptized person can baptize.

2. Eucharistic Consecration

The Orthodox deny the Catholic doctrinal position (developed primarily by the scholastics and defined at Trent) for which the conversion of bread and wine into the Body and Blood of Christ happens at the moment in which the words of Jesus are said. They instead teach that it is the epiclesis (the invocation of the Holy Spirit over the Eucharistic offering) that brings about this conversion. This also entails the fact that, for the Orthodox, the epiclesis consigns grace to the consecrated elements while—according to them—in the Catholic vision there would be greater emphasis on the celebrating minister, who says the words and acts *in Persona Christi*. Thus, the formulas of the Sacraments in the East remain 'deprecative,' while in the west they have become 'indicative.' Moreover, the Orthodox consecrate leavened bread instead of unleavened, retaining that this aspect is (in contrast to Catholics)[40] of fundamental importance.

---

[40] In this regard, it is possible to mention the position of Saint Thomas Aquinas, according to whom, for the validity, it is necessary that the bread that is to be consecrated is made of wheat, while regarding liceity the use or not of unleavened bread depends on the rite, given that even leavened bread can be consecrated. The Latin Church offers unleavened bread, and thus the priest of the Latin Church that consecrates leavened bread does so validly, but illicitly, and by doing so, sins because of disobedience to the Church. The same goes for the eastern priest who consecrates unleavened bread if in his rite fermented bread is used. The Angelic Doctor adds certain reasons of fittingness that it is better to use unleavened bread. The second of these reasons is that the bread is a sign of the body of Christ, which was conceived without corruption (without sin) and leavened bread in Scripture is often a symbol of corruption ("Beware of the leaven that is, the hypocrisy of the Pharisees" [Luke 12:1]). This position is expressed in *ST* III, q. 74, a. 4.

The "Synthetic" Principle

3. Eucharistic Communion and Adoration

The Orthodox deny the practice of Communion under only one species, a practice that was introduced over time and defended by the Council of Trent against the Protestants. The Orthodox always distribute consecrated bread and wine together. Moreover, they do not admit that a lay person may distribute communion, which instead happens in the Catholic Church after the post-conciliar reform. The denial of separating the Eucharistic Species can be one of the reasons for which the Orthodox do not solemnly adore the Sacrament outside of the Mass, a practice that has become very widespread among Catholics in the second millennium. Since the Host alone is displayed and adored, without the consecrated wine, even this separation can appear improper to our Orthodox brothers, along with the reason that, in general, they prefer hiding the Mystery (hence, the iconostasis) rather than displaying it publicly.

4. Matrimony

For the Orthodox, the minister of this Sacrament is the priest: not even deacons can celebrate Matrimony. The theology of the Latin west, which affirms that the spouses are themselves the ministers of the Sacrament, is rooted—according to the Orthodox—in a juridical medieval vision, which considers Matrimony to be a contract, and this is why the ministers of the Sacrament would be the contracting parties. Paradoxically, for the Orthodox the celebration of Matrimony with the rite of coronation of the spouses (which for them represents the essential element of the Sacrament, while for Catholics it is the consent) can happen only once in a lifetime. In fact, even in the case of a successive Matrimony after a death of a spouse, such wedding ceremonies are celebrated with a different rite, which does not include this coronation. We say paradoxically because the Orthodox Church allows a liturgical celebration of marriage even after a divorce and not only after the death of a spouse. This is not conceded in all cases, but only in some, for instance when a divorce happened following infidelity, and—in any case—second and third marriages (never the fourth) are only granted to the innocent spouse. The rite however is different from the true and proper nuptials. Rather than a Sacrament, it is considered a sacramental, even with a penitential character, that nonetheless carries out the function of recognizing a new union on the part of the Orthodox Church, a reason for which the "divorced and remarried" can receive sacramental Communion.[41]

---

[41] As regards this aspect, it must be said that the Orthodox Church has demonstrated less

5. Confirmation

In the Catholic Church the ordinary minister of this Sacrament is the bishop, while the priests can confirm as extraordinary ministers if delegated. On the other hand, for the Orthodox the priest is the ordinary minister of Confirmation, which he carries out in the parish using the Holy *Myron* (chrism) consecrated by the bishop. They retain that to reserve Confirmation for the bishop is a practice introduced in the Middle Ages. Such a practice would have also upset the natural order of administering the Sacraments of Christian initiation—Baptism-Confirmation-Eucharist—given that Confirmation would be postponed until the first occasion in which a bishop could make it to the parish. By contrast, Orthodox priests give all three of these Sacraments to infants.

6. Chants and Sacred Music

While for the Orthodox it is practically impossible to celebrate Worship without singing (even in the Eucharist celebrated "without the people"),[42] using musical instruments in this context is likewise excluded. This is always motivated by the Tradition: even if it is true that in the Scriptures musical instruments are mentioned even in the service of worship, for the Fathers the human voice alone must be used to praise God, as Christ and the Apostles did at the Last Supper (see Mark 14:26). For the Orthodox, the Catholic Church began using instruments through the influence of the Carolingians, and this represents an unjustifiable mixing of sacred and profane music.

3.1.3. Dogmatic and Theological Development

As is understandable, the Orthodox reject virtually all the doctrinal develop-

---

attachment to the Tradition. There are documented historical studies that demonstrate a development of the Orthodox matrimonial practices, due primarily to concessions in response to pressures exercised by civil authorities. The relationship between the Church and state is another point of difference between the Catholic Church (which has in the pope a principle of autonomy and liberty) and the Orthodox Church. However, here such a question must be set aside.

[42] In Orthodox churches, however, there is only one altar, as is now customary in recently constructed Catholic churches. Obviously, the Orthodox did not accept the influence of the Cluniac movement, which starting from the eleventh century has given rise to the multiplication of lateral altars for the personal celebration of the Mass by the monk-priests. In general, the Orthodox prefer concelebration.

The "Synthetic" Principle

ments that occurred in the Catholic world after 1054 as effects of Scholasticism and the councils of the second millennium. Therefore, this does not merely concern the *Filioque* or the Petrine primacy of jurisdiction. In general, not only do the Orthodox not accept many other dogmas—even if many of these are not declared heretical, they are not accepted—but above all they reject the concept of doctrinal development. For the Orthodox, generally speaking, such a development simply does not exist: there is divine Revelation, given once for all, which includes its understanding consigned by the Holy Spirit to the Apostles the day of Pentecost. When the ecumenical Councils (of the first millennium) defined dogmas, they did so—according to the Orthodox perspective—only to contrast the heresies that emerged on occasion, not to reach a greater understanding of Revelation. Thus, the dogmas do not offer any doctrinal progression, representing only the expression of a new cultural mediation, due to the circumstances—namely, the battle against heresy.[43] For Catholics, on the other hand, the dogmas do not just carry out this "negative" function of opposing error, but also a positive function of deepening the understanding of the truth revealed by God once and for all.

Dogmatic development, properly understood,—which can be called "true progress"[44]—is therefore possible, and even necessary. The Holy Spirit guides the Church into ever greater knowledge of the truth (see John 16:13), even if new truths are not added to it.

Consequently, even the profile of theology appears distinct in the two Churches. While for Catholics, theology is a science (see the next chapter), it is a science of faith; for the Orthodox it is rather a spiritual state of high contemplation, which requires tranquility (*esichia*) and lack of passions (*apatia*). Thus, while the Catholic Church more readily recognizes the title of "theologian," in the Orthodox Church such a title is officially recognized only for a few great saints, such as the Apostle Saint John, Saint Gregory of Nazianzus (or, more precisely, Saint Gregory the Theologian, as he is also called by the Third Council of Constantinople) and Saint Symeon the New Theologian. In order to be called a theologian, it is not enough to possess technical knowledge and to master the method proper to a science—even less does one become a theologian by acquiring a doctorate. Theologians are very rare saints who have reached, by grace and a life of prayer and asceticism, a superior state of spiritual life, which also allows for a profoundly sapiential immer-

---

[43] It is striking that this purely "negative" concept of dogma is very similar to that of the Modernist movement, which has little to do with the theology and spirituality of the Orthodox.

[44] See Blessed Antonio Rosmini (d. 1855), *Theosophy*, no. 1525.

The Missing Synthesis: The Orthodox and the Protestants

sion into the divine mysteries. For this reason, while Catholic theologians generally emphasize the possibility of intellectually reflecting on the divine mysteries after they have been revealed—and thus harmonizing faith and reason—the Orthodox by contrast do not seek such a harmonization. While partially availing themselves of classical philosophy in theology, they voluntarily tread the path of apophaticism, or negative theology, which rather than being expressive about God, loves to be silent in contemplation before the ineffable Mystery, affirming what God is not. Along the same lines, Orthodox theologians generally do not emphasize the knowability of God through natural reason.

3.1.4. Dogmas

There are several Catholic dogmas that are clearly rejected by the Orthodox, while others are not accepted. Here again without pretense of exhausting the theme, we can mention a few according to subject matter.

1. The Trinity and the Beatific Vision

In general, the Orthodox preserve the methodological approach of the Greek Fathers in Trinitarian theology, which consists in two main points: radical apophaticism, and the emphasis of the divine unity as a "consequence" of the "Monarchy" of the Father—that is, the emphasis of the fact that the Father is the First Person and, as such, is the principle of unity of the Triad. This second aspect entails an emphasis on the properly Trinitarian character of the Christian God, also appreciated today by many Catholic theologians. As regards their radical apophaticism, on the other hand, they make recourse to the doctrine of divine energies, distinct from the essence. The essence of God is and always remains absolutely unknowable, while the divine energies are the (uncreated) mode in which God manifests and communicates Himself to humanity. This does not only apply to the relationship of humanity with God in this life, but also in the next life. Not even in Heaven do the saved see the divine essence, but they communicate with God through the energies. We can say that the Orthodox maintain apophaticism even for eternal life. By contrast, Catholics, following above all Augustine, have developed a Trinitarian theology that is centered on the unicity of the divine nature, in which the Three should then be contemplated. Thus, the principle of unity is not in the Father, but in the divine essence. Gathering together the teachings of both the Latin and Greek Fathers, like different rivers into a basin, the Scholastics perfect the concept of Person in God. They, moreover, do not know the doc-

The "Synthetic" Principle

trine of energies; thus, the Catholic Church has defined as a dogma of faith[45] that the saved in Heaven directly know, in an intuitive way, the divine essence itself (beatific vision), which is denied to them on earth. For the Orthodox, the same mentality that has produced what is, for them, the error of the *Filioque* (see Chapter Six) is also the source of scant consideration of the Holy Spirit in Catholic theology. This accusation can find some basis, but only up to a certain point. If it is radicalized to the point of saying that the Catholic Church has not curated any reflection and adoration toward the Third Person, then it is wrong. Indeed, many current Catholic theologians—who place great emphasis on the action of the Paraclete in the world, the Church, and the souls of the faithful—offer a remedy to the pneumatological deficiencies of the past.

2. Salvation and Purgatory

Although, strictly speaking, the Catholic Church has not solemnly defined dogmas in the soteriological field, it can be said that she professes some doctrines about salvation as commonly held truths. Among these we can mention vicarious expiation and satisfaction, on which—starting from and basing themselves on the great Doctor Saint Anselm—medieval and modern theologians have widely reflected. The Orthodox clearly do not accept these theological insights of the second millennium and argue for an older patristic version, for which Christ's suffering and death on the Cross, more than being interpreted in light of justice and as a redemption paid by Christ for the human race, represent the defeat of the devil and the destruction of the power of death and sin over the human race. Catholics also teach these concepts, integrating them, however, with those mentioned above, not seeing opposition but complementarity between them. Moreover, the Orthodox do not love to speculate on the "motives of the Incarnation," preferring an ecstatic contemplation of the incarnate Word.

The Catholic soteriological vision is—in the eyes of the Orthodox—marked by a clear juridicism (particularly on account of Saint Anselm), for which, not only does a fault correspond to each sin, but also a penalty to be paid. If such a penalty is not paid on earth, it must be paid after this life before entering Paradise. The doctrine of Purgatory was perfected in the Middle Ages, and it is for this reason that the Orthodox do not recognize it. Although there are some scriptural passages that lend it support, they retain that there is no biblical basis for it. Therefore, they affirm that after death

---

[45] See Benedict XII, *Benedictus Deus* (1336) (*DS* 1000–1002).

The Missing Synthesis: The Orthodox and the Protestants

souls are immediately placed in an intermediate state either of salvation or of damnation, which will then be ratified with the final Judgment. However, they do not accept the idea of a "place/period" of purification of the unsatisfied punishments of committed sins. It is, anyhow, very interesting that they know the practice of the praying for the dead, but this is not for the purpose of "getting them out" of Purgatory sooner, but rather to purify the unatoned sins of those who are saved, or to soften the torments of those who are damned. This leads us to see that even in the faith of the Orthodox there is space for admitting that there remains something to be purified after this life—only that such a purification is done by the Church and not the souls of the individuals.

3. Transubstantiation

For Catholics, transubstantiation is a dogma of the faith (see Chapter Eleven). The Orthodox believe in the Eucharistic presence of Christ and in the transformation of bread and wine into the Body and Blood of the Lord, as the Fathers teach. They hold, however, that there is no need to explain such a change, especially with the help of philosophical categories. They prefer to preserve the incomprehensibility of the Mystery, while firmly believing in it. Thus, they reject the term and theology of transubstantiation, which was developed by Latin Scholasticism and then accepted and defined by the conciliar Magisterium of the second millennium.[46]

4. Mary

The dogmas of the divine Maternity of Mary and of her perpetual Virginity are both professed by the Orthodox, with both being defined in the first millennium. Catholics have, toward the end of the second millennium, defined two other Marian dogmas (see our chapter on Mary). Concerning the Immaculate Conception, the Orthodox generally reject the precise formulation of this doctrine, defined as a dogma by Blessed Pius IX in 1854. Nonetheless, they are not opposed to the possibility of maintaining such a doctrine as a theological opinion. Many believe, however, that affirming the immaculateness of Mary could separate Our Lady from the unity of the people of God—a theme of fundamental importance for Orthodoxy, which

---

[46] It is still possible for the Orthodox to use this term (see, for example, their Synod of Jerusalem held on March 20, 1672, in order to curb the protestantization of the Orthodox Church), but not in a binding way like Catholics.

The "Synthetic" Principle

in any case reserves very high devotion for Mary.[47]

In regard to the dogma of Mary's Assumption into Heaven, defined by Pius XII in 1950, the Orthodox contest two elements: first, its advisability; and second, the foundation in Revelation and the theological interpretation. The Orthodox Churches liturgically celebrate the Dormition of Mary, in which they also include her Ascent into Heaven. Thus, they agree with the essence of the dogma.

However, in conformity with their idea of dogmatic definitions, they say that in 1950 there was no heresy that contested this doctrine—thus it is not apparent why the Pope had to define it (non-advisability). As regards the content, the doctrine of Mary's Dormition among the Orthodox implies, in the first place, that Mary died. This is not always clear in the Catholic interpretation of this dogma, and Mary's death is even denied by some Catholic authors. Second, for Catholics the Assumption is a consequence, above all, of the immaculateness of Mary, while the Orthodox, for understandable reasons, connect it to her divine Maternity.[48]

5. *The Pope*

At a terminological level, Catholics only attribute the term "Pope" to the Bishop of Rome, to emphasize his uniqueness. The Orthodox, however, also use it for other prelates—for example, the Patriarch of Alexandria. Historically, the title reached Rome from Egypt. Moreover, the Patriarch of Constantinople claims the title as the Bishop of the New Rome,[49] a title that

---

[47] It should be said that the Second Council of Nicaea, accepted by the Orthodox, speaks of "our immaculate [*achrántou*] Lady, the Holy Mother of God," without, however, entering into the details of the doctrine. It is, nonetheless, present, at least *in nuce*, in many of the Fathers, even if the specification of it leading up to the proclamation of the dogma passed through a doctrinal development that the Orthodox, as we have seen, do not believe they can accept. Concerning the possible separation that this doctrine would create between Mary and the rest of humanity or the Church, one would also need to note such a distance between the most immaculate Jesus Christ and the Mystical Body of which He is the Head, and the humanity of which He is the new Representative (the Second Adam). But it does not seem that the Orthodox derive such a consequence.

[48] In reality, the dogma of the divine Maternity is also the most fundamental dogma in Mariology for Catholics: it is the root of the other Marian privileges. The difference is only in the connection, direct or indirect, that the Assumption has with her Maternity. For the Orthodox the connection is direct, while for Catholics it is mediated by the immaculateness: Mary ascends into Heaven because She has not sinned (however, She did not sin because She is the Mother of God).

[49] The title appears in canon 3 of the Council of Constantinople, which assigns the second place of honor to Constantinople, after Rome.

The Missing Synthesis: The Orthodox and the Protestants

the "old" Rome never accepted.[50] The Orthodox, on their part, do not accept papal titles like that of the Supreme Pontiff or the Vicar of Christ, which they consider undue, because they express a primacy of the Pope—with respect to the other bishops—that is not merely one of honor.

Obviously, what is more important than titles is doctrine. Catholics believe in the dogma of the primacy of the jurisdiction of the Pope over all the Church, and over all the bishops (see the Council of Florence and Vatican I). This means that he possesses a true authority that is supreme, full, immediate, ordinary, and universal.[51] Not only the faithful and the simple priests, but also the bishops are thus held to obedience to the Pope, who can issue norms that bind the whole Church in all the world. The Orthodox accept the primacy *of honor* of the Bishop of Rome, because this is the See of Peter, first among the Apostles. But they categorically deny juridical primacy as it conflicts with Orthodox ecclesiology, which considers the Churches as *autocephalous*, that is, subject to their own bishop, who is under no obedience to any other bishop. While synodal communion between the Churches is heavily emphasized, it remains the case that no bishop (despite the prominence given to Patriarchs and Metropolitans) can dictate law to another and, even less so, to all other bishops. Difficult cases are confronted in a synodal fashion.

Another Catholic dogma (defined at the First Vatican Council) that the Orthodox resolutely reject is that of the infallibility *in docendo* of the Supreme Pontiff, when he teaches *ex cathedra*. The Orthodox note that there is no trace of this doctrine in the first millennium, and that it began to be developed by scholastics (particularly by the Franciscans) only starting in the thirteenth century. Since the development of doctrine is impossible, then it is also impossible in this case that the Church could reach a greater clarity of vision through time, by meditating on the words of Christ spoken to Peter. The difference between Catholics and the Orthodox here does not concern the concept of doctrinal infallibility, but its applicability (or not) to one individual. The Orthodox believe in infallibility *in docendo*, but they attribute it only to Scripture and to the dogmas defined by the ecumenical councils, because they are an expression of the faith of the whole Church.[52] Catholics

---

[50] New Rome is again attributed to the See of Constantinople twice in canon 28 of the Council of Chalcedon. But both the pontifical legates present at the Council, and then Pope Leo the Great, while approving the conciliar texts as a whole, rejected this canon.

[51] "The bishop of the Roman Church [...] is the head of the college of bishops, the Vicar of Christ, and the pastor of the universal Church on earth. By virtue of his office he possesses supreme, full, immediate, and universal ordinary power in the Church, which he is always able to exercise freely" (*Codex Iuris Canonici*, can. 331).

[52] It may also be noted that the distinction between the "teaching Church" and the "learn-

The "Synthetic" Principle

agree on all of this, but because for them there cannot be an ecumenical council if it is not at least accepted by the Pope—who for them is the head of the College of bishops—they hold that the prerogatives of the whole body of bishops also belong to its head alone. Thus, the faculty that the bishops have of binding the faith of the Christians with irreformable pronouncements also pertains to the head of the bishops, who can then define dogmas infallibly. The fundamental concern of the Orthodox regarding the dogma of papal infallibility is that it may contradict the principle of synodality (collegiality), which is, to say the least, central to Orthodox ecclesiology. If an individual can do everything by himself then it appears that the college is useless or superfluous.

3.1.5. Ecclesiastic Discipline

In general, the Orthodox evaluation of Catholic discipline gives rise to two observations that are not always easily harmonizable: on one hand, the disciplinary practice of the Catholic Church is held to be overly juridical, having appropriated in an overly acritical way the spirit of the *ius romanum* and, as a result, places an undue emphasis on rules, canons, Canon Law, and disciplinary sanctions. On the other hand, it is not unusual for the Orthodox to argue that Catholic discipline is, at least on certain points, overly accommodating, if not lax. Perhaps this second observation is not justified as a description of the way Catholics intend penitence in itself, but only concerns what has been observed from the practice of the last few decades.

Also regarding discipline, we shall limit ourselves to a few notes, which will be expressed in a general way, and thus easily susceptible to imprecision in details. But we are only interested in offering an overview through a few examples.

1. Clerical Celibacy

The practice of the Orthodox Church observes the Tradition of the first millennium in admitting married men to the presbyterate, which is something the Catholic Church has not done in her Latin rites for many centuries,

---

ing Church," or between the Shepherds who teach and the baptized who learn, is greatly mitigated, if not truly non-existent, in Orthodox ecclesiology. The preservation of the faith—learning it, teaching it, and defending it—is a task of all the baptized. Catholics agree with this statement, but they maintain that certain persons (especially bishops) receive from Christ, through the Sacrament of Holy Orders, a special ministry (service!) in this regard, which is nonetheless for the sake of all the Church.

The Missing Synthesis: The Orthodox and the Protestants

exceptions excluded. Bishops in the Orthodox Church, however, are chosen from among the celibates, and thus they are generally chosen from among monks. As with Catholics, Orthodox cannot marry after ordination, but only before. In this sense, both Churches share the practice of not having "priests who can marry"—as is nonetheless often said about the Eastern Church—but rather "married men who can be ordained priests." In fact, the Orthodox have married men who then become priests, but never vice versa. Moreover, men who have married a divorcee or widow, or have been married a second time, are never admitted to Holy Orders. For the Orthodox, in fact, married men that are ordained deacons or priests are supposed to give an irreproachable witness to married life (see 1 Tim 3:2–5, 12).

2. Fasting and Abstinence

The Catholic practice of the Western rites in this regard (in the rules issued and even more in the concrete observance) has become extremely bland in recent times. By contrast, the Orthodox maintain a living sense of penance, and the days of fasting are frequent during the year. Fasting does not only regard meat, but even other things such as fish, eggs, wine, etc. Moreover, they maintain the "Jewish" prescription of the Council of Jerusalem (see Acts 15:20), whereby they abstain from consuming blood. Whereas Catholics have progressively reduced the prescribed days of fasting, the Orthodox maintain the customs of the first millennium, and they thus have four penitential periods during the year.[53]

With respect to the Eucharistic fast as well, the Orthodox condemn the laxity of the Catholic rules,[54] especially those in recent times in which the period of abstaining from food before receiving Eucharistic Communion has been reduced to just one hour. By contrast, the Orthodox maintain the old practice for which whoever wants to receive Communion must abstain from

---

[53] The four penitential periods are: Great Lent, corresponding to the Latin Church's Lent; the Fast of the Apostles, from the end of the octave of Pentecost to the solemnity of Peter and Paul (June 29); the Dormition Fast, the first fifteen days of August; and the Nativity Fast, from November 15 to December 24, namely, the forty days before the solemnity. Moreover, there are penitential days every Wednesday and Friday of the year, the vigils of the great liturgical feasts, and certain other anniversaries.

[54] However, the most recent Pan-Orthodox Synod, held in the week of Pentecost 2016 (June 17–26), has issued a document titled "The Importance of Fasting and Its Observance Today," in which, while confirming the traditional rules, the possibility of "easing the burden of" the traditional norms in this matter, based on the principle of "philanthropic oikonomia," and that of "pastoral care, is left to the discernment of the local Orthodox Churches (no. 8).

any food or drink from the time of waking up in the morning. If the Divine Liturgy is celebrated in the evening, a fast of only six hours can be tolerated. There is no shortage of faithful and very devoted Orthodox who will undergo even one or two full days of fasting before receiving Holy Communion.[55]

3. Religious Orders and Monasticism

In the Catholic Church there are many forms of consecrated life: from monastic orders to orders of knights, to mendicants, to clerical institutes, to the most recent forms. In the rise of new charisms and new forms of consecrated life, Catholics see a series of new "irruptions" of the Holy Spirit in history and thus, albeit with discernment, they approve and encourage them. The Orthodox, on the other hand, despite their partiality for the Holy Spirit, do not have forms of consecrated life other than monasticism, male and female—again remaining anchored to the older practice on this point.[56] It is true that various modalities of monastic life exist (cenobitism, anchoritism, etc.), but we are dealing here with only one form of consecrated life, which is different from that, for example, of the Catholic religious orders, and similar to western monasticism, albeit with its own particularities. The Catholic multiplication of institutes and charisms is critiqued by the Orthodox as an undue fragmentation of the spiritual life of the consecrated. Likewise, a number of elements that the Catholics have inserted into consecrated life are criticized; elements that for the Orthodox are of worldly origin and date back to the medieval and modern eras. The change that it is most under attack is the one concerning the Catholic women's orders and institutes, in which an emotive spirituality has progressively been added, which thinks of Christ as the mystical Groom of the religious sister. This creates an asymmetry between the consecrated life of women and men, given that a consecrated male cannot structure his own spiritual life in the same perspective. Quite a few Orthodox state that the numerical proportions have been affected by it. In the Catholic Church, in fact, the number of nuns is much higher than the number of male religious.

---

[55] This is in agreement with the suggestion of the Neo-Greek theologian Nicodemus the Hagiorite (d. 1809) in his *Commentary on the 13th Canon of the Sixth Ecumenical Council*: "... fasting before partaking of Communion is not decreed by the divine Canons. Nevertheless, those who are able to fast even a whole week before it, are doing the right thing" (in *The Rudder [Pedalion] of the Metaphorical Ship of the One Holy Catholic and Apostolic Church of the Orthodox Christians*, trans. D. Cummings [Chicago: The Orthodox Christian Educational Society, 1957], 307).

[56] See Saint John Paul II, *Orientale Lumen* (1995), §9.

3.1.6. Spiritual Life and Devotion

The attitude of adoring contemplation is the attitude that the devoted Orthodox believer seeks with fervor. It is based on the firm conviction that God in Himself is unknowable, and we can only access what He, by revealing Himself, wants to share with us. The effort of the human being, his or her initiative and capacity, is absolutely secondary.[57] This is why Orthodox Liturgy, as is true for the eastern liturgies in general, is very rich with words and symbols, precisely to signify that nothing that human beings can express can ever exhaust the greatness of the Omnipotent God. Since there is naturally much in common in the spiritual approaches of the Orthodox and Catholics, there are also differences, of which we will recall only a few.

1. Meditation

Especially since the era of the Counter-Reformation (e.g., Saint Ignatius of Loyola), in the Catholic Church it is common to pray with "discursive" meditation, in which the mind (the imagination and the other faculties) is actively employed in the effort to understand one's relationship with God. The Orthodox, on the other hand, greatly prefer "contemplative" prayer, consisting in the denial of such discursive effort, and to remain in a silent love before the Mystery. In reality, in the Catholic environment, both aspects are sought,[58] while our Orthodox brothers and sisters emphasize the second at the expense of the first. The devotion to silent contemplation has led the Orthodox to value highly the Hesychast prayer, also called the "Jesus Prayer" or "prayer of the heart," consisting in the unceasing repetition of a Christological invocation, which favors contemplative prayer, and which does not focus on images or sentiments, as does, by contrast, "discursive" meditation. The Orthodox often recite this prayer with the help of a "rope," generally made of knotted wool,

---

[57] It is for this reason that Orthodox spirituality is more focused on the Resurrection of Christ than on his Passion. Moreover, it does not love to cultivate a spirituality of the Passion, a spirituality that is oblative and concerns vicarious expiation. In these forms, the Orthodox see the risk of wanting to substitute for Christ, or almost hold that his Sacrifice was not sufficient, which is one reason why our sacrifice would need to be added in order to save sinners. In general, in Orthodox spirituality, one prays more for one's own sins than for those of others, and this is so, certainly not out of egoism, but for a particular interpretation of humility, namely, the smallness of the human being before God. This is a particular point where, coming from completely different perspectives, the Protestants and Orthodox find points of convergence.

[58] See Saint John of the Cross, *Subida del Monte Carmelo* 14.7.

which can appear similar to Catholic rosary beads. In reality, while with the Rosary, Catholics seek the meditative and imaginative prayer of the "Christological mysteries" (the important events in the earthly life of Christ), the Orthodox unceasingly repeat the Christological formula,[59] seeking to focus the mind on the words of the prayer and not on images, which according to them—being inevitably subjective—can easily deceive the soul.

2. Devotion

The Orthodox do not practice—and even hold to be harmful—various devotional forms developed in the Catholic Church in the second millennium. Among these we can recall the devotion to the Holy Wounds of Jesus and the Stations of the Cross, but also the crèche (nativity scene) and devotion to the Baby Jesus in general, as well as the spirituality focused on the Sacred Heart of Jesus. All these practices are considered sentimental—an element that the Orthodox always view with suspicion, seeking a more "objective" devotion. In regard to the devotion to the Sacred Heart, they also advance doubts of a dogmatic nature. Perhaps having in mind the Christological letters of Saint Cyril of Alexandria to Nestorius, the Orthodox are suspicious of any form of devotion that might "isolate" a part of Christ—in this case, the Sacred Heart—from the whole of the Mystery of Jesus. To the Orthodox it can seem that this approach leads to two distinct acts of adoration: one to the humanity of the Lord and another to His divinity, something that is rejected by Saint Cyril himself.[60] Moreover, the historical origin of the development of the devo-

---

[59] "Lord Jesus Christ, Son of God, have mercy on me a sinner": a Christological version of the prayer of the tax collector in Luke 18:13.

[60] Saint Cyril of Alexandria writes in his *Third Letter to Nestorius*: "We adore one Son and Lord Jesus Christ. We do not set up a division and distinguish the man and God [. . .]. But we refuse to say of Christ, 'Because of the one who clothed Him with flesh, I worship the one clothed; because of the invisible, I adore the invisible.' It is abhorrent to say this also, 'The one assumed, is called God as the one assuming Him.' Whoever says these things, severs Him again into two christs, and in turn sets the humanity and divinity apart also. Whoever says these things admittedly denies the union, according to which one is worshipped together with the other, not as one in another. Indeed God is not associated with another, but one Christ Jesus is meant, the only begotten Son, Who is revered along with His flesh by one act of adoration" (in *FCNT*, vol. 76, trans. John I. McEnerney [Washington, DC: CUA Press, 1987], 85 [with our corrections]). In the list of the 12 anathemas that concludes the Letter, no. 8 confirms that: "If anyone ventures to say that the assumed man must be worshipped and glorified along with God the Word, and bears the same title with Him, as the one in the other, for the "with" always being added will force (one) to understand this, and does not rather honor Emmanuel with one worship and apply one glory to Him, according as the Word was

tion to the Sacred Heart is based in the seventeenth century, with the private revelations to Saint Margaret Mary Alacoque (d. 1690): thus, it concerns yet another innovation that occurred in the second millennium. Obviously, similar devotions to Mary are also rejected (e.g., the Immaculate Heart).

3. Sacred Images

Sacred images are very important in liturgical and spiritual life, both for Catholics and for the Orthodox. Here too, however, there are some differences. The Orthodox do not make use of statues but rather icons, namely, two-dimensional images, usually painted on wooden boards, but also frescoed or mosaiced on the walls of the churches. Three-dimensionality is admitted in the bas-relief, usually in wood, but it retains mostly a two-dimensional image—whereas a statue is clearly three-dimensional in the fullest sense. Even here, the origin of the custom is, above all, historical; it coincides with the most frequent practice of the first millennium. But the Orthodox authors go further and furnish justifications in the fields of spiritual theology and the theology of icons. The icon would avoid, better than the statue, the risk of paganizing the Christian faith; the pagans, in fact, would represent their own gods in the form of statues. In the second place, the icon does a better job than the statue of removing the risk of imitating reality, namely, the risk of naturalism; it better preserves the supernatural character of what is represented and impels the soul beyond the natural world. Moreover, the icon is a powerful aid in contemplation, but it discourages sentimentalist and popular devotionalism, which instead—according to the Orthodox—is stimulated by the statues of a religious character, which could favor phenomena of superstition even to the extreme of magic. With its tri-dimensionality, the statue would give the illusion of finding oneself before the person represented (Christ, Mary, an angel, a saint), drawing attention to the object rather than its prototype. The bi-dimensionality of the icon, on the other hand, clearly manifests its character as a pure image, while referring as such to the model (or prototype) that is in Heaven. Thus, the statue could paradoxically end up attracting attention to itself, while the icon must refer to another.[61]

---

made flesh, let him be anathema" (DS 259).

[61] It is noteworthy that westerners have also developed two-dimensional representation and, among other things, have introduced the art of stained glass that is not present in Orthodox tradition, who possess a rich iconographic presence on the walls and columns of their churches, and do not need to decorate their windows too. Western stained glass also has a beautiful theology behind it, about which one can read the brief but significant insights of Benedict XVI in his *Homily at the Mass*

The "Synthetic" Principle

4. New Spiritual Movements

Being that they are "new," the Orthodox have not developed spiritual movements like Protestant Pentecostalism or the corresponding Charismatic Renewal that is present today in the Catholic Church. The charismatic movements did not take off in the Orthodox Church—despite some attempts that failed miserably. The great flourishing of new movements and new spiritualities that have happened in the Catholic Church since the middle of the twentieth century is not present and is certainly not seen in a good light by our Orthodox brothers and sisters.

3.1.7. Concluding Reflections

Many contemporary Catholics believe, at a basic level, that full communion with Orthodoxy is easy to accomplish: it would be sufficient to agree on the *Filioque* and the primacy of the Pope's jurisdiction, because the rest would already be the same. There is no shortage of ecumenical and dogmatic theologians who even suggest that the Catholic Church can and should give up the above-mentioned dogmas, in order to favor full communion with the Orthodox Churches. This of course is not a viable path to follow, because these are defined dogmas of the faith, and thus they will forever be a part of the deposit of faith, and we Catholics believe them by divine and Catholic faith. Thus, renouncing them is impossible. Their interpretation can, and must, be worked on, even if this should be understood correctly as a hermeneutic, and not as a deconstruction and dissolution of the doctrine.

The preceding pages have nonetheless shown us something else; namely, that the differences with our Orthodox brothers and sisters are not limited to the *Filioque* and to the Petrine primacy. There are many differences; some are secondary and surmountable, but others are of great importance. More than anything else, however, is that the fundamental approach is different. For what regards the perspective of our current treatment, we must note that the Orthodox—even if it is clear that they are much "closer" than the Protestants—have developed a thought and a practice that does not always respect the fundamental principle of *et-et*. If we had the possibility of expanding into a more general treatment, we could show that the theological thought has actually been influenced significantly by historical motives. However, such a treatment must unfortunately remain undeveloped. Sticking briefly to what we have expressed above, we note that the fundamental theological thought

---

celebrated in the Cathedral of New York, April 19, 2008.

The Missing Synthesis: The Orthodox and the Protestants

of the Orthodox presents different points of strength, but also a number of relevant weaknesses.

The most important point of strength appears to be the love and solid adherence to the Tradition. We Catholics today can benefit greatly from this example. To many of us, it can only be good to have brothers and sisters that constantly recall the principle of apostolic and patristic Tradition. The Tradition—by contrast to what some in the Catholic Church think today—is not the enemy of the present and the future, but it is the only force that can lead us through them in the right way. We must sincerely thank our Orthodox brothers and sisters for the witness of faith and of love for the Sacred Tradition that they have offered us for a thousand years now.

However, here we also encounter the great weakness of Orthodox thought: the concept of Tradition that our brothers and sisters maintain is not sufficient. And this is not because it does not respect the principle of *et-et*. Certainly, the Orthodox venerate *both* Scripture *and* Tradition (*et-et*)—in this way their thought is complete. But they do not manage to sufficiently complete their own interpretation of the concept of Tradition, remaining bound to a purely conservative aspect. Tradition is only what it was, and not also what it is and what it will be. We could say: Tradition is only the Apostolic Tradition that is found in the Fathers, but it is not also the process of transmission, the *Traditio vivens*, which in each era guards the deposit that was given once for all, precisely by incessantly expressing all its riches, both those already discovered, and those that, from time to time, the Holy Spirit helps the Church to uncover. For the Orthodox, the Holy Spirit has nothing more to say, because He has said everything with Revelation, and it is in its complete interpretation as it was already given to the Apostles at Pentecost. Therefore, all we need to do is preserve it. But can one only preserve the Word of God in this way? Is it not also perhaps true, as a famous author of the 1900's made known, that the manna cannot be preserved, otherwise it rots (see Ex 16:20), and instead it needs to be gathered fresh each day? And note well: this does not mean that something else is gathered, or that there is an increase in the deposit of faith, or that the Holy Spirit adds new truths. It is not this at all! It is always manna that is gathered, always the same food, not something else. But it needs to be gathered each day, in each age. Thus, Revelation is one and concluded: The Holy Spirit adds nothing and takes nothing away from the Word of Christ (see Rev 22:18–19). But this Word is a treasure so great that no one can pretend to put it in a glass case, in a museum—immortalized, certainly, but also inert. The deposit of faith is, rather, a chest that contains precious treasures; it is a perfect dowry, which lacks nothing and thus has no need of addition; it is a complete and harmonious whole, and thus nothing

The "Synthetic" Principle

can be taken from it. However, such a treasure is so great that we need time and many capable people in order to extract all of its content from the chest, and to also admire each individual piece in all its details. The treasure does not change, but it is our "proficiency" in it, our capacity to understand it and to better express it with time that changes, like the good wine (see John 2:10). Put briefly, we disciples of the kingdom must be wise scribes, who know how to draw things both new and old from the treasure (Matt 13:52).

Doctrinal progress, affirmed and practiced by Catholics, and clearly rejected by the Orthodox, is the true point of separation[62]; it is at the root of the Orthodox rejection of the *Filioque*, of the Petrine juridical primacy, and of other dogmas and practices that mark the differences between the Churches. The emphasis on the first millennium on the part of the Orthodox, and the rejection of everything that came after 1054, seems to be vitiated by a pique of ecclesiastical politics, which was later structured as theological thought as well. We say this with respect, only for love of the truth. The same honesty that led us to open the chapter by noting a few existential (not essential) defects in the Catholic Church of today, invites us to ask our Orthodox brothers and sisters to be able to be self-critical with respect to the way their theological thought has been conditioned by ecclesiastical (and civil!) politics. Pitting the first and second millennium against one another is at its core a senseless thing to do. It is also difficult to justify the many developments that have in fact occurred in the Orthodox practice and doctrine, even though the principle of development is denied. If *transubstantiatio* can be rejected because it was created by the theologians of the second millennium, how does one then justify the Nicene *homoousios*? If *homoousios* was permissible, then so is *transubstantiatio*. Moreover, the fact that the former term is the fruit of an eastern council, while the second is that of a western council, only moves the problem from the historical perspective (first and second millennium) to the geographical one (East or West). However, such a mode of proceeding is not truly theological but—precisely—(geo)political.

In conclusion, the ecumenical path between Catholics and Orthodox—something necessary to which the Holy Spirit calls us—cannot be serious, and

---

[62] Naturally, we defend doctrinal development here as it is healthily understood by the ecclesial Tradition, not as it is interpreted and practiced by certain theologians, who see in it the justification for carrying out a substantial change of the doctrine of the faith and of morals. The attitude of our Orthodox brothers and sisters works as a cure-all against such a misunderstanding of doctrinal development. The Orthodox can always help us understand progress in the true and proper sense, as it was incisively described by Pope Saint Stephen I in the year 256 in the *Epistola ad Cyprianum* 1: "*Nihil innovetur nisi quod traditum est*" ("Let nothing be introduced except what is already handed down": DS 110).

above all, will not be possible if the doctrinal questions are not addressed with clarity. In the meantime, let us proceed securely in our collaboration, esteem, and *affective* communion with the Orthodox. However, *effective* communion is based on truth and on faith. Neither the Orthodox nor the Catholics will be able to call themselves satisfied with a communion that is the fruit of agreements of ecclesiastical politics. The Holy Spirit must instead lead us, together, to the whole truth. This is not obtained by offering discounts on doctrine or annulling/relativizing dogmas. Rather, it is possible only by truly opening our mind and heart to Christ, who is the Truth in Person. The unity of the Church is a supernatural endowment guaranteed by the Head of the Church, Jesus. For this reason, even the visible unity of Christians is not a fruit of political agreement between "sister Churches,"[63] but rather a unity created by the Spirit of Christ, with Whom we seek to collaborate by remaining in Jesus, that is, in the Truth. Since the Truth is incarnate, it is reasonable to affirm that the "structural" principle of Christ Himself, namely, the *et-et*, must also be the principle around which the discussions on these particular points revolves.[64]

3.2. Protestants

As mentioned above, if our task were that of proposing an accurate description of Protestant theology, we should first distinguish the different groups, which here for brevity we are forced to consider under the same title. That is, we would have to distinguish Lutheranism from Zwinglianism, and from Calvinism, and all of them in turn from Anglicanism. And this is just to refer to the original large traditions of Protestantism. Secondly, we would have to consider the peculiarities of the Protestant denominations and groups that have been detached from the three principle branches: the Waldensians,[65] Mennonites, Baptists, Quakers, Methodists, Swedenborgians, the Darbyans (or Plymouth Brethren), the Mormons, Irvingists, the Adventists, the Pentecostals, etc.

---

[63] Directions on the appropriate or improper use of this expression are put forth by the text of the Congregation for the Doctrine of the Faith, *Note on the Expression "Sister Churches,"* June 30, 2000.

[64] Rereading the previous pages, the reader will also be able to recognize unaided the numerous violations of the *et-et* in the doctrine and practice of the Orthodox: either the first or the second millennium; either the Fathers or the scholastics; either the infallibility of the pope or the whole episcopal College; either the Petrine or the Episcopal authority; etc.

[65] The original Waldensian movement was born well before the modern era, making its head Peter Waldo of Lyon (d. ca. 1206). But in 1532, at the Synod of Chanforan, the Waldensians recognized themselves as an expression of Protestantism, uniting themselves to the Protestants of Geneva.

The "Synthetic" Principle

Obviously, we are not taking on the task of presenting the various differences between the existing forms of Protestantism. More modestly, we want to outline certain fundamental traits of the doctrine that—also with some divergences—is generally accepted by the Protestant world, and which thus distinguishes it from the Catholic Church. Even in this case, this will allow us to note the great challenge presented by Protestantism against the principle of the Incarnation that is at the basis of Catholicism, namely, the principle of *et-et* (both/and).

3.2.1. Fundamental Principles

Among the fundamental principles of Protestantism are that of *sola Scriptura* ("Scripture alone") and *sola fide* (justification happens "by faith alone"). The first coincides with a strong Biblicism, which excludes Tradition and the Magisterium; the second coincides with the celebrated Lutheran thesis of justification by faith alone without works.

1. Biblicism

A common point for all Protestants is the denial of the apostolic Tradition as a source of knowledge of divine Revelation. Retrieving a position that was already taken by John Wycliffe (d. 1384) and Jan Hus (d. 1415), Martin Luther (d. 1546) proclaims the principle of *sola Scriptura*, that in the Bible alone is found the Word of God; therefore, it is not found in the Tradition. Protestant Biblicism thus affirms that the Bible is the unique norm of truth, and the unique source of the faith and, consequently, theology. The Bible does not require authorized interpreters, neither the Pope—who is judged by Scripture—nor the councils, nor the Fathers of the Church. It is interpreted by itself. The Bible judges everyone and everything, without being judged by anyone (*norma normans, non normata*). When Luther says that the Bible is interpreted by itself, he means, in fact, that the individual reader interprets it. The reader of Scripture does not need, in order to understand it, the Tradition, the Magisterium, the Fathers, and the Doctors of the Church. It is enough that the person reading it has faith in the Word of God, and he or she will understand the content of the Sacred Page. If one observes what this principle—called the "free examination" of the Scriptures—has concretely produced, it will be noted that the internal fractioning within the Protestant world is a consistent application of it. If, in fact, each person personally interprets the Bible, he or she will believe to be true, and will profess, exactly what *he or she* has claimed to understand. And this is why, from the begin-

The Missing Synthesis: The Orthodox and the Protestants

ning, Protestantism broke apart into hundreds of different denominations, all obviously convinced to be the ones that correctly interpret the Word of God. For the purpose of condemning this attitude, the following Latin couplet was coined early on: *"Hic liber est in quo ponit sua dogmata quisque / Invenit et pariter dogmata quisque sua"* ("This [the Bible] is the book in which each seeks his own doctrine—and in fact each finds it in there").

Luther and the Protestants in general thus reject the Tradition both as a source (apostolic Tradition), and as an instrument for the preservation and interpretation of Revelation (*Traditio vivens*, ecclesiastical Magisterium).[66] And for Luther, Tradition is an evil. He had great veneration for the earliest times of the Church—it could be called an "archeologist" tendency—for which the Tradition does not appear, in his eyes, as a positive element of preserving what is original, or a better understanding of the same, but rather a departure from the purity of its origins, and thus a betrayal.

It is true that the rigidity of Luther concerning *sola Scriptura* was subsequently mitigated by several Protestant theologians. Already Georg Calixtus (d. 1656)[67] proposed a reconciliation concerning the theme of the sources with his theory of the *consensus quinquesaecularis*, according to which the Church and the faith are based on the Bible and on the Tradition of the first five centuries. The necessity of recognizing some role for the ecclesiastical Tradition comes from the simple observation of the fact that the very canon of Scripture (the list of its recognized books) is not found in the Bible and is known only through the ecclesial Tradition. However, Luther felt himself free to personally interpret even the canon; in fact, since the Letter of James was not acceptable to him, he called it an "epistle of straw," moving it to the back of the Protestant Bible along with other New Testament books, while expelling some Old Testament books from the canon. Many Protestant the-

---

[66] A problem that is not possible to deal with here concerns the acceptance of the first ecumenical councils, which defined dogmas concerning Christ and the Trinity, on which—along with different interpretations between them—the first reformers converged. Luther, for example, rejects the term *homoousios* defined by the Council of Nicaea (325), but in substance he recognizes its content: the divinity of Jesus Christ. The ex-Augustinian brother proposed a Christology based, all things considered, on the Chalcedonian dogma. Naturally he did not recognize the true and proper authority of the ecumenical councils, though at least concerning the central dogmas of the faith, albeit with some errors, he felt in tune with the teaching proposed there. We could draw from this that for him a correct interpretation of Scripture is possible on the part of the Church and not only the individual. However, the theme is complex and reflection on this should be postponed to another occasion.

[67] See his *De veritate unicae religionis christianae et autoritate antiquitatis ecclesiasticae dissertationes*.

The "Synthetic" Principle

ologians, nonetheless, today recognize that the Church and her preaching already existed before the redaction of the New Testament, which is in fact their fruit. Thus, the Bible itself comes from the Tradition! However, frequently the Protestants that admit some role for Tradition limit its influence only to the apostolic era. There was an apostolic Tradition, in its time, from which the Bible also came, but such a Tradition today is not in the hands of anyone; it remains only in the past. Therefore, even an ecclesiastical Magisterium, which had the pretense of interpreting the Bible in an authoritative manner, would have no reason for being. The "dogma" of the Biblical reader's personal inspiration thus endures almost unchanged.

2. Justification

Luther has a pessimistic vision of fallen humanity: original sin (see Chapter Three) has left in humanity such consequences that the latter cannot do anything that does not represent sin. Because of the wound created by the sin of Adam, human beings find themselves in such a condition that whatever they do, even the good, is always sinful. The human being is thus completely excluded from grace, cannot cooperate with it and, thus, cannot cooperate in his or her own salvation. The only attitude that is possible for the sake of being saved is total passivity; and the only possible co-*operation* with grace consists, paradoxically, in a non-*operation*, for which grace must do everything and we nothing. In fact, whatever we did would be a sin that would be an obstacle to grace. Thus, salvation happens *sola gratia* (by divine grace alone), and without human cooperation. For Luther, this absolute passivity coincides with faith: the person believes in what God has told him or her, namely, that Christ takes away our sins and gives to us His justice. The revelation of the remission of sins is the most central dogma believed by the faith, its true content. Again, the faith is not the fruit of human effort, or of human reasoning. For Luther, reason is even an enemy of faith, its greatest obstacle, to the point that in the (hypothetical) moment in which human reason was completely annulled one would have the fullness of faith. Lutheran pessimism reaches such a point as to hold that even in faith the person does not contribute anything—there is no cooperation. Even regarding the faith, the person is not a positive agent; it is God that makes the gift, and it is also He who is active in the gift. It could be said that it is God that "believes" in the faith of the human being, giving faith to the will of the latter, without it being an act imputable to him or her. Thus, the faith is entirely the work of God, and even here the human being does not carry out any work for his or her own salvation, not even to believe.

Being essentially negative, the faith also has in itself a pessimistic dimen-

The Missing Synthesis: The Orthodox and the Protestants

sion. The person of faith is desperate on account of his or her own irresolvable condition as a sinner, and allows himself or herself to fall passively in trust of the promises of God, passively accepting the imputation of the justice of Christ ("fiducial" faith). To believe does not mean to accept the dogmas, but to subjectively hold that they apply to me. To believe is to believe that divine justification has reached me.[68] It is in this way that justification "*sola fide*" ("by faith alone") and not by works—the cornerstone of Protestant doctrine—occurs. Nothing that a human person can do, none of a person's works, can justify him or her; faith alone can do it, precisely because it is not a human work.

In the background of Lutheran thinking there is a sort of horror for any possible form of "Phariseeism": that is, for the pretense that a human being can in any way claim rights or merits before God. Rather, the human being, according to the reformer, is absolutely bare and poor. Nothing good or valid is his or her own; all he or she possesses is sin. That is the work of the human being, which is always a work "of the flesh." For Luther, any pretense of claiming the goodness of an action or its merit are the attempt to "possess" one's own salvation. By contrast, he proposes *sola gratia*: the human being does not have and cannot have anything; he or she can only be saved in an absolutely passive way. From this perspective also derives the particular interpretation of how justification comes about in the human being, namely, in what such justification consists: it is the famous thesis of "forensic" justification.

For Luther, the justification of the sinner is similar to the absolution that a judge gives in a tribunal (in Latin *forum*, from which "forensic" derives). When the judge hands out the sentence of acquittal, the defendant is considered to be innocent. It does not matter whether or not he is actually guilty, since the judge has declared him innocent, or just. This is how Luther describes the justification of faith: God declares us just, imputing to us the merits of Christ (the only real merits of a human being), even if we really are guilty and remain so. A peculiarity of the Protestant perspective is that redemption only works verbally but not efficaciously. We are *declared* just, but we do not become so in reality. This is consistent with Lutheran thought: if we were to

---

[68] This subjective aspect, which we could generously define as "relational" or "personalistic," is evidenced in other parts of Lutheran thought. For example, with respect to the doctrine of the Real Presence of Christ in the Host, Luther accepts such a Presence only *in usu* or, namely, at the moment in which *I* receive Communion, but not before or after. This is because Luther: (1) does not think according to scholastic ontology, but rather according to nominalism; and (2) he says that Jesus is there "for you." Thus, an ontological transubstantiation would not make sense, nor would it make sense to think that Jesus is in the Host in moments that are different from this presence *in* it *for you* (consubstantiation: see the chapter on the Eucharist).

The "Synthetic" Principle

also become just, then we would possess justice in ourselves, but Luther has established that the human being cannot possess anything good. Note, then, that justice must remain extrinsic, externally imputed to the human being, but not given to him or her in a real way. God says that we are just—and we believe it through faith—but we are not truly just. It is difficult to understand how this can be harmonized with the passage of 1 John 3:1–2.[69] In any case, Luther summarizes his perspective through the famous formula according to which the human being is *"simul justus et peccator"* ("just and sinner at the same time"). This formula is of paramount importance not only for understanding the Protestant doctrine of justification but in order to understand the Protestant mental universe as a whole.

To sustain that the human being is *simul justus et peccator*—for what pertains to the first aspect (the doctrine of justification)—means that sins are never truly taken away. They remain forever, both original sin with the concupiscence that derives from it, and personal sins always remain in the human being, even if justification has reached the person. Sin remains, but God does not apply its effects, that is, the offense that is directed at the Lord and the consequent situation of hostility toward Him. Thus, the sin remains, but its effects are not imputed. Justification is the non-imputation. The sins will be eliminated only on the Day of Judgment.

For what concerns the second aspect, the formula *simul justus et peccator* reveals, above all, the nominalist and, thus, anti-ontological mentality of Luther. There is no objective destruction of sin, no actual and effective renewal of the human being. There is only the *speaking* of the word of absolution or acquittal, but such a word does not truly absolve; it does not liberate in reality. Moreover, this fundamental formula also discloses the anti-logical attitude of Luther. It is not surprising, given that he holds that reason is an obstacle in the sphere of faith (for this reason, such logical consistency between the two assumptions is astonishing!). The anti-logical attitude is

---

[69] In fact, the biblical text affirms: "See what love the Father has bestowed on us that we may be called the children of God. Yet so we are. The reason the world does not know us is that it did not know him. Beloved, we are God's children now . . ." Thus, we are not merely called just (children of God), but we really are just, and we are so now in this life. It is not by accident that the Council of Trent makes reference to this biblical text against the Lutheran doctrine of justification (see *Decretum de iustificatione*, January 13, 1547, ch. 7 [DS 1529]). The First Letter of John was recognized also by Luther, who had by contrast tried to exclude some New Testament books from the biblical canon, finally deciding to put them at the end of it. Luther excluded some Old Testament books calling them "apocryphal," i.e. non-inspired. Some recent Protestant Bibles, however, include these books in an appendix.

The Missing Synthesis: The Orthodox and the Protestants

revealed by the fact that the formula *simul justus et peccator* patently violates the principle of non-contradiction, for which "it is impossible that the same attribute, at the same time, pertain and not pertain to the same object and under the same aspect."[70] Thus, while under a superficial glance the principle of *simul justus et peccator* could appear as an application of the *et-et*, in reality, it clearly contradicts it. The principle of *et-et*, in fact, puts together distinct, and not reciprocally contradictory, elements. The principle does not violate human reason, but helps it to be elevated and perfected. *Simul justus et peccator*, on the other hand, is a consequence of the Protestant *aut-aut* (either/or), which juxtaposes humanity and God. Since salvation is *either* a human work *or* a divine one, a choice needs to be made. Naturally, God, and not the human being, will be chosen as the Author of salvation. This implies the exclusion of the human being and his or her cooperation, since nothing in the human being can be good. For this reason a theology must be devised that in some way affirms justification without it being considered a good that the human being truly receives. Thus the formula *simul justus et peccator*.

The justice that we receive is, according to Luther, extrinsic. It is the justice of Christ, and it only belongs to Him and never to us. The scholastic idea of grace, understood as a supernatural *habitus* that is steadily present in the human being, is entirely scorned by the German reformer. The theology of grace as a *habitus* would be a way of making it a human reality, something that we handle, of which we are the owners. Justification, however, does not consist in this but rather in the fact that, by watching us, God sees in us (because he wants to see) not ourselves, but rather Christ. Again, this is not a real fact; we are not Christ, nor are we like Christ. It is the mercy of God who wants to see us in this way, even if we are not really this way. For this reason, God imputes on us the justice of Christ and considers us as if we had satisfied divine justice for our sins, while only Christ satisfies it. We never do. Justification is a shining mantle (the justice of Christ) mercifully spread over soiled ragamuffins. The mantle certainly does not clean them, but covers their filth, even if below they remain the same.

3.2.2. Dogmas

1. Predestination

Concerning predestination, a difficult point of Christian doctrine, the modern reformers latched on to theological positions that were already known and

---

[70] Aristotle, *Metaphysics* 4.3.1005 b 19–20.

The "Synthetic" Principle

condemned by the Catholic Church.[71] To understand the Protestant perspective concerning predestination, one must start from the conviction of Luther for whom, after sin, the human being no longer possesses freedom. The German reformer wrote a work entitled *De servo arbitrio* (*On the Bondage of the Will*), to oppose the idea that the sinner still maintains a free will, that is, the possibility of choosing—in particular, of choosing the good. Rather, in Luther's judgment, any act that the human being carries out, either good or bad, is carried out in a necessary way, either because of the divine decree of grace and mercy toward those predestined for salvation, or because of the decree of judgment and condemnation for the damned. This is consistent with the fundamental perspective on justification that does not allow any human merit. On account of this, the human being cannot do anything good that assures him or her of Heaven, but also nothing evil that forces him or her to hell. Here again there is an *aut-aut*: the cause of predestination is either the human being or God. Naturally, Luther chooses God. Only God is the arbiter of the destiny of human beings; God decides the individuals' condemnation or salvation. In the case of the just, He wills it and makes it happen that they desire and carry out the good; in the case of the damned, God acts so that they desire and carry out evil. Thus, this does not merely involve divine permission, but a true disposition on the part of God.[72] Luther maintains that God also arranges for the damnation of a certain number of people in order to manifest

---

[71] In particular, the thesis of Gottschalk of Orbais (d. 867) condemned at the Council of Quiercy in May of 853 (DS 621–624); moreover, those of Florus of Lyon (d. 860), Prudentius of Troyes (d. 861), Remigius of Lyon (d. 875), and John Scotus Eriugena (d. 877), condemned by the Fourth Council of Valence of January 8, 855 (DS 625–633). Still, the error of Hus (which he took from Wycliffe), condemned at the Council of Constance on February 22, 1418, *Errores Joannis Hus*, nos. 3, 5, and 6 (DS 1203, 1205–1206).

[72] Luther does not accept the classical theological distinction between an antecedent and consequent will of God. This classical doctrine is illustrated by Saint John Damascene (d. 749), *De fide orthodoxa* 2.29: "Also one must bear in mind that God's original wish was that all should be saved and come to His Kingdom. For it was not for punishment that He formed us but to share in His goodness, inasmuch as He is a good God. But inasmuch as He is a just God, His will is that sinners should suffer punishment. The first then is called God's antecedent will and pleasure, and springs from Himself, while the second is called God's consequent will and permission, and has its origin in us. And the latter is two-fold; one part dealing with matters of guidance and training, and having in view our salvation, and the other being hopeless and leading to our utter punishment, as we said above. And this is the case with actions that are not left in our hands. But of actions that are in our hands the good ones depend on His antecedent goodwill and pleasure, while the wicked ones depend neither on His antecedent nor on His consequent will, but are a concession to free-will" (in *NPNF*, Second Series, vol. 9, trans. E.W. Watson and L. Pullan [Peabody, MA: Hendrickson Publishers, Inc., 1994], 42).

The Missing Synthesis: The Orthodox and the Protestants

the greatness of His wrath in punishing sin. Huldrych Zwingli (d. 1531) has a similar opinion, and he writes that those who carry out evil "are destined by divine Providence [which for him is synonymous with predestination] to eternal condemnation in order to serve as an example of his justice."[73]

John Calvin (d. 1564) maintains and even radicalizes the perspective that God is responsible not only for the absolute predestination of some toward Heaven and of others toward Hell, but also for the respective good or evil carried out by the different individuals. He writes:

> We call predestination God's eternal decree, by which He determined with Himself what He willed to become of each man. For all are not created in equal condition; rather, eternal life is fore-ordained for some, eternal damnation for others. Therefore, as any man has been created to one or the other of these ends, we speak of him as predestined to life or death.[74]

Naturally, Calvin knows the teaching of Saint Paul for whom God "wills everyone to be saved" (1 Tim 2:4), but resolves the aporia by affirming that God wants the salvation of all only through an external call, which is, however, inoperable and ineffective for those who are not predestined; while for the elect there is the true call, the inner one, which is effective, and even necessary and irresistible.

2. Redemption

The Protestant soteriological doctrine is also in harmony with the fundamen-

---

[73] Huldrych Zwingli, *De Providentia* (1530) 4.112.

[74] John Calvin, *Institutiones christianae religionis* (1536) 3.21.5 (in *The Institutes of the Christian Religion*, vol. 2, trans. Ford Lewis Battles [Philadelphia: The Westminster Press, 1960], 926). Calvin applies and reformulates in a way that is original to his perspective of predestination, a principle of medieval theology, which had been put forth to support the doctrine of the Immaculate Conception of Mary (see our chapter on Mariology). He says that predestination happens *"ante praevisa merita vel demerita."* This means that God establishes the decree of predestination regardless of the merits or demerits of the human being, which He also knows in advance. However, predestination is not linked to such merits or demerits; rather, according to Calvin, the latter are the consequence of the former. Although there can be points of contact with certain aspects of the Catholic doctrine about predestination, we are actually dealing with incompatible models of thought. As will be seen in its own place (see Chapters Five and Twelve), for Catholics, human cooperation is required by God, even if it is true that predestination depends only on Him (see *ST* I, q. 23, a. 5).

The "Synthetic" Principle

tal pillar of the Lutheran doctrine of justification. However, it also features peculiar traits. The fact that the human being cannot earn anything makes it so that only Christ can carry out salvation, without any cooperation on the part of human beings (*solus Christus*). The principle that the human being can do nothing for his or her own salvation is—paradoxically—applied even to the very humanity of Christ, which would not be salvific. If Christ is the Savior, and if for Him one speaks of merits, then it is due to the fact that the divinity of the *Logos* abides in His humanity. It could be said that even for Jesus it is true that God does everything, and the human being does nothing. Thus, the humanity of Christ, instead of an instrument conjoined to the divinity (see Chapter Four) or an instrument that really cooperates in the redemption of humankind, is for the Lutherans only the place in which God reveals His merciful grace.

Luther offers a unique interpretation of two passages of the New Testament, which actually are, at first glance, not easy to understand. The first passage is that of Gal 3:13: "Christ ransomed us from the curse of the law by becoming a curse for us, for it is written, 'Cursed be everyone who hangs on a tree.'" Here the Apostle appears to sustain that Jesus was cursed by God, insofar as it is in our favor. Luther commented on this passage as follows:

> All the prophets saw that Christ will be the greatest bandit of them all, the greatest murderer, adulterer, thief, sacrilegious one, blasphemer, etc., that there ever was on the earth, because it is no longer his own person that he bears [...] but a sinner [...]; the one that has [!] and that carries all the sins of all in his body. Not that he personally committed all these sins, but rather that he has taken the ones that we have committed into his body, for the purpose of making satisfaction for them through his blood.[75]

What is striking is that Jesus does not only take our sins *upon* Himself—as Catholic doctrine also teaches. For Luther, Jesus takes them *into* Himself. For this reason, since the sins do not belong to Him "personally," from another point of view they become His, to the extent that Jesus can be defined as a bandit, murderer, etc.

---

[75] Martin Luther, *Commentary on the Letter to the Galatians, ad locum* (*D. Martin Luthers Epistel-Auslegung*, ed. Hartmut Günther: *Der Galaterbrief*, ed. Hermann Kleinknecht – second edition [Göttingen: Vandenhoeck & Ruprecht, 1987], 168 [our translation]). In the same work, he notes that Christ "was a wretch and a sinner among all sinners," He who not only carries but even "has committed the sins of the whole human race"!

The Missing Synthesis: The Orthodox and the Protestants

A second Pauline passage that lends just as much support to the Protestant interpretation of soteriology is 2 Corinthians 5:21: "For our sake he made him to be sin who did not know sin, so that we might become the righteousness of God in him." Here too, if one so desires, Saint Paul can be interpreted as teaching that Jesus has become a sinner by taking on our sins in Himself. We shall see later how the Pauline soteriology should be properly understood from a Catholic perspective. Here we shall focus only on the characteristically Protestant perspective.

Luther holds that there is a total identification of Christ with the sinners of every place and time. The entire world of sin, along with the entire arc of time, is assumed in Christ. Jesus does not carry upon Himself, but rather in Himself, all the sins of each place and era. For Luther—who was always in search of the "God of mercy"[76] since he was continuously afflicted by his own sins—this doctrine would have been consoling, along with his version of justification. In fact, if all the sinners of every time are in Jesus, then each of us is also in Him, including me. Thus, faith in Jesus will be able to guarantee to me that His justice is applied to me, seeing as His merits spring forth from Jesus becoming a sinner for me, that is, to carrying me within Himself. This perspective confirms the absolute lack of our cooperation in salvation: everything happens for the sole fact that Christ has taken us into Himself. Nothing else is required for our salvation.

This soteriological doctrine is known by the name of "penal substitution." It is a substitution insofar as Christ substitutes Himself for us and takes our place as a sinner. It is penal because redemption occurs insofar as Christ accounts for the just penalty due to the sins of all human beings. It has been noted that the starting point for Protestant soteriological thought is the doctrine of Saint Anselm (see Chapter Four). Anselm developed the theme of "satisfaction" to be offered to the divine justice that has been offended by sin. The Protestants emphasize the theme of the negativity of sin and its consequences. Redemption consists in the fact that the wrath of God the Father toward sins and sinners is placed on Jesus, punishing Him in our place. The

---

[76] It is known that Luther's search started from the anxious question, "*Wie bekomme* [or *kriege*] *ich einen gnädigen Gott?*" ("How do I find a gracious [merciful] God?"). Here we shall not analyze the theme of Luther's psychological tension toward his own sins as an element that had a great influence on his theological thought. Such an aspect should however be kept in mind if one wants to reflect in a complete way on the origins of the Protestant Reformation. Recently, an old debate about the way Luther's life ended has resurfaced: there is testimony from that time according to which he committed suicide, even if historians debate its reliability. On this too, we must leave it to the reader to take a deeper look.

Father now sees them all received into Jesus. Thus, He no longer sees His Son in Him, but sin; and He punishes Him with wrath, to satisfy His justice. After having taken out the punishment on Christ, the Father is now appeased and forgives. The justice and merits of Christ then come to be imputed extrinsically to the predestined.

3. Mary

The original Reformers certainly professed the divine maternity of Mary and the virginal conception of Christ. The *Formula of Concord* of 1577, a fundamental document of the Protestant faith, calls Mary "Mother of God." Also, among the Anglicans, these fundamental Marian dogmas were not originally disputed (aside from some occasional isolated thinkers) even though—concerning this and other themes—the tendencies of the *High Church* and that of the *Low Church* need to be distinguished. The controversy concerning the perpetual virginity of Mary arises and gradually builds in the Protestant world, but it does not appear at the beginning.

Regarding the Immaculate Conception, Luther initially held the same doctrine as the Catholics. Later, however, he preferred not to say anything further on the matter. Here, we can see how his conception of justification seems to contradict this doctrine, since even the immaculateness of Mary would not be conceived as an absence of the contagion of original sin, but as a perfect extrinsic attribution or imputation of the merits of the Son. Obviously, not even Mary can claim any merit before God. Luther affirms that between Mary of Nazareth and Mary Magdalene there is no true difference. Both are the same before God—sinners in need of the grace of God. Calvin would be even more explicit, clearly rejecting the doctrine of the Immaculate Conception and attributing to Mary the state of sin.[77] In spite of this, both reformers praise the faith and humility of Mary, and hold her as our model of Christian life.

Concerning Mary's Assumption into Heaven, Luther found that in Scripture there were some who had been said to have been assumed into Heaven (Elijah and perhaps Moses). Thus, he did not directly deny this Marian dogma. In reality, however, on the basis of the principle of *sola Scriptura*, he sustained that it should not be made into an article of faith, given that there is no mention of the Assumption of Mary in the sacred text. Therefore, he

---

[77] This position has prevailed in the formula of faith called the *Declaratio Thoruniensis* of 1645, in which it is affirmed that "All human beings, excepting Christ, are born in original sin, even the most holy Virgin Mary."

suppressed the related liturgical feast, branded as a "papist" custom.[78] Instead, Luther resolutely denied Mary's celestial role, regality, and salvific influence,[79] on the basis of the principle of *solus Christus*.

The same principle also inspires the gradual rejection of Marian devotion, understood as a request for Our Lady's intercession. If initially Luther could still invoke Mary and invite prayer toward her, it was the development of his thought in a way that was more coherent with his starting principles which led him to declare Marian devotion banned. For the older Luther, Mary's prayer is worth nothing more to God than any other Christian's prayer. Everything, in fact, depends on God and on Christ, and thus the different degrees of sanctity between Christians are abolished (as we shall see, the ecclesiastical sacramental hierarchy is also abolished), and the canonization and veneration of Saints is eliminated.[80] Thus, Mary is not the Mediatrix between Christ and us. This drastic position certainly affirms the principle of *solus Christus*, but it contrasts with that of *sola Scriptura*. In fact, Mary is presented in the Bible as the one who intercedes with her Son, even obtaining what at first glance He does not seem to want to consider (see John 2:1–12). Moreover, in the Bible itself, there are more than a few accounts, in both the Old and New Testaments, in which it is seen that the prayer of the righteous obtains grace from God. Because of this inconsistency, little by little, several Protestants have recovered a certain amount of attention toward Mary, even if one cannot speak of a practice of Marian devotion among these separated brothers and sisters. They are probably still impacted by the memorable tirade of Luther who, in his *Sermon on the Day of Mary's Birth* of 1522, harshly critiqued the devotion to Mary, typical of papists, that obscures the centrality of Christ. Moreover, the reformer concludes with a phrase that—alas!—would also be affirmed today by a certain number of Catholics: rather than going to places of pilgrimage, it would be better to aid the afflicted! Even here we see

---

[78] Luther utilized this adjective in a pejorative sense, to indicate all the doctrines and customs of the Roman Church.

[79] An influence taught by the Catholic Church, for example in the Second Vatican Council, *Lumen Gentium*, §60: "The maternal duty of Mary toward men in no wise obscures or diminishes this unique mediation of Christ, but rather shows His power. For all the salvific influence of the Blessed Virgin on men originates, not from some inner necessity, but from the divine pleasure. It flows forth from the superabundance of the merits of Christ, rests on His mediation, depends entirely on it and draws all its power from it. In no way does it impede, but rather does it foster the immediate union of the faithful with Christ." Luther, on the other hand, in his *Commentary on the Magnificat*, denies to Mary the title of Queen of Heaven, and he was followed shortly after by Calvin in his *Harmonia Evangelica*. The Anglicans also held this position from the beginning.

[80] See the *Confessio Augustana* redacted in 1530 by Philip Melanchthon (d. 1560), art. 21.

the principle of *aut-aut*, for which *either* one has devotion *or* one gives charity. But there is no reason for such an opposition.

4. Church

The Lutheran concept of Church is marked by a spiritualism and a rejection of authority. Ecclesiological spiritualism denies the corporate character of the Church, understood as a stable structure, organized by laws, having adequate means for achieving its purposes. It needs to be remembered that, following his excommunication by the Pope, Luther, in addition to writing a defense against the papal bull excommunicating him, burned it along with the *Corpus Iuris Canonici*. The deed is significant. Luther rejected not only the particular excommunication of his person and ideas; he rejected the idea of a Church that could excommunicate or, better, of a Pope who is in charge of other Christians and can judge them based on objective norms. Consequently, even the principle of authority is denied. On this view, everyone is equal in the Church, and no one is superior to the rest (see below on the Sacrament of Orders). Thus, the Church is the assembly of all *believing* Christians on the earth. There remains a visible (but not corporeal) aspect of the Church, because the Christians are on the earth; but more important is the spiritual, invisible, Church, which God alone knows, comprised of those who truly believe in the Gospel.[81] Therefore, the Church is a spiritual unity, a communion of saints. Spiritual and interior Christianity is the true Church, not the material and exterior one. The principle of *aut-aut* is again at work.

5. Purgatory

All Protestants agree in the rejection of the Catholic doctrine of Purgatory. Since one may be justified without works, the merits of Christ alone are enough to lead the elect to Heaven. Thus, no *post mortem* purification is necessary. Moreover, for Protestant Biblicism, there is no passage of Scripture that speaks explicitly of Purgatory[82] and that is enough to disqualify this Catholic dogma. Purgatory is an invention of papists, on the basis of which they have

---

[81] This ecclesiology survives to this day, in those authors married to the idea—of a Protestant framework—that Christianity would not be a religion but a faith. It is true that the two concepts are distinct, but there is no need to oppose them such to say that one *either* has faith *or* practices religion.

[82] The Second Book of Maccabees is held by Catholics as an important reference to the doctrine of Purgatory; Luther, however, does not admit this book into the canon of the Old Testament.

created certain useless and damaging things, which are nonetheless sources of profit for them: Masses for the dead, indulgences, confraternities. Moreover, for Luther, Purgatory is not only *not* a truth of the faith, it is even a "*larva diaboli*" ("mask of the devil").[83]

3.2.3. The Sacraments

1. General Sacramental Theology

The principle of *solus Christus*, united to that of salvation *sola fide*, also determines Protestant thought concerning the Sacraments. Salvation is an exclusive work of God in Christ, with which the human being does not cooperate. Moreover, nature is fundamentally corrupted by original sin and thus cannot serve as a proper instrument of grace, as is instead the case in the Sacraments, in which—according to the Catholic conception—material elements serve as vehicles of divine grace. Faith alone is required for justification, thus the Sacraments are not necessary in themselves. Rather, for Luther, in a proper sense only Christ is true Sacrament—a thesis accepted in the last few decades by various Catholic theologians, also because it is possible to offer an explanation of it in line with the faith of the Church. According to this view, the other Sacraments are the means toward Christ. The external signs of the Sacraments (bread, wine, water, etc.) are actually none other than the flesh of Christ, the humanity of Christ or, namely, the place where God is present in His grace.

Speaking of Protestant soteriology, we have said that the humanity of Christ is considered a sign of salvation more than an active principle of it. This Christological doctrine influences the understanding of the Sacraments, leading to the conclusion that the Sacraments—which represent the humanity of Jesus—do not have any causal efficacy, that is, they do not "produce" grace, but they are only a sign of its being offered. They are the "place" in which God carries out salvation, but they do not generate it. The only *vehiculum gratiae Dei* ("vehicle of the grace of God") is, for Protestants, the Word. Thus, it cannot be the sacramental sign. Justification does not happen through the Sacraments, but rather through the faith that is expressed in them. For this reason, preaching is considered, in itself, more important than the Sacraments, and indeed it can go so far that the Sacraments are said to be important because they resonate what is preached. Luther even says that preaching is incomparably more important than the consecration of bread and wine.

---

[83] Martin Luther, *Smalcald Articles* [1536] 2.11.

The "Synthetic" Principle

Calvin would be more radical than Luther. For the Genevan, the only benefit of the Sacraments (which he reduces to two) consists in the fact that they make salvation known. The difference between the two reformers is this: for Luther, there is no distance between the sign and the reality signified, because the Sacrament is the "place" in which grace is offered; for Calvin, on the other hand, between sign and reality there is a distance, and grace is carried out outside the Sacrament, even if on occasion of its celebration.

Finally, the most extreme of all in this regard was Zwingli, who neither accepted the sacramental theology of Luther nor that of Calvin. For him, the Sacraments are pure ceremonies, used to affirm one's faith before the Church (he calls them *Bekenntniszeichen*, "signs of profession" [of the faith]), and with which one commits to it.

For what regards the number of Sacraments, which for Catholics are seven,[84] in the *De captivitate babylonica* (*On the Babylonian Captivity of the Church*) of 1520, Luther admits three of them: Baptism, the Eucharist, and Penance; but in other contexts, he only admits two. On the other hand, in the same work he had already diminished the consistency of the third Sacrament, for the fact that it does not have a sensible sign. Even though Luther recommended Confession, for him it really does not have the effect of taking away sins, but only of recalling Baptism.

Another peculiarity of Protestant sacramental theology lies in the way in which it understands *verbum*, the Word that accompanies the Sacrament—which Catholics call the "form"—in relation to the "matter," or sensible sign. Luther cites the celebrated expression of Saint Augustine: "*accedit verbum ad elementum et fit sacramentum*" ("the Word is added to the [visible] element, and thus is formed the Sacrament").[85] However, while Catholics see in the *verbum* the formula with which the Sacrament is celebrated (e.g., in the Eucharist: "This is my Body"), Luther instead understands it as the word of preaching, or the Gospel. The word, as a central element of the Sacrament, is thus not the "form" of the Catholics, but the Word of the promise and covenant of God in us. The Sacraments are thus signs of the Gospel, of the will of God toward us. Therefore, the apparent respect for the *et-et* concerning the Sacraments disappears. We Catholics maintain that a Sacrament is constituted both of a material element and a formal one. Even in Luther there is a duality (*verbum et elementum*), but this does not express the law of *et-et*, because this law implies that the two elements are united as a synthesis. Instead Word

---

[84] The sevenfold enumeration of the Sacraments was dogmatically defined by the Council of Trent, *Decretum de Sacramentis* (1547), can. 1 (DS 1601).

[85] Saint Augustine of Hippo, *In Evangelium Ioannis tractatus* 80.3.

and Sacrament, according to Luther, do not form a unified whole, since the second is only a sign that refers back to the first. For Catholics, the duality of the Sacrament is structural, but in Protestant thought there are two distinct entities that refer to one another, and not a component synthesis.

2. Baptism

The observations made about the Sacraments in general can be applied to the first Sacrament. The water of Baptism does not have any value in itself; it cannot purify from sin. However, God has commanded in Scripture that this sign be carried out; thus, it should be done. The various reformers then developed the theology of Baptism on the basis of the peculiarity of their general sacramental theologies. Luther emphasized that Baptism takes away sins, but not original sin, which, while remaining in the human being, is not imputed to him or her by God. In Baptism, the divine Word ensures the human being in regard to his or her future purification in Heaven. The faith proper to the Sacrament is thus the Protestant faith in extrinsic justification. This, more than the Sacrament, is what saves. The human being remains in sin, but now he or she is also under the promise made by God of future purification. This promise consoles the person, and sustains him or her in the battle against concupiscence. It is for this reason that in the true Christians one can note an improvement in moral works (which nonetheless do not save!). As for the Baptism of babies, Luther permits it, slightly expanding his understanding of *sola Scriptura*. In fact, infant Baptism comes from Tradition and not from the Bible, but Luther recalled that Jesus in the Gospel says not to keep the little ones from coming to Him, and for this reason it is an acceptable tradition.

Like Luther, Calvin maintained a certain objective character of Baptism insofar as it is a liberation from sins. Zwingli, on the other hand, affirms that salvation is not linked to it in any way. Baptism does not purify in any sense. It is only a sign of the profession of faith, and of commitment in the Church. Calvin also maintained infant Baptism, for a different reason than Luther. For Calvin, since the little Hebrew children had to be circumcised, so must the little Christians be initiated (in any case, a biblical argument). Finally, Zwingli justifies infant Baptism insofar as it would be a *Bundeszeichen* ("sign of the covenant").

3. Eucharist

Luther believed in the Real Presence of Christ in the consecrated species. However, he believed it in a mistaken way, for different reasons: (1) He

The "Synthetic" Principle

believed in the Real Presence only *in usu*: there is the Presence only in the moment in which the Sacrament is received (Communion), not *ante usum* or *post usum*, before or after (in a word, Christ is not present *extra usum*). Thus, all the practices of Eucharistic adoration and the conservation of the sacred Species should be abolished. (2) He believed that Christ becomes present by *consubstantiation*. This theory wishes to replace the Catholic faith in transubstantiation.[86] For Catholics, the substance of the bread and wine are transformed at the consecration into the substance of the Body and Blood of Christ. Consequently, after the consecration, there is no longer the substance of bread and wine, because it is transformed into another. By contrast, for Luther, the substance of the bread and wine remain, and to it there is added that of the Body and Blood of Christ. (3) He held a notion of the Real Presence, according to the *ubiquism*: God is present everywhere, and at the same time disconnected from any particular thing; He is present *for the human being* or, namely, for me and for you, through His Word. The ubiquity of God is transmitted to the humanity of Christ (for Luther, this happened following the Ascension); consequently, the presence of the humanity of Christ in the world coincides with that of God. Putting together the mentioned aspects, it follows that God is present for us where the Word of Christ resounds, and this happens in the Lord's Supper, where the Word of Christ is pronounced "for us." The point is that the Word of Christ also resounds for us in Baptism and in preaching, and thus it is not easy to distinguish the Eucharistic presence of Christ from other types of presence.

Also, concerning the sacrificial value of the Holy Mass, Luther's vision is incompatible with the Catholic one, and the reformer lashed out at the papists over this point with particular vehemence. The Eucharist is a Supper, not a Sacrifice. In the Supper, the Word of the Gospel, directed toward all human beings, is offered to the individual as the Word of justification. It is faith in the Word that justifies, not the merits of the Passion of Christ that would be sacramentally renewed each time that the Mass is celebrated, as Catholics held. The only sacrificial aspect of the Supper regards the offerings, not Christ. The sacrifice is the offering, or what is offered, which is done with the bread and wine. According to Luther, asserting that the Mass is the true Sacrifice of Christ represents one of the greatest blasphemies, because it sup-

---

[86] In *De captivitate babylonica*, the ex-Augustinian sustains that transubstantiation is impossible, superfluous, and requires too many miracles to be realized. The main argument that he nonetheless offers against transubstantiation, in various writings, is that he intends to liberate the faith from the invasion of Aristotelian philosophy. It can be objected that his proposal may not improve the situation very much.

poses that the death of Jesus on the cross was not sufficient for the salvation of all; which is one reason why He would have to return to sacrifice Himself each time that the priests celebrate the Eucharist.[87]

Finally, concerning the effects of the Eucharistic Sacrament, Luther limits them to the remission of sins alone, thus placing at a secondary level the Real Presence and ecclesial communion. For Catholics, all the effects of this Sacrament—among all, the most important is the gift and preservation of the *unitas Ecclesiae*—are linked to and depend on the Real Presence. Moreover, the remission of sins is understood by Luther in the extrinsic way that we have already described, while for Catholics, sins are truly remitted.[88]

4. Holy Orders

A firm point of Lutheran doctrine is that there is a single priesthood, the baptismal priesthood of all the faithful. This is clearly already expressed in the two works of 1520: *To the Christian Nobility of the German Nation* and *On the Babylon Captivity of the Church*. For Luther, the Sacrament of Orders is an invention of the Roman Church or, namely, of the Church of the Pope, while the Church of Christ ignores it. The words that Christ spoke at the Last Supper: "Do this in memory of me," do not represent for him an institution of a new Sacrament, which consecrated the Apostles as the first priests, as Catholics affirm. Luther gives more emphasis to the final verses of the Gospel of Matthew, in which the risen Christ gives the Apostles the mandate to preach and baptize. This is, for the reformer, the true *munus* of the priests, and since these things can and must be done by all Christians, then all Christians are priests. The so-called sacred ministers are none other than persons delegated by the community to carry out these ministries full-time. However, they do not have an ontological distinction with respect to the others, given by a presumed Sacrament of Orders.

---

[87] However, it seems certain that the Eucharistic theology of Luther arrives at these arguments later on. The starting point is experiential; namely, the scandal over how certain ecclesiastical figures enriched themselves on donations of money linked to the celebrations. The Catholic doctrine affirms that the merits of Christ are applied to souls, the living and the dead, each time that it is celebrated. This encourages that the Holy Masses are celebrated for many intentions and these celebrations are linked to an offering. Luther probably wanted to take away from the churchmen the possibility of profiting on the faith of Christians.

[88] See *ST* III, q. 79, a. 3 and 4. Against Luther, the Council of Trent establishes: "If anyone says that the principal fruit of the most Holy Eucharist is the forgiveness of sins, or that no other effects come from it, let him be anathema" (*Canones de ss. Eucharistiae sacramento* (1551), can. 5 [DS 1655]).

The "Synthetic" Principle

This theology of the priesthood is consistent with that of justification, in which the true gift is the faith, which also renders Baptism efficacious through imputation, and in which the human being cannot possess anything of his or her own, nor does he or she become truly configured to Christ. Moreover, it is in line with the principle of *solus Christus*, which is one reason why there is only one Mediator and Priest—Christ—and there are no other intermediaries. However, this vision is also consistent with the Lutheran Eucharistic doctrine, which rejects the sacrificial aspect. The priests of the Church cannot be "celebrators of the Mass." Calvin further emphasizes this point, saying that the command of Christ in the Last Supper ("Do this . . .") regards the distribution of the Eucharistic Sacrament, which is absolutely not a Sacrifice. He writes: "Christ ordered dispensers of his gospel and his sacred mysteries to be ordained, not sacrificers to be inaugurated, and his command was to preach the gospel and feed the flock, not to immolate victims."[89] Calvin still maintained a certain hierarchical (not ontological) distinction in the Church, something that Zwingli would reject. In *De vera et falsa religione* (*Commentary on True and False Religion*), the latter affirms that whoever preaches the Gospel is a bishop. The New Testament sign of the imposition of hands is interpreted with various nuances by the three reformers, but in substance they agree that it does not constitute a sacramental ordination.[90]

5. Matrimony

Matrimony is also not considered a Sacrament by the Protestants. In 1522, Luther dedicated a writing entitled *Vom ehelichen Leben* (*On Conjugal Life*) to this theme. He teaches therein that, like eating, drinking, and sleeping, Matrimony is a primary necessity for human beings. It is part of our nature, and thus a purely natural and human institution, regulated by human (civil) norms. Matrimony is not recognized as having the true nature of a Sacrament, nor as being endowed with its specific grace of state. The teaching of Saint Paul in Ephesians 5 is understood in a symbolic way: Matrimony is

---

[89] John Calvin, *Institutiones christianae religionis* 4.19.28 (*The Institutes of the Christian Religion*, 1476).

[90] However, in more recent times, many Protestant exegetes and theologians have admitted that the New Testament gives the deed of the imposition of hands a stronger significance than was recognized by the fathers of the Protestant Reformation. Therefore, here too the Biblicism of the reformers is not complete, because they do not read the message of the Bible in its full depth, but only partially. Other elements of the New Testament, such as, for example, the constitution of the Twelve, are also taken more seriously today by a considerable number of scholars in the Protestant environment.

an allegory of the relationship of Christ and the Church, not a Sacrament.[91] Matrimony was willed by God and inserted into creation from the beginning. Christ confirmed it but brought nothing new to it; much less did he transform it into a Sacrament.

Concerning the indissolubility of the bond, although Luther affirms that divorce is illegitimate for Christians as a matter of principle, at the practical level he recognizes a rather high number of exceptions and reasons that allow it, to the point of pronouncing it, in fact, licit. Thus, the solubility of the conjugal bond becomes a part of the Protestant perspective.

3.2.4. Spirituality and Discipline

1. Eucharistic Spirituality

It is clear from what we have said above that the practice of Eucharistic devotion is alien to the Protestant mentality. This involves not only acts of worship towards the consecrated Host, which have known a constant consolidation over the centuries among Catholics—solemn exposition and benediction, Eucharistic processions, *Corpus Domini*, visiting the tabernacle, spiritual communion, etc.—but also applies to the Holy Mass, which for Luther does not have impetratory or propitiatory effects, nor does the Church have the power or right to apply the merits of Christ to a particular soul. Thus, there is no space for the celebration of the Mass in intercession for the dead (for the souls in Purgatory).

2. Cult of Saints, Relics, and Images

We have already treated the Protestant rejection of devotion to the Virgin Mary when treating of the Marian dogmas. As for the aversion to the cult of the saints, its roots precede the reformers. Well before Luther, the Waldensians and the Albigensians had already opposed the veneration of the saints. It is well known that among the most painful pages of Protestant history is the fact that squadrons of Lutherans went about destroying churches and statues of Mary and the saints (recently, some Protestant confessions have asked pardon for this). The theological motive is the *solus Christus*: Scripture tells us that one alone is the Lord and Mediator between God and human beings; consequently, every other figure should be suppressed.[92] It is conceded that

---

[91] John Calvin is in agreement (see *Institutes of the Christian Religion* 4.19), for whom the Catholic interpretation of Eph 5 is due to gross ignorance (*crassae ignorantiae hallucinatio*).
[92] See *Confessio Augustana* (*Augsburg Confession*), art. 21.

The "Synthetic" Principle

the saints may be models to imitate, but not that they are intercessors; therefore, one should not pray to them because this would obscure the primacy of Christ. It would be even less licit to venerate the relics of the saints, which likewise came to be destroyed in notable quantities by the followers of Luther and Calvin.[93] It is obvious that the sacred images of Mary and the saints must also be banned. In this regard, Protestantism continues the work of the iconoclasts of the eighth century.

3. Indulgences

The doctrine of indulgences is a point that Luther contested from the beginning. It appears that the practice (and abuse) of indulgences on the part of certain churchmen was the unleashing cause, in the external forum, of the reaction of the ex-Augustinian friar. For Catholics, indulgences are linked to the power that the Church received from Christ for remitting sins. This is normally done through the Sacrament of Confession. But sins, in addition to the faults that are remitted by the Sacrament, also entail the so-called "temporal" penalties due to the sins themselves. Such penalties are not removed with the absolution of the priest. The penitent and/or the Church must thus satisfy the penalties of the sins in other ways, such as prayer, alms, and penance. However, the Catholic Church holds that it has received an infinite treasury from Christ, namely, the merits of the Passion (to which the merits of Mary and the Saints are added).[94] It holds that the legitimate pastors can make use of such a treasure to alleviate the penalties of sins already pardoned. Such a practice is called an indulgence. Everything that is summarized here obviously cannot be part of the Protestant system, where one is justified by faith alone and not through works. Moreover, the sin itself remains even in the justified, and one cannot pretend to take away the penalties of sins that are not truly removed. Finally, the annulment of the ecclesiological principle of authority also makes it so that for Luther no one in the Church has a power (in this case, of granting indulgences) that all the other baptized would not have. Thus, for Protestantism, indulgences are impossible from the theological point of view. From the practical point of view, they represent an invention of the papists for exacting money from the faithful.[95]

---

[93] It may be recalled, for example, that the French Calvinists (called "Huguenots") destroyed the relics of Saint Irenaeus of Lyon.

[94] See Clement VI, *Unigenitus Dei Filius* (1343) (DS 1025–1027).

[95] It is known that some in the past believed it possible to somehow "buy" indulgences. This was abused by a certain number of churchmen, which so scandalized Luther. While his

The Missing Synthesis: The Orthodox and the Protestants

4. Clerical Celibacy

Luther believed that the act of introducing obligatory celibacy for priests in the Latin Church was contemptuous toward Matrimony, which is established by God. It is understood immediately that the Lutheran position in this matter is based on a misunderstanding. The Church, in fact, in no way intends the celibacy of clerics as a negative judgment on marital life (allowed, moreover, to the priests of the eastern Rites). Luther also failed to sufficiently consider the example of Christ and Saint Paul in this regard. The reformers also agree on the fact that clerics cannot be obligated to celibacy and must be left free. On the other hand, no ontological difference between ministers and the faithful is affirmed in the Protestant perspective; therefore, it becomes more difficult from that perspective to motivate the renunciation of the marital state. By contrast, for Catholic doctrine, the ordained priest is ontologically configured to Christ. This offers a motive of great suitability and advisability, which the Latin Church has made its own by deciding to admit to the priesthood only those who—freely—decide to be celibates. Christ, in fact, was celibate for the Kingdom. It appears very advisable, then, that those who are configured to Him in a special way with the Sacrament of Orders make the same choices, even about this.

3.2.5. Concluding Reflections

From the proposed overview, four fundamental principles of Protestantism have emerged. We can add a fifth: glory should only be given to God (this means to confirm again that the human being cannot take on any merit). Here are these principles together again: *sola Scriptura* (by Scripture alone); *sola fide* (by faith alone); *sola gratia* (by grace alone); *solus Christus* (Christ alone; or *solo Christo*, "through Christ alone"); *soli Deo Gloria* (glory to God alone). There is no need to spend much time demonstrating that these principles represent the fundamental assumption of Protestantism, and thus that they could all be expressed by stating the unifying principle: *aut-aut*. The Word of God is found *either* in Scripture *or* the Tradition; thus, one needs to choose, and Luther chose Scripture, erasing the Tradition. Justification happens *either* by faith *or* through human works, so faith alone saves. Salvation is the fruit *either* of divine grace *or* human merit, so grace alone saves. Honor should be manifested *either* to Christ alone *or* also to Mary and the saints, so, obvi-

---

scandal is more than understandable, he should have distinguished the objective doctrine from the misuse practiced by human beings.

The "Synthetic" Principle

ously, Christ is chosen. Finally, glory should be given to God *or* to a human being—it is also clear here, given such an alternative, whom one must choose. The fundamental error of Protestantism is thus the dialectical opposition, the denial of the human-divine synthesis carried out by the Word in the Incarnation. It is significant that the reformers did not take their thinking all the way, applying it to Jesus Himself, as *either* God *or* man. They stopped before crossing this threshold, even if they applied the *aut-aut* to the soteriological work of Christ. A strongly pessimistic view of the human being derives from the basic Protestant approach. Above all, however, from the theology of Luther derives a fundamental element not only of modern Christianity, but of Modernity in general—the principle of subjectivism. Luther was very influenced by the Ockhamist nominalism of Gabriel Biel (d. 1495), thus inheriting an anti-ontological mentality. He applied this basic philosophy to practically all aspects of his theological thought—justification, redemption, the Eucharist, etc. In the background of his theology, one can almost always make out the rejection of the objective in favor of the subjective. This seed would then develop in a thousand different ways for all Modernity—even outside the Church—to this day.

3.2.6. Brief Considerations on Ecumenism

It is significant that Protestant thought has had such success in recent decades, even among Catholic thinkers. There is no shortage of theologians who have reinterpreted Catholic doctrines in light of Protestant ones, seeking in different cases to present them as equivalent—as substantially coinciding—despite "different languages" utilized by the different parties.

It is also surprising to read the assumption of this standpoint in a Vatican document (which in this case does not include the ritual formula of the Pope's approval). We are referring to the *Joint Declaration on the Doctrine of Justification*, signed in 1999 by the Pontifical Council for Promoting Christian Unity and by the Lutheran World Federation. One can read in this document that "a consensus in basic truths of the doctrine of justification exists between Lutherans and Catholics. In light of this consensus the remaining differences of language, theological elaboration, and emphasis in the understanding of justification [...] are acceptable."[96]

In reality, however, while the text of the *Declaration* may speak a bit triumphantly of a "consensus," we should speak, more realistically, of a positive

---

[96] Pontifical Council for Promoting Christian Unity–Lutheran World Federation, *Joint Declaration on the Doctrine of Justification*, October 31, 1999, §40.

The Missing Synthesis: The Orthodox and the Protestants

step toward a consensus. This clarification is offered by a text that accompanies the Declaration, prepared with the intervention of the Congregation for the Doctrine of the Faith. In introducing a whole series of "clarifications," this document states: "The Catholic Church is, however, of the opinion that we cannot yet speak of a consensus such as would eliminate every difference between Catholics and Lutherans in the understanding of justification. [. . .] On some points the positions are, in fact, still divergent." And it continues: "So, on the basis of the agreement already reached on many aspects, the Catholic Church intends to contribute towards overcoming the *divergences that still exist* by suggesting, below, in order of importance, a list of points that *constitute still an obstacle to agreement* between the Catholic Church and the Lutheran World Federation."[97] The study of such clarifications can be left to the reader. Here we would like to emphasize that the text of the just cited *Response* openly contradicts that of the *Joint Declaration*. And it could not be otherwise, given that the *Declaration* claims to mitigate the substantial differences at the doctrinal level to mere questions of language or of theological explanation. However, we are not just dealing with questions of language or explanation, but with views that are incompatible. Thus, if the *Response* in fact corrects the *Declaration*, it is symptomatic that the 'irenistic' spirit of a certain ecumenism has entered even into a Vatican text, however low its magisterial force.

On the other hand, it is necessary to be very clear: Protestantism and Catholicism, while having many things in common, are two forms of Christianity that are not only different—they are incompatible. Protestantism is based on the dialectic of *aut-aut*; Catholicism is based on the synthesis of *et-et*. This is one reason why it is pointless to attempt to reconcile them in a sophistical way. This cannot be what true ecumenism means. True ecumenism does not hide the difficulties and, while emphasizing everything that unites us, it can still face up to what divides us. The concrete experience—as we have said—of the Catholic Church today has encompassed many aspects of Protestantism, in the way of thinking and in pastoral practice. However, this syncretism between denominations whose DNA is so different certainly cannot represent a step forward in the ecumenical effort, which is, in itself, necessary. We must be guided by what the Second Vatican Council says with clarity:

---

[97] Congregation for the Doctrine of the Faith–Pontifical Council for Promoting Christian Unity, *Response of the Catholic Church to the Joint Declaration of the Catholic Church and the Lutheran World Federation on the Doctrine of Justification*, June 25, 1998, foreword (emphasis added).

The "Synthetic" Principle

> The way and method in which the Catholic faith is expressed should never become an obstacle to dialogue with our brethren. It is, of course, essential that the doctrine should be clearly presented in its entirety. Nothing is so foreign to the spirit of ecumenism as a false irenicism, in which the purity of Catholic doctrine suffers loss and its genuine and certain meaning is clouded. At the same time, the Catholic faith must be explained more profoundly and precisely, in such a way and in such terms as our separated brethren can also really understand.[98]

The Council tells us that the mode of expressing the Catholic faith must not be an obstacle to ecumenical dialogue. Many today understand this in the sense that there would be need of curtailing from the profession of faith, or at least relativizing in their importance, all of those Catholic doctrines that cannot be harmonized with the thought of other Christians. But the Council says the opposite! It explains that the way to not impede the ecumenical path is that whereby "doctrine should be clearly presented in its entirety." It affirms: "Nothing is so foreign to the spirit of ecumenism as a false irenicism, in which the purity of Catholic doctrine suffers loss and its genuine and certain meaning is clouded." We are not impeding ecumenism when we face up to the problems and say clearly what we believe. It is necessary to do this. We impede it when we hide our ideas. This, in addition to representing something lacking with respect to truth, also constitutes a sin against charity, because to hide one's own thought of faith implies not nurturing respect and trust toward our separated brothers and sisters. We must trust our Christian brothers and sisters, and open up to them clearly in mind and heart. Dialogue happens when people speak the truth and trust one another.[99] Otherwise it is called negotiation, and not ecumenism.

Therefore, in presenting Orthodoxy and Protestantism, although we manifest respect and love for our brothers and sisters in other confessions of faith who are baptized and believe in Christ, we must also recognize that, for us Catholics, they err concerning various points.[100] It is absolutely necessary,

---

[98] Second Vatican Council, *Unitatis Redintegratio* (1964), §11.

[99] See Saint Paul VI, *Ecclesiam Suam* (1964), §83–85, 91, 113–14.

[100] This affirmation may sound scandalous to some today. And the scandal would have to be the pretense of safeguarding, on our part, the fullness of truth concerning God, only partially possessed by other Christians. The supposition of "having the truth in our pockets" can bother many Catholics today, who are corrupted by the spirit of the time. It is typical of contemporary relativism to have a skeptical approach to the theme of truth. In the context of a widespread cultural climate, no one should be allowed to affirm that his or

in accord with that *parrhesia* to which Pope Francis often calls us, for us to communicate clearly to them what we believe and we can thus, together with them, face the differences between us, not to erect walls but to build bridges. However, no bridge is built if the banks of the river are not clearly marked out. Thus, in this book we propose to show that Catholic doctrine is the one that expresses and manifests in itself, better than all, the great principle and great reality of the Incarnation of the Word, the central pivot of the whole Christian faith, which sums up in itself the Revelation of the true God. With this, we wish to support Catholics in their faith, and at the same time be honest with our beloved non-Catholic brothers and sisters.

4. The "Synthetic" Principle of *Et-Et* (Both/And)

We have already mentioned the Christological foundation of our exposition. It is determined by a Trinitarian Christocentrism. Now, we must seek to better describe the use of the principle in Catholic theology. First, however, it may be useful to recall that it is possible to make recourse to other methods in theology, and that ours is not the only one, even if we consider it better.

4.1 Other Approaches

The scholastic approach to theological method prioritizes Theocentrism. It is God at the center and fulcrum of theology (which is, precisely, the "science of God"). From this perspective, Christ is the most important element within

---

her position is more correct, or better, than that of others. One should only note the existence of various positions, without being able to identify the hierarchical scale between them, on the basis of their respective degree of truth. If one accepts this perspective, then a Catholic will also be able to be scandalized by the claim of full truth advanced by the Catholic Church. However, the true Catholic knows that he or she must not conform to worldly thought, in this case to relativism, but rather renew his or her own mind (see Rom 12:2). While it appears politically incorrect today, it is necessary to remain in the perspective of truth, and to evaluate doctrines of the various Christian communities on the basis of this point of view. This in no way goes against fraternal charity, but it is actually a manifestation of it. When Saint Paul reproved Saint Peter (see Gal 2:11–14), he did so on the basis of the primacy of the truth, which exposed the error. And in doing so, the Apostle to the Gentiles did not sin against charity but put it into practice. Benedict XVI writes in *Caritas in Veritate* (2009), §1: "To defend the truth, to articulate it with humility and conviction, and to bear witness to it in life are therefore exacting and indispensable forms of charity."

The "Synthetic" Principle

the framework of actions that God (the Trinity) performs in the world. This approach has its own value entirely and has produced innumerable fruits. Our proposal does not aim to subvert it, but only to integrate it. We could say that what we are proposing is a new version of the scholastic approach, not a substitution. We are also remaining Theocentric, but in a way that is Theocentric *and* Christocentric at the same time. The biblical icon of our method is encountered in the Book of Revelation, written by Saint John:

> At once I was caught up in spirit. A throne was there in heaven, and on the throne sat one whose appearance sparkled like jasper and carnelian. [. . .] From the throne came flashes of lightning, rumblings, and peals of thunder. Seven flaming torches burned in front of the throne, which are the seven spirits of God. [. . .] Then I saw standing in the midst of the throne and the four living creatures and the elders, a Lamb that seemed to have been slain. He had seven horns and seven eyes; these are the [seven] spirits of God sent out into the whole world. (Rev 4:2–3, 5; 5:6)

He who sits on the throne and the Lamb are described in a similar way, with the image of the seven spirits of God. They sit on the same throne. Furthermore, the twenty-four elders and the four mysterious beings that surround the celestial throne direct adoration at each with the same adoration (see Rev 4:4–11 and 5:6–11). The two adorations, provided separately, in the end converge in a single act of *latria*, where we read:

> Then I heard every creature in heaven and on earth and under the earth and in the sea, everything in the universe, cry out: / "To the one who sits on the throne and to the Lamb / be blessing and honor, glory and might, / forever and ever." / The four living creatures answered, "Amen," and the elders fell down and worshiped. (Rev 5:13–14)

God and Christ (the sacrificial Lamb) are therefore equal in being (*homoousia*: equality of essence[101]), given that they sit on the same throne, and equal in the adoration that they receive (*homotimia*: equality of tribute[102]).

---

[101] As will be discussed in its own place, that the Son is *homoousios* ("consubstantial") with the Father is a dogma of the faith, defined by the First Council of Nicaea in the year 325.

[102] The criterion of *homotimia* was used especially by Saint Basil the Great (d. 379) in his *De Spiritu Sancto*, in order to argue in another way the ontological equality of the Third Person with the other Two Persons of the Trinity. We can say that this criterion is anticipated regarding God and Christ in Saint John's Revelation.

The "Synthetic" Principle of *Et-Et* (Both/And)

Thus, the sacred text has no reservations in speaking simply of the "throne of God and of the Lamb" (Rev 22:1, 3).

Another image is also very significant. Describing the celestial Jerusalem, the holy author affirms that it is not illuminated by the sun or by the moon because "the glory of God gave it light, and its lamp was the Lamb" (Rev 21:23). The light shines in the lamp and through the lamp. Although they are distinct, these two elements are always together. If we observe a similar instrument of illumination, we will note that the flame and the lamp are not the same, but the flame burns in the lamp, while the lamp contains the flame and filters its light. The image is powerful: God and Christ, while distinct, are a single, indissoluble mystery.[103] We cannot understand who Christ is if not against the Trinitarian backdrop, basing ourselves on the doctrine of the Father and the Son. However, we also do not receive the light of the Trinitarian doctrine if not through the lamp, which is the Lamb. That is why our method does not replace, and is not opposed to, the classical Theocentric method, but simply develops it within a process of organic continuity and not of dialectical opposition.

Other methodological approaches have been attempted in more recent times. In particular, there has been an anthropological approach, which at least in certain cases would perhaps be better defined as anthropocentric, and which has had and continues to have quite a bit of success in terms of popularity among theological circles. In short, it is a way of proceeding that does not start from God, but rather from the human being, and seeks to inductively ascend to God. Being that we are not able to fully analyze the question here, we shall only offer a few considerations: (1) The inductive method had never been used by theologians prior to the twentieth century; even if that fact in itself does not show that it is incorrect to proceed in this way, it is at least a significant red flag. (2) It is true that the human person possesses a capacity to receive Revelation and divine grace (*homo capax Dei*), but this capacity is not natural, or at least, human beings are not capable of carrying it out with their own strength; it is a capacity given by God, freely implemented by Him, and consequently, God

---

[103] Still with reference to a luminous symbol—the candelabrum with seven lamps (see Zech 4:1–2 and Rev 4:5)—Saint Maximus the Confessor (d. 662) writes: "The lamp placed on the candelabrum is the light of the Father, that true light, which illuminates every human being who comes into the world [see John 1:9]. It is our Lord Jesus Christ who, taking on our flesh, came and was called a lamp, that is, wisdom and connatural word of the Father. It is this lamp that the Church of God shows with faith and love in preaching, and which is held high and shines on the eyes of the people in the holy life of the faithful and in conduct inspired by the commandments" (*Quaestiones ad Thalassium* 63 [our translation]).

The "Synthetic" Principle

and His descent toward us is at the center more than our tending toward Him from "below"; the two things are not opposed, but the primacy is on the first aspect.[104] (3) We must not forget that humankind is impoverished, because of sin, and therefore the spiritual faculties of the human soul, while preserved, are wounded (see Chapter Three), and this is the reason why with less strength and making various mistakes, they continue to tend toward God, if drawn by Him in grace. For these and other reasons, we hold that the anthropological/anthropocentric method in theology must be discarded.

In sum, it seems that in theology too, and not just in spiritual and liturgical life, the great principle taught by the founder of western monasticism should remain valid: theologians, like monks, "may place nothing ahead of Christ."[105] Applied in a theological way, this Christocentrism implies recognizing Christ as *the* Principle and *the* Foundation of theology, given that He is *the* Principle and *the* Foundation of the faith. Moreover, the faith, when it is worthy of this name, respects the Christological criterion. This was taught by Saint Irenaeus, who recalled that the *et-et* is the orthodox position. None of the heretics, in fact, truly teach that the Word is made flesh. In one way or another, every form of heresy is an attempt to break or at least weaken the wonderful Christological synthesis.[106]

4.2. The Concept of "Synthesis"

At this point we must better clarify the concept of synthesis, as it should be understood for Catholics. We shall do this by means of a few points.

1. What Does "Synthesis" Mean?

It does not mean *mixture*. The elements held together remain distinct and

---

[104] Although they are distinct from it, in some way some other methods of recent theology are linked to the "fundamental option" of anthropological method, such as the hermeneutic, analytic, correlative, and liberation methods. Each of them contains interesting and correct aspects, but their basic approach tends to overturn the hierarchy of the *et-et* at the methodological level. It is true that one needs to keep in mind both God and man, the idea and the linguistic expression, transcendence and immanence, ontology and history, doctrine and experience, etc.; however, the problematic point of these new theologies consists above all in the fact that they upset the order of precedence between the various elements.

[105] See Saint Benedict of Norcia (d. 547), *Rule* 72.1.12.

[106] Clearly, Saint Irenaeus is referring particularly to Gnostics, but his affirmation is one of principle: "According to the opinion of no one of the heretics was the Word of God made flesh" (*Adversus haereses* 3.11.3, in *ANF*, vol. 1, 427).

identifiable. Through the Incarnation, in Christ both the divine nature (He is God) and the human nature (He is man) are found. The Incarnation is not a mixture between the divine nature and the human nature, from which a third human-divine nature would derive; rather, the Subject (He) unifies the distinct elements without reducing them. Synthesis also does not mean *overlapping*, juxtaposition, or a simple combination, such as when you put two books side to side on a shelf, and you can move and separate them at any time. Synthesis understood in a Christian way indicates an *indissoluble unity between realities that remain distinct*. In Christ, therefore, the divine nature and the human nature are united in an inseparable way. The union of the two natures is not a simple connection but a true indissoluble unity. Thus, synthesis in Christianity is putting together, in an inseparable way, elements that come to be preserved in their individuality, while entering to form part of a unity, constituting this unity.

2. How Does the Synthesis Happen?

It does not happen through a natural combination but rather through a supernatural union. It is not natural that divinity and humanity unite in Jesus Christ; the union happens because God so wishes it and carries it out. In fact, the Johannine formula does not say "the flesh became Word,"[107] but "the Word became flesh." Created nature does not possess in itself the ability to elevate itself to a synthesis with the Spirit. The real synthesis between Spirit and matter happens because the Spirit wills it and carries it out. In this sense, Christianity does not discard all types of evolutionary perspectives, but only self-referential, materialist, and thus atheist evolutionism (see Chapter Three). This affirms, among other things, that Christianity recognizes the real distinction between the two orders: the natural order and the supernatural one. The supernatural order is the world of the divine, of God, of His grace, and of His Revelation. The natural order is the world of things created by God. These two orders are and remain distinct and incommensurable, even if they are not dialectically opposed to one another; they are called to a synthesis through the will and work of God.

---

[107] See *ST* III, q. 16, a. 7 by the title: *Utrum haec sit vera: "Homo factus est Deus"* ("Whether this phrase is true: 'Man became God'").

The "Synthetic" Principle

3. What Does the Synthesis Imply for the Spirit and for Matter?

According to the Christian perspective (despite some more recent proposals that move in an opposite direction, even among certain Catholic theologians), the synthesis of Spirit and matter does not imply any novelty, any change, or any gain for the Spirit (i.e., for God); while it implies a radical change, the greatest novelty as well as an incalculable profit is for the creature, which is elevated to a higher plane, which can be called the order of grace. In other words, whether God does or does not carry out the synthesis with matter, for Him nothing changes. He is immutable, not the subject of any change (which would be an imperfection), and He would be totally and perfectly actualized in His being and beatitude, even if He had not created the world and had not united a human nature to Himself. Instead, the "synthetic" work of God represents an extraordinary novelty for the creature,[108] in particular, for humankind. For the latter, it entails rising up to a dignity to which it cannot aspire on its own ability. Entering into the synthesis with the Spirit, in grace, allows the human being to reach his or her ultimate supernatural end: eternal beatitude.

4. Is It a Synthesis in a Hegelian Sense?

With that said, it also becomes clear that, in using the word synthesis, we wish to distinguish it from the Hegelian use of the term, which indicates a third element after the thesis and the antithesis; namely, the idea that a thesis and antithesis have equal value and are then overcome[109] in what is born anew from their opposition. According to what we have already seen—namely that synthesis in Christianity is putting together, in an inseparable way, elements that come to be preserved in their individuality—the Hegelian theory of thesis-antithesis-synthesis only appears to be a translation into

---

[108] We are referring to the supernatural synthesis of Spirit and matter that happens in the Incarnation and in grace. At the natural level, the synthesis is not a novelty for the human creature, because the human being is "synthetic" *per se*, being naturally composed of soul and body.

[109] G.W.F. Hegel (d. 1831) uses the word *Aufhebung*, which is difficult to translate, to indicate the passage from the dialectic of thesis-antithesis to the moment of synthesis (see *Enzyklopädie der philosophischen Wissenschaften*). *Aufhebung* describes simultaneously maintaining and taking away, preserving, removing, and elevating. Synthesis is, on the one hand, the preservation of the thesis and antithesis but, on the other hand, an overcoming or cancelation, or a mixture in the superior unity of the synthesis.

The "Synthetic" Principle of *Et-Et* (Both/And)

other words of the formula *Verbum caro*. In reality, it represents one of its biggest misunderstandings.

5. Is the Synthesis Necessary?

It depends on what is meant by the word "necessary." If by necessary we mean, philosophically, that which cannot be, if not in the way in which it is, then the synthesis is not necessary. Being an initiative and work of God, God is not compelled to carry it out. He performs it in a sovereignly free way. If instead we understand the word in a relative sense, then it means that the synthesis between Spirit and matter is extremely reasonable and suitable for us. We can then say that this synthesis is necessary, and that God foresaw it and willed it when, always in an entirely free way, He decided to create the world, and humankind in particular (concerning the necessity, or not, of the Incarnation of the Word, see the following chapter).

6. Is the Synthesis Foreseen from the Beginning of Creation?

It depends what is meant by "foresee." If "foresee" indicates God's knowledge, then the response is affirmative. God knows everything always, and thus from eternity He knows that He will carry out the synthesis between Spirit and matter. If, however, it is meant that, "when" He decides to create, God foresees that creation will have an absolute need of the synthesis (which would imply a sort of "right" on the part of the creatures to receive the supernatural synthesis), then the answer is negative. God certainly would have been able to create the world and rational creatures in it while deciding to never carry out the synthesis between Spirit and matter, and to never elevate creation to the order of grace. This follows from the fact that grace—as the term itself suggests—is a gratuitous supernatural gift of God, which is not due in any way to the creature. In concrete reality, Revelation teaches that God did not want to act in this way, and for this reason He created in view of the world's elevation to the level of grace; however, He would have surely been able to act in a different way, if He had so willed.[110]

---

[110] See Pius XII, *Humani Generis* (1950), §26 (DS 3891): "Others [theologians] misrepresent the gratuity of the supernatural order, since God, they say, cannot create intellectual beings without ordering and calling them to the beatific vision." Pius XII does not say that God had acted in this way, but that He could have done so if He had wanted. To sustain the contrary involves removing the gratuitous and supernatural character from grace. Thus, we can say that we know from Revelation that God does not create rational

The "Synthetic" Principle

7. Are There More Ways of Carrying out the Synthesis, or Only One Way?

The question can be reformulated as such: Is the Incarnation of the Word the only possible way, or could God have acted differently? We shall provide greater details about this question in the following chapter when we take on the classical question of the *Cur Deus homo*, that is, the motive for which the Word becomes incarnate. However, from here we can affirm that nothing can be imposed on God by our thought. The good theologian, just as he or she never says, "God cannot," equally avoids saying "God must." Such a theologian will not usually use similar expressions, which would limit God, and when it is necessary to make recourse to these, he or she would do it always in a prudent and shrewd way, being very clear what he or she means. Thus, we can respond to the initial question: if God wanted, He could have carried out the synthesis in ways different from how He in fact did. However, this response is based on a hypothesis. The reality is what matters most, and in reality and in history God carried out the synthesis through the Incarnation of the Word.

4.3. The Dipolar[111] Nature of the Christian Faith

From what has been presented to this point, it has emerged that the preeminent principle of the Christian faith, always preserved in the doctrine and practices of Catholic life, is the *et-et*, which can also be applied to other pairs, such as Spirit-matter, invisible-visible, grace-nature, freedom-law, subjective-objective, intention-action, etc. This structural principle of all the Catholic faith rests on the decision and action of God, who has created, at the natural level, a spiritual-corporeal world and who, at the level of grace, has redeemed it from sin through the assumption of a human nature on the part of the divine Word. One cannot preach an *aut-aut* with respect to Jesus Christ, saying that He is either God or man, immortal or mortal, eternal or temporal, and so forth. With Him, one must preach the *et-et*. Since the whole Christian faith is based on Jesus Christ, it is obvious that such faith receives its own intimate structure from its Principle and Foundation. We shall now

---

beings without calling them to the supernatural order. The so-called "pure nature" does not exist historically. But it is of fundamental importance to emphasize that it could have existed, if God had willed it.

[111] Translator's note: The word in the original Italian version is "*bipolare*," which indicates a two-poled structure or nature. We have chosen to translate this word as "dipolar" instead of the more literal "bipolar" in order to avoid confusion with the meaning and connotations of the psychological use of the term in English.

The "Synthetic" Principle of *Et-Et* (Both/And)

see that in each aspect of dogmatic doctrine this principle is always verified, and this structure is always discovered,[112] and the Catholic Church has safeguarded this principle in its own classical teaching.

From this perspective, it is interesting to note that it is precisely the faith as such that possesses this dipolar structure, conforming adherents both to its Principle and Foundation, Jesus, and to its recipient, humanity. In effect, the Christian faith is not for an angel, a creature that is purely spiritual and that enjoys the *visio Dei* in Heaven; rather it is for the human being, a spiritual-corporeal creature. Scripture teaches that the creature that lives in the presence of his or her Creator does not live by faith, but precisely by vision itself, because the concept of faith presupposes the absence of vision of what is believed: "For in hope we were saved. Now hope that sees for itself is not hope. For who hopes for what one sees? But if we hope for what we do not see, we wait with endurance" (Rom 8:24–25).[113] This does not mean that the creatures that are already in Heaven (angels and saints) are dealing with a God that is different than that for human beings on earth. The Holy Trinity is the only God, both for angels and for human beings, and Jesus Christ is the only Lord of both, as for all those who live in Heaven and those on earth there is "the same Spirit" (see 1 Cor 12:4). However, this greatly changes the relation that one has with God. Some see Him, love Him, worship Him in His presence; others, while not having seen Him, believe in Him, awaiting and seeking to merit the moment that they will be able to meet Him and to be with Him always. That being the case, faith is for the earth-goers (which the Medieval theologians called *viatores*, wayfarers), and not for the heavenly spirits or for the holy souls in Paradise (the *comprehensores*, those who embrace, cling to, and hold on [to God]). Thus, the faith is constituted in a

---

[112] The original project of this volume was much more ambitious. It also aimed to find the golden principle of *et-et* in Christian morality, spirituality, and finally, in the laws and customs of the Catholic Church. Little by little, as the writing of the work advanced, it became clearer and clearer that such a project would have to be divided into parts, being limited for now to dogmatic theology. But it is easy to intuit that Catholic morality is equally structured on that principle. In fact, it always puts freedom and law together, the moral subject and the objective action, norm and conscience. The bipolarity is also discovered in special morals, as when, for example, it is taught that the conjugal act is both unitive and procreative, etc. Perhaps, considering the title of this dogmatic treatment, one could foresee the title of a second work dedicated to morals: *Love is a Synthesis*. However, we cannot foresee when and if it will be possible for the author of this volume to dedicate himself to the preparation of the other work. If this opportunity is not given to him, others will be able to attempt, even better than he, the drafting of a "synthetic" moral theology.

[113] The New Testament uses the word "hope" to indicate faith several times: see Benedict XVI, *Spe Salvi* (2007), §2.

The "Synthetic" Principle

basic way with the dipolar structure Spirit/matter both because it is founded on Christ, God and man, and because it is offered to human beings, creatures composed of soul and body.

In light of the previous reflections, before proceeding further, it is good to further propose some brief clarifications on how the principle of *et-et* should be understood.

1. Limit of Et-Et

As has been said, this principle concerns the faith—thus a reality that lasts as long as the world lasts. The world is structured on the basis of a harmony of distinct elements, channeled by God into a unity. Certainly, being a principle of reality, the *et-et* must in some ways apply to Heaven, but it cannot be asserted that it always applies, or that it explains not only the earth but also Heaven as a whole. For example, it is true that the *et-et* also applies to God because He is both One and Three. And it is true that, at the end of time and always, the saints will be in Heaven both in soul and in body. But the principle comes into crisis when one considers the divine Trinity, and one sees that in this case there are three "*et*" and not two: God is *at the same time* Father, *and* Son, *and* Holy Spirit. For what regards the angels, the *et-et* is not applied to their nature, because they are pure spirits, who lack any material body.[114] Thus, it does not need to be supposed that the *et-et* is a principle that explains all existing reality. However, it explains the Catholic faith quite well, and it does apply to a large part of heavenly realities. Therefore, it cannot be claimed that the divine Mystery can be exhausted in the principle of *et-et*. In fact, no doctrine, no theology—in a word, no human formulation, however true—can in itself exhaust the revealed mysteries.

2. Axiological Difference

As has emerged from the preceding pages, recognizing that the realities of faith have a dipolar or composite structure does not imply that the different elements have the same value. By contrast, there is always an element that has more value than the others, but this does not change the existence or importance of other factors. Human and divine nature go together in the unique concrete Person of the incarnate Word. This does not mean that the human

---

[114] Nonetheless, according to the Thomistic doctrine, the principle of *et-et* also applies to the angels; that is to say, not that of soul-body, but rather that of essence and existence, which only coincide perfectly in God.

The "Synthetic" Principle of *Et-Et* (Both/And)

nature has the same value as the divine, but that the superiority of the divine does not exclude the human. Nature and grace: grace is a higher reality, but nature is called to participate in grace, and is not cancelled out by it. The Holy Mass is both Sacrifice and Supper, but the sacrificial aspect is much more important. There are many more examples.

3. Logical Consistency

The Christian faith is a gift of the *Logos*, and thus it is deeply logical, not in the sense that the dogmas of faith are the result of rational inferences, but in the sense that the truth of faith, though it surpasses rational truth, does not contradict it. The logic of God is much higher than that of human beings, but this does not mean that the first contradicts the second. The human intellect, our little *logos*, is created by the divine *Logos* in its own image. It follows from this that the Catholic *et-et* never descends into a form of irrationalism; namely, the oxymoronic reconciliation of contraries.[115] It does not violate the principle of non-contradiction,[116] which we shall gladly cite a second time

---

[115] According to Nicholas of Cusa (d. 1464), the inviolability of the principle of non-contradiction would be valid only in creation, while invalid in God, who would be superior to any logic, and in Him would coincide the opposites that are irreconcilable in the world (*coincidentia oppositorum*). Later, that which referred only to God was also applied by Renaissance thinkers such as Marsilio Ficino (d. 1499) and Giovanni Pico della Mirandola (d. 1494) to the world and to humanity, opening the way to the syncretistic thought that was typical of the era. Although Nicholas of Cusa was an author of a far superior character than such epigones, it needs to be recognized that his proposal should be discarded. Indeed, in nature, there is the indispensable principle of non-contradiction as a reflection of the profound divine rationality. It can be seen, for example, in the precision with which one needs to define the omnipotence of God. The fact that God is omnipotent does not mean that He can do everything in an absolute sense, but that He can do absolutely everything that does not imply an irresolvable contradiction. If the terms are not made clear in this way, it is easy to become to the victim of the sophists, who propose questions of the type: Can God create a boulder so heavy that he cannot lift it? It is clear that any response one gives to such a question will be limiting to the divine omnipotence, if the definition one has of omnipotence is not clear. This means that logic is also valid for God, even if He is superior to any human logic (see Isa 55:8–9).

[116] In this sense, and only in this sense, we could say that there is also a legitimate Catholic *aut-aut*, which applies between irreconcilable realities. Jesus himself uses this *aut-aut*: "No servant can serve two masters. He will either hate one and love the other, or be devoted to one and despise the other. You cannot serve God and mammon" (Luke 16:13; see also Matt 6:24). The Catholic Church remains faithful in rejecting the unacceptable violation of the principle of non-contradiction. Thus, for example, it cannot affirm Luther's *simul justus et peccator*, because the human being is either in grace or not. For this reason, Dante Alighieri wrote the celebrated verses: "... ch'assolver non si può chi non si

The "Synthetic" Principle

in the version of it given by Aristotle: "It is impossible that the same attribute, at the same time, belong and not belong to the same object and under the same aspect."[117] Not violating this principle is not only a philosophical demand, or one of simple common sense; Revelation itself invites us to avoid this error. Christ says: "Let your 'Yes' mean 'Yes', and your 'No' mean 'No.' Anything more is from the evil one" (Matt 5:37). Moreover, Saint Paul interprets and applies to himself the words of the Master, as follows: "So when I intended this, did I act lightly? Or do I make my plans according to human considerations, so that with me it is 'yes, yes' and 'no, no'? As God is faithful, our word to you is not 'yes' and 'no.' For the Son of God, Jesus Christ, who was proclaimed to you by us, Silvanus and Timothy and me, was not 'yes' and 'no,' but 'yes' has been in him" (2 Cor 1:17–19). The word of Christians cannot be "yes" and "no" at the same time: one cannot violate the principle of non-contradiction. Thus, the Catholic *et-et* is never applied to terms that are objectively irreconcilable, while it often links aspects that seem so, but in reality are not, since in some cases it can be difficult to recognize that the opposition is not strict.[118]

In the end, it should be kept in mind that the principle of *et-et* is not imposed on reality or on the Word of God but is drawn from them. The classical assertion—"*Sensus non est inferendus sed efferendus*" ("The sense should not be attributed but obtained")—is valid both in exegesis and theology. The *et-et* is not a principle that we thought up while "sitting at the desk" and then imposed on the natural world and Revelation. On the contrary, it was discovered in both. Therefore, where the world and the Word of God do not

---

pente, / né pentere e volere insieme puossi / per la contradizion che nol consente" (*Inferno* 27. 118–120; "for who repents not cannot be absolved, nor yet can one at once repent and will, the contradiction not permitting it!": trans. Courtney Langdon [Cambridge: Harvard University Press, 1918], 311).

[117] Aristotle, *Metaphysics* 4.3.1005 b 19–20.

[118] An example of a case in which it is difficult to recognize that the opposition is not insuperable is the case of Mary, Virgin and Mother. In itself, it is very difficult to think that virginity and maternity are not absolutely irreconcilable. Perhaps it is also for this reason that some contemporary theologians reinterpret the virginity of Mary in a, as they write, "non-biological" sense. On the other hand, we emphasize that normally, at the natural level, the two things are opposed, but not at the supernatural level because God can carry out the miracle—which he indeed has done—of making Mary conceive and give birth in a virginal way (see Chapter Seven). Even this unique miracle, while impossible at the biological level, does not violate the logical principle of non-contradiction. It is useful to recall Saint Ambrose of Milan (d.397), *De Mysteriis* 53: "If we seek the natural order, the woman cannot conceive but by being united to a man. It is thus clear that the Virgin conceived outside of the natural order" (our translation).

present such a characteristic, it is always necessary to surrender to reality, instead of forcing the real into a preconceived scheme. Even the theology we are presenting here strives to grasp the *et-et* because it is there—we do not seek to insert it where it is missing. And for this reason, it also has an apologetic function: on one hand, it shows that such a principle is present in a determinate manner in the doctrine of the faith, and thus it is evidence of the faith's intrinsic reasonability; on the other hand, it confirms that Catholic doctrine is, among the various Christian doctrines, that which better corresponds to this intimate structure of the revealed Word, preserves it, and promotes it.

4.4. Confirmation from the Liturgy

To prove all of this, it will be useful to make reference to the presence of the *et-et* in liturgical texts, given that "*lex orandi, lex credendi*" ("the rule of prayer is the rule of belief").[119] The *et-et* is continually present in the Latin liturgical texts. It is enough to browse the prayers of the Missal in the original language to recognize it. Unfortunately, the missals in the national languages are often, if not always, translated in a way that loses the evidence of the principle. Thus, for a very brief presentation of examples, we shall try to browse the *editio typica* (official edition in Latin) of the Missal approved by Saint Paul VI, which contains many prayers of the great liturgical Tradition, and not merely the Roman Tradition.

To be concise and effective, we shall present a minimal selection of prayers of the Missal, limiting ourselves to the time of Advent alone, citing the original text. Our translation attempts to be strictly literal, even if less elegant than the official translations. In this way we can showcase the presence of the *et-et* in the liturgical texts, especially in the original Latin.

---

[119] The original formula of this principle is that of Prosper of Aquitaine, *Indiculus de Gratia* 8 (DS 246): "*Ut legem credendi lex statuat supplicandi*" ("So that the rule of prayer determines the rule of belief"). The *Indiculus* is attributed today by scholarship to Saint Prosper (d. ca. 455), while in the past it was attributed to Pope Celestine I (d. 432).

The "Synthetic" Principle

USCCB Translation	Editio Typica	Literal Translation
May the sacrifice of our worship, Lord, we pray, be offered to you unceasingly, to complete what was begun in sacred mystery and powerfully accomplish for us your saving work.	**Dominica III Adventus** *Super oblata* — Devotionis nostrae tibi, Domine, quaesumus, hostia iugiter immoletur, quae et sacri peragat instituta mysterii, et salutare tuum nobis potenter operetur.	We ask You, Lord, to always be offered the victim of our devotion, which may **both** realize what was instituted of the holy mystery, **and** may powerfully work your salvation within us.
Grant, we pray, almighty God, that the coming solemnity of your Son may bestow healing upon us in this present life and bring us the rewards of life eternal.	**Feria quarta Hebd. III Adv., Collecta** — Praesta, quaesumus, omnipotens Deus, ut Filii tui ventura sollemnitas et praesentis nobis vitae remedia largiatur, et praemia aeterna concedat.	Grant, we pray, O Almighty God, that the coming solemnity of Your Son give to us **both** help for the present life **and** eternal rewards.
May your grace, almighty God, always go before us and follow after, so that we, who await with heartfelt desire the coming of your Only Begotten Son, may receive your help both now and in the life to come.	**Feria sexta Hebd. III Adv., Collecta** — Praeveniat nos, omnipotens Deus, tua gratia semper atque subsequatur, ut, qui adventum Unigeniti tui summo cordis desiderio sustinemus, et praesentis vitae subsidia et futurae pariter consequamur.	May Your grace always precede us, almighty God, and accompany us, so that we, who await the coming of Your Only Begotten with the highest desire of the heart, may obtain help for **both** the present **and** the future life.

The "Synthetic" Principle of *Et-Et* (Both/And)

	Die 19 decembris *Collecta*	
O God, who through the child-bearing of the holy Virgin graciously revealed the radiance of your glory to the world, grant, we pray, that we may venerate with integrity of faith the mystery of so wondrous an Incarnation and always celebrate it with due reverence.	*Deus, qui splendorem gloriae tuae per sacrae Virginis partum mundo dignatus es revelare, tribue, quaesumus, ut tantae incarnationis mysterium **et** fidei integritate colamus, **et** devoto semper obsequio frequentemus.*	O God, who have deigned to reveal to the world the splendor of your glory through the birth from the Blessed Virgin, grant, we pray, **both** that we adore with full faith, **and** we always honor with devout homage, the mystery of the wonderful Incarnation.
	Die 21 decembris *Super oblata*	
Be pleased, O Lord, to accept the offerings of your Church, for in your mercy you have given them to be offered and by your power you transform them into the mystery of our salvation.	*Ecclesiae tuae, Domine, munera placatus assume, quae **et** misericors offerenda tribuisti, **et** in nostrae salutis potenter efficis transire mysterium.*	Accept well-disposed, O Lord, the gifts of Your Church, which compassionately You **both** have given us to offer, **and** which You powerfully transform into the mystery of our salvation.

As we said earlier, we have limited ourselves to presenting examples chosen exclusively from the liturgical season of Advent. Considering the Missal in its totality, there would obviously be many more texts. We add that we have only presented here the prayers that materially present both sides of the *et-et* in the original text. However, there are many other prayers, even if we stay in the season of Advent, which, while not materially presenting the *et-et*, express it clearly in their own way.[120] If the reader then has the patience to run

---

[120] Limiting ourselves again to the Advent season, see *Post Communionem* of the First, Second, and Third Sunday; *Collecta* of the Monday of the First and Third week; *Collecta* of the Tuesday of the Third week, *Post Communionem* of the Tuesday prior to December 16; *Collecta* of the Wednesday of the First week; *Post Communionem* of December 21 and

through the entire Missal in Latin, he or she will be faced with evidence that the *et-et*, both written literally or implicitly expressed, will be found in a high number of texts of prayer, including the prefaces (again, however, one needs to consult the original Latin, because it is not always evident in translation). We can conclude that the liturgical texts effectively confirm the very great importance that the Catholic Church recognizes in the *et-et*, making of it a fundamental principle, not only of theological-doctrinal expression, but also of her own official prayer.

5. Method of Treatment

The method of the present treatment is based on some basic aspects and choices, which have already been partially revealed in the previous pages. We must now express them more clearly, along with certain others that will now be made explicit.

5.1. Alethic Approach

Our perspective is that truth exists and that human beings—along with all their known limitations—have access to it. The human mind has the possibility of knowing the truth in the natural realm with its own capacities (nonetheless granted by God the Creator); and he or she also has the possibility of receiving divine, supernatural Truth if it comes to be communicated from on high. Thus, the human being can know the Truth about God and about what He wishes to reveal. Consequently, theology is not the realm of opinion, but rather that of healthy debate and engagement, a search for Truth in an ever more perfect way.

Moreover, theology does not study the sources of faith merely out of a historical interest; for example, simply to identify the beliefs of the Christians of the second, sixth, or twelfth centuries—beliefs that would change with time and would no longer be relevant today. Certainly, the historical approach to texts is necessary, but it is not everything. There must be an "alethic" approach (from the Greek *aletheia*, meaning "truth"). The theologian studies the sources to discover and learn in a deeper way the Truth, which is always "relevant" and never "overcome." The Truth is always young and never ages, because it lives in the eternal present of God, and at a lower level, it

---

22; *Super oblata* of December 24. Some of the prayers are repeated more than once in the various days of the season.

lives in created realities. For this reason, the Truth is not conditioned *per se* by the flow of time, being only the breadth of our knowledge of it that is so conditioned. The Truth is perennial. Even *a parte hominis*, once achieved it does not fall into silence. Naturally, it can always be known more and more. "Perennial philosophy" (*philosophia perennis*) and "perennial theology" (*theologia perennis*) thus have their own reason for being if understood in this sense. On the one hand, they remain perennially valid in their sure and established achievements, because the Truth does not change; on the other hand, they also remain open to knowing the Truth even more, because the Truth is never completely encompassed in human expression, insofar as there are always aspects waiting to be grasped, elements already known that can be understood further, deductions to be made, and applications to be carried out.

5.2. Ecclesiality

Consequently, the theologian, as a believer, is above all one that takes a position in favor of the Truth, namely, in favor of Christ. The theologian is not a passionless scientist, even if he or she is a scientist—a qualification many today would like to deny! He or she is a scientist of faith, that is, a person of faith that systematically studies the faith—his or her faith and that of the Church. Thus, the theologian is also a person of the Church, fully incorporated into the community of believers, who wishes to serve through his or her ministry of study, teaching, and the publication of texts.[121] Without idolizing the historical form of the Church of the era in which the Catholic theologian lives, he or she is fully recognized as a member of the community, as a "child of the Church," whose legitimate guides he or she also respects. This does not take away from the scholar an analytical and even, when appropriate, critical spirit; however, he or she exercises this spirit within the Church and for the sake of Church, even when its affirmations result in denying deviant aspects in ecclesiastical practice. Thus, theology will not be a solipsistic exercise of a narcissistic thinker sitting at his or her desk (as we have previously recalled, citing Pope Francis). Theology is scientific to the extent to which it is also "believing," that is, a rational activity directed at the faith, on the part of people of faith, in (and for) the community of believers.[122]

---

[121] Concerning the ecclesial vocation of the theologian, see Congregation for the Doctrine of the Faith, *Donum Veritatis* (1990).

[122] For the theologian, Benedict XVI said, "scientific rationality and lived devotion are two necessarily complementary and interdependent aspects of study" (*Address at Heiligenkreuz Abbey*, September 9, 2007). Two years prior, addressing the International Theological Commission (ITC), he stated: "The Revelation of Christ is [...] the fundamental norma-

The "Synthetic" Principle

5.3. Ecclesial and Ecumenical Parrhesia

Theology must have the courage to speak, and to do so according to the Truth that it has known. Within the Church, the theologian must be prophetic, in the correct sense of the word. The prophet is one who calls upon the people to follow him or her in observing the Word of God. Precisely with "eyes fixed on Jesus, the leader and perfecter of faith" (Heb 12:2), the theologian will always remember that "Jesus Christ is the same yesterday, today, and forever" (Heb 13:8), from which the exhortation also follows: "Do not be carried away by all kinds of strange teaching" (Heb 13:9). The prophetic role of the theologian, and of theology, does not consist in predicting the future, and much less in putting pressure on ecclesiastical authorities so that one's own plans be carried out and be placed on the agenda. Ecclesiastical politics are not the theologian's profession! He or she must not have an ideology to push. The theologian is above all a disciple, a hearer of the Word. Thus, he or she is also an apostle, called to announce the Word received as a gift from God—according to the ways pertaining to his or her scientific profession. Behold, the need for *parrhesia*, often recommended by Pope Francis. The theologian must know to call the community of which he or she is a part, and which he or she loves and serves, back to fidelity to God and to His Truth. For this reason, every theology that bows down to a worldly ideology represents a true failure: "Do not conform yourselves to this age but be transformed by the renewal of your mind, that you may discern what is the will of

---

tive starting point for theology. Theology must always be exercised in the Church and for the Church, the Body of Christ, the only subject with Christ, and thus also in fidelity to the Apostolic Tradition. The theologian's work, therefore, must take place in communion with the living voice of the Church, that is, with the living Magisterium of the Church and under her authority. To consider theology a private affair of the theologian is to underestimate its very nature. It is only within the Ecclesial Community, in communion with the legitimate Pastors of the Church, that theological work has meaning; it certainly requires scientific competence but likewise, and no less, the spirit of faith and the humility of those who know that God is alive and true, the subject of their reflection, who infinitely exceeds human capacities. Only with prayer and contemplation is it possible to acquire the sense of God and the docility to the Holy Spirit's action that will make theological research fruitful for the good of the entire Church and, I should say, of humanity. Here one might object: But is theology thus defined still a science and in conformity with our reason and its freedom? Yes. Not only are rationality, a scientific approach and thinking in communion with the Church not exclusive of one another but they go together. The Holy Spirit guides the Church to all truth (see Jn 16:13); the Church is at the service of truth and her guidance is an education in truth" (*Address to the Members of the International Theological Commission*, December 1, 2005).

God, what is good and pleasing and perfect" (Rom 12:2).[123]

This *parrhesia* is also necessary at the level of ecumenical and interreligious dialogue. As we have already seen, the Second Vatican Council has given many clear principles on how ecumenism should be practiced by Catholics. If the spirit of dialogue is to be maximized, as well as the sentiments of Christian and human fraternity, it is still true that ecumenism and interreligious dialogue are not a laboratory for experimenting with new "chemical mixtures" so that sooner or later we can create a formula that appeases everyone. Therefore, the Catholic theologian, with the humility of one who knows that the Truth possessed is not merited, but rather a gift, must combine the demands of Truth with a sincere love for separated Christians and all other people. He or she cannot escape this duty, under penalty of falling into nonsense. A theology that plays around with removing dogmas or contesting certain moral doctrines has certainly declared its own uselessness by these very acts, and the only thing left to do is that it be left to fade away.

5.4. Criteria to Identify the Truth of the Faith

However, it will be asked: How can the Catholic theologian be so certain that the interpretation of the sources given by the Tradition of the Catholic Church corresponds to the Truth? Why is the correct interpretation of the Bible that of Augustine and Thomas, and not that of Luther and Calvin? Here the theologian knows that he or she must refer to a principle that Scripture itself mentions; namely, the principle of allowing oneself to be guided in the faith by accredited figures. Earlier, we were referring to chapters 12 and 13 of the Letter to the Hebrews, which urge us to keep our gaze fixed on Christ and on the faith that He gives us and perfects. What is the correct way of doing this? It is in the same context of those chapters that the answer is revealed to us. At the beginning of chapter 12, the author of the letter says that we ought to remain solid in the faith "surrounded by so great a cloud of witnesses" (Heb 12:1). He refers here to the examples of faith that he has cited in the preceding chapter of his writing. And in chapter 13, verse 7, which introduces what we reported above, he says: "Remember your leaders who spoke the word of God to you. Consider the outcome of their way of life

---

[123] One can bow to the worldly ideology of the moment not only by saying what the mass media wants to hear or by trying to please journalists more than Christ. One can also "sell oneself" to ecclesiastical powers, hoping to gain some benefit: a chair, a rector, an episcopal promotion, etc. This is also spiritual worldliness, directed within the Church. In these cases, the Word of God is put in the service of the interests of the "ruler" of the moment, in view of attaining "human, all too human" purposes.

and imitate their faith." We can recall an analogous text of Jeremiah: "Stand by the earliest roads, / ask the pathways of old, / 'Which is the way to good?' and walk it" (Jer 6:16).

Various other biblical passages could be cited, but there is no need. We can already observe from them that the faith is never individual, even if it is personal. If faith is the prerogative of an individual who believes, it always remains the faith of the Church, which is also in me. Thus, the role of the Church—and accredited witnesses in her—is essential. Among them, the Apostles are at the top level, and on a level that is lower but still of essential importance are a group of witnesses, guides, and leaders, who give us the true faith, the true interpretation of the Word of God. How can we recognize them?

Saint Vincent of Lérins, in a famous passage, offered us a rule for discerning "the truth of the Catholic faith from the perverse falsity of heresy":

> Also in the Catholic Church itself we take great care that we hold that which has been believed everywhere, always, by all [*quod ubique, quod semper, quod ab omnibus creditum est*]. For that is truly and properly "Catholic," as the very force and meaning of the Word show, which comprehends everything almost universally. And we shall observe this rule if we follow universality, antiquity, consent. We shall follow universality if we confess that one Faith to be true which the whole Church throughout the world confesses; antiquity if we in no wise depart from those interpretations which it is plain that our ancestors and fathers proclaimed; consent if in antiquity itself we eagerly follow the definitions and beliefs of all priests [bishops] and doctors alike.[124]

St. Vincent affirms that the criterion of orthodoxy in the faith is the true universality—however well expressed by the principle of *et-et*, which holds together *in unum* the healthy Catholic complexity: a plurality without pluralism. In order to remain within the catholicity of the faith—continues St. Vincent—it is necessary to refer to three criteria: the universality of what the entire Church professes everywhere; antiquity, maintaining the spirit of the faith of the Fathers; and the general consensus, referring to the masters of the faith.

---

[124] Saint Vincent of Lérins, *Commonitorium* 2.6 in *Commonitory of St. Vincent of Lerins*, trans. T. Herbert Bindley (New York: E.S. Gorham, 1914), 26.

5.5. A Choice against the Current

What Saint Vincent has taught us is, thus, to listen to the Church and particularly the accredited teachers within it. Let us remember one of the initial motivations for this chapter: the Church is in urgent need of teachers! We are therefore making a choice here that is contrary to a large part of current theological literature. In fact, the current tendency frantically seeks novelty;[125] incessantly compiles updated bibliographies; it shies away from "dated" texts, unless they are of some criticizing theologian, in which case those texts are always considered "current" and "prophetic." Otherwise, it suffices that a book of theology is twenty or at most thirty years old in order for it to be considered "overcome" (in a Hegelian sense). We do not at all despise the research and the constant updating of theologians. However, in this book we shall make a different choice from the prevalent tendencies of today. We will only cite witnesses that are "dated" and, according to some, "surpassed." In the entire arc of the book no author will be mentioned explicitly (aside from a few carefully chosen exceptions[126]) who has died less than two hundred years ago[127] starting from the initial date of the redaction of this volume (2010). Thus, authors who died after 1810 will not be cited. Now, this choice should be explained.

1. Why Is No Theologian of the Last Two Hundred Years Cited?

Not citing authors who are not at least two hundred years old does not mean rejecting the whole of the theology of the last two hundred years. Nor does it mean that it is being ignored. Professional theologians will find many implicit references to recent and very recent authors and themes in this book. As a personal defense of myself, it should be made known that for a good number of years I have offered a course of theology at the licentiate level, dedicated

---

[125] And by contrast: "Novelty is never in itself a criterion of truth, and it can be praiseworthy only when it confirms the truth, and leads to rectitude and virtue" (Pius XII, *Menti Nostrae* (1950), §117 [our translation]).

[126] For example, we have already made quick references to Hegel, who died in 1831. The exception is justified because in very different ways he has had an absolutely determining influence on various currents of contemporary thought, including theology. However, we have cited the philosopher of Jena certainly not as an authority, but rather in a critical way.

[127] The motivation of the choice to make this the date of the author's death—rather than birth—can be explained with a reference to Sir 11:27-28: "at the end of life one's deeds are revealed. / Call none happy before death, / for how they end, they are known."

to the great themes and figures of the theology of the twentieth century. It is thus something about which I would know. However, the choice is motivated by the fact that, on the one hand, we do not want to enter directly into the polemics between schools of thought and authors, many of which are still going on. This book takes a side, but not in that sense. It sides with the perennial faith, and not one or another contemporary theologian. On the other hand, the necessity of learning from accredited teachers must be noted and, so that such an acknowledgment may be secure, also the need for time. It would not be difficult to propose a list of names, also among recent and even living authors, which probably merit the title of teacher (or doctor) in the faith. However, because this is not certain, the Church needs time for discernment. Nonetheless, where the Church has already pronounced, by beatifying and canonizing, such a temporal limit comes down to us automatically; the blessed and saints, in fact, being recognized by the Church, are certainly models of life, but also teachers in the faith.[128] This clearly does not imply that every single word written by a saint is *ipso facto* an expression of the Truth; however, it indicates a general reliability of teaching.

2. Why Two Hundred Years?

A date limit was necessary for selecting authors, for the reasons stated above. Now, a temporal distance of two hundred years was suggested by the Apostolic Constitution *Quo Primum Tempore*, with which Saint Pius V published a new Missal in 1570. Superficial interpretations affirm that this Pope imposed his own Missal to the entire Church, abrogating all other liturgical rites. In reality, Saint Pius V established that the rites being replaced by the new Missal were only those in practice by the Churches that "were not older than two hundred years."[129] That which is two hundred years old is thus considered "traditional" and, therefore, in some measure "reliable." Having found this temporal indication in the Magisterium, it is possible to proceed while maintaining the indicated criterion of citation: no author who died less than two hundred years ago. The *Catechism of the Catholic Church* also made this choice; indeed, it does not cite anyone (who is not either a saint, blessed, or holder of the Magisterium) of the last two centuries.[130]

---

[128] It is due to the value of personal and doctrinal testimony of these exemplar Christians that we place the title of Saint or Blessed before the name of these cited authors.

[129] Saint Pius V, *Quo Primum Tempore* (1570), §8 (our translation).

[130] There is a single exception: The *Catechism* cites an author who died in 1890, John Henry Newman, who at the time of the publication of the *Catechism* (1992) was not yet beati-

With specific reference to recent theology, the temporal limit of two centuries is also indicated by Pope Benedict XVI:

> In our time *in the past 200 years* we see the same thing. There have been great scholars, great experts, great theologians, teachers of faith who have taught us many things. They have gone into the details of Sacred Scripture, of the history of salvation but have been unable to see the mystery itself, its central nucleus: that Jesus was really the Son of God, that at a given moment in history the Trinitarian God entered our history, as a man like us. The essential has remained hidden! One could easily mention the great names in the history of theology *over the past 200 years* from whom we have learned much; but the eyes of their hearts were not open to the mystery.[131]

Surprisingly, the Pope confirms one of the initial observations of this chapter: a great part of recent theology has greatly developed in its scholarship, but very little in its adoration. Many facts are known, but the Mystery is hidden. Moreover, to indicate an approximate period of time, Pope Benedict also applies the same number, the last two hundred years. Even we take much in this book from the theology of the last two hundred years, recognizing how much good there is in it, within the limits of our capacity and knowledge. However, we are leaving aside its protagonists, even those among them who deserve our praise, preferring that it be the Church to tell us in the future which of the many and famous authors that we are used to reading were truly teachers of the faith. This is not to say that this choice should be made in every book of theology, but it seems the right choice for this book, because of its intended audience and its purpose (indicated in the general introduction to the volume).

3. What about the Magisterium?

Naturally, the Magisterium of the Church is excluded from this rule and will thus be cited in its most recent documents. However, we shall not make use of the private writings of the popes, both those published before elec-

---

fied. However, today, Newman also enters into criterion we indicated, being that he was declared Blessed by Benedict XVI on September 19, 2010 (and later canonized by Francis on October 13, 2019).

[131] Benedict XVI, *Homily at Mass for the Members of the International Theological Commission*, December 1, 2009 (emphasis added).

tion to the Pontifical Throne, and those that were published when they were already pope (including interviews with journalists). Those remain the writings of private authors—interesting, but not magisterial. The documents of the Vatican Congregations will be cited, because they represent an arm of the Papal Magisterium; while other texts will be left aside, such as those of the International Theological Commission or the present Pontifical Biblical Commission,[132] which, while being established alongside the Congregation for the Doctrine of the Faith, do not publish magisterial documents.

5.6. The Importance of Saint Thomas Aquinas

Many names of ancient, medieval, and modern authors will be encountered by browsing the pages of this volume and going through the footnotes. It is not enough to refer to only one teacher. Even in this treatment a healthy plurality is good. On the other hand, part of our method includes recognizing a hierarchy of values. Now, from the Magisterium of the Church and from personal study, we learn that Saint Thomas Aquinas must be given a privileged place, as he is the Master of all Catholic theologians, the author in which the Catholic synthesis has reached heights that were previously unknown, and are unparalleled even to this day.[133] This does not imply, obviously, that there is nothing to say after him! However, the Angelic Doctor remains the starting point and essential reference point for Catholic theology. We could say that for the essential formation of the priests of today, the *Catechism of the Catholic Church* and the *Summa Theologiae* of Saint Thomas are the fundamental texts. That is not to say that there is no need to read anything else, but that these texts cannot be ignored. Thus, Saint Thomas will be present and determinant in the whole arc of our treatise, both when explicitly cited and when operating in the background. In fact, beyond the solutions to the individual questions,

---

[132] By contrast, the older Pontifical Biblical Commission, in the profile that it had before the reform of the Curia carried out by Saint Paul VI, put forth texts that were held to be official teachings. However, this is no longer the case today.

[133] Accordingly, Pope Leo XIII attests in *Cum Hoc Sit* (1880): "Everything that was said or wisely discussed by pagan philosophers, the Fathers and Doctors of the Church, and the eminent men that flourished before him [Thomas], was not only assimilated by him, but was augmented, brought to completion, and ordained with such luminous perspicuity of form, with such accurate argumentation, and with such propriety of language that *he left the ability of imitating him to posterity, but seems to have removed their ability to overcome him*. His greatness consists in the fact that his doctrine, structured and deployed according to completely clear principles, is not only suited to the needs of a single era but of all times, and especially suitable to refute the errors that perennially re-appear" (our translation [emphasis added]).

Method of Treatment

what counts most is Aquinas's way of thinking. Such a *forma mentis* must be—along with the necessary adaptations and modernizations—the basic "scheme" of thought for each Catholic theologian, even if the latter chooses another great author as his or her own main teacher, which remains entirely acceptable.[134]

The irreplaceable role of Saint Thomas for Catholic doctrine was sanctioned by the ecclesial Magisterium itself. The first thing that catches the eye is the fact that he has been, in the two-millennium history of the Church, the only theologian that is explicitly recommended, and not simply cited, in the texts of an ecumenical council. Vatican II actually refers to him as a guide on two occasions.[135] On the other hand, it is well known that while the Council of Trent did not cite Saint Thomas explicitly in its documents, it drew profusely from the doctrine of the Angelic Doctor. Historians recall that, during the conciliar sessions, two thick books were open on the altar, as if to symbolize the illumination that the doctrine contained within them provided the minds of the conciliar Fathers: the Bible and the *Summa*.[136]

Several Popes officially declared approval of the theological doctrine of Saint Thomas; a complete anthology of these pronouncements would take us beyond our scope here. We shall therefore limit ourselves to a few examples. Pope John XXII (d. 1334), who canonized Saint Thomas in 1323, said: "He

---

[134] Saint Pius X, in the Motu Proprio *Doctoris Angelici* (1914), confirms that the thought of Saint Thomas is the criterion according to which other authors are also evaluated: "If on some occasions We or Our predecessors have approved with special praise the doctrine of another author or of a saint, and if we have also hoped that this doctrine will be divulged and defended, then it is because it has been proven that it is in harmony with the principles of Saint Thomas, or at least that it does not absolutely contradict them" (our translation). On the legitimacy of following other schools, see Clement XII, *Apostolicae Providentiae Officio* (1733), §1 (DS 2509).

[135] "In order that they may illumine the mysteries of salvation as completely as possible, the students should learn to penetrate them more deeply with the help of speculation, under the guidance of St. Thomas" (Second Vatican Council, *Optatam Totius* [1965], §16); "The Church is concerned also with schools of a higher level, especially colleges and universities. In those schools dependent on her she intends that by their very constitution individual subjects be pursued according to their own principles, method, and liberty of scientific inquiry, in such a way that an ever deeper understanding in these fields may be obtained and that, as questions that are new and current are raised and investigations carefully made according to the example of the Doctors of the Church and especially of St. Thomas Aquinas, there may be a deeper realization of the harmony of faith and science" (Second Vatican Council, *Gravissimum Educationis* [1965], §10).

[136] "What is more clearly demonstrated by the esteem that the Church has always given to such a Doctor, than the fact that only two volumes, Scripture and the *Summa Theologiae* have been shown on the altar of the Tridentine Fathers, so that they could be inspired by them in their deliberations?" (Pius XI, *Studiorum Ducem* [1923], §11 [our translation]).

The "Synthetic" Principle

illuminated the Church of God more than any other Doctor; whoever studies for a year only the books of him will obtain a greater profit than one who follows the teachings of another for one's whole life."[137] Leo XIII (d. 1903) declared that, "Among the Scholastic Doctors, the chief and master of all towers Thomas Aquinas, who, as Cajetan observes, because 'he most venerated the ancient Doctors of the Church, in a certain way seems to have inherited the intellect of all.'"[138] Saint Pius X (d. 1914) wrote that "after the blessed death of the holy Doctor, there has not been in the Church any Council where he was not present with his precious doctrine."[139] And in *Pascendi Dominici Gregis*, he added: "let Professors remember that they cannot set St. Thomas aside, especially in metaphysical questions, without grave detriment."[140]

Benedict XV (d. 1922), without mincing words, identified Thomistic doctrine with Catholic doctrine: "The Church declared the teaching of Thomas to be her own."[141] Pius XI (d. 1939) attributed the title of "principal master" of Catholic schools to Saint Thomas.[142] Pope Pius XII (d. 1958) also offered beautiful praise of the Common Doctor: "The method and principles of Saint Thomas prevail over all the rest, both for forming the intelligence of younger persons, and for leading already formed souls to penetrate the truths into their most hidden meanings." And he continues: "Being moreover in full harmony with divine Revelation, such a doctrine—that of Thomas—is thus uniquely efficacious in solidly establishing the foundations of the faith, as well as for grasping the fruits of true progress."[143] Saint John XXIII (d. 1963) sang the praises of Saint Thomas in the *Motu Proprio* with which he elevated the Roman Athenaeum "Angelicum" of the Dominicans to the status of a Pontifical University. Pope Rancalli writes: "We believe that the greatest contribution given by the [Dominican] Order to the defense of the faith and to the propagation of the Gospel, was that from its ranks arose Thomas Aquinas, Doctor of the Church, and Universal Doctor of the Church." The Pontiff adds:

---

[137] John XXII, *Consistory Speech of 1318*.

[138] Leo XIII, *Aeterni Patris* (1879), §17. Pope Leo also cites an expression of his predecessor Innocent VI (d. 1362): "His teaching above that of others, the canonical writings alone excepted, enjoys such a precision of language, an order of matters, a truth of conclusions, that those who hold to it are never found swerving from the path of truth, and he who dare assail it will always be suspected of error" (§21).

[139] Saint Pius X, *Doctoris Angelici* (1914) (our translation).

[140] Saint Pius X, *Pascendi Dominici Gregis* (1907), §45.

[141] Benedict XV, *Fausto Appetente Die* (1921), §7: "*Thomae doctrinam Ecclesia suam propriam edixit esse.*"

[142] Pius XI, *Studiorum Ducem*.

[143] Pius XII, *Inaugural Discourse of the Fourth International Congress of Thomist Philosophy*, September 14, 1955 (our translation).

We strongly desire, for the development of Christian life, that the doctrines of Thomas Aquinas are studied in-depth, as a treasure, and that his writings are shared extensively, because they are not inferior in any way to the doctrines and institutions of our time; [. . . moreover] we are persuaded that if studies of the doctrine of the Angelic Doctor are enhanced, the decisions of the Fathers of the Second Vatican Ecumenical Council will be better understood.[144]

Saint Paul VI (d. 1978) invited everyone to make direct contact with the texts of Aquinas:

There is no escape from the fact that, often, the distrust or aversion to Saint Thomas depends on a superficial and episodic approach and, in some cases, from a complete lack of direct reading and study of his works. Thus, We, like Pius XI, also recommend to each person who wants to be formed in a mature knowledge concerning the position to take in such subject matter: *Go to Thomas!* Seek and read the works of Saint Thomas—we wish to repeat—not only for finding in such rich treasures sure nourishment for the spirit, but also, and even before this, to personally recognize the incomparable depth, abundance, and importance of the doctrine that it contains.[145]

Saint John Paul II (d. 2005) emphasizes that "the Church has been justified in consistently proposing Saint Thomas as a master of thought and a model of the right way to do theology," and he adds:

Saint Thomas was impartial in his love of truth. He sought truth wherever it might be found and gave consummate demonstration of its universality. In him, the Church's Magisterium has seen and recognized the passion for truth; and, precisely because it stays consistently within the horizon of universal, objective, and transcendent truth, his thought scales "heights unthinkable to human intelligence." Rightly, then, he may be called an "apostle of the truth."[146]

---

[144] Saint John XXIII, *Dominicianus Ordo* (1963). See also his *Discourse to the Fifth International Thomistic Congress*, September 16, 1960.

[145] Saint Paul VI, *Lumen Ecclesiae* (1974), §3 (our translation; the reference is to Pius XI, *Studiorum Ducem*).

[146] Saint John Paul II, *Fides et Ratio* (1998), §43–44 (the internally quoted texts are taken from Leo XIII and Saint Paul VI, respectively).

The "Synthetic" Principle

> It should be clear in the light of these reflections why the Magisterium has repeatedly acclaimed the merits of Saint Thomas' thought and made him the guide and model for theological studies. This has not been in order to take a position on properly philosophical questions nor to demand adherence to particular theses. The Magisterium's intention has always been to show how Saint Thomas is an authentic model for all who seek the truth. In his thinking, the demands of reason and the power of faith found the most elevated synthesis ever attained by human thought, for he could defend the radical newness introduced by Revelation without ever demeaning the venture proper to reason.[147]

Given the role that the Magisterium recognizes for the Common Doctor, Benedict XVI draws attention to the fact that:

> It is not surprising that, after St. Augustine, among the ecclesiastical writers mentioned in the *Catechism of the Catholic Church* St. Thomas is cited more than any other, at least 61 times! He was also called the *Doctor Angelicus*, perhaps because of his virtues and, in particular, the sublimity of his thought and the purity of his life.

And then, with special reference to the theme of *et-et* and of the "synthetic" perspective, Pope Benedict continues:

> In short, Thomas Aquinas showed that a natural harmony exists between Christian faith and reason. And this was the great achievement of Thomas who, at that time of clashes between two cultures, that time when it seemed that faith would have to give in to reason, showed that they go hand in hand, that insofar as reason appeared incompatible with faith it was not reason, and so what appeared to be faith was not faith, since it was in opposition to true rationality; thus he created a new synthesis which formed the culture of the centuries to come.[148]

---

[147] Saint John Paul II, *Fides et Ratio*, §78.
[148] Benedict XVI, *General Audience*, June 2, 2010. The Pope dedicated another two "Wednesday Catechesis" sessions to Saint Thomas on the 16th and 23rd of June in 2010.

5.7. "Nexus Mysteriorum"

A final note on method concerns the importance of the link between the mysteries of faith (*nexus mysteriorum*),[149] called also "*analogia fidei*" ("analogy of faith"), an expression that is found in Romans 12:6 and is often translated "proportion to the faith." Although recent Calvinist theologians have suggested different ways of understanding the *analogia fidei*, in Catholic theology it indicates the harmonious proportion between the truths of the faith, which cannot enter into conflict with one another.[150] The *Catechism of the Catholic Church* speaks of it in this way: "By 'analogy of faith' we mean the coherence of the truths of faith among themselves and within the whole plan of Revelation" (CCC §114).

The criterion of the analogy of faith applies both in the biblical and theological spheres. At the biblical level, it is observed when we read Holy Scripture as a unity of the Old and New Testaments, a unity for which it is more than licit, indeed it is necessary, to compare passages of different books and eras that deal with the same argument in order to illuminate its understanding. Even the necessary exegetical contextualization must not lose sight of the fact that the Bible is a unitary book; it is the Word of God in written form, in which there is no contradiction. The connection of the mysteries is also observed in theology, in which the different elements of the faith illuminate each other, being distinct parts of a unified organism, the doctrinal *corpus*, which corresponds to the *corpus* of reality and of the Truth, and expresses it.

Furthermore, the criterion of the *analogia fidei* underpins what today is called the "hermeneutic of continuity,"[151] or the interpretation of the doctrinal

---

[149] The expression is found in the First Vatican Council, *Dei Filius* (1870), ch. 4 (DS 3016).

[150] In negative form, the principle implies that—with all the truths linked to one another—the negation of a single dogma should be detrimental to the entire organism of the faith: "For if any one part of Catholic truth be given up, another, and another, and another will thenceforward be given up as a matter of course, and the several individual portions having been rejected, what will follow in the end but the rejection of the whole?" (Saint Vincent of Lérins, *Commonitorium*, 23, 14).

[151] This is a synthesis of a more precise expression of Benedict XVI, of which it is worthwhile to provide a very important passage that relates to this theme: "The question arises: Why has the implementation of the Council [Vatican II], in large parts of the Church, thus far been so difficult? Well, it all depends on the correct interpretation of the Council or—as we would say today—on its proper hermeneutics, the correct key to its interpretation and application. The problems in its implementation arose from the fact that two contrary hermeneutics came face to face and quarrelled with each other. One caused confusion, the other, silently but more and more visibly, bore and is bearing fruit. On the one hand, there is an interpretation that I would call '*a hermeneutic of discontinuity and*

The "Synthetic" Principle

development in the Church as process of (generally harmonious) continuity and not of rupture or contradiction. This implies that the Fathers and Doctors are linked—as different as the historical forms of their theologies may be—as authors that, in the fundamental continuity of the *Traditio*, always remain connected. They are different, but not contradictory, and concurrent to a higher understanding of the faith.

Still, the hermeneutic of continuity must be applied to the magisterial teachings of different eras, especially of the ecumenical councils, which do not ever represent a rupture or a reversal of direction, but a deepening and an advancing that is in line with the uninterrupted Tradition. It is for this reason that, in our treatise, we shall not look at any council as essentially breaking with a previous one or, more importantly, as "superior" to the previous ones. There has been and continues to be in contemporary Catholic theology a widespread mentality according to which the Second Vatican Council would represent—despite its apparent will to present itself as non-dogmatic and pastoral—a "super-Council" or a "super-dogma." On each theme of theology, according to this perspective, we would need to refer mainly to Vatican II (of which a certain kind of interpretation is given), even if the last Council has not expressed significant teachings on that specific theme.[152] Rather, we shall cite the Second Vatican Council regarding those themes on which it represents a non-negligible reference point, but we do not feel compelled to treat it as a "super-dogma." Above all, we shall respect the bond of this Council with the whole doctrinal Tradition of the Church, avoiding seeing a dialectical moment in it: almost the birth of a new doctrine and a new Church, according to a pernicious "hermeneutic of rupture."

It is clear from what we have mentioned that in this volume we shall follow a mixed method, which is derived (here too) from putting together

---

rupture'; it has frequently availed itself of the sympathies of the mass media, and also one trend of modern theology. On the other, there is the '*hermeneutic of reform,*' of *renewal in the continuity of the one subject-Church* which the Lord has given to us. She is a subject which increases in time and develops, yet always remaining the same, the one subject of the journeying People of God. The hermeneutic of discontinuity risks ending in a split between the pre-conciliar Church and the post-conciliar Church" (*Address to the Roman Curia*, December 22, 2005 [emphasis added]). The whole final part of this extraordinary address should be contemplated carefully.

[152] Various theologians said they were scandalized by the fact that Benedict XVI's encyclical *Spe Salvi* did not cite the Council even once. However, the Second Vatican Council said nothing essential about the theme of which that encyclical spoke (Christian hope), and thus it cannot be a duty to cite it on every occasion. It would be like expecting the Council of Trent, or that of Florence, to always be cited even when the theme that is being discussed is not significantly touched on by the documents of these councils.

various methods, both old and new, which have been utilized in the history of theology. A first element of our method, corresponding to the analogy of faith, consists in seeking the links between the sources, so that, illuminating each other, they may help us to understand the mysteries of the faith. Approaching biblical, patristic, theological, and magisterial sources by theme is based on the most solid tradition of theological method. Most often we will not made explicit, but will keep in mind, the necessary connection between the sources according to theological *loci* (see the following chapter) and theological *notae*, which are currently out of fashion and yet necessary for theological precision and the proper evaluation of the doctrinal value of the various sources. However, we will not bore the reader by indicating such values from time to time, but we will seek to consider them in the background.

This classical method will be coupled with historical attention, typical of the most recent period. It may concern the contextual interpretation of sources, both for the Fathers, and for the Scholastics. Also in this case, the attention owed to the more recent hermeneutic approach will be respected, but it will often remain implicit; it would not be suited to the literary genre of this work to always make it explicit.

Therefore, our method does not only proceed in a conceptual way—that is, by theme—but also in a historical-salvific direction. With all of this, we hope to achieve a Catholic synthesis not only in regard to content, but in regard to method, in a such a way as to favor, as much as possible, an internal reconciliation of theology—which has lived for some time in a period of suffered fragmentation, due in part to the passage from more classical methodological paradigms to other more recent paradigms, which were often formulated in opposition to, and not in harmony with, those of the past. In particular, there was the passage from the so-called "essentialist" paradigm (which proceeds through concepts or themes) to the historical-salvific one (which analyzes the development), as well as the change of perspective from deductive to inductive theology. It seems to us that the principle of *et-et* also offers possibilities for development in the methodological field, because it is basically a principle of conceptual theology (for the sake of precision, correlative theology), but which due to its very nature can or, rather, must hold together the historical-salvific approach, accordingly integrating the deductive dimension with the inductive dimension as well. Naturally, since the *et-et* provides for a hierarchization, at the level of method the aspect of revealed content prevails over that of the receiving subject, as the God who reveals is greater than the human being who is the hearer of the word.

2

Revelation, Faith, Theology

Our approach emerges clearly from Chapter One: Trinitarian Christocentrism, founded on the central principle of Christianity, "*Verbum caro factum est*" ("The Word became flesh") (John 1:14). The historical event of the Incarnation involves two fundamental aspects and values (or effects). The Incarnation both carries out our salvation in the incarnate Son, and it reveals supernatural truths to the human race. It is a salvific and revelatory event. We shall consider various soteriological aspects in a later chapter, but here we want to begin from a theme that has become classic in soteriology, the theme concerning the motivation for the Incarnation. We shall then focus on the theme of Revelation and, consequently, faith and theology.

1. The Reason for the Incarnation of the Word

The Word has become flesh, which should be interpreted in the sense that He has become man. Here, a question arises in medieval theology: *Why* did the Word become man? The question was posed in these terms by Saint Anselm of Canterbury (d. 1109), who entitled one of his famous works precisely *Cur Deus Homo* ("Why [has] God [become] Man?"). Revelation tells us that the Word became flesh. Does it also tell us why this happened? It seems so, even if in this regard there is no definitive agreement among theologians. All Christians believe that the Word has become flesh; that is, they do not doubt the

Revelation, Faith, Theology

fact of the Incarnation.¹ In this sense, the fundamental fact is held in common.

But the question of why is also interesting. If we ask the average Christian about the reason why the Son became incarnate, he or she will answer that the Word became man for our sins, for our salvation. This implies that the Incarnation happens in view of the death on the cross² and of the atonement for the sins of humanity, accomplished by Christ with the offering of his life, as Scripture teaches (see Mark 10:45; Rom 3:25; 1 John 2:2; 4:10; 1 Pet 1:18-19; etc.). In fact, according to Saint Thomas Aquinas, Scripture teaches that the reason the Word became flesh is to atone for the sins of Adam, the first man, and for all other sins that were committed thereafter. Thus, he concludes, although the question is difficult, it must be held as the more certain opinion that if humanity had not sinned, the Word would not have become flesh.³ Saint Thomas follows the line of thought of Saint Anselm, who had reached a similar conclusion for a different reason, which Aquinas corrects in part. Saint Bonaventure (d. 1274) also advocates for the so-called "conditional thesis," that is, that the Word would not have been incarnate if Adam had not sinned. Among other reasons for the thesis, he adds this: "Such an opinion [the conditional one] enflames in a greater way the affection of the faithful. Because it greater excites the devotion of the faithful soul that God has become incarnate to wash away one's sins rather than to bring to fulfillment a work already begun."⁴

Blessed John Duns Scotus (d. 1308) distanced himself from these theologians, and instead sustained the "unconditional thesis": the Word would have

---

[1] It is significant that the CCC §461, emphasizes that the Incarnation is "the fact [*factum*] that the Son of God assumed a human nature in order to accomplish our salvation in it."

[2] Tertullian of Carthage (d. 220) summarizes the earthly activity of the incarnate Word, which he understands as entirely directed toward the death on the cross, with the expression *mori missus*—"sent (into the world) to die": *De carne Christi* 6.6.

[3] See *ST* III, q. 1, a. 3; in addition, see the stance of *ST* III, q. 31, a. 1: "Christ assumed human nature in order to cleanse it of corruption. But human nature did not need to be cleansed save in as far as it was soiled in its tainted origin whereby it was descended from Adam. Therefore it was fitting that He should assume flesh of matter derived from Adam, that the nature itself might be healed by the assumption" (our translation). Saint Thomas's prudence in his discussion of the question emerges again from his *Super I ad Timotheum*, I, 4, in which he writes: "We do not know what God would have arranged if the fact of sin had not happened; however, the holy Fathers affirm that [the Word] would not have become incarnate if humanity had not sinned. And so it also seems to me" (our translation). Therefore, not only Scripture, but also the Fathers, to whom is added the Master of all Catholic theologians, maintain this opinion (see also his *Compendium theologiae*, ch. 200).

[4] Saint Bonaventure, *In III Sententiarum* 1.2.2.

become incarnate even if Adam had not sinned.[5] Although the reasons he provides in support of his perspective are questionable (as Benedict XVI seems to also say[6]), from that point on theologians who faced the question about the reason for the Incarnation would be divided into "Thomists" and "Scotists," though they often supported their positions with different arguments than those of Thomas and Scotus, and sometimes emphasized the theories that they were starting from. Thus, whoever thought that the Word would not have been incarnate in the absence of sin, would be called a Thomist; whoever sustained that the Incarnation would have happened in any case, would be called a Scotist.

The position with the most supporters throughout the history of theology is that of Thomas. The Fathers of the Church and many theologians before

---

[5] "If the fall [of Adam] were the cause of the predestination of Christ, it would follow that the supreme act of God would be extremely conditioned, since the glory of all humankind is not comparable in intensity to the glory of Christ. Now it seems highly unreasonable that God would leave out such an eminent work on account of the good behavior of Adam, that is, if Adam had not sinned. And it cannot be admitted that such an elevated good is occasioned in the creatures solely on account of a lesser good" (Blessed John Duns Scotus, *Opus Oxoniense* 2.7.4 [our translation]).

[6] "First of all, he [Scotus] meditated on the Mystery of the Incarnation and, unlike many Christian thinkers of the time, held that the Son of God would have been made man even if humanity had not sinned. He says in his '*Reportatio Parisiensis*': 'To think that God would have given up such a task had Adam not sinned would be quite unreasonable! I say, therefore, that the fall was not the cause of Christ's predestination and that if no one had fallen, neither the angel nor man in this hypothesis Christ would still have been predestined in the same way' (in III Sent., d. 7, 4). This *perhaps somewhat surprising thought* crystallized because, in the opinion of Duns Scotus the Incarnation of the Son of God, planned from all eternity by God the Father at the level of love is the fulfillment of creation and enables every creature, in Christ and through Christ, to be filled with grace and to praise and glorify God in eternity" (Benedict XIV, *General Audience*, July 7, 2010, our emphasis). The reason Scotus sustained his thesis is that the souls of human beings are predestined from eternity. Thus, even the human soul of Jesus would have to be predestined from eternity to the union with the Word. The only biblical passage on which Scotus would have been able to base this second reason appears to be 1 Pet 1:20: "He was known before the foundation of the world but revealed in the final time for you," even if it can also be interpreted in a different way from what it seems to say at first glance. On the other hand, the opinion of the holy doctors Anselm and Thomas is supported by many biblical passages. Ultimately, one could respond to Scotus that the human soul of Christ was certainly always predestined to the Incarnation from eternity, but this is due to the fact that God always knew, while not willing it, that humanity would sin. Thomas himself responded to the future observations of Scotus, writing "If Christ were not to have been incarnate, God would have decreed men's salvation by other means. But since He decreed the Incarnation of Christ, He decreed at the same time that Christ should be the cause of our salvation" (*ST* III, q. 24, a. 4, ad 3 [our translation]).

Saint Thomas already held this line of thought, and Saint Thomas affirms that the conditional thesis is not only a theological opinion, but it represents the teaching of Holy Scripture, and thus, the Word of God itself. Despite this, the Angelic Doctor prudently leaves open the possibility of holding the opposing thesis. In recent times, the thesis of Scotus has regained much favor. Theologians who hold it today say that, although it is true that in Scripture the majority of passages affirm that Christ came for our sins, there are a few key texts in which the opposite is taught. These texts indicate that all of creation was predestined for fulfillment in Christ, and thus that the Incarnation of the Word should not be considered as the mending of a man-made tear in the plot of the divine plan, but as an event willed in advance by God. In fact, it is absolutely the most important event in history. Regarding this second consideration, the Thomists agree that even if the Incarnation happened to repair human sins, it remains the central event of history—alongside the Triduum of the Passion, Death, and Resurrection of Christ.

Here we do not wish to make a detailed analysis of the biblical passages that are for or against each thesis, but we would like to express two simple considerations.

1.1. New Creation

For the Scotists, the Incarnation is mainly understood as the event toward which creation tends. In the formation of Adam from the clay, God already looked to Christ who would one day become the Second Adam (they cite a celebrated passage by Tertullian that relates to this).[7] From this perspective, Christ, the God-man, primarily represents the fulfillment of creation. Creation would be called to the elevation of grace in Jesus Christ from the beginning. The Incarnation cannot be imagined as a spare tire or a patch sewn to cover a tear—things that are not necessary if no wheel is pierced, or no outfit torn. For the Scotists, thinking of the Incarnation primarily as an event of reparation of sin means reducing its importance. The Incarnation is not an event that is related to another event (the sin of Adam); it is an absolute event, not linked to conditions. For this reason, the Scotist thesis can also be

---

[7] *"Quodcumque limus exprimebatur, Christus cogitabatur homo futurus"* ("Whatever was the form and expression which was then given to the clay [by the Creator] Christ was in His thoughts as one day to become man"). He continues: "Thus, that clay which was even then putting on the image of Christ, Who was to come in the flesh, was not only the work, but also the pledge and surety, of God" (Tertullian of Carthage, *De resurrectione carnis* 6.3.5 in *ANF*, vol. 3, trans. Peter Holmes [Peabody, MA: Hendrickson Publishers, 1994], 459).

called the thesis of the "Unconditional Incarnation." That is to say that the Incarnation happens unconditionally, regardless of whatever event happens or does not happen in history. From the beginning, creation tends toward the Incarnation. Some recent theologians actually hold that creation exists as a means in view of an end, an end that would be precisely the Incarnation. Creation would have no other meaning than to be as a preamble in view of the future Incarnation. Adam is created only because one day his humanity will be assumed by Christ.[8]

One can counter this perspective with the fact that Sacred Scripture speaks of the work of Christ as ushering in a "new age" (Matt 19:28, which has in Greek "*palingenesia*," meaning "regeneration"). It is said also that in Christ each of us can become a "new creation" (2 Cor 5: 17; Gal 6:15). In this regard, the meaning of "new" must be clarified; it should be understood as a renewal of something that already exists, not as an absolute novelty. The new creation is not the creation (possibly also through material and/or spiritual evolution) of a humanity or cosmos that did not previously exist and that are now a substitute for the previous humanity and cosmos, or which exist alongside them. The cited passages of Saint Paul are directed to people who lived far from God, thus belonging to the first fallen creation in Adam, and who have been renewed by Christ. They are new creatures not according to nature, because they always remain human, members of the human family created by God; but rather, they are new creatures according to grace. Being a new creature implies the continuation of the "creature," not its destruction and substitution with another. Saint Irenaeus (d. ca. 202) says it clearly: the Word assumed our human flesh and not the flesh of another humanity, because He did not want to create a new Adam—to create a new humanity—but He wanted to restore that same humanity that was lost in Adam.[9]

The new creation is therefore the re-creation of creation itself, not its abolition. This understanding respects the principle of synthesis, for which the coming of God (of the Spirit, in matter and in creation) does not annul that same creation but elevates it while preserving it, maintaining it in being.[10]

---

[8] It is not unusual for similar extremes to be supported with citations of the Eastern Fathers, and these theologians' interpretation of such writings seems, to us, forced.

[9] Saint Irenaeus of Lyon, *Adversus haereses* 3.21.10. In this sense, it also needs to be noted that many recent theologians use the Christological title of "New Adam," but Scripture never makes recourse to such a title; it speaks of Jesus as a "Second Man" (1 Cor 15:47) (which, given the context, clearly means "Second Adam"), and as a "Last Adam" (1 Cor 15:45). Using "New Adam" does not thus correspond to Scripture and could at least in some cases be an indication of an underlying theological ideology.

[10] Let us note again the distance from the thought of Hegel, who imagines elevation as an

Revelation, Faith, Theology

In the work of the new creation, Christ does not cancel out the preceding creation, because God is never the cause of non-being.[11]

Keeping this in mind while still maintaining the Scotist position is possible, but it leads to some doubt. If the Incarnation is an event foreseen as an integral part of the plan of creation and the elevation of the cosmos—and above all of the human being—a certain dynamic image of the salvific process follows from this: a movement, a *fieri*, a becoming carried out by God; and this is very close to our modern sensibilities, strongly marked by models of evolutionary thought. On the other hand, it appears to be an overly strong link between nature and grace. From this perspective, a nature that does not receive the grace offered through the Incarnation is, deep down, without meaning. And this seriously jeopardizes the distinction between the natural and supernatural orders, which in fact was the object of several theological treatises in the twentieth century; treatments that have tended to blur, and in some cases to completely deny, any distinction between the two orders. Moreover, such a position offers a "primitive" (so to speak) idea of God, because it imagines Him as a craftsman who works on a project in various phases, not able to carry it all out at the same time. If it is true that even in the first chapters of Genesis one finds descriptive images of God who creates the human being like a potter who first kneads the clay (the body) and then breathes a soul into it, it is well known that these anthropomorphic images cannot be taken literally.[12] They indicate the composition, in human nature, of two elements that, even if united, are distinct: the soul and the body. Thus, they do not mean that God did not know or could not create the complete human being immediately.

In sum, following the Scotists, one could reach the supposition that God is not deep down capable of immediately creating something perfect. Crea-

---

ontological transformation: in synthesis, the thesis and antithesis are found but also lost. The synthesis is a *novum* that absorbs the previous elements into itself, and is not their preservation. This does not concern synthesis in the Christian sense, as we have described it, but something else entirely.

[11] "*At ille ad quem non esse non pertinet non est causa deficiendi, id est, tendendi ad non esse, quia ut ita dicam, essendi causa est*" ("The One to whom non-being does not pertain, is not the cause of becoming less, that is, of tending toward non-being, because He is, if it can be said so, the cause of being": Saint Augustine of Hippo, *De diversis quaestionibus octoginta tribus* 21 [our translation]).

[12] Concerning the interpretation of Gen 1–3 that is not strictly literal, see Biblical Commission, *De charactere historico priorum capitum Geneseos*, June 30, 1909, quaestio 5 (DS 3516); Second Vatican Council, *Dei Verbum* (1965), §12. On the historicity of Gen 1–3, despite the fact that not every single narrative detail should be taken literally, see Biblical Commission, *Epistola Secretarii Commissionis de Re Biblica ad card. Suhard* (1948) (DS 3864); Pius XII, *Humani Generis* (1950) (DS 3898–3899).

The Reason for the Incarnation of the Word

tion would not be perfect from the beginning, but would have to move along toward its fulfillment in the Incarnation of the Word. Nonetheless, it is true in a certain sense that creation is not perfect from the beginning, but this is so in a relative sense. God tells Adam to cultivate the earth and commands the human beings to grow and multiply (see Gen 1:28). The idea of taking care of the earth and the growth of humankind certainly imply something empty that is to be filled, or better, possibilities to be realized, and thus to some extent imperfections or shortcomings (the current absence of goods that will be achieved). But this concerns relative imperfections (or, namely, possibilities of development relative to certain aspects), not a constitutive imperfection of creation. On the contrary, Catholic faith teaches that the world was created by God in the beginning as good and complete (see Gen 1: 31; 2:2 "God looked at everything he had made, and he found it very good [. . .] he rested on the seventh day": goodness and completion), and that the imperfections and disorder are the fruit of the sin added to creation by humankind. The Catholic doctrine also affirms that at the beginning various gifts of grace were offered to humankind. Does the fact that the human being was certainly called to grow in grace imply that this grace itself had to grow? Was it an insufficient grace? And if so, why would God have given it?[13] Does it perhaps have to be thought that God needs time to increase his grace in such a way that it can become mature, that it can reach its maximum possible unfolding in the grace of the Incarnation? This would imply not only that God would not be capable of creating a perfect world from the beginning—and thus He would have created it imperfect; but would not evil then be His fault?—but it would also imply that even in giving grace He, so to speak, would need to learn, would require time to develop experience. This way of presenting the question naturally represents a simplification for educational purposes, but deep down it refers to seriously considered problems. It is not that Scotus and his followers had the intention of affirming such things, but that these and other doubts emerge from their position.

The Scotists certainly would have been right if Scripture spoke of a total reconstruction, or of the perfecting of creation in an absolute sense. But this is not the case. Revelation speaks of the restoration of the same work

---

[13] To the facile objection that could be posed here, concerning the figurativeness and partiality of the grace given in the Old Testament with respect to the fullness in the New, we shall respond with similar ease, noting also that the historical-salvific development, given concretely in the succession of the two Testaments, is determined by the sin of Adam, which does not entail a diminution of God's grace in itself, but diminishes the creature's capacity to receive it and bear fruit in it. Hence, the long divine pedagogy leading up to Christ becomes necessary (*a parte hominis*).

created as good by God at the beginning, and subsequently ruined by the sin of humanity.[14] Thus the Thomistic thesis appears more consistent. The Word has become flesh primarily to redeem humanity, to atone for the sins of human beings, to recover the dignity of the human being and to return order to the cosmos. In the remote and ultimately hypothetical possibility that the human had not sinned, then, the Word would not have become flesh. But this does not in any way imply that the Word would not have had a part in the salvation of humanity.

1.2. The Salvation of the Angels

A second reflection concerns the place of the angels in the divine plan. The formula *Verbum caro* speaks of the Word becoming a human being, not an angel. The Word assumes a human nature, not an angelic nature. As we shall see further on (Chapter 3), the good angels do not need redemption from sin, because they have never committed it; the evil ones cannot receive the grace of redemption and are eternally condemned to estrangement from the Creator.[15] Although the heavenly spirits owe everything to the Word—because He is their Creator and because they permanently receive the gift of being in Heaven from Him—it needs to be said that the incarnate Word has not poured out his Blood for them, but for human beings: "Surely he did not help angels but rather the descendants of Abraham" (Heb 2:16). Scripture speaks various times of the Blood of Christ as a means of atonement and as a price paid for the redemption of human beings. It never speaks this way for the angels. There is no doubt that the celestial spirits form a part of creation. And yet, if it were true—as the Scotists prefer—that creation was ordered, from the beginning,

---

[14] This is how it is understood, for example, in the ancient *Letter of Barnabas* (composed between AD 70 and 130), which affirms in chs. 5–6: "Furthermore, my brethren, if the Lord endured suffering for our souls, although He is the Lord of the whole world, to Whom God said at the foundation of the world: 'Let us make human beings in our image, after our likeness' (Gen 1: 26) . . . Again I will show you how He refers to us. He made a second creation in the last days. And [in this connection] the Lord says: '*Behold, I make the last thing as the first*'. . . . See, then, we have been recreated . . . Because He Himself was going to be manifested in the flesh and dwell among us" (in *FCNT*, vol. 1, trans. Francis X. Glimm, Joseph M.F. Marique, and Gerald G. Walsh [New York: Cima Publishing Co., Inc., 1947], 197–200 [emphasis added]).

[15] "It is the *irrevocable* nature of their choice, and not a defect in the infinite divine mercy, that makes the angels' sin unforgivable. 'There is no repentance for the angels after their fall, just as there is no repentance for men after death' [St. John Damascene, *De Fide orth*. 2, 4: PG 94, 877]" (CCC §393).

The Reason for the Incarnation of the Word

toward the Incarnation, what is to be thought about that part of creation that has not obtained a particular benefit from it? The good angels were already saved in Heaven before the Incarnation of the Word, in fact, before the creation of humanity. Certainly, it can be hypothesized that the heavenly spirits have received benefits deriving from the Incarnation in advance but this argument—which is quite valid for understanding the Immaculate Conception of Mary (see Chapter Seven)—is not applicable to the angels. In fact, in the case of Mary, it refers to her having been preserved from original sin, from the sin that marks each human being, in view of the merits of her Son, Jesus. This concerns a unique and unrepeatable grace, conceded by God in a world where there is sin and no human being escapes it. By contrast, the holy angels are beings who have already escaped sin and are confirmed in salvation; otherwise they would be in Hell like the demons, the fallen angels.

Thus, there is a significant part of creation that does not seem to be oriented toward the Incarnation in a decisive way. The Word is made flesh, is made material, is made a human being; this indicates the Incarnation is directed toward the work of redemption, of the reacquisition of the material and human world, created good by God at the beginning and ruined by us through sin. To say that the Word is made flesh implies that this coming of God onto earth has, in particular, the aim of this dimension of creation, which has irretrievably ruined itself by its own hands, and which, nevertheless, God loves and does not want to leave to be lost. The Incarnation is the concrete way in which God takes back this dimension of the cosmos: the world of humankind, which has condemned itself to estrangement from Him.

Thus, the angels represent a serious obstacle to the Scotist interpretation of the formula *Verbum caro*. Consequently, it is no wonder that in a part of contemporary theology there has been an attempt to gradually erase the study of angels, leading to its abolition altogether. We are referring to that part of contemporary theology that is focused in a special way on the human being, producing the so-called "anthropological turn." In this theological perspective, God naturally remains the declared primary interest, but the human being becomes the privileged point of reference. God is discussed mediately, that is, through His earthly interlocutor, the human being. The human being is studied in order to find some way to ascend back to God. The human being comes to be placed at the center of theology. In this perspective, the authors generally prefer the Scotist thesis concerning the reason for the Incarnation, even if they do so for different reasons than those of Scotus. Having placed humanity at the center, they see it as the apex of creation and as the end of the action of God Himself. Salvific history points towards the human being, in this case the man, Jesus Christ. For these recent theologians, the event in which the Word becomes man cannot be an accidental, conditional fact. They cannot conceive that the Word might act and work in a perfect way in this world without making Himself man, or at least that humanity can reach its fulfillment without being assumed by the Word. In a certain sense, even for the Word the human being becomes the center of all. An anthropocentrism that is so accentuated certainly cannot admit great importance to the angels, who instead represent a disturbing element in this theological perspective, as something that is interposed between God and humanity. Thus, various contemporary authors have stopped discussing celestial spirits, and in certain cases they have even explicitly denied their existence.[16]

In conclusion, we must remember that those who sustain the position that is called Scotist are not, in fact, to be considered heretical. It would be heretical to deny the fact of the Incarnation or to deny its salvific value. Though the Thomist position is the preferred stance of the Fathers and Doctors,[17] the Church has not taken a definitive position on this point, and this leaves space for the investigation of theologians and the possibility of thinking of it in one way or another. Nonetheless, for the reasons presented and for various others,[18] the opinion that the Word has become incarnate mainly to repair the sin of Adam is certainly preferable.

1.3. Response to an Objection

But here is a possible objection: In preferring the Thomistic position, do we not invalidate the cardinal principle of our entire exposition? In Chapter One,

---

[16] The crisis of angelology is also found in the fact that the majority of theological faculties have substituted the course concerning God the Creator, or concerning creation, with a course on theological anthropology. Anthropology is, of course, an important part of the doctrine of creation, but it does not exhaust the subject by itself, given that the Creed professes that God is the Creator of "all things visible and invisible" (DS 125, 150). To cast the theme of angels out of theological formation means to condemn it to oblivion and to relegate it to the mere level of devotion, which—without the support of an adequate theology and, consequently, of correct preaching to the faithful—can easily slip into paganized forms, as can be seen from the modern-day existence of a very broad New Age literature concerning the angels.

[17] A single example, among many, is represented by the *De Incarnatione* of Saint Athanasius of Alexandria (d. 373), which clearly is a precursor to the position of Saint Thomas.

[18] It seems that one could say that the strength of the Thomist position lies in the fact that it is mainly based on Scripture, while Scotus—though written against a biblical backdrop—actually leans more heavily on a theological deduction, starting from the predestination of the soul of Christ or, namely, from the glory realized by the Incarnation in a human nature.

we sought to show that the incarnate Word is the fundamental synthetic principle of faith and of theology, and now, at the beginning of Chapter Two, we are affirming that the incarnate Word is a historical accident, an optional figure who intervenes only because, and only after, humanity has sinned. How, then, could the centrality of Christ still be maintained?

We can respond to this briefly in the following ways: (1) Faith and theology, which depend on Revelation, are completely established on the Christocentrism of the *Verbum caro*. Revelation teaches us that the Word has been made flesh, and it is on this most central hinge that both the faith, as a response to Revelation, and theology as faith seeking understanding, turn. (2) In Revelation, there is no speaking about *what would have happened*, but rather *what happened*. Theologians contemplate hypotheses of the type "what would have happened if" not to substitute something else in place of the concrete historical-salvific economy, but only to better understand it. Thus, the hypothesis "if Adam had not sinned" is precisely that, and not a reality to pit against history. Adam actually sinned; this is the only historical event that in fact happened, and it is what counts. God has acted the way He has acted in *this* salvation history, not in another hypothetical one. However, the hypotheses lead us to better appreciate the value and significance of the choices of God for us in history. (3) Thus, in history, in Revelation, and in the faith that actually *exist*—and not in those hypothetical ones that do not exist—the Word became flesh because Adam sinned, that is, mainly to redeem humankind. Revelation, the faith, and theology, thus, completely pivot on the principle *Verbum caro*, namely, *et-et*. (4) There is also an original *et-et*, prior to the question of sin, namely, the two-pole structure of human nature (soul-body). A wound is inserted in it; a wound that puts the harmonic Spirit-matter unity in tension. This helps us to appreciate even more the *Verbum caro*, which heals such wounds and reestablishes the harmony of the synthesis. If Adam had not sinned, the Word would have maintained such a creatural synthesis without being incarnate, just as He had created it before becoming incarnate. If the fracture does not occur then there is no reason to mend it, just like when one does not fall ill, one does not need to take medicine to heal.

Therefore, we can comfortably maintain the classical thesis about the reason for the Incarnation, without it jeopardizing the fundamental centrality of the synthetic principle of the Incarnation, expressed with the *et-et*. We can therefore proceed by considering various aspects manifested by the remarkable union between the Word and flesh in Jesus Christ.

2. *Verbum* (Word)

2.1. The Word as Reason

Before anything else, let us look at the two terms: *Verbum* and *caro*. *Verbum*—*Logos* in the original Greek of John's Gospel—indicates discourse, reason, word, and science. At the center of the Christian faith we thus find Reason. And not just human reason, otherwise Christianity would only be one more version of rationalism, in which human reason is absolutized. At the center of Christianity, instead, we find the eternal Reason. That it is such, the same Saint John tells us at the beginning of the first chapter of his Gospel: "In the beginning was the Word, / and the Word was with God, / and the Word was God" (John 1:1). "In the beginning" should be understood as a way of indicating eternity. The Word exists from the beginning, that is, always.[19] Moreover, it is clearly said that He is God, and God is eternal. Thus, this does not concern human intelligence, but divine Reason.

Christianity is the religion that adores a God who is called Reason, *Logos*. It is not then an irrational religion, without reason, or even a religion that fights against reason (fideism). Christianity adores divine Reason and thus also knows to travel the paths of human rationality, without falling into rationalism (the use of reason without God, or against God) because of it.

Saint John Paul II defined faith and reason as two wings by which the human spirit is elevated to knowledge of the truth.[20] It follows that the Christian uses reason and does so *both* to know natural objects (through philosophy and the sciences, or even through simple common sense), *and* to reflect on objects of supernatural knowledge, given to him or her by God through Revelation.[21] In this second case, we are dealing with theology, the science that applies human reason to revealed mysteries that are in themselves superior to reason. To be more precise, one needs to speak of sacred or supernatural theology, because Christians also know and practice natural theology, or philosophical theology, also called theodicy. This concerns a purely natural, philosophical knowledge of God, carried out by the use of reason alone, prescinding from Revelation.

---

[19] Against the heretic Arius, the First Council of Nicaea (AD 325) defined as false the doctrine according to which "There was a time when He [the *Logos*] was not" (DS 126).
[20] See Saint John Paul II, *Fides et Ratio* (1998), §1.
[21] See *ST* I-II, q. 109, a. 1; First Vatican Council, *Dei Filius* (1870), ch. 4 (DS 3015).

Verbum (Word)

2.2. Natural Theology

Since God is Reason, Christians do not fear utilizing this faculty of the human soul, in which they see a clear reflection of the divinity. The small *logos*—our intelligence—is a limited participation in the great divine *Logos*. For this reason, Catholic faith is a faith that values reasonability in the theological sphere and in the more disparate spheres of knowledge.[22] Historical evidence is found in the fact that Christianity, in all eras and places, in addition to carrying out missionary preaching of the Word of God, has given impetus to all disciplines of human knowledge.

> Thomas [Aquinas] recognized that nature, philosophy's proper concern, could contribute to the understanding of divine Revelation. Faith therefore has no fear of reason, but seeks it out and has trust in it. Just as grace builds on nature and brings it to fulfillment, so faith builds upon and perfects reason. Illumined by faith, reason is set free from the fragility and limitations deriving from the disobedience of sin and finds the strength required to rise to the knowledge of the Triune God. Although he made much of the supernatural character of faith, the Angelic Doctor did not overlook the importance of its reasonableness; indeed he was able to plumb the depths and explain the meaning of this reasonableness. Faith is in a sense an 'exercise of thought'; and human reason is neither annulled nor debased in assenting to the contents of faith, which are in any case attained by way of free and informed choice.[23]

The queen of all rational disciplines, at least according to the classics, is philosophy. In this sphere, Christians have held—inheriting Greek thought in particular[24]—that God is knowable by pure reason as regards His existence

---

[22] See Benedict XVI, *Conferral of the First "Ratzinger Prize": Address of His Holiness Benedict XVI*, June 30, 2011: "If Christ is the Logos, the truth, human beings must respond to him with their own logos, with their reason. To arrive at Christ they must be on the path of the truth. They must open themselves to the Logos, to creative Reason, from which their own reason derives and to which it refers them. From this it may be understood that Christian faith, by its very nature, must bring theology into being, must question itself on the reasonableness of faith—although of course the concept of reason and that of science embrace many dimensions—and in this way the concrete nature of the connection between faith and reason must be fathomed ever anew."

[23] Saint John Paul II, *Fides et Ratio*, §43.

[24] See John Paul II, *Fides et Ratio*, §§36–48.

and some of His natural attributes, prescinding from the supernatural Revelation of the mysteries hidden in God. Scripture confirms this possibility (see Wis 13:5; Rom 1:19-20), as does the Magisterium of the Church.[25]

2.2.1. Certain but Limited Knowledge

It is clear that certain but limited knowledge of God can be reached with natural theology. One can know the existence of God as well as some of His attributes (non-Christian philosophers and thinkers have also succeeded at this), but there can be absolutely no knowledge of truths that are above the capacity of human reasoning; these truths are known only if God reveals them. Still—after He reveals these truths—we can make use of reason in regard to them (supernatural theology) in order to seek to better understand what we believe. However, reason can never exhaust the mystery of truths such as the Holy Trinity, the Incarnation of the Word, the perpetual virginity of Mary, Eucharistic transubstantiation, etc.

2.2.2. Christian Faith and Philosophy

Christian thought has made use of natural reason from its beginning. Believing does not imply ceasing to use one's mind, but to use it in a new and better way. Thus, for example, Benedict XVI writes:

> Faith by its specific nature is an encounter with the living God—an encounter opening up new horizons extending beyond the sphere of reason. But it is also a purifying force for reason itself. From God's standpoint, faith liberates reason from its blind spots and therefore helps it to be ever more fully itself. Faith enables reason to do its work more effectively and to see its proper object more clearly.[26]

The use of reason for apologetics is first witnessed in the early days of the Church. Both the Jews and the Pagans accused the Christians—as members of a new religion that was at that time considered only a superstition or idolatry—of various philosophical-theological errors and moral crimes. The first Fathers of the Church responded to various accusations against Christians, and at the same time to the accusations made against the Christian conception of God. This is the period of the so-called *Apologies*, such as the two

---

[25] See First Vatican Council, *Dei Filius*, ch. 2 (DS 3004), which will be cited further along.
[26] Benedict XVI, *Deus Caritas est* (2005), §28.

written by the philosopher and martyr Saint Justin (d. ca. 165). But other names should also be remembered, such as Saint Clement of Alexandria (d. ca. 215) and Origen (d. 254), who not only continued to defend Christianity against accusations of certain pagan philosophers (see Origen's *Contra Celsum*), but also took inspiration from Saint Justin himself in emphasizing that the Christian faith is not in fact opposed to philosophy, to a rational search for the truth, but that Christianity is in fact the "true philosophy," while classical Greek philosophy is a "preparation" (as Saint Clement puts it). The Gospel of Christ is the true philosophy toward which rational philosophy tends, just as the Old Testament tended towards it in a different way.[27] What Saint Clement affirmed in writing was later verified concretely in the existence of many philosophers and lovers of wisdom who, like Saint Justin before them, passed from the rational search for the truth to the acceptance of the Truth in Person, Jesus Christ, and became Christians. The most famous example is that of Saint Augustine of Hippo, who struggled for many years of his youth in the search for a philosophical school that could give him the truth, a truth he found in the Christian faith, which satisfied his "restless heart."[28]

This openness to philosophy on the part of Christian thought developed according to two paths (*et-et*): on one hand, faith was aided by philosophy to better understand itself; on the other hand, faith aided philosophy to reason better and thus kept philosophy clear of various errors. In the first case, we are dealing with supernatural theology, namely, the reflection that starts from the Revelation of God and from its acceptance in faith, and then uses intellectual means, particularly philosophy, to give reasons for itself and to seek deeper understanding of the mysteries of God. In the second case, we have both "Christian philosophy" and the so-called natural theology, which from Gottfried Leibniz (d. 1716) onward has also assumed the name of "theodicy." We shall bypass the theme of Christian philosophy here and focus our attention only on the two forms of theology, beginning with natural theology.

2.2.3. Proofs of God's Existence

Throughout the centuries, Christian thought has developed not only a rational defense against the attacks coming from various sides, but also a positive proposal, consisting in a philosophical reflection aimed at achieving a rational

---

[27] See Saint John Paul II, *Fides et Ratio*, §38; Benedict XVI, *General Audience*, April 18, 2007.
[28] Saint Augustine of Hippo, *Confessions* 1.1.1.

demonstration of the existence of God. There were many different attempts at this. The three most celebrated are: (1) the so-called "ontological proof" (an expression coined by Immanuel Kant, d. 1804) of Saint Anselm of Canterbury (d. 1109), called by the latter simply *"unum argumentum"* ("the single argument"); (2) the "five ways" of Saint Thomas Aquinas (d. 1275); and (3) the thesis of Leibniz about the "best of all possible worlds." These three proofs of the existence of God are the most famous, but they are not the only ones, and they are not in all cases the best. In fact, the Leibnizian argument shows itself to be excessively rationalistic and was ridiculed by Voltaire (d. 1778) in his well known romance the *Candide*. We shall begin with an exposition of this third argument and then go on to the other proofs.

1. Leibniz

The philosopher of Hanover seeks to demonstrate the "justice of God" (theodicy) despite the evils that we see present in the world. He holds that the existence of evil does not constitute an argument against the existence of an omnipotent and just God. In his work *Essais de théodicée* of 1710, he starts from the affirmation that "God is the first reason of all things."[29] From the beginning, it is easy to notice a weak point in the argumentation. Wanting to demonstrate the existence of God against those who use evil as a pretext for denying it, Leibniz starts from the assertion, taken for granted, that God exists and that He is the reason for all things. This way, what should be the end-point for the demonstration is found as a starting axiom, with or without which everything that follows in the reflection stands or falls. Thus, we can say that Leibniz's proof of the existence of God is not really such a proof at all. If anything, the brilliant thinker has provided a proof of the possibility of the existence of God despite the evil that exists in the world; that is, he has tried to show that discovering the evil of the world does not necessarily lead to the denial of God's existence. However, he does not demonstrate that God exists, given that he starts precisely from this premise.

The second—and most important—cornerstone of his argument is this claim: "this supreme wisdom, united to a goodness that is no less infinite, cannot but have chosen the best."[30] Basically, Leibniz says that if we attribute to God the divine characteristics, among which are supreme goodness and

---

[29] G.W. Leibniz, *Theodicy: Essays on the Goodness of God, the Freedom of Man, and the Origin of Evil*, trans. E.M. Huggard (Peru, IL: Open Court Publishing, 1985 [1st ed., London: Routledge & Kegan Paul Limited, 1951]), 127, §7.

[30] Leibniz, *Theodicy*, 128, §8.

wisdom, we cannot do anything other than affirm that such a God always chooses what is best. Thus, the philosopher introduces the idea of "possible worlds" that God could have created, among which He chose the actual world, which He decided to create because He saw that it was the best of all. According to Leibniz, for whatever evils this world might contain, they are certainly less than the evils that would be present in other possible worlds. This reflection undeniably has its own charm, yet it misses the mark, because it starts from the presupposition that God exists and that He is wise and good. The existence and attributes of God must be *demonstrated* by natural theology and not taken as postulates (as in supernatural theology).

2. Saint Anselm

More consistent in this sense—even if still imperfect—is the *unum argumentum* of the Magnificent Doctor. Even in this case, the existence of God is presented deep down as a presupposition but, in contrast to Leibniz, Saint Anselm makes the effort to demonstrate through reasoning that, at least in theory, he is open to the possibility that God does not exist. In his work entitled the *Proslogion* (1077–1078), he starts by noting that all people conceive of God as "That than which a greater cannot be conceived" ("*id quo maius cogitari nequit*"). Therefore, God exists, at least in the minds of those who think so. But—he continues—to exist in reality, and not only in the mind, represents a greater perfection than to exist only in thought. Thus, if God is "That than which a greater cannot be conceived," it follows that He must also really exist, otherwise one could think of a being greater than Him, that is, a being that exists not only in thought, but also in reality.[31] Now such an argument, however ingenious, remains inconclusive, as pointed out by the monk Gaunilo of Marmoutiers (d. 1083) in the *Liber pro insipiente*.[32] In fact—Gaunilo notes—imagining or thinking of a perfect island that exists really does not imply that the island exists in itself outside of thought, even if it is thought as existing. Saint Anselm responds with the *Liber apologeticus*, in which he clarifies that the *unum argumentum* is valid only for God and not for other created beings. The most perfect Being (God) must exist

---

[31] The Magnificent Doctor clearly grasps the extreme consequences of this principle, when he teaches that not only is God that which is the greatest that the human being can think about, but that He is also that which is greater than anything that the human being can think: "Thus, Lord not only are you that which nothing greater can be thought, but you are also something greater than what can possibly be thought" (Saint Anselm of Canterbury, *Proslogion* 15, [our translation]).

[32] The complete title is *Quid ad haec respondeat quidam pro insipiente* (ca. 1078).

really, otherwise He is not that to which we are referring.

With his proof, Saint Anselm is deep down responding primarily to fools who affirm the non-existence of God. He starts from the concept of God, which is also found in the mind of atheists and, on the basis of it, he demonstrates the logical inconsistency of their argumentation. From this standpoint, the *unum argumentum* (also accompanied by the answer to Gaunilo) is always valid and we must be thankful to the Magnificent Doctor for having provided such a solid philosophical response, which shows the theoretical absurdity of atheism. However, agnosticism, today referred to as a "weak thought" or "relativism," is not eradicated by this. Saint Anselm has in fact shown the logical absurdity of atheism understood as the presumption of affirming with certainty that God does not exist, but he has not yet proved the existence of God.

3. Saint Thomas

Thus, we reach the proof, or rather the proofs, that are rightly the most widely known in the history of Christian thought: the celebrated "five ways" developed by Saint Thomas for reaching the rational demonstration of the existence of God. This actually concerns paths that were already traveled by previous thinkers, but the merit of the Angelic Doctor is that of having presented them in a comprehensive, concise, and clear way, making out of what was scattered and fragmented a great argument that is refracted over five different and concordant paths. What unites them is the *a posteriori* procedure, in contrast to the *a priori* approach that we encountered in Leibniz and Saint Anselm. Saint Thomas himself criticizes that approach, recalling that something which is demonstrated in thought does not for this reason exist in reality as well.[33] Since God is not evident to us,[34] it follows that we must arrive at knowledge of Him through the things known to us. Therefore, we must move from created entities back to the Creator—from effects to the Cause. This is possible because created things, though they are limited and imperfect, have their own logic, and thus manifest a *logos*. Our intellect, the little *logos* that is in the human being, can grasp the link between the logic of

---

[33] See *ST* I, q. 2, a. 1, ad 2. In the body of the article, the saint also responds indirectly to Saint Anselm's defense of his thesis in response to the criticisms of Guanilo, a defense from which we have salvaged some usefulness.

[34] The philosophical trend of "ontologism" holds that our mind is in immediate cognitive contact with subsisting Being (God), and thus striving to prove the existence of God would be a useless effort. Not only does this position go against the teaching of Scripture and the Church, but even at the purely rational level it clashes with experience, through which God is not at all evident to us.

Verbum (Word)

creatures and the Creator *Logos*. In Saint Thomas this unity between *Logos* and *logoi* is drawn out over the registry of being, or what is called the "*analogia entis*" ("analogy of being"). This indicates that, while the being of God and of humanity are different, there is continuity between them because the creatures, the beings, exist insofar as they participate (though in a partial and imperfect way) in the being of God. The *a posteriori* direction of the Angelic Doctor is in harmony both with Scripture (see the passages of Wisdom and Romans cited above), and with the teaching of the Magisterium: "The same Holy Mother Church holds and teaches that God, the beginning and end of all things, can be known with certitude by the natural light of human reason from created things."[35]

The five ways are based on five fundamental aspects of reality and the experience we have of them; thus, we can see the connection for ourselves. These aspects are: the mutability of all things; their being produced by another; their non-necessity; the fact they are not perfect to the maximum degree; and their tending towards ends. Through these ways, the Angelic Doctor demonstrates not only that atheism is absurd and contradictory (as Saint Anselm does), but that agnosticism and polytheism are too. Existing things do not have any truly rational explanation if they are not traced back to that most perfect, subsisting, absolute, and unconditioned Being, who explains the existence and subsistence of finite beings. This subsisting Being is what everyone calls "God" or, namely, He is what is understood when people use the word God. Naturally, Saint Thomas does not pretend that God can be known perfectly starting from creatures, because they are finite, while God is infinite. But we can start from the former to show that He exists, because from the existence of an effect the existence of the cause can clearly be deduced.[36]

The five ways are presented by the Common Doctor in *Summa Theologiae* I, q. 2, a. 3:

(1) The first way is that which Saint Thomas derives from motion or movement (which must be understood in the Aristotelian sense as any change). We shall take the example of movement as it is commonly understood today,

---

[35] First Vatican Council, *Dei Filius*, ch. 2 (DS 3004). A few years later, for the purpose of anti-ontologism, this teaching would also be presented in the *Decretum* of the Holy Congregation of Studies of July 27, 1914, which approved the known twenty-four theses of Thomistic philosophy. The twenty-second thesis reads: "We do not perceive with immediate intuition that God exists, and neither do we demonstrate it *a priori*, but only *a posteriori*, that is, 'by means of the things that were made' (Rom 1:20), with a proof drawn from the effects to the cause" (DS 3622).

[36] See *ST* I, q. 2, a. 2, ad 3.

the change of position from one place to another. Every object, in itself, can be moved, even if it is still. When this occurs, it is because the object is moved by another, which is already in movement. No object is capable of moving itself, but it needs to be moved by another. In turn, the latter, to be in motion and so move the former, must be moved by something else. For example, a still marble is set in motion by another marble that clashes against it; but that in its turn was put in motion by a finger, which had flung it forward. Now, if we had to imagine that this chain of beings that transmitted the movement were infinite, we would have to conclude that it is impossible for the movement to exist. Or, to give another example, consider unlit matches that are lit by the passage of flame from one to another (changing from a cold to a hot state). However many matches are used for this game, we understand that at the beginning there must be a first flame from which the chain begins. This chain must be—however long it is—limited and finite. An infinite chain, in this case a beginning-less chain, cannot exist in the material world and would never lead to the lighting of that match that I now hold in my hands, because the flame that burns on the match that I have in my hands could never have reached the here and now if it had to pass through an infinite chain of passages. The infinite, in fact, never arrives at the end![37] But if here between my hands I have the lit match, there is an end here, however temporary. Well, this says that the chain of passages can be even very long but not infinite, and that, if I go backwards, I will find a point beyond which there is nothing else: that is the beginning of the chain that reaches me. Thus, if there are things that move and change, it is because at the beginning of the chain of movements and changes there is a First Mover, and this is normally called God. This proof is applied to all passages from "potency" (possibility) to "act" (reality) that we see in beings.

(2) The second way is developed on the basis of the notion of an efficient cause, that is, on that which produces something else, such as two parents who bring a baby into the world. If one goes backwards, it will be seen that those parents in their turn were begotten, and so forth, all the way back to the first human parent. If it were postulated that the chain of births of human beings is infinite, the previous discourse would apply, and I would not exist. Thus, at the origin of all efficient causes, there is a first efficient Cause, not caused by anything else, and this is called God.[38]

---

[37] In this sense, it will be useful to recall the lesson that derives from the paradoxes of Zeno of Elea (d. 431 BC), even if he proposed them in a skeptical sense, while we avail ourselves of them precisely for the procedure of a *reductio ad absurdum* that, *sub contrario*, manifests the reasonableness of the five Thomistic ways.

[38] We need to recall again that this process of going backwards does not imply that God is part of the created order, as the first element over and above the others. In a work of his

Verbum (Word)

(3) The third way is based on contingency, that is, on the non-necessity of created things. This means that it is not necessary that they exist; they can exist, or not, and above all, before they came into existence they were not, and one day they will no longer be. The pen that is on my table was produced in a factory perhaps a year ago; before then, it did not exist. One day, for one reason or another, it will be destroyed and will cease to be. Even if it helps me in my work, nonetheless it is not a necessary object in an absolute sense. The world existed and moved along even without my pen, and it will do so after it is destroyed. This line of thinking is also valid for all the elements that we find in the world. We think of the trees, the mountains, the planets, and the stars . . . there was a time in which these things did not exist and, going further and further back, we see that there was a time in which none of them existed (modern science has long confirmed these philosophical reflections). Can we thus say that there was a time in which absolutely nothing existed? No, because if there were, then nothing would exist now. In fact, as was said in the second way, everything that begins to exist comes from a cause that precedes it. Thus, it needs to be recognized that, even when nothing existed of the beings of the cosmos, there existed a first and eternal Being from which all others were drawn into existence. This Being will be the only necessary one, the only one that cannot not exist, and the One that all people call God.

(4) The fourth way takes its cue from various degrees of perfection that are found in things. There are works of art that are more beautiful or less beautiful, just as there are foods that are more tasty or less tasty, and so forth. On what basis do we human beings establish this hierarchy of values? In the current mentality, marked by relativism, such a hierarchy is often held as purely subjective and arbitrary: each one establishes it for oneself, without any objective reason, according to the slogan: "Beauty is in the eye of the beholder." Despite such often-circulating statements, the fact remains that the number of those who eat pasta or meat for lunch is infinitely greater than the number of those who are fed with paper confetti, even if their color makes them beautiful to see and recalls the joy of the carnival. Why? Because

---

youth, Saint Thomas distinguishes three types of efficient cause, remembering that God is cause of all things not essentially, but rather causatively: efficient causality exists in a univocal, equivocal, and analogous sense. A univocal cause: cause and effect are identical or of the same species (as in our example of father and son); equivocal cause: there is only a vague resemblance between cause and effect (a scribble by a human hand); analogous cause: cause and effect have a relative similarity or likeness in relation to existence and a substantial dissimilarity with respect to the essence. Thus, the analogical way allows us to indicate the link, despite the great dissimilarity, between God and creatures, Being and beings. For the passage of Saint Thomas, see *Scriptum super Sententiis* I, d. 8, q. 1, a. 2.

true food is much better and nourishing, and this is so objectively and not only on account of the will of the one who prefers it to the paper. Whoever is not blind from the intellectual point of view, knows very well that values are objective and not arbitrary, although tastes can make certain aspects prevail over others, without affecting the underlying objectivity (one can enjoy the works of Michelangelo over those of Giotto, but in both cases we are confronted, objectively, with beauty expressed through figurative arts).[39] We thus assign a degree of beauty, goodness, truth, etc., to things on the basis of a reference to a supreme degree, which surpasses all beautiful, good, and true things. The more these things approach perfection, the more we call them beautiful, good, and true. Therefore, there is a First Value, which shares with all beings its own attributes. This most perfect First Value is not only a fruit of imagination, but truly exists because—as Saint Thomas says, citing Aristotle—what is maximum in truth is also maximum in being. This fourth way, while being fully valid, appears less compelling than the others, because it is *a posteriori* in its beginning and its development, starting from the qualities that are in things that actually exist, but in its conclusion appears to yield to an *apriorism*.[40]

(5) The final way, rather, is very powerful, and the experimental sciences confirm it more and more in our own time. Saint Thomas notes that inanimate things, those that do not have knowledge and freedom and thus cannot choose, act for the realization of an end. We can, for example, recall what happens in the world of ants and bees, which manifest extraordinary rationality in what they do, both individually and in a group: an inexplicable

---

[39] In this sense, we note that it is possible to have a taste for contemporary works of art, but such an appreciation is not directed at the work itself, which is often very poor, if not banal or monstrous, but rather, to the idea that is expressed through it. That is to say, there has been a shift with regard to the object of artistic taste, resulting in the involution of contemporary art. Since the latter almost never expresses objective beauty and virtuosity, the taste of the person is not directed toward the artistic product, but rather the ideology that it conveys. From this it is confirmed that human taste is objective, so much that in order to enjoy contemporary art, one needs to not focus on the product of the art but on the idea of the artist. This is why contemporary art is conceptual and elitist, being accessible only in its hidden meaning—to be found through study and reflection—and not in the phenomenal beauty, toward which the artistic taste of the human being naturally inclines.

[40] However, we advise the reader that the question, referred to only briefly here, is very complex and has been debated by various currents of Thomism in the twentieth century. The basic question is that of establishing if the link with the ontological proof of Saint Anselm is only verbal or substantial. Moreover, this concerns clarifying whether the fourth way should be interpreted mainly through the way of causality, transcendentality, or participation. These are issues that we cannot even touch upon here.

fact, given that the insects do not have a mind, they do not reason, they do not have awareness of their own existence, and they do not choose. They carry out, so to speak, a "program" that they find in themselves. The Angelic Doctor says that what is lacking intelligence does not tend toward an end (for example, to construct a beehive with precise hexagonal cells that make the best use of the available space) if it is not directed by a being that possesses intellect and knowledge, just as an arrow that tends towards the target only because it was directed by an archer. But all that exists reveals a finality that is not explicable solely on account of immanent causes and, through the principle of the chain of causality, refers back to the first final Cause of all things. Now, the supreme Being who orders all natural things to their own ends is called by everyone, God.

4. Divine Attributes

The proofs set forth by Saint Thomas rationally demonstrate the existence of God, the perfect and subsisting Being, but also some of His attributes, such as His unicity, eternity, intellect, power, and capacity to direct and attract creatures to Himself. It is impossible, rather, to demonstrate philosophically that God is One and Triune. Only supernatural Revelation grants us this truth, unreachable to the capacities of the created intellect alone.

Finally, we note that with the Thomistic synthesis the chapter on "theodicy" is not definitively concluded. Other proofs can and must be thought up, through the sound and right use of the natural reason, in a special way in our time, enriched by the many new instances of scientific knowledge that the Angelic Doctor did not have at his disposal. However, the basic criterion taught to us by him remains firm; the position for which the only efficacious proofs are those that are *a posteriori*—those that start from reality, from creation, and ascend to the Creator.

Outline of the Five Ways

	Perspective	God	Divine Attribute
First Way	From Change	First Unmoved Mover	Subsisting Being Itself (*Ipsum Esse Subsistens*)
Second Way	From Production	First Cause	Creator
Third Way	From Contingency	Unique Necessary and Absolute One	Eternal
Fourth Way	From the Degree of Value	First Value	Most Perfect
Fifth Way	From Finality	Final Cause	Provident

N.B. From the divine attributes that are deduced from the aforementioned proofs, the attribute of the divine unicity can be shown: God is One. This is because a plurality of gods cannot be reconciled with the attributes presented above, because—for example—God would not be perfect if there were other gods (perfection, by definition, can belong to one alone). In polytheism, in fact, even if a sort of superior god or father of the gods is often contemplated, the fact remains that such a figure does not possess all of the attributes of the divinity, which are divided among the gods.

Finally, we note that these arguments are ontological/metaphysical. However, there are other ways of rationally demonstrating the existence of God, such as the scientific way (admiring the order, harmony, and mathematical structure of creation, which presupposes a creative Intelligence) and the historical way (the miracles and prodigious signs, the testimony of martyrs and saints, artistic and cultural achievements—this way is especially valid for showing the greatness of Christianity,[41] but it also reflects back on

---

[41] Numerous currents of recent theology have questioned (or have reread, in a way that is not merely philosophical) the *analogia entis*, that is, the possibility of demonstrating the existence and main attributes of God by means of natural reason. This is probably due to the assimilation that occurred between the *analogia entis* and apologetics as a whole,

Verbum (Word)

the God who with His grace produces these realities).

2.3. The Word Precisely as Word

The Greek *Logos* is also translated as "Word." The term should be understood, in general, as an expression of one's own thought and the communication of it to another. The dialogical character of the Trinity is manifested in the *Logos*-Word. By grace, it is communicated to creatures. In His eternal Word, God speaks with angels and human beings; He addresses the Word to them. This Word is the author and mediator of supernatural Revelation. As is necessary, the eternal Word is translated into human words, which then come to be put into writing in the Bible and are also found, handed down, in ecclesial Tradition. But these channels—written and oral—of Revelation exist only because there is the Word of which they are a pallid and yet coherent expression. Thus Christianity, more than being a religion of the book, is the religion of the Word, and this Word is a divine Person. Christianity requires us to entrust ourselves to the Word, the incarnate Word, Jesus Christ. We entrust ourselves because we believe the words spoken by the Word (the obedience of faith is to be given to God who reveals Himself).[42]

Naturally, these words have content—they teach a truth and a path to follow. The act of faith is thus not only trust in God, but also the acceptance as true of dogmatic and moral doctrines. It is necessary to know such doctrines, even by heart, so that they can be translated into life.[43] Following

---

which certainly includes the task of demonstrating the truth of theism, but not only that. Apologetics is also concerned, in fact, with demonstrating the truth of Christianity and of the (Catholic) Church. Given that contemporary theology has often been marked by temptation both toward rationalism and fideism, the denial of apologetics as a whole has also led to the denial of its first part: the philosophical demonstration of God. However, it must not be forgotten that apologetics is a discipline that often avails itself of proofs taken from Revelation, and this clearly presupposes faith. On the other hand, the *analogia entis* is based on natural reason alone. In his *Oath against Modernism*, Saint Pius X (d. 1914) prescribed that whoever assumed an ecclesiastical office should swear, as a first point: "I profess that God, the beginning and the end of all things, can be known with certainty and, indeed, also demonstrated through the natural light of reason from 'the things that have been made' [*Rom 1:20*], namely, from the visible works of creation, as the cause from its effects" (*Sacrorum Antistitum* [1910] [DS 3538]).

[42] See Second Vatican Council, *Dei Verbum*, §5.

[43] Thus wrote Saint Augustine of Hippo, *Enarrationes in Psalmos* 118/11.1: "It is not a law to be retained in [Christians'] memory but neglected in their lives. It is a law *they will know through their own understanding and observe* by loving choice in the wide freedom of love." In *The Works of Saint Augustine: A Translation for the 21st Century*, vol. III/19, trans. Maria Boulding (Hyde Park: New City Press, 2002), 388 [emphasis added to highlight the *et-et*]).

recent theological disputes, a perspective in theology is often imposed according to which methods and criteria would be more valid than content, research of the "sense" more than research of the truth. In other words, one would not need to approach the Word of God—wanting to grasp the "notional truths" to be learned, to profess them, and bring them to actualization in life—but only inspirations for the method to follow and creatively apply according to various times and existential situations. This perspective has crept into catechesis, which has become experiential and no longer notional; that is, it is dedicated to seeking perspectives of life instead of teaching the truth of the faith and morals.[44] Among other things, the Year of Faith (2012–2013), promulgated by Benedict XVI, had the scope of rediscovering both aspects of faith: the experiential side and the notional side. Hence, the Pope's recommendation to study the *Catechism*, twenty years after its promulgation and fifty years after the Second Vatican Council.[45]

2.4. The Word as Truth

Since the Word reveals truths, it is inevitable to also emphasize that *Logos* is inseparably linked to *Aletheia*, that is, to Truth. Indeed, Christ said of Himself: "I am . . . the truth" (John 14:6). Now, we can consider at least two meanings of this term: the philosophical meaning and the properly theological meaning.

From the standpoint of the history of philosophy, the search for the meaning of the notion of truth was given direction by Aristotle in the *Met-*

---

[44] However, there are also useful aspects in experiential catechesis. Here too, rather than contraposing the two aspects, they would need to be reconciled in a synthesis. This appears to be the attempt made by Saint John Paul II, with the Apostolic Exhortation *Catechesi Tradendae* (1979), in which the Pope indicates the meaning and aim of catechesis both in bringing to personal communion with Christ, and in teaching the doctrine of Christ. This involves combining the existential quest for the face of Christ with the doctrinal certitude of the baptized. A fragment of the spirit that inspires the entire exhortation is found at §55: "A certain memorization of the words of Jesus, of important Bible passages, of the Ten Commandments, of the formulas of profession of the faith, of the liturgical texts, of the essential prayers, of key doctrinal ideas, etc., far from being opposed to the dignity of young Christians, or constituting an obstacle to personal dialogue with the Lord, is a real need, as the synod fathers forcefully recalled. We must be realists. The blossoms, if we may call them that, of faith and piety do not grow in the desert places of a memory-less catechesis. What is essential is that the texts that are memorized must at the same time be taken in and gradually understood in depth, in order to become a source of Christian life on the personal level and the community level."

[45] See Benedict XVI, *Porta Fidei* (Apostolic Letter, "Motu Proprio Data," for the Indiction of the Year of Faith), October 11, 2011.

aphysics and at the beginning of the treatise *De Interpretatione*. In the latter, the Stagirite limits the application of the qualifications of "true" and "false" to apophantic or declarative discourse, that is to say, to affirmative or negative propositions, excluding from the study of the question other parts of human discourse. He, thus, initially considers truth as only a property of a declarative proposition.

From Platonism comes an ontological meaning of truth that will also be found again in Aristotle's *Metaphysics*. From this standpoint, the theme of truth is not only drawn out in relation to human discourse, but regards being or reality. Thus, the term "true," more than being opposed to "false," ends up determining the opposite of what is "apparent." This approach has often pushed the Platonic tradition toward contempt for empirical entities, insofar as they are endowed with a lower reality, because they are copies of the transcendent Ideas; in the Aristotelian line of thought, the material entities were valued much more, both at the level of knowledge and the ontological level. Despite such differences, it remains common for both currents that the notion of truth must be understood on the basis of the idea of conformity or correspondence.[46] "True" is, in the final analysis, that which corresponds to reality, or to being. Aristotle prefers a more logical connotation of the truth,[47] while Platonism recognizes a more ontological value,[48] but in both cases it is the conformity between what is existing and what is known that is the focal point for speaking of "truth."

The Scholastics happily welcomed a similar teaching. For Saint Thomas, the truth is defined as *"adaequatio rei ad intellectum"* ("conformity of the thing to the intellect") or *"adaequatio rei et intellectus"* ("conformity of the thing/

---

[46] The notion of truth as conformity or correspondence with reality was prevalent over every other understanding until the twentieth century, in which other solutions were proposed: truth understood as coherence, as conformity to rules, as practice, as existence, etc. Nonetheless, even in the twentieth century, there were thinkers who maintained the concept of truth as correspondence, especially among philosophers who were very attentive to the logical-mathematical sciences.

[47] In fact, for Aristotle, the truth is first and foremost a property of thought: "The true is the affirmation of what is really conjoined and the denial of what is really divided; the false, on the other hand, is the contradiction of this affirmation and denial. . . . In fact, the true and the false are not in things . . . but only in thought" (*Metaphysics* 6.1027b [our translation]).

[48] This becomes undeniably evident in the doctrine of Augustinian Christian Platonism, regarding the "eternal truths" postulated by the epistemological theory of "illumination." It should not be forgotten, however, that even in Aristotle an ontological connotation of truth is to be found: "Each thing, inasmuch as it possesses being, also possess truth" (*Metaphysics* 2.993b).

reality and the intellect").⁴⁹ However, scholastic philosophy is not reduced to repeating, in a more systematic way, the teaching of classical Greek thought. It is affected by the fundamental influence of Christian Revelation, which teaches that the truth is a Person and not only a notion of logical correspondence. The truth is the Person of the *Logos* made flesh. In the final analysis, the truth is God Himself. If, on the one hand, this can make the theological concept of truth lean more toward the Platonic tradition (truth in an ontological sense) then, on the other hand, it remains in contrast with it insofar as Platonism proclaims that sensible entities represent an estrangement from the truth, which would belong only to the supersensible world of Ideas.⁵⁰ The Christian dogma of creation of all things by God through His eternal *Logos*—a dogma that we also find revealed in the fundamental Prologue of Saint John (see John 1:2–3), the biblical text that speaks with greater clarity of Christ as the eternal *Logos* incarnated in time—compels the attribution of truth in an ontological sense, and not merely a logical sense, even to sensible things, which were created good by God (see Gen 1:31) and which correspond to archetypal ideas, present in the divine intellect, on the basis of which the beings were created. The Incarnation of the Word in material and sensible flesh represents the Christian argument *par excellence* of the goodness and truth of material and sensible things.⁵¹

For the Christian theologian, an exclusively philosophical concept of truth cannot suffice, although a good philosophical concept of truth is also necessary. The theologian has in the bow of his or her particular science certain arrows that philosophy cannot and must not utilize, at least in a direct way. These arrows are the revealed supernatural dogmas. From supernatural Revelation he or she knows that Christ, the incarnate *Logos*, has said "I am … the truth" (John 14:6). From here derives for him or her the task of cooperat-

---

[49] Saint Thomas Aquinas, *Scriptum super Sententiis* I, d. 19, q. 5, a. 1 and *ST* I, q. 16, a. 2, ad 2, respectively (our translations). The formulation of this classical axiom is attributed to Isaac Israeli ben Solomon (also known by the Latin name of Isaac Iudaeus), a Jewish physician and philosopher born in Egypt (ca. 850) and who died in Tunis (932 or 941). However, the notion of truth as a conformity between intellect and reality comes, as we have already noted, from Greek philosophy. It is already found implicitly in Parmenides of Elea (d. 450 BC), *Fragments* 3 and 8.

[50] Saint Thomas, while recognizing that God is eternal Truth (insofar as in God knowing intellect and essence coincide), does not adopt the Augustinian theory of illumination and of eternal truths: "*Sola veritas una quae in Deo est et quae Deus est, est aeterna et immutabilis*" ("Only the unique truth that is in God, and that is God, is eternal and immutable": *Scriptum super Sententiis* I, d. 19, q. 5, a. 3 [our translation]). See also *ST* I, q. 16, a. 7.

[51] See the discussion between the iconoclasts and the iconodules that took place around the Second Council of Nicaea in the year 787.

ing with the Truth (see 3 John 8: *cooperatores veritatis*), collaborating with the divine incarnate Person of the *Logos*. He or she will do this in two ways: both with a dialogical relationship with the Truth-Person, and with scientific work concerning the truth that is expressed in propositions of the faith, revealed by God. All of this will be discussed later. In conclusion, the incarnate Word is the divine personal Truth that is manifested in the flesh (in the world of phenomena and in human history) and who is expressed in the truths that he has expressed with his mouth in human terms, because his knowledge was not limited only to his contemporaries, but was usable—through appropriate human and intellectual mediations—for centuries to come.

2.5. The Word as Love

Some recent theologians speak of the divine Word not only as Reason, but also as love. Traces of this line of thought are found in magisterial texts of Pope Benedict XVI. He speaks of Jesus Christ as the "incarnate love of God," the One in whom the novelty of the New Testament is found, which is "not so much in new ideas as in the figure of Christ Himself, who gives flesh and blood to those concepts—an unprecedented realism."[52] The classical teaching of the Church and of theology, based on Revelation, recalls that the Word is Reason, and the Holy Spirit is Love (see Chapter Six). Insofar as personal characteristics are concerned, "to-be-Reason" and not "to-be-Love" is proper to the Word, the Second Person of the Trinity. But what Pope Benedict intends to say does not contradict this teaching. Indeed, he is speaking on a different level: not that of the Trinitarian nature of God in itself, but rather that of the salvific economy.[53] In his actions for us, the incarnate Word has shown the divine love for human beings—that love that is in God, and which, at the personal level, is the Holy Spirit. This is clear not only in the Encyclical *Deus Caritas Est*, cited here, but even more so in *Caritas in Veritate*, in which Benedict points out that "in the truth, charity reflects the personal yet public dimension of faith in the God of the Bible, who is both *Agápe* and *Lógos*: Charity and Truth, Love and Word."[54]

If it is permissible to speak in some way of the *Logos* as love as well, it can

---

[52] Benedict XVI, *Deus Caritas est*, §12.

[53] For further confirmation, Benedict XVI, in §13 of the same encyclical, proposes the application to the Eucharist, in which "the Logos, eternal wisdom, ... now truly becomes food for us—as love." This indicates a state of the *Logos* in the economy, not His personal characteristic in the Trinity.

[54] Benedict XVI, *Caritas in Veritate* (2009), §3. In §1, one finds the definition, "God, Eternal Love and Absolute Truth."

only be done if one is referring to the manifestation of divine love, offered to us in the history of Jesus, the Word incarnate. On the other hand, it cannot be said that the Word is Love (with a capital letter) in Person, insofar as this incommunicable prerogative belongs to the Holy Spirit.

2.6. The Word as Son

We have already considered various characteristics proper to the Word: God, Reason, Word, and Truth. Always remaining anchored to the first chapter of the Gospel of Saint John, we find a further clarification. Again, at verse 14 it says, "And the Word became flesh / . . . and we saw his glory, / the glory as of the Father's only Son." To better understand these words, let us recall verse 18 of the same chapter, which says: "No one has ever seen God. The only Son, God, who is at the Father's side, has revealed him." So, on one hand it is said that no one has ever seen God—and this is certain. On the other hand, however, it is said that there is Someone who has made God known to us; even if we have not seen Him with our own bodily eyes, we have known Him. The one who has accomplished this is the "only Son, God, who is at the Father's side."[55] In verse 14 we found a similar expression: "The Father's Only Son."

To recapitulate: the Word is God, eternal, the divine Reason, the Word, and eternal Truth. Then it is specified again that the Word is the Only Begotten God, that is, God in the form of the Only Begotten. The concept of begetting or generation requires one who begets and another that is begotten. John says that the Begetter is the "Father" (see John 1:14). Here we have God-Word who insofar as He is Only Begotten is begotten by Another, whom Saint John calls the Father (John 1:14, 18). Since God cannot be begotten by anyone but God,[56] it is clear that—since the Word is called God (John 1:1, 18)—even the Father who has begotten Him must be God (this is analogous to the fact that a human being can be begotten only by another human being, not by an inferior animal or by a vegetable). The Father has begotten His only Son as the Word. Here again is an important clarification: the Word is also the Son. In speaking of "being-begotten," Saint John implicitly refers the name of Son to the Word as well. He identifies the Word and the Son: they are the same Subject. The Word is God, begotten from the Father, and thus

---

[55] Unfortunately, various translations in the national languages render this verse as "only (-begotten) Son." But Saint John in Greek does not say Son, but rather "only-begotten *God*" precisely.

[56] The Creed recalls it once again: "God from God, light from light, true God from true God" (DS 125).

He is the Son; this Word-Son becomes flesh. All of this refers back to the fundamental mystery of the Most Holy Trinity, of which we will speak further on. This intimate mystery of the one and triune Divinity is inaccessible to the human mind and is known only through supernatural Revelation, remaining undeducible to natural human reflection.

> Of course, the mystery of God always remains beyond our conception and reason, our rites and our prayers. Yet, through his revelation, God actually communicates Himself to us, recounts Himself and makes Himself accessible. And we are enabled to listen to His Word and to receive His truth. This, then, is the wonder of faith: God, in His love, creates within us—through the action of the Holy Spirit—the appropriate conditions for us to recognize his Word. God himself, in His desire to show Himself, to come into contact with us, to make Himself present in our history, enables us to listen to and receive Him.[57]

For this reason, we must now briefly deal precisely with Revelation, the foundation of the faith and of theology. The exposition on divine Revelation is to be found under the second fundamental term of the binomial *Verbum caro*, for reasons that we will explain below.

3. *Caro* (Flesh)

After having briefly covered the meanings of Word, let us go on to *caro*, "flesh." The Word is made flesh. This term will indicate all that is human and historical that has been personally assumed by the eternal Son of God. The Word as such lives in the dimension of eternity and immutability. All that is historical, limited, and changing is linked to the human nature that He has assumed in his Person. In the following chapters of this book we shall speak of all the consequences that this entails at the Christological and soteriological level, of ecclesiological and sacramental doctrine, and so forth. In this chapter, we shall concentrate on only three aspects: (1) Revelation, because it—although it began well before the Incarnation—has concretely reached its apex and perfection in the historical reality of Jesus Christ; (2) faith, which is the historical and personal acceptance of Revelation on the part of human beings; and finally, (3) theology, which is the reflection on the faith carried

---

[57] Benedict XVI, *General Audience*, October 17, 2012.

out by believers throughout history. These three realities, although they also have a very strong link with the Word as the eternal *Logos*, are dependent in a stricter way on the historicity of the incarnate Word.[58] Therefore, we shall proceed in the first instance with Revelation.

3.1. Divine Revelation

3.1.1. "Re-velatio"

The term Revelation, or the verb "to reveal," derives from Latin and indicates, simply, to discover, to undress, or to uncover. The main meaning of Revelation lies therefore in this: God discloses Himself, uncovers Himself, makes Himself known. However, we need to add a second meaning of the term, inspired by the composition of the Latin word *revelatio*, which can also indicate a repeated veiling, a re-veiling. *Velatio* normally indicates taking the veil (for example, in the monastic investiture). But there is also a more ordinary sense of the term, which consists in the simple opposite of unveiling. If to reveal is to remove the veil, that is, to clarify, to show, "*re-velare*" means to cover it again, to perform the *velatio* again. Revelation, then, is both an unveiling, and a "re-veiling." God speaks, makes Himself known: Revelation unveils. But even in His manifestation, God remains wrapped in His transcendent and ineffable mystery. Revelation never completely reveals the mystery, rendering it completely visible to our eyes. It makes it known to us with certainty, yes. But it does not remove its properly mysterious character. It replaces a thick blanket that prevents it from being viewed with a thinner veil, which in its transparency allows us to see, even if only in a way that is not completely distinct, and not in all its details. Nonetheless, what we see is true and truly known, albeit imperfectly. Saint Paul refers to this when he writes: "At present we see indistinctly, as in a mirror, but then face to face. At present I know par-

---

[58] In particular, it was the Second Vatican Council that emphasized the historical character of Revelation, which was not only constituted by the communication of true doctrines (words), but also by the historical interventions of God. The Constitution *Dei Verbum* teaches: "This plan of revelation is realized by deeds and words having an inner unity: the deeds wrought by God in the history of salvation manifest and confirm the teaching and realities signified by the words, while the words proclaim the deeds and clarify the mystery contained in them" (*Dei Verbum*, §2). The *et-et* of deed and words together should be noted: if a purely knowledge-related conception of Revelation is limiting, a purely historical perspective, which values only historical events, is just as limiting. Such events, in fact, are interpreted correctly by words, while words are verified in events. For this reason, the Council speaks of words and deeds having "an inner unity."

tially; then I shall know fully, as I am fully known" (1 Cor 13:12). And, making recourse to 2 Cor 5:6–7, the First Vatican Council recalls:

> For, divine mysteries by their nature exceed the created intellect so much that, even when handed down by revelation and accepted by faith, they nevertheless remain covered by the veil of faith [*fidei velamen*] itself, and wrapped in a certain mist, as it were, as long as in this mortal life, 'we are absent from the Lord: for we walk by faith and not by sight.'[59]

3.1.2. Old and New Testament

We find a second *et-et* regarding Revelation concerning its two phases. The Word of God is delivered to us through a historical process that includes both the Old and the New Covenants. Revelation is the Old and New Covenant combined. In written form, they are codified in the two parts of the one Bible, the Old and New Testament. Revelation, however, although codified in the sacred text, is a process carried out by God that overcomes the mere biblical text, even if it is correctly expressed in it. The unity of the two phases is essential in the Catholic concept of Revelation. Denial of it corresponds to a rupture of the synthesis between the Old and New Covenant, which are held together by their end-point: Jesus Christ, prefigured in the words, signs, events, and figures of the Old Covenant, and given in the New Covenant. One may recall the ancient heresy of Marcion of Sinope (d. 160), who radically opposed the two testaments and claimed that the "god" of the Old Testament was not the same true God of the New Testament. In the Old Testament was a vindictive and punishing god who had nothing to do with the merciful Father of Jesus. He believed that Christianity had to be pure, something which for him meant not having any relation with the Jews and especially Judaism. Marcion had fundamentally radicalized the Pauline message according to which justification comes from faith in Christ and not from works of the Law of Moses. However, since the New Testament often cites the Old Testament, he found himself in need of cutting out his own rule ("canon") of the Scriptures, eliminating from the New Testament everything that was in contrast with his thought. The Church strongly rejected this heresy from the time of the early Apologists. It is significant that it reappears, albeit in a nuanced way, in Luther. In spite of Luther's extraordinary respect for the whole Bible, we have seen that the German reformer's search was based pre-

---

[59] First Vatican Council, *Dei Filius*, ch. 4 (DS 3016).

cisely on the question about a way to find a merciful God and not a just God. Moreover, Luther also radicalized the Pauline teaching concerning the relationship between faith and works. Finally, he also carved out his own canon within the biblical canon, which nonetheless includes almost the whole Old Testament. However, the principle of cutting out passages or biblical books that get in the way of one's thought is fundamentally the same.

In the Catholic perspective, on the other hand, the Old Testament is true Revelation, even if partial, of the one and true God. The Old Covenant has a pedagogical function of preparation for the fullness of truth and grace that will be offered by Jesus Christ (see John 1:17). The New Testament carries the Old Testament to its fulfillment, and uncovers its hidden riches, but it does not cancel it out. Here it is necessary to quote a famous expression of Saint Augustine: "*Novum Testamentum in Vetere latet et Vetus Testamentum in Novo patet*" ("The New Testament is hidden in the Old, and the Old Testament comes to full light in the New.")[60]

3.1.3. Object

Another *et-et* regards the content that is transmitted, namely, the object of Revelation. In the first place, the last two ecumenical councils have clarified that such an object is *both* God Himself, *and* the decrees (or the mystery) of His will for us.[61] Therefore, God does not speak *either* of Himself alone *or* for us alone, but both. And He does so *both* by communicating doctrine *and* by carrying out signs. Concerning the revealed doctrines—still with respect to the object of Revelation—we find another bipolarity, eminently made explicit by the Council of Trent, which teaches that the Gospel of Christ, preserved and preached by the Church, is "*fontem omnis et salutaris veritatis et morum disciplinae*" ("source of all saving truth and norms of conduct.")[62] The Council of Trent also makes recourse in a concrete way to the *et-et*, recalling that the Word of God is neither a generic exhortation nor the transcription of a mere religious feeling. It has certain contents, and these are divided between truths

---

[60] This is the common way of rendering the exact quotation, which is as follows: "*Multum et solide significatur, ad Vetus Testamentum timorem potius pertinere, sicut ad Novum dilectionem: quamquam et in Vetere Novum lateat, et in Novo Vetus pateat*" ("Often and with solid arguments it is taught that fear pertains more to the Old Testament, as love pertains to the New; though even in the Old the New is hidden, and in the New the Old is manifest" (Saint Augustine of Hippo, *Quaestiones in Heptateuchum* 2.73 [our translation]). On the relationship between the two Testaments, see Second Vatican Council, *Dei Verbum*, §16.

[61] See First Vatican Council, *Dei Filius* (DS 3004); Second Vatican Council, *Dei Verbum*, §2.

[62] Council of Trent, *Decretum de Libris Sacris et Traditionibus Recipiendis* (1546) (DS 1501).

of faith (dogma), and truths concerning the behavior that must be observed to please God (morals). If the question must be raised as to which of the two parts represent the primary term of the pair, there is no doubt that it is the dogma. For classical Catholic thought, in fact, the good is sought by the will (moral action) following the knowledge of the truth. It is for this reason that recent popes, particularly Benedict XVI and Francis, have more often emphasized the fact that Christianity is not a system of moral norms, but above all the knowledge (doctrinal and experiential) of the face of Christ, from whom the validity and obligatory character of the moral precepts also follow.[63]

The bipolarity concerning content is also expressed in a second place in the fact that Revelation speaks *both* of God *and* of the salvation of humankind. The most recent ecumenical council clearly attests to it: "By this revelation then, the deepest truth about God and the salvation of man shines out for our sake in Christ, who is both the mediator and the fullness of all revelation."[64] The end of Revelation is not only noetic—knowledge of truth—but also salvific. And the salvific aspect is hierarchically prevalent, insofar as God is manifested to us for the purpose of saving us. The knowledge of the truth is in view of the eternal salvation of human beings (this hierarchical order is also expressed in 1 Tim 2:4).

One can also appreciate the clear Christocentrism in the previous citation of Vatican II: Jesus is the Mediator and fullness of all Revelation (therefore not only of the New Testament). *Dei Verbum* §4 adds that Jesus Christ is the Word made flesh and that in Him the Revelation reaches its own definitive fulfillment. The same passage emphasizes very well the Trinitarian background of the Christological Figure: God has sent His Son into the world, who has perfectly revealed to us knowledge of Himself, of the Father, and of the Holy Spirit. The Trinitarian Christocentrism, the fulcrum of our treatise, is presented as the central criterion of Revelation itself. And this is why it is also the backbone of our theology, not a pillar conjured up at the drawing board or work desk, but indicated by the Word of God.

---

[63] One text among many: "Christianity, before being a moral or an ethic, is the event of love, it is the acceptance of the Person of Jesus. For this reason the Christian and Christian communities must first look and make others look to Christ, the true Way that leads to God" (Benedict XVI, *General Audience*, November 14, 2012).

[64] Second Vatican Council, *Dei Verbum*, §2. At §6, the Constitution confirms again that "Through divine revelation, God chose to show forth and communicate Himself and the eternal decisions of His will regarding the salvation of men. That is to say, He chose to share with them those divine treasures which totally transcend the understanding of the human mind [First Vatican Council, *Dei Filius* (DS 3005)]."

3.1.4. Channels

A fourth bipolarity in the Catholic understanding of Revelation is that which concerns the so-called "sources" of Revelation, which here we prefer to call "channels" that belong to a common source. As was seen in the previous chapter, Protestants and Catholics have very different ideas about this point. For Luther, there is the principle of *sola Scriptura*, while for us the *et-et* is applied while recognizing that the Word of God is found both in Sacred Scripture and in the Apostolic Tradition.[65] Here, Apostolic Tradition means not only the process of transmitting the doctrine of Christ on the part of the Apostles, but also the true and proper contents of faith, which form an integral part of the *depositum fidei*, that is, of the treasure of the faith, even if materially they are not found written in the New Testament. The Catholic Church recognizes that the entirety of Revelation, in the image of its center and culmination who is Christ, is composed of a fruitful synthesis of Scripture and Tradition. Today it is common to hear the expression "Word of God" used, even by Catholics, to refer to the Bible alone. But the Bible is the Word of God in written form, and certainly not the only channel of the Word of God. Thus, in using the expression, one should be careful not to imply a reduction of the Catholic concept of Revelation.[66]

Since each synthetical pair is also hierarchically organized, it becomes legitimate to ask, between the Bible and Tradition, which is the primary term. In the current context, it is likely that most would respond that the Bible is. It is actually the Tradition. The latter is first both chronologically, and hierarchically. It is first chronologically, because the Bible is put into writing on the basis of apostolic oral preaching. Saint John attests to such a "partiality" of the Scripture in the Scripture itself, noting at the end of his Gospel: "It is this disciple who testifies to these things and has written them, and we know that his testimony is true. There are also many other things that Jesus did, but if these were to be described individually, I do not think the whole world would contain the books that would be written" (John 21:24–25). Therefore, the same Scripture presents itself as a partial writing of the preceding Tradition concerning Jesus, evidently an oral Tradition. The exegetes are in agreement—

---

[65] See the Council of Trent, *Decretum de Libris Sacris et Traditionibus Recipiendis* (DS 1501). As we have already seen, the Bible itself actually suggests that there is a surplus of teaching with respect to its own written text. For example, Saint Paul in 2 Thess 2:15 exhorts his brethren with the words: "Therefore, brothers, stand firm and hold fast to the traditions that you were taught, either by an oral statement or by a letter of ours."

[66] The First Vatican Council uses the fitting expression *"Dei Verbo scripto et tradito"* ("the Word of God, written and transmitted": *Dei Filius, Prooemium* [DS 3000]).

Caro (Flesh)

despite differences in the details—in establishing the date of redaction of the books of the New Testament several years after the death and Resurrection of Christ, when the early Church was already in a state of consolidation and development.[67] In the years preceding the composition of the biblical texts, it was the oral Tradition that preserved and disseminated the *depositum fidei*. Thus, it has a chronological priority over Scripture.

Moreover, the Tradition also has a hierarchical priority because it has a wider scope than Scripture. Various truths of the faith and various apostolic practices, contained in the Tradition, were not written down by the sacred writers in the biblical books. For example, Saint Basil attests to this:

> For were we to attempt to reject such customs as have no written authority, on the ground that the importance they possess is small, we should unintentionally injure the Gospel in its very vitals; or, rather, should make our public definition a mere phrase and nothing more. For instance . . . to sign with the sign of the cross those who

---

[67] While it is correct to note the temporal separation between the first preaching and the initial writing of the *kerygma*, the (up to this point) consolidated tendency to date the books of the New Testament rather "late" with respect to the events that they narrate and interpret should nonetheless undergo greater scrutiny. An almost "dogmatic" presupposition of the majority of Bible scholars is that almost all of the New Testament was written, or at least redacted in its final form, after AD 70, the year in which the Romans destroyed the Temple of Jerusalem. The proponents (few, but valid) of an older dating of the New Testament books draw attention to a series of elements that instead speak in favor of a composition of texts in a more fully apostolic era. For example, it is noted that in the so-called "synoptic apocalypses" (Mark 13; Matt 24; Luke 21), the eschatological events that accompany the final coming of Christ are connected exactly with the destruction of the Temple. Now, if the synoptic Gospels were written/redacted after 70, the authors/redactors would have known that the Temple had fallen and yet Christ had not returned: it is hardly credible that they would have left such "apocalypses" in the mode in which they are presented, because this would have represented the attestation of a mistaken prophecy on the part of Jesus (the exegetes often say that the prophecies "put in the mouth" of Jesus are *ex eventu*, that is, they represent the community's acknowledgement of what happened later: Why in this case would the sacred writers have left a prophecy that did not take account of the events?). Concerning the Gospel of John, it is to be noted that in 5:2 the evangelist attests that "there is" (not "there were") a pool in Jerusalem called Bethesda. It is known that it too was demolished in AD 70. Why would he still speak of it in the present tense? These are only two examples. Here we do not want to take a position with regard to any exact dating (that is the task of specialists), but it may be hoped that in the future the mainstream biblical scholars will be both more open at least to *discussing* such arguments without prejudice, and also to adequately considering the fact that the work of "redaction" of a biblical text does not exclude the fact that it may report old traditions, even if sometimes applied to current circumstances.

have trusted in the name of our Lord Jesus Christ? What writing has taught us to turn to the East at the prayer? ... Moreover we bless the water of baptism and the oil of the chrism, and besides this the catechumen who is being baptized. On what written authority do we do this? Is not our authority silent and mystical tradition? ... Time will fail me if I attempt to recount the unwritten mysteries of the Church.... [For] the very confession of our faith in Father, Son, and Holy Ghost, what is the written source?[68]

This should not lead us to suppose a "material insufficiency" of Scripture,[69] for the simple reason that Scripture does not have the task of transcribing every single aspect of the *kerygma* (announcement) concerning Christ and God. Scripture is not insufficient. However, Scripture alone is not enough with respect to the contents of the faith. The preceding oral Tradition, partially fixed in Scripture, contains instead the whole of apostolic preaching (both what was then also transmitted in writing, and that which remained in oral form, but still as constitutive of the *depositum fidei*), and above all it represents the authority for interpreting it authentically: this is why we speak of a living Tradition. Like Christ, the preoccupation of the first Christians was not that of writing books, but of announcing the Kingdom of God and the Gospel. Therefore, it should not be surprising that the orality of the kerygmatic announcement prevails over the biblical text in importance. On the other hand, even after its redaction, if Scripture is not always preached, it remains a dead letter. It is only in missionary life and evangelization of the Church that it remains, in every era, a living word. This is the main reason for the general failure—among its many particular merits—of broad areas of modern and contemporary exegesis. The absolutizing of a single aspect (the historical-literal sense of the texts) has turned exegesis into an operation that in certain cases bears a better resemblance to the dissection of a corpse than the rational contemplation of a living organism. On the need for a complete biblical exegesis, Benedict XVI writes:

---

[68] Saint Basil the Great, *De Spiritu Sancto* 27.66–67, in *NPNF*, Second Series, vol. 8, trans. Blomfield Jackson (Peabody, MA: Hendrickson Publishers, Inc., 1994), 41–43).

[69] Scholars note that the original schema of the Decree on apostolic traditions of the Council of Trent contained the wording *partim-partim*, which was eliminated from the final text. The schema said that the truth of the Gospel is contained partially in the Bible and partially in the oral traditions. This supposes the material insufficiency of Scripture, i.e., that this (as well as Tradition) would not contain all the truths necessary for salvation. Instead the Tridentine Decree said simply that the Gospel truth is found both in the Bible and in the Tradition, without further specifications.

"Only where both methodological levels, the historical-critical and the theological, are respected, can one speak of a theological exegesis, an exegesis worthy of this book" [Benedict XVI, *Intervention at the Fourteenth General Congregation of the Synod* (14 October 2008): *Insegnamenti* IV, 2 (2008), 493; cf. *Propositio* 25]. The Synod Fathers rightly stated that the positive fruit yielded by the use of modern historical-critical research is undeniable. While today's academic exegesis, including that of Catholic scholars, is highly competent in the field of historical-critical methodology and its latest developments, it must be said that comparable attention need to be paid to the theological dimension of the biblical texts, so that they can be more deeply understood in accordance with the three elements indicated by the Dogmatic Constitution *Dei Verbum*.[70]

It needs to be added that Scripture, even if materially more limited, is necessary because it has a less elusive character, so to speak, with respect to the oral Tradition. To find Tradition, one needs to make recourse to certain "theological places," which we shall mention later, even if it often remains difficult to determine with certainty what the content of the *Traditio* is. By contrast, this is much easier for the canonical text of the Bible, which without doubt is the Word of God. Again, our hierarchization of the two elements of this *et–et* does not imply in any way the depreciation of the second element with respect to the first. It should be recalled that the Council of Trent affirms that Scripture and Tradition should be venerated with equal sentiment and reverence.[71] The Second Vatican Council, then, reminds students and scholars that "Sacred theology rests on the written word of God, together with sacred Tradition, as its primary and perpetual foundation."[72]

---

[70] Benedict XVI, *Verbum Domini* (2010), §34. The three levels of study marked by *Dei Verbum* had been recalled immediately before this paragraph: "1) the text must be interpreted with attention to *the unity of the whole of Scripture*; nowadays this is called canonical exegesis; 2) *the living Tradition of the whole Church* is to be taken into account; and, finally, 3) respect must be shown for the *analogy of faith*".

[71] Council of Trent, *Decretum de Libris Sacris et de Traditionibus Recipiendis* (DS 1501): the books of the Old and New Testaments, as well as the traditions concerning faith and customs are to be received "with the same sense of loyalty and reverence" ("*pari pietatis affectu ac reverentia*").

[72] Second Vatican Council, *Dei Verbum*, §24. In this same paragraph there is contained a directive that was quite popular after the Council: "so the study of the sacred page is, as it were, the soul of sacred theology." According to the premise, we can say that, for theology, there is need to contemplate, without separation, both the soul and the body, and thus, *both* the sacred biblical pages, *and* the corpus of the Tradition.

With these premises, in what follows we shall add some conceptual details regarding the two channels of Revelation.[73]

3.1.5. Sacred Scripture

1. A Book both Human and Divine

There are naturally many questions of a specialized nature concerning the description of the scriptural source, but here we shall mention only the principal ones that are of a purely theological interest, thus leaving aside philological, linguistic, and historical questions. The first thing to recall in this regard is that the Bible is both a human word, and the Word of God. If it is forgotten that the Bible is a human word, culturally and historically conditioned, one runs the serious risk of drawing the Jewish-Christian conception of Scripture close to the Islamic conception of the Koran, considered the book that Allah wrote in Heaven and that Muhammad received ready from on high. The Bible, instead, was written on the earth, by human authors called "hagiographers" (or sacred writers). Such sacred writers, insofar as they are human beings who are also "true authors," make use of their own language, their own cultural and scientific knowledge, and were thus historically conditioned like any other human author. But it would be an even greater error to consider the Bible as only a human book. It is also, and above all, a divine book—or, rather, a divine collection of books. The Bible is the Word of God.

2. Inspiration and Inerrancy

Although it is true that there are true human authors of the various biblical books, it is also true that the principal Author of the Scriptures is God Himself, who has inspired the sacred writers.[74] This concerns the theme of

---

[73] Note that recent theology, inspired by the Second Vatican Council, *Dei Verbum*, §9, does not use the terminology of two "sources," but identifies Christ as the unique Source of Revelation. Although this emphasizes the Christocentrism of Revelation, we must still find an adequate way of expressing the synthesis of the bipolarity. We propose here the terminology of the two "channels" that belong to the great Source, Jesus Christ.

[74] As regards God as Author, note how Saint Augustine of Hippo expresses it in *Contra adversarium legis et prophetarum* 1.17.35: "As God is the one and true Creator of goods both temporal and eternal, in the same way He is Author of the two Testaments: because the New is prefigured in the Old and the Old is realized by the New" (our translation). The doctrine regarding God as the true Author of the Bible is found in the following ecumenical councils: Florence, *Cantate Domino* (1442) (DS 1334); Trent, *Decretum de Libris Sacris et de Traditionibus Recipiendis* (DS 1501); Vatican I, *Dei Filius*, ch. 2 (DS

"biblical inspiration," that is, the fact that God has enlightened the sacred writers with a special grace, whose effect consists in the fact that the books of the Bible are exempt from errors in matters of faith ("biblical inerrancy"). *Dei Verbum* teaches that "Sacred Scripture is the word of God inasmuch as it is consigned to writing under the inspiration of the divine Spirit"[75]; and that "Those divinely revealed realities which are contained and presented in Sacred Scripture have been committed to writing under the inspiration of the Holy Spirit."[76] The most relevant biblical texts concerning inspiration are 2 Pet 1:16–21 and 2 Tim 3:14–17.

3. Literal and Spiritual Sense

Sacred Scripture is thus a book that is *both* divine *and* human: to not recognize this fundamental theological fact entails reducing the study of the Bible to the historical-critical method alone, which seeks the literal sense of the texts, but excludes access to the spiritual sense.[77] Scripture possesses, in fact, various senses, which are gathered into two categories: the literal sense and the spiritual sense.[78]

3006); and Vatican II, *Dei Verbum*, §11. Saint Thomas Aquinas, *Quaestiones Quodlibetales* VII, q. 6, a. 3 explains that the main Author of Sacred Scripture is the Holy Spirit; the human being is instead an instrumental author: "*In nulla scientia, humana industria inventa, proprie loquendo, potest inveniri nisi litteralis sensus; sed solum in ista Scriptura, cuius Spiritus Sanctus est auctor, homo vero instrumentum*" ("In no human-created science can one, properly speaking, find anything but the literal sense; [one can find it] only in the [Sacred] Scripture, whose Author is the Holy Spirit, with the human being then being an instrument" [our translation]).

[75] Second Vatican Council, *Dei Verbum*, §9.

[76] Second Vatican Council, *Dei Verbum*, §11. In the same paragraph, biblical inerrancy is also described: "Since everything asserted by the inspired authors or sacred writers must be held to be asserted by the Holy Spirit, it follows that the books of Scripture must be acknowledged as teaching solidly, faithfully and without error that truth which God wanted put into sacred writings for the sake of salvation."

[77] Modern exegetical techniques actually do not find the literal sense as understood by the ancients, but rather the simple sense "of the letter." According to classical Catholic exegesis, however, even the literal sense has a "theological" content, which actually in modern exegesis is often reduced to what the exegete takes with his or her own reflections, without reference to the doctrine of the Church.

[78] CCC §118 cites a famous medieval couplet, without mentioning its author, which expresses the four primary senses of Scripture: "*Littera gesta docet, quid credas allegoria, moralis quid agas, quo tendas anagogia*" ("The Letter speaks of deeds; Allegory to faith; The Moral how to act; Anagogy our destiny"). It was a widespread couplet in the thirteenth century, of which there is a version that substitutes the last part with "*quid speres anagogia*" ("Anagogy, what you must hope"). According to specialists, the first formulator of it was

When, again, not some one interpretation, but two or more interpretations are put upon the same words of Scripture, even though the meaning the writer intended remain undiscovered, there is no danger if it can be shown from other passages of Scripture that any of the interpretations put on the words is in harmony with the truth. And if a man in searching the Scriptures endeavors to get at the intention of the author through whom the Holy Spirit spoke, whether he succeeds in this endeavor, or whether he draws a different meaning from the words, but one that is not opposed to sound doctrine, he is free from blame so long as he is supported by the testimony of some other passage of Scripture. For the author perhaps saw that this very meaning lay in the words which we are trying to interpret; and assuredly the Holy Spirit, who through him spoke these words, foresaw that this interpretation would occur to the reader, nay, made provision that it should occur to him, seeing that it too is founded on truth. For what more liberal and more fruitful provision could God have made in regard to the Sacred Scriptures than that the same words might be understood in several senses, all of which are sanctioned by the concurring testimony of other passages equally divine?[79]

Here again, this does not concern an opposition, but a hierarchical integration. The principal sense is the literal, understood by the sacred writer, because it is on this that one must base one's search for the spiritual sense[80]:

Augustine of Dacia (also called Augustine of Denmark, d. 1285) in *Rotulus Pugillaris* I. Clearly, the literal sense corresponds to the first category, and the remaining three form the category of the spiritual sense. Saint Thomas Aquinas gave to the theme terminological and conceptual precision that lasts until this day, and it is in fact approved by the CCC §§115–119. Saint Thomas treats of the question particularly in *Quaestiones Quodlibetales* VII; *Super Epistolam ad Galatas lectura* IV, *lectio* 7 (concerning Gal 4:21–24); *ST* I, q. 1, a. 10.

[79] Saint Augustine of Hippo, *De doctrina christiana* 3.27.38, in *NPNF*, First Series, vol. 2, trans. James Shaw, ed. Philip Schaff (Peabody, MA: Hendrickson Publishers, Inc., 1994), 567. In *De Genesi ad litteram* 1.1.1, he writes: "In all the sacred books, we should consider the eternal truths that are taught, the facts that are narrated, the future events that are predicted, and the precepts or counsels that are given" (in *St. Augustine: The Literal Meaning of Genesis*, vol. 1, trans. John Hammond Taylor [New York: Newman Press, 1982], 19).

[80] "Since God speaks in Sacred Scripture through men in human fashion, the interpreter of Sacred Scripture, in order to see clearly what God wanted to communicate to us, should carefully investigate what meaning the sacred writers really intended, and what God wanted to manifest by means of their words" (Second Vatican Council, *Dei Verbum*, §12).

"*Omnes sensus fundentur super litteralem*" ("all [scriptural] senses are based on the literal").[81] If the spiritual sense was sought apart from the literal, one would inevitably fall into biblical allegorism, which could interpret every detail of the narrative in an arbitrary way. If this was a temptation in certain eras, in the present time the opposite tendency is predominant: that of focusing only on the literal sense (if not only on the sense "of the letter," or philological sense[82]), relegating the spiritual interpretation to the pure personal devotion of the reader. However, the great theological Tradition of the Fathers and Doctors has operated differently.[83] If the Bible is only studied with the historical-critical method, without a theological approach, it becomes a dead book.[84] The Bible, on this view, speaks of something that happened in its time, a long time ago, but now is no longer relevant. The Word of God no longer resounds in it, and it becomes nothing more or less than an ancient book written in the Near East. Thus, the salvific character and purpose of the Bible are lost. It is reduced to a noetic container, not of truths revealed by God, but rather of the religious conceptions of the Jews and early Christians. Moreover, the character of Revelation is annulled and with it the consequent personal salvific relationship with God, which the Bible seeks to provide. Thus, it loses its character of being "nourishment" of the faith, emphasized by *Dei Verbum* §21.

4. Correct Hermeneutic

To read the Bible properly, two elements are necessary: The Holy Spirit and the Church. The Holy Spirit is its Inspirator, a reason for which the Bible

---

[81] *ST* I, q. 1, a. 10, ad 1 (our translation).

[82] Thus, the following note of Saint Thomas Aquinas is instructive, *Super Matthaeum* XXVII, *lectio 1*: "*Officium est enim boni interpretis non considerare verba, sed sensum*" ("The task of a good interpreter is not that of focusing on the words, but on their meaning" [our translation]).

[83] "A significant contribution to the recovery of an adequate scriptural hermeneutic . . . can also come from renewed attention to the Fathers of the Church and their exegetical approach. The Church Fathers present a theology that still has great value today because at its heart is the study of sacred Scripture as a whole. Their example can teach modern exegetes a truly religious approach to sacred Scripture" (Benedict XVI, *Verbum Domini*, §37). In the rest of the paragraph, the Pontiff also speaks positively of medieval exegesis.

[84] See the careful analysis in this regard in *Verbum Domini* §35. Among the many observations worthy of attention proposed there by the Pope, we shall only mention the following: "The lack of a hermeneutic of faith with regard to Scripture entails more than a simple absence; in its place there inevitably enters another hermeneutic, a positivistic and *secularized hermeneutic* ultimately based on the conviction that the Divine does not intervene in human history."

must "be read and interpreted in the sacred Spirit in which it was written" ("*Sacra Scriptura eodem Spiritu quo scripta est etiam legenda et interpretanda sit*").[85] The Church is then the vital context in which the Scripture is born (particularly the New Testament, but if one intends the word Church with reference to the Assembly/Community or People of God, this is equally true for the Old Testament). It is thus impossible to interpret Scripture correctly if one places oneself outside the context in which it has arisen, and outside the community that safeguards it and keeps it alive, through prayer, preaching, and study.

> It is important that the criteria indicated in Number 12 of the Dogmatic Constitution *Dei Verbum* receive real attention and become the object of deeper study. A notion of scholarly research that would consider itself neutral with regard to Scripture should not be encouraged. As well as learning the original languages in which the Bible was written and suitable methods of interpretation, students need to have a deep spiritual life, in order to appreciate that the Scripture can only be understood if it is lived.[86]

5. Canon

In the matter of interpretation, the "final say" is the "judgment of the Church, which carries out the divine commission and ministry of guarding and interpreting the word of God."[87] It should not be forgotten that the very composition of the Bible, that is to say, the exact list of the books that comprise it (called the "canon") is known to us by the teaching authority of the Church that has defined it. Without the Church, we could not even distinguish the books that are inspired by God and inerrant in matters of faith, from other works—even of religious and theological value—which are not the Word of God in a proper sense. Therefore, Augustine even goes so far as to say: "*Ego vero Evangelio non crederem, nisi me Catholicae Ecclesiae commoveret auctoritas*" ("I would not believe the Gospel, if the authority of the Catholic Church did

---

[85] Second Vatican Council, *Dei Verbum*, §12.
[86] Benedict XVI, *Verbum Domini*, §47.
[87] Second Vatican Council, *Dei Verbum*, §12. In the background is this pronouncement of Trent: "No one . . . may twist Holy Scripture . . . according to his own mind, contrary to the meaning that Holy Mother the Church has held and holds—since it belongs to her to judge the true meaning and interpretation of Holy Scripture" (Council of Trent, *Decretum de Vulgata Editione Bibliorum et de Modo Interpretandi Sacram Scripturam* [1546] [DS 1507]).

not so lead me").⁸⁸ There are numerous ecclesiastical pronouncements about the biblical canon from the early centuries, but the dogmatic definition of it occurred in the Council of Trent, moved by the necessity of clearly expressing the Catholic faith with respect to the Protestant position, which had opted for a reduced canon. The fact that it is a true and proper dogmatic definition of this list (that the Council provides) is clear from the final threat of excommunication:

> If anyone does not accept all these books in their entirety, with all their parts, as they are being read in the Catholic Church and are contained in the ancient Latin Vulgate edition [of Saint Jerome], as sacred and canonical and knowingly and deliberately rejects the aforesaid traditions, let him be anathema.⁸⁹

3.1.6. Sacred Tradition

1. Traditio/Paradosis

Moving now to the channel of Apostolic Tradition, we immediately note the Latin origin of the term, from the verb *tradere*, that is, to deliver, transmit, or hand down. It is thus a Latin translation of the Greek term *paradosis*, from the verb *paradidomi*, which has the same meaning as *tradere*. The New Testament already uses *paradidomi* numerous times and in various senses, for example, to indicate that God the Father has sent His Son for our salvation (see Rom 8:32), or that Christ Himself is sent for us (see Gal 2:20). The term can also be used to indicate the handing over, or betrayal, on the part of Judas Iscariot (see Matt 26:25). However, the New Testament also uses this word in the way that will become technical in Christian theology, that is, with reference to the passing down of faith and the customs taught to us by Christ and the Apostles. Thus, for example, we have the words of Saint Paul in the First Letter to the Corinthians: "Hold fast to the traditions, just as I handed them [*paredoka*] on to you" (11:2); "I received from the Lord what I also handed on to you" (11:23); and "I handed on to you as of first importance what I also received" (15:3).

---

⁸⁸ Saint Augustine of Hippo, *Contra epistolam Manichaei quam vocant Fundamenti* 5.6 (our translation).
⁸⁹ Council of Trent, *Decretum de Libris Sacris et de Traditionibus Recipiendis* (DS 1504).

2. Act and Content

Even from the few examples (taken from many) that we are citing now, we can see a constitutive bipolarity of the *Traditio*: it consists *both* of an act, *and* a content. There is Tradition as an act of transmitting or handing down. And this can be done in two ways: by mouth or in writing. But naturally there is something that is transmitted; thus, there is the Tradition as content that is handed down. In the post-Tridentine era, the emphasis mainly fell on the concept of Tradition as a content and much less as a process. This can be taken to the extreme to make Tradition coincide with the documents of the ecclesiastical Magisterium. For this reason, the Second Vatican Council has brought balance to the discussion by deepening the theme of Tradition as a living exercise, in the Church, of handing down.[90] By keeping the two aspects together, the character of Tradition as synthesis is manifested in a better way. However, it needs to be added that the Council, not needing to express itself in a systematic way, left the area open to certain interpretations that move in an opposite direction from the counterreformation theologians. While the latter concentrate on the content, various recent interpretations can almost unilaterally emphasize the process of transmission to the detriment of the transmitted content. This interpretation is facilitated by the fact that the Constitution *Dei Verbum* seems here and there to overlap *tout court* the concept of Apostolic Tradition with the simple and incessant transmission of doctrine in the Church. Although the text distinguishes Scripture, Tradition, and Magisterium well, the risk of making the latter two coincide as if they were the same reality (called the *traditio vivens*), if it is not based in the letter of the Council, could be so in the general orientation of its dictate. For this reason, the theology of the twenty-first century is faced with the important task of drawing heavily on the teaching of Vatican II about Tradition, specifying unambiguously how it is connected with the preceding Magisterium, in particular the Council of Trent. It is necessary to keep alive the bipolarity of *et-et* within the concept of *Traditio*: it is both Apostolic Tradition in the sense of fixed contents handed down from the Apostles, which thus form part of the *depositum fidei*, and the incessant ecclesial action of transmission. In the

---

[90] For example, *Dei Verbum*, §8: "The Church, in her teaching, life and worship, perpetuates and hands on to all generations all that she herself is, all that she believes." The fact that the Tradition is found mainly, but not only, in the magisterial pronouncements, is a well-known doctrine, also summarized by the *Catechismus* of Saint Pius X (d. 1914), §890: "Where are the teachings of Tradition kept? ... The teachings of Tradition are kept chiefly in the Councils' decrees, the writings of the Holy Fathers, the Acts of the Holy See and the words and practices of the sacred Liturgy" (translation: *ewtn.com*).

Caro (Flesh)

synthesis, this bipolarity cannot be cancelled out, in a sort of Monophysitism (see Chapter Four) applied to the theme of Tradition.

3. *Subject*

Moreover, the constitutive link of Tradition with those who are authorized by God to carry out this process of the transmission of revealed content should be noted. Such authorized ministers are first and foremost the Apostles, witnesses of the Resurrected One, sent by Him (see Matt 28:19–20); then, there are the bishops consecrated by the Apostles as their successors. Finally, in a general sense, all of the Church is the subject of the *Traditio*. In the New Testament, we find various passages in which the necessity of safeguarding and transmitting the deposit of faith is attested, such as 1 Timothy 6:20 and 2 Timothy 1:14. In 1 Timothy 6:3, Saint Paul lashes out against whoever "does not agree with the sound words of our Lord Jesus Christ and the religious teaching." Clearly, the deposit is a collection of the "sound words of our Lord" and is a "doctrine." Thus, the deposit has a notional content. These sound doctrines sustain the existential aspect: the Apostle exhorts Timothy to "Compete well for the faith" (6:12). And he concludes: "O Timothy, guard what has been entrusted to you.[91] Avoid profane babbling and the absurdities of so-called knowledge. By professing it, some people have deviated from the faith" (6:20–21). Such safeguarding is not a fruit of ability or human technique alone, a sort of conservativism or, worse, "fixism." The Tradition understood as a safeguarding of the deposit of faith is a work first and foremost of the Holy Spirit: "Guard this rich trust[92] with the help of the holy Spirit that dwells within us" (2 Tim 1:14). Moreover, Saint Paul takes care to ensure that, even after the first sub-apostolic generation,[93] the transmission will continue: "And what you heard from me through many witnesses entrust to faithful people who will have the ability to teach others as well" (2 Tim 2:2).

---

[91] In Greek, *paratheke*, that is, "deposit."

[92] Again, this is *paratheke*. There seems to be a tendency to not want to translate this Greek word with its natural English counterpart.

[93] The command of the Apostle to safeguard the deposit of faith is affirmed and recommended again from the earliest stages of ecclesiastical history. A witness to this is the ancient *Letter of Barnabas*, which in chapter 19 describes the "way of light"; in order to travel in this way, the following indication—among others—is given: "Keep the teachings [deposit] which you have received, adding nothing and subtracting nothing" (no. 11: *FCNT*, vol. 1, 220). If this is part of the path of light, evidently whoever manipulates the *depositum fidei* finds himself in the way of darkness.

4. Tradition and Traditions

We can also note that the word "deposit" is used in the singular and not the plural. This indicates that, even before the apostolic preaching was put into writing, there were not several traditions but one Tradition alone. Naturally, there were many forms and various modes of passing on the *kerygma*, and in this sense, there was certainly a variety of traditions. But these were not and are not anything other than reflections of the great and unique Apostolic Tradition. The unity is, in the Tradition, originary, and the traditions develop over time and in various places, almost like buds coming from a plant. The opposite is not true; that is, we do not have a primitive community that follows various traditions, which—for one reason or another—would then flow together, perhaps even by force, into uniformity of doctrinal orthodoxy. A plurality of Christianities in the early days is a myth of modern historiography, born in a Protestant environment for apologetic reasons: for the Protestant Reformation, in fact, which presents itself as an alternative form of Christianity to the Catholic form, and which moreover recognizes immediately from within itself a widespread splintering into many groups, it is comforting to believe that such a pluralism corresponded to an original condition of the Church (or better of the Churches), before a presumed authoritative imposition of doctrinal orthodoxy. But the New Testament does not speak of Tradition in these terms, and this is even more true of the Fathers, who constantly refer to the deposit handed down by the Apostles, as a unique and not pluralistic source of the unity for the faith and the Church—and this does not exclude the fact that there are different tendencies in the New Testament, which are nonetheless situated within a fundamental unity.

With all that has just been said, reference has also been made to the theme of Tradition/traditions. The capitalization, or not, of the terms already indicates a different level of importance between the two. The traditions are the customs that the Church develops over time: they can arise, change, and even disappear. Although they are normally intimately linked to Revelation, they are not strictly necessary elements in the life of the Church, but rather represent local applications of the faith, of liturgy, of ecclesiastical discipline, and of devotion. For this reason, it is also possible for them to become corrupted, incorporating within themselves elements that are opposed to the Gospel. When this happens, they should be reformed.

5. Plurality and Pluralism

When good variation comes about, it is a varied refraction of the one Gospel, and it represents a treasure. However, when the multiplication of traditions is not just numerical and accidental, but rather one of substance (that is to say, when it affects the *depositum fidei*), then we are faced with damaging pluralism, and the very term "traditions" (Italian "*tradizioni*") is used abusively, instead becoming "betrayals" ("*tradimenti*"). Therefore, when the good variation or "plurality" deteriorates into pluralism, it is necessary to intervene with recourse to the unity and uniqueness of the source of the true *Traditio*. This is the classical criterion indicated by Saint Vincent of Lérins (d. ca. 450), and that we have already cited in the previous chapter: "In the Catholic Church itself, all possible care must be taken, that we hold that faith which has been believed everywhere, always, by all" [*quod ubique, quod semper, quod ab omnibus creditum est*].[94]

More than two centuries prior, Saint Irenaeus of Lyon had already emphasized the uniqueness of the Tradition, as well as its public and "pneumatic" character. Against the Gnostics, who followed esoteric traditions, Saint Irenaeus emphasized that the *kerygma* is publicly preached by the Church. Among Catholics there is no "exoteric" doctrine—reserved for the public—and an "esoteric" doctrine, for initiates, the spiritual elites. The Gospel is preached equally to all, even if not all bear the same fruit. *Traditio*, however, is public and offered without distinction. Secondly, Saint Irenaeus emphasized that it is unique thanks to its content, which he called the *regula fidei* ("rule of faith") or *regula veritatis* ("rule of the truth"). Finally, the Tradition is "pneumatic" because, as we have mentioned above, it is the Holy Spirit (*Pneuma*) that guarantees the uncorrupted transmission, from hand to hand, of the message of Christ through the Church.[95]

3.2. The Magisterium of the Church

3.2.1. In Service of the Word

The elements that have emerged from presenting the basic truths concerning the Tradition lead to a final point that is intimately connected with the the-

---

[94] Saint Vincent of Lérins, *Commonitorium* 2.5–6.
[95] For various aspects, see Saint Irenaeus of Lyon, *Adversus haereses* 1.10.2; 3.3.1-4; 24.1. Also worth mentioning is the emphasis Saint Irenaeus places on the importance of episcopal succession, as an uninterrupted chain from the Apostles that comes to us through the consecration of the bishops, the custodians of the deposit.

ological doctrine concerning Revelation: the ecclesiastical Magisterium. We should immediately clarify that the teaching of the Magisterium is not the Word of God, but serves it with a mainly interpretive function; not as a simple opinion, but rather with an authoritative judgment that binds the faith of Catholics.[96] The exercise of the "office of teaching" ("*munus docendi*")[97] is thus intimately linked to the Word of God, because it represents its authoritative explanation and transmission on the part of the Shepherds of the Church, but it does not contain teachings in addition to divine Revelation, which is considered concluded, as the classical formula states, "with the death of the last Apostle." In fact, when the apostolic phase of the Church ended, and with the passage into the era of bishops, the public Revelation of God ended: no new supernatural truth is to be expected, given that the Word of God is contained precisely in the deposit of faith delivered by the Apostles to their successors so that they would keep it intact and pass it on, without adding anything new to it, nor depriving it of any of its treasures.[98]

3.2.2. The Completeness of Revelation

The firm conviction that Revelation should be considered complete with the death of the Apostles has been the object of dispute in recent theology. However, it is of vital importance because it concerns the value of Revelation and the certainty with which it can be accepted. If, in fact, Revelation were not concluded, but rather in perpetual becoming, it would remain indefinite and uncertain. A clear and firm faith could not be founded on it, but the

---

[96] "Sacred Tradition and Sacred Scripture form one sacred deposit of the Word of God, committed to the Church.
. . . The task of authentically interpreting the Word of God, whether written or handed on, has been entrusted exclusively to the living teaching office [*Magisterium*] of the Church, whose authority is exercised in the name of Jesus Christ. This teaching office is not above the Word of God, but serves it, teaching only what has been handed on" (Second Vatican Council, *Dei Verbum*, §10).

[97] See the good summary provided by cc. 747–755: "*De Ecclesiae munere docendi*" of the *Codex Iuris Canonici*.

[98] Taking inspiration from *Dei Verbum* §7, we could say that in the apostolic age the Scriptures and Apostolic Tradition were formed, and they constitute the channels of Revelation and are the Word of God. That era having ended with the death of the last Apostle, the era of the bishops begins: the era in which we are now and will be until the end of time. In this era, the bishops, as the successors of the Apostles but not the Apostles themselves, continue to write and orally teach the Word of God, but these writings (encyclicals, pastoral letters, etc.) are not added to the Bible, as the *traditio vivens* (Magisterium) does not materially add to the Apostolic Tradition.

field would be left open for any change or even any distortion. It is true—as we noted in the first chapter—that the Catholic Church supports doctrinal development. But this is understood as an organic development, that is, as a full coming to light of what was already completely contained in the beginning (see Saint Vincent of Lérin's analogy of the human body[99]). Thus, there is a doctrinal corpus that in its essential elements is constituted from the beginning, even if throughout the centuries this organism grows, developing what it possesses at least in germ from the beginning. On the other hand, if it is believed that Revelation is still open, then at any moment new organs or limbs could be added to this body, distorting it. This is why Saint Pius X condemned a proposition of the modernists, which precisely affirmed the incomplete character of Revelation. In the Decree *Lamentabili*, the following statement is condemned as erroneous: "Revelation, constituting the object of the Catholic faith, was not completed with the Apostles."[100]

The reason for this stability of the deposit of faith resides once again in the Christological Figure. The deposit left by the Apostles, in fact, corresponds to the Gospel given by Jesus Christ, whose Word does not pass away (see Matt 24:35) because He is the Word of God in Person, the Mediator and fullness of all Revelation, as has been said. The Doctor of the Church Saint John of the Cross (d. 1591) emphasized this point well:

> The chief reason why the prayers in question were lawful under the old dispensation, and why it was necessary for prophets and priests to seek visions and revelations from God was, that the faith was not then revealed, that the evangelical law was not established; and therefore that it was necessary for men to enquire of God in this way, and that He should answer them at one time by visions, revelations, and locutions, at another by figures and similitudes, and again by other and different ways of communication. For all the answers, locutions, and revelations of old were mysteries of the faith, or matters pertaining or tending thereto. . . . But now that the faith of Christ is established, and the evangelical law promulgated in this day of grace, there is no necessity to consult Him as before, nor that He should answer and speak. For in giving to us, as He hath done,

---

[99] See Saint Vincent of Lérins, *Commonitorium* 3.1.
[100] Holy Office, *Lamentabili* (1907), no. 21 (DS 3421). Proposition no. 59 is also condemned. It affirms that "Christ did not teach a determined body of doctrine applicable to all times and all men but, rather, inaugurated a religious movement adapted or to be adapted to different times and places" (DS 3459).

His Son, Who is His only Word, He has spoken unto us once for all by His own and only Word, and has nothing further to reveal. [...] And, therefore, he who should now enquire of God in the ancient way, seeking visions or revelations, would offend Him; because he does not fix his eyes upon Christ alone, disregarding all besides. To such a one the answer of God is... I have spoken all by my Word, my Son; fix thine eyes upon Him, for in Him I have spoken and revealed all, and thou wilt find in Him more than thou desirest or askest.... He is My whole voice and answer, My whole vision and revelation, which I spoke, answered, made, and revealed.[101]

3.2.3. The Tasks of the Magisterium

The Magisterium of the Shepherds of the Church has these tasks: preserving the integrity of the Word of God, which was perfectly and definitively passed on by Christ; deepening its knowledge of the Word; and handing it on with fidelity. Vatican II teaches that the ecclesiastical Magisterium "*listening to [the Word of God] devoutly, guarding it scrupulously and explaining it faithfully* in accord with a divine commission and with the help of the Holy Spirit, [it] draws from this one deposit of faith everything which it presents for belief as divinely revealed."[102] Here the text points out the magisterial task: "*pie audit, sancte custodit, fideliter exponit.*" This is thus the relationship of the Magisterium with the Word of God: religious listening or listening done in obedience of the faith; holy safeguarding, which preserves the deposit from corruption; and faithful exposition, which does not concede to the fashion of the moment but remains in the truth of Christ. The Shepherds of the Church thus have the mandate of being "heralds of the faith,"[103] announcers of the Word. They cannot behave as owners of the deposit, but only as its guardians. An owner manages as he wishes; a guardian respects and preserves the property of another.

---

[101] Saint John of the Cross, *Subida del Monte Carmelo* 2.22.3–5, in *The Works of Saint John of the Cross*, trans. David Lewis, 2nd ed. (London: Thomas Baker, 1891), 183–184. This does not imply the inadmissibility of so-called "private revelations." Concerning these, see CCC §67.

[102] Second Vatican Council, *Dei Verbum*, §10 (emphasis added).

[103] "*Fidei praecones,*" as in Second Vatican Council, *Lumen Gentium* (1964), §25, dedicated to the *munus docendi* of bishops. The English translation found on the Vatican website, translates this expression as "preachers of the faith," though the Latin word *praeco* is better translated as "herald."

3.2.4. The Living and Faithful Magisterium

The Magisterium guarantees that the Tradition never devolves into traditionalism. The Tradition is living, because it is kept in life by the unceasing authoritative teaching of the Word on the part of the ministers of the Church. Traditionalism fixes the faith in trite formulas, correct from the material point of view, but a dead letter from the standpoint of a proclamation. In the face of the risk of traditionalism, there have often been reactions in recent times that propose the subversion of dogmatic and moral formulas—a solution worse than the evil it intends to cure. The Church's formulas are to be kept immutable because they express the faith that is to be preserved immutably. However, they are not dead, or items in a museum to be held in glass cases that are to be admired without being touched. On the contrary, the dogmatic and moral formulas must always be kept identical to their own content and at the same time they must continuously be kept alive and young in kerygmatic preaching. Here we see an *et-et* once again, according to which the deposit of faith must both be fixed in immutable formulas and must be always re-proposed in a living way by the Church. At the official level, this is done with the Magisterium of bishops; but there is also the more ordinary level of preaching and catechesis, which must not disconnect themselves from defined dogma and morals, but rather preach them again and again, also making use of new adapted languages, while still preserving the same meaning and even the traditional expressions of the language of the faith, alongside explanations in the language of today.[104]

> Consequently the understanding, knowledge, and wisdom of each and all—of each churchman and of the whole Church—ought to grow and progress greatly and eagerly through the course of ages and centuries, provided that the advance be within its own lines, in the same sphere of doctrine, the same feeling, the same sentiment [*sed in suo dumtaxat genere, in eodem scilicet dogmate, eodem sensu eademque sententia*].[105]

---

[104] This is not about forgetting—or worse, criticizing—the formulas and terminology that the Church has slowly and painstakingly developed. It is not a matter of substituting words such as the Trinity, nature, Person, atonement, Sacrament, etc. It is about using these words—yes, always continuing to use them!—explaining them nonetheless with words of the current language and with examples from daily life as well, preserving the original meaning intended by the classical categories. Only in this way, very slowly and with discernment, will new categories and terms be able to be added, not in the place of, but alongside the classical and established ones ("things new *and* old").

[105] Saint Vincent of Lérins, *Commonitorium* 23.54, in *The Commonitory of Saint Vincent of*

3.2.5. Forms of Exercise

The Magisterium of the Church is usually divided into two forms of exercise: ordinary and extraordinary. The latter can be exercised in a solemn or non-solemn way.

1. Ordinary

The ordinary Magisterium is present in all the pronouncements of the Shepherds of the Church that are not intended to bind the faith of believers, that is, those that do not require a total adhesion of the intellect and will on the part of the baptized, even if the greater part of what is taught through this magisterial form is obligatory for the faith: not, however, because it is sanctioned at that moment, but rather because it was already so. The ordinary Magisterium is the normal and everyday mode of exercising the *munus docendi* in the Church. For this reason, the other form is called extraordinary, because it is somewhat exceptional, occurring only from time to time.

2. Extraordinary

(1) There is a pronouncement of the extraordinary Magisterium both when a Roman pontiff issues a dogmatic definition *ex cathedra* and when an ecumenical council defines a dogma (see Chapter Eight). Given the rarity and the celebratory apparatus that usually accompanies these dogmatic definitions, one can also speak of a solemn Magisterium. (2) However, the extraordinary Magisterium can also be carried out in a non-solemn way and in this case, it is called the Ordinary Universal Magisterium.[106] Although the wording

---

Lerins, trans. T. Herbert Bindley (New York: E.S. Gorham, 1915), 90. In the opening speech of the Second Vatican Council, Saint John XXIII stated: "What interests the Council more than anything is that the sacred deposit of Christian doctrine is safeguarded and taught in a more efficacious way. . . . The twenty-first ecumenical council . . . wants to impart the entire, not diminished or distorted, Catholic doctrine. . . . It is necessary that this certain and immutable doctrine, to which we must give faithful assent, is deepened and presented according to what is required by our times. In fact, one thing is the deposit of faith, that is, the truths that are contained in our venerable doctrine, and another thing is the mode in which they are announced, always nonetheless in the same sense and the same meaning [*eodem tamen sensu eademque sententia*]" (*Gaudet Mater Ecclesia*, October 11, 1962, §5–6 [our translation]).

[106] To clarify the exercise of this form of Magisterium, Saint John Paul II, with the Apostolic Letter *Ad Tuendam Fidem* (1998), modified certain canons of the *Codex Juris Canonici*, which, in the version that was originally approved, were not expressed as completely as

includes the adjective "ordinary," in reality this is a form of execution of the extraordinary Magisterium, that is, of the Magisterium that binds the faith of believers to its own formulations. These are teachings that, while not having been defined in a solemn occasion, are part of the Church's Creed, and have always been taught everywhere and by everyone. Thus, in this case, "ordinary" does not mean "of little importance," but it indicates the uninterrupted continuity in proposing a given teaching. Therefore, these are not revisable affirmations; rather, they are certain.[107]

3.2.6. Object, Infallibility, and Possibility of Error

1. Object

The foregoing suggests that, in the case of a teaching that comes in the form of the ordinary Magisterium, it is possible—even if it is improbable and very rare—for there to be some error in the proposed texts. This is acknowledged for both theological and historical reasons. On the contrary, the extraordinary Magisterium is clothed in the charism of infallibility, for which the dogmas defined by the Church are certainly inerrant in matters of faith and morals (the proper object of the Magisterium[108]), due to the special assistance of the Holy Spirit.

---

they should have been. As regards the different degrees of the exercise of the Magisterium and the assent that is due to them by the faithful, the new *Professio Fidei* and *Iusiurandum fidelitatis in suscipiendo officio nomine Ecclesiae exercendo* are also important, as is the explanatory doctrinal note of these two texts, published on June 29, 1998, by the Congregation for the Doctrine of the Faith.

[107] A recent example of this is represented by the Apostolic Letter *Ordinatio Sacerdotalis* (1994), in which Saint John Paul II recalls that the Catholic Church has the faculty of ordaining only men (*viri*) as priests, and thus never women. Although, technically speaking, the Pope did not define a dogma, he writes in §4: "in order that all doubt may be removed regarding a matter of great importance, a matter which pertains to the Church's divine constitution itself, in virtue of my ministry of confirming the brethren I declare that the Church has no authority whatsoever to confer priestly ordination on women and that this judgment is to be definitively held by all the Church's faithful." We shall return to this theme in Chapter Ten (in a section concerning the Sacrament of Holy Orders).

[108] The proper object of the Magisterium is the "*res fidei et morum*" ("matter of faith and morals"). Thus, the Magisterium should not pronounce on everything! If pronounced on matters outside of its competence, the faithful would not be held to a deference of soul in regard to these teachings. Moreover, theologians distinguish between the "primary object" and the "secondary object" of the Magisterium. The primary object is the matter of faith and morals contained in the *depositum*; the secondary object are the contents of faith and morals that are not found directly or explicitly taught in the same deposit, but which are necessary for defending and deepening it. This concerns those "truths that are necessarily connected to divine revelation . . . either for historical reasons or by a

2. Infallibility

Infallibility is a gift that Christ gives, in the Holy Spirit, to the Church. That the Church does not err in the sphere of faith and morals is guaranteed by God: it is part of that supernatural endowment that the Groom wished to grant His Bride.

(1) The first form of infallibility is thus that *in credendo*, in faith. Vatican II reminds us—recalling Saint Augustine—that the totality of the faithful (*universitas fidelium*: indicates the Church as a whole, and not the arithmetic sum of each individual member) "cannot err in matters of belief" (*"in credendo falli nequit"*).[109]

(2) To preserve the purity of this faith, God has also arranged in the Church an *infallibilitas in docendo*, namely, a magisterial function that is granted only to the Shepherds, which guarantees certainty in believing, matters of faith, and morals.[110] As emphasized above, there are different modes in which this second form of infallibility is exercised and manifested. *Lumen Gentium* §25 recalls these different modes.

(3) The First Vatican Council dogmatically defined what specifically concerns the infallibility *in docendo* of the Supreme Pontiff:

> The Roman pontiff, when he speaks *ex cathedra*, that is, when, acting in the office of Shepherd and Teacher of all Christians, he defines, by virtue of his supreme apostolic authority, a doctrine concerning faith or morals to be held by the universal Church, possesses through the divine assistance promised to him in blessed Peter the infallibility with which the Divine Redeemer willed his Church to be endowed in defining the doctrine concerning faith or morals; and that such definitions of the Roman pontiff are therefore irreformable of themselves, not because of the consent of the Church [*ex sese non autem ex consensu Ecclesiae*].[111]

---

logical relationship" (Saint John Paul II, *Ad Tuendam Fidem*, §3). The Magisterium has the ability to pronounce on both its primary and secondary object in an infallible way.

[109] Second Vatican Council, *Lumen Gentium*, §12.

[110] Like the Magisterium itself, infallibility only relates to matters proper to the *munus docendi* and not just any object: "This infallibility with which the Divine Redeemer willed His Church to be endowed in defining doctrine of faith and morals, extends as far as the deposit of Revelation extends, which must be religiously guarded and faithfully expounded" (Second Vatican Council, *Lumen Gentium*, §25).

[111] First Vatican Council, *Pastor Æternus* (1870), ch. 4 (DS 3074).

The text clearly delineates the exercise of this extraordinary power—which on the other hand is used very rarely by the Pontiffs, insofar as it binds the faith of Catholics—while it emphasizes that the infallibility of the pope is not separate from that of the Church, being by contrast a manifestation of it. It is true that the infallibility of the pope should be considered "personal," in the sense that it is a faculty of each individual pope and not generically of the "papacy." But this does not mean that the pope can make use of such a faculty in an arbitrary way. The infallibility that—in certain conditions—he enjoys is, the First Vatican Council states, the infallibility with "which the Divine Redeemer willed his Church to be endowed." If, therefore, it is heretical to deny the dogma of papal infallibility, it would also be an error to believe that the pope exercises his magisterial *munus* according to his own pleasure, or in accord with his own, personal theological leanings.[112] The Magisterium is an ecclesial service to the Word of God, not the prevailing of personal opinions over this Word. Moreover, the supreme power over the whole Church that the Roman pontiff has received from Christ is a power for the service of Christ Himself and his brothers (see Luke 22:32), not permission to "lord it over" (1 Pet 5:3) the sheep of the flock of Christ doctrinally or in disciplinary matters.[113]

---

[112] In an exemplary way—while being a noteworthy theologian—Benedict XVI pronounced these words in his *Homily at the Holy Mass at the beginning of his Petrine Ministry*, April 24, 2005: "My real programme of governance is not to do my own will, not to pursue my own ideas, but to listen, together with the whole Church, to the word and the will of the Lord, to be guided by Him, so that He himself will lead the Church at this hour of our history." And in the *Homily at the Holy Mass of His Possession of the Seat of the Bishop of Rome*, May 7, 2005, he reiterated: "The power of teaching in the Church involves a commitment to the service of obedience to the faith. The Pope is not an absolute monarch whose thoughts and desires are law. On the contrary: the Pope's ministry is a guarantee of obedience to Christ and to his Word. He must not proclaim his own ideas, but rather constantly bind himself and the Church to obedience to God's Word, in the face of every attempt to adapt it or water it down, and every form of opportunism."

[113] In the past, and also during the discussion at Vatican I concerning the definition of papal infallibility, the theological question about the possibility of a heretical Pope was posed. Certain authors deny that it can even occur; many admit it as a theoretical hypothesis, extremely difficult to occur, etc. The case of a Pope that is formally a heretic should also be distinguished from that of one that is materially a heretic, or from the case of one who might have some confusion or be deceived in good faith about some point of doctrine. On a historical level, there are some cases that can be recalled, such as that of Pope Honorius (d. 638), who was later excommunicated by the Third Council of Constantinople (680–681; see Chapter Four), with the condemnation confirmed by Pope Leo II (see DS 563); or the case of Pope John XXII (d. 1334), whose eschatological ideas were corrected by his successor Benedict XII (see DS 1000–1002; see Chapter Twelve). One point that can be agreed upon is that—granting the remote hypothesis of a formally heretical Pope—no one in the Church has the legal authority to depose him. This is based

3. Extrincism and Historicism

If the dogma is always certain and valid, because it is infallibly taught, this does not mean that there is no positive development of dogma. With respect to the theology of dogma it is possible to fall into two extremes: the extrincism of a certain number of post-Tridentine theologians, and the historicism of the modernists. (1) The first sees a complete separation between history and dogma, on account of which history does not have any influence on the dogmatic formulations or, if it does, it should nonetheless be completely set aside when it comes to understanding and deepening the content of faith expressed by the dogma. (2) At the opposite extreme, the modernists affirm that dogma is entirely historically conditioned, and so it is not only understood simply as an expression of the Church in a certain moment, but it is also destined to be surpassed, once the particular historical context in which it was produced has changed. The latter would be a concept of evolution rather than the progress of dogma, an error already rejected by Saint Vincent of Lérins,

---

on the principle "*Prima Sedes a nemine iudicatur*" ("The First See is judged by no one") (*Codex Iuris Canonici*, can. 1404). However, the *Decretum Gratiani* 1.40.6 says "he cannot be judged by anyone, except in the case in which he distances himself from the faith [*a fide devius*]". To hold that an ecumenical council—this is the opinion, for example, of Cajetan (d. 1534)—or the Sacred College of Cardinals alone could depose a heretical pope would be a thesis of a "conciliarist" flavor, that is to say, one which allows—at least in exceptional circumstances—the superiority of the college over its head. On the other hand, a heretical pope could not be canonically deposed by anyone (for this reason Bellarmine [d. 1621] opined that such a pope would automatically fall from the See). This does not mean that the Church would not have to react in other ways: (1) by availing themselves of the faculty, reserved to all the faithful, of not consenting to doctrines that evidently clash with the Catholic faith; (2) by manifesting this absence of consent in suitable ways and without losing due respect to the Supreme Pontiff on account of his office; (3) with supplications to God and offerings of penance that the Holy Spirit may enlighten the mind of the Pontiff and that the latter may withdraw from his error; (4) by exercising, particularly through the cardinals, moral suasion, to solicit the pope either to resign voluntarily, or even better, withdraw from his error; etc. Naturally, all of this is purely theoretical in nature. In her 2000 years of history, the Catholic Church has known many dramas, including certain popes with uncertain faith on some point, perhaps even materially, but never formally heretical. It is to be hoped that the Holy Spirit wants to continue in the future to preserve the Church from such a disaster. N.B. The heresy is material when one denies or calls articles of faith into doubt without having awareness or intention of it (for example, if one said that Jesus is a human person, only intending to say that He is a true human being and not to deny that He is only a divine Person: in this case, materially, the writing would be heretical, but there would not be awareness and a will to deny the faith). On the other hand, heresy is formal when it is conscious and deliberate, and involves a certain obstinance on the part of the person. Only in the second case is heresy a delict against the faith.

Caro (Flesh)

who, as we have seen, distinguishes "progress" from "change."[114] The modernists accepted that there could be such an evolution of the dogma that would involve complete change, rather than just progressive development.

3.2.7. Doctrinal Development

The Catholic Church permits progress or doctrinal development (some authors speak equally of a "[homogeneous] evolution of dogma" while having in mind development). Such a development is due, above all, to four factors: (1) Revelation is expressed in human words and not only in the Bible. Given that human language is limited, it cannot express the infinite definitively, which is one reason why a constant process of honing dogmatic language also leads to the development of the very understanding of dogmatic content itself. (2) The Holy Spirit accompanies the disciples to the truth in its entirety (see John 16:13). Through the centuries, there is an incessant continuation of the study, meditative reflection, prayer, and practice of what is "written" in Revelation. This produces a slow but constant deepening of the understanding of the deposit of faith, without new truths being added to it. This entails the accumulation of greater and greater knowledge of the deposit that was received as complete from the beginning.[115] (3) Heresies and errors against the faith push the Church to better consider certain aspects of its own doctrine, both to defend it and to promote it. (4) New theological theories are evaluated by the Magisterium, which can approve them or reject them, and in this way new light is shed on the understanding of Revelation.[116]

As we emphasized in the previous chapter with reference to Saint Vincent of Lérins, in order for dogmatic development to be healthy, it is

---

[114] For example, in this well-known text: "Let that which was formerly believed darkly be understood clearly by thy exposition. Let posterity by thy aid rejoice in truths understood which antiquity venerated without understanding them. Yet teach still the same things which thou didst learn, so that although thou speakest in a new fashion, thou speakest not new things" (Saint Vincent of Lérins, *Commonitorium* 22.53, in *Commonitory of Saint Vincent*, 89). In 23.54, Saint Vincent explains: "For progress implies a growth within the thing itself, while change turns one thing into another."

[115] "Regarding the substance of the articles of faith [dogmas] there was no development [*augmentum*] throughout the course of time: since later Fathers believed all the truths that were contained, albeit implicitly, in the faith of their Fathers before them. On the other hand, regarding what is made explicit, the number of articles increased, since the later Fathers knew explicitly things that the earlier ones had not known in an explicit manner" (*ST* II-II, q. 1, a. 7 [our translation]).

[116] A classic case is the admission into the language of faith of the term, formulated by theologians, of "transubstantiation" to indicate the Eucharistic change (see Chapter Eleven).

necessary for it to be organic; that is, it happens in an analogous way to that of the development of a human body, which in growing does not undergo genetic mutation, much less substantial change, and does nothing else but grow in those elements that it possesses in itself from the beginning, without addition or subtraction.[117]

3.2.8. Hermeneutic of Continuity

Finally, it is necessary to present a practical criterion for evaluating magisterial texts, which emerges from what has been said about organic development. The texts of the more recent Magisterium and older texts are found in a sort of hermeneutical circle, for which the documents of the past are reread in light of the more recent ones, and vice versa. Which is the hierarchically principal movement in this hermeneutical *et-et*? Is it that which examines the documents of yesteryear in light of those of today, or that which interprets today's documents in light of the living Tradition of the past? If the Magisterium must embody an organic development, for which "new things" emerge from those already existing,[118] then it is clear that primacy should be recognized for the hermeneutic that places what is said in the more recent documents within the great framework of the doctrine that was previously presented. What is said today must be interpreted in light of what was said before, and consequently it must agree with it. To give primacy to the inverse dynamic would imply the very serious risk of a hermeneutic that, instead of interpreting and re-proposing the Magisterium of the preceding centuries, considers it overcome.

3.3. Faith

3.3.1. Grace and Freedom

Faith is the response that the human being gives to God who reveals Himself. Such a response is not a simple human act, like a response given out of simple

---

[117] See Saint Vincent of Lérins, *Commonitorium* 23.6-9. A notable contribution was given by Saint John Henry Newman (d. 1890) to the study of doctrinal development, particularly in the work *An Essay on the Development of Christian Doctrine*, in which he describes seven general criteria that allow one to distinguish between true organic or homogeneous development of dogma, and other forms of doctrinal evolution that distort the revealed content. The seven criteria are: (1) Preservation (or Unity) of Type; (2) Continuity of Principles; (3) Power of Assimilation; (4) Logical Sequence; (5) Anticipation of Its Future; (6) Conservative Action upon Its Past; and (7) Chronic Vigor.

[118] See the Second Vatican Council, *Sacrosanctum Concilium*, §23.

courtesy when a person asks us something. For Catholic doctrine, faith is—alongside hope and charity—a theological virtue, that is, it is grace that God has infused into the soul of the human being,[119] who is moved to accept as true the words spoken by God and to wholeheartedly trust in Him. It is very important in our day to emphasize, especially within western culture, that faith is first and foremost a grace of God, and only in a subordinate way a work and choice of the human being.[120] Saint Paul clearly attests to the divine origin of faith in the human being: "For by grace you have been saved through faith, and this is not from you; it is the gift of God" (Eph 2:8). Significantly, the Second Synod of Orange (in 529), recalling that faith is a gift of God, also observes that whoever held faith as a natural activity of the human being would automatically say that everyone is a believer:

> If anyone says that the increase as well as the beginning of faith and the very desire of faith [*credulitatis affectum*] . . . proceeds from our own nature and not from a gift of grace . . . such a one reveals himself in contradiction with the apostolic doctrine [Phil 1:6 and 1:29 are cited, as well as the above-mentioned Eph 2:8]. For those who say that the faith by which we believe in God is natural declare that all those who are strangers to the Church of Christ are, in some way, believers.[121]

---

[119] "No man can 'assent to the Gospel message'. . . 'without the illumination and inspiration of the Holy Spirit'. . . Wherefore faith . . . is in itself a gift of God" (First Vatican Council, *Dei Filius*, ch. 3 [DS 3010]). See Second Vatican Council, *Dei Verbum*, §5. Concerning the theme of the priority of grace as a gift with respect to the merit of the human being, see Saint Augustine of Hippo, *De praedestinatione sanctorum*.

[120] See *ST* II-II, q. 6, a. 1. With this, we do not wish to deny that there is a hook for theological faith in the very anthropological structure, insofar as humans, even at the simple natural level, perform a multitude of acts of trust or natural faith, often even in an unreflective way (for example, when one uses an elevator, one entrusts one's own physical safety to the honesty and competence of whoever has constructed it and who reviews it, people who are probably not even known to the person using it). Such a hook, nonetheless, does not represent the source from which full theological faith flows, but at most it is the "landing field" for it. See, more in general, the treatment concerning grace in Ch. 5.

[121] Second Synod of Orange, *Canones de Gratia*, can. 5 (DS 375). This local Synod has universal importance because it was confirmed by Pope Boniface II, *Per Filium Nostrum* (531) (DS 398–400). This Synod was cited both by the First Vatican Council and by the Second Vatican Council. Based on the fact that faith is not natural, while religions represent a search for the divine that is carried out with human capacities, the Congregation for the Doctrine of the Faith has clarified that "For this reason, the distinction between *theological faith* and *belief* in the other religions, must be *firmly held*" (*Dominus Iesus* [2000], §7).

We thus have a first synthetic pair for which faith is a grace of God and a free adherence on the part of the human being. Primarily grace, but also freedom.

With faith being a positive response to the Word of God, which makes us know the Truth, faith and truth should always go together. Faith is the knowledge of the truth given by God, not a simple opinion or human research. "Today more than ever, we need to be reminded of this bond between faith and truth, given the crisis of truth in our age."[122]

3.3.2. Love and Duty: The Obedience of Faith

Holy Scripture describes the adherence of the human being to God in faith as an act of obedience, as the "obedience of faith" (Rom 1:5; 16:26). In this sense, one can speak of faith—in addition to the fact that it is an act of love—as an act of duty: "We are bound to yield by faith the full homage of intellect and will to the God who reveals."[123] Faith is professed wholeheartedly, that is, with all the faculties of the soul. Thus, it is an intellectual and volitional act, which leads to the adherence of the intellect to the revealed truth, and to the voluntary adherence to God and to His will. Saint Thomas wrote that "to believe is an intellectual act of assent to Divine truth commanded by a free will moved by God through grace."[124]

Thus we find a second way of expressing the binary synthesis in the act of faith, recognizing that it is both an act of love and of duty, and that it leads to an internal adherence both to revealed notional truths (*fides quae creditur*),[125] and it implies a personal adherence to the One who reveals them (*fides qua*

---

[122] Francis, *Lumen Fidei* (2013), §25.

[123] First Vatican Council, *Dei Filius*, ch. 3 (DS 3008). And the Second Vatican Council confirms it: "'The obedience of faith' (Rom. 16:26; see 1:5; 2 Cor 10:5–6) 'is to be given to God who reveals, an obedience by which man commits his whole self freely to God, offering the full submission of intellect and will to God who reveals', and freely assenting to the truth revealed by Him" (*Dei Verbum*, §5).

[124] *ST* II-II, q. 2, a. 9 (our translation). The Council of Trent, *Decretum de Iustificatione* (1547), ch. 6, says that human beings are disposed to justification "by believing to be true what has been divinely revealed and promised" (DS 1526).

[125] Such truths are expressed in formulas or articles of faith. Saint Thomas reminds us that "*actus credentis non terminatur ad enuntiabile sed ad rem*" ("the act of believing is not terminated [with adherence] to an utterance [the formula], but rather to a reality [expressed by the formula]": *ST* II-II, q. 1, a. 2, ad 2 [our translation]). This does not mean that the formulas are not necessary, because only through them—the human language that God has chosen to speak—is it possible to turn to the signified reality. To eliminate the formulas means to eliminate the possibility of the act of faith.

creditur).¹²⁶ For this reason, believing is both an intellectual act of knowing the truth, and a volitional act of love.¹²⁷ In fact, the fundamental reason for believing resides in the authority of God:

> The Catholic Church professes that this faith, which is the beginning of man's salvation, is a supernatural virtue whereby, inspired and assisted by the grace of God, we believe that what he has revealed is true, not because the intrinsic truth of things is recognized by the natural light of reason, but because of the authority of God himself who reveals them, who can neither err nor deceive.¹²⁸

That faith always requires, despite its reasonability, an act of will, is due to the fact that it adheres to objects (truths) that are not *per se* evident, according to the definition offered by the Letter to the Hebrews 11:1: "Faith is the realization of what is hoped for and evidence of things not seen."¹²⁹ Thus one can also identify in the virtue of faith the pair "certainty and obscurity," where certainty is predominant: to believe is to know and hold what God has said as certain; nevertheless, the light of faith always remains in obscurity for the intellect, an obscurity that will only be taken away in the beatific vision (see Chapter Twelve). A small window always remains open, through which questions and, sometimes, difficulties can peek through. However, spiritual and ecclesial experience sustain the believer in dispelling the shadows.¹³⁰

3.3.3. Intellect and Will: Hearing and Vision

Despite the fact that faith is both an act carried out under the motion of the will that pushes the intellect to adhere to Revelation, God did not will that belief would be an act without reasons, a fideistic act. It is no accident that Saint Augustine was able to define faith as "to think (while) assenting" ("*cum*

---

¹²⁶ See CCC §150.
¹²⁷ See Francis, *Lumen Fidei*, §§26–28.
¹²⁸ First Vatican Council, *Dei Filius*, ch. 3 (DS 3008).
¹²⁹ See *ST* II-II, q. 4, a. 1. Concerning the correct way of translating these biblical words in the modern languages (and concerning the understanding that follows the translation), see Benedict XVI, *Spe Salvi* (2007), §7.
¹³⁰ "We may all be tempted by the disbelief of Thomas [the Apostle]. Suffering, evil, injustice ... does not all of this put our faith to the test? Paradoxically the disbelief of Thomas is most valuable to us in these cases because it helps to purify all false concepts of God and leads us to discover his true face" (Benedict XVI, *Urbi et Orbi Message*, April 8, 2007).

assensione cogitare").¹³¹ Thus, while the fundamental motive of faith does not consist in the result of human reasoning, God has offered to us reasonable signs of credibility of His Word, called "external proofs of Revelation," which are mainly the miracles of Christ and the saints, the fulfillment of prophecies, and the characteristics of the Church.¹³² Therefore, we can say that the person believes both through the inner aids of grace, and through the proofs of credibility of the historically verifiable Revelation. This opposes both fideism and rationalism, and maintains a healthy harmony between faith and reason. No one will be able to say that believers are gullible or credulous. Faith comes about from the combination of listening to the Word (*"fides ex auditu"* ["faith comes from what is heard"]: Rom 10:17) and the vision of light or, namely, the signs of credibility (*"videmus stellam eius in oriente et venimus adorare eum"* ["We saw his star at its rising and have come to do him homage"]: Matt 2:2).¹³³

3.3.4. Salvific Necessity and Meritorious Will

Holy Scripture adds that faith is necessary for the eternal salvation of the human being: "Without faith it is impossible to please [God]" (Heb 11:6). We shall focus on the theme of the salvation of those who do not have faith in another chapter. For it to be salvific, the act of faith must be meritorious and, consequently, it cannot be imposed. Although the human person must assent to Revelation, this does not imply the inevitability of faith, as is confirmed by the fact that all persons who come into contact with His Word have the duty to believe in God, but not all in fact do. Faith is a free act. Thus, we can identify the pair "necessity and voluntariness" of the act of faith.

3.3.5. Unity and Plurality

Faith then has a character of both unity and plurality. In fact, the one faith is refracted through many spiritualities, various theologies, and various inculturations. However, this polyhedral element must always be manifested within the constitutive and primordial unity of the faith, which is one: "one Lord, one faith, one baptism" (Eph 4:5). Saint Irenaeus wrote:

---

[131] Saint Augustine of Hippo, *De praedestinatione sanctorum* 2.5. See *ST* II-II, q. 2, a. 1.

[132] First Vatican Council, *Dei Filius*, ch. 3 (DS 3009).

[133] The union between hearing and seeing in the faith is founded Christologically by Francis, *Lumen Fidei*, §§29–32 (see also §37).

The Church, having received this preaching and this faith, although scattered throughout the whole world, yet, as if occupying but one house, carefully preserves it. She also believes these points [of doctrine] just as if she had but one soul, and one and the same heart, and she proclaims them, and teaches them, and hands them down, with perfect harmony, as if she possessed only one mouth. For, although the languages of the world are dissimilar, yet the import of the Tradition is one and the same. For the Churches which have been planted in Germany do not believe or hand down anything different, nor do those in Spain, nor those in Gaul, nor those in the East, nor those in Egypt, nor those in Libya, nor those which have been established in the central regions of the world. But as the sun, that creature of God, is one and the same throughout the whole world, so also the preaching of the truth shines everywhere, and enlightens all men that are willing to come to a knowledge of the truth. Nor will any one of the rulers in the Churches, however highly gifted he may be in point of eloquence, teach doctrines different from these (for no one is greater than the Master).[134]

Therefore, in the pair "unity and plurality" of the faith, the primacy should clearly go to the first term.[135] "Since faith is one, it must be professed in all its purity and integrity. Precisely because all the articles of faith are interconnected, to deny one of them, even of those that seem least important, is tantamount to distorting the whole."[136]

3.3.6. Person and Community

A further aspect regards the faith-Church relationship, implied by the fact that faith has another twofold characteristic: it has a personal side and a communal side. This theme is broad and touches various aspects: personal holiness, Gospel witness, the ecclesial missionary task, the relationship with

---

[134] Saint Irenaeus of Lyon, *Adversus haereses* 1.10.2, in *ANF*, vol. 1, trans. James Donaldson and Alexander Roberts (Peabody, MA: Hendrickson Publishers, Inc., 1994), 331. With all the emphasis today on the necessity of the inculturation of the faith, it can sometimes be forgotten that the Churches of a certain region of the world cannot preach differently from the others, otherwise the shepherds would consider themselves greater than the Good Shepherd.

[135] See *ST* II-II, q. 4, a. 6; Francis, *Lumen Fidei*, §47.

[136] Francis, *Lumen Fidei*, §48. See Francis, *Evangelii Gaudium*, §39: "The integrity of the Gospel message must not be deformed."

pastoral activity, etc. Several of these themes will be taken up again in the subsequent chapters. Here we shall only recall that doctrinal unity is not the only unity, but the first criterion of ecclesial communion. It is enough to recall the text of Acts 2:42–46, which draws an ideal picture of the first Christian community. Such an effective and affective communion—it is said—is based on certain objective elements, among which the first that is mentioned is perseverance in the teaching (doctrine) of the Apostles (v. 42).

> This [ecclesial] unity, in fact, is primarily a *unity of faith*, supported by the sacred deposit whose main custodian and defender is the Successor of Peter. Strengthening brothers and sisters in the faith . . . is the first and fundamental task that Jesus conferred upon the one seated on the Chair of Peter. It is a binding service on which depends the effectiveness of the Church's evangelizing action to the end of time.[137]

Therefore, the theme of faith can never be marginalized in the name of "prophetic" or "pastoral" angles. There is no prophecy without the faithful proclamation of the Word of God, just as there is no opposition between doctrine and the care of souls.[138] Here, the salutary *et-et* must be preserved once again!

3.3.7. "Credere Deo, Credere Deum, Credere in Deum"

In short, the act of faith can be described with a formula of Augustinian inspiration that has become classic: for the Catholic faithful, to believe means "*Credere Deo, credere Deum, credere in Deum*" ("to believe God, to believe in God as God, to believe in God.")[139] Saint Thomas explains that "*credere Deum*" indicates the object of faith, what is believed, the content of faith—God and all things in relation to Him. "*Credere Deo*" indicates the reason why we believe, that is, because of the fact that we trust that God, in speaking to us, does not deceive us. These two expressions are linked above all to the role of the intellect in the act of faith. Finally, for what regards the will, we have

---

[137] Benedict XVI, *Address to the Members of the Congregation of the Faith on the Occasion of the Plenary Assembly*, January 15, 2010.

[138] See Benedict XVI, *Homily at Holy Mass for the Opening of the Year of the Faith*, October 11, 2012.

[139] See *ST* II-II, q. 2, a. 2, based on Saint Augustine of Hippo, *In Evangelium Ioannis Tractatus* 29.6.

the "*credere in Deum*," that is, the fact that we confide in God, and thus our will leads our intellect to give its assent. Although we have three expressions here, in reality the fundamental dipolar character of the act of faith is maintained, given that—on the one hand—we do not have three distinct acts of faith, but rather one act alone composed of these elements and—on the other hand—the three elements are subdivided in a dipolar fashion, given that two regard the intellect and one the will.

The question about whether the intellect or the will is prevalent when it comes to believing has been much discussed. We prefer the idea that the intellect has (*a parte hominis*!) a principal role, even if the will cannot in any way be considered merely auxiliary.[140] To affirm the primacy of the intellect and the necessary knowledge of doctrines does not, in our view, imply any rationalism. We recall with Benedict XVI:

> Today too the Creed needs to be better known, understood, and prayed. It is important above all that the Creed be, so to speak, 'recognized.' Indeed, knowing might be merely an intellectual operation, whereas 'recognizing' means the need to discover the deep bond between the truth we profess in the Creed and our daily existence, so that these truths may truly and in practice be—as they have always been—light for our steps through life, water that irrigates the parched stretches on our path, life that gets the better of some arid areas of life today. The moral life of Christians is grafted on the Creed, on which it is founded and by which it is justified.[141]

In conclusion, the Catholic doctrine manifests the internal act of faith as an act that involves all the spiritual faculties of the human soul. Protestantism, on the other hand, with its theory of fiducial faith alone[142] ("*credere in Deum*") exposes itself to the error of voluntarism. By no accident, the "reasons

---

[140] See *ST* II-II, q. 2, a. 1, ad 3; q. 4, aa. 2–3 and 5. In the first of these texts, Saint Thomas teaches that the faith is an act of the intellect (*actus intellectus*) but that happens insofar as it is determined by the will (*a voluntate determinatur*). Such a determination (a word to be taken seriously) is such that in the *Summa contra gentiles* III, ch. 40, the Angelic Doctor writes: "In the knowledge of faith, the will has the principal task; in fact, the intellect gives assent of faith to things that are proposed to it because it is moved not by the very evidence of the truth, but rather by the will." Thus, the faith remains an act of intellect and in this sense the intellect remains principal in the act of faith; but the mover of this act is the will.

[141] Benedict XVI, *General Audience*, October 17, 2012.

[142] A conception condemned by the Council of Trent, *Canones de Iustificatione* (1547), can. 12 (DS 1562).

of belief" and, more generally, philosophy and the ratiocinative powers of the human person are not valued highly in this approach, marked as it is by a strong anthropological pessimism that we have touched on in the previous chapter. If original sin irreparably ruined the human person, then human reason and will are also wounded in an irreparable way. Positing an *aut-aut* about which of the two to choose, Luther prefers the will over the intellect, (unconsciously) opening the path for all the successive thinkers and currents of thought that, in the arc of Modernity and leading up to this very day, have progressively eroded the rational foundation of the faith, understanding the latter above all as sentiment.[143] This did not prevent the existence, and even expansion, of a Protestant theology that is also still marked by rather evident methodological limits. Therefore, to conclude the chapter, let us offer a brief outline of the nature of theology from a Catholic point of view.

3.4. Supernatural Theology

3.4.1. Philosophy and Theology

Supernatural theology works in an inverted direction with respect to natural theology, which is based on reason alone. Supernatural theology can and must be based on Revelation, which, as we have seen, is handed down to us both through Scripture and Apostolic Tradition. The believer accepts in faith the Word of God, and reflects on it with the aid of natural reason:

> If the reason illumined by faith inquires in an earnest, pious, and sober manner, it attains by God's grace a certain understanding of the mysteries, which is most fruitful, both from the analogy with the objects of its natural knowledge and from the connection of these mysteries with one another and with man's ultimate end. But it never becomes capable of understanding them in the way it does with truths that constitute its proper object.[144]

Thus, while theodicy, or natural philosophical theology, must proceed

---

[143] Instead, "faith involves the entire person: thoughts, affections, intentions, relations, bodiliness, activity, and daily work" (Benedict XVI, *General Audience*, May 31, 2006). For this reason, in the faith we do not find only the Revelation of God, but also perfect human fulfillment: "The definitive fulfillment of every authentic human aspiration rests in Jesus Christ" (Benedict XVI, *Address to the Participants of the Plenary Assembly of the Congregation for the Doctrine of the Faith*, February 10, 2006).

[144] First Vatican Council, *Dei Filius*, ch. 4 (DS 3016).

a posteriori, supernatural theology—commonly called in the Catholic sphere simply theology, sacred doctrine, or the science of the faith (*scientia fidei*)—proceeds *a priori*, holding the truths revealed by God as principles on which it is based and from which it proceeds toward further reflections and deductions. It also follows from this that philosophy and theology are quite distinct disciplines, a distinction that corresponds in the intellectual field to what subsists in reality between the natural and supernatural orders.[145] But the distinction does not involve an opposition between philosophy and theology:

> However, though faith is above reason, there can never be a real discrepancy between faith and reason, since the same God who reveals mysteries and infuses faith has bestowed the light of reason on the human mind, and God cannot deny Himself, nor can truth ever contradict truth....
>
> Not only can there be no conflict between faith and reason, they also support each other since right reason demonstrates the foundations of faith and, illumined by its light, pursues the science of divine things, while faith frees and protects reason from errors and provides it with manifold insights.[146]

The fruitful relationship between faith and reason was illustrated by Saint John Paul II, in the encyclical *Fides et Ratio* of 1998, to which we refer the reader. Here we recall simply that the relationship between these two modes of knowledge must be kept in a healthy balance, which is reached by recognizing the limits and characteristics of each, a recognition that avoids the extremes both of fideism (the acceptance of the Word of God in the faith, without and against reason: "*credo quia absurdum*" – "I believe because it is absurd"),[147] and

---

[145] "The perpetual common belief of the Catholic Church has held and holds also this: there is a twofold order of knowledge, distinct ... in its principle, because in the one we know by natural reason, in the other by divine faith; [and distinct] in its object, because apart from what natural reason can attain, there are proposed to our belief mysteries that are hidden in God that can never be known unless revealed by God" (First Vatican Council, *Dei Filius*, ch. 4 [DS 3015]).

[146] First Vatican Council, *Dei Filius*, ch. 4 (DS 3017 and 3019).

[147] This summary formula expresses a thought of Tertullian of Carthage, who in *De carne Christi* 5.4, wrote: "*Crucifixus est Dei Filius, non pudet, quia pudendum est; et mortuus est Dei Filius, prorsus credibile est, quia ineptum est; et sepultus resurrexit, certum est, quia impossibile*": "The Son of God was crucified: there is no shame in it, because it is shameful; and the Son of God has died: this should absolutely be believed, because it is unseemly; and that he was buried and rose is certain, because it is impossible" (our translation).

that of rationalism: I believe to the extent to which I comprehend it with natural reason as well (but in this case one can no longer speak of belief or faith).

3.4.2. The Superiority of Sacred Theology

Having recalled the non-oppositional distinction between faith and reason, and likewise that between theology and philosophy, it must also be said that in Catholic doctrine, theology is for obvious reasons considered a superior form of knowledge to that of the merely human sort (historical, philosophical, scientific). This is so because the truth revealed by God is far and away superior in its degree of certainty than what can be reached by human efforts alone. If much is to be admired and even learned from the intellectual efforts of the philosophers, even non-Christian ones, who have been able to reach many aspects of the truth, then we cannot forget that theology is the science that applies human reason to the truth delivered from on high, from God. The exercise of natural reason alone cannot deduce that truth which, in its origin and in the process with which it is transmitted, is not mixed with error and which, moreover, reveals aspects of reality and of history. The peculiarity of theological science consists then in applying reason to the faith, that is, to what God teaches supernaturally in His Revelation. Theology is the practice of *"credo ut intelligam"* ("I believe so that I may understand"). Richard of Saint Victor (d. 1173) exhorts:

> Let us always commit ourselves, within the limits of what is fair and possible, to understand with reason that of which we are convinced by faith.... It must seem to us therefore very little to have an authentic faith in eternal realities when it is not granted us to have these truths of faith corroborated with the testimony of reason.[148]

This passage also shows, in the second part, the other aspect of theology as *"intelligo ut credam"* ("I understand in order to believe"). The first aspect is that of believing, not that of reasoning: first there is the faith accepted based on the authority of God who reveals and does not deceive us; then there is the refection that is applied to it (*scientia fidei*). One could reformulate a well-known saying in this way: *"Primum credere, deinde theologari"* ("First believe, then theologize").[149] However, in the second place, the more one reflects on

---

[148] Richard of Saint Victor, *De Trinitate*, prologue (our translation).
[149] The original is *"primum vivere, deinde philosophari"* ("first live, then philosophize"), generally attributed to Thomas Hobbes (d. 1679), even if the concept is found in previous authors.

the faith, the more one realizes that theology as reason applied to Revelation helps us to believe more, and to believe better, because it shows us the internal logic of the faith itself, how deeply reasonable it is—due to the fact that the God who reveals is *Logos*. And thus the diptych of Augustinian origin is fulfilled: "*credo ut intelligam, intelligo ut credam.*"[150] Or, it also can be said with the other diptych, which has an Anselmian framework: "*fides quaerens intellectum et intellectus quaerens fidem*" ("faith seeking understanding, and understanding seeking faith").

3.4.3. "Fides Quaerens Intellectum"

A classical definition of theology has been borrowed from this Anselmian expression: "*fides quaerens intellectum*" ("faith that seeks understanding [of itself]"). Note a famous passage of the Saint:

> I do not try, O Lord, to penetrate Your depths, because my intellect is unequal to it, but I desire to in some way understand Your truth that my heart believes and loves. And I do not seek to understand in order to believe, but I believe in order to understand [*non enim quaero intelligere ut credam, sed credo ut intelligam*]. For I do not think I could understand if I had not first believed.[151]

Recognizing the role of reason in theology is of fundamental importance, but so is submitting it to faith. Theology is not the rational demonstration that allows us to believe in what God has said. First comes faith, possessed by all believers, even those who do not know theology, or even those who were illiterate. The faith that saves is not that which is deepened in books of theology, but it is the living faith, understood both as an adherence to revealed truth (*fides quae creditur*), and as a personal entrustment to the living and true God (*fides qua creditur*). This distinguishes Catholic faith from all other forms of gnosis, a very ancient heresy that considers as saved those who know, with the consequence of exalting the theologian above all ecclesiastical authorities. The Catholic concept of theology cannot accept this perspective. It entails the superiority and priority of faith over reason, while recognizing the whole value of the latter. In fact, natural reason, applied to the mysteries of faith, allows strengthening and better understanding, as much as is possible,

---

[150] See Saint Augustine of Hippo, *In Ioannis Evangelium Tractatus* 29.6; Augustine, *Epistola* 120.

[151] Saint Anselm of Canterbury, *Proslogion* 1 (our translation).

the doctrine of divine faith, brought to us by God Himself in Revelation. We see then why, despite the many definitions of theology that have been given throughout the centuries, there remains to this day preference for what is considered the classical definition. Theology is the *scientia fidei*, science of faith, or *fides quaerens intellectum*. This definition contains in a very concise formula all of the qualifying elements of this most special science that is supernatural theology, or sacred doctrine.

3.4.4. The Necessity of Faith

From all of this, it follows that it is impossible to study and to write Catholic theology without faith, and without faith understood in its twofold aspect of *fides quae* and *fides qua creditur*. To pretend to "do" theology while eliminating faith, or suspending one's own assent to faith, represents an intellectual exercise that many have tried, but which has never borne any good fruit. There is no shortage, especially in the modern era, of authors who have considered it necessary to produce a theology that prescinds from the faith. This methodological option would guarantee—so they say—an objectivity of thought and scientificality. But to cast out the faith from theology means eliminating the proper object of this science, its presupposition and its method![152] For Catholics, supernatural theology can be done only by people of faith (who profess the *fides quae* and persevere in the *fides qua creditur*), who reflect on the faith of the Church that they share and profess, for the sake of the Community of believers.

3.4.5. Ecclesial Horizon

The Congregation for the Doctrine of the Faith published a very important document in 1990, to which we refer the reader, entitled *Donum Veritatis*. The subtitle reads: "On the Ecclesial Vocation of the Theologian." The document reminds theologians that it is impossible to do theology without faith and outside—or worse, against—the Church. Theology is a service commended by the Church; it can be defined even as a charism given by the

---

[152] See Saint Pius X, *Sacrorum Antistitum* (1910): "I reject the opinion of those who maintain that an instructor who teaches a historical theological discipline or writes about these things must first of all discard any preconceived opinion about the supernatural origin of Catholic Tradition or about the help promised by God to preserve forever all revealed truth; [and that] therefore he must interpret the writings of the individual Fathers on purely scientific principles to the exclusion of all sacred authority and with the same freedom of judgment with which any profane document is studied" (DS 3547).

Holy Spirit to certain ones among the baptized (see 1 Cor 12:28); it is well known that the charisms are given not for the edification of oneself or one's own fame, but for the service of the entire Mystical Body of Christ, which is the Church (see 1 Cor 12:7).[153] Theology is thus an ecclesial mission that is carried out in that particular form of love that is intellectual charity. The theologian seeks to deepen understanding of the mystery of the faith so that all believers (the theologian included) can believe better in what they believe and can have better arguments, if needed, for rendering reason for their own faith (see 1 Pet 3:15).

On the necessity of a faith that is lived "ecclesially" on the part of the theologian, Pope Francis expresses himself in this way:

> Since faith is a light, it draws us into itself, inviting us to explore ever more fully the horizon which it illumines, all the better to know the object of our love. Christian theology is born of this desire. Clearly, theology is impossible without faith; it is part of the very process of faith, which seeks an ever deeper understanding of God's self-disclosure culminating in Christ. . . . Theology also shares in the ecclesial form of faith; its light is the light of the believing subject which is the Church. This implies, on the one hand, that theology must be at the service of the faith of Christians, that it must work humbly to protect and deepen the faith of everyone, especially ordinary believers. On the other hand, because it draws its life from faith, theology cannot consider the Magisterium of the Pope and the bishops in communion with him as something extrinsic, a limitation of its freedom, but rather as one of its internal, constitutive dimensions, for the Magisterium ensures our contact with the primordial source and thus provides the certainty of attaining to the word of Christ in all its integrity.[154]

3.4.6. "Theology on Bent Knee"

The professional theologian must, just like and in some sense more than other baptized persons, cultivate an intense spiritual life made of Sacraments, of prayer and asceticism. With the expression of Hans Urs von Balthasar (d.

---

[153] Concerning the value and ecclesial destination of the charisms, see the Congregation for the Doctrine of the Faith, *Iuvenescit Ecclesia* (2016), §§5, 7, 13, etc.

[154] Francis, *Lumen Fidei*, §36.

1988), we say that true theology is a "theology on bent knee."¹⁵⁵ In this regard, Benedict XVI has declared:

> Hans Urs von Balthasar was a theologian who put his research at the service of the Church, since he was convinced that theology could not but have ecclesial connotations. *Theology, as he conceived it, had to be married to spirituality;* only in this way, in fact, can it be profound and effective.
>
> Reflecting on this precise aspect, he wrote: ". . . As long as theology was the work of saints, it remained prayerful theology. This is why its rendering in prayer, its fruitfulness for prayer and its power to generate prayer were so immeasurably immense." These words lead us to reconsider the proper place of research in theology. Its need for a scientific approach is not sacrificed when it listens religiously to the Word of God and lives the life of the Church, strong in her Magisterium. *Spirituality does not attenuate the scientific charge, but impresses upon theological study the right method for achieving a coherent interpretation.* . . . In a word, von Balthasar deeply understood that theology *can only develop in prayer that accepts God's presence and entrusts itself to Him in obedience.*¹⁵⁶

"Since the object of theology is the Truth which is the living God and His plan for salvation revealed in Jesus Christ, the theologian is called to deepen his own life of faith and continuously unite his scientific research with prayer."¹⁵⁷

3.4.7. The Ends of Theology

The main purpose of theology as a science is to know. Nonetheless, this is

---

[155] See Hans Urs von Balthasar, "Theologie und Heiligkeit," in *Verbum Caro, Schriften zur Theologie*, I (Einsiedeln: Johannes, 1960), 195–224. We are citing a very recent author—in contrast with our methodological choice—because this particular aspect of his thought he has been borrowed in an appreciative way in various texts of the Magisterium (see the next footnote). This does not imply adherence to all aspects of his theological proposal, even if it is of considerable interest.

[156] Benedict XVI, *Message for the Centenary of the Birth of Fr. Hans Urs von Balthasar*, October 6, 2005 (emphasis added). The same Pontiff has expressly borrowed the saying "theology on bent knee" in his *Address at Heiligenkreuz Abbey*, September 9, 2007. Pope Francis has also borrowed the expression on at least two occasions.

[157] Congregation for the Doctrine of the Faith, *Donum Veritatis* (1990), §8.

inseparably linked to another end, which is to love. Theology serves, in the first place, knowing God better in the mysteries revealed by Him. This knowledge would be in vain if it did not lead to loving better, if it did not represent a contribution to the constant conversion of Christians to their Lord. From here it can be seen that theology possesses two joint aspects in its purpose: it does not serve only knowledge or only love, but it serves *both* knowledge *and* love. This does not mean that the two aspects are on the same level. One of the two precedes the other in the chronological order and in the order of value. The main aspect is knowledge.[158] In fact, theology is the *intellectus fidei* (understanding of faith) or *scientia fidei* (science of faith). Classical philosophy (Aristotle) teaches that one can only love what one knows, and thus knowledge must precede love for love to be genuine. Only knowledge tells us what is true; the will can then choose and love it. The recognition of the fact that there are two elements that make up the end of theology is found in both Saint Thomas Aquinas and in Saint Bonaventure (d. 1274).[159] Although they had different ideas about the primacy of one or the other aspect, both agree in recognizing that theology serves both knowledge and love: God, first and foremost, and then one's neighbor.[160] Their disciples have sometimes over-emphasized one or the other form of thought, ending up saying that theology either serves for knowing God, or loving Him and becoming better human beings. In the first case, they speak of a "Dominican School," and in

---

[158] On the other hand, love is impossible without knowledge: "We must know God if we are to know how to love God; and if someone is to know how to love his neighbor as himself he must first, by loving God, learn to love himself. But how can he do that, if he does not know God and does not even know himself?" (Saint Augustine of Hippo, *Enarrationes in Psalmos* 118.8.2, in *The Works of Saint Augustine: A Translation for the 21st Century*, vol. III/19, 373.

[159] The Seraphic Doctor places greater emphasis on the aspect of love, without denying that of knowledge. See, for example, Saint Bonaventure, *Commentaria in libros Sententiarum* 1.3 (*quaestio* 3 is dedicated precisely to the theme of whether theology is a speculative or practical science). See Bonaventure, *Breviloquium, Prologus*, 5. Saint Thomas, on the other hand, places the speculative/contemplative end above that of love: see *ST* I, q. 1, a. 4.

[160] For example, the Angelic Doctor, while reaffirming the primacy of theology as a science, writes that "There is a double perfection: the first relative to the intellect, and it is present when one possesses an intellect capable of judging and discerning rightly concerning what is proposed to it. The second perfection is that of love, and this is possessed by charity, which is possessed when one finds oneself entirely united to God.... Now, Sacred Scripture has this characteristic, that in it there are found not only realities on which to speculate, as in geometry, but also realities that one experiences with love.... In the other sciences it is enough that the person is perfect with respect to the intellect, but in this science, rather, it is required that the person be perfect with respect to the intellect and love" (*Super Epistolam ad Hebraeos Lectura* 5, 2 [concerning Heb 5:8–14] [our translation]).

the second case of a "Franciscan School." But Saint Thomas also says that theology aids one in becoming good, and Saint Bonaventure does not forget that to become good it is necessary to better know God and His Christ. The two great Doctors are thus much more balanced than some of their disciples: for Saint Thomas, theology is a science that is both speculative and practical, but nonetheless more speculative than practical; for Saint Bonaventure, it is the other way around.

Here we choose the Thomist position, which seems more correct, and thus we contend that theology is first and foremost for knowing and then also for loving. In fact, true knowledge aids the progress of holiness. Thought is followed by a corresponding action, and thus a solid and strong Church, and faithful and convinced Christians, will correspond more easily to a healthy and true theology, despite the sins of individuals that have always happened and will always happen (it is "necessary": Greek *anágke* in Matt 18:7). Theology deals more with the divine than the human, and thus its first and last end is not about us—our behavior, our moral goodness, or even our eternal salvation—but is turned completely toward God. In this sense, it is a science without ulterior motives, in other words, it is "gratuitous." Theology is open to the whole truth of God; it does not have to be "useful" (even if it is so), and it is not aimed at finding practical criteria for the life of the individual and the Church (even if it does this!). All of this actually does happen, but as a later effect: we could say that it occurs in an almost unconscious and unexpected way. In fact, for those who seek God above all things, all the rest will be given to them (see Matt 6:33).[161]

3.4.8. The Object

1. Subject

Before discussing the object of theology, it is necessary to make a brief ref-

---

[161] Thus, theologians can make a distinction between the primary end and secondary ends of theology. The primary end, for Thomists, is knowing. Then there are secondary ends that facilitate ecclesial unity, foment spiritual life, support pastoral action, decipher signs of the time, etc. From our point of view, if the secondary ends are sought as primary ones, that is, if theology is considered as a useful science for resolving problems, theology itself will fail and will provide weaker aid for achieving such goals, or no help at all. Instead, the more theology is carried out "gratuitously," concentrating on the Word of God while not having in view a problem to resolve, but for the desire of better knowing the One who has created and redeemed us, the more the secondary ends will be, as an effect, achieved in a better way, as fruits of the truth and love, which are never "pragmatic," "self-interested," or "useful."

erence to the fact that God is first and foremost the personal Subject of theology. This means that He is the only One who possesses perfect knowledge of Himself. God shares this knowledge with the blessed of Heaven (and it is thus called the "*scientia beatorum*").[162] The theology that we human beings produce here on earth, as "*viatores*" ("wayfarers"), is an obscure participation in this science of the blessed. Thus it happens through descending degrees of participation. It is important to say that in theology, in any degree of it, God is always and above all the personal Subject.[163]

2. Object

The object of theology can also be understood based on the end of theology. A classical formula identifies it as "*Deus sub ratione deitatis*" ("God from the standpoint of His divinity,"[164] that is, "God *qua* God"). We have discarded the "anthropological method" from the beginning, even if it is very much in vogue in the theology of the past few decades. In theology, everything must revolve around the object—as for every other science—and in this case the object of study is God and everything that is in relation to God and His plan of salvation (this includes humanity as well, but never as the center of the *scientia fidei*). The proper object of supernatural theology is God known through Revelation and received in faith. Faith knows that what God reveals is true and overcomes all human truths acquired "from below," that is, those truths acquired by the exercise of natural reason alone.[165] This makes Catho-

---

[162] See *ST* I, q. 1, a. 2.

[163] "God is never simply the 'object' of theology; he is always its living 'subject' as well" (Benedict XVI, *Address at Heiligenkreuz Abbey*); see Benedict XVI, *Homily at the Eucharistic Concelebration with the Members of the International Theological Commission*, October 6, 2006; *Address to Members of the International Theological Commission*, December 3, 2010.

[164] See *ST* I, q. 1, a. 6.

[165] See Saint Bonaventure, *De reductione artium ad theologiam*, a very well-respected work in which the Seraphic Doctor defends the idea that all other forms of human knowledge are subordinate, or "brought back" as the title says, to that knowledge which, alone, can make us understand what the Scripture teaches, namely, sacred theology (see no. 7). At no. 26 he concludes: "*Patet etiam, quomodo omnes cognitiones famulantur theologiae; et ideo ipsa assumit exempla et utitur vocabulis pertinentibus ad omne genus cognitionis*" ("It is thus evident in what manner all forms of knowledge serve theology; and that it assumes examples and utilizes terms that pertain to all disciplines"). It is the concept that is expressed in the classical formula "*philosophia ancilla theologiae*" ("philosophy is the handmaiden of theology"). To be of service is not a reason for the shame of the other sciences, but rather for their honor, because they serve the science of the faith that proceeds through "*via illuminativa*" (no. 26), that is, with the knowledge that descends from God, while the former come along through the way of pure natural reasoning.

lic theology the queen of all the scientific disciplines, even though in modern times it was instead considered the degraded Cinderella among them. While the other disciplines are based only on intellectual research and approach natural truths through successive degrees—through a path that knows enormous obstacles, difficulties, and errors—theology is based on certainties. What God says is indeed surely true, since He "can neither err nor deceive."[166] From the height of this knowledge, not merited or conquered from below—but rather gratuitously received from on high through a historical process of Revelation through witnesses accredited by God—theology can also illuminate the path of the other disciplines, whose methods and value nonetheless remain intact.[167]

3. Theocentrism and Christocentrism

It is important here to add that the reflection of the twentieth century has led to a decisive contribution on the theme of the object of theology, thanks to its attention to the history of salvation and, in particular, the mystery of Christ. The present volume, as is now quite clear, welcomes this progress, while focusing the whole reflection on the center of theology, which we consider Jesus Christ as God and man, the Word incarnate. It remains true that the object of theology is God in His intimate mystery and in the truths that He has revealed. Theology speaks of God, the God who is the "Father of our Lord Jesus Christ" (2 Cor 1:3; Eph 1:3; 1 Pet 1:3). Consequently, the mystery of Christ and that of God are entirely one, to the point that for Christians one does not speak of God apart from Christ, just as one does not speak of Christ apart from God (Trinity). Therefore, the classical formula *Deus sub ratione deitatis* should be maintained and at the same time deepened in the perspective of Trinitarian Christocentrism outlined in the previous chapter. If this formula means—as it in fact does—God in Himself and for us, then we have in the formula itself the two fundamental elements of the question: the Trinity and Jesus.

---

[166] First Vatican Council, *Dei Filius*, ch. 3 (DS 3008).

[167] Taking philosophy as an example, Leo XIII (d. 1903) teaches that even after Christ, the exercise of it does not become useless, but instead remains necessary and facilitated by the light of Christian Revelation: "For, not in vain did God set the light of reason in the human mind; and so far is the super-added light of faith from extinguishing or lessening the power of the intelligence that it completes it rather, and by adding to its strength renders it capable of greater things" (Leo XIII, *Aeterni Patris* [1879], §2).

3.4.9. Limits

1. Reason

In addition to recognizing the greatness of theology as the queen of the other sciences, it is also necessary to highlight its limit, consisting in the fact of being a science that applies human reason to supernatural mysteries. The human person does not have an infinite capacity, but the mysteries, being divine, have infinite value. The human mind can only reason in a temporal way, that is, according to reasoning done in steps, based on a chronological scheme of "before and after," or of "cause and effect," etc., while God is eternal, atemporal, and in Him there is no "before" and "after," but only an eternal being present to Himself.

2. Original Sin

We must add to this that original sin, even without taking the faculty of reasoning away from humanity, has wounded it, reducing its capacity, and thus fallen humanity encounters further obstacles to knowledge of God than did the original human being, who possessed his spiritual faculties fully intact. Concerning original sin and its consequences (see Chapter Three).

3. Language

The human intellect, finite and historical, expresses thought (concepts, judgments) by making recourse to language, which also has a limited and historical nature. Language thus represents another limit proper to theology, which certainly speaks of God according to truth, but which can never exhausts His mystery.

4. Provisionality and Certainty

Even from the standpoint of its own limits, theology reveals itself as the science of the faith. Saint Paul writes that we "walk by faith, not by sight" (2 Cor 5:7). Theology—as the science of faith, faith that is both true and provisional—cannot be other than a true and certain science, but also partial and provisional. The "definitive" knowledge of God will not be reached in this life of faith, but only in the "intuitive" contemplation of the face of God in Heaven (see Chapter Twelve). This does not mean, however, that the truths of faith are not really truths, or that the God of Heaven is totally different from the God known on earth. It means that the truth of that same God is still known very imperfectly here, but perfectly in Heaven (see 1 Cor 13:12)—understood as degrees of the same truth.

3.4.10. Analogous Language

Because of what we have just said, the question of theological language arises: How can we adequately speak about God?

1. Univocal and Equivocal Language

If we use our words and human concepts for God in the same sense that we use them for created realities, we make use of language that is called "univocal": such as when recourse is made to the word "good" to indicate a quality of both the human being and God, and in the same sense. This usage is to be excluded because of the fact that God infinitely surpasses the human being. If we instead use words relating to created beings and the Creator in a completely different sense, we use what is called "equivocal" language: when, for example, it is said (according to the equivocal use of language) that God is "good," the word is used in a totally different manner than when it is applied to a human being, or to food. This mode of speaking should also be excluded from theology, otherwise there would be no relation between God and what we know and say about Him.

2. Analogy

Theology is thus expressed in a language that is defined as "analogical": analogy is a mode of speaking in which a certain likeness or similarity is recognized between God and human beings, even if the dissimilarity is greater.[168] Thus, both the divine transcendence and the possibility of knowing and speaking the truth about God are preserved.

Classically, analogical language developed as a *via adfirmationis, via negationis*, and a *via eminentiae* (way of affirmation, way of negation, and way of eminence). One starts by affirming a truth, "God is good," then proceeds to deny the univocal sense of the expression: "God is not good if we understand good as the goodness of which the human being is good." Then, one explains the reason for the denial: "God is indeed infinitely better (has infinitely more

---

[168] "Between Creator and creature no similitude can be expressed without implying a greater dissimilitude" (Fourth Lateran Council, *Firmiter* [1215] [DS 806]).

goodness) than the human being," that is, His goodness is super-eminent with respect to ours, even if it would not be true to say that He is good in a *totally* different sense from how we can be good. The decisive concept is that of "participation." It is necessary to always keep this balance in the concept of theological language. In certain eras, there was an imbalance in favor of the way of affirmation, while today there is a strong return toward the way of negation (which in Greek terminology is called "apophaticism"). But these are parts of a linguistic process that is kept in check only if it is kept intact as a unified whole. We cannot pretend to know too much about God, but neither must we think—with excessive and thus disordered humility—that the mystery of God is such that we cannot truly know anything of it. If that were so, God would not have revealed Himself.

3.4.11. "Loci Theologici"

1. Primary Sources

We have already noted that theology is carried out on the faith that accepts Revelation. Thus the *"loci theologici,"* that is, the primary and proper sources, are Sacred Scripture and the Apostolic Tradition: the channels through which Revelation reaches us. However, we have also recalled that, in the Christian conception, Scripture is not a book written in Heaven that is placed, already complete, in the hands of a prophet. Divine Revelation happens through a historical process of witness. This is true not only for the constitution of the "channels" of Revelation, but also for the correct interpretation of it, which requires an ecclesial "milieu." Hence the theme of the sources of theology is broadened, including secondary sources that support and clarify the "two sources" or "channels" of the proper and primary ones.

2. Secondary Sources

The first place among the secondary sources belongs to the Magisterium of the Church, which is so connected with Scripture and Tradition that they could not be truly understood without the former.[169] In the sixteenth century, a well-known Spanish Dominican theologian, Melchor Cano (d. 1560) wrote a work entitled *De locis theologicis* in which he identified ten sources (called "places" ["*loci*"]) of theology, with different values. He divided them into seven proper sources and three extraneous sources. The proper sources are Scripture

---

[169] Second Vatican Council, *Dei Verbum*, §10.

Revelation, Faith, Theology

and the Apostolic Tradition (*loci* that "contain Revelation")—which we have called here primary sources—and then the teaching of the Catholic Church, the ecumenical councils, the Roman Church (that is, the pope), the Fathers of the Church, and the recognized Doctors (he calls these sources "that interpret Revelation"). Finally, the three extraneous, supporting sources are natural reason, the philosophers, and the customs that emerged in the history of the Church. At present, various theologians propose other sources that can be integrated with the list of Cano, for example: beauty (art), the liturgy, and the life of the saints. To make things clearer, we can compare the list of Cano with our own way of dividing the sources:

Melchor Cano	Our Proposal

1) Proper Sources
   A. Which Contain Revelation
      Sacred Scripture
      Apostolic Tradition
   B) Which Interpret Revelation
      Catholic Church
      Ecumenical Councils
      Roman Church
      The Fathers
      Doctors of the Church
 	
2) Additional Sources
    Natural Reason
    Philosophy
    History
	1) Primary Sources
	    Apostolic Tradition
	    Sacred Scripture
	
	2) Secondary Sources
	    Ordinary and Extraordinary Magisterium
	    The Fathers
	    Doctors of the Church
	    Liturgy
	    The Saints
	
	    Philosophy and Common Sense
	    History
	    Beauty

There are ten *loci* in both cases. We unite three of the *loci* of Cano under the magisterial *locus* (obviously, the theologian will keep in mind the different degree of authority of the individual interventions of the Magisterium, as well as the fact that this must always express the faith of the Catholic Church—the third *locus* of Cano). Moreover, we put together natural human knowledge, both systematically developed (philosophy), and instinctively deduced (common sense). We add three *loci* that Cano does not consider directly but which are included by him, more or less explicitly, in others: liturgy, saints, and beauty.

3.4.12. Internal Subdivision and Fundamental Unity of Theology

Finally, let us mention the internal division of theology, which includes many branches of specialization. Theology is and remains a unitary science, as we have recently begun to rediscover after a few decades of a strong fragmentation of theological knowledge. Within this unitary science, nonetheless, there have almost always been distinctions of different spheres; distinctions that in the beginning were less evident and that have been perfected with the passing of time. The internal subdivision of theological science can be done by branch or by treatment. The branches are different sectors: biblical exegesis, biblical theology, fundamental theology, dogmatic theology, liturgical theology, moral theology, spiritual theology, pastoral theology, canon law, missionary theology, ecumenical theology, etc. The treatises are generally parts within the branches: thus, in dogmatic theology we find the Trinity, Christology, Mariology, Sacramental theology, Ecclesiology, Eschatology, etc. The more centuries that pass, the more theology acquires new knowledge and the number and length of books dedicated to this or that fragment of sacred doctrine expands. Even if this is good it also still involves the fragmentation of theological knowledge, and thus we must fight with all our strength to maintain the fundamental unity of theology as a reflection of the unity of faith, which comes from the one Revelation of the one true God.

3.5. Appendix: A Text of Pope Benedict XVI concerning Theology

Responding extemporaneously to a question posed by a priest, Benedict XVI outlined the task of theology and of theologians today. The words spoken by the Pope in that occasion represent a true source of inspiration, so much so that we want to share them now in full:

> There is actually a theology that wants above all to be academic, to appear scientific and forgets the vital reality, the presence of God, his presence among us, his talking today not just in the past. Even St. Bonaventure distinguished two forms of theology in his time and said: "There is a theology that comes from the arrogance of reason, that wants to dominate everything, God passes from being the subject to the object of our study, while he should be the subject who speaks and guides us." *There is really this abuse of theology, which is the arrogance of reason and does not nurture faith* but overshadows God's

presence in the world. Then, there is a theology that wants to know more out of love for the beloved, it is stirred by love and guided by love. It wants to know the beloved more. And this is the true theology that comes from love of God, of Christ, and it wants to enter more deeply into communion with Christ. In reality, temptations today are great. Above all, it imposes the so-called "modern vision of the world" (Bultmann, "*modernes Weltbild*"), which becomes the criterion of what would be possible or impossible. And so, because of this very criterion that everything is as usual, that all historical events are of the same type, the newness of the Gospel is excluded, the irruption of God is excluded, the real news that is the joy of our faith.

What should we do? *I would say first to all theologians: have courage.* And I would like to say a big 'thank you' to the many theologians who do a good job. There are abuses, we know, but in all parts of the world there are many theologians who truly live the Word of God. They are nourished by meditation, are living the faith of the Church and want to help so that faith is present in our today. To these theologians I would like to say a big 'thank you.' *And I would say to theologians in general: 'Do not be afraid of this ghost of science!'* I have been following theology since 1946. I began to study theology in January '46 and, therefore, I have seen about three generations of theologians, and I can say that the hypotheses in that time, and then in the 1960s and 1980s, were the newest, absolutely scientific, absolutely *almost* dogmatic, and have since aged and are no longer valid! Many of them seem almost ridiculous. So, *have the courage to resist the apparently scientific approach, do not submit to all the hypotheses of the moment, but really start thinking from the great faith of the Church,* which is present in all times and opens for us access to the truth. Above all, do not think that positivistic thinking, which excludes the transcendent that is inaccessible is true reason! This weak reasoning, which only considers things that can be experienced, is really an insufficient reasoning. We theologians must use a broader reason which is open to the greatness of God. We must have the courage to go beyond positivism to the question about the roots of being. This seems to me of great importance. Therefore, we must have the courage to use the great, broader reason and we must have the humility not to submit to all the hypotheses of the moment and to live by the great faith of the Church of all times. There is no majority against the majority of the Saints. Saints are the true majority in the

Caro (Flesh)

Church and we must orient ourselves by the Saints!

Then, to the seminarians and priests I say the same. *Do not think that Sacred Scripture is an isolated Book*; it is living in the living community of the Church, which is the same Subject in all ages and guarantees the presence of the Word of God. The Lord has given us the Church as a live Subject with the structure of the bishops in communion with the pope. This great reality of the bishops of the world in communion with the pope guarantees to us the testimony of permanent truth. *We trust this permanent Magisterium of the communion of the bishops with the pope*, which represents to us the presence of the Word. Besides, we also trust in the life of the Church while, above all, exercising critical thought.

Certainly theological formation—I would like to tell seminarians—is very important. In our time, we must know Sacred Scripture well, in order to combat the attacks of the sects. We must really be friends of the Word. We must also know the currents of our time to respond reasonably in order to give—as St. Peter says—"reason for our faith." Formation is very important. But *we must also be critical. The criterion of faith is the criterion with which to see also theologians and theologies.* Pope John Paul II gave us an absolutely sure criterion in the *Catechism of the Catholic Church. Here we see the synthesis of our faith, and this Catechism is truly the criterion by which we can judge whether a given theology is acceptable or not*. So, I recommend the reading, the study, of this text, so we can go forward with a critical theology in the positive sense. That is critical of the trends of fashion and open to the true news, to the inexhaustible depths of the Word of God, which reveals itself anew in all times, even in our time.[170]

---

[170] Benedict XVI, *Vigil on the Occasion of the International Meeting of Priests*, June 10, 2010 (emphasis added).

3

The Creator

Both in natural theology and in the exposition that falls under the Latin term *Caro* (flesh), the previous chapter brings out the importance of the theme of creation for the Christian view of the world, as well as the influence of original sin on the cosmos and history (see the discussion of the motive for the Incarnation). We shall now study these two doctrines from a dogmatic standpoint.

1. Creation and the Attributes of the Creator

1.1. The Creator

The Christian doctrine on creation says, above all, that the world has a transcendent origin and therefore also has a meaning, finality, and value. The world is not the result of chance, but exists because it originated from an efficient Cause: God. The doctrine of creation is thus in the first place the doctrine of God's existence. The fact that the world has been created by God entails the fact that creation is in itself good (value), and that God has created it for a reason (finality and meaning). By reflection, this necessitates the goodness and intelligence of the Creator.

Moreover, the doctrine of creation frees humankind from the fear of cosmic forces. There is a superior God, the God who is the creator of everything: He is the One to whom the creative act must refer, and not the celestial powers that in the various ancient theogonies and cosmogonies are often violent forces that crush human beings with their presence and actions. The doctrine of creation in the Christian sense frees the world from the influence of these forces, declaring them non-existent. In this sense, such a doctrine is primarily a doctrine of the oneness of God[1]: God is one and there are no others (the denial of polytheism is the element that distinguishes the biblical recounts of creation from all other ancient accounts of a similar nature).

1.2. "Denumification" and Secularization

This doctrine also carries out what is called the "denumification"[2] of the world: it frees the world from the tutelary deities such as gods of water, air, nymphs, satyrs, elves, and any other kind of invention of the non-Christian religious mentality.[3] The denumification of the cosmos, a cosmos that is traced back to a single God and Creator, frees man's approach to nature from the burden of

---

[1] The Christian faith "believe[s] God is one, who created and completed all things and made all that is from that which is not": The Shepherd of Hermas, "The Mandates," 1.1, in *The Apostolic Fathers: A New Translation and Commentary*, vol. 6, trans. Graydon F. Snyder (London: Thomas Nelson & Sons, 1968), 63. This is the first patristic formula that speaks of creation from nothing and links it to the theme of the unity of God. The Shepherd is a very ancient text, composed around AD 120–140.

[2] Translator's note: Although we could not find a use of the term denumification in English, we opted for an Anglicization of the relatively uncommon Italian technical term *denumificazione* to express this idea.

[3] For Saint Ignatius of Antioch (d. ca. 107) such a denumification becomes definitive with the Incarnation of the Word: "A star shone forth in heaven above all the other stars, the light of which was inexpressible, while its novelty struck men with astonishment. And all the rest of the stars, with the sun and moon, formed a chorus to this star, and its light was exceedingly great above them all. And there was agitation felt as to whence this new spectacle came, so unlike to everything else [in the heavens]. Hence every kind of magic was destroyed, and every bond of wickedness disappeared; ignorance was removed, and the old kingdom abolished" (*Ad Ephesios* 19, in *ANF*, vol. 1, trans. James Donaldson and Alexander Roberts [Peabody, MA: Hendrickson Publishers, Inc., 1994], 57). Origen of Alexandria (d. 254) follows this line of thought in *Contra Celsum* 1.60 [at the birth of Christ, the Magi pass from divinization of demons to the adoration of Christ], as does Saint Athanasius of Alexandria (d. 373), *De Incarnatione* 8.47: "And formerly daemons used to cheat men with apparitions, pre-occupying founts or rivers or trees or stones, and thus struck the foolish with awe by their juggleries. But now, by the Divine Manifestation of the Word, their pretense has ceased. For by the simple use of the sign of the cross a man drives away their deceits" (*De Incarnatione Verbi Dei*, trans. T. Herbert Bindley [London: Religious Tract Society, 1903], 140).

terror and superstition[4]—which also made possible the birth of science in the modern sense. If plants, animals, and any other element are not in fact protected by a tutelary god, the human being can feel free to study them (science) and utilize them for his or her purposes (technology). Science and technology—at least as they are understood in the modern sense—are thus only able to arise thanks to Christianity.[5] The fact that they are often placed in opposition to faith, particularly the Christian faith, is due to the mistaken assumptions of modernity and postmodernity (which has influenced the personal inclinations of many people of science), and not science as such, which is a daughter and ally of the Christian faith. God is one, the Creator of nature and the Giver of grace. When science and faith succeed in carrying out their own tasks in their respective orders, there cannot be any well-supported opposition between them, but rather a fruitful and enriching collaboration.[6] This is demonstrated at the historical level by the existence of a large number of scientists, both of the past and of the present, who were also people of faith. Among them are many priests and religious.[7]

It should also be clarified that the positive denumification of the world does not necessarily lead to secularization, which is another thing entirely. Secularization is a rupture of the synthesis between Spirit and matter, because it not only postulates the justified distinction between nature and grace, natural

---

[4] Francis, *Laudato Si'* (2015), §78, speaks of a "demythologized" nature.

[5] Serious historical studies demonstrate that the birth of the sciences in the modern sense is due to medieval thought, which, in many fields, brought Christian intellectual development to a climax. This, among other reasons, is further confirmation that the Middle Ages cannot justifiably be considered an obscurantist era.

[6] It is stated in this way by the First Vatican Council, *Dei Filius* (1870), ch. 4: "Though the faith is above reason, there can never be a real discrepancy between faith and reason, since the same God who reveals mysteries and infuses faith has bestowed the light of reason on the human mind, and God cannot deny himself, nor can truth ever contradict truth" (DS 3017). "Not only can there be no conflict between faith and reason, they also support each other since right reason demonstrates the foundations of faith and, illumined by its light, pursues the science of divine things, while faith frees and protects reason from errors and provides it with manifold insights" (DS 3019).

[7] We can cite the names of some of the many holy scientists in the history of the Church: Saint Hildegard of Bingen (d. 1179), proclaimed Doctor of the Church in 2012; Saint Albert the Great, Doctor of the Church (d. 1280); Blessed Nicolas Steno (d. 1686); Saint Giuseppe Moscati (d. 1927); Blessed Francesco Faà di Bruno (d. 1888). In addition, there are yet many other scientists who are not beatified or canonized (for some of them the cause of beatification is in process). Having opted not to cite more recent names in accord with our method, we shall at least recall the bishop Nicolas d'Oresme (d. 1382); the priest Mikołaj Kopernik (Nicolaus Copernicus, d. 1543); the Protestant scholar Johannes Kepler (d. 1630); and Galileo Galilei (d. 1642), who, despite what is stated in a certain secularist recount of history, was a convinced Catholic.

The Creator

and supernatural, but it separates them, and ends up understanding the world without God. Denumification is thus a positive process, a direct consequence of the doctrine of creation. Secularization, on the other hand, is a denial of creation, because it conceives of the world as if it were not created by God.[8]

1.3. "Creatio ex Nihilo"

A central element of the Christian doctrine of creation is that God has created all things from nothing (*ex nihilo*).[9] The doctrine of creation is then also the doctrine of the omnipotence of God. For the Catholic faith, creation should be understood *both* in terms of causality *and* participation. God is the first cause of all beings, for which reason every being exists only insofar as it is created by God. God is subsisting Existence itself (*ipsum Esse subsistens*),[10] while every other being possesses an essence that is distinct from its own act of existing. Thus, creation happens because the subsisting Act of Being (God) shares His existence with the things He creates: and precisely this is the act of creating, because nothingness ceases inasmuch as there is now participation in Being.[11]

A second fundamental element is that God created each thing with/through His Word (see, for example, Gen 1:3; Ps 33:6).[12] This speaks to the intrinsic rationality of creation, given that the creative Word is the divine Reason.

1.4. The Natural Law

From the previous point it follows that in created nature there is an intimate rationality, a logical law, imprinted by the Creator into the cosmos. This

---

[8] "But if the expression, the independence of temporal affairs, is taken to mean that created things do not depend on God, and that man can use them without any reference to their Creator, anyone who acknowledges God will see how false such a meaning is. For without the Creator the creature would disappear" (Second Vatican Council, *Gaudium et Spes* (1965), §36).

[9] The classical formula goes "*ex nihilo sui et subiecti*" and refers to the philosophy in use during the Scholastic period, in which *subiectum* is "that-which-underlies." Without entering here into a detailed explanation, the formula means that God created with an act that has its entire energy, origin, and power in Him and that absolutely nothing pre-existed this act, because what exists is caused by the divine creation. It also follows from this that only God is capable of creating from nothing (see *ST* I, q. 45, a. 5, ad 1).

[10] See *ST* I, q. 3, a. 4; I, q. 4, a. 2.

[11] See *ST* I, q. 44, a. 1.

[12] "The New Testament reveals that God created everything by the eternal Word" (CCC §291).

law, called natural law, corresponds to the very being of God, who possesses Reason in Himself, and creates with/through His own divine Reason, the *Logos*. Therefore, there is in the cosmos a logical natural law, which is reflective of the very nature of God, in which the perfect *Logos* subsists eternally. Consequently, natural law is not simply a "positive" law, that is, one that depends only on the decree of the divine will, as for instance Duns Scotus took it to be.[13] This would imply that God could have established a completely different law from that which actually subsists. As a pure hypothesis, one must keep open this possibility, for which God would have been able to impress upon the cosmos a different law entirely—we should call it one that is "illogical" or "less logical." He could have done this, if He willed to do so. We must say this because we cannot fix limits on God, except what would imply an insoluble contradiction. However, at its core, it is unthinkable why God would ever want to will something so absurd. The only law fit to be imprinted into the cosmos is the natural law that God has in fact impressed upon it.[14] This is because He has not created an illogical cosmos, but rather He has created with and through His *Logos*. Thus, natural law is not a "positive" law, decided on the basis of authority alone; it is an ontological law, or rather it corresponds to being: to the being of God, of which it is a pallid reflection, and to the being of things, of the nature created by God.[15]

---

[13] He absolutizes the role of the divine freedom, linking it to the exercise of His will and not His intellect as well. This position was criticized in a catechesis of Benedict XVI: "An idea of innate and absolute freedom—as it evolved, precisely, after Duns Scotus—placed in the will that precedes the intellect, both in God and in man, risks leading to the idea of a God who would not even be bound to truth and good. The wish to save God's absolute transcendence and diversity with such a radical and impenetrable accentuation of his will does not take into account that the God who revealed himself in Christ is the God 'Logos,' who acted and acts full of love for us. Of course, as Duns Scotus affirms, love transcends knowledge and is capable of perceiving ever better than thought, but it is always the love of the God who is 'Logos'" (*General Audience*, July 7, 2010). See Benedict XVI, *Address at the University of Regensburg*, September 12, 2006, in which he already explicitly criticized the position of Scotus.

[14] This does not lead to the "greatest of all possible worlds" of Leibniz (see the previous chapter), both because God, willing it, could have created even greater worlds, and because human freedom contributes in the concrete determination of the "quality" of the world.

[15] Therefore, humans should not oppose natural law with their own formulations of positive laws. Today there is the pretense that democratic regimes can establish, with respect to any matter, however serious, what is or is not permissible, on the basis of a majority vote. Against such a view, and in support of a different belief that must be proper to Catholic politicians and voters, see the Congregation for the Doctrine of the Faith, *Doctrinal Note on Some Questions Regarding the Participation of Catholics in Political Life* (2002). On the relationship between natural law and democracy, see also Benedict XVI, *Visit to the Bun-*

The Creator

This is also the reason that each human being, even if not a Christian, for the sole fact of being human and thus possessing reason (the little created *logos* within us), can know and recognize natural law, which obliges each human being, not only those who know Christ and believe in Him.[16] Saint Paul attests to this:

> For when the Gentiles who do not have the law by nature observe the prescriptions of the law, they are a law for themselves even though they do not have the law. They show that the demands of the law are written in their hearts, while their conscience also bears witness and their conflicting thoughts accuse or even defend them (Rom 2:14–15).

This last point is also demonstrated by experience, or rather, by the observation of history as a whole, in which innumerable cases of humans manifesting an understanding of the natural law can be noted. Without dwelling on it here, we shall propose only two examples:

(1) The first example comes from the law of the pagan world. It is well-known that pagan civilizations, along with splendid accomplishments in many areas, also carried the baggage of a high degree of moral dissolution. Thus, it is to be noted that the practice of homosexuality and even pederasty were quite widespread, at least in certain eras and amongst certain peoples. Despite this, however, those people never legalized a sort of "matrimony" for homosexual persons; an evident indication that, despite widespread depravation, ancient humanity still had open eyes concerning nature and its law.[17]

(2) A second example comes from Greek literature. In the tragedy entitled *Antigone*, Sophocles (d. 406 BC) recounts that Antigone, daughter of Oedipus, harshly rebuked Creon, king of Corinth, because the latter had prohibited the burial of her brother Polyneices. Antigone, having arranged to

---

destag: Address of His Holiness Benedict XVI, September 22, 2011.

[16] A biblical example is the narration of Exodus 1, in which pharaoh orders the Egyptian midwifes Shiphrah and Puah to kill the newborn males of the Hebrews, but these women—with shrewdness—go around the command to disobey it. An example taken from the classics is the attestation of Marcus Tullius Cicero (d. 43 BC), *De inventione* 2.161: "The law of nature is that which is not born of opinion [*non opinio genuit*], but implanted in us by a kind of innate instinct: it includes religion, duty, gratitude, revenge, reverence and truth" (trans. H.M. Hubbell [Cambridge, MA: Harvard University Press, 2014], 329).

[17] Although this did not always happen: "Julius Caesar, for example, recounts [*De Bello Gallico* 6.23] that at one point among the Germans, theft, which is expressly contrary to the natural law, was not considered wrong" (*ST* I-II, q. 94, a. 4 [our translation]).

give him the honors due to the dead, defended herself before the unjust sovereign with words that reveal understanding of a fundamental fact: a moral law exists that is not provided by the gods but is part of the world itself. And for Antigone, burying the dead is a work of justice commanded by such a law. Behold these verses of the great Athenian tragedian:

> I heard it not from Heaven, nor came it forth
> From Justice, where she reigns with Gods below.
> They too have published to mankind a law.
> Nor thought I thy commandment of such might
> That one who is mortal thus could overbear
> The infallible, unwritten laws of Heaven.
> Not now or yesterday they have their being,
> But everlastingly, and none can tell
> The hour that saw their birth.[18]

For Saint Thomas, the first precept of natural law, on which all others are based, is "*Bonum est faciendum et prosequendum, et malum vitandum*" ("Good is to be done and sought, while evil is to be avoided.")[19] Human practical reason apprehends in a natural way the good to be done, observing its own natural inclinations, which is why the order of precepts of natural law also follows the order that is proper to human inclinations. It follows from this that the natural law is based *both* on the objective order of nature *and* on human rationality, and the latter is capable of interpreting this law and drawing precepts from it.[20] The rights of the human person are rooted in natural law and not created by human beings,[21] which is why the presumed "rights" that are in place today, if they oppose the law of nature, should be held as arbitrary whims, and not true and proper rights. The immutable objectivity of the law of nature does not imply an absolute fixedness. Indeed, no norm of natural law can be modified by human beings—this is clear. However, there are also—especially in the sphere of social doctrine—particular judgments about contingent facts. Thus, the natural moral law is not a "closed system"

---

[18] Sophocles of Colonus, *Antigone*, vv. 450-457, in *Sophocles: The Seven Plays in English Verse*, trans. Lewis Campbell (London: Oxford University Press, 1912), 16.

[19] *ST* I-II, q. 94, a. 2 (our translation). See Leo XIII, *Libertas Praestantissimum* (1888) (DS 3247).

[20] See Saint John XXIII, *Pacem in Terris* (1963) (DS 3956); Sacra Congregatio pro Doctrina Fidei, *Persona Humana* (1975), §4.

[21] See Saint John XXIII, *Pacem in Terris* (DS 3970; where it is added that specific duties also correspond to rights); Sacra Congregatio pro Doctrina Fidei, *Quaestio de Abortu Procurator* (1974), §10.

but rather "remains constantly open to the new questions which continually arise."[22] The immutable law in itself is always discovered anew and applied to the cases that history presents.

To summarize what has been said up to this point: the doctrine of creation is also a doctrine of its Author. Creation reveals at least the following attributes of God: He exists; He is one, rational, transcendent, and good; He creates freely by His will[23]; He has created a good world, has made it according to Reason (rationality), and for a reason (purpose/finality); He has impressed a law into the cosmos; and, finally, the evil that is in the world does not come from Him.

1.5. Other Specifications Concerning Creation

1. A Doctrine of Faith

Creation is a doctrine of faith. The idea can also be reached by reason alone; however, according to Saint Thomas,[24] human reason is not capable of offering apodictic arguments to demonstrate it. We know with certainty the truth of creation by faith, since God has revealed it. Moreover, human reason is not incompatible with the idea of creation: in fact, it is very helpful for explaining the phenomena of the world; not so much *how* they occur, but rather with respect to *why* they exist.

2. Time

The world was created with time: thus, it is not eternal. Saint Augustine affirms: "The world was made not in time but together with time."[25]

---

[22] Congregation for the Doctrine of the Faith, *Libertatis Conscientia* (1986), §72. See *ST* I-II, q. 94, a. 5 (an article dedicated to "If the Natural Law Can Change").

[23] Through both Blessed Pius IX and the First Vatican Council, the Magisterium of the Church spoke against the opinion of certain theologians of the nineteenth century who, influenced by idealist philosophy, hypothesized a necessity of creation inherent to the divine being, thus calling the freedom of the creative act into question (see DS 2828; DS 3025).

[24] *ST* I, q. 46, a. 2. In his youth, however, the Angelic Doctor had been more open to the capacity of human reason to demonstrate the work of creation (see *Scriptum Super Sententiis*, II, d. 1, q. 1, a. 2).

[25] Saint Augustine of Hippo (d. 430), *De civitate Dei* 11.6, in *FCNT*, vol. 14, trans. Gerald G. Walsh and Grace Monahan (New York: Fathers of the Church, Inc., 1952), 195; see *De Genesi ad litteram* 4.5.12.

3. *A Work of Love*

God loves the world. Since He created it freely and without any obligation,[26] God loves what He has done: if He had not loved it, He would not have created it. Obviously, this means that God loves the world as He has created it (good); He does not love the evil that has subsequently entered into the world (see Wis 2:23–24).

4. *"Continuous Creation"*

God is transcendent, but not absent from His creation. God and the world are really distinct, but this does not imply that God, after the creation, is disinterested in the world and is not present to it (a worldview known as "deism"[27]). God is at the same time, and according to different relationships, both transcendent and immanent to the world ("theism"). He transcends it in being while He is present to it with His action. In this sense, we also speak of "continuous creation": creation is not only the act with which God draws things from nothing and puts them into existence, but it is also the act with which He maintains them in being. If God did not maintain in being the existing things ("beings"), they would simply cease to exist: "In him we live and move and have our being" (Acts 17:28).[28] With this, the deist (Enlightenment) and pantheist/panentheist (Idealism) philosophies are excluded from the Catholic perspective. The former postulate the total transcendence of God with respect to the world, and thus a certain sovereign disinterestedness on His part with respect to the governance of the cosmos; the latter confuse the being of God with his activity in the world. By contrast, for Christian thought:

> The Maker of existing things must be the same as their Provider, for it is neither fitting nor logical that one should be their creator and another their provider, because in such a case they would both be

---

[26] This is related to the question about the reason for creation. *Catechism of the Catholic Church* §319 summarizes the response as follows: "God created the world to show forth and communicate his glory. That his creatures should share in his truth, goodness and beauty—this is the glory for which God created them."

[27] This is a theory condemned by Blessed Pius IX, *Syllabus* (1864), §2 (DS 2902).

[28] "In light of the faith and reason, it needs to be said that creatures are held in existence by God.... The conservation of the world is the continuation of the creative act" (*ST* I, q. 104, a. 1 [our translation]). Second Vatican Council, *Gaudium et Spes*, §36: "Without the Creator the creature would disappear." The theme of continuous creation is strictly connected with that of divine Providence (this theme will be discussed later).

The Creator

definitely wanting—the one in the matter of creating and the other in that of providing. Hence, God is both Creator and Provider.[29]

Beyond holding all beings in existence, God acts in numerous other ways in the world He has created, without identifying with it.

5. Autonomy

This also implies a certain autonomy of creation with respect to God. This concerns a relative autonomy, that is, based on the relation that things have with their Creator, not an absolute autonomy, as secular thought so wishes it. The human being, as a creature pertaining to the natural order, possesses a natural finality, which nonetheless is not the highest end toward which he or she may tend, because the final end is always one alone, namely, eternal salvation (a supernatural gift, which surpasses the intrinsic possibilities of the natural order). However, the fact that the *final* end is one alone[30] does not mean that the final end is also the *only* end. In reality, there are also natural ends toward which creation is directed.

6. Work

In all of this, a fundamental role is played by the human being who, according to Genesis, is the highest *earthly* creature made by God (angels, as they are celestial creatures, are superior to human beings: see Ps 8:6; Heb 2:7). God has placed the entire terrestrial world beneath humanity and given the latter the task of cultivating and safeguarding the former, that is, of advancing the attainment of creation's natural end. In the design of God, this work is always understood with reference to the final supernatural end.[31] Work is the ordinary means established by God as a means for achieving those ends.[32]

7. Work of the Trinity

Since God is one but also triune, and given that all that God carries out *ad*

---

[29] Saint John Damascene (d. 749), *De fide orthodoxa* 2.29, in *FCNT*, vol. 37, trans. Frederic H. Chase, Jr. (New York: Fathers of the Church, Inc., 1958), 260.

[30] See Second Vatican Council, *Gaudium et Spes*, §22.

[31] See Second Vatican Council, Gaudium et Spes, §57.

[32] One should recall here the spirituality of work developed and taught by Saint Josemaría Escrivá de Balaguer (d. 1975), the founder of *Opus Dei*.

extra, that is, outside of his own nature, is done with a common action of the three divine Persons, creation should be understood as a common work of the Holy Trinity.[33] The divine nature that has created the world is in fact a nature that is one in essence and three in Persons (for more on the doctrine of the Trinity, see Chapter Six). It follows from this that in some way creation bears the Trinitarian imprint. Saint Augustine speaks of "*vestigia trinitatis*" ("traces of the Trinity")[34] present in creation. However, it needs to be noted that such traces can be sought and eventually found only after God has made known through Revelation the mystery of His intimate life, which is precisely Trinitarian. A human being that did not know this mystery, could not in any way deduce it by observing creation, because the mysteries hidden in God are known to us only through divine Revelation; otherwise, they remain inaccessible to natural reason.

2. The Heavenly Spirits

2.1. Invisible Creation

The symbols of the faith (or "creeds") from the beginning affirm the doctrine of the creation of the world by God (Father) almighty. The standard formula is the one we find as early as the first ecumenical Council of Nicaea, "God ... creator of all things, visible and invisible."[35] This formula indicates that everything that exists—without exception—was created by God. No being has a different origin than the one, almighty God.[36] This also implies that for Christianity matter is good, because it is created by God. The goodness of matter derives from the goodness of the One who has made it.[37]

---

[33] "God has made all through the Word and the Wisdom [here this indicates the Holy Spirit]" (Saint Theophilus of Antioch [d. ca. 185], *Ad Autolicum* 1.7). In Chapters Four and Five, a famous expression of Saint Irenaeus of Lyon (d. ca. 202) will be cited, in which he speaks of the Son and Spirit as the "two Hands" of the Father.

[34] Saint Augustine of Hippo, *De Trinitate* 9–15.

[35] DS 125. The term Creator corresponds to the Greek *Poietes*: the Latin translation is *Factor*.

[36] "We firmly believe ... that there is only one true God ... the one principle of the universe, the creator of all things, visible and invisible, spiritual and corporeal, who by His almighty power from the beginning of time made at once out of nothing both orders of creatures, the spiritual and the corporeal, that is, the angelic and the earthly, and then the human creature, who, as it were, shares in both orders, being composed of spirit and body" (Fourth Lateran Council [1215], *Firmiter* [DS 800]).

[37] The Council of Florence, *Cantate Domino* (1442), teaches that God created "out of his

The Creator

In the previous chapters, on several occasions, we have used the term "matter" to refer to creation, distinguishing it from "Spirit" in reference to God; but at the same time we have cited the angels several times, created beings that are nonetheless immaterial. For this reason, it is good to clarify that in the use that we have made of the word "matter," we did not intend to affirm that God has created only matter and not also the spiritual world. The term matter was utilized consistently with the scheme with which we translated the formula *Verbum caro*, using the words "Spirit" and "matter": in this case, Spirit with the uppercase "S" refers to God; and matter refers to creation, which is composed both of the visible and the invisible. On the other hand, this can be intuited from the fact that *Verbum caro* was not only translated with "the Word became flesh," but also "the Word became man." As we will show in Chapter Four, the Incarnation of the Word involved the assumption by Him of a complete human nature, and not only a material body, but also the soul or human spirit. In this sense, we have used, alongside other pairs, that of Spirit/matter. This certainly not to deny invisible creation, but to make explicit, in terms that are easy to understand, the meaning of the fundamental revealed axiom: *Verbum caro*, in addition to grasping its value as a perfectly achieved synthesis of Spirit and matter, God and the world, etc. Using the word in this way, we do not classify angels under the term "matter" in the literal sense since, as pure spirits, they do not have bodies. It could be said that, in relation to the most perfect Spirit, God, even these created spirits can be defined in a sense on the material side of things given the great distance of nature and perfection from the divine nature and perfection.[38] Thus,

---

bounty, made all creatures, spiritual as well as corporeal. They are good since they were made by Him who is the Highest Good, but they are mutable because they were made out of nothing. [The Church] asserts that there is no such thing as a nature of evil, because all nature, as nature, is good" (DS 1333).

[38] An example of a creative or analogical use of the words "flesh" and "spirit," or of a use that—with the terms explained well—applies them to realities that in themselves could not be described with them, if they were meant in the strictly literal sense, is found in an ancient homily by an unknown second-century author (see *Liturgy of the Hours*, "Office of Readings," Thursday of the Thirty-Second Week of Ordinary Time): "Brothers, if we do the will of God the Father, we shall be members of the first spiritual Church that was created before the sun and the moon. . . . You surely cannot be ignorant of the fact that the living Church is the body of Christ; for Scripture says: God made man male and female. Now the male signifies Christ, and the female signifies the Church, which, according to both the Old and the New Testament, is no recent creation, but has existed from the beginning. At first the Church was purely spiritual, even as our Jesus was spiritual, but it appeared in the last days to save us. For the spiritual Church was made manifest in the body of Christ, in order to show us that if we uphold its honor in the outward, visible form, and do not defile it, we shall,

Saint Gregory the Great states: "In comparison with our body they are spirits; compared with the supreme and unlimited Spirit, they are corporeal."[39]

This linguistic use could also help to keep the two spheres of creation strictly linked, that is, the spiritual and the corporeal, often kept at a great distance from each other in the common consciousness of many. We must not forget that for as much as angels are superior to human beings, and for the fact that we usually do not experience their presence and action (except in an indirect way through the benefits that they procure for us), it remains true that the material/corporeal world is strictly linked to the spiritual/incorporeal world. Angels and human beings form part of a single creation, and heavenly spirits are thus in this sense much closer to us than they are thought to be. This is the case at least for those heavenly spirits that are also "angels," and thus sent to bear messages. Scripture and the theological Tradition indeed recognize other heavenly spirits that always remain close to the throne of God and are not sent to us.

2.2. Celestial Hierarchy

Within the invisible creation, there exists a hierarchy of heavenly spirits. In the Bible we find various orders of the choirs of angels: Cherubim, Seraphim, Thrones, Dominions, Principalities, Powers, Virtues, Archangels, and Angels. The principal author referenced for this theme is Pseudo-Dionysius the Areopagite (AD fifth or sixth century), who composed a work entitled *De Coelesti Hierarchia* (The Celestial Hierarchy), to which many subsequent authors refer. He distinguishes three angelic orders:[40]

---

through the Holy Spirit be made its members in the true, spiritual sense. For the body of the Church is a copy of the Spirit, and no one who defaces the copy can have any part in what the copy represents. In other words, brothers, you must preserve the honor of the body in order to share in the Spirit. For if we say that the body is the Church and the Spirit is Christ, it follows that anyone who dishonors his body, dishonors the Church. Such a man will have no part in the Sprit, which is Christ. But if the Holy Spirit is joined to it, this body can receive an immortal life that is wonderful beyond words, for the blessings God has made ready for his chosen ones surpass all human powers of description."

[39] Saint Gregory the Great, *Moralia in Job* 2.3. The full citation says: "*Eorum itaque scientia comparatione nostrae valde dilatata est, sed tamen comparatione divinae scientiae angusta: sicut et ipsi illorum spiritus comparatione quidem nostrorum corporum, spiritus sunt, sed comparatione summi et incircumscripti spiritus, corpus.*"

[40] See also *ST* I, qq. 108–109. Other classical authors who speak of various angelic choirs include Saint Bernard of Clairvaux (d. 1153), in the *De consideratione* (especially book 5), and Saint Robert Bellarmine (d. 1621), who is inspired by the former, in the *De aeterna felicitate sanctorum*.

1) Seraphim, Cherubim, and Thrones assist at the throne of God.
2) Dominions, Virtues, and Powers are occupied with the governance of the cosmos.
3) Principalities, Archangels, and Angels carry out various divine assignments such as delivering announcements, combating Satan and his angels, and acting as guardian angels.

However, if we consider the heavenly spirits that are angels, we see that it is true that they are "in Heaven"; Revelation nonetheless shows their frequent presence and action on earth.

2.3. Angelic Missions

The word *angel* literally means "messenger."[41] The angels are creatures that continuously deliver announcements and gifts of God to human beings and creation.[42] Being creatures, their ontological difference with respect to the Creator is infinite. Thus, while being heavenly spirits, they are much closer to us than they are to God.[43] This derives from the unity of creation in its two aspects, visible and invisible. The doctrine of the Church also recognizes the role of the "guardian angel": every human being is granted the personal and continuous care of a heavenly spirit.[44] Finding a basis in certain biblical

---

[41] Saint Augustine of Hippo distinguishes in a few words the functional aspect (the service) from the ontological aspect (the nature) of angels: "'Angel' is the name of a function, not of a nature. If you inquire about the nature of such beings, you find that they are spirits; if you ask what their office is, the answer is that they are angels" (*Enarrationes in Psalmos* 103.1.15, in *The Works of Saint Augustine: A Translation for the 21ˢᵗ Century*, vol. III/19, trans. Maria Boulding (Hyde Park: New City Press, 2002), 125.

[42] "Those who transmit messages of lesser importance are called angels, while those who announce things of great value are called archangels. . . . For the same reason, to them [the archangels] are attributed personal names, which describe their proper action" (Saint Gregory the Great, *Homiliae in Evangelia* 2.34.8). Scripture reveals the names of three archangels: Michael, Gabriel, and Raphael, who in the current liturgical calendar are celebrated on the same day, September 29.

[43] The First Synod of Braga (AD 561) condemned the opinion of the Manichaeans and the Priscillianists, according to whom "the human souls or the angels come from the substance of God" (DS 455), thus clearly repeating that the angels are creatures of God that are infinitely inferior to Him, however superior to human beings, and rank "between God and corporeal creatures" (*ST* I, q. 50, a. 1, ad 1).

[44] "Every believer has an angel that accompanies him": St. Basil the Great (d. 379), *Adversus Eunomium* 3.1, in *FCNT*, vol. 122, trans. Mark DelCogliano and Andrew Radde-Gallwitz (Washington, D.C., CUA Press, 2011), 186. St. Gregory of Nyssa (d. 394), *De Vita Moysis* 2.6, adds: "There is a doctrine that has credibility because it belongs to the Tra-

The Heavenly Spirits

passages, various Fathers and theologians have held that there are guardian angels of the various Churches (or dioceses), nations, regions, and cities.[45] A large number of saints have had mystical experiences of the angels or their own guardian angels, even in certain cases reaching a very deep relationship with them, formed from many conversations.

2.4. Materialism and Pantheism

We can say that the angels are material in the sense that they are creatures, but not in the sense that there are no immaterial realities, an idea completely abhorrent to the Christian faith. If in fact there existed only matter, there would only be two alternatives: (1) spirit is matter (pantheism); or (2) what is spiritual does not exist; from which would follow, on the one hand, the denial of the existence (or at least of the eminently spiritual and incorporeal nature) of God and the angels and, on the other hand, the reduction of the intellectual and volitional processes of the human being to reactions of the brain in

---

dition of the Fathers, which says: ever since our fallen nature declined due to sin, God has not looked upon our misery with indifference, but has placed an angel, one who has an incorporeal nature; and that on the contrary the corrupter of human nature engineered something similar, damaging the life of every person through a perverse and evil demon. Consequently, the human being is found between two beings that accompany him having opposing goals and can choose which one wins out" (our translation). St. Jerome of Stridon (d. 420), *In Evangelium Matthaei* 3.18: "The worth of souls is so great that from birth each one has an angel assigned to him for his protection" (in *FCNT*, vol. 117, trans. Thomas P. Scheck [Washington, DC: CUA Press, 2008], 209). From the sixteenth century onward, the liturgy has celebrated the feast of the guardian angels on October 2.

[45] "When God made the world in the beginning He put in charge certain hierarchies of celestial powers from which humankind was ruled and governed. Moses indicates that this has been done in the canticle of Deuteronomy, where he says, 'When the Most High assigned the nations their heritage, when he parceled out the descendants of Adam, He set up the boundaries of the peoples after the number of the sons of God' (Deut 32:8)" (Origen of Alexandria, *Explanatio Symboli* 13 [our translation]). "We recall that many spiritual powers exist, which are called angels or presiders of the Church. For example, as John says, the angels of the Church in Asia (Rev 1:20) [other biblical examples follow]": St. Hilary of Poitiers (d. 368), *Tractatus super Psalmos* 129.7 (our translation). Again, St. Basil the Great, *Adversus Eunomium* 3.1: "[Angels] share a nature that is absolutely the same. Yet some of them preside over the nations, whereas others accompany each individual believer" (in *FCNT*, vol. 122, 186). St. John Damascene, *De fide orthodoxa* 2.3: the angels "watch over the parts of the earth and are set over nations and places" (in *FCNT*, vol. 37, 207). These affirmations are based on biblical texts, including Dan 10:12–14, 20–21 and 12:1 and are confirmed by other mystical phenomena, such as the apparition of the "angel of Portugal" to the three shepherds of Fatima.

The Creator

the presence of material objects (as in Hobbes and Hume),[46] given that every spiritual component in the human being would have to be denied.

In a 1986 catechesis, John Paul II summarized and rejected various erroneous conceptions regarding creation, already condemned by the First Vatican Council, which also included an emphasis, in the second and third points below, on the Christian rejection of materialism and pantheism:

> The First Vatican Council reiterates the following truths: 1) The one True God is Creator and Lord "of things visible and invisible" (DS 3021); 2) Against the faith is the affirmation that only matter exists (materialism) (DS 3022); 3) Against the faith is the affirmation that God is essentially identical with the world (pantheism) (DS 3023); 4) It is against the faith to hold that creatures, even spiritual ones, are an emanation from the divine substance, or to affirm that the divine Being with its manifestation or evolution becomes each thing (DS 3024); 5) Against the faith is the conception according to which God is the universal or undefined being who in His self-determination constitutes the universality of beings distinct in genera, species, and individuals (DS 3024); 6) It is likewise contrary to faith to deny that the world and the things all contained in it, both spiritual and material, according to their substance were created by God from nothing (DS 3025).[47]

Let us also add that the preceding reflections about the reason for the Incarnation of the Word (see the previous chapter) have relied on the argument that the angels were not (at least directly) beneficiaries of it, because Christ assumed a material body and the soul of a human being, not an angelic nature. We could not, thus, contradict ourselves and place angels

---

[46] The reference is to Thomas Hobbes (d. 1679), for whom everything, even God and the soul, is corporeal (see his work *Leviathan, or the Matter, Forme, and Power of a Common Wealth Ecclesiastical and Civil*, published in 1651, a philosophical work in which many chapters of theological subject matter are also found). Furthermore, we also recall David Hume (d. 1776), author of essays on such themes as *A Treatise of Human Nature* (1738–1740) and *An Enquiry Concerning Human Understanding* (1748). It is interesting to note that recent scholars, including non-Christians, not only do not identify cerebral matter and its activities with thought, but explicitly speak of the necessity of a higher, spiritual component, which directs this activity, whose effects cannot be traced to neurons alone. The "mind" (the functioning of the brain) is not explained, that is, on the basis of cerebral matter alone. Obviously, there is no shortage of neo-materialist scientists and philosophers who affirm the contrary.

[47] Saint John Paul II, *General Audience*, January 29, 1986 (our translation).

in the realm of materiality. Nonetheless, we certainly include them in the framework of creatures.

2.5. Reconciliation between Heaven and Earth

This reflection on the theme of the angels may continue by keeping in mind a passage of Saint Paul, according to whom in the blood of Jesus Christ, that is, in his sacrifice on the cross, God has intended to reconcile to Himself all things, "those on earth or those in heaven" (Col 1: 20). This passage can certainly indicate the fundamental reconciliation between Spirit and matter (God and human beings) carried out by the Word incarnate. The use of the plural here is interesting: things that are on earth and those in heaven.[48] This seems to suggest a broader reconciliation than that between God and humanity. Perhaps we can see a reference here to celestial creatures, who are, as we shall note, of many different species, which we normally gather under the name of angels.[49] They are beings that did not know separation from God due to man's original sin: they are beings that remained with God in Heaven, while on account of Adam a radical rupture occurred between God and the world. This aspect prompts us to add to what we have said that, from the ontological perspective, the angels are part of creation and thus, with the right clarifications made, we can insert them into the category "matter," if we intend to continue to make use of the pair Spirit/matter. But from the moral perspective, the angels of Heaven have never known the radical break with God that is due to the sin of humanity.

2.6. Good and Evil Angels

It is well-known that, according to Catholic doctrine (based on certain biblical passages: see John 8:44; 2 Pet 2:4; Jude 6), a certain number of angels, namely, Satan and the other rebellious angels—created good by God in the

---

[48] In addition to its use in the already cited First Council of Nicaea and the Fourth Council of the Lateran, the expression in the plural is found, for example, in the following: the First Council of Constantinople (DS 150); the First Vatican Council (DS 3002, 3024, 3025); and Saint Paul VI, *Credo of the People of God* (1968), §8. According to CCC §328, the existence of heavenly spirits is a truth of the faith.

[49] This is the common use, but it needs to be repeated that not all heavenly spirits are angels, that is, not all are sent into the world as messengers of God. Thus, Saint Gregory the Great states: "Those holy spirits of the heavenly homeland are always spirits, but they are not always called angels, since only those who exercise the office of messengers are angels" (*Homilae in Evangelia* 2.34.8 [our translation]).

beginning⁵⁰—suffered definitive estrangement from God due to a sin of rebellion.⁵¹ These angels are not found in Heaven with God, nor will they ever be found there. The Catholic doctrine teaches that there is no longer any possibility of redemption for them, because they are definitively fallen from grace and salvation. The "transformation" of a certain number of heavenly spirits into demons is described with the image of a fall, on the basis of the words of Christ: "I have observed Satan fall like lightning from the sky" (Luke 10:18). It is then described in Rev 12:7–9:

> Then war broke out in heaven; Michael and his angels battled against the dragon. The dragon and its angels fought back, but they did not prevail and there was no longer any place for them in heaven. The huge dragon, the ancient serpent, who is called the Devil and Satan, who deceived the whole world, was thrown down to earth, and its angels were thrown down with it.

When Saint Paul speaks of a reconciliation between heavenly and terrestrial realities, he is not referring to the rebellious angels, who cannot be reconciled to God. He is referring instead to the heavenly spirits that remained faithful to God, and from whom the human being is also separated on account of sin. Thus, sin is not just a dramatic break between God and humanity, between creature and Creator; it also entails a split within the created world: between rational terrestrial beings (humans) and heavenly ones (angels).⁵²

Moreover, the sin of the human being carries with it a wound of the

---

[50] The devil is neither a god of evil opposed to the God of good, nor the principle of darkness that is naturally opposed to the Principle of light. The Church has expressed herself against this (very ancient) dualism on many occasions. The Synod of Braga condemns those who say that the devil was not originally a good angel created by God (see DS 457) and Pope Innocent III taught, "We believe that the devil became evil, not by constitution, but by his free choice" (*Eius Exemplo* [1208]: DS 797). The Fourth Council of the Lateran affirmed: "For the devil and the other demons were indeed created by God naturally good, but they became evil by their own doing. As for man, he sinned at the suggestion of the devil" (DS 800). Among the rites of the Church is the rite of exorcism, which bishops, or priests appointed by them, perform in cases of possession or harassment by the devil against a believer, or the infestation of places. See *Rituale Romanum*, "De exorcizandis obsessis a daemonio."

[51] The rebellion was due to the pride of wanting to be like God: "The angel, without any doubt, sinned by desiring to be like God" (*ST* I, q. 63, a. 3 [our translation]).

[52] A trace of this is also found in Genesis 3:24, where the Cherubim are to prevent the man and woman from reentering Eden after their sin. The spirits remain faithful to God, performing for Him the task of keeping the fallen creature at a distance.

entire material cosmos, which affects all non-rational corporeal creatures. This is attested by Saint Paul in the Letter to the Romans:

> For creation awaits with eager expectation the revelation of the children of God; for creation was made subject to futility, not of its own accord but because of the one who subjected it, in hope that creation itself would be set free from slavery to corruption and share in the glorious freedom of the children of God. We know that all creation is groaning in labor pains even until now. (Rom 8:19–22; see below, paragraph 5.1.10)

3. The Human Being

3.1. Angels and Humans: Genera and Species

The previous section was entitled, "The Heavenly Spirits," in the plural, while for this section we have used the singular, "the human being." This is because, in addition to the fact of being composed of matter and spirit, there is another element that distinguishes human beings from angels. Human beings are individuals that belong to the same species, namely, the human race. For classical philosophy, the genus of human being is animality: the human being pertains to the genus of the animals. The species to which human beings pertain is rational animality. Thus, the human being, each individual human being, is defined as a "rational animal."[53] This classical definition holds together the bipolarity of the human being: insofar as it has a body, the human being is an animal (very similar to other species of animals), but with respect to the other animals, this animal possesses a distinctive peculiarity: a rational soul. As for the heavenly spirits, they cannot be defined as animals because they do not have bodies. They are certainly rational, but their nature is not composite like ours.[54] Moreover, at least according to Saint Thomas Aquinas—called the

---

[53] This is a simplification of an anthropological definition of Aristotle (d. 322 BC), who in *Politics* 1.1253 a 9–10, defines the human being as an "animal endowed with *logos*," that is, endowed with reason, but also with the word with which his or her thought is communicated (language).

[54] The Ecumenical Council of Vienne has solemnly rejected as contrary to the Catholic faith any doctrine or thesis that holds that "the substance of the rational and intellectual soul is not truly and of itself the form of the human body," and thus concludes that anyone who affirms "that the rational and intellectual soul is not of itself and essentially the form of the human body is to be censured as heretic" (*Fidei Catholicae* [1312] [DS 902]). Refer-

Angelic Doctor precisely because of his magnificent theology of the angels—while each human being belongs to the indicated species of rational animal, each angel would constitute a species of its own. That is to say, while each human being is a rational animal, no individual human being exhausts in itself all of this species because every other human being is always of the same species. On the other hand, only Saint Michael the archangel possesses the species of "Michael-ness": no other angel can claim to pertain to the same species, even if it certainly pertains to the same genus as Saint Michael, as heavenly spirits. This is why one can speak of *the* human being while it is preferable to speak of heavenly spirits in the plural. For human beings, the multiplication concerns the individuals, not the human species, which is one. For the angels, on the other hand, there are as many species as there are individuals. The reason for Saint Thomas's position on this is simple: the individuals that belong to the same species are distinguished between them by matter (the body), which is the "principle of individuation." Since angels do not have a body, it is impossible for more than one angel to be distinguished within the same species. It follows that each angel forms a species of its own.[55]

3.2. Genesis 1

We have noted the classical philosophical definition of the human being; but what definition of the human being can be gleaned from divine Revelation? In this regard the first chapter of the Bible, Genesis 1, is fundamental. There we find the following description:

> Then God said: Let us make human beings in our image, after our likeness. Let them have dominion over the fish of the sea, the birds of the air, the tame animals, all the wild animals, and all the creatures that crawl on the earth. / God created mankind in his image; / in the image of God he created them; / male and female he created them. / God blessed them and God said to them: Be fertile and multiply; fill the earth and subdue it. Have dominion over the fish of the sea, the birds of the air, and all the living things that crawl on the earth." (Gen 1:26–28)

---

ring to the philosophical terminology of matter and form, the Council therefore defined the inseparably composite character of the human being's nature.

[55] *ST* I, q. 50, a. 4.

The Human Being

The definition of the human being that biblical Revelation gives is "image of God." We shall now seek to briefly express the implications of this definition.

3.2.1. The Summit of Visible Creation

The human being is not simply one material creature among others. In different but not opposed ways, the first two chapters of Genesis imply that the human being is the summit of visible creation.[56] The superiority of the human being transcends all other earthly creatures.

3.2.2. A Creature Willed in Advance

In the passage cited here, the human being is the only creature whose creation is preceded by God speaking to Himself. Reading the verses that precede the quote given above, it can be recognized that God simply says, "let there be" and then things come into existence. However, in the case of the human being, God first speaks to Himself. This is evidence that the choice to create the human being is of particular value and importance for the Creator. There is no other earthy creature of which God says that He wants to create it in His image.

3.2.3. "Let Us Make"

When God speaks to Himself, He says: "Let us make," in the plural. Jewish exegesis as well as recent Christian exegesis see in this the attestation of a majestic plural, or also the speaking of God to His celestial court, which one imagines is comprised of heavenly spirits. Some scholars hypothesize the presence in the biblical text of remnants of polytheism, according to which God would be speaking to other gods; however, this hypothesis should be rejected because the text of Genesis 1 is clearly monotheistic. The Fathers of the Church very often interpreted the "let us make" not only as a majestic plural, but as an implicit reference to the Holy Trinity: God the Father

---

[56] In Genesis 1, the human being is created last, after all the other creatures, as the summit of the divine poietic work. Moreover, while God says that the other creatures are "good," He says that the whole creation is "very good" (v. 31) only after He has created man. In Genesis 2, the formation of Adam from the earth is presented first, but in other words the text emphasizes humanity's superiority over inferior creatures: the man gives names (that is, he exercises authority) over the other animals and only when he sees the woman does he recognize her as equal to himself. Thus, no other earthly being can be considered equal to him.

would be speaking here with the Son and the Holy Spirit.[57] Modern exegesis generally denies the interpretation of the Fathers, because the mystery of the Trinity is not revealed in the Old Testament, but rather the New—which in the strict sense is true. However, we must also say—if it can be expressed in this way—that the Trinity is not "born" in the New Testament, given that the Trinity is eternal. Thus, the God who created—we know this thanks to the New Testament—is not a different God than that revealed in Jesus Christ. Therefore, the Trinity has created everything that exists, including the human being. The literal sense of the text thus does not refer to the Trinity, and it should instead be understood according to modern Jewish and Christian exegesis. Nonetheless, the literal sense is not the only sense of Scripture, which is why the "let us make" certainly does refer to the Trinity as well. It follows from this that the definition "image of God" should be taken not only as referring to the one and indivisible nature of God, but also to the Trinity of divine Persons.

3.2.4. Biblical Anthropology

We recall that Saint Augustine in his *De Trinitate*, in reflecting on the divinely revealed dogma of the triune God, seeks out the traces (*vestigia*) of the Trinity in the created world. And he recognizes that the "place" in which a pallid image of the Trinitarian mystery of God can be found in this world is above all the human being, who Scripture defines as having been made in His image. In particular, Augustine finds a powerful image of the Trinity in the capacities or faculties of the human soul. The soul is the most noble part of the human being and in it the image of God is reflected in a special way—and this does not exclude the possibility of finding such an image in other anthropological dimensions as well. This also explains why no other creature, even if very similar to human beings at the bodily level, is defined as image of God: this is because it lacks a soul, the little created *logos*, the created spirit that informs the body of the human being and makes it the only animal that "has *logos*."[58]

---

[57] See Augustine of Hippo, *De Genesi ad litteram* 3.19.29. In 11.39.53, Augustine applies the same Trinitarian exegesis to Genesis 3:22. However, this Trinitarian exegesis is much earlier: see *The Letter of Barnabas* 5.4; Saint Justin Martyr, *Dialogus cum Tryphone Iudaeo* 45.61–2; Saint Theophilus of Antioch, *Ad Autolicum* 2.18; Saint Irenaeus of Lyon, *Adversus haereses* 4.20.1 and 5.1.3.

[58] "Man was made to the image of God in that part of his nature wherein he surpasses the brute beasts. This is, of course, his reason or mind or intelligence or whatever we wish to call it. Hence, St. Paul says, *Be renewed in the spirit of your mind, and put on the new man* [Eph 4:23–24], *who is being renewed unto the knowledge of God, according to the image of*

Various recent authors emphasize the difference between the Semitic anthropology of the Old Testament, which sees the human being as a unity more than a composite, and the Greek anthropology, which instead considers the human being as a synthesis of *psyche* and *soma*, soul and body. However, in the Patristic and later theological traditions, these models are not opposed to one another[59]—a view also taught by the Magisterium of the Church.[60] In fact, even the biblical text clearly presents the two fundamental elements of the human creature, while Greek thought also speaks of the unity of these two elements. This is most notable in Aristotelian thought, in which the soul is the "form" of the material body.[61] Thus, a good number of recent theologians also find that the two anthropologies are not in fact opposed, but rather shed light on one another.

3.2.5. God's Representative in the World

It follows that the human being is given by God the power to have dominion over the lower creatures: animals, plants, and the earth. The immense superiority and incomparable dignity of the human being with respect to the lower forms of life should be emphasized, especially in our time.

We live in an era in which there is talk of "animal rights," while very often human rights are trampled on. In reality, animals do not possess rights, because they are not persons. Only the human being possesses inalienable rights, which are connected to the dignity of personal being. These are rights that are not granted by anyone (for example, the state) but are inherent. They should be respected by all and they cannot be taken away. Only the human

---

his Creator [Col 3: 10]. By these words he shows wherein man has been created to the image of God, since it is not by any features of the body but by a perfection of the intelligible order, that is, of the mind when illuminated" (St. Augustine of Hippo, *De Genesi ad litteram* 3.20.30, in *St. Augustine: The Literal Meaning of Genesis*, vol. 1, trans. John Hammond Taylor (New York: Newman Press, 1982), 96.

[59] For example, St. Augustine of Hippo, *De civitate Dei* 19.3.1: "... man as neither the soul alone nor the body alone but the combination of body and soul" (in *FCNT*, vol. 24, 192).

[60] See, for example, St. John Paul II, *General Audience*, April 16, 1986, especially §4–5.

[61] This view of the human being has also been adopted by the Magisterium of the Church, not in the sense that a human philosophical doctrine has been introduced into the doctrines of faith, but rather that this doctrine with its terminology has been placed in the service of the explanation and verbal expression of the revealed truth: "The unity of soul and body is so profound that one has to consider the soul to be the 'form' of the body [Council of Vienne, already cited by us]: i.e., it is because of its spiritual soul that the body made of matter becomes a living, human body; spirit and matter, in man, are not two natures united, but rather their union forms a single nature" (CCC §365).

being was called by God to be His collaborator in exercising dominion, as a sort of vicar, over the creation whose Lord is always God. Here we see a return to the theme of human work, to which we have already alluded: a work that constitutes a true and proper "natural vocation" of the human being. This does not take away the fact that, in grace, human work also becomes a means of sanctification. The fact that the human being is called to exercise dominion over the earth does not imply that his or her dominion can be equated with a dictatorship. He or she must exercise the authority that God has granted for the sake of building up creation.[62] This same creation must not be crushed or abused. Therefore, everything of which many persons today are sensitive—such as respect for animals and an ecological sense—is valid in itself, even though this sensitivity often reaches the point of exaggeration by subordinating human beings to inferior creatures. If we remain, however, within the right limits, the concept of creation and the dignity of the human being are not elements that are dangerous to the environment, but rather elements of its rightful governance and respect. The true ecology is a Christian ecology,[63] which holds together the two aspects (bipolarity): the superiority of the human being, and love and respect for nature—a nature created by God.

3.2.6. Differentiation between Man and Woman

The text of Genesis that we have cited states that God created man, and then immediately adds that He created them male and female. This implies three aspects:

1. Differentiation

In the first place, human nature, beyond being composite (soul-body), is also differentiated.[64] The differentiation does not only concern the body (mascu-

---

[62] This is the overall meaning of Pope Francis' encyclical, *Laudato Si'*.
[63] For several decades the figure of Saint Francis of Assisi (d. 1226) has been utilized as a model of environmentalism and pacifism. The historical reality is very different: see Pope Francis, *Homily at Saint Francis Square, Assisi*, October 4, 2013, §2: "Franciscan peace is not something saccharine. Hardly! That is not the real Saint Francis! Nor is it a kind of pantheistic harmony with forces of the cosmos . . . That is not Franciscan either! It is not Franciscan, but a notion that some people have invented! The peace of Saint Francis is the peace of Christ."
[64] This is what the current and all-pervasive gender ideology does not accept. On the irreconcilability between this and the text of Gen 1:27, see Benedict XVI, Discourse to the Roman Curia, December 21, 2012. Also see the clear words of Pope Francis, Meeting with the Polish Bishops, July 27, 2016: "We are experiencing a moment of the anni-

line-feminine)—a differentiation that is common with the other animals. It also regards the spirit, or soul, particularly in that part that is called psychological. Thus, the differentiation of the human being is better expressed by the man-woman binomial than the male-female binomial, even if the translations of the biblical text generally use the latter. Translations aside, what is important here is that human nature is not exhausted in man alone, or in woman alone. Human nature essentially comprises individual men and women. There are no intermediate differentiations between these two.

2. Equal Dignity

A second aspect consists in the fact of the equal dignity of man and woman. This equality is not assigned by culture or politics: it is inherent to the human creature as such. There is a difference of tasks and functions (also emphasized by Scripture) between man and woman, but there is no ontological superiority—i.e., in the order of essence—of man over woman. According to Saint Paul, the husband carries out the function of head in relation to the wife (see Eph 5:23), but this does not imply that he has the right to tyrannize his wife. It is true that, on account of original sin, the relationship between the husband and wife has deteriorated (see Gen 3:16), but this is not the case in the original plan of God. The fact that the husband has the authority of headship over his wife (not every man over every woman!), indicates that he must certainly guide her and that she must obey him (see Eph 5: 22) and must respect him (see Eph 5: 33). However, it also means that the husband must love the wife as himself (see Eph 5:33), following the example of Christ, Head of the Church, who gave his life for his Spouse (see Eph 5:25). When the man interprets the authority that God has given him over his wife as the right to tyrannize, unhappiness always follows, and sometimes even the failure of the marital relationship.

3. Nuptiality

Finally, the text shows a certain original nuptiality of man and woman. The two are made to complement each other (as is seen even better in Genesis 2)

---

hilation of man as the image of God.... Behind all this there are ideologies.... And one of these—I will call it clearly by its name—is [the ideology of] "gender." Today children—children!—are taught in school that everyone can choose his or her sex.... Pope Benedict's observation should make us think. 'This is the age of sin against God the Creator.'"

and to fill the earth through procreation. Matrimony is not a purely cultural fact that emerges with the passing of time within certain groups of people and not others. In fact, forms of marriage are found in all the civilizations of every age and place, albeit with certain proper characteristics and, in some cases, deviations. Marriage between a man and a woman is described by Scripture as an institution that pertains to the very order of human life. Thus, natural law does not know any other form of marriage but that in which two individuals complement each other because they are of different sex, and for this reason are also able to procreate. The current trend—which in some countries has already become legislation—to legitimize the so-called "marriages" between persons of the same sex is contrary to the order created by God and the natural law imprinted by Him into the world.[65]

3.2.7. "In the Image and Likeness"

When God speaks with Himself in deciding to create the human being, He says He wants to create him in His image, and also in His likeness. Is there a difference between these two terms? The Fathers of the Church do not agree in explaining the difference between image and likeness. In our time, a certain number of exegetes and theologians hold that these terms are simply synonymous. However, the text uses two Jewish words (*selem* and *demut*) that indicate

---

[65] It is well-known that homosexuality is a phenomenon that seems to be reported in practically all eras and cultures. We also know that among some peoples it was not morally condemned to the degree that it was in others. However, we have noted previously that even in those cultures where moral judgment was rather permissive, marriage between people of the same sex was never mentioned. What we see today, therefore, is an absolutely novel phenomenon in human history, tied to the new way in which Modernity conceives legislative activity. In our day, laws are no longer retained as a normative translation and/or application to specific cases of the natural order, grasped by human reason—a translation aimed at the good of the community (*"ordinatio rationis ad bonum commune ab eo, qui curat communitatis habet promulgata*—an ordering of reason addressed to the common good, promulgated by him who is responsible for the community": *ST* I-II, q. 90, a. 4 [our translation]). The typically modern phenomenon of democracy, which certainly brings with it various valid aspects, has often introduced a purely "positive" concept of law: the validity of a law does not come from the rational motivations that sustain it (which in fact are no longer invoked by the legislator): it is valid solely on account of the one who promulgates it (in general, the parliament). The parliamentary debate, then, is no longer considered a dialogue that tends toward mediation regarding the concrete way of translating the known truth into state law, for the common good. On the contrary, it often tends toward pleasing factions of people or influential groups in order to avoid losing their support. The theme of the truth of natural law has now disappeared from a large portion of the political and legislative debate: it is the political manifestation of the "dictatorship of relativism."

The Human Being

different things. *Selem* indicates precisely an image, for example, a statue; while *demut* is a term that (especially in the book of the prophet Ezekiel) is used to indicate a comparison. The first has a more static significance, the second a more dynamic one. The better explanation identifies "image"[66] as the nature of the human being, and "likeness" as the grace that God wants to grant this creature, in such a way that he or she becomes more and more a likeness of his or her Creator, growing in holiness.[67] This is confirmed by the fact that the above text shows that God decides to create the human being in His image (i.e., to constitute human nature), and also plans to endow him or her with a likeness, that is, with the supernatural gift of grace. However, immediately after, the cited text uses only the word image to indicate the creation of the human nature, not yet endowed with the gift of grace, which God will grant immediately afterward. This is not a matter of saying that God creates a "pure nature" (a technical expression that means purely natural nature, not called by God to elevation by grace), but also concerns distinguishing terminologically what is distinct in reality, without being separate: the order of nature (the human being in the image of God) and the order of grace (the human being in the likeness of God). When the human being commits sin, the grace is lost, that is, the likeness is lost; but human nature, the image, is not lost. This interpretation is confirmed by the recent Magisterium of the Church.[68]

---

[66] For the sake of brevity, it is usually said that the human being is the "image of God," and it is in this sense that we are expressing ourselves in these terms as well. In reality, however, only Christ is the image of God (see Col 1:15). The human being is the being created "*in the* image" of God. Saint Thomas notes: "In man there is some likeness to God, which derives from God as his exemplar. But this is not a likeness of equality, because the exemplar infinitely surpasses the copy. Thus, it must be said that in man there is an image of God that is not perfect, but rather imperfect. This is what it means in Scripture when it says that man is made 'in the image of God,' because the preposition 'in' indicates an approximation that is aimed at a reality [that remains] distant" (*ST* I, q. 93, a. 1 [our translation]).

[67] Saint John Damascene, *De fide orthodoxa* 2.12: "'according to His image' means the intellect and free will, while the 'according to His likeness' means such likeness in virtue as is possible" (in *FCNT*, vol. 37, 235). Saint Thomas distinguishes two meanings of the term likeness: likeness as nature and likeness as virtue (supported by grace). This prevents us from thinking that some human faculties are to be catalogued as images and others as likeness. As for likeness as virtue, he writes that it "indicates a certain perfection of the image. In fact, we say that the image is similar or not to the original, inasmuch as it represents it perfectly or imperfectly" (*ST* I, q. 93, a. 9 [our translation]).

[68] Second Vatican Council, *Gaudium et Spes*, §22: Christ is "the perfect man. To the sons of Adam he restored the divine likeness that had been disfigured from the first sin onward" (DS 1322). "Even after losing through his sin his likeness to God, man remains an image of his Creator" (CCC §2566).

The Creator

We can draw from this that the biblical definition of the human being as the "image of God" is a definition of general anthropology, while the theological definition of the human being in light of the mystery of predestination and salvation is "image and likeness of God." If we want to define what the human being is in light of God, it is enough to indicate his or her nature as a rational being, made in the image of God. If we want to define the human being also in light of the destiny to which God, in a totally gratuitous way, wants to call him or her, and in light of the grace that is conferred to reach such a destiny, then we will say that the human being is a rational being created by God and called by God to be sanctified, to grow in grace, and to reach glory: "image and likeness of God."

3.3. Genesis 2

The next chapter of the book of Genesis contains other anthropologically relevant aspects. We read:

> then the LORD God formed the man out of the dust of the ground and blew into his nostrils the breath of life, and the man became a living being. The LORD God planted a garden in Eden, in the east, and placed there the man whom he had formed. Out of the ground the LORD God made grow every tree that was delightful to look at and good for food, with the tree of life in the middle of the garden and the tree of the knowledge of good and evil. . . .

> The LORD God then took the man and settled him in the garden of Eden, to cultivate and care for it. The LORD God gave the man this order: You are free to eat from any of the trees of the garden except the tree of knowledge of good and evil. From that tree you shall not eat; when you eat from it you shall die. The LORD God said: It is not good for the man to be alone. I will make a helper suited to him. So the LORD God formed out of the ground all the wild animals and all the birds of the air, and he brought them to the man to see what he would call them; whatever the man called each living creature was then its name. The man gave names to all the tame animals, all the birds of the air, and all the wild animals; but none proved to be a helper suited to the man. So the LORD God cast a deep sleep on the man, and while he was asleep, he took out one of his ribs and closed up its place with flesh. The LORD God then built the rib that he had taken from the man into a woman. When he brought her to the man, the man said: / "This

one, at last, is bone of my bones / and flesh of my flesh; / This one shall be called 'woman,' / for out of man this one has been taken." / That is why a man leaves his father and mother and clings to his wife, and the two of them become one body. The man and his wife were both naked, yet they felt no shame. (Gen 2:7–9, 15–25)

The text confirms numerous aspects present in Genesis 1, which we shall not repeat. The narrative style is more popular and fable-like, and this leads scholars to retain that the text is more ancient than Genesis 1. Let's clarify that fable-like does not mean mere fiction, just as more ancient is not always the same as more historical. Nonetheless, what interests us is the revealed content of the text, staying out of the discussions among specialists.

3.3.1. The Man–Material Cosmos Relationship

1. "Adam"

The text specifies that the first human being (Hebrew: *adam*) is formed from the earth (*adamah*). The human being has a constitutive link with matter, which becomes part of his own being, in the corporeal part. This ontological link with the material cosmos is at the root of what we have already seen when citing Saint Paul above: all material creation, the physical cosmos, suffers a wound because of the man who sinned (see Rom 8; we shall return to this again further on). This is due to the mysterious link that God the Creator established between the human being, a spiritual-corporeal creature, and the rest of material creation. For one of his or her components, the human being comes from matter, and being material, pertains to matter. However, what makes the human being a living being is this breath that God introduces directly into him or her, and which we call soul, or created spirit.

2. Evolutionism

Here we can briefly mention the question of the eventual "descent of the human being from the monkey," as says the popular understanding of the theory of evolution, applied to the human being. What is truly important here for the faith is to affirm that the human being is a creature willed and made by God, not the product of accidental and blind evolution. The human being, even more so than the cosmos, was not born by accident: "We are not some casual and meaningless product of evolution. Each of us is the result of a thought of God. Each of us is willed, each of us is loved, each of us is necessary."⁶⁹ The Christian worldview cannot accept a different response from this. Moreover, the biblical texts indicate an action by God that is not progressive but immediate in the creation of the human being. However, it is also true that Scripture does not wish to give us information of a scientific nature concerning *how* the natural phenomena occurred. However, creation, which gives rise to nature, is not simply a natural phenomenon like those billions and billions of phenomena happening continually in the micro and macro cosmos. Creation is their beginning and reason for being. The creative act is an intervention of God. Moreover, the human creature is the being that is superior to all the rest, so it is not fitting to think that it emerges from inferior beings. Genesis 2, in fact, seems to say that the other animals represent a reduction of the human being, rather than the human being an improvement of the non-rational animals.⁷⁰

Nonetheless, nowadays there is no shortage of Catholic scholars who affirm the possibility of a harmonization between faith in creation as a work of God with the theory of evolution. In this regard, we must recall as a minimal reference point the limit placed by Pius XII, according to whom, even if one wants to affirm the descent of the human body from inferior forms of animal life,⁷¹ it must be maintained that the rational souls are directly

---

[69] Benedict XVI, *Homily at the Mass of Imposition of the Pallium and Conferral of the Fisherman's Ring for the Beginning of the Petrine Ministry of the Bishop of Rome*, April 24, 2005. See also the broad and meditated openness of the same Pontiff in *Meeting with the Clergy of the Dioceses of Belluno-Feltre and Treviso*, July 24, 2007. However, St. John Paul II, *Message to the Plenary of the Pontifical Academy of Sciences*, October 22, 1996, had already said: "New understandings lead to no longer considering the theory of evolution as a mere hypothesis" (§4). The Church believes that she can accept the scientific evolutionary thesis—to the extent to which it is demonstrated—because the possibility that God has introduced evolutionary processes into His creation does not endanger the dogma of faith in God as the creator of everything. The soul of the human being, however, is kept outside of the field of creatures that God may have brought about through an evolutionary process, directed by Him. Only the corporeal component of the human being could eventually derive from evolution.

[70] This must be understood not as if some humans had regressed to stages of an inferior life, losing their rational soul, but in the sense that animals possess some or many characteristics that human beings also have, but not all of their characteristics.

[71] Saint John Paul II confirms it again, *General Audience*, April 16, 1986: "From the standpoint of the doctrine of the faith, we do not see any difficulty in explaining the origin of man *as a body*, through the hypothesis of evolution. We must, however, add that the *hypothesis proposes only a probability, not scientific certainty*. The doctrine of the faith, rather, invariably affirms that the spiritual soul of man is created directly by God. It is therefore possible according to the hypothesis mentioned, that the human body, according to the order impressed by the Creator upon the energies of life, has been gradually prepared in the forms of antecedent living beings. The human soul, however, from which

infused by God, because they are created immediately by Him (i.e., without the mediation of nature).[72] The human soul represents an element of transcendence with respect to the whole material cosmos. Its eminent dignity, dependent upon its heightened faculties (intellect, will, freedom) that are not found in any other form of terrestrial life, make it a sign, an incomparable image of God the Creator within the material world. The human soul cannot come from others but only from God. Thus, it is confirmed that although the human being is not only soul, but a combination of spirit and matter, it is in the spiritual part that we must identify the place of superiority over other life forms. Soul and body go together, but the soul is infinitely more valuable than the body.[73]

3.3.2. Eden

God plants a garden in Eden and places man there. It should be noted that man is created from the ground and then moved to the land of Eden (which means "delight"). This shift may well indicate the gift of grace.[74] Man is created from the ground (natural order) and immediately elevated to the delight of friendship with God (supernatural order). Just as it was said in

---

man's humanity definitively depends, being [the soul] spiritual, cannot have emerged from matter" (§7 [our translation and emphasis]).

[72] Pius XII, *Humani generis* (1950; DS 3896); see Saint Paul VI, *Credo of the People of God*, §8; CCC §366: "The Church teaches that every spiritual soul is created immediately by God—it is not 'produced' by the parents—and also that it is immortal."

[73] There is also another question, that regarding the comparison between monogenist and polygenist theses. Monogenism argues that God created a single human couple from which all individuals descend (see Acts 17:26); polygenism postulates the existence of more couples. On this point, the teaching of Pius XII is that Christians do not enjoy the same freedom of thought in regard to this issue that he allowed regarding the human body originating from evolution. Pius XII gives the reason for his teaching based on the dogma of original sin, which is communicated through generation (see below). However, he uses a prudent formula, saying that "it is in no way apparent how [polygenism] can be reconciled" with what the faith teaches us about original sin (*Humani generis*, DS 3897). In theory, therefore, polygenism could be accepted if it were conceived in a way that was not inconsistent with dogma. In this regard, we note: (1) to this day, the texts of the Magisterium have always expressed themselves in favor of the monogenist thesis, faithful to the biblical and traditional information; (2) the commendable efforts of recent theologians for finding a way of reconciliation with dogma have been, to this point, in vain; and (3) the sciences themselves today tend very often toward monogenism rather than polygenism.

[74] The Garden of Eden is to be understood both as a place in the literal sense, and as a symbol in the spiritual sense; see Saint Augustine of Hippo, *De Genesi ad litteram* 8.1.1. Likewise about the tree of life: 8.5.9–10; and that of the knowledge of good and evil: 8.6.12.

The Creator

Genesis 1 that man must have dominion over the world and work in it, so here it says that man must look after and cultivate the garden. Work continues, but now it is also elevated to be a means of sanctification, which allows the human being to reach a supernatural end, in addition to maintaining its value with respect to the natural end of building up and developing the material cosmos. The Garden of Eden should not only be cultivated, but also cared for; this suggests that grace, or friendship and closeness with God, should be carefully protected, lest it be lost.[75] This interpretation of Eden as an elevation to the supernatural order is confirmed by the fact that as soon as sin occurs the human beings are cast out from the garden (see Gen 3).

3.3.3. The Edenic Commandment

The Lord gives a commandment in Eden: obedience to the divine will is the concrete mode in which the human being safeguards friendship with God.[76] The Fathers of the Church assumed two positions with respect to this Edenic commandment: some held that it concerns a temporary test, with which God would have tested Adam's fidelity; for others, such a commandment would express a fundamental law to be observed always, a restatement of the law of nature for which the creature must obey the Creator. In fact, this second position should be preferred: ethics is not a superstructure that is added to human life, but rather a constitutive dimension of it. Natural ethics corresponds to the law set by God in the cosmos, a cosmos of which the human being forms a part. To act against this law is not only to act against the will of God, but at the same time to act against one's own being, dignity, and destination. However, this does not exclude the other aspect entirely; in fact, the commandment, while it expresses an objective norm, is also an opportunity for a test. Thus, we also have an *et-et* in this respect, where the commandment has a primary place, insofar as it is an objective and stable norm, and it is coordinated to the second aspect of the commandment as a proof of fidelity.

---

[75] "Man had to work and take care of paradise. This work however would not have been very burdensome, as was the case after sin; but pleasant, on account of the experience of the forces of nature. Even this care did not have trespassers as its object: its scope was that man would care for paradise for himself, lest he should lose it by sin. Paradise was thus ordered toward the good of man and not vice versa" (*ST* I, q. 102, a. 3 [our translation]).

[76] This law is also confirmed by Christ: "You are my friends if you do what I command you" (John 15:14).

3.3.4. The "Preternatural" Gifts and Immortality

In Eden, in the state of original grace, the human being was endowed with certain gifts, called "preternatural" by modern theologians. The last verse of the above-cited passage says that the man and his wife were naked, and yet did not feel ashamed. This is called the gift of the "absence of concupiscence," i.e., the absence of any disordered desire that inclines one to commit evil. Saint Thomas dedicates an extensive study to the original justice of the human being.[77] He denies that the original justice allowed Adam to see God as He is in Himself, unless he were raptured in ecstasy.[78] However, Adam had a knowledge of God more perfect than our own, because his vision was not yet obscured by sin and thus he was better able to grasp the reflection of the Creator in creatures. Moreover, God had granted the knowledge of things necessary for life, and this in both the natural and supernatural sphere.[79] In addition, there was original holiness, through which "the human being in the state of innocence possessed in some way all the virtues. In fact, the perfection of the primitive state was such as to entail the subordination of the reason to God, and of the inferior powers to reason."[80]

Yet even more than these gifts, the Angelic Doctor focused on the supernatural gift of grace, through which the human being enjoyed the privilege of immortality. This was a gift of grace because "the body of Adam was not incorruptible on account of an intrinsic strength of immortality; but rather there was in the soul a power conferred by God in a supernatural manner, with which the soul could keep the body immune from any corruption, so long as it remained subject to God."[81]

---

[77] See *ST* I, qq. 94–102.

[78] See *ST* I, q. 94, a. 1.

[79] See *ST* I, q. 94, a. 3.

[80] *ST* I, q. 95, a. 3 (our translation).

[81] *ST* I, q. 97, a. 1 (our translation). Let us also cite another passage of the Angelic Doctor in this regard: "That which is produced by natural causes is said to be natural. Now, the intrinsic causes of nature are matter and form. However, the form of man is the rational soul, which is immortal *per se*. Thus, from the standpoint of his form, death is not natural for man. On the other hand, the matter of man is a body composed of contrary elements: and this is necessarily corruptible. Thus, from this standpoint death is natural for man. However, this corruptibility of the human body derives from a necessity of the matter: for it was necessary that the human body be the organ of touch, and therefore a means in between the objects of touch; and this could not be, as Aristotle explains, if it were not composed of contrary elements. However, this is not a condition imposed by form: for, if it were possible, with the form being incorruptible, it should be better to provide it with incorruptible matter. To provide an example: that the saw is composed of iron fits well

4. Divine Providence

From the first two chapters of the Bible emerge not only the profile of the human being but also and above all the profile of the human being's Creator, who not only draws everything that exists out of nothing, but also preserves in being what He has created. Consequently, the Christian perspective of God is not the one described by the famous image of the Enlightenment thinkers: the Creator who gives the famous "kick" to the world, to put it in movement, and then withdraws from it; or the "watchmaker" God who produces a perfect mechanism, capable—once wound—of functioning in an autonomous way. God, by contrast, is present to His creation and governs it. The governing of the world is called Providence. We can distinguish two types of divine Providence.

4.1. Providence as "Continuous Creation" ("creatio continua")

The first form of Providence generally concerns the "continuous creation": the conservation in being of beings and their governing. In this first sense of the word, Providence consists in making it so that things exist and carry out their own functions, pursuing their own ends. However, one needs not imagine that, as the popular Italian adage goes, "*non cade foglia che Dio non voglia*" ("a leaf does not fall without God willing it"). From a certain point of view this is true, because deep down everything is traceable to the Creator;[82] but from another point of view it is not, because the Christian concept of the divine governance of the world includes the fact that God has created and maintains in being natural processes, which are carried out by their own natures. For example, the succession of days and seasons, the growth of plants and fruits, and the falling of rain and snow happen because God maintains in being the processes and natural movements that are their origin, not because in each instance of rain God creates the drops of water and decides where

---

with its form, and with its operation, making it able to saw with hardness; but that it is subject to rusting depends on the requirements of this matter, and not on the purpose of the one who made it; for if the artisan could, he would make it with an iron that is not subject to rust. Now, God who has created man is omnipotent. And therefore out of a gratuitous gift, He removed from the first man the necessity of dying that derived from this matter. But this benefit was withdrawn due to the fault of our first parents. Thus, death is natural for the condition of the matter: but it is a punishment for the loss of the divine gift which preserved it from death" (*ST* II-II, q. 164, a. 1, ad 1 [our translation]).

[82] As stated by Saint Augustine of Hippo, *De Genesi ad litteram* 5.21.42, who recalls Matthew 6:30 and 10:29.

they must fall. The Catechism expresses it in this way:

> God is the sovereign master of his plan. But to carry it out he also makes use of his creatures' co-operation. This use is not a sign of weakness, but rather a token of almighty God's greatness and goodness. For God grants his creatures not only their existence, but also the dignity of acting on their own, of being causes and principles for each other, and thus of co-operating in the accomplishment of his plan. (CCC §306)

In this work of governing the world, as we have seen, God calls the human being to be His collaborator at the natural level, and in a particular way in work.[83] To summarize, the governance of the world belongs to God, but He makes use of "secondary causes" in its development. *Both* God *and* creatures cooperate in the realization of the divine plan for the cosmos.

4.2. Providence in the History of Salvation

Secondly, Providence is carried out in the governance of salvific history. Here the divine interventions directly regard the human being (an individual or a group) and are ordered according to a plan that grows in intensity with the passage of time, while respecting the response of the creature to which it is directed.

4.2.1. Toward the Elect People

We see that in salvific history two main phases are distinguished, strictly interconnected with each other and with increasing value: the Old and New Testament. Two peoples chosen by God in the midst of all other people correspond to these two phases: the People of Israel in the old covenant, and the new People of God, the Church, in the new and definitive covenant (see Jer 31:31–34; 32:40; Ezek 16:60; 37:26; Luke 22:20; 1 Cor 11:25; 2 Cor 3:6; Heb 8:13; 9:15; 12:24; 13:20; see Chapter Eight). Divine Providence has guided a centuries-old salvific history, until it reaches the central event of all human history: the Incarnation of the Word. This Providence raised up the patriarchs, the judges, kings, prophets, and priests of the Old Testament to prepare for the coming of the One who, in His Person, reassumes and completes all the ancient figures.

---

[83] See Second Vatican Council, *Gaudium et Spes*, §34–35.

4.2.2. Toward Individuals

This salvific Providence works not only in the great moments and figures of the history of salvation, but also in the small personal history of the individual believer, and often in very concrete and daily situations, as the experience of many saints attests, but also that of innumerable other Christians, especially the poor and those of pure heart and simple faith.[84]

4.2.3. The Infallibility of Providence, and Human Freedom

This second sense of divine Providence in particular encounters and clashes with human freedom, which God includes in salvific history. It is the conviction of believers that Providence does not impose its designs on human beings, thus preserving their freedom.[85] This is because Providence "of the second type," the historical-salvific sort, does not go against Providence "of the first type," the sort that maintains in existence what God has created. Since the Creator has made the human being free, He does not suppress this freedom even when it is misused to oppose the divine plan. Nonetheless, like every divine action, Providence is infallible, and thus fulfills its plans in one way or another.[86] Hence the conviction of faith, as it is expressed by Jacques Bossuet (d. 1704), that "God writes straight with crooked lines" Imagining life as a piece of paper in which the human being is entrusted with the task of tracing the lines and God is the One who writes. However, human beings often trace crooked lines: their response to the divine call is very disappointing. God allows human beings to draw crooked lines, yet he always manages

---

[84] A literary example is Renzo from chapter 17 of *I Promessi Sposi* who, meditating on his woes, says to himself: "Providence has helped me so far; it will also help me in the future." Then he himself becomes an instrument of it by helping some poor people, and bursting into the famous expression: *"La c'è la Provvidenza!"* or "There is the Providence!"; and "he immediately shoved his hand into his pocket, emptied it of the few coins he had, put them in the nearest hand he found, and went on his way" (our translation). The whole chapter is a hymn to Providence, just like, in the background, the entire Manzonian masterpiece, of which it is said that it could be summarized by the idea of Christian Providence, which knows how to draw good out of evil. According to a well-known critic of the twentieth century, divine Providence is the true protagonist of the novel.

[85] The problem is also intertwined with that of divine prescience, which knows in advance which people will choose to be evil. The classical response to the difficulties is in Saint Augustine of Hippo, *De Genesi ad litteram* 11.9.12.

[86] "By his providence God protects and governs all things that he has made ... for 'all are open and laid bare to his eyes' (Heb 4:13), even those things that will be done by the free action of creatures" (First Vatican Council, *Dei Filius*, ch. 1 [DS 3005]).

to find a way to write straight with these lines. From the infallibility of God in carrying out His will, and from the fact that His will desires the good, it can be deduced that Providence is able to even draw good out of the evil that human beings introduce into the world and into history. This does not imply that God desires evil, but only that He permits it in light of a greater good. This is what has happened since the first sin in human history. God did not want Adam to sin. Under the temptation of the devil, the man did it. God permitted it because He wanted to safeguard the freedom of His creature, and also because He knew He could draw out a greater good from that evil: thanks to the Incarnation of the Word, in fact, the human being will be elevated to a degree of grace even greater than that in the state of original justice.

> The eternal Father, by a [most] free and hidden plan [*liberrimo et arcano consilio*] of His own wisdom and goodness, created the whole world. His plan was to raise men to a participation of the divine life. Fallen in Adam, God the Father did not leave men to themselves, but ceaselessly offered helps to salvation, in view of Christ, the Redeemer.[87]

4.3. Providence and the Evils Present in the Cosmos

4.3.1. The Origin of the Evil in the World

Nonetheless, there are evils in the world that are not the direct fruit of the free will of human beings: earthquakes, volcanic eruptions, congenital diseases, and so forth. The existence of these evils, which provoke suffering and death, do not depend on the choice of one or more human beings; they simply happen. In reality, Christian faith also sees in these, even if not the direct fruit of free will, at least an indirect fruit of that same freedom; by sinning, the first human being has condemned creation to suffer the consequences of sin until the end of times. Creation is no longer in its state of original perfection: "For creation was made subject to futility, not of its own accord but because of the one who subjected it, in hope that creation itself would be set free from slavery to corruption and share in the glorious freedom of the children of God" (Rom 8:20–21). The disorder that is in the world, introduced by the sin of the human being and not by the Creator, produces all of those terrible fruits that are not directly the fault of the human being, in the sense that they derive from the original choice with

---

[87] Second Vatican Council, *Lumen Gentium* (1964), §2

which Adam condemned himself and the whole human race, and with it all of creation, to a fall, to disorder, and to evil.

4.3.2. Why God Allows Evil

If then one asks in what way Providence acts with respect to all of this—why Providence has allowed such a contagion within creation, such that there is not a single day without a natural disaster or the loss of thousands of lives through disease—one may shrewdly respond along with Saint Augustine: "God ..., being Himself supremely good, would [never] permit any evil to be in His works, were not His power and goodness such that even out of evil He can do good."[88] And Saint Thomas glosses this point: "So it belongs to the infinite goodness of God to allow some evil to derive certain goods from it."[89]

Now this might seem like a theoretical and dissatisfying response, especially these days, in which the dominant hedonistic culture makes us perceive evil with even more acute sensibility than in earlier times. But, in fact, this response also corresponds to experience. We see, for example, how much love the presence of a disabled child or a bedridden elderly person produces in a family in terms of attention, deeds of compassion, even the humblest services, vigils, and sacrifices. That family can certainly refuse to respond to evil with good in the way that God intended by permitting that evil. This does not take away the fact that, if the people react to the evil with good (see Rom 12:21), it is understandable why Providence would allow that evil.

However, whoever does not love, or whoever rejects suffering and sacrifice, is not capable of responding to the question about the existence of evil: for such a person, it will always remain an unsolvable problem. This might even lead us to say that, in the moments in which humanity is more corrupt, God allows a higher number of sicknesses, wars, and natural disasters. The latter, more than being true and proper divine punishments, are medicines (medicines, it is known, are sometimes bitter, but they are useful). God would permit a greater number of similar occurrences because these, by bringing about suffering, create the possibility of greater love, sacrifice, expiation, reparation, repentance, and prayer. And this, precisely, in the eras in which there is greater need for such things, is always because God desires the salvation

---

[88] Saint Augustine of Hippo, *Enchiridion de fide, spe et charitate* 3.11, in *FCNT*, vol. 4, trans. Bernard M. Peebles (New York: Cima Publishing Co. Inc., 1947), 376.

[89] *ST* I, q. 2, a. 3, ad 1 (our translation). Leo XIII teaches in *Libertas Praestantissimum* (1888): "God Himself in his Providence, though infinitely good and powerful, permits evil to exist in the world, partly that greater good may not be impeded and partly that greater evil may not ensue" (DS 3251).

of people and not their ruin (see Ezek 33:11). Thus, an event that according to human judgment is destructive can be the way in which God saves from a true catastrophe: the loss of eternal life. This can be hypothesized in general, although extreme prudence is required in trying to identify a precise divine intention, completely clear to us, in any particular event.

4.3.3. Providence and Fatalism

Based on what has been said about divine Providence, it can be said that the conception of life called "fatalism" is irreconcilable with Christian faith. Fatalism holds that the only thing governing the cosmos and human life is fate, and as a result nothing can be done to change the course of events, which are already predetermined and pre-established. This perspective negates the concept of history, but above all it takes away freedom and merit—or demerit—from the human being's own actions. For this reason, such a theory has been rejected by the ecclesiastical Magisterium on different occasions.[90] The Christian perspective teaches that God infallibly carries out His plan without overriding the freedom of the creature, but rather by preserving it, as can also be seen from the following theme.

5. Original Sin

We have now reached the treatment of the doctrine of original sin, which beyond the shadow of a doubt, and despite the contrary voices of the last decades, is among the most important dogmas of the Catholic faith. In fact, original sin is a doctrine revealed by God that is closely connected to the concrete development of salvific history (that is, the concrete mode in which divine Providence has unfurled its design concerning humanity). Without this doctrine, one cannot understand redemption, the marvelous work of Jesus Christ, who shed His Blood as price to obtain it for us. Moreover, without original sin, the mystery of evil in the world cannot be understood. Original sin is not a simple doctrine of theologians (a *"theologoumenon"*): it is a truth that is supernaturally revealed by God (a revealed dogma) and is defined by the Catholic Church in her extraordinary and solemn Magisterium (a defined dogma). Moreover, up until recent times, this

---

[90] See Saint Leo the Great, *Quam Laudabiliter* (447) (DS 283); First Synod of Braga, *Anathematismi contra Priscillanistas* (561), §9 (DS 459); Council of Constance, *Errores Iohannis Wyclif* (1415), §27 (DS 1177); Pius II, *Cum sicut Accepimus* [*Errores Zanini de Solcia*] (1459), §4 (DS 1364).

The Creator

doctrine was always, in all eras, a *tranquilla possessio* (undisputed truth) among the Christian people, who, as the Second Vatican Council recalls, when in their spatial-temporal universality profess a doctrine as definitive, cannot be in error.[91]

At the biblical level, the dogma of original sin was revealed both in the Old Testament and the New, with the perfection proper to each. The most important texts are chapter 3 of Genesis and chapter 5 of Saint Paul's Letter to the Romans. However, the theme of original sin, whether directly or indirectly, explicitly or implicitly, pervades all of Scripture: it is one of the threads that weaves the texture of the sacred texts from top to bottom.[92]

5.1. Genesis 3

With the narrative style typical of the first chapters of Genesis, Genesis 3 describes original sin in this way:

> Now the snake was the most cunning of all the wild animals that the Lord God had made. He asked the woman, "Did God really say, 'You shall not eat from any of the trees in the garden'?" The woman answered the snake: "We may eat of the fruit of the trees in the garden; it is only about the fruit of the tree in the middle of the garden that God said, 'You shall not eat it or even touch it, or else you will die.'" But the snake said to the woman: "You certainly will not die! God knows well that when you eat of it your eyes will be opened and you will be like gods, who know good and evil." The woman saw that the tree was good for food and pleasing to the eyes, and the tree was desirable for gaining wisdom. So she took some of its fruit and ate it; and she also gave some to her husband, who was with her, and he ate it. Then the eyes of both of them were opened, and they knew that they were naked; so they sewed fig leaves together and made loincloths for themselves. (Gen 3:1–7)

---

[91] "The entire body of the faithful, anointed as they are by the Holy One (see 1 John 2:20 and 27), cannot err in matters of belief [*in credendo falli nequit*]. They manifest this special property by means of the whole peoples' supernatural discernment in matters of faith when 'from the Bishops down to the last of the lay faithful' [St. Augustine] they show universal agreement in matters of faith and morals" (Second Vatican Council, *Lumen Gentium*, §12).

[92] It is true that Jesus did not speak of it directly, but indirectly he did several times. As a single example, see His conversation with Nicodemus in John 3.

5.1.1. The Serpent

First and foremost, note that the text introduces alongside the man and woman a snake, qualified as the most cunning of all creatures. Cunning here should be understood not as a simple shrewdness, but as malice, as the narration that follows shows. Genesis 3 does not reveal the identity of the serpent: for this we must wait for the Book of Revelation, which will speak of "The huge dragon, the ancient serpent, who is called the Devil and Satan, who deceived the whole world" (Rev 12:9). With this, Scripture, which should be read as a unified whole, ends by revealing that the human being has sinned on account of the temptation of the devil (see also Wis 2:24).

5.1.2. The Temptation

The temptation takes place as a dialogue between Satan and the woman. From this encounter, Christian spirituality draws out the lesson that one never should put oneself in dialogue with temptation, but should instead reject it immediately and firmly. Despite the fact that he is fallen, the devil remains a being of angelic nature, which is superior to our own nature (see Ps 8:6; Heb 2:7), thus we cannot claim to defeat him or resist him if we try to face him. The grace of God leads us to avoid this disastrous encounter, which, if it does happen, will always end with the defeat of the human being. Thus, Saint James says: "So submit yourselves to God. Resist the devil, and he will flee from you. Draw near to God, and he will draw near to you" (James 4:7–8).

When the demon tempts, we must not dialogue with him, but resist his attacks and, supported by grace, turn towards God.[93] The Genesis narrative, by showing that temptation comes from the devil, also exonerates God from any accusation of submitting us directly to temptation. Earlier in his letter, James writes: "No one experiencing temptation should say, 'I am being tempted by God'; for God is not subject to temptation to evil, and he himself tempts no one" (James 1:13). However, God *allows* us to be tempted (see Job 1:12; 2:6; see also what we have just said about the permission of evil by Providence).

---

[93] With specific reference to the baptismal ritual, Saint Ambrose of Milan (d. 397) writes in *De mysteriis* 2.7: "For he who renounces the devil, turns toward Christ, recognizes Him by a direct glance" (in *FCNT*, vol. 44, trans. Roy J. Deferrari [Washington DC, CUA Press, 1963], 7).

5.1.3. The Historical Character of Original Sin

Original sin is a historical event, like the fall of the Berlin Wall; although the episode of Eden has two peculiarities compared to any other event in history: (1) it has universal consequences, which go beyond the normal cause-and-effect relationship that every historical event produces, being in relation to other successive facts that happen or are modified because of it; and (2) the way in which original sin is narrated does not correspond to the literary genre of historiography: especially, but not only, modern historiography. Like the first two chapters, the third chapter of Genesis recounts the beginning of sacred history, framed in the broader context of the history of salvation that God directs. The character of sacred history implies the historicity of the narrated events, which are not simply religious myths but rather events that really happened (see CCC §390). However, these events happened within a sacred dimension, constituted by the fact that they are integrated into the history of salvation and thus do not have purely secular significance.[94] Hence, these historical events also convey an element of mystery (God acts in them and the human being responds to God, positively or negatively). This also makes it the case that the consequences of these events are not only natural, but also of the supernatural order, as is particularly the case with original sin.

5.1.4. Disobedience

Within the narrative genre typical of the ancient and eastern world, Genesis says that the first parents of the human race, seduced by the devil, disobeyed an explicit command of the Creator with an act of rebellion. The text describes this with the image of seizing a forbidden fruit. In this regard, given that the text speaks of the tree of the knowledge of good and evil—an evil that in Latin is called *malum*, the same word that is used to indicate an apple—the popular imagery has created the scene of Eve taking and eating an apple. However, the Bible only speaks of a fruit, without specifying which fruit. More important is the fact that fruit is the image that Genesis uses, which should not necessarily be taken literally, while instead we must at all costs take the meaning intended by the text literally: at the beginning of human history, the first man and the first woman sinned against the Creator by disobeying a command. This is a historical fact, even if we do not know the details of how it occurred,

---

[94] See the responses to various questions on the matter by the Pontifical Biblical Commission, *De Charactere Historico Priorum Capitum Geneseos* (1909) (DS 3512–3519).

or what type of sin the two committed (theologians have formulated various hypotheses throughout the centuries—e.g., theft, unchastity—but there is no agreement between them).

5.1.5. Pride

Even if we do not know the exact sin committed in its species, we know in general from the biblical text that it is a sin guided by pride[95]: wanting to be like God with respect to knowledge of good and evil. This is exactly the proposal that the serpent makes, the proposal that is accepted: if you eat, you will become like God. It is very probable that the knowledge of good and evil means making themselves judges of what is good and what is not, that is, deciding in an autonomous manner the rules of moral conduct, without listening either to God or seeking the natural law fixed by Him in the cosmos.[96] The fact that wanting to be like God in regard to good and evil is a sin implies that it is God alone who establishes natural and moral law, who establishes what is good or bad. Now, the human being wants to be like Him, and independently establish such a distinction. It is autonomy (becoming a law to oneself) against heteronomy (receiving the law from others).

5.1.6. Loss of Innocence, Beginning of Concupiscence

The first immediate consequence that the text highlights is the loss of the original innocence, which was still intact at the end of the second chapter. Although the man and the woman were previously without evil or concupiscence, and indeed they were naked but felt no shame, now concupiscence, the first consequence of original sin, enters into the heart and mind of the human being and pollutes them: the two now recognize their own nudity and cover themselves. This deed should not be understood here positively as an expression of a healthy modesty (which is a virtue), but as a consequence of the evil

---

[95] In the human being "the disobedience was caused by pride": *ST* II-II, q. 163, a. 1 (our translation). It is to be recalled that pride is, according to Thomas Aquinas, the root of the sin of Satan. The devil thus succeeded in making the human being fall into the same trap that ruined him. The Angelic Doctor in the *Compendium theologiae*, I, ch. 190, writes that Eve sinned by pride, curiosity, gluttony, and through an erroneous evaluation of God by giving credit to the words of the devil; moreover, she sinned through disobedience.

[96] "The first man sinned principally by desiring to be like God with respect to the knowledge of good and evil, namely, willing to determine what is good and what is evil and, at the same time, to know in advance what would be good and evil for himself in the future" (*ST* II-II, q. 163, a. 2 [our translation]).

The Creator

look that from that day forward becomes a common and daily experience of being human. From this detail of the text, one intuits that original sin has led to the immediate loss of divine likeness, as we have said, and thus the loss of the original justice, with all of its gifts, both preternatural and supernatural.

5.1.7. "Natura Lapsa"

However, the human being did not return to the simple natural order: the following verses of the text show that the natural order (the image), which is never lost (not even in sin), is now damaged, polluted, and no longer as intact as it had been when it came forth from the hands of the Creator.[97]

1. Trial and Judgments

As soon as God "becomes aware" of what the man has done, a trial begins, and its defendants are the woman, the man, and the serpent. After a brief interrogation, in which the right of defense is granted to the man and the woman but not to the serpent, God issues His judgments. Here is the text:

> Then the Lord God said to the snake: / Because you have done this, / cursed are you / among all the animals, tame or wild; / On your belly you shall crawl, / and dust you shall eat / all the days of your life. / I will put enmity between you and the woman, / and between your offspring and hers; / They will strike at your head, / while you strike at their heel. / To the woman he said: / I will intensify your toil in childbearing; / in pain you shall bring forth children. / Yet your urge shall be for your husband, / and he shall rule over you. / To the man he said: Because you listened to your wife and ate from the tree about which I commanded you, You shall not eat from it, / Cursed is the ground because of you! / In toil you shall eat its yield / all the days of your life. / Thorns and thistles it shall bear for you, / and you shall eat the grass of the field. / By the sweat of your brow / you shall eat bread, / until you return

---

[97] The condition of the human being in sin comes to be called the "*natura lapsa*—fallen/corrupt nature" (Saint Augustine uses this expression several times, for example in *Sermo 182*.3.3). For a brief presentation, see Saint Thomas Aquinas, *Compendium theologiae* I, chs. 192–194. Without using the expression, the doctrine of *natura lapsa* is confirmed by the Council of Trent, *Decretum de Peccato Originali* (1546), §1 (DS 1511). Saint John Paul II discussed this theme in his *General Audience* of May 14, 1980: the text is accompanied by a long note, no. 1, which presents the phases of the Magisterial teaching about the original integrity of the human being, the *natura lapsa*, concupiscence, and death.

to the ground, / from which you were taken; / For you are dust, / and to dust you shall return." (Gen 3:14–19)

The serpent is cursed by God, and thus the devil is to be considered personally cursed. His title could be "the cursed by God," or even the enemy of God. The human being and the woman are not personally cursed and thus they are not to be considered so, even in sin. God condemns, without reservation, what they have done and condemns the tempting serpent without appeal, but He does not condemn the man and the woman without appeal. For the human beings the possibility of re-entering intimacy with God remains open: one day they will be able to be absolved by the same God who now condemns them. It should be noted that, speaking to the man, God says "Cursed is the ground because of you!" On the one hand, this confirms that creation undergoes punishment deriving from the sin of the human being (see Rom 8), but, on the other hand, one can argue the thesis that original sin is transmitted from generation to generation. In fact, we must not forget that Adam had been drawn from the earth (*adam* from *adamah*). He thus carries the curse in the flesh of his body and passes it on to his descendants.

2. Etiology

The reference to the fact that the serpent crawled on its belly instead of walking like other animals is a cultural element that scholars call "etiology."[98] What follows represents instead a true and proper prophecy, as the Christian tradition always interpreted it up until very recent times.

3. "Protoevangelium"

The "*protoevangelium*"[99] is the "first announcement" of the good news of

---

[98] From the Greek word *aitía*, cause. An etiology is the explanation of a cause. In this case, it is explained why the serpent, unlike all the other animals, crawls on the ground and has no legs. The answer of that ancient culture is this:because it was cursed by God. It is easy for us to laugh at these etiologies, but they reveal an inquisitive spirit about nature and an attentive observation of it, which we modern people have lost. They also reveal a deep religious sense. Of course, these answers are not satisfactory today, but their value also lies in the fact that they put the world and God in constant relation. And also from this standpoint, although we cannot accept the specific details of it, we modern people have much to learn from the spirit underlying the ancient etiologies.

[99] It seems that the first to use the term "protoevangelium"—used in our time also by the CCC §§410-411—was the Protestant theologian Lorenz Rhetius in 1638. As for the doctrine expressed by this term, it dates back to the time of the Fathers of the Church.

Christ. Verse 15 speaks of enmity between the woman and the serpent, and between their respective descendants. The traditional interpretation of this text is applied to Mary, adversary and conqueror of the devil, and to Christ as the descendant of the woman (Mary, the New Eve[100]), who will be the Redeemer of the human race from original sin. Even in a condemnation text such as Genesis 3, God's mercy is revealed, and this vehemently foretells the Incarnate Word's future work of redemption, a work in which the serpent—who believed himself to have achieved victory over the human race—will be definitively defeated by a descendant of the human race (who is also God): Jesus, the son of Mary.

5.1.8. The Effects of Original Sin on Human Relationships

Original sin does not only trigger a war (that is endless on this earth) between Satan and humanity and bring about the loss of the gifts of original justice—which is an effect of the loss of friendship with God, the absolutely graver wound—the original fault also produces two other series of negative consequences: the first is the cracking of relationships between human beings, as can be seen from the fact that now the relationship between Adam and Eve will be marked by the tension of the woman's instinct towards the man, and by man's dominion over the woman.[101] One can interpret this woman's instinct toward the man as an attempt to prevail over the male role, to take command of the family and no longer obey her husband, as the law of nature imposes. This is clearly a moral disorder. As is also the dominion that the man now exercises over the woman, overwhelming her. The man will become overbearing and unfortunately also violent toward the woman, both to contain the disorderly tendencies in her, and because he is a slave to his own passions;

---

[100] "For what the virgin Eve had bound fast through unbelief, this did the virgin Mary set free through faith" (Saint Irenaeus of Lyon, *Adversus haereses* 3.22.4, in *ANF*, vol. 1, trans. James Donaldson and Alexander Roberts (Peabody, MA: Hendrickson Publishers, Inc., 1994), 455. The ancient hymn *Ave Maris Stella* plays on the name of Eve (Latin *Eva*), specular of the word "Ave," the greeting of the Archangel to Mary. The hymn sings: "*Sumens illud Ave / Gabrielis ore / funda nos in pace / mutans Evae nomen*—Receiving that *Ave* / from the mouth of Gabriel / immerse us in peace / changing the name of *Eva*" (our translation).

[101] According to Saint John Paul II, *General Audience*, June 4, 1980, even the shame that Adam and Eve felt in being naked is indicative of the fact "that the original capacity to communicate to each other, of which Gen 2:25 speaks, is broken. The radical change of the meaning of original nudity leaves us to suppose negative transformations of that whole man-woman interpersonal relationship" (§2 [our translation]). Gen 3:16 is then interpreted in the sense that we are presenting here, in the *General Audience* of June 18, 1980.

he will now interpret the authority that nature gives him over his wife as a right to lord over and tyrannize her. Marital relationships and, in general, the relationships between the two sexes, are not entirely ruined but are sullied and wounded by these immoral attitudes: a consequence of sin.[102]

5.1.9. The Effects of Original Sin on Human Nature

1. Childbirth and Work

A second series of consequences regards the wound introduced into the material world by human sin. In the first place, this wound is experienced in the very material component of the human being: from this day forward, childbirth will be painful, and the man will find many difficulties in his work, which will be burdensome and often will lead to annoyance or even hatred. Giving birth and working are not a consequence of original sin but, because of sin, suffering and fatigue will inevitably mark them from that point forward.[103]

2. Diseases and Death

Sin also introduces sickness and every type of suffering that comes with it. The curse of God includes death: "and to dust you shall return." The doctrine of the Church teaches that, in the absence of original sin, Adam would not have died.[104] In fact, as Saint Paul says, "the body is dead because of sin" (Rom 8:10).[105] And Saint Ambrose: "To speak truly, death was not inherent in nature, but became natural only afterward. In fact, God did not establish death from the beginning,

---

[102] See Saint John Paul II, *Familiaris Consortio* (1981), §3 and §9.

[103] See Saint Augustine of Hippo, *De Genesi ad litteram* 8.8.15 (on work); 9.3.6 (on childbirth).

[104] CCC §1008 expresses the permanent doctrine: "*Death is a consequence of sin*. The Church's Magisterium, as authentic interpreter of the affirmations of Scripture and Tradition, teaches that death entered the world on account of man's sin [Cf. Gen 2:17; 3:3; 3:19; Wis 1:13; Rom 5:12; 6:23; DS 1511]. Even though man's nature is mortal, God had destined him not to die. Death was therefore contrary to the plans of God the Creator and entered the world as a consequence of sin [Cf. Wis 2:23-24]. 'Bodily death, from which man would have been immune had he not sinned' [Second Vatican Council, *Gaudium et Spes*, §18] is thus 'the last enemy' [1 Cor 15:26] of man left to be conquered." In a note, the CCC recalls the teaching concerning this theme of the Council of Trent (see DS 1511). The doctrine however is very ancient: see the Fifteenth Synod of Carthage, *De Peccato Originali* (418), ch. 1 (DS 222).

[105] Romans 8:10 is interpreted through this lens by St Augustine, *De Genesi ad litteram* 6.23.34.

but He gave it as a remedy. It was for the penalty of the first sin."[106]

This teaching of the Church has been challenged in recent times by some theologians, who say that it is absurd to think that Adam and Eve would have remained forever in Eden without ever reaching Heaven. However, this objection fails immediately if it is noted that in the absence of sin Adam certainly would not have died the death that we know, that is, the death marked by the fear of the afterlife, by the terror of being alone and, above all, by physical sufferings of old age and sickness. In fact, God says that from that point (i.e., sin) forward there will be sickness, sufferings, and difficulties of all types, and then He adds that there will also be death. Just as no one interprets the former as evidence of the fact that before sin Adam did not have a real body liable (in theory) to get sick, or that he did not need to work (now he will *continue* to do so, but with fatigue), so too no one should interpret the words of God concerning death as if no end of earthly life for the human being was foreseen by the Creator. Certainly, even without the sin of Adam and Eve, they and everyone who was born after them would have gone to Heaven one day. However, they would not have died, they would not have experienced the end of earthly life as a day of mourning, darkness, and suffering, but as the most beautiful, the brightest, the most serene, and the day for which they were most grateful.[107] After all, this is the way in which so many saints have died even after original sin: this because the saint is one who is so renewed by Christ the Redeemer that, while continuing to carry the weight of original sin (concupiscence), he or she has almost returned to a state of original justice (as a personal state, and certainly not in terms of the state of the surrounding world).[108] But also many other faithful, however simple, and often in the midst of great sufferings,

---

[106] St. Ambrose of Milan, *De excessu fratris sui Satyri* 2.47 (our translation).

[107] Saint Augustine, *De Genesi ad litteram* 9.6.10, speaks of being "removed to a better life not by death but by a transformation" (in *St. Augustine: The Literal Meaning of Genesis*, vol. 2, 76) And in the *De peccatorum meritis et remissione et de baptismo parvulorum* 1.2.2, he writes: "Adam, if he had not sinned, would have been transformed into a spiritual body and would have passed without the trial of death to that incorruptibility that is promised to those who are believers and holy" (our translation).

[108] A single example: Konrad von Marburg (d. 1233), confessor of St. Elizabeth of Hungary (d. 1231), recounts the last moments of her death in this way: "Before her death I heard her confession. When I asked what should be done about her goods and possessions, she replied that anything which seemed to be hers belonged to the poor. She asked me to distribute everything except one worn out dress in which she wished to be buried. When all this had been decided, she received the Body of our Lord. Afterward, until vespers, she spoke often of the holiest things she had heard in sermons. Then, she devoutly commended to God all who were sitting near her, and as if falling into a gentle sleep, she died" (*Epistula ad Pontificem*, in *Liturgy of the Hours*, "Office of Readings," November 17).

have experienced death with a smile on their face—so great is the power of redeeming grace and those who accept it in faith!

5.1.10. The Effects of Original Sin on the Cosmos

The wound introduced into the material cosmos also regards creation itself, as has already been stated. Sin mars the relationship between the human being and the cosmos, as well as that with natural processes. As for the former, it is evident that the human being often casts aside the hat of a loving steward and puts on that of its destroyer. However, the material world also attacks humanity (earthquakes, tidal waves, volcanic eruptions, animal attacks, etc.), wounding and killing it. Obviously, the world, not being animate like the human being, does not have any moral culpability in all of this. In the passage quoted above, Saint Paul says that creation was subjected not by its own will but by the fault of humanity (see Rom 8:19–22). However, in addition to creation's aggression toward humanity, it seems that the consequences of sin also concern the consistency and quality of natural processes. In a world that, in spite of everything, is still splendid—a visible proof of the greatness of its Creator—it seems that there has been a decrease and a degradation that is often verifiable in particular cases.

5.2. Romans 5

In the New Testament, the most important passage with respect to original sin is Romans 5:12–21:

> Therefore, just as through one person sin entered the world, and through sin, death, and thus death came to all, inasmuch as all sinned—for up to the time of the law, sin was in the world, though sin is not accounted when there is no law. But death reigned from Adam to Moses, even over those who did not sin after the pattern of the trespass of Adam, who is the type of the one who was to come.

> But the gift is not like the transgression. For if by that one person's transgression the many died, how much more did the grace of God and the gracious gift of the one person Jesus Christ overflow for the many. And the gift is not like the result of the one person's sinning. For after one sin there was the judgment that brought condemnation; but the gift, after many transgressions, brought acquittal. For if, by the transgression of one person, death came to reign through that one, how much more will those who receive the abundance of grace and of the gift of justification come to reign in life through the one

person Jesus Christ. In conclusion, just as through one transgression condemnation came upon all, so through one righteous act acquittal and life came to all. For just as through the disobedience of one person the many were made sinners, so through the obedience of one the many will be made righteous. The law entered in so that transgression might increase but, where sin increased, grace overflowed all the more, so that, as sin reigned in death, grace also might reign through justification for eternal life through Jesus Christ our Lord.

The Church has defined that the doctrine of original sin is certainly taught in this passage of Saint Paul.[109] After all, it is not difficult to recognize this with plain common sense as well. The verses immediately preceding this pericope speak of Christ's work of reconciliation, carried out through His death for us sinners. Verse 8, for example, says "But God proves his love for us in that while we were still sinners Christ died for us," and verse 10 even calls us "enemies" of God, because in effect we were rendered such by sin. Here, a reader of Saint Paul may have at least two questions: Why were we all enemies of God, if aside from Adam and Eve, no one else had disobeyed God? Moreover, if we were all sinners (that is, every single person of every era, no one excluded), how is it possible that the death of one man alone can save all? Verses 12–21 respond specifically to these fundamental questions.

5.2.1. In Light of Christ

The great novelty of this Pauline passage is not the teaching on original sin itself (which is already found in Gen 3), but its explanation in light of the mystery of Christ, an explanation that was obviously impossible in the Old Testament, before the Incarnation of the Word. Knowing the mystery of Christ incarnate, dead and risen, Saint Paul (and we along with him) can now better understand the mystery of original sin, for which Christ has come among us and died to heal.

5.2.2. The Spreading of Original Sin

The Apostle begins responding to the second question: Why are all human beings sinners? And he responds that this has happened because the sin of Adam and Eve is transmitted to all of their descendants. Let us recall from Genesis 3:20 that "The man called his wife 'Eve', because she became the

---

[109] See Council of Trent, *Decretum de Peccato Originali*, §4 (DS 1514).

mother of all the living." From the first created couple all other human beings were born and are born marked by their fault, which then is transmitted through physical generation.[110] Parents transmit original sin to their children, as they have received it from their parents. History has happened this way, and it will happen this way until the end of time. This better explains what we said above, recalling the teaching of Pius XII on monogenism; the Pope said that he did not see how the other hypothesis (polygenism) could harmonize with the doctrine of the transmission of original sin through generation.

5.2.3. Originating and Originated Sin

This also allows us to recall the known distinction between "originating original sin" and "originated original sin," where the first expression indicates the sin of Adam and Eve, while the second refers to the sin itself inasmuch as it is transmitted to their descendants. Every human being receives from the very first instant of his or her conception the mark of this negative inheritance. In this regard, it is helpful to note two numbers of the *Catechism*:

> How did the sin of Adam become the sin of all his descendants? The whole human race is in Adam (*"sicut unum corpus unius hominis"*) "as one body of one man" [St. Thomas Aquinas, *De Malo* 4, 1]. By this "unity of the human race" all men are implicated in Adam's sin, as all are implicated in Christ's justice. Still, the transmission of original sin is a mystery that we cannot fully understand. But we do know by Revelation that Adam had received original holiness and justice not for himself alone, but for all human nature. By yielding to the tempter, Adam and Eve committed a *personal sin*, but this sin affected the *human nature* that they would then transmit *in a fallen state* [Cf. Council of Trent: DS 1511–1512]. It is a sin which will be transmitted by propagation to all mankind, that is, by the transmis-

---

[110] See Fifteenth Synod of Carthage, *De Peccato Originali* (418), can. 2 (DS 223); Council of Trent, *Decretum de Peccato Originali*, §3 (DS 1513); Council of Trent, *Decretum de Iustificatione*, ch. 3 (DS 1523); Pius XI, *Casti Connubii* (1930) (DS 3705). When CCC §404 says that sin is spread by "propagation," it does not intend to deny that this propagation occurs concretely through generation. It only wants to refute the theory that sin is spread through imitation, as the Pelagians of each age hold. Thus, in fact, Saint Paul VI uses the term in *Credo of the People of God*, §16: "We therefore hold, with the Council of Trent, that original sin is transmitted with human nature, 'not by imitation, but by propagation.'" Finally, it must be emphasized that although original sin is passed on through generation, this does not mean that the human reproductive act is in itself a sin.

The Creator

sion of a human nature deprived of original holiness and justice and that is why original sin is called "sin" only in an analogical sense: it is a sin "contracted" and not "committed"—a state and not an act (CCC §404).[111]

Although it is proper to each individual [Cf. Council of Trent: DS 1513], original sin does not have the character of a personal fault in any of Adam's descendants. It is a deprivation of original holiness and justice, but human nature has not been totally corrupted: it is wounded in the natural powers proper to it, subject to ignorance, suffering, and the dominion of death, and inclined to sin—an inclination to evil that is called concupiscence (CCC §405).

5.2.4. In the Face of Death

Saint Paul teaches that sin has also introduced death into the world, as we have already seen, and thus everyone dies because everyone has sinned (in Adam). Death is empirical proof that we participate in that sin that merited God's condemnation of death. All those who die are thus sinners.[112] It also follows from this that all human beings are called to accept the necessity of death (and to live accordingly), because they are born sinners. It is clear that this universal call to accept the fact of our future death and to modify our life on the basis of it is not met with consistent behavior from every single

---

[111] On the basis of this text, it can also be argued that the thesis on the extent of sin by "propagation" does not exactly correspond to the concept of diffusion by "physical generation." It is enough to say, as here, that Adam was established as the head of humanity and that is why his sin was passed on to all of his descendants, without postulating the necessity of a direct genetic line of all people from two human beings. Although this explanation is acceptable, another element of this same text of the *Catechism* compels us to still prefer the classical thesis. It actually says, "It is a sin which will be transmitted by propagation to all mankind, that is, by the transmission of a human nature deprived of original holiness and justice." How does the transmission of human nature occur if not through generation? Moreover, the concept of "transmission to one's own descendants" is better explained with the thesis of a transmission by generation. Still, the CCC says "this sin affected *the human nature* that they would then transmit in a *fallen state*." With the thesis of a universal propagation based solely on the chief role of Adam, we can explain well that human beings are born *without* the grace given to Adam. But this does not explain as well why they are born *with* a wounded humanity. Therefore, the other explanation is possible, but the more classical one still appears better.

[112] Obviously, Christ and Mary are exempt. We can, however, pose the question: Given that they have not contracted original sin, why did they die? For the response, see Chapters Four and Seven.

individual. This is because one of the paradoxical consequences that sin leaves in us is precisely that of wanting to deny the existence of sin and its most dramatic consequence, death. But this also happens because original sin is a mystery of which the non-Christian is unaware. All human beings experience frailty, suffering, and all the realities deriving from original sin, but only Christians know its cause. Nonetheless, many religions contemplate doctrines that in some respects mirror the Christian doctrine of original sin. Thus, it can be said that "what divine revelation makes known to us [concerning sin] agrees with experience. Examining his heart, man finds that he has inclinations toward evil too, and is engulfed by manifold ills which cannot come from his good Creator."[113]

5.2.5. "In Quo Omnes Peccaverunt"

The small phrase "inasmuch as all sinned" of verse 12 was always the center of attention. Among authors of antiquity, we must remember Saint Augustine, who sees original sin revealed here, which passes from Adam to all of his descendants. Saint Augustine makes use of the Latin version of this text, which goes "*in quo omnes peccaverunt.*" He understands the "*in quo*" in an entirely legitimate way as "in which," and thus he rendered the meaning of the phrase in this way: in Adam all have sinned[114]—and behold the clear affirmation of original sin. In the twentieth century, however, various exegetes believed that the interpretation of Saint Augustine was not justified on the basis of the original Greek text of the Letter to the Romans (where the Latin *in quo* corresponds to a Greek phrase that is difficult to translate: *eph'ho*). Therefore, according to various scholars, the last part of verse 12 would not just be about Adam, but would have to be understood as referring to all human beings and thus should be translated: "for the fact that all have sinned"; or "the condition being such that all have sinned."[115] If we refer, however briefly, to this theme for specialists, it is because from these exegetical studies some theolo-

---

[113] Second Vatican Council, *Gaudium et Spes*, §13.

[114] See St. Augustine of Hippo, *De Genesi ad litteram* 10.16.29.

[115] However, as such this reading would run the risk of endorsing the Pelagian thesis, in which sin would only be transmitted to the human being if each individual sinned. Rather, the doctrine of the Church teaches that the sin of Adam stains every human being, well before he or she is able to consciously take any action: to the sin of Adam "everyone born, without exception, is subject before being liberated through baptism" (*Epistula tractoria ad Ecclesias Orientales* [410] [DS 231]). This is why "even little children, who in themselves have not yet been able to commit any sins, are in consequence baptized truly for the remission of sins" (Fifteenth Synod of Carthage, *De Peccato Originali*, can. 2 [DS 223]).

gians have come to conclude things of the sort: "Original sin is an invention of Saint Augustine!" Thus, they forget that this doctrine is already found in Genesis 3, and in other biblical passages, and that the patristic Tradition, even before Augustine, understood Romans 5 in the same way as he did.[116] The Council of Trent then declared unequivocally that the doctrine of original sin is no doubt expressed in Romans 5. In fact, however one wants to understand verse 12, the doctrine emerges clearly from the whole cited passage.

But what is meant by "death reigned from Adam to Moses, even over those who did not sin after the pattern of the trespass of Adam" (that is, already before the promulgation of the Law); or by the passage "by that one person's transgression the many died"? Indeed, what is meant by these three claims of Saint Paul: "by the transgression of one person, death came to reign through that one"; "through one transgression condemnation came upon all"; "through the disobedience of one person the many were made sinners"? It is clear that if a theologian has decided, *a priori*, to deny the dogma of original sin, he or she will always find a way to circumvent these or other expressions that are clear as day. The dogma of original sin is too important a matter to be denied or even softened. It is at the center of the doctrines that better clarify, as far as possible, the mystery of human life and death, and also the mystery of the redemption carried out by the incarnate Word. "The Church, which has the mind of Christ [Cf. *1 Cor* 2:16], knows very well that we cannot tamper with the revelation of original sin without undermining the mystery of Christ" (CCC §389). This doctrine is not a human creation—neither that of Saint Augustine or anyone else. It is part of the supernatural Revelation of God, clearly attested in Scripture and the Tradition.

---

[116] It is true that St. Augustine, being committed to the long fight against the Pelagian heretics, was the one among the Fathers who had best developed this doctrine, and the very expression "original sin" might be traced back to him. This does not mean that he had invented the doctrine and that, therefore, it was not revealed. Rather, it already belonged to the Apostolic Fathers, then to the holy Fathers Irenaeus, Cyprian, and Ambrose, as well as Tertullian, all of whom wrote prior to Saint Augustine. Saint Cyprian, for example, presided over a council in Carthage in 252, in which it was established that young children were to be baptized for the remission not of their sins, evidently nonexistent, but of the sins of others (*aliena peccata*). Saint Augustine was accused already during his life of having "invented" the dogma of original sin. He defended himself, saying: "It was not I who invented original sin, which the Catholic faith believed from ancient times. You on the other hand, who deny it, are undoubtedly a new heretic" (*De nuptiis et concupiscentia* 2.12.25 [our translation]). In *Contra Iulianum*, 1.3.5–19, furthermore, he cites a wide array of testimonies that precede him, which taught the doctrine of original sin. We can mention, for example, St. Pacian of Barcelona (d. ca. 391), *Sermo de baptismo* 5, which decades before Augustine, interpreted "*in quo omnes peccaverunt*" in exactly the same way.

5.2.6. Adam and Christ

While Genesis 3 is concerned with giving a symbolic narration of the historical event of original sin, Saint Paul instead only takes up its significance within salvation history, and he does this by contrasting the two figures—and especially the different behaviors—of Adam and Christ, who are explicitly put into relation with each other.[117] Adam is the first man, who sinned and condemned us all. Christ—as 1 Cor 15:47 says—is the second man (it can also be translated as "Second Adam"), the one who not only did not sin (and thus lived in his humanity how Adam should have lived) but is also focused on freeing his human brothers and sisters, all descendants of the first Adam, from the consequences of Adam's sin. It needs to be recognized that this implies the doctrine of universal salvation in Jesus Christ. As all people, and not only Christians, have become sinners on account of Adam, so all those who are saved—even those who, in their earthly life, for reasons independent of their will, were not Christians—are saved only by the work of Christ, which has universal value (see Acts 4:12). Thus, the universal character of original sin also speaks of the universality of the redemptive and salvific work of Christ the Lord.

5.2.7. The Universality of both the Condemnation and the Redemption

Considered from this perspective, the consistency of the doctrine of original sin is further reinforced. In fact, Saint Paul does not have as his primary aim here to describe, much less defend, this doctrine. Here the Apostle is focused above all on Christ's work of reconciliation, and he frames it within the great history of salvation that begins with Adam (with the announcement of the "*protoevangelium*"). It is interesting that in making the comparison between Adam and Christ, Saint Paul makes use of the doctrine of original sin as something already known and established (*tranquilla possessio*). Here he responds above all to the question about Christ: Why is it that one saves all? This is his primary interest. In responding, he essentially gives this reply: if it was possible that all were condemned by the work of one alone, would it not then be possible that all come to be saved by the work of one alone?[118] Thus,

---

[117] On the relationship between Adam and Christ in Romans 5, see Benedict XVI, *General Audience*, December 3, 2008.

[118] To those who object that it would not be "just" that the sin of the first parents be passed to inculpable descendants, we should counter that—from their perspective—neither is it

The Creator

the reality that all of humanity is sinful in Adam is not the fact to be demonstrated here, but it is a reality that it is assumed as obvious, and it is a fact that Saint Paul connects to the new teaching concerning Christ the Redeemer. Let us read a text by Saint Pacian:

> Someone will perhaps say to me: It was just that the sin of Adam passed onto those who came after, because they descended from him through generation. However, have we perhaps been generated by Christ so that salvation descends to us from Him? Indeed, this is the case and it will be understood immediately. In the last times Christ took from Mary his soul and his flesh. This is the flesh that He came to save, which was not abandoned in the underworld, and which He united to his spirit and made his own. These are the nuptials of the Lord, carried out with one flesh alone, so that Christ and the Church, according to that great mystery, would be two in one flesh. From these nuptials the Christian people is born, while the Spirit of the Lord descends from on high. The heavenly seed is infused and united to the substance of our souls; we thus begin to develop in the womb, then, coming to the light, we enter into the life that is given to us by Christ. For this reason, the Apostle says: "The first man, Adam, became a living being, the last Adam a life-giving spirit" (1 Cor 15:45). In this way Christ generates in the Church by means of his priests, as is expressed by the same Apostle: "For I became your father in Christ Jesus through the gospel" (1 Cor 4:15).[119]

"just" that the merits of the Passion *of Christ* benefit us in atoning for *our* sins. Here the wise observation of Job finds a new application, from a rereading with the "eyes" of the New Testament conception of God: "We accept good things from God; should we not accept evil?" (Job 2:10; similar passages: Ex 4:11; Deut 32:39; 1 Sam 2:6; Lam 3:38; Sir 11:14; Isa 45:7). There is an ontological solidarity among human beings, as natural in Adam as it is supernatural in Christ, which comes to be denied by contemporary individualism, which believes the connections between human beings to be only accidental relations and not constitutive of the being of the human person. We will come back to the topic again in the following chapters. In the meantime, we can read what Saint Paul VI teaches in *Indulgentiarum Doctrina* (1967), §4–5: "There reigns among men, by the hidden and benign mystery of the divine will, a supernatural solidarity whereby the sin of one harms the others just as the holiness of one also benefits the others.... A testimony of this solidarity is manifested in Adam himself, whose sin is passed on through propagation to all men. But of this supernatural solidarity the greatest and most perfect principle, foundation, and example is Christ himself to communion with Whom God has called us. Indeed Christ 'committed no sin,' 'suffered for us,' 'was wounded for our iniquities, bruised for our sins ... by his bruises we are healed.'"

[119] Saint Pacian of Barcelona, *Sermo de baptismo* 5–6 (our translation).

5.2.8. Abundance of Sin, Overabundance of Grace

The Apostle, in instituting the parallel between Adam and Christ, nonetheless adds that the two respective effects are similar (in their opposition), but not of equal value:

> But the gift is not like the transgression. For if by that one person's transgression the many died, how much more did the grace of God and the gracious gift of the one person Jesus Christ overflow for the many. And the gift is not like the result of the one person's sinning. For after one sin there was the judgment that brought condemnation; but the gift, after many transgressions, brought acquittal. For if, by the transgression of one person, death came to reign through that one, how much more will those who receive the abundance of grace and of the gift of justification come to reign in life through the one person Jesus Christ. (Rom 5:15–17).

We cannot explain this passage point by point here, but after this passage Saint Paul himself summarizes what is most important with the words, "where sin increased, grace overflowed all the more" (v. 20). This does not only mean that in Christ we have restoration in the order ruined by the sin of Adam and the restitution of the divine likeness that humanity had lost. In Him we have even more: the grace given to us in Christ is a grace even superior to what was received in Eden. Sin has been abundant (how much it has multiplied and expanded over the millennia!), but grace has been superabundant. The human being is elevated in Christ to a dignity even greater than that of original justice. In other words, fallen nature (*"natura lapsa"*) is not simply brought back to its original state of intact nature (*"natura integra"*)—as it came forth from the hands of God—nor is it brought to the state of nature elevated by grace, as in Eden. The grace of Christ exceeds the grace of friendship with God that was given to Adam and Eve in Eden.

5.2.9. Consequences regarding Baptism

The recognition of the general involvement of humanity in the sin of Adam, and the universal value of Christ the redeemer, also implies two consequences for the Sacrament of Baptism: (1) all human beings are called to receive Baptism, which, by grafting men on to Christ, gives salvation (Matt 28:19: "Go, therefore, and make disciples of all nations, baptizing them in the name of the Father, and of the Son, and of the holy Spirit")—from this first consequence is also derived the importance of the mission of evangelizing the nations; (2) it gives support to the Church's practice of baptizing babies: though they cannot have committed any personal sin—because there cannot be sin where there is no awareness—the Church baptizes them in order to wash away original sin—the reason why Christ instituted Baptism (see Chapter Ten). It is no accident that Saint Paul dedicates the verses that follow in Romans 6 to the theme of Baptism.

5.2.10. "Felix Culpa"

The two preceding paragraphs, read together, bring us back to the theme of divine Providence. God certainly does not will evil but permits it both to respect human freedom and because, in his Providence, He is capable of drawing an even greater good from the evil. This general law of Providence is seen applied in a supreme way and verified in the case of the original sin of Adam and Christ's work of redemption. The *Praeconium Paschale* ("Easter Proclamation"), the long hymn that the deacon sings or recites on the Easter Vigil, makes use of the sublime expression *"felix culpa"* ("happy fault"), which summarizes everything we are saying. A fault can never be happy in itself, because it is evil. However, in this case, because of the guilt, we have received the immeasurable gift of the descent of the Word among us (He would not have come in the flesh if Adam had not sinned: see Chapter Two), and we have been elevated to a dignity that humanity had never known. The *Catechism* summarizes these aspects very well:

> *But why did God not prevent the first man from sinning?* St. Leo the Great responds, "Christ's inexpressible grace gave us blessings better than those the demon's envy had taken away" [St. Leo the Great, *Sermo* 73, 4: PL 54, 396]; and St. Thomas Aquinas wrote, "There is nothing to prevent human nature's being raised up to something greater, even after sin; God permits evil in order to draw forth some greater good. Thus St. Paul says, 'Where sin increased, grace abounded all the more'; and the Exsultet sings, 'O happy fault that earned so great, so glorious a Redeemer!'" [St. Thomas Aquinas, *STh* III, 1, 3, *ad* 3; cf. *Rom* 5:20]. (CCC §412)

6. THE BIPOLARITY OF THE DOCTRINE OF CREATION

Many elements emerge from the present chapter in which the principle of

The Bipolarity of the Doctrine of Creation

et-et may be appreciated. Without claiming to have compiled a complete list, let us recall only a few:

1) Creation is composed both of visible and invisible realities. The invisible realities are superior in the hierarchical order.
2) Consequently, there are both simple, purely spiritual beings, and material beings.
3) The human being, almost a middle term between the two above-mentioned orders of creatures, is constituted with an eminently synthetic nature in his or her bipolarity: the human is unitary but composite. While being a single person, a human being's nature is inseparably composed of soul and body. The soul is more important than the body (but without the body there is no human being).
4) Creation is both an originary moment in which God draws all things from nothing, and God's continuous creation, or permanent conservation, of the existence of the individual creatures.
5) Humanity is differentiated: it is both male and female. The single and indivisible human nature has within it this insuppressible bipolarity. Here, the hierarchy between the two depends on the point of view. If viewed from the standpoint of authority, the husband has—according to Scripture—authority over the wife. However, if looked at in relation to creation, the woman prevails, because her generative function has greater likeness to the creatio continua, which stands over the first creative act. Thus, if there is need of both a man and a woman for the creatio "*ex nihilo*" of a new human being, it is nonetheless the woman who maintains the child in being during pregnancy and then, after birth, nurses and cares for the child. However, it is necessary to recall—especially in this case that deals with persons—that the hierarchy existing between members of the *et-et* does not imply that the second member is a mere accessory or of little value. The second member always remains necessary and important.
6) Divine Providence is active both in the cosmos and in the history of salvation, with the latter being the primary term of this bipolarity.[120]

---

[120] This is at the origin of the fact that the liturgical calendar of the Church integrates elements of both cosmic time (the day and night, the week, the seasons, the Ember Days, and the year) and salvation history, especially the "Christological mysteries," such as the birth of Jesus, the baptism at the Jordan, the Transfiguration, the Passion, Easter, etc. In correspondence with the hierarchy that exists—at the level of the interventions of Providence—between cosmic and historical aspects, the historical-salvific events are also more important than cosmic rhythms in the liturgical calendar. This explains why in the two

The Creator

We leave it to the reader to seek out other synthetic dualities relating to the theme treated in this chapter. It seems to us that our emphases indicate with sufficient clarity that the principle of *et-et* is evidently present in the theology of creation.

---

earthly hemispheres the solemnities and liturgical feasts remain fixed on the same date even though the seasons are inverted. For example, the feast of Easter—which has clear symbolic links with spring—is held on the same date in the southern hemisphere, even though it is autumn there.

4

The Redeemer

It becomes clear from what was said in the previous chapter that human beings find themselves, after Adam's sin and because of it, in a different condition than what God had planned for them. God's plan foresaw that the human being, created good and gifted with the grace of the state of original justice, would persevere in obedience to God's law until one day being assumed into the eternal glory of Heaven. This growth of the human being toward the ultimate supernatural end would have happened not in opposition to the natural aspects of his or her life and the attainment of natural human ends, but in perfect harmony with them. Moreover, the ordered growth of the human being in goodness and in holiness would not have been the simple fruit of his or her own efforts, but of the cooperation between the human and the divine: both the gift of grace from on high and the free decision of the human being from below. Saint Irenaeus of Lyon (d. ca. 202) says that before sin, the Son and the Holy Spirit, whom he calls the two Hands of the Father, accompanied the creature along this path of growth in perfection.[1] However, when the first sin was committed, everything seemed lost. Adam and Eve were outside of Eden, outside of the state of grace, and even the material

---

[1] See Saint Irenaeus of Lyon, *Adversus haereses* 5.5.1; 5.16.1; 5.28.4. With a certain *vis polemica*, Saint Augustine of Hippo (d. 430), *Enarrationes in Psalmos* 118.18.1, emphasizes that the image of the Hands is not to be understood in the literal or anthropomorphic sense, but as a reference to the work of God, which is always done with/through the Word.

cosmos was marked, on account of them, by the wound of sin. Faced with such crooked lines, how can Providence draw straight? Does God not then have to give up on his plan for the "divinization" of the human being?

The response to these questions is not comprised of concepts but of a Person: the Person of the incarnate Word, Jesus of Nazareth, the Messiah (i.e., Christ).[2] God carries out His plan in Him. Providence finds a truly wondrous mode of preserving God's plan for creation (the divine plan of salvation is one and one alone!). God does not change His salvific plan, but He carries it out in a new way, through the Incarnation, life, Passion, Death, Resurrection, and Ascension of the incarnate Son Jesus Christ and, subsequently, through the sending of the Consoler, the Spirit. Therefore, we must now focus on the work carried out by the two Hands of the Father of putting humankind back on track so that it may resume the royal road of grace. We shall dedicate this chapter and the one that follows to this theme, first discussing the Son, and then the Holy Spirit.

1. Jesus Christ, True God and True Man

1.1. Salvation and Redemption

It was said in Chapter Two that the theological explanation that seems to better correspond to Revelation is the one according to which the Word would not have been incarnate if, hypothetically, Adam had not sinned. This does not imply that the Word would not have been the Savior of Adam and the whole human race if the first parent had not disobeyed. Here, an important clarification concerning the meaning of the terms "to save" and "to redeem" needs to be introduced. They are often used as synonyms: to say that Jesus is the Savior and Redeemer of human beings is basically the same. This is true, because the work of salvation and redemption *de facto* happens as in a unitary whole in the life of Jesus Christ. However, *de jure*, the two terms should be distinguished.

1.1.1. Salvation

"To save" means to lift up and bring to fulfillment. *Salvus*, in Latin, indicates being well. The Roman greeting "*salve!*" corresponds to "be well!" God saves

---

[2] "The real novelty of the New Testament lies not so much in new ideas as in the figure of Christ himself, who gives flesh and blood to those concepts—an unprecedented realism" (Benedict XVI, *Deus Caritas est* [2005], §12).

us in the sense that He makes us be well. However, this well-being should not be understood in the secular sense of well-being, but rather as the true and definitive well-being, which coincides with being eternally and not just provisionally fulfilled and happy. This can only happen when we reach our final supernatural end in God. Paradise is our final (or "eschatological") end, and God's work of salvation consists in this: He gives us the grace that allows us, if we cooperate with it, to be elevated and brought to our definitive fulfillment in Heaven. The Word is the Savior of the human being, whether or not the latter sins. In fact, the human being is not capable of reaching eschatological fulfillment by his or her own efforts alone. Thus, Saint Irenaeus says that the Word and the Spirit accompany Adam in his growth. It is an image in a way taken from the natural world, where mothers and fathers accompany the good growth of their children. It is extremely interesting that Irenaeus uses an expression that indicates the particular way in which the human being cooperates with the grace of the Word. He says that the human being, to obtain the salvation accomplished by God, must live *logikos*, that is, logically, or according to the *Logos*.[3] Various doctrinal contents that we have already discussed are implied in this expression.

In summary: God creates with and through the *Logos*, thus creation is *logical*. The logic of creation is expressed in the natural law, which is logical and rational. The human being is gifted with a small created *logos*: the rational soul. With intelligence, the human being is capable of recognizing the logic of the law of nature and living according to it. Adam, prompted by divine grace, could only live logically, that is, according to God's law. Thus, sin, in addition to being an act of pride and rebellion, is also an act of foolishness: an absolutely illogical behavior. In Eden, the *Logos* accompanied, along with the Spirit, the ordered and "logical" growth of the human being in the good, with this growth aimed at sanctification and a definitive "deification" in Heaven.

But with sin everything seems lost. How can man reach eschatological Paradise if he is now driven out of the earthly paradise? How does he reach eternal glory having lost earthly grace? How does he sign an eternal spousal agreement with God in Heaven, if man is no longer His friend on earth, and is even His enemy (see Rom 5:10)?

---

[3] See Saint Irenaeus of Lyon, *Adversus haereses* 5.8.2. Even earlier in Saint Justin Martyr (d. ca. 165), the expression "to live according to the Word [*kata Logon*]" is found (*II Apologia* 8.2).

1.1.2. Redemption

The divine solution to the human situation consists in the mystery of the Incarnation of the Word, entirely directed at the salvation of the human being, as the Creed states: "For us men and for our salvation."[4] However, could not the Word also carry out this salvation without becoming incarnate and dying? He certainly could have, because He already did so before original sin. What changed was not the divine power of the Word and the Sanctifying Spirit. What changed was the receptive capacity of the creature, who went from being righteous to being sinful. Sin can be compared to the sale of a slave. The human being, on account of not wanting to serve God, becomes a slave to sin (see John 8:34). We know that if someone wants to re-possess a man who has been sold as a slave, he must buy the man back. This is the meaning of the word "*redimere*," which in Latin means to buy back. The work of redemption is the work with which Christ buys us back, redeeming us from sin, death, and Satan. For this reason, Scripture speaks of the Blood of Christ as the "price of our redemption": the Blood, that is, the life (see Lev 17:11) of the Lord, is the highest price paid by God to buy us back. Now, the entire life of Christ, and especially the Holy Triduum of His Passion, Death, and Resurrection, is the mystery of redemption, recapitulation, and the salvation of the human race. Thus, it is clear that salvation and redemption are *de facto* synonymous, and one can practically use either expression indifferently to refer to the work of the Lord Jesus. This happens because the way in which God has *de facto* carried out the salvation of humanity is in His incarnate Son. We must not forget, however, that the Incarnation has a primarily redemptive purpose: Christ was born to die for us![5]

---

[4] First Council of Constantinople (381) (DS 150).

[5] Tertullian of Carthage (d. ca. 230), *De carne Christi* 6.6 (previously cited), summarizes in two words the meaning of the coming of the Word among us: "*mori missus*—sent to die." In this sense, we clearly see—as Saint Bonaventure (d. 1274) suggested—how the preference for the Thomistic position concerning the question of *cur Deus homo* reveals the greatness of God's love for us much better. Let us present once again (but this time in the original Latin) the citation of the Seraphic Doctor that was offered in the second chapter: the conditional thesis "*fidelem affectum magis inflammat. Plus enim excitat devotionem animae fidelis, quod Deus sit incarnatus ad delenda scelera sua quam propter consummanda opera inchoata*—it more greatly inflames the affection of the faithful. In fact, it excites more the devotion of the faithful soul that God became incarnate to erase her sins than it would to carry to completion His work" (*In III Sententiarum* 1.2.2). The Scotists say that their position better reveals the love of God, who from eternity has predestined us to be saved in the *incarnate* Son. We say, rather, and the opinion seems to us to be more expressive of Scripture and Tradition, that the Father has predestined us to be saved by the work

1.2. The Value of Christ's Life

1.2.1. The Will of the Father, the Will of Jesus

Although Jesus' Paschal Triduum represents the summit of the work of salvation and redemption, it is with His entire earthly life that Christ has redeemed us. In the Passion and death on the cross, the Lord has poured out His Blood to the last drop. This expresses in the most dramatic and visible way what the Lord did from the first instant of his conception in the virginal womb of Mary. The Lord came to die, but this death did not happen only on the day in which He commended His spirit on the cross; the entire life of Jesus was a continual death. For this reason, we must recall again that Jesus is the Second Adam (see 1 Cor 15:47), that is, the first man after the first Adam who appeared on the earth without being contaminated by sin.[6] He is thus free from the stain of sin, Immaculate.[7] This means that when we speak of

---

of His Son (the *Logos*) and the Holy Spirit (His two Hands). Being that the "condition" of sin has occurred, the plan of God is maintained in a new form: it will always be the Son to save us, but in a new way, through His Incarnation. To the Scotists, this opinion appears harsh because—they say—our sin would obligate the Word to become incarnate. But the Thomist position does not speak in any way of obligation: the Word does not have to become incarnate at all, just as He is not obligated to redeem us or even to save us. Everything is a gift of grace and thus our position best emphasizes the love God has for us. Moreover, even if the Thomist position appears harsh, the Scotist position is actually much harsher, because for Scotists the Word, who would become incarnate anyway, would then be "forced" to undergo the "accidental" Passion. In conclusion, it must also be said that Thomists and Scotists agree on what remains absolutely central: Jesus Christ is the only Savior and Redeemer of the world. The dispute focuses on what purpose is pre-eminent in the Incarnation: the Scotists say that the Incarnation is first and foremost salvific and then, as a result of the specific situation of humankind, also redemptive. The Thomists say that the primary purpose of the Incarnation is the redemptive one, since the Word would have carried out the salvific work (however concretely achieved by Christ) without the Incarnation, in the hypothesis in which humanity had not sinned.

[6] "He in fact took on a human nature without sin, in the purity that it had in the innocent state" (*ST* III, q. 14, a. 3 [our translation]). Chronologically, the first human being without original sin who appeared on the earth after Adam is obviously Mary. But her Immaculate Conception was due to the anticipation of the future merits of her Son (see Chapter Seven); thus, even if she is the first in chronological order, Mary is second in the axiological order.

[7] "Immaculate, He [Christ] willed to arise from the Immaculate woman, because he had to wash away everyone's stains—*de . . . immaculata immaculatus procederet, omnium maculas purgaturus*" (Saint Bernard of Clairvaux, *Sermo II super Missus est* 1 [our translation]). We can also recall the Roman Canon, which defines the consecrated Species on the altar, that is, the Eucharistic Jesus, "*hostiam puram, hostiam sanctam, hostiam immaculatam*—pure victim, holy victim, spotless [immaculate] victim."

The Redeemer

His "death," we must recall that for Jesus death is not the ultimate experience, which is lived in darkness, doubt, terror, and pain. Dying, for Him, means giving His life to obey the Father, what Adam should have done and what every human being should do. This pertains to His humanity. Since He is not only a man (see John 1:14), we have already said that in His case (and this time, only in His case!), dying is not simply obediently accepting the will of God, but it is deciding to give His life—a life over which death has no power (see John 10:17–18). The entire life of Christ was lived as dying:[8] as obedience to the will of the Father who delivered Him to death for our salvation (see Rom 8:32), and as a free decision of the incarnate Word to give His life as the price for our redemption (see John 10:15; 1 Pet 1:18–19). The will of the Father that sends His Son into the world as a victim for the atonement of our sins (see Rom 8:32; 1 John 4:10; etc.) and the will of the Son to give his life for this same purpose (see Matt 20:28; 26:28; John 10:14-18; etc.) coincide perfectly, and actually are one will alone. The Father and Son are two "consubstantial"[9] Persons, that is, Two who are the same nature, who also have the same will, which is why there cannot be any opposition between what the Father wills and what the Son wills. In Jesus, both God and man, this will is lived with a twofold act, corresponding to His twofold nature: human and divine. As God, the Word wants to give His own life freely; as man, with His human will, He wants to obey the divine will. Thus, Christ's life, understood as a constant will to give His own life until the end, is the fruit of the convergent action of two wills present in the one Person: the divine will and the human will, which are proper to the two natures of Christ, Whose Person is that of the Word or the eternal Son of the Father (see further along, the Third Council of Constantinople).

---

[8] Based on the example of Christ, we understand one of the fragments of Saint Irenaeus of Lyon, in which we read: "The business of the Christian is nothing else than to be ever preparing for death" (Frag. 11, in *ANF*, vol. 1, trans. James Donaldson and Alexander Roberts [Peabody, MA: Hendrickson Publishers, Inc., 1994], 570). Dying indicates the death that is obedience to the divine will, of which the perfect exemplar is Christ: "The Son calls himself a servant of the Father because of His obedience to the Father"; "The sin committed because of the tree was taken away by the obedience accomplished on the tree, obedience to God by which the Son of man was nailed to the tree," which is why "Evil is to disobey God; good, rather, is to obey" (Irenaeus, *Demonstratio apostolicae praedicationis* 51 and 33 [our translation]).

[9] See Council of Nicaea I (DS 125).

1.2.2. One Man Alone Saves All

This explains why the actions of Jesus' life have a universal salvific value. One objection, which was posited by the work of the philosopher Gotthold Ephraim Lessing (d. 1781), concerns the universal application of the salvific effect of the life of an individual, Jesus of Nazareth, to the existence of all other human beings, of every time and place.[10] When it is affirmed that the salvation carried out by Jesus Christ has universal value, it indeed means precisely this: the work of a man, an individual human being, who lived twenty centuries ago for around thirty years in a rather remote location of the Roman Empire, impacts the life of every other individual, living in every time and place. Moreover, this is not just speaking of a moral effect, as if the life of Christ merely represented a good example to imitate (in this case, at least so far, its influence would not be considered universal, though universality would in theory remain achievable in the future). When we Christians speak of the universal salvific value of the life of Christ, we give the expression a higher value than a purely moral one, while not excluding that. We affirm that the work of Christ objectively produces something new, which concerns all of humanity, at least from the standpoint of the offer, if not its acceptance. This means that the life of Christ adds a new element into the world and history and that it is offered to every single individual, whether that person knows it or not, and whether that person accepts it or not.[11]

This is possible because Jesus is not only a man, but He is the incarnate Word, and thus in Him, in His unique Person, there are two natures: divine and human. The human acts of Christ, then, are not the acts of just any human being, which always have a limited value, however great and famous such a person might be. The human acts of Christ belong to the Person of

---

[10] In chapter 15 of his 1777 work, Über den Beweis des Geistes und der Kraft, Lessing wrote: "Contingent truths of the historical type can never become the proof of necessary truths of the rational type.... This, precisely this, is the ugly broad ditch [*garstig breiter Graben*] that I cannot cross, despite the fact that often and with every effort I have tried to jump over it" (our translation). Therefore, even the historical action of Jesus could not—in his judgment—in any way be elevated to be the truth and permanent reality of human history and religion. Therefore, the historic event of the crucifixion of an individual two thousand years ago cannot represent *the* salvation for all in every time and in every place. Note that Lessing had a rationalistic approach to religion.

[11] *ST* III, q. 1, a. 4: "It is certain that Christ came into this world not only to take away that sin which is handed on originally to posterity, but also in order to take away all sins subsequently added to it; not that all are taken away (and this is from men's fault, inasmuch as they do not adhere to Christ ...), but because He offered what was sufficient for cleansing from all sins" (our translation).

the Word, who is God. Thus, everything that Christ does as a human being is done by the divine Person of the Word, in the human nature that He has assumed in the Incarnation.

1.2.3. Jesus' Humanity as an Instrument of the Divinity

Thus, traditional theology says that Christ's humanity is an instrument that is conjoined to His divinity.[12] A conjoined instrument means two things: inasmuch as it is an instrument, the humanity of Jesus is used by the Word to act and to suffer (as a painter uses the brush to trace the marks on a canvas); inasmuch as it is conjoined, this instrument is acquired by the Word and is not something extrinsic to Him (thus, it is better compared to a hand joined to a body). The painter, after finishing a painting, puts the brushes back: they are only instruments, not a part of him. The humanity of Christ, on the other hand, is a conjoined instrument: Christ never gets rid of it, not even when all of human history will be completed at the end of time. The Incarnation is a point of no return: the Word, becoming flesh, decided to become man forever, not merely for a defined—even if very long—period. For all eternity the Word will remain in the indissoluble state of Incarnation. The Creed says this with the words: "And his kingdom will have no end."[13]

Since Christ's humanity is an instrument of his divinity, and the Person that "sustains" both natures is one, the actions that Jesus carries out as man have the divine Word as their Subject. In other words, if we ask *what* is acting when Jesus teaches, eats, sleeps, is mistreated by persecutors, and so forth, we respond: His human nature.[14] The divine nature, eminently spiritual (God is Spirit) does not carry out these actions or suffer the Passion. But, if we ask *Who* does or suffers these things, then we say that it is the divine Word. In fact, the humanity of Jesus is the Word's, and Jesus is He—the Son of the

---

[12] See Saint John Damascene (d. 749), *De fide orthodoxa* 3.15; *ST* III, q. 49, a. 1, speaks of the humanity as *instrumentum divinitatis*. The expression "conjoined instrument" is in Saint Thomas Aquinas, *Summa contra gentiles* IV, ch. 41.

[13] Against the heretic Marcellus of Ancyra (d. 374), the First Council of Constantinople (DS 150) includes these words in the symbol of the faith. Marcellus taught that, after the Final Judgment, the Word would have dissolved His personal union with the human nature assumed in the Incarnation. This is because he believed that at the end of time the Son and the Holy Spirit would be reunited in the Father, in order to form a single God without distinction of Persons. Marcellus therefore believed that the abandonment of the assumed humanity is an inevitable transition, before the Word would be "dissolved" at the personal level in the divine essence.

[14] All of these things "would not have been true" if Christ had not assumed a true human body, and therefore a true humanity (see *ST* III, q. 5, a. 2).

eternal Father made man. Consequently, the human actions of Jesus are true human actions carried out by a true human nature, but these human actions do not pertain to a human person (as happens with each of us), but to God in the Person of the Son (see further along, the Council of Ephesus). This is why these actions take on an infinite value,[15] which transcends the boundaries of space and time. The claim of the salvific universality of the life of Christ can be grounded only in the doctrine of the Incarnation, which recognizes that Jesus is not a man like other men, but rather God made man.[16]

1.2.4. "The Last Adam"

A final introductory question should now be addressed. If we distinguish (without separating) the aspect of salvation from that of redemption in the inseparable unity of the life of Christ, and we recognize that the redemption is carried out with Christ's gift of His Blood (that is, of His life), in what does salvation consist? Redemption is the reacquisition of a human being from slavery, and this is paid with the great price of the Lord Jesus' Sacrifice. Salvation is the elevation and eschatological fulfillment of human nature. So what particular aspect of Christ's life offers us salvation? We can respond by recalling again the title that Saint Paul uses for Jesus in the First Letter to the Corinthians (15:47): that of "Second Man," which can be also translated "Second Adam." Now let us add that in the same passage the Apostle also calls Jesus the "Last Adam" (15:45), where "last" is expressed with the Greek word *eschatos*. As is clear, the Apostle evidently creates a comparison between the persons and work of Adam and Christ, which is why in the Christian Tradition an understanding has always developed not only of Adam on the basis of Christ, but also of Christ (especially his work) on the basis of Adam—as a reversal of what Adam had done.

As was said, "Second Adam" means above all that Christ is the first man after Adam who has appeared on this earth without being mired in original sin. From this privileged position, He was able to carry out His life as a total

---

[15] "Everything that was accomplished in the flesh of Christ was salvific for us by virtue of the united divinity" (Saint Thomas Aquinas, *Compendium theologiae*, ch. 239 [our translation]).

[16] It is therefore no wonder that when the doctrine of the Incarnation is questioned or even denied, the claim of the universal salvation in Christ also inevitably falls away and they begin to talk about the existence of many salvific paths established by God for human beings. Only God can save human beings, and if Jesus is not God, He cannot be *the* Savior of the world. On these basic doctrines, see the Congregation for the Doctrine of the Faith, *Dominus Iesus* (2000).

gift to the Father for us. In His human nature, Christ lived as Adam should have lived but did not. Thus, Jesus shows in Himself humanity as it should be, "He reveals the human being to the human being."[17] However, Christ is much more than Adam, and not only because He is God. Even as a man, Christ surpasses Adam, for at least two reasons: (1) Being the Word incarnate, humanity was raised in Him to a sublime dignity, which it did not have in Adam: however, this aspect regards only Him and not us; as was said in Chapter Two, Christ makes a new creation but not a new creature. The fact that in Him humanity was raised to a level of existence never experienced before concerns *His* humanity. (2) Christ has not only reproduced Adam in Himself with respect to original and immaculate justice, but He has led the life of the human being to its fulfillment. This is expressed by the Pauline title "Last Adam," which means the man who has reached definitive perfection. Jesus did not fall, He did not discontinue—although He was tempted (Mark 1; Matt 4; and Luke 4)—His ordered human growth in grace. His Resurrection and Ascension into Heaven make Christ the first case of a man that entered into the glory that God intended for His creature from the beginning. The human being from the beginning was called to the triumphant entrance into Paradise, but on account of original sin no one reached it, nor could anyone reach it. That is why Jesus is the Firstborn of the resurrected (see Col 1:18): the absolute first to have entered into the new life of the resurrection. The Ascension of Christ marks the moment in which resurrected man is admitted into the heavenly court for the first time. Faith tells us that this is not a solitary case: He is not the Only Begotten of the resurrected, but the Firstborn. He is not the only one to have been called to this destiny, but the first among many brothers and sisters, for whom He has opened the path (see 1 Cor 15:20–23; John 14:2–3).

1.2.5. Jesus "Grew in Grace"

This is the work of salvation achieved by Christ: He lived a perfect human life, without sin, full of all virtues, consistent with His twofold nature. In this way, as Scripture says, Christ in His humanity grew not only in age and wisdom but also in grace (see Luke 2:52). This growth in grace does not imply any imperfection or lack of grace. Christ always possessed the maximum degree of

---

[17] Second Vatican Council, *Gaudium et Spes* (1965), §22. This theme was taken up and developed often in the Magisterium of Saint John Paul II, beginning with his first encyclical, *Redemptor Hominis* (1979), §8 and §10.

grace, since His conception in the most pure womb of the Ever Virgin Mary.[18] His growth pertains to His humanity, which, growing and always responding perfectly to the grace that dwelled within Him in fullness, became more and more perfect. This ordered growth reaches its definitive culmination with His Resurrection and Ascension into Heaven. Now human nature is saved, that is, fulfilled: it reaches the supernatural destiny willed by God for the human being—"it is well." And this is the work of Christ the Savior.

1.3. The Person and Natures of Christ

It can be inferred from what we have just seen that the work of Christ has its value because it is He, and no other, who performs it. Thus, before examining the doctrine of salvation ("soteriology") we must first expound upon that of Jesus' Person ("Christology"). Before studying the function of Jesus as Messiah and Savior, we must recall the Church's teaching on His being. We shall summarize here the essential elements of Christological dogma, which were established by six ecumenical councils, held in the first millennium of the Christian era, and in opposition to various heresies.

1.3.1. Like the Father, Jesus Is True God (First Council of Nicaea)

Arius (d. 336), a priest of Alexandria in Egypt, preached that Jesus would not be in all things equal to the Father, that He would not be God like the Father. Arius believed that the Son was not God like the Father, but rather an intermediate being between the Father and creatures: a sort of super-creature. The Alexandrian heretic thus affirmed that the Son was not eternal, saying that "there was a time in which he was not," which is the equivalent of saying that the Word was created. This doctrine is clearly erroneous because it denies the teaching of both Scripture and the Tradition on Christ. For this reason, the first ecumenical council in history,[19] the First Nicene Council

---

[18] See *ST* III, the entire *quaestio* 7, and in particular articles 9 and 12.

[19] An "ecumenical council," as opposed to a "local" council or synod, is a gathering of bishops, the doctrine of which represents the faith of the Church. The requirement for establishing the ecumenicity of a council is the approval of the pope. We only call a council "ecumenical" when it has been, if not also convened and presided over by the pope, at least approved as such, that is, as an ecumenical council, even long after its celebration, by a legitimate Roman Pontiff. According to some, the first ecumenical council in history would not have been that of Nicaea I, but the council held by the Apostles themselves, which is spoken of in Acts 15. We believe, however, that the

The Redeemer

(AD 325) defined as a dogma of faith that Jesus Christ is "consubstantial with the Father," in Greek: *homoousios to Patri*. Consubstantial means that the Father and the Son are the same substance, a word that indicates nature or essence ("what something is"). Thus, both the Father and the Son are of a divine nature and are the divine nature. The word *homoousios* prevents us from thinking that this nature is divided between them, or that it is the sum of the Father and the Son. This is true for human beings: human nature is precisely the totality of individual human beings. But this is not the case for the divine nature. To say "consubstantial" means that the Father and the Son, while really distinct as Persons, mutually belong in the indivisible divine nature, that is, they are the unique divine nature, they are one, they are God. God is and always remains One, but the divine nature is entirely possessed both by the Father and by the Son. In this way, the First Nicene Council excludes the possibility that the Son, Jesus Christ, is not God in the full sense of the term. It is thus impossible that He is a creature,[20] however exalted, and it is also impossible that He is not eternal.

1.3.2. Like His Mother, Jesus Is a True Human Being (First Council of Constantinople)

Apollinaris (d. 390), bishop of Laodicea, was very satisfied with the dogmatic definition of the First Nicene Council. In fact, he was an avid anti-Arian and strongly believed in the divinity of Christ. However, he emphasized this to such an extreme that he also fell into heresy, albeit in the opposite extreme to that of Arius. Before stating what "Apollinarianism" consists in, let us note that the entire history of Christological councils is a fluctuating history, at one point emphasizing the divinity of Christ and then His humanity, and at another point emphasizing the unity of His Person and then the duality of His natures. In fact, the dogmatic definitions of the first millennium of the Church manifest the ideal synthesis (*et-et*) of Christianity, which—as we have

---

expression "ecumenical council" cannot refer to this gathering, because the acts, or the decisions made by the Apostles in this reunion, are part of divine Revelation, actually found in Scripture. The decisions of the ecumenical councils, on the other hand, being acts of the ecclesiastical Magisterium, did not add anything to the Revelation of God, which is concluded with the death of the last Apostle (see Chapter Two). They only explain the doctrine revealed once and for all by God in a new way. Nevertheless, with an analogy like the one that exists between the college of the Apostles and that of the bishops, it can be said that the practice of convening synods and episcopal councils derives from the "council" of the Apostles at Jerusalem.

[20] Obviously, the human nature of Christ is created. We are referring here to His divine nature.

seen—occurs perfectly in Jesus Christ in a primordial and perfect way. The Church's doctrine faithfully reflects the complexity of the mystery of Christ, unlike the heretics, who either emphasize the divinity at the expense of the humanity or emphasize the humanity at the expense of the divinity.[21]

Let us return to Apollinaris. In arguing against Arius, who denied the divinity of Christ, he emphasized His divinity to such an extent that he did not recognize a truly complete humanity in Him. Apollinaris did not deny that the Word was truly made flesh, but he interprets the Johannine passage (see John 1:14) literally, holding that the Word did not assume a complete human nature, composed of body and soul, but only a human body. Apollinaris does this because it seems to him impossible that in Christ there was a rational soul that guides the body, given that the Word Himself guides Jesus' humanity. Thus, according to Apollinaris, since Jesus is the divine *Logos*, His humanity does not need a natural soul, a small created *logos*. But in this case, one could not truly speak of Jesus as a man. Human nature (as we have seen in Genesis 1–2) is a composition of soul and body. If there were not also a human rational soul in Jesus Christ, He would not truly be a complete man—He would not even be a man at all. The consequences of this would be very serious for us, because an axiom of patristic theology affirms "what is not assumed is not healed"[22]; thus, if Christ had not assumed a true human soul, He would have redeemed only the body and not the soul of the human being. And thus, His salvific work would have been in vain. This is why the second ecumenical council, the First Council of Constantinople (AD 381), while not directly concerned with the question because it mainly had other heretics in mind (the "Macedonians" or "Pneumatomachians"), added a rich section on the life and work of Jesus to the Creed already defined at Nicaea. In this way it indirectly emphasized that Jesus was a true man, something denied by the heresy of Apollinaris. We can see the additions below, comparing the two texts:

---

[21] In fact, as we said in Chapter One, the meaning of the word heresy (from the Greek *airesis*) corresponds to "choice." The heretic chooses to emphasize only part of the truth, denying or reducing the other part. Thus, every choice that he or she makes against the constitutive polarity of Christianity, against the *et-et*, is heresy, that is, an error in the teaching of the faith, a reduction of Revelation.

[22] "*Quod non assumptum non sanatum*" (Saint Gregory of Nazianzus [d. 390], *Epistula 101*.32).

The Redeemer

Credo of the First Council of Nicaea	Credo of the First Council of Constantinople
DS 125 (*versio graeca*) We believe in one God, the Father almighty, creator of all things, visible and invisible. And in one Lord Jesus Christ, the Son of God, the Only-Begotten generated from the Father, that is, from the being of the Father, God from God, light from light, true God from true God, begotten, not made, consubstantial with the Father, through whom all things were made, those in heaven and those on earth, who for us men and for our salvation came down and became flesh, was made man, suffered, and rose again on the third day, ascended into heaven and will come to judge the living and the dead. **DS 126** And in the Holy Spirit.	**DS 150** (*recensio graeca*) We believe in one God, the Father almighty, creator of heaven and earth, of all things visible and invisible. And in one Lord Jesus Christ, the only begotten Son of God, generated from the Father before all ages, light from light, true God from true God, begotten not made, consubstantial with the Father, through whom all things were made. For us men and for our salvation he came down from heaven and became flesh from the Holy Spirit and the Virgin Mary and was made man. For our sake, too, he was crucified under Pontius Pilate, suffered, and was buried. On the third day he rose again, according to the Scriptures, ascended into heaven, and is seated at the right hand of the Father: and he will come again in glory to judge the living and the dead: to his kingdom there will be no end. And in the Holy Spirit, the Lord and Giver of life, who proceeds from the Father, who together with the Father and the Son is adored and glorified, who has spoken through the prophets. And in one, holy, catholic, and apostolic Church. We acknowledge one Baptism for the forgiveness of sins. We await the resurrection of the dead and the life of the world to come. Amen.

In conclusion, the First Council of Nicaea says that Jesus is consubstantial with the Father (as regards His divinity) and the First Council of Constantinople recalls that He is also of the same nature as His Mother, Mary Most Holy, as regards the true humanity that He took from her. The Gospels, in fact, speak of the virginal conception of Mary, in which there was no intervention on the part of man, with Saint Joseph being (see Chapter Seven) for Jesus only a putative father (that is, retained as such) and a legal father (which gives Him His name and inserts Him into the tribe of David, to which Joseph belongs).

1.3.3. Christ Is One (Council of Ephesus)

The duality of divinity and humanity in Christ must not make us forget that He is "one and the same."[23] The fact that two natures really subsist in Him does not imply a division in His being, but only a distinction between the natures, which, however, are held in an indissoluble unity by the Person of the Word who possesses both.

1. "Unio Hypostatica"

Actually, the union of the two natures in Christ is called a "hypostatic union," where the *"Hypostasis"* ends up referring to what we call the "Person" of Christ. Unfortunately, there were some who did not know how to find this harmonious and synthetic unity between the two distinct natures (*et-et*), and therefore thought that in Christ the distinction between God and man was marked to such a degree as to imply the existence in Him of two persons, two sons. This was the error of the heretic Nestorius (d. 451), the patriarch of Constantinople, who probably was motivated by good intentions, but whose position remains unacceptable. His great adversary was the patriarch of Alexandria in Egypt, Saint Cyril (d. 444), who made every effort

---

[23] Saint Cyril of Alexandria often emphasized the unity of Christ in his correspondence with Nestorius. For example, in his *III Epistula* he writes: "For the Lord Jesus Christ is One, according to the Scriptures"; "One Christ Jesus is meant, the only begotten Son, who is revered along with His flesh by one act of adoration" (in *FCNT*, vol. 76, trans. John I. McEnerney [Washington, DC: CUA Press, 1987], 85–87). In his *Tomus ad Flavianum*, Saint Leo the Great wrote, in regard to Jesus: "For, as we must often be saying, He is one and the same [*unus idemque*], truly Son of God, and truly Son of Man" (in *NPNF*, Second Series, vol. 14, trans. Henry Percival [New York: Charles Scribner's Sons, 1900], 203–204). The expression "one and the same" would later be used by the Council of Chalcedon (see below).

to see the Nestorian doctrine condemned. This happened in the Council of Ephesus (AD 431), in which Saint Cyril of Alexandria played a crucial role. Even before the Council, there had been a close discussion and exchange of letters between the two patriarchs, letters dense in theological content. In the end, the Council of Ephesus officially accepted the position of Saint Cyril, in particular the one expressed in his Second Letter to Nestorius, and it excommunicated the latter. This is a difficult issue to summarize briefly, so we shall only recall one aspect, which is nonetheless the most important, and which was of all the aspects the spark that lit the fuse for the outbreak of the Nestorian controversy.

2. "Theotokos"

Denying the unity in Christ and speaking of a non-ontological unity (i.e., no unity according to being) in Him, Nestorius also denied the unity between the human and divine characteristics of the Lord. He imagined a union of God and man as something, so to speak, superficial, eventually even provisional (extrinsic union): If He so wished, the Word could at any time withdraw from Jesus. Nestorius imagined Jesus as a man who could subsist autonomously, and who the Word united to Himself by benevolence, but not in an ontological way with an indissoluble union in the Person. As a consequence, even the characteristics proper to the two natures would have to remain not only distinct—which is certain—but also separate. According to Nestorius, one should never use language that could insinuate a union of such characteristics. Reasoning in this way, he denied that one could use for Mary the title Mother of God, in Greek *Theotokos*, a title already used at that time in the Church. Nestorius, however—who wanted to strongly separate the two natures of Christ—affirmed that Mary is only the Mother of Christ (*Christotokos*), since she had certainly generated the human nature of Jesus, but not the Mother of God (*Theotokos*), since she did not generate the divine nature. Nestorius' reasoning works only in appearance. It actually represents a heresy, because it denies the hypostatic union of the two natures of Christ in the one Person. This is why Saint Cyril strongly defended the affirmation that Jesus Christ is "one and the same," both when titles are used that refer to His divinity, and when those referring to His humanity are used. The Subject is one, even if the natures are two; therefore, everything that pertains to the two natures, even if distinct, is united and affirmed of the one Son, or Word incarnate.

3. "Communicatio Idiomatum"

This mode of expression, which Nestorius denied, is called a *"communicatio idiomatum,"* that is, a communication of properties. It is not merely a manner of speaking but something that really finds its basis in Jesus on account of the Incarnation. The unity in Christ is such that one can and must affirm *both* divine *and* human aspects of the same Subject. It is true, for example, that the divine nature in itself did not die on the cross because it is immortal, and that only the human nature died. But it was not merely the case—nor should it be said—that on the cross "the human nature of Christ died," but rather, "the Lord died on the cross." And who is the Lord, if not the Word incarnate? The *communicatio* has its basis in the Person, who possesses both natures and to whom the qualities and acts of both refer. Therefore, one can and must say that the eternal Son of the Father died on the cross for us, as a victim in "expiation for our sins" (1 John 2:2). Or again, that "the Word became flesh" (John 1:14), even if the Word did not become flesh, but rather it is the flesh that is assumed by the Word. Thus, it can and must be said that Mary is certainly the Mother of God, because that human nature that she begot is the human nature of the Word incarnate. Mary did not give birth to a human nature in the abstract: she conceived and gave birth to the Word incarnate. Even if it is obvious that Our Lady did not conceive the divine nature of the Word, it is still true that She deserves the full title of Mother of God. Nestorius denied the *et-et* of the relationship between the one Person and the two natures. His heresy greatly emphasized the humanity of Jesus, making it totally distinguishable from the Word, and affirming two persons and two sons in Christ. Saint Cyril and the Council of Ephesus reaffirmed the rightful equilibrium of the truth.[24]

---

[24] A similar heresy to Nestorianism is Adoptionism, for which Jesus was a complete man, who at a certain point had been "adopted" by God. Against this view we must reiterate that Jesus's humanity was never subsistent, not even for an instant, without being assumed by the Person of the Word. St. Augustine of Hippo (d. 430) explains that *"Ipse namque unus Christus et Dei Filius semper natura, et hominis Filius qui ex tempore assumptus est gratia: nec sic assumptus est ut prius creatus post assumeretur, sed ut ipsa assumptione crearetur*—He, in fact, is the only Christ and always the Son of God by nature, and Son of man who [as nature] has been assumed in time by grace; He was not assumed in the manner of being first created and then assumed, but was created by the same assumption" (*Contra Sermonem Arianorum* 8.6 [our translation]). Saint Leo the Great (d. 461), *Licet per Nostros* (449), reformulates it as such: *"Natura quippe nostra non sic adsumpta est, ut prius creata post adsumeretur, sed ut ipsa adsumptione crearetur*—For our nature was not assumed in such a way that it was first created and then assumed, but (in such a way) that it was created by that very act of assumption" (DS 298). Saint Fulgentius of Ruspe (d. 533), *De Fide Trin-*

1.3.4. Christ Is Twofold (Council of Chalcedon)

The Council of Ephesus was well-received, not only by the many bishops who were advocating the true faith, but also by some who, although citing Saint Cyril, actually distorted his teaching. These heretics pushed the pendulum of heresy to the opposite extreme from Nestorius, emphasizing the divinity of Christ to the point of dissolving His humanity. Therefore, they are called "Monophysites," because they affirmed only one (mone) nature (physis) in Christ: the divine nature. The most widely known representative of this position was the monk Eutyches (d. ca. 454), archimandrite in Constantinople, who retrieved certain expressions from the writings of Saint Cyril, and then radicalized them. In particular, he retrieved the expression of Cyril for which there would be "only one nature" (mia physis) in Christ. Though Cyril's mode of expression could have been misunderstood (as indeed happened), if his writings are read carefully, one will note that Cyril's doctrine does not affirm only one nature in Christ, but only one being, against Nestorius. Thus, Eutyches held that in Christ there was not only one Person but truly only one nature, with the consequence that the Incarnation would not really have been such. Christ, according to the Monophysites, would not truly be human, but only truly God. Eutyches professed, paradoxically, that there would have been two natures before the hypostatic union, but only one after the union. This heresy was condemned by the fourth ecumenical council, the Council of Chalcedon (AD 451), which, along with the preceding three councils, represents the dogmatic cornerstone of the ecclesial doctrine concerning Christ.[25] After having reiterated, with Ephesus, that Christ is one and the same, the Council also reaffirms the clear subsistence in the one Person of the two natures, and clarifies through four adverbs the manner in which these natures relate, insofar as it affirms that the natures of Christ stand together "without confusion, or change, without division or separation," [26] from which, nonetheless, it is deduced in a positive way that in Christ there are two "united and distinct" natures. Thus, the excommunication of Nestorius by Ephesus was confirmed, and the same condemnation was imposed on Eutyches. Both

---

itatis ad Petrum diaconum 18: "Take it as certain and without any doubt that the flesh of Christ was not conceived in the womb of the Virgin prior to being assumed [*susciperetur*] by the Word" (our translation). See also St. Gregory the Great (d. 604), *Quia Caritati Nihil* (601) (DS 479) and *ST* III, q. 33, a. 3.

[25] In effect, the first four councils have an importance that is difficult to overvalue. St. Gregory the Great attested: "Just as (I do for) the four books of the holy Gospel, I profess that I accept and venerate the four councils" (*Consideranti Mihi* [591] [DS 472]).

[26] Council of Chalcedon, *Symbolum Fidei* (451) (DS 302).

of them attempted to suppress the bipolarity of the Catholic *et-et* in the Christological sphere. Let us recall that Pope Leo the Great was the champion of Chalcedon, as Saint Cyril had been for Ephesus. A letter of Saint Leo—written and addressed two years earlier to Flavian (June 13, 449), the patriarch of Constantinople—was read and approved by the Council. Therefore, even though it is titled Lectis dilectionis tuae, it is commonly referred to as the Tomus ad Flavianum or Tomus Leonis. This text is of the utmost importance for the history of theology and the ecclesiastical Magisterium.

1.3.5. The Unity in Christ Is Due to the Person (Second Council of Constantinople)

The fifth council, the Second Council of Constantinople (AD 553), is the most complex from a historical standpoint. Three already defunct bishops were excommunicated by the Council, and Pope Vigilius was subjected to unacceptable pressures from the imperial authority to approve the conciliar decisions. Beyond these events, the doctrinal nucleus of the Council consists in its having specified the way in which the hypostatic union of the two natures takes place. In the background of such a clarification, there is the doctrine of *enhypostasis*, which was a theological thesis that was perfected in the sixth century. This doctrine affirms that the *Logos*, in taking on flesh, has hypostatized (personalized) the human nature in His divine *Hypostasis*, and therefore the human nature of Christ, while perfect and individual, does not have its own *hypostasis*. This does not represent an imperfection, because this is how the human nature of Christ reaches the summit of its ontological realization and salvific efficacy. Thus, the human nature of Christ is not divinized only by grace or by participation (as Nestorius believed), but ontologically. Being the flesh of the *Logos*, it is the source of divine life. As regards the great value of this council for the concept of "Christological synthesis," we refer the reader to what we said in Chapter One.

1.3.6. In Christ There Are Two Wills and Two Natural Operations (Third Council of Constantinople)

The sixth council, the Third Council of Constantinople (AD 680–681), represents the final fundamental element of the Christological doctrine of the Church.[27] It revolves around opposition to certain monophysite heretics, who

---

[27] A complete treatise of conciliar Christology should also contemplate the Second Nicene Council (AD 787), which discussed the consequences of Christology in the liturgical

had not yet given up their error, despite the definitions of Chalcedon. They considered themselves empowered by the Second Council of Constantinople, which they said rehabilitated Eutyches, given that it had once again emphasized the unity in Christ and excommunicated authors who took a Nestorian line. These heretics, however, affirmed monophysitism in a new way, preferring to speak of a single will and single operation in Christ. Thus, they were called "monothelites" (one will alone) and "monoenergites" (one operation alone). In Jesus there would not be, under this conception, two wills and two operations (human and divine) but only one will and operation—obviously the divine ones. By contrast, the Council, as a natural consequence of what is said in Scripture, the Fathers, and the preceding councils, affirms the opposite: Christ is one, but since there are two natures, there are also two wills, and two operations. Christ possesses a divine will and a human will, and thus He acts with divine and human actions, the unity of which is guaranteed by the unicity of the Person that performs and presides over each. Here the name of Saint Maximus the Confessor (d. 662) should be recalled, for with his theological reflection he prepared the way for the conciliar pronouncements.

1.3.7. "One Person—Two Natures"

While these considerations provide scarce historical-dogmatic data, they clearly show the two elements that constitute the fundamental Christological formula: "one Person—two natures." The ecclesial doctrine concerning Christ, and His ontological constitution, sees in Him the unique case of a true human being, or else an individual of a human nature like ours, who is nonetheless not a human person, because in the unique and unrepeatable case of this man, the personal character—we might say the character of the individual subject, the individual subsistence and all other ways we want to define the term "person"—is provided by the divine Person of the Word.[28] In the present theological context, it is necessary to repeat it: Jesus is a true man, but He is not a human person. However, Jesus is a Person: He is the Word incarnate. This is why everything that Jesus says and does belongs to the Word of God: it is the Word or Son who says it and does it. When Jesus speaks, it is the Word of God who speaks with a human language; and when Jesus acts, it is the Word who acts through His humanity. Thus, Christ is the definitive Revealer, because there cannot be a superior Revelation to that

---

sphere in regard to the use of icons.

[28] See the broad demonstration of St. Thomas Aquinas, *Quaestio disputata de unione Verbi incarnati*, art. 2.

given by God in Person, who uses our human language to reveal Himself and His will. Therefore, Christ is, moreover, the one and perfect Mediator between God and human beings, because there can be no superior mediation than that which God Himself carries out with the humanity that He assumed in the Person of the Word.

1.3.8. "Unus de Trinitate"

This confirms again that it is not possible to proclaim the doctrine concerning Christ, and to deepen it with theological study, if the mystery of Christ is separated from the mystery of the Holy Trinity. Jesus of Nazareth is *"unus de Trinitate"* ("one of the Trinity").[29] He is the Son, and the Son does not subsist without the Father. The background before which the figure of Christ stands is that of the divine Trinitarian nature:

> It is therefore necessary to return to God the Creator, to the God who is creative reason, and then to find Christ, who is the living Face of God. Let us say that here there is a reciprocity. On the one hand, we have the encounter with Jesus, with this human, historical and real figure; little by little, He helps me to become acquainted with God; and on the other, knowing God helps me understand the grandeur of Christ's Mystery which is the Face of God. Only if we manage to grasp that Jesus is not a great prophet or a world religious figure but that he is the Face of God, that he is God, have we discovered Christ's greatness and found out who God is.... As a result, these two topics penetrate each other and must always go together.[30]

1.4. Elements of Christology in the New Testament

These dogmatic elements of the councils and the great theologians are based on Scripture and the apostolic Tradition, even if the councils and Fathers often reformulate the teachings of Revelation by making recourse to new expressions. The content of what is said is still the same.[31] Here we want to

---

[29] See Second Council of Constantinople, *Anathematismi de Tribus Capitulis* (553), §5 (DS 426).

[30] Benedict XVI, *Meeting with the Clergy of Rome*, February 22, 2007.

[31] The intention of the ecumenical councils is not that of adding something to the faith, but rather of safeguarding, deepening, and communicating the revealed doctrine, as well as defending it against errors. The above-cited symbol of the faith of Nicaea (DS 125) teaches: "And in one Lord Jesus Christ, the Son of God, the Only-Begotten generated from the Father, that is, from the being of the Father." From this proposition, we high-

recapture certain elements of the New Testament in which the two natures of Christ in the one Person are clearly revealed. To be properly developed, such an argument would require many pages, but here we intend to present only a few notes.

1.4.1. Divine Nature

1. Christology "from Above"

The divine nature of Christ is clearly taught in many passages of the New Testament. We can once again recall John 1, in which Jesus is identified with the eternal Word made flesh; or we can note the Christological hymn of Philippians 2, which speaks of the divine condition of the Son, who in becoming incarnate assumes the form of a servant, that is, the form of a man. In both cases, we are faced with two examples of "descending Christology" (also called "Christology from above"): that is, a presentation of Christ that follows the dynamics of the descent—from the height of His divine condition, He descends to us, becoming man.

2. "I Am"

A second example is in the use of the formula "I Am" in an absolute way. Many times, Jesus in the Gospels says "I am . . ." finishing the sentence with a complement: the gate of the sheep; the way, the truth, and the life; the good shepherd; etc. But in some cases, Christ simply says "I Am" (see John 8:24–29, 58; 18:5–6; perhaps also 6:20). Here Jesus clearly refers to a passage of the Old Testament where God revealed Himself to Moses by saying: "'I am who am.' Then he added, 'This is what you shall tell the Israelites: I AM sent me to you'" (Ex 3:14). God presents Himself to Moses with the name "I AM." This is the same name used by Jesus, who presents Himself as the same God who had spoken to Moses in ancient times.

---

light here the words "that is" (in Greek, *toutestin*): the intention of the conciliar Fathers was not to teach anything different from Scripture, but to express in new terms, approved by the Church, the same biblical message, thus preserving the content throughout different eras. Scripture teaches that Jesus is the Only-Begotten Son of the Father (see John 1:18): this revealed doctrine means, in other words, that He is "from the being of the Father." Professing this does not imply a change in biblical faith, but rather an expression of it in a new way, and thus a preservation of it.

3. "Abba"

Jesus' relation as God the Son with respect to God the Father can also be seen in various passages. Let us recall here only the habit that Christ had of addressing God using the intimate term "Abba," an Aramaic diminutive that children of that time used in an affectionate way toward their fathers, and which we could translate as "Dad." In the twentieth century, a wide consensus developed among scholars, according to which no Israelite would have ever dared to address God with a term so familial and personal. Jesus did so, and this indicates a relationship of total filial closeness that we call "ontological": Jesus is not simply a man who prays, but He is the eternal Son who is in the bosom of His Father, and He is God like the Father (see again John 1). Many other examples could be given, but it is not necessary here. The New Testament clearly reveals the divine nature of Christ.

1.4.2. Human Nature

Likewise, Christ's real human nature is revealed in an indubitable way. The evangelists Matthew and Luke, for example, report two different genealogies of Jesus, and they should not be taken in a strict sense as faithful descriptions of descent, but rather have the value of affirming that Jesus is the true King of Israel, and moreover, that He is truly a member of the human race, inserted as such within a human lineage, within a "family tree." Jesus takes His flesh from Mary, as emphasized by Luke 1:31 ("you will conceive in your womb and bear a son") and Matthew 1:20 ("conceived in her").[32] Thus, there are many examples of actions, reactions, and human passions of Christ in the four Gospels: Jesus eats, drinks, sleeps, prays, walks, sits, cries, and loves; He is seen and touched, slapped, crucified; and He dies. Thus, in John 8:40, He defines Himself as "*a man* who has told you the truth that I heard from God." (emphasis added).

1.4.3. One Person

Despite the duality of nature in Christ, He is always presented in the Gospels as a single Subject, as one Person. This is precisely what makes the interpretation of certain Gospel verses difficult for those who do not consider this

---

[32] The ancient work *De ecclesiasticis dogmatibus*, which today is commonly attributed to Gennadius of Massilia (Marseille, d. ca. 496), 2, states: "The Son of God is born, taking His flesh from the body of the Virgin, not bringing it with Himself from Heaven" (our translation).

The Redeemer

fact when comparing different verses. In fact, in some cases Christ presents Himself as equal to the Father: "The Father and I are one" (John 10:30); in others, He says He is less than the Father: "The Father is greater than I" (John 14:28). This happens precisely because Christ sometimes speaks in reference to His divine nature, for which He is equal to the Father, and other times He refers to His human nature, in which He is inferior to the Father.[33] And in both cases he confidently uses the Subject in the singular, "I."[34] This reveals that it is only one Person who possesses these two natures.

---

[33] Saint Cyril of Alexandria, in his *Third Letter to Nestorius*, writes: "*We do not allocate the statements of our Savior in the Gospels either to two Hypostases or indeed to two Persons*, for the one and only Christ is not twofold, even if He be considered as from two different entities, which had been made into an inseparable unity, just as, of course, man also is considered to be of soul and body yet is not twofold, but rather one from both. But, because we think rightly, *we shall maintain that the statements as man and also the statements as God have been made by one person*. When as God He says about Himself, "He who has seen me, has seen the Father," and, "I and the Father are one," we think of His divine and ineffable nature according to which He is one with His Father through identity of substance and is His likeness and image and the brightness of His glory. But when, not despising the full measure of His humanity, He said to the Jews, "But now you are seeking to kill me, one who has spoken the truth to you," again nevertheless even from the full measure of His humanity we recognize the Word who is God in both equality and likeness to His Father. If we must believe that, although He was God by nature, He was made flesh, that is to say, He was made man animated by a rational soul, what reason would anyone have for being ashamed at statements by Him, if they had been made by Him as man? For if He declined the words which are proper to a man, what necessary reason was there for Him becoming man as we are? For what reason would He, who descended for us into a voluntary emptying of Himself, decline words proper to the emptying? *Therefore to one Person must all the statements in the Gospels be ascribed, to the one incarnate Hypostasis of the Word, for the Lord Jesus Christ is one, according to the Scriptures*" (in *FCNT*, vol. 76, 87 [with our corrections; emphasis added]).

[34] "When something is said about the Lord Jesus Christ, particularly in prophecy, which seems to imply some lowly condition unworthy of God, we must not shrink from ascribing it to Him, who did not shrink from uniting Himself to us. In fact the entire creation is at His service, because the entire creation was made by Him, but if we do not keep His unity with us in mind, we may be very disconcerted. We consider His sublime godhead, we hear the text: 'In the beginning was the Word, and the Word was with God, He was God. He was with God in the beginning. Everything was made through Him, no part of created being was made without Him' (John 1:1–3); we contemplate the super-eminent divinity of God's Son, which transcends every nobility found among creatures. Yet then we hear Him in some scriptural text apparently groaning, praying, and confessing. We shrink from ascribing these words to Him, because our minds, so recently engaged in contemplation of His divinity, balk at descending to His humility. We think that it would be an affront to Him if we were to admit that words spoken by a man could be His words—His, to whom words were addressed when we prayed to God. Our minds often come to a standstill, and attempt to alter the meaning. The only scriptural passages we

1.4.4. Christological Titles in the Acts of the Apostles

Additional support for the ecclesial doctrine is found in the New Testament in what is called the "Christological titles," that is, the functional appellations with which Christ is designated by the biblical writings of the New Covenant. There are many of these titles, and it is impossible to adequately discuss the theme here. We shall offer a single example, considering the "seven kerygmatic sermons" contained in the book of the Acts of the Apostles (see Acts 2:14–36; 3:11–26; 4:8–12; 5:29–32; 10:34–43; 13:16–41; 17:22–31). Five of these sermons were given by Saint Peter, and two by Saint Paul. Putting aside exegetical distinctions, we can say that these texts contain the first announcement (*kerygma*) of the Apostles after Jesus' Resurrection, starting from the day of Pentecost. They are very rich texts, but here we only note—putting the seven texts together—the names and titles given to Christ: "Jesus"; "The Nazarene"; "Man Accredited by God"; "Christ"; "Lord"; "Servant of God"; "Author (or Ruler) of Life"; "Savior"; "Judge of the Living and the Dead"; "Stone"; and perhaps also "Holy and Just One" (depending on the interpretation of the passages, that is, whether they are attributed to Jesus as man or to God the Father). Some of these titles are very noble, others instead indicate the service that Jesus carries out for God. The title of Lord (*Kyrios*) is particularly interesting. It is used very often in the New Testament and is perhaps the oldest of all the titles. Exegesis has shown that in the Septuagint (ancient Greek version of the Old Testament), the divine tetragrammaton YHWH (that is, the name with which God reveals Himself to Moses) is translated

---

can think of are those which bring us back to Him and keep us firmly with Him. When this happens our meditation needs to wake up and be more alert in faith, remembering that He whom we were just now contemplating in the form of God took upon Himself the form of a servant, and that bearing the human likeness, sharing the human lot, He humbled Himself and became obedient to the point of death; and that as He hung on the cross He willed to make the words of a psalm His own, crying, 'My God, my God, why have you abandoned me?' (Ps 21:2 [22:1]).... According to the flesh our Lord is the son of David; but in His godhead He is David's Lord and David's Creator. He exists not only before David came to be, but before Abraham, from whom David was descended, and before Adam, from whom all our race derives, and even before heaven and earth, in which all creation is comprised. Let no one, then, on hearing these words, maintain, 'This is not said by Christ'... Does the Gospel not make this plain to us? We read there, certainly, 'In the beginning was the Word, and the Word was with God; He was God; everything was made through Him'; but with equal certainty we read there that Jesus was overcome by sadness, that Jesus was tired, that He slept, that He was hungry and thirsty, that Jesus prayed—indeed, that He persevered in prayer all night" (Saint Augustine of Hippo, *Enarrationes in Psalmos*, 85.1, in *The Works of Saint Augustine: A Translation for the 21ˢᵗ Century*, vol. III/18, trans. Maria Boulding [Hyde Park: New City Press, 2002], 221–222).

precisely with *Kyrios*. It has likewise been established that the New Testament, when it cites the Old, makes recourse in ninety percent of the cases not to the original Hebrew, but rather to the Greek translation of the Septuagint. Thus, the authors of the New Testament were familiar with that version of the Old Testament and knew very well that *Kyrios* indicates, in that translation, God. Making use of this word for Jesus, they are affirming that He is God, the same God of the Old Testament. These exegetical observations are also accepted by the *Catechism*:

> In the Greek translation of the Old Testament, the ineffable Hebrew name YHWH, by which God revealed himself to Moses [Cf. *Ex* 3:14], is rendered as *Kyrios*, "Lord." From then on, "Lord" becomes the more usual name by which to indicate the divinity of Israel's God. The New Testament uses this full sense of the title "Lord" both for the Father and—what is new—for Jesus, who is thereby recognized as God Himself [Cf. *1 Cor* 2:8]. (CCC §446)[35]

Here we find, therefore, the supporting evidence that has been mentioned: we see that to the same individual, Jesus (Person), titles are attributed that refer to His humanity—such as "the Nazarene," "the man accredited by God," "Servant of God," and "Christ"—while other titles clearly imply a dignity that surpasses that of human beings—"Author of Life," "Savior," "Judge of the living and the dead" (recall that in the Bible only God judges the living and the dead), and "Lord."

1.5. Open Christological Questions

Essential facts about biblical and conciliar Christology were offered in the previous paragraphs. However, there are many questions, older and more recent, that engage scholars of Christology. For various reasons, we cannot adequately address these questions here. It is worth recalling a general principle that was put forth by Saint Thomas. Since He is both man and God, Jesus possesses—as has been stated—two natural intellects and two natural wills, united harmoniously in the unique Person. A question posed by medieval theologians consisted in asking whether Jesus was a *viator* or a *comprehensor*. The Angelic Doctor responds:

---

[35] See also *CCC*, §§447–451.

Jesus Christ, True God and True Man

One is called a wayfarer ["*viator*"] who tends toward [eternal] beatitude [in heaven], and one is called a comprehensor who has already reached it [i.e., beatitude]. . . . However, the perfect beatitude of the human being refers to the soul and the body . . . : to the soul, for what is proper to it, and it consists in seeing God, and in the enjoyment of Him; to the body inasmuch as it "will rise spiritual, full of power, glorious and incorrupt," as Saint Paul says. Now, prior to death, Christ with his intelligence saw God perfectly, and thus enjoyed the beatitude proper to the soul. However, as for the remainder, beatitude was lacking to him, because his soul was passible, and his body was passible and mortal. . . . Thus, he was comprehensor for the possession of beatitude proper to the soul, and at the same time he was wayfarer ["*viator*"] insofar as he tended toward beatitude where he lacked it.[36]

In substance, Thomas says that Jesus was *both* wayfarer *and* comprehensor, or one could say—"*simul viator et comprehensor.*" In this case the expression is licit and not erroneous, in contrast to the "*simul justus et peccator*" that Luther attributed to the baptized. In fact, while the Lutheran expression violates the principle of non-contradiction, the other expression respects it, because Jesus is both wayfarer and comprehensor, but at different levels, and not from the same perspective.[37] The co-presence of the two natures in a personal unity, and of these two existential states in the one Jesus, should be the starting point and the basic inspirational criterion for confronting the many open questions of Christology.

It has become common today among a certain number of scholars of Christology to put into doubt, if not completely deny, various points of Christological dogmatic content, such as:

- The real Incarnation of the divine Word
- The personality of Jesus Christ as solely divine
- His virginal conception
- The fullness of His divine nature
- The fullness of grace of Jesus insofar as He is human

---

[36] *ST* III, q. 15, a. 10 (our translation).

[37] Saint Thomas clearly demonstrates this in *ST* III, q. 46, a. 7–8, in which, on one hand, he affirms that Christ enjoyed the beatific vision even during the bitter Passion, but *from another point of view*, He did not enjoy it as a "wayfarer" (he uses precisely the Latin word *viator*).

- The perfect filial and messianic self-understanding of Christ
- The beatific vision of the soul of Christ, even while on earth
- The perfect knowledge of the soul of Christ (albeit with a distinction between different types of knowledge)
- The historical and bodily character of His Resurrection

We have listed only the most relevant points of the Christological sphere, and not even all of them, without mentioning soteriological aspects, which are also frequently debated if not denied by a certain number of scholars, even Catholic ones. In the last decades, the Congregation for the Doctrine of the Faith has had to intervene several times in Christological matters. Immediately after the Second Vatican Council, in 1966, the CDF observed:

> The venerated Person of Our Lord Jesus Christ is called into question when, in the elaboration of the doctrines of Christology, certain concepts are used to describe His nature and His person though they are difficult to reconcile with that which has been dogmatically defined. A certain Christological humanism is twisted such that Christ is reduced to the condition of an ordinary man who, at a certain point, acquired a consciousness of his divinity as Son of God. The virginal birth, miracles, and the resurrection itself are admitted only as concepts, reduced to a purely natural order.[38]

A few years later, in 1972, the Congregation considered it necessary to publish a Declaration "for safeguarding the belief in the mysteries of the Incarnation and of the Most Holy Trinity against some recent errors." We refer the reader to this document, which succinctly expresses both the primary truths of the faith concerning Christ and the Trinity, and the most common recent errors in the matter.[39]

The Congregation has also censured a certain number of Christological works, or those containing aspects of Christology, which are more representative of such errors.[40] Additionally, it published the Declaration *Dominus Iesus*

---

[38] Sacra Congregatio pro Doctrina Fidei, *Epistula ad Venerabiles Praesules Conferentiarium Episcopalium* (1966), §5.

[39] See Sacra Congregatio pro Doctrina Fidei, *Mysterium Filii Dei* (1972).

[40] See Sacra Congregatio pro Doctrina Fidei, *Declaratio circa librum R.P. Iacobi Pohier: "Quand je dis Dieu"* (1979); *Letter to Rev. Fr. Edward Schillebeeckx, O.P., Regarding His Christological Positions* (1980); Congregation for the Doctrine of the Faith, *Notification concerning the text* Mary and Human Liberation *by Fr. Tissa Balasuriya, OMI* (1997); *Notification concerning the writings of Fr. Anthony De Mello, SJ* (1998); *Notification on the*

right in the heart of the Great Jubilee of the year 2000,[41] the Jubilee dedicated to Christ, who is "the same yesterday, today, and forever" (Heb 13:8). It is significant that the text of the Letter to the Hebrews, which emphasizes the permanence of the mystery of Christ, adds immediately after: "Do not be carried away by all kinds of strange teaching. It is good to have our hearts strengthened by grace and not by foods, which do not benefit those who live by them" (v. 9).

During the years of the Second Vatican Council, the following slogan became widespread in certain sectors of Christology: "Overthrow Chalcedon." This clearly refers to the fourth ecumenical council, which we considered above. However, more generally, Chalcedon stood for the dogmatic-ontological Tradition of the Church. The Chalcedonian perspective of Christ—"one Person in two natures"—had to be "reversed" for some theologians, if one wanted to give real impetus to Christology. It was necessary, according to this perspective, to develop a Christology "from below," which did not consider Jesus as God made man, but rather as the man chosen by God. This approach led to many severe errors, as can be intuited from the aforementioned activity of the Congregation for the Doctrine of the Faith. In reality, to construct a solid contemporary Christology, and to take on the many exciting themes that are still open, it is not at all necessary to overthrow Christological dogma. On the contrary, it needs to be maintained and we must walk the royal road drawn out by it. This is not a matter of being "conservative," in the sense of only repeating what was already said. However, new responses, if they are to be *true* responses and not merely original ones, cannot deny the truth already acquired, but only deepen it and apply it to new questions that arise. If this is true of theology in general, then it is also true of Christology. Even if for the sake of the approach of this treatment we must abstain from analyzing very recent authors, we believe that this general criterion will be helpful for those who are beginning to develop their own theological perspective.

2. Jesus Christ, the Only Savior of the World

Jesus' work of salvation and redemption can be summarized in the category

---

book Toward a Christian Theology of Religious Pluralism *by Fr. Jacques Dupuis, SJ* (2001); *Notification regarding the book* Jesus Symbol of God *by Fr. Roger Haight, SJ* (2004); *Notification on the works of Father Jon Sobrino, SJ:* Jesucristo liberador. Lectura histórico-teológica de Jesús de Nazaret *and* La fe en Jesucristo. Ensayo desde las víctimas (2006).

[41] See Congregation for the Doctrine of the Faith, *Dominus Iesus* (2000).

of Mediator or Priest.[42] Saint Paul teaches that there is no other Mediator between God and human beings: "For there is one God, and one mediator between God and men, the man Christ Jesus; Who gave himself a ransom for all" (1 Tim 2:5–6 [KJV]). The rupture between God and humanity is only truly healed by the Blood of Christ, who has given His life, Who has given Himself in ransom—that is, in the repurchase of all human beings—because all are slaves of sin and in need of redemption. Let us immediately clarify that the office of Mediator pertains to the human nature of Christ, as the citation of Saint Paul emphasizes. The mediation happens between the divine nature and the human nature in Christ, Who is one Person, but the office of being Mediator pertains to the human nature of Christ, and not His divine nature.[43]

2.1. Unique Mediation and Participated Mediations

The uniqueness of the mediation of Christ does not exclude, but rather includes, other participated mediations,[44] which, however, only have value as partial and imperfect extensions of the one true mediation of Christ. Thus, God chooses and consecrates many mediators throughout the history of salvation, both in the Old and in the New Testament: patriarchs, kings, judges, prophets, priests, Apostles. Still today, after the fulfillment of the earthly mystery of Christ, God continues to send mediators, such as the ecclesial Hierarchy and, greater yet, Mary Most Holy and the saints, who intercede for us. All these participated mediations do not in any way obscure Christ's role as unique Mediator, but rather they exalt it, just like the assistance of a large court does not diminish, but rather reinforces, the prestige and majesty of the one king.[45]

> No one, therefore, can enter into communion with God except through Christ, by the working of the Holy Spirit. Christ's one, uni-

---

[42] "The office proper to the priest is that of being a mediator between God and the people ... thus it is maximally fitting for Christ to be a Priest" (*ST* III, q. 22, a. 1 [our translation]).

[43] See *ST* III, q. 26, a. 2.

[44] "The unique mediation of the Redeemer does not exclude but rather gives rise to a manifold cooperation which is but a sharing in this one source" (Second Vatican Council, *Lumen Gentium* [1964], §62). See *ST* III, q. 26, a. 1.

[45] Regarding the Most Holy Mary, *Lumen Gentium* §60 says: "The maternal duty of Mary toward men in no wise obscures or diminishes this unique mediation of Christ, but rather shows His power. For all the salvific influence of the Blessed Virgin on men originates, not from some inner necessity, but from the divine pleasure. It flows forth from the superabundance of the merits of Christ, rests on His mediation, depends entirely on it and draws all its power from it. In no way does it impede, but rather does it foster the immediate union of the faithful with Christ."

versal mediation, far from being an obstacle on the journey toward God, is the way established by God Himself, a fact of which Christ is fully aware. Although participated forms of mediation of different kinds and degrees are not excluded, they acquire meaning and value *only* from Christ's own mediation, and they cannot be understood as parallel or complementary to His.[46]

2.2. Reconciliation and Liberation

Christ's work of mediation can rightly be called, with Saint Paul, "reconciliation."[47] In fact, this category is important, even if its value is not always sufficiently emphasized. Let us read a few passages:

> But God proves his love for us in that while we were still sinners Christ died for us. How much more then, since we are now justified by his blood, will we be saved through him from the wrath. Indeed, if, while we were enemies, we were reconciled to God through the death of his Son, how much more, once reconciled, will we be saved by his life. Not only that, but we also boast of God through our Lord Jesus Christ, through whom we have now received reconciliation. (Rom 5:8–11)

> For the love of Christ impels us, once we have come to the conviction that one died for all; therefore, all have died. He indeed died for all, so that those who live might no longer live for themselves but for him who for their sake died and was raised.... So whoever is in Christ is a new creation: the old things have passed away; behold, new things have come. And all this is from God, who has reconciled us to himself through Christ and given us the ministry of reconciliation, namely, God was reconciling the world to himself in Christ, not counting their trespasses against them and entrusting to us the message of reconciliation. So we are ambassadors for Christ, as if God were appealing through us. We implore you on behalf of Christ,

---

[46] Saint John Paul II, *Redemptoris Missio* (1990), §5. On account of this, "those solutions [regarding the theme of participated mediation] that propose a salvific action of God beyond the unique mediation of Christ would be contrary to Christian and Catholic faith" (Congregation for the Doctrine of the Faith, *Dominus Iesus*, §14).

[47] See *ST* III, q. 49, a. 4: The Passion of Jesus is the cause of our reconciliation with God both because it takes away sin, and because it is a "most acceptable [*acceptissimum*] sacrifice" to God.

be reconciled to God. For our sake he made him to be sin who did not know sin, so that we might become the righteousness of God in him. (2 Cor 5:14–15, 17–21)

And you who once were alienated and hostile in mind because of evil deeds he has now reconciled in his fleshly body through his death, to present you holy, without blemish, and irreproachable before him. (Col 1:21–22)

In the past few decades, a part of Catholic theology has willingly emphasized the theme of salvation in Christ as "liberation."[48] This theme too has its roots in the New Testament, where it indicates above all the liberation from the slavery of sin and death, more than the liberation from oppressive agents within human society. However, the liberation carried out by Christ finds its deep root in the work of the reconciliation of the human being with God and, consequently, with other human beings. The human being is freed from sin and for this reason returns to friendship with God, lost at the beginning. This reconciliation is not the work of the sinner, but the work of God: "God was reconciling the world to himself in Christ" (2 Cor 5:19). The purpose of the reconciliation is not earthly social peace, but supernatural peace with God: "We have peace with God through our Lord Jesus Christ" (Rom 5:1). However, since Christian faith always holds together the *et-et*, we see that earthly peace is not a value opposed to supernatural peace, but is rather its direct consequence.[49] Reconciling the human being with God, Christ establishes the true necessary presupposition for peace among human beings. The

---

[48] For a correct perspective about the theme, so that it can be discussed in conformity with Revelation, see Congregation for the Doctrine of the Faith, *Libertatis Nuntius* (1984) and *Libertatis Conscientia* (1986).

[49] This is why the Church seeks dialogue with everyone on the theme of peace, even with representatives of other religions—as in the famous "Days of Prayer for Peace in Assisi"—and this not because all religions are equal, but because from spiritual life, correctly understood, the effort for peace between people also derives. The Catholic Church feels particularly responsible for this, by virtue of a *doctrinal* teaching and not out of a mere social option, since the Church, in Christ, "is like a Sacrament or as a sign and instrument both of a very closely knit union with God and of the unity of the whole human race" (Second Vatican Council, *Lumen Gentium*, §1). The full unity of the human race is realized when it is reunited in the one Church of God and it is in intimate union with Him (see §13). In our time, the Church holds that the dialogue and work for peace between people represent a sort of *praeparatio evangelica* with respect to the recognition of the one true God and the entrance of human beings into communion with Him, and with herself. However, the inverse dynamic is also true: the more human beings are united to God, the more they are disposed to build a stable peace.

same Saint Paul deduces this consequence, applying it to the case of the division between the Israelites and the "Gentiles" (or, pagans). The Apostle reports the following hymn:

> For he is our peace, he who made both one and broke down the dividing wall of enmity, through his flesh, abolishing the law with its commandments and legal claims, that he might create in himself one new person in place of the two, thus establishing peace, and might reconcile both with God, in one body, through the cross, putting that enmity to death by it. He came and preached peace to you who were far off and peace to those who were near, for through him we both have access in one Spirit to the Father. (Eph 2:14–18)

2.3. Jesus the Priest

Redemption is thus a work of reconciliation and liberation. Thanks to Christ, the human being can live in peace with God and his or her neighbor. In what way has Christ obtained this for us? We have already said that He did it by re-purchasing sinners with the price of His Blood, with the price of His life. Here Scripture uses the category of "sacrifice." But for Christ in particular the title of Priest needs to be used, and not only that of Lamb (sacrificial victim).

2.3.1. The (High) Priest and Priests

Priest is another word that the New Testament uses to refer to the office of Mediator that is carried out by Christ. The Revelation concerning the priesthood of Jesus is found in the Letter to the Hebrews.[50] Before giving it a brief glance, we must recall that, in speaking of Jesus the Priest, we must not think at first according to our current concept of priesthood, which indicates the ordained, ministerial, or hierarchical priesthood carried out in the Church by those baptized who received the Sacrament of presbyteral or episcopal Orders (see Chapter Eleven). The priesthood of the latter certainly derives from the priesthood of Christ, and is a participation in it.[51] Thus, when we speak of the priesthood of Christ, we think of something much more eminent in compari-

---

[50] The fact that this is the only book of the New Testament that explicitly utilizes the title of Priest for Jesus should not make us forget that the revelation of the priesthood of Christ is nonetheless expressed in other texts of the New Testament as well.

[51] "The priesthood of Christ is shared in various ways both by the ministers and by the faithful" (Second Vatican Council, *Lumen Gentium*, §62).

son to the priesthood of the ministers of the Church, who nonetheless possess an extraordinary dignity.

2.3.2. Mediation

The priesthood of Christ consists precisely in this work of perfect mediation between God and humanity. Christ carries out such a mediation in a dual way: (1) In an ontological way, primarily through the Incarnation: the hypostatic (personal) union between God and man in the incarnate Word marks the reconciliation between the two natures, divine and human, and allows the transmission of grace from the divinity to the humanity of Jesus.[52] (2) In a moral (meritorious) way: living in such a way as to offer to the Father a worthy reparation for the sin of Adam and all other human beings. Here Christ merits our redemption and obtains for us the recovery of friendship with God, at least in the form of an offer of grace (this offer will then have to be received by each individual). Even in this case, the priestly office is precisely that of Jesus' human nature, not that of his divine nature.

2.3.3. The Letter to the Hebrews

The Letter to the Hebrews makes reference to both of these aspects,[53] even if it emphasizes the latter aspect more. It compares the priesthood of the Old Testament with the priesthood of Jesus. In the Old Testament, only men from the tribe of Levi were priests.

1. Levitical Priesthood

It is well-known that the people of Israel were subdivided into twelve tribes, which descended from the twelve sons of the patriarch Jacob. By the will of God, only human beings of the tribe that derives its name from Levi, thus called Levites, could carry out the priestly function. This function consisted of numerous tasks, but the most important and demanding was the service in the Tabernacle (during the exodus from Egypt) and then, once they reached the Promised Land, the service in the Temple, God's Dwelling. In the Temple, the priests specifically

---

[52] "The habitual grace [of Christ], given for the holiness proper to that man, is an effect consequent of the [hypostatic] union . . . ; this means that that man has the fullness of grace and truth, precisely by virtue of the union whereby he is the Only Begotten of the Father" (*ST* III, q. 6, a. 6 [our translation]). Concerning the theme of the grace of Christ as man, see the various articles of *ST* III, q. 7.

[53] The first chapter of this letter shows that Jesus is not only a man, but also the Son of God.

carried out sacrificial worship, described in great detail in the Book of Leviticus. This involved the sacrifice of animals or vegetables, as well as the offering of incense, burned in a large brazier. On the sacrificial altar of Jerusalem, innumerable animals were immolated, and their blood flowed in streams. The sacrificial practice is present in almost all religions, even in very different forms. It forms part of human religiosity, even at the purely natural level, to present gifts and immolated victims to God. Even in the religion of Israel—a preparation closer and less imperfect than others to the perfect Christian Worship—God willed that the practice of sacrifice remain, while often reminding them, through the prophets, to unite a pure heart to the sacrificial action: that is, the sacrifice is no substitute for the moral responsibility of living as God commands.[54]

2. Priesthood of Melchizedek

Based on the sacrificial practice of Israel, the anonymous author of the Letter to the Hebrews develops a parallelism between the work of the high priest of the Hebrews in the great solemnity of the Day of Atonement (Hebrew: *yom kippur*), and the work of Christ, whom he defines as High Priest "in the manner of Melchizedek," or "according to the order of Melchizedek" (see Heb 7). This expression is understood by recalling an episode of the Book of Genesis. Abraham is (after the whole narrative of Gen 1–11) the first man that God called (see Gen 12) after the drama of original sin, re-starting with him a long path of preparation toward the reconciliation achieved by Christ. Abraham is thus the father of the entire Old Testament, but in a broader sense it can be said that he is the father who had faith in the one true God for the first time after Adam and the first human beings: therefore, whoever believes in the one God is a son of Abraham. Genesis recounts the following brief episode in this regard:

> When Abram returned from his defeat of Chedorlaomer and the kings who were allied with him, the king of Sodom went out to greet him in the Valley of Shaveh (that is, the King's Valley). / Melchizedek, king of Salem, brought out bread and wine. He was a priest of God Most High. He blessed Abram with these words: / "Blessed be Abram by God Most High, the creator of heaven and earth; / And blessed be God Most High, / who delivered your foes into your hand." / Then Abram gave him a tenth of everything. (Gen 14:17–20)

---

[54] Among the many prophetic texts in this regard, it is sufficient to cite Hosea 6:6: "For it is loyalty that I desire, not sacrifice, / and knowledge of God rather than burnt offerings," which is also taken up by Jesus (see Matt 9:13).

Melchizedek is a figure wrapped in mystery: we know nothing about him, except what we read in these few lines and in Psalm 110:4. Aside from being a king, Genesis states he was a priest of God Most High, and that he blessed Abraham. In the Bible, the one who blesses is superior to the one who receives that blessing (see Heb 7:7). Abraham recognized the superiority of Melchizedek, and thus he paid the latter a tenth of all his goods (also those who pay tithes recognize the superiority of the one to whom it is paid).

3. Priesthood of Jesus

Now, this is precisely where the Letter to the Hebrews begins to explain in what sense Jesus is Priest. This concerns an important novelty in Revelation, as Benedict XVI recalled:

> [The Letter to the Hebrews] introduced a new way of understanding the Old Testament as a Book that speaks of Christ. The previous tradition had seen Christ above all, essentially, in the key of the Davidic promise, the promise of the true David, of the true Solomon, of the true King of Israel, the true King since he was both man and God. And the inscription on the Cross truly proclaimed this reality to the world. . . .
>
> However, the Author of the Letter to the Hebrews discovered a citation which until then had gone unnoticed: Psalm 110 [109]:4, "You are a priest forever after the order of Melchizedek." This means that not only does Jesus fulfill the Davidic promise, the expectation of the true King of Israel and of the world, but He also makes the promise of the real Priest come true. In a part of the Old Testament and especially in Qumran there are two separate lines of expectation: of the King and of the Priest. In discovering this verse, the Author of the Letter to the Hebrews realized that the two promises are united in Christ: Christ is the true King, the Son of God in accordance with Psalm 2:7, from which He quotes, but He is also the true Priest.
>
> Thus the whole of the religious world, the whole reality of sacrifices, of the priesthood that is in search of the true priesthood, the true sacrifice, finds in Christ its key, its fulfillment. And with this key it can reinterpret the Old Testament and show precisely that also the religious law abolished after the destruction of the Temple was actually moving towards Christ. Hence it was not really abolished

but renewed, transformed, so that in Christ all things might find their meaning. The priesthood thus appears in its purity and in its profound depth.

In this way the Letter to the Hebrews presents the theme of the priesthood of Christ, of Christ the priest, at three levels: the priesthood of Aaron, that of the Temple; Melchizedek; and Christ himself as the true priest. Indeed, the priesthood of Aaron, in spite of being different from Christ's priesthood, in spite of being, so to speak, solely a quest, a journey in the direction of Christ, is nevertheless a "journey" towards Christ and in this priesthood the essential elements are already outlined. Then [comes] Melchizedek ... who is a pagan. The pagan world enters the Old Testament. It enters as a mysterious figure, without father or mother the Letter to the Hebrews says it simply appears, and in this figure can be seen the true veneration of the Most High God, of the Creator of the Heavens and of the earth. Thus the pagan world too experiences the expectation and profound prefiguration of Christ's mystery. In Christ himself everything is recapitulated, purified and led to its term, to its true essence.[55]

In summary, what the Letter to the Hebrews says about Christ the Priest is that He has a higher priesthood than that of Aaron, that is, higher than the Levitical priesthood of the Old Testament. And it argues such a superiority by recalling that, on the great Day of Atonement, the high priest of the Hebrews enters into the innermost and most sacred part of the Temple, bringing the blood of the immolated victims on the altar before God—in fact, the innermost part of the Temple of Jerusalem was the place that preserved the ark of the covenant, which had accompanied the Hebrews during the exodus and on whose cover the presence of God dwelled. No one had access to this part of the Temple except the high priest, who could enter only once a year to carry out the solemn rite of atonement (see Lev 16:34; Heb 9:7). Now the author of the Letter says that Christ, unlike the Hebrew high priest, did not need to enter into the presence of God every year to offer blood, because He did this once and for all (see Heb 9:12). This indicates that the Sacrifice of Christ is perfect and definitive, and there is no need to repeat it as was done with the imperfect sacrifices of the old law, because it obtained the redemption of the human race once and for all: one sacrifice alone saves human beings throughout the whole world and in all times.

---

[55] Benedict XVI, *Meeting with the Parish Priests of the Diocese of Rome: Lectio Divina*, February 18, 2010.

4. Priest and Victim

Moreover, the Letter says that Christ, unlike the priest of the Temple, does not carry the blood of others—the blood of animals—but He presents to God His own blood in expiation, that is, His life. It is this unique sacrifice that is truly and definitively pleasing to God. Thus, Christ possesses a priesthood that is greatly superior to that of the Mosaic law: it is He who is the High Priest of our faith. The priesthood of Jesus should not be understood as a continuation of the Levitical priesthood (see Heb 8:4; Jesus belongs to the regal tribe of Judah, to which David belonged). The priesthood of Christ is then understood as a superior priesthood to that; in the line of the mysterious character of Melchizedek. Since Abraham publicly recognized his inferiority to Melchizedek, and given that Levi, who is the leader of the Hebrew priesthood, is a descendant of Abraham, Hebrews says that Levi paid tithes to Melchizedek while he was still in the loins of Abraham (see Heb 7:9–10). That is to say, in Abraham the Mosaic priesthood recognized its own inferiority with respect to that of Melchizedek. Since Christ embodies this priesthood, the Letter thus confirms that the priesthood of Jesus is greater than the Levitical priesthood of the Temple. The priesthood of Christ consists in a gift, in the offering of the sacrifice pleasing to the Father for our salvation. As we have seen, Hebrews also notes another, fundamental difference: while the priest of the Hebrews presents the blood of others, Christ presents His own blood. Thus, He is not only Priest, but also sacrificial Victim. In Jesus, Priest and Victim are identical.

2.4. Lamb of God (Victim)

We have thus reached another fundamental aspect of the salvific work of Jesus: He is the "Lamb of God" (John 1:36), who "takes away," that is, who bears upon Himself (Latin: *tollere*) the "sin of the world" (John 1:29). The depiction of Jesus as Lamb or Victim[56] refers again to the Old Testament, specifically to the practice of atoning for sins through ritual sacrifices. With the Letter to the Hebrews, we have learned that those sacrifices were actually figures or types arranged by God to prepare human beings for the one true Sacrifice, that of the one true Lamb, Jesus. Therefore, those sacrifices were always renewed, because it was not possible to redeem human beings from sin through them, something that instead the Sacrifice of the Lord accomplished. The title of Lamb is applied many times by the New Testament to

---

[56] See *ST* III, q. 22, a. 2.

Christ, in particular in the writings of Saint John: his Gospel and the Book of Revelation; although there is also a passage of Saint Peter, in which he writes: "[Know] that you were ransomed from your futile conduct, handed on by your ancestors, not with perishable things like silver or gold but with the precious blood of Christ as of a spotless unblemished lamb" (1 Pet 1:18–19). Before explaining its content, let us recall that there are texts in the Old Testament that already prepare for this Revelation.

2.4.1. The Fourth Song of the Servant of YHWH

We want to cite here the so-called "Fourth Song of the Lord's Servant," a text that is found in the Book of the prophet Isaiah.[57] This text speaks of a future servant sent by God, who will suffer for the sins of the people. He will bear the sins of others on his shoulders. Here we cite the key verses:

> But the Lord laid upon him
>   the guilt of us all.
> Though harshly treated, he submitted
>   and did not open his mouth;
> Like a lamb led to slaughter
>   or a sheep silent before shearers,
> he did not open his mouth. (Isa 53:6–7)

Isaiah foresaw the coming of one sent by God, who will bear the sins of others on his shoulders, and he compared him to a meek lamb who silently allows himself to be led to slaughter, as Christ would do during His Passion. A beautiful episode concerning this citation of Isaiah is recounted in the Acts of the Apostles (8:29-40): an Ethiopian was reading this very passage out loud, and the deacon Philip, hearing him, asked if he understood the meaning of the passage that he was reading. The Ethiopian replied sincerely: "How can I, unless someone instructs me?"—a response, if the aside is allowed, which

---

[57] We find in this prophetic book four texts called "Servant Songs" (Isa 42; 49; 50; 52–53), which present the figure of a Servant of God, chosen and called by the Lord to be a covenant with the people of Israel, and a light for all nations. Through Him, God will offer salvation and Revelation to all peoples. The Servant is distinguished by the gifts with which God crowns him and for his obedient disposition towards the divine commandments. This figure certainly refers to the People of Israel, but also to a single individual. Thus, in the Christian Tradition, these songs were always interpreted as prophecies regarding Jesus Christ. The Fourth Song is especially impressive for its precise predictions regarding the Lord's Passion.

The Redeemer

calls the Protestant principle of "free examination" into question. Specifically, that Ethiopian man wanted to know if Isaiah, writing such words, was talking about himself or someone else. Philip, then, starting from this point, announces the Gospel of Christ to him. Therefore, the Church clearly understood from the beginning that those words of Isaiah represent a prophecy regarding Christ, the Lamb of God.[58]

2.4.2. The "Corpus Ioanneum"

Saint John the Apostle uses the image of the Lamb many times in his work, having seen it realized in Jesus. He reports the way in which the other John, John the Baptist, the Precursor of Christ, used to indicate the Master to his own disciples: "Behold, the Lamb of God, who takes away the sin of the world" (John 1:29), an expression that Catholic priests say during the celebration of the Eucharist, when they show to the people the consecrated Host prior to Communion. The Apostle proceeds to use the term various times in the Book of Revelation of which he is traditionally considered the author: a great vision in which he contemplates the Heavenly City, where God reigns seated on His throne, and on His knees stands a Lamb (see Rev 5:6) who at the same time is immolated (thus, dead, sacrificed) and standing on His feet (which alludes to the victorious Resurrection of the crucified Christ). The image is extraordinary: it is difficult to think of an immolated victim who is at the same time living and victorious, but this is precisely the mystery of Christ, dead and risen.[59] His Sacrifice (immolation) has a permanent value and thus even in the glorified state He remains and always will remain the Crucified One, "the One who has been sacrificed." In this way, we also understand why the risen Christ presented Himself alive to the Apostles after death, with his body still bearing the holes produced by the nails and the lance during the Passion (see Luke 24:39-40; John 20:27). The Resurrection marks the victory of the One who was crucified, not the negation of His crucifixion.[60] In the

---

[58] "Christ is the suffering servant mentioned by the Prophet Isaiah (cf. Isa 52:13–15), who gave himself as a ransom for many (cf. Matt 20:28)" (Benedict XVI, *General Audience*, August 11, 2010).

[59] The fact that the Lamb of the Book of Revelation is to be identified with Jesus Christ can be seen, among other things, in the attestation of Rev 14:1: "Then I looked and there was the Lamb standing on Mount Zion, and with him a hundred and forty-four thousand who had his name and his Father's name written on their foreheads." Thus, it refers to the Son.

[60] It may be noted that, although Christ is now in the risen state, the Church prescribes that an image of the crucifix, and not the risen Jesus, is to be placed on the altar of the Eucharist (see *Institutio Generalis Missalis Romani: Editio Typica Tertia Emendata* [2008],

Book of Revelation, the Lamb is also the One who opens the seven seals of the mysterious book that is in Heaven (see Rev 5). Thus, in so doing, He guides all of human history successfully into port and presides in the Final Judgment, a power of the risen Christ that is recognized from the time of the first preaching of the Apostles (see Acts 10:42; 1 Cor 4:4; 2 Tim 4:8).

The Book of Revelation clearly expresses the redemptive value of the Blood of Christ, because it affirms that "Salvation comes from our God, who is seated on the throne, / and from the Lamb" (7:10), and in particular that those who are found in Heaven with white clothing (a sign of purity), are there because they "have survived the time of great distress; they have washed their robes and made them white in the blood of the Lamb" (7:14). The description most likely refers to the martyrs (the perfect Christians, who have passed with fidelity through the great tribulation), but the Church has known from the beginning that it also applies to every faithful Christian. God does not ask of everyone the supreme testimony of martyrdom by blood, but all must pass through the tribulation that the life of faith always requires from the faithful believer. Therefore, since ancient times, those who are baptized are clothed in the alb, a long white tunic, which indicates the splendor of the soul purified by the Blood of the Lamb through the Sacrament. The alb remains the liturgical vestment for all the baptized, from lay persons to the Pope. It signifies the condition of being a new creature, that is, a creature purified by the Blood of the Lamb, who is now able to participate in divine Worship, to adore the Ancient of Days (see also Dan 7:9) who sits on the throne, and the Lamb standing upright at the center of it, thus imitating on earth the great heavenly Liturgy that Saint John describes in the Book of Revelation.

2.5. Prophet

2.5.1. The Prophets and Christ

Together with the office of High Priest and Victim, which express His personal Sacrifice, Christ also carries out the offices of King and Prophet. When we speak of the prophetic office of Christ, we do not wish to simply place Jesus in the large ranks of God's messengers. This is how the Koran understands it,[61] not the New Testament. Certainly, in the Bible, Jesus is sent by God, by

---

§308). This is because—even though He is now victorious in glory—the Holy Mass is (see Chapter Eleven) primarily the memorial of His Passion and Death (it is a sacramental Sacrifice).

[61] In 3:45–47, the Koran defines Jesus as "son of Mary, eminent in this world and in the

the Father. However, He is not merely one among the other envoys, but rather He is the envoy *par excellence*. A very important text of the Old Testament predicts that God will send a great prophet, on par with Moses (see Deut 18:15). This prophecy was fulfilled in a super-eminent way in Christ (see Acts 3:22): not only is Jesus on par with Moses, but He is superior to him (see Matt 5:21–48; 19:8; John 1:17; 6:32; 2 Cor 3:7–18). The same Lord implicitly recognized for Himself the title of Prophet (see Mark 9:37; Matt 10:40; 15:24; Luke 4:18, 43; 9:48; 10:16; John 3:17; 4:34; 5:24; etc.). Jesus knows well that He is superior to the prophets and says so (see Matt 12:41–42). He claims His superiority even over Abraham (see John 8:58) and over Moses (see above), as well as over Jonah (see Matt 12:41), thus provoking disdainful reactions from many of His listeners. The title of Prophet, nonetheless, is suitable for Him by virtue of a certain continuity with the mission of His imperfect predecessors.

2.5.2. The Essence of Propheticism

But who is a prophet? Often it is believed that a prophet is someone who predicts the future, or one who knows things that are hidden to most (the Samaritan woman of John 4 believes Jesus to be a prophet because He has demonstrated that He knows hidden aspects of her life). Certainly, these elements are found in the prophets,[62] but they actually manifest something more essential. The essential aspect of the prophetic office is to always speak the truth in the name of God.

The prophet is one who is chosen by God to communicate the truth to human beings, whether they like it or not, at opportune or inopportune times (see 2 Tim 4:2). When such a mission is carried out, then there is the presence of prophets, even when they do not receive from God revelations of future events, or the capacity of reading the souls of persons who they encounter. Thus, the greatest of the prophets, and the last of them, Saint John the Baptist, neither performed miracles nor foretold the future. However, he always proclaimed the truth. Above all, he proclaimed the presence of Christ,

---

other, one of the closest [to God]." For Islam, Jesus is the penultimate prophet, second only to Mohammed, who is the final and definitive prophet of Allah. The Koran explicitly rejects the Christian faith, according to which Jesus is God (see 5:17). Allah "is too high and glorious to have a son" (4:17; see 6:101). Finally, the Koran accepts a Gnostic legend, according to which, in the moment of the death on the Cross, God took Jesus away from His tormentors, invisibly replacing Him with another man (see 4:157–158).

[62] Thus Saint Thomas wrote that "the name prophet is given to one who speaks or sees from afar, in the sense that such a one knows and proclaims distant events" (*ST* III, q. 7, a. 8 [our translation]).

the presence in his time of the long-awaited Messiah of God. Therefore, Saint John the Baptist was the greatest of the prophets, because he not only proclaimed truths from God, but first and foremost the Truth in Person, Christ. Saint John the Baptist also demonstrated this faithful attitude toward the truth in the episode that cost him his life: he died as a martyr of his prophecy, that is, of his ministry of truth. In fact, he was beheaded for having clearly spoken the truth to Herod regarding his concubinage (see Mark 6; Matt 14; Luke 3). We can observe that *diakonia* (service) to the truth also involves *martyria* (testimony at a great cost) to the truth.

2.5.3. Christ the Prophet

Christ is the Prophet *par excellence*, because He not only reveals the truth in a definitive way (He is the "eschatological" Revealer), but because He is the Truth in Person (see John 14:6), and He is the Truth who makes the human being free: "Jesus then said to those Jews who believed in him, 'If you remain in my word, you will truly be my disciples, and you will know the truth, and the truth will set you free'" (John 8:31–32). Therefore, we discover that the prophetic office of Christ has a liberating power, and thus also that the Revelation He carries out is part of His work of salvation. Christ's word of truth has a power of liberation because the greatest oppression for the human being is slavery to sin. To know the word of Christ is to know that truth according to which the human being is freed: "'Amen, amen, I say to you, everyone who commits sin is a slave of sin. . . . So if a son frees you, then you will truly be free'" (John 8:34, 36).

The definitive knowledge that Christ gives us is first and foremost the perfect knowledge of the face of God. When we say perfect knowledge, we do not mean to sustain that there is nothing left to discover and that the mystery of God is completely revealed. On the contrary, God remains *re-veiled* until we arrive at direct vision in Heaven. In this sense, "we know partially and we prophesy partially" (1 Cor 13:9). But in another sense our knowledge is perfect, because Christ brought the work of Revelation to completion: concerning God, He taught us everything that had been planned for us to know so that we could adore Him in truth. The Trinitarian face of God, revealed to us by the Lord Jesus, is not a provisional image, or a metaphor to use for a pedagogical purpose. God is the Most Holy Trinity. The one God is Father, Son, and Holy Spirit. The face of God *per se* corresponds to the face of God communicated to us by Jesus:[63] "For God who said, 'Let light shine out of

---

[63] In the current theological language, this is said in following way: "The economic

darkness,' has shone in our hearts to bring to light the knowledge of the glory of God on the face of [Jesus] Christ" (2 Cor 4:6). This refers to the human face of Jesus, on which the divinity shines as well: thus, the prophetic office also (as the priestly one) belongs to the humanity of the Lord.

The link between the knowledge of the truth and salvation is particularly clear in a passage of Saint Paul that reveals the will of God for the human race: He "wills everyone to be saved and to come to knowledge of the truth" (1 Tim 2:4). The theme of salvific knowledge is then also developed by the Apostle Saint Peter in his Second Letter, in which, among other things, the theme of false prophets is mentioned (2 Pet 2), as is above all that of true *gnosis*, of true knowledge of Christ (see 2 Pet 1:2–3, 5–6, 8; 2:20; 3:18).

Finally, let us recall that the prophetic office of Christ also has salvific value because it enables us to follow the path of salvation. We follow this path by listening to the voice of Truth (see John 18:37; Rev 3:20), by living in the truth of Christ, by observing His word, and by imitating His behavior (see 1 Cor 11:1; Eph 5:1). But in turn, we too are made prophets by participation in His prophetic ministry. The baptized person participates in the priesthood of Christ: Christ, through Baptism, enables us to participate in divine Worship. Now, we see that the baptized person is not only a priest, but also a prophet: he or she is entrusted by Christ with the task of giving testimony to the Truth. This is done through evangelization, catechesis, mission, and also in all the thousands of occasions of personal, familial, and social life in which we are called to speak the truth—indeed with charity—but also with great clarity and force.[64]

2.6. King

2.6.1. The Messiah in the Old Testament

Christ carries out a third salvific ministry in His human nature: the royal one. Here we encounter the fundamental title of Messiah. In the Old Testament, the Messiah is the Anointed One of the Lord. "Anointed One" indicates a man chosen and consecrated by God, because the anointing with oil, a material symbol of what is done by the divine Spirit, is the sign of vocation and consecration. In the Old Testament, the ones considered as anointed by God are the king, priest, and prophet, but in a particular way the king, with a special distinction for David, who was the greatest ruler in Israel's history.

Trinity is the immanent Trinity."

[64] On various occasions and in various contexts, Pope Francis has insisted on the virtue of evangelical *parrhesia* (frankness). See, for example, *Evangelii Gaudium* (2013), §259.

Although all these figures are messianic in their own way, an expectation nevertheless develops in the Old Testament for one Messiah in particular, considered the new and definitive king of Israel. For this reason, he will be expected as a member of the line of David, belonging to the tribe of Judah. The Messiah will reproduce in himself the perfect characteristics of the king and will be the great liberator of the people. The Gospels take up this legacy and convey the perception of this expectation on the part of the people. On the other hand, we need to recall that more than one person presented himself as the awaited Messiah and gathered followers for a short time (see Acts 5:34–39). Thus, in the days of Jesus there was widespread uncertainty, which was mixed in with the anxiety of waiting. The people waited for the Messiah, while others, especially those who held religious power, were very watchful and suspicious, and tried to act with political prudence given that Palestine was under Roman rule at that time.

2.6.2. Jesus' Messianicity

It was in this context that the royal office of Jesus was carried out. He had to affirm His messianicity, demarcating it from reductive conceptions of it. Many times, the people called Him "Son of David," or a descendant of the king and his successor (it is a messianic title). Jesus did not deny the title of Messiah,[65] but clarified that He is much greater than David (see Mark 12:35–37 and parallel passages). Thus, when one speaks of the kingship of Christ, one needs to distinguish well the different meanings that it implies. Is Jesus the king of Israel? In what sense? Is His kingship broader than that and, if so, what are its limits? Is it a spiritual or temporal power, or both?

1. Facing Pontius Pilate

Pontius Pilate's interrogation of Jesus is particularly interesting in this regard. In fact, the Sanhedrin, that is, the supreme Jewish council presided over by the High Priest, also wanted to know if Jesus was the Messiah (see Mark 14:61); but the conversation with Pilate grants us a broader glance at Christ's kingship:

---

[65] In the nineteenth century, the thesis of a "Messianic secret" (German: *Messiasgeheimnis*) was advanced, according to which Jesus ordered that word not spread that He was the Messiah, inasmuch as He did not recognize Himself as such. The progress of biblical and theological studies has clearly shown the inconsistency of this theory. It is enough to mention the way in which Jesus triumphantly entered Jerusalem (see Mark 11:1–11 and parallel passages): an act of an evidently regal character.

The Redeemer

> So Pilate went back into the praetorium and summoned Jesus and said to him, "Are you the King of the Jews?" Jesus answered, "Do you say this on your own or have others told you about me?" Pilate answered, "I am not a Jew, am I? Your own nation and the chief priests handed you over to me. What have you done?" Jesus answered, "My kingdom does not belong to this world. If my kingdom did belong to this world, my attendants [would] be fighting to keep me from being handed over to the Jews. But as it is, my kingdom is not here." So Pilate said to him, "Then you are a king?" Jesus answered, "You say I am a king. For this I was born and for this I came into the world, to testify to the truth. Everyone who belongs to the truth listens to my voice." (John 18:33–37)

Pilate is not interested in religious questions: he does not want to know if Jesus is the religious Messiah, but only if He claims to be the political king of Palestine, thus threatening the power of the Roman emperor. But even in this circumstance, Jesus wants to clarify the sense of His kingship. The response question, "Do you say this on your own or have others told you" means this: Are you asking me if I am king like your emperor, or do you want to know according to the concept of kingship that comes from God, the concept that the Jews (the "others") know from Scripture? However, Pilate replies, annoyed, that he is not a Jew: he is not interested in religious questions. When Jesus ensures that His interlocutor has a clear understanding of the response that He is about to give him,[66] He then says that He is not a king of this world. Jesus does not deny being a king, but He refutes attributing the title to Him without making us understand the way in which it applies to Him.[67]

We have already said that He did not deny the title of Messiah, Son of David, but He wanted it to be understood that He is infinitely superior to David. It is not Jesus who would be king in the manner of David; it is David who was only a pallid figure of the true King. Thus, in this case Jesus does not deny being King but clarifies that He has no interest in driving out the

---

[66] "The Lord of course knew both what He himself asked and what that man would answer, but nevertheless He wanted it to be said, not that He might know himself but that what He wanted us to know might be written down" (Augustine of Hippo, *In Evangelium Ioannis Tractatus* 115.1, in *FCNT*, vol. 92, trans. John W. Rettig [Washington, DC: CUA Press, 1995], 21).

[67] "Not that he was afraid to confess Himself a king, but 'you say' was so balanced that He neither denies himself [to be] a king (for He is a king whose kingdom is not of this world) nor does He say that He is such a king whose kingdom is thought to be of this world" (Augustine of Hippo, *In Evangelium Ioannis Tractatus* 115.3, in *FCNT*, vol. 92, 23–24).

Roman emperor from the throne and taking His place. He has a kingship infinitely superior to that of Caesar, and Caesar's kingship, like every other authority, derives from His. He will say this immediately afterward to Pilate: "You would have no power over me if it had not been given to you from above" (John 19:11). Nonetheless, the kingdom of Christ is not an earthly kingdom, but rather a heavenly one. The earthly kingdoms are only small irradiations of His infinite majesty. Therefore, Jesus says that His kingdom does not belong to this world. Pilate presses again, asking if He is king. At this point Jesus can solemnly confirm His kingship. The words that He pronounces make clear that His kingship resides in His human nature and not His divine one.[68] In fact, He says: "For this I was born and for this I came into the world" (John 18:37), in this way linking His kingship to His birth in time.[69]

2. Characteristics of Jesus' Kingship

The kingship of Christ has the following characteristics: (1) it is superior to all forms of kingship, and all human kingships derive from His, in various orders and degrees; (2) His kingdom is not a political one, but a spiritual one: Christ reigns, above all, over the hearts of those who belong to the truth and obey His voice; and yet, nonetheless, given the principle of *et-et*, (3) the kingship of Christ develops, through Christians, also as a social kingship.[70]

---

[68] "We cannot but see that the title and the power of King belongs to Christ as the man in the strict and proper sense, too. For it is only as man that He may be said to have received from the Father 'power and glory and a kingdom,' since the Word of God, as consubstantial with the Father, has all things in common with Him and, therefore, has necessarily supreme and absolute dominion over all things created" (Pius XI, *Quas Primas* [1925] [DS 3675]).

[69] "Whence it is clear that He here spoke of his temporal nativity whereby he came incarnate into the world, not that one without beginning whereby he was God" (Augustine of Hippo, *In Evangelium Ioannis Tractatus* 115.4, in *FCNT*, vol. 92, 24).

[70] "It would be a grave error ... to say that Christ has no authority whatever in civil affairs, since, by virtue of the absolute legal right over all creatures committed to Him by the Father, all things are in His power. Nevertheless, during His life on earth He refrained from the exercise of such authority, and although He Himself disdained to possess or to care for earthly goods, He did not, nor does He today, interfere with those who possess them. To this, the words well apply: 'He does not take away mortal things who gives the reign of heavenly things' (Hymn '*Crudelis Herodes*' in the Office of Epiphany). Thus the dominion of our Redeemer embraces all men. To use the words of Our immortal predecessor Pope Leo XIII: 'His empire includes not only baptized persons who, though belonging to the Church by right, have been led astray by error or have been cut off from her by schism, but also all those who are outside the Christian faith; so that truly the whole of mankind is subject to the power of Jesus Christ' (Encyclical *Annum Sacrum*

The Redeemer

In contemporary exegesis there is substantial agreement on the fact that the center of Jesus' preaching was the theme of the kingdom of God, or the kingdom of Heaven. The nearly total absence of a broad reflection on the theme of the King of this kingdom is therefore striking. If one disconnects Jesus' preaching about the kingdom from His role of King, the concrete risk is that of making Jesus recede into a simple prophetic role of announcing a kingdom in which He is not implied as the protagonist. It is necessary to hold the two aspects together: Jesus is both the Announcer of the kingdom and its Sovereign.[71] Therefore, since the patristic age, it was recognized that the kingdom and Jesus are identical.[72]

3. "The" Christ

In conclusion, the fundamental title of "Christ" is mainly linked, at the historical level, to the kingly office of Jesus. "Christ" is the Greek equivalent of the Hebrew word Messiah: both refer to the Anointed One of God. Since the Messiah was above all the Messiah-King, then the "Christhood" of Jesus is above all linked to His kingly office. However, it is necessary not to forget that the priest and prophet were also the anointed of the Lord. Thus, we must recognize that in Jesus the title Christ expresses the fullness of the three offices: kingly, priestly, and prophetic. In Him, these ministries reach the unsurpassable summit and perfect realization with respect to which the other anointed ones remain partial and preparatory shadows and figures. This fullness of the "Christhood" of Jesus of Nazareth made it such that Jesus was not only called Christ but rather *the* Christ *par excellence*. Hence, from the beginning the title became like a second name of Jesus. In itself, a title applies to many persons without being the name of any of them: lawyer or professor is applied to many, and none of the representatives of these categories can claim to be *the* lawyer, or *the* professor, as if they were the best, or as if there were no others. But for Jesus one does not simply say that He is *a* Christ, but *the* Christ of God, the Messiah. Thus, Christ becomes His second name, which is added to the name given to Him by Saint Joseph as His legal father.

[1899])" (Pius XI, *Quas Primas* [DS 3679]).

[71] See once again the symbol of faith of the First Council of Constantinople: "His kingdom will have no end" (DS 150).

[72] See Origen of Alexandria, *Homiliae in Matthaeum* 14.7: "Christ is Himself the Kingdom": here the Alexandrian uses the famous conception of the kingdom as *autobasileia*. See also Tertullian of Carthage, *Adversus Marcionem* 4.8; Saint Hilary of Poitiers, *In Matthaeum* 12.17 (". . . *ipse sit regnum caelorum* . . ."); etc. See also Saint John Paul II, *Redemptoris Missio* (1990), §§16 and 18; Congregation for the Doctrine of the Faith, *Dominus Iesus*, §18 (and note 73).

3. The Value of Jesus' Sacrifice: Soteriological Categories

With great clarity, Sacred Scripture affirms that the death of Jesus redeemed us from sin and death. Christian thought has always sought to better understand the way in which this happened and the value of the Lord's Sacrifice. Scripture itself utilizes certain expressions such as "sacrifice" or "expiation," whose exact meanings need to be specified. Christian Tradition has then added other "soteriological" (having to do with salvation) categories, such as "satisfaction" or "vicarious substitution" (in German *Stellvertretung*), or even "penal substitution." What do these terms mean? Do they represent better explanations of Revelation, or are they undue additions that lead away from the truth? We shall provide a quick explanation of the soteriological categories below.

3.1. Battle, Ransom Price, and Victory (Redemption)

In a first model, Salvation is presented as an onerous combat. Christ fights and wins, redeeming imprisoned human beings. The victory, however, is achieved at a high cost: in order to liberate us, He gives His precious blood, His life. Thus, victory actually seems to be a defeat: Christ dies. However, it is precisely in His death that the defeat of the enemy of human beings, the devil and sin, takes place. Revelation 5:5 defines Jesus as the victorious lion of the tribe of Judah. Saint Paul specifies: "You have been purchased at a price" (1 Cor 6:20, repeated in 7:23). The Church is the people that God has acquired in the Sacrifice of Christ (see Acts 20:28; 1 Pet 2:9). Let us look at a few significant passages on the theme of the price of our redemption:

> Mark 14:24: "This is my blood of the covenant, which will be shed for many."

> Ephesians 1:7: "In him we have redemption by his blood, the forgiveness of transgressions, in accord with the riches of his grace."

> Hebrews 9:12: "He entered once for all into the sanctuary, not with the blood of goats and calves but with his own blood, thus obtaining eternal redemption."

> Hebrews 9:13–14: "For if the blood of goats and bulls and the sprinkling of a heifer's ashes can sanctify those who are defiled so that their flesh is cleansed, how much more will the blood of Christ,

who through the eternal spirit offered himself unblemished to God, cleanse our consciences from dead works to worship the living God."

1 Peter 1:18–19: "Realizing that you were ransomed from your futile conduct, handed on by your ancestors, not with perishable things like silver or gold but with the precious blood of Christ as of a spotless unblemished lamb."

3.2. Sacrifice

The idea of redemption is strictly connected, because of what has been said, with the idea of sacrifice. Saint Thomas defines a sacrifice as that which is done to render unto God the honor He properly deserves, for the sake of appeasing Him.[73] A sacrifice is an offering accompanied by immolation: to offer something to God and to perform an act on it that destroys it (e.g., to burn incense or to immolate a lamb).[74] The Angelic Doctor also applies the notion of sacrifice to the Passion of Christ, which He endured voluntarily as a self-offering to God out of love. In fact, these two elements—self-offering and love—are decisive in speaking of a true Christian Sacrifice; otherwise there would only be an external deed, while the true Sacrifice also, and especially, involves the intention of the one who performs it, in addition to the immolation of what is offered. Thus, Saint Thomas declares that "the offense [to God] is taken away only by love"[75] and thus the redemption of human beings is not accomplished without the charity of Christ's Heart.

A little earlier, we discussed Christ as the Lamb of God, the sacrificial Victim. Redemption is carried out through His personal Sacrifice. Jesus became a true sacrificial Victim for us. The difference with the animal victims

---

[73] See *ST* III, q. 48, a. 3, cited below. Appeasing God does not have the same meaning in the Christian world as it does in other religions: we are not dealing—*sit venia verbis*—with a "blood-thirsty" God, but with a loving Father. Nonetheless, there is divine justice, which demands satisfaction, as well as a righteous divine anger, of which Scripture speaks, which is not a disordered passion but represents God's rejection of sin. The concepts will be further clarified as we proceed.

[74] "One speaks properly of a sacrifice when a [sacrificial] act is performed over what is offered to God: animals, for example, are killed; bread is broken, eaten, and blessed.... Oblation instead directly indicates the offering made to God, even if no act is performed over it.... Thus every sacrifice is an oblation, but not vice versa" (*ST* II-II, q. 85, a. 3, ad 3[our translation]; see Thomas Aquinas, *Super Psalmos* 39, 4). We shall return to this theme in the context of the Eucharist in Chapter Eleven.

[75] Saint Thomas Aquinas, *Summa contra gentiles* III, ch. 157; see Thomas Aquinas, *Scriptum super Sententiis* IV, d. 15, q. 1, a. 3; *ST* III, q. 79, a. 5.

The Value of Jesus' Sacrifice: Soteriological Categories

immolated in the worship of the Temple of the Old Testament is in the fact that the latter victims were unaware—that is, they did not consciously desire to immolate themselves to redeem human beings from sin—while Christ was the conscious Victim. He sacrificed Himself because He wanted to; He offered His life to the Father for us. In the Gospel of John He says: "I consecrate myself for them [the disciples]" (17:19), which clearly expresses self-offering, the Sacrifice of Himself.[76] In a text that we have cited, Jesus indicates the voluntariness of His Sacrifice, saying: "I lay down my life in order to take it up again. No one takes it from me, but I lay it down on my own. I have power to lay it down, and power to take it up again" (John 10:17-18).

Saint Paul refers to the Sacrifice of Christ with just as much clarity:

> Ephesians 5:2: "Live in love, as Christ loved us and handed himself over for us as a sacrificial offering to God for a fragrant aroma."

> Galatians 2:20: "Insofar as I now live in the flesh, I live by faith in the Son of God who has loved me and given himself up for me."[77]

The Letter to the Hebrews presents passages of great importance, which we reference without further comment: Hebrews 7:24–27; 9:11–15, 24–28; 10:9–14. It is enough to suggest that the reader read these passages while keeping in mind what we have just explained above regarding the teaching of this biblical book.

The Sacrifice that brings salvation to human beings has thus been fulfilled in the Passion and death of Christ:

---

[76] "When Jesus says: 'I consecrate myself,' He makes Himself both priest and victim. Bultmann was right to translate the phrase: 'I consecrate myself' as 'I sacrifice myself.' Do we now see what happens when Jesus says: 'I consecrate myself for them'? This is the priestly act by which Jesus—the Man Jesus, who is one with the Son of God—gives Himself over to the Father for us. It is the expression of the fact that He is both Priest and Victim. I consecrate myself—I sacrifice myself: this unfathomable word, which gives us a glimpse deep into the heart of Jesus Christ, should be the object of constantly renewed reflection. It contains the whole mystery of our redemption. It also contains the origins of the priesthood in the Church, of our priesthood" (Benedict XVI, *Homily in Chrism Mass*, April 9, 2009). In fact, well before Bultmann, a much more authoritative author already interpreted John 17:19 in this sense: "'For them I sanctify myself.' I sanctify, states, that is: I consecrate myself and I offer myself as an immaculate Host [Victim] of sweet odor" (Saint Cyril of Alexandria, *In Evangelium Ioannis* 4.2 [our translation]).

[77] Here the Apostle recalls the self-Sacrifice of Christ with the verb "to give/deliver," which recurs in the words of the Eucharistic institution (see 1 Cor 11:24, in which the word "given/delivered" in itself is missing, but is implied, as is clear from the parallel text of Luke. On the institution narratives, see Chapter Eleven).

> A sacrifice properly so called is something done for that honor which is due to God alone, in order to appease Him. . . . Christ in the Passion sacrificed Himself for us and this action, that is the voluntary enduring of the Passion, was most acceptable to God, since it proceeded from charity. Thus it is evident that the Passion of Christ was a true Sacrifice.[78]

3.3. Atonement (Expiation) and Propitiation

By offering Himself for us, Christ atones for our sins. What does it mean to atone/expiate? In common language, this verb has taken on the meaning of "paying the penalty," suffering punishment. When one says "I must expiate," what is meant is "I must suffer a penalty on account of an evil I have committed." If we apply this meaning of the verb personally to Christ, we could not say that He atones for sin, because He is without sin and does not have to suffer any punishment. Let us then see what Revelation says about Jesus' atonement.

3.3.1. The Old Testament

The theme of atonement is present since the Old Testament. God allowed the Israelites to offer the blood of a victim in atonement: "Since the life of the flesh is in the blood, and I have given it to you to make atonement on the altar for yourselves, because it is the blood as life that makes atonement" (Lev 17:11). This passage is based on the Old Testament principle of "life for a life" (Lev 24:18; Deut 19:21), that is to say, the offering of one life is valid as a substitution for another. The life (blood) of a goat or other animal immolated in atonement saves the life of the sinner. It is obvious that the sin was not committed by the goat! Moreover, in the liturgy of *yom kippur*, the "scapegoat" on which the sin of the people is placed is not the animal immolated in the Temple, but the one sent into the desert (see Lev 16).

The concept of atonement is found again in the above-cited "Fourth Servant Song." Here we find the concept expressed with the terms of "vicarious atonement." This means that one atones for another, in the place of another. "Yet it was our pain that he [the Servant] bore, / our sufferings he endured" (Isa 53:4); "But he was pierced for our sins, / crushed for our iniquity. / He bore the punishment that makes us whole, / by his wounds we were healed" (Isa 53:5).

---

[78] *ST* III, q. 48, a. 3 (our translation).

The Value of Jesus' Sacrifice: Soteriological Categories

3.3.2. The New Testament

As has been said, the identity of the Servant is no longer mysterious in the New Testament: the Servant is Jesus. Thus, it is Jesus who atones for our sins in our place. Saint Paul attests: "God set forth as an expiation,[79] through faith, by his blood, to prove his righteousness because of the forgiveness of sins previously committed" (Rom 3:25). Saint John also touches upon the theme:

> 1 John 2:2: "He [Christ] is expiation [*hilasmos*] for our sins, and not for our sins only but for those of the whole world."

> 1 John 4:10: "In this is love: not that we have loved God, but that he loved us and sent his Son as expiation [*hilasmos*] for our sins."

The Letter to the Hebrews, which we have already mentioned several times, says that Christ became High Priest to atone [*hilaskestai*] for the sins of the people (see Heb 2:17). The same text, as has been said, compares the Tabernacle of the mercy seat (called the Holy of Holies in Heb 9:3) and the new tent into which Jesus enters, not with the blood of animals but with His own (see Heb 9:12), which thus has expiatory value *par excellence* and is sprinkled on the new mercy seat, which is Jesus Himself, as Paul says in Romans 3:25, which was just cited.

3.3.3. Vicarious Atonement, Not Penal Substitution

The character of atonement and propitiation (to appease God) of Christ's work should not be separated from what has been said concerning the voluntariness of His personal Sacrifice: Christ offered Himself as a Victim of expiation because He wanted to do so, not because He was forced. Christ's atonement consists in purifying our sins and is perfected by the fact that He bears our punishment. He suffered because He wanted to do so, not because He had to do so. He does not have to do so because He is without sin: "[He] has similarly been tested in every way, yet without sin" (Heb 4:15; see *ST* III, q. 15, a. 1). Thus, the Passion of Christ is not a punishment that the Father

---

[79] The Greek word used here by the Apostle (*hilasterion*) is reminiscent of the Hebrew term *kapporet*, which indicates the mercy seat, that is, the cover of the ark of the covenant kept in the innermost part of the Temple of Jerusalem. On such a mercy seat, the blood of immolated victims was sprinkled as a sign of atonement. Thus, Saint Paul says that the *kapporet*, an instrument of atonement, was an image of Christ, the true Atoner.

imposed on the incarnate Son. It is the weight of *our* faults that the Father asks the Son to carry upon Himself (consider the Lamb that *"tollit"*—carries upon Himself—the sins of the world). The Son voluntarily carries out the design of the Father. It is not a matter of "penal substitution,"[80] of the condemnation of the innocent Jesus in the place of the guilty humans. This is a matter of a vicarious expiation or atonement: something happens and as a result, the one who must atone does not atone, because someone else voluntarily (out of love) purifies the sins in that person's place. Even in the Old Testament, atonement (*kippur*) is not the suffering of a punishment, but rather doing something that avoids it. Atonement purifies the person from sin and thus such a person is not punished.

3.3.4. Atonement and Propitiation

In conclusion, "to atone" means to purify, cover, or wash away. The sins of human beings are covered by the Blood of Christ, in the sense that sinners are purified: their sins are no longer, because they were washed away. "To propitiate" indicates what is connected with atonement: God is appeased, that is, He looks upon the human being benevolently,[81] with favor, precisely because He recognizes in the person a creature that was purified by the atonement of Christ. The Sacrifice of Jesus has an atoning (or expiatory) and propitiatory value: it purifies sinners and renders God propitious towards them.

---

[80] Penal substitution is the theory that derives from the interpretation that Martin Luther (d. 1546) gives to Galatians 3:13, a text that we cited in Chapter One (see the section concerning Protestants, specifically regarding redemption). This entails the fact that the Father vents His righteous anger on Christ, because He now sees in Christ the worst sinner in history! According to this theory, Christ would save us by replacing us in suffering the penalty that we deserve for our sins. The doctrine of vicarious atonement, far from saying that Jesus takes our sins *into* Himself, learns from Scripture that He takes them *upon* Himself: that is, He carries them on His shoulders, without making them His own. Some authors wanted to compare the Lutheran theory of penal substitution with the theology of satisfaction (see below) of Saint Anselm of Canterbury (d. 1109). That Saint Anselm does not affirm at all that the Father punished the fault in the Son, Who would suffer passively, can be seen in the following passage: "God the Father . . . did not deliver to death an innocent person for a guilty one. In fact, He did not force Him to die against His will, nor did He permit that He be killed, but He Himself [the Son, Jesus] of His own free will, endured death to save human beings" (*Cur Deus homo* 1.8 [our translation]).

[81] As was said in Chapter One, this new way of God looking at the person corresponds to a real and objective change that Christ produces in that same person, who becomes righteous after being a sinner. Thus, it is not an extrinsic imputation of a righteousness that is only that of Christ, and never becomes our own, as the Luther doctrine of justification hypothesizes.

The Value of Jesus' Sacrifice: Soteriological Categories

3.4. Satisfaction

The soteriological category of 'satisfaction' is not found in Scripture, even if it is based on it. It became a classical category for explaining the work of salvation in Christ, especially thanks to Saint Anselm of Canterbury, who baptized it with his book *Cur Deus homo*. To satisfy, in Latin *satis facere*, means to "make enough, to make sufficient." The basic idea is that what Christ did for our salvation was sufficient. In this sense, satisfaction becomes synonymous with redemption.[82] And what was necessary to satisfy? According to the Magnificent Doctor, it was necessary to repair the honor of divine majesty, offended by sin.

> Whoever does not render God this due honor takes from God what is His and dishonors God, which is the same as sinning. So long as he does not give back what he has taken away, he remains in sin. And it is not enough to merely return what was taken away, but for the offense caused he must render more than he has taken away.... Thus, whoever sins must return to God the honor that was taken away; and this is the satisfaction of which every sinner is indebted to God.[83]

Adam's disobedience (and then of all human beings) represents a crime of lèse-majesté: the divine majesty is offended by the rebellion of the creature. Justice demands that the human being repair the damage done. However, for Anselm, the human being—who also has the obligation to satisfy the divine honor—cannot do it, both because everything that can be given to God is already owed to Him by His creature, and because the human is now in sin and his or her works are marked by the fault. Finally, the human being cannot satisfy, he or she cannot do enough to repay God, because God is infinite. For this reason, the gravity of the offense that injures the divine honor is also infinite. However, the human being, a finite creature, cannot do anything that has infinite value. This is why—Anselm states—Christ comes, God and man, to satisfy as God and man.

Cur Deus homo is a great classic of theological literature, which here—for the sake of brevity—we cannot give due space. Various recent theologians

---

[82] Just as Saint Thomas said (see Chapter Two) that Christ became incarnate to redeem the sin of Adam, he also attested that He came to satisfy: "The Son of God, having assumed flesh, came into the world to satisfy for the sin of the human race. One satisfies for the sin of another when one bears the penalty due to the sin of another" (*ST* III, q. 14, a. 1 [our translation]).

[83] Saint Anselm of Canterbury, *Cur Deus homo* 1.11 (our translation).

have strongly critiqued Anselm's theology of satisfaction, in which—they believe—an image of God prevails that is much too similar to that of a medieval feudal lord. We cannot analyze these criticisms here; we can only say that in most cases they are unfair. If one attentively reads the text of Anselm, one recognizes that it has many more merits than limitations (though limitations are clearly present, as in any human work). The soteriological category of satisfaction, granted that it is properly understood, cannot be eliminated. It is certainly true that there is a divine justice, along with divine love that is always greater. Love, however, does not do away with justice, but rather justice is a minimum level of love: without justice, there is no love.[84] It is an expression of love to not want to save the human being without justice. Thus, it is true that salvation also involves a just penalty for sin. It is not true that the category of *satisfactio* gives us a mistaken view of God, as if He were an offended lord, who pretends—childishly and proudly—to be repaid for his offended honor. Satisfaction is certainly, in its origin, a juridical concept (already present in Roman law), but in Christianity it is reread in light of the Revelation of God, the merciful Father. In fact, the satisfaction of the Christian God is a work not only of justice, but justice and love at the same time. Justice is reaffirmed because the human being, Jesus Christ, is the One who satisfies. However, the greater love is revealed in the fact that it is God Himself who takes the initiative—in His assumed humanity—of satisfying, giving such satisfaction to us in Christ. In Christ, the human being has done enough as restitution for sin, in fact, much more than enough is accomplished. The merit of Christ is not only sufficient (*satis*) but superabundant: it has universal value, the power to save every human being of every age. Saint Thomas—with an expression that we have already cited—reminds us that "the offense [to God] is taken away only by love."[85] It is the love of the priestly Heart of Christ[86] that takes

---

[84] "Justice is the primary way of charity or, in Paul VI's words, 'the minimum measure' of it" (Benedict XVI, *Caritas in Veritate* [2009], §6).

[85] Saint Thomas Aquinas, *Summa contra gentiles* III, ch. 157 (our translation).

[86] "Jesus knew and loved us each and all during his life, his agony and his Passion, and gave himself up for each one of us: 'The Son of God ... loved me and gave himself for me' [Gal 2:20]. He has loved us all with a human heart. For this reason, the Sacred Heart of Jesus, pierced by our sins and for our salvation, 'is ... considered the chief sign and symbol of that ... love with which the divine Redeemer continually loves the eternal Father and all human beings'" (CCC §478; the citation comes from Pius XII, *Haurietis Aquas* [1956] [DS 3924], an encyclical entirely dedicated to the cult of the Sacred Heart of Jesus). Concerning the words of the CCC, for which Jesus "loved us all with a human heart," even if the text is not cited, it certainly refers to this passage of the Second Vatican Council, *Gaudium et Spes*, §22: "The Son of God ... worked with human hands, He thought with a human mind, acted by human choice and loved with a human heart."

away the offense caused to the divine honor and so makes satisfaction for us. With his usual precision, Aquinas gathers the essential facts of the issue in these terms:

> One who fully satisfies for an offense is one who offers to the offended what the latter loves in an equal or superior manner to the hate he has for the suffered offense. Now, Christ, accepting the Passion out of charity and obedience, offers to God a good superior to that required to compensate all the offenses of the human race. First, for the greatness of the charity with which He wanted to suffer. Second, for the nobility of His life, which was the life of the man-God, and which He offered as satisfaction. Third, for the universality of His sufferings and for the magnitude of the accepted pains....[87]

Therefore, the satisfaction theory reminds us that sin has *both* an aspect of fault, *and* an aspect of penalty,[88] and thus redemption passes *both* through the vicarious atonement of our faults, *and* through the satisfaction of the penalties due to them. Satisfaction, then, also possesses in itself a bipolarity, being *both* a work of justice *and* of love.

3.5. Excursus: The Value of Suffering in Christianity

Jesus has redeemed us and placed us back on the path of salvation through His Passion and death on the cross. This implies that He has redeemed us through His suffering. The cross of Jesus is a source of inspiration and an interpretative key for the mystery of suffering. Saint Ignatius of Antioch (d. ca. 107) held that the death of Jesus "is the source of our faith and the patience with which we suffer."[89] He *probably* based this on Colossians 1:24, in which Saint Paul affirmed: "Now I rejoice in my sufferings for your sake, and in my flesh I am filling up what is lacking in the afflictions of Christ on behalf of his body, which is the church." It is from the sorrowful Passion of Christ that Christian thought has always drawn inspiration for its appraisal of human suffering.

---

[87] *ST* III, q. 48, a. 2 (our translation).

[88] "For the perfect cancellation of sins there must be two things, because there are two elements of sin: the mark of sin and the debt of the penalty. The mark of the sin is taken away by grace, which converts the heart of the sinner to God; the debt of the penalty disappears totally with the satisfaction that the human being renders God" (*ST* III, q. 22, a. 3 [our translation]; see also *ST* III, q. 48, a. 4).

[89] Ignatius of Antioch, *Ad Magnesios* 9.1 (our translation).

3.5.1. Difference between Evil and Suffering

The first necessary distinction is that between evil and suffering. Evil indicates any sort of privation, or something missing in any sphere of reality.[90] Sickness is evil because it is a lack of a good that should be present: health. Sin is evil because in its place there should be virtue and grace. Death is evil because it is a privation of the good of life, and so forth. But when we speak of suffering, we enter into the mystery of evil understood from the standpoint of the conscious subject. Even a plant or an animal undergoes evil if it gets sick or dies. But it does not suffer, it simply undergoes evil. By contrast, the human being undergoes evil and suffers because, as a rational animal, the human being is aware of the evil that he or she suffers. In him or her the evil also becomes a subjective, personal experience. It follows, among other things, that the same evil—for example, to be the victim of a theft—can be experienced in various ways, with very different reactions on the part of different people: a person very advanced in the spiritual life can even rejoice for having suffered a theft, not for the act in itself, but because this fact is helpful for maintaining a heart that is detached from material goods, or because such a person immediately offers the loss to God in atonement for sins; while another person could suffer greatly for it to the point of losing peace.

3.5.2. Redemption in, and of Suffering

We have seen that the Book of Genesis explains the origin of evil: the sin of the human being. This explanation, profoundly true, still does not yet give meaning and positivity to human suffering. Knowing the remote cause of evil does not transform it into a good. In Jesus Christ, such a transformation happens—and here we find again the wonderful work of divine Providence (see Chapter Three), that does not want evil or ever authorize anyone to commit it—not even as an exception—but rather allows it to occur and draws a greater good out of it.

Jesus had the capacity—because He is God—to enter into the mystery of human suffering and to use the suffering as an instrument of universal salvation. Jesus, states John Paul II, has redeemed us through suffering; but, in so doing, He redeemed suffering itself and, given that it now has a meaning, it is no longer useless.[91] Jesus had the ability to turn evil into a good. This is why

---

[90] "What else is that which is called evil, if not a privation of a good [*privatio boni*]?" (Saint Augustine of Hippo, *Enchiridion de fide, spe et caritate* 3.11 [our translation]).

[91] "In the Cross of Christ not only is the Redemption accomplished through suffering, but

suffering has become so important in Christian spirituality.⁹²

Here again we experience the Catholic principle of *et-et*: we recognize that suffering is both an evil and a possible instrument of salvation. Moreover, we also encounter the two levels, natural and supernatural, distinct but always united. At the natural level, evil remains a privation of a good. But at the level of grace, at the supernatural level, it is possible to draw good from evil. This also explains the attitude of the believer in the face of suffering. We do not seek out evil and we do not self-inflict it—we are not masochists. Evil remains evil for the Christian too. However, we accept evil and the suffering that it entails, because we see in it a providential design of God in Christ. When evil arrives, without us seeking it, we accept it with love and, if we have sufficiently progressed in the paths of the Spirit, even with joy. Not because we enjoy suffering, which no one of sane mind enjoys, but because we can "suffer-with" Jesus. When in our life something happens that makes us suffer, in the light of faith we discover in this a gift of the Lord: He esteems us and deems us worthy to carry a small amount of the weight of His cross.⁹³ It is Christ Himself who has invited us to this attitude of life, "whoever does not take up his cross and follow after me is not worthy of me" (Matt 10:38; see also Matt 16:24; Mark 8:34; Luke 9:23).

3.5.3. To Suffer with Joy

The importance of our participation in the suffering of Christ was emphasized by Saint Paul: "Now I rejoice in my sufferings for your sake, and in my flesh

---

also *human suffering itself has been redeemed*. Christ—without any fault of His own—took on Himself 'the total evil of sin.' The experience of this evil determined the incomparable extent of Christ's suffering, which became the price of the Redemption" (Saint John Paul II, *Salvifici Doloris* [1984], §19).

⁹² "In bringing about the Redemption through suffering, Christ has also *raised human suffering to the level of the Redemption*. Thus each man, in his suffering, can also become a sharer in the redemptive suffering of Christ"; "Thus to share in the sufferings of Christ is, at the same time, to suffer for the kingdom of God.... Through their sufferings, in a certain sense they [those who suffer with Christ] repay the infinite price of the Passion and Death of Christ, which became the price of our Redemption" (John Paul II, *Salvifici Doloris*, §§19 and 21).

⁹³ "In so far as man becomes a sharer in Christ's sufferings ... to that extent *he in his own way completes* the suffering through which Christ accomplished the Redemption of the world. Does this mean that the Redemption achieved by Christ is not complete? No. It only means that the Redemption, accomplished through satisfactory love, remains *always open to all love* expressed *in human suffering*. In this dimension ... the Redemption which has already been completely accomplished is, in a certain sense, constantly being accomplished" (John Paul II, *Salvifici Doloris*, §24).

The Redeemer

I am filling up what is lacking in the afflictions of Christ on behalf of his body, which is the church" (Col 1:24). We note two things in this witness: (1) Saint Paul is very advanced in the spiritual life and thus does not say merely "I accept the sufferings," but in fact "I rejoice" in suffering for you (referring to the brothers and sisters in the faith). This experience was shared by all the saints: not only can one accept the cross of Jesus, but one can carry it with joy, even if it causes suffering (*both* cross *and* joy). Some saints were worried if for one day the cross was lifted from their shoulders: "I suffer because I do not suffer," said Saint Gerard Majella (d. 1755) in such moments. (2) Saint Paul says that he suffers *for* the brothers and sisters and *in favor* of the Mystical Body of Christ, which is the Church. Suffering received with joy and lived with love obtains grace from God, grace that is shared especially with brothers and sisters in faith, the Church (see "the communion of saints" in Chapter Eight). Thus, in the two thousand years of the history of the Church, there have always been people ("souls," in older language[94]) who have voluntarily offered themselves to the Lord as victims of expiation for the Church. Several of these souls have also clarified the focus of their offering: the Pope, or priests, or missionaries who carry the Gospel in distant lands at the risk of their lives. The latter was the choice, for example, of Saint Thérèse of the Child Jesus (d. 1897), who is venerated as the patroness of the missions, even though she was a cloistered nun who not only never went to a place of mission but never even left her convent in Lisieux. However, by offering her life to the Lord for missionaries, she too worked in a very concrete way in those lands so distant from her.[95]

---

[94] It is a very good thing that Benedict XVI has reprised the language that calls Christians "souls," against the tendency of the last decades to discredit such a mode of expression: "The last keyword that I should like to consider is "zeal for souls" (*animarum zelus*). It is an old-fashioned expression, not much used these days. In some circles, the word 'soul' is virtually banned because—so they say—it expresses a body-soul dualism that wrongly compartmentalizes the human being. Of course, the human person is a unity, destined for eternity as body and soul. And yet that cannot mean that we no longer have a soul, a constituent principle guaranteeing our unity in this life and beyond earthly death. And as priests, of course, we are concerned for the whole person, including his or her physical needs—we care for the hungry, the sick, the homeless. And yet we are concerned not only with the body, but also with the needs of the soul: with those who suffer from the violation of their rights or from destroyed love, with those unable to perceive the truth, those who suffer for lack of truth and love. We are concerned with the salvation of men and women in body and soul. And as priests of Jesus Christ we carry out our task with zeal." (Benedict XVI, *Homily in Chrism Mass*, April 5, 2012).

[95] Saint John Paul II, *Redemptoris Missio*, §78, speaks of prayer and sacrifices as forms of cooperation with the work of missionaries.

3.5.4. Oblative Spirituality

Thus, any suffering in life, even the smallest, can have great value if it is redeemed by Christ in us, which means if we accept it with joy, for the love of God and neighbor, and offer it in a spirit of faith. The concrete mode of redeeming suffering in ourselves is to offer it with love to God. The traditional formula of devotion is expressed with the words of the sort: "I accept this suffering for your love, O Lord, and I offer it to you." This oblative spirituality (i.e., spirituality that offers up suffering) was always very important in the life of Christians, up until our days in which it has unfortunately often been shelved. Benedict XVI recalled its importance:

> There used to be a form of devotion—perhaps less practiced today but quite widespread not long ago—that included the idea of "offering up" the minor daily hardships that continually strike at us like irritating "jabs," thereby giving them a meaning. Of course, there were some exaggerations and perhaps unhealthy applications of this devotion, but we need to ask ourselves whether there may not after all have been something essential and helpful contained within it. What does it mean to offer something up? Those who did so were convinced that they could insert these little annoyances into Christ's great "com-passion" so that they somehow became part of the treasury of compassion so greatly needed by the human race. In this way, even the small inconveniences of daily life could acquire meaning and contribute to the economy of good and of human love. Maybe we should consider whether it might be judicious to revive this practice ourselves.[96]

3.5.5. Active and Passive Virtues

We can ask ourselves why, in recent times, this oblative spirituality has been cast aside by most Christians. It is likely due to the recent forgetfulness of the so-called "passive" virtues (mortification, penance, obedience, contemplation) in favor of the "active" ones (the apostolate, organization, social action). That is to say, in our day many Catholics tend to concentrate especially on "acting" and very little on "undergoing," forgetting that Christ redeemed us *both* by acting *and* by undergoing. Even a portion of the clergy has often been involved in this "activism," as various recent documents of the Magisterium

---

[96] Benedict XVI, *Spe Salvi* (2007), §40.

The Redeemer

note. Activity is certainly an essential component of the cooperation of Christians with the Lord: He Himself sends the Apostles to evangelize, baptize, and care for His people (see Matt 28:19-20). However, there is not only the apostolate of activity, which remains essential in every age, but also (*et-et*) the apostolate of suffering and contemplation, which is even more important (see Mark 3:14; Luke 10:38-42) and thus, in the bipolarity of the terms, occupies the primary hierarchical position. The cultivation of the "passive" virtues is not optional in Christian spirituality. For example, the catechetical tradition (which summarizes the teaching of Scripture) also includes among the spiritual *works* of mercy "to bear wrongs patiently" (see Col 3:12–13). Patience is a passive virtue but is combined here with activities of spiritual love. In fact, even undergoing or suffering is acting, because the will chooses to undergo suffering for love of God and neighbor, just as the human will of Christ chose to adhere to His divine will, which directed Him to the Passion (see Mark 14:36). As soon as the phenomenon of the overvaluation of active virtues to the detriment of passive ones appeared, Pope Leo XIII intervened firmly.[97] Unfortunately, despite his efforts, this too-partial perspective of Christian life has nevertheless spread in large sectors of the Church today. It is therefore necessary to correct this trend, and to return to teaching and putting the Christian value of suffering and patience into practice.

3.5.6. Penitential Spirituality

In the text that was cited, Benedict XVI also spoke of "exaggerations and perhaps unhealthy" things that may have been present in oblative spirituality. The Holy Father refers to cases of excessive zeal, which in practice could result in the confusion, if not the ruin, of the Christian sense of suffering; that is, transforming it from an acceptance of suffering full of love, to seeking it out suffering for its own sake. In fact, Christian spirituality has also seen the development of the phenomenon of passive virtues being practiced not only when they were necessary, but in a systematic way. It has been recognized that in order to be ready when the moment arrives, one also has to constantly train oneself. Therefore, the practice of penance and deliberately chosen renunciations began very early. The simplest and most popular expression of this attitude consists in small penances (Italians use the word "*fioretti*," literally "little flowers"): more

---

[97] See Leo XIII, *Testem Benevolentiae* (1899). This is an apostolic letter that the Pope sent to the archbishop of Baltimore, in which he rejects so-called "Americanism," which among other things held that the passive virtues were adapted to bygone times but not to our own times.

intense efforts at prayer or of renouncing little, unnecessary goods, particularly in certain times of the liturgical year.[98] This spirituality is entirely legitimate and the saints have always practiced it, since apostolic times (see Acts 13:2-3; 14:23; Jesus Himself announced that His disciples would fast: see Luke 5:35). Since all good things can degenerate, even this excellent spirituality in certain times—Benedict XVI recalls—has known cases of exaggeration. However, we generally do not run this risk today. While avoiding any exaggerations, it is necessary to reinforce and renew penitential and oblative spirituality in our time.

3.5.7. Consoling the Afflicted

Christ thus taught His disciples the value of suffering. However, this does not imply that Christians are uninterested in the evils of the world, that they do not seek to make it, as much as is possible, a "better world."[99] On the contrary, the appreciation of the human value of suffering and the fact of knowing how to live it as a moment of grace has led to the development within Christianity of compassion (Latin *"cum-passio,"* "to suffer-with"), which has been put into practice through innumerable works of charity. Places such as Lourdes or the *"Casa Sollievo della Sofferenza,"* the hospital founded by Saint Pio of Pietrelcina, are just two examples taken from a seemingly infinite list, which the holiness of life of many believers has written in the last two thousand years. Finally, let us recall that among the Sacraments of the Church there is one explicitly instituted by Christ for the suffering: the Anointing of the Sick (see Chapter Ten).

3.6. The Death and Descent into Hell of Jesus

To complete the picture of this Christological chapter, let us end by carrying out a quick investigation of the apical moment of the earthly life of Christ: the Holy Triduum of the Passion, death, and Resurrection.

---

[98] Let us recall that the liturgical calendar of the Church also includes days and entire periods of "planned" penance, such as Ash Wednesday, Good Friday, Advent, Lent, and vigils. Planning penance, even establishing it with ecclesiastical law, is not bad if it is done *cum grano salis*.

[99] "Hence, while earthly progress must be carefully distinguished from the growth of Christ's kingdom, to the extent that the former can contribute to the better ordering of human society, it is of vital concern to the kingdom of God" (Second Vatican Council, *Gaudium et Spes*, §39).

The Redeemer

3.6.1. The Gravity of Sin, and the Cruelty of Crucifixion

Jesus of Nazareth was condemned to death by Pontius Pilate, Roman procurator (or prefect) of Judaea. Thus, the capital sentence was carried out by crucifixion—probably the cruelest punishment ever devised by humankind.[100] The death of Jesus was extremely painful from a physical point of view, and particularly dishonorable from the moral perspective given that crucifixion was reserved for slaves and evildoers, not people of high class, especially not if they were citizens of Rome. Beyond the historical aspects, what interests us here is especially the significance of the Lord's death for the faith. The cross, as a terrible punishment, reveals above all the gravity of humanity's sin, because of which Christ "had to" suffer (see Matt 16:21; Mark 8:31; Luke 24:26; John 11:51; Acts 3:18; etc.).[101]

3.6.2. A Sign of God's Love

The crucifixion shows the measure without measure of God's love for us. "[God] did not spare his own Son but handed him over for us all" (Rom 8:32; see *ST* III, q. 47, a. 3). The *Exultet* sings with gratitude for this love, and addressing the Father says: "O wonder of your humble care for us! O love, O charity beyond all telling, to ransom a slave you gave away your Son!" The love of the Father is also the love of the Son, who also wants to die for us: "I will lay down my life for the sheep" (John 10:15). The love of the Father and the Son is a Person in God (see Chapters Five and Six): the Person of Love, or Gift, Whose name is Holy Spirit. Thus, at the moment in which Jesus dies, He does not only let out a last breath in the sense that His human soul is separated from His body, but also because He breathes out the Spirit, Whom He will then send out from the Father to the Church after the Resurrection and Ascension. "Jesus cried out in a loud voice, 'Father, into your hands I commend my spirit'; and when he had said this he breathed his last [Spirit]" (Luke 23:46).

---

[100] Marcus Tullius Cicero (d. 43 BC) defines crucifixion as "the most cruel and horrible of punishments," as well as an "extreme and supreme punishment that is reserved for slaves" (*In Verrem* 2.5.165 and 169).

[101] To clarify what it means to say that Christ "had to" suffer the Passion, that is, in what way the Passion was "necessary," see *ST* III, q. 46, a. 1.

3.6.3. The Cause of Our Redemption

The death of Christ effectively achieves our redemption. The merit of the self-oblation that the incarnate Son makes to the Father obtains the remission of sins for the entire world. Here we can, with Saint Thomas, take up an aspect touched upon in the previous chapter: just as the fault of one alone wounded all his descendants (we sinned "in" Adam), so the merit of one alone, Christ, saves all those who are associated with Him:

> Christ was granted grace not only as an individual Person, but also as the Head of the Church [see *ST* III, q. 7, aa. 1 and 9; q. 8, aa. 1 and 5], i.e., in a way such that from Him it would overflow on all His members. Thus, the actions carried out by Christ are referred to Him and His members together as the actions of another man in a state of grace are referred to him personally. Now, it is evident that any man in grace, in suffering for justice, merits salvation for himself; and this according to that passage of Matthew 5: "Blessed are they who are persecuted for the sake of righteousness" [Matt 5:10]. Therefore, Christ with His Passion merited salvation not only for Himself, but for all His members.[102]

This is what recent exegesis and theology call "corporate personality": a typical perspective of the biblical world—and, in general, of ancient cultures—for which individual and community have mutual belonging and form a sort of "mystical" community for which the individual is in the many, and the many are in the individual (see Chapter Eight for the discussion of the Mystical Body).

3.6.4. The Exemplar Cause of Christian Life

The death of the Lord is an example of life, and a spur for believers, who learn to give their whole life to God, and to die with love on the cross, a cross they have carried throughout the entire span of their existence. For this reason as well, the representation of the crucified Lord is a fundamental element of the Christian spiritual life. It is found at the center of the altar of the Sacrifice of the Mass, in houses, in public places, and is even worn by believers.[103] It

---

[102] *ST* III, q. 48, a. 1 (our translation); see also *ST* III, q. 19, a. 4.

[103] By extension, this is true both of the representation of the holy cross, and the images of Mary, the angels, and the saints: see the Second Council of Nicaea, *Definitio de sacris*

The Redeemer

adorns the Rosary and liturgical objects. Finally, the sign of the cross is the gesture that clearly distinguishes the Christian. This sign is made on one's own body while the Persons of the Most Holy Trinity are invoked.

3.6.5. Jesus' Death: Christological Perspective

As regards the death of Christ, it was a real human death, and thus it involved the separation of the soul from the body, as the Gospels show by saying that Jesus released His spirit from His body. Jesus truly was in a state of death for about three days[104] until His Resurrection. In the state of death, His human nature knew the paradox[105] that all the dead know: the separation of the soul from the body. In the unique case of Jesus, however, the soul and the body, while separated from one another, were always the humanity of the Word, because they were hypostatically united to the divine nature. This means that the human nature of Jesus, even in the state of death, is always the human nature assumed by the Person of the Son. While during His earthly life (and after, in the resurrected life) soul and body were united and the divine Person possessed them this way, during His death the Word continued to assume them, albeit separately.[106] The dead body of Christ in the tomb was always the body of the Word, and this is also the case with His soul. Jesus' death was a real death, as the New Testament highlights by emphasizing that He was "buried" (therefore it was not an apparent death). The Lord's body was sealed in the bare rock of a tomb just outside Jerusalem, and there it awaited, incorrupt, His Resurrection.

3.6.6. Descent into Hell

What about Jesus' soul? Some texts of the New Testament mention the fact that in those three days between the death and Resurrection, Christ "also went

---

imaginibus (787) (DS 600).

[104] The figure of three days is correct if we count as the Jews did, including the day of the death itself in the calculation, and not starting with the next day, according to the common method in modern times. Otherwise, one needs to say that Christ remained in the tomb around a day and a half.

[105] The separation of the soul from the body is paradoxical because it is unnatural. It was introduced into the world as a consequence of the sin of Adam, as we saw in the previous chapter.

[106] "Although He died as a man and His holy soul was separated from His incorrupt body, the divinity remained inseparable from both, that is, from the soul and the body" (Saint John Damascene, *De fide orthodoxa* 3.3 [our translation]). See *ST* III, q. 50, a. 2–3; *ST* III, q. 52, a. 3.

The Value of Jesus' Sacrifice: Soteriological Categories

to preach to the spirits in prison" (1 Pet 3:19). With the soul alone—though still assuming the body that was in the tomb—the Word went to proclaim to certain spirits the salvation He had obtained, that is, to souls separated from bodies and thus dead human beings (see 1 Pet 4:6) who waited in a "place" that Saint Peter calls "prison." Here the Christian Tradition has clarified the terms by utilizing the expression *limbus patrum*, the Limbo of the Fathers, not to be confused with the Limbo of Infants, which will be discussed in the final chapter of this book. The Limbo of the Fathers was a place, or better said, a state of waiting.[107] The spirits of the Limbo are the souls of the Fathers, that is, of the righteous ones who lived before Christ, who had merited Heaven by the conduct of their life, but could not enter the eternal reward because the gates of Eden were still guarded by the Cherubim placed there by God after the sin of Adam (see Gen 3:24). According to Tradition, Adam and Eve were also found in the state of Limbo.[108] They and all their descendants now receive the proclamation that the wait is over. Christ Himself goes to bring this Gospel of liberation: the gates of Heaven are opened once again. Thus, an ancient Psalm can be read anew in a Christological way:

> Lift up your heads, O gates; / be lifted, you ancient portals, / that the king of glory may enter. / Who is this king of glory? / The Lord, strong and mighty, / the Lord, mighty in war. / . . . The Lord of hosts, he is the king of glory (Ps 24:7-8, 10).

Christ is the mighty Lord who has brought victory in His battle against Satan, sin, and death. For this reason, in the face of His triumph, the ancient gates, closed for so long, must open. He will cross the threshold first (Last Adam), but after Him, and thanks to Him, many others will follow (He is the Firstborn of those who will rise). Thus, Christ's descent into hell is not a "going to the dead," a sharing of the experience of the darkness of the dead, as John Calvin (d. 1564) wanted when he imagined the soul of Christ suffering the

---

[107] It is highly probable that Jesus Himself spoke of it, calling it "Abraham's bosom," in the parable recounted in Luke 16 (see Chapter Twelve).

[108] For the mainstream of the Tradition, Adam and Eve were saved by Christ even though they were guilty of original sin. Saint Irenaeus of Lyon attests to this in *Adversus haereses* 3.23.2. In 3.23.8 he adds: "Thus, they all lie who deny his [Adam's] salvation . . . because they do not believe that the sheep that had been lost was found. In fact, if it has not been found, the entire human race is still under the power of perdition." In the same text, Irenaeus believes that it was Tatian the Syrian (d. 180) who introduced for the first time "this opinion, or rather ignorance and blindness," by affirming that Adam had been condemned to eternal Hell.

penalty for wrongs, namely, the penalty of the damned of Hell (but the "hell" where Christ went is not the same as the Hell of the damned!). The cross is the most radical point of self-emptying or humiliation (the cross is *kenosis*: emptying or total dispossession, as is said in Phil 2:7–8). After the cross, the ascent toward the Father has already begun (see Rom 10:7). The descent into the underworld is actually the first step of an ascent to the heavenly spheres. The Word goes into the Limbo of the Fathers not as a dead one among the dead, but as the Victor who liberates the dead (see Col 2:15; Rev 1:18).[109] This is also seen from the fact that the *Apostle's Creed*—an ancient profession of faith preceding the fourth century—places the descent into hell and the Resurrection together in one article: "He descended into hell; on the third day he rose again from the dead."[110]

The mystery of the descent into hell shows that Christ's redemption is also universal in a retroactive way. Truly, Jesus is the center of history, and with His power He saves even those who lived on the earth before Him. The power of the salvific mediation of Jesus is extended not only to all places, but also to all times. This does not imply that He saves every individual, but only those who, in every place and time, "were joined to His Passion through faith informed by charity."[111]

3.7. The Resurrection and Ascension of Christ

The paradox of death is definitively overcome by the glorious Resurrection on the third day, the first after the Sabbath. The Resurrection of Christ, occurring on a Sunday, made it so that this day (*dies dominicus/dominica* ["the Lord's day"]) took the place of the Hebrew Sabbath as the weekly feast day for the new People of God, the Church.[112] Sunday is the day in which the Christian, exceptions aside, suspends all activities done for profit, and dedicates the day

---

[109] "The divine nature descended among the dead, not to be restrained by death according to the law of mortal creatures, but to open the gates of death for those who thanks to Him would rise. It is as if a king went to a prison and having entered inside, opened the doors, untied the chains and shackles, broke locks and bolts, led out to freedom those who were imprisoned, and brought light and life back to those who sat in darkness and the shadow of death (see Ps 106:10). We shall say then that the king, certainly, was in prison, but nonetheless He was not in the condition of those who were held in prison: those who were captives had to suffer the penalties, but He came there to remit the penalties" (Origen of Alexandria [d. 254], *Explanatio Symboli* 15 [our translation]).

[110] CCC §633 summarizes it in this way: "Jesus did not descend into hell to deliver the damned, nor to destroy the Hell of damnation, but to free the just who had gone before him." (Cf. Council of Rome [745]: DS 587; Benedict XII, *Cum dudum* [1341]: DS. 1011; Clement VI, *Super quibusdam* [1351]: DS 1077; Council of Toledo IV [625]: DS 485; *Mt* 27:52–53).

[111] *ST* III, q. 52, a. 6.

[112] See Saint Justin Martyr (d. ca. 165), *I Apologia* 67.

The Value of Jesus' Sacrifice: Soteriological Categories

more intensely to God, family, and rest. All of this happens because Christ rose on that day.

3.7.1. The Historical and Physical Character of Jesus' Resurrection

The first fundamental aspect to recall concerning the Resurrection of Jesus is its historicity and physicality. The Resurrection is a historical fact that happened in time, the day after the Sabbath that followed the burial of Christ. It concerns His true biological body.[113] Even if the scriptural sources do not describe the event in itself, because there were no eyewitnesses who were in Christ's tomb when He rose, it does not take away the fact that it really happened—as the eyewitnesses of its effects could ascertain.[114] Such consequences of this fact are the following: the finding of the empty tomb, the vision of the angels who announced the Resurrection, the finding of the linens that covered the dead body of Christ,[115] but above all the numerous apparitions of the Risen One Himself. The historicity of the Resurrection of Christ is a point on which the Christian faith stands or falls:

> But if Christ is preached as raised from the dead, how can some among you say there is no resurrection of the dead? If there is no resurrection of the dead, then neither has Christ been raised. And if Christ has not been raised, then empty [too] is our preaching; empty, too, your faith (1 Cor 15:12–14).

It is also necessary to emphasize a notable aspect of the post-Resurrection appearances of Jesus. While before the Resurrection (that is, during His

---

[113] "The body of Christ after the resurrection was a true body and of identical nature as before. If it were a phantasmal [*phantasticum*] body, the resurrection would not have been true but apparent" (*ST* III, q. 54, a. 1 [our translation]; see ST III, q. 54, a. 3).

[114] The four Gospels report the facts by varying some details and circumstances, but they all agree on the fundamental aspects. For example, Matthew and Mark speak of the apparition of only one angel, while Luke and John speak of two; but the fact of an angelic apparition (or perhaps more than one) remains. The disagreement on secondary aspects can be explained quite easily, as many scholars have shown.

[115] From certain details of Saint John's narration (see ch. 20 of his Gospel), some recent scholars have affirmed that the way in which the linens were found, specified by the Greek verbs used in the Johannine text, would in itself represent a sign of the credibility of the resurrection. To adequately explain this very fascinating theory would require a large extension to this paragraph, which unfortunately would not meet the conciseness of the present treatment.

mortal life) Christ was visible to all His contemporaries, the appearances of the Risen One were reserved only to His "own," namely, to those who followed Him during His earthly life and ministry. He appeared to Peter, to the Apostles, to the women, and also one time to more than five hundred faithful gathered together (probably for Sunday Worship: see 1 Cor 15:3–8), but He never appeared to Pontius Pilate, Annas and Caiaphas, to the soldiers who mistreated Him, and so forth. This means at least two things: (1) Only those who welcomed Christ "before" see Him "afterwards"; everyone saw Him but only some followed Him. Now, Christ only allows Himself to be seen by those who did. This probably also implies that after death the only ones who will see the Lord in Heaven are those who welcomed Him as much as they could during their earthly life. (2) The choice of Christ has a very exact value: all could see Jesus in mortal life, but the witness of the Risen Christ is entrusted only to the Apostles and the Church. Prior to this, anyone could approach Jesus: disciples, friends, family, enemies, Jews, Samaritans, and pagans. From the Resurrection onward, one comes into contact with Christ only through the apostolic ministry, which is kept alive in Jesus' Church. One comes into contact with Jesus only through the Church, or at least, this is the ordinary way that the Lord has established.

3.7.2. *Transcendent and Mysterious Character*

Although it is a historical fact, the Resurrection has a transcendent and mysterious significance, which is why for some decades the adjective "metahistorical" has been applied to it in order to indicate an event that both happens in, and transcends, time. In fact, the Resurrection of Jesus does not consist simply in coming back to life, as is the case with Lazarus, the friend that Jesus brought back to life (see John 11). The Resurrection of Jesus does not consist in returning to earthly life, to then die again afterwards. The Risen One is no longer subject to death: "We know that Christ, raised from the dead, dies no more; death no longer has power over him" (Rom 6:9). Resurrection means that Jesus enters into a new state of life (Last Adam) never before experienced by a human being. Jesus enters into a new life, with new characteristics: resurrected life. The transcendent character of the Resurrection is also present in the fact that it is a Trinitarian work (see further along).

3.7.3. *Characteristics of the Resurrected Body*

We do not know in detail how human life will be after the resurrection or what the qualities possessed by a resurrected human being will be. However,

The Value of Jesus' Sacrifice: Soteriological Categories

the Gospels give us some indications. Even during His earthly life, Jesus, insofar as He is God,[116] carried out exceptional signs, such as walking on water, multiplying bread and fish, bringing the dead back to life, etc. However, it is never narrated that before His Resurrection Jesus, for example, entered into a room locked from within, which instead happens after the Resurrection (see John 20:19); nor did it happen before that His disciples did not recognize Him when they met Him, which was the first reaction that they all have—in the Gospel accounts—upon seeing the risen Jesus. Such points lead us to infer that the risen body must possess certain qualities that it did not possess before the Resurrection.

In particular, we see that spatial and corporal limits are no longer an obstacle for the risen body, which can present itself when and where the person wants, even in places that are very far apart, and that it can appear in various forms.[117] It should be noted that the Apostles and the other disciples, who also knew Him very well, generally did not recognize the Master when He showed Himself after the Resurrection. This suggests that the physical aspect of Christ has in some way changed. They knew Him with the face of a first-century Palestinian Semite. Now He appears with a renewed face, the traits of which we do not know but which must be different than they were before the Resurrection.[118]

---

[116] Jesus carried out in life certain signs that surpassed the ordinary nature of things insofar as He is the Word and not through strictly natural powers: see *ST* III, q. 13, a. 3; *ST* III, q. 43, aa. 2 and 4. Saint Leo the Great, *Tomus ad Flavianum* 4, had said that the divine nature "shines forth with miracles," while the human nature "succumbs to injuries" (DS 294).

[117] "This authentic, real [risen] body possesses the new properties of a glorious body: not limited by space and time [*non amplius in spatio et tempore positum est*] but able to be present how and when he wills (Cf. *Mt* 28:9, 16–17; *Lk* 24:15, 36; *Jn* 20:14, 17, 19, 26; 21:4).... The risen Jesus enjoys the sovereign freedom of appearing as he wishes: in the guise of a gardener or in other forms (Cf. *Mk* 16:12; *Jn* 20:14–16; 21:4, 7)" (CCC §645). When the Catechism speaks of the relation of the risen body to space and time, we believe it means that it is no longer subject to these limits, as the rest of the text clarifies, and not that it no longer possesses any sort of spatial-temporal individualization (see Chapter Twelve). For Saint Thomas, the ascent of Jesus into Heaven is a "locomotion" and from this point of view it should be attributed to the (already risen!) humanity of Christ "which is contained in place and subject to motion" (*ST* III, q. 57, a. 2 [our translation]; see also *ST* III q. 57, aa. 4–5). It is exactly this, among other things, that explains why—in the Eucharistic doctrine—one needs to distinguish between the local presence of Christ and His sacramental presence (see Chapter Eleven). If the risen Christ did not have some "place" (however different it is from our own) then the clarification that He is not in the consecrated Host locally, which is also maintained by the post-conciliar Magisterium, would no longer be necessary.

[118] It is clear—and it should be reiterated—that we do not know anything exact in this regard, but it is intriguing to recall an iconographic clue. In the first centuries, the few representations of Christ that we possess represent Him according to the idealized stylistic features of a Greco-Roman shepherd, a shaven man, dressed in a tunic, who carries a

The Redeemer

Saint Paul calls the risen body a "spiritual body" (1 Cor 15:44; see below).

3.7.4. The Heavenly High Priest

On the Lord's resurrected body there are signs of the nails that pierced His hands and feet, and of the lance that pierced His side. It is precisely the appearance of the stigmata that in many cases allows the disciples to recognize Jesus. This fact is very significant: the Risen Christ is and will forever remain the resurrected Crucified One. He lives immortal with the signs of His Passion[119] and carries them on His resurrected body in Heaven, at the right hand of the Father. By showing His stigmata to the Father, Christ permanently obtains the redemption and forgiveness of the sins for all human beings. The Father, looking at the stigmata of Jesus, forgives every crime, even the gravest ones. The risen Christ thus continues His ministry as High Priest: that is, He offers Himself to the Father for our sake. The Letter to the Hebrews, the *magna carta* of Jesus' priesthood, reveals it:

> but he, because he remains forever, has a priesthood that does not pass away. Therefore, he is always able to save those who approach God through him, since he lives forever to make intercession for them (Heb 7:24–25).

We can even dare to imagine Jesus who, at the right hand of the Father, holds His pierced hands open and intercedes for us[120]: a priestly deed *par excel-*

---

sheep on His shoulders; or He is presented as a child-master (equally shaven). The depictions of Christ with long hair and a beard, which we are accustomed to, begin in the sixth century, and not by chance: in fact, the Mandylion of Edessa was found, a depiction of the face of Christ that was considered "*acheiropoieta*" (not painted by human hand: thus the image would have been imprinted miraculously and would be a most faithful reproduction of the face of Jesus). Several scholars hypothesize that the Mandylion coincides with the Shroud of Turin. The fact that Christ was represented in the first centuries as without a beard and long hair, that is, different from how the Apostles knew Him in His earthly life, could be due, in addition to symbolic motives, to the fact that the Apostles passed down that they had seen the Lord with a new face after His Resurrection. In this sense, Michelangelo Buonarroti (d. 1564) may not have depicted the Christ of the celebrated *Last Judgment* in the Sistine Chapel just in a symbolic way (as the Greek god Apollo), but rather in a theological manner: the risen Christ assumes features that go beyond those of a first-century Palestinian Semite and represent the perfect man (Last Adam).

[119] See *Missale Romanum*, "*Praefatio paschalis III*": "He is the sacrificial Victim who dies no more, the Lamb, once slain, who lives for ever." The original Latin is more beautiful: "*Qui immolatus iam non moritur, sed semper vivit occisus.*"

[120] See *ST* III, q. 54, a. 4 (third reason in the *respondeo*).

lence, which the priests of the Church humbly imitate in the Liturgy, holding the palms of their hands turned toward God.[121] They can do this because Jesus the Priest works in them and they celebrate the divine Worship *"in Persona Christi"* ("in the Person of Christ") (see Chapters Nine through Eleven). Is there anything the Father could deny us if His dead and risen Son, the High Priest, requests it of Him? "And whatever you ask in my name, I will do, so that the Father may be glorified in the Son" (John 14:13); "Amen, amen, I say to you, whatever you ask the Father in my name he will give you. Until now you have not asked anything in my name; ask and you will receive, so that your joy may be complete" (John 16:23–24; see also John 15:16; Matt 21:22).

3.7.5. The Resurrected Crucified One

From the preceding point also follows the aspect of continuity in the one life of the incarnate Word in its two stages: mortal life and resurrected life. This does not mean two lives, but one human life that makes the qualitative leap from earthly and mortal existence to one that is celestial and immortal.

1. Cross and Resurrection

First, this continuity means that one cannot refer to the Crucified One as in opposition to the Risen One, or the Risen One as in opposition to the Crucified One. We adore the Lord Jesus Christ, who is *both* crucified *and* risen. Thus, when Christians recognize their fundamental symbol in the cross, they do not at all disavow Christ's Resurrection. The fact that prayer opens and closes with the sign of the cross, and that the representation of the crucifix is placed on the altar in the Holy Mass, does not come at the expense of our faith in the Risen One, but it is the recognition of the salvific value of the Passion and death of the Lord and of the fact that He reached the Resurrection and opened up this future possibility to us by passing through the cross. "What you sow is not brought to life unless it dies" (1 Cor 15:36); "Unless a grain of wheat falls to the ground and dies, it remains just a grain of wheat; but if it dies, it produces much fruit" (John 12:24).

It should also be said that the main emphasis falls on the fact that Jesus was crucified and then rose, not vice versa. It is the Passion that above all has

---

[121] In the Rite of the extraordinary form proper to the Order of Preachers (Dominicans), at the moment of the *"Unde et memores,"* the priest spreads out his arms, imitating the exact position of Christ on the cross. This gesture is also found in the extraordinary form of other rites: for example, in the Ambrosian Rite and in the Rite proper to the Carthusians.

The Redeemer

redeemed us, with the Resurrection being the consequence and the confirmation of the work carried out by the incarnate Son. Although both members in the bipolarity are necessary, the fact that the crucifixion is hierarchically preeminent is demonstrated by the choice of the Church to mark houses, churches, vestments, etc., with the sign of the cross. The sign of the cross, as was said, was also chosen as a fundamental sign of the Christian: a sign of recognition and profession of the faith. It is thus the crucifix, as has been noted, and not the statue of the risen Jesus (N.B., not even in the Easter Season!), that is placed on the altar of the Eucharist, "source and summit" of the life of the Church (see Chapters Nine and Ten). All of this should always have visible consequences both in the spiritual life and in the Church's liturgical celebration.

2. *"Animal Body" and "Spiritual Body"*

Second, continuity implies that the risen body is a body of flesh, which Jesus defined as having "flesh and bones" (Luke 24:39), not an apparent or evanescent body.[122] Here we can borrow the expression of Saint Paul, who distinguishes the "animal" body (that of earthly life) from the one that is "spiritual." We note that the Apostle proposes this terminology in a text in which he speaks precisely of the resurrection, both that of Jesus and of Christians (see 1 Cor 15). Moreover, he uses these expressions in describing a process of continuity: just as one sows a seed in the earth and it dies, and a new life arises from it (that of the plant), so too one sows an animal body and it (re)-arises as spiritual, with greater splendor. The subject is always "body," an indication of continuity. The expression "spiritual body" therefore does not indicate an immaterial body, but a material body that is nonetheless now totally subjected to the spirit (the soul) and the Spirit (God): a body that no longer resists the action of the S/spirit in any way and is totally pervaded by it.

3.7.6. Resurrection as a Work of the Trinity

The Resurrection of Jesus is therefore a Trinitarian event: an event in which the Father raises up the Son (see the texts in which it is said that "God raised him up" [Acts 2:24; etc.]); but the Son also raises Himself up ("I lay down my life in order to take it up again.... I have power to lay it down, and power to

---

[122] Saint Thomas notes that flesh and blood "fall within the definition of the human being. Thus, it is impossible for the human nature to subsist without sensible matter" (*ST* III, q. 4, a. 4 [our translation]). Therefore, if Christ is risen as a human being, He maintains a true human body, even if glorified.

The Value of Jesus' Sacrifice: Soteriological Categories

take it up again" [John 10:17–18]). Finally, the Resurrection is an event of the Spirit, who fills the mortal humanity of the Son with new life (see Acts 2:33). This grafting, so to speak, of the Spirit to the humanity of Jesus, represents the gift of the Father to the humanity of the incarnate Son. We must not forget that, during the earthly life of Jesus, the Spirit already dwelled within Him in fullness, making Him the Anointed, *the* Christ of God.[123] The novelty that occurs here, however, concerns the entry of the body of Jesus into the new state of the Resurrection. This body, now definitively "spiritual," also becomes a principle of the outpouring of the Holy Spirit over the Church. Various passages of Scripture refer to this, among which are the following:

> Acts 2:32–33: God raised this Jesus; of this we are all witnesses. Exalted at the right hand of God, he received the promise of the holy Spirit from the Father and poured it forth, as you (both) see and hear.

> John 16:7: [Jesus said:] It is better for you that I go. For if I do not go, the Advocate [the Holy Spirit] will not come to you. But if I go, I will send him to you.

> John 7:36–39: What is the meaning of his saying, "You will look for me and not find [me], and where I am you cannot come"?

> On the last and greatest day of the feast, Jesus stood up and exclaimed, "Let anyone who thirsts come to me and drink. Whoever believes in me, as Scripture says: / 'Rivers of living water will flow from within him.'" / He said this in reference to the Spirit that those who came to believe in him were to receive. There was, of course, no Spirit yet, because Jesus had not yet been glorified.[124]

> 1 Corinthians 15:45: The last Adam [became] a life-giving spirit.[125]

---

[123] Among the Fathers of the Church, there are two opinions about the moment of the Anointing: the older Fathers think that it happened when the Spirit descended upon Christ at the moment of the Baptism in the Jordan, while starting from the fourth century—also in response to Arianism—there was a shared conviction that Jesus was fully anointed in His humanity from the time of His conception in Mary's womb.

[124] "There was ... no Spirit yet" does not mean that the Holy Spirit did not exist, but that He had not yet been sent over the Church in fullness, because Jesus was not yet risen when He pronounced those words. Regarding the eternity of the Holy Spirit, who is true God, see Chapter Five.

[125] Understood in its context, this verse means precisely that Jesus pours out the Holy Spirit

The Redeemer

3.7.7. *The Apologetic Value of the Resurrection*

Jesus' Resurrection is proof of His messiahship: it shows that He truly is *the* Christ of God and that He is also God Himself in Person. The Resurrection was always considered the greatest proof of the divinity of Jesus Christ:

> Matt 12:39–40 (see also Matt 16:4): An evil and unfaithful generation seeks a sign, but no sign will be given it except the sign of Jonah the prophet. Just as Jonah was in the belly of the whale three days and three nights, so will the Son of Man be in the heart of the earth three days and three nights.

> Acts 2:36: Therefore let the whole house of Israel know for certain that God has made him both Lord and Messiah, this Jesus whom you crucified.

> Acts 3:14–15: You denied the Holy and Righteous One and asked that a murderer [Barabbas] be released to you. The author of life [Jesus] you put to death, but God raised him from the dead; of this we are witnesses.

> Acts 17:31: He [God] has established a day on which he will "judge the world with justice" through a man [Jesus] he has appointed, and he has provided confirmation [!] for all by raising him from the dead.

This is why the Resurrection underpins not only our faith, but also our hope.[126] We do not know in detail what Heaven is like, but we know for certain that Heaven exists (it consists in being with Christ) and that Christ wants to welcome us and present us to His Father:

> Do not let your hearts be troubled. You have faith in God; have faith also in me. In my Father's house there are many dwelling places. If there were not, would I have told you that I am going to prepare a place for you? And if I go and prepare a place for you, I will come

---

through His glorified humanity.

[126] "There is a God, and God can create justice in a way that we cannot conceive, yet we can begin to grasp it through faith. Yes, there is a resurrection of the flesh. There is justice. There is an 'undoing' of past suffering, a reparation that sets things aright. For this reason, faith in the Last Judgment is first and foremost hope" (Benedict XVI, *Spe Salvi*, §43).

back again and take you to myself, so that where I am you also may be. (John 14:1-3)

The Resurrection of Jesus is a pledge of our future resurrection (see 1 Cor 15:20–24). We too are called to rise in soul and body, although for us, on account of sin, an "intermediate state" is placed between the judgment of the soul (that happens at the moment of death) and the resurrection of the body and its reunion with the soul, which instead happens at the end of time (see Chapter Twelve).

3.7.8. Catholic Optimism

The reality of the Resurrection, a foundation of Christian faith and hope, is also at the base of a typically Catholic attitude, namely, optimism. To be Catholic means to be an optimist, a trait that differentiates Catholicism from large strata of traditional Protestantism, which by contrast are marked by a certain theological and spiritual pessimism. To be optimistic does not mean failing to see the harshness of daily reality or, worse, disregarding it. Neither does it mean being idealistic, which would be contrary to the fundamental law of the Incarnation. Instead, it is precisely from this law of the Incarnation that Catholic optimism takes shape, to then be definitively confirmed by the Resurrection of Jesus. The Incarnation tells us, in fact, that God loves us immensely, that He takes care of us and intervenes in our favor even in the most desperate situations: "If God is for us, who can be against us? He who did not spare his own Son but handed him over for us all, how will he not also give us everything else along with him?" (Rom 8:31–32). The Resurrection then demonstrates that whoever is with God always wins in the end. The world can attack the Catholic with all its force and often can come out victorious in individual battles, but in the end, God is stronger than all the rest, even stronger than death, as is seen in the glorious destiny of the Messiah. From this derives trust and, indeed, Catholic optimism, which is based on the Catholic concept of redemption as an effective and not merely forensic justification of the sinner. In Christ, God makes us once again pure and able to perform meritorious acts for salvation. Thus, thanks to the risen Redeemer, we can look at humanity and the future with more optimism, albeit not in a naïve way.

3.7.9. Presence of the Risen Christ

The reality of Jesus' Resurrection is also at the base of His action and presence in the Church and in the world, through the work of the Holy Spirit, whom He sends from the Father. The presence of Christ is real because He is contemporary to every era of history, being the One who risen no longer dies. He is the Living One who accompanies the journey of humanity in every moment.

> The historical character of the mystery of Christ's Resurrection and Ascension helps us to recognize and understand the transcendent condition of the Church which was not born and does not live to compensate for the absence of her Lord who has "disappeared" but on the contrary finds the reason for her existence and mission in the invisible presence of Jesus, a presence working through the power of his Spirit. In other words, we might say that the Church does not carry out the role of preparing for the return of an "absent" Jesus, but, on the contrary, lives and works to proclaim his "glorious presence" in a historical and existential way.[127]

The reality of His presence is differentiated in various degrees. The highest degree of the presence of the Risen One in the world is the Eucharistic presence, which—as Paul VI explains[128]—is called real not by exclusion but *par excellence*: this means that all degrees of the presence of the Lord are real, but that His presence is found in the highest degree in the Eucharist, because the Lord is not present only with His grace, with His action, or with His loving gaze, but He is present in Person (see Chapter Eleven). This gradation of Christ's presence is also assumed by the Second Vatican Council, when it lists certain ways in which Christ makes Himself present in the Liturgy (see Chapter Nine), implying that these ways do not have the same value and that Christ is not present in all of them with equal intensity, although all of them are real modes of His presence.[129]

---

[127] Benedict XVI, *Homily on the Solemnity of the Ascension on Pastoral Visit to Cassino and Monte Cassino*, May 24, 2009.

[128] See Saint Paul VI, *Mysterium Fidei* (1965), §40.

[129] "Christ is always present in His Church, especially in her liturgical celebrations. He is present in the Sacrifice of the Mass, not only in the person of His minister, 'the same now offering, through the ministry of priests, who formerly offered Himself on the cross,' but especially under the Eucharistic species. By his power he is present in the Sacraments, so that when a man baptizes it is really Christ himself who baptizes. He is present in his word, since it is he himself who speaks when the Holy Scriptures are read in the Church.

3.7.10. *Ascension into Heaven*

The Resurrection is not the terminal moment in the parabola sketched by the human existence of Christ. There are two further stages, one of which has taken place—the Ascension into Heaven—and the other which is yet to come—the *parousia*, namely, the glorious return of Christ at the end of time. We shall now look at the first of these two moments, leaving treatment of the return of Christ for the final chapter.

The Ascension of Jesus is narrated by Saint Luke, both in his Gospel (see Luke 24:50–53) and in the Acts of the Apostles (see 1:6–11), which he also authored. He informs us that after the Resurrection a period of forty days passed in which the risen Jesus continued to manifest Himself to the Church, and to instruct the Apostles concerning what they had to do and teach (see Acts 1:3). The fact that only Saint Luke gives us detailed information on the Ascension has led some modern scholars to doubt the historicity of this event, which is not reported by the other hagiographers (but see Mark 16:19). However, there are indeed other indications in the New Testament. For example, in the Gospel of John, when Jesus appears to Saint Mary Magdalene, He tells her to not hold onto Him because He—although risen—has not yet ascended to the Father (see 20:17). Moreover, Saint John (see 20:26) clarifies that eight days after the Resurrection, Jesus was still with His disciples and convinced the incredulous Saint Thomas of His corporeality. Furthermore, Saint Paul writes: "What does 'he [Christ] ascended' mean except that he also descended into the lower [regions] of the earth? The one who descended is also the one who ascended far above all the heavens, that he might fill all things" (Eph 4:9–10). We could mention other passages as well. Thus, with the Resurrection, the journey of Jesus is not completed. He then ascends to the Father.

From the soteriological standpoint, Jesus' "being seated at the Father's right hand signifies the inauguration of the Messiah's kingdom" (CCC §664). From the Christological point of view, the Ascension is the fact that the glorified humanity of Christ has been admitted, so to speak, into the Holy Trinity. As Son, the Second Person, Jesus has always been and always will be "at the right hand" of the Father. Even when He became incarnate, the divine Word did not leave the bosom of the Trinity, because the Incarnation does not consist in a local movement of the Word, that is, a movement from one place to another, from Heaven to earth. It instead consists in the assumption in His

---

He is present, lastly, when the Church prays and sings" (Second Vatican Council, *Sacrosanctum Concilium* [1963], §7).

The Redeemer

Person of a human nature, created in the womb of the Virgin Mary. Now His human nature, glorified by the Resurrection and always united personally to the Word, reaches, so to speak, the "place" where the Person who assumed it always is and remains. The man enters into the Sanctuary of Heaven: "one of us," that is, a human being, "stands in Their midst," among the Persons of the divine Trinity.[130]

3.7.11. The Ascension and the Effusion of the Holy Spirit

This mystery marks the further confirmation of the divinity of Christ and of our hope of eternal salvation. Our High Priest was admitted into the heavenly Sanctuary to intercede for us. Standing at the right hand of the Father, the risen Christ sends from the Father, and with the Father, the Holy Spirit over us. For this reason, the risen Jesus tells His disciples to wait for the One who He will send from on high once He has ascended into Heaven (see Luke 24:49; Acts 1:4–5): only in the power of the Spirit will the Apostles be able to spread the Gospel. Therefore, without the Ascension and the sending of the Spirit of truth, the work of Christ will not be complete, and the Church cannot begin its journey in history.

3.7.12. The Ascension of Christ and the Attraction of Believers

The Ascension of Jesus sets into motion the effusion of every grace that descends from on high. This grace, brought by Jesus' Spirit, is aimed at elevating human beings, and guiding them toward Heaven, purifying and drawing them in. Grace purifies, directs, and above all attracts. Jesus spoke of this work that He would carry out after the Ascension: "And when I am lifted up from the earth, I will draw everyone to myself" (John 12:32).[131] From this point of view, the mystery of the Ascension also demonstrates all of its value

---

[130] Of course, this does not imply that the Trinity becomes a "quaternity," given that Christ is not a human person, as we have said: "For the Holy Trinity has had no person or hypostasis added to it, even by the Incarnation of God the Word, One of the Holy Trinity" (Second Council of Constantinople, *Anathematismi de Tribus Capitulis* [553], §5 [DS 426]).

[131] It is true that these words are applied first and foremost to when Jesus was elevated from the earth with the crucifixion. In fact, the evangelist says in the verse that immediately follows: "He said this indicating the kind of death he would die." However, this is applied equally well to the Ascension. The grace that attracts flows out from the Sacrifice of Jesus on the cross, and it is poured out on believers by the Holy Spirit, sent by Christ who has ascended into Heaven.

The Value of Jesus' Sacrifice: Soteriological Categories

in the liturgical sphere, given that in the celebration of Christian Worship, the orientation or direction of the heart is of fundamental importance (see Chapter Nine). During Worship, Christians do not speak to one another, because they speak to God through the High Priest, Christ. They do not look to one another, but they look to Christ, Who they await and Whose glorious return they implore. Therefore, since the early centuries of the Church, the resurrected Christ was depicted in the apse in the basilicas. The ancient mosaics present Christ as the Pantocrator who looks out from His tribune of Heaven, where He was seated following His Ascension: He looks at us and draws us to Himself. He is the One who comes (*marana tha!*: 1 Cor 16:22; see Rev 22:20); in the meantime, He directs us to Himself so that we may convert from mistaken paths and meet Him with joy.

Finally, this reference to Worship reminds us of the intimate link between the Ascension and the Sacraments of the Church. In a famous passage, Pope Saint Leo the Great teaches that "What was visible of our Redeemer has passed into the Sacraments"[132] The Sacraments are the continuation of the presence and work of Christ in the midst of His disciples.

---

[132] Saint Leo the Great *Sermones* 74.2, in *NPNF*, Second Series, vol. 12, trans. Charles Lett Feltoe (Peabody, MA: Hendrickson Publishers, 1994), 188 (with our corrections).

5

The Sanctifier

1. Jesus and the Spirit

In addition to the Father, a third figure appears in the life of Christ: the Holy Spirit. The Spirit is present from the first instant of His conception in the virginal womb of Mary (see Luke 1:35). The Holy Spirit accompanies Christ throughout His earthly life and mission and, as was said in the previous chapter, it is the Spirit who anoints the humanity of Jesus, which is a reason why the Nazarene is *the* Christ of God.[1] Moreover, the Spirit is present in Jesus' teaching, given that the Master spoke of the Holy Spirit on more than one occasion. In this first part of the chapter we will consider these two aspects: the presence and action of the Spirit in the life of Jesus, and the teaching of Jesus concerning the Holy Spirit.

1.1. The Presence and Action of the Holy Spirit in the Life of Jesus

1.1.1. The Holy Spirit in the Earthly Life of Christ

The Holy Spirit is present from the beginning of the earthly life of Jesus[2]: the Incarnation, although a work of the Son alone with respect to its final stage, is

---

[1] "Jesus is Christ, 'anointed,' because the Spirit is his anointing, and everything that occurs from the Incarnation on derives from this fullness (Cf. *Jn* 3:34)" (CCC §690; see also CCC §727).
[2] This treatment will be enriched with further elements in the next chapter, dedicated to the Trinity.

The Sanctifier

certainly a work of the whole Trinity as regards the initiative and execution.[3] The Gospel says explicitly that the Word becomes incarnate by the work of the Holy Spirit in the virginal womb of Mary (see Matt 1:18, 20; Luke 1:35). The simultaneous presence of the incarnate Son and the Spirit since Jesus was in the womb of Mary can also be inferred from the fact that as soon as Mary's cousin Elizabeth was greeted by the Virgin she was filled with the gift of the Holy Spirit (see Luke 1:41). This means that the incarnate Word, present in the womb of Mary, sent the Spirit over Elizabeth. It also happens that the Spirit brings people to the incarnate Word, such as the elderly Simeon, a righteous man in whom the Holy Spirit dwelt, and who was moved by the same Spirit to go to the Temple on the occasion of the presentation of the infant Jesus in that holy place (see Luke 2:25–27).

According to the Baptist, Jesus is the One who baptizes "with the Holy Spirit" (Mark 1:8; see Matt 3:11; Luke 3:16). At the moment of Christ's baptism, a special manifestation of the Spirit occurs under the form of a dove who descends upon Him (see Mark 1:10; Matt 3:16; Luke 3:22). Immediately after, Jesus is compelled by the Spirit to go into the desert (see Mark 1:12; Matt 4:1; Luke 4:1). Luke notes that Jesus' return to Galilee, after the temptation, was also guided by the Spirit (see 4:14), and he is the only evangelist who reports in detail the episode of the synagogue of Nazareth, in which Jesus read and gave commentary, applying the passage of Isaiah 61:1–2 to Himself: "The Spirit of the Lord is upon me, because he has anointed me" (4:16–21).

The Baptist will later attest not only to having seen the Spirit, in the form of a dove, descend and remain upon Jesus (see John 1:32), but also to having received in advance the revelation of this event, as a criterion for recognizing the Messiah (see John 1:33). In this sense, Matthew sees in Jesus the fulfillment of the prophecy regarding the Servant of YHWH of Isaiah 42:1–4: "Behold, my servant / ... I shall place my Spirit upon him" (Matt 12:18).

The works of Christ are also explicitly linked to the action of the Holy Spirit several times. Indeed, Jesus Himself attributes His exorcisms to the Spirit of God who works in Him (see Matt 12:28).

1.1.2. The Holy Spirit and Jesus' Disciples (Election, Mission, Prayer)

Regarding the prayer of Christ, we note that it is always addressed to the Father (*Abba*) and never to the Spirit. The Holy Spirit is not the "You" who Jesus addresses in prayer; however, at least once, the Gospels tell us that Jesus

---

[3] See Saint Augustine of Hippo, *De Trinitate* 2.10.18; *ST* III, q. 23, a. 2; *ST* III, q. 32, aa. 1–2.

addresses the Father while "rejoicing in the Holy Spirit" (see Luke 10:21). And soon afterwards, He assures the disciples that the Father will give the Holy Spirit to them, if they ask Him (see Luke 11:13). Saint Paul teaches in two distinct passages that we too can call God *Abba*, and this is possible because Jesus gives us the gift of the Spirit (see Rom 8:15; Gal 4:6). The very prayer of true worshipers of God, Jesus states, will be carried out "in Spirit and truth" (John 4:23), because God Himself is Spirit (see John 4:24). Jesus even relates the future preaching of the Church to our theme: in fact, the Lord says to the disciples that it will be the Spirit of the Father who speaks in them (see Mark 13:11; Matt 10:20; Luke 12:12). And, thus, in the Acts of the Apostles, we see that Jesus had chosen the Apostles in the Holy Spirit (see Acts 1:2).

1.1.3. The Holy Spirit in the Death and Resurrection of Jesus

According to a widely attested interpretation,[4] the Holy Spirit is also present at the moment of Christ's death, because Luke relates: "Jesus cried out in a loud voice, 'Father, into your hands I commend my spirit' [Ps 31:6]" (Luke 23:46); and Matthew: "Jesus cried out again in a loud voice, and gave up his spirit" (Matt 27:50). This would also be the sense of the passage of Hebrews 9:14 in which we read that "the blood of Christ, who through the eternal [S]pirit offered himself unblemished to God, [will] cleanse our consciences from dead works." The "eternal Spirit" that this refers to is the Third Person of the Trinity,[5] present and cooperating in the Sacrifice of Christ on the cross.[6]

Lastly, let us recall the presence of the Holy Spirit in the Resurrection of Jesus (see the previous chapter). The New Testament also teaches that the Resurrection of Jesus itself was a work of the Spirit. We can limit ourselves here to recalling the single passage of Romans 1:3–4, which speaks of Jesus "established as Son of God in power according to the spirit of holiness through resurrection from the dead."

---

[4] Taken up in CCC §730.
[5] See Saint John Paul II, *Dominum et Vivificantem* (1986), §40.
[6] Regarding the presence and cooperation of the Spirit in the death of Christ, the Liturgy and Magisterium leave little room for doubt. For example, Leo XIII, in *Divinum Illud Munus* (1897), says that the Holy Spirit was present in all the work of Christ and "especially in the Sacrifice of Himself." In the celebration of the Eucharist, a prayer reserved to the priests says: "*Domine Jesu Christe, Fili Dei vivi, qui ex voluntate Patris, cooperante Spiritu Sancto, per mortem tuam mundum vivificasti*" ("Lord Jesus Christ, Son of the living God, who by the will of the Father, and the cooperation of the Holy Spirit, through your death gave life to the world").

The Sanctifier

1.2. Jesus' Teaching Concerning the Holy Spirit

The object of Jesus' teaching is above all the mystery of the Father and His own mystery as Son; nonetheless, there is no shortage of teachings concerning the Spirit (see Mark 3:28–29; Matt 12:31–32; 28:19; Luke 12:10; etc.). Moreover, Jesus qualified His words as "spirit and life" (John 6:63).

1.2.1. "Ruah" in the Old Testament

Jesus' teaching concerning the Holy Spirit is spoken against the backdrop of the Revelation of the Old Testament, which Christ confirms and brings to perfection. In the biblical books preceding the coming of the Lord, the word spirit (*ruah* in Hebrew) has numerous meanings: wind or air, breath, the human soul or the breath of life (see Gen 6:17), and it can even refer to spiritual beings or angels. We could say that the word *ruah* indicates everything that is impalpable, invisible, vital, and dynamic. This explains why the term was used in the Old Testament to also indicate the "Spirit of God," an expression which, basically, indicates God Himself. It is clear that in the Old Testament there are various texts in which it is possible to see a preparation for the revelation of the Third divine Person, a revelation that nonetheless is only presented clearly in the New Testament.

1.2.2. "Pneuma" in the New Testament

The New Testament is in continuity with the Old because, in the New Testament, the word spirit (*pneuma* in Greek) likewise assumes the same meaning, including the divine meaning. However, Jesus teaches that "Spirit of God" is not only an expression to indicate God as such. The Holy Spirit is, along with Him and the Father, a Third One in God. This is to be noted, for example, in the last words that the risen Christ pronounced before ascending to Heaven, where He distinguishes the three Persons, putting them, at the same time, on the same level of dignity: "Go, therefore, and make disciples of all nations, baptizing them in the name of the Father, and of the Son, and of the holy Spirit" (Matt 28:19). This will be explored further in the next chapter.

1.2.3. The Cooperation of the Holy Spirit and the Sending on the Part of Jesus

The Lord qualifies His mission as a mission carried out along with the Spirit: (1) To His opponents who accuse Him of being able to cast out demons because a demon was in Him, He responded that He actually casts them out with the "[F]inger of God" (Luke 11:20), namely, with the power of the Holy Spirit (see Matt 12:28). Thus, Jesus acts by cooperating with the Holy Spirit. (2) We encounter another example of this in the miracle of the "*ephphatha*" ("be opened!") (see Mark 7:31–37): Jesus healed a deaf and mute person by means of a real reforming of the ears and tongue (it seems to reflect the work of the Creator, when He formed Adam of old) and, before carrying out the miracle, He looked to heaven, that is, toward the Father (see Matt 6:9) and sighed deeply, that is, He let out the Holy Spirit (see John 20:22), who carried out the healing. (3) A final example, among others, is represented by an episode that happened after Jesus had risen from the dead. He appeared to the Apostles and breathed on them, while instructing them to forgive the sins of others (see John 20:22–23). Such a breath indicated the outpouring of the Third Person, as Jesus explicitly states: "Receive the holy Spirit" (v. 22). From these examples, it is clear that the Holy Spirit intervenes in the world by cooperating with Jesus, but is also sent by Jesus, passing through His humanity. Before the Resurrection, this happens in a hidden way and through particular interventions, while after the glorification of Christ's humanity, there is an explicit and universally directed outpouring that begins with Pentecost (see Acts 2:33).

1.2.4. The Trinitarian Dynamic of Christ's Works

Regarding the relations between the Father, Son, and Spirit, and their coordination in the salvation of human beings, the four sayings concerning the Advocate (or Paraclete) contained in the Gospel of John are decisive (see John 14:16–17; 14:26; 15:26; 16:7, 13–15). These four passages all refer to the Holy Spirit as the Paraclete (or Advocate, or Consoler). We will return to these texts in the next chapter. Here, we want to note two things: (1) Christ reveals that He and the Father together send the Holy Spirit; and (2) while the mission of Jesus, the Son, is something that already happened—Jesus uses verbs in the past tense—for the Spirit, the mission is to come (future tense verbs are used). The Trinitarian dynamic outlined in these passages is that the Father sends the Spirit who is of the Son, because the Father and the Son have everything in common. Therefore, the Spirit is the Spirit of both. For this reason, it is said that the Son will also send the Spirit, and He will send Him from the Father. The important verb "to proceed" is used: the Spirit proceeds from the Father. Thus, this verb will become a technical term in Trinitarian theology, as will be noted in the next chapter. From all this, it follows that the Spirit is an integral "part" of the mystery of God the Trinity. He is sent to us by the

Father and the Son, and this is the case because eternally, in the Trinity, He proceeds from the Father and the Son.

1.3. The Names of the Holy Spirit in the New Testament

The New Testament uses many names to indicate the Third Person of the Trinity. Here is a catalogue of them compiled by Saint Gregory of Nazianzus (d. 390):

> He is called the Spirit of God (1 Cor 2:11), Spirit of Christ (Rom 8:9), Mind of Christ (1 Cor 2:16), Spirit of the Lord (Wis 1:7), and Lord Himself (2 Cor 3:17), Spirit of adoption (Rom 8:15), of Truth (John 14:17), of freedom (2 Cor 3:17), Spirit of Wisdom, understanding, counsel, strength, knowledge, and fear of the Lord (Isa 11:2).... He is the Finger of God (Luke 11:20), Fire (Acts 2:3).[7]

There are even more names Saint Gregory omits,[8] such as Spirit of the promise (Eph 1:13) and Spirit of glory (1 Pet 4:14). These titles do nothing but confirm what was said in the preceding paragraphs: the Holy Spirit has an indissoluble link with the Son and the Father, and also possesses divine power like Them.

Regarding the personhood of the Paraclete and His properties within the divine nature, see the following chapter. Here we will dwell more extensively on the action attributed to Him "*ad extra*," that is, within space and time. Thus, the rest of the present chapter is dedicated to bringing to light the Holy Spirit's multiform action of grace in the entire cosmos and, in particular, in the Family of God that is the Church.

2. The Spirit's Action in the Church and in the World

The Holy Spirit, sent by the risen Christ, carries out many functions, mainly in the Church, but also in the entire cosmos. They can be grouped under

---

[7] Saint Gregory of Nazianzus, *Oratio* 31.29 (our translation).
[8] In addition to the names, the symbols used by the Scripture and the Fathers to designate the Person and work of the Spirit are instructive. A list accompanied by a brief explanation is offered by the CCC §§694–701. The following symbols are taken into consideration: water, anointing, fire, cloud and light, seal, hand, finger, dove.

The Spirit's Action in the Church and in the World

the category of "continuation and fulfillment" of the work of Christ,[9] as for example the Third Eucharistic Prayer of the Missal of Paul VI assumes:

> You are indeed Holy, O Lord,
> and all you have created
> rightly gives you praise,
> for through your Son our Lord Jesus Christ,
> by the power and working of the Holy Spirit [*Spiritus Sancti operante virtute*],
> you give life to all things and make them holy,
> and you never cease to gather a people to yourself,
> so that from the rising of the sun to its setting
> a pure sacrifice may be offered to your name.

The Constantinopolitan Creed (see DS 150) professes that the Holy Spirit is the Lord and Giver of Life. The term "Lord" indicates His divinity, which we shall return to in the following chapter. "Giver of life" indicates that He gives both natural and supernatural life.[10] The fact that the Spirit is involved in creation is already seen from the first verses of the Bible: "In the beginning, when God created the heavens and the earth, the earth was formless and void, and darkness covered the abyss, and the Spirit [*ruah*] of God was hovering over the waters" (Gen 1:1–2 [our translation]). This is why the Psalm confirms: "By the Lord's word the heavens were made; / by the breath [Spirit] of his mouth all their host" (Ps 33:6). Finally, the Liturgy absorbed this biblical message in the hymn "*Veni Creator Spiritus*" ("Come, Creator Spirit"). While it is true that the work of creation is attributed to the Father, it is also true that the Son and Spirit are not excluded from it, because God always works with His two Hands.[11]

---

[9] "The Spirit *prepares* men and goes out to them with his grace, in order to draw them to Christ. The Spirit *manifests* the risen Lord to them, recalls his word to them and opens their minds to the understanding of his Death and Resurrection. He *makes present* the mystery of Christ, supremely in the Eucharist, in order to reconcile them, to *bring them into communion* with God, that they may 'bear much fruit' (*Jn* 15:8, 16)" (CCC §737).

[10] The Holy Spirit is "(uncreated) Gift from which as from a living source derives all giving of gifts vis-a-vis creatures (created gift): the gift of existence to all things through creation; the gift of grace to human beings through the economy of salvation" (Saint John Paul II, *Dominum et Vivificantem*, §10).

[11] It is well-known that this image is from Saint Irenaeus of Lyon (d. ca. 202), *Adversus haereses*. A small anthology of passages: "There is only one God, the Creator . . . He is Father, He is God, He is the Founder, He is the Maker, He is the Creator, who made those things by Himself, that is [!], through His Word and His Wisdom [here this means the

The Sanctifier

As for the dispensation that the Spirit makes of supernatural life, the first element to mention is His role in Revelation. As the Constantinopolitan Creed recalls, the Third Person of the Trinity "has spoken through the prophets."[12] He has an active role not only in the creation of the world, but also in the revelation of the true face of God and, in doing so, He remains in a certain sense hidden:

> "No one comprehends the thoughts of God except the Spirit of God" [1 Cor 2:11]. Now God's Spirit, who reveals God, makes known to us Christ, his Word, his living Utterance, but the Spirit does not speak of himself. The Spirit who "has spoken through the prophets" makes us hear the Father's Word, but we do not hear the Spirit himself. We know him only in the movement by which he reveals the Word to us and disposes us to welcome him in faith. The Spirit of truth Who "unveils" Christ to us "will not speak on his own" [John 16:13]. Such properly divine self-effacement explains why "the world cannot receive [him], because it neither sees him nor knows him," [John 14:17] while those who believe in Christ know the Spirit because he dwells with them. (CCC §687)

The second part of this text highlights the link between the Spirit's work of Revelation and His presence of grace in Christians (regarding the theme of Revelation, see Chapter Two). He is the Giver of life because He gives to us precisely the "life in the Spirit," that is, the grace that sanctifies us and makes us able to carry out our Christian mission.

Therefore, our treatment will now examine the Catholic concept of grace

---

Holy Spirit]" (2.30.9, in *ANF*, trans. James Donaldson and Alexander Roberts [Peabody, MA: Hendrickson Publishers, Inc., 1994], 406); "The Father being in no want of angels, in order that He might call the creation into being, and form man, for whom also the creation was made; nor, again, standing in need of any instrumentality for the framing of created things, or for the ordering of those things which had reference to man; while, (at the same time,) He has a vast and unspeakable number of servants. For His *Offspring* [here meaning that the Son and the Holy Spirit are not creatures] and His *Hands* do minister to Him in every respect; that is, the Son and the Holy Spirit, the Word and Wisdom; Whom all the angels serve and to Whom they are subject" (4.7.4, p. 470 [with our variations]); "By the Hands of the Father, that is, the Son and the Holy Spirit, man, and not (merely) a part of man, was made in the likeness of God" (5.6.1, in *ANF*, 531).

[12] "By 'prophets' the faith of the Church here understands all whom the Holy Spirit inspired in living proclamation and in the composition of the sacred books, both of the Old and the New Testaments" (CCC §702). This interpretation of the *Catechism* is corroborated by an ancient symbol of faith (fourth century), which reads as follows: "We believe in the Holy Spirit...who has spoken through [in] the law and the prophets and the evangelists" (*Symbolum maius Ecclesiae Armeniacae* [DS 48]).

The Spirit's Action in the Church and in the World

and then will explore the principal modes by which the Holy Spirit extends the presence and action of Christ in the Church and in the world.

2.1. The Spirit, the Giver of Life: Grace

Grace in the Christian sense is the grace of Christ obtained through the merits of His humanity, poured out over human beings insofar as He is God and the Head of the Mystical Body. Christ's gift of grace is poured out through the action of the One who is the uncreated Gift in Person: The Holy Spirit. We have already identified grace in the divine "likeness," granted to the human being immediately after being created, and then lost on account of original sin (see Chapter Three). On account of the redemption of Christ, the Holy Spirit gives back to humanity the likeness that was lost in the beginning.[13]

The role of the Holy Spirit in the dispensation of the grace of Christ is fundamental. Christianity, understood as the path of grace and sanctification, is a "living in the Spirit," a journey in the paths of the Holy Spirit. The link between Christ and Spirit in the life of faith is unequivocally indicated by Saint Paul: "Now those who belong to Christ [Jesus] have crucified their flesh with its passions and desires. If we live in the Spirit, let us also follow the Spirit" (Gal 5:24–25). The same Apostle reaffirms such an indissoluble link in describing the Christians of Corinth by the beautiful metaphor of being a letter written by Christ, through the hand of the Apostle, with the ink that is the Holy Spirit: "[You are] shown to be a letter of Christ administered by us, written not in ink but by the Spirit of the living God, not on tablets of stone but on tablets that are hearts of flesh" (2 Cor 3:3).

Thus, we shall proceed further by briefly presenting the fundamental facts concerning the ministry of grace, dispensed by the Holy Spirit—the Spirit of Christ.

2.1.1. The Gratuitousness of the Divine Gift

The Latin word *gratia* (in Greek, *charis*) indicates a gratuitous reality, that is, a gift given gratuitously by God. This means that the gift of grace is above all an initiative of God, more than a response of His to our action or to our merit (an element that is nonetheless not excluded, on account of the well-

---

[13] See Saint Irenaeus of Lyon, *Adversus haereses* 5.6.1; 5.8.1; Irenaeus, *Demonstratio apostolicae praedicationis* 5. CCC §720 notes that "with John the Baptist, the Holy Spirit begins the restoration to man of 'the divine likeness,' prefiguring what he would achieve with and in Christ."

known principle of *et-et*). The absolutely gratuitous and prevenient character of divine grace thus implies that it is in no way due to the creature. Grace is part of the supernatural order of reality, not the natural order. It is poured out over nature, presupposes it, purifies it, and elevates it without suppressing it or changing it in its very being. Nonetheless, this gift from on high, although it is the only thing that makes the attainment of one's ultimate end possible, is—as already mentioned—in no way due to the creature. If God so decreed, He could undoubtedly refrain from pouring out His grace on the world and on human beings.

2.1.2. *"Potentia Oboedientialis"*

The theological Tradition gives us the Thomistic affirmation, of incalculable value, for which grace presupposes nature and brings it to fulfillment.[14] We see the principle of *et-et* wonderfully realized here: it is not a case of *either* grace *or* nature, but rather that *both* grace *and* nature contribute to the salvation of the human being. The fact that grace is not due to nature, and that the natural order can subsist even without grace, means neither that nature can be led to the final end without grace, nor that grace is something added to nature in an extrinsic way, that is, as a mere decoration or superstructure, only placed on top of nature to embellish it. On the contrary, nature is created by God in such a way that, if He freely chooses to give grace, nature is not opposed to such a gratuitous supernatural gift.[15] Nature does not demand this gift, nor is it owed to nature; yet the Creator establishes the natural order by inserting into it a passive capacity to receive grace, if He chooses to give it.[16] This fact

---

[14] See *ST* I, q. 1, a. 8, ad 2.

[15] This is the true meaning of the expression for which the human being is *"capax Dei"* ("capable of God"): not that the creature can with his or her own natural capacities rise to the supernatural level, but that—if grace is given to the human being—human nature is such that it is not repugnant to receiving grace, but rather is capable of accepting the gift. The human being is capable of God because God has created (nature!) him or her as a fundamentally religious being. It is this constitutive openness to the mystery that God has placed in the human being by creating him or her, which *can* (but not *must*) be filled by grace, if it is granted (see CCC §§27–30).

[16] If it is permissible to make use of an image, we shall say that the creation of nature can be compared to the construction of a hotel complex equipped with everything necessary, built by a person of great importance. A heliport is also set up on the hotel, in case the builder one day decides to visit the hotel that he has built. A heliport is a place arranged in such a way that, if a pilot wants to land his helicopter there, he can do so in the best way. But the person with the helicopter is not obliged to land there, nor is it the hotel's right that the builder will land there simply because he has equipped it with a heliport.

implies that, while giving origin to two distinct orders of reality (natural and supernatural), God manifests the intention of giving grace to nature, and thus already predisposes it to receive that grace, even if such a passive capacity, or predisposition, is not a grace as such but rather nature.

This purely passive capacity is called, in traditional theological language, *potentia oboedientialis*, that is, the possibility of docilely obeying the divine gift if granted from on high. Since the *potentia oboedientialis* is impressed in the created nature by the Creator, it is not repugnant to it to receive the gift of elevating grace. This means that supernatural salvation is not a work whereby God does violence to His creation but is an elevation above the natural in a way that is not opposed to the being of the creature. The creature is made by God in such a way that he or she *can* be elevated to a higher level, that of grace. The active role of grace and the passive role of nature (at least in the beginning) must always be recognized.[17] Saint Augustine (d. 430) expresses such a "landing place" of grace in us with this exhortation: "Make of yourselves a hollow space, take the water of heaven upon you. The places below [the humble] are filled, the heights [the proud] dry up. Grace is a rainfall" ("*Vallem facite, imbrem suscipite. Depressa implentur, alta siccantur. Gratia pluvia est*").[18]

2.1.3. The Cooperation of Nature with Grace

If what has been said is the case, how can it be that both grace and nature contribute to human salvation? If only grace is active, is not salvation an imposition on the part of God? Are we not faced with a "soteriological imperialism"? The Catholic doctrine strongly rejects such a perspective when—in contrast to Protestantism—it teaches the doctrine of merit. What we have said above about the activity of grace and the passivity of nature should be understood, in general, about the process of giving grace to nature, and the

---

It can be said that it is reasonable to expect a visit and the contrary could seem strange; nonetheless, if it did not happen, there would be nothing paradoxical about it. God places in human nature the capacity to receive grace, but his does not mean that the existence of this passive capacity implies the gift of grace, attracts it, or determines it.

[17] "One cannot prepare oneself to receive the light of grace, except through the gratuitous help of God, who moves one interiorly" (*ST* I-II, q. 109, a. 6 [our translation]).

[18] Saint Augustine of Hippo, *Sermo* 131.3 (our translation). The image of the hollow space is taken up centuries later by Saint Alphonsus de Liguori (d. 1787) in the work *La pratica di ben governare: Riflessioni utili ai vescovi*, in which he writes: "No one can be a channel, who is not hollow first" (ch. 2, *incipit* [our translation]). This reference is very useful in an era such as ours, in which the active virtues are greatly highlighted (evangelization, the apostolate, etc.), while the passive ones are, at times, neglected (see in the previous chapter the reference to the *Testem Benevolentiae* of Leo XIII).

reciprocal relationship between the natural and supernatural orders. That is to say, it concerns God's initiative in granting grace, which is totally gratuitous and not based on any previous merit of the human being, or on some obligation linked to natural being. However, when we speak of the grace of salvation, that is, of the definitive fulfillment, a different perspective enters into play. In fact, here we do not speak of the initiative with which God, based exclusively on His love, comes to encounter us in grace. Here we are speaking of the terminal point, that is, the arrival of the human being at his or her final supernatural end (eternal salvation). This is where cooperation comes in, the *et-et* of grace and nature.

Once grace is given by God, it requires a free response on the part of the rational creature. Saint Augustine puts it this way: "The One who made you without you, does not justify you without you."[19] Salvation will remain a work of grace, but to guarantee that the human being wants to be saved, God requires and accepts a paltry collaboration, which produces a "merit."[20] The doctrine of merit does not imply that eternal salvation is what is due to the human being for his or her good works: What good work can, in the proper sense, merit Paradise? However, this doctrine implies the infinite respect of God for His creature, which He already demonstrated when He permitted sin, despite it being against His will. Not only in sin, but also and especially in grace, God loves the freedom of the human being whom He has created. He loves that human beings use it to choose the good.

2.1.4. Prevenient Grace

However, it is good to clarify what we have said here as well. We do not imagine that the human being is left alone to struggle between good and evil, to autonomously choose between good and evil. If we thought that, we would fall into the error of thinking that the human being merits grace and, in the

---

[19] Saint Augustine of Hippo, *Sermo 169*.11.13 (our translation).

[20] Merit should be understood as the reward that should be given by right for a good work. On the contrary, a "penalty" is what one must receive by right for an evil work. Saint Thomas distinguishes a merit *"de condigno"* from one *"de congruo."* The first derives from strict justice, and it is the just reward that is due in proportion to the work accomplished. The second is a reward given in friendship, in a free way, which exceeds the measure of what would correspond to pure justice. In the sphere of grace, merit is clearly *de congruo*, because with respect to the good works of the Christian, God grants rewards that infinitely exceed what the human being has done. With it being a reward given in friendship, we can understand why a person in mortal sin, that is, someone who is not in friendship with God, cannot merit in a supernatural way. See *ST* I-II, q. 109, a. 5; *ST* I-II, q. 114, aa. 1–10.

The Spirit's Action in the Church and in the World

end, merits in the proper sense also his or her eternal salvation. If we imagine a man placed in a neutral situation, in which he alone chooses to follow God and the good, and is inserted with his autonomous decision into the world of grace, we place the merit of his right decision before the divine gift. Thus, rather than God acting before the man with grace, it would be the man who chooses to enter into it. Would grace still be an initiative of God, or rather the destiny that the man chooses for himself? Therefore, Revelation and ecclesial doctrine teach that, in actuality, when one chooses the good, this is done already under the influence of grace, without which no one could choose the good.

> We also believe and profess for our salvation that in every good work it is not we who begin and afterward are helped by God's mercy, but He himself, without any previous merits on our part, first instills in us faith in Him and love for Him, so that we may faithfully seek the Sacrament of Baptism and, after Baptism, we may with His help accomplish what is pleasing to Him.[21]

When someone chooses the good, this means that this person is already attracted by grace (even if he or she is still living in sin). In fact, no one can carry out acts that have salvific value without the grace of God preceding, sustaining, and accompanying it:[22] "Without me you can do nothing" (John 15:5). Let us read how Saint Bede the Venerable (d. 735) commented on the conversion of the Apostle Saint Matthew:

> Jesus saw a man called Matthew sitting at the tax office, and he said to him: "Follow me.". . . "And he rose and followed him." There is no reason for surprise that the tax collector abandoned earthly wealth as soon as the Lord commanded him. Nor should one be amazed that neglecting his wealth, he joined a band of men whose leader had, on Matthew's assessment, no riches at all. Our Lord summoned Matthew by speaking to him in words. By an invisible, interior impulse flooding his mind with the light of grace, he instructed him to walk in his footsteps. In this way Matthew could understand that Christ, Who was summoning him away from earthly possessions, had incorruptible treasures of Heaven in his gift.[23] On this point,

---

[21] Second Synod of Orange (year 529), *Conclusions Drawn up by Bishop Caesarius of Arles* (DS 397).

[22] See *ST* I-II, q. 109, aa. 9–10.

[23] Saint Bede the Venerable, *Homilia* 21, in *Liturgy of the Hours*, Office of Readings for the

there was in the first centuries a very bitter dispute among the followers of Pelagius (d. 420) on one side, and ecclesial orthodoxy on the other, represented especially in that era by Saint Augustine. The Doctor of the Church from Hippo arose as the great defender of the true Catholic concept of grace. Recent scholars point out that in the excitement of a very heated dispute, he sometimes used exaggerated expressions to counterbalance the extremes of the Pelagians, such as the famous "massa damnata" ("condemned mass") when referring to humanity fallen into sin.[24] Besides this, it should be recalled that the position of Saint Augustine nonetheless expresses the essence of the ecclesial dogma, as was also officially recognized by the Magisterium.

2.1.5. Pelagianism and the Life of the Church

The clearly anti-Pelagian position of Saint Augustine must be maintained in every era, but perhaps especially in our own, in which Pelagianism often presents itself as a luring temptation in various forms. For example, we have already mentioned the current tendency of many Christians toward activity (evangelization, organization, social action) and their scarce esteem for the passive virtues, prayer, and contemplation. Also symptomatic of this tendency is the fact that in the last several decades the contemplative religious orders have seen significant decline; in fact, there has been much more esteem for a

---

Feast of St. Matthew (emphasis added).

[24] For example: "The cause of the condemnation of the whole mass of mankind lies here. The first man who committed the sin was punished along with the human race that was rooted in him, and so punished that no individual at all was to be freed from this just and merited punishment save by mercy and unmerited grace, and the human race as a whole was to be so divided that in those of the one portion would be revealed the power of mercy and grace and in the others the rigor of justice and retribution. Both justice and mercy were not to be revealed in all because, if all were to remain in the punishments of a just condemnation, merciful grace would appear in none and, on the other hand, if all were to be transferred from darkness to light, in no one would be revealed the truth that retribution was due. And, if there are more to reveal justice than mercy, that was to make clear that it was justice which all incurred. And although, if all paid the penalty, no one could have found fault with the justice of the One who justly demanded retribution, yet so many have been pardoned in order to give them ground for the utmost gratitude for the unmerited gift of the pardoner" (Saint Augustine of Hippo, *De civitate Dei* 21.12, in *FCNT*, vol. 24, trans. Gerald G. Walsh and Daniel J. Honan [New York: Fathers of the Church, Inc., 1954], 371). And in the *Contra Iulianum* 3.4.10, he writes: "God does not withdraw the good of his work from this mass of perdition" (our translation).

The Spirit's Action in the Church and in the World

concept of active religious life rather than contemplative religious life.²⁵

It has been opined that it is no longer useful, as in the past, to be enclosed in a monastery, because the task of the Christian, even a religious, is to go out into the world. While it is clear that ecclesial activity is of enormous value and importance, we must be attentive to the creeping Pelagianism, which leads us to structure ecclesial life mainly, if not exclusively, from the standpoint of doing and organizing.

As an example, we shall mention the fact that, in the last several decades, in almost all the dioceses of the world, there has been a strong decline in vocations to the priesthood. The response to this fact is often (but not always!) sought by organizational means: sociological investigations concerning the phenomenon, models and statistical projections, planning for the future redistribution of remaining clerics, pastoral programs for the fusion of parishes, meetings of vocational ministry teams, etc. All of this is useful. However, we have not always remembered the words of the Lord: "The harvest is abundant, but the laborers are few; so ask the master of the harvest to send out laborers for his harvest" (Matt 9:37–38). Christ tells us to pray for vocations, to beg for them as a gift of grace. Vocation ministry must certainly be done, and done well; but before, during, and after the "doing" there must be the "praying" ("*ora et labora*" ["pray and work"]: yet another *et-et*, whose internal hierarchy is quite clear).

This is only one example among many that shows that in the Church today—which continues to condemn Pelagianism²⁶ as a heresy—many do not realize (probably in good conscience) that they have become Pelagian in their own way of thinking: that is, that human action would make the Church, and

---

²⁵ The sharp decline of new men and women religious has also affected the more active orders, but it seems that the contemplative orders have undergone an even more drastic decrease in numbers. The exception seems to be those communities that, with a prophetic spirit, have had the courage to remain firmly bound in the practice of daily life (even with some necessary adaptation) to the demands of the original rule of their founders. It seems that being demanding attracts young candidates to religious life more than being compliant with a worldly spirit. However, from the first steps, a demanding attitude generally produces a better group of candidates. The Second Vatican Council, *Perfectae Caritatis* (1965), §1, and *passim* (see *Lumen Gentium* [1964], §§43–47) reminded the Church that religious life is a "splendid sign of the heavenly kingdom" and this on the example of the Master, Who is followed in a particularly close way by the practice of the evangelical counsels. Thus, the religious must manifest the future hope with their life, and remind everyone with their example (see *Lumen Gentium*, §13), that we live on the earth to one day be in Heaven. It is important to recall this, particularly in the present ecclesial context.

²⁶ See the strong expressions of Francis, *Evangelii Gaudium*, §94 against the "spiritual worldliness" that can also present itself under the form of a "self-absorbed promethean neopelagianism of those who ultimately trust only in their own powers and feel superior to others."

···357

The Sanctifier

that know-how could keep it prosperous. This is one of the ways of affirming that the human being can do good without the help of divine grace.

2.1.6. Pelagianism and the Liturgy

The Liturgy also frequently suffers today, because its *gratuitous* character is not recognized—to worship God because it is right and beautiful to do so. The Liturgy is understood—often in good conscience—more as a useful *means* to gather the faithful and to experience a communal moment. But this can also be done by mere human effort: it is enough to organize a feast and gather the people in the parish buildings or on the grounds, instead of remaining in the church. By contrast, the Liturgy is a sacred convocation: it is God who gathers His own, to be with them and to fill them with true joy. For this reason, the Liturgy is not an object at our disposal to be manipulated at will. Changing the rite or inserting new things into it from time to time implies, after all, a Pelagian approach to divine Worship: here it is man who acts, not God Who gives. Man is at the center and carries out the rite (activity), while he should instead receive it from God through the authority of the Church (passivity). Since obedience is a passive virtue—which is downplayed in our time—this helps us to understand why many priests no longer carry out the liturgical rite as established by obeying liturgical norms[27] (concerning the Liturgy, see Chapter Nine).

2.1.7. Grace and Freedom

The previous digressions, while seemingly redundant, help us to clarify another aspect of the doctrine of grace: that of human freedom. Saint Paul tells us that Christ has called us to freedom; he then goes on to clearly explain his teaching: "You were called for freedom, brothers. But do not use this freedom as an opportunity for the flesh; rather, serve one another through love" (Gal 5:13; see also Gal 5:1). Living according to the flesh does not only mean violating the Sixth Commandment but generally living according to human thought, in the lowest sense of the expression. Freedom is an extraordinary gift of God—in the face of freedom, even He has decided to yield!—but this gift was given for living according to God's plan, not according to the mentality of this world. Divine grace, encountering our freedom, liberates it further, makes it freer, and gives it the capacity to act for the sake of that for which it was given to us: to do good.

---

[27] See Congregation for Divine Worship and the Discipline of the Sacraments, *Redemptionis Sacramentum* (2004), §§29–33.

The Spirit's Action in the Church and in the World

1. Freedom as Absolute Autonomy

This point is particularly relevant in the modern world, which has emphasized the concept of absolute freedom. In our culture, freedom is understood as self-determination, the ability of each individual to choose whatever they wish and desire. Such a concept of freedom is profoundly anti-Christian. Freedom is not a faculty without content, depending on an indeterminate will. Freedom is linked (in addition to the will) to the intellect (*et-et*), which provides the object that the will chooses and pursues. Freedom and the will, therefore, cannot be irrational. Recall the words of Saint Irenaeus (cited in Chapter Four) regarding the fact that the human being should live "according to the *Logos*." The grace of Christ, given to us through the Holy Spirit, rehabilitates us, enabling us to use our freedom to choose the good desired by the will, a good that is first known by the intellect. In this way, we see again that morality cannot be autonomous. Human freedom does not consist in creating the moral law, but in following the law that it comes to recognize. Only in this way will the good that is carried out be objective. Again in the fifth chapter of Galatians (v. 22), Saint Paul provides a list of what are, objectively, the fruits of the Spirit: when one truly lives in accordance with them, this is a sure sign that he or she is living in the grace of the Holy Spirit. Saint Paul cautions those who pretend to create their own values: "You were running well; who hindered you from following [the] truth?" (Gal 5:7).

2. The Freedom of the Children of God

Here we note the link with the Holy Spirit in particular, which re-enables us to live the freedom of the children of God. Saint Paul says: "Now the Lord is the Spirit, and where the Spirit of the Lord is, there is freedom" (2 Cor 3:17). To live according to the Holy Spirit is not to live according to one's own tastes. Jesus says that the Christian, "who is born of the Spirit," is like the wind: "The wind blows where it wills, and you can hear the sound it makes, but you do not know where it comes from or where it goes; so it is with everyone who is born of the Spirit" (John 3:8). But these words should not be misunderstood as if Christ were authorizing us to do whatever we want, merely because we are reborn by the grace of the Holy Spirit. On the contrary, Saint Paul has just told us: "the Lord is the Spirit" and we know that the Third Person is also called the "Spirit of Christ" (Rom 8:9; 1 Pet 1:11), that is, the Spirit of the *Logos* and the "Spirit of Truth" (John 14:17; 15:26; 16:13; 1 John 4:6). With all of this we understand that the Spirit of love in

Christianity is not in fact the Spirit of doing-what-you-want.[28] The action of the Spirit within us instead allows us to again live according to the Lord, i.e., according to the *Logos*. Those who speak of a life "according to the Spirit" understood as a freedom of self-determination or an autonomous morality of the believer, forget the principle of *et-et*, for which we follow both the Spirit of love, and the Word of truth. In Christianity, the only acceptable concept of love is that of loving according to truth.[29]

2.1.8. Filial Adoption

The main fruit of grace in the human being is that of giving back to him or her the supernatural life that was lost through sin (divine likeness). In this sense, we speak of the process of human "deification"—the human being's progressive elevation by divine grace, which elevates the creature to a dignity superior to that of the order of nature. The human being, in itself a simple and at the same time marvelous "rational animal" and creature of God, becomes in grace a bearer of divine life.[30] In this sense, the Apostle Saint Peter states:

> His divine power has bestowed on us everything that makes for life and devotion, through the knowledge of him who called us by his own glory and power. Through these, he has bestowed on us the precious and very great promises, so that through them you may come to share in the divine nature (2 Pet 1: 3–4).

Regarding this gift of grace, three things need to be noted: (1) It happens through faith and Baptism, as Christ says: "Whoever believes and is baptized will be saved; whoever does not believe will be condemned" (Mark 16:16; see also Gal 3:26–27). Therefore, the gift of grace passes through the reception of the first Sacrament, which takes away original sin, gives supernatural faith,

---

[28] How often and how inaccurately is the famous phrase of Saint Augustine of Hippo cited: "*Dilige, et quod vis fac*" ("Love and do what you want": *In Epistolam Ioannis ad Parthos Tractatus* 7.8). This phrase means exactly the opposite of what many believe it to mean: it means that when you love with true love, the love of Truth, then you will only want good things and thus you will be able to do whatever you want, because your heart will suggest to you to carry out only good works. In fact, immediately afterward, the Saint continues: "If you are silent, be silent for love; if you speak, speak for love; if you correct, correct for love; if you pardon, pardon for love; may the root of love be in you, so that from this root nothing can proceed except the good" (our translation).

[29] See Benedict XVI, *Caritas in Veritate* (2009), §1 and *passim*.

[30] We must remember especially Saint Elizabeth of the Trinity (d. 1906), whose spirituality and teachings revolve around her "perceiving the indwelling" of God the Trinity.

restores the divine likeness, and inserts one into the Church. (2) The gift of grace produces the justification of the sinner, which is a real and objective event (see below). (3) The grace of divine likeness is given to us in the form of filial adoption, through which we truly become sons (or daughters) in the Son. The natural Son of God, the eternal Word, becoming incarnate, has entered fully into the human family, making Himself one of us in addition to being our Head. The grace of the Word is poured out in a new way (and will always continue to be poured out this way) as the grace of the *incarnate* Word. The divine likeness is not given to us now simply as the grace of the *Logos*, but reaches us, through the Spirit, as the grace of Christ, the *Logos* made flesh.[31] Here we see what we discussed in Chapters Two and Four: God carries on with His unique original salvific plan and at the same time carries it out in a new way. The grace conferred by the *Logos* to Adam, the divine likeness, now—after sin—reaches us through the crucified and glorified humanity of Christ, the Word incarnate. The Holy Spirit, sent in the beginning by the *Logos*, now reaches us by the incarnate *Logos*, as passing through the marks of His glorious Passion.[32] Thus we are not only made again in likeness to God, but we also become brothers and sisters of Christ, and thus adopted children of the Father. He is the Son by nature and renders us sons (and daughters) by grace.[33] From this it follows that—even if it can be said that God is in

---

[31] After the Incarnation, the *Logos* does not carry out any salvific work separately from His humanity, as is emphasized by the Congregation for the Doctrine of the Faith, *Dominus Iesus*, §10: "It is likewise contrary to the Catholic faith to introduce a separation between the salvific action of the Word as such and that of the Word made man. With the Incarnation, all the salvific actions of the Word of God are always done in unity with the human nature that He has assumed for the salvation of all people. The one Subject which operates in the two natures, human and divine, is the single Person of the Word. Therefore, the theory which would attribute, after the Incarnation as well, a salvific activity to the Logos as such in his divinity, exercised 'in addition to' or 'beyond' the humanity of Christ, is not compatible with the Catholic faith."

[32] "The Risen Christ, as it were beginning a new creation, 'brings' to the Apostles the Holy Spirit. He brings Him at the price of his own 'departure': *He gives them this Spirit as it were through the wounds of His crucifixion*: 'He showed them his hands and his side.' It is in the power of this crucifixion that He says to them: 'Receive the Holy Spirit.' Thus there is established a close link between the sending of the Son and the sending of the Holy Spirit. There is no sending of the Holy Spirit (after original sin) without the Cross and the Resurrection" (Saint John Paul II, *Dominum et Vivificantem*, §24 [emphasis added]).

[33] Jesus emphasizes this difference because He never says together with us "our Father." While the Father is one and unique, there is a difference in how He is the Father of Jesus (by nature, from eternity) and how He is our Father (by grace, through faith and Baptism). Thus, the Master says. "This is how *you* are to pray: / Our Father . . ." (Matt 6:9); and also: "I am going to my Father and your Father" (John 20:17, emphasis added).

The Sanctifier

some sense, as Creator, the Father of all human beings—in the proper sense (however much this truth may be unwelcome in our cultural context marked by radical theoretical egalitarianism), God is truly the Father only of Christians, who are adopted in the grace of the Spirit through Baptism, which is a sacramental immersion in the death and Resurrection of the Son.[34]

2.1.9. The Justification of the Sinner

Among the main effects of grace, we have mentioned the justification of the sinner, a very important theme of the Pauline epistolary, which was at the center of attention during the Protestant Reformation—as was noted in Chapter One. Here, we cite only a few passages of the Doctor of the Church Saint John of Avila (d. 1569), who stresses, against the Lutherans, the objectivity of justification and, consequently, the fact that it is a reality given effectively to human beings:

> You must not think that, for the fact that Christ is called "our justice" (1 Cor 1:30) ... those who are in grace do not have their own justice in themselves. ... To say that sin remains in the human being, according to the true *ratio* of sin, and that through the love of Jesus Christ our Lord the human being is released [only] from the penalty due to that sin, does not do the Scriptures justice and is not suitable to the dignity of Jesus Christ. In fact, given that the penalty due to sin is for the human being the lesser evil with respect to the fault of the sin itself ... it cannot be said that Christ "will save his people from their sins" (Matt 1:21), if He does it in such a way that through His merits He no longer imputes a penalty but does not take away the fault itself.
>
> [Concerning the Lutheran position:] Surely, a judge would receive no esteem if he did not punish or if he loved certain evil doers only because they live with his son. In fact, this would demonstrate that the son is not a perfect lover of goodness because he loves the

---

[34] Saint Augustine of Hippo, *De sancta virginitate* 7, recalls: "Those born of their flesh are not Christians, but become such afterwards through the motherhood of the Church" (in *FCNT*, vol. 27, trans. Charles T. Wilcox, Charles T. Huegelmeyer, John McQuade, et al. [New York: Fathers of the Church, Inc., 1955], 150–151). Even before him, this was already attested by Tertullian of Carthage (d. 220), *Apologeticum* 18.5: "Christians are not born, they become" (our translation); there is also the articulate explanation of Saint Athanasius of Alexandria (d. 373), *Oratio II contra Arianos* 21.59.

wicked, and that the father is not a lover of justice because he tolerates and loves those who he instead should punish, without regard for anyone. Those who must be pleasing servants of Jesus Christ our Lord must not have the iniquity of mortal sin, because He is the Head... In fact, it would be a frightening monster who had the head of a man and the body of a brute animal.[35]

2.1.10. Grace and the Moral Life

The concept of a new life in Christ implies that the Christian life is certainly an *"imitatio Christi"* ("imitation of Christ"), but not only this. The Christian is not only one who attends the school of Jesus and strives to follow His moral example (again, this could be pure Pelagianism). In reality, the imitation and following of Christ are possible, as well as necessary (a free response, merit), only because the grace of the Spirit has already renewed the sinner, putting him or her on the path paved by the Master, and sustaining all the progress he or she makes on this path, which is both exciting and challenging at the same time. Following Christ is not then only an external repetition of behavior, but an intimate transformation of the person.[36] This does not only concern following Christ, but also being *in* Him. The doctrine of grace projects a mystical dimension of the Catholic understanding of the moral life. Saint Paul goes in this direction when he writes to the Christians of Philippi to not only reproduce exteriorly the behaviors of Jesus, but to reproduce in themselves the "attitudes" of Christ (see Phil 2:5). The Greek word used by Saint Paul is *phronein*, which, rather than indicating a momentary state, refers to the more stable thoughts and decisions of the human soul. Here as well there is an *et-et*: the moral life unfolds both with internal acts and external ones. A legalistic morality of scrupulous observance of precepts is not enough, but neither is an interior morality of intentions that is not lived out.

2.1.11. The Theological Classification of Grace

1. Created and Uncreated Grace

How does divine grace transform the sinner to be just and make him or her to live a new life in Christ? Traditionally, a distinction has been made in

---

[35] Saint John of Avila, *Audi, filia*, chs. 88–89 (our translation).

[36] See Council of Trent, *Decretum de Iustificatione* (1547), can. 11 (DS 1561).

the "gracious" activity of God between "uncreated grace" and "created grace."[37] The first expression usually indicates God Himself and His eternal love that predestines all to salvation. The second case refers to God who gives Himself to the human being through an indwelling in the heart of the just (see John 14:23; 1 Cor 3:16), "informing" them to Himself.[38] "Created grace" also indicates the effect that the indwelling of God produces in the just, that is, the effect of being a new creature.[39] This implies that grace, on one hand, is a personal reality more than a "thing": it is none other than the Holy Trinity who dwells in us; on the other hand, however, grace is also a possession given to the creature,[40] who is not just nominally, but really a son of God, who is in the new life in Christ—with all of concrete consequences that this entails.

2. Habitual and Actual Grace, the Charisms

This reality is also commonly called "habitual grace" or "sanctifying grace" (gratia gratum faciens): a reality that stably inheres in the person and transforms him or her (sanctification or deification). It is the new life that unites us to God. From sanctifying grace comes the supernatural infused virtues and the seven gifts of the Holy Spirit. Theologians also speak of the gratiae gratis datae—the charisms—given by God above all for the edification of the Church.[41] Additionally, "actual grace" is distinguished from all this, and consists in the illuminations and aids that are granted to the person at specific times.[42]

---

[37] See *ST* I-II, q. 110, a. 1: "When it is said that one has the grace of God, this means to indicate a gift supernaturally produced by God in the human being [created grace]. However, sometimes the very eternal love of God is called [uncreated] grace" (our translation). A useful clarification concerning the concept of created grace is in ST I-II, q. 110, a. 2, ad 3.

[38] "To inform" here does not refer to the communication of news, but it is a technical term that indicates that with the indwelling of grace, God is present in the heart of the just and "configures" such a person to Himself. Often, recourse is made to the terminology of grace as a formal (or in recent times, a quasi-formal) cause, to attempt to describe more precisely such a configuration.

[39] Grace has the effect *both* of healing the person wounded by sin, *and* of making him or her able to carry out the good in the supernatural order (see *ST* I-II, q. 109, a. 2).

[40] Grace is a "quality of the soul" of a supernatural type: see *ST* I-II, q. 110, a. 2.

[41] See Congregation for the Doctrine of the Faith, *Iuvenescit Ecclesia* (2016), §5, and *passim*. *ST* I-II, q. 111, a. 1 says that sanctifying grace reunites the person to God, while that *gratis data* is granted to the person in order that he or she can help another person return to God. In the hierarchy of this bipolarity, the first pole is greater than the second (see *ST* I-II, q. 111, a. 5).

[42] Prior to Saint Thomas (see *ST* I-II, q. 111, a. 1), and even in the early texts of the Angelic Doctor, there was a tendency to have actual grace and *gratia gratis data* coincide.

3. Operant and Cooperant Grace

To illustrate the distinction between operant and cooperant grace, we shall cite the text of Saint Thomas itself:

> As we have already noted [see *ST* I-II, q. 109, aa. 2–3, 6, 9], by grace two things can be meant: first, the help with which God moves us to want the good and to carry it out; second, the gift of a habit infused in us by God. In both senses, grace is rightly divided into operant and cooperant. In fact, the accomplishment of an effect is not attributed to the moved subject, but to the one who moves it. Thus, if the effects are considered in which our mind does not move, but is only moved, while God alone is the mover of it, the operation is to be attributed to God: then one speaks of operant grace. Instead, in the effects in which our mind both moves and is moved, the operation is not only attributed to God, but also to the soul; and thus one speaks of cooperant grace. Thus, there is in us a dual act. The first is the interior act of the will. And with respect to this act the will is moved, while God is its mover ... But there is another, exterior act; and since it is commanded by the will, ... the operation of this act is attributed to the will. Since God helps us in such act as well ... with respect to it grace is called cooperant.[43]

4. Prevenient and Subsequent Grace

Grace can be distinguished as prevenient and subsequent on the basis of its effects. Saint Thomas recalls that grace has five primary effects: healing the soul, making it so that the soul wills the good, working in such a way that the willed good be effectively carried out, persevering in the good, and finally reaching eternal glory.[44] Now, the grace that produces the first effect is clearly prevenient with respect to that which produces the second, because—as we have already noted in various places—the supernatural good is carried out only if one is justified. If the grace of healing the soul does not come first, there cannot be the effect that this same person wants the good and achieves it: thus, this second effect is a subsequent grace. In its turn, the second effect is prevenient of the third, and the third is subsequent to the second. Therefore, it is to be noted that the same effect is considered a prevenient or subsequent grace in relation to the other effects connected to it.

---

[43] *ST* I-II, q. 111, a. 2 (our translation).
[44] See *ST* I-II, q. 111, a. 3.

5. Sufficient and Efficacious Grace

Finally, a distinction can be made between "sufficient grace" and "efficacious grace." The second is intrinsically efficacious because God so wills: it is the grace that arouses the consent of our will. Sufficient grace is not intrinsically efficacious: it can remain without effect, insofar as it only confers the capacity of acting, without making us perform the act.[45] In the *Commentary on the First Letter to Timothy*, Saint Thomas says that Christ is propitiation for our sins "*pro aliquibus efficaciter, sed pro omnibus sufficienter, quia pretium sanguinis eius est sufficiens ad salutem omnium, sed non habet efficaciam nisi in electis propter impedimentum.*"[46] Therefore, when grace is sufficient, it is possible for human freedom to interpose an impediment that renders it ineffective, not in itself but rather in us.

Here we can recall two classic expressions of theology and Catholic doctrine, which highlight the importance both of human freedom in the acceptance of grace, and the fact that this freedom should not place an obstacle in the way of grace: (1) A first expression concerns in particular the grace conferred through the Sacraments, which is certainly granted to those who "do not place an obstacle" ("*non ponentibus obicem*").[47] (2) A second classical expression affirms: "*Facienti quod est in se, Deus non denegat gratiam*" ("to one who does what is in oneself [i.e., what one can], God does not deny grace").[48] Free will is thus fully involved, even if "doing what one can"—if it concerns the supernatural order—is supported by grace.[49]

In fact, our acts cannot *per se*, insofar as they are natural, reach an end

---

[45] A text in which such a distinction appears to be present is Philippians 2:13: "God is the one who, for his good purpose, works in you both to desire and to work." Concerning efficacious grace, then, one can cite Ezekiel 36:27: "I will put my spirit within you so that you walk in my statutes, observe my ordinances, and keep them"; and in the New Testament, John 10:28: "I give them eternal life, and they shall never perish. No one can take them out of my hand."

[46] Translation: "For some in an efficacious way but for all in a sufficient way, because the price of His blood is sufficient for the salvation of all, but it has efficacy only in the elect and this on account of some obstacle" (*Super I ad Timotheum* II, *lectio* 1 [our translation]).

[47] Council of Trent, *Decretum de Sacramentis* (1547), can. 6 (DS 1606).

[48] See *ST* I-II, q. 112, a. 3.

[49] This is said in order to avoid the Semipelagian error, whose formulator is commonly believed to be Saint John Cassian (d. 435). For Semipelagians, human beings can accomplish the passage toward God by themselves; they can be disposed to grace with only their natural force of free will. St. Thomas rejects this view in *ST* I-II, q. 112, a. 2: "No preparation is required on man's part, that, as it were, anticipates the divine help, but rather, every preparation in man must be by the help of God moving the soul to good" (our translation). Here, the mature Thomas writes with greater clarity than he had done in his youth in the *Scriptum super Sententiis* II, d. 28, q. 4. This latter text is not semipelagian (see ad 2) as some believed, but it is less clear than that of the *Summa*. See also *ST* I-II, q. 113, aa. 3 and 5.

that surpasses them.⁵⁰ Thus, each human act that has salvific value is moved, accompanied, and led to fulfillment by the actual grace of God. Christ has said this clearly: "without me you can do nothing" (John 15:5). Saint Paul echoes: "Not that of ourselves we are qualified to take credit for anything as coming from us; rather, our qualification comes from God" (2 Cor 3:5). Venerable Pope Pius XII glosses: "Holiness begins from Christ; and Christ is its cause. For no act conducive to salvation can be performed unless it proceeds from Him as from its supernatural source."⁵¹

2.1.12. Gifts and Fruits of the Holy Spirit

The theological and catechetical tradition has identified in Scripture different "gifts" (see Isa 11:2–3) and "fruits" (see Gal 5:22) of the Holy Spirit that enrich the supernatural life of human beings renewed in the image of, and through the grace of, Christ the Lord. The *Compendium of the Catechism of the Catholic Church* (Appendix, B. Formulas of Catholic Doctrine) enumerates them as follows:

THE SEVEN *GIFTS* OF THE HOLY SPIRIT	THE TWELVE *FRUITS* OF THE HOLY SPIRIT
1. Wisdom 2. Understanding 3. Counsel 4. Fortitude 5. Knowledge 6. Piety 7. Fear of the Lord	1. Charity 2. Joy 3. Peace 4. Patience 5. Kindness 6. Goodness 7. Generosity 8. Gentleness 9. Faithfulness 10. Modesty 11. Self-Control 12. Chastity

---

⁵⁰ J.B. Bossuet (d. 1704) summarizes the need for sufficient and efficacious grace with beautiful concision in *Avertissement sur le livre des réflexions morales*: we need to admit two types of grace "of which one [sufficient] leaves the will without excuse before God; the other [efficient] does not allow for self-glorification."

⁵¹ Pius XII, *Mystici Corporis* (1943), §51.

The Sanctifier

2.2. Doctrinal Errors and Theological Discussions about Grace

Divine grace is granted by the Holy Spirit to sanctify human beings. We need to take these two aspects together: the end—to sanctify—and the recipients of this sanctification—human beings. Grace is therefore understood as a divine, supernatural work, which comes to be offered to and welcomed by a human nature, with its own characteristics, especially that of freedom. To deny or reduce one of the two aspects (bipolarity), or to invert their proper order (hierarchy), would entail—as a rupture of the *et-et*—erroneous views about grace. If grace is above all the grace of Christ, that is, the unique and unrepeatable grace that is in Christ and that from Him, as the Head of the Church, is shared with His members in the Mystical Body, consequently the grace given to Christians will have to be structured and understood according to the bipolarity of the union of the human and divine. Moreover, as always, the right hierarchy of values will have to be maintained between the gratuitous initiative of God and the human reception of the gift. There have been, throughout the Church's history, various misunderstandings in this regard; as such, it is not surprising that the Magisterium and the great theologians have always rejected them.

2.2.1. Pelagianism and Semipelagianism

1. Pelagianism

A first error—already mentioned above—was that of Pelagius and the Semipelagians. Here the bipolarity of divine and human is denied, because it is held that the human being is not marked by original sin: for this reason, according to Pelagius, the natural faculties of the human being remain integrated and capable of autonomously choosing the good, without the need for grace. As was seen in the Chapter Two, Saint Augustine battled strenuously against this grave error, which takes away from Christ His role as the Redeemer of the human race, reducing Him to a mere example of life. Pelagius, moreover, also denies divine predestination: one saves oneself by choosing the good with one's free will and thus achieves eternal salvation. It necessarily follows that the natural capacities of the human being are capable of obtaining what is supernatural—which is, in reality, impossible.

2. Semipelagianism

As for the Semipelagians, they do not believe that human beings can reach heaven by their own capabilities, and thus they affirm that grace is necessary

The Spirit's Action in the Church and in the World

to reach the ultimate supernatural end. In this sense, they do not deny the bipolarity of grace and freedom. However, according to them, grace comes only at a second moment, namely, when the human being has chosen the good in an autonomous way. Thus, grace is not prevenient, but only accompanies the person, making him or her to persevere in the good until the end. The error lies in the inversion of the hierarchy that, in sound doctrine, instead affirms the primacy of grace.

3. Response of the Magisterium

The Magisterium expressed itself against Pelagianism on more than one occasion: (1) Pope Saint Zosimus, *Epistula Tractoria* (year 418, DS 231); (2) Fifteenth Synod of Carthage (year 418; DS 222–230); (3) Pseudo-Celestine I (actually Saint Prosper of Aquitaine), *Indiculus* (ca. 431; DS 238–249); (4) Council of Ephesus (431)[52]; (5) Second Synod of Orange (year 529; DS 370–397); (6) Pope Adrian I, *Institutio Universalis* (letter to the Spanish bishops, between 785 and 791; DS 596 [concerning predestination]); (7) Council of Trent, *Decretum de Iustificatione*, chs. 1–3 (DS 1521–1523 [against the conceptions of Luther and Calvin, but it also rejects Pelagianism]).

In the majority of cases, the excommunications of the Pelagians are valid against the Semipelagians as well. Moreover, we shall cite a passage that specifically rejects Semipelagianism:

> If anyone contends that God awaits our will before cleansing us from sin, but does not confess that even the desire to be cleansed is aroused in us by the infusion and action of the Holy Spirit, he opposes the Holy Spirit himself speaking through Solomon: "The will is prepared by the Lord" (Prov 8:35, LXX) and the Apostle's salutary message: "God is at work in you, both to will and to work for his good pleasure" (Phil 2:13).[53]

2.2.2. The "Quaestio de Auxiliis"

1. Molina and "Middle Knowledge"

In the post-renaissance era, excessive Pelagian optimism was revived in a

---

[52] In itself, this Council was convened against Nestorius (see Chapter Four), but it also excommunicated the Pelagians by approving the anti-Pelagian letter of a synod held in 426–427.

[53] Second Synod of Orange (AD 529), can. 4 (DS 374).

The Sanctifier

moderate and non-heretical form by the Jesuit Luis de Molina (d. 1600), who, to reconcile the omnipotent divine plan with human freedom, proposed the theory of *"scientia media,"* a mode of knowledge with which God could foresee all human actions, not only those that will occur, but also those which, while they can occur, will never occur, even while such a foresight does not take away the freedom with which such actions will be carried out.[54] On this view, God can foresee a human being's adherence to grace, but such a decision remains totally autonomous and free on the part of creature: divine prescience is a pre-knowledge, not a pre-determination. This adherence would be based on the human capacity to believe, love, and hope. Moreover, under this conception, there would be a sort of sufficiency in the human being for the sake of a self-orientation toward grace, but this would not take away the fact it was "established" by God. Molina affirms that original sin has certainly damaged the human being, but only insofar as he or she lost the gifts and the virtues that Adam possessed in Eden; not with respect to freedom, which would still be capable of choosing the good. The human being could carry out the good in the natural order without grace (God nonetheless is not entirely excluded, on account of *scientia media*). Moreover, for Molina, the impulse of grace is not irresistible and does not necessarily determine the human will. This endangers the distinction, upon which Saint Thomas had insisted, between sufficient and efficacious grace. In fact, for Molina, the human being can always reject divine grace. He thus formulates the thesis of "simultaneous concurrence," for which we must always contemplate two causes: divine grace and the free human disposition, which depends on the creature. There were theologians of the Dominican Order who considered the theses of Molina to be Semipelagian and the *quaestio de auxiliis* ensued.

2. Báñez and "Physical Predetermination"

The dispute heated up intensely in 1595, when the Dominican, Domingo Báñez (d. 1604), a confessor of Saint Teresa of Avila for a period of time, accused Molina of Semipelagianism.[55] Molina responded by accusing Báñez

---

[54] See Luis de Molina, *Liberi arbitrii cum gratiae donis, divina praescientia, providentia, praedestinatione et reprobatione concordia* (1588), commonly known as the *Concordia*. It is called *media* because this divine *scientia* (knowledge) would stand between the knowledge of intelligence, with which God knows all the possibilities of His own omnipotence, and the knowledge of vision, with which He knows what He freely carries out.

[55] This was done in the work, written along with some colleagues of Salamanca, *Apologia fratrum praedicatorum*. In 1600, he then wrote *De vera et legitima concordia liberi arbitrii cum auxiliis gratiae Dei efficaciter moventis humanam salutem*, in which already from the

of Calvinism, inasmuch as the Dominican theology of grace seemed to him to involve such an influx of divine grace on the human being as to annul the cooperation of the creature, falling into the trap of Calvin's theory of double predestination (see Chapters One and Twelve). Báñez, referring to Saint Thomas, believes that the sovereignty of God should be emphasized above all. God "physically predetermines"—that is, in a real and efficacious way— the act of the creature, which remains, however, equally free. Grace not only encounters the free human choice but precedes and causes it. Moreover, there is a divine prescience, which knows in advance the future merits of the person who accepts grace. There is also a true predestination, which determines those to whom God will give efficacious grace.

3. Evaluation

It can be said that Báñez defends a theology of grace in which God decides His plan *ante praevisa merita*, before (and independently from!) the merits that He nonetheless foresees; while Molina would speak of a *post praevisa merita*, for which God intervenes with His grace because, examining the heart of the human being, He sees within it the freely adhering will. Molina's system highlights human freedom well but errs in ignoring the hierarchy of the *et-et*, almost putting divine and human action on the same level. Báñez, rather, highlights God's sovereignty very well, even if he leaves himself open to the risk of breaking the bipolarity, presenting human freedom as a simple word more than a reality. The Church, however, has held that the two systems, by not becoming true and proper heresies, have not fallen into the trap to which they were exposed. The Magisterium has left space for theological liberty on the question, while preserving the fundamental elements of the discussion.

4. The Intervention of the Magisterium

Pope Paul V effectively decided to declare both theologies legitimate, at the same time prohibiting their representatives from accusing each other of heresy.[56] The text of a discourse of the Pontiff to the legate of the King of Spain, Philip III, is very interesting in this regard. It states:

---

title—in which he speaks of a true and legitimate *concordia*—he shows himself to be in polemic with Molina.

[56] See Paul V, *Formula pro Finiendis Disputationibus de Auxiliis* (1607) (DS 1997).

Both parties [Molinists and Bañezians, that is, Jesuits and Dominicans] agree in substance with Catholic truth, namely, that God causes us to act with the efficacy of his grace ... and He bends and changes the wills of men, and about this there is question; but they disagree only as to the manner; because the Dominicans say He predetermines our will physically, that is, really and efficiently, while the Jesuits maintain that He does so congruently and morally: opinions that can both be defended.[57]

2.2.3. Jansenism

1. Michael Baius

Another error to consider regarding the theological understanding of the grace of the Holy Spirit is Jansenism. Its precursor was the Belgian, Michael Baius (Michel de Bay, d. 1589). His doctrine concerning grace also comes in a certain sense from Pelagianism, but it then turned toward Protestantism. Baius attributed to human beings the natural ability to correspond to grace, before original sin. But he reaches a very pessimistic theology as regards man after sin: free will is now irredeemably corrupt. Baius claimed that his position of fallen man was rooted in the writings of St. Augustine. Since before the fall, the good that humanity performed corresponded to the integrity of its nature, if it had persevered, eternal salvation would have been, not grace, but a simple reward due to him, given the fact that, in the state of intact nature, the natural works were sufficient to attain eternal salvation. Humanity previously had—to say it in Thomistic terms—a *de condigno* merit. After sin, however, whatever it does, humanity cannot merit anything. Consequently, it is saved without any merit, the only merit being that of Christ (and here we see the affinity to Lutheranism). Baius' theology was condemned by Saint Pius V in 1567.[58]

---

[57] Paul V, *Allocutio Legato Regis Hispaniae Destinata* (1611) (DS 1997a). Following the discourse, the Pope also positively teaches what the doctrine of the Church is in this regard. It is that—he says—of the Council of Trent, which has rejected both Pelagius and Calvin and "teaches the Catholic doctrine according to which it is necessary that the free will be moved, stirred up, and assisted by the grace of God and that it can freely assent and dissent." The Pope recalls that the Tridentine Council had intentionally avoided going into the particulars of exactly how this happens.

[58] See Saint Pius V, *Ex Omnibus Afflictionibus* (1567) (DS 1901–1980), which contains and reproves about eighty theses of Baius.

2. Cornelius Jansen

Jansenism receives its name from Cornelius Jansen (d. 1638), a Dutch theologian and bishop, and author of a work called *Augustinus*, in which he believes to be expressing the position of the great saint from Hippo concerning the theme of the relationship between grace and freedom. The work was published posthumously in 1640 and condemned some years later; consequently, Jansen was not excommunicated in his lifetime. The ecclesiastical condemnation did not prevent the birth of a true and proper movement, which was not only theological, but also philosophical, spiritual, and political.

Jansen presented a pessimistic view, like Baius and the Protestants. For him, human beings were so corrupted by original sin as to be invariably determined to do evil. Without grace, anything that human beings do, even good things, are sins.[59] Having or not having grace depends only on an iron-clad divine predestination (see Calvin). This reduces the role of human freedom to practically zero. Naturally, with these ideas Jansen voluntarily opposes the ideas of the Jesuits. They relied on Molinism, with its optimistic view of the human being, to develop their own missionary campaign, tending to maximally increase the boundaries of the Church, increasing the number of the baptized (see earlier, the work of Saint Francis Xavier, d. 1552). The Jansenists, on the other hand, proposed a small Church, even of élite: an ark of a few chosen ones. Here, spiritual life comes to be connoted above all by the fear of a God who is the absolute arbiter of human destinies, more than a love toward the God of mercy.

3. Famous Jansenists

It is in this field that the moral Jansenism of Antoine Arnauld (d. 1694) "collides" with the devotion to the Sacred Heart of Jesus—enthusiastically spread, not coincidentally, by the Jesuits—which was based on the apparitions of Christ to Saint Margaret Mary Alacoque (d. 1690). Arnauld's sister Angèlique (d. 1661) was the Abbess of Port-Royal des Champs, which became one of the most important centers of the elaboration of Jansenism (the name

---

[59] We noted earlier that if a human being is not in God's grace, he or she cannot obtain merits for eternal life. This, however, does not mean that everything that the sinner does is a sin. The sinner can do many good works, which nevertheless, if they are outside of grace, do not produce supernatural fruits, but only natural ones. Nothing prevents such natural fruits from being considered by God as a title of merit, as signs of a good will, to give a sinner eternal salvation. However, this depends on God, since the good works in themselves do not produce supernatural fruit if they are not within a life lived in God's grace.

The Sanctifier

of Port-Royal would be maintained even when the monks were transferred to Paris). Among the mentors of the abbey were Jean-Ambroise Duvergier de Hauranne, called Saint-Cyran (d. 1643). We must recall that the philosopher Blaise Pascal (d. 1662) joined the Port-Royal movement: his defense of Jansenism against the Jesuits is recounted in the famous *Provincial Letters*.

4. The Intervention of the Magisterium

Jansen's *Augustinus* was condemned first by Urban VIII in 1642[60] and, with greater precision concerning the contested doctrines, by Innocent X in 1653.[61] The errors of Jansen's followers were condemned in 1690 by the Holy Office.[62]

2.3. The Universal Expansion of the Kingdom of Christ

In the proper sense and in a direct way, the effusion of the Spirit on the part of the risen Christ is addressed to the Church, as is inferred from the narrative of the day of Pentecost (see Acts 2:1–13). Grace is poured out over Mary and the Apostles gathered in prayer in the Upper Room: that day the "Catholic" (that is, universal) Church was all contained in one room (see v. 1) and the Spirit of Christ descended precisely there for the first time. As we have seen, the justification of the sinner occurs in an ordinary way from faith and Baptism, elements that are inseparable from the dimension of ecclesial life. The adopted child of God is always a member of the Mystical Body of Christ that is the Church.

The outpouring of the Spirit at Pentecost, focused on the Church, however, has an irrepressibly universal tendency.[63] We can cite a prophecy from the Old Testament, in which God promises: "I will pour out my spirit upon all flesh" (Joel 3:1). It is no coincidence that this passage was explicitly cited by Saint Peter in the speech that he gave immediately after the effusion of the Holy Spirit (see Acts 2:14–36) to the crowd that gathered because of the roar that was felt in the surroundings when the Consoler had come down in the form of tongues of fire. In his discourse, St. Peter evokes this passage from the prophet Joel, saying that the prophecy has just been fulfilled. The

---

[60] See Urban VIII, *In Eminenti Ecclesiae* (1642).

[61] See Innocent X, *Cum Occasione* (1653) (DS 2001–2007). See also Alexander VII, *Ad sanctam beati Petri sedem* (1656) (DS 2010–2012).

[62] See Holy Office, *Errores Iansenistarum* (1690) (DS 2301–2332).

[63] "The Spirit manifests Himself in a special way in the Church and in her members. Nevertheless, his presence and activity are universal, limited neither by space nor time" (Saint John Paul II, *Redemptoris Missio* [1990], §28).

Spirit descended on the Church, on which He will always dwell in fullness, but from the Church and through her He wants (if it is acceptable to express ourselves in these terms) "to bounce" to the whole world and to all people.[64] The gift of the tongues that the Apostles receive in that moment is a sign that this is His will. They would have to preach the Gospel of Christ, in the strength of the Spirit, to all peoples of the world (see Matt 28:19–20).[65] This is where they get their title of Apostles, that is, envoys (ones who are sent).

2.3.1. "Missio ad Gentes"

A primary aspect to consider among those fruits produced by the Spirit in the Church, which have a deeply universal character, is the *missio ad gentes*, that is, the preaching of the Gospel to the peoples that do not know Christ. The ministry of the Apostles was, from the beginning, played on two fields: *ad intra* and *ad extra Ecclesiae*. Within the Church, the Apostles, as eye-witnesses of the Resurrection, have played the roles of highest authorities, masters of the faith, founders of new communities, keepers of correct doctrine, and dispensers of the mysteries of Christ (especially the *fractio panis* [breaking of the bread], which would later be called the Eucharist or Holy Mass). Outside of the Church, the Apostles, from the beginning as well, have been missionaries, bringing—we can say with an expression that is a bit antiquated—"the good news," or simply the Gospel (from Old English "gōd[good]-spell"; Greek *euangelion*: "good news," "good announcement"). The missionary task is constitutive of the apostolic ministry. The mission is not only an activity performed for a certain time, but it is a constitutive part of the mandate given by Christ to the Apostles.[66] Since in turn the

---

[64] "Salvation, which always remains a gift of the Holy Spirit, requires man's cooperation, both to save himself and to save others. This is God's will, and this is why He established the Church and made her a part of His plan of salvation" (John Paul II, *Redemptoris Missio*, §9 and *passim*).

[65] "The different versions of the 'missionary mandate' contain common elements as well as characteristics proper to each. Two elements, however, are found in all the versions. First, there is the universal dimension of the task entrusted to the apostles, who are sent to 'all nations' (Matt 28:19); 'into all the world and . . . to the whole creation' (Mark 16:15); to 'all nations' (Luke 24:47); 'to the end of the earth' (Acts 1:8). Secondly, there is the assurance given to the apostles by the Lord that they will not be alone in the task, but will receive the strength and the means necessary to carry out their mission. The reference here is to the presence and power of the Spirit and the help of Jesus himself" (John Paul II, *Redemptoris Missio*, §23).

[66] "Evangelizing is in fact the grace and vocation proper to the Church, her deepest identity. She exists in order to evangelize, that is to say, in order to preach and teach, to be the

The Sanctifier

Apostolic role is essential in the Church, it follows that the evangelizing (and re-evangelizing[67]) mission of the Church makes up part of the very essence of the Church.[68] We can make two observations in regard to the *missio ad gentes*:

(1) The first observation is that this mission cannot be understood in a Pelagian way, as a human initiative: "The mission of the Church, like that of Jesus, is God's work or, as Luke often puts it, the work of the Spirit."[69] Christ gives this mandate to the Apostles and to the Church in general, but orders them not to move from Jerusalem, that is, not to start to go around the world to preach until after they have received the One who the risen Jesus will send from the Father (see Luke 24:48; Acts 1:4–5). The mission takes place in the power of the Spirit, of that Power that Christ gives after ascending to the right hand of the Father. This does not concern a human initiative, but our collaboration with a grace that comes from God. The Holy Spirit uses us as instruments of spreading the Kingdom of Christ in the world through the preaching of the truth, the celebration of the Sacraments, and the example of charitable works.

(2) A second aspect follows from this: the mission cannot be interpreted in a "horizontalist" way, as a simple activity of human solidarity consisting in educating the illiterate, in the care of the sick, in the construction of infrastructure, etc. Naturally, the mission involves all of these things, because the Gospel is *both* deifying power (supernatural order) *and* humanizing force (natural order). Missionaries often find themselves before people whose fundamental rights are being tread upon. Other times, they find people who have

---

channel of the gift of grace, to reconcile sinners with God, and to perpetuate Christ's Sacrifice in the Mass, which is the memorial of His death and glorious resurrection" (Saint Paul VI, *Evangelii Nuntiandi* [1975], §14).

[67] Unfortunately, certain lands that are already evangelized are now experiencing long periods of regression in the faith. In certain places (e.g. Turkey), once flourishing for the Church, it is hardly possible to find any Catholic today. Currently, while in Africa, Christianity, and especially Catholicism, are in constant growth, in the western world (America, Europe, and, culturally speaking, some countries in Oceana) they seem to be in great crisis. From this standpoint, we understand clearly both the various magisterial interventions of Saint John Paul II on the theme of the new evangelization (see, for example, *Christifideles Laici* [1988], §34), and the initiative of Pope Benedict XVI, who in June 2010 instituted the Pontifical Council for the Promotion of the New Evangelization, which has as its end the counteraction of the process of secularization of the countries of ancient evangelization and the re-igniting of the life of ecclesial faith in them (see his *Ubicumque et Semper* [2010]). In October 2012, moreover, the meeting of the Synod of Bishops in Rome was dedicated to this same theme.

[68] See Second Vatican Council, *Lumen Gentium*, §17.

[69] Saint John Paul II, *Redemptoris Missio*, §24.

no possibility of fully developing the wonderful faculties given to us by God. In the face of countless situations of the degradation of human dignity that they have witnessed, the missionaries feel compelled to intervene by the commandment of charity toward one's neighbor. However, this does not take away the fact that their mission remains primarily supernatural and spiritual. They bring what human beings need most—the truth, which satisfies better than bread (see Matt 4:4). Saint John Paul II identified and clearly condemned three conceptions of the kingdom of God that involve grave consequences in the missionary realm:

> Nowadays the kingdom is much spoken of, but not always in a way consonant with the thinking of the Church. In fact, there are ideas about salvation and mission which can be called "anthropocentric" in the reductive sense of the word, inasmuch as they are focused on man's earthly needs. In this view, the kingdom tends to become something completely human and secularized; what counts are programs and struggles for a liberation which is socio-economic, political and even cultural, but within a horizon that is closed to the transcendent. Without denying that on this level too there are values to be promoted, such a notion nevertheless remains within the confines of a kingdom of man, deprived of its authentic and profound dimensions. Such a view easily translates into one more ideology of purely earthly progress. The kingdom of God, however, "is not of this world . . . is not from the world" (John 18:36).

> There are also conceptions which deliberately emphasize the kingdom and which describe themselves as "kingdom-centered." They stress the image of a Church which is not concerned about herself, but which is totally concerned with bearing witness to and serving the kingdom. It is a "Church for others" just as Christ is the "man for others." The Church's task is described as though it had to proceed in two directions: on the one hand promoting such "values of the kingdom" as peace, justice, freedom, brotherhood, etc., while on the other hand fostering dialogue between peoples, cultures and religions, so that through a mutual enrichment they might help the world to be renewed and to journey ever closer toward the kingdom.

> Together with positive aspects, these conceptions often reveal negative aspects as well. First, they are silent about Christ: the kingdom of which they speak is "theocentrically" based, since, according to

them, Christ cannot be understood by those who lack Christian faith, whereas different peoples, cultures and religions are capable of finding common ground in the one divine reality, by whatever name it is called. For the same reason they put great stress on the mystery of creation, which is reflected in the diversity of cultures and beliefs, but they keep silent about the mystery of redemption. Furthermore, the kingdom, as they understand it, ends up either leaving very little room for the Church or undervaluing the Church in reaction to a presumed "ecclesiocentrism" of the past, and because they consider the Church herself only a sign, for that matter a sign not without ambiguity.

This is not the kingdom of God as we know it from Revelation. The kingdom cannot be detached either from Christ or from the Church. As has already been said, Christ not only proclaimed the kingdom, but in Him the kingdom itself became present and was fulfilled.[70]

Though recognizing the many oppressions of human beings that missionaries have encountered, the Church does not forget that the real power of liberation is, above all, the Truth (See John 8:32). That is why the Church has received the Spirit of Truth. Thus, it seems incorrect, generally, to put social action before the Gospel proclamation. It is true that—as they say—if someone is dying of hunger, we need to first give him a piece of bread and then nourish him with the Word of the Gospel. But it can also be understood that there is more than one way to give a piece of bread. Saint Teresa of Calcutta (d. 1997) transformed every gesture of charity into an act of evangelization. Thus, more than putting one before the other, the proclamation of the Gospel and works of charity should always go together, remembering that the first is the most important aspect. Man needs Christ more than anything else. While anyone who intends to do good can give him the other things—because they are natural realities—only the Church can give someone Christ, especially through preaching and the Sacraments. If the Church were to stop giving Christ, and giving Him clearly and explicitly, who else could give Him to the world?

2.3.2. The Salvation of Non-Christians

Considering the theme of mission, we encounter a second point of discussion especially prevalent in modern times. The Holy Spirit gives grace, the super-

---

[70] John Paul II, *Redemptoris Missio*, §§17–18.

The Spirit's Action in the Church and in the World

natural life, the justification of believers. The sinner, through faith and through Baptism, becomes part of the family of God that is the Church. All this implies that in order to be saved we need to believe, to be baptized, and to be incorporated into the Church. That is why the mission is always characterized as one of the greatest acts of charity that the Church is able to accomplish. Bringing the truth is the greatest act of love, especially if what is brought is the truth of the Gospel of Christ, which is the Truth in Person. Listening to the Word of preaching, human beings can reach the faith and ask to be baptized, becoming new friends of God. Thus, the door to eternal salvation is opened.[71]

The universal work of the Spirit therefore tends toward catholicity, understood here in the geographic and temporal sense—the expansion of the Church in all places and all times. One wonders, however, what happens to those who, having never received the visit of the missionaries, dies in ignorance of Christ and of the true faith: Are they all condemned to Hell? This position has never been that of Catholic doctrine, although in certain periods this opinion was given more credence than in others. In reality, we have already seen (see Chapter Four) that Scripture refers to a state of waiting for the righteous souls who died before the Incarnation of Christ (*limbus patrum*). They are saved. They were saved by virtue of Christ the Redeemer, even if they were not aware of Him. The salvation of Christ, therefore, has a universal character: anyone who is saved is saved only because of the work of Christ. This is true both for those who knew and believed in Him, and for those who have never heard His name pronounced. This does not imply, however, any religious indifference, as if human beings did not have to seek the truth and, in particular, the true religion, and could instead live as if each religion were equally valid.[72]

The Church manages to maintain the *et-et* even in such a complex theme as that of the salvation of non-Christians. And the *et-et* also maintains the fundamental characteristic of the different value of the individual aspects of

---

[71] See Second Vatican Council, *Lumen Gentium*, §14; Benedict XVI, *Porta Fidei* (2011), §1 and *passim*.

[72] See Gregory XVI *Mirari Vos* (1832) (DS 2730–2732) and Blessed Pius IX, *Quanto Conficiamur Moerore* (1863) (DS 2865–2867); Pius IX, *Syllabus* (1864), *propositiones* 15–18 (DS 2915–2918). The doctrine concerning religious freedom of the Second Vatican Council is clearly not indifferentist. In fact, while about non-Christian religions the Council declares, "The Catholic Church rejects nothing that is true and holy in these religions," on the other hand, it is immediately afterward noted, "Indeed, she proclaims, and ever must proclaim Christ 'the Way, the Truth, and the Life' (John 14:6), in Whom men may find the fullness of religious life, in Whom God has reconciled all things to Himself" (*Nostra Ætate* [1965], §2).

a question. Here the greater affirmation is this: in order to obtain eternal salvation, the human being must believe in the one true God and in Him Who God has sent, Jesus Christ our Lord (see John 17:3). Faith invariably leads to the request to be baptized, and therefore, as we have seen, faith and Baptism are necessary for salvation. The main affirmation is that, in order to be saved, one must practice the true religion, Christianity, and be incorporated to the true Church, the Catholic Church.[73]

Another affirmation is juxtaposed with the previous one: it is possible that a non-Christian is saved. These two affirmations only appear to be contradictory, because saying that a non-Christian can be saved does not mean that the person can be saved without Christ and without the Church. And it does not even mean to deny the necessity of Baptism for salvation, because in certain cases it is possible to receive the grace belonging to Baptism, that is, the justification of the sinner, without receiving the sacramental sign[74] (see Chapters Nine and Ten). In this regard, the Church has always believed that if a catechumen—that is, one who already professes the Christian faith and is preparing to receive Baptism—dies before receiving the Sacrament, he is saved by faith and by the desire (*votum* in Latin) to receive the Sacrament necessary for salvation—an explicit *votum*, because the person was voluntarily preparing to be baptized. Traditional theology thus also spoke of the possibility of an implicit *votum*, which under certain conditions is sufficient for salvation. Ultimately, this would also be the case for the righteous of the Old Testament who, if they had known the true faith, would have been baptized. Even after the coming of the Lord, an incalculable number of people have not been reached in any way by the Gospel, or else they have heard of Christ and the Church, but not in such a way as to be able to embrace the true faith. People in this case are not culpable for their non-adherence to the true religion. Such people, however, can and must use their natural faculty of intellect to seek the truth and the good and, in conscience, follow what they know.

---

[73] See Second Vatican Council, *Lumen Gentium*, §13: "All men are called to belong to the new people of God. Wherefore this people, while remaining one and only one, is to be spread throughout the whole world and must exist in all ages, so that the decree of God's will may be fulfilled.... All men are called to be part of this catholic unity of the people of God." And at §17: "In this way the Church both prays and labors in order that the entire world may become the People of God, the Body of the Lord and the Temple of the Holy Spirit, and that in Christ, the Head of all, all honor and glory may be rendered to the Creator and Father of the Universe."

[74] Some form of faith, even implicit, is instead always demanded, as Hebrews 11:6 teaches: "But without faith it is impossible to please him, for anyone who approaches God must believe that he exists and that he rewards those who seek him."

Here the role of the Holy Spirit, the great Illuminator,[75] enters into play.

When human beings know the truth, even partially, and sincerely strive to follow it and to do good according to a right conscience, they are already under the influence of the Holy Spirit, Who in a mysterious way puts them into contact with the mystery of Christ, the *Logos*, the Truth incarnate. This universal work of the Paraclete is an "evangelical preparation"[76]: the Third Person prepares human beings to embrace "all truth" (John 16:13) when it is preached to them. If this does not occur, the merit of having sincerely sought the truth and the good, having striven to cultivate an upright conscience, remains within them. The Second Vatican Council proposed in a new way this perennial doctrine. It has preferred to omit the terminology of *votum*, but has maintained the essence of the doctrine in question.[77]

2.3.3. Religious Pluralism and the Need for the Church

In addition to what we have said, there is a further specification of noteworthy importance and topicality. In the last few decades, the question that we have just discussed has been put forth in a new way by a rather substantial number of theologians, belonging to various Christian denominations. The so-called "theology of religious pluralism" has begun to develop, based on the conviction that the existence of many religions in the world would not only be something existing *de facto* (it is a fact that there are many of them), but rather *de iure* (by right), as if to say that God would want, and not just tolerate, that there are many religions. The various religions, with their founders, would thus be multiple ways—and declared by some to be equally valid—for approaching the divine mystery, which remains superior to all particular determinations, marked by different factors, like the time period and culture of origin. The

---

[75] The sequence of Pentecost, *Veni, Sancte Spiritus*, attributes to the Third Person the titles of "Light of the hearts" ("*lumen cordium*") and "most blessed Light" ("*lux beatissima*"). The hymn, *Veni, Creator Spiritus* (attributed to Rabanus Maurus, d. 856) prays: "*accende lumen sensibus*" usually translated as, "guide our minds with thy blest light."

[76] See Eusebius of Caesarea (d. 339), *Praeparatio Evangelica* 1.1.

[77] "Those also can attain to salvation who through no fault of their own do not know the Gospel of Christ or His Church, yet sincerely seek God and moved by grace strive by their deeds to do His will as it is known to them through the dictates of conscience. Nor does Divine Providence deny the helps necessary for salvation to those who, without blame on their part, have not yet arrived at an explicit knowledge of God and with His grace strive to live a good life. Whatever good or truth is found amongst them is looked upon by the Church as a preparation for the Gospel. She knows that it is given by Him who enlightens all men so that they may finally have life" (Second Vatican Council, *Lumen Gentium*, §16).

various authors are distinguished from one another by the fact that each one proposes nuances or clarifications, but in the end the view that unites them is the one described.

Clearly this theology is unacceptable for the Catholic faithful, who believe that there is one God and one Lord Jesus Christ, who is not one of the manifestations of the divine, an "avatar,"[78] but the *Verbum caro*, that is, *the* definitive Revelation of the mystery of God and *the* salvation of humanity in Person. These fundamental elements of the faith have always been taught, and confirmed again in the Declaration *Dominus Iesus*, published in August 2000—a very brief text, but one of great importance, whose reading is highly recommended. The Catholic faith, as was said, absolutely admits that non-Christians can be saved under certain conditions, always through the mediation of Christ and the Church (this is called the "inclusivist model," because it also includes non-Christians in salvation). It thus refutes the "exclusivist model," which gives an extreme interpretation of the dogma "*Extra Ecclesiam nulla salus*" ("Outside the Church there is no salvation"),[79] understanding it as "outside of visibly and formally belonging to the Church, absolutely no one is saved,"[80] with the latter interpretation being too restrictive, and not corresponding to the way in which the Magisterium itself understands the dogma.[81] However, the Church with just as much force

---

[78] In Hinduism, the term indicates the apparition or descent of a divinity to earth. This concept is not compatible with Christianity, not only because it is framed within polytheism, for which there are various *avatars* of the various gods, but also because the same god is manifested various times in multiple ways and in different circumstances. An *avatar* is thus *one* manifestation of a god, not *the* true, unique, and definitive manifestation of God in the world, as it is in the Christian concept of the Incarnation.

[79] "*Salus extra Ecclesiam non est*" (Saint Cyprian of Carthage, *Epistola [LXXIII]ad Iubaianum* 21). For the adoption of this principle by the Magisterium, see DS 575; 792; 802; 870; 1351; 2867; 2730–2731; 2785; 2999; 3304; 3821.

[80] Whoever gives this interpretation takes as its basis—inappropriately—the formulation given by the Fourth Lateran Council, *Firmiter* (1215), which teaches: "There is indeed one universal Church of the faithful outside of which no one at all is saved [*extra quam nullus omnino salvatur*]" (DS 802).

[81] The Magisterium has always rejected such a radical reading of the dogma. For example, Blessed Pius IX, in the allocution *Singulari Quadam* (1854), teaches: "Because of the faith, one must, it is true, hold firmly that outside the Apostolic Roman Church no one can be saved, insofar as it is the only ark of salvation: whoever does not enter into it will drown in the flood; nonetheless, however, it must equally be held certainly that those who are subjected to a lack of knowledge concerning the true religion, if this cannot be overcome, they are not implicated in any fault for this in the eyes of the Lord" (our translation). During the pontificate of Pius XII, a *Letter to the Archbishop of Boston* sent by the Holy Office was published (1949), which says: "In order that one may obtain eternal salvation, it is not always required that he be incorporated into the Church actually as a member,

The Spirit's Action in the Church and in the World

denies the "pluralist model," described above, because it cannot in any way abdicate the fundamental claim of Christianity, to be the only true religion desired by God, to which all people are called, as the Second Vatican Council also recently recalled in continuity with the Tradition of the faith.[82]

2.3.4. The Universal Attraction of the Spirit toward Christ, and Missionary Zeal

Moreover, Vatican II stressed that the salvation of non-Christians—which remains a more difficult goal for various reasons,[83] thus the missionary zeal of the Church should not decrease—always happens through the work of the Holy Spirit and the mediation of the Church. Now, what the Holy Spirit does is not simply put human beings into contact with God (a God superior to all religious forms). Vatican II clarifies that the Spirit, in His action of universal diffusion, places people in contact with the Paschal Mystery of Christ,[84] that is, with His Death and Resurrection. We mentioned above the role of the Spirit as the Illuminator who puts persons in touch with the Truth. But this Truth or *Logos* is incarnate: it is Christ, crucified and risen. The salvation of human beings passes through the redemptive Passion of the immolated Lamb. Thus, those who are saved "outside the Church," are not saved by themselves, but by the Blood of Christ, even if they only knew Him under the form of Truth and Love, and not with the name that He took when He became man.[85] Since Christ has a Mystical Body and a Bride, the

---

but it is necessary that at least he be united to her by desire and longing. However, this desire need not always be explicit, as it is in catechumens; but when a person suffers from invincible ignorance, God accepts also an implicit desire, so called because it is included in that good disposition of soul whereby a person wishes his will to be conformed to the will of God" (DS 3870).

[82] The Second Vatican Council undoubtedly incorporates the dogma: "Basing itself upon Sacred Scripture and Tradition, it [the Council] teaches that the Church, now sojourning on earth as an exile, is necessary for salvation. Christ, present to us in His Body, which is the Church, is the one Mediator and the unique way of salvation. In explicit terms He Himself affirmed the necessity of faith and Baptism (see Mark 16:16; John 3:5), and thereby also affirmed the necessity of the Church, for through Baptism as through a door men enter the Church. Whosoever, therefore, knowing that the Catholic Church was made necessary by Christ, would refuse to enter or to remain in it, could not be saved" (*Lumen Gentium*, §14).

[83] See Pius XII, *Mystici Corporis* (DS 3821).

[84] Second Vatican Council, *Gaudium et Spes*, §22.

[85] A Gregorian antiphon recognizes that where there is true love, love that is accompanied with the truth, there is God: *Ubi caritas est vera Deus ibi est* ("where love is true, God is there": this is the version that is found in the oldest manuscripts, instead of the other one,

Church, He never is separated from her, as He never abandons His humanity. Thus, wherever Christ is, there is His Bride. It follows from this that not only is no one saved without Christ, whether they know it or not, but also no one is saved without the mediation of the Church, even if they were not formally incorporated into her.

It must be repeated that none of this in any way leads to religious indifferentism, which holds that—given that even the non-baptized who are in good conscience can be saved—it remains basically true that any religion would save (or even no religion at all). Without the Gospel of Christ and the grace of the Holy Spirit, in fact, the sinner gropes in the darkness of error. Thus, without Christ, the Spirit, and the Church, forming a right conscience and honest activity is very difficult. From this it follows that those who, with effort and not without grace, succeed, must be admired, and the Lord will take into account the fact the such a person has achieved this result while having received much less than the Christian (see Luke 12:47–48). But this path is difficult, and not many cross it. Despite the fact that today's sensibilities run in the opposite direction, it must be recalled that theologically it is probable that many are lost because the Gospel was not preached to them, at least not in an adequate way. Thus, the possibility of the salvation of non-Christians must not let us forget the possibility of their damnation (which is also the case with Christians, if they are unfaithful): from this it follows that the Church can never withdraw from its fundamental missionary duty.[86]

---

used for a long time, which says: *ubi caritas et amor, Deus ibi est*).

[86] "But often men, deceived by the Evil One, have become vain in their reasonings and have exchanged the truth of God for a lie, serving the creature rather than the Creator [see Rom 1:21, 25]. Or some there are who, living and dying in this world without God, are exposed to final despair. Wherefore to promote the glory of God and procure the salvation of all of these, and mindful of the command of the Lord, 'Preach the Gospel to every creature' [Mark 16:15], the Church fosters the missions with care and attention" (Second Vatican Council, *Lumen Gentium*, §16). Vatican II then dedicated an entire decree to the theme of missions, titled *Ad Gentes* (1965). On the twenty-fifth anniversary of the promulgation, Saint John Paul II wished to dedicate to the missionary theme the encyclical *Redemptoris Missio*, which we have cited several times above; this is the encyclical in which he begins with the important words: "The mission of Christ the Redeemer, which is entrusted to the Church, is still very far from completion. As the second millennium after Christ's coming draws to an end, an overall view of the human race shows that this mission is still only beginning and that we must commit ourselves wholeheartedly to its service" (§1).

2.3.5. Ecumenical and Interreligious Dialogue

1. The Importance and Risk of Dialogue

After the Second Vatican Council, the pastoral choice of dialogue with the representatives of other Christian confessions ("ecumenical dialogue") and non-Christian religions ("interreligious dialogue") was added to the task of missionary proclamation, a task that has been constitutive of the life of the Church from the beginning.[87] This novelty carries with it both riches and danger.[88] The riches consist in the fact that this pastoral choice of the Church, we must believe, is willed by the Holy Spirit. Ecumenical and interreligious dialogue represent a concrete path that the Spirit of Christ has indicated to the Church in the context of our era. The risk that the practice of dialogue carries is that of forgetting the far superior value of proclamation: to non-Catholics, of the fullness of truth and the means of salvation, which are found in their integrity in the Catholic Church (see Chapter Eight); and to non-Christians, of the very knowledge of Christ.

2. Dialogue and Proclamation

Not that many years ago, the Holy See issued a document called *Dialogue and Proclamation*, precisely to remind us that the recent pastoral path of dialogue does not replace the two-thousand-year-old, and constitutive, evangelizing and missionary action of the Church, but joins it, or better yet the dialogue

---

[87] A more accurate differentiation between these two forms of dialogue should be proposed, but this is not possible in this treatment. The fundamental texts of the Second Vatican Council are, for ecumenism, *Unitatis Redintegratio* (1964), and for interreligious dialogue, *Nostra Ætate* (1965).

[88] Speaking generally of dialogue as a pastoral option of the Church in our time, Saint Paul VI, in his first encyclical, *Ecclesiam Suam* (1964), expresses both the beauty and the risks of the dialogue: "If we want to be men's pastors, fathers and teachers, we must also behave as their brothers. Dialogue thrives on friendship, and most especially on service. All this we must remember and strive to put into practice on the example and precept of Christ. But the danger remains. Indeed, the worker in the apostolate is under constant fire. The desire to come together as brothers must not lead to a watering down or whittling away of truth. Our dialogue must not weaken our attachment to our faith. Our apostolate must not make vague compromises concerning the principles which regulate and govern the profession of the Christian faith both in theory and in practice. An immoderate desire to make peace and sink differences at all costs (irenism and syncretism) is ultimately nothing more than skepticism about the power and content of the Word of God which we desire to preach. The effective apostle is the man who is completely faithful to Christ's teaching" (§§87–88).

represents a modality of the proclamation.[89] The principle of *et-et* requires that both the dialogue and the proclamation coexist, but it also prescribes that the two do not have the same value. The evangelical mandate of Christ regards the proclamation, not dialogue (see Matt 28:18–20). As shocking as this truth may be today, it is equally evident according to the texts of Scripture and Tradition. The task for which the Holy Spirit gives strength to the Church is that of announcing Christ.[90] Dialogue is carried out alongside this work, and in a sense is part of it, but it does not replace it. Dialogue is not for the purpose of seeking the truth together with others, because the Church has always had the basic claim to possess the Truth already,[91] since it is the Mystical Body and the Bride of Christ.

3. Specifications about Dialogue

Let us note the following points concerning dialogue:

(1) Dialogue can be of great help because the same men of the Church deepen ever more the truth that is already fully possessed, also stimulated by the comparison with other perspectives concerning Christianity or religion. This is not to change the Christian faith based on the comparison with other faiths or beliefs, but to believe always more in that same faith that has been handed down intact from the Apostles, or even to better announce Christ to the world.

(2) Dialogue helps us to better know the members of other Christian denominations and other religions, and to forge ties of esteem and friendship,

---

[89] See Pontifical Council for Interreligious Dialogue, *Dialogue and Proclamation* (1991). Saint Paul VI said that dialogue is a form of proclamation in *Ecclesiam Suam*, §66.

[90] The document of the Congregation for the Doctrine of the Faith, *Nota Doctrinalis de Quibusdam Rationibus Evangelizationis* (2007), is worthwhile reading. The text shows the incorrectness of the mental approach that is very widespread today, even in some sectors of the Church, which is described like so: "Often it is maintained that any attempt to convince others on religious matters is a limitation of their freedom. From this perspective, it would only be legitimate to present one's own ideas and to invite people to act according to their consciences, without aiming at their conversion to Christ and to the Catholic faith. It is enough, so they say, to help people to become more human or more faithful to their own religion; it is enough to build communities which strive for justice, freedom, peace and solidarity. Furthermore, some maintain that Christ should not be proclaimed to those who do not know Him, nor should joining the Church be promoted, since it would also be possible to be saved without explicit knowledge of Christ and without formal incorporation in the Church" (§3).

[91] The same thing can be said even better this way: "Let us never forget St Augustine's experience: it is not we who possess the Truth after having sought it, but the Truth that seeks us out and possesses us" (Benedict XVI, *General Audience*, November 14, 2012).

based on the common humanity and the religious sense that binds us all. This is very important and allows us to overcome any attitude of an undue "religious war," which does not express the genuine essence of the faith, and to collaborate for the good of humanity.

(3) Dialogue—this only applies to the ecumenical one—accompanies a person on the road that, with the guidance of the Holy Spirit, leads all human beings to unity in a single faith, a single Baptism, and a single Church. This is because it allows us to highlight those elements that Catholics have in common with non-Catholics and start from what already unites us in order to face with serenity and truth the doctrinal points that divide.

(4) We must not get the idea, however, that by dialoguing we are building a new religion together, or that the latter will emerge out of our dialogue, as a new faith, a new Church, that will finally place everyone in agreement. Catholics do not recognize another true Church or true faith other than their own, even if they acknowledge all elements of truth and goodness that are present elsewhere and consider them as good seeds that the Word has sown in the world, so that one day they might sprout up to full maturity, which always consists in adhering to Christ and the Church.

(5) These clarifications do not imply that the dialogue is, on the Catholic side, a simple tactic for directing as many people as possible into the Church, without really being committed to dialogue. On one hand, it is the will of Christ that the Church does all that she can so that all people are put in the condition of *freely* choosing to enter into full communion with her. On the other hand, this does not imply that the Church does not put herself into play or discussion when she dialogues. She is not disposed to revise the faith that comes to her from Christ, but she is well disposed to revise the concrete modes in which she has lived and preached the faith.[92] For example, Pope John Paul II has fully confirmed the defined dogma of the primacy of honor and jurisdiction of the Bishop of Rome, but in dialogue with the Christian East, has said that the concrete *mode of exercise* of this primacy—unchangeable in itself—can be an object of discussion.[93] Another example of this attitude, albeit of a different nature, is represented by the apostolic constitution *Anglicanorum Coetibus*,[94] which opens the doors of the Catholic Church to groups of Anglican faithful and ministers: they must integrally accept the Catholic doctrine as it is expressed in the *Catechism of the Catholic Church*, but they may make use of special celebratory and disciplinary *modalities*.

---

[92] See Saint Paul VI, *Ecclesiam Suam*, §43–59.
[93] See Saint John Paul II, *Ut Unum Sint* (1995), §95.
[94] See Benedict XVI, *Anglicanorum Coetibus* (2009).

2.3.6. Testimony of Charity

Another way in which the Spirit spreads the presence of Christ in a universal way in the world is the charity of the Church. As is known, the Church has always been concerned not only with the salvation of souls (charity in the spiritual order), but also with material welfare (charity in the material order). Obviously, in this particular bipolarity, the primacy goes to the first pole, eternal salvation. The history of charity is absolutely one of the brightest chapters ever written by the persons of the Church in the history of humanity. In her traditional doctrine, the Church—encountering them in the Scripture—has enumerated fourteen works of charity, or mercy, subdividing them between the spiritual and material spheres. This list is found again in the *Compendium of the Catechism of the Catholic Church* (Appendix, B. Formulas of Catholic Doctrine):

THE SEVEN WORKS OF CORPORAL MERCY	THE SEVEN WORKS OF SPIRITUAL MERCY
1. Feed the hungry	1. Counsel the doubtful
2. Give drink to the thirsty	2. Instruct the ignorant
3. Clothe the naked	3. Admonish sinners
4. Shelter the homeless	4. Comfort the afflicted
5. Visit the sick	5. Forgive offenses
6. Visit the imprisoned	6. Bear wrongs patiently
7. Bury the dead	7. Pray for the living and the dead

2.3.7. The Fruit of Holiness and Martyrdom

Last but not least, the most beautiful fruits that grow on the tree of the Church, through the Holy Spirit, are the martyrs and saints. We shall discuss them here because they represent not only the treasures of holiness of the Church (action of the Holy Spirit *ad intra*), but also the great call and the great testimony that the Church gives to the world. The saints possess such a charm as to be able to convince anyone that what the faith says is true. Their witness is like a living proof of the existence of God and of the truth of the Catholic faith. Tertullian wrote the famous phrase: "The blood of the martyrs is the seed of the Church."⁹⁵ In this regard, Benedict XVI expresses it as follows:

> I did once say that to me art and the Saints are the greatest apologetic for our faith. The arguments contributed by reason are unquestionably important and indispensable, but then there is always dissent somewhere. On the other hand, if we look at the Saints, this great luminous trail on which God passed through history, we see that there truly is a force of good which resists the millennia; there truly is the light of light.⁹⁶

The Holy Spirit produces the great witness of the faith, a witness that is able, if necessary, to express itself even in the spilling of blood. This is where we get the word "martyr," indicating witness (in Greek *martys*). In Revelation, it is Jesus Himself who is defined as "the faithful witness" (Rev 1:5) and in one of the letters that he dictated to St. John, the risen Christ tells the recipient, "Remain faithful until death, and I will give you the crown of life" (Rev 2:10). Being a martyr means always and unconditionally following Jesus. It means taking up one's cross daily and following him (see Luke 9:23). When this faithful following is crowned with the bloody sacrifice of life, which reproduces in the Christian the exact destiny of the Lord, the Church recognizes the title of martyr, not because other Christian faithful are not witnesses, but because the martyr is the witness *par excellence*.

The Church sees very well, however, that Jesus says to take up one's cross "daily" and this implies that martyrdom can also be bloodless (this is often called "white martyrdom"): it is a life of daily fidelity to the will of God, which even if it is not crowned with the supreme self-sacrifice for the faith, always remains a life of exemplary witness,⁹⁷ sustained by the grace of that divine Spirit that is Holy and that makes others holy. In all of these cases, the Church recognizes

---

[95] "*Sanguis martyrum, semen christianorum*" (Tertullian of Carthage, *Apologeticum* 50.13 [our translation]).

[96] Benedict XVI, *Meeting with the Clergy of the Diocese of Bolzano-Bressanone*, August 6, 2008. This is expressed in a similar way by Saint John Henry Newman (d. 1890) in ch. 5 of the work *Apologia pro vita sua*.

[97] The expression "white martyrdom" is used with caution and only in an analogical way with respect to martyrdom of blood, which is martyrdom in the true and proper sense. This is also because, to speak of "white martyrdom," we need to find ourselves before an exceptional exemplification in the life of faith and not simply an example of the life of a "good Christian." The term will apply, then, to those faithful who have lived virtue in a heroic way, even if their terrestrial existence has not been crowned by martyrdom.

The Sanctifier

the title of saint and, in lower degrees, of blessed, venerable, and servant of God. The existence of saints, and particularly of martyred saints, not only represents a witness *ad extra Ecclesiae*, but also a warning *ad intra*. They constantly remind us that Christianity can never be "gentrified" and that, when this happens, there is a betrayal of the essence of the faith. The fact that in each era there are Christians willing to die for the faith and actually shed their blood for Christ reminds all of us that it is not right to be mediocre in the faith (see Rev 3:16), to simply model our behavior on a person who is considered civil in a certain era and culture (see Rom 12:2), and to water-down the demands of following the Lord. The saints and the martyrs, then, continuously call us back to our duties and our vocation.

3. Magisterial Pronouncements

We shall conclude this chapter with a brief review of the magisterial teachings concerning the Holy Spirit. This is not an exposition that touches on all aspects, because those concerning the "intimate life" of the Trinity, that is, the relations between the Persons in God, will be discussed more in the following chapter. We are therefore proposing only an overview of the ecclesial teachings concerning the themes about which we have focused in this chapter, that is to say, those regarding the "economic" action (in the world and in the Church) of the Holy Spirit.

3.1. The Holy Spirit in Creation

The fact that the Holy Spirit cooperates in creation was interpreted from the first centuries as a sign of His divine nature. Pope Damasus I (d. 384) wrote: "We likewise profess that the Holy Spirit (is) uncreated and of one majesty, of one essence [*usia*; in this form it is transliterated from Greek in the original Latin of Damasus], of one power with God the Father and our Lord Jesus Christ. Nor is He deserving of creaturely injury, (He) who was sent to create."[98]

The Second Council of Constantinople (AD 553) proposes an interesting Trinitarian formula in which it says: "For one (is) the God and Father from Whom [Greek *ex*] all things (are), one (is) the Lord Jesus Christ through Whom [*diá*] all things (are), and one is the Holy Spirit in Whom [*en*] all things (are)."[99] It is interesting to note that a similar, but not perfectly identical, formula is found in Saint Paul: "For from [*ex*] him [God] and through

---

[98] Saint Damasus I, *De Trinitate Divina* (fragment 1: DS 145).
[99] Second Council of Constantinople, *Anathematismi de Tribus Capitulis*, §1 (DS 421).

[*diá*] him and for [*eis*] him are all things." (Rom 11:36). While the Apostle says that all things are "toward, for" God, the Second Constantinopolitan Council—making the triunity of the Pauline formula explicit—says that all things are created "in the" Holy Spirit. St. Leo IX (d. 1054), putting together the Pauline text and that the Second Council of Constantinople, writes (in Latin and no longer in Greek): "the Creator of all creatures, from Whom [*ex*], through Whom [*per*], and in Whom [*in*] all things (are), those in Heaven and on earth, those visible and invisible."[100]

The two perspectives, of the "in" and of the "toward, for," are harmoniously put together and explained—like the other prepositions—in a text by Leo XIII:

> The Church is accustomed most fittingly to attribute to the Father those works of the Divinity in which power excels, to the Son those in which wisdom excels, and those in which love excels to the Holy Spirit. Not that all perfections and external operations are not common to the Divine Persons; for "the operations of the Trinity are indivisible, even as the essence of the Trinity is indivisible," because as the three Divine Persons "are inseparable, so do they act inseparably."[101] But by a certain comparison and a kind of affinity between the operations and the properties of the Persons, these operations are attributed or, as it is stated, "appropriated." . . .
>
> In this manner the Father, Who is "the principle of the whole Godhead," is also the efficient cause of all things . . . , of [ex] Him are all things: of Him, referring to the Father. But the Son, the Word and Image of God, is also the exemplar cause, whence all creatures borrow their form and beauty, their order and harmony . . . ; by [per] Him are all things: by Him, referring to the Son. The Holy Spirit is the ultimate cause of all things, since . . . (He) is the Divine Goodness and the mutual Love of the Father and Son, completes and perfects, by His strong yet gentle power, the secret work of man's eternal salvation . . . in [in] Him are all things: in Him, referring to the Holy Spirit.[102]

To say "in Him" or "for, toward Him" is thus the same: the expression indi-

---

[100] Saint Leo IX, *Congratulamur Vehementer* (1053) (DS 680).

[101] The two citations come from Saint Augustine of Hippo, *De Trinitate* 1.4.

[102] Leo XIII, *Divinum Illud Munus* (1897) (DS 3326).

The Sanctifier

cates that all creation—but in particular human beings and especially those who are friends of God—is filled with the presence and action of the Holy Spirit[103] and tends toward Him as toward its own final cause. The Holy Spirit, in other words, carries creation to eschatological fulfillment.[104]

3.2. The Holy Spirit in the History of Salvation

In addition to the already mentioned inspiration of the "prophets," i.e., the holy writers of the Scripture, the Holy Spirit has intervened in many ways in the history of salvation, as we have seen. The intervention that is most important, because it is the greatest work carried out by the Trinity *ad extra*,[105] is certainly the Incarnation, which is of the Word alone,[106] but in which the Holy Spirit intervenes. Leo XIII writes:

> Now this work [the Incarnation], although belonging to the whole Trinity, is still appropriated especially to the Holy Spirit. . . . Not only was the conception of Christ accomplished, but also the sanctification of His soul, which, in Holy Scripture, is called His 'anointing.' . . . Wherefore all His actions were 'performed in the Holy Spirit,' and especially the Sacrifice of Himself. . . . Considering this, no one can be surprised that all the gifts of the Holy Spirit inundated the soul of Christ.[107]

The presence and action of the Spirit in the life of Christ was not only at the beginning, but permanently—from the Incarnation until the extreme Sac-

---

[103] See Second Vatican Council, *Gaudium et Spes*, §11: The Spirit *"replet orbem terrarum"* ("fills the earth").

[104] Second Vatican Council, *Gaudium et Spes*, §26: The true good of the social order should be promoted and "God's Spirit, Who with a marvelous providence directs the unfolding of time and renews the face of the earth, is not absent from this development [*huic evolutioni adest*]." Note, however, that the Holy Spirit always maintains His divine transcendence over the world; the Church has condemned the thesis (see Synod of Sens [1140/1141], *propositio* 2 [DS 722]) that holds the Holy Spirit to be the Soul of the World spoken of by the Platonists in philosophy, and which—though with other names—is evoked in the contemporary religiosities of New Age and Next Age.

[105] "Among the external operations of God, the highest of all is the mystery of the Incarnation of the Word" (Leo XIII, *Divinum Illud Munus* [DS 3327]).

[106] "The Incarnation of the Godhead has taken place, not in the Father or the Holy Spirit, but only in the Son" (Innocent III, *Eius Exemplo* [1208] [DS 791]).

[107] Leo XIII, *Divinum Illud Munus* (DS 3327). The reported citation is from Saint Basil the Great (d. 379), *De Spiritu Sancto* 16.39.

rifice of the cross. Moreover, the Spirit carries out the "Christification" or anointing of Jesus and fills His human soul with all the gifts of grace, to the maximum degree. We can see gathered here in brief the various biblical facts that were expressed in the first part of the chapter.

Despite the role of the Spirit in the Incarnation of the Word, the Magisterium clarifies that the title of "Father of the Son" cannot be applied to Him: in fact, the Father of the Son is the One who eternally generates Him in the divine nature, not the One (the Spirit) who intervenes in the creation of the humanity that the Word assumes.[108] However, it is said that the Word is incarnate "by [Greek, *ek*; Latin, *de*] the power of the Holy Spirit."[109] If it is observed that "and by Mary" is added immediately afterwards, it is understood that the first expression makes reference, in a parallel manner to the second, to the human nature of Christ, which comes both from the Holy Spirit and from Mary (see Chapters Four and Seven). Thus, it can be said that the Spirit is the origin of Christ as regards His human nature, but not in His Personhood as the Son in the Trinity: in this respect, it is the Father who is the Son's principle of origin (see the next Chapter).

The Magisterium also recalls other interventions of the Holy Spirit in the life of Jesus, particularly the descent at the Baptism in the Jordan, and the death of the Lord. A beautiful text from the fourth century focuses on the fullness of the gifts of grace that the Holy Spirit, "that reposes in Christ," pours out into His humanity:

> We must first treat the sevenfold Spirit that reposes in Christ. The Spirit of wisdom: Christ (is) "the power of God and the wisdom of God" (1 Cor 1:24). The Spirit of understanding: "I will give you understanding and instruct you in the way you should go" (Ps 32:8). The Spirit of counsel: "And his name shall be called messenger of great counsel" (Isa 9:6, LXX). The Spirit of strength, as said above: "the power of God and the wisdom of God" (1 Cor 1:24). The Spirit of knowledge: [we are] Apostles "because of the excellence of the

---

[108] "Yet we must not believe that the Holy Spirit is the Father of the Son because Mary conceived by the overshadowing of the same Holy Spirit, lest we should seem to affirm that the Son has two fathers—which it is certainly impious to say" (Eleventh Synod of Toledo [675] [DS 533]).

[109] First Council of Constantinople (DS 150). The Fourth Lateran Council (AD 1215) uses with regard to Christ the beautiful expression "*Spiritus Sancti cooperatione conceptus*" ("conceived with the cooperation of the Holy Spirit": *Firmiter* [DS 801]). Pius XII says that the human nature of Jesus "*ex Spiritus Sancti virtute concepta est*" ("was conceived by the power of the Holy Spirit": *Haurietis Aquas* [1956] [DS 3923]).

knowledge of Christ Jesus" (Eph 3:19; Phil 3:8). The Spirit of truth: "I (am) the way, the truth, and the life" (John 14:6). The Spirit of the fear (of God): "The fear of the Lord is the beginning of wisdom" (Ps 111:10; Prov 9:10).[110]

Finally, the Second Vatican Council recalls that the risen Christ pours out the Spirit on the Apostles, and that the Paraclete accompanies the mission of the Church since the day of Pentecost.[111] This leads to the following point.

3.3. *The Holy Spirit in the Church*

This theme was touched upon by the Magisterium, especially in recent times,[112] given the rediscovered sensibility for the relationship between pneumatology (theology of the Holy Spirit), and ecclesiology, due also to the dialogue with the Orthodox, who place a high value on this aspect.

A first reference is found in Leo XIII, who speaks of the Holy Spirit as Soul of the Church: "That the Church is a divine institution is most clearly proved by the splendor and glory of those gifts and graces with which she is adorned and whose author and giver is the Holy Spirit. Let it suffice to state that, as Christ is the Head of the Church, so is the Holy Spirit her soul." Pope Pecci concludes by citing Saint Augustine: "What the soul is in our body, that is the Holy Spirit in Christ's Body, the Church."[113]

In continuity with this teaching, the Second Vatican Council declared that the Holy Spirit, "Giving the [ecclesial] Body unity through Himself and through His power and inner joining of the members, this same Spirit produces and urges love among the believers."[114] The connection of the members is understood as unity in the apostolic doctrine, in communion, in the *fractio*

---

[110] See Synod of Rome, *Decretum Damasi* (382) (DS 178).

[111] See Second Vatican Council, *Lumen Gentium*, §§19, 21, 24.

[112] However, there is no shortage of older references. For example, in 787 the Second Council of Nicaea says, in passing, that the Holy Spirit "dwells" in the Church (*Definitio de Sacris Imaginibus* [DS 600]). Even earlier, the Sixteenth Synod of Toledo (year 693) said that the Catholic Church is "brilliant in virtues, and resplendent in the gifts of the Holy Spirit" (*Symbolum*, art. 36 [DS 575]).

[113] Leo XIII, *Divinum Illud Munus* (DS 3328); the citation of St. Augustine of Hippo is from *Sermo* 267.1.4. On the theme of the Spirit as Soul, see Pius XII, *Mystici Corporis* (1943) (DS 3807–3808).

[114] Second Vatican Council, *Lumen Gentium*, §7. The description of the Spirit as Soul of the Church is explicitly resumed later in the same number, citing in a footnote Leo XIII and Pius XII.

panis, and in prayer.¹¹⁵ Given the importance of the doctrine, the Holy Spirit guarantees special assistance to those who hold the *munus docendi* in the Church, namely, the Magisterium.¹¹⁶ The Holy Spirit dwells within the Church, guides her to the whole and entire truth, unifies her in communion and services, and gives her charisms¹¹⁷ and hierarchical gifts,¹¹⁸ as well as gives her the fruits that are her own.¹¹⁹ Thus, "the Church is compelled by the Holy Spirit to do her part that God's plan may be fully realized."¹²⁰ "Led by the Holy Spirit, Mother Church unceasingly exhorts her sons 'to purify and renew themselves so that the sign of Christ can shine more brightly on the face of the Church.'"¹²¹ This means that every single baptized person is called to cooperate with the grace of the Holy Spirit. We shall conclude, therefore, with some references to this.

3.4. The Holy Spirit in the Life of the Baptized

The baptized have received, with the Sacrament of the faith, justification. The Council of Trent taught that the justice given to the individual faithful is a gift from the Holy Spirit, Who "'apportions to each one individually as He wills' and according to each one's personal disposition and cooperation."¹²²

---

¹¹⁵ Second Vatican Council, *Lumen Gentium*, §13, with a clear reference to Acts 2:42.

¹¹⁶ "In carrying out their task, the Shepherds of the Church enjoy the assistance of the Holy Spirit; this assistance reaches its highest point when they teach the people of God in such a manner that, through the promises of Christ made to Peter and the other Apostles, the doctrine they propose is necessarily immune from error" (Congregation for the Doctrine of the Faith, *Mysterium Ecclesiae* [1973], §3 [DS 4534]). See First Vatican Council, *Pastor Æternus* (1870), ch. 4 (DS 3070); Second Vatican Council, *Lumen Gentium*, §25.

¹¹⁷ The Holy Spirit subjects the charismatic gifts to ecclesial evaluation: "What has a special place among these gifts [given by the Spirit to the Church] is the grace of the Apostles to whose authority the Spirit Himself subjected even those who were endowed with charisms" (Second Vatican Council, *Lumen Gentium*, §7). See Congregation for the Doctrine of the Faith, *Iuvenescit Ecclesia* (2016), §8: "He who has received the gift to lead in the Church has also the responsibility of keeping watch over the good exercise of the other charisms." In *Testem Benevolentiae* (1899), Leo XIII had rejected the conception of those who, feeling themselves endowed with powerful charisms given by the Spirit, believed to proceed alone in the Christian life under "a kind of hidden impulse" and without the guidance of the Magisterium (DS 3342).

¹¹⁸ "The Holy Spirit unfailingly preserves the form of government established by Christ the Lord in His Church" (Second Vatican Council, *Lumen Gentium*, §27).

¹¹⁹ Second Vatican Council, *Lumen Gentium*, §4. See also Second Vatican Council, *Gaudium et Spes*, §42.

¹²⁰ Second Vatican Council, *Lumen Gentium*, §17.

¹²¹ Second Vatican Council, *Gaudium et Spes*, §43.

¹²² Council of Trent, *Decretum de Iustificatione*, ch. 7 (DS 1529).

The Sanctifier

The justified person then becomes inhabited by the Holy Spirit as long as he or she remains just, that is, in grace.[123] On the other hand, it is the same Paraclete Who moves the sinner, directing him or her to the desire to be purified of sins and to be made just.[124]

The Holy Spirit is "the very source of every gift and created grace"[125] and since He dispenses His seven gifts to human beings (see the list above), He is called the "sevenfold" Spirit.[126] "He makes them fit and ready to undertake the various tasks and offices that contribute toward the renewal and building up of the Church."[127] The Spirit of Christ is therefore also the source of the different vocations that Christians receive:

> Now, the gifts of the Spirit are diverse: while He calls some to give clear witness to the desire for a heavenly home and to keep that desire green among the human family, He summons others to dedicate themselves to the earthly service of men and to make ready the material of the celestial realm by this ministry of theirs. Yet He frees all of them so that by putting aside love of self and bringing all earthly resources into the service of human life they can devote themselves to that future when humanity itself will become an offering accepted by God.[128]

---

[123] "The beginnings of this regeneration and renovation of man are by Baptism. In this Sacrament . . . the Holy Spirit enters in (the soul) for the first time and makes it like to Himself. . . . For He not only brings to us His divine gifts, but is the Author of them and is Himself the supreme Gift. . . . God by grace resides in the just soul as in a temple. . . . Now this wonderful union, which is properly called 'indwelling' . . . is attributed in a special manner to the Holy Spirit. For, while traces of divine power and wisdom appear even in the wicked man, charity, which, as it were, is the special mark of the Holy Spirit, is shared only by the just" (Leo XIII, *Divinum Illud Munus* [DS 3330–3331]).

[124] This is taught more than once in canons 4–8 and 17 of the Second Synod of Orange (DS 374–378; 387) and is repeated by the Council of Trent, *Decretum de Iustificatione*, ch. 5 (DS 1525); *Doctrina de Sacramento Paenitentiae* (1551), ch. 4 (DS 1678) as well as by the First Vatican Council, *Dei Filius* (1870), ch. 3 (DS 3010).

[125] Pius XII, *Mystici Corporis* (DS 3807).

[126] See Synod of Rome, *Decretum Damasi* (DS 178); Pope Siricius (d. 399), *Directa ad Decessorem* (385) (DS 183). The Council of Trent does not use the expression "sevenfold Spirit," but it cites four of the seven gifts that He distributes, for He is the "Spirit of wisdom and understanding, the Spirit of counsel and piety" (*Doctrina et Canones de Communione sub Utraque Specie et Parvulorum* [1562] [DS 1726]). Finally, we recall that the hymn *Veni, Creator Spiritus*, sings: "*Tu septiformis munere / Digitus paternae dexterae*" [Thou who art sevenfold in Thy grace / Finger of the Father's right hand].

[127] Second Vatican Council, *Lumen Gentium*, §12.

[128] Second Vatican Council, *Gaudium et Spes*, §38.

The strong eschatological orientation of the action of the Paraclete in the soul of the just is clear from the text: He orients us toward the Throne of God in Heaven, toward the heavenly Jerusalem, where those who have persevered in life in His grace will be able to see the face of God—Father, Son, and Holy Spirit.[129]

---

[129] See CCC §1137

6

The Trinity

1. Entering into the Divine Sanctuary

In the previous chapters, we considered God as the Creator, Redeemer, and Sanctifier. This does not merely refer to three activities (creating, redeeming, and sanctifying) that God carries out *ad extra*, that is, outside of His own Being, in the world, and in history. This concerns activities that, while being "external" to His divine nature (they happen in the created world), correspond to that same divine nature, because *"omne agens agit sibi simile"* ("every agent produces an effect similar to itself"[1]). Therefore, if God acts as Creator, Redeemer, and Sanctifier, that is, if God shows a Trinitarian character in history and in the world, He is also triune in Himself. Recent theology has had the merit of emphasizing the importance of the "salvific economy." Although this is undoubtedly an element that is not to be undervalued, it should not be the only focus either. From the "economic Trinity" one must proceed to the "immanent Trinity": "It is true that the mystery of the Most Holy Trinity was revealed to us in the economy of salvation, and most of all in

---

[1] *ST* I, q. 115, a. 1. In its context, the expression refers to creatures, not to God. But it is preceded by this observation: "Activity, which is none other than rendering a thing to be actual, is an essential property of act insofar as it is act" (our translation). God is pure Act, Act of all acts (see *ST* I, q. 3, a. 1); thus, the aforementioned principle also applies, and with greater perfection, to Him. On the other hand, did we not already see in Chapter Two that God created human beings in His image? And was it not also said, always with reference to Scripture, that from created works, by analogy, one traces back to the Creator? Thus creation—i.e., what God realizes outside of Himself—bears the fingerprints of its Creator.

Christ. . . . But by this revelation there is also given to believers some knowledge of God's intimate life."[2]

From the activity *ad extra* of God, the Trinitarian face of God may be understood. It is a process that is similar to natural theology, but it involves an opposite procedure. Natural theology proceeds "from below," from finite beings, and it goes back to their transcendent Origin. With natural reason, it is thus possible to know God as Being and in some of His characteristics (see Chapter Two). Supernatural theology, on the other hand, proceeds "from above," from Revelation, which—as was also seen in Chapter Two—is expressed in salvation history, in deeds and words intimately linked to one another, which God continues to unfold. In such a history of Revelation and salvation, God shows Himself and reveals Himself in His Trinitarian character: a conception that cannot be reached by natural reason alone, because of the fact that—as will be repeated time and again in this chapter—the actions of God *ad extra* are always carried out by God as a single nature, by God as God. Thus, only the existence of God can be deduced from creation. However, when reason encounters Revelation, it stands before a new object: the revelation of the intimate nature of God, of the Sanctuary of Trinitarian life, to which access is now given, albeit through the veil of faith and not in direct view.

In summary: we know that there is one God in Three (which we call Persons) because it was God who lifted the veil that hid the knowledge of His inner life. We enter with veneration into the Sanctuary of the intimate life of God, only because God opens up the possibility to us, revealing His Trinitarian Mystery: the one God who is truly Father, Son, and Holy Spirit.

2. The Old Testament Pedagogy

The mystery of the Most Holy Trinity was only revealed in the New Testament, while the Old Testament was more dedicated to emphasizing the unity of God, thus freeing Israel from polytheism. However, God is eternally Trinity: that is why, even in the period of the long pedagogy leading toward Christ (the Old Testament), He acted and spoke as a Trinitarian God, while not clearly revealing His most intimate nature. On account of this, after reading the New Testament, it is possible to reread the Old Testament and identify traces or prefigurations of the future Revelation of the Trinity. We have already noted one of these traces, commenting on the words "Let

---

[2] Congregation for the Doctrine of the Faith, *Mysterium Filii Dei* (1972), §5 (DS 4522).

us make" in Genesis 1:26 in the chapter dedicated to creation. Let us look at some others.

2.1. The Hebrew Name "Elohim"

God is called by many names in the Old Testament. One of these is *El*, which means the Strong, the Powerful. In the plural, *El* becomes *Elohim*. This very name, in the plural, is the first divine name that we encounter in the canonical ordering of the Bible. In fact, Genesis 1:1 says: "In the beginning, when God [*Elohim*] created the heavens and the earth." After that of YHWH, *Elohim* is also the most frequently used name in the Old Testament: in fact, it is found 2,750 times. The meaning is practically identical to *El*, the Powerful, but it slowly takes on monotheistic significance, the "One God." It is used, along with *Adonai*, as a substitute name for God in Israel, considering that YHWH was not allowed to be pronounced on account of its sacredness. This term is also used in the Bible to speak of the gods of other peoples (for example, in Ex 20:23: "You shall not make alongside of me gods of silver, nor shall you make for yourselves gods of gold."), but in these cases *elohim* is accompanied by qualifications like "gods of the Egyptians," or is accompanied by an article. Among other things, this is the name used in the texts that describe the commitment that God makes with the human being in the covenants (see, for example, Gen 17:7-8; Lev 11:45; Num 15:41). Finally, this is the name with which the human being chooses YHWH as his or her God: "[Jacob said: If] I come back safely to my father's house, the LORD shall be my God [*Elohim*]" (Gen 28:21).

One should not insist too much on the fact that the plural *Elohim* is used much more than the singular *El* and that it is, after YHWH, the most used name for God in the Old Testament. However, the Christian eye sees in the preference for the plural form not only an expressive form typical of the Semitic environment, but also an allusion to the fact that God is singular and plural at the same time (One and Triune): and so a word is chosen in the plural precisely to emphasize the uniqueness and unity of the God of Israel compared with the ancient polytheisms.

2.2. The Paternity of God

In the Old Testament, the concept of God the Father does not yet have that fullness that it would acquire thanks to Christ. In spite of this, we find that God is Father and is called so especially in a metaphorical sense, that is, in relation to Israel's election (see Isa 1:2: "Hear, O heavens, and listen, O earth, / for the

The Trinity

Lord speaks: / Sons have I raised and reared, / but they have rebelled against me!"; Deut 8:5: "So you must know in your heart that, even as a man disciplines his son, so the Lord, your God, disciplines you"). Three streams run together in revealing the paternity of God:

1. God Is Father of the Chosen People

Exodus 4:22–23 contains all the successive developments in seminal form, and the paternity of God is conceived there in a collective way. The text states: "Israel is my son, my firstborn. I said to you: Let my son go, that he may serve me. Since you refused to let him go, I will kill your son, your firstborn." Here, 'firstborn son' means a very beloved son. It is the election that makes Israel the son of God. This choice corresponds analogously to generation in the human sphere.

2. God Is the Father of the Righteous

Not even the chosen people are all saints, which is why the idea arises that God is especially the Father of the righteous. From the moral perspective, His paternity is understood here in a personal sense. Wisdom 2:13 says that the righteous one "professes to have knowledge of God / and styles himself a child of the Lord." Sirach 23:4 expresses the prayer of the righteous one: "Lord, Father and God of my life, / do not give me haughty eyes."

3. God Is Father of the Messiah-King

This aspect takes the first two and elevates them. All the kings of the ancient East were considered "sons of (a) god," but in the non-biblical religions, a physical generation was imagined, through the union of a god with a woman. This was not the case for Israel, where the Messiah-King (David *par excellence*) is recognized as a son of God by election. The most famous text is the oracle of the prophet Nathan:

> When your days have been completed and you rest with your ancestors, I will raise up your offspring after you, sprung from your loins, and I will establish his kingdom. He it is who shall build a house for my name, and I will establish his royal throne forever. I will be a father to him, and he shall be a son to me. If he does wrong, I will reprove him with a human rod and with human punishments; but I will not withdraw my favor from him as I withdrew it from Saul who

was before you. Your house and your kingdom are firm forever before me; your throne shall be firmly established forever (2 Sam 7:12–16).

The permanence of the Davidic dynasty is prophesied in this text, and there is a glimpse of the future figure of a son (or, a descendent) of David, who will be particularly beloved by God (Christians know that the reference is to Jesus). The text is important because it shows that God presents Himself as Father of the Messiah-King. Similarly, there are two important texts from the book of Psalms: in Psalm 2:7, the King speaks and says, "I will proclaim the decree of the Lord, / he said to me, 'You are my son; / today I have begotten you'"; and in Psalm 89:27–28, God Himself speaks, saying, "[David] shall cry to me, 'You are my father, / my God, the Rock of my salvation!' / I myself make him the firstborn, / Most High over the kings of the earth."

2.3. Dabar

This Hebrew term means *Word*. It is central in the revelatory processes, both in the Old Testament and the New. In the latter, the Word becomes flesh, and thus assumes a certain visibility (see 1 John 1:1–3), while in the Old Testament there is greater emphasis on the fact that God cannot be seen. On Sinai, Moses does not see God, but he hears His Word (see Ex 20:1) and the "ten words" (the Ten Commandments; see Ex 34:28) are given to him. However, it is also true that in the meeting tent Moses had some sort of vision of God: "Since then no prophet has arisen in Israel like Moses, whom the Lord knew face to face" (Deut 34:10). But this is not a vision in the true and proper sense, because God cannot be seen, as is clear in the passage of Exodus 33:18–23, in which Moses says to God:

> Then Moses said, "Please let me see your glory!" The Lord answered: I will make all my goodness pass before you, and I will proclaim my name, "Lord," before you; I who show favor to whom I will, I who grant mercy to whom I will. But you cannot see my face, for no one can see me and live. Here, continued the Lord, is a place near me where you shall station yourself on the rock. When my glory passes I will set you in the cleft of the rock and will cover you with my hand until I have passed by. Then I will remove my hand, so that you may see my back; but my face may not be seen.

Thus, when Scripture says that Moses spoke face-to-face with God, it suggests a relationship of unique intimacy, not a vision in the exact sense of the term. The Word is the means through which God reveals Himself. But the Word is not only—in the Old Testament—a verbal expression, a communicative means. It has already taken on a "personal" or "hypostatic" aspect. In the Old Testament, the Word is the creative Word (see Gen 1:3: "Then God said [i.e., pronounced the word]: Let there be light, and there was light"; see also Ps 33:6) and a preserving Word in respect to what is created, as is seen in Psalm 147:15–18, in which the Word conserves natural processes: "He sends his command to earth; / his word runs swiftly! / Thus he makes the snow like wool, / and spreads the frost like ash; / He disperses hail like crumbs. / Who can withstand his cold? / Yet when again he issues his command, it melts them; / he raises his winds and the waters flow." Finally, in the following text, the "personification" of the Word is even clearer, and it almost approaches the concept of Incarnation in the New Testament:

> For when peaceful stillness encompassed everything
>   and the night in its swift course was half spent,
> Your all-powerful word from heaven's royal throne
>   leapt into the doomed land,
>   a fierce warrior bearing the sharp sword of your inexorable decree,
> And alighted, and filled every place with death,
>   and touched heaven, while standing upon the earth.
> (Wis 18:14–16).

2.4. Ruah

This Hebrew term—already mentioned in the previous chapter—is used in the Old Testament both as an attribute and as a work of God. *Ruah* (in the Greek of the Septuagint, *pneuma*) means wind, breath, or vital breath. It can simply mean life: the human being lives so long as YHWH communicates His Spirit to him or her. The Spirit is a divine power that gives life to everything and is thus omnipresent and omniscient (see Wis 1:7: "For the spirit of the LORD fills the world, / is all-embracing, and knows whatever is said"; Ps 139:7: "Where can I go from your spirit? / From your presence, where can I flee?").

In the Old Testament, the messianic time (the era in which the Messiah will come) is described as a particular action of the Spirit, Who will renew human beings to such an extent as to make a "new creation." Let us look at a few passages that are worth considering:

Ezekiel 11:19: "And I will give them another heart and a new spirit I will put within them. From their bodies I will remove the hearts of stone, and give them hearts of flesh."

Ezekiel 18:31: "Cast away from you all the crimes you have committed, and make for yourselves a new heart and a new spirit."

Ezekiel 36:26-27: "I will give you a new heart, and a new spirit I will put within you. I will remove the heart of stone from your flesh and give you a heart of flesh. I will put my spirit within you so that you walk in my statutes, observe my ordinances, and keep them."

Isaiah 32:15: "Until the spirit from on high / is poured out on us. / And the wilderness becomes a garden land / and the garden land seems as common as forest."

Isaiah 44:3: "I will pour out water upon the thirsty ground, / streams upon the dry land; / I will pour out my spirit upon your offspring, / my blessing upon your descendants."

Isaiah 59:21: "This is my covenant with them, / which I myself have made, says the LORD: / My spirit which is upon you / and my words that I have put in your mouth / shall not depart from your mouth, / nor from the mouths of your children. / Nor the mouths of your children's children / from this time forth and forever, says the LORD."

Joel 3:1-2: "It shall come to pass / I will pour out my spirit upon all flesh. / Your sons and daughters will prophesy, / your old men will dream dreams, / your young men will see visions. / Even upon your male and female servants, / in those days, I will pour out my spirit."[3]

There is also a tendency toward the personification of the Spirit, but it is less pronounced than it was in the case of the Word (see, for example, Wis 1:5–7, which was partially cited earlier: "For the holy spirit of discipline flees deceit / and withdraws from senseless counsels / and is rebuked when

---

[3] In the speech given immediately after Pentecost, Saint Peter affirms that this prophecy of Joel is fulfilled exactly at the moment in which the Holy Spirit descends over Mary and the Apostles in the Cenacle (see Acts 2:14–21). See the previous chapter.

unrighteousness occurs. / For wisdom is a kindly spirit,[4] / yet she does not acquit blasphemous lips; / Because God is the witness of the inmost self / and the sure observer of the heart / and the listener to the tongue. / For the spirit of the LORD fills the world, / is all-embracing, and knows whatever is said.").

2.5. Divine Plural

There are texts in the Old Testament that, as we recalled at the beginning, prove to the Christian eye to be explicit references to the Trinity. Among these are the one that we already mentioned twice, that is, Genesis 1:26 ("Then God said: Let us make human beings in our image, after our likeness."). The Fathers of the Church and the ecclesial writers saw there the adumbrated revelation of the Trinity.[5] Today, the interpretation that has the greatest following among the exegetes is that of the Jewish rabbis: the plural indicates a deliberation of God together with the celestial court (the angels). Here, God is similar to a king who consults with his ministers prior to acting. Another exegesis that is often proposed is that the plural is a *plurale maiestatis*: the name used of God used here (*Elohim*) is—as we said—in the plural form. The same is true for other passages such as Genesis 3:22 ("Then the LORD God said: See! The man has become like one of us, knowing good and evil!") and Genesis 11:6–7 ("Then the LORD said: If now, while they are one people and all have the same language, they have started to do this, nothing they presume to do will be out of their reach. Come, let us go down and there confuse their language, so that no one will understand the speech of another."). Another case is Isaiah 6:8 ("Then I heard the voice of the Lord saying, 'Whom shall I send? Who will go for us?' 'Here I am,' I said; 'send me!'"), where God first speaks in the singular and then in the plural. The current exegesis interprets

---

[4] Texts like this could have misled a Father (see Saint Irenaeus, referenced in the previous chapter) who identified Wisdom with the Holy Spirit. But the majority position of the Tradition recognizes the Old Testament Wisdom in the Word. It is true, however, that the Wisdom is the Spirit, in the sense that She is divine. Saint Paul also plays on this double use of the name of Spirit in 2 Cor 3:17.

[5] Along with the passages cited in Chapter Two, see Tertullian of Carthage (d. 220), *Adversus Praxean* 12.1, in *FCNT*, vol. 3, trans. Alexander Roberts and James Donaldson (Grand Rapids: W.B. Eerdmans Publishing Company, 1980), 606: "I ask you how it is possible for a Being who is merely and absolutely One and Singular, to speak in plural phrase, saying, 'Let us make man in our own image, and after our own likeness'; whereas He ought to have said, 'Let me make man in my own image and after my own likeness,' as being a unique and singular Being? . . . Or was it to the angels that He spoke, as the Jews interpret the passage, because these also [like heretic Christians] acknowledge not the Son?"

this passage, as with the previous ones, with reference to the seraphim mentioned at v. 2: "Seraphim were stationed above." Now, we recognize that at the literal level the Jewish rabbis and modern exegetes are probably right on this point. However, we must add that Scripture cannot only have a literal meaning (see Chapter Two). Thus, the interpretation of the Fathers and the Doctors is entirely justified: in the light of the New Testament, they saw implicit references to the Trinity in some passages of the Old Testament. Obviously, this interpretation was precluded before the coming of Christ.

2.6. Theophanies

We read in Genesis 18:1–5:

> The LORD appeared to Abraham by the oak of Mamre, as he sat in the entrance of his tent, while the day was growing hot. Looking up, he saw *three men* standing near him. When he saw *them*, he ran from the entrance of the tent to greet *them*; and bowing to the ground, he said: "Sir, if it please you, do not go on past your servant. Let some water be brought, that you may bathe your feet, and then rest under the tree. Now that you have come to your servant, let me bring you a little food, that you may refresh *yourselves*; and afterward you may go on your way." "Very well," *they* replied, "do as you have said" (emphasis added).

Exceptions aside,[6] the Fathers have interpreted this passage as an example of Trinitarian theophany. According to many recent scholars, this would, instead, be a theophany of YHWH accompanied by two angels (see Gen 19:1), and not of the Trinitarian Persons. We find another theophany in Isaiah 6:3: "'Holy, holy, holy is the LORD of hosts! / All the earth is filled with his glory!'" God appears to Isaiah, showing Himself on a throne and surrounded by seraphim who say "holy" three times. According to recent exegesis, this happens because in Hebrew there is no absolute superlative, which is substituted by repeating the positive form of the adjective multiple times. On the other hand, the ecclesiastical writers see in this triple repetition of the adjective a trace of a Trinitarian revelation: God is three times holy, because each Person of the Trinity is holy.[7]

---

[6] Saint Augustine of Hippo (d. 430), *De Trinitate* 3.11.22, argues that, generally speaking, the theophanies of the Old Testament are to be attributed to the angels and not directly to God.

[7] For example, see Saint Basil the Great (d. 379), *Contra Eunomium* 3.3.

In conclusion, we must emphasize that the Old Testament prefigurations of the Trinity are rather scarce, especially if one only focuses on the literal sense of Scripture. For this reason, among others, it was not possible to understand them before the New Testament. This is no wonder because, in the writings of the old covenant, God has as His main purpose educating the Israelites in the adoration of the one God. In the divine pedagogy of Revelation, the dogma of the divine unity was taught first. Later, in the New Testament phase, the Lord also revealed His own intimate life, that is, the reality of the Trinity.

3. The New Testament Fullness

In the New Testament, divine Revelation is completed. God reveals His Mystery to us in Jesus Christ. Trinitarian Revelation is carried out by one of the three divine Persons, the Son made man, who is perfectly capable of revealing to us His divine nature, His personality, and that of the other two Persons. If we understand the term "theology" not as *scientia fidei*, but etymologically as "to speak of God" (*theos-logos*), we can say that Jesus is the first and most perfect Trinitarian Theologian.[8] The Trinity is not a theological perspective of Matthew, John, Paul, Augustine, and Thomas: it is the "theology" of Jesus Christ. Certainly, Jesus never wrote a treatise or gave an academic class on the Trinity, but from His words and deeds, the will to teach the Trinitarian nature of God is clearly evident. On the other hand, Jesus was condemned by the Sanhedrin for a Trinitarian declaration, or at least a "binitarian" one, that is, because He affirmed that He was the Son of God. It was not, in fact, for His preaching on the paternity of God that He was condemned, given that—although Christ characterized it in a new way—it is in continuity with the Old Testament. Instead, what determined His condemnation was His proclamation of being in an ontological, and not merely moral, relation to the heavenly Father, namely, claiming to be God like the Father, while being distinct from Him.[9]

---

[8] See Saint Gregory of Nazianzus (d. 390), *Oratio 31*.8.
[9] There is no agreement between recent scholars on the exact meaning of Jesus' self-proclamation before the Sanhedrin, during the religious trial. For some, He proclaimed Himself only as Messiah and not God in an ontological sense. However, since proclaiming Himself Messiah did not entail a condemnation of death, these scholars must then explain why Jesus was declared guilty of blasphemy and sentenced to capital punishment. They say that in His particular state (chained, slapped, humiliated, and of [presumed] Galilean origin), proclaiming Himself Messiah implied an offense to God and a contradiction of

3.1. The Trinity in the Life of Jesus

The first way in which the New Testament reveals the Most Holy Trinity is by bringing out the presence and action of the Three in the earthly life of Christ. We must not forget that one of the fundamental principles of Trinitarian theology consists in recognizing that the actions of God *ad extra* (in the world and in history) are always unitary and thus Trinitarian, because they are precisely actions of God, who is Trinity. This principle was not superimposed on Scripture, but is drawn from it, as we shall briefly illustrate here.

3.1.1. The Annunciation

At the Annunciation, the Father is the principal agent ("an angel was sent by God"), He acts through the Holy Spirit, and the Son becomes incarnate. Note the narration, in which we have highlighted the presence of the Three:

> In the sixth month, the angel Gabriel was sent from *God* to a town of Galilee called Nazareth, to a virgin betrothed to a man named Joseph, of the house of David, and the virgin's name was Mary. And coming to her, he said, "Hail, favored one! The Lord is with you." But she was greatly troubled at what was said and pondered what sort of greeting this might be. Then the angel said to her, "Do not be afraid, Mary, for you have found favor with God. Behold, you will conceive in your womb and bear a son, and you shall name him Jesus. He will be great and will be called *Son of the Most High*, and the *Lord God* will give him the throne of David his father, and he will rule over the house of Jacob forever, and of his kingdom there will be no end." But Mary said to the angel, "How can this be, since I have no relations with a man?" And the angel said to her in reply, "The *holy Spirit* will come upon you, and the *power of the Most High* will overshadow you. Therefore the child to be born will be called

---

prophecies. Thus, the self-proclamation in that case would have represented a blasphemy, to be punished by death. These interesting theories are nonetheless contradicted by the fact that, to the question of the high priest, "Are you the Messiah?," Jesus responded immediately "I am" (Marcan narrative: Mark 14:53–65). After this response, however, there was no reaction on the part of the members of the Sanhedrin, who rose up only after Jesus added, "and you will see the Son of Man seated at the right hand of the Power and coming with the clouds of heaven." Evidently, in these words there is something more than the simple proclamation of being the Messiah, a self-proclamation on Jesus' part that unleashed the scandal of the Sanhedrin and condemned Him to death.

holy, the *Son of God*." (Luke 1:26–35 [emphasis added])

3.1.2. The Baptism in the Jordan

The outpouring of the Holy Spirit over the incarnate Son marks the beginning of a new creation carried out by the Father:

> It happened in those days that Jesus came from Nazareth of Galilee and was baptized in the Jordan by John. On coming up out of the water he saw the heavens being torn open and the *Spirit*, like a dove, descending upon him. And a *voice* came *from the heavens*, "You are my beloved *Son*; with you I am well pleased." (Mark 1:9–11 [emphasis added])

Although the Father is not explicitly named, the Voice from heaven says, "my Son": consequently, He is the Father of that Son.

3.1.3. The Miracles Carried Out by Jesus

Miracles are signs willed by the Father.[10] The Father carries them out by means of the incarnate Son (John 5:36: "The works that the Father gave me to accomplish, these works that I perform testify on my behalf that the Father has sent me"; see also John 5:19–23). Thus, everything that the Son does, He does in the Holy Spirit, who not only descends, but remains over Him for His entire earthly life, as is attested by John the Baptist: "I saw the Spirit come down like a dove from the sky and remain upon him. I did not know him, but the one who sent me to baptize with water told me, 'On whomever you see the Spirit come down and remain, he is the one who will baptize with the holy Spirit'" (John 1:32–33). This last text is also Trinitarian: there is God (the Father) who sends the Baptist, the Spirit who descends and remains, and the incarnate Son upon whom He descends.

---

[10] This is also seen in the fact that, at the wedding feast at Cana, Jesus responded to His mother, who requested a prodigious intervention, "My hour has not yet come" (John 2:4), a sign that He carried out miracles by following the plan of the Father. This is confirmed directly by Acts 2:22: "You who are Israelites, hear these words. Jesus the Nazorean was a man commended to you by God with *mighty deeds, wonders, and signs, which God worked through him in your midst*, as you yourselves know" (emphasis added).

3.1.4. The Exorcisms

Exorcisms are carried out by the incarnate Son but with the "Finger of God," thus with the Spirit of the Father. As was mentioned in the previous chapter, this identification emerges clearly by comparing the two parallel Gospel texts that report the same phrase of Christ with a significant variation:

> Luke 11:20: "But if it is by the *finger of God* that (I) drive out demons, then the kingdom of God has come upon you" (emphasis added).

> Matthew 12:28: "But if it is by the *Spirit of God* that *I* drive out demons, then the kingdom of God has come upon you" (emphasis added).

3.1.5. Passion and Death

During the Passion and in the moment of death, the incarnate Son is in continual dialogue with the Father. This is seen in the prayer of Gethsemane: "He said, 'Abba, Father, all things are possible to you. Take this cup away from me, but not what I will but what you will'" (Mark 14:36). The Spirit also presents Himself at the moment of Jesus' death: "Jesus cried out in a loud voice, 'Father, into your hands I commend my spirit'; and when he had said this he breathed his last" (Luke 23:46). Here the Son delivers the S/spirit to the Father, as was already said in Chapter Four.[11] The expression that Jesus pronounces at the moment of His death is a citation of Psalm 31:6 that says: "Into your hands I commend my spirit; / you will redeem me, LORD, God of truth." This psalm was also cited by the protomartyr Stephen at the moment of his death.[12] An aforementioned passage from the Letter to the Hebrews also highlights the role of the Spirit: "how much more will the blood of Christ, who through the eternal Spirit offered himself unblemished to God, cleanse our consciences from dead works to worship the living God" (Heb 9:14).

---

[11] The dual interpretation of the word "spirit" is made possible by the fact that the Gospel does not use the Greek work *psyche* (soul, human life), but rather *pneuma*, corresponding to the Hebrew *ruah*. Thus, it can also refer both to the created spirit (soul, human life) that is in Jesus as man, and to the Spirit that is in the Son in the unity of the divine nature. In the first case, the meaning of the text is simply that Jesus, as man, entrusted Himself to God at the moment of death; in the second, there is a Trinitarian meaning.

[12] Acts 7:59: "As they were stoning Stephen, he called out, 'Lord Jesus, receive my spirit.'" It is interesting that, speaking this way, Saint Stephen recognized that Jesus is God. Naturally, in the case of Saint Stephen, the spirit is only his human soul.

The Trinity

3.1.6. Resurrection

In the Resurrection, the Father raises the Son from death (see Acts 2:24: "God raised him up") and gives Him the Holy Spirit in fullness, Whom the glorified Jesus then pours out over the Church (see Acts 2:32–33: "God raised this Jesus; of this we are all witnesses. Exalted at the right hand of God, he received the promise of the holy Spirit from the Father and poured it forth, as you [both] see and hear").

3.1.7 The Ascension and Seating at the Right Hand of God

The presence of the Three is also taught by the New Testament regarding the new phase of the life of Christ that now exceeds the narrow confines of earth: it is His life as the Risen One, glorified in Heaven. Here we can recall the apocalyptic vision of Saint John, who contemplated Christ as already ascended to Heaven and attested the presence of the Father and of the Holy Spirit as well:

> At once I was caught up in spirit. A throne was there in heaven, and on the throne sat one whose appearance sparkled like jasper and carnelian. Around the throne was a halo as brilliant as an emerald.... From the throne came flashes of lightning, rumblings, and peals of thunder. *Seven flaming torches* burned in front of the throne, which are *the seven spirits of God*. In front of the throne was something that resembled a sea of glass like crystal. In the center and around the throne, there were four living creatures covered with eyes in front and in back.... Day and night they do not stop exclaiming: / "Holy, holy, holy is the Lord God almighty, / who was, and who is, and who is to come." / ... Then I saw standing in the midst of the throne and the four living creatures and the elders a *Lamb* that seemed to have been slain. He had seven horns and seven eyes; these are the [seven] *spirits of God* sent out into the whole world.... Then the angel showed me the *river of life-giving water*, sparkling like crystal, flowing from the throne of God and of the Lamb." (Rev 4:2–3, 5–6, 8; 5:6; 22:1 [emphasis added])

The passage is beautiful and extremely rich. For our current scope, let us note that the one who is seated on the throne is the Father. The Lamb is obviously the incarnate Son, who is standing (indicating the Resurrection), but also "seemed to have been" sacrificed (that is, He is not dead, but has the signs of his immolation—like the risen Christ who, appearing to His disciples, showed the signs of the nails). The seraphim (the beings studded with eyes, as the spirits who see God more closely) sing, as in Isaiah 6:3, "Holy, holy, holy"—thus the Trinitarian interpretation of that passage of the Old Testament is also confirmed. The Holy Spirit can be identified with the seven spirits of God sent over all the earth, which are described as having seven eyes and the seven horns of the Lamb[13]: in fact, the Spirit, who is the Unction of Christ (see Chapters Four and Five), is poured over the Church by the risen Christ. The Holy Spirit, then, is also portrayed by the river that springs from the throne of the Father and of the Son.[14]

Based on the brief exposition provided, it is clear that Jesus is not only the Revealer of the Trinity, but He is the One who, in each instant of earthly life, intimately and personally lives the Trinitarian life—the Trinity is at work in the life of Jesus of Nazareth. Thus, in Him, the Trinity, besides being a doctrine, is life. The "Trinitarian theology" of Jesus is not reflected and inductive, but direct and immediate. It is the original triadology. Every other Trinitarian theology is a faint reflection and a more or less clumsy attempt to intellectually understand what the immediacy of intimate and personal contact with the Father and Holy Spirit is for the incarnate Son.

3.2. The Teaching of the New Testament on the Holy Trinity

The New Testament highlights the paternity of God better than the Old to the extent that a fundamental element of the Revelation accomplished by

---

[13] As seen in the previous chapter, the Paraclete is also called the "sevenfold Spirit." Not all exegetes agree that the seven eyes and the seven horns of the Lamb represent the Holy Spirit. Some have, for example, proposed that they symbolize the perfect science of Christ, God and man. Although this interpretation remains possible, due to the fact that the four living beings are full of eyes—which can easily indicate the fullness of knowledge they have of God—we prefer the one we have proposed, because the passage cited speaks of the seven torches lit before the throne, which are the seven spirits of God, and it adds that the horns and eyes of the Lamb are those same spirits sent over all the earth. It seems that these two elements are reconciled better with the interpretation that identifies the spirits with the sevenfold Spirit, than with the knowledge of Christ. The knowledge, on the other hand, is well-symbolized by the eyes, while the horns in the Bible would instead indicate vigor, which would express the nature of the Holy Spirit as *dynamis*: an element that is clearly revealed in the New Testament.

[14] It is meant in this way in CCC §1137 (which we have cited for this reason at the end of the previous chapter), saying that this image of the river is "one of the most beautiful symbols of the Holy Spirit [*Rev* 22:1; cf. 21:6; *Jn* 4:10-14]."

The Trinity

Christ is precisely the merciful paternity of God. This emphasis in the New Testament occurs mainly in two ways: (1) in teaching that God is Father of the believers; and (2) in teaching that He is Father of Jesus. These two teachings in the preaching of Jesus are often interwoven.

3.2.1. God as Father of Believers

The qualification of God as Father is based on His goodness. We see three passages on this theme in the Gospel of Saint Matthew:

> Matthew 5:44–45: "But I say to you, love your enemies, and pray for those who persecute you, that you may be children of your heavenly Father, for he makes his sun rise on the bad and the good, and causes rain to fall on the just and the unjust."

> Matthew 6:25–32: "Therefore I tell you, do not worry about your life, what you will eat [or drink], or about your body, what you will wear. Is not life more than food and the body more than clothing? Look at the birds in the sky; they do not sow or reap, they gather nothing into barns, yet your heavenly Father feeds them. Are not you more important than they? Can any of you by worrying add a single moment to your life-span? Why are you anxious about clothes? Learn from the way the wild flowers grow. They do not work or spin. But I tell you that not even Solomon in all his splendor was clothed like one of them. If God so clothes the grass of the field, which grows today and is thrown into the oven tomorrow, will he not much more provide for you, O you of little faith? So do not worry and say, 'What are we to eat?' or 'What are we to drink?' or 'What are we to wear?' All these things the pagans seek. Your heavenly Father knows that you need them all.

> Matthew 10:29–31: "Are not two sparrows sold for a small coin? Yet not one of them falls to the ground without your Father's knowledge. Even all the hairs of your head are counted. So do not be afraid; you are worth more than many sparrows."

An exemplary case of the paternity of God toward human beings is the parable of the "prodigal son and the merciful father" (see Luke 15:11–32), which aside from being part of Revelation is also a cornerstone of world literature. Facing accusations because He allowed Himself to be approached by tax-collectors and sinners, Jesus defends Himself through the parable, stating He is acting like God, that is, with abundant mercy toward sinners. Jesus and God behave, among men, like a father who is always disposed to welcome the son who has offended him and become estranged from him. Father and Son are united in the way in which they approach sinners, which opens the path to understanding that they are united in their being.[15]

3.2.2. God as the Father of Jesus

We already highlighted the way in which Jesus saw His relationship with the Father in the chapter on the Redeemer, especially by mentioning his use of the word "*Abba*." Here we shall briefly add some aspects:

1. The Parable of the Murderous Vineyard Tenants

The passage is in Matthew 21:33-44 (see parallels in Mark 12:1–12 and Luke 20:9–19). It can be said that this text is a true and proper allegory, that is, each narrative elements corresponds to a historical fact and/or a moral teaching (in the parable, on the other hand, what matters is the core, the principal teaching, beyond the details). The son who is killed outside the vineyard is clearly Jesus, who will be crucified outside the doors of the city (the "vineyard of Israel"). Therefore, with this allegorical parable, Jesus attributed to Himself such a qualification before God that the prophets that came before Him are only servants in comparison. The relationship of Jesus with the Father is unique: He is not only a servant, and not even just any son of God, but He is the beloved and unique Son of the Father.[16] With this parable, Jesus' presentation of God's paternity goes beyond the understanding of God the Father that was offered by the Old Testament.

---

[15] Saint Augustine of Hippo, *Sermones* 112/A.6, sees the two divine Persons revealed in the parable, noting that the man of the narrative wraps his arm around the prodigal son. Augustine notes: "The arm of the Father is the Son" (let us recall that for Saint Irenaeus, the Son is one of the two Hands of the Father). It is true that with this interpretation, Augustine goes beyond the strictly literal sense and moves into the allegorical; but it is also true that, although it must be based on the literal, the spiritual sense also expresses the content of Scripture.

[16] The analysis of other allegorical elements can be found, for example, in Saint Thomas Aquinas, *Super Matthaeum* 21, *lectio* 2.

2. The Sending of the Son into the World on the Part of the Father

God's love for us is the motive for His sending the Son:

In this way the love of God was revealed to us: God sent his only Son into the world so that we might have life through him. In this is love: not that we have loved God, but that he loved us and sent his Son as expiation for our sins (1 John 4:9–10).

Father and Son are typical terms with which Saint John refers to the God of the Old Testament and Jesus Christ. The Father loves the Son (see John 3:35). Father and Son are one (see John 10:30). Thus, the Father is the horizon and constant foundation of all that the Son is, says, and does (see John 5). The Father is the One who knows the Son and makes Him known, and vice versa, to the point that knowing the Father and knowing the Son produces the same outcome on the part of the believer:

Matthew 11:27: "All things have been handed over to me by my Father. No one knows the Son except the Father, and no one knows the Father except the Son and anyone to whom the Son wishes to reveal him."

John 5:23-24: "So that all may honor the Son just as they honor the Father. Whoever does not honor the Son does not honor the Father who sent him. Amen, amen, I say to you, whoever hears my word and believes in the one who sent me has eternal life."

John 14:8-11: "Philip said to him, 'Master, show us the Father, and that will be enough for us.' Jesus said to him, 'Have I been with you for so long a time and you still do not know me, Philip? Whoever has seen me has seen the Father. How can you say, "Show us the Father"? Do you not believe that I am in the Father and the Father is in me? The words that I speak to you I do not speak on my own. The Father who dwells in me is doing his works. Believe me that I am in the Father and the Father is in me, or else, believe because of the works themselves.'"

Let us repeat that the works that Jesus carries out are the works of the Father; therefore, they—along with the Father Himself—bear witness to the sending of the Son into the world by the Father:

> "But I have testimony greater than John's. The works that the Father gave me to accomplish, these works that I perform testify on my behalf that the Father has sent me. Moreover, the Father who sent me has testified on my behalf." (John 5:36-37)

On what occasions has the Father given this testimony? In the Gospels, the Father sometimes let His voice be heard and defines Jesus as "His Son":

After the baptism in the Jordan, in Mark 1:11: "And a voice came from the heavens, 'You are my beloved Son; with you I am well pleased.'"

At the Transfiguration, in Mark 9:7: "Then a cloud came, casting a shadow over them; then from the cloud came a voice, 'This is my beloved Son. Listen to him.'"[17]

Therefore, it is reasonable that the synoptic Gospels call Jesus the "Son of God" many times.[18] We shall cite only a few texts:

> Mark 1:1: "The beginning of the gospel of Jesus Christ [the Son of God]."

> Mark 15:39: "When the centurion who stood facing him saw how he breathed his last he said, 'Truly this man was the Son of God!'"

> Matthew 16:15–16: "He said to them, 'But who do you say that I am?' Simon Peter said in reply, 'You are the Messiah, the Son of the living God.'"

> Luke 1:35: "And the angel said to her in reply, 'The holy Spirit will come upon you, and the power of the Most High will overshadow you. Therefore the child to be born will be called holy, the Son of God.'"

---

[17] A similar example is the episode reported in John 12:20–36, in which Jesus asked the Father to glorify His name: "Then a voice came from heaven, 'I have glorified it and will glorify it again'" (v. 28). However, here the title Son is not explicitly used by the heavenly voice. Nonetheless, it is implied because Jesus asks the *Father* to glorify His name.

[18] For an overview of the biblical theology, including the development of the meaning of this title in the transition from the Old Testament to the New, see CCC §§441–445.

The Trinity

The Gospel of John, which we have already cited several times, also adds a fundamental distinction between us and Jesus: the latter is "the Son" (in Greek, *ho Hyios*), while we are "sons" (*tekna*).[19] The New Testament insists on emphasizing that the mission of the Son in the world is aimed at realizing our adoptive sonship (*hyiothesia*). For this reason Saint John, both in his Gospel and in his First Letter, says that believers are generated by God (see John 1:12–13[20]; 3:3; 1 John 2:29).

3.2.3. The Sending of the Spirit of the Son into the World on the Part of the Father

The syntagm "Holy Spirit" (used 70 times) is, in a certain sense, a novelty of the New Testament, because in the Old Testament it is found very few times. In the Writings of the New Covenant, the Holy Spirit is mentioned primarily in reference to the effects produced by His work in the world. For example, the Acts of the Apostles show the effect of the operation of the Holy Spirit in the first evangelization, to the point that the Book of Acts was called by some the "Gospel of the Holy Spirit."[21] It is true that more than one time in Acts, the Holy Spirit is understood as a divine energy (see Acts 4:8; 11:24; 13:9). However, in various other cases, He has a marked personal character and presents the traits of a Person and not only a divine

---

[19] *Hyios* is a Greek term reserved to the Son (see, for example, John 3:16, 18; 5:25; 20:31), while *tekna* is for those who become sons by grace (see 1:12; 12:33; in a way also 8:39; in 12: 36, *hyios* is also used for human beings, but in the plural).

[20] The text reads: "But to those who did accept him he gave power to become children of God, to those who believe in his name, who were born not by natural generation nor by human choice nor by a man's decision but of God." It is important to know that there is a version in the singular of this text, which then would go as such: "Who [Jesus] not by natural generation nor by human choice ... but by God was generated." The version in the singular is not found in the manuscripts we possess of the Gospel of John, which report the text in the plural; it is instead mentioned by various Fathers of the Church, since the second century (note that the oldest manuscripts of John's Gospel that we have are from the fourth century!). If the original version were in the singular, then this text would not be applied to the divine filiation of believers, but to the virginal generation of Christ in the womb of Mary. Some exegetes of the twentieth century have proposed a solution that seems interesting to us, because it respects the *et-et*: whatever was the original version of this Johannine verse, the two meanings (the virginal generation of Jesus or the adoptive filiation of believers) both remain true and connected to one another. The first is preeminent: since Jesus is the incarnate Word—conceived virginally by Mary—we too can, by His work, be conceived "virginally," that is, in a spiritual way, as adoptive sons of God.

[21] The wording was accepted by Saint John Paul II, *Letter to the Families of Rome*, December 8, 1997.

The New Testament Fullness

impersonal energy. Let us look at some texts in this regard:

> Acts 1:16: "My brothers, the scripture had to be fulfilled which the holy Spirit spoke beforehand through the mouth of David, concerning Judas, who was the guide for those who arrested Jesus."

> Acts 7:51: "You stiff-necked people, uncircumcised in heart and ears, you always oppose the holy Spirit; you are just like your ancestors."

> Acts 13:2: "While they were worshiping the Lord and fasting, the holy Spirit said, 'Set apart for me Barnabas and Saul for the work to which I have called them.'"

> Acts 15:28: "It is the decision of the holy Spirit and of us not to place on you any burden beyond these necessities."

> Acts 16:6–7: "They traveled through the Phrygian and Galatian territory because they had been prevented by the holy Spirit from preaching the message in the province of Asia. When they came to Mysia, they tried to go on into Bithynia, but the Spirit of Jesus did not allow them."

> Acts 20:22–23: "But now, compelled by the Spirit, I am going to Jerusalem. What will happen to me there I do not know, except that in one city after another the holy Spirit has been warning me that imprisonment and hardships await me."

The Holy Spirit with His divine power exercises an action of grace in the hearts of believers (see Gal 4:6). Saint Paul also mentions the ecclesial (charismatic) dimension of the gift of the Spirit:

> There are different kinds of spiritual gifts but the same Spirit; there are different forms of service but the same Lord; there are different workings but the same God who produces all of them in everyone. To each individual the manifestation of the Spirit is given for some benefit. To one is given through the Spirit the expression of wisdom; to another the expression of knowledge according to the same Spirit; to another faith by the same Spirit; to another gifts of healing by the one Spirit; to another mighty deeds; to another prophecy; to another discernment of spirits; to another varieties of tongues; to another

The Trinity

interpretation of tongues. But one and the same Spirit produces all of these, distributing them individually to each person as he wishes.

As a body is one though it has many parts, and all the parts of the body, though many, are one body, so also Christ. For in one Spirit we were all baptized into one body, whether Jews or Greeks, slaves or free persons, and we were all given to drink of one Spirit. (1 Cor 12:4–13)

The passage—after a clearly Trinitarian introduction (Spirit—Lord [Jesus]—God [Father])—shows how Saint Paul recognizes the fundamental role of the Holy Spirit in the life of the Church. But what does Saint Paul mean when he speaks of the Spirit? A divine energy, or a divine Person? A brief examination of his writings is sufficient to show that for him too, the Holy Spirit is the Third in God, after the Father and the Son. Let us consider three types of texts.

1. The Spirit Dwells

(1) Romans 8: 9-11: the general idea of this passage, as of the whole eighth chapter of the letter, is that salvation is accomplished because the Spirit is present in us and dwells within us. (2) 1 Corinthians 3:16-17: the context of the passage is the exhortation of Saint Paul to unity. This exhortation makes recourse to the rhetorical figure of a building. The underlying idea is that the Spirit dwells within us as in a temple, and thus we are the temple of the Spirit. (3) 1 Corinthians 6:19: the context is the correction of some faithful regarding their vice of impurity. This is evil first and foremost because it is an offense to Christ, since our bodies are members of Him (see v. 15). Moreover, it is an offense against the Holy Spirit, given that our body is His temple. The teaching of previous passages is therefore confirmed. In this passage, Son and Spirit are on the same level of importance, because to offend One or the Other is considered a sin of equal gravity; or better said, offending One also offends the Other. From these three texts we deduce that the Holy Spirit is presented as God, because in the Old Testament only God dwells in the Temple.

2. The Spirit Makes Us Children of God

(1) Romans 8:14–16: the context is again Romans 8 (description of life according to the Spirit). The idea here is, however, different: we are made adopted children of God by means of, or by the work of, the Spirit. (2) Galatians 4:4–6: the context of the pericope is the teaching according to which

the protection of the Law has passed and we are now children of God. The idea of the passage is that the Holy Spirit works similarly to the Son, making it possible for us to call God by the name of Father. This is equivalent to saying that the Spirit makes us sons and daughters, because He introduces us into the divine sonship. From these two texts we deduce that the Holy Spirit performs our divine adoptive filiation and therefore He is God, because only God can divinize man. Naturally with the word "divinize" we mean that He elevates and sanctifies us, in the adoptive sonship.

3. The Spirit Freely Chooses to Whom He Gives Charisms

(1) 1 Corinthians 12:4–11: the context of this chapter is the theme of "the community and charisms." The idea of this pericope—that we have cited above—is that the Holy Spirit works as He wants, that is, with supreme liberty. Since freedom is a personal characteristic, it follows that the Holy Spirit is understood in this passage as a Person. (2) 1 Corinthians 2:13: here the Spirit is presented as a master or a pedagogue, therefore with clear personal characteristics. There are even more Pauline passages in which the personality of the Third Person in God emerges: see 1 Corinthians 2:10–11; 6:11; 2 Corinthians 1:21–22.

3.2.4. The Paraclete

In the New Testament, the sending of the Spirit—in His various forms—is always done in view of the glorification of the Son. He is the "Spirit of Christ," the "Spirit of Jesus," and the "Spirit of Truth," in addition to being the "Spirit of God [Father]." The strict relation between the Son and the Spirit (aside from what was already discussed in the previous chapters), is also evident from four unique texts of the Gospel of John. They are unique because, in them, the Holy Spirit is called by a name that is not used anywhere else in Scripture: "Paraclete," that is, "Advocate" or "Consoler." We read these texts through two lenses: that of listening to what they tell us about the relation of the Paraclete to the Father and of what they teach about the relationship between the Paraclete and the Son. We shall cite each text and then comment on what it reveals about these Trinitarian relations.

1. John 14:15–17

"If you love me, you will keep my commandments. And I will ask the Father, and he will give you another Advocate to be with you always, the Spirit of truth, which the world cannot accept, because it neither sees nor knows it. But you know it, because it remains with you, and will be in you."

The Paraclete-Father relation is expressed by the verb 'to give' (*didomi*) in the future tense. The Father is the One who "will give" the Paraclete; consequently, the Paraclete is the One who "will be given" by the Father. The Father has an active role, and the Paraclete has a passive one. About the Paraclete-Son relationship, the Son will pray the Father to give the Paraclete: the relationship between the Two is indirect.

2. John 14:26

"The Advocate, the holy Spirit that the Father will send in my name—he will teach you everything and remind you of all that [I] told you."

Here, the verb "to send" (*pempo*) is in the future tense; the Father is the One who "will send" the Paraclete, and the Paraclete is the One who "will be sent" by the Father: once again, the activity and passivity correspond to the Father and the Paraclete, respectively. About the relationships with the Son, Jesus says that the Paraclete will be sent in His name, and that "He will teach . . . and remind" us about the teaching of the Son: here, this directly concerns the relation of the Paraclete with believers, but the Spirit-Son link is equally evident, because the Spirit instructs the believers according to the message of Christ.

3. John 15:26

"When the Advocate comes whom I will send you from the Father, the Spirit of truth that proceeds from the Father, he will testify to me."

About the relationship with the Father, the verb *ekporeuomai* or "proceed" is of the utmost importance. Unlike the previous two cases, this verb is not transitive. It follows that the Father is the One from whom the Paraclete proceeds, and the Paraclete is the One who proceeds from the Father. To proceed means to start from (*ek*) one point and move toward another. It is of tremendous relevance that here the verb is not in the future tense, but rather in the present (it is not "will proceed" but "proceeds"), because it indicates a permanent and present state and not an event that will occur later in the economy of salvation.[22] Regarding the relationship to the Son, Jesus says that He will send the Paraclete, and the Paraclete will be sent by the Son. Moreover, the

---

[22] In other words, the Spirit will be sent into the world, after the glorification of Christ; but the Spirit already proceeds now (and always) from the Father. The personal existence of the Paraclete is not totally identified with His historical mission.

Paraclete will witness the Son and therefore the Son will be witnessed by the Paraclete. Note that here the activity of both the Father and the Son is preached: the Paraclete proceeds from the Father, and the Son will send the Paraclete.

4. John 16:7–15

But I tell you the truth, it is better for you that I go. For if I do not go, the Advocate will not come to you. But if I go, I will send him to you. And when he comes he will convict the world in regard to sin and righteousness and condemnation: sin, because they do not believe in me; righteousness, because I am going to the Father and you will no longer see me; condemnation, because the ruler of this world has been condemned.

I have much more to tell you, but you cannot bear it now. But when he comes, the Spirit of truth, he will guide you to all truth. He will not speak on his own, but he will speak what he hears, and will declare to you the things that are coming. He will glorify me, because he will take from what is mine and declare it to you. Everything that the Father has is mine; for this reason I told you that he will take from what is mine and declare it to you.

This passage does not have an explicit revelation of the relationship of the Paraclete with the Father, but at verse 13 it says that the Paraclete will refer to what "He hears" (verb *akouo*). From whom does He hear? At verse 14, Jesus says that the Spirit will take of what is His (Jesus'), and He (the Spirit) will announce it. It is an expression that mirrors the previous one: the Spirit hears from the Son, that is, He takes what He says to us from the Son. However, at verse 15, Jesus adds that everything that is of the Father is His, and this is why the Spirit will take from Jesus. It is evident from all of this that the Paraclete, hearing Jesus, hears the Father, even if not directly. The Paraclete hears the Father through the Son. In the second place, for what concerns the relationship with the Son, it says in the text that the Son goes away and the Paraclete comes, because it will be Jesus—after His departure—to send Him to us. The Paraclete hears the Son. He will glorify the Son. And finally, it says that the Paraclete takes from the Son in order to give to us (Revelation/grace).

5. In Summary

Recalling now what emerges from the set of the four cited passages, we note the following: (1) Four relationships emerge between the Paraclete and the

Father, indicated by the verbs "give," "send," "proceed," and "hear." It follows that the Paraclete is not identifiable with the Father because He does not give Himself, send Himself, proceed from Himself, or listen to Himself. The Holy Spirit is a distinct Person from the Father. (2) When we then consider what emerges about the Paraclete-Son relationship, we reach the same conclusion: Son and Spirit appear as clearly distinct, because it is not possible for the Son to pray to the Father to send Himself, referring to Him in the third person,[23] nor is the Son sent in his own name, and so on. (3) Let us now add a further reflection, comparing the Father-Paraclete relationship to the Father-Son relationship, following the verbs we found in these four texts: we find "give" in John 3:16[24] in reference to the Son; "send" (*pempo* or *apostello*) is found about thirty times in John[25] in reference to Jesus; the verb "proceed-*ekporeumai*" in reference to the Son cannot be found, but the synonym *exerchomai* can[26]; finally, we find the verb "hear" in reference to Jesus in the Gospel of John.[27]

Therefore, in the Gospel of John, Son and Spirit are qualified in relation to the Father with the same verbs or with synonyms. This tells us that the Paraclete has a similar relation with the Father as that of the Son with the Father. However, the Son and the Spirit are not the same Person, because we notice two differences: the first is that the verbs used for the Son are in the past tense, while for the Spirit they are in the future tense; and the second is that the Father-Son relation is always immediate and direct, while in the relation between the Father and Spirit, the Son is always included.

Therefore, the four passages about the Paraclete reveal that: (1) the Holy Spirit is not the Father or the Son, but a third Person alongside the first Two; (2) with respect to the first Two, He is passive ("He proceeds from," "He is given," "He is sent"); and (3) He is in a personal situation similar to that of the Son with respect to the Father, and so He is not inferior to the Son (but He is not the Son). All of this means that—just as we could detect the divine nature

---

[23] That is, He could well have said, "Here I am, send me" (see Isa 6:8), but it does not make sense to say, "And I will ask the Father, and He will give you another Advocate," if He is talking about Himself.

[24] "For God so loved the world that he *gave* his only Son, so that everyone who believes in him might not perish but might have eternal life" (emphasis added).

[25] For example, in John 3:17: "For God did not *send* his Son into the world to condemn the world, but that the world might be saved through him" (emphasis added).

[26] John 8:42: "Jesus said to them, 'If God were your Father, you would love me, for *I came from* God and am here; I did not come on my own, but he sent me'" (emphasis added). See also John 13:3.

[27] John 5:30: "I cannot do anything on my own; I judge as I *hear*, and my judgment is just, because I do not seek my own will but the will of the one who sent me" (emphasis added). See also John 7:16–17.

of the Holy Spirit in Saint Paul's writings—so His distinct personality emerges in Saint John as well. The Holy Spirit is God like the Father and the Son, and yet He is distinct from the Father and the Son. We could at this point reformulate the first chapter of the Gospel according to John—in which we read that, "In the beginning was the Word, / and the Word was with God, / and the Word was God" (John 1:1)—this way: "In the beginning was the Holy Spirit, and the Holy Spirit was with God, and the Holy Spirit was God."[28]

3.3. Other Trinitarian Texts of Saint Paul

We shall conclude the biblical exposition with the citation of some other Pauline texts. The hymn of Ephesians 1:3–14, which we are only quoting in part, is certainly Trinitarian:

> Blessed be the God and *Father* of our Lord Jesus Christ, who has blessed us in Christ with every spiritual blessing in the heavens. [...]
>
> In love he destined us for adoption to himself through Jesus Christ, in accord with the favor of his will, for the praise of the glory of his grace that he granted us in the beloved [i.e., *Son*]. [...]
>
> In him you also, who have heard the word of truth, the gospel of your salvation, and have believed in him, were sealed with the promised holy *Spirit*. . . . (emphasis added)

A little further along in the same letter, there is another passage that is probably Trinitarian: "the God of our Lord *Jesus Christ*, the *Father* of glory, may give you a *[S]pirit* of wisdom and revelation resulting in knowledge of him" (Eph 1:17). Still in Ephesians, we find two more passages:

> Ephesians 2:18–22: "[F]or through him we both have access in one *Spirit* to the Father / So then you are no longer strangers and sojourn-

---

[28] As theologically daring as this proposal might seem, it is supported by the fact that Saint Gregory of Nazianzus behaves the same way regarding other evangelical expressions; that is, not caring, as he writes, whether it "seems too bold to someone" (*Oratio 31*.3 [our translation]).

The Trinity

ers, but you are fellow citizens with the holy ones and members of the household of God, built upon the foundation of the apostles and prophets, with *Christ Jesus* himself as the capstone. Through him the whole structure is held together and grows into a temple sacred in the Lord; in him you also are being built together into a dwelling place of God in the *Spirit*."(emphasis added)

Ephesians 4:4–6: "One body and one *Spirit*, as you were also called to the one hope of your call; one *Lord*, one faith, one baptism; one God and *Father* of all, Who is over all and through all and in all" (emphasis added).

Other Pauline Trinitarian texts include 2 Thessalonians 2:13–14 and Titus 3:4–7.[29] We shall conclude the Trinitarian citations of Saint Paul with the passage from 2 Corinthians 13:13, which has become relevant in the liturgy, being the first greeting among the options proposed by the Roman Missal of Paul VI at the beginning of Mass. While the Pauline Greek text leaves the verb implicit—which to be grammatic'ally correct should be in the plural—the liturgical version uses the singular (Latin "*sit*") to highlight the unity of nature of the Trinity. The biblical text says: "The grace of the *Lord* Jesus Christ and the love of *God* and the fellowship of the *Holy Spirit* (be) with all of you." In the Letter of Paul, it is not an initial greeting, like in the Mass, but a final greeting and blessing. The passage is clearly Trinitarian, with Jesus Christ (that is, the Son), God (that is to say, the Father), and the Holy Spirit being placed on the same level, exactly like the clearest Trinitarian passage in the whole New Testament, or the final one of the Gospel according to Matthew, in which the risen Christ says to His own: "All power in heaven and on earth has been given to me. Go, therefore, and make disciples of all nations, baptizing them in the name of the Father, and of the Son, and of the holy Spirit" (Matt 28:18–19). It is no coincidence that these words of Christ are the formula adopted by the Church for Baptism: "I baptize you in the

---

[29] Here are the two texts, respectively: "But we ought to give thanks to God for you always, brothers loved by the Lord, because God chose you as the firstfruits for salvation through sanctification by the Spirit and belief in truth. To this end he has [also] called you through our gospel to possess the glory of our Lord Jesus Christ"; "But when the kindness and generous love / of God our savior appeared, / not because of any righteous deeds we had done / but because of his mercy, / he saved us through the bath of rebirth / and renewal by the holy Spirit, / whom he richly poured out on us / through Jesus Christ our savior, / so that we might be justified by his grace / and become heirs in hope of eternal life."

name of the Father, and of the Son, and of the Holy Spirit." Note that Christ does not say "in the names," but rather "in the name."[30] There are three names, which correspond to three Persons; nevertheless, the Church baptizes in a single name—the name of God, who is Father, Son, and Spirit.[31]

4. The Mystery of the Trinity, as Treated by Christian Thinkers

From the earliest times of the Church, Christians, accepting in faith the Revelation of God, one and triune, have reflected on the divine Trinity, thus forming the branch of Christian knowledge called Trinitarian theology. The first development they achieved was that of choosing the technical terms with which to refer to the Mystery of God. Some of these terms—such as the verb "to proceed"—are taken from Scripture; others—such as "Trinity" itself—were introduced by the Fathers of the Church to express the content of the Revelation in a clear and concise way. We would now like to give a brief overview of the Trinitarian theology of the Church.

4.1. Fathers of the Church and Ecclesiastical Writers

4.1.1. Saint Justin of Nablus (d. ca. 165)

He was pagan by birth and had studied the Greek philosophical conception of the eternal *Logos*, subsequently becoming a philosopher. Converting to Chris-

---

[30] Saint Thomas Aquinas comments: "He says 'in the name' and not 'in the names,' and on the one hand it refutes those heretics who do not make any distinction [between the divine Persons], because it says: 'in the name *of the Father and of the Son.*' But on the other, Arius is also refuted by it because of the fact that we say in the singular 'in the name'" (*Super Matthaeum* 28 [our translation]).

[31] The baptismal liturgy is understood as an affirmation of the divine equality of the three Persons by Saint Ambrose of Milan (d. 397) in *De mysteriis* 38, when he recalls the profession of faith made by the one being baptized and says to him or her: "You have descended then (into the water); remember what you replied (to the questions), that you believe in the Father, you believe in the Son, you believe in the Holy Spirit. You do not have in your response: 'I believe in a greater and a lesser and a lowest (person).' But you are bound by the same guarantee of your own voice to believe in the Son exactly as you believe in the Father, to believe in the Spirit exactly as you believe in the Son, and if you make an exception, it is that, dealing with the death on the Cross, you only believe it of Jesus Christ" (in *FCNT*, vol. 44, trans. Roy J. Deferrari [Washington, DC: CUA Press, 1963], 15 [with our corrections]).

tianity, he came to know and believe in the incarnate and revealed *Logos*. Saint Justin saw the universal Truth in the *Logos*, which led him to sense the fruitful connection between good philosophy as natural knowledge and wisdom, and Christian Revelation, which is a supernatural gift. Each human being, possessing reason, participates in some way in the *Logos*, the universal principle of rationality. The Greek philosophers were thus able to grasp various truths, because they gathered the seeds of the *Logos* spread out over the world.[32] For this reason, "the truths which men in all lands have rightly spoken belong to us Christians."[33] But Saint Justin concentrates on the incarnate *Logos* and on the Trinitarian Revelation, inaccessible to natural human speculation, given to us by God. The Saint reports the order—in the technical term, *taxis*—of the Trinitarian Persons, as is found in Scripture:

> Our Teacher of these things is Jesus Christ, who was born for this end [the creation and our salvation], and who was crucified under Pontius Pilate, procurator of Judea, in the reign of Tiberius Caesar. We shall prove that we worship Him with reason, since we have learned that He is the Son of the living God Himself, and believe Him to be in the second place, and the Prophetic Spirit in the Third.[34]

As we can see, he supports the idea that the *Logos* was generated by the will of the Father in view of creation (and then of salvation). But this does not mean that Justin was a forerunner of the future Arian heresy, which would deny the full divinity of the Son; on the contrary, he recognizes without a doubt that the Son "as the First-born Word of God, is also God."[35] The idea of a generation of the Son from the Father in light of what the Former would do for the world (create and save) is found in various second-century authors. This is due to the imperfection of a Trinitarian theology that was still being formed; and this imperfection would be eliminated definitively by later Fathers of the Church. However, what is defective in this early period is not faith in the Trinity—whose divinity and tri-personality are clearly professed by these Fathers, even if they do not always have a way of extending it in depth with respect to the Holy Spirit—but only the rational speculation (theology) on the mystery that was revealed and believed by them. We can say

---

[32] See Saint Justin of Nablus, *II Apologia* 10.1–3.

[33] Saint Justin, *II Apologia* 13.4, in *FCNT*, vol. 6, trans. Thomas B. Falls (New York: Christian Heritage, Inc., 1948), 133–134.

[34] Saint Justin, *I Apologia* 13.3, in *FCNT*, vol. 6, 46.

[35] Saint Justin, *I Apologia* 63.14, in *FCNT*, vol. 6, 103.

that in this phase, theology does not correspond, in every single aspect, to the faith of those who practice it, in the sense that theology cannot yet translate faith perfectly into its own categories. However, the faith, in the majority of the authors, corresponds to Revelation.

4.1.2. Tatian the Syrian (d. ca. 180)

This ecclesiastical writer emphasized the unity of the Persons in the one God (monotheism). To explain the distinction of the divine Persons, Tatian presents the image of a fire that starts another without diminishing: something similar would have happened with the generation of the Son from the Father.[36] For him, as for his teacher Saint Justin, the *Logos* is generated by the will of God the Father. According to Tatian, the *Logos* exists in potency in the Father, is immanently in Him, and is actualized at the moment of creation. He is the primal work of the Father, generated inwardly by Him, Who then outwardly generates the world. However, Tatian clarifies that the Word is not a simple potency existing in God, but He was generated as a distinct Person. The Spirit seems to be understood more as a divine force in us than as a personal entity, given that Tatian never speaks explicitly of the Holy Spirit as the Third in God. However, it is hard to share the position of those patrologists who completely deny the presence of the Holy Spirit in the theology of Tatian. He actually has a very interesting theory, for which there are two spirits, an inferior one and a superior one. The inferior spirit is spread out into matter and is inferior to the divine Spirit, because it is "similar to the soul."[37] The superior Spirit is not the soul but lives close to the soul. While being divine, we cannot say with absolute certainty that it corresponds to the Holy Spirit as Christian faith identifies it: in fact, it seems that Tatian tends to identify it with the *Logos* or with an energy of the *Logos*.[38] This evidently concerns an

---

[36] Tatian the Syrian, *Oratio ad Graecos* 5: "God was in the beginning, and we have learned that the beginning is the power of the Word [see John 1:1]. The Lord of all things, being Himself the substantial principle of each thing, was alone because creation had not yet happened; consequently, every power of visible things was with Him, and He had all things with Himself thanks to the power of the *Logos*, and the *Logos* that was in Him came to light. It was by the will of the simple nature of God that the *Logos* originated. The *Logos*, which did not come in vain, is the primal work of the Father.... As many fires are lit from a single torch, and the light of the first torch is not diminished on account of the lighting of the many torches, so too the fact that the *Logos* originated by the power of the Father does not render the One who originated Him deprived of *Logos*" (our translation).

[37] Tatian, *Oratio ad Graecos* 4.

[38] See Tatian, *Oratio ad Graecos* 12–13, 15. Tatian speaks of the action of the divine Spirit in

imperfect theology of the Holy Spirit, because it does not account very well for the biblical passages described above.

4.1.3. Athenagoras of Athens (d. ca. 190)

The main focus of this writer, venerated as a Saint by Orthodox Christians, was that of demonstrating the oneness of God, in contrast to pagan polytheism. In spite of this, in his writings the distinction of the Persons of the Trinity is very clear, and he makes use of various concepts that designate the Son (Mind, Wisdom) and the Spirit (Emanation, in Greek, *aporroia*). Athenagoras speaks of the three Persons as united in power and distinct in order (*taxis*). He does not use a precise theological vocabulary in every case: for example, he says that the Son is the Idea and operative Force of creation—two concepts that, nonetheless, can also be understood in an entirely orthodox way. In fact, Athenagoras also speaks unequivocally of "God the Father, God the Son, and the Holy Spirit"[39] and clarifies that the difference between the Three is not a difference in nature, but rather in order: "The difference is in the class (*taxis*),"[40] that is, in the fact that each Person is denominated as being in the first, second, or third place, without this implying a diminution of nature, as if the second would be "less God" than the first. In his work, we see an explicit profession of Trinitarian faith: "We speak of God, of the Son, His Word, and of the Holy Spirit; and we say that the Father, the Son, and the Spirit are united in power. For the Son is the intelligence, reason, and wisdom of the Father, and the Spirit is an effluence, as light from fire."[41]

Finally, in chapter 10 of his work *A Plea for the Christians*, albeit with some theological shortcomings, he provides some interesting reflections on the Mystery of the Trinity:

> We acknowledge one God, Who is uncreated, eternal, invisible, impassible, incomprehensible, illimitable. He is grasped only by mind and intelligence, and surrounded by light, beauty, spirit, and indescribable power. By Him the universe was created through His

---

the human being: various elements of his exposition can be harmonized with the much more precise explanation that his contemporary Saint Irenaeus gives. Thus, the question should be pursued more in-depth.

[39] Athenagoras of Athens, *Legatio pro christianis* 10, in *Early Christian Fathers*, vol. 1, trans. Cyril C. Richardson (Philadelphia: The Westminster Press, 1953), 309.

[40] Athenagoras, *Legatio pro christianis* 10, in *Early Christian Fathers*, vol. 1, 309.

[41] Athenagoras, *Legatio pro christianis* 24.2, in *Early Christian Fathers*, vol. 1, 326.

Word, was set in order, and is held together. [I say "His Word"], for we also think that God has a Son. Let no one think it stupid for me to say that God has a Son.... The Son of God is His Word in idea and in actuality; for by Him and through Him all things were made, the Father and the Son being one. And since the Son is in the Father and the Father in the Son by the unity and power of the Spirit, the Son of God is the mind and Word of the Father.... He is the first offspring of the Father. I do not mean that He was created, for, since God is eternal Mind, He had His Word within Himself from the beginning, being eternally wise. Rather did the Son come forth from God to give form and actuality to all material things, which essentially have a sort of formless nature and inert quality.[42] ... Indeed we say that the Holy Spirit Himself, who inspires those who utter prophecies, is an effluence from God [see Wis 7:25] flowing from Him and returning like a ray of the sun. Who, then, would not be astonished to hear those [the Christians] called atheists who admit God the Father, God the Son, and the Holy Spirit, and who teach their unity in power and their distinction in rank?[43]

4.1.4. Saint Theophilus of Antioch (d. ca. 185)

Unlike Saint Justin and Athenagoras, Saint Theophilus did not seek to establish a relationship with Greek culture to the extent that he placed himself in open polemic with the pagan world and its literary production. He was the first to use the Greek term *Trias*, which would then become the Latin *Trinitas*—the fundamental technical term of Trinitarian theology: "The three days prior to the luminaries are types of the Triad [*Trias*]: of God and His Logos and His Sophia."[44] His doctrine on the two stages of the Word is important. The two stages go from the immanent *Logos* (*endiathetos*), that is, contained in the bosom of the Father before being pronounced, to the spoken *Logos* (*proforikos*), when God generates Him to create the world by means of Him. Let us cite an expression from his work *Ad Autolicum* 2.10:

> Therefore God [Father], having His own Logos innate [*endiathetos*] in His own bowels, generated Him together with His own Sophia,

---

[42] The term is uncertain in the original text.
[43] Athenagoras, *Legatio pro christianis* 10, in *Early Christian Fathers*, vol. 1, 309–310.
[44] Saint Theophilus of Antioch, *Ad Autolicum* 2.15, trans. Robert M. Grant (Oxford: Clarendon Press, 1970), 53.

The Trinity

> expelling Him forth before everything else. He used this Logos as His servant in the things created by Him [Father] and through Him [Word] He made all things. He [Word] is called Beginning because He leads and dominates everything fashioned through Him. It was He, Spirit of God and Beginning and Sophia and Power of the Most High, who came down into the prophets and spoke through them about the creation of the world and all the rest. For the prophets did not exist when the world came into existence; there were the Sophia of God which is in Him and His holy Logos who is always present with Him.[45]

At first, the text seems a little confused and appears to identify Word and Spirit, but in the end, it makes it clear that this is not the case. Moreover, it seems that the Spirit is co-present to the Father while He is issuing the Word, something that would eliminate the Trinitarian *taxis*, if this expression did not simply want to affirm the eternity of the Third Person, who is not negated by the fact that he proceeds from the Others. However, it must be emphasized that the Holy Spirit does not have an active role in the generation of the Son, even if He is eternal like the Father and the Son. Thus, when Saint Theophilus says that the Father will generate the Son along with the Wisdom (which here is the Spirit), he only means that the Father will both generate the Word and give rise to the Wisdom, and that the Wisdom, from a chronological standpoint, does not come after the Word.

Let us also cite *Ad Autolicum* 2.22, in which Theophilus reprises his fundamental thesis on the Father-Son relationship:

> The Logos is always innate in the heart of God [*endiathetos*]. For before anything came into existence He had this as His Counsellor, His own Mind and Intelligence. When God wished to make what He had planned to make, He generated this Logos, making Him external [*proforikos*], as the firstborn of all creation. He did not deprive Himself of the Logos but generated the Logos and constantly converses with His Logos.[46]

With this distinction, Theophilus wants to demonstrate the *Logos* as the Reason and the Word of the Father: as Reason (or Mind) He is immanent to the Father, as the Word He is begotten, issued, and uttered; as long as He

---

[45] Theophilus of Antioch, *Ad Autolicum* 2.10, in Grant, 39–40 (with our corrections).
[46] Theophilus of Antioch, *Ad Autolicum* 2.22, in Grant, 63.

is only Reason He is not distinct from the Father, but when He is also Word He is distinct from the Father and is the Firstborn of creation. The merit of this proposal is that it distinguishes the two aspects of the *Logos* well, that is, Reason and Word. Its limitation lies in the possibility of stating the non-eternity of the personal distinction of the *Logos*, because it would affirm the non-eternity of His generation/emanation from the Father. As we have seen, it is a common limitation in various second-century authors, because it is one thing to believe in the Trinity by accepting the Word of God in faith, but another to offer a reasonable explanation through theological science. Faith is a gift from God, while the science of faith is a human construct, which requires time and proceeds through successes and failures.

4.1.5. Saint Irenaeus of Lyon (d. ca. 202)

Saint Irenaeus, the first systematic theologian in the history of Christianity, explains that God has created everything through the Word, without resorting to intermediate powers, since He does not need anything.[47] He is the God of both Testaments, because He leads the sole economy (that is, the historic execution of the divine plan). Creation and redemption came to be read, by Irenaeus, in a Trinitarian way. As we said in Chapter Two, the "let us make" in Gen 1:26 is explained by Irenaeus like so: it is the Father who speaks of His Hands, that is, of the Son and the Holy Spirit. Creation and salvation are united because everything is done by the one God with His Hands (this is opposed to the heretic Marcion [d. 160], who hypothesized the existence of two gods—one of the Old Testament and one of the New). Saint Irenaeus is primarily interested in the action of the Trinity *ad extra*, more than its nature *ad intra*, which is why he does not focus on an analysis of the generation of the Son, and therefore he does not reprise the terminology of the "immanent" and "spoken" *Logos*. He writes:

> The Church . . . has received from the Apostles and their disciples this faith: (She believes) in one God, the Father Almighty, Maker of heaven, and earth, and the sea, and all things that are in them;

---

[47] Let us cite the following passage again: "There is one God Almighty, who made all things by His Word, and fashioned and formed, out of that which had no existence, all things which exist. . . . He did not make by angels . . . For God needs none of all these things, but is He who, by His word and Spirit, makes, and disposes, and governs all things, and commands all things into existence" (*Adversus haereses* 1.22.1, in *FCNT*, vol. 1, trans. Alexander Roberts and William Rambaut [New York: Charles Scribner's Sons, 1903], 347).

and in one Christ Jesus, the Son of God, Who became incarnate for our salvation; and in the Holy Spirit, Who proclaimed through the prophets the dispensations of God, and the advents . . . of the beloved Christ Jesus."[48]

This passage shows the Trinitarian view of Irenaeus clearly, but also his special attention to the economy of salvation: the Three in God are distinguished by mentioning their activity *ad extra*. Nevertheless, Irenaeus manages to say at least something on the so-called "immanent Trinity," that is, on the Trinity *ad intra*: "One God, the Father, not made, invisible, Creator of all things; above Whom there is no other God, and after Whom there is no other God. And, since God is rational, therefore by (the) Word He created the things that were made; and God is Spirit, and by (the) Spirit He adorned all things."[49]

A reflection of Irenaeus on the eternity of the Son and on the eternal generation is found in *Demonstratio* 43:

> Because, for God, the Son was (as) the beginning before the creation of the world; but for us (He was) then, when He appeared; and before that He was not for us, who knew Him not. Wherefore also His disciple John, in teaching us Who is the Son of God, Who was with the Father before the world was made, and that all the things that were made were made by Him says thus: "In the beginning . . ." [John 1:1–3]. Showing with certainty that the Word, Who was in the beginning with the Father, and by Whom all things were made, this is His Son.[50]

This passage is important for three reasons: (1) it affirms the coeternity of the Son with the Father; (2) it highlights the necessity of the manifestation of the Trinity so that humanity may know the intimate nature of God; in fact, before the Son appeared, for us He was non-existent, because it was impossible for us to know Him *as Son* without the economy of Revelation; and (3) it sets forth, more or less consciously, an argument that will be fundamental

---

[48] *Adversus haereses* 1.10.1, in *FCNT*, vol. 1, 406.

[49] Irenaeus of Lyon, *Demonstratio apostolicae praedicationis* 5, in *Irenaeus's Demonstration of the Apostolic Preaching*, trans. J. Armitage Robinson (Aldershot: Ashgate, 2002), 2. See also no. 6. This concerns attributes that are always deduced from the economy, but still preached as immanent.

[50] Irenaeus of Lyon, *Demonstratio apostolicae praedicationis* 43, in Robinson, 14.

in the history of Trinitarian theology, that is, that the Father can be eternal Father, and that He can only be eternally Father if He eternally has a Son, because if the Son only began to exist from a certain point onward, it follows that the Father had not always been Father, since one is not a father if one does not have a child.[51] The conclusion is discussed coherently in *Demonstratio*, 47: "So then the Father is Lord and the Son is Lord, and the Father is God and the Son is God; for that which is begotten of God is God."[52]

4.1.6. Tertullian of Carthage (d. ca. 230)

Tertullian introduced terms such as *substantia*, *natura*, and *Persona* into Trinitarian theology; he is therefore the great creator of the Latin Trinitarian vocabulary. We must also attribute to him the Latin term *Trinitas*, which occurs ten times in his work *Adversus Praxean*. Through his theory of the missions of the Word and the Spirit, he favors, like no one before him, going from the study of the "economic Trinity" (*ad extra*) to the "immanent Trinity" (*ad intra*); that is, from the study of the action of the triune God, we move on to the intellectual contemplation of the nature of the Trinity.

His deepest and most extensive discussion of the Trinity is found in *Adversus Praxean*, a work written against Praxeas, one of his contemporaries who was a Modalist heretic.[53] In this work, Tertullian uses certain cosmic analogies to speak of the Trinitarian mystery; that is, he takes some examples of "triadology" from the natural world, not to reduce the mystery of God, but only to aid our understanding and show that the Trinitarian dogma, while never com-

---

[51] Tertullian of Carthage, who we will focus on next, says it clearly when he writes: "Now a father makes a son, and a son makes a father ... A father must have a son, in order to be a father; so likewise a son, to be a son, must have a father" (*Adversus Praxean* 10.2–3, in FCNT, vol. 3, 604). And the principle is applied in an explicitly Trinitarian way in Novatian (see *infra*), *De Trinitate* 31.184: "He who is before all time must be said to have been always in the Father; for no time can be assigned to Him who is before all time. And He is always in the Father, unless the Father be not always Father" (in FCNT, vol. 5, trans. Alexander Roberts and James Donaldson [Buffalo: The Christian Literature Company, 1888], 645).

[52] Irenaeus of Lyon, *Demonstratio apostolicae praedicationis* 47, in Robinson, 15

[53] Modalism is a Trinitarian heresy that does not recognize the real personal distinction between the Father, Son, and Spirit, believing them to be only names, masks, or 'modes' through which the one God is manifested in history. On this view, God would not have a Trinitarian nature. This implies—ultimately—that God, in showing Himself to us, lies, revealing Himself differently from how He really is. For the Church, when God reveals, He neither deceives, nor is deceived (see First Vatican Council, *Dei Filius* [1870], ch. 3 [DS 3008]).

pletely comprehensible, is not in itself unreasonable. He proposes three cosmic analogies: (1) Root/trunk/fruit: the tree is a single reality, but three parts of this single reality can be distinguished, namely, the roots, the trunk, and the fruit. (2) Source/stream/irrigation: the same thing happens with rivers. The river is a unitary and indivisible reality and yet the three marked parts are distinguished. (3) Sun/ray/heat: this latter cosmic image was more successful than the others and was taken up by the great Doctors, Saint Bonaventure and Saint Thomas. This is because—among the three—it is the one that conveys a greater sense of spirituality, given that in the ancient and medieval world it was believed that light was immaterial.[54] Thus, the image of light (which arises from the sun, is brought by the ray, and reaches us as heat) seems less inadequate for describing the spiritual and incorporeal divine Trinity.

Tertullian had the merit of maintaining the unity of the Three in the one substance, however, he committed the theological error of proposing a view with strong subordinationist notes, in which the Father is greater than the Son and the Spirit. He argued that the Son and Spirit are neither coeternal nor equal to the Father, while also affirming that the Son and Spirit come from the one divine substance. Here is a text that exemplifies this: "For the Father is the entire substance, but the Son is a derivation and portion of the whole, as He Himself acknowledges: 'My Father is greater than I.'"[55] For Tertullian, the Son is God, because the divine essence did not split in two at the time of His generation; but the Son does not have all of the divine essence: He only participates in it. In his comment on the announcement to Mary, we find confirmation of this: Tertullian highlights the fact that the angel does not say to Mary "God will come upon you," but rather, "The Holy Spirit will come upon you," and he erroneously deduced: "By not directly naming God, he wished that portion of the whole Godhead to be understood, which

---

[54] Here we encounter the great theme of the metaphysics and theology of light, which we cannot even touch. We shall limit ourselves to citing the name of Robert Grosseteste (d. 1253), bishop of Lincoln, theologian, and scientist, who is considered the true founder of scientific thought in medieval Oxford. He was prolific in the study of light on the physical, philosophical, and theological levels, and he was strongly influenced by the Platonic tradition.

[55] Tertullian of Carthage, *Adversus Praxean* 9.2, in *FCNT*, vol. 3, 603-604. The later Fathers would better clarify that some of the expressions that Christ uses in the Gospels are attributed to His divine nature, and others to His human nature, as we have shown in Chapter Four. Tertullian is wrong because he applies an expression that Christ uses to refer to His humanity to the invisible nature of Christ. The correct exegesis is found, for example, in Saint Leo the Great, *Tomus ad Flavianum*: "To say 'I and the Father are one' (John 10:30) and to say 'The Father is greater than I' (John 14:28) is not by any means of the same nature" (DS 295). We have cited other texts in the chapter about the Redeemer.

was about to retire into the designation [*nomen*] of 'the Son.'"⁵⁶ In simpler terms, the Son is incarnated in Mary, and He would not be entirely God, but a part of God, that part which is present in the Son. It is true, however, that these forced conclusions can be derived from the context of opposition to the Modalists: affirming that the Word is God, but not God exactly like the Father, prevented the conclusion that the Father and Son were not distinct but merely two faces or modes of the one God, as the heretics wanted.

Despite the evident shortcomings in his Trinitarian theology, Tertullian is considered the precursor of the Nicaean *homoousios*, that is, of the full affirmation of the divinity of Christ. This is so because he spoke of "*trinitas unius divinitatis, Pater et Filius et Spiritus Sanctus*—a Trinity of one sole divinity, the Father, the Son, and the Holy Spirit"⁵⁷: even if the Carthaginian theologian did not give a correct interpretation of this expression, the terms would be specified after him and would remain as technical words for expressing the proper faith in the Trinity. In short, on this point, as on others, Tertullian proves to be an excellent lexicographer of the Latin theological dictionary, but not always a theologian of the highest caliber when it comes to explaining the terms.

4.1.7. Novatian of Rome (d. 258)

Novatian was the first theologian of the Church of Rome who wrote in the Latin language. He was a schismatic and anti-Pope, and the condemnation of his works meant that most of his writings would be lost. In his *De Trinitate*, he offered the first systematic presentation of the Trinitarian doctrine against Modalism, although this work mainly discusses Jesus Christ as true God and true man as well as the Father-Son relation. This confirms the fact that, after and because of Tertullian, Western theology had begun to move toward the future outcomes of the First Nicaean Council. In fact, Novatian dedicated the central and most consistent part of his work to showing that Jesus is truly God, in addition to being truly man.

One of the fundamental ideas in his work is the simplicity and transcendence of God.⁵⁸ Starting from this point, he proposes a non-material concept of the divine substance, against the orientation of Tertullian, who—as we have mentioned—divided it into parts. It also follows that Novatian understood the Father-Son relation in more ontological terms than his predecessors did, who based themselves more on the economy of salvation. But this "ontologi-

---

⁵⁶ Tertullian, *Adversus Praxean* 26.3–4, in *FCNT*, vol. 3, 622.

⁵⁷ Tertullian, *De pudicitia* 21.16 (our translation).

⁵⁸ See Novatian of Rome, *De Trinitate* 5.29; 6.36.

cal" turn (that is, toward a consideration of the being of God) cannot obscure the fact that Novatian's *De Trinitate* is the work that cites Holy Scripture the most with respect to all other works that were concurrent to it or that preceded it which dealt with the same subject matter. This means that his theology of the Trinity *ad intra* continued to be based on the way in which the Trinity is shown *ad extra*, narrated in Scripture. Novatian, nevertheless, inevitably suffered from the influence of other earlier authors: for example, although he abided the distinction between "immanent" and "uttered" logos, he affirmed that the "prolapsic" state of the Son with respect to the Father, or that His "being outside" of the Father, is a temporal and not eternal state.[59] However, he also managed to intuit the eternal generation of the Word by the Father—which would be affirmed clearly only from Origen on.

Novatian understood the procession of the Son not from the divine substance (like in Tertullian) but from the "being-without-principle" of the Father (the so-called "innascibility") and from His capacity to give rise to others. This excludes a second principle in God, because only the Father, as "non-generated," "non-originated" from anything, can be Principal. Although it may seem that such a statement must lead to Subordinationism (that is, believing that the Son is inferior to the Father), this reflection actually gives Novatian his foundation for affirming the equality of natures between the Father and Son, precisely because it excludes the substance from the generative process. Thus, he speaks of "*communio substantiae*—communion of nature"[60] between Father and Son.

As regards the Holy Spirit, however, he takes a step back with respect to Tertullian, who—even if with a fragmented divinity—had recognized the personality of the Third One in God. Novatian limits himself to narrating the activity of the Holy Spirit, without defining His properties very much. This narration touches on, among other things, points of high spirituality and poetry.

4.1.8. Origen of Alexandria (d. 254)

Origen had a fundamental role in the ancient theological development of the Eastern Church, comparable to that of Saint Augustine in the Latin Church. In his Trinitarian theology, the Three are all eternal; in fact, they are above and precede eternity itself. Origen emphasizes the dynamic relationship between

---

[59] This is paradoxical, given that this author intends to refute Modalism, a representative of which was Marcellus of Ancyra (d. ca. 374; mentioned in Chapter Four), who would support the same theory.

[60] Novatian of Rome, *De Trinitate* 31.192.

The Mystery of the Trinity, as Treated by Christian Thinkers

the Father, Son, and Holy Spirit, Who are united by the substantial possession of being (which for Origen is the same, in the Platonic sense, as the good), and above all by a unity of will and action. The Father is characterized by innascibility (He is *agennetos* ["ungenerated"]). He possesses all the powers and perfections that then pass to the other two Persons. Thus, the Father possesses them to a supreme degree. Both the Son and the Spirit proceed from the Father, but in a different way: the Son by generation, a non-corporeal generation for which "from the Invisible and Incorporeal was generated the Word and Wisdom."[61] The generation of the Son does not provoke any alteration of nature of the Father. The Son is coeternal and consubstantial with the Father. In the era of Origen—as we have seen and as he writes himself—there was not yet clarity in the field of Trinitarian theology about the procession of the Holy Spirit. Origen wondered whether or not He is generated, and thus, whether He is also a Son. For Origen it is nonetheless certain that the Spirit is uncreated and consubstantial with the Father and the Son "because the entire Trinity is one and incorporeal."[62] He says that the Spirit originates from the Father through the Son.[63]

Origen's Trinitarian theology was nonetheless interpreted as subordinationist, in that he stated that the Father reaches all beings, making them participants in the being that He is, the Son reaches all rational creatures rendering them participants of Himself (*Logos*), and the Spirit reaches only the baptized, whom He sanctifies. For Origen, only the Father is "God-by-Himself" ("*autotheos*"), while the Son is *deuteros theos*, that is, He is "second God." The Father transcends all, is the principle, because everything comes from Him. However, it should be recalled that Origen wrote His works a hundred years before the First Council of Nicaea defined the doctrine of the consubstantiality of the Son and the Father. What is lacking is not his faith in the divinity of the Second Person, but rather his theological vocabulary and, in the end, some aspects of his theology (understanding of the faith).

As evidence, remember that in his works we find the first clear affirmation that the Father and the Son are coeternal, and that the generation of the Son is eternal and not in connection with creation. It should be noted that Irenaeus, Tertullian, and Novatian had said that the Son preexists creation, which does not mean *per se* that the Son is coeternal to the Father. Novatian, Origen's contemporary, had affirmed that the Word "is always in the Father, so that the Father is always Father," but it was Origen who recognized clearly

---

[61] Origen of Alexandria, *De principiis* 4.28 (our translation).
[62] Origen, *De principiis* 4.32 (our translation).
[63] See Origen, *De principiis* 1.3.

that God is not God before being Father; on the contrary, He is always Father of the Son. The personality of the Son, although coeternal to the Father, is still connected to the economy of salvation: He is the Image who reveals the Father to us. In fact, for Origen as well, the main focus is not the study of the "immanent Trinity," but the economy of salvation. As regards the Holy Spirit, the Alexandrian theologian argues that, while not being a simple creature, He is the first of beings made by the Father through the Son, in a descending scale of ontological quality. Thus, the Father is more powerful than the Son, and the Son is more powerful than the Spirit. This also derives from the idea that the *Logos* completely exhausts the task of mediating between God and the world. The Spirit may appear as a divine energy for the sanctification of human beings. Despite this descending scale, the fact remains that Origen uses the term *Hypostasis* (which will then be specified as Person) for all Three.[64]

4.1.9. Saint Hilary of Poitiers (d. 368)

After Saint Augustine, Saint Hilary of Poitiers is the greatest Trinitarian theologian of the ancient West. His *De Trinitate* (in twelve books, written around the years 356–360) is the basis of the reflections of many others, including the holy Doctors Ambrose (d. 397) and Jerome (d. 420) and above all, Augustine himself. The starting point for Saint Hilary's reflection is the baptismal formula (see Matt 28:18). *De Trinitate* is an anti-Arian work, which affirms the unity of nature between the Father and Son and their distinction on basis of the "relation of origin." He calls the Father *auctor*, the Son *imago*, and the Spirit *donum*. The Son is not a *flatus vocis*, a pure name: He has real consistency and real subsistence, and thus Saint Hilary deemed the cosmic metaphors of older theologies insufficient. He chose the metaphor "light from light," drawing on the Nicene Creed. The Son is not a creature, because in God generation means that the One who generates gives all of what He has. The reason for this lies in the simplicity of the divine nature. Thus, texts such as John 14:28 ("The Father is greater than I") cannot be interpreted as an argument in favor of Subordinationism. The Father is greater only as principle, but the Son—even though He receives everything from the Father—is not inferior to Him, precisely because He receives everything. For Saint Hilary,

---

[64] And among other things, he writes: "There is no difference in the Trinity, but rather in the fact that what is called a gift of the Spirit is made known by the Son and is carried out by God the Father" (Origen, *De principiis* 1.3). In summary, there is a frequent oscillation between expressions that explain the Trinitarian dogma well and others that diminish it.

the Holy Spirit is also God, and not a creature.[65] He is the gift of life of the risen Christ to human beings.

As important as Hilary's work is, we can already conclude this overview, since we shall find various aspects of his thought again, taken up and perfected, in the Trinitarian theology of Saint Augustine.

4.1.10. Saint Athanasius of Alexandria (d. 373)

The main works of Saint Athanasius include *De Incarnatione Verbi*, the *Epistulae ad Serapionem* and, above all, the *Orationes contra Arianos*, in which he summarizes and condemns the thought of Arius and presents his own Trinitarian theology. In the third *Discourse* (*oratio*), the Saint debates the opinion that the Word comes from the will of the Father and not from His nature. Athanasius responds simply by citing the *homoousios* defined at Nicaea, the Council at which he assisted as a young deacon while accompanying his patriarch, and which he then strenuously defended once he in turn became the patriarch of Alexandria in Egypt.

Taking up the language of Origen, Saint Athanasius calls the Son "*apaugasma*" ("Image, Splendor"), and also "*charakter*" ("Imprint") of the Father. Moreover, he uses the biblical titles of Truth, Wisdom, and Light for the Son. On the basis of these, he proposes the following line of reasoning: God cannot subsist without what is proper to Him; now, truth, wisdom, and light are proper to Him. Therefore, the Son is coeternal to the Father. The coeternity of the Father and Son is based on the completeness of the divine essence of the Father: human beings generate after having been born (and after they grow into adults), because their nature is incomplete; but God is always complete, and thus He must have always generated His Son. The generation is based on nature and not on the will or grace of the Father. This does not mean that the Father is forced to generate, and that the generation of the Son was not free. It instead means that freedom and necessity coincide in God. The Son "cannot" not be eternal like the Father, yet the generation of the Son from the Father is an expression of perfect freedom and, at the same time, strict necessity.

The Word is "the true Son, the only God from the true God"[66]; "the *Logos* has become man so that we may become gods,"[67] that is, "adoptive

---

[65] See Saint Hilary of Poitiers, *De Trinitate* 12.55–56.

[66] Saint Athanasius of Alexandria, *Orationes contra arianos* 1.39 (our translation).

[67] Athanasius, *De Incarnatione Verbi* 54.3 (our translation). He thus clarifies: "We also become sons, not as He [the Son] does according to nature and in truth, but according to

sons of the Father."⁶⁸ Saint Athanasius battled not only against Arianism but also against Modalism, which could at first glance seem strengthened by the Nicene *homoousios*. His great credit is to have attributed—accepting the Nicene wording—the *ousia* of which the Son participates fully (*homoousios*, precisely) not to the Father as such, but rather to the substance of the Father, that is, to the common essence of the three Trinitarian Persons. It follows that the distinction between Father and Son does not intervene at the level of substance or nature, but rather exactly at that of personhood. In the work *De Synodis*, Saint Athanasius explains that the Son is everything that the Father is, except what pertains to the Father as Father.⁶⁹

The Alexandrian patriarch completed his Trinitarian theology in the *Letters to Serapion*: he affirms the full divinity of the Holy Spirit, Who belongs to the one, eternal, and immutable Trinity. The one Trinitarian God acts with a unity of operation in creation and salvation: that is, the works that God carries out *ad extra* are always Trinitarian works, done by God, that is, by the Three together.

4.1.11. The Cappadocian Fathers

The holy Doctors Athanasius and Hilary were great defenders of the First Council of Nicaea against the Arians; however, neither of them delved into the consequences of the *homoousios*, or gave speculative explanation to the problem of the unity/distinction in God, with the same level of depth as the three Cappadocian Fathers: the Saints Basil of Caesarea (called Basil the Great, d. 379), Gregory of Nazianzus (d. 390), and Gregory of Nyssa (d. 394). They developed their reflection starting from the controversy with Eunomius of Cyzicus (d. ca. 392), an Arian bishop and theologian, who gave "Ungenerated" as a general definition of God. It followed that for Eunomius, the Son, being generated, could not be considered God in the full sense.

The Cappadocians start from the distinction of the triad of Persons, which they consider the proper subject matter of Trinitarian theology, and from this triad they try to go back to the notion of unity of nature. With this, they establish the fundamental movement of Greek Trinitarian theology, which

---

the grace of the One who has called us; and thus, although earthly human beings, we are called gods, not like the true God or His *Logos*, but as it pleased God that we be made similar by grace" (*Orationes contra arianos* 3.19 [our translation]).

[68] Athanasius, *Orationes contra arianos* 1.39; 3.9 (our translation).

[69] "Everything that you find that is said of the Father, you shall also find said of the Son; everything except His being Father" (Athanasius, *De Synodis* 49 [our translation]).

starts from reflection on the Persons (starting from the Father as "Monarch," that is, "only Principle" of the divinity—that which is called doctrine of the divine "monarchy"), while the Latins normally begin from the unicity of divine nature and its works—a method that is actually chosen also by some Greeks, such as Saint Athanasius and Saint Didymus the Blind (d. 398).

The Cappadocians managed to formulate an adequate Trinitarian theology primarily because they distinguish the term "hypostasis" from that of "*ousia*," contraposing them rather than identifying them as synonyms. They forged the Greek expression "*mia ousia, treis hypostaseis*—one substance, three Hypostases/Persons" (Saint Basil). In this way, the term *homoousios* would no longer be misunderstood as it was by the Sabellians (Sabellius was a Modalist). Another merit of the Cappadocians is that of having definitively applied the *homoousios* of Nicaea not only to the Son, but also to the Holy Spirit, precipitating (with the First Council of Constantinople, AD 381) the defeat of the Macedonians, deniers of the divinity of the Third Person. In the following section, we shall consider some of the distinguishing features of the Cappadocians.

1. Saint Basil the Great (d. 379)

He is the reference figure for the group. His most important works for Trinitarian theology were *Contra Eunomium* and *De Spiritu Sancto*. Eunomius was, along with Aëtius of Antioch (d. 367), the founder of Anomoeanism, a radical form of Arianism, which affirmed that the Son is not "similar" to the Father, but rather totally "dissimilar (*anomoios* in Greek). Saint Basil starts from the arcana of divinity and therefore from the impossibility of defining the divine substance as such.[70] The divine nature cannot be defined; God comes to be known only through the Son and the Spirit. Saint Basil notes that Jesus Christ reveals Himself in different ways, and He does so in view of teaching different aspects of Himself, given that no word can say everything about Him. The same must be said of the Father: for example, the word "ungenerated" does not exhaust the discussion on the First Person. In fact, "ungenerated" cannot be the name of the substance of the Father, because it is a negative and not positive term (it says what the Father is not, not what He is).[71] On the other hand,

---

[70] "It is impossible to superimpose any definite concept upon the immaterial because of our persuasion that it is above every concept" (Saint Basil the Great, *Epistle 38*.3, in *FCNT*, vol. 13, trans. Agnes Clare Way [New York: Fathers of the Church, Inc., 1951], 86–87).

[71] See Basil, *Contra Eunomium* 1.5.

The Trinity

Scripture does not speak of "ungenerated or generated" but of Father and Son,[72] and it is impossible to understand the passage of John 12:45 ("whoever sees me sees the One who sent me") if the Father and the Son do not have the same nature, a unity of nature that Eunomius denied. For Saint Basil, the likeness between the Father and Son does not lie in activity, but rather in nature. It is the unity of nature that also makes their activity common.

Here, the Cappadocian takes the second key step in developing Trinitarian theology by asking: In what way are the Three distinct Persons one God? Father, Son, and Spirit—he responds—are distinct according to their "personal properties" (*idioteta ton prosopon* in Greek) but they are one because of their "community of nature" (*kata to koinon tes physeos*).[73] The characteristic of the personal properties is "of showing the otherness in the identity of essence," that is, we would say, to identify the Person within the indivisible divine nature.

In the famous *De Spiritu Sancto*, Saint Basil opposes the Pneumatomachians (followers of Macedonius of Constantinople, d. 362) by affirming the divinity of the third Person.[74] He notes that the New Testament uses various prepositions for the Father, the Son, and the Holy Spirit (from, through, in) but in such a way that a difference in nature between the Three cannot be deduced. Moreover, the Saint introduces an argument that would then become classic: that of the "*homotimia*" or "*isotimia*," that is to say, equality in dignity and honor. This means that, for Saint Basil, we need to observe the faith of the Church, guarded and celebrated in the holy Liturgy. In the liturgical Tradition, he encounters the equality of honor given to the three divine Persons, from which it follows that the Holy Spirit is believed to be God like the Father and the Son, given that the Church pays to the Spirit the same Worship of adoration that she gives the first Two.

The Holy Spirit brings to perfection the creation carried out by the Father through the Son, and He distributes the salvific gifts (grace). Moreover, we find, perhaps for the first time, the idea of creation not as the solo work of the Father and the Son, but as a true and proper Trinitarian work: in creation, in fact, the Father acts as principal cause, the Son acts as efficient cause, and the Spirit acts as perfecting cause. The Spirit is in fact capable of

---

[72] See Basil, 1.16ff.

[73] These concepts are developed in the important *Epistle 37*, addressed to his brother, Saint Gregory of Nyssa.

[74] See also the third and fifth chapters of the book *Contra Eunomium*. For example, in 3.3, he writes: "If His nature is holiness, as for the Father and the Son, in what way would He be a third extraneous nature?" (our translation).

divinization. Between the Father, Son, and Spirit there is therefore no difference in degree—and Holy Scripture actually never speaks of the "first, second, and third." If, therefore, we speak at the theological level of *taxis* in God, it is not done in the Arian or Macedonian way—in the subordinationist sense—but only to respect the order of articulation used by Christ in the Gospel (see Matt 28:19–20).

2. Saint Gregory of Nazianzus (d. 390)

In his Trinitarian teaching (which we get above all from *Orationes* 27–31), Saint Gregory of Nazianzus places the unity of the nature of the three Persons in the primary place and highlights the divinity of the *Logos* and his "co-equality" with the Father. According to him, the Hypostases are distinguished based on their origins, and indeed the Father is ungenerated,[75] the Son is generated by the Father,[76] and the Holy Spirit proceeds from the Father through the Son. It is no wonder that in the Middle Ages, Gregory of Nazianzus was considered the starting point for the study of Trinitarian relations: in fact, he specified that the names of the Persons indicate the relative differences, namely, the reciprocal relationships between the Three.

Against Macedonius, Gregory then expanded the study of the mystery of the Holy Spirit. He affirms the divinity of the Third Person in no uncertain terms, because He is consubstantial with the other Two.[77] Saint Gregory reads John 15:26 ("The Spirit of truth that proceeds from the Father") differently than his close friend Saint Basil, that is, not as an attestation of the work of sanctification (the action of the Spirit *ad extra*) but as a Revelation of the origin *ad intra* of the Third Person. Thus he, borrowing from Scripture, introduces the word "procession" (*ekporeusis*) into Trinitarian theology, as a technical term to describe the mode of existence of the divine Persons. The three Persons are distinguished by *agennesia—gennesia—ekporeusis* (absence of generation—generation—procession). The Father is without principle, un-generated; the Son is generated by the Father; the Holy Spirit proceeds (but is not generated). Unlike Basil, for Gregory of Nyssa, what is proper to the Father is not having an origin in anyone; what is proper to the Son is being generated by the Father; and what is proper to the Spirit is proceeding from the Father (through the Son). For the Nazianzene, all Three are God on account of the "monarchy,"

---

[75] "Who is this Father who has never begun to be Father? It is He who has not even begun to exist" (Saint Gregory of Nazianzus, *Oratio 29*.5 [our translation]).

[76] See Gregory of Nazianzus, *Oratio 30*.20.

[77] See Gregory of Nazianzus, *Oratio 31*.3.

The Trinity

that is, because of the fact that the Father is the one Principle of the whole divinity. Hence, even though the Three are coeternal, it does not mean that they are *anarchoi* (without principle): only the Father is without principle, while the Son and Spirit have their principle, in different ways, in the Father. Thus, "three different properties, one divinity alone."

3. Saint Gregory of Nyssa (d. 394)

The brother of Saint Basil, Saint Gregory of Nyssa participated actively in the First Council of Constantinople (AD 381), held when Saint Gregory of Nazianzus was patriarch of that city, and contributed to the development of the Creed. He was the most speculative Trinitarian theologian of the Cappadocians. The Council Fathers of the First Council of Constantinople dubbed him the "column of orthodoxy." The most important of his dogmatic writings is the *Oratio Catechetica Magna*, written around 385. This work is the first great essay of systematic theology in which the exposition of the main dogmas is accompanied by a metaphysical foundation, presented along with the biblical one. He is also the author of the *Contra Eunomium*, a work in four books that is one of the most effective refutations of Arianism.

Like his brother Basil, Saint Gregory takes John 1:12 as his starting point, and makes this claim: in God there is no before and after, thus the generation of the Son must be eternal.[78] The Nyssean bishop openly proclaims the divinity of the Holy Spirit, reasoning as follows: the perfecting of the soul, which culminates in divinization, is a work of the Holy Spirit, and He could not divinize the human being if He were not God. Thus, if Scripture attributes this work to the Third Person, it means that He is God. Saint Gregory makes recourse to two images to describe the Trinity: the first, which is inadequate, is that of three human beings—Peter, James, and John—three individuals who are of one essence, one nature alone (they are all "human"),[79] even if they are so in the different properties of their persons; in fact, for the Saint, one should not say "three human beings," because they have the same human nature. This image is misleading if applied to the Trinity, because the way in which Father, Son, and Spirit are the same nature, compared to three human individuals

---

[78] "Be it sufficient to conceive the Father as existent before the Son only at the level of causality, and one should not think that the life of the Father was separated and identified before the generation of the Son" (Saint Gregory of Nyssa, *Contra Eunomium* 1.25 [our translation]). "The One who is truly Father is always Father" (1.38). The fact that in God there is no before and after is said in 1.24 and *passim*.

[79] As for this, Gregory of Nyssa simply re-proposes what was written to him by his brother Saint Basil the Great, in *Epistula 38*.

being all "human," is very different. The other image, which is not misleading, but imperfect, is that of a lamp that transfers its light to another and, through this, to a third (it is a new version of that proposed by Tatian). If one imagines the origin of the Son and the Spirit in this way, he says, the Monarchy of the Father is not affected. The Word is then described as an intermediary between Father and Spirit, the latter being, for this reason, called both Spirit of God (Father) and Spirit of Christ by Scripture. This implies a dependence in being of the Spirit with respect to the Son. What sort of dependence is this? The Nyssean, at the end of the first book of *Contra Eunomium*, says that Son and Spirit are always with the Father, with only a difference of order (*taxis*), because as the Son is united to the Father and receives being from Him, without however being temporally posterior as regards His Hypostasis, the Son is conceived before the Spirit only with respect to the cause (the Father).[80] Therefore, to say that the Three are coeternal and equal in *physis* (nature), does not deny a difference that "regards the situation of cause and caused," that is, the situation of the One in God who is Principle of the Other. The processions in God are therefore *immediate*—that of the Father to the Son—and *mediated* by the Son—that from the Father to the Holy Spirit. The clarification of Saint Gregory of Nyssa on the fact that the procession of the Spirit is from the Father "through the Son" marks in our days the formula that expresses the rule of faith in the Orthodox Church (for further specifications, see, further along, the *excursus* on the *Filioque*).

4.1.12. Saint Cyril of Alexandria (d. 444)

Among the Eastern Fathers, Saint Cyril, one of the successors of Athanasius on the patriarchal chair of Alexandria, is the one who dealt most with the Trinitarian Mystery, leaving us two vast works: *Thesaurus de Sancta et Consubstantiali Trinitate* ("Book of Treasures Concerning the Holy and Consubstantial Trinity") and *De Sancta Trinitate* ("Dialogues on the Trinity"), both written against the Arians. His theology has a strongly polemical character, fervently denouncing the positions of Arius, Nestorius, and Macedonius. As was already done by Saint Athanasius with *De Synodis* with respect to the First Council of Nicaea, Saint Cyril also defends the new ecclesial theological

---

[80] "Just as the Son is linked to the Father and, although He has His own existence from Him, He is not posterior in substance, so also the Holy Spirit is in contact with the Only-Begotten One, who is held to have existed before the subsistence of the Spirit only from the theoretical point of view of causality [*aitia*]" (Gregory of Nyssa, *Contra Eunomium* 1.42 [our translation]).

language, introduced by the first ecumenical councils, against the accusation of being unbiblical. He defends it because the meaning of such language is true and universally recognized, and also allows one to enter into the depth of the teaching of Scripture itself.

Cyril emphasizes the rigorous identity of the divine nature in the three Persons. They are one God and when They act *ad extra* there is a unity of operation. In God, there is no other distinction than that of the Hypostases and the names that indicate the hypostatic (personal) characters. The names of Father and Son are relative names, for which "each of the two exists, or not, along with the other; if one exists, then the other for which the first is called, and is what it is, would undoubtedly exist as well."[81] In each of the Three there is the integral divine nature along with what is proper to the Person or "hypostatic property." This causes Each to remain what He is, while possessing the other Two in the divine nature: "The Father is in the Son and in the Spirit, and the Son and Spirit are in the Father and One in the Other."[82] As for the divinity of the Holy Spirit, he states: "The Spirit of the Son is holy not by participation or by an extrinsic relation with Him, but rather by nature and identity."[83]

Saint Cyril also agrees with Saint Athanasius about the unity of works and of will of the Three *ad extra*. In fact, "for the communion in the unity of nature, each thing is of Everyone: presence, words, participation, works, glory, and everything that adorns the divine nature."[84] In acting *ad extra*, there is however a certain order (*taxis*), which corresponds to that of the processions *ad intra*.

5. The Best Trinitarian Theologies of the West

Among the great authors that we have presented, and among others still that could be added, two great giants of Latin theology stand out. They have offered us the most complete proposals of Western—and not only Western—Trinitarian theology. Naturally, we are referring to the unmatched saints and doctors Augustine of Hippo and Thomas Aquinas. We would now like to summarize the results of their theological reflections on the Most Holy Trinity.

---

[81] Saint Cyril of Alexandria, *De sancta Trinitate* 4.510 (our translation).
[82] Cyril, *De sancta Trinitate* 7.641 (our translation).
[83] Cyril, *De sancta Trinitate* 7.658 (our translation).
[84] Cyril, *De sancta Trinitate* 7.642 (our translation).

5.1. Saint Augustine of Hippo

Saint Augustine resumed the Trinitarian theology of Tertullian after two centuries, and he did so in such a way that Latin theology would be updated in light of the developments of the Eastern Fathers. Among the many merits of his monumental work *De Trinitate*, there is that of having precisely and definitively established the meaning of the key words of Trinitarian reflection. *De Trinitate* is a book that took the Hipponate bishop a great deal of effort and that—as he says in the prologue of the work—he began writing as a young man and published as an old man. In fact, he almost certainly began it in 399, and finished it between 420 and 426, making it a work of at least twenty years. The work was completed in two blocks (books 1–12 and 13–15). The first block was taken from the author by some friends who were anxious to read it and was then published without his permission.

There were three main questions that Saint Augustine intended to resolve with his book: (1) Why, while saying that the Father is God, the Son is God, and the Holy Spirit is God, do we not say that there are three gods? (2) If the works *ad extra* of the Trinity occurred jointly, how does one understand those works that seem to be accomplished by a single Person: the Incarnation, which is the work of the Son alone; the voice on Mount Tabor, which belongs to the Father; and the descent of the Holy Spirit at Pentecost? (3) What are the personal properties of the Holy Spirit, and what is the distinction in God between generation and spiration?

It is clear that Saint Augustine can pose these questions and resolve them based on the solution to previous problems, which were already given by earlier authors; indeed, he begins where others left off. In his book, therefore, we do not find a broad demonstration of the divinity of the Son and the Spirit, which was taken as a given by this point. Let us now give a strict summary of this great work, following the tripartite structure identified by a great contemporary scholar of Saint Augustine.

5.1.1. Exposition of Dogma (Books 1–4)

1. Method

Unlike Eastern theology, which generally starts from the Monarchy of the Father or from the hypostatic Triad, Saint Augustine sets as his starting point the investigation into the one divine nature, which is by essence the Trinity. As the Cappadocians have set the methodological norm for Eastern Trinitarian theology (beginning with the Three Persons), Augustine has done so for

The Trinity

Western Trinitarian theology, up to the twentieth century (beginning with the one nature). Moreover, instead of starting from the "economic Trinity," he began with the "immanent" one. This does not imply, however, that for Augustine the Mystery of the Trinity can be known without Revelation. The method in question, rather, is always based on the fact that we know the Trinity only through supernatural Revelation, accepted in faith. When faith is placed in a state of coherent and organic reflection on itself, the science of faith arises (see Chapter Two). It is within the latter, that is, theology, that we can choose to proceed in one sense or the other: from God as one to God as triune or vice versa.

2. Divine Simplicity and Relations

The first attribute of God is that of substance (or essence, *ousia*). Unlike a creature, whose substance is always united to accidents,[85] God is substance free from accidents; that is, He is substance in which all properties are identified with the essence itself.[86] This has significant repercussions for the problem of the identification of the Persons. The distinction cannot be based on substance (which is one), or on absolute perfections (for example, infinitude or goodness), because in God these coincide with substance. The divine substance, in fact, is simple: all properties are identified with it. And thus, in God, being wise or being luminous is the same as being. Thus, Augustine says that a divine attribute—for example, wisdom—cannot identify a Person, because if divine wisdom were only the Son, then "before" His generation the Father would not be wise; and if it is said that wisdom is a property of the Father, then the Son-Wisdom would be a simple quality of the Father. Wisdom, then, is not a relative quality of a Person, but an absolute quality of God, Who is thus identified with His essence. It follows that the distinction of the Persons does not reside in any accidental quality. But it also does not reside in numeric multitude (that with which individuals of the same species are distinguished, like the three men of which Gregory of Nyssa spoke, drawing on Basil's use of this image) because in God there is no extension. Thus, for Saint Augustine, the one principle of distinction of the Persons in God is relation. As we have said, this was a solution already glimpsed by the Cappadocians, but now perfected by him.

---

[85] Elements that are not constitutive of nature, which rely on nature to subsist. For example, the fact that a man is short or tall, or has blond hair or brown, are all accidental aspects, which do not define the nature of man.

[86] "For there is nothing else of this essence besides the Trinity" (Saint Augustine of Hippo, *De Trinitate* 7.6.11, in *FCNT*, vol. 45, trans. Stephen McKenna [Washington, DC: CUA Press, 1963], 238).

3. Works "ad extra"

Saint Augustine also developed another presupposition: the works *ad extra* of the Trinity occur inseparably, that is, the Three act together. But then how can we say that only the Son is incarnate? Does it not need to be said that all Three are incarnated? With a statement that is both concise and accurate, the Doctor replies: "*Humanam illam formam ex virgine Maria Trinitas operata est sed solius Filii Persona est*—the Trinity wrought that human form from the Virgin, but it is the Person of the Son alone."[87] The Saint interprets the voice of the Father on the Tabor and the descent of the Holy Spirit at Pentecost in a similar way, with the fundamental difference, however, that in the Incarnation human nature is assumed forever by the Word, while the voice and tongues of fire (or the dove that appears after the Baptism of Christ in the Jordan) are forms used provisionally for a particular ministry.

5.1.2. Defense of Dogma (Doctrine of Relations: Books 5–7)

1. Relations and "Circumincessio"

From the unity of being and the divine works, the exposition goes on to the distinction of the Persons. Against the Arians, the author says: in God there are no accidental perfections; but this does not lead to the Arian position for which everything that is thought about God is thought according to substance, with the consequence that the begotten Son—Who is distinct from the unbegotten Father—cannot be of the same substance. Instead, Saint Augustine says that not only is there the predicament of substance, but also of relations, which are not pure accidents in God, as they are among human beings. Creatural relations are accidental, but divine relations are not. Relations in God are not substantial (otherwise there would be a God—a separate divine substance—for every divine relation), but they are not accidents either, because they are eternal and immutable. This position is based on the principle that the Saint explains in *De civitate Dei*, written at the same time as the last three books of *De Trinitate*: "It is what it has—with the exception of the real relations in which the Persons stand to each other."[88] Therefore, all

---

[87] Saint Augustine of Hippo, *De Trinitate* 2.10.18, in *FCNT*, vol. 45, 73.
[88] Augustine, *De civitate Dei* 11.10.1, in *FCNT*, vol. 14, trans. Gerald G. Walsh and Grace Monahan (New York: Fathers of the Church, Inc., 1952), 202. This Augustinian assertion contains, in a nutshell, the teaching that would then be expressed by the formula

the divine perfections are identified with the divine being, and each Person is mutually present in the other—this doctrine would be called *circumincessio* by the Latins and *perichoresis* by the Greeks. However, in God, absolute perfections and mutual relations must be distinguished: the former refer to themselves (*dicuntur a se*), and the latter refer to the other (*dicuntur ad alium*). The first are common to the Three, and the second establish the distinction of the Persons.

2. Identification of the Three

The identity of the Father is then (the relation of) paternity, that of the Son is filiation, and that of the Spirit is passive gift. These relations are real and thus involve a real distinction between the correlative terms (the Father is not the Son, etc.). This concerns immutable and subsistent relations that, being simultaneous, are coeternal. The Father has always been Father, and so forth for the Son and the Spirit. "Father" indicates relation to the Son, and "Son" indicates relation to the Father; the Father would not be called Father if not for the fact that He has a Son. These are not denominations that refer to substance, because neither Father nor Son refer to themselves, but to the "other-than-self"; yet these relations are not accidental, because that which is called Father or Son is eternal and immutable, and the relation itself is thus eternal and immutable.[89] The three relations that are in God are not substantial; that is, it is not the case that a nature corresponds to each relation, otherwise one would fall into the heresy called Tritheism, which postulates the existence of three divine substances, and hence of three gods. These relations, however, are not accidental either, otherwise one would fall into the aforementioned Sabellian Modalism. The fact that they are neither substantial nor accidental does not imply that they are only entities of reason (that is, that they are imagined by us without being real). How would we need to define them? Saint Augustine does not give a direct answer (which would be done later by Saint Thomas), but he paves the way for it. Augustine, in fact, speaks of "*subsistentia personarum*—subsistence of the Persons."[90] Therefore, he does not define the divine Person as "subsistent relation," but introduces

---

of Saint Anselm of Canterbury (d. 1109) for whom everything is one in God "*ubi non obviat aliqua relationis oppositio*—where there is no opposition of relation" (*De processione Spiritus Sancti* 2 [our translation]). The Council of Florence, *Cantate Domino* (1442) will later quote this Anselmian affirmation (DS 1330).

[89] See Augustine, *De Trinitate* 5.5.6.

[90] Augustine, *De civitate Dei* 11.10.1 (our translation).

the fundamental term, *subsistentia*, which will be enhanced later.

3. "Filioque"

Looking deeper, then, at the procession of the Holy Spirit, Saint Augustine holds that the relationship between the Father and the Son with the Holy Spirit is identical and thus he uses the formula "*ex Patre Filioque*" ("[the Spirit proceeds] from the Father and the Son"): this means that the Father and Son are together the unique Principle from which the Holy Spirit has origin in God.[91] The procession of the Son is His generation from the Father; the procession of the Spirit is the active donation on the part of the Father and the Son. Thus, the Holy Spirit is not Son by proceeding from the Father, because "the Spirit came forth, not as born, but as given."[92] The Spirit proceeds *principaliter* from the Father—originally, as from a source. The Son is "Principle from Principle," that is, since He has received everything from the Father, from the Father He also receives being Principle of the Holy Spirit: "For if whatever He has, the Son has from the Father, then certainly He has from the Father that the Holy Spirit also proceeds from Him."[93] Thus, the Father remains the source of the whole divinity (called the "Monarchy" doctrine by the Eastern Fathers).

4. Personal Names

Saint Augustine focuses on the names proper to the Persons. He finds three for Each: the names of the First are Father, Principle, and Ungenerated. Only the first name is biblical, the others are from the Tradition. All three are relative—even Ungenerated—because, although it is in the negative form, it expresses a relation that is absent ("not-generated"), thus it falls within the category of relation. For the Second in God, the names are those of Son, Word, and Image. All three are biblical names and clearly relative: the Son refers back to the Father, the Word to the Mind, the Image to the Exemplar. Finally, for the Third, the names are Holy Spirit, Gift, and Love. According to authoritative specialists, the most noteworthy contribution of Saint Augustine to Trinitarian theology is found in this part, dedicated to the names of the Third One in God. Of the three names only the first (Holy Spirit) is biblical, and, moreover, all three names in themselves could also

---

[91] See Augustine, *De Trinitate* 5.14.15.
[92] Augustine, *De Trinitate* 5.14.15, in *FCNT*, vol. 45, 205.
[93] Augustine, *De Trinitate* 15.26.47, in *FCNT*, vol. 45, 517; see also Augustine, *De Trinitate* 15.17.29.

The Trinity

apply to the Father or the Son, or even the whole Trinity.

5. *The Spirit as Love*

Augustine, to resolve the dilemma, starts from Revelation that teaches that the Holy Spirit is Spirit of the Father and the Son. Then he considers the works that the same Revelation attributes *ad extra* to the Spirit: to bestow the gifts of God on human beings and to spread charity in their hearts. Now if the Spirit bestows the gifts of God, He himself is the Gift in God (here, Augustine moves from the "economic Trinity" to the "immanent Trinity"); and if He spreads love, then He is the Love in God. Moreover, Augustine continues, if the Scriptures are studied more intently, one notes that they attribute these two names to the Spirit: "God is love" (1 John 4:16); "If you knew the gift of God" (John 4:10); "You will receive the gift of the holy Spirit" (Acts 2:38)—these passages refer, according to Augustine, to the Third One in God. In fact, in the Bible, He is the Spirit of the Father and the Son and thus, when it says "God is Love," it is understood as the Love common to the Father and the Son that is the Holy Spirit. Naturally, the possibility remains of also using the name of love to refer to the Father and Son, something that distinguishes this name of the Third Person from the names of the other Two (Ungenerated and Generated), which are applied only to Them.

The African Doctor explains the reason for this difference: we use human concepts to speak of God. Now, while a relation that is called generation exists in our world, a relation that comes from a substance in a different way than a generation and that can be called a procession, does not. That is why it is more difficult to connote the Holy Spirit with a created name that is taken from our experience (we have an experience of generation, but not of procession).

6. *The Spirit as Gift*

As for the name Gift, Augustine notes that we find the relational character of the Third Person in this name, which is not found in the name Holy Spirit. If there is a Gift, there is a Giver,[94] just as if there is a Son, there is a Father. The Holy Spirit then refers to the Father and the Son as He is the Gift of Love of Both, and thus Saint Augustine also calls Him the Embrace, Communion, and Gentleness.[95]

---

[94] See Augustine, *De Trinitate* 5.11.12.
[95] See Augustine, *De Trinitate* 6.10.11.

7. The Concept of Person

Saint Augustine's doctrine of relations is brilliant but imperfect. Indeed, it lacks a definition of Person,[96] along with a study of analogy that permits the application of this concept to the human being, the angel, and the Three of the Trinity. The definition of Person would be perfected by later authors: in the West, especially Saint Severinus Boethius (d. ca. 525) and Saint Thomas; in the East, particularly Leontius of Byzantium (d. ca. 544).

5.1.3. Illustration of Dogma (Books 9–15)

1. "Capax Dei"

Another great effort of Augustine is that of finding some sensory images that may aid in the understanding of the transcendent reality. According to various experts in the thought of Augustine, the human being "in the image of God" is the central theme of Augustinian philosophy, theology, and spiritual doctrine. The divine image is a permanent characteristic of the human being, which corresponds to the human rational soul. The image in the human beings consists in the fact that they are *capax Dei*,[97] due to their capacity for knowing and loving. By virtue of being made in the image of God, the human being is in the image of the Trinity and for this reason there must be traces of the same Trinity in the human being.

2. "Vestigia Trinitatis"

Indeed, Saint Augustine believes that he can also find visible traces of the Trinity in the external human being, especially in the sense of sight, and he does so by identifying the trinomial reality/vision/intention; or even sensitive memory/the inner vision/will, but these are rather poor *vestigia trinitatis*, because the identity of substance is lacking in these triads. To find a true image of the Trinity, one needs, in his judgment, to study the interiority of men. The triads that he identifies by studying the human soul are *mens/notitia/amor* (mind/knowledge/love; book 9), *memoria/intelligentia/voluntas sui* (self-memory/self-intelligence/self-love) when the object is oneself (book 10), and *memoria/intelligentia/voluntas Dei* (memory of God/intelligence of God/love of God) when the object is God (books 14–15). The word pro-

---

[96] See further along, note 112.
[97] See Augustine, *De Trinitate* 14.8.11.

ceeds from the human mind, and love proceeds from the mind that is known through the word—so too it occurs in God. The three human faculties are inseparable and yet each of them is a substance, and together they are one single substance, just as it is with God.[98]

3. Psychological Analogy

The Saint nonetheless recognizes the weakness of this "psychological analogy," because, even though it is by means of these three distinct powers, it is always the one *I* of the human subject that remembers, understands, and loves. I possess memory, intelligence, and love, but these three faculties do not completely coincide with my being, nor are they me. They are predicated of a single human person, while the divine nature is instead three Persons. Therefore, there are the following differences between Trinitarian image and Trinitarian reality: (1) The "Trinitarian" structures of the human rational nature do not coincide perfectly, but only analogously with the way in which the divine Trinity is the essence of the Divinity. (2) While memory, intellect, and will operate separately, the three divine Persons always operate with a unique and indivisible action. (3) While in the human being the memory, intellect, and will are *functions* of a human person, in God the Three *are* Persons. (4) Therefore, to remember, to know, and to love are, in God, proper to each Person, although Each possesses them in a different way according to His own relation to the Others. Ultimately, the psychological analogy of Saint Augustine has its own value, but only *a posteriori*, that is, if one already knows Revelation; otherwise no one, starting from the three functions of the human mind, could formulate a doctrine of the Trinity.

5.2. Saint Thomas Aquinas

For the sake of brevity, we shall not present the important Trinitarian theologies of great medieval masters such as Saint Anselm of Canterbury (d. 1109), Richard of Saint Victor (d. 1173), and Saint Bonaventure (d. 1274). We shall limit ourselves to summarizing the treatment on the Trinity contained in the *Summa Theologiae* of Saint Thomas Aquinas. As is the case with other spheres of his theology, the Trinitarian theology of Saint Thomas brings together the best of the preceding Tradition with an extraordinary capacity for synthesis, lucidity of vision, depth of intuition, and accurate vocabulary, not to mention his use of very helpful categories of the "new" Aristotelian philosophy, which

---

[98] See Augustine, *De Trinitate* 9.5.8.

in the Middle Ages progressively replaced Neoplatonism, the main philosophy of reference for the Fathers.

The Angelic Doctor engages with the mystery of the Trinity in several works: in the *Scriptum Super Sententiis* (I, dd. 2–32); in the *Summa Contra Gentiles* (IV, chs. 2–26); in the *Compendium Theologiae* (I, chs. 37–67); and in the *Summa Theologiae* (I, qq. 27–43). The latter is his most mature work. It discusses the Trinity in seventeen questions: the first (I, q. 27) is dedicated to the divine processions, the second (I, q. 28) is dedicated to the divine relations, and the others (I, qq. 29–43) are dedicated to the study of the Persons. The rigor of the treatise's structure is evident: everything starts with the fundamental fact—the processions—upon which the relations depend. The relations that identify the Persons are then studied: paternity, filiation, and passive spiration. It is obvious that the study is concluded by treating the Persons, focusing deeply on various themes. In the *Summa Theologiae*, Saint Thomas maintains the basic approach of Saint Augustine, starting with the unity of the divine nature, in which the eternal processions occur, and going on from there to study the existence of three Distinct-Ones or Persons in God: Father, Son, and Holy Spirit.

5.2.1. Processions

1. Psychological Analogy

As for Saints Augustine and Anselm, for Saint Thomas the best theological approach to the Trinity consists in considering the structure of a spiritual being,[99] which exists in three ways: in its being as a reality; in its thought as a known object; and in its will as a loved object. Thought and will are immanent operations that are in the subject as its very life. The Angelic Doctor speculatively explores the Augustinian psychological analogy, thanks to the epistemological theory and the anthropological view of Aristotle. Aristotle explained the cognitive and volitional processes of the human being in this way: the intellect knows an object by reproducing it immaterially in itself through the idea/concept, or mental word, which is the "fruit" of the action of knowing. The will tends toward the known object: this tending is the "fruit"

---

[99] In addition to the Revelation about the human being made in the image of God (see Chapter Three), this method is also underpinned by another foundation in Scripture: "For the Spirit scrutinizes everything, even the depths of God. Among human beings, who knows what pertains to a person except the spirit of the person that is within? Similarly, no one knows what pertains to God except the Spirit of God" (1 Cor 2:10–11).

The Trinity

of the act of the will, that is, of loving. Now, if these processes were considered not in relation with an object that is external to the subject, but rather to the subject itself, then we have a thinking subject that produces an idea of itself in itself, in which it knows and contemplates itself and, with the will, loves itself. The thinking subject thus becomes a thought object and both are joined in a common term that is love.

2. Divine Processions

Saint Thomas applies this psychological analogy to the Trinity, to clarify the divine processions. God, who is most simple Spirit and most perfect Act, performs in His immanence the works of knowing and willing, which are thus addressed to Himself. In the case of God, the terms of the action of knowing and willing are not—as for human beings—simple modifications of the soul, but rather, subsistent realities, that is, the Persons of the Word and of the Holy Spirit. The procession of the Son from the Father takes place through the intellect and is analogous to the generation of the idea on the part of the human mind.[100] The procession of the Holy Spirit, rather, occurs through the appetition (desire), and it corresponds to what occurs in the human soul when it loves itself. The difference between God and the human being is that the human being loves himself, while in God there are two lovers (Father and Son), yet there is only one subsistent Love that emerges from Them. The second procession in God comes jointly from the Father and from the Son.[101] Therefore, the Son is "God-known" and the Spirit is "God-loved," or "God-who-knows-Himself" and "God-who-loves-Himself."

5.2.2. Relations

1. Divine Substance and Relations

The two processions in God (generation and spiration) establish real relations between the One who proceeds and the Principle from whom He proceeds. The relations are real because, although it is so within the identity of nature, a real and non-imaginary connection is present between the Principle and the One who proceeds from Him. That is, in God, there really is the One who gives and the One who receives the identical divine nature, which is to say

---

[100] See *ST* I, q. 27, a. 2.
[101] See *ST* I, q. 27, a. 3.

that the divine nature is really given and actually received, though its unity remains intact.[102]

In God, this real relation coincides with the essence because in Him essence and existence coincide and therefore the three Persons have a single, common existence, which is identical to the essence. Thus, there are no perfections proper to the Persons (see Augustine), because the Person is not something (i.e., a substance), to which a quality (an accident) can be inherent. The Person in God is not something, but "a pure being in relation to something."[103]

2. Real Relations

Saint Thomas calls the four real relations in God: "paternity," "filiation," "spiration," and "procession." They are constituted as a 'consequence' of the two divine processions: each procession actually gives rise to two relations. The procession of the intellectual type (which is called "generation") gives rise to the relations of paternity and filiation, and the volitional procession[104] gives rise to spiration (which can also be called "active spiration") and to procession (or "passive spiration"). Therefore, each procession gives rise to two relations: one of the Principle that originates the procession, and another of the One who proceeds from the Principle. The fact that each real relation is identified with the divine nature does not mean that the relations are identical to each other; in fact, they are not identical to each other when they are reciprocally opposed.

5.2.3. Persons

1. "Naturae Rationalis Individua Substantia"

The most brilliant point of Thomas' Trinitarian theology is the concept of

---

[102] See *ST* I, q. 28, a. 1; see Thomas Aquinas, *Quaestio de potentia*, q. 8, a. 1: "*Oportet dicere in divinis relationes reales esse.* [...] *Per sola relativa distinctio in divinis personis attenditur. Haec tamen distinctio non potest esse rationis tantum,*" ("It is necessary to say that in God the relations are real [...] There is an only relative distinction between the divine Persons, a reason for which such a distinction cannot only be one of reason" [our translation]).

[103] Thomas Aquinas, *Quaestio de potentia* 2, 5: "*Ipsae relationes quibus Personae ad invicem distinguuntur, sunt ipsa divina essentia secundum rem*—The relations on the basis of which the Persons are distinguished from each other are, as regards substance, the very divine essence" (our translation). See also *ST* I, q. 28, a. 2.

[104] Procession that, for Saint Thomas, does not have a proper name: see *ST* I, q. 27, a. 4.

the divine Person. Following Saint Severinus Boethius, Saint Thomas defines person in the general sense as "individual substance of a rational nature" ("*naturae rationalis individua substantia*").[105] He then distinguishes human, angelic, and divine persons. Obviously, the person in the most perfect sense is the divine Person, because in God everything is perfect. In God, "Person" means "subsisting relation" ("*relatio subsistens*"), that is, the term of Person used in the Trinitarian doctrine indicates in God a relation that subsists in the divine nature.

2. "Subsistens in Rationali Natura"

In light of this specification, the Angelic Doctor perfected the concept of person in general, which he says is the noblest reality in the universe.[106] There are three essential coefficients of the person: subsistence,[107] incommunicability,[108] and spirituality (intellectual nature). Person is one who subsists in the order of the spirit: "*Omne quod subsistit in intellectuali vel rationali natura, habet rationem personae*—everything that subsists in an intellectual or rational nature is defined as a person"[109]; the person is the "*subsistens in rationali natura*—what is subsisting in a rational nature."[110] To subsist means "to exist by itself and in itself," to have a proper "act of existence." It is not required, therefore, for substance to be part of the definition (and of the reality) of the person.

Having clarified the distinction between the concept of person and that

---

[105] Saint Severinus Boethius, *Contra Eutychen et Nestorium* [*De duabus naturis et una Persona Christi*] 3. Different editions report "*naturae rationabilis*" instead of "*naturae rationalis*."

[106] See *ST* I, q. 29, a. 3.

[107] Saint Severinus Boethius, in the cited work, proposes important reflections about *esse* and *subsistere*, also referring to the confusion that can emerge when one goes from Greek to Latin terms.

[108] Richard of St. Victor offers the following definition, which highlights the aspect of incommunicability, that is, of the individual peculiarity: "*Persona est intellectualis naturae incommunicabilis existentia*" ("Person is an incommunicable existence of intellectual nature": *De Trinitate* 4.22, [our translation]). About the concept of *existentia*, it has nothing to do with existentialist philosophies of the twentieth century, because Richard understands it in an ontological sense, with the *existentia* being the substance connoted by the origin. "*Existere*" means "*ex aliquo sistere, hoc est substantialiter ex aliquo esse*" ("to subsist from someone, that is, to exist substantially from someone": *De Trinitate* 4.12 [our translation]).

[109] Saint Thomas Aquinas, *Summa contra gentiles* IV, ch. 35 (our translation). By virtue of its precision, this definition exceeds the classical (and always valid) definition of Boethius and applies (analogically) to divine, angelic, and human persons.

[110] *ST* I, q. 29, a. 3 (our translation).

of substance—a distinction that is not so clear at the terminological level in the Boethian definition, which makes it harder to use in the Trinitarian sphere—Saint Thomas connects the concept of person with that of relation, drawing from the writings of Saint Augustine. It follows that "person" can also be a relational subsistence or a subsistent relation. In the created world, this never occurs: the relations between the creatures are, in fact, always accidental and thus cannot be the stable foundation of personhood. But it does occur in God: paternity, filiation, and passive spiration are three subsistent relations, or three Persons.

3. "Relatio Subsistens"

The distinction in God can only happen by relations of origin, and such relations in God are not accidents inherent to a nature, but are the divine substance itself, and thus, they are subsisting like the divine substance itself. Consequently, just as the Deity is God, so the Father is God, etc. Thus, divine Person "*significat relationem ut subsistentem*—signifies a relation as subsisting".[111] As was said, the divine Person is defined as "*relatio subsistens*" ("subsistent relation"). Saint Thomas thus succeeds in an enterprise that seemed impossible: overcoming the Trinitarian theology of the great Augustine. The Angelic Doctor effectively managed to give a response to a problem left unsolved by Augustine, who recognized honestly that he did not know how to define a divine Person.[112]

4. Relations of Opposition

Thomas then proceeds to demonstrate that there are three Persons in God. There are as many Persons in God as there are real oppositions connected to the relations.[113] The personal distinction arises where the relations are

---

[111] *ST* I, q. 29, a. 4 (our translation).

[112] "*Dictum est tamen 'tres Personae,' non ut illud diceretur, sed ne taceretur*" ("'Three Persons' is said more to not remain silent than to express that reality": Augustine, *De Trinitate* 5.9.10, in *FCNT*, vol. 45, 185). This Augustinian apophatism with respect to the concept of divine Person is still present in Saint Anselm of Canterbury, *Monologion* 79: "*Ecce patet omni homini expedire ut credat in quandam ineffabilem trinam unitatem et unam trinitatem. Unam quidem et unitatem propter unam essentiam; trinam vero et trinitatem, proter tres 'nescio quid'*" ("It is thus evident how it is opportune for each one to believe in an ineffable trinal unity and in one Trinity. One and a unity on account of the one essence; but trinal and Trinity on account of three 'I do not know what[s]'" [our translation]).

[113] Evidently, Saint Thomas bases this on the assertion of Saint Anselm, which we have already cited: in God all is a unity—"*ubi non obviat aliqua relationis oppositio*."

reciprocally in opposition to one another. Paternity and filiation are in opposition to one another. Active and passive spiration are as well: but active and passive spiration are not in opposition to the paternity and the filiation. Thus, though there are four real relations in God, only three are in opposition to one another (thus, they are defined "relations of opposition"), and consequently only three are Persons, who are identified and distinguished exactly by relations of opposition. The reciprocal oppositions are the following: there is the opposition between paternity and filiation (thus, the first two Persons are identified) and there is an opposition of the passive spiration or procession (the Third Person).[114] There is no relation of opposition between paternity and active spiration, and between filiation and active spiration. As was said numerous times since Saint Augustine, the active spiration is common to the Father and Son. That is to say, Father and Son are distinguished because of their relative opposition of being Father and Son. On the other hand, the two are not in opposition to one another with respect to the active spiration of the Holy Spirit: in fact, together they are a single Principle of the Holy Spirit. Instead, the passive spiration, that is, the relation of "proceeding-from" is in opposition to the active spiration (Father and Son together, as Cause, for the Greeks; or Principle, for the Latin theologians, of the Holy Spirit), and thus this passive spiration identifies the Third One in God.

5.2.4. Missions and Notions

Saint Thomas discusses several other aspects, particularly the "missions" *ad intra* and *ad extra* of the divine Persons, as well as the so-called Trinitarian "notions." We must, however, stop here, leaving these other aspects of Thomistic Trinitarian theology up to the personal study of the reader, as remarkable as they are. Nonetheless, the reader should not think that the doctrines of the notions and missions are of little importance, for the fact that we have to forego presenting them here. We recommend that the reader independently study this part of Saint Thomas's Trinitarian theology, while we can at least partially justify our omission by recalling that Chapters Three, Four, and Five have presented the economic activity of the Three as Creator, Redeemer, and Sanctifier.

In conclusion, we dare to propose two illustrative tables of the theological explanation furnished by Thomas Aquinas, recalling that the certainty of faith, which is based on the Word of God, consists in recognizing one God in three Persons: the Father, the Son, and the Holy Spirit. Theological explanations are important intellectual approximations to the mystery, which never

---

[114] *ST* I, q. 30, a. 2.

have the pretense of exhausting it or of being definitive. Nonetheless, they aid in showing the reasonableness of the faith, the content of which always surpasses any theological explanation, without declaring the latter useless.

TABLE 1: PROCESSIONS AND RELATIONS

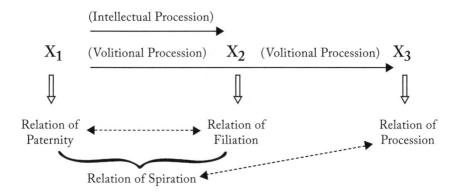

TABLE 2: OPPOSITION OF RELATIONS

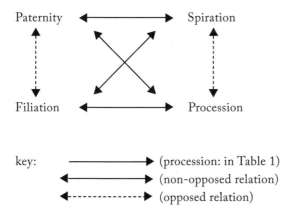

6. Magisterial Pronouncements

We propose here a brief review of the main teachings of the Magisterium on Trinitarian doctrine, leaving those concerning the theme of the *Filioque* for the end of the chapter.

6.1. The One and Triune God

The fact that God is one and triune is attested from the most ancient Symbols of the faith. The profession of Trinitarian faith is an original fact of the life and teaching of the Church. Naturally, the most ancient Symbols are less articulate than later ones, which benefitted from a Trinitarian theology that had matured over time. This also explains the progressive use of a more technical language, as well as the broad reference to the "immanent Trinity" with respect to the oldest professions of the faith. However, we need to say that even in the late patristic era, we already find Symbols of the faith that are based on deep theological speculation.[115] The most meaningful case is probably that of the Creed called, from its first words, *Quicumque vult*. Saint Athanasius was believed for a long time to be its author, and therefore, the name of Athanasian Symbol is also used. Today, critics are divided on its attribution: some scholars think the text was written by Saint Martin of Braga (d. ca. 580), some think it was written by Saint Ambrose of Milan (d. 397) or Saint Vincent of Lérins (d. ca. 450), and others think it was Saint Fulgentius of Ruspe (d. 533). The imprint of Augustinian theology is, however, quite evident:

> Whoever wishes to be saved must, before all else, hold the Catholic faith:
> for unless one maintains it whole and inviolate, he will certainly perish in eternity.
> This, then, is the Catholic faith: We worship one God in the Trinity and the Trinity in the unity,
> Without confusing the Persons or separating the substance;
> for indeed the Person of the Father is one, (the Person) of the Son another, (the Person) of the Holy Spirit another;
> but the divinity of the Father, the Son, and the Holy Spirit is one, (their) glory equal, and (their) majesty coeternal.

---

[115] For example, in the Synod of Rome (680), we find the complex expression: "*Non trium nominum subsistentiam, sed trium subsistentiarum unam substantiam*—not a subsistence of three names, but one substance of three Subsistences" (*Omnium Bonorum Spes* [DS 546]).

As the Father is, so is the Son, (and) so is the Holy Spirit:
uncreated the Father, uncreated the Son, uncreated the Holy Spirit;
infinite the Father, infinite the Son, and infinite the Holy Spirit;
eternal the Father, eternal the Son, and eternal the Holy Spirit;
and yet (they are) not three eternal beings, but One eternal;
just as (they are) not three uncreated beings or three infinite beings,
> but One uncreated and One infinite being.

In the like manner, omnipotent (is) the Father, omnipotent the
> Son, omnipotent the Holy Spirit;

and yet (there are) not three omnipotent beings but One omnipotent being.

Therefore the Father (is) God, the Son (is) God, the Holy Spirit
> (is) God.

and yet (there are) not three gods but one God.

In the same way, the Father (is) Lord, the Son (is) Lord, the Holy
> Spirit (is) Lord;

yet (there are) not three Lords, but there is one Lord;

for just as we are compelled by Christian truth to confess each
> Person individually as God and Lord,

just so the Catholic religion forbids us to say that there are three
> gods or three lords.

The Father was not made by anyone; nor was He created or
> begotten;

the Son is from the Father alone, neither made nor created but
> generated;

the Holy Spirit (is) from the Father and the Son, neither made nor
> created nor generated, but proceeding.

Therefore, (there is) one Father, not three fathers; one Son, not
> three sons; one Holy Spirit, not three holy spirits.

And in this Trinity, (there is) nothing before or after, nothing
> greater or lesser,

but all three Persons are coequal and coeternal with each other.

And so, in all things, as was said already above, both the unity in
> the Trinity and the Trinity in the unity must be worshipped.

Let anyone, therefore, who wishes to be saved think of the Trinity
> in this manner.[116] . . .

This is the Catholic faith: unless one has believed it faithfully and
> firmly, he will not be saved. (DS 75–76)

---

[116] We are omitting the Christological section of the Profession.

The Trinity

As regards the more elaborate professions of faith, one can see, for example, the Definition *Firmiter* against the Albigenses and Cathars of the Fourth Lateran Council (ch. 1: DS 800–801). Let us cite a rather exemplary passage from the second chapter, dedicated to the reprobation of the errors of Joachim of Fiore (d. 1202):

> [We] believe and confess with Peter the Lombard[117] that there is one highest, incomprehensible, and ineffable reality, which is truly Father, Son, and Holy Spirit; the three Persons together, and each Person distinctly; therefore in God there is only Trinity, not a quaternity, because each of the Persons is that reality, that is, that divine substance, essence, or nature which alone is the beginning of all things, apart from which nothing else can be found. This reality is neither generating nor generated nor proceeding, but it is the Father who generates, the Son who is generated, and the Holy Spirit who proceeds, so that there be distinctions between the Persons but unity in nature.... What [*quod*] the Father is, this very same reality is also the Son, this the Holy Spirit, so that in the orthodox and Catholic faith we believe them to be of one substance. For the Father gives His substance to the Son.... One cannot say that He gave Him a part of His substance and retained a part for Himself, since the substance of the Father is indivisible, being entirely simple. Nor can one say that in generating, the Father transferred His substance to the Son, as though He gave it to the Son in such a way as not to retain it for Himself, for so He would have ceased to be substance.[118]

---

[117] A medieval theologian (d. ca. 1160), author of the celebrated *Liber Sententiarum*, which earned him the title of Master of the Sentences. In the work, he collects biblical and patristic references, ordering them by themes. His *Sententiae* were so successful that they became the obligatory textbook in the theological faculties up until the sixteenth century, when it was substituted by the *Summa* of Saint Thomas. It is significant that he is explicitly cited by an ecumenical council.

[118] Fourth Lateran Council, *Firmiter* (1215), ch. 2 (DS 804–805). Note that, 800 years in advance, the text rejects an opinion that was affirmed in some Trinitarian theologies of the 1900s, which interprets the generation of the Son from the Father as a sort of *kenosis* (in Greek, "emptying") of the First Person, who would shed the divine substance to give it completely outside Himself—and this would be the generation of the Son. The Son, "then," would restore the entire substance to the Father and this generous restitution, along with the first generous divestiture of the Father, would constitute the perfect Love in God (Holy Spirit). It seems to be a rereading of the Augustinian Trinitarian theology in an idealistic interpretive key. But such a position cannot be maintained.

Another text that expresses the Trinitarian teaching of the medieval councils well is the Decree for the Jacobites (Coptic and Ethiopian) of the Council of Florence:

> First, then, the holy Roman Church, founded on the words of our Lord and Savior, firmly believes, professes, and preaches one true God, almighty, immutable, and eternal, Father, Son, and Holy Spirit; one in essence, three in Persons; unbegotten Father, Son begotten from the Father, Holy Spirit proceeding from the Father and the Son. . . . These three Persons are one God, not three gods, because there is one substance of the three, one essence, one nature, one Godhead, one immensity, one eternity, and everything (in them) is one where there is no opposition of relationship [*ubi non obviat relationis oppositio*].[119]

6.2. The Persons and Relations

The Magisterium confirms that the divine Persons are distinguished by their relations, that is, if considered according to the aspect of a reciprocal relationship. This teaching is found in many texts, including the Eleventh Synod of Toledo in the year 675 (see DS 528) and the Sixteenth Synod held in 693 in the same city, which clearly grasps what Augustine says about relative names (see DS 570) and about the triad *memoria/intellegentia/voluntas*; moreover, this synod presents the important distinction between *alius* and *aliud*:

> Although, according to essence, the Father (is) will; the Son (is) will; the Holy Spirit (is) will, nevertheless, we must not believe that They are one according to relation [*secundum relativum*]; for the Father is one as He relates to the Son; the Son is another as He relates to the Father; and the Holy Spirit, who because He proceeds from the Father and the Son, is another as He relates to the Father and the Son; not something other [*aliud*]; but Another [*alius*]; because They who have one being in the nature of the divinity have a particular property [*specialis proprietas*] in the distinction of Persons.[120]

---

[119] Council of Florence, *Cantate Domino* (1442) (DS 1330).
[120] Sixteenth Synod of Toledo, *De Trinitate Divina* 30 (DS 573). The distinction goes back much earlier. For example, we find in *Epistula 101*.1.20 of Saint Gregory of Nazianzus—whose Latin translation was cited by the Fourth Lateran Council—that although "another [*alius*] is the Father, another the Son, another the Holy Spirit, They are however not diverse realities [*aliud*]" (our translation).

The Trinity

The personal properties are also affirmed. For the Father it is being ungenerated, for the Son it is being generated, and for the Spirit it is to be proceeding: "While then these Three are One and this One Three, each of the Persons retains His own characteristics [*proprietas*]: the Father has eternity without birth; the Son has eternity with birth; the Holy Spirit has procession with eternity but without birth."[121]

It has already been stated that the Eastern ecclesial writers greatly emphasize the Father's personal property of being the unique Principle of the divinity. The doctrine of the Monarchy of the Father did not find any special acceptance by the Magisterium of the Church. The only trace that is found is in a very ancient text of Pope Saint Dionysius (d. 268), who—being originally from *Magna Graecia* (Terranova da Sibari, in Calabria, Italy)—was of Greek culture and language. As was the custom in those early times, even in the Roman Church, he wrote in Greek: "It is quite appropriate now for me to speak against those who are tearing apart, destroying, and annihilating the most venerable proclamation of God's Church, the (divine) Monarchy [*monarchia*], by making it three powers [*dunameis*], divided hypostases, and three gods [*theotas*].... The doctrine of that foolish Marcion, which cuts and divides the Monarchy into three principles [*archas*] is a diabolical teaching."[122]

Instead of the eastern theology of the Monarchy, the Magisterium preferred the Augustinian theology of the Father as "Principle of the Trinity."[123] Naturally, this does not imply that the doctrine of the Monarchy is mistaken, but only that the Magisterium believed that the theology of the Principle better explained the revealed doctrine: perhaps because it allows us to speak of the Father and the Son as unique Principle of the Spirit, with the Father being "Principle without Principle" and the Son being "Principle from Principle."

6.3. Mutual Indwelling

As we have mentioned, Christian theology specified—with a foundation in Revelation (see John 14:10–11)—that the Three are One in the Other, within

---

[121] Eleventh Synod of Toledo, *De Trinitate Divina* 35 (DS 532). Other attestations in this regard: the First Synod of Toledo, *Regula Fidei contra Errores Priscillianorum* (400) (DS 188); Saint Leo the Great, *Quam Laudabiliter* (447) (DS 284); Saint Hormisdas, *Inter Ea Quae* (521), ch. 9 (DS 367); Third Synod of Toledo, *De Trinitate Divina* (589) (DS 470).

[122] Saint Dionysius of Alexandria, *De Trinitate et Incarnatione*, year 262, Ch. 1 (DS 112). In Ch. 3 (DS 115) he uses for a third time the term, speaking of the "holy proclamation of the Monarchy."

[123] The expression is from Saint Augustine of Hippo, *De Trinitate*, IV, 20, 29, and it is explicitly cited by Leo XIII, *Divinum illud munus* (DS 3326).

the indivisible divine nature. On one hand, the Persons are distinct in such a way that They cannot be intermingled; on the other hand, on account of the unity of nature, They carry out a reciprocal immanence, which the Latin writers call *circumincessio* or *circuminsessio*, and the Greek writers call *perichoresis* ("rotation").

On this theme, the clearest magisterial text is probably found in the Florentine Council, which simply cites Saint Fulgentius: "Because of this unity the Father is entirely in the Son, entirely in the Holy Spirit; the Son is entirely in the Father, entirely in the Holy Spirit; the Holy Spirit is entirely in the Father, entirely in the Son."[124]

6.4. The Works "Ad Extra"

The Magisterium also confirms this traditional point of Trinitarian theology: the works of the Trinity *ad extra* are always common, because the works are produced by the nature, which in God is one alone. Thus, the three Persons always act together in the world, even if a particular work — which is carried out by all Three—is appropriated to One or Another because it corresponds more to the particular character (personal property) of that Person.

The unity of action is emphasized well by Pope Vigilius (d. 555), who reminds us that we are baptized "in the name," not "in the names" of the Father, Son, and Spirit. This is because the Trinity is one divinity alone that possesses "one operation [*una operatio*]." He adds: "For in the Godhead nothing is differentiated, since only the manifest uniqueness of the Persons is subject to distinction."[125] The Eleventh Synod of Toledo affirmed that the three Persons "are inseparable both in what they are and in what they do" (DS 531). The following text is also very clear: "All the works of the Trinity are always inseparable, and there is nothing in the Holy Trinity that is contrary or dissimilar or unequal."[126]

Even the Incarnation of the Word, although its outcome is only of the Second Person, is a common work of the Holy Trinity. Both aspects are highlighted by the Sixth Synod of Toledo:

---

[124] Council of Florence, *Cantate Domino* (DS 1331): this is a citation of Saint Fulgentius of Ruspe, *De Fide Trinitatis ad Petrum diaconum* 1. In the *De Trinitate et Incarnatione* of Saint Dionysius there are important allusions to this doctrine.

[125] Vigilius, *Professio fidei* (DS 415). Also speaking of "*una operatio*" are Popes Pelagius I, *Humani Generis* (557) (DS 441) and Saint Agatho, *Consideranti Mihi* (681) (DS 542 and 545).

[126] Synod of Cividale in Friuli (AD 796/797), *De Trinitate Divina* (DS 618).

> Only the Son came forth from the secret and mystery of the Father for the redemption of the human race.... Though the entire Trinity cooperated in the formation of His assumed humanity—since the works of the Trinity are inseparable—yet He alone, in the singularity of Person, not in the unity of the divine nature, became man. In this is something special to the Son, not something common to the Trinity: for if the nature of man had been confused with the nature of God, the entire Trinity would have assumed a body.[127]

The "appropriations," instead, attribute to one particular Person that which is in itself a work of all Three: the works of power (such as creation) are attributed especially to the Father; the works of wisdom (such as Trinitarian Revelation) are attributed to the Son; and the works of love (such as the Incarnation of the Word), are attributed to the Spirit.[128]

7. The Trinity and the Principle of *Et-Et*

7.1. Relativization of the Et-Et

From the very first chapter, we have noted that the principle of *et-et* pervades the entire Catholic faith, but it must be learned from Revelation—that is, it should be observed where it is present and not imposed on reality where it is not. In fact, we noted that the highest Reality, God, eludes all categorization. Though we can find the *et-et* also in Him, because He is *both* One *and* Three, it is also true that there are not only two Persons: *both* Father *and* Son. They are three, and so the fundamental axiom is surpassed in the Trinity. That is a good thing! It avoids the temptation of wanting to exhaust the mystery of God in our reflections, categories, and systems—though all these intellectual realities are *per se* fruitful and precious.

---

[127] Sixth Synod of Toledo, *De Trinitate et de Filio Dei Redemptore incarnato* (638) (DS 491). And the Eleventh Synod of Toledo (675) would say: "We do not, however, say that the Virgin Mary gave birth to the unity of this Trinity, but only to the Son, who alone assumed our nature in the unity of His Person" (DS 535). The Sixteenth Synod of Toledo (693) would then say, "Wherefore, although the works of the Holy Trinity are inseparable, we nevertheless profess in faith ... that the entire Trinity has not assumed flesh, but only the Son of God" (DS 571).

[128] See Leo XIII, *Divinum Illud Munus* (1897) (DS 3326). According to Leo XIII, the attribution happens "by a certain comparison and a kind of affinity between the operations and the properties of the Persons."

On the other hand, this does not mean that the *et-et* is a principle that should be forsaken. As we have expressed, it is the principle that permeates the Catholic faith, which certainly has its first and ultimate foundation in the One and Triune God, but has its efficient, exemplar, and final cause in Jesus Christ, God and man. It is underpinned by the fundamental bipolarity of Christ, structuring the entire faith that is, not by accident, called Christian. The believer in the Trinitarian God is not called "Trinitarian" but rather "Christian." It seems trivial, but it is not. Christ, God and man, gives the name to God's children by adoption.

Moreover, the principle of *et-et* actually structures the Christian *faith*. Now faith is a companion on the path of the human being as *viator*, not a dimension of the *comprehensor*, that is, of the blessed in Heaven. The comprehensors no longer have faith, because they see. Thus, the comprehensors, by fixing the eye of the soul on the nature of God, do so by means of the *lumen gloriae*, not through the *lumen fidei* (see Chapter Twelve). No longer needing faith in their contact with God, which is immediate, they no longer need the *et-et* either, just as they no longer need the Sacraments. They contemplate the mystery of God in all its simplicity, in its marvelous absence of composition, which is one reason why they no longer live in the regimen of faith that they experienced when they lived in the world of complexity and composition: a faith that manifests the principle of harmonization of the earthly and created composition precisely in the *et-et*.

And so, we also better understand what Saint John says: "Beloved, we are God's children now; what we shall be has not yet been revealed. We do know that when it is revealed we shall be like him, for we shall see him as he is" (1 John 3:2). In Heaven we shall be adjusted to the divine simplicity and will no longer need the *et-et* of faith, although we will preserve the *et-et* of soul and risen body in our glorified nature. However, on earth this principle is precious, nay, vital to us. It alone marks the path of redemption. It alone speaks of the human being who is spirit and matter, and heals its composition that, after sin, is wounded. This is why the reality of the Holy Trinity does not call the *et-et* into question: it is God the Trinity who, with only the Son becoming incarnate, has given us this fundamental vision of the world, history, and faith. This is the only vision that is able to lead us, one day, before the One who surpasses every perspective and category.

7.2. The *Et-Et Found Again*

Without contradicting what was just said, we can nonetheless note (not impose) the existence of other "synthetic" aspects even in the Trinitarian doctrine. It has already been noted that God is both One and Triune. It should be added that the Persons are, consequently, both personally distinct, and the same reality at the level of nature. In fact, we find here the perfect prototype of the *et-et*, which provides for the non-admissibility of statements in which the principle of non-contradiction is violated. In fact, at first sight to affirm that the Three are three and simultaneously One alone, would seem to violate fundamental logic. Instead it reaffirms it, because the two aspects are only in apparent, and not true contradiction, inasmuch as they do not affirm the two things from the same point of view, but with respect to different aspects. God is One as regards the essence, and Triune as regards the Persons. Therefore, God can simultaneously be both, and this is reasonable. The One who is above and beyond all human logic is not against logic and reasonableness. Therefore, each Person is both absolutely distinct from the other Two and in the other Two (*circumincessio*) and the same nature as Them.

Taking the divine processions into account, we can observe that in God it is possible both to come from no one (the Father), and to come from a Principle (Son and Spirit). Moreover, in God, it is possible to come from Another both by intellectual generation (the Son) and by volitional procession (the Holy Spirit). Furthermore, in God it is possible to come from a unipersonal Principle—the Son proceeds from the Father alone—or to come from a bi-personal Principle—as the Spirit who proceeds from the Father and the Son, as from a unique Principle. This last note leads us to discuss the theme of the *Filioque*, which we shall do next.

It is precisely the *Filioque* that allows us to find a final presence of the *et-et* in the Trinity. Does the Spirit proceed from the Father or from the Son? In fact, it is not necessary to choose: He proceeds from both the Father and from the Son. The hierarchy within the bipolarity is also respected, given that Augustine teaches that the Spirit proceeds mainly from the Father, which does not imply, as we know, that the Son is optional in such a procession. Since the Holy Spirit is the One who unites Father and Son as reciprocal Love, we have an extremely important confirmation of the *et-et* in the heart of the Trinitarian unity itself.

7.3. Hierarchy between Unity and Trinity

To conclude this section on the "synthetic" theology of the Trinity, we must mention the hierarchy between the terms of the bipolarity. They are in this case the Unity of nature and the Trinity of Persons. Which of these two elements should be considered the primary, without downgrading the second? It is possible to respond that the first element is the divine unity. We Christians are monotheists. Our monotheism is, properly understood, very different from that of the Jews and Muslims, because it is a Trinitarian monotheism. Nonetheless, it is true monotheism. "I believe in one God" are the first words of the Symbol of the faith. The divine nature is unique and the nature defines what a thing is. The Trinitarian doctrine illustrates the peculiar characteristic of this nature, which possesses a real relational triad in Itself. But God is first and foremost One, as is seen by the fact that all God's works *ad extra* are carried out by Him as from the divine nature and—for this reason—are always connoted as common to the Persons as well. Therefore, we consider Latin theology, which has traditionally studied the Trinity starting from the Unity, to be better. There is one God, in three Persons. One can reasonably proceed with a different method: to start from the Trinity of Persons and from there move to the Unity. It is our opinion that this second investigative method is more apt when it comes to going from the "economic Trinity" (God "with us") to the "immanent Trinity" (God "in Himself"), and that is why we have also followed this method, placing Chapters Three, Four, and Five before the present one. But when we move on to the study of the immanent Trinity, then we must begin from the unity of God in order to understand the Trinity as an internal characterization of the nature. Of course, this does not imply that the Trinity of Persons is an insignificant aspect (we are not Modalists!). As always, the *et-et*, in affirming the hierarchy of terms, maintains both of them as necessary.

8. Excursus: The *Filioque*

8.1. Historical Data

8.1.1. Ctesiphon

Although many authors do not mention it, the first testimony of the *Filioque* is found in an eastern Synod, held in 410 in Ctesiphon, in modern-day Iraq. At this Synod, the Symbol of the Nicene faith of 325 was accepted and there was a significant addition to the article dedicated to the Holy Spirit: "We profess the living and Holy Spirit, the living Paraclete [who is] of the Father and the Son." In any case, this attestation, for contingent reasons, did not spread.

8.1.2. Synods of Toledo

In the West, the introduction of the *Filioque* was the result of the Synods of Toledo, starting from that of 589, after the conversion of the Visigoth Arians

The Trinity

to Catholicism.[129] Intuitively, the new clause is due to the firm will to reject Arianism, which preaches the inferiority of the Son with respect to the Father. But if the Spirit also proceeds from the Son, clearly the Son is equal in divinity to the Father. The new formula was reiterated by the following Fourth Synod of Toledo in the year 633,[130] and the Sixth Synod of Toledo in 638, which used the very word *Filioque* for the first time.[131] In spite of this, the formula of the Constantinopolitan Symbol remained unchanged. The Eighth Synod of Toledo added the *Filioque* to the Creed in 653. Other synods held later in the same area would maintain the recitation of the Symbol with the *Filioque*.

8.1.3. The Carolingians

In the Kingdom of the Franks, the Spanish texts were known, received, and valued. Particularly in the Carolingian period, the theme of the Most Holy Trinity was debated in various eighth-century synods, especially in contrast with the Adoptionist heresy. The theological collaborators of Charlemagne were convinced of the opportunity to oppose the heretics as had been done in Spain, that is, by making recourse to the *Filioque*. In this case, reaffirming that the Son is Principle of the Holy Spirit contributes to maintaining that Jesus Christ is One of the Holy Trinity, which is one reason why it does not make sense to argue that He was an inferior god or a mere man who was later adopted by God, as the heretics affirm. Among Carolingian theologians, we can mention Saint Paulinus of Aquileia (d. 802) and Blessed Alcuin of York (d. 804). Saint Paulinus presided in a synod in 796–797 in his city of residence as the patriarch of Aquileia, that is, Cividale in Friuli, where the *Filioque* was added to the Creed for the first time in a Frankish area. It seems, however, that the inclusion of the Creed in liturgical use (in the Mass) was only formalized in the Kingdom of the Franks in 799.[132]

8.1.4. Pope Leo III

The addition of the *Filioque* to the Creed sparked disputes and even accusa-

---

[129] "The Holy Spirit proceeds from the Father and the Son [*a Patre et a Filio*]" (Third Synod of Toledo, *De Trinitate Divina* [589] [DS 470]).

[130] "*Ex Patre et Filio*" (Fourth Synod of Toledo, *Symbolum Triado-Christologicum* [633], ch. 1 [DS 485]).

[131] "*De Patre Filioque procedentem*" (Sixth Synod of Toledo, *De Trinitate et de Filio Dei Redemptore Incarnato* [DS 490]).

[132] This is attested by Walafrid Strabo (d. 849), *Ecclesiasticarum rerum exordiis et incrementis liber*, ch. 22. Similarly, Blessed Alcuin of York, *Adversus Felicem* 1.9.

tions of heresy, especially on the part of the Eastern monks. Pope Saint Leo III (d. 816) was also involved in the debate, and he pronounced in favor of the doctrine of the *Filioque*, but believed it was a mistake to put it in the Symbol of the faith acting autonomously, as they did in the kingdom of the Franks. To emphasize his opposition to the inclusion of the clause into the Constantinopolitan Creed, he placed silver tablets in the papal Basilicas of Saint Peter and Saint Paul, bearing the text of the Creed in Greek and Latin, without any addition—a fact that Orthodox theologians still mention today in order to declare that this is the true faith (even of Catholics), contrary to later developments. However, it must be emphasized that Leo III had explicitly approved the doctrine of the *Filioque*, and only rejected the insertion of the term in the text of the Symbol.

8.1.5. Benedict VIII and Michael Cerularius

The culmination point would be reached in 1014, during a synod presided over by Pope Benedict VIII (d. 1024) along with the neo-emperor Saint Henry II (d. 1024). During this synod, Henry noticed that in Rome they sang the Creed without the *Filioque*, contrary to the established custom in the kingdom of the Franks. The emperor asked the Pope why, and after much insistence, he ultimately succeeded in convincing the Pontiff to have the *Filioque* added to Roman practice as well. This innovation represented the starting point for Patriarch Michael Cerularius (d. 1059) to reopen the schism with the Latin Church—a schism that had already been opened by his distant predecessor Photios (d.893) but was later closed. The schism of Cerularius, however, remains to this very day, and marks the separation between the Catholic Church and the Orthodox Churches.

The reason for the schism, which was already expressed by Photios and then repeated by Michael Cerularius, is that the Latin Church had committed an appalling crime of adding something to the Symbol of faith, going against the principle of inviolability of the Nicene Creed: a principle affirmed by various Fathers and by the ecumenical councils themselves.[133] Such an addition, as they say, would also present a grave error in Trinitarian doctrine, because it would introduce a double Principle into the Trinity. Evidently, they were not convinced by what Saint Augustine said in that regard. The Latin

---

[133] However, regarding this matter, the defenders of the *Filioque* have always put forward the historical observation that the Council of Constantinople itself added clauses to the Nicene Creed. Naturally, they were explanatory clauses that deepen and better explain the faith without changing it, and this is also true of the clause regarding the *Filioque*.

The Trinity

Church tried to reconcile with the Eastern Church in the Second Council of Lyon in the year 1274 and then again in the Council of Florence in 1439. Although in both cases they came to an agreement during the councils, after their conclusion, the decrees and decisions were rejected by the Eastern Churches.

8.2. Theological Elements

8.2.1. Biblical Elements

At the biblical level, the *Filioque* is revealed in a form that is implicit but also rather clear, particularly (but not exclusively) in the "sayings of the Paraclete," which we considered above.[134] John 16:7 is very significant. Jesus (the Son), referring to the Holy Spirit, says: "I will send him to you." Regarding this passage, it should be noted that the current tendency of various exegetes and theologians is to interpret these passages only in an "economic" sense. That is to say that these passages would exclusively attest to the temporal mission of the Holy Spirit in the world, with respect to which Jesus is the Principle of sending. But there is a certain resistance to applying these passages to the "immanent Trinity." Now, it is true that the immediate sense of the text is the one reported (i.e., the "economic" one). But we should not forget that our only access to the immanent Trinity is the economic Trinity; moreover, we should not forget that the economic Trinity corresponds—despite all the distinctions of the case—to the immanent Trinity, because God acts according to the way in which He is. It is true that the economic Trinity does not exhaust the hidden mystery of the immanent Trinity, but it still corresponds to it. Thus, if the Son is the origin of the economic mission of the Holy Spirit, this happens (and we are told about it) because in the divine nature He is also the Principle of the Third Person. Denying this theological inference would seriously expose one to the risk of Modalism, for which the Persons and their reciprocal relationships are not real (i.e., they do not subsist really in God, but are only economic, only shown to us).

---

[134] It is impossible to provide a biblical overview on the topic here. Let us just mention that for Saint Paul, the Holy Spirit is also "Spirit of the Son" (see Gal 4:6; Rom 8:9). Commenting on this expression, Saint Augustine of Hippo would say: "Why, then, should we not believe that the Holy Spirit proceedeth also from the Son, seeing that He is likewise the Spirit of the Son?" (*In Evangelium Ioannis tractatus* 99.7, in *NPNF*, First Series, vol. 7, trans. John Gibb and James Innes [Peabody, MA: Hendrickson Publishers, Inc., 1994], 383).

8.2.2. Saint Augustine

The great representative of western patristic theology, including the theme of the *Filioque*, is Saint Augustine, even if there are other attestations before and after him. The first clear affirmation of the doctrine is found in the fourth book of the *De Trinitate*, where—take note!—he inferred the *Filioque* precisely by applying to the immanent Trinity what is found in the economic Trinity, that is, by observing the temporal missions of the Son and Spirit. He writes: "And as for the Holy Spirit to be the Gift of God is to proceed from the Father, so to be sent is to be known as proceeding from Him. Neither can we affirm that the Holy Spirit does not proceed from the Son [*et a Filio*]."[135] Nonetheless, as we have already said, Augustine clarifies two things: first, that the Father and the Son are not two Principles of the Spirit's spiration, but a single Principle[136]; and second, that the Spirit proceeds "*principaliter a Patre*" ("principally from the Father").[137] This last statement is understood in the sense that the Son receives everything from the Father, even being Principle of the Holy Spirit.

8.2.3. The Eastern Fathers

The Eastern Fathers generally prefer to avoid the formula of *Filioque* and speak instead of a procession of the Spirit from the Father *through* (in Greek, *dia*) the Son, not, however, denying a role of the Second Person in the active spiration of the Third.[138] Nonetheless, there is no shortage of texts of the Eastern Fathers that also move in the direction of the *Filioque*, such as this one by Saint Cyril of Alexandria: "For even if the Spirit exists in His own *Hypostasis*, and moreover is considered by Himself insofar as He is the Spirit and not the Son, yet He is not therefore alien from the Son, for He is called the Spirit of Truth and Christ is the Truth, and the Spirit proceeds from Him, just as undoubtedly He also proceeds from the Father."[139]

---

[135] Saint Augustine of Hippo, *De Trinitate* 4.20.29, in *FCNT*, vol. 45, 167–168 (with our corrections).

[136] See Augustine, *De Trinitate* 5.14.15.

[137] See Augustine, *De Trinitate* 15.17.29; 15.26.47.

[138] See, for example, Saint Basil the Great, *De Spiritu Sancto* 16.38; 18.47; Saint Gregory of Nyssa, *Ad Ablabium quod non sint tres dei* 21.

[139] Saint Cyril of Alexandria, *III Epistula ad Nestorium*, in *FCNT*, vol. 76, trans John I. McEnerney (Washington, DC: CUA Press, 1987), 89. Saint Cyril does not use the Greek term *exerchetai* but rather the synonym *procheitai*.

The Trinity

8.2.4. The Middle Ages and the Ecumenical Councils

The medieval theologians accepted, defended, and elaborated on the doctrine of the *Filioque*. On the other hand, this doctrine is no longer a theological thesis but a dogma of faith, confirmed by two ecumenical councils. The Second Council of Lyon expressed itself in the following terms: "We confess faithfully and devoutly that the Holy Spirit proceeds eternally from Father and Son, not as from two principles, but from one, not by two spirations, but by only one."[140] And the Council of Florence: "The Holy Spirit is eternally from the Father and the Son, and He has His essence and his subsistent being at once from the Father and the Son, and He proceeds eternally from Both as from one Principle and one spiration."[141] This council also clarifies the nature of the different formulations in the East and West: "We declare that when the holy Doctors and Fathers say that the Holy Spirit proceeds from the Father through the Son, this tends toward that understanding which signifies that the Son, like the Father, is also what the Greeks call 'Cause' and the Latins 'Principle' of the subsistence of the Holy Spirit."[142]

Notable medieval authors on the theme of the *Filioque* include Saint Anselm of Canterbury, author of *De processione Spiritus Sancti*; Rupert of Deutz (d. 1129), who wrote the *De Spiritu Sancto et operibus eius*; Richard of Saint Victor, who spoke in his *De Trinitate* of the Holy Spirit as of the *Condilectus* (Co-beloved) of the Father and the Son; and naturally Saint Thomas Aquinas, who focused on the *Filioque* in various works, among which we shall only mention *Contra errores graecorum* here. These and various other authors confirmed Augustinian theology and paved the way for the dogmatic conciliar definitions, which we have referred to above.

---

[140] Second Council of Lyon, *De Processione Spiritus Sancti* (1274) (DS 850).

[141] Council of Florence, *Laetentur Caeli* (1439) (DS 1300).

[142] Council of Florence, *Laetentur Caeli* (DS 1301). The text continues by confirming Augustinian theology again: "And since the Father Himself has given to His only begotten Son, in generating Him, all that the Father has except being the Father, the Son Himself eternally has from the Father, from Whom He is eternally generated, precisely this: that the Holy Spirit proceeds from the Son." Therefore, it can no longer be said that the theology of Saint Augustine in regard to the *Filioque* is debatable or even mistaken, because the solemn Magisterium of the Catholic Church made this doctrine its own. The same teachings are repeated once again by the same Council, in the Bull *Cantate Domino* (DS 1331).

8.2.5. Distinction between Liturgical Custom and Dogmatic Assent

In conclusion, although the ecumenical cause is certainly important to us, we must remember that for us Catholics the *Filioque* is not a theological thesis that is subject to free discussion, but rather a dogma of the faith, and therefore it is undeniable. It is certainly possible to recite the Creed without inserting this clause (as the Catholics of the Eastern Churches in communion with Rome do: in this sense, Saint John Paul II has sometimes recited the Nicene-Constantinopolitan Creed without the *Filioque*, along with representatives of Orthodox Churches). On the other hand, what is not possible is to expunge the *Filioque* from the *depositum fidei*.

At the doctrinal level, it is permissible to use various formulae: the Spirit "proceeds from the Father"; "from the Father and from the Son"; "from the Father through the Son." But underlying the different formulations there must be a common doctrine: that the Third One in God proceeds from a single Principle, which is the Father and/with the Son. For this reason, the late Eastern formula, coined by Photios and absent in the Greek Fathers, according to which the Holy Spirit "proceeds from the Father *alone*," does not appear compatible with this dogmatic content. On the other hand, it is enough to observe that the Father is never "alone," insofar as He is always Father because, and only if, the Son is always with Him. It is precisely for this reason that the formula "proceeds from the Father"—if properly understood—can be admitted. In fact, if the Holy Spirit proceeds from the Father, and the Father is such because He has the Son, it is implicit that the procession of the Holy Spirit has as His origin the Father and/with the Son.

There is no difficulty in maintaining the custom of two distinct liturgical customs. But there cannot be two different dogmatic faiths if there is to be the communion of the one Church.

7

The Mother of God

1. The Placement of the Treatise on Mary

After having discussed God both in His unity and in His main properties, and having presented the essential points about the three divine Persons and their reciprocal relations, we see this as an opportune place for a chapter on the Blessed Virgin Mary, who Saint Thomas Aquinas defined, with a marvelous image, as the *Triclinium totius Trinitatis*:

> Like all the Saints, St. Thomas had a great devotion to Our Lady. He described Her with a wonderful title: *Triclinium totius Trinitatis*; *triclinium*, that is, a place where the Trinity finds rest since, because of the Incarnation, in no creature as in Her do the three divine Persons dwell and feel delight and joy at dwelling in Her soul full of Grace. Through Her intercession we may obtain every help.[1]

1. Link with the Trinity

The first valid reason we can speak here of the Blessed Virgin Mary, before other themes, is Her unique and unrepeatable link with the Holy Trinity, to which we dedicated the previous chapter. Our Lady is rightly called Daughter

---

[1] Benedict XIV, *General Audience*, June 23, 2010. Saint Thomas Aquinas uses the expression *totius Trinitatis nobile triclinium* in the *Expositio salutationis angelicae* 1. However, he did not create the title, but he adopted it from the Sequence *Salve Mater Salvatoris*, composed by Adam of Saint Victor (d. 1192).

of the eternal Father, Mother of the divine Son, and Spouse and Temple of the Holy Spirit.

2. Christocentrism

A second reason for this placement consists in the Christocentrism that has been adopted for our entire treatise, which emerges from the first pages of this work. Effectively, Mary is directly connected to Christ. "Mariology"—the theology of Mary—is mainly a consequence of Christology.[2] Mary is great because She is the Mother of Christ the Lord. All of Her privileges derive from Her divine Maternity, including the fullness of grace with which She is adorned.

3. Full of Grace

Thirdly, the Virgin Mary is the masterpiece of all creation. We have already presented the Catholic faith concerning the creation of the human being and concerning grace (see Chapters Three and Five). Creation reaches its culmina-

---

[2] Theologians speak of "Christotypical Mariology" when the study of Our Lady is done primarily on the basis of the link between Her and Christ, while they speak of "ecclesiotypical Mariology" when Mary is seen primarily as a Disciple of the Lord and as the most eminent Member of the Church. In the past, the first one was considered Catholic, and the second was considered Protestant. Today things have changed because, with the Second Vatican Council having included its own Mariological treatment in the ecclesiological constitution *Lumen Gentium*, many Catholic theologians have also felt the need to develop an ecclesiotypical Mariology. We must recall that the Second Vatican Council wanted to dedicate to Our Lady a document of Her own, and that the inclusion in *Lumen Gentium* was only due to the desire not to multiply the number of published documents—not to an underlying theological decision. Moreover, there was no agreement among the conciliar Fathers on the question, with them being split in half on this inclusion. After several vicissitudes, the voting that decided in favor of including a Mariological chapter in the ecclesiological constitution came about with a marginal difference of only 35 votes in favor (1114 yes; 1074 no; 5 null votes must be subtracted from the difference of 40). We cannot rule out the possibility that many of the Fathers who voted affirmatively did so for the aforementioned practical reasons. We shall add that the chapter of *Lumen Gentium* that treats of Our Lady is entitled "The Blessed Virgin Mary, Mother of God, in the Mystery of Christ and the Church": first of all, she is called Mother of God, a Christotypical and not ecclesiotypical title; secondly, the consideration of Her in the mystery of Christ precedes consideration of Her in the mystery of the Church. Saint John Paul II, *Redemptoris Mater* (1987), §5, writes that the Council "by presenting Mary in the mystery of Christ, also finds the path to a deeper understanding of the mystery of the Church." All of this is not to deny the ecclesiotypical aspects of Mary, but to remind us that the Second Vatican Council did not decide in favor of an ecclesiotypical Mariology, as is often maintained. Finally, Mariologists today prefer to speak of a multifaceted approach to the mystery of Mary: anthropological, Christological, ecclesiological, cultural, etc.

tion in Mary: She is the perfect Woman, the New Eve. And for what regards the supernatural order, the Archangel Gabriel calls her "full of grace" (Luke 1:28 , RSVCE). There is no other creature in the world who has ever possessed, who possesses, or who will possess more grace than Mary. Naturally, this fullness is relative to Her being *only* a creature. Mary is the only human being who is only a creature and who possesses the fullness of grace, as a gratuitous gift from on high. In an absolute sense, the fullness of grace does not belong to Her, but to Jesus Christ, who, as man, is creature, but not only a creature. The fullness of divinity abides in Him (see Col 2:9), thus the highest degree of grace in absolute terms is found in Christ, not Mary; yet Mary receives from Christ the fullness of the grace that adorns Her. After Christ, the privileged place is that of Mary. Thus, She is the summit of creation and of the new creation in Christ.

4. Mother of the Church

Finally, it seems good to include here the exposition of the Mariological doctrine because Our Lady is also Mother of the Church[3] and the perfect model for every Christian, in addition to being an image and anticipatory prophecy of the resurrection, which is the destiny for those who will be saved.[4] Thus, the discussion of Mary allows us to connect the doctrine of the Trinity with that of the Church, which we shall see in the next chapter.

2. Mary and the Trinity

2.1. Mary and the Individual Divine Persons

2.1.1. Appropriations

The link between Mary and the Trinity is evident from the fact that She is Mother of God, and the Christian God is the Most Holy Trinity. The

---

[3] "For the glory of the Most Holy Virgin and for our consolation, we proclaim Mary Most Holy the Mother of the Church, that is to say, Mother of all Christian people, both the faithful and the Shepherds, who call Her most loving Mother; and we wish that from now on She be honored and invoked by all Christian people with this most grateful title" (Saint Paul VI, *Closing Speech of the Third Session of the Second Vatican Council*, November 21, 1964 [our translation]).

[4] Rupert of Deutz (d. 1130) says that Mary is, with respect to the Church, "the most exalted, the greatest, the preeminent part, the most elect part" (*Commentaria in Apocalypsim* 1.8.12 [our translation]).

mystery of Mary is rooted in the mystery of the Trinitarian God. As was mentioned, the Tradition attributed to Mary the titles of Daughter of the eternal Father, Mother of the divine Son, and Spouse and Temple of the Holy Spirit. With respect to these titles, one must bear in mind the clarification we already presented during our treatment of the Trinity: the actions of God ad extra—except, as regards its final stage, the Incarnation of the Son—are operations that are common to the three Persons. Therefore, we must not hypothesize here an action proper to God as Father of Mary, or of the Spirit as the Spouse of Mary. These are attributions that are given on account of greater consonance between the individual graces granted to Mary and the personal properties of the divine Hypostases.

In the case of divine Motherhood, however, things should be further clarified, because on one hand it concerns an attribution to the Son, but on the other hand, it does not. When it is said that Mary is Mother of God, indeed, we are referring to the Incarnation only of the Son (not the Father or the Spirit) in Her. In this sense, it is not a simple attribution to the Son of an operation *ad extra*, but rather this operation in its final stage is proper (not only appropriated) to the Son alone. With his usual genius, Saint Anselm discusses the matter:

> Indeed, God assumed a human nature not in such way that the divine nature and the human nature were one and the same but in such way that the Person of God and the person of the man [who thus does not exist] were one and the same. But this [assumption of a human nature] can occur only in the case of one person of God. For it is incomprehensible that different Persons be one and the same Person with one and the same man. For if one man were one Person with several other distinct [divine] Persons, then [here would be an instance in which] a plurality of Persons who are different from one another would have to be one and the same Person—something impossible. Therefore, when God is incarnate with respect to any one of His Persons, it is impossible that He be incarnate with respect to another of His Persons as well.[5]

If we speak, on the other hand, of the Incarnation as an intervention of God in the world, it is a Trinitarian work. Therefore, when we speak of Mary

---

[5] Saint Anselm of Canterbury (d. 1109), *Epistula de Incarnatione* 9, in *Complete Philosophical and Theological Treatises of Anselm of Canterbury*, trans. by Jasper Hopkins and Herbert Richardson (Minneapolis, MN: The Arthur J. Banning Press, 2000), 283.

as Mother of the divine Son, that title implies the proper action of the Son becoming incarnate while, for the divine nature, it refers to the decision and action that has led the Logos to become flesh, which is a decision and work of God, and thus is common to the three Persons.

2.1.2. Daughter of the Father

Therefore, a special fatherhood of Mary is attributed to the Father, just as creation is attributed to Him. Mary is the beloved creature of the Father: the most exalted creature from Whom the Father wished to take humanity so that it may be assumed by the Son in view of our redemption. By offering a human nature to the Son of the Father, Mary uses Her freedom to cooperate (*fiat*: Luke 1:38) in the plan of salvation that passes through the redemption.

The attribution of the title of "Daughter of the Father" to Mary appears more than fitting, given that the Father possesses the attribute of Creator, and creation was a work of the divine omnipotence. Now, among creatures—as we have said—there is none more perfect than Mary. Consequently, the creative omnipotence of God shines more brightly in Her than in any creature.

2.1.3. Mother of the Son

It is proper to the Son alone to become incarnate by taking His flesh from Mary. Thus, the *Logos* is the Son of the Father as regards divinity, but also of the Mother relative to His humanity. This is based on the *communicatio idiomatum*, which we spoke of in Chapter Four (Council of Ephesus, against Nestorius). Mary is Mother of the Son not because She has generated Him eternally—this generation, in fact, happens in God for all eternity and not in time, and it belongs to the Father alone. However, She has generated Him in time, because She has generated the humanity that He has assumed, and thus She has generated in the world the incarnate Person of the Son of God.[6] Thus, as has been noted, She is called Mother of God fully and truthfully.

---

[6] After the Council of Ephesus, a text was written to reunite the Fathers of the Council and the Eastern Bishops, gathered under the guidance of Patriarch John of Antioch (d. 442). The text, known as *Formula unionis*, was signed by the parties involved in 433. It states: "We acknowledge that our Lord Jesus Christ . . . was begotten of the Father before the ages in respect to His divinity, but in the final days the same was born for our sake and for our salvation of the Virgin Mary in respect to His humanity. . . . We acknowledge that the holy Virgin is the God-bearer because the God-Word took flesh and became man, and, from His very conception, He made one with Himself the temple [the body] taken from Her" (DS 272).

The Mother of God

Moreover, it is again confirmed that the Greek title of *Theotokos*—literally "She who gives birth/generates God," which in Latin is rendered with *Deipara* or *Dei genetrix*—is the fundamental Marian title, on which all other such titles depend.

2.1.4. Bride of the Holy Spirit

Moreover, Our Lady is called Bride of the Holy Spirit, because in the Gospel according to Luke the angel Gabriel explicitly says: "The holy Spirit will come upon you, and the power of the Most High will overshadow you. Therefore the child to be born will be called holy, the Son of God" (Luke 1:35). The angelic announcement links the mysterious impregnation in the virginal womb of Mary Most Holy to the action of the Holy Spirit. By analogy with the natural process of human generation, the Tradition has thus attributed the title of Bride of the Holy Spirit to Mary.[7] Of course, this is again just an attribution: if the Spirit were Mary's Spouse in the proper sense, He would be the Father of Jesus, that is, one would have to say that the Spirit is the Father of the incarnate Word, which is impossible, because the Father of the Word is the First Person, not the Third.[8] What is attributed to the Person of the Holy Spirit is to create the humanity that the Son assumes, drawing it from the humanity of Mary. On the other hand, it has been said (and we shall repeat it) that apart from the assumption of humanity, which is done only by the Son, everything that happens in the Incarnation is a common work of the Father, Son, and Holy Spirit, and thus the mysterious impregnation of the most pure womb of the Ever-Virgin Mary is a

---

[7] Saint Francis of Assisi (d. 1226) writes in a prayer: "Holy Virgin Mary, there is no one like Thee born in the world among women, Daughter and Handmaid of the Most Highest King, the Heavenly Father, Mother of Our Most Holy Lord Jesus Christ, Spouse of the Holy Spirit" (translation: *franciscan-archive.org*). Saint Louis-Marie Grignion de Montfort (d. 1716) attests that "God the Holy Spirit entrusted His wondrous gifts to Mary, His faithful Spouse, and chose Her as the Dispenser of all He possesses" (*Traité de la vraie dévotion à la Sainte Vierge* [*True Devotion to Mary*], no. 25, in *God Alone: The Collected Writings of St. Louis Marie de Montfort* [Bay Shore, NY: Montfort Publications, 1997], 296). Saint John Paul II, *Redemptoris Mater*, §26, teaches: "The Holy Spirit had already come down upon Her, and She became His faithful Spouse at the Annunciation, welcoming the Word of the true God."

[8] "[Jesus] is God generated from the substance of the Father before all ages; and He is man born from the substance of a mother in time" (*Symbolum Quicumque vult* [DS 76]). "[Jesus is] Son of Mary and Son of God" (Ignatius of Antioch, *Ad Ephesios* 7.2, in *FCNT*, vol. 1, trans. Francis X. Glimm, Joseph M.F. Marique, and Gerald G. Walsh [Washington, DC: CUA Press, 1947], 90). "Mary brought to light one Son alone, Who, being the only Son of the Father, is also the only Son of His earthly Mother" (Blessed Guerric of Igny [d. 1157], *Sermo I in Assumptione beatae Mariae* [our translation]).

common work as well. Just as the Trinity created human beings in the beginning, created Adam and Eve, so the Trinity created Mary, the New Eve; and the humanity of Jesus, the Second and Final Adam.

2.1.5. Temple of the Holy Spirit

Another way of describing the relationship of Mary with the Holy Spirit is the way that gives Her the title of Temple. In recalling Her relationships with the three divine Persons, the Second Vatican Council chose this title: Mary "is endowed with the high office and dignity of being the Mother of the Son of God, by which account She is also the beloved Daughter of the Father and the Temple of the Holy Spirit."[9] The title emphasizes God's work of dwelling in Mary by grace (see in the previous chapter, the texts relating to the theme "The Spirit Dwells").

2.1.6. Handmaid of the Trinity

The fact that the Trinity works in a common way in the life of Mary does not mean, however, that this common action does not happen with a personal characterization. In this sense it is God who acts in Mary, but it is the Trinitarian God; thus, the common and unique action is internally characterized by a real threefold reflection of the one divine nature. This does not involve divisions in the divinity, but it certainly can be the basis, on the part of the creature (Mary in this case), for a relationship with God that is characterized by this harmonious and inalienable plurality of the one and most simple divine nature. This gives origin, for Mary, to a relationship with God that certainly is one and indivisible, but which is lived in the three-dimensionality of an experience of spiritual life that is Trinitarian. Thus, in addition to being the Mother of God, Mary is also the Handmaid of the Trinity, and is thus the first who lived a spiritual life that was completely Christian.

2.1.7. Guardian of the Mystery

Although She was formed in the strictly monotheist religiosity of the People

---

[9] Second Vatican Council, *Lumen Gentium* (1964), §53. See also, Saint John Paul II, *General Audience*, January 10, 1996, which at §5 shows the link between the Marian titles "Bride" and "Temple." In Italy, "Temple of the Holy Spirit" (*"Tempio dello Spirito Santo"*) is also the translation usually proposed for the Litany of Loreto, which invokes Mary as *Vas spirituale* ("Spiritual Vessel").

of Israel, the Daughter of Zion was the first to know that the Mystery of the one God has a Trinitarian inner life. Our Lady was the first creature in history to know and believe that God is One and Three. She was the first to have a spiritual life characterized by the complete and perfect doctrine of God. Thus, She is the star that guides the path of faith and the spiritual life of all believers. Our Lady is not only an example of faith because Her faith was perfect with respect to the abandonment to the will of God (*fides qua*)—though this aspect is certainly fundamental. Her faith is also a perfect model for us for the doctrinal aspect (*fides quae*): even before the Apostles and disciples were chosen and instructed by Christ, Mary was the first guardian of the most concealed mystery of God, that which regards His intimate Trinitarian life. She knew before Peter and the other Apostles that God is Father, Son, and Holy Spirit. She knew before them that the Son had become incarnate for our salvation. She knew in Herself before any other the omnipotent action of the Holy Spirit. Mary was not only the Tabernacle that guarded the Lord within herself,[10] but also the first Guardian of the Christian faith, in its dual aspect of personal trust and doctrinal profession. For this reason, the Christian Tradition always continues to see in Her the Guardian and Defender of the faith, and it has expressed this in a marvelous antiphon that was found in the Missal and Breviary preceding the last liturgical reform: "*Gaude, Maria Virgo, cunctas haereses tu sola interemisti in universo mundo*" ("Rejoice, Virgin Mary, you alone have destroyed all the heresies in the whole world").[11]

2.2. The New Eve

The Marian title of New Eve is based on the "*Protevangelium*" (Gen 3:15), traditionally considered a prophecy about the future coming of the Redeemer from the Woman descended from Eve (see Chapter Three). Despite the philological difficulties that the translation of this text has encountered (on which we do not need to focus), it is important to point out that from the earliest times of the Church, Mary was also considered in reference to Eve.

---

[10] "She became in some way a 'tabernacle'—the first 'tabernacle' in history" (Saint John Paul II, *Ecclesia de Eucharistia* (2003), §55).

[11] *Breviarium Romanum* (1568), "Commune Festorum beatae Mariae Virginis," *Antiphona in III Nocturno*. The antiphon actually goes back to at least the eighth century, but it was added by Saint Pius V (d. 1572) to the Breviary with the addition of the words "*in universo mundo.*"

2.2.1. *Christological Value*

We have already previously referred to this Marian title, which is very old (second century). It was used for the first time by Saint Irenaeus of Lyon (d. ca. 202),[12] who was also the first Father of the Church to reflect broadly on what Saint Paul says regarding Christ when he calls Him the Second and Last Adam.[13] In the context of his reflections on Christ, Saint Irenaeus recognized that it is also possible to coin a similar title for Mary, calling Her the New Eve.[14] Here the relationship is analogous; thus, it involves points of similarity and points of difference with Adam and Eve. (1) The latter were husband and wife, while Christ and Mary are Son and Mother. The first point of difference lies here. (2) The second difference is what Saint Paul already notes in his letters (at least regarding Christ): Adam and Eve were sinners, whereas Christ and Mary are immaculate. This is a strength of the parallelism, which is deliberately posed as antithetical.

In fact, Saint Paul and Saint Irenaeus make recourse to this comparison precisely to emphasize the radical difference between the first human beings, on the one hand, and Jesus and Mary on the other. Adam sinned and condemned all; Christ did not sin and saved all. Eve sinned, marring herself and contributing to the ruin of others; Mary did not sin, remaining immaculate and cooperating in the salvation of others. In fact, it should be stated that in the Scriptures and in classical theology, original sin in a proper sense is not that of Eve but that of Adam. Eve was the cause of Adam's sin and thus she

---

[12] Even though he did not use the title of New Eve, Saint Justin Martyr (d. 165), an immediate predecessor and a contemporary of Irenaeus, instituted a parallelism between Eve and Mary: see *Dialogus cum Tryphone Iudaeo* 100.

[13] The reflection on Mary the New Eve was then developed by many Fathers and ecclesiastical writers. Here is an example: "Evil came from the woman, likewise good was obtained through the woman; given that, if by the work of Eve we have fallen, it is by the work of Mary that we now stand; by Eve we are prostrate, by Mary we rise; Eve led us to slavery, Mary obtained freedom for us; Eve caused us to be enslaved for a long time, Mary renewed us; Eve caused our condemnation on account of the fruit of the tree, Mary acquitted us with the fruit of another tree, since Christ was hung like a fruit on a tree [the cross]" (Saint Ambrose of Milan [d. 397], *Sermo 45*.2 [our translation]).

[14] See Saint Irenaeus of Lyon, *Adversus haereses* 3.22.4. Also found there is the famous phrase: "What the virgin Eve had bound fast through unbelief, this did the virgin Mary set free through faith" (in *ANF*, vol. 1, trans. James Donaldson and Alexander Roberts [Peabody, MA: Hendrickson Publishers, Inc., 1885], 455). This very old perspective is the basis of the devotion to Mary, born in the German-speaking world, of "*Knötenloserin*" ("loosener of knots") depicted by J.G.M. Schmidtner (d. 1705) in a painting today preserved at Augsburg. The title implies that Mary is able to untangle even the most difficult problems.

cooperated in the ruin of the whole human race. By analogous antithesis, Mary is not the cause of salvation of the whole human race, a cause that is Christ, but She cooperates with Her Son in its redemption.

2.2.2. Anthropological Value

Saying that Mary is the New Eve does not refer only to Her behavior, which perfectly cooperates with that of Christ for salvation. Mary is also the New Eve in the sense that She is the "reformed" or renewed Eve, as Christ is the Second Man, or Second Adam, because He is a man without sin, as was the case at the beginning of creation. In Mary, then, we find the perfect woman, just as in Christ we find the perfect man. In Her, we find woman as God the Creator intended her in His plan. This is the anthropological value: in Mary we see Eve as she should have been. We read in a speech of Saint Andrew of Crete (d. 740):

> The shame of sin has obscured the splendor and mystique of human nature; but when the Mother of Beauty *par excellence* is born, this nature recovers, in Her person, its ancient privileges and is shaped according to a model who is perfect and truly worthy of God. . . . Today the reform of our nature begins, and the aged and weary world, subject to a completely divine transformation, receives the first fruits of the second creation.[15]

2.2.3. Pneumatological Value

Finally, there is the pneumatological aspect, that is, the one concerning the Holy Spirit with respect to the grace that He dispenses. Mary is the perfect woman from the vantage point of nature (natural order) but also from the standpoint of grace (supernatural order). In Her, grace reaches its summit, because it does not encounter any obstacle in a creature that does not have original sin—consequently, She is not affected by concupiscence. And, given Her election as the Mother of God, She is endowed by the Creator with the greatest gifts of nature and grace. In this sense, Our Lady is a model of the Christian, but it must be added that She is an unreachable model.[16] We who

---

[15] Saint Andrew of Crete, *Sermo I de Nativitate Mariae* (our translation).

[16] "After saying that Mary is a 'type of the Church,' the Council adds that She is her 'outstanding model,' an example of perfection to be followed and imitated. Indeed, Mary is an 'outstanding model' because Her perfection surpasses that of all the other members of

are sinners can partially resemble Her, but we will never be like Her; not only because She is Mother of God—no one else could be that—but also because She is (in addition to Christ) the only one whom we know for sure to be Immaculate.[17] For this reason Pius XII (d. 1958) wrote: "The holy Mother of God was, at the very moment of Her Immaculate Conception, so filled with grace as to surpass the grace of all the saints."[18]

2.3. The Privileges of Mary Most Holy

2.3.1. Predestination

It is clear from what has been said why Mary was granted privileges that no other creature ever possessed nor would ever possess; privileges that we shall look at later in this chapter. They derive from a mystery of predestination, which was highlighted well by Blessed John Duns Scotus (d. 1308), who is known for having been an advocate of the Immaculate Conception of the Virgin. Our Lady was predested from eternity to be the Mother of God. This mystery of predestination makes of Her the summit of all creation and the specially beloved creature of the Most Holy Trinity. This does not contradict what the Tradition sustains regarding the Incarnation of the Son. We saw that the Son became incarnate primarily to heal the sin of Adam, and in the hypothetical case of the latter not having sinned, we have to believe it absolutely more probable that the *Logos* would not have become incarnate. But in this case—one might object—Mary would not have been the Mother of God; instead Her eternal predestination to this office implies that God decided from eternity to become incarnate! Although this problem is difficult—as are virtually all theological questions related to predestination, one of the most unfathomable mysteries of faith—we can nonetheless respond by noting the following:

(1) The fact that God *knows* in His omniscience that the human being will sin does not imply that the human being must sin; the sin remains a free choice even if the divine foreknowledge knows it in advance and thus can predestine Our Lady to become the Mother of the Word incarnate. In itself,

---

the Church" (Saint John Paul II, *General Audience*, August 06, 1997, §4). The expression "unreachable model" has been used for Mary by Saint John Paul II in the *Homily at the Mass in Piazza del Campo (Siena, Italy)*, September 14, 1980, §2.

[17] Even if we someday manage to deduce from Revelation, with certainty, that others were preserved from original sin (for example, the prophet Elijah or Saint Joseph [see below]), Mary's uniqueness as Mother of God would remain.

[18] Pius XII, *Ad Caeli Reginam* (1954) (DS 3917).

therefore, the eternal predestination of Mary and the redemptive character of the Incarnation are doctrines that do not contradict each other.

(2) Divine predestination is infallible, but this does not take away the fact that God includes conditionality in it. God predestines, from eternity, Mary to be the Mother of Christ *in the case in which*, and at the same time *knowing infallibly that*, man will freely sin. The conditionality is relative to the fact that God *knows* that man will *freely* sin. Thus, the infallibility of predestination is due to this infallible knowledge on the part of God, while the freedom of Adam's deed is preserved by the conditionality that God includes in His decree of Our Lady's predestination.

(3) Faced with these speculative complications, some might be inclined to think that the Scotist thesis (which we have rejected) about the motive for the Incarnation resolves all these problems through a simpler response: it would be enough to say that the Incarnation is not linked to sin. However, such an opinion actually implies other significant problems, as has been mentioned before when dealing with this issue. Moreover, theology does not consist in finding the simplest path at all costs, but in explaining what God has revealed to us in words and deeds. And we have recalled, with Saint Thomas Aquinas, that Scripture always affirms that Christ came to heal sin.

2.3.2. Regality

The eternal predestination of Mary to be the Mother of God, the Ark of the new and eternal covenant, the perfect creature, the One full of grace, and the Triclinium of the entire Trinity, implies that from eternity God also predestined Her to be the summit of creation: not only of what is visible but also what is invisible. Saint John Damascene (d. 749) writes: "Mary really did become Lady of all created things, since She was accounted Mother of the Creator."[19] That is why the Virgin Mary is not only Mother of the Church and the perfect human creature, but She is also elevated above all creatures, even those who in themselves are superior by nature, namely, the celestial spirits. This is one reason why the faith of the Church sees in Mary the Queen not only of all the saints, but also the Queen of angels, the Queen of Heaven, and the Queen of the entire universe.[20] It is no wonder that Saint

---

[19] Saint John Damascene, *De fide orthodoxa* 4.14, in *FCNT*, vol. 37, trans. Frederic H. Chase, Jr. (Washington, DC: CUA Press, 1958), 363.

[20] A Marian liturgical memorial with this title is celebrated on August 22. Pope Pius XII introduced it with the encyclical *Ad Caeli Reginam*. In the text it is emphasized that the regal dignity of Mary is based primarily on the divine Maternity (see DS 3913). The Pope then adds that the regality of Mary is—like that of Christ—not only a birthright, but also

Thomas wrote that "the Most Holy Virgin, on account of being Mother of God, obtains from the infinite Good that is God a dignity that is in a certain sense infinite."[21]

3. Mary and Christ

3.1. The "Infancy Narratives"

3.1.1. Natural Link

The link of Mary to Christ, Son and Word of God, is mentioned even in the first pages of the Gospel. The evangelists Matthew and Luke, albeit in different ways (understandably), offer us in the first chapters of their writings the "Infancy Narratives," so called because they describe the first years of Jesus' life. In these texts, the link between Jesus and Mary is showcased in a very clear way. Even in the natural order, there is a very close bond between a mother and her child, whom she carries in her womb for nine months. This should not be overlooked, because such a bond is not established with anyone else in the world, not even with the natural father. The mother is occupied with breastfeeding and still today, despite the fact that the role of women in western society has changed greatly, it is usually she who spends the most time with the child, nourishing, taking care of every need, and educating. Virgil recalls that the child begins to know the world starting with his mother's smile[22]: indeed, that is the first thing that one learns to recognize in this life. But in the case of Our Lady and Christ, the link is even stronger and is also at the supernatural level.

---

an acquired right (see DS 3914). It is a birthright because She is the Mother of God. It is an acquired right insofar as Mary earned Her own queenship with Her cooperation in the salvific work of Her Son (see DS 3915–3916).

[21] *ST* I, q. 25, a. 6 (our translation).

[22] "*Incipe, parve puer, risu cognoscere matrem*" ("Begin, o little child, to know the mother by a smile": Virgil [Publius Vergilius Maro, d. 19 B.C.], *Bucolic*, "Fourth Eclogue"). In the fourth Eclogue, Virgil celebrates the future birth of a divine child, who will bring peace to the empire. Since his work was published (ca. 38 B.C.) before the birth of Jesus, Christian scribes saw a sort of pagan prophet in Virgil, who had predicted the future birth of Christ from Mary. He was considered as such for the whole Middle Ages and thus Dante Alighieri (d. 1321) chose him, in the *Divine Comedy*, not only as master of the poetic style but also as a "holy pagan" who accompanies him through Hell and Purgatory.

3.1.2. Supernatural Conception

1. Matthew

The Gospels indeed teach that something happened in Christ's conception in Mary's womb that went beyond all common natural laws. Saint Matthew simply reports the fact with the following words: "Now this is how the birth of Jesus Christ came about. When his mother Mary was betrothed to Joseph, but before they lived together, she was found with child through the holy Spirit" (Matt 1:18). He adds that the virginal conception of Christ from Mary was foretold in the Old Testament, and it is in this regard that he quotes a famous prophecy of the prophet Isaiah: "the young woman, pregnant and about to bear a son, shall name him Emmanuel" (Isa 7:14 = Matt 1:23).[23] Immanuel means "God is with us." Saint Joseph, betrothed to Mary, is entrusted by an angel, who appears to him in a dream, with the task of being the legal father of the child, which implies that it will be he who gives the name Jesus (which means "God saves") and that the child will officially belong to the Israelite tribe of the father, namely, the tribe of Judah, the same tribe of the great king David. To avoid misunderstandings, in the closing of his recount, the evangelist repeats: "[Joseph] did as the angel of the Lord had commanded him and took his wife into his home. He *had no relations with her* [did not *know* her] until she bore a son, and he named him Jesus" (Matt 1:24–25, emphasis added). "To know" in the Bible also indicates the sexual act, which thus was not the cause of Jesus' conception. From where, then, does this child come? The angel says it clearly to Saint Joseph in the dream: "Do not be afraid to take Mary your wife into your home. For it is through the holy Spirit that this child has been conceived in her" (Matt 1:20).

Thus, in the space of very few verses Saint Matthew repeats three times that Jesus was not conceived through a man's intervention, and that Saint Joseph is only His legal, or "putative" (i.e., held as such) father. Mary, on the other hand, is explicitly called "His Mother" (Matt 1:18). The special link between Mary and Christ is clearly affirmed, as is the supernatural origin of this Man's conception from His mother alone without the intervention of any

---

[23] "The Old Testament does not contain a formal announcement of the virginal maternity, fully revealed only in the New Testament. Nonetheless, the oracle of Isaiah (Isa 7:14) prepares the Revelation of this mystery, and it has been clarified in this sense in the Greek translation of the Old Testament. Citing the prophecy thus translated, the Gospel of Matthew proclaims its perfect fulfillment by means of the conception of Jesus in the virginal womb of Mary" (Saint John Paul II, *General Audience*, January 31, 1996, §7 [our translation]).

human father. Holy Scripture attributes the miracle of this conception to the Holy Spirit.

2. Luke: Birth of the Baptist

The same revealed doctrine is found again in Saint Luke, who narrates with quite a bit of detail how the events came to pass. At the very beginning of his Gospel, Luke declares that he wants to report the content of the scrupulous research he has conducted, to present in an orderly sequence the result of his investigation that, on several occasions, is not found in the writings before his Gospel, which were already circulating (e.g., the Gospels of Mark and Matthew, with which there are many points of convergence, but with respect to which he also adds new details). Saint Luke begins by recounting the birth of Saint John the Baptist, the Precursor of Christ, which was also miraculous, even though the Baptist was conceived in a natural manner, by his parents. The miracles that accompany this birth consist in the fact that the parents were already very advanced in years and did not think themselves capable of having children, because the mother, Saint Elizabeth, was sterile (Luke 1:7). The miracle here consists in the divine intervention through which a sterile woman conceives a son. However, the conception occurs in a natural way, with the Hebrew priest Saint Zechariah being John's father (Saint John thus belongs to the priestly tribe of the Levites).

A second miracle concerns Saint Zechariah himself: he also receives an angelic vision, but he doubts the promise of a son who will be given to him. As a result, he is deprived of speech and becomes mute until he gives to the son the name told to him by the angel: John, which means "God is favorable" (Luke 1:8–20, 59–66). This miracle only appears punitive. It was actually interpreted as a sign: the father will remain without voice until that boy is born who will call himself "a voice of one crying out in the desert,"[24] echoing a prophecy of Isaiah (Isa 40:3–5; see Luke 3:1–6; Matt 3:1–3; Mark 1:1–4; and especially John 1:19–23).

---

[24] So Saint Augustine of Hippo comments in *Sermo* 293.2: "Zechariah is silent and loses his voice until John, the precursor of the Lord, is born and restores his voice. The silence of Zechariah is nothing but the age of prophecy lying hidden, obscured, as it were, and concealed before the preaching of Christ. At John's arrival Zechariah's voice is released, and it becomes clear at the coming of the one who was foretold. The release of Zechariah's voice at the birth of John is a parallel to the rending of the veil at Christ's crucifixion. If John were announcing his own coming, Zechariah's lips would not have been opened. The tongue is loosened because a voice is born" (in *Liturgy of the Hours*, "Office of Readings of the Nativity of St. John the Baptist," June 24).

The Mother of God

3. Luke: The Annunciation

As for the birth of Christ, Saint Luke describes the announcement that the angel Gabriel makes to Mary of the future miraculous birth of Her Son, while requesting for Her free consent. The angel calls Her "full of grace" [NABRE renders it, "favored one"], a designation that leaves Mary pensive about its meaning.[25] The angel clarifies that Our Lady has "found favor with God," which means that what will happen in Her is a fruit of the mysterious divine design, which has prechosen Her for the incomparably great task of giving a human nature to the Son of God, becoming His Mother. Before such an announcement, the Virgin Mary remains—if it is permissible to express it this way—with Her feet firmly grounded. From time immemorial, it has never been seen that a virgin can give birth. And She says: "How can this be, since I have no relations with [I do not know] a man?" (Luke 1:34). To "know" here has the same meaning as it does in Matthew. The Virgin Mary attests to Her state of perfect virginity: She still does not live with Her betrothed, Joseph.[26] But the announcement of the angel refers to an

---

[25] Full of grace, in Greek *kecharitomene* (literally, "rendered full of grace," or "filled with grace"), is a term that is not found elsewhere in ancient literature. This is a passive participle, without an article, used as a proper name. This means that Mary is not only a woman full of grace, but one whose being full of grace is Her personal *status*: She is *the* Full of grace and this is "the name of Mary in the eyes of God" (Saint John Paul II, *General Audience*, May 15, 1996, §2 [our translation]). It is thus a title that becomes Her name, such as "Christ" for Jesus. The archangel Gabriel calls Our Lady by the title that expresses the place that Mary has in God's plan. Only afterward does he also pronounce Her proper name ("Do not be afraid, Mary"), but he does so in referring to Her humanity, the humanity that Our Lady manifested by asking, specifically, how it was possible for Her to have a son without the cooperation of a man. If he thinks of Her as a creature, the archangel sees that Mary is inferior to him by nature, because She is a human being. But if he considers Her in the order of grace, he cannot call Her by name, because with Her being predestined to be the Mother of his God, he owes Her respect and reverence, as the servant of the king owes to the queen mother.

[26] Nonetheless, it is not only this, namely, the fact that She has not *yet* known Her husband. Mary implicitly attests to wanting to remain in a state of virginity: "At first sight, Mary's words would seem merely to express only Her present state of virginity: Mary would affirm that she does not 'know' man, that is, that She is a virgin. Nevertheless, the context in which the question is asked: 'How can this be?,' and the affirmation that follows: 'since I do not know man,' emphasize both Mary's present virginity and Her intention to remain a virgin. The expression She uses, with the verb in the present tense, reveals the permanence and continuity of Her state" (Saint John Paul II, *General Audience*, July 24, 1996, §1 [translation: *ewtn.com*]). On Mary's vow of virginity, see the clarifications of *ST* III, q. 28, a. 4. The fleeting annotation of the Doctor of the Church Saint John of Avila (d. 1569) is also significant. He writes that Jesus preferred that His Mother "were

event that happens, if She consents, now. Hence, Mary's sensible question. In fact, no one could imagine, before it happened, the miracle of the virginal conception of the Word. Such a mystery of faith is undeducible, that is, it cannot be foreknown before its actual happening.[27] Not even the "Full-of-Grace" could imagine having been predestined for a conception that bypasses the laws of nature. Mary's question does not represent a lack of faith, but rather an attestation to the fact that, if one may pardon the expression, She was not at all a lunatic or naive. Although She is everything that Scripture and Tradition tell us about Her—the most sublime creature about which we could speak and that, in speaking of Her, the end of the praise that She justly deserves can never be reached[28]—Mary is and remains a woman who is very grounded, as Her own words attest. This is exactly why, as a true Mother, She sees and also provides for the smallest and most concrete necessities of all Her children, as is seen in the episode of the wedding at Cana (see John 2:1–11).

4. The Importance of Mary's "Fiat"

Returning to the narration, we see that the angel responds to Mary's question, confirming the very doctrine that we found in Matthew's Gospel: "The holy Spirit will come upon you, and the power of the Most High will overshadow you" (Luke 1:35). Gabriel recalls as support the conception of Saint John on the part of Saint Elizabeth, not to put the two births on the same level, but rather to show the *crescendo* in the divine action: if Saint John, however great, who is still only a man, was born in miraculous circumstances, how much greater is the One whom the Baptist is called to announce? Thus, it is evident that the birth of the Baptist is a preparatory event to the birth of the Messiah in its miraculous aspect as well, which is infinitely surpassed by the virginal conception of Christ. The narrative concludes with Mary's acceptance of the task for which She has been predestined by God. Only then does the angel depart from Her, because he has carried out his mission: The Word, in the very instant in which Mary said "yes," Her "*fiat*" ("let

---

married, preferring to be considered Joseph's son, rather than men saying awful things about His most holy Mother" (*Audi, filia*, ch. 8 [our translation]).

[27] See Saint Irenaeus of Lyon, *Adversus haereses* 3.19.3: "Because he [man] never expected that a virgin could conceive, or that it was possible that one remaining a virgin could bring forth a son, and that what was thus born should be '*God with us*'" (in *ANF*, vol. 1, 449).

[28] This is expressed by the classic adage: "*De Maria numquam satis*" ("Concerning Mary, nothing [that will be said] will be enough": Saint Bernard of Clairvaux [d. 1153], *Sermo de nativitate Mariae* [our translation]).

it be done"), and not an instant prior, becomes incarnate in Her most pure womb. Thus, the One who is the Foundation of the *et-et* is also the first that respects it: the divine will is not enough for the Incarnation; there is need *both* of God's will, communicated by the angel, *and* the consent of the creature, who was predestined and prepared for this event. Mary's "yes" is thus the guarantee of human freedom before God.[29] She—under the action of grace—used freedom in the right way, for the reason for which the Lord granted it to human beings: to always say yes to Him, not being forced, but out of love.[30] The moment in which Mary accepts the divine plan has been represented in art and literature innumerable times. Among the most significant passages, we should at least mention this famous homily of Saint Bernard of Clairvaux:

> You have heard, O Virgin, that you will conceive and bear a son; you have heard that it will not be by man but by the Holy Spirit. The angel awaits an answer; it is time for him to return to God who sent him. We too are waiting, O Lady, for your word of compassion; the sentence of condemnation weighs heavily upon us.
>
> The price of our salvation is offered to you. We shall be set free at once if you consent. In the eternal Word of God we all came to be, and behold, we die. In your brief response we are to be remade in order to be recalled to life.
>
> Tearful Adam with his sorrowing family begs this of you, O loving Virgin, in their exile from Paradise. Abraham begs it, David begs it. All the other holy patriarchs, your ancestors, ask it of you, as they dwell in the country of the shadow of death. This is what the whole earth waits for, prostrate at your feet. It is right in doing so, for on your word depends comfort for the wretched, ransom for the captive, freedom for the condemned, indeed, salvation for all the sons of Adam, the whole of your race.
>
> Answer quickly, O Virgin. Reply in haste to the angel, or rather through the angel to the Lord. Answer with a word, receive the Word

---

[29] "The Annunciation was to ask the Virgin's consent in lieu of the whole human race" (*ST* III, q. 30, a. 1 [our translation]).

[30] "The Father of mercies willed that the Incarnation should be preceded by the acceptance of her Who was predestined to be the Mother of His Son, so that just as a woman contributed to death, so also a woman should contribute to life" (Second Vatican Council, *Lumen Gentium*, §56).

of God. Speak your own word, conceive the divine Word. Breathe a passing word, embrace the eternal Word.

Why do you delay, why are you afraid? Believe, give praise, and receive. Let humility be bold, let modesty be confident. This is no time for virginal simplicity to forget prudence. In this matter alone, O prudent Virgin, do not fear to be presumptuous. Though modest silence is pleasing, dutiful speech is now more necessary. Open your heart to faith, O blessed Virgin, your lips to praise, your womb to the Creator. See, the desired of all nations is at your door, knocking to enter. If He should pass by because of your delay, in sorrow you would begin to seek Him afresh, the One whom your soul loves. Arise, hasten, open. Arise in faith, hasten in devotion, open in praise and thanksgiving. Behold the handmaid of the Lord, She says, be it done to me according to your word.[31]

3.2. The Marian Dogmas

3.2.1. "Per Mariam ad Jesum" and Vice Versa

From this overview of the infancy narratives of Christ, we can see clearly that the mystery of Mary derives from that of Christ and is ordered to it. Here we can cite a traditional adage that unfolds in a symmetrical way: on one hand, the Tradition says, "*per Mariam ad Jesum*" ("through Mary to Jesus"). In fact, the entire mystery of Mary emanates from and tends toward the mystery of Christ, and thus whoever comes into contact with Our Lady cannot stop at Her but will immediately be directed toward the center of faith: Jesus. On the other hand, the adage is completed with: "*per Jesum ad Mariam*" ("through Jesus to Mary").[32] While the first part can be accepted by everyone, the second might scandalize some: would Jesus only be a means to the end that is Mary? Clearly the adage should not be interpreted in this way. Christ is always the endpoint for all.[33] The saying actually means: whoever truly encounters

---

[31] Saint Bernard of Clairvaux, *Sermones de tempore: De laudibus Virginis Matris* 4.8–9 (in *Liturgy of the Hours*, Advent Season, "Office of Readings of December 20").

[32] CCC §487 expresses the reciprocity of the two parts of the adage, without mentioning it: "What the Catholic faith believes about Mary is based on what it believes about Christ, and what it teaches about Mary illumines in turn its faith in Christ."

[33] Saint Louis-Marie Grignion de Montfort (who, as an aside, also maintains the dual principle on which we are commenting) points out that Jesus Christ must be the ultimate end of all devotions (see *Traité de la vraie dévotion à la Sainte Vierge*, nos. 61–67 [in *God Alone*, 307–310]).

Christ, that is, encounters Him not partially, as a simple man, but as God incarnate, cannot but consider the mystery of that Mother whom God has chosen for Himself, who virginally generated Him in the flesh.

Thus, the principle of *et-et*, which the Protestants unfortunately do not see, is also found in this adage. The fact that Mary always leads us to Jesus is key, but it is also true that whoever encounters Jesus in an integral way cannot but encounter His Mother. Whoever is with Jesus to the end, and not merely to a certain extent, finds the Mother of God, like Saint John, the faithful disciple who followed the Lord all the way to the cross and there found the Lord's Mother, who for this reason was entrusted to him by the Master (see John 19:25–27). With this, we see that the link between Jesus and Mary does not only concern the beginnings of the life of Christ, but the entire arc of His existence, from beginning to end, even if it is the case that during His public ministry Mary accompanied Her Son in a more reserved and hidden way. Nonetheless, the Mother always accompanies the Son, from the cradle to the cross.[34] Anyone who meets Jesus on the way will always find Him alongside Mary, and he or she will learn from Mary the right way to be a disciple: always remaining with Jesus, in good times and bad.

3.2.2. Mother of God

1. The Dogma

The first and greatest Marian title is thus that of *"Theotokos"* or *"Deipara"* ("Mother of God"). This title was solemnly defined by the Church at the Council of Ephesus (AD 431), in the context of the struggle with the Nestorian heresy of which we already spoke in Chapter Four. Mother of God is a title that is not found literally in Scripture but is justified on the basis of it. Nestorius held that the title of *Theotokos* did not have a biblical foundation, because the Gospel says that Mary is Mother of Jesus, not of God. Therefore, he proposed *"Christotokos"* ("Mother of Christ"). But Saint Elizabeth, in the Gospel, asks Mary: "And how does this happen to me, that the mother of my Lord should come to me?" (Luke 1:43). From our treatment in the chapter on Christology, we know that "Lord" is equivalent to God (YHWH). Thus, in

---

[34] "In accepting with complete availability the words of the Angel Gabriel, who announced to Her that She would become the Mother of the Messiah, Mary began Her participation in the drama of Redemption. Her involvement in Her Son's sacrifice, revealed by Simeon during the presentation in the Temple, continues not only in the episode of the losing and finding of the 12-year-old Jesus, but also throughout His public life" (Saint John Paul II, *General Audience*, April 2, 1997, §1).

the Gospel, there is a clear foundation for the title *Theotokos*, given that Saint Elizabeth does indeed greet Mary as "Mother of my God."

2. Explanation

Matthew 1:25 says that Mary "bore a son" (see Matt 1:21). *Who* is this son? We know that He is the divine Word. Mary conceived and gave birth to the eternal Son of God come in the flesh. If one asked *what* Mary gave birth to, one would have to respond: the human nature of Christ, because obviously She did not generate the divine nature. But who, when visiting a mother who has just given birth to a child, would ever ask her "what have you given birth to?" Such a phrase would sound offensive. Instead everyone asks the name: "what's his name?" This question means: to *whom* have you given birth? The Son of Mary is not only a human nature; He is a Person. And this Person is not a human but a divine Person, He is God. That is why, while only having materially begotten the humanity of Jesus and not His divinity, Mary has full title to being not only "Mother of Christ" but also "Mother of God." We have already said that this is all based on the *communicatio idiomatum* found in Jesus, true God and true man.

3.2.3. Immaculate

1. The Dogma

All of the other titles, offices, and privileges of the Virgin Mary derive from the title and office of Mother of God. First of all Her Immaculate Conception, a doctrine present from the earliest times of the Church, but defined as a dogma rather recently[35] by Blessed Pope Pius IX (d. 1878) in 1854.[36]

---

[35] One reason for the definition being delayed for so long is that, throughout the centuries, the doctrine was professed by some, but also questioned—or not adequately understood—by others, including even excellent theologians. In the seventeenth century, however, Pope Alexander VII (d. 1667) anticipated the decision of Pius IX, while not defining the dogma *ex cathedra*, and expressed this doctrine in a more descriptive way than it would be by his successor: "The soul of the Blessed Virgin Mary in its creation and its infusion into the body was blessed by the grace of the Holy Spirit and preserved from original sin" (*Sollicitudo Omnium Ecclesiarum* [1661] [DS 2017]).

[36] Blessed Pius IX, *Ineffabilis Deus* (1854). Four years later, in 1858, the Virgin Mary appeared to Saint Bernadette Soubirous (d. 1879), and confirmed the papal pronouncement when She presented herself with the words: "I am the Immaculate Conception." The supernatural character of the apparitions of Lourdes was officially recognized by the bishop of Tarbes on January 18, 1862.

The greeting of the angel, "Hail, favored one! [one full of grace!]" (Luke 1:28), is the biblical reference that is the background of this doctrine, which is also widely attested by Tradition.[37] The theological reasoning goes that, if Mary is called "Full of Grace" and if the angel ensures Her that "the Lord is with you," this presupposes that She does not have any sin. She could not in fact be in the fullness of grace if there were any blemish in Her. Thus, Saint Bernard states: "How could the angel proclaim Her full of grace, if She had something, even something small, that was not from grace?"[38] Revelation 12:1 is also often cited, in which a vision is narrated of a "woman clothed with the sun." Today, however, exegetes often see only an image of the heavenly Church in it; this is an interpretation that seems to us to be reductive of the wide symbolic scope of the text, which admits multiple levels (*et-et*) of reading.

2. Explanation

This doctrine, defined infallibly by the Church, teaches that the Virgin Mary never knew the contagion of sin, neither personal sin nor original sin. She was preserved immaculate, that is, without blemish, from the first instant of Her conception.[39] The Immaculate Conception of Mary is a privilege that was granted to Her by God in view of Her divine Maternity. Since She had to be the Mother of God, that is, since She had to give humanity to the Word in the Incarnation, this humanity had to be pure and uncontaminated:

(1) It would have been impossible for the Word to assume a flesh of sin. Moreover, He had to reproduce in Himself the integral human being as it

---

[37] In a passage in which he says that no saint lived without sinning (at least in a venial way), Saint Augustine of Hippo excludes only the Virgin Mary: "Therefore, I make an exception of the Blessed Virgin Mary, in whose case, out of respect for the Lord, I wish to raise no question at all when the discussion concerns sins—for whence do we know what an abundance of grace for entirely overcoming sin was conferred on Her who had the merit to conceive and bear Him who undoubtedly was without sin?" (*De Natura et Gratia* 36.42, in *FCNT*, vol. 86, trans. John A. Mourant and William J. Collinge (Washington, DC: CUA Press, 1992), 53–54. In the Eastern Tradition, Mary is called *Panagia*, the "All Holy."

[38] Saint Bernard of Clairvaux, *Sermo super Missus est* 1 (our translation).

[39] The liturgical Tradition of the Church celebrates the memorial of the parents of the Blessed Virgin Mary on July 26. The names are not known from Scripture, but they come from apocryphal texts: Saints Joachim and Anne. The conception of Mary happened in a natural way, through the cooperation of both parents, while the apocryphal texts sustain also that Saint Anne (as was the case later with Saint Elizabeth) was sterile and thus there was a double miraculous intervention: the overcoming of Anne's sterility and the preservation of the new creature, Mary, from the contagion of sin. The Church pronounced infallibly only on this last point.

left the hands of the Creator at the beginning.⁴⁰ But if He had inherited a flesh of sin, this would have been impossible. Thus, He predestined Mary to be exempt from the contagion of the fault of Adam and Eve. From Her, the Word took an immaculate humanity. Since the Son had to be immaculate, His Mother was immaculate as well.

Regarding this last point, Saint Andrew of Crete expressed it in this way: "The body of the Virgin is a land that God worked, the first fruits of the mass of Adam's descendants divinized by Christ, the image that is truly a likeness of the primitive beauty, the clay kneaded by the hands of the divine Artist."⁴¹ The metaphor of the pure earth was already found much earlier in Saint Irenaeus: "And as the protoplast himself, Adam, had his substance from untilled and as yet virgin soil . . . so did He who is the Word, recapitulating Adam in Himself, rightly receive a birth, enabling Him to gather up Adam [into Himself], from Mary, who was as yet a virgin."⁴²

(2) In the eleventh century the monk Eadmer of Canterbury (d. 1126), a friend and biographer of Saint Anselm of Canterbury, developed an argument that was then taken up by the most famous defender of the dogma of the Immaculate Conception, Blessed Duns Scotus. The argument is summarized in three Latin words, whose subject is Christ and whose object is the Immaculate Conception of His Mother: "*potuit, decuit, ergo fecit*" ("[Christ] had the power, it was fitting, therefore He did it").⁴³

(3) One hundred years after the proclamation of the dogma, Pius XII wanted to proclaim a Marian Year, announced by the encyclical *Fulgens Corona*, in which the Pope emphasized two relevant aspects for understanding why Mary was preserved Immaculate. The first reason consists in God's love for Her: "If we consider the burning and sweet love which Almighty God without doubt had, and has, for the Mother of His only begotten Son, for what reason can we even think that She was, even for the briefest moment of time, subject to sin and destitute of divine grace?"⁴⁴ Secondly, the Immaculate Conception is justified because its hypothetical absence would call into question the wording of the "*Protevangelium*," whereby there would always be enmity between the woman and the serpent:

---

⁴⁰ See *ST* III, q. 31, a. 2.
⁴¹ Saint Andrew of Crete, *Sermo I de Dormitione Mariae* (our translation).
⁴² Saint Irenaeus of Lyon, *Adversus haereses* 3.21.10 (in *ANF*, vol. 1, 454).
⁴³ See Eadmer of Canterbury, *Tractatus de conceptione Beatae Mariae Virginis* 10.
⁴⁴ Pius XII, *Fulgens Corona* (1953) (DS 3908).

Now, if at any time the Blessed Mary were destitute of Divine grace even for the briefest moment, because of contamination in Her conception by the hereditary stain of sin, there would not have come between Her and the serpent that perpetual enmity spoken of from earliest Tradition down to the time of the solemn definition of the Immaculate Conception, but rather a certain subjection.[45]

A hypothesis in which She was at one point not free from sin would make it impossible to speak of Mary as the seed of a new creation and as the pure earth from which the Second Adam was drawn.

3.2.4. Ever-Virgin

1. The Dogma

The third Marian dogma officially recognized by the Magisterium of the Church[46] is that of the perpetual Virginity of Mary, the most solid biblical foundation of which is the attestation of Mary: "How can this be, since I have no relations with a man?" (Luke 1:34).

When the Magisterium proclaims Mary Ever-Virgin, it means the word "virginity" in the most common and, if you will, "biological" sense. Generally, the texts avoid entering too much into details, because this would not be fitting and is not, in general, necessary. But on at least one occasion, the Magisterium was rather explicit:

> If anyone does not, following the holy Fathers, confess properly and truly that holy Mary, ever virgin and immaculate, is Mother of God, since She conceived really and truly of the Holy Spirit, without seed [*absque semine*], God the Word himself, who, before all ages, was born of God the Father, and that, in the latter age, She gave birth to Him without corruption, Her virginity remaining

---

[45] Pius XII, *Fulgens Corona* (not quoted in the DS selection of the text).
[46] Mary is called Virgin or Ever-Virgin by various ecumenical councils: Constantinople I (381), Ephesus (431), Chalcedon (451), Lateran IV (1215), Lyon II (1274), Florence (1439), and others. Commonly, for greater precision of expression, the text indicated as giving a dogmatic definition of the Perpetual Virginity of Mary is the second canon of the *Anathematismi de Tribus Capitulis* of the Second Council of Constantinople (553): "If anyone does not confess the two births of the Word of God, one from the Father before the ages ... the other [in which the Word ...] was made flesh from Mary, the holy and glorious Mother of God ever Virgin, and was born of her, let him be anathema" (DS 422).

equally inviolate after His birth, let him be condemned.[47]

2. Explanation

The privilege of Perpetual Virginity is connected to the divine Maternity in that it expresses a consequence of the fact that Jesus Christ, born of Mary, is truly the Son of God and the Second Adam.

(1) Concerning the first aspect: the fact that Jesus is Son of God implies that He possesses the highest degree of purity, a purity that is also manifested in His virginity.[48] Christ is *the* Virgin *par excellence*, which is why He was born of the Virgin Mary.

(2) As regards the second aspect, Saint Irenaeus—quoted above—says that just as in the beginning God formed Adam from the virgin earth (because it was not yet cultivated by human hands), so the Second Adam took humanity from the Virgin Mary.[49] The Latin liturgy, therefore, often used not only the title of Virgin but also Ever-Virgin (*Sempervirgo*), based on the Greek *Aeiparthenos*.[50]

(3) The doctrine of the Perpetual Virginity of Mary teaches not only that Mary was Virgin before the birth (*ante partum*)[51]—as we already saw citing the Gospel sources—it also affirms perpetual, and therefore permanent, Virginity: both during the birth (*in partu*)[52] and after birth (*post partum*).[53] Saint

---

[47] Lateran Synod (649), can. 3 (DS 503). This throws out the absurd theories, proposed by imprudent theologians, about the nature and origin of the virile seed that God, according to their theory, placed in the womb of the Virgin to miraculously fertilize it.

[48] The Gospels make it very clear that Christ did not marry. In that culture, this represented a very rare (though not unique) fact, which could even give rise to suspicions. That mischievous thoughts might have been made by some of Jesus' adversaries about Him can be intuited from Matt 19:10–12, in which the Lord seems to respond to them.

[49] See Saint Irenaeus of Lyon, *Adversus haereses* 3.21.10.

[50] For example, the title is used by Saint Epiphanius of Salamis (d. 403) in the *forma longior* of the symbol of faith, presented in his catechetical work *Anchoratus* around the year 347. It is then found in the above-cited Second Council of Constantinople.

[51] This means that the conception of Christ was virginal: see *ST* III, q. 28, a. 1.

[52] See *ST* III, q. 28, a. 2. The Virginity *in partu* and *post partum* was denied by Tertullian of Carthage (d. 220), *De carne Christi* 23; *De monogamia* 8; and by Jovinian of Rome (d. ca. 405), who originated the formula "*Virgo concepit, sed non Virgo generavit*" ("A Virgin conceived but a virgin did not generate [give birth]"). He was excommunicated in a synod in Milan presided over by Saint Ambrose, in 390. Concerning Tertullian, Saint Jerome [d. 420], in *Adversus Helvidium de perpetua virginitate Beatae Virginis* 19, discredits the question, writing: "Regarding Tertullian, I say nothing more than that he was not a man of the Church" (in *FCNT*, vol. 53, trans. John N. Hritzu [Washington, DC: CUA Press, 1965], 36).

[53] See *ST* III, q. 28, a. 3. The threefold specification was perfected in Africa in the fifth

The Mother of God

Augustine expresses the same concept with an equally classic formula, "*Virgo concepit, Virgo peperit, Virgo permansit*" ("A Virgin conceived, a Virgin gave birth, and She remained a Virgin").[54] It is clear that this implies certain miraculous interventions of God.

A first intervention consists in the virginal conception, as we have said. Another consists in giving birth in such a way that, by mysterious divine intervention, it does not take away the virginity of the one giving birth,[55] but confirms and seals it—even increases it, as the Patristic and theological Tradition holds. Since Christ is purity in Person, His passage from the Mother's womb to the external world does not blemish the virginal integrity of Mary, but, on the contrary, confirms and elevates it to a greater dignity, according to the assertion: that which is even purer (Christ) by passing through what is less so, does not render it less pure, but rather more so.[56] And the Liturgy says that

---

century. In the seventh century, Saint Ildefonsus of Toledo (d. 667) writes, in his work *De virginitate S. Mariae contra tres infideles*: "Virgin before the coming of the Son, Virgin after the generation of the Son, Virgin with the birth of the Son, Virgin after the Son was born" (our translation). Saint John Damascene, *Sermo VI de Nativitate Beatae Virginis Mariae*, defines Our Lady as "that pearl of virginity that was a Virgin before the birth, during the birth, and after the birth" (our translation).

[54] Saint Augustine of Hippo, *Sermo 51*.11.18 (our translation). In similar terms, Saint Zeno of Verona (d. 371), *Tractatus* 1.5.3, notes that Mary was "*Virgo post connubium, Virgo post conceptum, Virgo post Filium*" ("Virgin after the nuptials, Virgin after the conception, Virgin after [having had] the Son"); 2.8.2: "*Virgo incorrupta concepit, post conceptum Virgo peperit, post partum Virgo permansit*" ("She conceived as an incorrupt Virgin, after the conception a Virgin gave birth, after the birth She remained a Virgin"). See also Peter Chrysologus (d. 450), *Sermo 117*.

[55] "A woman who has conceived and borne a son, shall be unclean seven days . . . she will remain three and thirty days in the blood of her purification . . . But far be it from us to have to entertain such a thought about the mother of our Savior . . . !" (Saint Jerome [d. 420], *Adversus Helvidium de perpetua virginitate Beatae Virginis* 10, in *FCNT*, vol. 53, 22). The Virginity *in partu* of Mary would have also had a biblical attestation if the first chapter of the Gospel of John at v. 13 had to be read with the pronoun in the singular, as various ancient authors report it: "He who . . . was" (rather than "they who . . . were": see Chapter Six). Keeping in mind that "of blood," as it is normally translated in the modern languages (though the NABRE translates it "by natural generation"), is not found in the Greek original, but rather the plural "of bloods," the text could be read in this way: "Who [Christ] not of bloods, nor of the will of the flesh, nor of the will of man, but of God was generated." "Of bloods" is borrowed from the Old Testament, and it indicates both the menstrual blood and the blood that remains after childbirth. Thus, if the subject of this verse of Saint John were effectively Christ, there would be a biblical text directly attesting to a birth that did not happen in the common way, that is, with the release of the woman's blood.

[56] "The Son of God [became] the Son of man, (the pure One opening purely that pure womb which regenerates men unto God, and which He Himself made pure)" (". . . *Purus*

Christ "did not diminish His mother's virginal integrity but sanctified it."[57] As for the *virginitas post partum*, it implies the fact that even after the birth of Jesus, Mary and Joseph lived out their marriage in perfect continence. Saint Francis de Sales (d. 1622) wrote about this:

> Both had vowed to preserve their virginity for a lifetime; and here God wants them to be united by the bond of Holy Matrimony, not to make them yield or repent of their vow, but to confirm and fortify each other to persevere in their holy purpose; thus, they continued to live together in a virginal way for the rest of their lives.[58]

3.2.5. Excursus: Other Children of Mary and Joseph?

Difficulties on this point have arisen that still persist to this day. In fact, the Gospels speak in some passages of brothers and sisters of Jesus (see, for example, Mark 6:3; Matt 12:47). How should these passages be interpreted? The Catholic response is that wherever Scripture uses the term "brothers," the reader should read "cousins," because in the language used by Jesus and the Apostles (Aramaic and occasionally Hebrew), there are not two distinct words

---

pure puram aperiens vulvam, eam quae regenerat homines in Deum, quam Ipse puram fecit": Saint Irenaeus of Lyon, *Adversus haereses* 4.33.11, in *ANF*, vol. 1, 509). Some scholars have wanted to attribute these words to the Church more than Mary. In addition to the fact that the two attributions are not opposed to one another, the reference to the feminine genital organ—which reflects the typical direct mode of expression of ancient people—frames the text within a certain concrete context which is that of the human body, the body of the Virgin, even if a metaphorical interpretation of the term is possible (Baptism, the baptismal font?). A medieval example of the same doctrine is: "Like the star emits its ray without corrupting, so, without breaking her integrity, the Virgin gave birth to the Son. The ray does not diminish the splendor of the star, the Son does not take away the integrity of the Mother" (Saint Bernard of Clairvaux, *Sermo II super Missus est* 17 [our translation]).

[57] "Lord, may the humanity of your Only-begotten help us, so that He, who, born of the Virgin, did not diminish the integrity of his Mother but sanctified it, divesting us of our sins, might make our offering acceptable to return to you" (*Sacramentarium Gregorianum-Hadrianum*, "Votive Mass of Saint Mary: Prayer over Gifts," translation from Michael Joncas, "Mary in the Mysteries of Christ During Ordinary Time: Liturgical References," *Marian Studies* 43 [1992], 72–131, at 101). This prayer is found in liturgical use at least since the eighth century and is also cited by the Second Vatican Council, *Lumen Gentium*, §57.

[58] Saint Francis de Sales, *Les vrais entretiens spirituels*, appendix III: "Sermon on the Virtues of Saint Joseph" (1622) (our translation). This sermon is not included in the official collection, though it is contained in the manuscript of the Visitation of Mans.

to indicate these categories of persons.⁵⁹ The words "brother" and "sister," therefore, also indicate cousins. The Orthodox and some Protestants have a different opinion.

The Orthodox recognize the perpetual virginity of the Mother of God, and so they do not hypothesize the existence of true brothers and sisters of Jesus. Nonetheless, they do not grasp the above-mentioned nuance of meaning of the terms brother and sister and thus claim that they are half-brothers and half-sisters, namely, sons and daughters of Saint Joseph from a previous marriage of which he remained the widower, thus being able to be married again to Mary.⁶⁰ This hypothesis, however, in addition to not respecting the mentality or context that is the background of the Gospels (that of the Semitic use of the words, even if the texts are written in Greek), is compelled to introduce a presumed marriage of Saint Joseph, about which the sources of Revelation say nothing.

Some Protestant groups, who consider their hypothesis to be more faithful to the biblical text, affirm instead that the brothers and sisters of Jesus of which the Gospel speaks would be true brothers and sisters, born after Christ, within a normal practice of marriage between Joseph and Mary.⁶¹ But

---

[59] John Calvin is in agreement on this point. He writes in *Concordance qu'on appelle Harmonie composée des trois Evangelistes* (or *Commentary on Matthew, Mark, Luke*): "The word brothers, we have formerly mentioned, is employed, agreeably to the Hebrew idiom, to denote any relatives whatever" (translation: ccel.org). Thus, he accepts the critique made in this regard by Saint Jerome in his *Adversus Helvidium* 13–19, where he demonstrates that the "brothers" are in reality cousins or kinsfolk.

[60] The claim about the children of Saint Joseph is not found in Scripture, but only in apocryphal writings, such as the *Protoevangelium of James* (second century), which has the intent of defending the Virginity of Mary and thus represents Joseph as an old widower, thus implying that, while going into a new marriage with Mary, he was no longer capable of consummating the marriage. The claim is then taken up again by the apocryphal *History of Joseph the Carpenter*, a text that cannot be dated before the sixth century. The fancifulness of this writing emerges clearly when reading it. A single example: it is said that Saint Joseph died at the age of 111, working until the last day. The day of his death is identified with the 26th of the month of Epep (or Abib) (July 20), a detail that reveals the influence of Egyptian religious beliefs, since the "resurrection" of Osiris was celebrated on the 26th of Epep. Saint Jerome refutes the hypothesis that Saint Joseph had had children from a previous marriage, because he affirms: "Joseph himself was also a virgin through Mary, so that a virgin son might be born of a virgin wedlock ... and it is not written down that he had a second wife ... the conclusion follows that he, who was deemed worthy to be called the father of the Lord, remained a virgin with Mary" (*Adversus Helvidium* 21, in *FCNT*, vol. 53, 39).

[61] This, for example, is the claim of the Anabaptists and many Protestant authors of our time. As we said in Chapter One, the early Protestant reformers and Anglicans believed the doctrine of the Perpetual Virginity of Mary.

this opinion has at least two weak points: first, just like the Orthodox, it does not respect the biblical text, which it intends to defend; second, this opinion does not have any corroboration in the Fathers and in the great theologians before Protestantism itself. Regarding the first of the two weak points, if the Gospels are viewed in their totality, there are important details that neither the Orthodox nor the Protestant theses can explain: (1) the total absence of references to brothers and sisters of Jesus in the Infancy Narratives; (2) the fact that Mary is always called "Mother of Jesus," but never the mother of any of those who the Gospels also call brothers and sisters of Him; (3) that Saint Joseph is called father of the Child and it is specified that he was in the sense that the people understood him to be so, but it is never said that he was the father of those other persons who, according to the Orthodox and Protestants, would be his children; and (4) the fact that Jesus on the Cross entrusts Mary to a disciple (John), which there would be no need to do if He had brothers and sisters, who certainly would have taken care of Her.

We can conclude with a text of Pope Paul IV (d. 1559):

> [The opinion is condemned according to which] the same (Lord) was not, according to the flesh, conceived in the womb of the most blessed and ever Virgin Mary by (the power of) the Holy Spirit but, like other men, from the seed of Joseph ... or that the same most blessed Virgin Mary is not the true Mother of God and did not always persist in the integrity of virginity, namely, before giving birth, in giving birth, and perpetually after giving birth [*ante partum, in partu et perpetuo post partum*].[62]

3.2.6. Assumption into Heaven

1. The Dogma

The fourth and, to this point, final dogma officially proclaimed by the Church is also the most recent: the Assumption of Our Lady into Heaven "in soul and body," at the end of Her earthly life. This doctrine, whose liturgical solemnity is celebrated on August 15, was defined by Pope Pius XII in 1950.[63] The most traditional biblical foundation is Revelation 12:1, in which Saint John sees a glorious woman in Heaven, a symbol—according to the greater part of the Tradition—both of the Church and of Mary. The doctrine of the Assumption

---

[62] Paul IV, *Cum Quorumdam Hominum* (1555) (DS 1880).
[63] See Pius XII, *Munificentissimus Deus* (1950) (DS 3900-3904).

implies that the body of Mary did not undergo decay on earth and that it cannot be found on earth, because it was glorified with Her soul in Heaven. Saint John Damascene states:

> It was necessary that She, who in childbirth had kept Her virginity unharmed, also preserved Her body without any corruption after Her death. It was necessary that She, who had carried the Creator made child in Her womb, would dwell in the divine tabernacles. It was necessary for the Bride of the Father to live in the Heavenly mansions. It was necessary that She who had seen Her Son on the cross, receiving in Her heart that sword of sorrow from which She had been immune in giving birth to Him, would contemplate Him sitting at the right hand of the Father. It was necessary for the Mother of God to possess what belongs to Her Son and be honored by all creatures as Mother and Handmaid of God.[64]

2. Explanation

There are various hypotheses concerning the passage of Mary from this world to the other.

(1) There are those who hypothesize a death entirely equal to that of other human beings. On the other hand, there is the eastern conception which speaks of the *Dormitio Mariae*, the Dormition of Mary: the end of Our Lady's earthly life would consist in falling into a sweet sleep, without knowing death as we experience it. We can cite a text of Saint Gregory of Tours (d. 594), which, while speaking of the separation of the soul from the body (in this sense, a true death), narrates the final day of Mary in such a way as to show the extraordinary nature of Her passing away:

> Although the blessed Mary had already been called [to live apart] from this world, finally the passage of Her life was completed, and all the Apostles gathered from their particular regions at Her house. When they heard that She must be taken from the world, they all kept watch with Her. And behold, the Lord Jesus came with his angels, and after taking Her soul He gave it to the angel Michael and left. At dawn the Apostles lifted Her body on a bed, placed it in a tomb, and kept guard over it, in anticipation of the arrival of

---

[64] Saint John Damascene, *Encomium in Dormitionem Dei Genitricis Semperque Virginis Mariae* 2.14 (our translation).

the Lord. And behold, again the Lord approached them. He took the holy body in a cloud and ordered it to be brought to Paradise, where, after regaining Her soul, Mary now rejoices with His elect and enjoys the goodness of eternity that will never perish.[65]

Beyond the narrative details (a delicate specification—"on a bed"—to emphasize that no one dared touch the body of the Virgin), this perspective is to be preferred to that which hypothesizes a common death for Mary, because it better corresponds to the role of Mary as New Eve: She "died" in the same way in which Eve would have "died" if she had not sinned (see Chapter Three). The death would not be marked by sin and by its consequences, and thus it would be a joyous passage to true life. Mary is without sin, and so She cannot die as we sinners do.

(2) It could, however, be objected that Christ Himself experienced death though He too was without sin; and, unlike Mary, He was also God and not only a human being. Indeed, He experienced the most tormenting and agonizing of deaths. We may, however, respond to this objection by saying that Christ died not because He had to (as we sinners do: see Rom 6:23), but rather because He willed to (see John 10:17–18), and in this way He achieved our redemption from sin and death. He voluntarily let Himself be swallowed up by death, so that death could be destroyed from within. For Mary all this was unnecessary, because Christ is the Redeemer. She certainly participated in the work of redemption but in a different way.

(3) The Tradition of faith developed the spirituality of Our Lady of Sorrows (which has a liturgical memorial on September 15[66]), that is, of Our Lady who suffers the Son's suffering along with Him, not in Her body, but in Her spirit, in Her Immaculate Heart. A biblical foundation of this spirituality is the word of the elderly Simeon who welcomed Mary and Joseph in the Temple of Jerusalem when they brought the Baby Jesus (born just a few days before) there for the first time. He prophesied to the Virgin: "and you yourself [your soul] a sword will pierce" (Luke 2:35). Several Western depictions of Our Lady of Sorrows show Her dressed in black, with a heart pierced by seven daggers: the number seven indicates perfection, thus Mary has suffered in the

---

[65] Saint Gregory of Tours, *De gloria beatorum martyrum* 4, in *Glory of the Martyrs*, trans. Raymond Van Dam (Liverpool, UK: Liverpool University Press, 1988), 22.

[66] The Liturgy enriches this memory with the marvelous sequence titled *Stabat Mater*, attributed to Blessed Jacopone da Todi (d. 1306). The strophes of the sequence are usually also sung in the pious practice of the *Via Crucis* ("Way of the Cross").

perfect way along with Her Son.⁶⁷ But the sword, Saint Simeon said, pierces the soul and not the body (as instead happens to Christ: see John 19:34). So while the Roman soldier strikes the physical heart of the Redeemer, tearing it open, the pain pierces the soul of Mary, sacrificial victim along with the unique Victim, the unique Lamb of God who takes away the sin of the world: Christ.⁶⁸ The Passion of Christ is in the soul (see Mark 14:34) and in the body, and it is a perfect Passion; that of Mary is only in the soul,⁶⁹ and it is a participation of the Mother in the redeeming Passion of the Son. For this reason, suffering in the body is not part of the vocation of Mary: She did not die a martyr in the strict sense, even if Her sufferings were comparable to martyrdom, as Saint Bernard affirms.⁷⁰ And that is why, even if Christ wanted to die by partaking in our dark death to the maximum degree, it is not necessary for Mary to die in this way. On the contrary, at the end of Her life of continuous offering to the Lord, She fell asleep in God to rise with Her Son in the new life.⁷¹

(4) Her resurrection was also corporeal, in the image of the Resurrection

---

[67] Saint Alphonsus Maria de Liguori (d. 1787) in his famous work *Le glorie di Maria*, part II, *Discourse IX*, enumerates and illustrates seven sorrows: (1) Saint Simeon's Prophecy; (2) the flight of Jesus into Egypt; (3) the loss of Jesus in the Temple; (4) the meeting of Mary and Jesus when He was going to death; (5) the death of Jesus; (6) the piercing of the side of Jesus, and His descent from the cross; and (7) the burial of Jesus (in *The Glories of Mary*, in *The Complete Works of Saint Alphonsus de Liguori*, vol. 8, ed. Eugene Grimm [Brooklyn, NY: Redemptorist Fathers, 1931], 493–537). At the beginning of the same *Discourse*, the Patron of moralists and Doctor of the Church writes that "Mary is the Queen of Martyrs, for Her Martyrdom was longer and greater than that of all the Martyrs" (p. 463; see our notes on "white martyrdom" in Chapter Five).

[68] Melito of Sardis (d. 180), in the homily *On the Passover* [*Peri Pascha*], 71, calls Mary "the good Ewe-Lamb" (literally, "the beautiful Ewe-Lamb," where the Greek adjective *kalos* indicates goodness and purity), explicitly linking this Marian title with the Christological title "Lamb of God": hence, the relationship between Christ the Victim and Mary the Victim.

[69] Saint Bernard of Clairvaux, cited by Saint Alphonsus Liguori, *The Glories of Mary*, II, *Discourse IX*, says that Mary was martyr "*non ferro carnificis sed acerbo dolore cordis*" ("not by the sword of the executioner, but by bitter sorrow of heart" [in *The Complete Works of Saint Alphonsus de Liguori*, vol. 8, 465]).

[70] "Do not marvel, O brothers, when it is said that Mary was a martyr in the spirit." In the same text, the Mellifluous Doctor adds: "The martyrdom of the Virgin is set forth both in the prophecy of Simeon and in the actual story of our Lord's Passion. . . . Truly, O blessed Mother, a sword has pierced your heart. For only by passing through your heart could the sword enter the flesh of your Son" (Saint Bernard of Clairvaux, *Sermones de tempore: in dominica infra octavam Assumptionis* 14 [transl. catholic.org]).

[71] The text of the dogmatic definition deliberately leaves the question undetermined by saying that Mary "having completed the course of Her earthly life [*expleto terrestris vitae cursu*], was assumed body and soul into heavenly glory" (Pius XII, *Munificentissimus Deus* [DS 3903]).

of Christ. And this fourth Marian dogma is also a consequence of the divine Maternity: just as the body of Christ, which is the body of the immortal *Logos*, could not remain in the sepulcher, so too the body that was the Tabernacle of the Most High on earth could not know terrestrial corruption.[72] For nine months Mary carried the Son of God, who received His body and blood from Her. That flesh and that blood, which have provided the material for the Incarnation of the *Logos*, could not decay in death. The light of the Risen Lord immediately illumined His Mother's journey towards the eternal Jerusalem. Thus, Saint Germanus of Constantinople (d. 733), imagining the scene in which Jesus descends from Heaven to take His Mother, attributes these words to the Lord: "It is necessary that where I am, you too will be, a Mother inseparable from your Son."[73]

3.3. Other Marian Titles

3.3.1. Queen

Aside from the four dogmas infallibly taught by the Church, she recognizes other titles and offices of the Mother of God. The fact that they have not yet been the subject of a solemn dogmatic definition does not imply that the Church does not consider these doctrines true, especially those that she has professed from time immemorial and that in some cases are also liturgically celebrated. We have already mentioned the role of Mary as Queen of the universe, with the liturgical memorial of August 22. This truth about Mary is celebrated in different ways in the prayer of Christians: (1) The Fifth Glorious Mystery of the prayer of the Rosary contemplates the Coronation of Mary in Heaven. (2) A famous ancient antiphon greets Mary with the words, "*Salve, Regina,*" ("Hail, holy Queen"), and another begins with the words "*Ave Regina coelorum*" ("Hail, Queen of the Heavens"). (3) The Litany of Loreto

---

[72] The Preface of the Holy Mass for the Solemnity of the Assumption, August 15, recites: "Rightly you would not allow Her to see the corruption of the tomb since from Her own body She marvelously brought forth your incarnate Son" ("*Corruptionem enim sepulcri eam videre merito noluisti, quae Filium tuum, vitae omnis auctorem, ineffabiliter de se genuit incarnatum*").

[73] Saint Germain of Constantinople, *Homilia III in Dormitionem* (our translation). The implied biblical reference is to John 12:26: "Whoever serves me must follow me, and where I am, there also will my servant be. The Father will honor whoever serves me." Nobody can ever serve the Lord better than the One who defined Herself as God's Handmaiden (see Luke 1:38), which is why it is no surprise that the Father would have also honored Mary at the end of Her earthly existence, leading Her to be alongside Her Son in Heaven.

contains different references to the regality of Mary: Queen of the angels, the patriarchs, the prophets, the Apostles, the martyrs, the confessors of the faith, the virgins, and all the saints. It continues, invoking Mary as Queen who was conceived without original sin, Queen assumed into Heaven, Queen of the holy Rosary, Queen of the family,[74] and Queen of peace. (4) The prayer of the *Regina Coeli* ("Queen of Heaven"), which substitutes for the recital of the *Angelus* during the Easter Season. (5) The beginning of the Supplication to the Madonna of the Rosary of Pompeii, composed by Blessed Bartolo Longo (d. 1926), which calls Mary "O August Queen of Victories, O Sovereign of Heaven and Earth."[75]

3.3.2. Mediatrix

There are many other Marian titles that the Church uses and recognizes, such as the aforementioned Mother of the Church, introduced by Paul VI at the end of the Second Vatican Council, or the title of Mary, Mediatrix of all graces. The aforementioned Supplication of Blessed Longo (part III) says: "Kindly design to hear us, O Mary! Jesus has placed in your hands all the treasures of His graces and His mercies."[76] And a little further along he adds the extraordinary affirmation: "You are omnipotent by grace" ("*Tu sei l'onnipotente per grazia*"). It is difficult to find a better and more concise definition of the office of the universal mediation of the graces performed by Our Lady. Only God is omnipotent by nature; Mary is a creature and is not omnipotent by nature. However, God in a completely free way, was pleased to entrust to Mary all of the treasures and graces that He gives to human beings. Thus, God wills to render Mary, by grace, in some way omnipotent, not in the sense that She takes on divine omnipotence—that is impossible—but rather that Her prayer is never ineffective at the throne of God[77]; and that God does not have to, but rather wants to pass all of His salutary influence on all human beings through Mary.

In regard to this Marian office too, we are before an irradiation of the

---

[74] This invocation has been added by Saint John Paul II: See *Angelus*, December 31, 1995.
[75] The original Italian text reads: "*Augusta Regina delle Vittorie, Sovrana del Cielo e della terra*" (trans. *ourladyofpompeii.org*).
[76] "*Degnati benevolmente, o Maria, di esaudirci! Gesù ha riposto nelle tue mani tutti i tesori delle sue grazie e delle sue misericordie*" (trans. *ourladyofpompeii.org*).
[77] "Omnipotent by grace" can thus be understood as an alternative version of the other classical expression: "*Quod Deus imperio, tu prece Virgo potes*" ("That which God can do by His power, that canst thou do by prayer, O sacred Virgin": cited, for example, by Saint Alphonsus Maria Liguori, *The Glories of Mary*, I, *Discourse VI*, in *The Complete Works of Saint Alphonsus de Liguori*, vol. 8, 465).

fundamental dogma of the divine Maternity of Mary: God did not have to, but rather He wanted to be born of Her and save humanity by assuming, as a conjoined instrument, a human nature drawn from Her. Thus, God wants to continue to give grace to human beings through the hands of the One He has chosen to be His Mother forever:

> For all the *salvific influence* of the Blessed Virgin on men originates, not from some inner necessity, but from the divine pleasure. It flows forth from the superabundance of the merits of Christ, rests on His mediation, depends entirely on it and draws all its power from it. In no way does it impede, but rather does it foster the immediate union of the faithful with Christ.[78]

3.3.3. Co-Redemptrix

In concluding, among the many Marian offices and titles used by the Church, we shall consider one that is currently at the center of an intense debate among theologians: the title of Co-Redemptrix of humankind. The discussion does not focus on the objective content that the title conveys, but on the verbal expression.

1. Doctrinal Content

When we speak of Marian co-redemption, the content refers to the cooperation of Mary in the Redemptive work of Christ, the only Mediator. There are no doubts about this. Let us quote, for example, Vatican II (our italics):

> Rightly therefore the holy Fathers see Her as used by God not merely in a passive way, but as freely *cooperating in the work of human salvation* through faith and obedience. For, as St. Irenaeus says, She "being obedient, became the cause of salvation for Herself and for the whole human race" (*Adversus haereses* III, 22, 4). Hence not a few of the early Fathers gladly assert in their preaching, "The knot of Eve's disobedience was untied by Mary's obedience; what the virgin Eve bound through her unbelief, the Virgin Mary loosened by Her faith" (ibid.). Comparing Mary with Eve, they call Her "the Mother of the living," (Saint Epiphanius of Salamis, *Panarion*, 78, 18) and

---

[78] Second Vatican Council, *Lumen Gentium*, §60. Note in particular the expression we have highlighted.

The Mother of God

still more often they say: "death through Eve, life through Mary."[79]

Predestined from eternity—by that decree of divine Providence which determined the Incarnation of the Word—to be the Mother of God, the Blessed Virgin was on this earth the virgin Mother of the Redeemer, and above all others and *in a singular way the generous associate and humble Handmaid of the Lord*. She conceived, brought forth and nourished Christ. She presented Him to the Father in the temple, and was united with Him by compassion as He died on the Cross. *In this singular way She cooperated by Her obedience, faith, hope and burning charity in the work of the Savior* in giving back supernatural life to souls. *Wherefore She is our Mother in the order of grace*.[80]

This maternity of Mary in the order of grace began with the consent which She gave in faith at the Annunciation and which She sustained without wavering beneath the cross, and lasts until the eternal fulfillment of all the elect. *Taken up to heaven She did not lay aside this salvific duty, but by Her constant intercession continued to bring us the gifts of eternal salvation.* By Her maternal charity, She cares for the brethren of Her Son, who still journey on earth surrounded by dangers and difficulties, until they are led into the happiness of their true home. Therefore the Blessed Virgin is invoked by the Church under the titles of Advocate, Auxiliatrix, Adjutrix, and Mediatrix. This, however, is to be so understood that it neither takes away from nor adds anything to the dignity and efficaciousness of Christ the one Mediator.[81]

2. *Terminological Expression*

On the basis of these texts of the most recent Council and numerous other reasons, various theologians, bishops, and cardinals have for several decades now been promoting a theological-spiritual movement so that a future dogmatic definition of the Church may infallibly proclaim that the Virgin Mother of God is Co-Redemptrix along with the one Redeemer, Christ. Theologians who instead oppose the definition do not call into question the cooperation of Mary in the work of the Son, but they believe that the title Co-Redemptrix

---

[79] Second Vatican Council, *Lumen Gentium*, §56.
[80] Second Vatican Council, *Lumen Gentium*, §61.
[81] Second Vatican Council, *Lumen Gentium*, §62.

is ambiguous and also damaging from an ecumenical standpoint. They add that the Second Vatican Council did not use the term in the documents and that this Marian title has not been used by the papal Magisterium in important documents since the time of Pius XII. Thus, it seems strange that some ask the Magisterium to solemnly define a dogma by making recourse to a term that the Magisterium itself has avoided for decades. That being the case, before being able to pronounce on the subject, it is necessary to explore all the related questions in greater theological depth.

4. Mary and the Church

4.1. Daughter and Mother

The link between Mary and Christ is the foundation and origin of Mary's link with the Church. Mary is not linked to Christ because She forms part of the Church, but She is linked to the Church because She is the Mother of Christ, whose Mystical Body is the Church. This shows once again that "ecclesiotypical" Mariology, while certainly rich in content, cannot be the starting point or the main perspective for approaching the mystery of Mary. The reference to the Church can and must be secondary to the more fundamental regard for the connection that unites Mary and Jesus. The holy Virgin is certainly also a member of the Church (in this sense, even for Her it is true that *"extra Ecclesiam nulla salus"*), because all Her being and Her mission are a gratuitous gift, a grace from Her Son, the Redeemer and Savior of the world. However, Mary is not only placed within the Church, but also above it, being the Mother of the Church.

Saint Augustine explained well that Mary is one of the faithful—the most perfect of them, and thus the first Christian—but also that She surpasses all of the faithful:

> That one woman [Mary], therefore, is both Mother and Virgin, not only in spirit, but also in body. She is mother, indeed, in the spirit, not of our Head, who is our Savior Himself, of whom She was rather born spiritually, since all who believe in Him (among whom She, too, is included) are rightly called children of the bridegroom, but She is evidently the Mother of us who are His members, because She has co-operated by charity that the faithful, who are members of the Head, might be born in the Church. Indeed, She is Mother of the Head Himself in the body. It behooved our Head to be born of a

virgin according to the flesh, for the sake of a wonderful miracle by which He might signify that His members would be born according to the spirit, of a virgin, the Church. Mary alone, therefore, is Mother and Virgin both in spirit and in body, both Mother of Christ and Virgin of Christ.[82]

Note the perfect application in the text of the principle of *et-et*, for which Mary can be simultaneously "daughter" and "Mother" of Christ (in different senses; thus this is not opposed to the principle of non-contradiction).

4.2. First of the Redeemed

Mary's relationship with the Church is thus twofold: on the one hand, She belongs to the Church, on the other hand, She guides her with maternal authority. Mary belongs to the Church because She is the first of the redeemed.[83] The redemption consists, as we know, in Christ's/God's reacquisition of the creature. We are redeemed from sin and death through the grace of Jesus' Incarnation and the merits of His Passion. Baptism and faith justify us, applying the merits of the Lord to each of us and washing away sin. Mary Most Holy is the first for whom the gift of redemption was granted; first from the chronological point of view—because She received the gift of Christ even before Christ came into the world—and from the point of view of the divine plan of salvation, that is, the intention of God.

In this sense, it can be said with Saint Augustine that Mary is one of us: both because of the human nature identical to our own, and by virtue of the fact that She was redeemed by Her Son, Jesus. But it must immediately be added that, if She is like us in these ways, in other ways She surpasses us infinitely, even if we consider Her mystery from the standpoint of Her belonging to the Church, to the community of the redeemed. In fact, in the natural order She is a human being like us, but She is the New Eve, that is, the most pure reappearance of humanity as it came forth from the hands of

---

[82] Saint Augustine of Hippo, *De sancta virginitate* 6, in *FCNT*, vol. 27, trans. Roy J. Deferrari (Washington, DC: CUA Press, 1955), 149.

[83] In Mary, the redemption was preventive, in view of the future merits of the Son. Thus, Blessed John Duns Scotus, *In III Sententiarum*, d. 3, a. 1: "There is no better way to call Christ the most perfect Redeemer, nor Mary the most perfect redeemed, than by affirming the preservation [of Mary] from original sin" (our translation). Pius XII, *Fulgens Corona*: "We easily perceive how Christ the Lord in a certain most perfect manner really redeemed His Mother, since it was by virtue of His merits that She was preserved by God immune from all stain of original sin" (DS 3909).

Mary and the Church

God in the beginning: without the contagion of fault or concupiscence. This is explained on the basis of the supernatural order, or that of grace, in which Mary is like us because She is also redeemed, but redeemed in a different way than we are; different, that is, because it is superior.[84] We are born in the sin of Adam (see Chapter Three), we are conceived in it[85] and, once purified in Baptism, we keep its mark for our whole life, namely, the concupiscence that inclines us toward evil, while not forcing us to commit it. For Mary, as we know, things went in a different way: She did not know any contagion of sin, having been preserved whole and intact in Her created nature, from the first instant of Her conception (Immaculate Conception). The grace of the redemption was carried out in Her in a preventive and non-curative way: it was carried out before the contagion of sin in order to avoid it, not afterward in order to heal the evil already contracted. Therefore, in Mary, unlike in our redemption, there is no shadow of sin or concupiscence.

4.3. Mother of the Redeemed

Secondly, Mary is in relation to the Church as her Mother. This is explained by the fact that She has brought Christ, His physical body, into the world. As we shall see in the following chapter, the Church is the Mystical Body of Christ, whose members are we faithful. In bringing the physical human body of the Lord into the world, the Virgin also gave birth in a mystical way to the Church, and thus She is the Mother both of the ecclesial Body as a whole and of each individual member.

Here we must repeat an undoubtable truth, which we have already recalled in Chapter Five, even if it is a little uncomfortable in our times. God is certainly the Father of all human beings from the standpoint of the natural order, because He is their Creator. However, in the perfect sense, God is Father in the order of grace only of the baptized, made adopted sons and daughters in the dead and risen Son and through the Holy Spirit. Thus, not all people are sons and daughters of God in the strict sense, but only Christians, while all are creatures of God and are very much loved by Him. Something similar must be said about the motherhood of Mary. In Her case, in a weaker sense, one can say that She is Mother of all human beings. While God is indeed the Father of all both by virtue of creation and by virtue of the love that He has for them, Mary is so only by virtue of love. Thus, Mary is the Mother of

---

[84] Second Vatican Council, *Lumen Gentium*, §53: Redeemed in a more sublime way [*sublimiore modo*] by reason of the merits of Her Son".

[85] "Behold, I was born in guilt; / in sin my mother conceived me," David sings in Ps 51:7.

everyone in the accommodated sense: this expression means that the Virgin loves all creatures made by Her Son, who is the creator *Logos*, and She desires the eternal salvation of all while She prays to obtain it. In the strict and proper sense, however, in the order of grace, Mary is only the Mother of the baptized, who enter into the Mystical Body of Christ to become part of it, thus acquiring a mysterious link with Her. This additionally applies to all the baptized who, like the Protestants, do not cultivate devotion to Mary. She is also the Mother of the sons and daughters who do not nurture a relationship with Her. She loves them very much, because by virtue of their Baptism they are creatures redeemed by Her Son, the elect of the Father, and the consecrated of the Spirit. She continuously intercedes for their perfect conversion.

4.4. *Advocate*

What was just said reminds us of the primary role that Mary performs as Mother and eminent and peerless member of the Church: that of intercession. Even from this standpoint, the life and work of Our Lady are perfectly conformed to following Her Son, of whom She is the perfect Disciple, as the One who always does the will of God.[86] We spoke in Chapter Four of the priestly office of Christ, which He exercised not only on the cross and with the constant offering of His whole life to the Father for us, but which

---

[86] The Gospels recount how one day Jesus was teaching the crowds and was summoned by His relatives: His Mother and "brothers." But the Lord responded that His mother and brothers were the disciples, thus indicating the priority of His mission to the Church, with respect to His natural duties toward family (likewise in Luke 2:49). This episode, however, does not at all diminish the importance of Our Lady. On this same occasion in the Gospel of Luke, Jesus says: "My mother and my brothers are those who hear the word of God and act on it" (Luke 8:21). The disciple who is obedient to the Word of God is the true relative of Jesus, because he or she is part of the Family of God, the Church. Mary is then doubly a relative of Jesus: from the natural standpoint, because She is His true biological Mother; and from the supernatural standpoint, because She is His perfect Disciple, who always listens to the Word of God and puts it into practice. That Mary has always listened to the Word of God is shown by Her prayer, the *Magnificat* (see Luke 1:46-55) of which Benedict XVI wrote: "The Magnificat—a portrait, so to speak, of Her soul—is entirely woven from threads of Holy Scripture, threads drawn from the Word of God. Here we see how completely at home Mary is with the Word of God, with ease She moves in and out of it. She speaks and thinks with the Word of God; the Word of God becomes Her word, and Her word issues from the Word of God. Here we see how Her thoughts are attuned to the thoughts of God, how Her will is one with the will of God. Since Mary is completely imbued with the Word of God, She is able to become the Mother of the Word Incarnate" (*Deus Caritas est* (2005), §41). The fact that Our Lady had not only meditated, but also lived the Word of God, is manifested by the fact that She always remained with Jesus, even under the cross.

He continues to exercise in Heaven as the High Priest who intercedes for sinners. The intercession of Mary is a participation in this office of Christ. In reality, the Lord deigns to associate all Christians with His priesthood, and through Baptism they become priests, prophets, and kings. In Mary, however, we find a degree of realization of this common priesthood of the faithful that cannot be found in any other Christian. In fact, Her office of intercession is distinct from that of other Christians for several reasons: (1) The perfection with which it is carried out and the acceptance it finds at the throne of God. Not even the greatest saint reaches the level of excellence that is found in the intercession of Our Lady, and no saint can obtain grace from the Lord with the same infallibility of the Virgin, the "Omnipotent by grace." (2) Christians address Her not only as a sister in the faith, like when a Christian says to another "pray for me"; they address Her as Mother and Queen. This type of supplication is not even addressed to the saints, whose patronage Christians also invoke, as older brothers and sisters in the faith and in the Church, as well as models of life. And, as the basis of the other two, (3) the intercession of Mary is not only the intercession of the most excellent member of the Church, but the proper office of the Mother of God assumed into Heaven in soul and body.

Therefore, we have an Advocate who is with the Father (see 1 John 2:1) who is Christ the Lord, High Priest. And we have an Advocate with the High Priest, who is Mary, Mother of God and of the Church. Advocate is what She is called by the ancient antiphon of the *Salve Regina*: "*eia ergo, Advocata nostra*" ("Come then, our Advocate"). The Latin word *ad-vocatus* is the perfect translation of the Greek *para-kletos*, which the New Testament applies both to Jesus and the Spirit (the "other Paraclete" of John 14:16). The intercession of Mary, Her office of Advocate at God's throne, shows once again Her unique and unrepeatable link with the Persons of the Trinity.

Regarding the intercession of Mary, we can cite a passage of Saint Louis-Marie Grignion de Montfort (d. 1716):

> Moses, by the power of his prayer curbed God's anger against the Israelites (see Ex 32:10), . . . how much greater, then, will be the prayer of the humble Virgin Mary, worthy Mother of God, which is more powerful with the King of Heaven than the prayers and intercession of all the angels and saints in Heaven and on earth?[87]

---

[87] Saint Louis-Marie Grignion de Montfort, *Traité de la vraie dévotion à la Sainte Vierge* [*True Devotion to Mary*], no. 27 (in *God Alone*, 297).

The same Saint emphasizes that the intercession of Mary entails a work of mediation. On one hand, all divine graces reach human beings through the hands of Mary; on the other hand, the spiritual offerings that human beings present to God are accepted by Him because they are presented to Him—embellished—by the hands of Mary:

> St. Bernard tells us that God, seeing that we are unworthy to receive His graces directly from Him, gives them to Mary, so that we might receive from Her all that He decides to give us. His glory is achieved when He receives through Mary the gratitude, respect and love we owe Him in return for His gifts to us.[88]

4.5. Image and Model of the Church

From what we have seen so far, we also understand the role of Mary as the perfect image and model of the Church. Mary achieves in fullness in Herself what the Church is by nature (that is, holy). It is as though Mary were the "incarnation" of holiness, of that note of the Church that for each baptized person is a task of purification that lasts one's entire life and unfortunately is often not completed. In Mary, holiness resembles, much more than in any other Christian, the constitutive holiness of the Church. Each baptized person is called to holiness[89] and, if faithful, strives to pursue it with an honest conduct of life, after having been regenerated to life in Christ through Baptism.

The fact of an original holiness is added to this progressive dimension of holiness: a holiness that, in Mary alone, is not only a conquest, the end of a

---

[88] Saint Louis-Marie Grignion de Montfort, *Traité de la vraie dévotion à la Sainte Vierge*, no. 142 (in *God Alone*, 333). The second aspect is illustrated by Montfort with a famous comparison: "Any good our soul could produce is of less value to God our Father, in winning His friendship and favor, than a worm-eaten apple would be in the sight of a king, when presented by a poor peasant to his royal master as payment for the rent of his farm. But what would the peasant do if he were wise and if he enjoyed the esteem of the queen? Would he not present his apple first to her, and would she not, out of kindness to the poor man and out of respect for the king, remove from the apple all that was maggoty and spoilt, place it on a golden dish, and surround it with flowers? Could the king then refuse the apple? Would he not accept it most willingly from the hands of his queen who showed such loving concern for that poor man?" (Saint Louis-Marie Grignion de Montfort, *Le secret de Marie* [*Secret of Mary*], no. 37 [in *God Alone*, 272]; similarly in *Traité de la vraie dévotion à la Sainte Vierge*, no. 147).

[89] "If therefore in the Church everyone does not proceed by the same path, nevertheless all are called to sanctity" (Second Vatican Council, *Lumen Gentium*, §32); "all the faithful of Christ of whatever rank or status, are called to the fullness of the Christian life and to the perfection of charity" (Second Vatican Council, *Lumen Gentium*, §40).

journey, but also a previous fact, an original gift. Thus, She is much more the icon of the holy Church than anyone else, because the holiness of the Church is first and foremost a gratuitous gift from on high that Christ gives to His Mystical Body, and then also the result of the faithful lives of the baptized. The first aspect, however, is not found in us, because we are born without original holiness; and the second is found only in an imperfect way. This is why the true image of the holy Church can only be the Mother of God: holy both through original gift (Immaculate Conception) and for Her own perfect conduct of life.

Blessed Isaac of Stella (d. 1169) offers us a good parallelism, which shows that Mary is the perfect figure of the Church, in which She encapsulates in Herself all of the characteristics that the Church possesses:

> They are many sons, yet one Son. Head and members are one Son, yet, many sons; in the same way, Mary and the Church are one Mother, yet more than one mother; one Virgin, yet more than one virgin. Both are mothers, both are virgins. Each conceives of the same Spirit, without concupiscence. Each gives birth to a child of God the Father, without sin. Without any sin, Mary gave birth to Christ the Head for the sake of His Body. By the forgiveness of every sin, the Church gave birth to the Body, for the sake of its Head. Each is Christ's Mother, but neither gives birth to the whole Christ without the cooperation of the other. In the inspired Scriptures, what is said in a universal sense of the virgin mother, the Church, is understood in an individual sense of the Virgin Mary, and what is said in a particular sense of the Virgin Mother Mary is rightly understood in a general sense of the virgin mother, the Church. When either is spoken of, the meaning can be understood of both, almost without qualification.[90]

4.6. *Sign of Hope*

Mary, as the image and model of the Church, is also the source of hope for wayfarers, the Christians who are still *"en route"* in this life. This is what is sung by Saint Bernard of Clairvaux in the prayer that Dante Alighieri (d. 1321) attributes to him in the *Divine Comedy*. The supreme Poet imagines the Saint giving a marvelous prayer to Mary, in which the following praise is also found:

---

[90] Blessed Isaac of Stella, *Sermo 51*, in *Days of the Lord: The Liturgical Year*, vol. 1, trans. Gregory LaNave and Donald Molloy (Collegeville, MN: The Liturgical Press, 1991), 95.

The Mother of God

> Here unto us
> thou art a noonday torch of Charity;
> and down below 'mong mortal men, thou art
> a living fount of Hope.[91]

The Mellifluous Doctor sings the greatness of Mary, saying that in Heaven ("Here unto us," that is unto the saints and angels of Paradise) She shines like a torch (ancient Italian "*face*"), which burns with love like the noon sun; while for mortals on earth, for the wayfarers, Mary is like a fountain from which the water of hope continuously and abundantly flows with vivacity. Vatican II seems to echo Dante's Saint Bernard when it teaches:

> In the interim just as the Mother of Jesus, glorified in body and soul in Heaven, is the image and beginning of the Church as it is to be perfected is the world to come, so too does She shine forth on earth, until the day of the Lord shall come, *as a sign of sure hope and solace* to the people of God during its sojourn on earth.[92]

On the other hand, to recall again the antiphon *Salve Regina*, we need to remember that in it Christians call Mary "*spes nostra*" ("our hope").

This hope ignited by Mary can be motivated in at least two ways: (1) In a more classic way: looking at Mary, the Christian renews his or her hope of going to Heaven, because he or she knows that Mary intercedes for sinners—as we ask in the *Hail Mary*: "pray for us sinners"—and that Her maternal intercession is powerful and saves many. (2) According to a more recent emphasis: since the Assumption of Mary represents the anticipation of our destiny to be risen with Christ. This second interpretation is not incorrect as long as it does not tend toward bringing Mary back into the mere flock of the Church, as one of the many people who will one day be assumed into Heaven. We must remember that on the one hand it is true that the Assumption of Mary, in the image of the very Resurrection of Christ, represents an anticipation of that to which we too are called. On the other hand, however, none of us will

---

[91] Dante Aligheri, Paradiso 33.10–12, in *Paradise*, trans. Courtney Langdon (Cambridge, MA: Harvard University Press, 1921), 385. In verses 19–39 of the same oration, the initials of each triplet (in the original Italian) form the acrostic "*Iosep Av*," a contraction of "*Ioseph, Ave*" ("Hail, Joseph"). The silent Spouse of Mary is silently present even in the prayer addressed to his Bride.

[92] Second Vatican Council, *Lumen Gentium*, §68 (emphasis added). The *Missale Romanum* of Saint Paul VI refers to Mary as a sign of consolation and hope both in the Preface of the Solemnity of the Assumption of Mary (August 15) and in Preface IV of the Blessed Virgin Mary.

ever arrive at the degree of glory to which Mary has been raised as the Queen of Heaven and earth. Nobody else is or will ever be the Mother of God, the Immaculate, the Ever-Virgin, the Assumed, the Mediatrix of all graces, the Mother of the Church, or the Queen of the universe. Mary was not only assumed first in body and soul into Heaven; Her Assumption, though in continuity with ours, will always remain qualitatively greater,[93] like Her degree in the celestial hierarchy: the first degree immediately after the supreme majesty of the Holy Trinity (in which we include Christ). This degree immensely surpasses that of all the angels and all the saints, over whom She is Lady.

Finally, let us recall that Benedict XVI reread the ancient Marian title of *"Stella Maris"* ("Star of the Sea") calling Our Lady "Star of hope."[94] This allows us to reread the texts of the Tradition concerning the Stella Maris as texts that speak of the relationship between Mary and Christian hope. Among such texts, we shall only cite the one that is, in all likelihood, the best-known:

> Oh, whoever you are that sees yourself, amid the tides of this world, tossed about by storms and tempests rather than walking on the land, turn not your eyes away from the shining of this star if you wish not be overwhelmed by the hurricane! If squalls of temptations arise, or you fall upon the rocks of tribulation, look to the star, call upon Mary. If you are tossed by the waves of pride or ambition, detraction or envy, look to the star, call upon Mary. If anger or avarice or the desires of the flesh dash against the ship of your soul, turn your eyes towards Mary. If, troubled by the enormity of your crimes, ashamed of your guilty conscience, terrified by dread of the judgment, you begin to sink into the gulf of sadness or the abyss of despair, think of Mary. In dangers, in anguish, in doubt, think of Mary, call upon Mary. Let Her be ever on your lips, ever in your heart; and the better to obtain the help of Her prayers, imitate the example of Her life. Following Her, you will not stray; invoking Her, you will not despair; thinking of Her, you will not wander; upheld by Her, you will not fall; shielded by Her, you will not fear; guided by Her, you will not

---

[93] This is analogous to Christ, who is the first among the risen, but not only in the chronological sense. No one will think that, after the final resurrection of the flesh, the blessed in Heaven will have the same dignity as Christ, just because they are risen; analogously, it should be thought of Mary, whose dignity no one will ever equal. This is all true, (1) insofar as Mary herself will always be subordinate to Christ; and (2) Christ is the cause of the resurrection (Assumption) of Mary as well as our own, while Mary is not the cause but the first and most perfect beneficiary.

[94] See Benedict XVI, *Spe Salvi* (2007), §49–50.

grow weary; favored by Her, you will reach the goal. And thus will you experience in yourself how good is that saying: 'And the Virgin's name was Mary.'[95]

4.7. Marian Devotion

In Her *Magnificat*, the Virgin had prophesied the veneration that would be rendered to Her in every age: "From now on will all ages call me blessed" (Luke 1:48). Given the unique prerogatives of the Mother of God, the immense devotion that the Christian people have always paid Her is not surprising, nor is the fact that this devotion has always grown with time and has also developed new forms to be practiced. Saint Paul VI wrote that the "Church's devotion to the Blessed Virgin is an intrinsic element of Christian worship."[96] It is true that there is no shortage, inside and outside of the Church, of those who are skeptical of Marian devotions (if not all, then at least a certain number of them). But, while it is true that there can be exaggerations, the phenomenon of Marian devotion in itself is healthy and is a constitutive part of an integral Christian spiritual life.

Orthodox Christians display an extraordinary devotion to the Mother of God. The eastern Tradition surrounds the Ever-Virgin with wonderful praises in its hymns[97] and paints Her in marvelous forms in its icons. Despite this, it is generally the Catholic Church that is considered the keeper of the strongest devotion to Mary, perhaps also on account of the popularity and many branches of devotion to Our Lady. In fact, Catholics take care of their direct relationship with the Mother of God in many different and concrete ways, and they feel She is very close to them as a tender Mother.

So many beautiful prayers and devotions developed, the most important of which were officially recognized by the Church. Among these we recall

---

[95] Saint Bernard of Clairvaux, *Sermo II super Missus est* 17, in *Liturgy of the Hours*, "Office of Readings of the memorial of the Most Holy Name of the Blessed Virgin Mary". The final annotation is understood by bearing in mind that, from very early on in the Church, the name "Mary" was interpreted precisely as "Star of the sea": see Saint Jerome, *Liber de nominibus hebraicis*, who writes: *Mariam, illuminatrix mea vel illuminans eos, aut smyrna maris vel stella maris*" ("Mary [means] my illuminatrix or she who illuminates them, myrrh of the sea, or star of the sea").

[96] Saint Paul VI, *Marialis Cultus* (1974), §56.

[97] May it be enough to mention the celebrated Hymn *Akathistos* (literally: "Unseated Hymn"; in the East, the sign of adoration and veneration is not to be on one's knees, but on one's feet). The hymn is a composition in Greek of the fifth century, which sings to Mary in twenty-four "stanzas"—as many as the letters of the Greek alphabet—with the first letter of each "stanza" following the order of that same alphabet, from *alpha* to *omega*.

first and foremost the reciting of the Rosary, "the compendium of the entire Gospel"[98]: a devotion so important that many Popes have written official documents about it. May it be enough to recall Leo XIII, author of numerous encyclicals on the Rosary, and Saint John Paul II who, with the apostolic letter *Rosarium Virginis Mariae* (2002), brought the number of "mysteries" of the Rosary to twenty. In fact, this prayer is carried out by reciting the *Hail Mary* many times while one meditates on a "mystery," namely, on an episode contained in Revelation (Scripture and Tradition), which mainly concerns Jesus and Mary. The meditation on each mystery is accompanied by the recitation of a "decade," that is, a group of prayers formed by the *Our Father*, ten *Hail Mary* prayers, and the *Glory Be*. Litanies or invocations are almost always added after the *Glory Be*, such as the one revealed by the angel to the shepherds of Fatima.[99] Up until the innovation willed by John Paul II, the mysteries of the Rosary were fifteen in number. However, they were only rarely prayed all in a row. In general, five are recited each day (at least by the majority of Catholics who pray the Rosary). There are also those who only pray one or two decades a day, as well as those who pray the entire crown of fifteen or twenty decades, although perhaps spread out throughout the day. The Church reserves a liturgical memorial to Mary under the title of Our Lady of the Rosary, on October 7.[100] In many countries, the recitation of the Rosary concludes with the Litany of Loreto, so called because it comes from the custom of the Holy House of Loreto[101] from as early as the first half of the sixteenth century. This litany was approved by Sixtus V in 1587 and successively integrated by the Roman Pontiff, who then added other invocations.

---

[98] Pius XII, *Philippinas Insulas* (1946).

[99] The invocation goes: "O my Jesus, forgive us our sins, save us from the fires of hell, lead all souls to Heaven, especially those most in need of Thy mercy."

[100] Moreover, the entire month of October and that of May are considered "Marian months," in which devotion to Our Lady is cultivated with prayers and "little flowers" (Italian "*fioretti*," meaning small penitential offerings). In addition, Saturday of each week is dedicated to Our Lady. When there are no other obligatory feasts or memorials prescribed, each Saturday the Holy Mass and the Liturgy of the Hours can be celebrated as a "Saturday Memorial of the Blessed Virgin Mary."

[101] This is a famous basilica in which is kept an ancient dwelling that the Tradition indicates was the home of Our Lady at Nazareth, and therefore the home of Saint Joseph and the Infant Jesus as well. It is believed to have been removed, transported to Italy, and remounted there. Archeological studies claim that the construction technique of the small building (for example, the engravings on the bricks) conforms to Galilean customs of the first century. Moreover, even the structure and dimensions of the little house perfectly correspond to those of the site of Nazareth, where Tradition locates the home of the Holy Family (where the Basilica of the Annunciation now stands).

Finally, we cannot forget to recall that all the saints of the Church were always great devotees of Our Lady. Some saints were distinguished for the particular ardor of their love for Mary. Here are just a few more recent examples: Saint Louis-Marie Grignion de Montfort, Saint Alphonsus de Liguori, Saint Maximillian Kolbe (d. 1941), Saint Pio of Pietrelcina (d. 1968). Saint John Paul II had chosen as an episcopal motto *"Totus Tuus"* ("Totally Yours"), referring to Mary Most Holy.[102]

5. Mariology and the "Synthetic" Principle

We shall only offer a few notes in order to present what will already be evident to the eyes of an attentive reader, namely, that in Mary the principle of *et-et* is verified magnificently.

5.1. Virgin and Mother

The fundamental fact, to which all other aspects are connected, is Her being both Virgin and Mother. What is impossible at the natural level miraculously becomes possible in the progression of the supernatural plan of God, and we learn it from divine Revelation. It could seem, however, that in this case the *et-et* goes against the principle of non-contradiction, but it is not so. In fact, a miracle is never the contradiction of the laws of nature, but an exceptional suspension, decreed by God for reasons known to Him.[103] Even when working miracles, God does not violate the principle of non-contradiction; for example, God does not perform such a miracle as a man being alive and dead at the same time. But this is not like what occurs with Mary. In Her, the

---

[102] The same Pontiff explained that the motto is inspired by the work of de Montfort: See Saint John Paul II, *Rosarium Virginis Mariae*, §15.

[103] "Miracles are not in contrast with the forces and laws of nature, but only entail a certain experiential 'suspension' of their ordinary function, not their annulment. Actually, the miracles described in the Gospel indicate the existence of a power that overcomes the forces and laws of nature, but which at the same time operates in line with the demands of nature itself, even if above its actual normal capacity. Is that not what happens, for example, in every miraculous healing? The potentiality of the forces of nature is carried out by divine intervention which extends it beyond the sphere of its normal possibility of action. This neither destroys nor frustrates the causality that God has communicated to things in creation, nor does it violate the 'natural laws' established by Him and inscribed in the structure of creation, but in a certain way exalts and ennobles the capacity of working or even of receiving the effects of the work of others" (Saint John Paul II, *General Audience*, January 13, 1988, §3 [our translation]).

supernatural intervention produces not only the conception of a son without the intervention of a man, but also preserves and consecrates the Virginity of the Mother in and after the birth. While it is absurd that someone could be living and dead at the same time and with respect to the same ambit (e.g., physical life or spiritual life), it is not absurd—unusual as it may be—that a woman could be Virgin and Mother simultaneously. This, of course, can only take place for the aforementioned supernatural suspension of the laws of nature[104] and it will be known (being undeducible) only if the One who has worked the unimaginable (but not unreasonable) prodigy gives news of it. In the binomial, the divine Maternity occupies the primary place and the Perpetual Virginity occupies the secondary.

5.2. Christotypical and Ecclesiotypical Interpretations

In Mary, then, we find other applications of the principle of *et-et*. She can be understood in a Christotypical way and in an ecclesiotypical way, where the hierarchy of the binomial is very much highlighted: the Christotypical approach is undoubtedly the primary one. This is also evident in the formulation of the *Catechism*, which dedicates twenty-seven paragraphs (§§484–511) to the main themes of Mariology within its own Christological section, and twelve paragraphs (§§963–975) to other aspects in the ecclesiological section, entitled "Mary, Mother of Christ, Mother of the Church." This arrangement makes clear that the ecclesiotypical keys are founded, first and foremost, on the relationship of Christ and Mary.[105]

5.3. Other Binomials

Moreover, Mary is simultaneously both: (1) Mother and Member of the Church; (2) Mother and "Daughter" (First-Redeemed, Disciple) of Christ; and (3) beneficiary and dispenser of grace (by divine will). Even more binomi-

---

[104] According to the text in the previous note, this miraculous suspension implies a strengthening of nature beyond its normal limit. In the case of Mary, the suspension of the laws of nature according to which, normally, a woman is a virgin *or* a mother, occurs through the supernatural strengthening of the human nature of Mary, which, being female nature, can generate a child in the womb. In this case, nature goes beyond itself, because (by grace) it generates alone, without the cooperation of a male human individual; but it does not go against itself, because it is precisely a nature that is capable of generating human life.

[105] The above-cited §487 of the CCC is very clear in this regard: "What the Catholic faith believes about Mary is based on what it believes about Christ, and what it teaches about Mary illumines in turn its faith in Christ."

als could be identified in what is rightly defined as the mystery of Mary. Mary, in fact, is mystery and, among the mysteries, not only one of the greatest, but probably one of the sweetest and most comforting for those who have faith. We shall mention a final binomial, which sets the stage for the following section: She was, at the same time, both the Virgin consecrated to God alone, and the most faithful Spouse of Joseph.

6. Excursus: Saint Joseph of Nazareth

In closing the fourth section, we recalled the names of some saints that are distinguished by their great love for Mary. We can also ask ourselves which saint loved Mary most of all. It is only at first glance that the answer seems difficult and in need of lengthy historical research. It is actually quite simple: the saint that loved Mary the most is Saint Joseph of Nazareth, Her most chaste Spouse. We would like to conclude this chapter on Mary by speaking of him, immediately after the part that we have dedicated to the relationship between Mary and the Church, because Saint Joseph is both the Spouse of the Virgin and the putative father of Christ, as well as the Patron of the universal Church. His patronage is clearly explained: when he was in this life, God the Father made him an image of Himself, making him His representative on earth, as the putative father of Jesus. Moreover, God the Father entrusted to Saint Joseph a task that He did not reserve for anyone else, a task that requires unlimited fidelity: He entrusted to Saint Joseph the care and custody of His most precious treasures, Jesus and Mary.[106] Thus, as he took care of the physical body of Christ while on earth, from Heaven he also watches over the Mystical Body of Christ, which is the Church.

The *"theology of Saint Joseph,"* developed over the centuries in many works (and which is little-known today), is justified by the unique relationship of the Patriarch with Jesus and Mary. Saint Bernardino (d. 1444) writes:

> A comparison can be made between Joseph and the whole Church of Christ. Joseph was the specially chosen man through whom and under whom Christ entered the world fittingly and in an appropriate way. So, if the whole Church is in the debt of the Virgin Mary, since, through Her, it was able to receive the Christ, surely after

---

[106] "He was chosen by the eternal Father to be the faithful foster-parent and guardian of the most precious treasures of God, His Son and His spouse." (Saint Bernardino of Siena, *Sermo de Sancto Joseph Sponso Beatae Virginis*, translation: *vatican.va*).

Her, it also owes to Joseph special thanks and veneration.[107]

By consensus of the Fathers and the Doctors, the foundation of the theology of Saint Joseph consists in his marriage to the Virgin Mary, who consequently had the assignment of the parental role toward the Word incarnate. We shall now look briefly at some elements of this theology.

6.1. Humility and Justice

Even from these clues, we realize what an extraordinary figure this man must have been, so beloved by God and predestined to such a high and difficult task, before which he himself wavered, considering himself, due to his exceptional humility, unworthy or incapable of it.[108] This is indeed the interpretation of the so-called "doubt" of Saint Joseph that traditionally appears most appropriate. It is recounted by Saint Matthew:

> Now this is how the birth of Jesus Christ came about. When his mother Mary was betrothed to Joseph, but before they lived together, she was found with child through the holy Spirit. Joseph her husband, since he was a righteous man, yet unwilling to expose her to shame, decided to divorce her quietly. (Matt 1:18-19)

The very thought of divorcing Mary in secret already denotes the delicacy of this Saint's soul: if he had publicly repudiated Her, Mary would have received the death penalty by stoning, as She would have been accused of adultery (see Deut 22:20–21). However, the point that has always been debated regards the reason for Saint Joseph's decision: did he want to repudiate Mary because he did not believe She was truly pregnant through the work of the Holy Spirit, and thus he believed She committed a sin of adultery? Or was it because he believed Her and therefore—being very humble—did not consider himself worthy of being the head of the family and educator of Israel's Messiah? The question is complex and cannot be adequately treated here, but the detail that points to the more credible solution is the term "righteous" (Greek: *dikaios*, which has as in its background the Hebrew term *zaddiq*),

---

[107] Saint Bernardino of Siena, *Sermo de Sancto Joseph Sponso Beatae Virginis*.
[108] From this standpoint, Mary and Joseph are quite similar. The former said of Herself that God "has looked upon his handmaid's lowliness" (Luke 1:48). God also looked at the extraordinary humility of Saint Joseph. Thus, the consequence should be similar and therefore we must say, not just of Mary, but also of the Craftsman of Nazareth, that all generations will call him blessed (see Luke 1:48).

attributed to the Craftsman of Nazareth in Matthew's account.

In Scripture, being righteous means much more than what the expression means for us. First and foremost, it is God who is righteous. Those who serve God very seriously and always do His will are also righteous. To say that Saint Joseph was righteous implies that he was a man of most solid faith and very much a friend of God, always ready to do His will. He certainly knew the oracle of Isaiah, which we have already recalled: "the young woman, pregnant and about to bear a son, shall name him Emmanuel" (Isa 7:14) and thus the thought that Immanuel would be born of a young girl, an unmarried woman, and thus a virgin, was not at all foreign to his mental horizon. It is to be noted that Saint Matthew, in the same context in which he narrates the so-called "doubt" of Saint Joseph and the vision of the angel who encourages him to take Mary and the Child with him, cites precisely this oracle of Isaiah, adding that all these things happened in order for that prophecy to be fulfilled.

We must also add that a righteous person of the Old Testament would not have dared transgress the law of God. Now, Deuteronomy prescribed death for young women who had premarital relations. A righteous one of Israel, therefore, if he were certain of such a transgression, could not have done anything but denounce the young sinner. Precisely such a denunciation would be consistent with his being righteous. Thus, we cannot believe that Saint Joseph would doubt the integrity of Mary. If this were so, as a righteous one he would have had to denounce Her. The Craftsman[109] of Nazareth, rather, had to believe Mary and doubt himself, that is, his capacity to assume so great a responsibility.[110]

To all appearances this interpretation is disproven by what follows:

> Such was his intention when, behold, the angel of the Lord appeared to him in a dream and said, "Joseph, son of David, do not be afraid to take Mary your wife into your home. For[111] it is through the holy Spirit that this child has been conceived in her. She will bear a son

---

[109] The Greek *tekton* is frequently translated as "carpenter," as Luther did (*Zimmermann* in German). The Vulgate translates is as *faber*, which can mean carpenter, smith, or mason. In English, the word craftsman better renders the generic meaning of the original Greek. Saint Joseph carried out a manual activity, but it is not certain what it was. Furthermore, it is plausible that he knew how to perform masonry, carpentry, and metallurgy, as was common in the ancient world.

[110] After having discussed various patristic opinions, Aquinas agrees with this solution. See Saint Thomas Aquinas, *Super Matthaeum* I, lectio 4.

[111] In the Greek text it is *gar* (here translated "for"), which can certainly be translated in this way, even if it is commonly translated as "in fact" or "indeed."

and you are to name him Jesus, because he will save his people from their sins." (Matt 1:20–21)

At first glance, the angel seems to tell Joseph not to think ill of Mary, because what is inside of Her truly comes from the Holy Spirit. Actually, however, the translation of the original is not exactly unexceptionable, even if this argument cannot be explored here in detail. In spite of this, the translation cited can also be correctly interpreted, understanding it like so: "Do not be afraid to take Mary for the fact that what is generated in Her comes from the Holy Spirit." Therefore, Saint Joseph was afraid because he believed that what was in Mary came from the Spirit and was not the result of adultery. Therefore, he was afraid to assume the paternity of the Messiah, of the Christ of God[112]: it was humility that motivated him, not suspicion. However, the angel conveys to him that this is the plan of God: Mary would have to give birth (She will be the true Mother of the Child) and he would thus have to provide the name, and therefore exercise parental authority over Jesus.[113]

6.2. *The Obedient Silence*

A second evident aspect of the figure of Saint Joseph is his silence. He never speaks a word in the Gospels. This information reveals his attitude toward the will of God: he is the faithful and obedient servant,[114] who follows the divine orders without discussion (see Ps 39:10). We note that Mary speaks at the angel's annunciation, asking how the conception of Christ within Her could be possible, since She does not know man. It was the Virgin's right to ask that question, since She was asked to express full consent to the divine plan. This does not involve any imperfection on Mary's side. On the contrary, the angel confirms to Joseph a fact that had already occurred and in which, according to what has just been said, the Saint himself believes: that what is in Mary comes from the Holy Spirit. Saint Joseph does not have to consent to this

---

[112] We also see this interpretation in Saint Bernard of Clairvaux, *Sermo II super Missus est* 14.

[113] To support Joseph's vocation, the angel cites that of Mary. This is the same scheme that Saint Gabriel uses with Our Lady: to support Her call to maternity, he cites the maternity of Saint Elizabeth.

[114] Remember that earlier we cited the parallelism between Eve and Mary that was instituted by Saint Irenaeus. With surprising expression, Remigius of Auxerre (d. 908) proposed the same between Adam and Joseph "*Per inobedientiam Adae omnes perditi sumus, per bonum obedientiae Joseph omnes ad pristinum statum revocamur*" ("For the disobedience of Adam we are all lost, through the obedience of Joseph we are all returned to the original state": *Homilia 4* [our translation]).

The Mother of God

event at all, because it already occurred. Thus, he cannot ask: How will this happen? The only question that he could pose in his position is: Why me? But such a question would imply—indeed—an imperfection, a seed of rebellion to the will of God, even if only of venial gravity, or a doubt about the Divine Wisdom, which has chosen him. But Saint Joseph does not concede any of this. The angel confirms the will of the Most High for him and he immediately, without any words or questions, obeys: "When Joseph awoke, he did as the angel of the Lord had commanded him and took his wife into his home" (Matt 1:24). He also conducts himself in the same way after the birth of the Child, when Herod seeks him out to kill him:

> When they had departed, behold, the angel of the Lord appeared to Joseph in a dream and said, "Rise, take the child and his mother, flee to Egypt, and stay there until I tell you. Herod is going to search for the child to destroy him." Joseph rose and took the child and his mother by night and departed for Egypt. (Matt 2:13–14)

And on the way back:

> When Herod had died, behold, the angel of the Lord appeared in a dream to Joseph in Egypt and said, "Rise, take the child and his mother and go to the land of Israel, for those who sought the child's life are dead." He rose, took the child and his mother, and went to the land of Israel. (Matt 2:19–21)

After all, the prompt obedience of Saint Joseph confirms once again that he was just, because "to be righteous is nothing other than to be perfectly united with the will of God, and to always be in conformity to it in all kinds of events, both prosperous and adverse."[115]

He remains silent even at the time of the presentation of the Baby at the Temple, a presentation prescribed by Mosaic Law (see Luke 2:22–38). The meeting with the two elders Simeon and Anna revolved around the role of Jesus and the cooperation of Mary. Saint Joseph observed silence again in the last Gospel episode in which he appears: the loss of the twelve-year-old

---

[115] Saint Francis de Sales, *Les vrais entretiens spirituels*, appendix III, "Sermon on the Virtues of Saint Joseph." He continues: "Nobody can question that Saint Joseph was always in all circumstances perfectly subject to the divine will. Do you see it? Look how the angel uses him at his pleasure." (our translation) The silence and justice of Saint Joseph are also connected by Saint John Paul II, *Redemptoris Custos* (1989), §17.

Excursus: Saint Joseph of Nazareth

Jesus in Jerusalem. It is on this occasion that Jesus clearly says that His true Father is not Joseph, but God. Indeed, His Mother said to Him: "Son, why have you done this to us? Your father and I have been looking for you with great anxiety"; but Jesus responds: "Why were you looking for me? Did you not know that I must be in my Father's house?" (Luke 2:48–49).

6.3. His Death

After this episode, Saint Joseph is not named again in the Gospels,[116] which do a Pindaric flight from Jesus being twelve years of age to about his thirties, when the Lord began His public ministry. We cannot know for sure what happened during that time. The most probable thing is that Jesus continued to carry out His "hidden life" awaiting His revelation to Israel and to the world. At that point Jesus began His adult life and did not need guardians any longer: Saint Joseph had performed his task well. This is why, even if the Gospels do not say anything in regard to it, the belief developed that the putative father of Jesus died before the beginning of the Lord's public ministry,[117] surrounded by the love and care of Mary and Jesus himself.[118] Since a believing Christian cannot imagine a more beautiful death than that in which Christ and Mary assist the dying one in person, Saint Joseph has commonly also been considered as the Patron of the "good death"[119]: that is, we turn to his patronage to obtain from the Lord a serene death, comforted by the presence of the Lord and Mary, and above all a death in a state of grace, which opens the way for access into Paradise.

6.4. Care of Christ and of the Church

The silence of Saint Joseph in the Bible and his relatively defiladed role should not deceive us: he is and remains a figure in the foreground of the

---

[116] The rhetorical question posed by those who were marveling at the work of Jesus is an exception: "Is he not the carpenter's [craftsman's] son?" (Matt 13:55). However, the question does not imply that Saint Joseph was still alive when it was posed.

[117] Support for this is found in the fact that, not only under the cross, but even before during Christ's public ministry, the Mother and the "brothers" appear, but never the "father" (see Matt 12:46–50).

[118] Thus sings the liturgical hymn *Iste, quem laeti colimus fideles* (author J. Escollar, d. 1700): "*O nimis felix, nimis o beatus / cuius extremam vigiles ad horam / Christus et Virgo simul astiterunt / ore sereno*" ("O, most happy, most blessed / of which, vigilant to his [last] hour / Christ and the Virgin assisted / with serene face"). It is sung similarly in the hymn *Salve, pater Salvatoris*, which is even earlier.

[119] See Benedict XV (d. 1922), *Bonum Sane* (1920).

Gospel narrative and of the spiritual life of the believing people, of which he is Patron.[120] The Church does not forget that he was the Guardian of the Redeemer, as recalls a title of an apostolic exhortation written by Saint John Paul II.[121] That is why Saint Joseph considers it his duty—in addition to caring for the physical body of Jesus on the earth—to also care for the Mystical Body, the Church.[122] He does this in particular through his powerful intercession. Among the saints, a great many have been devoted to Saint Joseph, to whose patronage and intercession they resorted with trust. Among them, the Doctor of the Church Saint Teresa of Avila (d. 1582) deserves a special mention. She dedicated twelve of the seventeen Carmelite monasteries that she founded to Saint Joseph, and this, according to what she wrote, was not by chance:

> I took for my advocate and lord the glorious St. Joseph and earnestly recommended myself to him. . . . I don't recall up to this day ever having petitioned him for anything that he failed to grant. . . . For with other saints it seems the Lord has given them grace to be of help in one need, whereas with this glorious saint I have experience that he helps in all our needs and that the Lord wants us to understand that just as He was subject to St. Joseph on earth—for since bearing the title of father, being the Lord's tutor, Joseph could give the Child command—so in Heaven God does whatever he commands. . . . I had the desire to persuade all to be devoted to [this glorious saint].[123]

The Liturgy dedicates two whole occasions to the Saint: the Solemnity of March 19, in which he is venerated under the title of Patron of the Universal Church, and the memorial of May 1, in which he is honored with the title "Saint Joseph the Worker."[124] The latter, among other things, emphasizes once

---

[120] With the Decree of the Sacred Congregation of Rites, *Inclytus Patriarcha Joseph* (1847), Blessed Pius IX extended the feast of the patronage of Saint Joseph to the whole Church. On December 8, 1870, acquiescing to the request of several Conciliar Fathers of Vatican I, the same Pontiff, with the Decree *Quemadmodum Deus Iosephum*, elevated Saint Joseph to the Patron of the Universal Church.

[121] Saint John Paul II, *Redemptoris Custos*. The pontifical document was issued on the centennial of the Encyclical *Quamquam Pluries* of Leo XIII, dedicated to the recitation of the Rosary and devotion to Saint Joseph.

[122] See Leo XIII, *Quamquam Pluries* (1889) (DS 3262-3263).

[123] Saint Teresa of Avila, *Libro de la vida* 6.6–8, in *The Book of Her Life*, trans. Kieran Kavanaugh and Otilio Rodriguez, in *Saint Teresa of Avila: Collected Works*, vol. 1, second edition (Washington, DC: ICS Publications, 1987), 79–80.

[124] Leveraging this aspect, Pius XI, in *Divini Redemptoris* (1937), writes: "We place the vast

again that work is a great path of sanctification.[125] At the liturgical level, it should be recalled that Saint John XXIII wanted to include, while the Second Vatican Council was still in progress, the name of Saint Joseph in the only Eucharistic Prayer in use at the time, the Roman Canon.[126] After the Council, the liturgical reform produced a Missal in which there are three other primary Eucharistic Prayers, in addition to some minor ones. It was Pope Francis who also added the name of Saint Joseph into the other main prayers.[127]

6.5. Hypothesis to Examine

1. Immaculate Conception

Finally, we need to note two questions that still require a long theological reflection, given that they are only hypotheses. The first regards the possibility that Saint Joseph, like Mary, could have been preserved from original sin in light of his vocation as Guardian of the greatest treasures of the Father: Jesus and Mary. It would indeed seem more fitting that the most pure and perfect creatures who ever appeared on the earth would be entrusted to a man without the disordered desires that are a consequence of concupiscence. If this hypothesis were verified, it would be the case that God decided that under the same roof with Jesus and Mary there lived a most pure man not only in behavior, but also in thoughts and desires (free of the concupiscence that comes from original sin). A biblical basis would again be the attestation of Saint Matthew according to which Saint Joseph was "righteous."[128] We

---

campaign of the Church against world Communism under the standard of St. Joseph, her mighty Protector. He belongs to the working-class, and he bore the burdens of poverty for himself and the Holy Family, whose tender and vigilant head he was.... In a life of faithful performance of everyday duties, he left an example for all those who must gain their bread by the toil of their hands. He won for himself the title of 'The Just,' serving thus as a living model of that Christian justice which should reign in social life."

[125] See Saint John Paul II, *Redemptoris Custos*, §22–24.

[126] See Sacred Congregation of Rites, *Novis Hisce Temporibus* (1962). The same Saint John XXIII had published an apostolic letter in Italian with the title *Le Voci* (1961), in which—after a broad overview on the liturgical and devotional teachings of the popes in regard to Saint Joseph, from Blessed Pius IX to his predecessor Pius XII—he invoked the patronage of the Craftsman of Nazareth over the Second Vatican Council.

[127] See Congregation for Divine Worship and the Discipline of the Sacraments, *Decretum* (2013) (the decree specifies that Pope Francis confirmed the decision already made by his predecessor Benedict XVI).

[128] Another question is posed at the biblical level that would easily be resolved if the immaculateness of Saint Joseph were actually demonstrated. We are referring to the word of Christ: "Among those born of women there has been none greater than John the Baptist"

have to remember that the hypothesis is not excluded *a priori* by the dogmatic definition of the Immaculate Conception of Mary, because the text speaks of a "singular privilege"[129] of Our Lady: consequently, even if this is a privilege presented more as unique than rare, the chosen formulation does not in itself absolutely exclude that God could have conceded to somebody else this entirely exceptional grace.[130]

2. Assumption in Soul and Body

The second hypothesis regards the possible assumption of Saint Joseph in soul and body to Heaven, which is based on both a reflection and a fact:

(1) The reflection consists in that, once the possible "Immaculate Conception" of Saint Joseph is ascertained, the assumption in soul and body would be a direct consequence of his having been created in a state of righteousness and of having persevered in it through his whole life. Nonetheless, even in the absence of such a premise, his role as putative father of Jesus could equally justify the grace granted by God of receiving His faithful "parent" in Heaven in both soul and body. In fact, for Mary, the Assumption is linked not only to her Immaculateness, but first of all to her divine Maternity. Moreover, it would be motivated by a commonality of eternal destiny for the three members of the Holy Family, none of Whom would have known the corruption of the grave. This is also because the Holy Family is an image of the Trinity on earth. Like

---

(Matt 11:11). Since it is true that the Baptist was born with original sin and was purified in the womb of his mother Elizabeth (Luke 1:44), it does not seem possible that Saint Joseph is the greater saint, given that Christ says otherwise. But in the same citation of Matt 11, Jesus continues: "Yet the least in the kingdom of heaven is greater than he." Therefore, Saint John the Baptist is the greatest born of women, but others are greater than him. Of course, among these are Mary, who by dogma of the faith we know to be not "among those born of women," even though she was naturally born of her mother and father. If Saint Joseph had also received the gift of immaculateness, the question would therefore be easily resolved. Commenting on the Matthean passage, Cornelius a Lapide (d. 1637), *Super Matthaeum*, ad locum, writes that "it is worthier to be the father and nurturer of Christ than His precursor" (our translation). Pope Benedict XIV (d. 1758), in *De servorum Dei beatificatione et beatorum canonizatione* 4.2.20, argues that Saint Joseph is "probably" superior in holiness to the Baptist. Other insights for untangling the question are found in the patristic texts reported by Saint Thomas Aquinas in *Catena Aurea*, ad locum, and in his *Super Matthaeum* XI, lectio 1.

[129] "*Singulari omnipotentis Dei gratia et privilegio*" (Blessed Pius IX, *Ineffabilis Deus* [DS 2803]).

[130] However, we need to say that, recalling a text of Pius XII, Saint John Paul II excluded the hypothesis of the immaculateness of Saint Joseph (see *General Audience*, June 12, 1996). Considering its low magisterial weight, the text of the Holy Pontiff does not, however, prevent theologians from continuing to reflect on the question.

the divine Trinity is entirely in Heaven, indivisibly, so it could be for the Holy Family, in soul and body: for Jesus and Mary, this is a dogma of the faith, for Saint Joseph, it is a theological hypothesis to be explored.

(2) It is a fact, which is far from insignificant, that there is no place in the world claiming to possess the relics of Saint Joseph.[131] This is remarkable, since the local Churches have always "competed" to obtain the relics of the saints. In certain eras, this has also led to the trade, and in some cases, the creation of false relics. Why did no one come to think of seeking or "creating" the relics of Saint Joseph, despite the fact that the devotion to the putative father of Jesus has always been so strong in the Church? This argument was used by Saint Francis de Sales, Doctor of the Church, who believed in the assumption of Saint Joseph:[132]

> What remains to be said now, if not that we must not think that this glorious Saint does not have much credit in Heaven to the One who has favored him so much to raise him in Heaven in body and soul; which seems to me to be all the more likely, since here on earth we have no relic, and it seems to me that no one can doubt this truth; in fact, how could He have refused this grace to Saint Joseph, the One [Jesus] who had been so obedient to him in His life? ... How could we doubt that our Lord did not bring to Heaven with Him, in body and soul, the glorious Saint Joseph, who had the honor and grace to carry Him so often in his blessed arms, arms in which our Lord was so pleased? ... Therefore, Saint Joseph is undoubtedly in Heaven in body and soul.[133]

---

[131] We mean relics of the body. In some places, objects are kept that are believed to have been his property; for example, the ring of Saint Joseph is kept at Perugia, while his staff is at the Camaldolese in Florence, and so on.

[132] Other authors that have spoken in this regard include Saint Bernardino of Siena, *Sermo de Sancto Joseph Sponso Beatae Virginis*; P. Poquet (d. 1408), *Dictamen de laudibus beati Joseph*; Blessed Bernardine of Feltre (d. 1494); Isidore of Isolanis (d. 1528), *Summa de donis Sancti Joseph*, year 1522. The theologian Jean Charlier de Gerson (d. 1429) on September 8, 1416, spoke in the presence of the Fathers of the Council of Constance the *Sermo de nativitate gloriosae Virginis Mariae et de commendatione virginei sponsi eius Joseph*, in which he argued for the sanctification of Saint Joseph in his mother's womb, his immunity from concupiscence, his resurrection with Jesus, and his assumption into Heaven.

[133] Saint Francis de Sales, *Les vrais entretiens spirituels*, appendix III, "Sermon on the Virtues of Saint Joseph" (our translation). Matt 27:52 affirms that, as soon as Jesus died, "tombs were opened, and the bodies of many saints who had fallen asleep were raised." Saint Thomas Aquinas, *Super Mattheum* XXVII, lectio 2, wondered whether they would resurrect to their former life, or whether they would rise again to enter Heaven. And he

Obviously, based on what has already been said, if the hypothesis were to be accepted, it would still be clear that Saint Joseph, although assumed into Heaven, would occupy an inferior place with respect to both Christ and Mary.

---

answers that, if the first were right, the miracle worked at the death of Christ would have been a loss for them, more than a benefit. Thus, they rose "*tamquam intraturi cum Christo in caelum*" ("like people who will enter into Heaven with Christ"). But this supposes that some have entered Heaven with their bodies well before the final judgment. Saint John XXIII recalled this Thomistic exegesis in the *Homily for the Canonization of Saint Gregorio Barbarigo*, May 26, 1960, and cited two saints that, presumably, may have been in some way assumed into Heaven with Christ. The Pontiff writes: "It is therefore due to the dead of the Old Testament, closest to Jesus—let us name two of the most intimate in His life, John the Baptist, the Precursor, and Joseph of Nazareth, his nurturer and guardian—it is due to them, so we can piously believe, the honor and the privilege of opening this admirable accompaniment through the ways of Heaven."

8

The Church

1. The Church in the Salvific Plan of God

The word "Church" in the New Testament corresponds to the Greek *ekklesia*, which means convened assembly.[1] In the Hebrew of the Old Testament, the term *qahal* is used. The very name of the Church implies that she is not established by herself, through human initiative, but is the fruit of an encounter, once again, between the greater element, which is the divine vocation, and the lesser one, that is, the free response of the human being. The Church is thus *both* the gift of God (principal aspect) *and* the response of the human being. Considered concretely, it is thus the fruit of a divine design, which is realized with the contribution of the members of this group of human beings who are identified as Church.

1.1. The Church: Society and Mystery

In the liturgical constitution of the Second Vatican Council, we find a beautiful text that speaks of the constitutive bipolarity of the Church and highlights the hierarchy between the two fundamental elements:

---

[1] Saint Cyril of Jerusalem (d. 386), *Catecheses mystagogicae* 18.24: "Well is the Church named *Ecclesia* [assembly], because it calls forth and assembles all men" (in *FCNT*, vol. 64, trans. Leo P. McCauley [Washington, DC: CUA Press, 1970], 132).

It is of the essence of the Church that she be both human and divine, visible and yet invisibly equipped, eager to act and yet intent on contemplation, present in this world and yet not at home in it; and she is all these things in such wise that in her the human is directed and subordinated to the divine, the visible likewise to the invisible, action to contemplation, and this present world to that city yet to come, which we seek. While the liturgy daily builds up those who are within into a holy temple of the Lord, into a dwelling place for God in the Spirit, to the mature measure of the fullness of Christ, at the same time it marvelously strengthens their power to preach Christ, and thus shows forth the Church to those who are outside as a sign lifted up among the nations under which the scattered children of God may be gathered together, until there is one sheepfold and one shepherd.[2]

1.1.1. Baptismal Adoption

The more essential character of the Church stands on the side of God, on the side of His convocation or supernatural call to form part of His People. We have already seen (see Chapters Five and Seven) that not all human beings are children of God in the proper sense; only the baptized are, that is, those elected to the grace of Baptism. Baptism carries out the purification of original sin, makes people adoptive children of God, and inserts a person into the supernatural Family of God: the Church. Each human being is born in the context of a natural family. Baptism is a new birth, which causes the individual to be reborn into a new family, the supernatural family formed by all those who, being adoptive children of God in Christ, also become brothers and sisters according to faith and Baptism, according to election and grace. Jesus says to Nicodemus: "Amen, amen, I say to you, no one can enter the kingdom of God without being born of water and Spirit. What is born of flesh is flesh and what is born of spirit is spirit. Do not be amazed that I told you, 'You must be born from above.'" (John 3:5–7). From the beginning, therefore, Christians have called each other "brothers and sisters," even if they belong to families, cultures, and different peoples from the natural and social standpoint. And from the beginning this fact, apparently harmless, has caused a revolution of unparalleled historical significance:

---

[2] Second Vatican Council, *Sacrosanctum Concilium* (1963), §2. The text abounds with implicit biblical (recorded in the footnotes) and magisterial references.

Those who, as far as their civil status is concerned, stand in relation to one another as masters and slaves, inasmuch as they are members of the one Church have become brothers and sisters—this is how Christians addressed one another. By virtue of their Baptism they had been reborn, they had been given to drink of the same Spirit and they received the Body of the Lord together, alongside one another. Even if external structures remained unaltered, this changed society from within. When the Letter to the Hebrews says that Christians here on earth do not have a permanent homeland, but seek one which lies in the future (see Heb 11:13–16; Phil 3:20), this does not mean for one moment that they live only for the future: present society is recognized by Christians as an exile; they belong to a new society which is the goal of their common pilgrimage and which is anticipated in the course of that pilgrimage.[3]

1.1.2. Social Character

The Church is first of all a family: the supernatural Family of God and our own. This means, as Pope Benedict XVI remarked in the preceding passage, that the Church is a society. The societal character is certainly not the only one, nor is it the most important constitutive element, but it represents one of the most important elements, as well as the element that is first grasped by the experience both of her members and those who do not form part of her. The most obvious and experiential approach with the Church consists in living within (or at least in relation to) a structured reality, which has its own laws, its own traditions, its own ends, and its own authorities.[4] It is obvious that there is much more than this, which does not take away the fact that these elements remain the most visible, and the ones with which most people deal.

---

[3] Benedict XVI, *Spe Salvi* (2007), §4.

[4] In this sense, the Cardinal and Doctor of the Church Saint Robert Bellarmine (d. 1621) wrote, against the Protestant error of a purely invisible and spiritual Church, that "the Church is an assembly of human beings, as visible and palpable as the Roman people, the Kingdom of France, or the Republic of Venice" (Saint Robert Bellarmine, *De controversiis*, Liber III: *De Ecclesia militante*, caput 2 [our translation]). This expression was criticized very much in the last few decades because it would highlight only the human and juridical aspect of the Church, forgetting the mysterious aspect. But Saint Robert had previously emphasized the elements of grace that are at the base of ecclesial life, writing that "the assembly of human beings, who profess the same Christian faith, and are bound together by the communion to the same Sacraments, under the rule of legitimate shepherds, and especially of the Roman Pontiff, the only Vicar of Christ on earth" (*De controversiis*, Liber III: *De Ecclesia militante*, caput 2 [our translation]).

The Church

That the Church has the form of a society is a fact that falls before the eyes of everyone; indeed, the existence is clear to all of a multitude of Catholic faithful, congregated (as was said from the earliest days of Christianity, see *Didaché*, IX, 4) from the four winds, subject and obedient to the leadership of a supreme Shepherd and other particular rectors, equipped with means, both spiritual and temporal, intended for the benefit of the community, and addressed to the supernatural end of the beatific vision.[5]

That is not all. These institutional elements are all necessary, because without them there would be no way of relating to the Church, and there really could not even be the use of the subject "the Church" to identify a historically and juridically well-defined reality. Excessive emphasis on the institutional elements of Church ("juridicism") is harmful, because it overshadows the element that is supernatural and pertains to grace, which is invisible to the eyes, but real. However, the undervaluation of the societal/institutional components of the Church is also an error, because the Church (at least the earthly one)[6] is a group of human beings, not angels. Human beings are not pure spirits, but embodied spirits, as we said in Chapter Three when discussing the indissoluble unity of soul and body in the human being. The human being, in his or her natural constitution does not need a merely spiritual Church, but a Church that is spiritual-corporeal. The corporeal element of the Church is her institutional, juridical, and societal aspect.

In this way the Lord wanted His Church: a real organized, visible, and religious society, with the powers proper to a perfect and sovereign society, with its own laws, with its own authority, with its own means and end. This is a fundamental truth of Catholic doctrine, which has its firm and clear roots in the New Testament and its evident reality in the history of the Church. But perhaps, precisely for this incontrovertible traditional manifestation, it is one of the most debated and combated truths in the great controversy about the true nature of the Church. There are those who would want her to only be spiritual and thus invisible, this alone would be of divine

---

[5] Alfredo Ottaviani (d. 1979), *Compendium Iuris Publici Ecclesiastici*, Pontificium Institutum Utriusque Iuris, 2nd ed. (Rome: 1948), 94 (our translation). We mention a recent author, because this passage of his was explicitly cited in the Magisterium of Saint Paul VI: see *General Audience*, May 25, 1966.

[6] It is interesting that the Second Vatican Council clarifies in *Lumen Gentium* §8 that the Church is "constituted and organized *in the world* as a society" (emphasis added).

origin, not minding the logical consequence that an invisible Church is no longer a Church at all.[7]

Far from being a limit in itself, the societal aspect of the Church guarantees her fully human aspect. For example: in order to be a full member of the Church, would it be enough, under normal circumstances, to simply have the intention in one's spirit to be part of the Church? Certainly not. The will to adhere is in fact essential, but—as is natural for the human being—it must be followed by the visible operation of sacramental and juridical incorporation into a community of believers (unless this step—though desired by the individual—is prevented by elements that are independent of his or her will). The juridical-societal aspect of the Church is thus a guarantee of objectivity for the believer himself (or herself), who is preserved from a risky disincarnated spiritualism, which always leaves doubt as regards the objective reality of what is felt inwardly.

1.1.3. Society for Sinners

Yet another aspect needs to be added to this. The juridical-institutional character of the Church is based on philosophical anthropology, on the natural constitution of the human being—soul and body—but also on theological anthropology, which not only confirms the philosophical fact about the spiritual-corporeal character of the human being, but adds a revealed element: original sin, which clarifies many aspects of concrete human life. The members of the Church are not only human beings, but also human beings born with original sin, who are certainly freed from it by Baptism, but in whom remains the inclination toward evil called concupiscence. In this sense, the members of the Church can, and indeed do, sin again. Even the members of the Church, although freed from the great sin of origin, are "sinners."[8] Therefore, they are

---

[7] Saint Paul VI, *General Audience*, May 25, 1966 (our translation). The same teaching is found in Pius XII, *Mystici Corporis* (1943), §65: "For this reason We deplore and condemn the pernicious error of those who dream of an imaginary Church, a kind of society that finds its origin and growth in charity, to which, somewhat contemptuously, they oppose another, which they call juridical. But this distinction which they introduce is false: for they fail to understand that the reason which led our Divine Redeemer to give to the community of men He founded the constitution of a Society, perfect of its kind and containing all the juridical and social elements—namely, that He might perpetuate on earth the saving work of Redemption—was also the reason why He willed it to be enriched with the heavenly gifts of the Paraclete."

[8] "Nor must one imagine that the Body of the Church ... is made up ... only of members conspicuous for their holiness" (Pius XII, *Mystici Corporis* [DS 3803]).

tempted to commit evil and this temptation is extended to all spheres of life; and this does not exclude their way of living and acting within the believing community. Concupiscence can often lead to a certain incorrect mode of living within the Church and thus "the wisdom of the law, by providing precise rules for participation, attests to the hierarchical structure of the Church and averts any temptation to arbitrariness or unjustified claims."[9]

1.1.4. Mysterious Character

The institutional component does not exhaust the entire essence of the Church, otherwise it would be nothing more than one association among many that arise among human beings and gather people together according to interests or necessities: nation states, political parties, sporting and cultural associations, and so forth. In the understanding of the Catholic faith, the Church far exceeds all these human groups, because although the Church is also a human group, she has not arisen by human choice, nor is she ruled by human forces alone. The Church arises from the divine will, from the election and convocation of the Trinity. In this sense, as Baptism causes a rebirth because it brings a "new man" into the world, namely, one renewed in the image of Christ, so the Church is like a re-creation, because God causes the rebirth of the human family, whose unity was destroyed by the original disobedience.[10] Creation is not formed on its own: it is God who calls all things

---

[9] Saint John Paul II, *Novo Millennio Ineunte* (2001), §45. We add that in certain eras there may have been too much emphasis on the institutional aspect of the Church, understood as a *Societas perfecta inaequalis*, a perfect society in which not all are equal, because there is a Hierarchy (N.B. "perfect" society is not understood in a moral sense, as if everyone in the Church were saint, but rather in a social sense: the Church is a society that possesses in itself all the necessary means to carry out its ends). This definition of the Church was not wrong but partial, as is the case with any other definition or concise description of her (in this sense, even "Communion," "Sacrament," or "New People of God" do not individually express the whole truth about her). In reaction to excessive "juridicism," a more mysterious and spiritual model of the Church was developed in the last few decades, at times undervaluing her institutional elements. The recent moral scandals, especially those concerning a small but severely deviant portion of the clergy, have however led to vehement calls for the Church to improve her *rules* for handling such cases. Thus, it is clear that the Church cannot do without her juridical and normative component, including penal law.

[10] This is traditionally illustrated with the two biblical episodes of the construction of the Tower of Babel and the coming of the Holy Spirit at Pentecost (see Gen 11:1–9 and Acts 1:1–13). While sin divides human beings, which is evident both from the multiplication of the various languages that breaks down the communication between them and from the cultures that oppose one another, grace restores their unity: the Apostles begin to

into being out of nothing. Thus, the Church is not constituted on her own, but it is God who constitutes her. And the analogy can be developed further if we recall the concept of "continual creation" from Chapter Three: not only did God create existing things at the beginning, but they continue to exist because He holds them in being. This also holds true for the Church: not only was she established by God at her beginning, but she is constantly vivified and governed by Him throughout history. All of this invites us to look at the supernatural and mysterious component of the Church, without stopping only at the first contact with the visible-institutional reality of the community of believers. The more essential aspect of the Church is the mysterious aspect, it is that gift of grace that is at the very center of her being and her mission.

1.1.5. Primacy of the Mystery

Therefore, the institutional and juridical-organizational aspect, while being co-essential to the spiritual and supernatural aspect and never truly separable from it, is inferior to the latter, and at its service. To understand this in a concrete way, it is enough to cite the last canon of the current *Code of Canon Law*. The *Code* contains the fundamental laws of the Church, to which other laws must also conform. After having presented in seven books all the main rules of the internal life of the Church, in her various and complex aspects, the *Code* ends by saying that in the Church the supreme law is always the salvation of souls: "*salus animarum suprema lex in Ecclesia.*"[11] Such an affirmation could, at first sight, seem even ironic, given that up to that point the *Code* had sought to specify all the juridical regulations regarding the Church: the last, brief statement could seem to produce a crack at the base of this canonical building. Moreover, such a principle would be out of place in any code of civil law, even if reformulated in a more secular way. But it is not out of place in the *Code of Canon Law*, nor does it undermine its solidity, because, actually, it confirms the particular character of the Church, which is a *societas sui generis* (a society of its own kind), and it manifests a principle that is obvious for the Catholic: rules are very important, but they are not the most important thing. The most important thing is the salvation of the soul, as Jesus taught (see Mark 8:36). In the Church there is always a need for organization and the giving of rules

---

miraculously speak other languages and communication between people is reestablished because everyone hears the Gospel of Christ from the mouth of His witnesses. God, who is One, brings the human race back to unity: "One body and one Spirit, as you were also called to the one hope of your call; one Lord, one faith, one Baptism; one God and Father of all, Who is over all and through all and in all" (Eph 4:4–6).

[11] *Codex Iuris Canonici*, can. 1752.

(and of respecting them!). However, the organization and rules are in view of the eternal salvation of Christians; otherwise, they would not make any sense.

1.1.6. Relation with the Trinity

The Church is thus not just a society, but also and primarily a mystery of grace. It is not by accident that the first chapter of *Lumen Gentium*, the dogmatic constitution of the last council dedicated to the theme of the Church, is entitled "The Mystery of the Church." The word mystery, which is of biblical origin, does not express something arcane and incomprehensible, but refers to a reality that is included in the salvific plan of God and comes from God. It is thus an invisible, transcendent reality, but one that is also manifested in a visible and historical way. *Lumen Gentium* explains the mysterious character of the Church by recalling first of all its character as "Sacrament," to which we shall return further along. The Church's relationship with the Most Holy Trinity is then presented. This is a theme that we have already touched on when discussing Mary Most Holy, the Daughter of Zion who, not by accident, is the perfect Image or Figure of the Church. The Church is in relation to the Father, the Son, and the Holy Spirit; to the tri-personal God who has willed the Church, founded her in Christ, and perennially gives her life through the action of the Holy Spirit. The Second Vatican Council places itself within the Tradition and expresses it by rereading the role of the Church in the divine plan, in light of the project that God has regarding man (Adam) from the beginning, and regarding the consequences of sin as a division between human beings and God and among themselves, as well as their reconstitution in unity by means of Christ and the Church. In the words of Saint Cyprian of Carthage: "A people made one with the unity of the Father, the Son and the Holy Spirit."[12]

1.1.7. Founder

A second reason the Church is mystery consists in the fact that it was founded by Jesus Christ in relation to the kingdom of God:

---

[12] Second Vatican Council, *Lumen Gentium* (1964), §4, which cites Saint Cyprian of Carthage (d. 258), *De oratione dominica* 23. Here we can leave out the discussions of theologians about how exactly this relation of the Church with the Trinity should be understood: mainly in a causal sense, or an exemplary sense.

> The Lord Jesus set her on her course by preaching the Good News, that is, the coming of the Kingdom of God, which, for centuries, had been promised in the Scriptures.... The Church, equipped with the gifts of her Founder and faithfully guarding His precepts of charity, humility and self-sacrifice, receives the mission to proclaim and to spread among all peoples the Kingdom of Christ and of God and to be, on earth, the initial budding forth of that kingdom. While she slowly grows, the Church strains toward the completed Kingdom and, with all her strength, hopes and desires to be united in glory with her King.[13]

Let us notice two aspects in this passage: (1) It confirms that the Church is not founded by herself, by human initiative: in fact, it says that her Founder is neither Peter, nor the Apostles or first bishops. The Founder of the Church is Christ (Peter is the rock on which Christ founds her [see Matt 16:18]). (2) The word "kingdom" is used in a dual sense: the kingdom of God in becoming, and the perfect and realized kingdom. The Church is already the kingdom of God in the first sense and with her activity she expands the kingdom of God in all the world. In this dynamic sense, the word "kingdom" expresses "the reigning" of Christ the King: Christ already reigns over Christians, and thus the Church already is the kingdom of Christ. By bringing the Gospel everywhere, she also brings herself and thus expands the confines of the kingdom/reigning of Christ. At the end of time there will be a perfect and actualized kingdom; that is to say, the definitive establishment of God's dominion over all who will be saved and the definitive exclusion from His kingdom of those who will be damned (see 1 Cor 15:20–28; Matt 25:31–46). In this second sense, for the time being, a distinction between the Church and kingdom is admitted—a distinction that is not admitted with respect to the first meaning of the term. But even this distinction regarding the second meaning is temporary and destined to terminate on the day of judgment, when the kingdom of God and the Church will perfectly coincide and all those who will be saved, even if in this life they were not able to visibly form part of the Church, will be members of the heavenly Church, members of the kingdom. This is further confirmation that, at least in Heaven, "there is indeed one universal Church of the faithful outside of which no one at all is saved."[14]

---

[13] Second Vatican Council, *Lumen Gentium*, §5.
[14] Fourth Lateran Council, *Firmiter* (1215), ch. 1 (DS 802).

The Church

1.1.8. Three States

This latter aspect reminds us that the concept of Church cannot stop at contemplating only the earthly face of the Church. In reality, the Church currently knows different states of life, or conditions of her members: there are Christians who are still in this life, the wayfarers, who form the "pilgrim" or "militant" Church; there are deceased Christians who have not yet entered into Paradise and are expiating for the faults of their earthly life: the "penitent" Church, or the Church "in purification"; finally, there are the Christians who enjoy the beatific vision of God in Heaven, and this is the "celestial" or "triumphant" Church.[15] We must emphasize that these are not three distinct and separate Churches, but the one Church, whose members temporarily experience distinct states of life: *viatores* (wayfarers), *purgantes* (in purgation), *comprehensores* (beholders).

If we then consider not only the saved human beings but all those who have vision of God in Heaven as partakers of the triumphant Church, then we must recognize the heavenly spirits as members of the Church,[16] understood here as the Family of God in Heaven. This doctrine is expressed very well in the Liturgy, the public and official Worship of the Church, which is an imitation of the Worship of adoration that the angels and saints direct to God in Paradise, described in the grandiose visions of Saint John's Book of Revelation. But it is not only this: the Liturgy of the Church on earth does not only imitate the heavenly one, but is objectively united to it in reality. That is to say, the Church firmly believes that, by offering divine Worship here on earth, she is united to the choirs of angels and saints.[17] An indication of this is the recital of the *Sanctus* at the end of the Preface in the Holy Mass. This hymn takes up a song that the Seraphim perform before the Throne of God, as the prophet Isaiah makes known to us (see Isa 6:1–3) and is confirmed by Revela-

---

[15] "*Habet autem haec Ecclesia tres partes. Una est in terra, alia est in caelo, tertia est in purgatorio*" ("This Church has three parts: one is on earth, another in Heaven, and the third in Purgatory": Saint Thomas Aquinas, *Expositio in Symbolum Apostolorum*, art. 9 [our translation]).

[16] "The Mystical Body of the Church is constituted not only of human beings, but also angels" (*ST* III, q. 8, a. 4 [our translation]).

[17] This is what can be called "a glimpse of Heaven on earth" (Benedict XVI, *Sacramentum Caritatis* [2007], §35), or also "the Worship of a wide open Heaven" (Benedict XVI, *General Audience*, October 3, 2012). Even earlier, Saint John Paul II, *Orientale Lumen* (1995), §11, had written: "The Liturgy is Heaven on earth, and in it the Word who became flesh imbues matter with a saving potential which is fully manifest in the sacraments: there, creation communicates to each individual the power conferred on it by Christ."

The Church in the Salvific Plan of God

tion (see Rev 4:8). Moreover, not only does the Church on earth unite herself to that in Heaven, but also *vice versa*: the angels and saints direct themselves toward their brothers and sisters who are still "on the way," to help them by their intercessory prayers and, during the Eucharist, to adore together their Lord Jesus who renders Himself truly present on the earthly altar, under the appearances of bread and wine consecrated by the priest.[18] In this regard, we can cite a beautiful text from Saint John Chrysostom (d. 407):

> [At the moment of the Eucharist] angels stand by the Priest; and the whole sanctuary, and the space round about the altar, is filled with the powers of Heaven, in honor of Him who lieth thereon. For this, indeed, is capable of being proved from the very rites which are being then celebrated. I myself, moreover, have heard someone once

---

[18] There are many saints and mystics who have stated that they have seen the angels descend from Heaven and adore Christ in the Eucharist during the celebration of the Holy Mass. But in addition to the mystics, the liturgical texts themselves allude to this. In the Roman Canon, the angelic intervention is expressed by the *Supplices te rogamus*: "Command that these gifts be borne by the hands of your holy Angel to your altar on high in the sight of your divine majesty. We entreat you, almighty God, that by the hands of your holy Angel this offering may be borne to your altar in heaven in the sight of your divine majesty" ("*Iube haec perferri per manus sancti angeli tui in sublime altare tuum in conspectu divinae maiestatis tuae*"). Saint Ambrose of Milan (d. 397) in the *De sacramentis* 4.6.27, cites part of a Eucharistic Prayer that is very similar to the Roman Canon, in which the prayer goes as follows: "We ask and pray that you accept this offering upon your sublime altar through the hands of your angels" (in *FCNT*, vol. 44, trans. Roy J. Deferrari [Washington, DC: CUA Press, 1962], 306). The Greco-Egyptian Liturgy of Saint Mark prays similarly: "Accept, O God, by Your ministering archangels at Your holy, heavenly, and reasonable altar in the spacious heavens, the thank-offerings of those who offer sacrifice and oblation" (in *ANF*, vol. 7, trans. James Donaldson [Peabody, MA: Hendrickson Publishers, Inc., 1994], 556). In the Byzantine Liturgy, starting from the sixth century, a hymn called the *Cherubikon* is sung at the moment of the so-called Great Entrance, namely, when the priest, in passing through the iconostasis, enters into the sanctuary to bring the oblates to the altar. The hymn is sung like so: "Let us the Cherubim mystically representing, and unto the life-giving Trinity the thrice-holy chant intoning, now lay aside all earthly care. That we may raise on high the King of all, by the angelic hosts invisibly attended" (in *The Orthodox Liturgy*, ed. Stavropegic Monastery of St. John the Baptist [New York: Oxford University Press, 1982], 61). But even before this, at the moment of the Little Entrance, a prayer is offered with these words: "O Master and Lord our God, Who established the heavenly orders and hosts of angels and archangels to minister unto Thy glory: Grant that the holy angels may enter with our entrance, to minister with us, and with us to glorify Thy goodness" (*The Orthodox Liturgy*, 42). Still in the Byzantine Rite, in the Mass of the Presanctified, when the procession is carried out with the already consecrated oblates, it is sung: "Now the heavenly Powers invisibly do minister with us" (*The Orthodox Liturgy*, 190).

relate, that a certain aged, venerable man, accustomed to see revelations, used to tell him, that he being thought worthy of a vision of this kind, at such a time [of the Holy Mass], saw, on a sudden, so far as was possible for him, a multitude of angels, clothed in shining robes, and encircling the altar, and bending down, as one might see soldiers in the presence of their King, and for my part I believe it.[19]

1.1.9. Eschatological Nature

All of this implies what today is called the "eschatological nature of the Church." The expression means that the Church can never totally triumph on the earth, but only in Heaven. The Church, like the Christian, lives in this world, but is not of this world, as Christ taught at the Last Supper (see John 17). Thus, she cannot conform to the thought of this world, but must always, in every generation of Christians, renew her own mind (see Rom 12:2), that is, live in the true freedom of the children of God. The eschatological character of the Church also implies that she is concerned not only with the living, those who are down here, but also the dead. Yes, the Church has a relationship with the dead: it is a relationship of fraternal love, based on reciprocal prayer. Thus, the Church prays for the deceased who are still on the way of purification, while the latter pray for their brothers and sisters who are wayfarers (*viatores*).

1.1.10. Communion of Saints

In the Liturgy and in private prayer the Church prays for the souls in Purgatory, trusting in this way to "shorten" the sufferings of the "period" of their definitive purification after death. In particular, the Church offers the Holy Sacrifice of the Mass for the aid of the souls suffering in Purgatory: this means that the Church applies the merits of the Passion, Death, and Resurrection of Christ to these souls.[20]

The Church, also, prays to the dead who are saints. In this case, they are not in need of our prayer, but they listen to it with brotherly love and, uniting it to their own prayers, present it at the Throne of God. The intercession of the saints consists in this: our elder brothers and sisters offer to God their

---

[19] Saint John Chrysostom, *De sacerdotio* 6.4 (in *NPNF*, First Series, vol. 9, trans. W.R.W. Stephens [Peabody, MA: Hendrickson Publishers, 1994], 76).

[20] The doctrine and practice of indulgences is also based on the communion of saints: see *ST* "Supplement," q. 25, a. 1. On indulgences, see Chapter Ten.

merits and prayers for the sake of their younger brothers and sisters, who have yet to reach the house of the Father. Those who are in a state of purification (Purgatory) also do the same. They are also traditionally called "holy souls," because, although still imperfect, they are infallibly destined to enter into Paradise (for the various aspects involved here, see the final chapter). These souls also pray for us, manifesting their bond of fraternal affection. All this wonderful and loving exchange of gifts is summarized in one aspect of the expression the "communion of saints" (discussed further below). In this case, the word "saints" does not only refer to the saints canonized by the Church, but all members of the Church: wayfarers, those in purgation, and the saints of Paradise. As members of the Church, the "saints" are, in grace, all brothers and sisters: they thus share their goods and exchange reciprocal favors. On earth, the communion of saints also provides for the exchange of material goods in addition to spiritual ones (*et-et*), given the spiritual-corporeal character, and the relative needs, of both the human being and the Church herself.

1.2. The People of God in the Old and New Testaments

The framing of the Church within the salvific plan of God implies the recognition of a fact that is seemingly in conflict with what was said regarding her Founder: that is, that the Church already existed, in a certain sense, before the coming of Christ. It is here that we encounter the apparent contradiction: How can Christ be the Founder of the Church if she existed before Him? The contradiction actually goes away if we consider that the Church coincides in concrete terms with the Catholic Church, founded by Jesus and governed by the successor of Saint Peter, the Bishop of Rome, and by the bishops in communion with him; but this concrete realization follows what we already said in Chapter Two about the motive for the Incarnation of the Word.

1.2.1. From the Origins

The Word has become incarnate because of original sin, in order to restore the lost divine likeness to the human being. If, hypothetically, sin never occurred, the Word would have brought about our salvation without having become incarnate. Because of sin, the Word achieves our salvation in a concrete form through His work of redemption in the humanity that He has assumed. It is clear that if we ask Who the Word is, the response will be Jesus of Nazareth. But this does not imply that the Word did not exist before the Incarnation. This can be applied to the Church, too, in an analogous way. If we ask what is the true Church that God wished as a constitutive part of His salvific plan for humanity, we shall respond that the Church of Christ "subsists in the Catholic Church, which is governed by the successor of Peter and by the bishops in communion with him."[21] In fact, the Church willed by God as a means of salvation for all human beings is the Catholic Church,[22] also called Roman.[23] But this does not mean that God did not have a people even before the incarnate Word founded the Church.

In the Old Testament, God chooses and convenes a people chosen among all others, the people of Israel. But even before calling Moses, even before Abraham, we see at the very beginning God says to the first human beings: "Be fertile and multiply" (Gen 1:28). Keeping in mind what was said in various places in the previous chapters, we can now summarize in this way: God creates human beings, elevates them to the plane of grace, directing them to a final supernatural end, eternal salvation. God wills that salvation be a personal fact (the freedom belongs to the individual!), yet it is also pleasing to Him to give a social dimension to salvation, as the Second Vatican Council recalls:

> At all times and in every race God has given welcome to whosoever fears Him and does what is right (see Acts 10:35). God, however, does not make men holy and save them merely as individuals, without bond or link between one another. Rather has it pleased Him to bring men together as one people, a people which acknowledges Him in truth and serves Him in holiness.[24]

Even in Adam there was a mysterious link that united human beings to one another in a supernatural community, namely, one of grace, so that each individual could merit his or her own salvation within a "communion of saints." This explains again how it is possible for the sin of one to affect all the rest. The "Church" of the earliest stages of humanity, the Church as a community of human beings in grace, originally willed and established by God Himself with His *Logos* and His Holy Spirit, is now shattered, as we already illustrated by recalling in a footnote the episode of Babel. God's plan does not change but now it will be carried out in new concrete ways. Here, therefore, is the beginning of the great preparation toward the renewal and even improve-

---

[21] Second Vatican Council, *Lumen Gentium*, §8.
[22] See Congregation for the Doctrine of the Faith, *Responsa ad Quaestiones de Aliquibus Sententiis ad Doctrinam de Ecclesia Pertinentibus* (2007), questions 1–3; Congregation for the Doctrine of the Faith, *Dominus Iesus* (2000), §16–17.
[23] See, for example, Pius XII, *Mystici Corporis, passim*.
[24] Second Vatican Council, *Lumen Gentium*, §9.

ment of the Church of the beginning in the Church in the proper sense, founded by Jesus.²⁵ And just as, in Him, our human nature not only has been restored in the grace of its origins, but has been elevated to an even greater dignity, so too Christ does not only reestablish the Church of the earliest times, but He establishes the Church as a perfect community of salvation. The call of Abraham represents the first step of a long journey of reestablishing the People of God. The election of Israel, the people of the Old Covenant, is the highest realization before Christ of this reestablishment. Perfection finally arrives with the work of the incarnate Word.

1.2.2. Analogy between Christ and the Church

What we have just presented presupposes an important aspect of the doctrine of the Church, that is, the analogy that she has with the Incarnation of the Word. We find a spiritual element and a corporeal element both in Christ and in the Church. In Christ and in the Church, there is both divinity and humanity; and, as in Him, in the Church the human and divine aspects are not of equal value. Both Christ and the Church are incarnated in their concrete mode of subsisting as a consequence of original sin.

However, we need to add three points of clarification: (1) This is an analogy, and so there are elements of similarity but also strong elements of dissimilarity; however, it is not a weak analogy. (2) To say that the Church

---

²⁵ "All know that the father of the whole human race was constituted by God in so exalted a state that he was to hand on to his posterity, together with earthly existence, the heavenly life of divine grace. But after the unhappy fall of Adam, the whole human race, infected by the hereditary stain, lost their participation in the divine nature (see 2 Pet 1:4) and we were all 'children of wrath' (Eph 2:3). But the all-merciful God 'so loved the world as to give His only-begotten Son,' (John 3:16) and the Word of the Eternal Father with the same divine love assumed human nature from the race of Adam—but as an innocent and spotless nature—so that He, as the new and heavenly Adam, might be the source whence the grace of the Holy Spirit should flow unto all the children of the first parent. Through the sin of the first man they had been excluded from adoption as children of God; through the Word incarnate, made brothers according to the flesh of the only-begotten Son of God, they receive also the power to become the sons of God (see John 1:12) As He hung upon the Cross, Christ Jesus not only appeased the justice of the Eternal Father which had been violated, but He also won for us, His brethren, an ineffable flow of graces. It was possible for Him of Himself to impart these graces to mankind directly; but He willed to do so only through a visible Church made up of men, so that through her all might cooperate with Him in dispensing the graces of Redemption. As the Word of God willed to make use of our nature, when in excruciating agony He would redeem mankind, so in the same way throughout the centuries He makes use of the Church that the work begun might endure" (Pius XII, *Mystici Corporis* I, prologue [§12]).

existed before Christ in the form of the People of God (first in Adam, then in Israel) does not imply that, after the foundation of the Church by Christ, there continues to be an alternative people to that of the Church, in which God would carry out salvation in an equal or at least similar way to what He does in His unique and indivisible Church.[26] The Word certainly existed before the Incarnation, but once this happened, He did not also subsist in a state of non-incarnation along with His state of being the incarnate Word: from the Incarnation on, the Word is always and only the Word incarnate, Jesus (see Chapter Four). Likewise for the Church: after the foundation by Christ, the new People of God subsists, in its fullness, only in the Catholic Church and not elsewhere. It follows from this that only the Church is the universal Sacrament of salvation, toward which the history of the People of God in the Old Testament tended. Thus, God calls all human beings to enter the Catholic Church.[27] (3) The analogy is clarified in *Lumen Gentium*, §8, with reference to the role of the Holy Spirit in the Church. This aspect will be dealt with later.

1.2.3. "Ecclesia ab Abel"

We thus understand how the two seemingly contradictory statements stand together harmoniously: the Church was established by Christ *and* the Church existed before the Incarnation of the Word. It is thus no wonder that the Fathers of the Church were able to speak of the *Ecclesia ab Abel*, of the Church that already began with Abel,[28] the first son of Adam, with whom the human family blessed by God began to be formed after the creation of the first couple. This patristic expression also implies the entire theme of the salvation of those who lived before Christ (and who then waited for Him in the *limbus patrum*) and all those who, even after He came, for reasons independent of their will, did not become members of His Mystical Body. This theme was already presented in Chapter Five, and we need not take it up again. But what is added here at the ecclesiological level sheds further light on such questions.

---

[26] One could apply to this the Pauline principle: "So whoever is in Christ is a new creation: the old things have passed away; behold, new things have come" (2 Cor 5:17).

[27] "All men are called to belong to the new People of God. Wherefore this people, while remaining one and only one, is to be spread throughout the whole world and must exist in all ages, so that the decree of God's will may be fulfilled. In the beginning God made human nature one and decreed that all His children, scattered as they were, would finally be gathered together as one (see John 11:52)" (Second Vatican Council, *Lumen Gentium*, §13).

[28] See Saint Augustine of Hippo (d. 420), *Enarrationes in Psalmos* 118.29.9.

1.2.4. Old and New People of God

Therefore, if we consider the Church in the historical continuity of her development, from Adam to the Last Judgment, we see that the most expressive category is that of the "People of God." Since the work of Christ represents the "new" creation with respect to the original one (see Chapter Four), we also speak of the "new People of God," with the understanding that the previous People (the Church in Abel and the Church in Israel) is not destroyed, but purified and elevated to a higher dignity.[29] And just as the old creation no longer exists alongside the new, but rather only one renewed and elevated creation exists after the coming of Christ, so too from the time that Christ established the Church onward, there are no longer other parallel peoples of God, because there is always one and only one People of God. The ancient promises made to the patriarchs of the Old Testament were not revoked, but they have found their fulfillment and are thus definitively realized in Christ.

Saint Paul states it clearly when he writes, referring to the Israelites: "In respect to the gospel, they are enemies on your account; but in respect to election, they are beloved because of the patriarchs. For the gifts and the call of God are irrevocable" (Rom 11:28–29). And what the Apostle adds immediately after confirms once again what we have said here so far about the continuity of the Church, from the beginning until today. He writes, addressing the Christians: "Just as you once disobeyed God but have now received mercy because of their disobedience, so they have now disobeyed in order that, by virtue of the mercy shown to you, they too may [now] receive mercy. For God delivered all to disobedience, that he might have mercy upon all" (Rom 11:30–32). This means that the earliest human beings, who made up the early People of God, sinned and became disobedient by living in sin and practicing all forms of paganism, both religious and moral. God elected Israel, which from that moment was, although in a temporary and imperfect way, the People obedient to God. Now that God has established His definitive People in Christ, the Israelites that do not enter in to form part of it are—Saint Paul says—"enemies in respect to the Gospel" and "disobedient." However, this refusal of theirs represented the good fortune of the pagans, of those who at the time of Israel were enemies of God, who disobeyed Him. In fact, on account of Israel's refusal, the Gospel was also preached to the pagans,

---

[29] In 2 Cor 3:9–10, Saint Paul says that the ministry of the Old Law was glorious, but that of the New Covenant is that much greater. In fact, he continues, the Old Law disappears in the face of the New Law, because the ministry of the New Testament has a "glory that surpasses it."

who received it with joy. What Saint Paul is saying about the Israelites does not, however, represent a condemnation without appeal, nor does he manifest hatred toward them by calling them enemies.[30] "Enemy" here does not indicate a subjective feeling of resentment on the part of the Christian toward the Jew, but an objective situation of the latter not accepting the Gospel—a fact highlighted by the Lord Himself (see Luke 19:44). For the Apostle, however, this too is part of the mysterious divine plan, which—being Providence—knows how to draw a greater good from evil:

> Hence I ask, did they stumble so as to fall? Of course not! But through their transgression salvation has come to the Gentiles, so as to make them jealous. Now if their transgression is enrichment for the world, and if their diminished number is enrichment for the Gentiles, how much more their full number. / Now I am speaking to you Gentiles. Inasmuch then as I am the apostle to the Gentiles, I glory in my ministry in order to make my race jealous and thus save some of them. For if their rejection is the reconciliation of the world, what will their acceptance be but life from the dead? (Rom 11:11–15; see also Rom 9:22–24).

That the sentiments of the Apostle—a recent convert from Judaism—were clearly not hostile to the Israelites, emerges clearly in another passage:

> I speak the truth in Christ, I do not lie; my conscience joins with the holy Spirit in bearing me witness that I have great sorrow and constant anguish in my heart. For I could wish that I myself were accursed and separated from Christ for the sake of my brothers, my kin according to the flesh. They are Israelites; theirs the adoption, the glory, the covenants, the giving of the law, the worship, and the promises; theirs the patriarchs, and from them, according to the

---

[30] To avoid doubt, the last Council clarified that the words of the Apostle cannot be interpreted in an anti-Semitic sense: "Although the Church is the new People of God, the Jews should not be presented as rejected or accursed by God, as if this followed from the Holy Scriptures. All should see to it, then, that in catechetical work or in the preaching of the Word of God they do not teach anything that does not conform to the truth of the Gospel and the Spirit of Christ. Furthermore, in her rejection of every persecution against any man, the Church, mindful of the patrimony she shares with the Jews and moved not by political reasons but by the Gospel's spiritual love, decries hatred, persecutions, displays of anti-Semitism, directed against Jews at any time and by anyone" (Second Vatican Council, *Nostra Ætate* [1965], §4).

flesh, is the Messiah. God who is over all be blessed forever. Amen (Rom 9:1–5).

The relationship between the two peoples of God, or better, between the two phases of the development of the one People of God, should be understood like the relationship between the biblical writings that correspond to them, gathered in the Old and New Testaments: a continuity in novelty, in a dynamic that goes from imperfect and temporary to perfect and definitive. However, what is imperfect is not cancelled out by the arrival of what is perfect, as is evident from the fact that the Church still reads and venerates the writings of the Old Covenant, because God spoke and speaks through them. At the historical level, then, we note that the converts to Christianity from the Jewish religion attest to not having needed to deny their own previous faith (as happens when there is a conversion from other religions) but to have simply passed to the fullness of faith in the same God of the Fathers,[31] a fullness that is lacking in the Jewish religion because it does not recognize Christ having come in the flesh and all the gifts that He brought with Him. But, if this can help our Jewish friends, the Lord Jesus, in bringing to perfect fulfillment the Revelation of the One and Triune God, has also said that the Trinity is "the God of Abraham, (the) God of Isaac, and (the) God of Jacob" (Mark 12:26).

2. What Is the Church?

The first part framed the Church within the salvific plan of God and also hinted at the experience that the human being, Christian or not, has of the Church. Now we must clarify the nature of this human-divine entity, keeping in mind three aspects that also emerged in the previous part: the fact that the Church is not only a society, but also a mystery of grace; the fact that the Church is principally from God as a gift, but also from human beings insofar as they respond to grace; and finally, the fact that Christ is always present in

---

[31] For example, Saint Teresa Benedicta of the Cross (whose secular name is Edith Stein, d. 1942), by interpreting the value of her Baptism, which ratified her conversion from Judaism to Catholicism, said: "I had ceased practicing my Jewish religion and I only felt like a Jew again after my return to God." The harmonic coexistence of belonging to the Jewish people and the convinced adherence to the Catholic faith of this Saint is also highlighted by Saint John Paul II, *Homily for the Beatification of Sister Teresa of the Cross*, Cologne, May 1, 1987; and *Homily for the Canonization of Blessed Teresa of the Cross*, Rome, October 11, 1998.

His Church, which has a (certainly not weak) analogy with the mystery of the Incarnation.

2.1. Extension of the Incarnation

2.1.1. Ecclesial Synthesis of Spirit and Matter

A rather classic way of describing the nature of the Church derives from the fundamentally Christocentric horizon of the Catholic faith. Christ has become incarnate once and for all, and His Incarnation is a permanent state of the Word, who for all eternity will never abandon the humanity He has assumed. The Word is and will always be in the state of incarnate Word (see Chapter Four). If the Church is considered against the backdrop of the permanent presence of the Word in her, we must then consider her as the "place" of the incarnate Word's presence. In this sense, the Church represents a sort of "extension" in time of the Incarnation. The Word (God, the Spirit[32]) has assumed matter in an indissoluble way, uniting a human nature to Himself. The eminently spiritual and supernatural mystery (grace), which is the most important element of the nature of the Church, is also found indissolubly linked to matter, to the humanity of which the Church is composed. We find analogously in the Church, the Bride of Christ, what we have said since the beginning of the volume about a dynamic of harmonic synthesis between Spirit and matter.

2.1.2. The Sacraments

This extension of the Incarnation regards not only the nature of the Church but also her activity, which is an always "incarnate" activity. The greatest case of this are the Sacraments (see Chapters Nine, Ten, and Eleven). They dispense supernatural and invisible grace through material and visible signs. But this principle of the Incarnation is truly extended to all aspects of ecclesial life and activity, down to the smallest details and the most particular aspects. In regard to the Sacraments, we note that they are truly an extension of the salvific Incarnation of the Word. We should recall in this regard a teaching of Saint Leo the Great (d. 461), who linked the Sacraments to the Ascension of Christ into Heaven. As we said in Chapter Four, ascending to the Father, the humanity of Christ is taken away from this earthly life and reaches its

---

[32] This is to be understood here not in the sense of the Holy Spirit, or Third Person of the Trinity, but rather as a generic term to indicate the divine nature, which is Spirit.

final destination. Of course, Christ is not far from us, He does not leave us orphans (see John 14:18), but His presence and action, from that moment on, are carried out in a different way. The highest point of the new presence of Christ among us is found in the Sacraments which, although they are not the only form of His presence among us, certainly represent the highest point of its intensity and reality, with a special distinction for the Eucharist (see Chapter Eleven). This is the reason Saint Leo the Great affirms that "What was... visible in our Savior passed into His Sacraments."[33] These words mean that the grace that Christ, during His earthly life, dispensed to human beings through the events of His life ("Christological mysteries"), and the merits that He obtained for us through His Passion and Death, now come to us transmitted, normally, through the Sacraments of the Church.[34] Given that the whole activity of the Church always maintains a sacramental character, one can understand why the Church herself is also called a "Sacrament" (see below).

2.1.3. "Christus Totus"

The link between the Church and Christ is so strong that Saint Augustine coined the expression "*Christus totus*" ("the whole Christ"),[35] to indicate the mystic union between the Groom and Bride, or between the Head and the members. Later on, Pope Saint Gregory the Great (d. 604) would also say that Christ and the Church form, in a certain way, a single Person.[36] That is not simply a patristic thesis, but a teaching of Scripture. When the risen Christ appears to Saul, the harsh persecutor of the Church, He does not present Himself by saying: "I am the Lord of the Church that you are persecuting," but rather, "I am Jesus, whom you are persecuting" (Acts 9:5). Saul (the future Saint Paul) did not persecute Jesus directly; he persecuted the Christians. Jesus, however, totally identifies Himself with the Church, both in suffering (being accepted or rejected), and in action (deciding and acting): "Whoever receives you receives me" (Matt 10:40; see John 13:20); "Whoever listens to you listens to me. Whoever rejects you rejects me" (Luke 10:16); "Whatever

---

[33] Saint Leo the Great, *Sermo 54*.2 (our translation).
[34] See CCC §§1115–1116.
[35] Saint Augustine of Hippo, *Enarrationes in Psalmos* 90.2.1, in *The Works of Saint Augustine: A Translation for the 21st Century*, vol. III/18, trans. Maria Boulding (Hyde Park: New City Press, 2002), 330.
[36] "Our Redeemer revealed Himself as one Person together with holy Church, whom He took to Himself" (Saint Gregory the Great, *Moralia in Job*, "Praefatio," 1.6.14, in *Gregory the Great: Moral Reflections on the Book of Job*, vol. 1, trans. Brian Kerns [Collegeville, MN: Liturgical Press, 2014], 70).

The Church

you bind on earth shall be bound in heaven, and whatever you loose on earth shall be loosed in heaven" (Matt 18:18; see 16:19); "Whose sins you forgive are forgiven them, and whose sins you retain are retained" (John 20:23). All of this is based on the fact that Jesus and His disciples are so united at the supernatural level that the Lord Himself describes us as branches linked to the Vine that is Him (see John 15:1–11). This leads us to the image of the Church as the Mystical Body of Christ.

2.2. Mystical Body of Christ

2.2.1. The Pauline Image

The Church is described in the New Testament as the "Body of Christ," of which the Lord is the Head and the Christians are the members. This is an image taken from the natural world, already used by non-Christian philosophers and orators, and applied by Saint Paul to the supernatural society of the Church (see Rom 12:4–5; 1 Cor 12:12–21; Eph 1:22–23; Col 1:17–18; 2:9–10). The Pauline use of this image implies:

(1) The catholic complexity of the Church, in which, despite its fundamental unity, various elements subsist: various ministries, various charisms, various vocations and missions, etc. The image of a body composed of many members and various organs, but all cooperating for a common health, is ideal for expressing the complexity of the ecclesial reality.

(2) The image of the body is determined by the Apostle as being a body "in" Christ (Rom 12:5) and "Christ's" (1 Cor 12:27; Eph 4:12). The body is not ruled and coordinated by itself: just as in the human body it is the head that sends orders to the members, so in the Church it is Christ who distributes the various tasks and gives unity to the body. If you take away the head, the whole body dies; if Christ is not at the head of the Church, she perishes. Saint Paul thus explicitly calls Christ the "Head of the body" (Col 1:18; 2:19; Eph 4:15).

(3) A body is composed of members that are not only distinct but also of different value (see Rom 12:4). This also applies to the Church, in which all ministries should be respected as a gift of God, but there are members that, from an objective standpoint, are more important than others: obviously the Head is at the top of the Hierarchy, then other members follow that participate in its fullness in various ways (see Col 2). However, Saint Paul clarifies that all members are necessary and cooperate for the unity and well-being of the body, thus no member can say to another that it is not needed (see 1 Cor 12)—something that showcases the principle of *et-et* very well, in which

What Is the Church?

"principal/secondary" is not equivalent to "essential/optional."

(4) The image of the body, moreover, speaks not only of a cooperation between the members, but also of their reciprocal belonging: they belong to each other (see Rom 12:5). This is so because all belong to Christ (see Gal 3:27–28).

2.2.2. The Adjective "Mystical"

The image of the body confirms that the Church cannot be conceived in either a purely human way (as a charitable organization), or in a purely spiritual way (lacking a visible and institutional component). The Fathers of the Church took up and developed the parallelism between the human body and the Body of Christ that is the Church. Then in the Middle Ages, the terminology was developed and honed, and the adjective "mystical" was added to the noun "body."[37] This specification helps to better distinguish the physical body of Jesus and the Eucharist, from the ecclesial body. The physical body of Jesus is risen, and stands at the right hand of the Father in Heaven; the Eucharistic Body is that same physical body, really present, but in a sacramental way (see Chapter Eleven) in the consecrated Host; finally, the Mystical Body is the Church: the mystical union—that is, the supernatural union—between believers and the Lord. Historical studies conducted in the twentieth century have brought to light the fact that before the Middle Ages, the expression Mystical Body was used in reference to the Eucharist: the change of terminology happened in the twelfth century and seems very appropriate because it avoids any possible misunderstanding about the reality of Christ's presence in the consecrated Eucharistic Species. Even the definition of Church gains something from this addition of the adjective "mystical." That is why

---

[37] Saint Thomas Aquinas highly enhanced the ecclesiological image of the Mystical Body (see *ST* III, q. 8, a. 1; *Expositio in Symbolum Apostolorum*, art. 9; *Super I Epistolam b. Pauli ad Corinthios*, X, *lectio* 4; XII, *lectio* 3; *Quaestio disputata de Veritate*, q. 29, a. 4). In the cited *De Veritate*, the Angelic Doctor emphasizes the metaphorical character of the image: "*In spiritualibus caput dicitur per transumptionem a capite corporis naturalis: et ideo consideranda est habitudo capitis ad membra, ut appareat qualiter Christus sit Ecclesiae caput*" ("In spiritual things head is said in a metaleptic sense with respect to the head of a natural body; and therefore to see how Christ is head of the Church we should consider how the head relates to the members [of a human body]" [our translation]). The difference between Mystical Body and physical body is described in *ST* III, q. 8, a. 3, in which Saint Thomas also clarifies another concept: that Christ is Head not only of Christians who are members *in act* of the Mystical Body, but also of all other human beings, insofar as they are members *in potency*. This is consistent with what was said in the Chapter Four about the universal kingship of Christ.

The Church

the Church has made this terminology her own and keeps it to this very day.[38]

2.2.3. Mystical Body and the Christological Principle

Pope Leo XIII connected the doctrine of the Church as Mystical Body to the Catholic *et-et*, which also applies to the nature of the Church:

> Precisely because it is a body is the Church visible: and because it is the body of Christ is it living and energizing, because by the infusion of His power Christ guards and sustains it, just as the vine gives nourishment and renders fruitful the branches united to it. And as in animals the vital principle is unseen and invisible, and is evidenced and manifested by the movements and action of the members, so the principle of supernatural life in the Church is clearly shown in that which is done by it. From this it follows that those who arbitrarily conjure up and picture to themselves a hidden and invisible Church are in grievous and pernicious error: as also are those who regard the Church as a human institution which claims a certain obedience in discipline and external duties, but which is without the perennial communication of the gifts of divine grace, and without all that which testifies by constant and undoubted signs to the existence of that life which is drawn from God. It is assuredly as impossible that the Church of Jesus Christ can be the one or the other, as that man should be a body alone or a soul alone. The connection and union of both elements is as absolutely necessary to the true Church as the intimate union of the soul and body is to human nature. The Church is not something dead: it is the Body of Christ endowed with supernatural life. As Christ, the Head and Exemplar, is not wholly in His visible human nature, which Photinians and Nestorians assert, nor wholly in the invisible divine nature, as the Monophysites hold, but is one, from and in both natures, visible and invisible; so the Mystical Body of Christ is the true Church, only because its visible parts draw life and power from the supernatural gifts and other things whence spring their very nature and essence. But since the Church is such by divine will and constitution, such it must uniformly remain to the end of time. If it did not, then it would not have been founded as

---

[38] It seems that the first magisterial document in which the expression Mystical Body is applied to the Church is the famous bull *Unam Sanctam* (1302) of Boniface VIII (DS 870).

perpetual, and the end set before it would have been limited to some certain place and to some certain period of time; both of which are contrary to the truth. The union consequently of visible and invisible elements because it harmonizes with the natural order and by God's will belongs to the very essence of the Church, must necessarily remain so long as the Church itself shall endure.[39]

As we have said, the expression "Mystical Body" is not found in Scripture, which speaks of the Church as a "Body" or "Body of Christ." However, the syntagm "Mystical Body" is still justified on the basis of Scripture, because Saint Paul does not just understand the Church from the social standpoint, using the rhetoric of the body already utilized by non-Christian authors; the Apostle also confers a new meaning to the image of the body, given that the Church is a mystery, which is understood on the basis of the mystery of Christ. Hence, the Church is a Body not only because she is an ordered society that obeys a Head ("moral body"), but also because she is mysteriously, supernaturally identified with Him. In 1947, Pope Pius XII wrote a magnificent encyclical on this theme, called precisely *Mystici Corporis*, in which he presents the biblical, patristic, and magisterial doctrine of the Church as the Mystical Body in a very wide-ranging way. The Pope also shares the reasons why it is not only opportune, but even necessary to add the adjective "Mystical" to the name "Body":

> There are several reasons why it [the syntagm "Mystical Body"] should be used; for by it we may distinguish the Body of the Church, which is a Society whose Head and Ruler is Christ, from His physical Body, which, born of the Virgin Mother of God, now sits at the right hand of the Father and is hidden under the Eucharistic veils; and, that which is of greater importance in view of modern errors, this name enables us to distinguish it from any other body, whether in the physical or the moral order.[40]

Therefore, saying that the Church is the Mystical Body of Christ allows for the specification that distinguishes the Church from a physical body[41] and from the Eucharistic Body of the Lord; it also evades the interpretation of the Pauline expression as having only the sense of a "moral body." Once again,

---

[39] Leo XIII, *Satis Cognitum* (1896) (reproduced with parts omitted in DS 3300–3301).
[40] Pius XII, *Mystici Corporis* I, 3 [§60] (DS 3809).
[41] On this, see *ST* III, q. 8, a. 3.

The Church

this clearly presses upon us the fact that the Church can only be understood in her mystery within the plan of God and the mystery of Christ. The Second Vatican Council confirmed the significance of this syntagm in dedicating §7 of the constitution *Lumen Gentium* to the ecclesiology of the Mystical Body.

2.3. Sacrament

Sacrament (in Greek, *mysterion*) is the first definition given in the dogmatic constitution on the Church of the last Council. We read there, right at the beginning, that "the Church is in Christ like a Sacrament or as a sign and instrument both of a very closely-knit union with God and of the unity of the whole human race."[42]

2.3.1. Sign and Instrument

This definition concisely contains several elements that we have already presented: Sacrament means first of all a sign of Christ. A sign is an indicator that refers to another. In fact, the Church is not an end in herself, but serves to bring human beings to Christ, and thus she refers to Christ. This aspect of the doctrine is already seen in the First Vatican Council, where it is taught that the Church is like a banner raised in the midst of the nations of the earth, to call all people to knowledge of the true God in Jesus Christ.[43]

The Church is not just an inert sign; it is also an instrument, that is, a reality that is utilized and contributes to the performance of an action, to the completion of a work. The category of Sacrament is therefore based on the analogy between the Incarnation and the Church: as Christ makes use of his physical body as an instrument conjoined to His divinity (see Chapter Four), so He makes use of His Mystical Body as an instrument to unite human beings with God and each other.[44] This purpose of the Sacrament Church

---

[42] Second Vatican Council, *Lumen Gentium*, §1.

[43] First Vatican Council, *Dei Filius* (1870), ch. 3 (DS 3014). The biblical foundation that is cited is Isa 11:12.

[44] It is significant that the Second Vatican Council recalls this very analogy in the context of the Constitution on the Sacred Liturgy, thus showing that the Church—Sacrament by analogy to Christ—manifests her character as His sign and instrument, above all, in sacramental celebration and the Liturgy: "[Christ's] humanity, united with the Person of the Word, was the instrument [*instrumentum*] of our salvation. Therefore in Christ 'the perfect achievement of our reconciliation came forth, and the fullness of divine Worship was given to us.' . . . The work of Christ the Lord in redeeming mankind and giving perfect glory to God . . . [was] achieved . . . principally by the paschal mystery. . . . For it was from the side of Christ as He slept the sleep of death upon the cross that there came

has already emerged previously and will not be taken up again here: the unity of human beings with God has been lost; this was also followed by a rupture between individuals and nations (Babel). The Church is the Sacrament of unity, that is, a sign and instrument that God uses to reconcile the fallen creature to Himself and thus also to reconcile individuals and peoples to each other (see Eph 2:14–18). This is why the Church is also defined with greater breadth as the "universal Sacrament of salvation,"[45] that is, sign and instrument of salvation of all human beings: an expression that reveals the positive meaning of the dogma that was defined in the negative form, "*Extra Ecclesiam nulla salus*" ("Outside the Church there is no salvation").

2.3.2. The Analogical Use of the Term

Concerning the application of this theological category to the Church, we must highlight that the text of *Lumen Gentium* says that the Church is in Christ "like"[46] a Sacrament. This implies that "Sacrament" is used in an analogous way to how it is applied to the seven Sacraments that the Church celebrates. As in any analogy, there is an element of continuity but also one, an even greater one, of dissimilarity. We shall dedicate the next chapters to the Sacraments.

2.4. Communion

2.4.1. "Communio"

The category of communion (in Greek, *koinonia*) is another possible way of defining the Church. In particular, it has been highly esteemed in the last decades, after the Synod of Bishops, in 1985, affirmed that the ecclesiology of communion—that is, the understanding of the Church on the basis of the category of *communio*—was the most important teaching of the last Council.[47] It is thus clear that several scholars have developed this perspective of

---

forth 'the wondrous Sacrament of the whole Church'" (Second Vatican Council, *Sacrosanctum Concilium*, §5).

[45] Second Vatican Council, *Lumen Gentium*, §48.

[46] "*Veluti*," which can be translated "like" or "so to speak." It is found in *Sacrosanctum Concilium*, §1.

[47] "The ecclesiology of communion is the central and fundamental idea of the [Second Vatican] Council's documents" (The Final Report of the Extraordinary Synod of Bishops, *The Church, in the Word of God, Celebrates the Mysteries of Christ for the Salvation of the World* [1985], II, C, 1 [translation: *ewtn.com*]). After the very first General Assem-

the Church as communion in their reflections, even if it must be said that they already worked on it before the Synod of 1985 (and probably had an influence on the Synod itself). In this regard, we must clarify two things: (1) The category of communion is certainly a valid perspective for understanding the documents of the Second Vatican Council, and for shedding further light on the mystery of the Church.[48] (2) The proposal of the Synod of Bishops of 1985 was never officially adopted by the Catholic Church (see note 47). The statement that communion is the central idea of the documents of the Second Vatican Council is only a respectable proposal for reflection offered by some bishops and not a pronouncement of the Church's Magisterium. On the other hand, after some years of theological ferment on the ecclesiology of communion, at present it seems to have lost its previous steam. Not that this disqualifies it, but not many specialists today present it as the true and primary ecclesiology of the Second Vatican Council. At the time in which we are writing this, the theme of the sacramentality of the Church is more "in vogue."

2.4.2. Hierarchical Communion and Communion in Charity

When we speak of the Church as Communion, there is a greater emphasis on the charity that unites the members of the Mystical Body of Christ, rather than the juridical and institutional link—which nonetheless is not denied. It is an ecclesiological model that wants to go to the deepest essence of the Church, to the root of the union between believers, which is the supernatural union with Christ. But this model also greatly emphasizes our response and

---

blies of the Synod, both Ordinary and Extraordinary (not in all cases the Special ones), were followed by the publication of a post-synodal apostolic exhortation of the Supreme Pontiff. The sole exception is represented by the Synod of 1985 itself, of which Saint John Paul II did not prepare any subsequent document. This reinforces the awareness that the Magisterium did not intend to make the proposals of that Synod its own. On the other hand, we cite it here only as an element of documentation, given the emphasis that some theologians have placed on the aforementioned synodal statement. In fact, we should recall that the Synod of Bishops is not a subject of the Magisterium, representing only a consultative body. The affirmations of a synod only become a magisterial expression if they are accepted in a later document by the Pope, or if the Pope expressly approves them. According to more recent norms, the Pope could also grant deliberative power to the synodal assembly so that the final document of the synod participates in the Ordinary Magisterium of the Pope, but only "once it has been ratified and promulgated by him" (Francis, *Episcopalis Communio* [2018], art. 18 §2; see also §1). Of course, more recent norms do not apply to previous synodal assemblies. Though such norms seem to be more open to concessions, it remains true that a Synod of Bishops is totally dependent on the Pope as per its magisterial power.

[48] See Congregation for the Doctrine of the Faith, *Communionis Notio* (1992), §1.

our dedication, so that the gift of communion, given from on high, is effectively received.

Therefore, in the ecclesiology of communion, four points stand out: (1) Generally, institutional aspects are not denied, but the spiritual aspects and those pertaining to grace are emphasized much more. (2) There tends to be emphasis on what the believers must do to construct a Church as a true communion of brothers and sisters. (3) From the previous two points it follows that it is preferable to emphasize the common call to holiness of all the baptized, not so as to deny the role of the Hierarchy, but to reread it in light of a greater shared responsibility and an esteem for all the charisms that the Holy Spirit gives to the Church. (4) The fact that some theologians have radicalized the model of communion in anti-hierarchal and democratic lenses does not imply that it is in itself invalid: it is important to know how to build upon the positive aspects without denying the fundamental Catholic *et-et*, and not to put elements of the Church that have objectively (in themselves and not regarding persons) different authorities and tasks, such as the sacred Hierarchy and the laity, on the same level. In particular, we must not forget that the Catholic concept of ecclesial communion is always understood in the sense of "hierarchical communion."[49] This expression entails, among other things, the fact that there is a need to effectively avoid identifying communion with a feeling of fraternity. Ecclesial communion is something quite objective and verifiable, linked to doctrine, to the Sacraments, and to the laws of the Church.[50]

2.4.3. Gift and Task

That the Church is Communion in herself means that God establishes her as a community of people who are united before all else with Him and, for this reason, also to each other. Communion is primarily a gift of grace and then a task. We must avoid reversing the terms so as not to fall into an ecclesiological form of Pelagianism that in the end would make us lose sight of the divine and supernatural character of the Church: a Church that would then be understood only as a group of persons who *strive* to remain united with God and each other (the Church as a "moral body"). Communion cannot be understood as a bottom-up initiative, whether of the individual or groups. In

---

[49] Second Vatican Council, *Lumen Gentium*, §§21–22.
[50] "Communion is a notion which is held in high honor in the ancient Church (and also today, especially in the East). However, it is not understood as some kind of vague disposition, but as an organic reality which requires a juridical form and is animated by charity" (Second Vatican Council, *Lumen Gentium*, "Preliminary Note of Explanation," §2).

this second case, it would not be a communal model but rather a "federative" model of the Church. If ecclesial communion were the result of a convergence of groups in unity (the "local Churches" which, remaining united, form the one and Catholic Church), the Church would not be that different from a federal state. But this is not the case with the Church, as if the individual local Churches had decided to converge under the presidency of the pope. It is true that the unity of the Church does not suppress, but rather preserves the so-called "legitimate differences,"[51] but this does not mean that they are autonomous. In reality, the differences are local expressions of the one Church, which precedes all the particularities (see below); they are not what produces the one Church, or what produces the Church-communion.

On the other hand, it is true that—having saved the primacy of the grace of the Church's supernatural vocation—the aspect of human response, of effort in communion, should also be sufficiently emphasized. This to avoid the opposite risk to that of ecclesiological Pelagianism, a sort of ecclesiological Quietism.[52]

2.5. Creature of the Holy Spirit

2.5.1. Once Again on the Relationship between Christ and Spirit

In addition to her being defined in reference to Christ, the Church is also defined by her equally indispensable dependence on the Holy Spirit. As was previously mentioned, the Church-Spirit relationship is not an alternative to the Christ-Church relationship, but it is its direct consequence. It is the Lord Himself who spoke to the Apostles about the future coming of the Holy Spirit over the Church after the Resurrection (see John 16:5–15). As soon as He rose, Christ commanded them not to begin preaching until He had sent the Spirit from the Father after the Ascension (see Luke 24:49). Pentecost is

---

[51] Second Vatican Council, *Lumen Gentium*, §13.

[52] Pius XII warned against these risks in the ecclesiological encyclical *Mystici Corporis*. On the one hand, the Pope recalled that without Christ we cannot do anything, let alone create the Church. On the other hand, that "marvelous though it may seem: Christ has need of His members" (DS 3805). Thus, he stigmatizes as "dangerous" the error of those who, while emphasizing our mystical incorporation into Christ, without simultaneously highlighting its respective bipolarity (*et-et*) of our response to grace, deduce "a certain unhealthy Quietism. They would attribute the whole spiritual life of Christians and their progress in virtue exclusively to the action of the Divine Spirit, setting aside and neglecting the collaboration which is due from us" (DS 3817).

the mystery of the Spirit that descends over the Church, giving her the new life of the risen Christ. The Holy Spirit is thus called by the New Testament, "Spirit of Christ" (Rom 8:9; Phil 1:19). The Son and Spirit are the two Hands with which the Father forms His creature.[53] The Spirit of Christ dwells in the believers as in a Temple (see 1 Cor 3:16–17; 6:19): He is the Giver of the life of Christ, the Life-Giver. Christ is the Life (see John 14:6), and the Spirit brings this Life into the hearts of believers. Christ is the true Image of God (see Col 1:15) and the Spirit restores to the sinful person, deformed image of the Creator, the likeness to its model (see 2 Cor 3:18; Rom 8:29). The Spirit of Christ brings nothing but Christ.

2.5.2. Ecclesiological Application

The Church gathers together these biblical teachings and in turn teaches in her own Magisterium that:

> Christ our Lord wills the Church to live His own supernatural life, and by His divine power permeates His whole Body and nourishes and sustains each of the members according to the place which they occupy in the Body, in the same way as the vine nourishes and makes fruitful the branches which are joined to it [see Leo XIII, *Sapientiae Christianae* and *Satis Cognitum*]. If we examine closely this divine principle of life and power given by Christ, insofar as it constitutes the very source of every gift and created grace, we easily perceive that it is nothing else than the Holy Spirit, the Paraclete, Who proceeds from the Father and the Son, and Who is called in a special way, the "Spirit of Christ" or the "Spirit of the Son" (Rom 8:9; 2 Cor 3:17; Gal 4:6).[54]

> For this reason, by no weak analogy, [the Church] is compared to the mystery of the incarnate Word. As the assumed nature inseparably united to Him, serves the divine Word as a living organ of salvation, so, in a similar way, does the visible social structure of the Church serve the Spirit of Christ, Who vivifies it, in the building up of the Body (see Eph 4:16).[55]

---

[53] See Saint Irenaeus of Lyon, *Adversus haereses* 5.1.3. This is an image already taken up in the previous chapters.

[54] Pius XII, *Mystici Corporis* 1, 2 [§§55–56] (DS 3806–3807).

[55] Second Vatican Council, *Lumen Gentium*, §8.

There were those who, in contemporary theology, saw in this last passage of the Second Vatican Council a denial of the perspective of the Church as an extension of the Incarnation (despite the clear incipit of the text). It is true there is a sort of sliding down, through which it starts with the analogy of Christ-Church and then concludes by expressing the relationship as Church-Spirit. But to understand the meaning of the text, it is not necessary to make recourse to an *aut-aut* (either/or), as if one thing excluded the other. The Church is both the extension of the Incarnation of the Word (Christotypical understanding) and the Temple inhabited and vivified by the Holy Spirit (Pneumatotypical understanding). In fact, the Spirit that inhabits the ecclesial Body is called "Spirit of Christ" in the text precisely to emphasize that the mission of the Spirit is distinct but not separate from that of the Incarnate Word.[56]

When the fundamental link between the mystery of Christ and the mystery of the Church is noted, it is impossible to forget the link between the Third Person of the Trinity and the Church. The presence of the Holy Spirit and His action are not accidental in the life of the Christian community. Just as there is no Christ (anointed) without the Spirit, there is also no Church without Christ and His Spirit. In contemporary theology, the effective title of the Church, "chrismated Body," (Italian *"Corpo crismato"*) was thus coined. The Church is the Mystical Body of Christ, anointed—like its Head—with the supernatural oil of the Messiah, of God's Anointed. Such an anointment is that of the Holy Spirit. Christ Himself says that the Church, established by Him, cannot act if He does not first give the Vivifier, that is, if the Holy Oil does not descend from the Head to its members. The Church is then also a Creature of the Spirit, Who works His wonders in her. The link with the Trinity is thus highlighted once again: the Church is willed in the plan of God the Father, established and purified by God the Son in His Blood, and filled with new life by God the Holy Spirit.

2.6. Other Images of the Church

The supernatural character of the Church is also noted by the fact that no image or definition manages to express all her elements. This happens because the human mind is incapable of grasping all the individual aspects of the Mystery with its own intellectual act, and thus, with a single verbal expression. Moreover, the very character of the truths of the faith—the character

---

[56] "When the Father sends His Word, he always sends his Breath. In their joint mission, the Son and the Holy Spirit are distinct but inseparable" (CCC §689).

of supernaturally revealed truths—implies that numerous other aspects of it remain still hidden in the deposit of Revelation, and not completely explored. The way to a sound development of doctrine (see Chapter Two) remains open in the ecclesiological sphere, like in other fields.

A list of the primary biblical images of the Church is found in *Lumen Gentium*, §6. We shall only cite a few examples, without going in-depth: the vineyard, the sheepfold, the field or tillage of God, the house of God, the heavenly Jerusalem. Given the complexity of the ecclesial mystery, some hold that a complete ecclesiology—as far as it is possible—could only come about from a simultaneous presentation of different images, or "models of the Church," none of which will be able to exhaust the entire discussion, while providing a specific element of a larger perspective of the whole.

3. How Is the Church Composed?

In this third part of the chapter, we shall briefly discuss the internal constitution of the Church, as it was willed by its Founder, Jesus Christ.

3.1. The Notes and Properties of the Church

3.1.1. "Notae" or "Proprietates"

Four fundamental attributes of the Church are taught in the Creed.[57] These attributes are usually called "notes" of the Church. The word "notes" means to indicate the essential properties of the Church. In the past, other categories were used; for example, in the fifteenth and sixteenth centuries, they used "*signa*" ("signs") and particularly in the sixteenth century, "*qualitates, indoles, rationes, praerogativae*" and more often "*proprietates.*" The word "*notae*" prevailed with the theologians Johann Eck (d. 1543), a great opponent of Luther,[58] and Saint Robert Bellarmine (d. 1621). The use of "*proprietates*" as a synonym for "*notae*" remains the custom to this day, even if the two terms originally had different meanings: "*proprietates*" indicated what is proper to the Church but is not known by those who are not part of it, insofar as it is

---

[57] For a treatment that is concise but still rather complete in its elements, see Saint Thomas Aquinas, *Expositio in Symbolum Apostolorum*, art. 9.

[58] Regarding Johann Eck, the *Enchiridion locorum communium adversus Lutherum et alios hostes Ecclesiae* should be recalled in this sense. It is a work from 1525, which had forty-six editions by 1576.

The Church

not—so to speak—clearly visible from the outside. On the other hand, "*notae*" indicated what is also known if the Church is observed from the outside, what distinguishes her and is visible to all, even non-Christians and non-believers. The notes are those properties of the Church that are capable of notifying, of giving knowledge and recognition of the Church. Since they are also properties, the two terms became synonymous in the end.

In the past, the theological treatment of the ecclesiological notes was presented from a primarily apologetic perspective: to demonstrate that the Roman Catholic Church is the one that possesses all the notes of the true Church of Christ. Today, a more dogmatic perspective is preferred: the notes are studied to understand what they teach us about the Church, more than to demonstrate to those outside the Catholic Church that she is the true Church founded by Christ. The apologetic emphasis of the treatment of the notes was a consequence of the polemic with the Hussites and Lutherans. According to them, the distinctive notes of the Church would be the Word of the Gospel and the Sacraments attested to in it. It is clear that this is a reductive perspective of the notes, which does not correspond to the Symbol of the faith. Thus, the so-called "*via notarum*" ("way of the notes") was developed as a true and proper apologetic way, similar to the five ways (see Chapter Two) with which Saint Thomas rationally demonstrates the existence and main attributes of God.[59] Also in this regard, it would be preferable not to oppose the two meth-

---

[59] The theologians Johann Eck, Stanislaus Hosius (in Polish, Stanislaw Hozjusz, d. 1579), and Saint Robert Bellarmine listed up to fifteen notes of the Church in their treatises. Thomas Bozius (d. 1610), in his work entitled *De signis Ecclesiae Dei contra omnes haereses* (1591), arrived at more than one hundred, including those called "*signa temporalis felicitatis*" ("signs of earthly success"), that is, the geographic and scientific discoveries as well as the technical applications carried out by Catholics, which would also show the superiority of the true Church over Lutheranism. Even some catechisms were affected by this approach, coming to as many as nineteen notes, as late as the eighteenth century. In this century, however, specifically in 1726, the theologian Honoré Tournély (d. 1729) established the apologetic scheme of the *via notarum* within the four notes of the Symbol. Finally, in the nineteenth century, some authors of the Roman theological School added the note of "Romanity" to the four of the Creed. It is significant that the First Vatican Council adopted the note of "Romanity" at the beginning of the constitution *Dei Filius*, where it calls the Church "Holy, Catholic, Roman," taking up the ancient text of the *Decretum Gelasianum* (a compilation of ancient documents put together at the beginning of the sixth century), which says: "The Holy Roman Church." However, it should also be said that the First Vatican Council did not intend to make a dogmatic definition on the fifth note of the Church. In the intentions of the First Vatican Council, the term "*Romana*" is a clarification of "*Apostolica*": in fact, in Rome there is the tomb of Peter and the See of his successor. To say "Roman" means to refer to the foundation of the Church on Peter, who had Rome as his definitive episcopal See. It does not then mean that the Church is limited to Rome and that it is like a guest or stranger in the other places of

odologies, but rather to integrate them in such a way that the treatment that deals with the notes of the Church could be *both* of a dogmatic sort *and* of a sound apologetic character, while giving primacy to the first aspect.

3.1.2. The Original Character and the Order of Listing

At the dogmatic level, recent theologians have posed a series of interesting questions not only about the study of the individual notes, but also about them as a whole. Some wonder if there is a temporal succession among the notes, that is, if the first two notes (One and Holy) were present since the time of the New Testament while the others (Catholic and Apostolic) arose gradually. The question must be answered negatively, because if the notes were not there from the beginning, they would lose their character as essential properties of the Church. Another question regards the order of presentation: Does the Symbol of faith list them in the correct order, or should this be changed? Various proposals have been set forth, and there is currently no consensus among scholars of ecclesiology. It seems that one could say that the note of unity should be kept first, because the first necessity is that of identifying the entity we want to discuss. That of holiness seems to fit well in the second position, because it speaks first of all of the intimate nature the Church receives from Christ, the Holy One par excellence. Moreover, it is in line with the teaching of the Second Vatican Council, which speaks of the vocation of holiness for the whole Church. Perhaps a door can be left open concerning the order of the other two notes, since apostolicity would also fit well in the third position, insofar as it is a sign and instrument for guaranteeing catholicity. But the order proposed in the Symbol also has good reasons to support it. In the absence of solid arguments, therefore, the order given by the Fathers of the First Council of Constantinople should be followed.[60]

---

the earth. The See of Rome is the center of the apostolic unity of the Church, because it is the See of the successor of Saint Peter. The Second Vatican Council preferred not to take up the note of "Romanity" and limited itself to speaking of the Catholic Church "governed by the successor of Peter and by the Bishops" (*Lumen Gentium*, §8). This did not diminish the role of the Pope, on whose prerogatives the Second Vatican Council widely pronounced, in full continuity with previous councils (see below).

[60] The reason why the question still seems debatable, even in the face of a solemn dogmatic pronouncement like this, is that the First Council of Constantinople certainly did not intend to define the order of the notes as such. According to various recent theologians, in fact, it has not even defined the four notes in themselves. To the last point, we respond that it is possible that the notes were not objects of a direct (infallible) dogmatic definition, but that they fall into the category of "undefined dogmas" (truths taught by God even if not yet defined by the Church), to the point of being added to nothing less than

3.1.3. Organic Unity

Remaining on a general level, some aspects must still be noted: (1) The four notes are distinct, but inseparable; for example, one cannot think of a holiness that is not linked to unity—schismatic or heretic saints do not exist![61] (2) The notes are united by the fact of being simultaneously gift and task. They are a gift already fulfilled, offered by Christ as a natural dowry of the Church—in this sense, the notes are as indefectible as the Church herself, that is, they can never be lost—but they are also a task: Christians are called to conform their own personal and organic-structural behavior to these objective gifts. That the notes are both gift and task is a magnificent manifestation of the *et-et*, because the same reality is both an already perfect gift (at the ontological level) and a task to be carried out (at the existential level).[62] (3) If the first two notes (One and Holy) are acknowledged to indicate above all the supreme vocation of the Church, called to unity and holiness, and the other two (Catholic and Apostolic) to refer to the supernatural endowment for the development of this vocation—the Word of truth, the sacramental celebration (above all the Eucharist), and the ministry of the Apostles and their successors—then it will be possible to see that the fundamental principle of *et-et* is verified not only in each individual note, but also in all of them as a totality.

3.1.4. One

The unity of the Church is first and foremost an essential gift of Christ, for which the Church is and will always remain One—she can never lose her unity. "It is a mystery that finds its highest exemplar and source in the unity of the Persons of the Trinity: the Father and the Son in the Holy Spirit, one God."[63]

---

the Symbol of faith! The notes as such, therefore, cannot be open to dispute, though their order can.

[61] We are referring to obstinate and unrepentant heretics. The inseparable unity of the notes is also among the reasons why Catholics do not recognize the title of "Churches" to other Christian communities that have lost apostolicity, that is, the link to the original apostolic foundation, which valid Ordination maintains. See Congregation for the Doctrine of the Faith, *Responsa ad Quaestiones de Aliquibus Sententiis ad Doctrinam de Ecclesia Pertinentibus*, question 5.

[62] "It is Christ who, through the Holy Spirit, makes his Church one, holy, catholic, and apostolic, and it is he who calls her to realize each of these qualities" (CCC §811).

[63] Second Vatican Council, *Unitatis Redintegratio* (1964), §2.

How Is the Church Composed?

1. Christ the Principle, the Spirit the Guarantor of Unity

The Spirit of Christ, the Spirit of love, is the divine Guarantor of ecclesial unity: "It is the Holy Spirit, dwelling in those who believe and pervading and ruling over the Church as a whole, Who brings about that wonderful communion of the faithful. He brings them into intimate union with Christ, so that He is the principle of the Church's unity."[64] One can glean from this that Christ is the Principle of the Church's unity: in fact, the Spirit unites in Him. At the Last Supper, Jesus Himself had said: "I pray not only for them, but also for those who will believe in me through their word, so that they may all be one, as you, Father, are in me and I in you, that they also may be in us, that the world may believe that you sent me" (John 17:20–21). Baptism, incorporating us into Christ, gives us the unity of His Mystical Body: "For in one Spirit we were all baptized into one body, whether Jews or Greeks, slaves or free persons, and we were all given to drink of one Spirit" (1 Cor 12:13); "one body and one Spirit, as you were also called to the one hope of your call; one Lord, one faith, one baptism" (Eph 4:4–5).

2. The Apostles, Sign and Instrument of Unity

Moreover, the Church is one because she is united to one visible principle of unity alone: the Apostles and their successors (unity linked to apostolicity). Christian authors have insisted on this point from the earliest centuries. In fact, unity is an objective gift, but also a task: Christians—who have received incorporation into the one Church—must remain in unity. The visible sign and instrument of this is adherence to the sacred Shepherds. In the year 250, Saint Cyprian of Carthage wrote a famous phrase in this regard:

> *Habere iam non potest Deum Patrem, qui Ecclesiam non habet matrem. Si potuit evadere quisque extra arcam Noe fuit, et qui extra Ecclesiam foris fuerit evadet.* ("He can no longer have God for his Father, who has not the Church for his mother. If anyone could escape who was outside the Ark of Noah, then he also may escape who shall be outside of the Church").[65]

Saint Cyprian knew that the unity of the Church is first of all a gift of

---

[64] Second Vatican Council, *Unitatis Redintegratio* (1964), §2.
[65] Saint Cyprian of Carthage, *De unitate Ecclesiae* 6, in *ANF*, vol. 5, trans. Robert Ernest Wallis (Peabody, MA: Hendrickson Publishers, Inc., 1994), 423.

God: it was he who stated the famous expression, cited by the Second Vatican Council, that the Church is *"plebs adunata de unitate Patris et Filii et Spiritus Sancti"* ("A people made one with the unity of the Father, the Son and the Holy Spirit").[66] For this reason, writing to Pope Cornelius, he attested: "The Catholic Church has been shown to be one, incapable of being rent or divided."[67] But what cannot be divided *in itself*, can be so *in us*. Hence, the ancient African Bishop's call to remain in the Church, portrayed as Noah's ark, the ark of true salvation.

3. The Successors of the Apostles

To remain in the ark, it is necessary to be faithful to those who govern it. That is why the link with the Apostles and their successors is crucial from the beginning of the Church's history. The bishop and martyr Saint Ignatius of Antioch (d. ca. 107) laid down the principle *"nihil sine episcopo"* ("nothing [is to be done by the faithful] without the bishop").[68] And Tertullian notes:

---

[66] Cyprian of Carthage, *De oratione dominica* 23; translation taken from the citation in the English version of the Second Vatican Council, *Lumen Gentium*, §4.

[67] Cyprian of Carthage, *Epistula 51.2*, in *FCNT*, vol. 51, trans. Sister Rose Bernard Donna (Washington, DC: CUA Press, 1964), 127.

[68] See Saint Ignatius of Antioch, *Epistula ad Trallianos* 2.2; *Epistula ad Smyrnenses* 8.1; *Epistula ad Polycarpum* 4.1. In several places in his letters, the saint also illustrates the principle he coined more broadly. For example: "Let all follow the bishop as Jesus Christ did the Father, and the priests, as you would the Apostles. Reverence the deacons as you would the command of God. Apart from the bishop, let no one perform any functions that pertain to the Church. Let that Eucharist be held valid which is offered by the bishop or by one to whom the bishop has committed this charge. Wherever the bishop appears, there let the people be; as wherever Jesus Christ is, there is the Catholic Church. It is not lawful to baptize or give Communion without the consent of the bishop. On the other hand, whatever has his approval is pleasing to God" (*Epistula ad Smyrnenses* 8.1–2, in *FCNT*, vol. 1, trans. Gerald G. Walsh [Washington DC: CUA Press, 2008], 121). "For, all who belong to God and Jesus Christ are with the bishop. And those, too, will belong to God who have returned, repentant, to the unity of the Church so as to live in accordance with Jesus Christ. Make no mistake, brethren. No one who follows another into schism inherits the Kingdom of God. No one who follows heretical doctrine is on the side of the passion. Be zealous, then, in the observance of one Eucharist. For there is one flesh of our Lord, Jesus Christ, and one chalice that brings union in His blood. There is one altar, as there is one bishop with the priests and deacons, who are my fellow workers. And so, whatever you do, let it be done in the name of God" (*Epistula ad Philadelphenos* 3, in *FCNT*, vol. 1, 114). "To the honor of Him who loves you, you must obey without any insincerity; for in this case one does not so much deceive a bishop who can be seen as try to outwit one who is invisible—in which case one must reckon not with a man, but with God who knows our hidden thoughts. It is not enough to be Christians in name; it behooves us to be such in fact. So, too, there are those who invoke the name of the bishop

"Opposition to the episcopate is the mother of schisms."[69]

4. Objective Elements of Unity

From these annotations we can deduce that the unity of the Church does not consist in mere communal sentiments. It is not simply loving and encouraging one another. These attitudes are a consequence, not the essence, of ecclesial unity. In this regard, it is useful to cite a passage of the Acts of the Apostles, in which the original community is concisely described:

> [The Christians] devoted themselves to the teaching of the apostles and to the communal life, to the breaking of the bread and to the prayers. Awe came upon everyone, and many wonders and signs were done through the apostles. All who believed were together and had all things in common; they would sell their property and possessions and divide them among all according to each one's need. Every day they devoted themselves to meeting together in the temple area and to breaking bread in their homes. They ate their meals with exultation and sincerity of heart, praising God and enjoying favor with all the people. And every day the Lord added to their number those who were being saved (Acts 2:42–47).

As the text points out, the sentiments, such as "joy" or the "sense of awe" are not enough to characterize the Church's communion. Saint Luke emphasizes the objective elements of communion: apostolic teaching (unity of faith), prayer, and particularly the Eucharistic Liturgy (unity of Worship), as well as the common life and the concrete acts that follow from it (unity of charity).

5. One Church, Divided Christians

Finally, there is need to mention two themes connected to that of ecclesial unity. The first one originates from the historical fact that, although ecclesial unity can never be lost, the Church is actually divided. To this we respond that the Church is not divided in herself, but in us. The Church never lost her unity, which remains concretely—along with other essential prerogatives—in

---

while their actions are without any regard for him" (*Epistula ad Magnesios* 3.2–4.1, in *FCNT*, vol. 1, 97).

[69] Tertullian of Carthage, *De Baptismo* 17, in *Tertullian's Homily on Baptism*, trans. E. Evans (London: S.P.C.K., 1964), 37.

the Catholic Church[70]; it is the Christians who have lost it. It is for this reason that we should speak of a "division of Christians" and not a "division of the Church."[71] An essential property of the Church did not fail, nor did the gift given by Christ. What fell short was the fidelity of believers of Christ to unity, taken as a task.

6. Unity and Plurality in the Church

Given our discussion of unity thus far, a question naturally arises: How do we explain, in light of the unity, the variety that is clearly present in the Church? As is clear for all to see, in the Church there are manifold religious congregations, spiritual and theological schools, customs and traditions, and so forth. Does this plurality contradict her unity? In the Catholic perspective of the Church, it does not at all. Rather, this plurality, for which we speak of *"varietates legitimae"* ("legitimate differences"),[72] manifests the one Church in many ways, like a prism reflects the one light through its many facets. There is a harmful "pluralism," which jeopardizes lived unity. This pluralism should be fought firmly, as should, for example, dogmatic or liturgical pluralism. However, there is also a positive "plurality," which is not opposed but rather encouraged, because it manifests the richness of the gifts and charisms given by the one Lord:

> There are different kinds of spiritual gifts but the same Spirit; there are different forms of service but the same Lord; there are different workings but the same God who produces all of them in everyone. To each individual the manifestation of the Spirit is given for some benefit. To one is given through the Spirit the expression of wisdom; to another the expression of knowledge according to the same Spirit; to another faith by the same Spirit; to another gifts of healing by the

---

[70] See Congregation for the Doctrine of the Faith, *Responsa ad Quaestiones de Aliquibus Sententiis ad Doctrinam de Ecclesia Pertinentibus*, question 2.

[71] This is why the Vatican dicastery for ecumenism is called the "Pontifical Council for Promoting Christian Unity," not "for Promoting the *Church's* Unity." Unity of the Church is an objective and indefectible gift of Christ, which will never be lost, and thus should not be promoted. What should be promoted is unity among believers. It is from this perspective that the question of the use of the expression "undivided Church" is also clarified. It is not uncommon to hear talk of the "undivided Church of the first millennium." If we refer to undivided Christians, the expression is acceptable, even if somewhat ambiguous. On the other hand, it is unacceptable if one presumes a loss in the ecclesiological note of unity, on account of historically determined divisions among Christians.

[72] Second Vatican Council, *Lumen Gentium*, §13.

one Spirit; to another mighty deeds; to another prophecy; to another discernment of spirits; to another varieties of tongues; to another interpretation of tongues. But one and the same Spirit produces all of these, distributing them individually to each person as he wishes. (1 Cor 12:4–11)

3.1.5. Holy

The Second Vatican Council teaches:

> The Church ... is believed to be indefectibly holy. Indeed Christ, the Son of God, Who with the Father and the Spirit is praised as "uniquely holy," loved the Church as His bride, delivering Himself up for her. He did this that He might sanctify her (see Eph 5:25–26). He united her to Himself as His own body and brought it to perfection by the gift of the Holy Spirit for God's glory.[73]

The second note is also a stable gift, or rather an "indefectible" gift to the Church: this means it will remain forever, just like the indefectible Church, which will remain throughout the existence of the world (see Matt 28:20).

1. Holiness in the Bible

In Holy Scripture, holiness is a prerogative of God: we have already cited Isaiah and Revelation, which tell of the vision of the Seraphim who sing before the Throne of God "Holy, Holy, Holy." In Hebrew, the term used is *qadosh*, which indicates the glory, almost the "heaviness" of God, and above all His transcendence, that is, His separateness from what is not holy, from what is profane. The same idea is found in Exodus 3:5 (Moses must take off his sandals, because the earth he treads on is holy, that is, it is separated from common ground that can be stepped on wearing footwear). In Greek, the word for holy is *hagios*, which comes from the verb *haxomai*, "to shudder," and at its base the meaning is the same: before God the human being experiences sacred fear. However, in the Old Testament the people of Israel are also called holy: "For I, the LORD, am your God; and you shall make and keep yourselves holy, because I am holy" (Lev 11:44). But, in this passage, the difference emerges: God is the Holy One, He is Holy by nature. The people, on the other hand, are not holy and must be made holy, in the image of God. Thus, for

---

[73] Second Vatican Council, *Lumen Gentium*, §39.

God, holiness is a stable gift, while for the people, it is a task to put into effect. This task, however, is not the fruit of human effort alone: it is the "holy" covenant that God makes with Israel to provide the possibility of sanctification (see the "Holiness Code," both cultic and moral, contained in Lev 17–26).

We are met with an analogous situation in the New Testament, where it can only be said of Christ, absolutely speaking, that He is Holy (see Luke 1:35; Heb 4:15; 7:26). But in Chapter Five we already considered the passages in which it is said that the Holy Spirit dwells in us and sanctifies us. That is why the New Testament also calls the baptized "holy" (see Rom 1:7; 8:27; 12:13; 15:25–26, 31; 16:2, 15; 1 Cor 1:2; 14:33; etc.). Christ, the only one who is Holy, gives us participation in His holiness; thus, He also gives us the task of living as "saints," that is, living in fidelity to Him. In giving a new version of the command of Leviticus 11:44, Jesus said, "so be perfect, just as your heavenly Father is perfect" (Matt 5:48). Thus, already in Scripture, the holiness of the Church is both a gift and a task.

2. The Communion of "Saints"

The note of the Church's holiness is also attested in Christian literature from ancient times. The aforementioned Saint Ignatius of Antioch, for example, at the beginning of his letter addresses himself to the "holy Church which is in Tralles in Asia."[74] Starting from the third century, the question was posed to the candidates for Baptism if they believe "in the Holy Spirit in the Holy Church." In the fourth century, the expression *"communio sanctorum"* ("communion of saints") entered into ecclesiastical language. According to various scholars, it was Saint Nicetas of Remesiana (d. after 414) who added this expression to the Roman baptismal Symbol (see his work *De explanatione Symboli*). Nonetheless, this expression experienced an immediate evolution of meaning. At first, the "saints" of this communion were understood as those of the beginning, which is why *"communio sanctorum"* meant being in communion with the Church of the Apostles, that is, with the faith transmitted by them, and it was a criterion of continuity in ecclesial life (a link between holiness and apostolicity). In the Middle Ages, on the other hand, *sanctorum* no longer referred to the "saints" but rather the *"sancta"* ("holy things"), especially the Sacraments. And this made the meaning shift toward the fact that one is in communion by validly and licitly receiving the Sacraments.[75] In this

---

[74] Saint Ignatius of Antioch, *Epistula ad Trallianos*, incipit, in *FCNT*, vol. 1, 102.

[75] Saint Thomas Aquinas, *Expositio in Symbolum Apostolorum*, art. 10: "*Haec communicatio fit per Sacramenta Ecclesiae*" ("this communication [of the grace of Christ] happens through

How Is the Church Composed?

regard, Pope Boniface VIII showed a good application of the *et-et* principle, which puts together the two meanings of the expression, by speaking of "the Church, on account of the unity of the Church's spouse, faith [first meaning], Sacraments [second meaning], and love."[76]

3. A Holy Church or a Sinful One?

Now all of this seems to be at odds with the experience of the Church that many Christians and non-Christians have had. Many times (too many times) in the Church we have come into contact not with holiness but rather sin. Especially in our days, we are even more aware of this sin, because of the mass media (and the particular way in which they choose the content of their focus), and due to a greater sensitivity with respect to cases of inconsistency, especially if it involves religious authorities.[77] A terminological clarification must also be made here. The expression "sin of the Church" is often used. In

---

the Sacraments of the Church." [our translation]). Article 10 comments on the part of the Apostles' Creed in which the communion of saints and the remission of sins are professed.

[76] Boniface VIII, *Unam Sanctam* (DS 871).

[77] In particular, the Catholic faithful and public opinion are, justly, struck by the infidelity of the priests. There is an impressive text on this by the Doctor of the Church, Hildegard of Bingen (d. 1179), which focuses, on the one hand, on the splendor that no one can take away from the Holy Church, and, on the other hand, on the gravity of the sin of the priests: "In the year of our Lord's incarnation 1170, I had been lying on my sick-bed for a long time when, fully conscious in body and in mind, I had a vision of a woman of such beauty that the human mind is unable to comprehend. She stretched in height from earth to heaven. Her face shone with exceeding brightness and her gaze was fixed on heaven. She was dressed in a dazzling robe of white silk and draped in a cloak, adorned with stones of great price. On her feet she wore shoes of onyx. But her face was stained with dust, her robe was ripped down the right side, her cloak had lost its sheen of beauty and her shoes had been blackened. And she herself, in a voice loud with sorrow, was calling to the heights of heaven, saying, 'Hear, heaven, how my face is sullied; mourn, earth, that my robe is torn; tremble, abyss, because my shoes are blackened!' And she continued: 'I lay hidden in the heart of the Father until the Son of Man, who was conceived and born in virginity, poured out his blood. With that same blood as his dowry, he made me his betrothed. For my Bridegroom's wounds remain fresh and open as long as the wounds of men's sins continue to gape. And Christ's wounds remain open because of the sins of priests. They tear my robe, since they are violators of the Law, the Gospel and their own priesthood; they darken my cloak by neglecting, in every way, the precepts which they are meant to uphold; my shoes too are blackened, since priests do not keep to the straight paths of justice, which are hard and rugged, or set good examples to those beneath them. Nevertheless, in some of them I find the splendor of truth.' And I heard a voice from heaven which said: 'This image represents the Church'" (*Epistula ad Wernerum de Kircheim* [translation: *vatican.va*]).

reality, from the theological point of view, a "sin of the Church" does not exist and cannot exist. The Church is and always remains holy from the objective standpoint. On the other hand, there is clearly "sin in the Church," and it coincides with transgressions by the baptized against God's law. The holiness of the Church, like her unity, can never be lost; what can be lost is the holiness within the Church, namely, the holiness of the individual members of the Mystical Body of Christ. When on March 12, 2000, Saint John Paul II wanted to make a prophetic gesture of reconciliation with the past, he asked forgiveness certainly not for the sins of the Church, which did not exist, but rather for the faults of the Church's children. Naturally, this necessary theological distinction does not take away the negative judgment about the sins and scandals, nor does it encourage the baptized to moral laxity.

Saint Ambrose recognizes that our sins do not affect the objective holiness of the Church, but nonetheless he strongly urges the baptized not to disfigure the immaculate face of the Bride of Christ in themselves: "Not in herself... is the Church wounded, but in us. Let us thus take care so that our fall does not become a wound for the Church."[78] And Saint Leo the Great insists on the holiness of the Mystical Body, to exhort believers to integral life conduct: "Realize, o Christian, your dignity. Once made a 'partaker in the divine nature,' do not return to your former baseness by a life unworthy [of that dignity]. Remember whose Head it is and whose Body of which you constitute a 'member.'"[79]

Finally, it is useful to recall that there are two ways of reacting to sin in the Church: anger or love. But of these two ways, the second is the correct one. To respond in anger does not help; only loving sinners—while still feeling all the sadness for their sin—is a way to resolve the scandal, especially if those who sin are those from whom we should least expect it: sacred ministers. And love does not manifest itself as an absence of justice (it is necessary to respect justice, even by imposing medicinal penalties on the guilty), but rather in the form of commiseration and prayer for those who have sinned, in addition to the resolution to be vigilant regarding one's own behavior. The following notes of Pius XII are always useful:

> And if at times there appears in the Church something that indicates the weakness of our human nature, it should not be attributed to her juridical constitution, but rather to that regrettable inclination

---

[78] Saint Ambrose of Milan, *De virginitate* 48 (our translation).
[79] Saint Leo the Great, *Sermo* 21.3, in *FCNT*, vol. 93, trans. Jane Patricia Freeland and Agnes Josephine Conway (Washington, DC: CUA Press, 1996), 79.

to evil found in each individual, which its Divine Founder permits even at times in the most exalted members of His Mystical Body, for the purpose of testing the virtue of the Shepherds no less than of the flocks, and that all may increase the merit of their Christian faith. For, as We said above, Christ did not wish to exclude sinners from His Church; hence if some of her members are suffering from spiritual maladies, that is no reason why we should lessen our love for the Church, but rather a reason why we should increase our devotion to her members.[80]

3.1.6. Catholic

We distinguish two uses of the term "Catholic": on the one hand is the theological use, which coincides with the catholicity as a note or property of the Church and is explored in the study of ecclesiology; on the other hand, there is a confessional use of this adjective, which is the more common use today. In this second acceptation, the word is used in reference to the Church that is in communion with the Bishop of Rome, which is one reason why in some countries such as the United States, the word "Roman" is still used when speaking of the Roman Catholic Church. In this sense, the Catholic Church is the Roman Church, which is distinct from other Christian confessions, such as the Orthodox Churches and the various Protestant and Anglican communities. Here, however, we want to concentrate on the theological use of the term.

1. "Kath'holon"

The word "catholic" is not found in Sacred Scripture and comes from classical Greek. In the texts of Aristotle (for example), *kath'holon* means "according to the whole, according to the totality." However, the fact that the term is not found in the Bible does not mean that the catholicity of the Church is never mentioned in Scripture—it only means that the Bible makes use of other expressions to make reference to such a catholicity. The Greek phrase *kath'holon* seemed, from very early times in the Church,[81] well-suited to expressing a particular aspect of the Church, because in classical logic it means that which is general, as opposed to that which is particular: the whole

---

[80] Pius XII, *Mystici Corporis* II, 4 [§66].
[81] We can cite again Saint Ignatius of Antioch, *Epistula ad Smyrnenses* 8.2: "Wherever the bishop appears, there let the people be; as wherever Jesus Christ is, there is the Catholic Church" (in *FCNT*, vol. 1, 121).

or set, in contrast to the detail or fragment. *Holon*, in fact, indicates precisely the whole or the entirety, and the preposition *katha* can, depending on the case, be translated with "down from" or "for, through, toward," or also "among" and "according to." However it is translated, the expressed idea is that *kath'holon* is an organic or complete whole, a whole that surpasses, which is more perfect than the simple sum of its parts. And thus "catholic" indicates completeness, perfection, universality, and so forth.

2. Quantitative and Qualitative Sense

When this word is applied to the Church, it is done in a dual sense: in both a qualitative and a quantitative sense. (1) At the quantitative level, the Church is Catholic because she extends, ideally, to the whole world: therefore, she must embrace the whole "quantity" of the world, so to speak.[82] In this sense, the catholicity of the Church is a task to be realized and it is also translated well with the word "universality": the Catholic Church is the Church destined to be universal in extension. (2) At the qualitative level, on the other hand, "catholic" indicates the perfection of the Church in quality, namely, the fact that she possesses the fullness of revealed truth and salvific grace. And this is the aspect of the gift given by Christ, which—despite all the human infidelity and all the attacks of her enemies—can never be lost. The Church is Catholic because it indefectibly keeps in herself the fullness of truth and the salvific means that were given to her by her Founder. On this basis, the Second Vatican Council taught that the Church of Christ subsists in fullness only in the Catholic Church (also used in a confessional sense here), although it recognized that many means of truth and grace are also found in the Orthodox Churches and Protestant communities.[83] Obviously, through the principle of

---

[82] "The Church is one: and that is what our ancestors called 'Catholic,' to show, even in the name, that it is everywhere. In fact, in Greek "according to the whole" is said: *kath'holon*" (Saint Augustine of Hippo, *Epistola ad Catholicos contra Donatistas* [= *De unitate Ecclesiae*] 2.2 [our translation]; see Augustine, *Contra Gaudentium Donatistarum episcopum* 2.2.2).

[83] "This is the one Church of Christ which in the Creed is professed as one, holy, catholic and apostolic. . . . This Church constituted and organized in the world as a society, subsists in the Catholic Church, which is governed by the successor of Peter and by the bishops in communion with him, although many elements of sanctification and of truth are found outside of its visible structure. These elements, as gifts belonging to the Church of Christ, are forces impelling toward catholic unity" (Second Vatican Council, *Lumen Gentium*, §8). This text of the Council was for a long time the center of attention of ecclesiology in that it replaced the "*est*" ("is") used by Pius XII in *Mystici Corporis* with "*subsistit in*" ("subsists in"). There was no shortage of authors who held that this substitution implied the will of the Council to no longer sustain the doctrine for which

et-et, the qualitative and quantitative senses are not mutually exclusive, but rather they together form the mystery of the Church's catholicity. Saint Cyril of Jerusalem holds the two aspects together:

> [*Quantity*] The Church is called Catholic because she is spread throughout the world, from end to end of the earth; [*Quality*] also because she teaches universally and completely all the doctrines which man should know concerning things visible and invisible, heavenly and earthly; and because she subjects to right worship all mankind, rules and ruled, lettered and unlettered; further because she treats and heals universally every sort of sin committed by soul and body, and she possesses in herself every conceivable virtue, whether in deeds, words or in spiritual gifts of every kind.[84]

The Second Vatican Council dealt with the Church's catholicity in *Lumen Gentium* §§13–17, in which it recalled both the quantitative and qualitative aspects. Regarding the former, it says, "All men are called to belong to the new people of God. Wherefore this people, while remaining one and only one, is to be spread throughout the whole world and must exist in all ages" (§13)—a text in which the quantitative extension of the Church is seen with respect to space and time (all peoples, all ages).[85] Then, concerning the qualitative aspect, it notes: "This characteristic of universality which adorns the people of God is a gift from the Lord Himself. By reason of it, the Catholic Church strives constantly and with due effect to bring all humanity and all its possessions back to its source in Christ, with Him as its head and united in His Spirit" (§13). Moreover, the Council includes in its discussion of catholicity the theme of varied incorporation or relation of human beings with the Church.

---

the Church of Christ is—*tout court*—the "Roman" Catholic Church. This theological position is nevertheless unsustainable, as was definitively clarified by the Congregation for the Doctrine of the Faith, *Responsa ad Quaestiones de Aliquibus Sententiis ad Doctrinam de Ecclesia Pertinentibus*, questions 1–3. The text also explains the true meaning of why "*est*" was replaced with "*subsistit in*."

[84] Saint Cyril of Jerusalem, *Catecheses mystagogicae* 18.23, in *FCNT*, vol. 64, 132.

[85] The Second Vatican Council does not put "space" and "time" in opposition, almost as if in the evangelizing and pastoral action of the Church one must choose between occupying spaces and waiting for times. The sound Catholic *et-et* must be observed in this case as well, although it is true that time is hierarchically more important, so much so that today the Church is absent in many places of the earth where it was once flourishing, and nevertheless it maintains its temporal continuity. However, both space and time must be cared for.

3. Catholic Church and Particular Churches

Finally, we should address the question of which aspect (qualitative or quantitative) is the primary one; in fact, as we know, the principle of *et-et* allows for two elements to stand together while having different value. Now, since the gift of grace is greater than the human response, in the notes of the Church the objective aspect surpasses the subjective in value: the gift surpasses the task. Thus, catholicity in a qualitative sense not only chronologically precedes the quantitative sense, but it is also its foundation. The first stands in relation to the second as nature to action (and it is known that *"agere sequitur esse"* ["action follows upon being"][86]). Therefore, the expression "Catholic Church" cannot be used to mean a confederation of particular Churches. The Church is Catholic from the first day she arose, even when the whole Church was contained in a single room on the day of Pentecost (see Acts 2:1). Benedict XVI emphasized this very clearly:

> The very act of the Church's birth is already "catholic" or universal. From the outset the Church speaks in all languages, because the Gospel entrusted to her is destined for all peoples, according to the will and mandate of the risen Christ (cf. Matt 28:19). The Church which is born at Pentecost is not primarily a particular Community—the Church of Jerusalem—but the universal Church, which speaks the languages of all peoples. From her other communities were to be born in every part of the world, particular Churches which are all and always actualizations of the one and only Church of Christ. The Catholic Church is therefore not a federation of Churches but a single reality: the universal Church has ontological priority. A community which was not catholic in this sense would not even be a Church.[87]

---

[86] Properly: *"Agere sequitur ad esse in actu"* ("To act is the result of a being which is in act"): Saint Thomas Aquinas, *Summa contra gentiles* III, ch. 69, 20 (our translation). See Thomas Aquinas, *Scriptum super Sententiis* III, d. 2, q. 1.

[87] Benedict XVI, *Homily on the Solemnity of Pentecost*, May 11, 2008. This teaching was reiterated with other words by the Supreme Pontiff in the *Address at the Ordinary Public Consistory* on November 24, 2012: "From its origins, then, the Church is oriented *kath'holon*, she embraces the whole universe.... The Church's universal mission does not arise from below, but descends from above, from the Holy Spirit: from the beginning she seeks to express herself in every culture so as to form the one People of God. Rather than beginning as a local community that slowly grows and spreads outwards, she is like yeast oriented towards a universal horizon, towards the whole: universality is inscribed within her.... Around the Apostles, Christian communities spring up, but these are 'the' Church

3.1.7. Apostolic

The note of apostolicity is intimately connected with that of unity and catholicity. In fact, this property of the Church regards her stable permanence in her own identity (relationship with unity), and also expresses her continuity in time in a way that mirrors her catholicity, which expresses above all her spatial extension. And just as within the catholicity—as was noted—the aspect of temporal diffusion is not lacking, so in the apostolicity the territorial aspect is present. In fact, the local Churches are always presided over by a bishop, a successor of the Apostles. The apostolicity of the Church guarantees that she remains identical to herself, faithful to the original project of her Founder, despite the changing of times and contexts, and the natural turnover of the Church's leaders. It is primarily a gift: the Church is gifted with the apostolic character by Christ. Her faith is the faith of the Apostles (the "deposit") and her hierarchical leaders are the successors of the Apostles in teaching, in celebrating the Sacraments, and in the authority of pastoral guidance (the so-called *tria munera*). This is why the apostolicity is—for every generation of Christians—always a task as well: to remain faithful to the fundamental process of "receiving and transmitting" (see 1 Cor 11:23; 15:1–3).

1. Apostolic Succession

The most important aspect of this note is that of "apostolic succession." This concerns the uninterrupted continuity that begins from the constitution of the Twelve Apostles by Christ and is perpetuated in the Church through episcopal Ordination (see Chapter Ten). Only the uninterrupted continuity of this succession guarantees the apostolicity of the Church, the link with the Twelve; and with this it preserves the Church in her original identity, despite changes in time and place. Saint Luke writes that, "When day came, [Jesus] called his disciples to himself, and from them he chose Twelve, whom he also named apostles" (Luke 6:13). Saint Paul says that the Apostles are a foundation of the Church, firmly built on the cornerstone that is Christ (see Eph 2:19–22). And Saint John recounts the vision of the heavenly City, whose walls "had twelve courses of stones as its foundation, on which were inscribed the twelve names of the twelve apostles of the Lamb" (Rev 21:14).

> which is always the same, one and universal, whether in Jerusalem, Antioch, or Rome. And when the Apostles speak of the Church, they are not referring to a community of their own, but to the Church of Christ, and they insist on the unique, universal and all-inclusive identity of the *Catholica* that is realized in every local church."

The Church

The *Catechism of the Catholic Church* (§§857–865) explains these and other passages of the New Testament by noting that there is a threefold meaning of the Church's apostolicity: (1) it always remains built on the foundation of the Twelve; (2) it safeguards and transmits the teaching of the Apostles, or the "deposit of faith"; and (3) it continues to be taught, sanctified, and governed, until the end of time, by the Apostles through their legitimate successors, namely, the validly ordained bishops.

2. The Indissoluble Link with the Origin

From the first centuries, the Fathers and ecclesiastical writers were aware of the fundamentally apostolic character of the Church and of the decisive importance of this aspect for discerning the true Church of Christ from other groups that also had reference to Him. Thus, Tertullian notes: "Every sort of thing must necessarily revert to its original for its classification. Therefore the Churches, although they are so many and so great, comprise but the one primitive Church, (originated) by the Apostles, from which they all (spring). In this way all are primitive, and all are apostolic, while they are all proved to be one."[88] Saint Irenaeus of Lyon also greatly emphasized the theme of "apostolic Tradition," which he understood both as a transmission of doctrine and a succession of ministry. In his times (the second century), he could still piece together the lines of succession of the bishops in the various Churches. He attests to this explicitly with these words: "It is within the power of all, therefore, in every Church, who may wish to see the truth, to contemplate clearly the Tradition of the Apostles manifested throughout the whole world; and we are in a position to reckon up those who were by the Apostles instituted bishops in the Churches, and [to demonstrate] the succession of these men to our own times."[89]

3. Apostolicity and Apostolate

We shall dedicate the next section to the brief exploration of the character of the ecclesial Hierarchy. For now, we can conclude through a final note that apostolicity—though it is mainly linked to the theme of apostolic succession—is and remains a note of the whole Church and thus does not pertain to

---

[88] Tertullian of Carthage, *De praescriptione haereticorum* 20.7–8, in *ANF*, vol. 3, trans. Peter Holmes (Peabody, MA: Hendrickson Publishers, Inc. 1994), 252.

[89] Saint Irenaeus of Lyon, *Adversus haereses* 3.3.1, in *ANF*, vol. 1, trans. James Donaldson and Alexander Roberts (Peabody, MA: Hendrickson Publishers, Inc., 1994), 415.

How Is the Church Composed?

the Shepherds alone. Although not everyone in the Church is a successor of the Apostles, the whole Church is nonetheless apostolic. This means that the character of apostolicity is present as a gift and is exercised as a task especially in the sacred ministers, but not only in them. Thus, the Catechism teaches:

> The whole Church is apostolic, in that she remains, through the successors of St. Peter and the other apostles, in communion of faith and life with her origin: and in that she is "sent out" into the whole world.... Indeed, we call an apostolate "every activity of the Mystical Body" that aims "to spread the Kingdom of Christ over all the earth" [*AA* 2] (CCC §863)[90]

3.1.8. *"Mysterium Lunae"*

Concluding this exposition of the four properties of the Church, we want to point out that they correspond to four properties of Christ Himself: (1) Jesus is one with His Father (unity: see John 10:30); (2) He is Holy *par excellence* (holiness: see Luke 1:35); (3) He is the universal Revealer, Mediator, and Savior, Whose work is valid for all people of all times (catholicity: John 1:18; 1 Tim 2:5–6; 1 John 2:2); and (4) Jesus is the One who is sent (in Greek, *"Apostolos"* ["Apostle"]) by the Father into the world (apostolicity: John 5:36; 10:36).

Thus it becomes clear that the patristic metaphor of the *"mysterium lunae"* ("mystery of the moon") suits the Church well.[91] Christ is the Son: Truth, perfect Holiness, and Light; the Church receives all that she is and all that she has from Christ. She is like the moon, which does not shine with its own light, but reflects the light of another.[92]

---

[90] The citation mentioned in the text is from the Second Vatican Council, *Apostolicam Actuositatem*, §2.

[91] "Deservedly is the moon compared to the Church.... This is the real moon which from the perpetual light of her own brother [the Sun, Christ] has acquired the light of immortality and grace. Not from her own light does the Church gleam, but from the light of Christ. From the Sun of Justice has her brilliance been obtained, so that it is said: 'It is now no longer I that live, but Christ lives in me' [Gal 2:20]" (Saint Ambrose of Milan, *Hexaemeron* 4.8.32, in *FCNT*, vol. 42, trans. John J. Savage [New York: Fathers of the Church, Inc., 1961], 156).

[92] Saint Thomas Aquinas developed the elements of his ecclesiology within the Christological section of the *Summa*, as if to suggest that the mystery of the Church can only be understood as a part and consequence of the mystery of Christ (see *ST* III, q. 8: a question dedicated to the grace of Christ as Head of the Church).

3.2. The Sacred Hierarchy

Another constitutive aspect of the Church, in addition to her notes, is the existence, by the will of her Founder, of the sacred Hierarchy within her.[93]

3.2.1. Heavenly and Earthly Hierarchies

1. Heavenly Hierarchy

Hierarchy is a Greek term, which indicates being the head (also in the sense of being the origin) of sacred things. The word is not found in classical Greek, but only in later Greek, and its diffusion in the Church is due to a fifth- or sixth-century author who presents himself with the pseudonym of Dionysius the Areopagite, an Athenian who converted upon hearing the preaching of Saint Paul (see Acts 17:34). The real identity of Pseudo-Dionysius is unknown, but some of his works have survived, among which are two with the following titles: *The Ecclesiastical Hierarchy* and *Celestial Hierarchy*. In these, on the basis of the concept of "order/ordering" (in Greek, *taxis*) he presents the arrangement of the celestial spirits (see Chapter Three) and the ecclesial

---

[93] Naturally, all baptized persons are a constitutive and essential aspect of the Church: sacred ministers as well as lay faithful. In order not to overextend the discussion, we shall focus here only on the Hierarchy, without intending to undervalue the importance of the other faithful. The Second Vatican Council reaffirmed the vocation of all the baptized to holiness and expressed the specific task of the lay faithful to "seek the kingdom of God by engaging in temporal affairs and by ordering them according to the plan of God. [The laity] live in the world, that is, in each and in all of the secular professions and occupations. They live in the ordinary circumstances of family and social life, from which the very web of their existence is woven. They are called there by God that by exercising their proper function and led by the spirit of the Gospel they may work for the sanctification of the world from within as a leaven. In this way they may make Christ known to others, especially by the testimony of a life resplendent in faith, hope and charity. Therefore, since they are tightly bound up in all types of temporal affairs it is their special task to order and to throw light upon these affairs in such a way that they may come into being and then continually increase according to Christ to the praise of the Creator and the Redeemer" (*Lumen Gentium*, §31). With that in mind, a discussion of the laity—which here must unfortunately be omitted—could be included in a possible future treatment of the Catholic moral truths, especially in the chapter that deals with the social doctrine of the Church. For an overview on the doctrine regarding the Catholic laity and the state of consecrated life, see CCC §§897–933. For guidelines on the identity and commitment of the lay faithful, see Saint John Paul II, *Christifideles Laici* (1988); Congregation for the Doctrine of the Faith, *Doctrinal Note on Some Questions Regarding the Participation of Catholics in Political Life* (2002); Pontifical Council for Justice and Peace, *Compendium of the Social Doctrine of the Church* (2004); Benedict XVI, *Caritas in Veritate* (2009).

ministers. The idea that the Hierarchy of the Church is ordered by the same principle as the angelic spirits are arranged in Heaven—according to inferior and superior degrees and corresponding to greater or lesser objective perfection—is interesting. This means that, in the celestial Hierarchy, the angels of superior nature preside over those of inferior nature.

2. Ecclesiastical Hierarchy

In the ecclesiastical Hierarchy, the baptized that have received a higher ministry preside over other faithful. This is an "objective" superiority or excellence; it is not, in all cases, individual or subjective as well. Sacred ministers objectively possess a superior ecclesial ministry,[94] which places them as leaders of the other faithful; this does not imply that they are in all cases superior to the others from the standpoint of personal holiness as well.[95] A second principle of this perspective (profoundly marked by Neoplatonism) is that the inferior orders receive divine gifts through the superior ones, that is, through the mediation of the latter. This applies both with respect to the heavenly spirits and to the Church. Thus, the inferior spirits receive divine illuminations through the superior spirits. Likewise, the lay faithful receive the graces of God through the mediation of the sacred ministers, who themselves are hierarchically ordered as bishops-presbyters-deacons.

3.2.2. Sacramental and Juridical Distinction

1. Sacramental Distinction

The Catholic Hierarchy is structured according to these three degrees of the Sacrament of Holy Orders: the episcopate, the presbyterate, and the diaconate. For a long time, these were called the major Orders, to distinguish them from the minor Orders, which—in the more ancient liturgical

---

[94] Thus, it was expressed by Gerbert of Aurillac [later Pope Sylvester II, d. 1003]: "*Nihil [est] in hoc saeculo excellentius sacerdotibus, nihil sublimius episcopis*" ("Nothing in this world is more elevated than priests, nothing more sublime than bishops": *Sermo de informatione episcoporum* [our translation]).

[95] For this reason, a theologian of the Orthodox Church recently considered having to contrast the term "hierarchy," an objective order of precedence in ministry, with that of "filiarchy," the subjective order of precedence in love. Whoever has a higher ministry is higher up in the hierarchical scale, while whoever is holier, is also higher in the "filiarchy." In obedience to the principle of *et-et*, it is not a bad thing that in the Church both the hierarchical and "filiarchical" scales are considered.

ordering—were received in preparation for the former. The current "ordinary form" of the Liturgy in the Roman Rite, approved by Paul VI, no longer includes the minor Orders but rather the "ministries" of lector and acolyte (which can be received also by laypersons who will not approach Holy Orders), while it maintains the major Orders, with the latter being of divine law. The highest degree of authority linked to the Sacrament of Holy Orders is that of the bishop.[96]

2. Juridical Distinction

However, there is another criterion for further distinguishing authority in the Church: the juridical criterion. From the juridical perspective, there are other hierarchical degrees, which do not depend on the reception of a Sacrament, but still confer a higher authority. All those who have received episcopal Ordination are bishops in the full sense through the Sacrament. But there is also a hierarchical distinction at the juridical level among the bishops, including archbishops, metropolitans, primates, and patriarchs. Furthermore, Canon Law recognizes particular prerogatives to the cardinals. All these distinctions are born historically (they concern "ecclesiastical law") and they have also undergone a certain amount of transformation in regard to the authority, rights, and duties that they confer.

There is also, however, a case of a ministry founded on the juridical order that does not depend on the historical evolution of the Church—that is to say, which was not introduced by her—but that pertains to the very constitution of the Christian community as it was willed by its Founder (and is thus of "divine law"). This ministry is the office of the Bishop of Rome, successor of Saint Peter, the Supreme Roman Pontiff. His superior authority does not derive from the Sacrament of Holy Orders, because from this perspective he is a bishop like all other bishops. This authority instead represents the highest degree of the hierarchical order from the perspective of the power of jurisdiction. This supreme power in the Church was willed by Christ Himself, as can be read in the famous passage of Saint Matthew:

> When Jesus went into the region of Caesarea Philippi He asked His disciples, "Who do people say that the Son of Man is?" They replied, "Some say John the Baptist, others Elijah, still others Jeremiah or one of the prophets." He said to them, "But who do you say that I am?" Simon Peter said in reply, "You are the Messiah, the Son of the living

---

[96] Second Vatican Council, *Lumen Gentium*, §21.

God." Jesus said to him in reply, "Blessed are you, Simon son of Jonah. For flesh and blood has not revealed this to you, but my heavenly Father. And so I say to you, *you are Peter, and upon this rock I will build my Church, and the gates of the netherworld shall not prevail against it.* I will give you the keys to the kingdom of heaven. Whatever you bind on earth shall be bound in heaven; and whatever you loose on earth shall be loosed in heaven." (Matt 16:13–19 [emphasis added])

These words are addressed to Peter, but they reveal the "primacy" that the Bishop of Rome—every successor of Saint Peter—possesses over the whole Church, as will be explained shortly. For now, suffice it to note that this juridical criterion of distinction within the Hierarchy comes not only from ecclesiastical law. It was not only the Church, in the arc of her own history, that introduced it—something that she certainly did as well, in terms of concretely shaping the historical forms of it. The juridical criterion, rather, belongs to the divine constitution of the Church, having been willed by her Founder, Jesus Christ.

3.2.3. The Slant of the Treatment

Based on what has been said, we can recognize that it is possible to speak of the ecclesiastical Hierarchy in a twofold perspective: that of the Sacrament of Holy Orders and that of the power of jurisdiction. The sacramental and juridical powers are therefore distinct. It is clear that the two aspects cannot be separated, but the starting point that is chosen in the exposition determines the standpoint from which the hierarchical ministries will be considered. For example, if one chooses to begin from the Sacrament of Holy Orders, it will first of all be noted that the pope is a bishop, placed at the head of the episcopal college. And then one goes on to the other aspect to highlight that, being the Bishop of Rome, he is also the successor of Saint Peter and thus receives the authority of being the head, and not only a member, of the college of bishops and therefore the supreme authority over the whole Church. If instead one starts from the juridical aspect, one will first of all notice the difference between the role of the pope and that of the other bishops, and then also emphasize the episcopal communion of the Supreme Roman Pontiff with the other members of the college of bishops.

Another important question concerns the theological discussion about the moment in which a bishop receives the power of jurisdiction: the priestly power *(munus)* is evidently given to him with the Sacrament of Holy Orders, but when is he given juridical power *(potestas)*—for example, the authority to lead a diocese? If one starts from the perspective of the Sacrament that gives the episcopacy, one will be led to say that it also confers ipso facto the power of government, which would, however, remain indeterminate as regards the place or the particular office in which such power is exercised. This means that when someone is ordained bishop, he receives from the Sacrament both the high priesthood and the juridical power of governance, but the latter, in order to be carried out, would have to be "determined"; that is, it would have to be specified what diocese that bishop will govern or what office he will exercise. Such a determination is made by the pope, who has the supreme authority of governance in the Church, and he is the one who grants them a particular office, thus determining the exercise of the juridical power that they already possess as bishops. On the other hand, if in order to analyze the theme one starts from the perspective of the power of jurisdiction, one will be led to affirm that the Sacrament only gives the high priesthood and not the power of jurisdiction, which is not only determined, but also conferred by the pope through the assignment of a bishop for a specific task (and, in fact, no bishop is ever appointed without contextually receiving at least a titular see, if not a real diocese).[97]

We have only proposed two examples here, but the difference of perspective also determines other aspects of the theological reflection on the Hierarchy. Both perspectives can be held and indeed they have been. It is important—whichever of the two is chosen—to present all the aspects and to give each its due value.

3.2.4. *The Apostle Peter*

The passage of Saint Matthew that we have cited above concerns the conferral of primacy to Peter. Peter appears in the New Testament as head of the group of the Twelve, commonly called Apostles. The Gospels are keen on emphasizing that, from the beginning, Peter was always the first of this group; he was the first called by Jesus when He chose His disciples—the closest collaborators in the work of God's kingdom. There are several other

---

[97] The discussion on the matter is very much open among theologians. The *"Nota Bene"* that concludes the "Preliminary Note of Explanation" of *Lumen Gentium* is limited to saying: "Without hierarchical communion the ontologico-sacramental function [*munus*], which is to be distinguished from the juridico-canonical aspect, cannot be exercised." It says that the two aspects (sacramental and juridical) are distinct, but it does not clarify whether that "cannot" refers to the determination of the power of governance that the bishop already has, or the conferral of that power. §2 of the same "Preliminary Note of Explanation," nonetheless, seems to lean toward the latter position.

clues that clearly bring out the unique role of Saint Peter:

(1) The name of Peter appears 114 times in the four Gospels and 57 times in the Acts of the Apostles, while the name John, traditionally identified with the Apostle that Jesus most loved, appears only thirty-eight times in the Gospels and eight times in Acts.

(2) In several Gospel passages, Peter forms—with James and John—a privileged group within the Twelve that is allowed by Christ to accompany Him to particularly important events, such as the miraculous resuscitation of Jairus' daughter (see Mark 5:37), the Transfiguration on Mount Tabor (see Mark 9:2), and the agony in Gethsemane (see Mark 14:33). Among these three, Peter is always named first. Also, when the Gospels report the entire list of the Twelve, we notice the same pattern: invariably, Peter is always mentioned first (and Judas Iscariot last). On one occasion, Peter considers himself so familiar with the Lord as to call Him aside and even begin to rebuke Him (see Mark 8:32).

(3) The Gospels report various accounts of Christ's call to Peter, as if to emphasize its importance (see Mark 1:16–17; Matt 4:18–19; Luke 5:1–11; John 1:40–42). Moreover, they agree in reporting that Christ gave Simon the new name of Cephas (the Aramaic word for rock), from which Peter (from the Greek word for rock) is derived (see John 1:42). Christ chose Peter's boat as a place to preach (see Luke 5:3). Jesus told Peter to find the coin in the mouth of a fish to pay the tribute (see Matt 17:24–27) and again asked him (along with John) to prepare the Upper Room for the Last Supper (see Luke 22:8). The latter detail assumes further importance, given that the Jewish Passover banquet was prepared by the head of the family or by his representative: Peter thus plays the role of representing the Head of the family of the Apostles and the Church, namely, Christ. During the Last Supper, Peter is the first to have his feet washed by Jesus (see John 13:6). On the same occasion, he demonstrates a certain authority over the disciple whom Jesus loved, almost ordering him to ask the Master to reveal the identity of the traitor (see John 13:23–24).

(4) The Gospels also mention three occasions in which Christ rebukes Peter: for his pusillanimity (Matt 14:31—and yet, here again he stands out, because he is the only one of the Apostles to get off the boat to meet Jesus by walking on the water); for his overly human mentality (see Mark 8:33); and for his inability to stay awake with Him (see Mark 14:37—it is significant that Christ rebukes three Apostles here, and yet it is Peter He addresses directly, as the representative of the others even in receiving correction). Now these rebukes of Christ, far from diminishing the importance of Peter, confirm it: he is always the most important Apostle for the Master and, thus, he has the greatest honors, but also the greatest responsibilities. And since more

is expected from the one who has received more (see Luke 12:48), Christ expects more from Peter than from the rest: hence, the corrections reserved to him, but also the assurance of a special prayer for him, the one who is called to confirm the faith of his brothers (see Luke 22:31–32).

(5) Peter would deny knowing the Lord three times during the Passion (see John 19:15–27), and—almost in a medicinal way—the risen Christ would ask Peter three times if he loves Him more than the others; and, on this same occasion, He would entrust the sheep of the ecclesial flock to him (see John 21:15–19).

(6) Peter's primacy also appears clearly in the Acts of the Apostles: after Jesus' Resurrection, he presides from the beginning over the apostolic college—without there being any election (see Acts 1:13, 15). Peter provides for and directs the choice of Matthias as a member of the Twelve to replace Judas Iscariot (see 1:15–26); he delivers the first proclamation to the people after Pentecost (see 2:14–41); he carries out the first miracle performed by an Apostle (3: 6–7); he is the representative of the Church before the Jewish authorities who persecute the new community (see 4:8; 5:29); he judges the case of the fraud of Ananias and Sapphira (see 5:1–11); he issues an anathema against Simon the Magician (see 8:20–23); he carries out the first missionary journeys to Lydda, Jaffa, and Caesarea (see 9:32–42; 10:23–24); he commands the admittance of pagans into the Church (see 10:48); the Church prays incessantly for him while he is in prison (see 12:5)—and he is miraculously freed (see 12:7–11); and he directs the so-called "Council of the Apostles" in Jerusalem (15:7–11). Therefore, according to Scripture, Saint Peter has a role and importance in the earliest Church that is not recognized for any other person.

(7) This is also attested by Saint Paul, when he states that, three years after his conversion, he—even though he was charged with announcing the Gospel directly by the risen Christ—went to Jerusalem to meet Cephas (see Gal 1:19). Moreover, the same Saint Paul mentions a detail that escaped the Gospel narrative, namely, that Saint Peter was the recipient of a privileged appearance of the risen Christ before the Lord appeared to the entire apostolic college (see 1 Cor 15:5).

3.2.5. The Role of Saint Peter and His Successor

We can also identify other important aspects of the above-cited passage of Petrine primacy from the Gospel of Matthew (16:13–19): (1) Christ does not speak such solemn words to anyone but Peter. (2) Christ indissolubly links the foundation of the Church to the role of Saint Peter, the rock/stone on which the Lord has decided to construct the entire ecclesial edifice. (3) If one takes away the rock on which a house rests, the house falls; so too, the Petrine ministry is not ancillary or secondary—if Peter falls, the Church falls too. (4) But Christ Himself promises: "The gates of the netherworld shall not prevail," which means that despite all of Satan's attacks against the Church and against Peter in particular, Peter and the Church will not fall, because Christ will keep the promise made to Simon, the fisherman of Galilee. (5) The ministry of Saint Peter is then qualified with the image of the keys and with that of loosing and binding, which we shall develop below.

1. The Power of the Keys (Opening and Closing)

The image of the keys recalls a passage of the Old Testament—Isaiah 22:22—which speaks of the steward of David's house, that is, the one who had the task and authority of opening and closing the doors of the king's house. The text of Isaiah says: "I will place the key of the House of David on his shoulder; / what he opens, no one will shut, / what he shuts, no one will open." The Book of Revelation (3:7) applies the same prophecy to the risen Jesus, referring to the doors of Heaven; as we saw in Chapter Four, Jesus is the One who has reopened the doors of Heaven, closed by sin. Moreover, Jesus will be the Judge of the living and the dead at the end of time: thus, it is said that when He opens the doors of the heavenly kingdom, no one can close them and, vice versa, if He closes them, no one will be able to open them. But as regards the kingdom *in via*, the Church, Jesus entrusts this power to Saint Peter, who is thus the Vicar of Christ on earth or, as Saint Catherine of Siena (d. 1380) liked to say: "sweet Christ on earth."[98]

The image of the keys placed on the shoulder may seem bizarre: keys are carried in pockets or in a bag. But the ancient Middle Eastern custom was different: the house owners usually carried the keys in sight, hanging from the shoulder—a visible sign of their status as owners, to be admired by those who passed by. A great biblical scholar of the first half of the twentieth century, visiting Palestine, was able to see some of these characters, as he reports in his extraordinary book on the life of Christ. The keys were thus chosen as a symbol of the popes, which is found in their coat of arms, as well as on the pontifical seals, and the flag of the Vatican City State, etc.

---

[98] In a letter addressed to the pope, Saint Catherine writes, "O my father, sweet Christ on earth" (Saint Catherine of Siena, *Epistula 185* [our translation]).

2. Loosing and Binding

Jesus also uses another image—implied in the symbol of the keys—of opening and closing: namely, the image of loosing and binding. What was said about the keys is valid here: no one else can modify what Peter decides for the Church on earth. Peter is the supreme visible authority of the Church. But here there is another interesting aspect. Jesus applies to Peter alone the phrase that He also says elsewhere to the other Apostles as a whole. A little later, in the same Gospel, we read: "Amen, I say to you, whatever you bind on earth shall be bound in heaven, and whatever you loose on earth shall be loosed in heaven" (Matt 18:18). By comparing the two citations, we infer that Saint Peter does not receive a power different from that of the other Apostles, but that he receives the power to do alone what the other Apostles can only do together (Peter included).[99]

3. The College of the Apostles and Its Head

Christ gives the Twelve, as a college, the power of binding and loosing. This same power of the whole apostolic college (which does not subsist without Peter) is also entrusted to Peter alone, who gathers in himself all the authority that Christ gives to "His own," and he is the only one among the Apostles who can exercise it alone. Peter, to be even more explicit, can decide to make use of his authority individually or collegially.

An exemplification of this lies in the fact that in the Church there are two ways of defining the doctrine of faith with a solemn and infallible act (see Chapter Two): through a dogmatic definition by an ecumenical council, or through a dogmatic definition by the pope—when he speaks "*ex cathedra*." In the first case, the entire episcopal college (which succeeds the college of the Twelve) defines the faith by acting as a group, however always "*cum Petro et sub Petro*" ("With Peter and under [the authority of] Peter").[100] In the second case, the pope—because he is the successor of Peter—is able to carry out the same act alone, because he is the only bishop who has the authority to do alone what the other bishops can do only together and under his leadership, that is, precisely as a college that has its head. But it should

---

[99] One of the most important applications of the principle of binding and loosing consists in the possibility of forgiving or not forgiving sins: "Whose sins you forgive are forgiven them, and whose sins you retain are retained" (John 20:23).

[100] The teaching found in the Second Vatican Council, *Lumen Gentium*, §22, can effectively be summarized with this classic formula.

be added that the Supreme Pontiff can still carry out acts that the college cannot, because he alone is head of the college.[101] There is a further distinction in the fact that the pope, by exercising authority over all the baptized, including bishops, has the power to judge everyone, from lay persons to cardinals, while no one can judge (in the juridical, and not moral sense) the Supreme Pontiff: "*Prima Sedes a nemine iudicatur*" ("The First See is judged by no one").[102]

3.2.6. From the Apostolic College to the Episcopal College

The reader may have noticed that in the previous section, we naturally went from the relationship between Peter and the Apostles to that between the pope and the bishops. Thus, we now need to consider how it is justified that the pope and the bishops believe they have to continue to exercise tasks that Christ conferred on Peter and the Apostles. This is possible on the basis of the aforementioned "apostolic succession," which was clearly intended by Christ, as can be inferred from this passage of Saint Matthew:

> The eleven disciples went to Galilee, to the mountain to which Jesus had ordered them. When they saw him, they worshiped, but they doubted. Then Jesus approached and said to them, "All power in heaven and on earth has been given to me. Go, therefore, and make disciples of all nations, baptizing them in the name of the Father, and of the Son, and of the holy Spirit, teaching them to observe all that I have commanded you. And behold, I am with you always, until the end of the age" (Matt 28:16–20).

1. The "Tria Munera"

The risen Christ gives the Apostles a participation in His own power, as can be seen from the conjunction "therefore" (in Greek, *oun*): "All power in heaven and on earth has been given to me. Go, *therefore*"—a sign that the sending of the Apostles in the world is linked to the power possessed by the glorified humanity of Christ. They will have to carry out three tasks: to make disciples of all peoples, to baptize them in the name of the Trinity, and to teach them to live as Christians.

These three tasks come to be called the *tria munera* in classical theology,

---

[101] See Second Vatican Council, "Preliminary Note of Explanation," §3.

[102] *Codex Iuris Canonici*, can. 1404. See also our Chapter Two, note 113.

The Church

namely, the three offices, tasks, or faculties of the Apostles: the "*munus docendi*" ("office of teaching") through which the Apostles are the teachers and heralds of the Gospel who safeguard and defend the Word of God; the "*munus sanctificandi*" ("office of sanctification"), through which the Apostles are priests who have the faculty of celebrating and regulating the Sacraments; and the "*munus regendi*" ("the power of governance"), through which the Apostles are rulers who have authority of governing and directing the baptized with laws and sanctions, provisions and initiatives.

2. The Transmission of the "Tria Munera"

So far, we understand what task Christ has conferred on the Apostles, but the question still must be answered: Why does the Church believe that the bishops succeed the Apostles in the exercise of the *tria munera*? The answer lies in the fact that, in the cited passage of Saint Matthew, Christ continues: "I am with you always, until the end of the age." The risen Christ lives in eternity and thus it is quite possible that He is present until the end of the world. But the Lord knew well that the Apostles would not live so long (see John 21:19, 23). How then can He say: I am with you until the end of the world? He can because—by virtue of apostolic succession—even if those who hold an office in the Church die, that office always remains, because there is someone who takes on the same role. Thus, Jesus will always be with the Apostles who preach, baptize, and govern the Church, because He will always be with those who, in every era, carry out the tasks given to the Apostles.[103] Therefore, in this concise formula, Christ foresees and establishes the succession of bishops in the ministry that He gives to the Apostles.

3. The Laying On of Hands

This is why the Apostles established certain individuals as their collaborators in the ministry and transmitted to them their own duties through the deed of laying hands on their head, a deed that in the Bible means "identifying oneself with," in addition to blessing. The laying on of hands indicates, according to the context: (1) blessing; (2) transmission of a power or authority; (3) sharing a responsibility, both for good and evil (thus the Israelites placed their sins onto animals that were immolated as a sacrifice for their sins: see Lev 16:21); and (4) communion between whoever performs the laying on of hands and the one over whom it is performed (see, for example,

---

[103] See Saint Thomas Aquinas, *Super Matthaeum*, XXVIII, lectio 1.

Num 8:10–12; 27: 18–23; Lev 1:4; 16:20–22; Deut 34:9). This deed was performed by Saint Paul (who in turn also received it: Acts 13:2–3) to establish Timothy as overseer of a Church (probably Ephesus): "For this reason, I remind you to stir into flame the gift of God that you have through the imposition of my hands" (2 Tim 1:6).[104] Hands are also laid upon the first deacons (see Acts 6:6).

3.2.7. The Petrine Primacy

The Supreme Roman Pontiff, as the successor of Saint Peter on the chair of the Church of Rome, possesses the Petrine primacy, namely, that primacy that Christ conferred to Saint Peter over all the Church and that was transmitted to his successors.

1. The New Testament

The personal primacy of the Apostle Peter is, as we have seen, a dogma clearly revealed by the Scripture. The primacy of his successor, the Bishop of Rome, has its roots, indirectly, in the New Testament itself:

(1) We find a first indication of it in John 21, a text that was written after the death of Saint Peter, as can be deduced from verse 19. This chapter of the Fourth Gospel speaks of the task conferred by Christ to Peter to guide His flock, and it does so not by presenting it as something of the past, but rather something that pertains to the present, the moment in which the evangelist is writing. Therefore, even if Peter is already dead at that time, the Gospel of John implies that the *munus* of Peter remains alive in the Church.

(2) The New Testament presents the foundation of the Church on the part of Christ as a reality destined to remain until the end of the world (see Matt 28:20). The Petrine ministry is no exception with respect to this permanence, given that—as we have seen—the Gospels clearly emphasize that the primacy of Saint Peter among the Twelve is a constitutive element of the Church.

---

[104] This text appears contradictory with respect to 1 Tim 4:14: "Do not neglect the gift you have, which was conferred on you through the prophetic word with the imposition of hands of the presbyterate." We do not intend to settle this complex question here, but the two texts can be reconciled if one hypothesizes that the laying on of hands by Saint Paul took place in a celebration of a collegial type, whose nature must be explored deeper, but which may well correspond to what we know of the ancient Liturgy. Another solution could be that the two texts refer to two distinct instances of laying of hands, which occurred at different times and with different meanings.

The Church

(3) The Acts of the Apostles emphasize the centrality of Rome in the original apostolic work: it is said explicitly that Saint Paul was, as a prisoner, taken to Rome, where he preached the Gospel despite being a prisoner, because he was allowed to live in a house under the surveillance of a soldier (see Acts 28:16). For what regards Saint Peter, the attestations of ancient writers report that he also went to Rome, preached there, and became a martyr like Saint Paul.[105]

(4) The New Testament recognizes that the ecclesial responsibility of the successors of the Apostles (e.g., Timothy and Titus) is linked to a seat, something that is therefore valid for Rome too, as the seat of Saint Peter and his successors.

2. Exercise of the Primacy since the Beginning

There has been awareness of all this since very early in the Church's history: a classic example of it is the fact that, as early as the year 95 or 96,[106] the Bishop of Rome, Saint Clement, wrote to the Church of Corinth with the purpose of resolving problems that arose there. It is clear, therefore, that from the beginning the successor of Peter on the Roman Cathedra (chair) has carried out a function of overseeing all the Churches, because he occupies the See of Peter, head of the apostolic college. For this reason, Saint Ignatius of Antioch, writing to the Christians of Rome, speaks of the Church "which holds the primacy of the community of love."[107] And at the end of second century, Saint Irenaeus of Lyon attests to the primacy of the Roman See in an indubitable way: "For it is a matter of necessity that every Church should agree [*necesse est omnem convenire ecclesiam*] with this Church [of Rome], on account of her preeminent authority [*propter potentiorem principalitatem*; it can also be translated, 'on account of her most excellent origin']."[108] Based on these assumptions, in the fifth century Pope Leo the Great was able to declare, in a homily on the anniversary of his consecration as the Bishop of Rome:

---

[105] See Saint Irenaeus of Lyon, *Adversus haereses* 3.1.1 and 3; Tertullian of Carthage, *De praescriptione haereticorum* 35; Lucius Caecilius Firmianus Lactantius (d. after 317), *De mortibus persecutorum* 2; Saint Eusebius di Caesarea (d. 340), *Historia Ecclesiastica* 5.8.3, and especially 2.14.6, etc.; Saint Jerome of Stridon (d. 420), *De viris illustribus* 1; etc.

[106] To understand just how ancient the practice of the primacy of the bishop of Rome is, remember that in the year 96, Saint Timothy was still alive. He, who was a direct disciple of Saint Paul, died the following year.

[107] Saint Ignatius of Antioch, *Epistula ad Romanos, incipit* (in *FCNT*, vol. 1, 107).

[108] Saint Irenaeus of Lyon, *Adversus haereses* 3.1–2 (in *ANF*, vol. 1, 415).

For the sturdiness of that faith which was praised in the leader of the Apostles endures. Just as what Peter believed in Christ remains, there likewise remains what Christ instituted in Peter. . . . This pattern of truth remains. Persevering in the fortitude he received, blessed Peter does not relinquish his government of the Church. He was ordained before the others so that, when he is called rock, declared foundation, installed as doorkeeper for the kingdom of heaven, appointed arbiter of binding and loosing (with his definitive judgments retaining force even in heaven), we might know through the very mysteries of these appellations what sort of fellowship he had with Christ. . . . So, if we do anything correctly or judge anything correctly, if we obtain anything at all from the mercy of God through daily supplications, it comes about as a result of his works and merits. In this see his power lives on and his authority reigns supreme. . . . Regard him [Peter] as present in the lowliness of my person [Leo]. Honor him. In him continues to reside the responsibility for all Shepherds, along with the protection of those sheep entrusted to them. His dignity does not fade even in an unworthy heir. On that account, the presence of my venerable brothers and fellow priests—though I have longed for it indeed and thought it something to be honored—has all the more sacred and devout a character if they redirect the reverence of this service, at which they have seen fit to be present, to the one whom they know to be not only the ruler of this see but the primate of all bishops. When we present our exhortations to your holy ears, consider that you are being addressed by the one [Peter] in place of whom we [Leo] exercise this function. It is with his affection that we admonish you. We preach to you nothing other than what he taught.[109]

3. Primacy of Honor and Jurisdiction

The papal primacy is twofold: it is a primacy of honor and jurisdiction. That the pope possesses primacy of honor within the episcopal *corpus* is a doctrine accepted also by the Orthodox Churches. The primacy of honor can be summarized in the formula for which the Bishop of Rome is *"primus inter pares"* ("first among equals"). This Latin formula identifies a person who represents a group of equals, namely, persons who are entirely at the same level. The

---

[109] Saint Leo the Great, *Sermones* 3.2–4, in *FCNT*, vol. 93, trans. Jane Patricia Freeland and Agnes Josephine Conway (Washington, DC: CUA Press, 1996), 22–24.

primus inter pares performs a function of coordination, but he is not superior by authority to the other members of the group. This perspective could be accepted if the ecclesiastical Hierarchy were discernable only according to the sacramental order. In this sense, it has been said, the pope is a bishop and *as a bishop* he is absolutely equal to all the others. But from this perspective, our Orthodox brethren could not easily justify the Hierarchy that they themselves acknowledge and value (Patriarchs, Metropolitans, etc.) *from the theological, and not merely practical perspective.*

The hierarchical degree is actually established on the basis of jurisdiction as well. And here the second important aspect intervenes, for which the Bishop of Rome is not only the bishop of that Church, but the supreme authority of the whole Church from the standpoint of his primacy of jurisdiction. That is why the doctrine of the Church has always condemned conciliarist tendencies. Conciliarism is the heresy that believes that the ecumenical council is superior in authority to the pope, thus denying the latter's primacy of jurisdiction. The bishops gathered in the Councils of Constance (1414–1418) and Basel (1431) fell into this error. Their affirmations were never approved by the Church; on the contrary, the Council of Florence (1439) explicitly condemned and censured their pronouncements on the matter.[110] The same Council, a few months prior, had already dogmatically defined the Petrine primacy:

> We define that the holy Apostolic See and the Roman Pontiff have the primacy over the whole world [*in universum orbem*] and that the same Roman Pontiff is the successor of blessed Peter, the prince of the Apostles and the true Vicar of Christ, the Head of the whole Church, the father and teacher of all Christians; and that to him, in the person of blessed Peter, was given by our Lord Jesus Christ the full power of feeding, ruling, and governing the whole Church.[111]

The bull *Exsurge Domine*, with which Leo X condemned many errors of Luther, also rejects the affirmation that the "Roman pontiff, the successor of Peter, is not the Vicar of Christ over all the Churches of the entire world."[112]

---

[110] See Council of Florence, *Moyses Vir Dei* (1439) (DS 1309).

[111] Council of Florence, *Laetentur Caeli* (1439) (DS 1307). The insistence on verbs (*pascendi, regendi et gubernandi*) that all have to do with the juridical aspect of Petrine governance is notable.

[112] Leo X, *Exsurge Domine* (1520), §25 (DS 1475). As a summary of the Council of Trent, in the Bull *Iniunctum Nobis* (1564), Pope Pius IV (d. 1565) proposes a broad profession of faith, which—among other things—reads: "I acknowledge the Holy, Catholic, and Apostolic Roman Church as the mother and the teacher of all the Churches, and I promise

4. The First Vatican Council

Finally, the teaching of the First Vatican Council is of fundamental importance. It reaffirmed Petrine primacy and solemnly defined the infallibility of pronouncements of the pope *"ex cathedra"* as a dogma of faith (see Chapter Two). For our purpose here, we can limit ourselves to emphasizing that the First Vatican Council, by explicitly citing the Council of Florence, reiterates the primacy of jurisdiction, and not simply honor, of the Supreme Pontiff and specifies that such a primacy is of "divine right," that is, it is conferred directly by Christ to Peter and his successors:

> We, therefore, teach and declare, according to the testimony of the Gospel, that the primacy of jurisdiction over the whole Church was immediately and directly promised to and conferred upon the blessed Apostle Peter by Christ the Lord.[113] ... Now, what Christ, the Lord ... established in the blessed Apostle Peter for the perpetual safety and everlasting good of the Church must, by the will of the same, endure without interruption in the Church.... Therefore, whoever succeeds Peter in this chair, according to the institution of Christ himself, holds Peter's primacy over the whole Church.... And so we teach and declare that, in the disposition of God, the Roman Church holds the preeminence of ordinary power over all the other Churches; and that this power of jurisdiction of the Roman pontiff, which is truly episcopal, is immediate. Regarding this jurisdiction, the Shepherds of whatever rite or jurisdiction and the faithful, individually and collectively, are bound by a duty of hierarchical subjection and of true obedience; and this not only in matters that pertain to faith and morals, but also in manners that pertain to the discipline and government of the Church throughout the whole world."[114]

---

and swear true obedience to the Roman Pontiff, successor of blessed Peter, chief of the Apostles, and Vicar of Christ" (DS 1868).

[113] The omitted text explicitly says what is implied in this proposition: "In manifest opposition to this very clear teaching of the Holy Scriptures, as it has always been understood by the Catholic Church, are the perverse opinions of those who wrongly explain the form of government established by Christ in his Church; either by denying that Peter alone in preference to the other Apostles, either singly or as a group, was endowed by Christ with the true and proper primacy of jurisdiction; or by claiming that this primacy was not given immediately and directly to blessed Peter, but to the Church and through her to him as a minister of the Church herself" (DS 3054).

[114] First Vatican Council, *Pastor Æternus* (1870), chs. 1–3 (DS 3053; 3056–3057; 3060).

3.2.8. The College of Bishops

It is very significant that the First Vatican Council, shortly after the concluding words of the previous citation, adds: "This power of the Supreme Pontiff, however, is far from standing in the way of the power of ordinary and immediate episcopal jurisdiction by which the bishops ... feed and rule individually, as true Shepherds, the particular flock assigned to them."[115] These words open the door to a further development that would be realized by the Second Vatican Council, in perfect continuity with the First Vatican Council. In fact, the last Council—once again reiterating all that has been taught about the primacy of the pope in previous centuries—broadened the scope to the consideration of the collegiality of the episcopal body, of which the pope is the head.

1. Truly Collegial Power

The college of bishops is the stable group or class of those who have received the Sacrament of Holy Orders in the degree of the episcopate and which are in hierarchical communion with the head of the college, the pope. The episcopal college also possesses supreme authority over the Church, but in a different way from the pope who additionally exercises supreme authority alone; the college can exercise it only in a truly collegial way. This implies that the college of bishops carries out an act that has characteristics of true collegiality, namely: (1) that the college subsists as such, that is, as a body united to its head; and (2) that the act carried out expresses the unity of faith and the authority of the college. Both these conditions can occur only and exclusively if the bishops that make up the college are in communion with the Supreme Pontiff. If the bishops are not in hierarchical communion with the pope, the college simply does not subsist, because it is like a dead body, which has no life when separated from its head. This is so for the first condition. Concerning the second, the role of the pope for guaranteeing the collegiality of an act is indispensable. Only the pope, in fact, has the authority of head of the college, which can then guarantee that the act carried out is an expression of the Catholic faith and of the collegial action of the bishops. No one else possesses such an authority.

2. Ecumenical Council

This is why, for example, a council is called ecumenical (i.e., general)—and,

---

[115] First Vatican Council, *Pastor Æternus*, ch. 3 (DS 3061).

consequently, its teachings bind the faith of the whole Church—only if the Supreme Pontiff has convened it, presided over it, or—if he could not—at least confirmed it. If there is no confirmation on the part of the pope, no council can be recognized as ecumenical, that is, as expressing a truly collegial act of the universal episcopate: "A council is never ecumenical unless it is confirmed or at least accepted as such by the successor of Peter; and it is prerogative of the Roman Pontiff to convoke these councils, to preside over them and to confirm them."[116]

3. *The* Sede Vacante

That the college of bishops cannot act without its head is seen also from the fact that in a period of "*Sede vacante*," that is, in the time between the death (or renunciation) of a pope and the election of his successor, there cannot be an intervention in any significant matter in the governance of the Church. Moreover, many offices stop (almost all the offices of the Roman Curia) and, if a council is in process, it is suspended automatically. The death of the pope marks almost a paralysis in the life of the Church. The faith is certainly not suspended, the Sacraments continue to be celebrated, and the bishops remain at the head of their dioceses; however, nothing can be done that has universal effect on the governance of the Church except for the election of the successor of the deceased pope.[117] This implies that the college of bishops cannot act without its head.[118]

Thus, the Second Vatican Council, which significantly developed the theme of episcopal collegiality, nonetheless specified that: "'College' is not

---

[116] Second Vatican Council, *Lumen Gentium*, §22.

[117] The specific mode of the election of the Roman Pontiff has undergone extensive historical development. The current *iter* for the Sacred College of Cardinals to follow was established, at a general level, by the apostolic constitution *Universi Dominici Gregis* (1996) of Saint John Paul II, to which Benedict XVI made certain modifications: in the first place with the apostolic letter *De Aliquibus Mutationibus in Normis de Electione Romani Pontificis* (2007); and later with the Motu Proprio *Normas Nonnullas* (2013).

[118] Hence, the Second Vatican Council has specified that, when it comes to episcopal collegiality, "It is not a distinction between the Roman Pontiff and the bishops taken collectively, but a distinction between the Roman Pontiff taken separately and the Roman Pontiff together with the bishops" (*Lumen Gentium*, "Preliminary Note of Explanation," §3). In fact, the college of bishops does not exist without the pope: without the pope there is no episcopal college, and thus we cannot consider as the two terms of the question the pope, on the one hand, and the college, on the other, as if they were each entities that could exist without the other. The pope (in pure theory!) could remain without the college, but not the college without the pope.

understood in a strictly juridical sense, that is as a group of equals who entrust their power to their president, but as a stable group whose structure and authority must be learned from Revelation."[119] This means that, even if the pope is chosen through a vote by the cardinals, he does not receive his power from them, but he receives it from Christ Himself. The voting only serves to indicate the one that Christ has chosen. This procedure is already found in the Acts of the Apostles, when the Eleven cast lots to determine who—among the two candidates for substituting Judas Iscariot in the college of the Twelve—would be *chosen by the Lord* ("You, Lord, who know the hearts of all, show which one of these two you have chosen" [Acts 1:24]). Thus, the episcopal college is not simply a group of equals that determines through oligarchical election—that is, through the cardinals, the chosen members of the college—who will be their president. This can happen in human societies, but not in the Church, which is a society *sui iuris* and *sui generis*. The pope is equal to the other members of the college through the received Sacrament: he is a bishop. But he is also superior to all others because only he is the Vicar of Christ on earth and the head of the college.

4. Visible Signs of the Distinction between the College and Its Head

This difference is expressed in many ways, not excluding the use of different signs. For example, the pope is the only bishop who has in his coat of arms the keys of Peter; and he is the only one who dresses completely in white. In the Liturgy, his "crosier," namely the high and noble staff on which he leans, is not curled on the top—as it is with other bishops—but instead it has the cross. In the past, these external signs of distinction were more numerous and solemn (we think of the gestatorial chair, the papal tiara, the flabella, the fanon, etc.). Although there has been some simplification in recent decades, in line with modern times, there still remain various signs that manifest the different position of authority of the pope with respect to that of other bishops.

5. Authority of the Episcopal College over the Entire Church

With all these necessary clarifications, it still remains true that the episcopal

---

[119] Second Vatican Council, *Lumen Gentium*, "Preliminary Note of Explanation," §1.

college has a true authority over the Church. It solemnly exercises this authority in the ecumenical council and in more ordinary forms in various ways. The Second Vatican Council sees in the bishops the Shepherds of the People of God, and it describes the importance of their ministry in these words:

> Bishops, therefore, with their helpers, the priests and deacons, have taken up the service of the community, presiding in place of God over the flock, whose Shepherds they are, as teachers for doctrine, priests for sacred worship, and ministers for governing. And just as the office granted individually to Peter, the first among the Apostles, is permanent and is to be transmitted to his successors, so also the Apostles' office of nurturing the Church is permanent, and is to be exercised without interruption by the sacred order of bishops. Therefore, the Sacred Council teaches that bishops by divine institution have succeeded to the place of the Apostles, as Shepherds of the Church, and he who hears them, hears Christ, and he who rejects them, rejects Christ and Him who sent Christ (see Luke 10:16).
>
> In the bishops, therefore, for whom priests are assistants, Our Lord Jesus Christ, the Supreme High Priest, is present in the midst of those who believe. For sitting at the right hand of God the Father, He is not absent from the gathering of His high priests, but above all through their excellent service He is preaching the Word of God to all nations, and constantly administering the Sacraments of faith to those who believe, by their paternal functioning (see 1 Cor 4:15) He incorporates new members in His Body by a heavenly regeneration, and finally by their wisdom and prudence He directs and guides the People of the New Testament in their pilgrimage toward eternal happiness. These Pastors, chosen to shepherd the Lord's flock of the elect, are servants of Christ and stewards of the mysteries of God (see 1 Cor 4:1) to whom has been assigned the bearing of witness to the Gospel of the grace of God (see 1 Cor 4:1) and the ministration of the Spirit and of justice in glory (see 2 Cor 3:8–9).[120]

---

[120] Second Vatican Council, *Lumen Gentium*, §§20–21.

6. Authority for Service

The bishops thus exercise the *tria munera*[121] in the Church for the sake of the whole People of God. An important aspect of the Second Vatican Council, indeed, is that of having clearly emphasized the, so to speak, "diaconal" character of the sacred Hierarchy. The pope and the bishops have true authority on the basis of which they are owed obedience. But they must first obey Christ and His Gospel. They are sacred ministers—and minister, in Latin, means servant. One of the pope's most significant titles is *"servus servorum Dei"* ("servant of the servants of God")[122]: it means that in the Church, the more one assimilates to Christ, the more one serves God and one's brothers and sisters. In fact, Christ, who is the true and only universal authority, says of Himself in John 5:30: "I do not seek my own will but the will of the one who sent me" (service of God); and, in Mark 10:45, He adds that the Son of Man "did not come to be served but to serve and to give his life as a ransom for many" (service of human beings). The Lord has thus applied to us what He said of Himself: "Rather, whoever wishes to be great among you will be your servant; whoever wishes to be first among you will be the slave of all" (service of human beings: Mark 10:43–44). Moreover, He teaches us to pray like so: "your will be done" (service of God: Matt 6:10).

Thus, the Second Vatican Council, reaffirming the characteristics of the sacred Hierarchy, explained its true authority, which must be recognized and appreciated by all the faithful, within the entire People of God and within the universal call to holiness of the baptized. The bishops are the heads in the Church, but they are heads called to work in view of the eternal salvation of souls, not to dominate them:

> Saint Paul: "But I call upon God as witness, on my life, that it is to spare you that I have not yet gone to Corinth. Not that we lord it

---

[121] Second Vatican Council, *Lumen Gentium*, §§25–27.

[122] Saint Augustine of Hippo, *Confessiones* 9.9.22, had called his mother Saint Monica "*serva servorum tuorum*" ("servant of your [God's] servants"). But the application of the title to the pope is due to Saint Gregory the Great, who wanted to respond, through this application, to the initiative of the Patriarch of Constantinople John IV (Nesteutes) (d. 595), who, with the support of the emperor, called himself an Ecumenical Patriarch. Since Christ says that "whoever wishes to be first among you will be the slave of all" (Mark 10:44), to define oneself as "servant of the servants" allowed the Pope, on one hand, to reaffirm his own primacy over all the bishops of the world and, on the other hand, to remind John IV that in the Church what counts more is carrying out the service received from Christ, not worrying about new titles to support one's own claim to greatness.

over your faith; rather, we work together for your joy, for you stand firm in the faith" (2 Cor 1:23–24).

Saint Peter: "So I exhort the presbyters among you, as a fellow presbyter and witness to the sufferings of Christ and one who has a share in the glory to be revealed. Tend the flock of God in your midst, [overseeing] not by constraint but willingly, as God would have it, not for shameful profit but eagerly. Do not lord it over those assigned to you, but be examples to the flock" (1 Pet 5:1–3).

7. The Obedience Owed to the Shepherds

From this perspective it is understood that the leaders of the Church are not in opposition or competition with the faithful. On the contrary, they are at their service, and their service consists in the exercise of the *tria munera*, for which they are the Teachers of the Gospel, Priests that administer the Sacraments, and Shepherds who direct the brothers and sisters toward the pastures of Heaven. It is for this reason that they also have a true authority and a right to be heard, revered, and obeyed, at least so long as they do not command things that—even minimally—go against the will of God.[123] In this case, they would turn from shepherds into wolves (see Matt 7:15—the false prophets are called wolves in sheep's clothing) and the sheep of Christ's flock must flee from them rather than listen to them (see John 10:8—the sheep do not listen to the "thieves and robbers"). But save for this exception, the baptized must always follow their legitimate Shepherds.

8. Authority and Charisms

Finally, the fact that the call to be bishops is a divine gift and not a human designation also implies the automatic dismissal of those theological proposals that want to see, within the life of the Church, a structural dialectic between the "institution" and the "charisms."[124] It is an indisputable fact that there have been many tensions in the history of the Church. But to make "*de*

---

[123] "It is obedience and obedience alone that shows us God's will with certainty. Of course our superiors may err, but it cannot happen that we, holding fast to our obedience, should be led into error by this. There is only one exception: if the superior commands something that would obviously involve breaking God's law, however slightly. In that case the superior could not be acting as a faithful interpreter of God's will" (Saint Maximilian Maria Kolbe [d. 1941], in *Liturgy of the Hours*, "Office of Readings," August 14).

[124] See Congregation for the Doctrine of the Faith, *Iuvenescit Ecclesia* (2016).

The Church

jure" what is *"de facto,"* almost as if Christ intended a Church always torn by internal struggles, is impossible to accept. On the contrary, the institutional aspect itself, being a gift of God, is one of the ecclesial charisms, which is only distinct from, but is not in opposition, to other charisms:

> The Church is built on the foundations of apostolic faith which continues to be ever present: the Apostles, in apostolic succession, are present in the Shepherds, whom we are, by the grace of God and in spite of our poverty. And let us all be grateful to God who has wished to call us to be in the apostolic succession and continue to build up the Body of Christ. Here an element that I think important appears: the ministries—the so-called "ministries"—they are called "gifts of Christ," they are charisms; that is, this opposition does not exist: on the one hand the ministry, as a juridical component, on the other charisms, as a prophetic, lively and spiritual gift, as a presence of the Spirit and of His newness. No! The ministries themselves are a gift of the Risen One and are charisms, they are articulations of his grace; one cannot be a priest without being charismatic. It is a charism to be a priest. It seems to me that we must bear this in mind. Being called to the priesthood, being called with a gift of the Lord, with a charism of the Lord. And thus, inspired by his Spirit, we must seek to live this charism of ours.[125]

Recent tendencies that oppose charism and institution, or hierarchy and prophecy, are thus unfounded. Just as the Church has her legitimate authority *both* in the Holy Father *and* in the entire college of bishops with and under him—without the need for introducing a competition into the harmony of the episcopal class—so the Church as a whole is based *both* on the Apostles *and* on the prophets, *both* on the teachers *and* on the shepherds (see Eph 2:20; 4:11–16). And these forces are not always distinct and separate: on the contrary, the charism is often mixed with the institution, not only because of the fact that the institutional ministers are charisms themselves, but because every prophecy—if it must remain stable in the Church—must sooner or later be institutionalized, as happened, for example, with the prophecy of Saints Francis of Assisi (d. 1226) and Dominic of Osma (d. 1221), resulting in the founding of the Franciscan and Dominican Orders, each with its own structure and its own internal hierarchical authorities. Thus, on the other hand, the institution is often prophetic, as frequently happens with the Magisterium

---

[125] Benedict XVI, *"Lectio Divina" with the Parish Priests of Rome*, February 23, 2012.

of the Church, which, remaining firm in the truth, assumes rather prophetic positions, as occurred, for example, with the encyclical *Humanae Vitae* (1968) of Paul VI. Therefore, an opposition between these forces does not correspond either to the historical reality, or to the nature of the Church as Christ intended and established.

9

The Sacraments in General and the Liturgy

The seven Sacraments form the most important part of divine Worship or sacred Liturgy with which the Church renders to God, through Christ, the honor and glory owed to Him, adores Him in His majesty, and thanks Him for the goods received while she prays to receive others. The Sacraments are salvific signs and acts of Worship through which God grants grace to the Church, and Christ continues His salvific presence among human beings through the Spirit who extends Christ's work in time and space. The Sacraments are also the most common and ordinary way of living the faith for most members of the Catholic Church. A decisive element for verifying religious practice among Catholics is precisely the frequenting of the Sacraments. One case is that of the Sunday Eucharist, a practice sanctioned by divine law (the Third Commandment)—an aspect discussed in moral theology. Another case of obligation is the need to go to sacramental Confession for grave sins before approaching the Eucharist (see 1 Cor 11:28–29; see Chapter Eleven). These two examples of obligation pertain to repeatable Sacraments; but obviously, before all of them, Revelation teaches that the first Sacrament, Baptism, which can be received only once, is essential for salvation (see John 3:3; etc.).

These few introductory notes already show the importance of the Sacraments for the faith and the practice of Christian (especially Catholic) life. It is no accident that the Sacraments have an importance in the Catholic Church that is not found in other Christian denominations, especially those born in the modern era. We shall therefore dedicate ourselves here, with the usual brevity, to providing an overview of the sacramental world of the Church.

1. The Notion of Sacrament in General

In the previous chapter we have already encountered the notion of Sacrament in reference to the Church, inasmuch as it is a sign and instrument of grace. We find the same meaning—but according to analogy—when we use the word in reference to the sacramental celebrations carried out by the Church. The Catechism states:

> The Sacraments are efficacious signs of grace, instituted by Christ and entrusted to the Church, by which divine life is dispensed to us. The visible rites by which the sacraments are celebrated signify and make present the graces proper to each sacrament. They bear fruit in those who receive them with the required dispositions. (CCC §1131)

1.1. Sign and Instrument

1.1.1. Meaning of "Sacrament"

Let us start with the Latin word *sacramentum*. It was introduced at a very early time in the Church's history as the counterpart to the Greek word *mysterion*. It is also well-known that it was Tertullian (d. 220) who introduced it into Latin theological language, using it a full 134 times in his works. In classical Latin, *sacramentum* refers to an oath like that made by a soldier (*"sacramentum militiae"* ["oath of military service"]) and by extension, enlistment in the army; a court or bail deposit and, by extension, a lawsuit, a claim, a note, or a bet; and it could also mean a bond or a pact (such as the *"sacramentum amicitiae"* ["bond of friendship"] or the *"sacramenta nuptialia"* ["the marriage bonds"]). Tertullian Christianized the term, applying it to Baptism in particular (understood as enlistment in the army of God and contextual oath of fidelity on the part of the neophyte), but also to other Sacraments, and even to God's plan of salvation, which he calls *"sacramentum humanae salutis"* ("Sacrament of human salvation"),[1] probably referring to Saint Paul, who uses the word "mystery" to indicate the hidden plan of God (see Eph 3:1–12; Col 1:26). But predominantly in Tertullian—and from him onward—*sacramentum* was used

---

[1] See Tertullian of Carthage, *Adversus Marcionem* 2.27.7.

to indicate the visible and efficacious signs celebrated by the Church, which today are commonly called the seven Sacraments, and which he also defined Christologically as "*sacramenta Christi*" ("Sacraments of Christ").[2]

The accentuation of the nature of "sign" is especially due to Saint Augustine (d. 430), who defined Sacrament as "sacred sign." In a well-known passage, Augustine writes: "A visible sacrifice, therefore, is a sacrament or sacred sign of an invisible sacrifice."[3] With these few words, he highlights the relationship, in the Sacrament, between a visible reality and an invisible reality, showing the profoundly Christian character of the Sacraments of the Church, in which, in conformity with the principle of the Incarnation and the composite structure of the human being, there is *both* an invisible component *and* a visible one. Moreover, Sacrament is understood precisely as the visible sign of an invisible reality that is, so to speak, "contained" in it. The same Father of the Church speaks of "symbolical actions of former and present times, which, because of their pertaining to divine things, are called Sacraments."[4] The definitive refinement of the category of Sacrament is due to Saint Thomas Aquinas, who emphasizes the aspect of efficacy, specifying the way in which the Sacraments cause grace.[5] This teaching was officially defined by the Church in her Magisterium:

> There are seven Sacraments of the New Law..., which differ greatly from the Sacraments of the Old Law. The latter, in fact, did not produce grace.... These Sacraments of ours, however, both contain grace and communicate it to those who worthily receive them.[6]

---

[2] See Tertullian of Carthage, *De praescriptione haereticorum* 40.7.

[3] Saint Augustine of Hippo, *De civitate Dei* 10.5, in *FCNT*, vol. 14, trans. Gerald G. Walsh and Grace Monahan (Washington, DC: CUA Press, 1952), 123.

[4] Saint Augustine of Hippo, *Epistula 138*.1.7, in *NPNF*, vol. 1 trans. J.G. Cunningham (Peabody, MA: Hendrickson Publishers, 1994), 483. The relationship between visible sign and invisible grace is then expressed in all those texts in which Augustine emphasizes the salvific efficacy of the Sacraments, as he does, for example, in *Epistula 85*.5 (on Baptism, valid also among the heretics).

[5] See *ST* III, q. 62, a. 1. Saint Thomas also proposes a definition of Sacrament that puts it in relation to the past, the present, and the future (see *ST* III, q. 60, a. 3). The first to provide the definition of Sacrament as a cause of grace was Peter Lombard (d. 1160), *Sententiae* IV, d. 1, 4. But Saint Thomas was the first to develop the notion in regard to the type of causality and also the fact that the grace offered is sanctifying grace (see Chapter Four).

[6] Council of Florence, *Exsultate Deo* (1439) (DS 1310).

If anyone says that the Sacraments of the New Law do not contain the grace they signify or that they do not confer that grace . . . let him be anathema.[7]

1.1.2. The Objective Efficacy of the Sacraments

The *Catechism* accepts the specification of the term and defines the Sacraments as "efficacious signs of grace." They are not just signs of an invisible reality, such as, for example, a person's good will to worship God. They are efficacious signs of God's grace. Thus, the text of the *Catechism* from which we began adds that, "The visible rites by which the Sacraments are celebrated signify and make present the graces proper to each Sacrament." The Sacrament is not only a sign of grace but produces the grace of which it is a sign. It is a cause of grace, and this grace is objectively produced by the Sacrament, without forgetting—as is also specified—that this grace can be accepted or rejected by individuals.

This objective character of sacramental grace was traditionally illustrated through the terminology of "*ex opere operato*" and "*ex opere operantis (Ecclesiae)*." The formula "*ex opere operato*" means "by the very fact that the action is carried out" (CCC §1128), and this means that Sacraments are celebrated validly if the objective conditions of validity are met. In other words, the Church is certain that a particular Sacrament is valid, that is, that it causes the grace that it signifies, if it is celebrated as it must be celebrated, that is, respecting the essential conditions for celebrating the Sacrament itself. There are three such conditions: (1) it must respect the "matter" and "form" of the Sacrament (which we shall discuss below); (2) the one who celebrates the Sacrament must be a true and proper minister of that Sacrament (for the Eucharist, for example, it is a validly ordained priest); and (3) the minister of the Sacrament must carry it out with the intention of doing what the Church does when she celebrates that Sacrament.[8] If these three necessary conditions are met, then by the very fact of being celebrated ("*ex opere operato*"), the Sacrament is valid and confers grace to the one who receives it with the necessary dispositions.

---

[7] Council of Trent, *Decretum de Sacramentis* (1547), can. 6 (DS 1606).
[8] For example, as regards the valid celebration of the Eucharist, there is the teaching of Innocent III, *Eius Exemplo* (1208): "We believe three things are necessary for this office: namely, a specific person, that is, a priest, who . . . has been properly constituted for this office by a bishop; those solemn words that are expressed by the Fathers in the canon; and the faithful intention [*fidelis intentio*] of the one who pronounces (these words)" (DS 794). See also Martin V, *Inter Cunctas* (1418) (DS 1262).

1.1.3. The Validity of the Sacraments

The doctrine of "*ex opere operato*" is very important: it reassures the faithful about the validity of the Sacraments they receive, even if the priest who celebrates them is an unworthy minister from the moral perspective. If he is a true (i.e., validly ordained) minister and carries out what he must, as he must, regardless of his personal state of conscience, the Sacrament is certainly valid. This is because in the Sacraments it is above all Christ who acts, with the minister as His collaborator; thus, the holiness of the Sacraments is not that of the minister, but that of Christ. Therefore, since the power that works in the Sacrament is not that of the human being, but that of God, He can make use of imperfect human instruments.

In the history of the Church, there is no shortage of those who instead held that the efficacy of the Sacraments depends on the holiness of the one who celebrates them. The dispute with the Donatists, followers of Bishop Donatus of Casae Nigrae in Numidia (d. 355), is classic in this regard. He held that the Sacraments celebrated by bishops and priests who had denied the faith during the persecutions out of fear and handed over holy books to the civil authorities, and then later returned to the Church, were invalid. Donatism is a more serious question than it may seem at first glance. And this is not only because it holds that the validity of the Sacraments is dependent on the moral dispositions of the minister—already a reason to approach it with great caution. But it is also serious because Donatism produces a dangerous ecclesiology, which places a spiritual, mystical, holy, "martyrial" Church in opposition (*aut-aut!*) with a Church of a second category that contains sinners, considering only the first worthy of its name.

There is no shortage of biblical passages that reject this perspective: not only the numerous Gospel passages about the mercy Christ had for sinners, but also others, such as the parable of the simultaneous growth of wheat and weeds in the same field (see Matt 13:24–30), taken up by Saint Augustine precisely through anti-Donatist lenses.[9] As regards the holiness of the ministers, in the First Letter to the Corinthians, Saint Paul—in subduing a conflict that arose in the community due to the creation of groups that identified themselves in reference to the one who baptized them, for which some said, "I belong to Paul" or "I belong to Kephas"—asks rhetorically: "Is Christ divided? Was Paul crucified for you? Or were you baptized in the name of Paul?" (1 Cor 1:13). The last rhetorical question is especially important: it positively shows

---

[9] See Saint Augustine of Hippo, *Epistola ad Catholicos contra Donatistas* [= *De unitate Ecclesiae*] 14.35, and also his other works on the Donatist heresy.

that one is not baptized in the name of the minister who celebrates the Sacrament, but in the name of Christ. Thus, the power of the Sacrament does not depend on its minister. Therefore, later on, Saint Paul reminds the believers that the Apostles should be considered as "servants of Christ and stewards of the mysteries of God" (1 Cor 4:1), emphasizing again the "relativity" of the minister, who acts as a servant, as an instrument.[10] The same is said in John 4:1–2: "Now when Jesus learned that the Pharisees had heard that Jesus was making and baptizing more disciples than John (although Jesus himself was not baptizing, just his disciples)," a text that shows that it is Jesus who baptizes, but He does so through the disciples (and it should be recalled that Saint Peter and Judas Iscariot were also among them: the former would deny him, although momentarily, and the latter would betray Him!). On the basis of these and many other texts, both of the Old and New Testament, the Catholic authors who were contemporary to the Donatists faced a long and exhausting dispute, which was ultimately won above all thanks to Saint Augustine, who dedicated much energy and various writings to eradicating this error.

We can share a few of his expressions as a simple example. Regarding the ecclesiological aspect—to avoid a "purist" concept of Church—Augustine says: "Clearly one must flee from the company of criminals, but we must not reject that of those who have amended [their behavior]."[11] Citing a letter of Saint Cyprian, he adds: "Even if we notice the presence of weeds, it must not however constitute such an impediment to our faith or charity, so as to make us abandon the Church because we discovered weeds in it."[12] With an argument that is valid with respect to any heretical or schismatic group, Augustine then places before the Donatists a fatal alternative for those who hold themselves to be the only pure Church and hold that the other Church—the one that welcomed back sinners—was no longer the true community of Christ. He writes in this regard: "Either one must affirm that the Church has already disappeared and there is no longer a Church from which their Donatus was born, or—and this is the truth—that if the Church continued, then the bad in it does not pollute the good."[13]

---

[10] We see from what is added immediately afterward by the Apostle that this does not imply a justification of moral laxity on the part of the sacred ministers: "Now it is of course required of stewards that they be found trustworthy" (v. 2); however, the principle of the objective validity of the Sacraments remains intact.

[11] Saint Augustine of Hippo, *Contra Gaudentium Donatistarum episcopum* 1.4.5 (our translation).

[12] Saint Augustine of Hippo, *Contra Gaudentium Donatistarum episcopum* 2.4.4 (our translation).

[13] Saint Augustine of Hippo, *Ad Donatistas post collationem* 29.50 (our translation).

The Notion of Sacrament in General

As for the ministry of the Sacraments, Augustine recalls that "the only consecration of the person in Baptism is of Christ"[14] and thus—on the basis of Scripture—the Saint does not tie the validity of the Sacrament to the moral uprightness of the priest who celebrates it. Saint Augustine, in various places in his works, holds insistently that Baptism is valid even if administered by a schismatic or heretic, provided there are the essential conditions. For example, he writes: "Accordingly, if Marcion consecrated the Sacrament of Baptism with the words of the gospel, 'In the name of the Father, and of the Son, and of the Holy Ghost,' (Matt 28:19) the Sacrament was complete, although his faith expressed under the same words, seeing that he held opinions not taught by the Catholic truth, was not complete, but stained with the falsity of fables."[15] And again:

> There is therefore "no fellowship between righteousness and unrighteousness," not only without, but also within the Church; for "the Lord knows them that are His," and "Let every one that names the name of Christ depart from iniquity." There is also "no communion between light and darkness" (2 Cor 6:14), not only without, but also within the Church; for "he that hates his brother is still in darkness" (1 John 2:9). And they at any rate hated Paul, who, preaching Christ out of envy and malicious strife, supposed that they added affliction to his bonds (Phil 1:15-16); and yet the same Cyprian understands these still to have been within the Church. Since, therefore, "neither darkness can enlighten, nor unrighteousness justify," as Cyprian again says, I ask, how could those men baptize within the very Church herself? I ask, how could those vessels which the large house contains not to honor, but to dishonor, administer what is holy for the sanctifying of men within the great house itself, unless because *that holiness of the Sacrament cannot be polluted even by the unclean* [*illa sanctitas Sacramenti nec ab immundis pollui potest*], either when it is given at their hands, or when it is received by those who in heart and life are not changed for the better?[16]

---

[14] Saint Augustine of Hippo, *De unico Baptismo contra Petilianum* 2.3 (our translation). In 5.7, the Saint recalls the text of 1 Cor 1, which we mentioned above.

[15] Saint Augustine of Hippo, *De Baptismo contra Donatistas* 3.15.20, in *NPNF*, First Series, vol. 4, trans. J.R. King (Peabody, MA: Hendrickson Publishers, Inc.), 442.

[16] Saint Augustine of Hippo, *De Baptismo contra Donatistas* 4.13.19, in *NPNF*, vol. 4, 455–456.

1.2. The Sacraments: Works of Christ

1.2.1. Extension of the Incarnation

Having emphasized the primary meaning of the Sacrament as an efficacious sign of grace, other aspects of it are not excluded. Above all, in recent times, sacramental theology has developed other ways of speaking about the Sacraments, but they have not yet passed the scrutiny of sufficient reflection and, above all, they have not been received into the living Tradition of the Church; thus, we shall not consider them here directly, but only in the background. A traditional path sees in the Sacraments an extension of Christ's Incarnation and thus of His presence among us.[17] Here, the fact that the word "Sacrament" is used analogously comes into play, and that it is thus applied to various realities and subjects: to the seven Sacraments, to the Church, but also to Christ himself, Who in reality is the *"princeps analogatum"* ("criterion of comparison"), namely, the fullness of sacramentality, of which the other realities that are called Sacraments participate through analogy. While in the first perspective the emphasis is on how the Sacraments produce God's grace, this second perspective emphasizes the link between the Sacraments and Christ, the incarnate Word, whose action they extend into the world. Just as Christ "went about doing good and healing all those oppressed by the devil" (Acts 10:38) during His earthly life, so now in His risen state, He continues to carry out the good of salvation through the work of the Holy Spirit in the Sacraments instituted by Him.[18]

Of particular relevance in this perspective is the fact that the Sacraments perpetuate the presence and action of Christ in every era and place in

---

[17] The conformation of the Sacraments to their Author is explained well by Saint Thomas Aquinas, *De articulis fidei et Ecclesiae sacramentis* 2: "*Sacramentum consistit in verbis et rebus corporalibus, sicut in Christo, qui est sacramentorum auctor, est Verbum caro factum. Et sicut caro Christi sanctificata est, et virtutem sanctificandi habet per Verbum sibi unitum, ita et res sacramentorum sanctificantur, et vim sanctificandi habent per verba quae in his proferuntur*" ("A Sacrament consists in words and corporeal things, just as Christ, who is the Author of the Sacraments, is the Word made flesh. And as the flesh of Christ is sanctified and has the power of sanctifying by virtue of being united to the Word, so also sacramental realities are sanctified and have the power of sanctifying by reason of the words pronounced in them" [our translation]).

[18] "Jesus' words and actions during his hidden life and public ministry were already salvific, for they anticipated the power of his Paschal mystery. They announced and prepared what he was going to give the Church when all was accomplished. The mysteries of Christ's life are the foundations of what he would henceforth dispense in the sacraments, through the ministers of his Church" (CCC §1115).

which they are celebrated. In this regard, we should cite that classical text of Saint Leo the Great who, preaching about Christ's Ascension into Heaven, a moment in which He withdrew from the sight of human beings, comments: "*Quod itaque Redemptoris nostri conspicuum fuit, in sacramenta transivit*" ("What was visible of our Redeemer has passed into the Sacraments").[19] With His Ascension, Christ withdraws from the sight of human beings and is no longer visible. But what was visible of Him, namely, that humanity with which He passed on the earth to benefit humans, is now present in a different way, in sacramental form. The Sacraments are the new way, inaugurated by the Paschal Mystery of Christ, through which the Lord is present to His disciples and acts for them. Thus, Paul VI wrote: "The Sacraments are the actions of Christ who administers them through men. And so the Sacraments are holy in themselves and they pour grace into the soul by the power of Christ, when they touch the body."[20]

1.2.2. Elements of the History of Salvation

This last citation allows us to go one step further, contextualizing the Sacraments within the history of salvation as a whole. In the words of Paul VI, we note that here the virtue, that is, the power of Christ that works in them, is added to the first perspective, which speaks of the virtue proper to the Sacraments (*ex opere operato*). These perspectives are not different, but the same: the objective virtue of the Sacraments is the virtue of Christ, produced by the Sacraments as causes of the grace. But the clarification is important: the Sacraments produce divine grace efficaciously, but this divine grace is Christological, that is, it comes from Christ, the Word incarnate, and it is connoted by the gift of Christ for us. In clearer words, this is not the grace of God, so to speak, "in general," but the grace given by God in Christ, through His Person and work.

> Christ produces the interior effect of the Sacrament, *both* as God *and* as man, but each in a different manner. In fact, as God He works in the Sacraments by authority. As man, on the other hand, He produces the interior effects of the Sacraments as a meritorious and efficient cause, but instrumentally. In fact . . . the Passion of Christ, suffered by Him according to His human nature, is the meritorious

---

[19] Saint Leo the Great, *Sermones* 74.2, in *NPNF*, Second Series, vol. 12, trans. Charles Lett Feltoe (Peabody, MA: Hendrickson Publishers, 1994), 188 (with our corrections).
[20] Saint Paul VI, *Mysterium Fidei* (1965), §38.

and efficient cause of our salvation: not as a principal, or authoritative, agent cause, but as an instrumental cause, in that His humanity, according to the explanations given, is an instrument of the divinity.[21]

This means that the Sacraments offer us salvific grace in the form of the grace of the redemption. Thus, these signs are better understood within the concrete history of salvation, as we understand them in this book. Also, the Sacraments form part of that fundamental correction that God makes of the concrete mode of carrying out His salvific plan as a consequence of original sin.[22] In Eden, there would not have been Sacraments, at least not the Christian Sacraments that we know.

> In the original state of innocence before sin, the Sacraments would not have been necessary. The reason this can be inferred comes from the rectitude of that state, in which the higher [parts of the human being] ruled over the lower parts, and in no way depended upon them. . . . It would have been opposed to such an order if the soul had to depend on something corporeal in order to be perfected in knowledge and grace, as happens presently in the Sacraments. Thus, in the state of innocence, the human being did not have need of the Sacraments, not only for the sake of remedying sin, but not even inasmuch as they are ordered toward perfecting the soul.[23]

These Sacraments were instituted by Christ as part of the concrete way of carrying out the salvific economy, once the human being had attempted the impossible, that is, preventing God's plan from being realized. The grace produced by the Sacraments is thus the grace of Christ, crucified, died, and risen. Receiving the Sacraments of the Church means receiving the gift of grace merited for us by the incarnate Son. This is emphasized by the fact that the Sacraments are celebrated on earth and not in Heaven, as is clearly stated in the Book of Revelation, in which Saint John, describing the heavenly Jerusalem, attests: "I saw no temple in the city, for its temple is the Lord God almighty and the Lamb" (Rev 21:22). This is even more noteworthy if one considers that the Book of Revelation describes the great heavenly Liturgy in good detail. In Heaven, therefore, the divine Worship of the Trinity does not

---

[21] *ST* III, q. 64, a. 3 (our translation and emphasis).

[22] See, Saint Thomas Aquinas, *Scriptum super Sententiis* IV, d. 1, q. 1, a. 2, which quotes Hugh of Saint Victor: "The Sacraments were instituted as medicine for sin."

[23] *ST* III, q. 61, a. 2 (our translation).

cease (on the contrary, it intensifies and is celebrated in a perfect way), but the divine Worship ceases to be carried out through the seven Sacraments, because divine grace is poured out on the elect directly by the Lord.

1.2.3. Number and Institution

We just mentioned that the seven Sacraments were instituted by Christ. These two affirmations—regarding their number and institution by Christ—are defined doctrine of the Church, even if there have been more than a few questions posed by theologians in this regard. The Council of Trent leaves no room for doubt about the Church's doctrine on the subject:

> If anyone says that the Sacraments of the New Law were not all instituted by Jesus Christ our Lord; or that there are more or fewer than seven ... or that any one of these seven is not truly and properly a Sacrament, let him be anathema.[24]

The doubts are generally motivated, on the part those who advance them, above all on the basis of the fact that in the Scripture there are explicit elements only for affirming that Christ instituted Baptism and the Eucharist, a reason why Luther (d. 1546), against whom the Council of Trent was directed, standing firm on his principle of *sola Scriptura*, only ended up recognizing two of the seven Sacraments. The other five would be celebrations of the Church, but not Sacraments in the strict sense (see Chapter One). The Catholic concept of Revelation must be posited against this. For this concept of Revelation, the Word of God is found not only in Scripture, but in both Scripture and Apostolic Tradition (see Chapter Two). It is true that Scripture does not tell us *how* and *when* Christ instituted the Sacraments, at least not all of them, but this does not mean that Revelation (Scripture and Tradition) does not tell us *that* Christ instituted them. An example may be enlightening: Scripture tells us directly and explicitly that Christ instituted the Eucharist the evening before His death, in the Upper Room, in the presence of the Apostles. But the same Scripture indirectly affirms that on that very occasion He also instituted the Sacrament of Orders, and that He established the Apostles themselves as ministers of the new covenant. This institution was carried out with the words: "Do this in memory of me" (see the following chapter). While the institution of the Eucharist is evident in itself, the understanding of these words of Christ as a formula for the institution of another

---

[24] Council of Trent, *Decretum de Sacramentis*, can. 1 (DS 1601).

Sacrament comes to us from the Tradition, which interprets Scripture. The same applies to John 20:22–23, a foundational passage for the Sacrament of Reconciliation, and James 5:14–15, which regards the Anointing of the Sick.[25] For the other Sacraments, there do not seem to be biblical passages that indicate the moment of their institution; nonetheless, the Tradition of the Church affirms without hesitation that such an institution dates back to Christ.

Among theologians, a distinction between an immediate institution and a generic institution of the Sacraments has also been advanced.[26] This means that Christ would have directly instituted (without mediation) some of the Sacraments, while He would have given power to the Apostles to institute others. Of the two theses, that of immediate institution seems more correct,[27] although with some clarifications. The immediate institution on the part of Christ fits better with other scriptural facts, especially with the attitude, found since the time of the first Fathers of the Church, of not wanting to modify in any way what the Apostles have passed down, not only in the doctrinal sphere, but also the sacramental one. A biblical foundation of this link with the Tradition is provided by Saint Paul with respect to the Eucharist (see 1 Cor 11:23). Moreover, the surety with which Saint James speaks to us about the Anointing of the Sick is better explained if it is supposed that it was well-known in the early community that the Sacrament was instituted by Christ Himself.

Naturally, there are two clarifications to be made. In sustaining the immediate institution, we are not saying that Christ established how the Liturgy must be carried out down to the smallest details. On the contrary: (1) the Lord

---

[25] Within this perspective, the Council of Trent, *Doctrina de Sacramento Extremae Unctionis* (1551), ch. 1, after having cited the passage of Saint James, explains: "By these words, as the Church has learned from the Apostolic Tradition handed down and received by her, he teaches the matter, the form, the proper minister, and the effects of this salutary Sacrament" (DS 1695).

[26] One could refer here to a further distinction between the question of the immediate or mediate institution of the Sacraments and that of the mode of institution regarding the degree of specification (in a generic way; in a specific way in an immutable form; in a generic way but in a mutable form). We leave it to the reader, if at all, explore this more in depth, since these theological theses are quite detailed.

[27] Saint Thomas affirms that Christ did not want to transfer to the ministers His "power of excellence," i.e., that power that would have made it so that the merits of the ministers would influence the Sacraments, and that the Sacraments would be conferred in their name. Moreover, the power of excellence would have conferred to them the power of instituting the Sacraments, and it would even have made it so that they could produce the sacramental effect by simply willing it without celebration of the external rite. Christ chose not to confer such a power "not on account of jealousy, but for the good of the faithful, so that they would not place their hope in man; and so that [the disciples] would not institute various Sacraments, which would give rise to divisions in the Church" (*ST* III, q. 64, a. 4, *corp.*, ad 1; see ad 3 [our translation]).

would have established only the essential elements of the Sacraments (those of "divine law," which the Church holds as immutable), while He would have left it up to the Apostles and their successors to determine all other aspects, what pertains to "ecclesiastical law," which can be changed by the authority of the Church.[28] Historical counter-proof is the existence of many liturgical rites and traditions, which are recognized as fully legitimate by the Catholic Church. Moreover, historical study reveals the evolution, which was at times very great, that the individual Sacraments underwent in their concrete celebratory form, even within the same liturgical tradition. (2) Christ would have instituted all seven Sacraments, but He would have postponed the beginning of their celebration until the sending of the Holy Spirit at Pentecost (see CCC §1076). In so doing, the Lord would have acted in full continuity with the order that He gave to the Apostles not to leave Jerusalem, that is, not to begin preaching the Gospel, before the sending of the Paraclete. Since the Sacraments are a fundamental part of the work of the evangelization and the foundation of the Churches, they could also be celebrated only after the sending of the Holy Spirit, Who brings the presence and power of Christ into the sacramental signs. If this interpretation were correct, we could speak of an immediate institution of the Sacraments on the part of Christ, with intrinsic reference to the future work of the Apostles and the Church.[29]

1.3. Bipolarity, Causality, Ends, and Effects of the Sacraments

We have yet to consider three general aspects of the Sacraments[30]: their struc-

---

[28] "Provided their substance is preserved—there has always been in the Church that power to determine or modify what she judged more expedient for the benefit of those receiving the Sacraments or for the reverence due to the Sacraments themselves" (Council of Trent, *Doctrina et Canones de Communione sub Utraque Specie et Parvulorum* (1562), ch. 2 [DS 1728]). And the current *Codex Iuris Canonici* establishes at can. 841: "Since the Sacraments are the same for the whole Church and belong to the divine deposit, it is only for the supreme authority of the Church to approve or define the requirements for their validity; it is for the same or another competent authority ... to decide what pertains to their licit celebration, administration, and reception and to the order to be observed in their celebration."

[29] The instruction of the Apostles on the Sacraments could be part of the formation that the Risen One gave them in the forty days that elapsed between the Resurrection and the Ascension; the exact content of this formation is not described in detail by the New Testament (see John 21:25; Acts 1:1–3) and is thus contained in the Apostolic Tradition itself, orally handed down in the Church.

[30] There is actually another element to consider, which, however, is only common to some Sacraments and not to all—that is, the "character." Thus, we shall speak of it in the next chapter when discussing the individual Sacraments that imprint it, and not in this general

turing on the basis of the *et–et* (a theme that also includes those of matter and form, as well as the identity and intention of the minister); the type of causality at work in them; their ends; and their effects. Finally, we shall mention the mystagogical catechesis and consequences of the sacramental economy for Christian life.

1.3.1. Dipolar Structure

Let us begin by considering the dipolar or composite structure of the Sacraments, for which they are each and always composed of a visible and an invisible element, both in the image of Christ and that of the Church. We can cite a famous expression of Saint Augustine here:

> *Ista, fratres, dicuntur sacramenta, quia in eis aliud videtur et aliud intelligitur. Quod videtur, speciem habet corporalem, quod intellegitur, fructum habet spiritalem*—These realities, brothers, are called Sacraments precisely because in them, one thing is seen and another is understood. What is seen is a visible aspect, and what is understood produces a spiritual effect.[31]

In the Sacraments we thus find a visible element and an invisible one. Augustine will also speak of *sacramentum*—to indicate the external sign—and of *res sacramenti*[32]—to indicate the invisible grace contained in it—although it would later be the Scholastic theologians who would make the technical sense of these and other categories very precise. This composite character of all the Sacraments once again manifests the fundamental Catholic principle of *et–et* and it does so not only on account of its dipolar character, but also with respect to the fact that the two aspects that comprise it, while both necessary, do not have the same value. Just as grace and nature are both necessary for a salvific act for the human being, with grace being of infinitely greater value than nature, so in the Sacraments both the *res* and the *sacramentum* are necessary; but the *res*, that is, grace, has an immeasurably greater value than the sacramental sign, which is nonetheless its vehicle and produces it. It is for this reason that—in certain cases and under certain conditions—the Lord gives the grace of the Sacrament even without the reception of the external sacra-

---

discussion of the Sacraments.

[31] Saint Augustine of Hippo, *Sermo 272*.1 (our translation).

[32] See, for example, Saint Augustine of Hippo, *De bono coniugali* 7, in which the expression *sacramenti res* is found.

mental sign. Thus, it is possible in certain circumstances to be saved (the grace of Baptism) without physically receiving the washing of regeneration; and it is possible—under certain conditions—to have spiritual communion with the Eucharistic Christ, without receiving the Eucharist in its sacramental form (see Chapter Eleven). In fact, the *sacramentum* is in view of the *res*. As a rule, the *res* is received through the *sacramentum*. However, in particular cases, God can grant the *res* even without such a mediation, if there is no real possibility of accessing it through the *sacramentum*. In this case, the connection between *res* and *sacramentum* would be guaranteed by the *votum*, that is, by the (explicit or implicit) desire to receive the Sacrament.

The material-spiritual bipolarity of the Sacraments is also understood on the basis of the one toward whom they were directed by God, namely, the human being, composed of soul and body. This is expressed by the classical axiom "*sacramenta sunt propter homines*" ("the Sacraments are for human beings").[33] Since human beings are composite beings, the Sacraments that are ordered to them will also be.

1.3.2. Matter and Form

The composite character of the Sacraments is also found in the celebratory part, in the concrete way in which they are "performed." We also find two elements here, which Saint Thomas calls "matter" and "form."[34] The matter is clearly a visible or at least objectively verifiable element; while the form is the word that, united to the matter, makes it a Sacrament of the Church. A very apt expression of Saint Augustine is also at our disposal here. He draws from the case of Baptism a general rule:

> *Detrahe verbum, et quid est aqua nisi aqua? Accedit verbum ad elementum, et fit sacramentum, etiam ipsum tamquam visible verbum*—Take

---

[33] The axiom again confirms the two aspects that we discussed above: the inseparable link between the Sacraments and Christ, as well as their place in the concrete history of salvation. In fact, *sacramenta sunt propter homines* insofar as Christ *propter nos homines . . . descendit de coelis*, as is professed by the Constantinopolitan Creed (DS 150): "For us men . . . He came down from Heaven."

[34] Leo XIII, in the letter *Apostolicae Curae* (1896), teaches that the principle of *et-et* is also in play with respect to the binomial "matter-form," that is, both the elements are necessary, but one is superior to the other: "Even if this signification [of the sacramental grace] must be found in the whole essential rite, namely, in the matter and form, nevertheless, it pertains in a special way to the form, since the matter is part not determined by itself but determined by the form" (DS 3315).

...631

away the word, and what is the water except [mere] water? The word is added to the elemental substance, and it becomes a Sacrament, also itself, as it were, a visible word.[35]

The expression that would remain classic is the central one: *accedit verbum ad elementum et fit sacramentum*. The word, the formula of prayer—the "form"—is united to the visible element—the "matter"—and thus the Sacrament is made. All seven Sacraments are composed of matter and form by divine institution. Thus, the validity of the celebration of the Sacraments depends on the effective conjunction of these two realities: if one of the two is missing there will not be a true Sacrament. For example, if the priest says the form of the Eucharist ("This is my Body . . . This is the chalice of my Blood") over matter that is different from that of this Sacrament (bread and wine), there will not be a true Eucharistic Sacrament. This is also true in the contrary situation: if the matter were right, but the correct formula was not pronounced by the priest.

The matter and form of the individual Sacraments are the following[36]: (1) For Baptism, natural water and the words "I baptize you in the name of the Father, and of the Son, and of the Holy Spirit." (2) For Confirmation, the laying on of hands accompanied by anointing with chrism (a mix of oil and perfume consecrated by the bishop) and the formula (in the ordinary form of the Roman Rite): "Be sealed with the gift of the Holy Spirit." (3) For the Eucharist, wheat bread and grape wine, and the words used by Christ in the Upper Room. (4) For Penance, also called Confession, or Reconciliation, the matter is the acts of the penitent (see the following chapter) and the form is the words "I absolve you from your sins, in the name of the Father, and of the Son, and of the Holy Spirit." (5) For the Anointing of the Sick, the matter is the oil of the sick blessed by the bishop, and the form—in the ordinary form of the Roman Rite—is: "Through this holy anointing may the Lord in his love and mercy help you with the grace of the Holy Spirit." (6) For Holy Orders, the matter is the laying on of the hands of the bishop over the candidate, and the form is the formula presented in the liturgical books, different for each of the three degrees of the Sacrament (episcopate, presbyterate, diaconate), which will be presented in the next chapter. (7) For Matrimony, there is not yet definitive agreement on the matter and form, even if it is certain that the consent of the spouses constitutes Matrimony, where consent is understood as

---

[35] Saint Augustine of Hippo, *In Ioannis Evangelium Tractatus* 80.3, in *FCNT*, vol. 90, trans. John W. Rettig (Washington, DC: CUA Press, 1994), 117.

[36] For greater detail, see the following chapter.

a "human act whereby spouses mutually bestow and accept each other"[37] in a definitive way. Thus, two aspects are distinguished in this consent: the internal consent, and its external expression, which for Saint Thomas is the matter of the Sacrament, just as washing in water is for Baptism.[38] It can be said that in Matrimony the form is the internal consent of the spouses, and the matter is the external expression of it (but this is only one opinion among others).

1.3.3. Intention of the Minister

Another element needs to be added to what has been said: the intention, on the part of the one who celebrates the Sacrament, to do what the Church does when she celebrates that Sacrament. This intention is also necessary for the validity of the Sacraments, as the Council of Florence teaches:

> All these Sacraments are accomplished by three elements: namely, by things as the matter, by words as the form, and by the person of the minister who confers the Sacrament with the intention of doing what the Church does [*cum intentione faciendi quod facit Ecclesia*]. If any of these is absent, the Sacrament is not accomplished.[39]

The necessity of the intention of the minister for validity is also explained on the basis of the principle of *et-et*, which already clarified the dipolar structure of the Sacrament in form and matter. The *et-et* also applies to the celebration that produces the Sacrament; it needs to be recognized that for valid celebration both the integral form of the Sacrament in itself (composed of form and matter) and the correct intention of the celebrant minister are necessary. The synthesis of spirit and matter, typical of the *et-et*, is thus verified twice in each Sacrament: (1) with respect to the Sacrament in itself, there is the material element of the matter and the spiritual element of the form; (2) with respect to the celebration that makes the Sacrament, there is the material element of the Sacrament considered as a union of form and matter (which we can call "material" because we are considering it from the concrete perspective of the celebration, in which form and matter both appear as visible/audible and concrete elements), and there is the spiritual element of the minister's intention.

This intention is characterized as *"intentio faciendi quod facit Ecclesia"*

---

[37] Second Vatican Council, *Gaudium et Spes* (1965), §48.
[38] See *ST* "Supplement," q. 45, a. 2.
[39] Council of Florence, *Exsultate Deo* (1439) (DS 1312).

("the intention of doing what the Church does"). In fact, the Sacraments are not arbitrary signs, but signs of God, Christ, and the Church. The minister does not celebrate in his own name, but in the Person of Christ and in the name of the Church. Thus, when he celebrates, he must have the intention of doing what the Church does each time that Sacrament is celebrated in her. There is no need, however, for him to internally renew this intention every time. If he does so, it is certainly helpful for the devotion with which the minister celebrates,[40] but for validity, it is enough that he has in general[41] the intention of acting as a minister of the Church when he celebrates the Sacraments of the faith.

1.3.4. Minister

It is commonly thought that only the priests (bishops or presbyters) can celebrate the Sacraments in the Church. This is true for most of the Sacraments, but not all. Others can be celebrated by laypersons, although this rarely happens (except in the case of Matrimony, where the ministers are always laypersons [see *infra*]). The ministers of the various Sacraments are: (1) For Baptism, the priest or deacon, but in case of necessity also a layperson, or even a heretic or non-believer, so long as he or she has the intention of doing what the Church does when she baptizes, and the minister performs the rite in with proper form and matter. (2) For Confirmation, the ordinary minister is the bishop, but in case of necessity, he can delegate a presbyter. (3) For the Eucharist, the priest (bishop or presbyter). (4) For Penance or Reconciliation, the priest (bishop or presbyter). (5) For Anointing of the Sick, the priest (bishop or presbyter). (6) For Holy Orders, only the bishop can perform it—without any exceptions. (7) For Matrimony, the Latin Church holds that the spouses

---

[40] That is why among the traditional prayers of preparation for the celebration of the Mass (which in the Missal of Saint Pius V were obligatory, while they are optional in the Missal of Saint Paul VI) there is also the *formula intentionis ante Missam*, which prepares the priest with these words: "*Ego volo celebrare Missam, et conficere Corpus et Sanguinem Domini nostri Jesu Christi, juxta ritum sanctae Romanae Ecclesiae . . .*" ("I intend to celebrate the Mass and consecrate [confect] the Body and Blood of our Lord Jesus Christ, according to the rite of the Holy Roman Church. . ."").

[41] One can distinguish an intention that is purely "habitual" from one that is "virtual." The latter appears to be the one required as a minimum for valid celebration. The intention is virtual when the act concretely carried out does not express an explicit volition of the ultimate end, but it is equally oriented toward it on account of a previous intention. Habitual intention is not a true and proper intention, but it is a disposition of the person: for example, a person in sanctifying grace is habitually disposed toward his or her ultimate supernatural end.

themselves are the ministers, while in the Eastern Church it is believed to be the priest (CCC §1623).[42] The Latin position seems more correct, given that what constitutes the Matrimony is not the priest's blessing—which only publicly ratifies the manifestation of the consent—but rather the consent itself (internal and external).

In summary, Holy Orders and Confirmation are reserved to bishops, even if it is possible for the bishop to delegate the latter to a presbyter. The Eucharist, Reconciliation, and the Anointing of the Sick are reserved to priests (both bishops and presbyters). Matrimony can be celebrated by all the baptized who are without impediment (it is prohibited, for example, for those who have received the Sacrament of Holy Orders[43]). Finally, Baptism is celebrated by a priest or deacon or, in the case of emergency, a layperson or even an unbaptized person. Consequently, we note that the deacon, who has also received the Sacrament of Holy Orders in its third degree, cannot perform anything that a layperson cannot: the only Sacrament that he can administer is Baptism (in fact, in Matrimony, just as with the priest, while he blesses the nuptials, he is not the minister of the Sacrament). This is because, although he is an ordained minister, the deacon does not receive the ministerial priesthood: he is a minister of the Church, but not a priest, except for the baptismal priesthood that he shares with all the baptized; he does not possess the hierarchical priesthood.[44]

---

[42] Note here that the text of §1623 has undergone two redactions. The first affirmed that "In the Eastern Liturgies the minister of this Sacrament (which is called "Crowning") is the priest or bishop who, after receiving the mutual consent of the spouses, successively crowns the bridegroom and the bride as a sign of the marriage covenant." The new version instead teaches that, "In the Tradition of the Eastern Churches, the priests (bishops or presbyters) are witnesses to the mutual consent given by the spouses, but for the validity of the sacrament their blessing is also necessary (Cf. CCEO, can. 828)." The current formulation brings the eastern theology of Matrimony closer to that of the Latin Church. In fact, the priest is no longer called "minister" but only "witness," and it confers a principal role upon the spouses, although it continues to affirm the necessity *ad validitatem* of the priestly blessing of the nuptials.

[43] In the Latin Church, bishops and priests are celibate. Deacons can be married, but not if they are ordained prior to Matrimony. If a married deacon becomes a widower, he cannot enter into a new marriage (however, especially if he has small children, the Holy See can concede a dispensation for him to enter into a second marriage—these, however, are exceptional cases). This is because, as a general rule (both East and West), one can receive Holy Orders after Matrimony, but not vice versa (in the case of priests, it is possible to receive a dispensation if they leave ministry, but in this case they will not exercise it anymore). Therefore, it is not exactly accurate to say that "deacons can marry," but rather that married men can be ordained deacons. The same practice is observed in the Eastern Churches that allow an "uxored" (married) presbyterate: married men can be ordained priests. However, even in the East, only celibates are chosen to be bishops.

[44] See Benedict XVI, *Omnium in Mentem* (2009), art. 2.

1.3.5. Causality

The type of causality proper to the Sacraments was also specified by Saint Thomas Aquinas. In fact, this involves holding together two affirmations: (1) that grace is caused only by God, and (2) that grace is caused by the Sacraments. Following the principle of *et-et*, the Catholic does not feel constrained to admitting only one of these affirmations, but can and must accept them both, making the due distinctions and putting things in their proper order with respect to value. The primary affirmation is that only God is Author of grace; the secondary affirmation is that Christ instituted the Sacraments, which were endowed with a participated capacity of producing divine grace. Here is the explanation of the Angelic Doctor:

> Some say that the Sacraments are causes of grace not in the sense that they produce it; but in the sense that God infuses it into the soul on the occasion of the Sacraments. . . . But, if it is considered rightly, this way [of explaining it] does not go beyond [considering the Sacraments as merely] a sign. . . . Thus according to the above-mentioned explanation, the Sacraments of the new law would be nothing more than signs of grace; while we have it on the authority of many saints that the Sacraments of the new law do not only signify, but cause grace. Thus, we must proceed differently, recalling that the agent cause is of two kinds: principal and instrumental. The principal one works by the power of its own form, impressing its own likeness on the effect: fire, for example, heats with its own heat. Well, in this way nothing but God can cause grace, because grace is none other than a participated likeness of the divine nature. . . . The instrumental cause, on the contrary, does not act by the power of its own form, but by virtue of the impulse with which it is moved by the principal agent. Thus, the effect does not resemble the instrument, but rather the principal agent: a couch, for example, does not share a likeness with the ax, but with the art in the mind of the craftsman. It is in this way that the Sacraments of the new law cause grace: they are in fact used by divine disposition to produce grace.[45]

This text is very important, because it clarifies that the Sacraments are not only occasions that God uses to give grace to those who partake of them. The Sacraments are instruments created by God, which He uses to give grace.

---

[45] *ST* III, q. 62, a. 1 (our translation).

We can add to Saint Thomas' examples that of a brush that is skillfully used by the painter. The painting that emerges from it could not be painted by the brush alone; but, moved about by the skillful hand of the artist, the brush produces the painting—it causes it. However, only the artist is the principal agent cause (without him, there is no art). The brush is an instrumental cause, which produces the painting insofar as it is used as an instrument by the painter—even in common language, one could say that the painting came out of Caravaggio's brush. Nonetheless, the painter could have chosen other brushes (the brushes are interchangeable, the artist is not), or he could have painted by making use of some other instrument, for example, his fingers. The Sacraments produce divine grace in the sense that God has chosen to use them to transmit His grace, producing it in and through them. However, just like the artist, He is not limited by the instruments He has chosen. Thus, while as a rule God offers grace through the Sacraments, He can also grant grace to human beings in other ways. This is expressed in classical theology through the assertion "*Deus virtutem suam non alligavit sacramentis.*"[46]

With respect to this principle, which in itself is certain but which is sometimes misinterpreted in contemporary theology, we need to make two clarifications: (1) The grace that God can give without the Sacrament is the same grace that He intends to give normally through the Sacrament.[47] For example, God can grant the grace of salvation to human beings who have not received Baptism, but in these cases, He nonetheless grants them the grace of Baptism, namely, the remission of sins in virtue of the merits of Christ and

---

[46] "*Deus virtutem suam non alligavit sacramentis quin possit sine sacramentis effectum sacramentorum conferre*" ("God did not bind his power to the Sacraments in such a way as to not be able to produce the effect of the Sacraments without them": *ST* III, q. 64, a. 7 [our translation]). It is important to emphasize that this affirmation is found in the context of an article in which the Angelic Doctor asks if angels can administer the Sacraments. He responds no, because it is up to human beings to be the ministers of them. Nonetheless, since God has not bound His own omnipotence to the Sacraments absolutely, He can also allow angels to give human beings the grace that is usually conveyed by the Sacraments. Therefore, the direction of the discourse—which clearly emerges from the context—is not that one can take the Sacraments less seriously! Saint Thomas, as a magnificent theologian, is defending divine freedom, not relativizing the value of the Sacraments. Rather, what he concedes is instead considered as hypothetical and exceptional. The principle also applies in other places in the Thomistic Opus (see, for example, *Scriptum super Sententiis* III, d. 3, q. 1, a. 1; IV, d. 1, q. 1, a. 2; *et alii*; *ST* I-II, q. 113, a. 3; III, q. 27, a. 1, etc.). By studying the various occurrences in their context, it is confirmed that Saint Thomas always uses the principle in a hypothetical and exceptional sense.

[47] This is understood as the grace to which the person can place an obstacle (*res*), not the grace linked necessarily to the sacramental sign (*res et sacramentum*) such as, for example, the character conferred by Baptism.

incorporation into His Mystical Body. (2) It is true that the artist can paint with other instruments than a brush, but in general He prefers it, because it is the most suitable instrument for painting. Thus, God can give grace in other ways, but normally He prefers the "main roads of grace" that He established, which are the Sacraments. The Sacraments, indeed, with their spiritual and corporeal character, correspond better to human nature, which is why God has instituted them. Since, then, they have medicinal powers, they are "medicines of immortality"[48] that God dispenses to the individual who is sick from original sin[49] and wounded by his or her own personal faults.

1.3.6. Purpose and Effects

Moving on now to the purpose of the Sacraments, we see that, in general, they have a dual purpose[50]: "To take away the faults of committed sins" and "to perfect the soul in what regards the Worship of God according to the Christian religion."[51] This explanation of the Angelic Doctor fits perfectly with the perspective of salvation history that we have been presenting from the beginning and with the principle of *et-et*. In the Sacraments, in fact, we rediscover the twofold end of salvation and redemption, according to the mode in which we have previously specified these categories. On one hand—that of redemption—the Sacraments, by applying the merits of Christ's Passion to us, purify us from sin; on the other hand—that of salvation—they elevate us and direct us toward God and heavenly glory by sustaining us along the path of sanctification through the grace that they produce and contain. There is no need to hold that the Sacraments have *either* a medicinal-redemptive end, *or*

---

[48] Saint Ignatius of Antioch, *Epistula ad Ephesios* 20, calls the Eucharist "the medicine of immortality and the antidote against death" (in *FCNT*, vol. 1, trans. Gerald G. Walsh [Washington, DC: CUA Press, 2008], 95).

[49] Since the Sacraments are symbolized by the water and blood that flowed from the pierced side of Christ (see John 19:34), their medicinal character can also be noted through a typology, proposed by Origen of Alexandria (d. 254), *Explanatio Symboli* 21: "If you also research why it is said that He emitted water and blood, not from another member, but from His right side, it seems to me that a woman is indicated by the rib. In fact, since the source of sin and death also came from the first woman, who was the rib of the first Adam (see Gen 2:22), so also the source of redemption and life springs from the rib of the Second Adam" (our translation).

[50] The Second Vatican Council explains this bipolarity through three expressions, which also refer to the ecclesial aspect of salvation: "The purpose of the Sacraments is to sanctify men, to build up the Body of Christ, and, finally, to give Worship to God" (*Sacrosanctum Concilium*, §59).

[51] *ST* III, q. 62, a. 5 (our translation).

a sanctifying-perfective one; they have both. The primary end is that of being a remedy of sin; indeed, they were instituted especially for this reason: to give to human beings, after the sin of Adam, a concrete and efficacious way of receiving saving grace, which would have been received in a non-sacramental way if Adam had not sinned.[52]

The Council of Florence (AD 1439), in the aforementioned bull, Exsultate Deo, mentioned the end of each of the seven Sacraments and also their effects, directly connected to the ends: (1) Baptism makes a person become spiritually reborn, because its effect is the remission of all original and current guilt and of any punishment related to those. (2) Confirmation increases grace in the person and strengthens his or her faith; its effect is courageous witness to Christ. (3) The Eucharist nourishes inwardly, feeding the new supernatural life and uniting the Christian people to Christ.[53] (4) Reconciliation carries out spiritual healing for those who fall into sin after the purification that happens in Baptism, given that its effect is precisely the absolution of sins. (5) Anointing of the Sick brings spiritual healing and, if it is beneficial to

---

[52] This superiority of the medicinal element of the Sacraments could be interpreted as an endorsement of a pastoral practice that distributes them with a certain facility to all. Although it is clear that we should not be Jansenists (see Chapter Five), receiving the Sacraments requires a conversion, a purification that, however imperfect, must be real and not only intentional; and this is so precisely because the medicinal aspect is fundamental. Thus, Saint Paul in the First Letter to the Corinthians encourages a good self-examination before access to the Eucharist. The fact that the latter is "medicine of immortality" does not mean that it can be received in immorality. This would be like taking a medicine while wanting to remain sick. Note that the first Sacrament is Baptism, without which the other Sacraments cannot be received. Baptism has the task of purifying sin, and it is only after purification has occurred that one can receive the other Sacred Signs. Not by chance, the Church has always been very open in giving Baptism, while she was very attentive in regulating access to other Sacraments, especially the Eucharist.

[53] "*O Sacramentum pietatis! O signum unitatis! O vinculum caritatis!*" ("O mystery of true faith! O sign of unity! O bond of love!": Saint Augustine of Hippo, *In Ioannis Evangelium Tractatus* 26.13, in *FCNT*, vol. 79, 271). The union with Christ is considered not only from the collective standpoint, but also the individual one, as is seen from these beautiful and concrete words of *Exsultate Deo*: "The effect that this Sacrament produces in the souls . . . is to unite them with Christ. For, since it is by grace that persons are incorporated into Christ and united to His members, it follows that those who receive this Sacrament worthily receive an increase of grace. And all the effects that material food and drink have on the life of the body—maintaining and increasing life, restoring health, and giving joy—all these effects this Sacrament produces for the spiritual life" (DS 1322; see *ST* III, q. 79, a. 1). On the other hand, it is a doctrine of the same Council of Florence that, of the seven Sacraments, five are directed to the individual perfection of each person, while the other two (Holy Orders and Matrimony) are aimed at the governance and multiplication of the whole Church.

salvation, can also bring corporeal healing. (6) Holy Orders has as its end that the Church is governed and can grow spiritually (today we would say qualitatively), thus its effect is to establish sacred ministers and to grant grace to the ordained so that they carry out their ministry irreproachably. (7) Marriage is directed toward the union of the spouses and to the material growth (numeric or quantitative) of humanity (natural society) and of the Church (supernatural society). Therefore, three goods of Matrimony are acknowledged: welcoming the children that God grants and educating them in the true faith; preserving the fidelity and union of the spouses; and generating the indissolubility, which is also proper to natural matrimony, but which elevated by sacramental grace is a sign of the union of Christ with the Church.

1.3.7. Moral and Catechetical Implications

In concluding this general discussion of the Sacraments, let us briefly consider two concrete implications of the sacramental economy in the life of faith of believers.

1. Moral

The sacramental economy confirms the dipolar structure of the faith, solidly linked to the very nature of its recipient, the human being, who is a union or synthesis of spirit and matter. The sacramental economy confirms the plan of creation, because it is a manifestation of the plan of redemption, tending toward the restoration, not the nullification, of creation, in addition to its elevation. The Sacraments thus confirm the Christian in the conviction that divine things are transmitted and reside in concrete, daily, and visible things. The extraordinary salvific graces of God ordinarily pass through rather common elements of creation: bread, wine, water, and oil. The Church has added other fundamental signs to these, with which she celebrates the sacramentals. The Church's Worship, itself, has a sacramental—that is, spiritual-corporeal—structure. Even the life of prayer and grace, as well as Christian moral life, have identical compositions of spirit and matter. The nature of sacramental Worship is not appropriate to angelic nature, but to human nature: it therefore includes visible and invisible aspects; and the moral life is not purely spiritual (morality of intentions) or mechanistically practical (morality of executions). In summary, the Sacraments on one hand confirm, and on the other hand are an impetus to live Christianity in the concreteness of the spirit-matter synthesis that was accomplished by the Incarnation and, in turn, to live according to the great principle of *et-et*.

2. Catechesis

The fact that Sacraments are carried out, concretely, through their celebration, has from ancient times led to the recognition of the importance that the Liturgy has in the very understanding of dogma, as is stated by the famous assertion: "*Lex orandi, lex credendi*" ("the law for prayer is the law for faith").[54] The Liturgy is not only an application of the doctrine of the faith, but the same doctrine of faith is enriched in the form (texts and gestures) of the Liturgy. If it is true that the texts and rites of the Liturgy are an expression of the dogma, then it is also true that the dogma draws from them its sources in a fruitful circularity. Recent theology greatly highlighted the importance of the Liturgy in the study of theology. The fruitful circularity mentioned above is also at the root of the fact that, historically, at least two forms of catechesis have been developed in Catholicism: the pre-sacramental and the mystagogical forms. The second form of catechesis prevailed above all in the first centuries, and the first—though even present from the beginning[55]—was further developed later on, up until the most recent times; indeed, it still seems to be the most commonly practiced one nearly everywhere, although in our days, greater attention is given to mystagogical catechesis. Pre-sacramental catechesis is based primarily on doctrine and prepares believers to receive the Sacraments: therefore, it is a catechesis that is done prior to the Sacrament and in view of it. This catechesis focuses primarily on the dogmas and moral truths of the Church. Mystagogical catechesis, however, was imparted, in the ancient Church, after reception of the Sacraments, and it constituted an explanation of the rites, instructing the neophytes in the sacramental doctrine of the Church. We still have several accounts of mystagogical catechesis held by the bishops for the neophytes of their Churches, generally in the week *in albis*, the week that follows Easter, in whose nighttime vigil celebration the catechumens had been baptized. We will not delve into the theological and historical details here. We can simply say that both types of sacramental catechesis are useful and necessary: *both* the pre-sacramental-doctrinal, *and* the post-sacramental-mystagogical.[56]

---

[54] As was noted in Chapter One, the original text is in the form of a subordinate clause: "*Ut legem credendi lex statuat supplicandi*" ("so that the rule of prayer determines the rule of belief": Pseudo-Celestine I [really Prosper of Aquitaine, d. 455], *Capitula seu Indiculus*, ch. 8 [DS 246]).

[55] Saint Ambrose of Milan (d. 397), for example, attests to this in *De mysteriis* 1.1–2, in which he says to the newly baptized that, upon having received the various teachings (both moral and biblical) prior to receiving the Sacraments, then—after having received them—they can listen to the teaching of the bishop on the Sacraments.

[56] Even in the ancient Church, in which mystagogical catechesis was preferred, the cat-

The Sacraments in General and the Liturgy

These references introduce us to the second part of the chapter, in which we intend to offer a glimpse of the theology of the Liturgy.

2. The Liturgy

2.1. A Question of Method

The Sacraments are "confected"[57] through a ritual celebration; consequently, recent theology has highlighted the fact that the study of sacramental theology cannot be separated from that of the so-called *scientia liturgica* ("liturgical science"). The joining of the two theological branches can be achieved in at least two ways: (1) It is possible to study the Sacraments by commenting on liturgical texts. In this case, sacramental theology is close to a scientific version of the mystagogical catechesis of the Fathers, who normally explained the Sacraments by beginning with the liturgical rite that had been celebrated. This methodological option better highlights a principle that we have encountered many times in the arc of our treatise: "*Lex orandi, lex credendi.*" Since the law of prayer (the texts and the liturgical gestures) determines the law of faith, it is necessary to study the doctrine on the Sacraments by basing oneself decisively on the euchological texts and on the cultic rituals. (2) A second possibility is what we shall explore here, and it consists in taking advantage of the liturgical texts and rites while studying the Sacraments insofar as they represent one of the *loci theologici*, to which we need to refer in order to discuss the sacramental doctrine. However, this is not the only *locus theologicus*, nor must it necessarily occupy the first place. In our approach, therefore, we shall proceed in a twofold way: on the one hand, we shall recall the texts and rites of the Liturgy in treating the dogmatic themes (this was done in all of the previous chapters); on the other—and this is what we are about to do now—we shall also develop within sacramental theology a theology of the Liturgy, to highlight the fact that the understanding of the Sacraments cannot only be

---

echumens were not at all deprived of doctrine in order to receive the Sacraments. The catechumenate generally lasted years, in which, among other things, the candidates for Baptism went to church every Sunday to listen to the biblical readings and the commentary of the bishop (homily). Likewise, though the preparatory catechesis has become more and more important, the Church has not stopped practicing the permanent catechesis of its faithful through different forms.

[57] In the Latin theological language, the expression *conficere sacramentum* is used. The verb *conficere* has the meanings "to do, to bring to completion, to accomplish, to carry out," etc. The English verb "confect" derives from it.

The Liturgy

doctrinal, but their theology must also include their celebration.

This second option can be justified by noting something that we purposely omitted in the previous chapters when we cited the assertion of Prosper of Aquitaine, "*lex orandi, lex credendi.*" The clarification that now intervenes causes us to note that the dynamics of the influence between dogma and liturgy is not one-way, but two-way. There is an *et-et* here too! It is not so that *either* the Liturgy forms the doctrine *or* the doctrine forms the Liturgy. Both are true, and the influence is reciprocal. Pius XII taught this in his important encyclical, *Mediator Dei*, which we shall cite several times in the following pages. It is the first papal text in history that discusses the theme of divine Worship in such a broad and organic away.

Discussing the relationship between dogma and Liturgy, Pius XII writes:

> On this subject We judge it Our duty to rectify . . . the error and fallacious reasoning of those who have claimed that the sacred Liturgy is a kind of proving ground for the truths to be held of faith, meaning by this that the Church is obliged to declare such a doctrine sound when it is found to have produced fruits of piety and sanctity through the sacred rites of the liturgy, and to reject it otherwise. Hence the epigram, "*Lex orandi, lex credendi*"—the law for prayer is the law for faith. But this is not what the Church teaches and enjoins. The Worship she offers to God . . . is a continuous profession of Catholic faith and a continuous exercise of hope and charity. . . . In the sacred Liturgy we profess the Catholic faith explicitly and openly, not only by the celebration of the mysteries . . . but also by saying or singing the Symbol of the faith . . . along with other texts, and likewise by the reading of Holy Scripture, written under the inspiration of the Holy Ghost. The entire Liturgy, therefore, has the Catholic faith for its content, inasmuch as it bears public witness to the faith of the Church.

Pope Pius XII rejected the theological opinion that interprets the statement of Saint Prosper unilaterally, as if the Liturgy determined faith and thus faith would be established after certain formulas had been tried in Worship to verify whether they are acceptable to the People of God. This is the position of those scholars who think, for example, that faith in the Trinity derived from the baptismal liturgical formulas of the ancient Church, more so than the reverse. Since—according to them—the ancient Church accepted these tested formulas in Worship, she would then also profess faith in the Trinity. Pius XII recalls, however, that the very opposite also occurs, that is, that the—preexisting—faith is expressed in Worship. It appears much more often that liturgical formulas are a prayerful expression of the Creed, than vice versa.

Then the Pontiff continues with a historical annotation:

> For this reason, whenever there was question of defining a truth revealed by God, the Sovereign Pontiff and the Councils in their recourse to the "theological sources," as they are called, have not seldom drawn many an argument from this sacred science of the Liturgy. . . . Similarly during the discussion of a doubtful or controversial truth, the Church and the Holy Fathers have not failed to look to the age-old and age-honored sacred rites for enlightenment. Hence the well-known and venerable maxim, "*Legem credendi lex statuat supplicandi*"—let the rule for prayer determine the rule of belief.

The Liturgy is *locus theologicus* for the doctrine; but this is true not because it creates the dogma but rather because it contains it, guards it, and hands it down. The faith of the Church is expressed in the Liturgy (which is why the heretics, in addition to denying the truth of the faith, have always changed the rites and liturgical texts that were opposed to their errors). Consequently, it is natural that in the case of a dogmatic definition or a doctrinal dispute, this locus is also examined, in which the belief of the Church is sought.

Finally, Pius XII offers the following important explanation:

> The sacred Liturgy, consequently, does not decide or determine independently and of itself what is of Catholic faith. More properly, since the Liturgy is also a profession of eternal truths, and subject, as such, to the supreme teaching authority of the Church, it can supply proofs and testimony, quite clearly, of no little value, towards the determination of a particular point of Christian doctrine. But if one desires to differentiate and describe the relationship between faith and the sacred Liturgy in absolute and general terms, it is perfectly correct to say, "*Lex credendi legem statuat supplicandi*"—let the rule of belief determine the rule of prayer.[58]

---

[58] Pius XII, *Mediator Dei* (1947), I, 3. Only some excerpts from the encyclical (here in the translation present on *vatican.va*) are reproduced in the DS, which is why we are quoting the text—which does not include paragraph numbers—with reference to the parts and sections into which editors usually divide it. Here is a summary of the individual parts: Introduction; I: The Nature, Origin, and Evolution of the Liturgy; II: Eucharistic Worship; III: The Divine Office and the Liturgical Year; IV: Pastoral Guidelines;

The Liturgy

To conclude, let us recall that Pius XII, in the apostolic constitution with which he defined the dogma of the Assumption of Mary, would repeat this teaching clearly: "The Liturgy of the Church does not engender the Catholic faith, but rather springs from it, in such a way that the practices of the sacred Worship proceed from the faith as the fruit comes from the tree."[59]

2.2. The Nature of the Sacred Liturgy

2.2.1. "Liturgy," "Worship," and Annexed Terms

1. Classical Greek

The word Liturgy has Greek origins: *leitourgia* derives from *leiton* and *ergon*. The first part comes from *laos* ("people") and means "public."[60] *Ergon* refers to action or operation. The compound word *leitourgia*, therefore, in classical Greek, means "public service, public work/function," or "ministry, service." It is true that it may also indicate a service of religious (pagan)[61] worship, but *leitourgos* refers per se to the public official, more so than to the priest, although some Greek authors have used it rarely in this second sense as well.[62] The Greek *leitourgia* is therefore rendered in Latin with *publicum opus*. It is a term that does not indicate functions that are mainly religious, but rather assignments or public works. Therefore, it could have been used in a wide range of applications: from democracy, to military service, to agriculture, to music. Everything that is done in public and for the sake of the public is, in some sense, "liturgy."

2. The Septuagint

The term would be reprised by the Septuagint, the Greek translation of the Old Testament, which was composed between the third and second century BC. The Septuagint chose the substantive *leitourgia* and the verb *leitourgein* to translate the Hebrew terms *sheret* and *abodah*, which refer to the Worship of God. An important change in meaning occurs here: while for classical

---

Epilogue.

[59] Pius XII, *Munificentissimus Deus* (1950) [§20] (this passage is not reproduced in DS).

[60] *Leiton* comes to be used in compound words as a synonym for *demosios*, which means "the public [sector], that which concerns the state."

[61] See Iamblichus of Chalsis (d. 330), *De mysteriis Aegyptorum, Chaldaeorum, Assyriorum* 9.2, where he uses the term even in reference to the astral divinities, subjected to the *dekanoi*.

[62] See Dionysius of Halicarnassus (d. 7 BC), *Antiquitates romanae* 2.22.

Greek the use of *leitourgia* for religious services is admitted—even if it is not the main meaning (which is instead related to the state, the *res publica)*—the Septuagint then reversed the accentuation and connected *leitourgia, leitourgien,* and *leitourgos* mainly to the priestly work of cultic offering to God. What remains unvaried in the passage of the meaning is the fact that, here too, it is maintained that the Liturgy is a public thing, not hidden or esoteric, but rather performed before the people (though this does not imply that each individual rite of the Liturgy must be visible to all). Secondly, the concept of benefit is also maintained: a "liturgy" is an action done for the people and in favor of the people, as is certainly the case with Worship toward God.

3. The New Testament

The New Testament uses the Septuagint as its text of reference, and it therefore inherits the same usage of these words. In the writings of the New Covenant, these liturgical terms are used on different occasions and in different contexts. Here is a brief overview, referring to: (1) Christ: Hebrews 8:1–2 (calls Him *ton aghion leitourgos*— "minister of the sanctuary [or: of sacred things]"); 8:6. (2) Angels: Hebrews 1:7 (they are called *leitourgoi*); 1:14 (called *leitourgika pneumata*—"ministering spirits"). (3) Paul: Romans 15:15–16 (he identifies himself as *leitourgos Christou Iesou*); Philippians 2:17. (4) Celebration of Worship: Acts 13:2 (the disciples *leitourgounton to Kyrio*—"they were worshipping the Lord"). (5) Works of charity: Romans 15:26–27; 2 Corinthians 9:11–12; Philippians 2:29–30.

4. The Word "Worship"

In the previous three points we have focused on the term Liturgy, which is preferred by scholars today, given the strong tendency to assume Greek words into Latin theology. We should not forget, however, that even though the Magisterium commonly refers to the Greek word, at the official level, the word Worship remains the preferred one, to the extent that the dedicated Vatican Dicastery is called the Congregation for Divine Worship and not the Congregation for the Liturgy. These are, of course, matters of detail, but they should not be completely ignored.

The word Worship is a translation of the Latin word *Cultus,* which derives from the verb *colo* ("cultivate"). It originally means, literally, the cultivation of the earth, but also has a generic figurative sense of "taking care of" and also of "inhabiting," "practicing," and "exercising." It will not be surprising, therefore, that even in classical Latin it also takes on a religious meaning—again, in the pagan context—given that it is necessary to take care of the gods and carry out religious practices and exercises. For example, Cicero (d. 43 BC) used the expression *colere deos* ("honor the gods") and Livy (d. 17) used *religiones colere* ("cultivate religious practices").

The term Worship, with respect to Liturgy, highlights less the public and assembly aspect of the action taken, and more so, its religious orientation towards the divinity. We could say that the underlying meaning is both anthropologically (the effort, the commitment to cultivate) and theologically oriented (one honors the gods). It is therefore more than natural that the Church has assumed this term and used it to make reference to the true Worship, to the true Liturgy, to the true religion.[63]

5. Other Terms

Finally, let us recall that other terms that come from Latin are very much used in the liturgical ambit:

(1) "Celebrate," which indicates the execution of the rite, derived from the Latin equivalent *celebro*, which means "to frequent, or to visit in crowds," "to celebrate in crowds," but also "to use often, to practice." The specifically cultic acceptation of the word derives from the first meaning, because it refers to an action of the group or assembly. In this sense, *celebro* also means "to make known, divulge" and thus "to solemnize, exalt." Divine Worship is therefore celebrated, because it is an action that usually presupposes a gathering of people, and it is a solemn action, which intends to manifest a reality. Uniting the two Latin words *colo*—from which *cultus* derives—and *celebro*, allows us to put together the different aspects of the terms Liturgy and Worship. Today "celebrate the Liturgy" is generally said, but it would be better if "celebrate divine Worship" were used more frequently, in that it is more complete from the standpoint of the specific content of the words.[64]

---

[63] "Every approach to a good and blessed life is to be found in the true religion, with which is honored [*colitur*] the only God, Who is acknowledged by the sincerest piety to be the source of all kinds of being, from which the universe derives its origin, in which it finds its completion, by which it is held together" (Saint Augustine of Hippo, *De vera religione* 1.1, in *The Works of Saint Augustine: A Translation for the 21st Century*, vol. I/8: *On Christian Belief*, trans. Edmund Hill (Hyde Park, NY: New City Press, 2005), 29 (with our corrections).

[64] We also note that today "celebrate" has taken the place of a verb that was used often in the past: "officiate." The latter term specifically indicates the minister that celebrates, focusing on his faculty and power to implement the sacred rites. Perhaps this is also why the word "celebrate" is preferred today, since it refers more to the whole of the liturgical assembly and not just to the sacred minister. The tendency of the post-conciliar liturgists was, in fact, strongly oriented toward highlighting the fact that the whole assembly is

(2) "Rite," from the corresponding Latin *ritus*, "rite, religious ceremony," but also "custom" or "mode, manner." The liturgical act is a rite, not only because it is an act of a religious nature, but also because it is performed in a certain way, according to custom. Therefore, in the word *ritus* is contained the sense of doing things as they should be done, as they have been handed down, that is, the way they have always been done. A rite is by its nature "immutable," in the sense that it is marked by a very slow, imperceptible mutation, precisely because human beings have a cultural, but also anthropological, need for ritual (i.e., repetition done according to the rules handed down). This also corresponds to the unceasing cosmic circularity.

(3) "Ceremony," which derives from the Latin *caerimonia*, "veneration, religious respect" and then "worship, practice or religious custom." In the past, this was a very valuable word in the liturgical ambit, but for several decades it has been shelved and viewed with suspicion. In recent times, the second meaning of the word—the liturgical act as practice—has caused this word to be put aside as focusing too much on "externals." However, it has been forgotten that the first use of the term expresses the inner state with which this practice is done: the sacred fear of divinity, the religious respect of the soul. They have focused on the ceremony understood only as a ritual exercise[65] and not also as referring to the proper internal disposition of the practitioner.[66] Perhaps taking the two meanings together (*et-et*) would also allow for the recovery today of an uncontroversial use of this word.

2.2.2. Definition

To define means to indicate the essence, what something is in its most proper reality. It is different than describing, which consists in reporting the characteristics that manifest a thing. It is important to distinguish a definition from a description in the liturgical realm as well. In this section, we would like to provide the definition, not the phenomenological description of divine Worship.

"liturgically in charge."

[65] It is used this way, for example, by Tacitus (d. ca. 120), *Annales* 3.58: "*in libris caerimoniarium*" ("in the ritual texts").

[66] As in Cicero, *De inventione* 2.161: "*Religio est, quae superioris cuiusdam naturae, quam divinam vocant, curam caerimoniamque affert*" ("Religion is to render worship and veneration to a superior nature that is called divine"). It is known that external worship comes to be called *cura*, while internal veneration is called *caerimonia*.

1. Description

It has become very common in our time to point to the words of *Sacrosanctum Concilium* §10 as the definition of Liturgy: "The liturgy is the summit [*culmen*] toward which the activity of the Church is directed; at the same time it is the font [*fons*] from which all her power flows."[67] The continuation of the same conciliar text offers other descriptive details, in order to further clarify the sense in which the Liturgy comes to be understood as *culmen et fons*. This binomial—which, incidentally, we do not regret at all, representing again one of many expressions of the *et-et*—was confirmed in two other documents of the same Council, even though in both cases it refers not to the Liturgy as a whole, but only to the Eucharistic Liturgy. In *Lumen Gentium*, the Eucharist is described as "fount and apex of the whole Christian life—*totius vitae christianae fontem et culmen*."[68] In *Presbyterorum Ordinis*, it is called "the source and the apex of the whole work of preaching the Gospel—*fons et culmen totius evangelizationis*."[69]

From these three quotes, we can observe: (1) The Second Vatican Council repeats the same expression in three separate documents, therefore, it has a certain importance. (2) Only the first time is "summit [*culmen*] and font [*fons*]" said, while in the latter two "fount [or source] and apex—*fons et culmen*" is used, inverting the terms. Since *Lumen Gentium* and *Presbyterorum Ordinis* are later, one has to suppose a specific desire to invert the order of expressing these two words. On the other hand, the second part of *Sacrosanctum Concilium* §10 was already placed within the perspective of a similar inversion in the order of the words.[70] We infer that, by describing Liturgy, the Fathers intended first to highlight its aspect of being a font, followed by the aspect of being an apex. In other words, after a less apt first formulation, they wanted to indicate a clearer hierarchy between the two subjects of this *et-et*. The Liturgy, especially the Holy Mass, is primarily the font of grace and then the destination at which one arrives to present the fruits of one's commitment: the primacy of the grace and the proper understanding of human cooperation

---

[67] Second Vatican Council, *Sacrosanctum Concilium* (1963), §10.
[68] Second Vatican Council, *Lumen Gentium* (1964), §11.
[69] Second Vatican Council, *Presbyterorum Ordinis* (1965), §5.
[70] The text thus reads: "From the Liturgy, therefore, and especially from the Eucharist, as from a font [*ut e fonte*], grace is poured forth upon us; and the sanctification of men in Christ and the glorification of God, to which all other activities of the Church are directed as toward their end, is achieved in the most efficacious possible way." Here the liturgical constitution places the fontal nature of grace in the primary place, followed by its nature as apex or end of the ecclesial activity.

The Sacraments in General and the Liturgy

(see Chapter Five) is much better expressed in this way. (3) Considered in their proper context, all three recurrences (and the last two with great clarity) make it clear that "font and apex" is a perfect theological description of the Liturgy, but not its definition. In other words, the Liturgy is manifested as the font of grace—because all the initiatives and works of the Church spring forth from it—and as destination of our Christian commitment. We begin from the celebration and return to it at the end of our labors.

In conclusion, *Sacrosanctum Concilium* §10, and the other two texts cited, represent an excellent description of the Liturgy, with privileged references to the pastoral and missionary perspective, but not a true and proper definition. The expression *fons et culmen*, in fact, speaks of the Liturgy only in reference to the Church and her action in the world. The expression does not make reference to God, Christ, and the Holy Spirit. It cannot, therefore, be a true definition of the Worship rendered to the Holy Trinity. Such a definition will have to be sought elsewhere.[71]

2. Definition

We do not need to travel far to find a true definition of the Liturgy. It is sufficient to go a little further back in the same liturgical constitution in order to find what we are looking for. The Council says:

> Rightly, then, the Liturgy is considered as an exercise of the priestly office of Jesus Christ. In the Liturgy the sanctification of the man is signified by signs perceptible to the senses, and is effected in a way which corresponds with each of these signs; in the Liturgy the whole public worship is performed by the Mystical Body of Jesus Christ, that is, by the Head and His members.[72]

The definition that tells us what the Liturgy is in its essence is: "*Iesu Christi sacerdotalis muneris exercitatio*" ("exercise of the priestly office of Jesus Christ"). Note that the definition is preceded by an appropriate *veluti* ("as"): we are always in the realm of theological analogy (see Chapter Two). We have here a distinct reference to Christ, without which the Liturgy could hardly be

---

[71] The *Catechism* implicitly confirms what we are saying, in that it cites *Sacrosanctum Concilium* §10 at CCC §1074, dedicated to the theme "Catechesis and Liturgy," therefore discussing a pastoral activity of the Church. It cites *Sacrosanctum Concilium* §7, which we shall cite next as a true definition of Christian Worship, at CCC §1070, in the context of the two paragraphs that aim to express the very nature of the Liturgy.

[72] Second Vatican Council, *Sacrosanctum Concilium*, §7.

defined as *Christian*.[73] Moreover, we have a qualified reference to the Church, His Mystical Body, without which it would be difficult to define it as a Christian *Liturgy*. There is also a magnificent *et-et* here: we should not choose between Christ and the Church, since Christian Worship is an action *both* of Christ *and* of the Church, and it appears superfluous in this case to indicate which of the terms is the most important.

Taking another look at the text just quoted, we note that it begins with the Latin word *merito*, that is, "rightly." The use of this term implies that the Council refers, by confirming it, to something that has been said previously. And this is indeed the case. With that "*merito*," the Council reconnects itself with what it wrote earlier regarding the Christ-Church link in divine Worship. However, what it wrote immediately beforehand is actually not an absolute novelty but a reprisal of a text of Pius XII. The "rightly," therefore, means that the Council wanted to confirm the teaching of Pope Pius XII on the nature of the Liturgy, drawing upon his teaching in *Mediator Dei*. Going back to the text, note that Vatican II did indeed offer its own definition of Liturgy—modifying the word order a little—by re-proposing the definition of Pius XII. Here is the 1947 text:

> The sacred Liturgy is, consequently, the public Worship which our Redeemer as Head of the Church renders to the Father, as well as the Worship which the community of the faithful renders to its Founder, and through Him to the heavenly Father. It is, in short, the Worship rendered by the Mystical Body of Christ in the entirety of its Head and members.[74]

---

[73] The reference to Christ already implies in itself the Trinitarian aspect (see Chapters One, Four, and Six), which in the present case of the definition of the Liturgy will immediately be brought to light by a quote of Pius XII.

[74] Pius XII, *Mediator Dei*, I, 1 (this definition is found in the selection of the DS, at no. 3841). Even what the Pope says immediately before the cited text, in regard to the different ways in which Christ is present in the Liturgy, is taken up again by *Sacrosanctum Concilium*, at the same no. 7. We need to point out an anomaly here: the text of the liturgical constitution draws completely from *Mediator Dei* in many places but, strangely, it never cites it explicitly. The study of the different preparatory outlines of the constitution revealed that the citations were initially there and that they were progressively eliminated. Perhaps one can justify this fact by noting that, at the time of *Sacrosanctum Concilium*—1963—only sixteen years had passed since the publication of the encyclical of Pius XII: a very short time, for which it could reasonably be thought that the texts of Pius XII on this subject were widely known, with no need to cite them explicitly. The fact remains, however, that such an idea had not entered the minds of the editors of the previous drafts, which had instead included many references to *Mediator Dei*. Moreover, considering only the four Constitutions, other texts of Pius XII were explicitly cited

The Sacraments in General and the Liturgy

We shall leave it up to the reader to compare the text of the Council with that of Pius XII—he or she will clearly notice the near total overlap between the two. Here, the reader will encounter one of the many examples of the "hermeneutic of continuity," for which it is absurd to think that Vatican II had wanted to propose a radically new doctrine and constitute a new Church with respect to the "pre-conciliar Church."[75]

Readers who compare the texts carefully will notice that Vatican II, in addition to retrieving Pius XII *in toto*, added an element. The Council refers to the "signs" through which the sanctification of human beings occurs in the Liturgy. Even this element, which appears to be a novelty of Vatican II, is actually only relatively so, and therefore also falls under the initial "*merito*." In fact, there is an earlier text that had appropriately highlighted the importance of liturgical signs, which Vatican II returns to appreciate here. Here is a text from the Council of Trent:

> As human nature is such that it cannot easily raise itself up to the meditation of divine realities without external aids, Holy Mother Church has for that reason duly established certain rites, such as that some parts of the Mass should be said in quieter tones and others in louder; and she has provided ceremonial such as mystical blessings, lights, incense, vestments, and many other rituals of that kind from apostolic order and Tradition by which the majesty of this great Sacrifice is enhanced and the minds of the faithful are aroused by those visible signs of religious devotion to contemplation of the high mysteries hidden in this Sacrifice.[76]

---

various times in *Lumen Gentium*, *Dei Verbum*, and *Gaudium et Spes* (which also cites John XXIII and the then-reigning Paul VI many times).

[75] Within a "hermeneutic of discontinuity," "the nature of a Council as such is therefore basically misunderstood. In this way, it is considered as a sort of Constituent [Assembly] that eliminates an old constitution and creates a new one. However, the Constituent Assembly needs a mandator and then confirmation by the mandator, in other words, the people the constitution must serve. The Fathers [of Vatican II] had no such mandate and no one had ever given them one; nor could anyone have given them one because the essential constitution of the Church comes from the Lord" (Benedict XVI, *Address to the Roman Curia*, December 22, 2005).

[76] Council of Trent, *Doctrina et Canones de ss. Missae Sacrificio* (1562), ch. 5 (DS 1746). Saint Thomas had already expressed himself in this sense: "Human beings carry out sensory activities not to solicit God, but to awaken themselves to divine things: such are the prostrations, genuflections, acclamations, and songs. These things are not done because they are needed by God, Who knows everything, and Whose will is immutable, Who welcomes directly the affection of the soul and not the movements of the body. But they are done for

The Liturgy

Note that both the cited councils make recourse to the same term: *signa* ("signs"), specifying that they are visible, sensible signs. Indeed, both councils place these signs in relation to the sanctification of the participants in divine Worship. Trent emphasizes that they help the minds of the faithful to rise up to God, contemplating the hidden realities in the Eucharistic Sacrifice.[77] Vatican II teaches that these signs sanctify the participants in the Liturgy. This leads us to discuss them a little more extensively.

2.2.3. Sacramental Character

We have encountered the category of Sacrament both in the ecclesiological chapter and in the first part of this chapter. Using the adjective "sacramental," we shall now refer to the concept of sacramentality as a union of the visible and invisible element, but with particular emphasis on the sensible sacramental sign. The Liturgy has a sacramental character because it uses different types of signs.

1. Mutability of Signs

The first distinction to be proposed in this regard is the one between the signs established by God (of "divine law"), which cannot be modified; and the signs

---

us, so that through these sensible acts our attention may be turned toward God and our affection set aflame. At the same time, with these acts we come to know that God is the Author of the soul and of our body, as we lend Him spiritual and corporeal acts of homage. Thus, it is not surprising that certain heretics, who deny that God is the Author of our body, condemn these corporeal gifts addressed toward God. From this we see how they forget to be human beings, thinking that they do not need the representation of things that are sensible for knowledge and for inner affection. . . . Thus, the convenience of also using certain corporeal acts to elevate our souls to God is evident. Worship of God consists precisely in lending these corporeal acts to God. In fact, we speak of cultivating [*colere*] the things that we give attention and care. . . . As we await God directly with our internal acts, we properly exercise Worship of God with similar acts. However, even external acts pertain to the Worship of God in that our souls, as we have said, are elevated to God with these actions" (*Summa contra gentiles* III, ch. 119 [our translation]).

[77] These teachings are further confirmed, with specific reference to the Eucharist, at *Sacrosanctum Concilium* §48, where—with an expression that turned out to be quite fortunate—it is taught that the Church desires that the faithful understand well, "*per ritus et preces*" ("through rites and prayers"), the sacred action in which they are participating. Leaving aside the use that has often been made of this expression after the Council, we must not fail to note the full consonance of views with the Tridentine Council. The rites and prayers established by Mother Church help the faithful to adequately participate in Worship, that is, with their minds turned toward God. We shall return to this theme later.

The Sacraments in General and the Liturgy

established by the Church ("ecclesiastical law"). This fundamental distinction is at the base of the power, which the Church has received, of enriching and modifying the historical form of the Liturgy.[78] That is to say, the distinction between immutable elements and elements that are subject to change, theologically justifies the development of liturgical forms (which also gives rise to different families of rituals), as well as the possibility of liturgical reform, which has occurred many times in the history of the Church, with more or less happy outcomes, depending on the particular case.[79]

---

[78] See Pius XII, *Mediator Dei*, I, 4; Second Vatican Council, *Sacrosanctum Concilium*, §21.

[79] Excellent reforms of the sacred Liturgy can be recalled, but also some that did not fare well, which, after a period of use, required revision. An example of an unfortunate reform that can be mentioned is the re-edition of the Roman Breviary, done by the humanist bishop Zaccaria Ferreri di Guarda (d. 1524), who was appointed by Pope Leo X (d. 1521). Ferreri produced a new edition of the hymns, which was very much affected by his extensive classical erudition and poetic skill. However, an adequate understanding and esteem, on his part, of the Liturgical Tradition, did not match the elegance of his Latin, nor did he seem to have an interest in studying that Liturgical Tradition, preferring to operate on the basis of his literary erudition alone. Later, Pope Clement VII (d. 1534) asked Cardinal Francisco Quiñones (d. 1540) to revise the Breviary, and he produced a work that was not much better, as he too operated from reductive ideological presuppositions, intending to bring the Liturgy back to its most ancient form, with a certain disdain for the development of the rites over the centuries. It even occurred that upon seeing the Breviary of Quiñones used in the cathedral for the ritual of the *Tenebrae* on Good Friday, the crowd at Zaragoza revolted against the canons, suspecting them to have become Huguenots! Despite the fact that this Breviary was officially approved by a Roman Pontiff (Paul III, in 1536), two of his successors were forced to reject it (Paul IV in 1558 and Saint Pius V in 1568). Between approval and definitive rejection, thirty-two years and five popes had passed, but in the end, the Church recognized with humility that she had made a mistake in the liturgical reform. But, while to err is human, to persevere is diabolical: *"Humanum fuit errare, diabolicum est per animositatem in errore manere"* (Saint Augustine of Hippo, *Sermo* 164.10.14). What Augustine says here is addressed to the Donatists, who feared correcting their mistake because they would have to disavow all they had taught up to that moment. Augustine says to them, inviting them to the humility necessary to come back: "Their answer should be, if they feared God, 'It was human to be mistaken, it's diabolical to remain in the mistake out of spiteful animosity. It would have been better if we had never gone wrong; but at least let us do the next best thing and finally correct our error. We deceived you, because we were deceived ourselves. We preached untruths, because we believed others who preached untruths.' They should say to their people, 'We have gone wrong together, let us together withdraw from our error. We were your leaders into the ditch, and you followed us when we led you into the ditch; and now follow us when we lead you back to the Church.' They could say that; they would be saying it to indignant people, saying it to angry people; but they too would sooner or later lay aside their indignation, and come, even though late in the day, to love unity" (in *The Works of St. Augustine*, vol. III/5, trans. Edmund Hill, 195–196). It is an invitation that is very good not only for those who erred on the dogmatic level, but also for those who have been deceived on the liturgical or moral level.

2. Different Types of Signs

There are four types of signs: (1) Cosmic signs, borrowed, so to speak, from creation: water, ashes, palm fronds, but also day (light) and night (darkness). (2) Social signs, like the breaking of bread, the sharing of the chalice, the washing of the feet, or the exchange of a sign of peace with a fraternal kiss or hug. (3) Signs of the Old Testament such as the anointing with oil, the laying on of hands, or the burning of incense. (4) Signs of the New Testament, which we shall describe more extensively below.

3. Signs of Christian Worship

The Church borrows different signs both from the cosmos and from history (human society and the Old Testament), adopting them to her own use. Some signs are specific to the New Covenant. Let us consider on the whole the principal signs used in the Christian Liturgy: (1) Word: Christian Worship is fundamentally oratio, prayer. Therefore, the Word has a determinant role. This sign is found both in the form of the Word of God (biblical readings) and in various types of euchological texts: orations, benedictions, litanies, exorcisms, Symbols of the faith, doxologies, hymns, songs, etc. (2) Gestures and movements: the body is a participant in the act of Worship (see later), therefore, corporeal gestures and movements, both of the ministers and the faithful, are an integral part of Christian Worship, which (being *propter homines* like the Sacraments) is corporeal-spiritual. (3) Natural elements: the Church uses many of them in Liturgical celebrations. Some, as we have seen, constitute the matter of the Sacraments (bread and wine, water, etc.). Others visibly express invisible realities and/or intentions of the worshippers (ashes, wax, fire, oil, perfume/balsam, incense, salt, etc.). (4) People: even the participants and officiants are living signs of the Liturgy, as noted in the above-cited *Sacrosanctum Concilium §7*. Through the persons as signs, Christ is shown, He is made present.[80] (5) Art: the beauty of the music, of the Liturgical architecture, and of sacred art are important signs of the presence of Christ in Christian Worship. This aspect has been highlighted by Benedict XVI:

---

[80] "Christ is always present in His Church, especially in her liturgical celebrations. He is present in the Sacrifice of the Mass, ... *in the person* of His minister ... but especially under the Eucharistic Species. ... He is present, lastly, when the Church prays and sings, for He promised: 'Where two or three are gathered together in my name, there am I in the midst of them'" (Second Vatican Council, *Sacrosanctum Concilium*, §7 [emphasis added]).

This relationship between Creed and Worship is evidenced in a particular way by the rich theological and liturgical category of beauty. Like the rest of Christian Revelation, the Liturgy is inherently linked to beauty: it is *veritatis splendor*. The Liturgy is a radiant expression of the paschal mystery, in which Christ draws us to Himself and calls us to communion. As Saint Bonaventure would say, in Jesus we contemplate beauty and splendor at their source. This is no mere aestheticism, but the concrete way in which the truth of God's love in Christ encounters us, attracts us and delights us, enabling us to emerge from ourselves and drawing us towards our true vocation, which is love.[81]

It is very important to know how to grasp the meaning of the signs of the Liturgy, which are very eloquent, and make it the object of meditation and of catechesis.

2.3. The Participation of the Faithful in Divine Worship

2.3.1. Purpose of the Liturgy

The proper end of the liturgical action has already emerged from the aforementioned texts. It is twofold: as divine Worship, the first and primary end of the Holy Liturgy is, naturally, the glorification of God in Christ. Second, the proper end of the Liturgy is the sanctification of human beings. We have already highlighted the primacy of the first of these, the latreutical end of this *et-et*, that is, of the adoration of God. The second end is also very important, namely, that of transmitting divine grace to the participants.

Based on this twofold end, we can mention two aspects, linked respectively to one or the other member of the binomial described:

1. The Liturgical Orientation

The Liturgy is Theocentric, Christocentric, and Pneumatocentric: the Protagonists and Center of orientation are the Three divine Persons. Consequently, Christian Worship is neither ecclesiocentric nor anthropocentric. Neither the individual person nor the community represent the central element. We celebrate God, not ourselves. This is why the inner orientation of the celebration cannot be anything other than that expressed by the Trinitarian doxology (formula of glorification), which is found at the end of the Eucharistic Prayer:

---

[81] Benedict XVI, *Sacramentum Caritatis* (2007), §35.

"Through Him [Christ], with Him, and in Him, O God, almighty Father, in the unity of the Holy Spirit, all glory and honor is yours, for ever and ever." The Christian Liturgy is either oriented toward the glorification of the Trinity above all else, or it simply does not exist.

Therefore, there cannot be any debate regarding the *internal* orientation of the liturgical action.[82] Today, there are various opposing opinions among liturgists about the *external* orientation during Worship. Here we cannot dwell on a wide historical and archeological discussion, but it is possible to show beyond any doubt, and against a widespread opinion, that in the past the Church never had the celebrant minister turned towards the faithful gathered in assembly.[83] It is Church Tradition that the minister and the faithful participants are physically turned in the same direction, toward east or toward the apse, during the Worship, or at least during the Eucharistic Liturgy.[84]

---

[82] "Whatever the position of the celebrating priest is, it is clear that the Eucharistic Sacrifice is offered to the One and Triune God.... It would be a grave error to imagine that the main orientation of the sacrificial action is the community. If the priest celebrates *versus populum* ... his spiritual attitude must always be *versus Deum per Jesum Christum*.... Even the Church, which takes concrete form in the assembly that participates, is entirely turned *versus Deum* as the first spiritual movement" (Congregation for Divine Worship and the Discipline of the Sacraments, *Responsa ad Quaestiones de Nova Institutione Generali Missalis Romani*, in *Communicationes* 32 [2000], pp. 171–172 [our translation]).

[83] In the rare cases in which the celebrating priest actually turned towards the nave, it was due to the particular conformation of the Church and of the altar and was absolutely not understood as a celebration "towards the people." On the other hand, even if they wanted to, the ministers and faithful could not have looked at each other anyway, since the ancient altar was often built near the apse and elevated on high steps. Sometimes the *bema* was also interposed between the presbytery and the nave. Furthermore, in order to separate the priest and the nave, the iconostasis (a wall with icons: still used today) was used in the East, while, in the West, structures such as a canopy or pergola (see the Patriarchal Cathedral Basilica of Saint Mark in Venice) were used. Often, during the Eucharistic Liturgy, curtains were drawn to protect the Mystery from view. Additionally, large candelabra and the crucifix completed the work of rendering the celebration almost invisible to the faithful, even if the priest were physically facing the assembly.

[84] Prayer toward the east was "handed down and recommended by the primary Priest [Christ] and by His sons [the Apostles]" (Origen of Alexandria [d. 254], *Homiliae in Numeros* 5.1.4 [our translation]); "From the east came atonement for you; for from there is the man Whose name is 'East', Who became a Mediator between God and man. Therefore, you are invited by this to look always 'to the east' whence 'the Sun of Righteousness' arises for you" (Origen of Alexandria, *Homiliae in Leviticum* 9.10, in *FCNT*, vol. 83, trans. Gary Wayne Barkley [Washington, DC: CUA Press, 1990], 199); "It is necessary to pray toward the East" (*Didascalia apostolorum* [third century] 12 [our translation]); "The Apostles ordered that one should pray to the east" (*Didascalia Addai* [Fourth Century], can. 1 [our translation]); "Invariably all standing and facing east to pray to God" (*Constitutiones apostolorum* [ca. 375] 2.57.14 [our translation]); "Having entered, therefore, that

The Sacraments in General and the Liturgy

The practice of the ordinary form of the Roman Rite, although it does not at all exclude physically celebrating *ad orientem*, today features the so-called celebration *versus populum* ("toward the people") as a general custom. That is, the priest finds himself face-to-face with the assembly, which is why he and the gathered community now have two different orientations: the minister looks at the assembly, and the assembly looks at him. In this way, we can say, the community looks at itself, remaining a little closed (at the level of a sign—the interiority depends on the individual and only God knows it) to the orientation toward God. The "mainstream" of the liturgists of recent decades argue that this way of celebrating is surely much better, because it facilitates communication, and therefore, the pastoral dimension of the Liturgy. They normally add that this was also the most ancient way of celebrating, which is an affirmation that we strongly contest, supported by evidence, although we do not have room to deal with the issue here.

Actually, the main end of glorifying God in the Liturgy is expressed much better by having a common orientation, of faithful and ministers *versus Dominum*, toward the Lord. Saint Augustine, at the end of his homilies, often said: "*Conversi ad Dominum*" ("turn toward the Lord"). The exhortation has a dual meaning: it indicates, on the one hand, the corporeal attitude, for which everyone must now turn toward the east or the apse, the symbol of Christ coming from the east (see Matt 24:27),[85] He who is the *Orientale Lumen*. On the other, it is a strong call to moral conversion, in which—while turning physically toward the Lord—we are called to that internal turn that is verified by a holy life.[86] Here too, we prefer not to oppose or separate, but to maintain the

---

you might recognize your adversary, whom you think you should renounce to his face, you turn toward the east. For he who renounces the devil, turns toward Christ, recognizes Him by a direct glance" (Saint Ambrose of Milan [d. 397], *De mysteriis* 2.7, in *FCNT*, vol. 44, trans. Roy J. Deferrari [Washington, DC: CUA Press, 1963], 7); "And so, while we are awaiting Him, we worship toward the east. This is, moreover, the unwritten Tradition of the Apostles" (Saint John Damascene [d. 749], *De fide orthodoxa* 4.12, in *FCNT*, vol. 37, trans. Frederic H. Chase, Jr. [Washington, DC: CUA Press, 1958], 353–354); etc.

[85] "To adore by looking toward the east is appropriate, first, because the movement of the heavens that manifests the divine majesty comes from the east. Second, (Edenic) paradise was located in the east, according to the Septuagint of Genesis, and we seek to return to paradise. Third, on account of the path of Christ, Who is the Light of the world and is defined as the Orient who rides in the heavens of the heavens toward the east (see Ps 68:34 *LXX*) and is expected to return from the east according to Matthew (24:27): like the lightning that comes from the east and appears even in the west, so will be the coming of the Son of man" (*ST* II-II, q. 84, a. 3, ad 3 [our translation]).

[86] This second aspect is especially highlighted by Saint Augustine of Hippo in *Sermo 130/A* [Dolbeau, 19], 12. Pius XII, *Mystici Corporis*, I, 1, writes: "The fundamental duty of man is certainly that of orienting [*dirigat*] himself and his life towards God."

unity of the *et-et*: there is no doubt that, among the two, the internal orientation of the soul is primary (what good would it do to turn physically toward the east, if one's heart were far from God?); nevertheless, there is no need to choose *either* the orientation of the soul *or* that of the body. Just as the human being is both soul and body, so should the person orient himself or herself both internally and externally toward the Lord.[87] Thus is also manifested the unity of the two ends of the Liturgy: giving the primacy precisely to the glorification of God, which also results in a more perfect sanctification of the human being in all his or her dimensions, even the bodily dimensions.[88] This brings us to the second aspect, linked to the constitution of the human being.

2. Sanctification of Time and Space

As a corporeal-spiritual being, the human person is sanctified in all his or her dimensions through the Liturgy. The second end of Worship, that is, the

---

[87] "The Worship rendered by the Church to God must be, in its entirety, interior as well as exterior. It is exterior because the nature of man as a composite of body and soul requires it to be so. . . . Every impulse of the human heart, besides, expresses itself naturally through the senses; and the Worship of God, being the concern not merely of individuals but of the whole community of mankind, must therefore be social as well. This obviously it cannot be unless religious activity is also organized and manifested outwardly. Exterior worship, finally, reveals and emphasizes the unity of the Mystical Body. . . . But the chief element of divine Worship must be interior. . . . *The sacred Liturgy requires, however, that both of these elements be intimately linked with each another.* . . . Otherwise religion clearly amounts to mere formalism, without meaning and without content" (Pius XII, *Mediator Dei*, I, 2 [emphasis added]).

[88] Given our particular theological context, it is necessary to insist again upon this point: "Christianity does not reject matter. Rather, bodiliness is considered in all its value in the liturgical act, whereby the human body is disclosed in its inner nature as a temple of the Spirit and is united with the Lord Jesus, Who himself took a body for the world's salvation. This does not mean, however, an absolute exaltation of all that is physical, for we know well the chaos which sin introduced into the harmony of the human being. The Liturgy reveals that the body, through the mystery of the cross, is in the process of transfiguration, pneumatization: on Mount Tabor Christ showed his body radiant, as the Father wants it to be again" (Saint John Paul II, *Orientale Lumen* [1995], §11). On the one hand, therefore, the liturgical act must be corporeal (rites, gestures that express the devotion of the soul); on the other, not all corporeal movements are worthy and admissible, but only those that express the cross's purification of our flesh from sin. Therefore, the various dance choreographies, which are so often introduced into divine Worship today, should be left aside, not least because they are not mentioned by the liturgical books, but above all for theological reason: such dances tend to exalt corporeality, not redeem it. They are forms of liturgical anthropocentrism. Saint John Chrysostom (d. 407), *Homiliae super Epistulam ad Colossenses* 12.5, says: "What need is there for dance? In the mysteries of the Greeks there are dances, in ours, rather, silence and order, respect and composure" (our translation).

The Sacraments in General and the Liturgy

sanctification of the person, does not therefore consider a human being as abstract or ideal, but a concrete person just as God has created him or her. This is why he or she needs visible signs to help elevate the soul toward God through corporeality. We have already sufficiently spoken about this. Instead, let us quickly touch on another aspect. In order to sanctify the human person, the Christian Liturgy sanctifies the fundamental dimensions of his or her terrestrial existence: space and time. It is not possible to discuss this theme in sufficient detail here, but we can at least give it a brief comment.

(1) The Liturgy sanctifies space not only with the Sacraments—of which we have spoken and will speak more in the chapters to come—but in other ways too: through the sacramentals, which are the celebrations instituted by the Church for a certain imitation of the Sacraments.[89] The sacramentals, in fact, combine material elements and prayer. The difference between the two is that the Sacraments work *"ex opere operato" (see above)*, while the sacramentals produce effects, especially, *"ex opere operantis Ecclesiae."*[90] The sacramentals are very important, because they consecrate or bless people (e.g., the abbatial blessing or the religious profession) and things, extending the sanctification of Liturgy to almost all spheres of human life (homes, schools, workplaces, transportation, fields, etc.). The sacramentals also include exorcisms, which intend to purify people and places that are under the influence of the devil.

(2) The liturgical sanctification of time is also done in a twofold way: through the Liturgy of the Hours (or Divine Office) and the Liturgical Year. The latter, from the ritual standpoint, is the ordering that the Church gives to her official prayer, subdividing it into annual, seasonal, and weekly periods and cycles. The center of the Liturgical Year is the Easter Triduum. From the theological point of view, the Liturgical Year is Christ himself Who is always present, with His mysteries, in the Church.[91]

The Divine Office is "the prayer of the Mystical Body of Jesus Christ, offered to God in the name and on behalf of all Christians" done by the ministers delegated to this by the Church.[92] With a certain lyricism, then, Pius XII teaches that the Liturgy of the Hours is the reproduction on earth of the hymn with which the angels of Heaven eternally adore the Trinity. This hymn, he says, was brought to earth by the Word when He became incarnate.[93]

---

[89] See Second Vatican Council, *Sacrosanctum Concilium*, §60.
[90] See Second Vatican Council, *Sacrosanctum Concilium*, §60.
[91] For greater detail, see Pius XII, *Mediator Dei*, III; Second Vatican Council, *Sacrosanctum Concilium*, §§102–111.
[92] Pius XII, *Mediator Dei*, III, 1.
[93] Pius XII, *Mediator Dei*, III, 1. Vatican II has also clearly revived the teaching of Pope Pius XII on this (though without citing it): "Christ Jesus, High Priest of the new and eternal

In this song of praise, Christ associates the Mystical Body with Himself. Thus, properly speaking, the Office is—compatibly with the general definition of Liturgy—the prayer of Christ Himself, raised up through our voices. Saint Augustine expresses the concept, writing:

> God could have granted no greater gift to human beings than to cause His Word, through whom He created all things, to be their head, and to fit them to Him as His members. He was thus to be both Son of God and Son of Man, one God with the Father, one human being with us. The consequence is that when we speak to God in prayer we do not separate the Son from God, and when the Body of the Son prays it does not separate its Head from itself. The one sole Savior of His Body is our Lord Jesus Christ, the Son of God, Who prays for us, prays in us, and is prayed to by us. He prays for us as our Priest, He prays in us as our Head, and He is prayed to by us as our God. *Accordingly we must recognize our voices in Him and His accents in ourselves.*[94]

The Church prays the Liturgy of the Hours every day to obey the command of Christ to always pray ceaselessly (see Luke 18:1; Eph 6:18; 1 Thess 5:17). The Divine Office sanctifies the entire day, extending into time the grace offered to the Church, particularly through the Eucharistic Sacrifice.[95]

2.3.2. Liturgy and Priesthood

What was just said about the Divine Office, in conformity with the general definition of Liturgy, makes it seem to us that the divine Worship of the Church is first and foremost an action of Christ as Priest, Head of the Mystical Body,

---

covenant, taking human nature, introduced into this earthly exile that hymn which is sung throughout all ages in the halls of Heaven. He joins the entire community of mankind to Himself, associating it with His own singing of this canticle of divine praise. For He continues His priestly work through the agency of His Church, which is ceaselessly engaged in praising the Lord and interceding for the salvation of the whole world. She does this, not only by celebrating the Eucharist, but also in other ways, especially by praying the Divine Office" (*Sacrosanctum Concilium*, §83).

[94] Saint Augustine of Hippo, *Enarrationes in Psalmos* 85.1, in *The Works of Saint Augustine: A Translation for the 21st Century*, vol. III/18, trans. Maria Boulding (Hyde Park, NY: New City Press, 2002), 221.

[95] Further insights are found in the Second Vatican Council, *Sacrosanctum Concilium*, ch. 4.

The Sacraments in General and the Liturgy

Who unites His members to Himself. From the theological standpoint, it is very important to understand that, when the Church celebrates the Liturgy, it is actually first of all Christ who celebrates. The Church celebrates inasmuch as she is associated with the celebrating activity of Jesus Christ. Thus, Christian Worship is defined as an exercise of the priesthood of the whole Christ, Head and members. Let us offer two points on this to consider.

1. Theological Description of the Activity of Worship

Pius XII described with great accuracy the way in which, in mystery, the Liturgical celebration takes place. He did so within the general definition of the Liturgy, which we presented above. While, indeed, Vatican II better highlighted the aspect of the signs, Pius XII's definition is more complete in the description of the exercise of the priesthood of Christ, when he notes: "The sacred Liturgy is, consequently, the public Worship which our Redeemer as Head of the Church renders to the Father, as well as the Worship which the community of the faithful renders to its Founder, and through Him to the heavenly Father." The activity of Worship is therefore performed like this: it is first and foremost Christ—Who as a true man also has the duty to adore God—to perform the role of Priest. Thus, as a man, He gives Worship to the Father. He is indeed the Second Adam, Who lives a perfect human life, which Adam had a duty to live and chose not to. While Adam preferred to follow himself, that is, he oriented himself toward himself rather than toward God, Christ on the contrary performed the fundamental duty of being human: orienting Himself and His life toward God. However, Christ did not do this just as an individual: He, in fact, is the Head of the Church, the Mystical Body. He is in the supernatural order what Adam was in the natural order: the progenitor. Thus, Christ associates to Himself, almost contains in Himself, all the living members of His Mystical Body, who for this reason adore the Father through Him, with Him, and in Him, as it says in the above-mentioned doxology: "*Per Ipsum et cum Ipso et in Ipso*"—Through Him [Christ], with Him, and in Him."

We must not forget, however, that Jesus is also God, as the above-cited Saint Augustine reminded us: Christ "prays for us as our Priest; He prays in us as our Head; He is prayed to by us as our God." Our adoration to the Father is not un-mediated, but mediated. And it is theologically described like so: we give Worship to Christ, our Head, as He is God incarnate. Adoring Him—Who as man and Priest adores the Father, while as God receives our adoration—we adore the Father through Christ. *Christian* Worship, therefore, has an irrepressible dimension of mediation. Christ is the Mediator between

God and human beings (see 1 Tim 2:5); nobody has access to the Father if not through Him (see John 14:6). This is why the liturgical prayers of the Church always end with the formula of Christological mediation: "Through our Lord Jesus Christ..." This final formula of prayers has two versions: a long one and a short one. The short one simply says, "Through Christ our Lord. Amen." It was introduced (as a conclusion of the orations) by the liturgical reform made after the Second Vatican Council. In the extraordinary form of the Roman Rite, that is, in the liturgical books preceding the reform that followed the Second Vatican Council, and which can be freely used today,[96] the long form is always used at the end of the orations. Instead, in the ordinary form of the Rite, approved by Saint Paul VI, the long formula is maintained only at the end of the main oration of the Holy Mass (the "Collect"), while for the others the short version is introduced. The long formulation reads: "Through our Lord Jesus Christ, your Son, who lives and reigns with you in the unity of the Holy Spirit, one God, forever and ever. Amen."[97] Although the brief formulation is theologically correct, the long version is preferable, not only because it better explains the dual nature of Jesus Christ, but also because it highlights a very important element, implied in Pius XII's description: the pneumatological dimension. The explicit mention of the Holy Spirit is an important strength of the long formula. That the Son incarnate Worships the Father, that we do the same towards Him and, through Him, towards the Father: all this happens—so to speak—in the Trinitarian "divine environment," which involves the active cooperation of the Holy Spirit in the liturgical action.

The fundamental priestly, or mediatory, element of the Christian Liturgy, now recalled, leads us to a second point.

2. The Liturgical Priesthood

The fact that Christ is the only Mediator, and the High Priest (see Heb 2:17; 3:1; etc.) of our faith and our Worship does not imply that there are no other forms of priesthood in the Church. On the contrary, as we already mentioned in previous chapters, the unique mediation of Christ is the cause of various participatory mediations, all stemming from His.[98] The dogmatic doctrine on the Sacrament of Holy Orders will be presented in the next chapter. Here we

---

[96] See Benedict XVI, *Summorum Pontificum* (2007); Pontifical Commission Ecclesia Dei, *Universae Ecclesiae* (2011).
[97] "*Per Dominum nostrum Jesum Christum Filium tuum qui tecum vivit et regnat in unitate Spiritus Sancti, Deus per omnia saecula saeculorum. Amen.*"
[98] See Second Vatican Council, *Lumen Gentium*, §62.

The Sacraments in General and the Liturgy

shall limit ourselves to mentioning that the Liturgical celebration of divine Worship includes the exercise of the priesthood of Christ and also that of the Church, which is participation in the former.

Now, there are clearly two different priesthoods in the Church: baptismal and ministerial. *Lumen Gentium* has a valuable text in this regard:

> Though they differ from one another in essence and not only in degree, the common priesthood of the faithful and the ministerial or hierarchical priesthood are nonetheless interrelated: each of them in its own special way is a participation in the one priesthood of Christ. The ministerial priest, by the sacred power he enjoys, teaches and rules the priestly people; acting in the Person of Christ, he makes present the Eucharistic Sacrifice, and offers it to God in the name of all the people. But the faithful, in virtue of their royal priesthood, join in the offering of the Eucharist. They likewise exercise that priesthood in receiving the Sacraments, in prayer and thanksgiving, in the witness of a holy life, and by self-denial and active charity.[99]

In this text, we observe several things: (1) The two priesthoods are presented as different participations in the one priesthood of Jesus Christ. (2) For this reason, they are not competitive, but are harmoniously ordered toward each other. (3) They are, however, quite distinct, not only from the standpoint of hierarchy, but also from that of essence: that is, they are truly two different things, having different natures. (4) The progression of the roles of the two priesthoods is present primarily (even if not exclusively) from the standpoint of the different liturgical functions that they perform.

The last aspect in particular is the one we would like to briefly focus on here. What the Council says—citing in the footnotes texts of Pius XII, including *Mediator Dei*—is a good synthesis of what Pope Pius XII had previously taught very extensively in his liturgical encyclical in 1947. Let us see, therefore, what the Pontiff wrote about the two priesthoods, for what regards their liturgical functions, especially in the celebration of the Holy Mass:

> That is why the visible, external priesthood of Jesus Christ is not handed down indiscriminately to all members of the Church in

---

[99] Second Vatican Council, *Lumen Gentium*, §10. It should be noted that the expression, "in essence and not only in degree" [*essentia et non gradu tantum*] comes, although not explicitly cited, from Pius XII, *Allocutio Cardinalibus atque Antistitibus* (1954), in which the Pope said: "*non gradu tantum, sed etiam essentia.*"

general, but is conferred on designated men, through what may be called the spiritual generation of Holy Orders. This latter [is] one of the seven Sacraments. . . . In the same way, actually that Baptism is the distinctive mark of all Christians, and serves to differentiate them from those who . . . are not members of Christ, the Sacrament of Holy Orders sets the priest apart from the rest of the faithful who have not received this consecration. For they alone, in answer to an inward supernatural call, have entered the august ministry, where they are assigned to service in the sanctuary.[100]

Here the Pope recalls the essential distinction between the baptismal and ministerial priesthoods, mentioning that only ordained ministers can officiate Worship at the altar. In fact, as the Holy Father specifies, the consecration of the Eucharistic Species is the prerogative of ordained priests alone: "The unbloody immolation [of the Mass] is performed by the priest and by him alone."[101] But in *Mediator Dei*, Pius XII greatly emphasizes that, having made this fundamental distinction,[102] the baptized have an active role, they really exercise their royal priesthood in Worship. They do it by offering Christ to the Father together with the minister. In other words, if it is only the ordained minister to consecrate the Eucharist, and thus place Christ on the altar in the state of the Victim, it is however the whole liturgical assembly to offer to the Father His incarnate Son in expiation for sins. This is expressed by Pius XII like so:

> The [ordained] priest acts for the people only because he represents Jesus Christ, Who is Head of all His members and offers Himself in

---

[100] Pius XII, *Mediator Dei*, I, 3.

[101] Pius XII, *Mediator Dei*, II, 1.

[102] Pius XII insists on this, urging bishops to be clear in this regard: "The fact, however, that the faithful participate in the Eucharistic Sacrifice does not mean that they also are endowed with priestly power. It is very necessary that you make this quite clear to your flocks" (*Mediator Dei*, II, 2). The doctrine of faith of the irrepressible difference between the two priesthoods in the Church was not denied only by Luther in the sixteenth century. Unfortunately, there are ambiguous lines in some sectors of recent theology, even in the Catholic sphere. In the last decades there has been the real risk of thinking that, in the end, the only priesthood in the Church is the baptismal one and that—contrary to the aforementioned dictate of Vatican II—the ministerial priesthood could not be ontologically distinguished from it. It was partially because of this ambiguity that Benedict XVI wanted to proclaim a special Year for Priests (see the *Proclamation Letter* of June 16, 2009), on the occasion of the 150th anniversary of the death of the holy *Curé d'Ars*. In the splendid *Homily in the Holy Mass for the Conclusion of the Year for Priests*, June 11, 2010, Pope Benedict also recalled that the priesthood is not simply an "office," but a Sacrament.

their stead. Hence, he [the priest] goes to the altar as the minister of Christ, inferior to Christ but superior to the people. The people, on the other hand, since they in no sense represent the divine Redeemer and are not mediator between themselves and God, can in no way possess the sacerdotal power.

All this has the certitude of faith. However, it must also be said that the faithful do offer the divine Victim, though in a different sense. . . . We are happy to recall one of St. Robert Bellarmine's [d. 1621] many statements on this subject. "The sacrifice," he says "is principally offered in the Person of Christ. Thus the oblation that follows the consecration is a sort of attestation that the whole Church consents in the oblation made by Christ, and offers it along with Him."[103] Moreover, the rites and prayers of the Eucharistic Sacrifice signify and show no less clearly that the oblation of the Victim is made by the priests in company with the people. . . . Nor is it to be wondered at, that the faithful should be raised to this dignity. By the waters of Baptism, as by common right, Christians are made members of the Mystical Body of Christ the Priest, and by the "character" which is imprinted on their souls, they are appointed to give Worship to God. Thus they participate, according to their condition, in the priesthood of Christ. . . .

In this most important subject it is necessary, in order to avoid giving rise to a dangerous error, that we define the exact meaning of the word "offer." The unbloody immolation at the words of consecration, when Christ is made present upon the altar in the state of a Victim, is performed by the priest and by him alone, as the representative of Christ and not as the representative of the faithful. But it is because the priest places the divine Victim upon the altar that he offers it to God the Father as an oblation for the glory of the Blessed Trinity and for the good of the whole Church. Now the faithful participate in the oblation, understood in this limited sense, after their own

---

[103] Saint Robert Bellarmine, *De Missa* 1.27. Today there are more than a few scholars who accept—against the Council of Trent—the opinion of the Orthodox that it is not the speaking of the words of Christ on the bread and the chalice that consecrates the Eucharist (on these questions, see Chapter Eleven). The text of Saint Robert, assumed into the papal Magisterium, proves enlightening on the issue: the oblation that follows the consecration does not produce transubstantiation (it already happened) but possesses the other meaning described by the Jesuit Doctor.

fashion and in a twofold manner, namely, because they not only offer the Sacrifice by the hands of the priest, but also, to a certain extent, in union with him. It is by reason of this participation that the offering made by the people is also included in liturgical Worship.[104]

Insofar as they are baptized, all Christians are "liturgical beings," with an active role in Worship. The theme of active participation deserves further examination.

2.3.3. Active Participation

1. Prior to the Second Vatican Council

The expression "active participation" (*actuosa participatio*) was not created by Vatican II, even if it occupies a central place in *Sacrosanctum Concilium*. It entered into magisterial language much earlier—in 1903, to be exact—in a *motu proprio*, written in Italian by Saint Pius X, on the theme of sacred music:

> Being that it is Our most intense desire that the true Christian spirit flourish in every way and is maintained in all the faithful, it is necessary to first tend to the sanctity and dignity of the temple, where the faithful gather to draw this spirit from its first and indispensable source, which is the active participation in the sacrosanct mysteries and the public and solemn prayer of the Church.[105]

The expression was reprised by Pius XI, again in reference to sacred music:

> In order that the faithful may more actively participate in divine Worship, let them be made once more to sing the Gregorian Chant, so far as it belongs to them to take part in it. It is most important that when the faithful assist at the sacred ceremonies, or when pious sodalities take part with the clergy in a procession, they should not be merely detached and silent spectators, but, filled with a deep sense of the beauty of the Liturgy, they should sing alternately with the clergy or the choir, as it is prescribed.[106]

---

[104] Pius XII, *Mystici Corporis*, II, 1.
[105] Saint Pius X, *Tra le Sollecitudini* [*Among the Cares*] (1903), introduction (our translation).
[106] Pius XI, *Divini Cultus* (1928), §9 (translation: *adoremus.org*).

The historical context clarifies the meaning of these requirements: the great polyphony or even the great orchestra concerts had often replaced Gregorian chant in Catholic Worship. These magnificent compositions had the limit of preventing any form of song to the faithful, while the Gregorian, at least in its most accessible and most famous parts, allowed the priest, the *schola cantorum*, and the faithful to alternate. The two Popes, therefore, recall the need to return to the use of Gregorian chant—without excluding other compositions—to encourage the active participation of the faithful, who would otherwise be forced to attend the Ministry as "silent spectators,"[107] practically as if they were in a theater. In this sense, the expression "active participation" is connected to an activity (to sing), but not to "activism." It is not a frenetic act, something to do for the sake of doing, but to praise and worship God through the Gregorian chants, namely the liturgical chants of highest value according to liturgical Tradition.

It is therefore implied that the most important aspect of active participation consists in the internal orientation of the soul toward God. This aspect is fully brought to light by the Magisterium of Pius XII:

> All the faithful should be aware that to participate in the Eucharistic Sacrifice is their chief duty and supreme dignity, and that not in an inert and negligent fashion, giving way to distractions and day-dreaming, but with such earnestness and concentration that they may be united as closely as possible with the High Priest.[108]

As can be seen, the concept of participation is consistent with the general definition of the Liturgy and with the description of the performance of the priestly role of the faithful in Worship. Pius XII also delineates exactly what constitutes "intimate contact" with Christ. The essence of active participation is to:

> Possess, as far as is humanly possible, the same dispositions as those which the divine Redeemer had when He offered Himself in sacrifice: that is to say, they should in a humble attitude of mind, pay adoration, honor, praise and thanksgiving to the supreme majesty of God. Moreover, it means that they must assume to some extent the character of a victim, that they deny themselves as the Gospel com-

---

[107] This expression of Pius XI would be reprised by Pius XII, *Mediator Dei*, VI, 2; by Sacred Congregation of Rites, *Instructio de Musica Sacra et Sacra Liturgia* (1958); and by Second Vatican Council, *Sacrosanctum Concilium*, §48.

[108] Pius XII, *Mediator Dei*, II, 2.

mands, that freely and of their own accord they do penance and that each detests and satisfies for his sins. It means, in a word, that we must all undergo with Christ a mystical death on the cross.[109]

Far from being entirely involved with things to be done during the rite, active participation is above all an internal state. However, as the *et-et* demands, to affirm the principality of the internal element does not at all exclude the importance of active participation in the external forum as well. The same Pontiff taught it clearly, through a document of the Roman Curia:

> Interior participation is the most important; this consists in paying devout attention, and in lifting up the heart to God in prayer.... The participation of the congregation becomes more complete, however, when, in addition to this interior disposition, exterior participation is manifested by external acts, such as bodily position (kneeling, standing, sitting), ceremonial signs, and especially responses, prayers, and singing.... When the papal documents treat of "active participation" they are speaking of this general participation, of which the outstanding example is the priest, and his ministers who serve at the altar with the proper interior dispositions, and carefully observe the rubrics, and ceremonies.[110]

It should be emphasized that the Magisterium understands active participation according to the *et-et*: it implies both the internal participation of the soul, and scrupulous observance of the liturgical norms (*ars celebrandi*) that entail a whole series of external signs and gestures.

2. In the Liturgical Constitution of the Council

Vatican II resumed and strengthened the teaching on the *actuosa participatio*. The Council says that the Shepherds must do everything possible so that the faithful take part in the liturgical action *scienter, actuose et fructuose* ("consciously, actively, and fruitfully").[111] Notice that the theme of "activity" is found at the center between that of awareness (to understand what is being done) and that of efficacy (to receive the grace and bear fruit in it). It is there-

---

[109] Pius XII, *Mediator Dei*, II, 2. See also II, 3.
[110] Sacra Congregatio Rituum, *Instructio de Musica Sacra et Sacra Liturgia*, §22 (translation: adoremus.org).
[111] Second Vatican Council, *Sacrosanctum Concilium*, §11.

fore not a mindless and purposeless activity. It is an activity supported by an adequate liturgical formation and above all by a constant internal orientation toward the Lord, the source of grace (see above). Only in this way is participation truly active and not representative of an unbridled and senseless liturgical activism, without content or direction. This is confirmed in Sacrosanctum Concilium §14, a key text:

> Mother Church earnestly desires that all the faithful should be led to that fully conscious, and active [*plenam, consciam, actuosam*] participation in liturgical celebrations which is demanded by the very nature of the Liturgy. Such participation by the Christian people . . . is their right and duty by reason of their Baptism. In the restoration and promotion of the sacred Liturgy, this full and active participation by all the people is the aim to be considered before all else; for it is the primary and indispensable source from which the faithful are to derive the true Christian spirit; and therefore pastors of souls must zealously strive to achieve it, by means of the necessary instruction, in all their pastoral work.

The Council also maintains the *et-et* because it highlights both the internal aspects of Worship and the visible, external ones. For example, again at §11, it is recommended that in divine Worship "the laws governing valid and licit celebration be observed."[112] The constitution, then, also motivates the future liturgical reforms based on the principle of favoring the active participation of the faithful.[113] We therefore see that external aspects (the laws) and internal aspects (active participation) always go together.

---

[112] The translation of §11 provided by *vatican.va*, which reads "something more is required than the mere observation of the laws," should be corrected. The original Latin text says something different: "*non solum observentur leges ad validam et licitam celebrationem*," where "*non solum observentur*" cannot be rendered with "something more is required," but must be translated as "not only is it necessary to observe." The meaning of the text is not that we should go beyond the observance of liturgical laws to look for "something more," but that we should respect them faithfully while adding something else (internal participation) to them. At §22 (subsection 3), the constitution, after having recalled that the regulation of the holy Liturgy belongs to the Apostolic See—and within certain limits, to the bishops—concludes: "Therefore no other person, even if he be a priest, may add, remove, or change anything in the Liturgy on his own authority." This confirms that *Sacrosanctum Concilium* does not aim to diminish the importance of observing liturgical laws and rubrics.

[113] Second Vatican Council, *Sacrosanctum Concilium*, §§21 and 30.

3. After the Second Vatican Council

The interpretation of the conciliar texts has not infrequently presented aspects that are clearly identifiable with the so-called "hermeneutic of discontinuity." This also occurs with respect to the theme of active participation. More than a few authors and pastoral workers have dissolved the harmonious union of the internal and external aspect of this participation, focusing their attention only on the second sphere. A certain activism and "liturgical creativity" derives from it. While the Magisterium teaches that we need to take internal and external participation together, the first—especially as described by Pius XII—has actually been shelved in a great many cases. It was thus decided to only focus on the external participation in the rite, and this led to the habit of many to "customize" or "contextualize" the celebration well beyond the possibilities already provided by the liturgical norms. The Magisterium of the Church has continued and continues to repeat that true active participation is both that of the soul and that of ritual gestures. Thus, the *ars celebrandi*—that is, celebrating as the Church establishes and, at the same time, celebrating whole-heartedly—is, along with the internal orientation of the spirit, a necessary element for a true, conscious, and fruitful participation in divine Worship:

> In the course of the Synod [of 2005], there was frequent insistence on the need to avoid any antithesis between the *ars celebrandi*, the art of proper celebration, and the full, active and fruitful participation of all the faithful. The primary way to foster the participation of the People of God in the sacred Rite is the proper celebration of the Rite itself. The *ars celebrandi* is the best way to ensure their *actuosa participatio*. The *ars celebrandi* is the fruit of faithful adherence to the liturgical norms in all their richness; indeed, for two thousand years this way of celebrating has sustained the faith life of all believers, called to take part in the celebration as the People of God, a royal priesthood, a holy nation (see 1 Pet 2:4–5, 9).[114]

It is with this that we can conclude our brief overview of the theological understanding of the Liturgy. The many other topics belonging to the *scientia liturgica* left aside, or only hinted at, need not be addressed here. It was sufficient to show that Worship must be understood not only from the historical, spiritual, pastoral, and juridical standpoints—undoubtedly perspectives of considerable importance—but also and especially from the truly theologi-

---

[114] Benedict XVI, *Sacramentum Caritatis*, §38.

cal standpoint.¹¹⁵ Even from the essential treatment offered, it very clearly emerges that, under many aspects, the mystery of Christian Worship is also a clear expression of the central principle of *et-et*.

---

[115] See Second Vatican Council, *Sacrosanctum Concilium*, §16, which cites these five perspectives of study for the liturgical formation of clerics and places the theological one in first place.

10

The Sacraments in Particular

For a long time, the word "Sacrament" had a broader sense than it has for us today. It also referred, in addition to the seven principal celebrations, to many other rites and customs of the Church in the sphere of the Liturgy and prayer.[1] Starting with Sicard of Cremona (d. 1215), the term began to be used only for the seven principal rites of the Liturgy, which are Sacraments *par excellence*. The theology of the "Master of the Sentences," Peter Lombard (d. 1160) gave an impetus to this choice, as of course, the works of Saint Thomas Aquinas did later. As we already saw in the previous chapter, the Council of Trent defined that in the Church the Sacraments in a full and proper sense are precisely seven in number (no more or fewer).

1. Subdivision of the Sacraments

We have emphasized, when discussing the Sacraments in general, that they are contextualized within the concrete history of salvation, which brings with it an aspect that in the Christological chapter we identified as "salvation," and another that is "redemption." In clearer terms, the Sacraments play, in the concreteness of the development of salvation history, both a positive role of promotion and growth and a curative role of healing and reconstruction. Saint Thomas also recalls these truths in order to justify the number of the

---

[1] For example, Saint Peter Damian (d. 1072) mentions twelve of them in *Sermo 69*, among which are the anointing of the king, the dedication of a church, and the institution of canons.

Sacraments. The Angelic Doctor says that they serve, on the one hand, to perfect the human being with respect to carrying out divine Worship and, on the other hand, to offer a remedy against the evil of sin. We could also reword this by saying that the Sacraments are, at the same time, *both* rewards[2] *and* medicine.[3] In agreement with this premise, Saint Thomas affirms that the seven Sacraments achieve these ends very well. In fact, on the one hand, they sustain and give a positive push to the supernatural life of the person; and, on the other hand, they represent remedies to the seven classes of sin into which human beings fall (or at least toward which they are inclined). On the positive side, just as in the life of each person there is a personal and a social aspect, so there are five Sacraments that regard the individual and two that are ordered to the good of the community. In the negative:

> Baptism is opposed to the absence of spiritual life; Confirmation is opposed to the spiritual weakness that is found in the young; the Eucharist is opposed to the instability of the soul with respect to sin; Penance is against the actual sin committed after Baptism; Extreme Unction is against the remainder of sins not completely removed by Penance, or sin remaining through neglect or ignorance; Holy Orders is opposed to the dissolution of the community; Marriage is opposed to personal concupiscence and against the voids that death opens in society.[4]

Therefore, there are different ways of listing or subdividing the Sacra-

---

[2] The Sacraments are a reward in the sense that they presuppose some merit on the part of the one who receives them: for example, receiving Baptism requires the previous acceptance of God in faith on the part of the one being baptized (or, in the case of the Baptism of children, on the part of the parents); to receive the Eucharist in a fruitful way one needs to be in the state of grace, as Saint Paul teaches (see 1 Cor 11:26–30). If such merit is not possessed, the reception of Communion does not heal, but on the contrary it makes one sicker, as is said in the hymn *Lauda Sion* of the Office of the Feast of *Corpus Christi*: "*Sumunt boni sumunt mali / sorte tamen inaequali / vitae vel interitus. / Mors est malis vita bonis / vide paris sumptionis / quam dispar exitus*" ("The good consume, the evil consume / with such an unequal outcome / of life and death / death for the evil, life for the good / see that for the same consumption / how different is the outcome" [our translation]).

[3] Even the medicinal character of the Sacraments is broadly attested both in Scripture (see the Eucharistic Blood of Christ "shed on behalf of many for the forgiveness of sins": Matt 26:28) and by the Tradition as well. We can cite as an example in this regard, "I ought always to accept Him [in the Sacrament], that He may always dismiss my sins. I, who always sin, should always have a remedy" (Saint Ambrose of Milan [d. 397], *De sacramentis* 4.6.28, in *FCNT*, vol. 44, trans. Roy Deferrari [Washington, DC: CUA Press, 1963], 306).

[4] *ST* III, q. 65, a. 1 (our translation).

ments: (1) Distinguishing between those that have primarily personal ends and those that have primarily social ones.[5] In this case, the second category would include Holy Orders and Matrimony, because the former serves to provide sacred ministers to the ecclesial Society, while the latter is aimed at sanctifying the union of spouses from whom children are born, who increase the number of people in society and in the Church. Consequently, the first category of the primary division would include the other five Sacraments, directed mainly at the growth and spiritual healing of those who receive them. (2) Ordering them according to the evil that they oppose, as is the case with the passage of Saint Thomas just cited. (3) Listing them, as some recent theologians like to do (but with a basis in the texts of Saint Thomas), in correspondence with the different phases of human life, for which the Sacraments would be the ritual expression of the natural life of the person. Baptism, for example, is likened to birth, the Eucharist to taking food, Confirmation to entrance into society as adults, etc.

There is a fourth way that we would like to propose: (4) The Sacraments could be distinguished on the basis of their repeatability or non-repeatability (there are indeed *both* repeatable Sacraments *and* unrepeatable ones).[6] There are three Sacraments that are not repeatable, that is, those that can be received only one time in someone's life: Baptism, Confirmation, and Holy Orders. Consequently, in the category of repeatable Sacraments, we find the Eucharist, Reconciliation, Matrimony, and the Anointing of the Sick. Matrimony is considered a repeatable Sacrament since in the case of the death of one of the spouses the other is free to remarry if he or she so desires. The first three Sacraments, on the other hand, are not repeatable because they impress a "character," which will be discussed below. This subdivision is also based on the general bipolarity of Christianity, which we already saw above in the Sacraments, in that they *both* elevate *and* cure.

In this fourth mode of listing them, we see that the sacramental signs *both* establish a new "being-something" *and* they keep alive, that is, they nourish and cure it according to the particular case. Baptism establishes the human being both as an adoptive child of God and as a member of the Church; Confirmation establishes the person both as a soldier for Christ and a witness to His resurrection; Holy Orders establishes the person as minister both of

---

[5] For example, the Council of Florence, *Exsultate Deo* (1439): "The first five [Sacraments] are ordered to the spiritual perfection of each person in himself, and the last two [are directed] to the governance and the increase of the whole Church" (DS 1311).

[6] The same Council of Florence also proposes this subdivision, which we shall cite shortly in the body of the text.

God and the Church. The other Sacraments serve to nourish these gifts, or to recover the grace necessary for their employment. This subdivision is also well understood according to the ecclesiological bipolarity: since the Church is *both* Society *and* Mystery, the non-repeatable Sacraments provide the ecclesial Society with its staff: the members in general (Baptism), the member-soldiers[7] (Confirmation), and the priest members (Holy Orders). The repeatable Sacraments, for their part, correspond to the Church's mystical character, because they concern the effective permanence of being "grafted onto Christ" by the work of grace, like the branches to the vine (see John 15).

We find a testimony of Tradition, in a text of Saint Pacian (second half of fourth century), which lends credit to this grouping of unrepeatable Sacraments:

> Christ, through the Spirit of God, through the ministry of the priest and the power of faith, gives birth to the new man, formed in the mother's womb and welcomed into the Church by the birth of the baptismal font. We must therefore accept Christ, so that He may

---

[7] In recent theology and, consequently, in current ecclesial language, the term soldier has become less and less acceptable, insofar as it was considered inadequate for describing the life of the Christian, better understood in terms of testimony. However, if properly understood, the term is quite valid, in addition to being able to boast a clear traditional foundation. For example: "When struggle and difficult situations catch up with the saints, and when at the same time they bear the insults of some and the advice of others, they defend themselves against the former with the shield of patience, and against the latter they cast the darts of their teaching. By the admirable art of their virtue they apply themselves to both kinds of combat, insofar as they teach their interior adversaries wisely and courageously disdain their exterior ones; their teaching corrects the former, and their tolerance shames the latter. Their patient disdain deals with enemies who rise up against them, while their compassion leads weak citizens back to safety. They resist the former lest they entice others, but they worry about the latter lest they completely lose touch with the upright way of life. Let us watch the soldier [*militem*] in God's camp as he battles both enemies" (Saint Gregory the Great [d. 604], *Moralia in Job* 3.39, in *Gregory the Great: Moral Reflections on the Book of Job*, vol. 1, trans. Brian Kerns [Collegeville, MN: Liturgical Press, 2014], 213). In more recent times, Pope Francis, *Evangelii Gaudium* (2013), §96 has referred to the right attitude of Christians in the Church, making recourse to the metaphor of a "mere private in a unit which continues to fight." After all, the military metaphor is biblically based: see, for example, Eph 6:10–17, which cites battle, armor, shield, and helmet. With a clear reference to the Pauline text, a very ancient author writes: "Please the leader under whom you serve, for from him you receive your pay. May none of you turn out a deserter. Let your Baptism be ever your shield, your faith a helmet, your charity a spear, your patience a panoply" (Saint Ignatius of Antioch [d. ca. 107], *Ad Polycarpum* 6.2, in *FCNT*, vol. 1, trans. Gerald G. Walsh [Washington DC: CUA Press, 2008], 126).

regenerate us. The Apostle John affirms this: "But to those who did accept Him He gave power to become children of God" (John 1:12). This birth cannot take place without the Sacrament of Baptism, of Confirmation and of Holy Orders. In fact, our sins are washed away with Baptism, and with the Confirmation we are infused with the Holy Spirit: we obtain both from the hand and the mouth of the Priest. In this way the entire person is reborn in Christ.[8]

2. The Sacramental Character

In sacramental theology, the word "character" refers to an invisible and permanent sign that is imprinted by some Sacraments on the human being, like a seal is imprinted on wax. Since nothing can eliminate this sign once it has been imprinted, the Sacraments that confer it can be celebrated only once in a lifetime (if the celebration was valid) and furthermore the character itself, precisely because it is indelible, remains forever, even if the person who has received it chooses later to deny the faith.[9]

With a term that has its foundation in Scripture, the character[10] can be called a "seal," even if it is distinct from the "sacramental seal" (or "seal of the confessional") in the strict sense, which is the secrecy that the priest is absolutely obligated to maintain about the sins he has heard in Confession. We could thus, in order to distinguish one from the other, call the former the "seal of the Sacraments." The word "character," however, is preferable, because it eliminates any possible ambiguity.

The *Catechism* associates the two terms and also recalls the New Testament basis of the character:

---

[8] Saint Pacian of Barcellona (d. ca. 391), *Sermo de Baptismo* 6 (our translation).
[9] Unfortunately, for some years now there have been Catholics who, having lost their faith, ask to be "debaptized." The most that can be done in these cases is to note in the parish register of Baptisms that the person asked to be no longer considered Catholic. In fact, it is not only impossible to eliminate the sacramental seal from the soul of these people, but it is in itself incorrect to completely delete the notation of Baptism on the register, because it is a historical event that did happen whether they like it or not. The Church, which granted the Baptism, has the right to preserve its memory even if the person wants to forget it. This guarantees, among other things, the person's rights if he or she wants to return to the Church.
[10] The original Greek term refers to an impression or an engraving (on a coin, for example). At the level of material recurrence, it is explicitly found only in Heb 1:3: Christ "is the refulgence of his [God's] glory, / the very *imprint* [character] of his being."

> *The seal* is a symbol close to that of anointing. "The Father has set his seal" [John 6:27] on Christ and also seals us in him [2 Cor 1:22; Eph 1:13; 4:30]. Because this seal indicates the indelible effect of the anointing with the Holy Spirit in the Sacraments of Baptism, Confirmation, and Holy Orders, the image of the seal (*sphragis*) has been used in some theological traditions to express the indelible "character" imprinted by these three unrepeatable Sacraments. (CCC §698)

Further along, the *Catechism* takes up other basic terms concerning this theme:

> The three Sacraments of Baptism, Confirmation, and Holy Orders confer, in addition to grace, a sacramental *character* or "seal" by which the Christian shares in Christ's priesthood and is made a member of the Church according to different states and functions. This configuration to Christ and to the Church, brought about by the Spirit, is indelible [Cf. Council of Trent (1547): DS 1609]; it remains forever in the Christian as a positive disposition for grace, a promise and guarantee of divine protection, and as a vocation to divine worship and to the service of the Church. Therefore these sacraments can never be repeated. (CCC §1121)

The *Catechism*, therefore, includes its own teaching on the sacramental character into the theme of grace and that of ecclesial incorporation. The sacramental character incorporates persons into the Church according to various states and functions, giving different participations in the priesthood of Christ. The character gives the following: (1) Disposing configuration to grace: the one who receives the character is "con-formed," that is, receives a particular form in which to receive the specific grace that he or she needs to carry out his or her particular ecclesial task, like a vessel that is given a specific form, suitable for the use that will be made of it. (2) The promise and guarantee of divine protection (see, for example, Matt 28:20). It is as if the one who is "sealed" by the Sacraments carries a sign that distinguishes him or her from the unsealed, which marks his or her belonging to Christ and to the Church and therefore recalls the special divine protection—it could be compared to a "safe conduct" in a warzone. (3) The vocation to divine Worship and to the service of the Church: in particular, Baptism qualifies one for the Liturgy (see the previous chapter), and Confirmation empowers one in the struggle for Christ and His mystical Bride. Holy Orders marks one for configuration to Christ and the total dedication to the ecclesial ministry (see further on).

We note that the impossibility of cancelling the character indicates the objectivity of this supernatural gift, which reconnects it with the principle *ex opere operato*. Where Baptism, Confirmation, and Holy Orders are validly celebrated, there is an objective impression of the character in the soul of the recipient of the Sacrament, beyond his or her personal merit and holiness. We can quickly retrace the primary magisterial pronouncements on the matter:

> Among these [seven] Sacraments, there are three, namely, Baptism, Confirmation, and Orders, that imprint an indelible character [*characterem ... imprimunt*] on the soul, which is a type of spiritual sign that is distinct from the rest. As a consequence they may not be repeated in the same person. The other four, however, do not imprint a character and allow for repetition.[11]

> If anyone says that in three Sacraments, namely, Baptism, Confirmation, and Orders, a character is not imprinted [*non imprimi characterem*] on the soul, that is, a kind of indelible spiritual sign by reason of which these Sacraments cannot be repeated, let him be anathema.[12]

> In the Sacrament of Orders, as also in Baptism and Confirmation, a character is imprinted [*character imprimitur*] that can be neither erased nor taken away.[13]

Based on the fact that the character is indelible, the Magisterium teaches the impossibility of the reiteration of the three mentioned Sacraments:

> Baptism, Confirmation, and Orders cannot be repeated without sacrilege.[14]

> Of these (seven Sacraments), Baptism, Confirmation, and Orders cannot be repeated (without sacrilege).[15]

---

[11] Council of Florence, *Exsultate Deo* (DS 1313).
[12] Council of Trent, *Decretum de Sacramentis* (1547), can. 9 (DS 1609).
[13] Council of Trent, *Doctrina et Canones de Sacramento Ordinis*, ch. 4 (DS 1767); see can. 4 (DS 1774).
[14] Pius IV, *Iniunctum Nobis* (1564) (DS 1846).
[15] Benedict XIV, *Numper ad Nos* (1743) (DS 2536).

The Sacraments in Particular

> The Sacraments of Baptism, Confirmation, and Orders, which imprint a character, cannot be repeated.[16]

It must be said that various theologians in recent times are rather skeptical toward these teachings, especially seeing in the background of the doctrine of the sacramental character an unacceptable "reifying" perspective—an objectification of the effect of certain Sacraments. The idea of an indelible sign that is imprinted on the soul is repugnant to some mentalities present in recent theology, marked by a spiritualist and subjectivist-existential tendency. Moreover, some of these scholars have stated that the doctrine of character did not even arise until the twelfth century, being unknown to the Church in earlier times. But, in fact, there is a consistent patristic basis for the doctrine of the sacramental character. For example, we can mention the following:

> [The faith] bids us bear in mind that we have received Baptism for the remission of sins . . . and that this Baptism is the seal of eternal life, and is the new birth unto God [*sigillum aeternae vitae et regenerationem*].[17]

> If the Sacrament of Christian Baptism, being always one and the same, is of value even when administered by heretics, and though not in that case sufficing to secure to the baptized person participation in eternal life, does suffice to seal his consecration to God; and if this consecration makes him who, having the mark of the Lord [*dominicus character*], remains outside of the Lord's flock, guilty as a heretic, but reminds us at the same time that he is to be corrected by sound doctrine, but not to be a second time consecrated by repetition of the ordinance.[18]

In what follows, we propose the presentation of the six Sacraments—leaving the discussion on the Eucharist for the next chapter—following the plan for presentation that we have proposed, structured on the basis of the principle of *et-et*, which reveals a bipolarity between the Sacraments, for

---

[16] *Codex Iuris Canonici* (1917), can. 732 §1; reprised identically in the *Codex* of 1983, can. 845 §1.

[17] Saint Irenaeus of Lyon (d. ca. 202), *Demonstratio apostolicae praedicationis* 3, in *Irenaeus's Demonstration of the Apostolic Preaching*, trans. J. Armitage Robinson (Aldershot, UK: Ashgate, 2002), 2.

[18] Saint Augustine of Hippo (d. 430), *Epistula 98.5*, in *NPNF* vol. 1, trans. J. G. Cunningham (Peabody, MA: Hendrickson Publishers, Inc., 1994), 408.

which there are both those that impress the character, and are therefore unrepeatable, and those that do not imprint it and can be received multiple times. In the cases in which we do not resume themes already touched upon in the previous chapter, it is because we believe that what was already stated about those matters is sufficient.

3. Unrepeatable Sacraments

3.1. Baptism

3.1.1. The Baptism of Christ in the Jordan

A first thing to note concerns the fact that the baptism of Christ in the river Jordan by Saint John the Baptist is a founding event with respect to the Sacrament of Baptism—but, it is not that Sacrament. Jesus did not receive the Sacrament of Baptism from John. On the contrary, the event is read by the Tradition as the moment in which the Lord sanctified the waters, immersing His most holy body in them, making them fitting for conveying the grace of the Christian Sacrament. Immersing Himself in the Jordan, Christ drowns the man of sin and gives us the possibility of being reborn to new life:

> Christ is illumined, let us shine forth with Him. Christ is baptized, let us descend with Him that we may also ascend with Him. . . . But John baptizes, Jesus comes to Him . . . perhaps to sanctify the Baptist himself, but certainly to bury the whole of the old Adam in the water; and before this and for the sake of this, to sanctify Jordan.[19]

> Christ *has appeared* (Titus 2:11) to the world, and having adorned the unadorned world, He filled it with radiant joy. He took upon Him the sin of the world and overthrew the enemy of the world. He sanctified the fountains of waters, and enlightened people's souls.[20]

---

[19] Saint Gregory Nazianzus (d. 390), *Oratio* 39.14–15, in *NPNF*, vol. 7, trans. Charles Gordon Browne and James Edward Swallow (Peabody, MA: Hendrickson Publishers, Inc., 1994), 357.

[20] Saint Proclus of Constantinople (d. 446), *Oratio 7*: "In sancta Theophania," 1, in *Proclus Bishop of Constantinople Homilies on the Life of Christ*, trans. Jan Harm Barkhuizen [Brisbane, AU: Centre for Early Christian Studies Australian Catholic University, 2001], 125).

That is why the Lord Jesus went to the river for baptism, that is why He wanted His holy body to be washed with Jordan's water. Someone might ask, "Why would a holy man desire baptism?" Listen to the answer: Christ is baptized, not to be made holy by the water, but to make the water holy, and by His cleansing to purify the waters which He touched. For the consecration of Christ involves a more significant consecration of the water. For when the Savior is washed all water for our baptism is made clean, purified at its source for the dispensing of baptismal grace to the people of future ages. Christ is the first to be baptized, then, so that Christians will follow after Him with confidence.[21]

Inspired by these teachings, a Dominican author from the seventeenth century interpreted the crossing of the Kidron stream (which Jesus did on the night in which He was betrayed, going to Gethsemane [see John 18:1]) in light of the baptism of Christ in the Jordan:

Jesus crosses the Kidron stream. The satisfaction that was owed to God was a torrent that neither angels nor men could cross. . . . It is therefore He who first crossed the torrent Who eliminated the difficulty of crossing it after Him. He sanctified the waters as with another baptism: it is the name He gives to the afflictions when He speaks to the sons of Zebedee. He did even more than this: with His own Person, He conferred divine qualities to the waters.[22]

3.1.2. The Necessity of Baptism

Baptism is the first of the Sacraments, also called *vitae spiritualis ianua* ("door of spiritual life"), or *ianua Sacramentorum* ("the door to enter into sacramental life").[23] Baptism is necessary along with faith for eternal salvation:

---

[21] Saint Maximus of Turin (d. 465), *Sermo 8*: "De sancta Epiphania," 2 (translation: *crossroadsinitiative.com*).

[22] Louis Chardon (d. 1651), Méditations sur la Passion de Notre-Seigneur Jésus-Christ, "Meditation for January 5" (our translation).

[23] "The 'door of faith' (Acts 14:27) is always open for us, ushering us into the life of communion with God and offering entry into His Church. It is possible to cross that threshold when the Word of God is proclaimed and the heart allows itself to be shaped by transforming grace. To enter through that door is to set out on a journey that lasts a lifetime. It begins with Baptism (see Rom 6:4)" (Benedict XVI, *Porta Fidei* [2011], §1).

The Lord himself affirms that Baptism is necessary for salvation [see John 3:5]. He also commands his disciples to proclaim the Gospel to all nations and to baptize them (*Mt* 28:19-20' cf. Council of Trend [1547] DS 1618; LG 14; AG 5). Baptism is necessary for salvation for those to whom the Gospel has been proclaimed and who have had the possibility of asking for this Sacrament. The Church does not know of any means other than Baptism that assures entry into eternal beatitude. (CCC §1257)

Therefore, under normal conditions, *both* faith *and* Baptism are necessary for eternal salvation. The normal conditions are given by the fact that the person has effectively had the possibility of knowing Christ and desiring His salvation. Whoever does not know Christ—or anyone to whom He has not been adequately preached or witnessed—can be excused for not having asked for Baptism and can be put in contact with the Paschal Mystery of Christ in ways that are known to the Holy Spirit:

> Therefore, all must be converted to Him, made known by the Church's preaching, and all must be incorporated into Him by Baptism and into the Church which is His Body. For Christ Himself "by stressing in express language the necessity of faith and Baptism (cf. Mark 16:16; John 3:5), at the same time confirmed the necessity of the Church, into which men enter by Baptism, as by a door. Therefore those men cannot be saved, who though aware that God, through Jesus Christ founded the Church as something necessary, still do not wish to enter into it, or to persevere in it" [*Lumen Gentium*, §14]. Therefore though God in ways known to Himself can lead those inculpably ignorant of the Gospel to find that faith without which it is impossible to please Him (Heb 11:6), yet a necessity lies upon the Church (1 Cor 9:16), and at the same time a sacred duty, to preach the Gospel. And hence missionary activity today as always retains its power and necessity.[24]

> Since Christ died for all men, and since the ultimate vocation of man is in fact one, and divine, we ought to believe that the Holy Spirit in a manner known only to God offers to every man the possibility of being associated with this paschal mystery.[25]

---

[24] Second Vatican Council, *Ad Gentes* (1965), §7.
[25] Second Vatican Council, *Gaudium et Spes* (1965), §22.

The Sacraments in Particular

3.1.3. Sacrament of Faith

Being a Sacrament of faith, Baptism requires the latter virtue. In the case of an adult catechumen, the faith is that of the very person being baptized, while in the case of the Baptism of children,[26] it is the Church herself that offers her faith, in particular through the representation of the parents and godparents.[27] Consequently, those who arrive at Baptism as adults are prepared with a previous catechetical journey, while those who receive it as babies must be formed in the faith through a later catechesis. In the ancient Church, Baptisms done in adulthood were much more frequent than they are today, which is why the catechumenate developed, as a way of preparation for the reception of the Sac-

---

[26] Even if there is no shortage of ancient polemics, it began in the modern era that the opportunity, and even the validity of so-called "paedobaptism," has been recurrently contested. But even in the Acts of the Apostles, there is talk of whole families who were baptized (see, for example, 16:33), which was a concrete way of obeying the Lord's command: "Let the children come to me; do not prevent them, for the kingdom of God belongs to such as these. Amen, I say to you, whoever does not accept the kingdom of God like a child will not enter it" (Mark 10:14-15). The custom of paedobaptism is very ancient and dates back to the Apostles themselves: *"Ecclesia ab Apostolis Traditionem suscepit, etiam parvulis baptismum dare"* ("The Church has received the Tradition from the Apostles to give Baptism even to little children": Origen of Alexandria [d. 254], *Commentarius in Epistolam ad Romanos* 5.9, in *FCNT*, vol. 103, trans. Thomas P. Scheck [Washington, DC: CUA, 2001], 367). With greater authority, the Council of Trent teaches the same: "In accordance with Apostolic Tradition, 'even children who of themselves cannot have yet committed any sin are truly baptized for the remission of sins'" (*Decretum de Peccato Originali* (1546), §4 [DS 1514]; the citation is from the Fifteenth Synod of Carthage of 418 [DS 223]). Finally, it is absolutely reasonable that Christian parents want their child to become as soon as possible an adoptive child of God and to be freed from original sin, a true and serious illness of the soul. The contemporary argument that parents want their children to choose (as adults) whether or not to be baptized, should for the sake of consistency also advise parents not to give their children any medication in case of illness: that is, they should want to wait for children to grow and decide for themselves whether or not to take care of themselves. In fact, we should not forget that for Christians the health of the soul is more important than that of the body: if, as is proper, the sick child is given medication to heal physical ailments, then he or she must immediately be given the spiritual medicine of Baptism.

[27] "In the Church of the Savior, infants believe by means of other people [*per alios parvuli credunt*], as they have derived those sins which are remitted them in Baptism from other people" (Saint Augustine of Hippo, *Contra duas epistolas pelagianorum* 1.22.40, in *NPNF*, vol. 5, trans. Peter Holmes and Robert Ernest Wallis [Peabody, MA: Hendrickson Publishers, Inc., 1994], 390). The words of Pope Innocent III in *Maiores Ecclesiae Causas* (1201) are also interesting: "Original sin, which is contracted without consent is remitted without consent by the power of the Sacrament (of Baptism); but actual sin, which is committed with consent, is by no means remitted without consent" (DS 780).

rament. There was, however—see the previous chapter—also the mystagogical catechesis, held by the bishop in the days following the celebration. In the catechumenate, the dogmatic and moral doctrines of Christianity were learned, while the so-called *disciplina arcani* ("discipline of secrecy") was observed with the Sacraments, maintaining the secrecy concerning the doctrinal meanings of the celebration, which were illustrated only to those who had already been initiated into the faith through the same Sacraments. This was one possible way to observe the call of Christ: "Do not give what is holy to dogs, or throw your pearls before swine" (Matt 7:6). Saint Paul also speaks of a certain progression in Christian formation: "Brothers, I could not talk to you as spiritual people, but as fleshly people, as infants in Christ. I fed you milk, not solid food, because you were unable to take it" (1 Cor 3:1–2; see Heb 5:11–14). The practice of *disciplina arcani* was also due to the slanderous rumors that the enemies of the Christians spread, especially about the ritual practices of the new religion. Thus Tertullian writes: "by whom could [rituals] be made known? Not, surely, by the guilty parties [Christians] themselves; even from the very idea of the thing, the fealty of silence being ever due to mysteries."[28]

3.1.4. Rite

The essential rite of Baptism prescribes contact of the baptized person with water, which is the proper and non-substitutable material element of the Sacrament, while the formula is pronounced: "I baptize you in the name of the Father, and of the Son, and of the Holy Spirit."[29] In the earliest Church, contact with water often occurred "by immersion," while later, but still soon after, the practice of pouring water on the head alone was also introduced ("by infusion" or in some cases "by aspersion or sprinkling"), especially for young children. Both immersion and the simple pouring are done three times, corresponding to the Persons of the Trinity, in whose Name the Baptism is

---

[28] "... *omnibus mysteriis silentii fides debeatur*" (Tertullian of Carthage [d. 220], *Apologeticum* 7.6, in *ANF*, vol. 3, trans. S. Thelwall [Peabody, MA: Hendrickson Publishers, Inc. 1994], 23).

[29] Recently, especially in Anglophone countries, an abuse has been introduced in which the formula is substituted with the following: "I baptize you in the name of the Creator, and of the Redeemer, and of the Sanctifier" and "I baptize you in the name of the Creator, and of the Liberator, and of the Sustainer." This is due to the influence of feminist theology, which substitutes the names of Father, Son, and Spirit, which are masculine, with neutral ones, in the sense that they could be either masculine or feminine. The Congregation for the Doctrine of the Faith, in a *Responsum* from February, 1, 2008, has declared that baptisms done with this formula are invalid and therefore have to be repeated the right way.

received. The rite of descending into water manifests what invisibly occurs: one descends into the waters of death with Christ, to ascend victoriously with Him, and thanks to Him, to a new life:

> Or are you unaware that we who were baptized into Christ Jesus were baptized into his death? We were indeed buried with him through baptism into death, so that, just as Christ was raised from the dead by the glory of the Father, we too might live in newness of life. / For if we have grown into union with him through a death like his, we shall also be united with him in the resurrection. We know that our old self was crucified with him, so that our sinful body might be done away with, that we might no longer be in slavery to sin. For a dead person has been absolved from sin. (Rom 6:3–7)

> You were buried with him in baptism, in which you were also raised with him through faith in the power of God, who raised him from the dead. (Col 2:12)

The Tradition has identified some preparatory figures of the mystery of Baptism in the Old Testament. The two most famous—indicated by the New Testament—are the ark of Noah and the passage through the Red Sea that was divided into two parts:

> God patiently waited in the days of Noah during the building of the ark, in which a few persons, eight in all, were saved through water. This prefigured baptism, which saves you now. It is not a removal of dirt from the body but an appeal to God for a clear conscience, through the resurrection of Jesus Christ (1 Pet 3:20–21)

> I do not want you to be unaware, brothers, that our ancestors were all under the cloud and all passed through the sea, and all of them were baptized into Moses in the cloud and in the sea. (1 Cor 10:1–2)

The rite is accompanied by various preparatory formulas, questions and answers, prayers, as well as explanatory symbols of the effects of the Sacrament, such as the white garment.

3.1.5. *Effects*

The main effect of the Sacrament of Baptism is the purification of the human being from all sin: both original sin, and—in the case of adults—all other sins committed up to that moment, with the relative penalties.[30] The sign of the white baptismal garment indicates that the baptized one is now "clothed ... with Christ" (see Gal 3:27). Indeed, Christ died precisely to render His Church "holy and immaculate" (see Eph 5:27). This reminds us of the second effect of Baptism: it grafts the human being to the Mystical Body of Christ, which is the Church. This would not be possible if the person were not first rendered unblemished. The Church, in fact, is immaculate and would not tolerate the grafting of sick members—they must be living members and not dead ones. With Baptism, therefore, the human being is made a "new creature" (see 2 Cor 5:17) by Christ and endowed with the sanctifying grace and the whole supernatural apparatus of graces, virtues, and charisms that are necessary for he or she to grow in the gift of faith now received. In summary, Baptism makes the human being an adoptive child (by grace) of God, brother of Christ and conformed to Him, and member of the ecclesial Body whose breath of supernatural life is the Holy Spirit.[31] We can say that the effects of this Sacrament imply the production *both* of a new relationship with God *and* with the Church. Both the effects are constitutive, and between the two the first has greater value: this allows—historically, or *de facto*—for there to be baptized persons who do not live in the full visible ecclesial communion, belonging to different Christian communities that are not united to one another.[32]

3.1.6. Baptism of Blood and of Desire

The Tradition of the Church also speaks of "Baptism of blood" and of "Baptism of desire [*votum*]." The foundation of these doctrines is the classic assertion that God has united salvation to the Sacrament of Baptism, but for His part, God is not bound by His Sacraments, and therefore in particular situations He can grant salvation even without the reception of the Sacrament (see the previous chapter). In these cases, however, what is received is not a general grace, but the grace of the Sacrament itself (though not the character), a Sacrament that thus always remains necessary in itself, just as God has established it.

---

[30] "The effect of this Sacrament is the remission of all guilt, original and actual, and also of all punishment due to the guilt itself" (Council of Florence, *Exsultate Deo* [DS 1316]).

[31] See Second Vatican Council, *Lumen Gentium* (1964), §§11, 31–32; *Apostolicam Actuositatem* (1965), §3.

[32] See Second Vatican Council, *Unitatis Redintegratio* (1964), §22.

The Sacraments in Particular

1. Baptism of Blood

"Baptism of blood" corresponds to the situations in which someone, though not yet baptized, dies for the Catholic faith. Traditionally, it is believed that the Holy Innocents were baptized in their own blood. They are the children who were killed by Herod in his search to kill the newborn Messiah (see Matt 2:16–18). The Office of Readings of the liturgical feast of the Holy Innocents (December 28) references one of the sermons of Saint Quodvultdeus (d. 450), a Carthaginian bishop who died in exile in Naples, who affirms:

> The children die for Christ, though they do not know it. The parents mourn for the death of martyrs. The Child makes of those as yet unable to speak fit witnesses to Himself. See the kind of kingdom that is His, coming as He did in order to be this kind of king. See how the Deliverer is already working deliverance, the Savior already working salvation. But you, Herod, do not know this and are disturbed and furious. While you vent your fury against the Child, you are already paying Him homage, and do not know it. How great a gift of grace is here! To what merits of their own do the children owe this kind of victory? They cannot speak, yet they bear witness to Christ. They cannot use their limbs to engage in battle, yet already they bear off the palm of victory.[33]

2. Baptism of Desire

As for "Baptism of desire,"[34] it is believed that the grace of Baptism is granted by God to those who desire Baptism and are preparing to receive it in the future, but die before receiving the Sacrament. The most common example is that of catechumens, who have explicit desire (*votum*) for Baptism: if they die without having received it, this does not occur because of a refusal of the grace of faith, which, on the contrary, they had accepted.

Theology has then developed the reflection on the "implicit desire" of Baptism, which is possessed by those who, while not knowing Christ, or not having sufficient knowledge to believe in Him, nevertheless strive to follow right conscience, that is, to live according to the known truth, which they constantly continue to seek, even at the cost of personal sacrifice. This good orientation of their existence is believed to be an implicit desire for Baptism,

---

[33] Saint Quodvultdeus of Carthage, *Oratio de Symbolo* 2.
[34] See *ST* III, q. 68, a. 2; Council of Trent, *Decretum de Iustificatione* (1547), ch. 4 (DS 1524).

because people like this, if they knew Christ, the fullness of truth and good, would certainly have the desire to adhere to Him and to the Church in an explicit way. The classic doctrine nurtures great hope that these people are saved, that is, that God grants them the grace of that Baptism that they certainly would have desired if they had adequately known it. This is also why the Church does not ever affirm that any individual is certainly in Hell: because the evaluation of the intimate sanctuary of conscience belongs to God alone. This does not imply a relativization of the gravity of sins objectively considered. Though the Second Vatican Council did not explicitly use the terminology of *votum*, it lends implicit support to the idea, as can be seen from re-reading the citations that we have proposed a little earlier. Faithful to the Second Vatican Council, the *Catechism* speaks explicitly of the doctrine of the *votum*.[35]

3.1.7. The Fate of Children Who Die without Baptism

The doctrine of the, at least implicit, desire/*votum* for Baptism constitutes a strong argument of hope for the salvation of many just and good people who have died without being spiritually reborn in Christ through reception of the Sacrament. The doctrine about the *votum* allows giving the maximum value possible to the choices made by people following an upright conscience. But what happens if someone dies so young—that is, as a baby—that he or she lacks self-awareness and cannot make any choice of conscience? What happens if such a child dies without Baptism? The question is complex because we need to respond to it while maintaining two truths revealed by God: (1) The universal salvific will that is due to God's infinite, merciful love; (2) The necessity of faith and Baptism for salvation. Neither of these two dogmas can be erased or ignored in response to the question.

The classic response placed the emphasis more on dogma (2), later reintegrating dogma (1), and therefore proposed the doctrine of *limbus puerorum*, the Limbo of Infants. Since Baptism and faith (or at least the desire of them) are absolutely necessary, a child cannot go to Heaven if he or she does not have them; after all, he or she cannot have desired them. Thus dogma (2) is maintained. Dogma (1) intervenes at a second step to affirm that God's mercy cannot allow these children to go to Hell because, although they inherited original sin, they did not commit any personal sin, therefore it would not correspond either to justice or mercy if they were damned forever. *Limbus puerorum* is therefore described neither as a place of torment, nor as a place of

---

[35] See CCC §§1259–1260.

heavenly bliss. It is a place of purely natural happiness: these children experience the joy that is due to the fulfillment of the ends proper to human nature, without the ultimate supernatural fulfillment in God. It is evident that this doctrine supposes a clear distinction between the order of nature and the order of grace.

In more recent theology, the order of factors is inverted, but in this case the product is also changed. Modern thinkers generally start from dogma (1) and then try to interpret dogma (2) in light of it. They believe that the *limbus puerorum* is only a "theologoumenon," that is, an explanatory theological hypothesis, which today should be set aside because it is incompatible with the infinite love of God. Having said this, they seek to also maintain dogma (2) as best as they can. Generally speaking, in these proposals, they tend to reduce the distinction between the natural and the supernatural. We shall return to this theme in Chapter Twelve.

3.2. Confirmation

3.2.1. The Link with Baptism

The second Sacrament of Christian initiation (with Baptism and Eucharist), and the second non-repeatable Sacrament, is Confirmation. In this case too, we can begin by recalling the baptism of Jesus in the Jordan, given that the Gospels, in the telling of the story, recall the descent of the Holy Spirit in the form of a dove. Thus the link between water and the Holy Spirit already seen in Baptism is again confirmed; but in this case it is known to subsist between the first and second Sacraments of initiation. In other words, Jesus' baptism at the Jordan shows not only the connection between the water and the Holy Spirit within the Sacrament of Baptism, but can be also interpreted as a sign of the connection between Baptism (symbolized by water) and Confirmation (symbolized by the descent of the Spirit on Jesus' wet body).

There is a very close bond between Baptism and Confirmation, as shown, for example, by three facts: (1) the rite of Baptism includes an anointing with chrism, the consecrated oil that is used for Confirmation; (2) in the East, Baptism and Confirmation are always bestowed together, even in the case of infants; and (3) the name Confirmation refers to the fact that the second Sacrament aims to confirm and seal the consecration and commitments of Baptism.

3.2.2. Confirmation in the New Testament

The administration of Confirmation is attested in the New Testament[36]:

> Now when the Apostles in Jerusalem heard that Samaria had accepted the word of God, they sent them Peter and John, who went down and prayed for them, that they might receive the holy Spirit, for it had not yet fallen upon any of them; they had only been baptized in the name of the Lord Jesus. Then they laid hands on them and they received the holy Spirit. (Acts 8:14–17)

> While Apollos was in Corinth, Paul traveled through the interior of the country and came [down] to Ephesus where he found some disciples. He said to them, "Did you receive the holy Spirit when you became believers?" They answered him, "We have never even heard that there is a holy Spirit." He said, "How were you baptized?" They replied, "With the baptism of John." Paul then said, "John baptized with a baptism of repentance, telling the people to believe in the one who was to come after him, that is, in Jesus." When they heard this, they were baptized in the name of the Lord Jesus. And when Paul laid [his] hands on them, the holy Spirit came upon them, and they spoke in tongues and prophesied (Acts 19:1–6).

According to Paul VI,[37] the Tradition of the Church also interprets the following passage in reference to Confirmation:

> Therefore, let us leave behind the basic teaching about Christ and advance to maturity, without laying the foundation all over again: repentance from dead works and faith in God, instruction about baptisms and laying on of hands, resurrection of the dead and eternal judgment. (Heb 6:1–2)

The reference to the laying on of hands after the mention of Baptism is interpreted with reference to the gesture done by the bishop in the rite of

---

[36] Holy Office, *Lamentabili*, (1907), §44, rejects the following modernist thesis: "There is nothing to prove that the rite of the Sacrament of Confirmation was employed by the Apostles. The formal distinction of the two Sacraments of Baptism and Confirmation does not pertain to the history of primitive Christianity" (DS 3444).

[37] Saint Paul VI, *Divinae Consortium Naturae* (1971).

Confirmation. We can add that, without excluding this, it could also refer to the other Sacrament that is celebrated by making this gesture, that is, Holy Orders. In this broader sense, which does not at all contradict the pronouncement of Paul VI but instead accepts it, the author of the Letter to the Hebrews cited both Baptism and the other Sacraments that are given with the laying on of hands: Confirmation and Holy Orders. That is, we would find here the triad of unrepeatable Sacraments, which infuse sacramental character. Given that what follows in the Letter to the Hebrews further develops the theme of the priesthood of Christ (in which the ministerial priesthood participates), our hypothesis may not be so far-fetched.

3.2.3. Rite

Although in the East the same baptizing priest also confers Confirmation, in the West the latter is usually celebrated after the child has reached the age of discretion and is usually administered by the bishop, though he can delegate a priest to administer the Sacrament in cases of necessity (it is good, however, that this does not usually happen). Unlike Baptism, the confirmand must present himself or herself in the state of grace for the reception of Confirmation.[38] The Sacrament requires the use of sacred chrism. The chrism is a holy oil mixed with perfume (or balsam),[39] which is consecrated by the Bishop at the Chrism Mass during Holy Week. Even when it is a priest administering Confirmation (both in the East and in the West), he can only do so with a chrism that was consecrated by a bishop. The celebrant, in addition to anointing the confirmand with the chrism, lays hands on him or her, invoking the descent of the Holy Spirit. The formula currently set for the ordinary form of the Roman Rite is: "Be sealed with the gift of the Holy Spirit." At the end, the bishop and the newly confirmed exchange the kiss of peace. As with Baptism, Confirmation also requires the presence of a sponsor (like a godfather or godmother), who

---

[38] The confirmands "should approach Confirmation fasting, they should be warned to make a Confession, so that in purity they may be ready to receive the gift of the Holy Spirit" (Synod of Orleans [511], cited by the *Decretum Gratiani* 3.5, can. 6 [our translation]).

[39] "Chrism made from oil, signifying purity of conscience, and balsam, signifying the fragrance of a good reputation" (Council of Florence, *Exsultate Deo* [DS 1317]). Similarly, Saint Pius X (d. 1914), *Catechismus*, §582: "In this Sacrament the oil, which is unctuous and strengthening, signifies the abounding grace which is diffused over the soul of the Christian to confirm him in his faith; and the balsam, which is fragrant and prevents corruption, signifies that the Christian, strengthened by this grace, is enabled to give forth a good odor of Christian virtue and preserve himself from the corruption of vice" (translation: *ewtn.com*).

assumes the responsibility of accompanying the confirmed along the path of Christian life, helping, encouraging, and if necessary, reproaching him or her.

It should be emphasized that the matter that is proper to the Sacrament, more than just the chrism itself, is the laying on of hands united with the anointing of the chrism on the forehead of the candidate. In fact, in the New Testament, Confirmation is administered by the Apostles without the use of consecrated oil, but only with the laying on of hands, which thus appears to be the true and proper matter of the Sacrament. However, in the ancient Church this gesture was accompanied by the sign of the chrism, because the bishop, before laying on his hands, anointed them with chrism.[40] Saint Paul VI indicates the matter and form of Confirmation with these words:

> The Sacrament of Confirmation is conferred through the anointing with chrism on the forehead, which is done by the laying on of the hand, and through the words: *Accipe signaculum doni Spiritus Sancti* ("Be sealed with the gift of the Holy Spirit")[41]

3.2.4. The Minister

A long-disputed question has concerned the minister of this Sacrament. In the East, it is believed that both the bishop and the priest are ordinary ministers of it, while in the West it is only the bishop. The Eastern doctrine was refuted by the Council of Trent.[42] But the Catholic Church recognizes that the priest can validly administer Confirmation as an extraordinary minister. Perhaps to avoid inconvenience, the Second Vatican Council speaks of the bishop as the "original" minister of Confirmation, rather than the ordinary minister.[43]

---

[40] Thus it is stated by Saint Hippolytus of Rome (d. 235), *Traditio apostolica* 21.3. Much later, it is taken as a given by the Second Council of Lyon, *Professio Fidei Michaëlis Palaeologi Imperatoris* (1274): "... the Sacrament of Confirmation, which bishops confer by the laying on of hands while they anoint the reborn [the baptized] ..." (DS 860).

[41] Saint Paul VI, *Divinae Consortium Naturae* (1971) (translation: *L'Osservatore Romano* [English edition], September 23, 1971).

[42] "If anyone says that the ordinary minister of holy Confirmation is not the bishop but any simple priest let him be anathema" (Council of Trent, *Canones de Sacramento Confirmationis* (1547), can. 3 [DS 1630]). This pronouncement is based on the Council of Florence, *Exsultate Deo* (DS 1318). Much earlier, Saint Innocent I (d. 417), *Si Instituta Ecclesiastica* (416), ch. 3, §6, had taught: "But in regard to the signing [Confirmation] of little children, it is evident that it may not be done by any other than a bishop" (DS 215), also adding a New Testament foundation that would be repeated by the Council of Florence, in the aforementioned text.

[43] See Second Vatican Council, *Lumen Gentium*, §26.

The Sacraments in Particular

According to Catholic doctrine, therefore, Confirmation conferred by a priest who is appointed by the bishop is valid. However, this should not represent the rule (as often happens today) but an exception, hence the extraordinary nature of the Confirmation that is conferred by a priest. In current pastoral practice, there are many places where certain priests receive a permanent delegation to confirm from the bishop. In reality, this Sacrament should normally be administered by a bishop and only in rare cases by a priest.[44]

3.2.5. Effects

If we now inquire about the effects of this Sacrament, we can identify them with the help of certain witnesses:

> The imposition of the hands is designated by the anointing of the forehead that by another name is called Confirmation, because through it the Holy Spirit is given for an increase (of grace) and strength [*augmentum et robur*].[45]

> In this Sacrament the Holy Spirit is given to the baptized to reinvigorate them [*ad robur*]. . . . The bestowing of the Holy Spirit does not happen without sanctifying grace [see *ST* I, q. 43, a. 3]. It is therefore clear that sanctifying grace is bestowed in this Sacrament. The remission of sins is proper to sanctifying grace; but it also has other effects. . . . Sanctifying grace is not just given for the remission of guilt [as in Baptism], but also for the increase [*augmentum*] and the stability [*firmitatem*] of justice.[46]

> With this Sacrament, the human being is spiritually advanced to the age of maturity.[47]

---

[44] Keeping that fact in mind, the Council of Florence, *Exsultate Deo*, says that it may occur "sometimes"— (*aliquando*)—"through a dispensation of the Apostolic See for a reasonable and very urgent cause" (DS 1318). Therefore, an exceptional fact should not become the norm: usually, the bishop should confirm. Likewise, Sacra Congregatio de Propaganda Fide, *Instructio pro Simplici Sacerdote Administrante Sacramentum Confirmationis* (1774) says that the Apostolic See attributes to a priest the faculty of confirming as an extraordinary minister "sometimes" (*quandoque*) and "for just reasons" (DS 2588).

[45] Innocent III (d. 1216), *Cum Venisset* (1204) (DS 785).

[46] *ST* III, q. 72, a. 7 (our translation).

[47] *ST* III, q. 72, a. 8 (our translation).

The effect of this Sacrament is that in it the Holy Spirit is given for strength, as He was given to the Apostles on the day of Pentecost, in order that Christians may courageously confess the name of Christ. And, therefore, those to be confirmed are anointed on the forehead, which is the seat of shame, so that they may not be ashamed to confess the name of Christ and chiefly His cross.[48]

[The faithful] are more perfectly bound to the Church by the Sacrament of Confirmation, and the Holy Spirit endows them with special strength [*robore*] so that they are more strictly obliged to spread and defend the faith, both by word and by deed, as true witnesses [*testes*] of Christ [49]

A first effect of Confirmation, which we do not have to return to the texts to demonstrate, is the bestowing of the character. The texts cited above mention the other effects. With Confirmation, the baptized person is established as a witness of Christ. What Christ said to the Apostles applies to him or her: "*Eritis mihi testes*" ("you will be my witnesses") (Acts 1:8). Great courage is needed to be a witness of Christ crucified and risen, for Jesus adds: "If they persecuted me, they will also persecute you" (John 15:20). This is why the effect of Confirmation is to provide strength[50] to overcome the shame of the cross and the courage to fight for Christ as His faithful soldiers. Confirmation perfects the gift of sanctifying grace, "increasing" the level of spiritual life, in view of the particular mission that the Lord entrusts to each person. As can be appreciated from the cited texts, there can be no opposition between being witnesses to the Risen One and being soldiers of Christ the King: the witness of Christ must be offered with strength and fidelity—characteristics of a good soldier. The confirmed one is *both* a witness *and* a soldier: *et testis et miles*. All of this contributes to the growth in perfection of the Christian, who with Confirmation reaches—from the objective point of view—perfection: namely, the complete maturation of the supernatural tools necessary for his or her work and salvation. For this reason, it is more fitting to receive Confirmation once one has reached the age of discretion, just as it is better to receive Baptism as a child. Indeed, just as the Sacrament of supernatural rebirth corresponds to the moment of natural birth, so the Sacrament of maturity is better conferred when the person is self-aware.

---

[48] Council of Florence, *Exsultate Deo* (DS 1319).
[49] Second Vatican Council, *Lumen Gentium*, §11.
[50] In Latin, *vis*, with the genitive *roboris*: from *robur*, which in a strict sense means "oak tree." The confirmed person is made spiritually strong like an oak tree.

In short:

> Confirmation is a Sacrament which gives us the Holy Ghost, imprints on our souls the mark of a soldier of Jesus Christ, and makes us perfect Christians. The Sacrament of Confirmation makes us perfect Christians by confirming us in the faith and perfecting the other virtues and gifts received in Baptism; hence it is called Confirmation.[51]

3.2.6. Necessity

Although receiving Confirmation is not strictly necessary for eternal salvation, the Church strongly recommends "receiving [it] promptly."[52] Under normal conditions, therefore, it is necessary for Christian initiation and should be conferred on all the baptized.[53] However, when death intervenes before it is possible to receive Confirmation, the lack of this Sacrament does not imply jeopardizing eternal salvation since, strictly speaking, Confirmation is not necessary to obtain eternal beatitude.

3.3. Holy Orders

The third and last of the non-repeatable Sacraments is that of Holy Orders. "The Sacrament of Holy Orders ... confers an *indelible spiritual character* and cannot be repeated or conferred temporarily [Cf. Council of Trent: DS 1767; *LG* 21; 28; 29; *PO* 2]" (CCC §1582).[54] This Sacrament is therefore another great sign of the objectivity of the sacramental order and of the fidelity of God, whose call and gifts are irrevocable (see Rom 11:29).

---

[51] Saint Pius X, *Catechismus*, §§577–578 (translation: *ewtn.com*).

[52] See *Codex Iuris Canonici*, can. 890.

[53] Benedict XIV, *Etsi Pastoralis* (1742), says that, although Confirmation is not necessary for eternal salvation, whoever does not complete it without due cause must be warned by their bishops that "they are bound by the guilt of grave sin if, being able to agree to confirmation, they refuse or neglect it" (DS 2523). Therefore, one must not arrive at contempt for the Sacrament from the fact that it is not, strictly speaking, necessary for salvaiton.

[54] The root of this paragraph of the *Catechism* is found in the Council of Trent, *Doctrina et Canones de Sacramento Ordinis* (1563), ch. 4: "But since in the Sacrament of Orders, as also in Baptism and Confirmation, a character is imprinted that can be neither erased nor taken away, the holy Council justly condemns the opinion of those who say that priests of the New Testament have only a temporary power and that those who have once been rightly ordained can again become lay persons if they do not exercise the ministry of the Word of God" (DS 1767).

3.3.1. The Old Testament

In the Old Testament, though the whole People of Israel is referred to as "a kingdom of priests" (Ex 19:6), a particular priesthood was also instituted. The Levitical priesthood was established at the service of the Temple and the altar. It gets its name from Levi, one of the twelve sons of Jacob, who gave their names to the tribes of Israel. The males born in the tribe of Levi were, *ipso facto*, members of the priestly classes, while the other Israelites could not access this dignity. In the Old Testament, in a certain sense, one is a priest from birth. This is not, however, a purely natural or cultural reality, but the fruit of a divine, salvific will manifested and sanctioned through a rite of institution (see Ex 29; Lev 8). The active exercise of the priesthood was regulated according to a beginning and an end:

> The LORD said to Moses: This is the rule for the Levites. Everyone twenty-five years old or more shall join the personnel in the service of the tent of meeting. But everyone fifty on up shall retire from the work force and serve no more. They shall assist their fellow Levites in the tent of meeting in performing their duties, but they shall not do the work. This, then, is how you are to regulate the duties of the Levites. (Num 8:23–26)

It should be noted that within the tribe of Levi, there was a special distinction for the descendants of Aaron (and of Moses). This explains, *sub specie contraria* (under a contrary form), the episode of the revolt of Korah, Dathan, and Abiram, who challenged the superiority of the special role reserved to Aaron in the priesthood and wanted to reduce the entire priesthood in Israel to the priesthood of all the people. They said to Moses and Aaron: "You go too far! The whole community, all of them, are holy; the LORD is in their midst. Why then should you set yourselves over the LORD's assembly?" (Num 16:3). In what follows in the narrative, God confirms—in a very dramatic way—that a real distinction subsists and is desired by Him. The episode is instructive for understanding the structure of the Levitical priesthood and as a figure of the new People of God, in which there are also two truly distinct priesthoods that cannot be reduced to one: that is, the ministerial priesthood (received through Holy Orders) cannot be reduced to the common priesthood of all the baptized.

In the Old Testament, there is also a second priestly line, which remains almost hidden up to the advent of Christ: it is the priesthood according to the line of Melchizedek (see Gen 14:17–20; Ps 110:4), which will be used by the

The Sacraments in Particular

author of the Letter to the Hebrews (see Chapter Four) in order to explain the priesthood of Christ.

3.3.2. The New Testament

As regards the New Testament, some elements at the biblical level have already emerged in Chapter Eight, where we discussed the foundation of the ecclesial Hierarchy on the part of Christ.

The Book of Revelation explicitly says that Christ, in founding the Church, has maintained that characteristic of Israel for which the People of God is entirely priestly: Christ "has made us into a kingdom, priests for his God and Father" (1:6). Saint Peter attests: "let yourselves be built into a spiritual house to be a holy priesthood to offer spiritual sacrifices acceptable to God through Jesus Christ"; likewise, Saint Peter: "you are 'a chosen race, a royal priesthood'" (1 Pet 2:5, 9). But as is the case with the Old Testament, in the New Covenant, the general "priestliness" of the new People of God does not exclude, but rather requires, another form of priesthood, possessed only by some of the faithful: the ministerial or hierarchical priesthood.

Though the New Testament does not speak of "order" or "orders"—terms that would be introduced later, under the influence of Roman culture—it does use terms that are adequate to indicate ministries that do not belong to all the faithful: "Apostles," "The Twelve," "bishops," "presbyters," "deacons," "managers" (*proistamenoi*), "guides" (*egoumenoi*), "shepherds" (*poimenes*), "cooperators" (*synergoi*).[55] As for the three degrees of the Sacrament, in many cases in the New Testament, the term bishop and the term priest appear as synonyms. The clear distinction and hierarchy of the three degrees is made clear by Saint Ignatius of Antioch, a very ancient witness to the Apostolic Tradition.[56]

These duties—especially the priestly duties—are conferred through an institution, that which we call the Sacrament of Holy Orders, established by

---

[55] It is interesting to note that the term "priest" (*hiereus*) in the New Testament is applied to Christ, to the Jewish or pagan priests, and to baptized Christians, but never to those whom we call ordained ministers. This means that the New Testament wants to emphasize that the priesthood of ordained ministers is distinct from any other form of priesthood, not only that of the Jews and pagans, but also the common priesthood of the faithful. As for Christ, (the perfection and origin of every priesthood) He is called the High Priest, thus emphasizing His uniqueness. Moreover, Hebrews 8:4 specifies that, if He were on earth, he would not even be a (Levite) priest. Calling Him *hiereus*, therefore, does not include Him in the priesthood of the Jerusalemite Temple.

[56] See Saint Ignatius of Antioch, *Ad Ephesios* 3.2–4.1; *Ad Magnesios*, 3.1; 6.1; 7.1; 13.1; *Ad Trallianos* 3.1; 7.2; *Ad Philadelphenos* 7.1; *Ad Smyrnenses* 8.1.

Christ during the Last Supper with the words, "do this in memory of me" (Luke 22:19; 1 Cor 11:24). This interpretation of the words of Christ has been confirmed by the Magisterium:

> If anyone says that by the words "do this in memory of me" Christ did not establish the Apostles as priests or that He did not order that they and other priests should offer his Body and Blood, let him be anathema.[57]

The Council of Trent, against the Protestant theses, definitively specified some other important points about the relationship between the New Testament and the Sacrament of Holy Orders: (1) That the New Testament undoubtedly teaches the existence of a visible and external priesthood, which consists above all in consecrating the Body and Blood of Christ and in the remittance of sins, and not simply in the preaching of the Word of God. (2) That Holy Orders is a true and proper Sacrament and that it is not a human institution (even if apostolic) but rather a divine one, because it has its origin from Christ Himself. (3) That, because of this, the Hierarchy of the Church is formed "by divine disposition" (*divine ordinatione instituta*), which consists of bishops, priests, and ministers, where by this last term we mean both the deacons and the ministers of a lower degree.[58]

3.3.3. The Relationship between Orders and the Priesthood

Our discussion thus far leads to another question concerning the relationship between the Sacrament of Holy Orders and the priesthood. It is, in fact, indisputable that the ministerial priesthood in the Church is conferred only and exclusively through the reception of sacred Ordination. It is only possible to be priests (bishops or presbyters) if ordained. However, it is also possible to be ordained without being consecrated as priests, as occurs in two cases: (1) in the ordinary form of the Roman Rite, when deacons are ordained; and (2) in the extraordinary form, when deacons or subdeacons are ordained, or one of the minor orders is received. Beyond the liturgical question of substitution, in the ordinary form, of the minor orders with the ministries of the lectorate and acolyte, the exquisitely dogmatic question is addressed by recalling a distinction that was already proposed in the ecclesiological chapter, where it

---

[57] Council of Trent, *Doctrina et Canones de ss. Missae Sacrificio* (1562), can. 2 (DS 1752).
[58] See Council of Trent, *Doctrina et Canones de Sacramento Ordinis*, cann. 1, 3, 6 (DS 1771, 1773, 1776).

has been noted that the ecclesiastical hierarchy is structured *both* through the Sacrament of Holy Orders *and* for the conferral of a juridical power. These two criteria are fully distinct but not separate, as was illustrated in that place through the example of the Roman Pontiff, whose juridical powers are nevertheless linked to his being a bishop (*of Rome!*), and we also appreciate this in the case of deacons, to whom we have just referred. They do not receive the priesthood, even if they are ordained ministers.[59] We could even go so far as to say that, especially in the ordinary form of the Roman Rite, there does not appear to be any peculiarity of authority in the deacon and no liturgical ministry that the deacon receives that cannot also be carried out by a layperson (albeit only in cases of necessity), if we leave out the faculty of blessing in a public and official form. On the contrary, various tasks of the bishop and presbyter cannot be carried out either by a layperson or a deacon, even in extraordinary cases. This makes it clear that, in the case of the deacon, the Sacrament of Holy Orders does not confer the priesthood, but only a higher hierarchical degree than the laical one. The ministry of service proper to the deacon is indicated precisely in the word "*diakonia*": "At a lower level of the hierarchy are deacons, who receive the laying on of hands 'not unto the priesthood, but unto a ministry of service.'"[60] Since, however, even the ministerial priesthood is conferred for service,[61] the peculiarity of the diaconate is not clear, even when it is qualified as "*diakonia* of charity," given that priests too (bishops and presbyters) must serve in love and for love. The most convincing way of speaking of the degrees of Holy Orders, therefore, consists in recognizing that they structure the ecclesiastical hierarchy with different degrees of participation in the power of Christ. In the case of the bishop, the fullness of the Sacrament of Holy Orders is conferred, that is, the high priesthood.[62] Presbyters receive a participation in the priesthood of Christ lower than that of bishops; that is, they do not possess the fullness of the Sacrament of Holy Orders, but are constituted cooperators of the episcopal

---

[59] The most recent magisterial document on the theme is the motu proprio of Benedict XVI, *Omnium in Mentem* (2009), which—out of desire for clarity—modified can. 1009 of the *Codex Iuris Canonici* of 1983 as follows: "Those who are constituted in the order of the episcopate or the presbyterate receive the mission and capacity to act in the Person of Christ the Head, whereas deacons are empowered to serve the People of God in the ministries of the liturgy, the word and charity" (art. 2).

[60] Second Vatican Council, *Lumen Gentium*, §29.

[61] "The ministerial priesthood is at the service of the common priesthood. It is directed at the unfolding of the baptismal grace of all Christians" (CCC §1547).

[62] See Second Vatican Council, *Lumen Gentium*, §20.

Order[63] and, as such, they receive priestly faculties that serve the fulfillment of this mission. The two most important faculties are that of consecrating the Body and Blood of Christ in the Eucharist, and that of absolving sins in Confession.[64] But we must not forget the *munus regendi*.[65] Of the deacons, the Catechism recalls that they are not priests, and that this degree of Orders, with respect to bishops and presbyters, "is intended to help and serve them" (CCC §1554). The proper character of the deacon, therefore, is not service in general, which pertains to all "ministers" (from the Latin *ministrare*, to serve). Their service is specific: they serve the Church by serving the bishop and the presbyter, helping them and collaborating with them, as far as possible, in apostolic action.[66] There are clear signs of this in the New Testament, in the Fathers and Doctors, and in the Liturgy.

In conclusion, Holy Orders structures the ecclesiastical Hierarchy in three degrees not only through differing participations in the priesthood of Christ (from which the diaconate is excluded), but also by conferring specific authority in the Church at the juridical level. In fact, the faculties of ordained ministers (which reside fully only in the bishops) involve three spheres, not only the sacramental one: the *munus docendi* (power/office in teaching), the *munus sanctificandi* (Sacraments), and the *munus regendi* (authority). The deacon does not receive a true and proper participation in the *munus sanc-*

---

[63] See Second Vatican Council, *Presbyterorum Ordinis* (1965), §2.

[64] See Second Vatican Council, *Lumen Gentium*, §28.

[65] In certain places, on account of a lack of priests, some bishops have decided to entrust parishes to deacons, non-ordained religious men or religious women, or even lay faithful. In this case, we are dealing with a purely functional leadership, which must cease as soon as there is a priest available. Deacons, non-ordained religious, and lay persons, in fact, cannot have a participation in the *munus regendi* of bishops, thus they cannot be, nor can they be called, "pastors." That is why the *Codex Iuris Canonici*, can. 517 §2, prescribes that, in these cases, it is necessary that a priest be nominated to supervise this temporary type of pastoral care for the parish.

[66] It should be noted that deacons also "serve . . . the people of God" (Second Vatican Council, *Lumen Gentium*, §29); nonetheless, their proper mode of serving the Church consists precisely in the ministry of privileged cooperation with the bishops and presbyters. In this sense, diaconal Ordination gives the deacon a special title of cooperation with priests that is superior to the cooperation (even though it is very important) of lay faithful with the Hierarchy. We cite in support a text of Saint Hippolytus Romanus (d. 235), *Traditio apostolica* 8: "In ordaining a deacon, only the bishop may lay hands, for the reason that he is not ordained to the priesthood, but to the service of the bishop, to carry out what will be commanded by him" (our translation). The attribution of the *Traditio apostolica* to Hippolytus is classical, but strongly debated in recent times, at least with regard to the completed state of the work. Beyond the question of authorship, the text is still a very ancient testimony of the Tradition.

tificandi. He receives, as the presbyter does, a participation in the *munus docendi*, in the sense that he can preach the Word (but cannot determine its meaning with apostolic authority, something reserved to bishops alone). He also receives a participation in the *munus regendi* (which is found in fullness in the bishop, subordinate in the presbyter, and also in the deacon as the bishop's cooperator), as an aid and servant (in an evangelical sense) of the bishop and, by extension, of the presbyter.[67] This participation in the *munera* of teaching and ruling in the Church, however, in the case of the deacon, is not original but derived, and applies to the extent needed for his cooperation with the bishop and presbyter. That is why, for the deacon, the terminology applying to priests is not used, namely, that they (bishops and presbyters) act *in Persona Christi capitis* ("in the Person of Christ the Head [of the Church]").[68] This does not take away the fact that deacons should also be understood and respected as members of the Hierarchy of the Church, because with the Sacrament of Holy Orders they receive, if not priestly powers superior to the laity, certainly an ecclesiastical authority superior to that of lay persons.[69] And, while this power deserves respect, on the other hand, it must always be exercised for service, since the priesthood and the deaconate are gifts of God to the Church, given for service. And precisely because the sacred ministers serve all, they must be respected by all and, when the case arises, we must obey their instructions (see Mark 9:35). "Pay attention to the bishop, if you would have God pay attention to you. I offer myself up for those who obey the bishop, priests and deacons."[70]

---

[67] Saint Ignatius of Antioch, *Ad Magnesios* 1.2, praises the deacon Sotio "since he is obedient to the bishop, as to the grace of God, and to the priests, as to the law of Jesus Christ" (in *FCNT*, vol. 1, trans. Gerald G. Walsh [Washington DC: CUA Press, 2008], 96).

[68] The classical terminology of *in Persona Christi* was used various times in the Second Vatican Council, *Lumen Gentium*, §§10, 21, 28, 37; *Presbyterorum Ordinis*, §§2, 12, 13. The various texts teach that priests act *in Persona Christi* mainly in the Holy Mass, but also that their ministry should generally be interpreted as carrying in themselves the Person of Christ, which is one reason why they should be treated with respect by the lay faithful (see *Lumen Gentium*, §37), for whom they carry out service.

[69] "All should respect the deacons as they would Jesus Christ, just as they respect the bishop as representing the Father and the priests as the council of God and the college of the Apostles: Apart from these there is nothing that can be called a Church" (Saint Ignatius of Antioch, *Epistula ad Trallianos* 3.1 [in *FCNT*, vol. 1, 102–103]; see Saint Ignatius of Antioch, *Ad Magnesios* 6.1).

[70] Saint Ignatius of Antioch, *Ad Polycarpum* 6.1 (in *FCNT*, vol. 1, 126).

3.3.4. Hierarchical Authority and Charisms

Power—or, more accurately, authority—and service are not opposed in the Church. There is no need to sustain, as was done in the not-so-distant past, that space must be given to the charisms in order to prevent power from taking over in the community of Christ. This is a false dichotomy. In the Church, there is place *both* for charism *and* authority: both contribute to the good of souls and are willed by Christ.[71] Moreover, the ministry of guidance in the Church is an original fact, which is clearly found in the New Testament, and which itself is a charism, if what is intended by the term is a gift given by the Holy Spirit for the edification of the community.[72] In the spirituality of the saints, even when they had to suffer because of decisions of the Hierarchy, there was never room for an opposition between charism and ecclesiastical authority. Two single examples taken from the Wednesday catecheses of Benedict XVI remind us of this. They are about Saint Francis of Assisi (d. 1226) and Saint Bridget of Sweden (d. 1373):[73]

> The *Poverello* of Assisi understood that every charism as a gift of the Holy Spirit existed to serve the Body of Christ, which is the Church; therefore he always acted in full communion with the ecclesial authorities. In the life of the Saints there is no contradiction between prophetic charism and the charism of governance, and if tension arises, they know to patiently await the times determined by the Holy Spirit.

> Bridget, moreover, knew well and was firmly convinced that every charism is destined to build up the Church. For this very reason many of her revelations were addressed in the form of admonishments, even severe ones, to the believers of her time, including the religious and political authorities, that they might live a consistent Christian life; but she always reprimanded them with an attitude of respect and of full fidelity to the Magisterium of the Church and in particular to the Successor of the Apostle Peter.

---

[71] See Congregation for the Doctrine of Faith, *Iuvenescit Ecclesia* (2016): the letter concerns the relation between hierarchical and charismatic gifts in the Church.

[72] Ministry is considered a charism by the New Testament: see 1 Tim 4:14; 2 Tim 1:6, in which the Apostle uses precisely the Greek word *charisma*. *Charisma* is a special grace for carrying out a mission received by God.

[73] Benedict XVI, *General Audience*, January 27, 2010 and October 27, 2010.

3.3.5. Matter

Concerning the matter of the Sacrament of Holy Orders, there was a gradual deepening of understanding on the part of the Magisterium. The Council of Florence had affirmed that the matter of Holy Orders is the *porrectio seu traditio instrumentorum*, namely, the conferral of explicative signs: for example, the chalice and paten to the presbyter.[74] But, in the Greek Rite, the *porrectio* is not carried out, yet the Church recognizes the validity of such ordinations. On the basis of this, Pius XII better clarifies that the matter proper to Holy Orders is the laying on of the bishop's hands over the head of the candidate:

> There is no one who does not know that the Roman Church always considered valid the ordination conferred in the Greek rite, without the handing over the instruments, so that at the Council of Florence . . . it was not imposed on the Greeks that they change the rite of ordination, or that they insert in it the handing over of the instruments; rather, the Church wished that even in the City (Rome) Greeks would be ordained according to their own rite. From all this it is gathered that according to the mind of the same Council of Florence, the handing over of the instruments is not required for the substance and validity of this Sacrament. . . . Since these things are so . . . we determine and ordain: the matter of the Holy Orders of the diaconate, priesthood, and episcopate is the laying on of hands alone.[75]

3.3.6. Form

In the constitution *Sacramentum Ordinis*, Pius XII, in addition to describing the matter of the Sacrament, also identifies the form. It consists in "the words determining the application of the matter, words by which the effects of the Sacrament—that is, the power of [Holy Orders] and the grace of the Holy Spirit—are unequivocally signified and, for that reason, are accepted and used by the Church."[76] Since the reform approved by Paul VI (currently called the ordinary form of the Roman Rite) happened since then, we shall present

---

[74] See Council of Florence, *Exsultate Deo* (DS 1326).
[75] Pius XII, *Sacramentum Ordinis* (1947), §§3–4 (DS 3858–3859).
[76] Pius XII, *Sacramentum Ordinis*, §4 (DS 3859). In the following number (DS 3860), the Pontiff, referring to the ritual today called the extraordinary form, also expresses the form for each degree of the Sacrament.

in what follows the form of the different degrees of Orders as indicated by the same Pontiff. The form of the Sacrament is contained in the prayer of Ordination, in which the formulas that constitute the essential words, and which are thus required for the validity of an Ordination, are identified. The formulas are presented in the plural for presbyters and deacons, supposing the consecration of several candidates; and they are in the singular for bishops:

> [Diaconate] Lord, send forth upon them the Holy Spirit, that they be strengthened by the gift of your sevenfold grace to carry out faithfully the work of the ministry.
>
> [Presbyterate] Almighty Father, grant to these servants of yours the dignity of the priesthood. Renew within them the Spirit of holiness. As co-workers with the order of bishops may they be faithful to the ministry that they receive from you, Lord God, and be to others a model of right conduct.
>
> [Episcopate] So now pour out upon this chosen one that power which is from you, the governing Spirit whom you gave to your beloved Son, Jesus Christ, the Spirit given by Him to the holy Apostles, who founded the Church in every place to be your temple for the unceasing glory and praise of your name.[77]

The form of the Sacrament, as we have said, is also essential for the Sacrament's validity. The invalidity of Anglican ordinations was declared by Leo XIII precisely on the basis of a defect of form. The Anglicans, separated from Rome through the schism of King Henry VIII (d. 1547), changed the liturgical rites. For Ordination, they chose the simple formula: "Receive the Holy Spirit." Leo XIII (d. 1903) taught that such words "certainly do not signify definitely the Order of the priesthood or its grace and power, which is preeminently the power 'to consecrate and offer the true Body and Blood of the Lord.'"[78] From this we learn not only that the priestly (episcopal and

---

[77] Saint Paul VI, *Pontificalis Romani* (1968) (catholicliturgy.com).

[78] Leo XIII, *Apostolicae Curae* (1896) (DS 3316; the internal quote comes from the Council of Trent). It is noteworthy that the erroneous understanding of the essence of the priesthood on the part of the Anglicans is also revealed by the change of the rite (then considered the matter of the Sacrament) with respect to the *traditio instrumentorum*. In the place of the chalice and paten, the Anglican Ordinal of 1552 introduced the conferral of the Bible. Thus, it saw in the bishops and presbyters substantially proclaimers of the Word, neglecting the *munera sanctificandi et regendi*.

The Sacraments in Particular

presbyteral) function finds its essential center in the Eucharistic Celebration,[79] but also that what we already noted cannot be overlooked: with Holy Orders one receives *both* the grace of the Holy Spirit *and* a true ecclesial power. These two elements are expressed in the form of Ordination of the Roman Rite, both in its ordinary and extraordinary form. For what regards the priestly power, the Catechism of Trent notes:

> This [priestly] power is twofold: the powers of Orders and the power of jurisdiction. The power of Orders has for its object the real Body of Christ our Lord in the Blessed Eucharist. The power of jurisdiction refers altogether to the Mystical Body of Christ. The scope of this power is to govern and rule the Christian people, and lead them to the unending bliss of Heaven. The power of Orders not only embraces the power of consecrating the Eucharist, but also fits and prepares the souls of men for its reception. It also embraces all else that can have any reference to the Eucharist.[80]

3.3.7. Essence of Priestly Ministry

1. Christotypical/Cultic Model

We still need to address the question of the proper identity of the priest, strictly connected to that concerning the effects of the Sacrament. From what we have seen, the form of the Sacrament speaks both of authority and the gift of the Holy Spirit. The reference to the grace of the Spirit highlights the supernatural character of the priestly ministry, which builds up the Church especially through the mysterious ways of the supernatural realm. Therefore, it pertains more to the mysterious component of the Church. From this perspective, the essence of priestly ministry is that of Worship: the bishop and the presbyter are above all ministers of the sacred Liturgy and the Sacraments,

---

[79] "*In sacrificio offerendo potissime sacerdotis consistit officium*" ("The priestly office consists above all in the offering of the [Eucharistic] Sacrifice" (*ST* III, q. 22, a. 4). "The proper and principal office of the priest was always and is that of sacrificing, in such a way that, where there is no true and proper power of sacrificing, one cannot speak of a true and proper priesthood" (Pius XII, *Allocutio cardinalibus atque antistibus* (1954), [our translation]). "In the mystery of the Eucharistic Sacrifice . . . priests fulfill their greatest task [*munus praecipuum*]" (Second Vatican Council, *Presbyterorum Ordinis*, §13).

[80] *Catechismus ad Parochos ex decreto Concilii Tridentini* (*Pii V iussu editus*; year 1566), §274 (in *Catechism of the Council of Trent for Parish Priests*, trans. John A. McHugh and Charles J. Callan [New York: Joseph F. Wagner, 1934], 320–321).

the grace of which edifies the Church, in mystery, by nurturing holiness in her members. For this reason, in describing the effects of the Sacrament, the *Catechism* recalls the title of *priest* first ("*sacerdos*," corresponding to the *munus sanctificandi*) and then the titles corresponding to the *munus docendi* and *regendi*: "The grace of the Holy Spirit proper to this sacrament is configuration to Christ as Priest, Teacher, and Pastor, of whom the ordained is made a minister" (CCC §1585).

2. *Ecclesiotypical/Pastoral Model*

As for the aspect of authority, it appears primarily linked to the Church as a society, thus the *munus* of reference would not be here the *sanctificandi* as much as it would be the *regendi* (or, in other versions of the same thesis, the *munus docendi*, through which the priest is a preacher of the Word). The essence of the priesthood would consist in its pastoral nature. Bishops and presbyters are guides of the community, of which they regulate life with opportune interventions aimed at fostering the affective and effective communion of the new People of God. In the twentieth century, theologians gave great attention to this second aspect, despite the fact that the societal character of the Church was not always adequately emphasized by some of them. In reality, the tendency was, in certain cases, to reduce the sacral and cultic character of the priesthood, in favor of a more functional perspective of ministry (the minister as coordinator within the community). If the risk that can sometimes be connected with the cultic model is to consider the *munus sanctificandi* as expressive of the "being" of the priest, and the other two *munera* as relevant only to priestly "activity"—with the consequence of creating a rupture between the three *munera*—the most recent functionalist tendencies have had the great limitation of considering the minister no longer as representative of Christ, but of the community, approaching the Protestant concept of ministry. Hence, for example, the change of terminology from "celebrant priest" to "president of the liturgical assembly." When it was taken to an extreme, this tendency—especially in Flemish and German-speaking areas—attempted a veritable desacralization of the priesthood, or "desacerdotalization" of the ordained ministry. In these radical proposals, the priests were understood as animators no longer of the Church, but rather the world, having to work for social, pacifist, feminist, proletarian, ecologist, etc., causes. Beyond such extremes, there remains the dilemma about which of the two models must be preferred: the Christological model of the priest as a cultic minister, or the ecclesiological model of the priest as president of a community?

The Sacraments in Particular

3. "Synthetic"/Representative Model

Faithful to the general approach of this treatise, we believe that is not necessary to exclude either of the models, and that the two models need to be integrated according to the principle of *et-et*. This principle, however, requires that one of the two sides brought together is superior to the other and, in the present case, certainly the Christological-Cultic model remains the more important (as well as being the more classical). An integration with the ecclesiological-pastoral model, therefore, will have to happen based mainly on the Christological model or, better yet, from within it. Among those who have walked this path we find the name of the private theologian Joseph Ratzinger, which we can cite here despite our choice of method of not mentioning recent theologians, because, concerning this point, he—after becoming Pope—recalled his private studies, citing them explicitly within a magisterial teaching:

> In a world in which the common vision of life includes less and less of the sacred, instead of which "functionality" becomes the only crucial element, the Catholic concept of the priesthood might risk losing its natural esteem, at times even within the ecclesial conscience. Two different conceptions of the priesthood are frequently compared and at times even set against one another, in theological milieus as well as in actual pastoral practice and the formation of the clergy. In this regard I pointed out several years ago that there is: "on the one hand a social and functional concept that defines the essence of the priesthood with the concept of 'service': service to the community in the fulfillment of a function . . . Moreover, there is the sacramental-ontological concept, which of course does not deny the priesthood's character of service but sees it anchored to the minister's existence and claims that this existence is determined by a gift granted by the Lord through the mediation of the Church, whose name is Sacrament" (J. Ratzinger, *Ministero e vita del Sacerdote*, in *Elementi di Teologia fondamentale. Saggi sulla fede e sul ministero*, Brescia 2005, p. 165). The terminological shifting of the word "priesthood" to "service, ministry, assignment," is also a sign of this different conception. The primacy of the Eucharist, moreover, is linked to the former, the ontological-sacramental conception, in the dual term: "priesthood-sacrifice," whereas the primacy of the word and of the service of proclamation is held to correspond with the latter. Clearly these two concepts are not contradictory and the

tension which nevertheless exists between them may be resolved from within [a quotation from *Presbyterorum Ordinis* §2 follows in the text].[81]

The proposal of synthesizing the two models consists in seeing in the priest the representative and the envoy of Christ to the brethren. In this way, the ontological-sacramental (Christological) and the pastoral-missionary (ecclesial) accents are held together in a fruitful way. Upon closer inspection, this solution had already been accepted, albeit briefly, by Saint John Paul II:

> The priest's fundamental relationship is to Jesus Christ, Head and Shepherd. Indeed, the priest participates in a specific and authoritative way in the "consecration/anointing" [= cultic priesthood] and in the "mission" [= pastoral priesthood] of Christ. . . . The priest's relation to the Church is inscribed in the very relation which the priest has to Christ, such that the "sacramental representation" to Christ serves as the basis and inspiration for the relation of the priest to the Church.[82]

3.3.8. *Episcopate-Presbyterate Distinction*

These clarifications allow us to also mention the theme of the real distinction between the first and second degree of Holy Orders (episcopate and presbyterate). Although we have up to now taken for granted that there is such a distinction, the theme has been debated for centuries and only recently, with Vatican II, has a decisive contribution to the solution of the question been made. A classical and medieval line, in which there are excellent representatives, held that there was no real distinction between the presbyterate and the episcopate at the sacramental level, but only at the hierarchical level. For example, in the Canons attributed to Saint Hippolytus, it is stated that "the bishop is equated in everything to the presbyter, except for the chair and the faculty to ordain."[83] Saint Jerome (d. 420) wondered: "except for ordination, what does the bishop do that the presbyter cannot also do?"[84] We could cite

---

[81] Benedict XVI, *General Audience*, June 24, 2009. The rest of the text explains very well the way in which the two perspectives are held together, through the category of "representation."

[82] John Paul II, *Pastores Dabo Vobis* (1992), §16.

[83] Saint Hippolytus Romanus, *Canones* 32 (our translation). Also in this case the attribution of the work to Hippolytus is not certain and various specialists do not accept it.

[84] Saint Jerome, *Epistola 146*.1 (our translation).

The Sacraments in Particular

other witnesses of the patristic era. Even the great Scholastics professed this doctrine. The Common Doctor, Saint Thomas, writes that it is only the bishop who ordains, just as only he confirms.[85] The analogy is relevant, because a little further, the Angelic Doctor affirms that "every Order . . . is directed to the Eucharist. And since the bishop does not have in this a power superior to the priestly power, the episcopate is not an Order."[86] Thus, it would seem that, just as the Apostolic See for good reasons can delegate the presbyter to confirm, something that only the bishop can usually do, so it could delegate him to also ordain (deacons or presbyters). It is understood that in this perspective the episcopate is only superior to the presbyterate according to authority and hierarchical power, but not sacramentally. Saint Bonaventure (d. 1274) likewise thinks the same.[87] Although this position is classical, and as such deserves great respect, given the number and quality of the authors who support it, today the tendency is to accept the teaching of Vatican II, which—although not wishing to pronounce itself definitively—clearly taught the sacramentality of the episcopate: "The Sacred Council teaches that by Episcopal consecration the fullness of the Sacrament of Holy Orders is conferred, that fullness of power, namely, which both in the Church's liturgical practice and in the language of the Fathers of the Church is called the high priesthood, the supreme power of the sacred ministry."[88]

Despite some historical cases to the contrary,[89] it remains established that

---

[85] See *ST*, "Supplement," q. 38, a. 1.

[86] *ST*, "Supplement," q. 40, a. 5 (our translation). However, he adds that the episcopate is an Order distinct from the presbyterate if it is considered from the point of view of the power relative to hierarchical acts carried out with respect to the Mystical Body.

[87] See Saint Bonaventure, *In IV Sententiarum*, d. 25, a. 1, q. 1.

[88] Second Vatican Council, *Lumen Gentium*, §21.

[89] There were a few cases in which the Apostolic See authorized an abbot to ordain subdeacons, deacons, and priests for his own monastery. The question is to this day not completely clear: if such abbots were ordained bishops, there would be no dogmatic issue; it appears, however, that they were only presbyters. We can recall the following cases: Boniface IX, with the bull *Sacrae Religionis* (1400), authorized the abbot of Saint Osyth (near London) to carry out such ordinations, though it must be said that the permission was withdrawn very early, with the bull *Apostolicae Sedis* (1403). Martin V, with *Gerentes ad Vos* (1427), authorized the abbot of Altzelle in Saxony for five years. Innocent VIII, with *Exposcit Tuae Devotionis* (1489), granted the abbot of Cîteaux permission to ordain deacons and subdeacons. There has been no shortage of historians who considered these documents "surreptitious bulls," that is, issued without the knowledge of the popes. Beyond this, what counts most is that these cases were very few and that these privileges were more or less quickly withdrawn. This is an indication of the fact that the Church—except for these few oversights—does not contemplate in her practice the possibility that a presbyter may carry out sacramental Ordinations, even if (as for the abbots) he possesses

in the Church the only one who can celebrate the Sacrament of Holy Orders, in all three of its degrees, is the bishop, with no exceptions.[90] Although the teaching of Vatican II was based on solid reasons, and theologically appears very reasonable and is thus preferable, the question of the sacramentality of the episcopate may still remain open to the discussion of theologians, given that the Council did not intend to dogmatically define its own teaching. What does not appear to be in question, rather, is the exclusivity of the power to ordain, which resides only in the bishops, who keep the apostolic succession uninterrupted, in turn ordaining other bishops and guaranteeing ministers (presbyters and deacons) to the Church for their pastoral and missionary needs.

3.3.9. Ordination of Women?

1. Arguments in Support

Despite the fact that the Church's pastoral and missionary necessities are urgent, Catholic doctrine prevents responding to these urgencies by expanding the ranks of the clergy through the ordination of women. The question has been widely debated in the second half of the twentieth century, parallel to the movements for the emancipation and promotion of women (feminism). There have been more than a few theologians and Church people who believe we should be open to this possibility. The underlying anthropological argument, which is brought to support by those who want women to be ordained, consists in affirming the equal dignity of men and women. On this view, denying ministry to women in some way presupposes that they are not on the same level as men. A historical argument is added to this: Christ did not include women among the Twelve due merely to a cultural prejudice. Jesus himself shared the negative prejudice toward women that was typical of His era and environment; or at least, He indulged it. But in our times, this prejudice has fallen away, therefore—so it is said—permission should be given for priestesses in the Catholic Church. There are also preparatory movements—or so they are understood by some—for example, the fact that, at the discretion of

---

the juridical power of an Ordinary and bears episcopal insignia.

[90] "The Pope, having the fullness of pontifical power, can appoint those who are not bishops to functions that belong to episcopal dignity, provided that such functions do not immediately relate to the real Body of Christ [the Eucharist]. This is why by his appointment a simple priest can confer the minor Orders and Confirmation—but not one who is not a priest. And neither can he confer the major Orders, which have an immediate relation with the Body of Christ, with respect to whose consecration the Pope has no superior power to that of a simple priest" (*ST*, "Supplement," q. 38, a. 1 [our translation]).

the local Ordinary, girls may now also serve at the altar during the Liturgy (this service has always been exclusive to boys, as "priests in potency," and therefore the girls were excluded). At the Synod on the theme of the Word of God (2008), there was the proposal—then dropped—to grant access to the instituted lectorate to women as well. On August 2, 2016, Pope Francis, following a request made to him by the 20th Plenary Assembly of the International Union of Superiors General, established a commission of theologians for re-studying the ordaining of women as deacons or "deaconesses." On the occasion of the 21st Plenary Assembly of the same Union (May 10, 2019), Francis communicated the results of the works of the commission. The Pope explained that an agreement had not been reached on several aspects of the issue among the scholars who were appointed members of the commission of studies. Francis also said that, in order for him to issue new rules in the sacramental ambit, a theological and historical foundation is needed. At the time of writing, it seems that diaconate for women will not be introduced in the Catholic Church. Still, Francis has promised that the investigation on this topic will continue.

2. Responses to the Arguments

With regard to the historical argumentation proposed by supporters of female ordination, it shows itself to be unfounded for two reasons: (1) Jesus clearly showed an attitude of respect and benevolence toward women, which seemed to set the bar in His context. Therefore, He did not share the widespread suspicion toward female figures of the culture of the time. (2) If it is true that in Israel—as in the majority of ancient cultures—the woman had a modest role in comparison to men, it is nonetheless true that the ancient world was more than used to seeing priestesses; in fact, it can be said that the ancient world was full of priestesses, given that many pagan religions had them.[91] And, although in Israel the priesthood was carried out only by male Levites, if Jesus had wanted to also institute priestesses in the community He founded, this would have been less scandalous for the Jews than other aspects of the new religion (especially Jesus' claim to be God: see John 10:33).

Regarding the anthropological argument, Catholic doctrine, based on Genesis, recognizes the full ontological and axiological equality between men and women. But when one speaks of the priesthood, one is not dealing with

---

[91] Although it seems that they did not offer sacrificial worship, being instead at the service of the divinity, at most performing certain ritual parts such as sacred dances, or sometimes sacred prostitution.

the dignity of the human person, but rather with the supernatural gifts of God, towards which neither man nor woman can make claims. Just as there is no right of the human being to supernatural grace, which precisely for this reason is a gratuitous gift, so there cannot be any right to a particular vocation and mission. These come from God and are not due to nature. Could one think that God actually calls women to the priesthood and the Church intervenes between the call and response with her contrary discipline? We must respond to this by noting that the will of God is not communicated to the individual, but to the Church. Moreover, the human being cannot penetrate the thoughts of God if God Himself does not communicate it to him or her (Revelation). In the texts of divine Revelation, it is evident that Christ—although He could freely do otherwise—wanted to call into the group of the Twelve only men (*viri*). The Church considers herself bound by this decision of her Founder, not having the authority to modify what Christ has established.[92]

3. Magisterial Interventions

Faced with numerous pressures, the popes of the twentieth century returned repeatedly to the subject. Here we recall only the two most relevant texts.

(1) Saint Paul VI had the Congregation for the Doctrine of the Faith publish the declaration *Inter Insigniores*, in which the importance of the role of women in society and the Church from the beginning of its existence is emphasized. It also called for greater participation of women in the various fields of the apostolate of the Church. Thirdly, in the face of requests coming from many places and in the face of the fact that the Communities of the

---

[92] The New Testament, on one occasion (Rom 16:1) speaks of the "deaconess" Phoebe. The term is then found again in some ecclesial writings of the first centuries. About this, we shall note briefly: (1) In no place is there talk of "presbyteresses" or "episcopesses." Therefore, there is no consideration by the New Testament of a priestly role for women. (2) It is highly probable—almost certain—that Phoebe was not ordained (we don't read of a laying on of hands). The term was probably formed from the masculine term (perhaps even an appellation of affection and esteem) by an analogy between certain services carried out by this woman and those of deacons: particularly the works of charity and some liturgical act, such as assisting and perhaps also anointing women during the rite of Baptism. It is in this line also that the deaconesses present in certain patristic writings are understood: they probably descended into the baptismal font together with the female catechumens, which was done by the deacon for the male catechumens, and they anointed the body of women with oil, something that would have been unseemly if done by a man. But the use of the term, which then disappears, does not imply an ordination, the rite of which there is no trace in the sources. In support of this interpretation, there is the fact that—as the Church took root and consequently adult Baptisms diminished—the deaconesses also disappeared: evidently, their intervention was not indispensable for paedobaptism.

The Sacraments in Particular

Reformation admitted a female "priesthood," the Congregation presents an examination of the biblical and traditional sources concerning the question. One of the observations affirms:

> The Catholic Church has never felt that priestly or episcopal ordination can be validly conferred on women. A few heretical sects in the first centuries, especially Gnostic ones, entrusted the exercise of the priestly ministry to women: This innovation was immediately noted and condemned by the Fathers, who considered it as unacceptable in the Church.[93]

A second observation:

> The same Tradition has been faithfully safeguarded by the Churches of the East. Their unanimity on this point is all the more remarkable since in many other questions their discipline admits of a great diversity. At present time these same Churches refuse to associate themselves with requests directed towards securing the accession of women to priestly ordination.[94]

The Declaration then examines the practice of Jesus and the Apostles and confirms what we expressed above. Finally, the arguments of those who affirm that the Church can and should move away from the practice followed by Christ and the Apostles are examined. To the issues already mentioned above, the Declaration adds the evaluation of the argument for which the Church has the possibility of changing sacramental rites. But it can be answered, of course, that this is only possible for the aspects that are not essential or constitutive of them: and the ordination of the *viri* alone is not among them, because it is an immutable element of "divine law."

On the positive side, the observation is added that bishops and priests act *in Persona Christi*: the priest is an image of Christ. The image must be similar to its model and "there would not be this 'natural resemblance' that must exist between Christ and His minister if the role of Christ were not taken by a man: in such a case it would be difficult to see in the minister the image of Christ. For Christ Himself was and remains a man."[95]

---

[93] Congregation for the Doctrine of Faith, *Inter Insigniores* (1976), I (DS 4590 only quotes the first phrase of the passage cited by us).

[94] Congregation for the Doctrine of Faith, *Inter Insigniores*, I (DS 4591).

[95] Congregation for the Doctrine of Faith, *Inter Insigniores*, V (DS 4600).

The observation concerning the vocational aspects is also interesting. The Declaration brings the theme of vocation—which often in our times is understood in an intimistic and almost individualistic way: "*my* perception of being called"—back to its proper context, which is the ecclesial one:

> It is sometimes said and written in books and periodicals that some women feel that they have a vocation to the priesthood. Such an attraction however noble and understandable, still does not suffice for a genuine vocation. In fact a vocation cannot be reduced to a mere personal attraction, which can remain purely subjective. Since the priesthood is a particular ministry of which the Church has received the charge and the control, authentication by the Church is indispensable here and is a constitutive part of the vocation: Christ chose "those He wanted" (Mark 3:13)....
>
> Women who express a desire for the ministerial priesthood are doubtless motivated by the desire to serve Christ and the Church. And it is not surprising that, at a time when they are becoming more aware of the discriminations to which they have been subjected, they should desire the ministerial priesthood itself. But it must not be forgotten that the priesthood does not form part of the rights of the individual, but stems from the economy of the mystery of Christ and the Church. The priestly office cannot become the goal of social advancement: no merely human progress of society or of the individual can of itself give access to it: it is of another order.[96]

Thus, the implicit "careerist" character of the request for a feminine priesthood is brought to light.[97] For these and other reasons, it is recognized that the Church does not have the authority to admit women to priestly ordination.

(2) A second important text on the matter is the apostolic letter *Ordinatio Sacerdotalis* of Saint John Paul II. It was written because, despite the pronouncements of Saint Paul VI, discussions and pressures on this issue con-

---

[96] Congregation for the Doctrine of Faith, *Inter Insigniores*, VI (DS 4603–4605; some of the phrases we included were omitted in the DS).

[97] The aforementioned document speaks of "jealousy": DS 4606. In saying this, we do not want to claim that all people who call for female priesthood do so out of jealousy, but only that such temptations could be in the background. For the sake of honesty, it must also be said that certain men seek access to the ordained priesthood for the wrong reasons (career, social advancement, economic security, seeking a leadership role, etc.).

tinued in the Church. John Paul II reprised the various arguments already examined and added others, including a Mariological argument:

> The fact that the Blessed Virgin Mary, Mother of God and Mother of the Church, received neither the mission proper to the Apostles nor the ministerial priesthood clearly shows that the non-admission of women to priestly Ordination cannot mean that women are of lesser dignity, nor can it be construed as discrimination against them. Rather, it is to be seen as the faithful observance of a plan to be ascribed to the wisdom of the Lord of the universe.[98]

In conclusion, making recourse to the infallibility proper to the Universal Ordinary Magisterium of the Church, the Pope teaches:

> Wherefore, in order that all doubt may be removed regarding a matter of great importance, a matter which pertains to the Church's divine constitution itself, in virtue of my ministry of confirming the brethren I declare that the Church has no authority whatsoever to confer priestly Ordination on women and that this judgment is to be definitively held by all the Church's faithful.[99]

3.3.10. Clerical Celibacy

A final aspect concerns clerical celibacy, in itself a matter of moral theology and of canon law more than dogmatic theology, being an ecclesiastical discipline more than an essential element of the Sacrament of Holy Orders. However, discussing it will be useful, to show the fittingness of this discipline for theological and not just functional reasons.

---

[98] Saint John Paul II, *Ordinatio Sacerdotalis* (1994), §3.
[99] The Universal Ordinary Magisterium—as mentioned in Chapter Two—is the constant teaching of the Church concerning a doctrinal aspect. Even if it has never been solemnly defined by an ecumenical council or by a Pope, this doctrine is proposed to the faithful as infallibly taught and thus is obligatory. That these words of John Paul II should be understood exactly in this sense is evident from the text, but it was then officially confirmed by a *Responsum ad Dubium* of the Congregation for the Doctrine of the Faith, dated October 28, 1995, which says that the inadmissibility of women to the priesthood was declared by Saint John Paul II as belonging to the deposit of faith.

1. The New Testament

At the Biblical level, the fundamental information is the following: (1) Jesus was celibate. (2) Some of the Apostles were married (for example, Scripture speaks of the mother-in-law of Saint Peter). (3) The New Testament does not say anything about the familial life of the Apostles after their call, therefore it is hypothesized that they would leave their wives to follow Christ alone, living in celibacy. This cannot be said with certainty, but some passages may provide a good scriptural basis (see, for example, Matt 19:27–30). (4) In the New Testament, the call of married men is contemplated, but there are never men who are already called to Christ but who later marry. (5) The Apostolic Letters speak of "married" men who govern the Churches (see, for example, 1 Tim 3:2–5). It is emphasized, however, that the bishop must be *unius uxoris vir* ("married to one wife").[100] This has been interpreted in various ways: from the prohibition of polygamy (which, however, concerns everyone), to the binding to one Church (against careerism), to the prohibition concerning remarriage if left widowed, or to being married only to the Church (renouncing the proper acts of the Marriage contracted before becoming bishops; or not ever having been married). Saint Paul, who coined the formula, was himself celibate. Let us focus on this expression of his, which deserves some attention.

2. "Unius Uxoris Vir"

The stereotypical formula of Saint Paul is a formula of covenant, as is noted by the comparison with 2 Corinthians 11:2: "For I am jealous of you with the jealousy of God, since I betrothed you to one husband [*uni viro*; in Greek, *eni andri*] to present you as a chaste virgin to Christ." The Church (of Corinth) was Bride to "one husband," Christ. The passage refers to a spiritual marriage and thus to a covenant. It is significant that Saint Paul did not use the stereotypical formula in Ephesians 5, where—while recalling the theme of the Christ-Church marriage—he does so by focusing primarily on marriage between men and women, between Christians. Instead, the Apostle uses "*unius uxoris vir*" in reference to the ordained ministry! Therefore, the minister must reproduce in himself the image of Christ, Bride of the Church and—like the Lord—must be the husband of only one wife. And note that in 2 Corinthians 11, the wife is indeed the Church, which is called "pure virgin." If this does

---

[100] The formula is used for bishops (see 1 Tim 3:2: in Greek, *mias ghynaikos andra*), for priests (see Titus 1:6), and for deacons (see 1 Tim 3:12). In 1 Tim 5:9, then, the reciprocal formula is used *unius viri uxor* ("wife of one man") for an elderly widow.

not exclude that the ministers of which the New Testament speaks could be (or have been) married, it does direct the interpretation of the formula toward a meaning of abstinence from conjugal relationships, if not precisely celibacy by choice: one way or another, the ordained minister must be married only to the Church.

This is why the exegesis of the Pauline formula that was offered by Saint Augustine, although it may appear fanciful, is actually quite serious. He wonders why polygamy was accepted in the Old Testament, while among Christians the Sacrament consists in the union between one man and one woman, which is why it is also not licit to ordain anybody but those who have had only one wife [*unius uxoris virum*]. And he answers: "as the many wives of the old Fathers signified our future Churches out of all nations made subject unto one husband, Christ [*uni viro subditas Christo*]: so our chief-priest [*antistes*, meaning the bishop], the husband of one wife [*unius uxoris vir*] signifies unity out of all nations, made subject unto one husband, Christ."[101] Now, although—as we shall say shortly—the Church has regulated the matter of celibacy only starting from the fourth century, we must remember that the synods that have dealt with the subject have done so by claiming to require ecclesial celibacy because it corresponds to the Apostolic Tradition!

3. Ecclesiastical Discipline

It is known that the first official decision of the Church on the matter goes back to the Synod of Elvira (Granada) held between 300 and 306.[102] It was asserted by well-known nineteenth-century scholars that the Synod of Elvira introduced for the first time in the history of the Church a practice that was previously unknown. Pius XI responds to this thesis:

> The law of ecclesiastical celibacy, whose first written traces pre-suppose a still earlier unwritten practice, dates back to a canon of the Council of Elvira, at the beginning of the fourth century, when persecution still raged. This law only makes obligatory what might in any case almost be termed a moral exigency that springs from the Gospel and the Apostolic preaching.[103]

---

[101] Saint Augustine of Hippo, *De bono coniugali* 18.21, in *NPNF*, vol. 3, trans. C.L. Cornish (Peabody, MA: Hendrickson Publishers, 1994), 408.

[102] See cann. 27 and 33 (DS 118–119).

[103] Pius XI, *Ad Catholici Sacerdotii* (1935), II, 4.

Also in the fourth century, the Popes Saint Damasus (d. 384) and Siricius (d. 399) would speak of an obligation of continence for clerics, which they attributed to the very teaching of Christ and the Apostles.[104] Likewise, Saint Leo the Great (d. 461) spoke of it in the following century. The first Ecumenical Council of Nicaea (AD 325), in can. 3, already resumed the prescriptions given at Elvira by prohibiting the clerics of the three degrees from having a woman with them unless it was a mother, sister, or aunt—namely, people above all suspicion. It is relevant that "wife" is not listed. This is interpreted as an attestation of the fact that members of the clergy were not to be married, or at least that they had to observe continence in their previous marriage.

For many centuries, however, at least *de facto*, the question remained open. In the meantime, a better reflection was developed, and further motivations for clerical celibacy emerged: conformity to Christ,[105] ritual purity,[106] total dedication to the ministry, etc. There are numerous texts of the Fathers that are in favor of clerical celibacy. The Pope who made a decisive commitment to its universalization, even *de facto*, was Gregory VII (d. 1085). The decisions of the Second Lateran Council of 1139 are also a consequence of his commitment: "we prescribe that nobody is to hear the Masses of those whom he knows to have wives or concubines."[107] After various other pronouncements, the Council of Trent would reconfirm the invalidity of the marriage contracts of those who were already ordained and affirmed the superiority of the state of life of celibacy or virginity for the kingdom over that of marriage.[108]

It can be said that priestly celibacy has always been, in some way, a stumbling block, not only on an existential level, but also on the level of doctrinal and canonical discussions. This very brief and incomplete sketch of the history of the issue shows that the Church tends to consider the practice of perfect continence on the part of ordained ministers a teaching with apos-

---

[104] See the Decretals *Directa ad Decessorem* (385) (DS 185); *Cum in Unum* and *Dominus Inter* of 386.

[105] This argument has a long Tradition and comes to be newly emphasized in the twentieth century by the apostolic exhortation *Menti Nostrae* (1950) and the encyclical *Sacra Virginitas* (1954) of Pius XII.

[106] Already present in the mentioned Decretals of Saint Damasus and Siricius, this argument becomes central at the Second Synod of Carthage in 390, which would become a privileged *testimonium* concerning celibacy all the way up to (and during) the Council of Trent.

[107] Second Lateran Council, *Canones* (1139), can. 7 (translation: *papalencyclicals.net*). The canon (which is missing in the DS) goes on to declare marriage contracts invalid for those who are already clerics.

[108] See Council of Trent, *Doctrina et Canones de Sacramento Matrimonii* (1563), cann. 9–10 (DS 1809–1810).

tolic origins, or at least a very suitable attitude, especially for the two priestly degrees of ordained ministry. Therefore, more than that of priestly celibacy, we would need to speak of perfect priestly continence, which implies, for someone who enters into Holy Orders already married, the choice—obviously taken in mutual agreement with his wife—to live in marriage without exercising sexuality. This path could also be feasible at the ecumenical level.[109] For those who go into ordination as celibates, they consciously choose to renounce marriage, having to live out their priesthood in perfect continence.[110]

4. Recent Magisterium

In the second half of the twentieth century, the attack on clerical celibacy became strong once again. Saint John XXIII lamented it:

> It pains us that . . . there is muttering by some concerning the will or fittingness for the Catholic Church to renounce what for centuries and centuries was and remains one of the most noble and pure glories of the priesthood. The law of clerical celibacy and the care for making it prevail always hearkens back to the battles of heroic times, when the Church of Christ had to fight, and succeeded, for the glorious trinomial, always an emblem of victory: Church of Christ, free, chaste, and Catholic.[111]

The Second Vatican Council has fully confirmed the validity of the discipline of celibacy for the clergy[112] and Saint Paul VI, in the wake of the Council, published the encyclical *Sacerdotalis Caelibatus* (1967), in which he examines the objections to celibacy and amply proposes the theological, his-

---

[109] Our Orthodox brothers could establish that even their "uxored" (married) clergy should live a marriage in which perfect continence is observed. This would allow Orthodox priests to more fully embody the image of Christ, Bridegroom of the Church. It would not eliminate, however, the practical problems, because of which the Catholic discipline still appears to be better.

[110] This approach to the problem could favor an opening, in the Catholic Church, to the practice of so-called *viri probati*: men of a certain age, practicing and committed to the Church, who could be ordained priests to make up for priest shortages in certain parts of the world. If it is true that this possibility is not excluded by dogma, it is still, however, to be discouraged for practical as well as theological reasons. In fact, real problems would be created that are greater than those that would eventually be solved.

[111] Saint John XXIII, *Allocution in the Second Session of the Roman Synod*, January 26, 1960 (our translation).

[112] See Second Vatican Council, *Optatam Totius* (1965), §10; *Presbyterorum Ordinis*, §16.

torical, and spiritual reasons that support it. It is the first time (and so far the only time) that a text of such breadth is dedicated to the theme—a fact that also indicates the attacks this discipline has suffered from many opponents. We can add a text of John Paul II:

> In virginity and celibacy, chastity retains its original meaning, that is, of human sexuality lived as a genuine sign of and precious service to the love of communion and gift of self to others....
>
> In this light one can more easily understand and appreciate the reasons behind the centuries-old choice which the Western Church has made and maintained—despite all the difficulties and objections raised down the centuries—of conferring the order of presbyter only on men who have given proof that they have been called by God to the gift of chastity in absolute and perpetual celibacy.
>
> The synod Fathers clearly and forcefully expressed their thought on this matter in an important proposal which deserves to be quoted here in full: "While in no way interfering with the discipline of the Oriental Churches, the Synod, in the conviction that perfect chastity in priestly celibacy is a charism, reminds priests that celibacy is a priceless gift of God for the Church and has a prophetic value for the world today. This Synod strongly reaffirms what the Latin Church and some Oriental rites require that is, that the priesthood be conferred only on those men who have received from God the gift of the vocation to celibate chastity.... The Synod does not wish to leave any doubts in the mind of anyone regarding the Church's firm will to maintain the law that demands perpetual and freely chosen celibacy for present and future candidates for priestly Ordination in the Latin rite. The Synod would like to see celibacy presented and explained in the fullness of its biblical, theological and spiritual richness, as a precious gift given by God to His Church and as a sign of the kingdom which is not of this world—a sign of God's love for this world and of the undivided love of the priest for God and for God's people, with the result that celibacy is seen as a positive enrichment of the priesthood."[113]

---

[113] Saint John Paul II, *Pastores Dabo Vobis* (1992), §29.

The Sacraments in Particular

Finally, let us also listen to Pope Benedict XVI:

> The fact that Christ Himself, the eternal Priest, lived His mission even to the sacrifice of the cross in the state of virginity constitutes the sure point of reference for understanding the meaning of the tradition of the Latin Church. It is not sufficient to understand priestly celibacy in purely functional terms. Celibacy is really a special way of conforming oneself to Christ's own way of life. This choice has first and foremost a nuptial meaning; it is a profound identification with the heart of Christ the Bridegroom who gives His life for His Bride.[114]

4. Repeatable Sacraments

We shall now go on to the treatment of those Sacraments that are repeatable because they do not imprint a character and thus they can be received multiple times in someone's life. Here we shall discuss three Sacraments: Matrimony, Penance, and the Anointing of the Sick. We shall dedicate the entire next chapter to the Eucharist, given its transcendent importance. Although the Eucharist is one of the seven Sacraments, it is nonetheless superior to all the rest; indeed, the other Sacraments are ordered toward the Eucharist. The Angelic Doctor teaches that "the Eucharist is, as it were, the perfection of the spiritual life and the end of all the other Sacraments," although it "is not indispensable for salvation like Baptism."[115] At the foundation of every Sacrament is the Passion of Jesus Christ, which has merited the grace that is infused in us by the Sacraments. In the Eucharist, the perfect sign of the Passion is found.[116] The Sacrament of the altar is thus the greatest of all the Sacraments:

> Absolutely speaking, the Sacrament of the Eucharist is the greatest of all the Sacraments. This results from three considerations. First, because it really contains Christ in Person.... Second, for the

---

[114] Benedict XVI, *Sacramentum Caritatis* (2007), §24.

[115] *ST* III, q. 73, a. 3 (our translation).

[116] "The Eucharist is the perfect Sacrament of the Passion of the Lord, in that it contains Christ himself Who has suffered.... This Sacrament was instituted in the [paschal] supper [of Jesus] because it would subsequently be the memorial of the Lord's Passion" (*ST* III, q. 73, a. 5 [our translation]).

order existing between the Sacraments: all the other Sacraments are indeed ordered to the Eucharist as their end.... Third, this results from the ritual of the Sacraments, in fact, the reception of almost all the Sacraments is completed with Eucharistic Communion.[117]

Let us therefore postpone our discussion on the Eucharist, and instead continue with the other three repeatable Sacraments.

4.1. Marriage

4.1.1. Natural Reality and Sacrament

Marriage, that is, the union of a man and a woman who become spouses, is a reality that has been found throughout human history and in all cultures. It is therefore, first of all, a natural reality that belongs to the law of nature. In Christianity, this natural reality is elevated to the level of grace, being established by Christ as a Sacrament.[118] Thus, a first aspect of the bipolarity of Marriage consists in the fact that, in Christianity, it is both a natural reality and a supernatural one. The values, goods, and natural ends of marriage in the Christian religion are confirmed and filled with grace.

4.1.2. In Salvation History

Marriage is mentioned more than a few times in the history of Salvation. The *Catechism* notes that it is found both in the first pages of Genesis and the last page of Revelation, as though the reality of matrimony were coextensive with biblical Revelation (see CCC §1602). Moreover, it is indeed no wonder that some contemporary authors have tried to reread the entire history of salvation in light of the category of "Covenant." God carries out the history of salvation by making covenants with the people and individuals. Matrimony is a pact/covenant between partners (a man and a woman), and thus to some extent we speak of God's nuptiality towards His people and toward His elect. At the apex of salvation history is Christ, Who would then found the Church, understood as His mystical Bride. On the basis of this biblical confirmation,

---

[117] *ST* III, q. 65, a. 3 (our translation).
[118] "If anyone says that Matrimony is not truly and properly one of the seven Sacraments of the law of the Gospel, instituted by Christ the Lord, but that it was devised in the Church by men and does not confer grace, let him be anathema" (Council of Trent, *Doctrina et Canones de Sacramento Matrimonii*, can. 1 [DS 1801]; see Council of Trent, *Decretum de Sacramentis*, can. 1 [DS 1601]).

some contemporary authors tried to make God's spousal relationship with us the fulcrum of systematic theology. Putting aside the specific content of these proposals, it is certainly clear that Marriage receives ample attention in the sources of Revelation.

4.1.3. Essential Natural Elements

As a natural reality, marriage has its origin in God the Creator. That is why it pertains to the order of nature that He established, and it cannot undergo essential changes, even if accidental aspects—especially regarding rituals and customs—can change from time to time and place to place. Here we refer to matrimony in normal conditions, without entering into the issue of particular cases.

1. Sexual Complementarity

A basic aspect of marriage from the natural point of view is that of the complementarity of the sexes. It is an incontrovertible biological fact that human beings are born sexually differentiated, in an objective and indubitable physical-psychic determination, linked to being male or female. The differentiated and complementary genital organs clearly indicate an immutable difference, but also a reciprocal reference. The law of nature for which the conjugal bond can only be sanctioned between individuals of a different sex is already written into the bodies of the persons, as well as in the natural sexual orientation for which the man tends toward the woman and vice versa.

2. Fecundity

A second aspect that is immediately linked to the first is procreation—namely, the fecundity of marriage. In normal conditions, the union of the man and woman tends by its nature toward the procreation of new human beings, as also happens in the subhuman animal world. Marriage thus has a clear procreative purpose, inscribed in corporeity itself, as well as in the spontaneous instinct of human beings to have descendants.

3. Indissolubility

From the second aspect, the third is derived: the permanence of the strict pact between spouses, for which they unite not *ad certum tempus* (for a limited time), but in perpetuity. This can also be called the indissolubility of marriage. It is based in the first place on the demands of children, who must be accompanied during their growth by paternal and maternal figures, as well as being based on the stability of the family unit that is created through marriage. It is useful to observe that many species of subhuman animals manage to reach independence immediately after birth, or at least rather quickly. In the subhuman animal world, therefore, the necessity of stability is often not needed, and sexual relationships are ordered mainly, if not exclusively, toward procreation, aimed at the continuance of the species. But in the human world there are superior characteristics and values. Among human animals, a bond is formed that is not only sexual but also affective. The stability of the human-social unit (family) that originates with the wedding is ordered not only toward the accompaniment of offspring, who need many years of care before they are capable of providing for themselves, but also toward the psychological and social demands of human beings.[119] By psychological needs, we mean here both sentimental (lower stratum of the human soul) and the intellectual and volitional (upper stratum) needs. In forming a marriage, the human being, in fact, undertakes not only to reproduce other human beings (procreative aspect), but also to live in a communion of life with the spouse (unitive aspect) that, as with the children, involves the just expectation of a stable family life.[120]

Being a fundamental life choice—which in optimal conditions is made only once—it involves the sentimental and emotional aspect in a strong way. The indissolubility of marriage guarantees to both spouses the psychological stability needed in the context of so radical a commitment of their affectivity. At the level of the superior stratum of the soul (intellect and will), the indissolubility is linked to the possibility of the human being to make definitive and incontrovertible acts in his or her existence. The dignity of the human person is clearly affirmed where it is capable of responsibility: assuming commitments and acting on them. The marriage commitment is among the highest that the human being can take on, and it once again distinguishes him or her from inferior animals who, not possessing the superior stratum of the soul, are incapable of such commitment, and thus incapable of responsibility.[121]

---

[119] See Pius XI, *Casti Connubii* (1930) (DS 3707).

[120] "The commandment 'do not commit adultery' finds its just motivation in the indissolubility of the Marriage in which the man and the woman ... unite.... Adultery, by its essence, contrasts with such a unity, in the sense in which this unity corresponds to the dignity of persons" (Saint John Paul II, *General Audience*, October 8, 1980, §6).

[121] A simple example: When a dog bites someone, one does not take it up with the animal but with the owner, who has not kept him at bay. The same is true if a skittish horse kicks someone. We cannot ask non-human animals to answer for their actions, to be responsi-

The indissolubility of marriage represents this typically human responsibility, which even at the natural level exalts human union over the merely reproductive mechanisms of inferior animals.

Finally, the indissolubility of marriage is also linked to the social needs of human beings—this both for the members of the family unit, and for others. Giving rise to the family, marriage remains as a perennial root of its stability, a stability that is a most important element of the wider stability of society.[122] Hence the classic saying that sees in the family the *"original cell of social life"* (CCC §2207). Wherever families are stable, society—even with its imperfections—is stable. In those societies where marriages are easily broken— and "broken families" formed—individuals lose their point of reference, to the detriment of social cohesion and the moral order.

4.1.4. Sacred Scripture

1. Confirmation and Elevation of the Natural Values

In Holy Scripture, all these elements are reaffirmed, and thus they also become part of sacramental Marriage, the grace of which is in view of the preservation and growth of these values.[123] The sexual complementarity of male and female is confirmed in Genesis 2:18, 21–23:

> The LORD God said: "It is not good for the man to be alone. I will make a helper suited to him." ... So the LORD God cast a deep sleep on the man, and while he was asleep, he took out one of his ribs and

---

ble; we expect it from human beings.

[122] "If in fact the tranquility, stability, and security of human commerce generally require that that contracts are not lightly proclaimed null, this is even more true for a contract of such importance, like that of marriage, whose firmness and stability are required by the common good of human society and the private good of spouses and their children" (Pius XII, *Discourse to the Roman Rota*, October 3, 1941 [our translation])

[123] Second Vatican Council, *Gaudium et Spes*, §48: "Authentic married love is caught up into divine love and is governed and enriched by Christ's redeeming power and the saving activity of the Church, so that this love may lead the spouses to God with powerful effect and may aid and strengthen them in sublime office of being a father or a mother. For this reason Christian spouses have a special Sacrament by which they are fortified and receive a kind of consecration in the duties and dignity of their state. By virtue of this Sacrament, as spouses fulfill their conjugal and family obligation, they are penetrated with the Spirit of Christ, which suffuses their whole lives with faith, hope and charity. Thus they increasingly advance the perfection of their own personalities, as well as their mutual sanctification, and hence contribute jointly to the glory of God."

closed up its place with flesh. The LORD God then built the rib that he had taken from the man into a woman. When he brought her to the man, the man said: / "This one, at last, is bone of my bones / and flesh of my flesh; / This one shall be called 'woman,' / for out of man this one has been taken."[124]

The aspect of fertility is confirmed in Genesis 1:28: "God blessed them and God said to them: 'Be fertile and multiply; fill the earth and subdue it. Have dominion over the fish of the sea, the birds of the air, and all the living things that crawl on the earth.'" Finally, the aspect of indissolubility is confirmed in Genesis 2:24: "That is why a man leaves his father and mother and clings to his wife, and the two of them become one body,"[125] the exegesis of which, in the sense indicated, was provided by Christ himself:

> Some Pharisees approached him, and tested him, saying, "Is it lawful for a man to divorce his wife for any cause whatever?" He said in reply, "Have you not read that from the beginning the Creator 'made them male and female' and said, 'For this reason a man shall leave his father and mother and be joined to his wife, and the two shall become one flesh'? So they are no longer two, but one flesh. Therefore, what God has joined together, no human being must separate" (Matt 19:3–6).[126]

2. Jesus and the Indissolubility of Marriage

This Gospel passage continues with a counter-question of the Pharisees (v. 7): "Then why did Moses command that the man give the woman a bill of divorce and dismiss [her]?" Moses had effectively permitted—if we express it in an anachronistic way—the possibility of divorce (see Deut 24:1–4), something that would eliminate the value of matrimonial indissolubility within our religion. The response of Jesus to the question is illuminating both because it confirms this indissolubility, and because it makes implicit reference to

---

[124] See the commentary on the text by Saint John Paul II, *General Audience*, November 7, 1979, and November 14, 1979.
[125] See Saint John Paul II, *General Audience*, November 21, 1979.
[126] Saint John Paul II broadly explained this Gospel pericope in several catecheses among those of the broad series he dedicated to the so-called "theology of the body," which actually contains multiple aspects: love and virginity, Marriage, the resurrection of the flesh, the redemption of the heart, etc. See, for example, *General Audience*, September 19, 1979; September 26, 1979; April 2, 1980.

another dimension of Marriage that is also present in the Scriptures. Christ tells them, "Because of the hardness of your hearts Moses allowed you to divorce your wives, but from the beginning it was not so" (v. 8). Jesus considers the possibility of divorce to be a concession made due to the wickedness and selfishness of human beings, but He reaffirms that God did not want this, because He placed in His creation an immutable law, of which the indissolubility of Marriage forms a part: "from the beginning it was not so." And not only in the beginning. What is original is always valid; thus Christ concludes by fully reestablishing the rule of indissolubility and thus eliminating the Mosaic concession: "I say to you, whoever divorces his wife (unless the marriage is unlawful) and marries another commits adultery" (v. 9).

We must say a few words on the statement, "unless the marriage is unlawful," which is found in this passage of Matthew, but not in the parallel of Mark 10:12. The Greek text of Matthew reads in this way: *parektos logou porneias*. At first sight, it would seem that Jesus admits at least a case in which divorce is licit: the case of *porneia*, a word that the Vulgate translates with *fornicatio* (*excepta fornicationis causa*). From the time of Saint Jerome, exegetes have offered various explanations of these words of Jesus. For modern Protestants and for the Orthodox, these words indicate that it is possible in some cases to divorce. The case would be in particular that of a spouse who is betrayed. Without dwelling here on analyzing the various exegetical proposals, we can say that the most acceptable holds that *porneia* should not be understood as adultery, but rather in the sense of "concubinage" or "illegitimate union" (as we saw, the NABRE translates it as referring to an "unlawful" marriage). Therefore, Jesus does not admit divorce if one of the spouses betrays the other; the Lord says that they can be separated only if they were never truly married, that is, if their union was illegitimate. In fact, in another place, Jesus distinguishes between true marriages and unions not ratified by marriage (see John 4:18). This interpretation explains better than others the general sense of the pericope of Saint Matthew, in which Jesus declares the Mosaic exception in favor of divorce to no longer be in force. And how could He declare exceptions to indissolubility no longer applicable, if He himself then made another one? Moreover, the reactions of the disciples to His words would not be understandable in that case either: "[His] disciples said to him, 'If that is the case of a man with his wife, it is better not to marry'" (Matt 19:10). Such a response is explained only if Jesus has just finished saying that there are no exceptions to the indissolubility of marriage.

3. The Weight of Original Sin

The other aspect implied by the text of Matthew emerges clearly if we ask a further question: Why are human beings, with respect to Marriage, selfish and hard of heart? The response brings the question back into the wider context of original sin, which we encountered in Chapter Three. Marriage in itself remains intact even if people who access it are sinners, and thus always exposed to sin. Let us recall that one of the consequences of original sin touched exactly the relationship between husband and wife, in which, because of the first sin, conflict arises: "To the woman he said: / ... Yet your urge shall be for your husband, / and he shall rule over you" (Gen 3:16). On the other hand, this conflict had already become evident from the fact that, before the divine interrogation, Adam had sought to exculpate himself by accusing his wife, from whom he already distances himself: "The woman whom you put here with me—she gave me fruit from the tree, so I ate it" (Gen 3:12).

4. Medicinal Value

The disorder of original sin affects all human reality, including the matrimonial reality, with varied and serious consequent evils. It is in this perspective that the medicinal value of Matrimony should be understood. If, in the original plan of God, it had values, goods, and ends oriented toward the growth of the individual, the couple, the family, and society, then all of this is now put at risk by concupiscence, a fruit of sin, which tends to ruin all positive realities and pushes the person to turn inward to selfish ends. In this new situation, the realities of faith also become medicinal and therapeutic. The Sacraments (as we shall see especially with the two specific Sacraments of healing) are not only propulsive and elevating, but also curative and medicinal: hence the classical perspective of Marriage as a *remedium concupiscentiae* ("remedy for concupiscence"). It is rightly noted, in the recent literature on Marriage, that neither *Gaudium et Spes* of Vatican II, nor the *Codex Iuris Canonici* of 1983 use this expression. One can infer from this that the Magisterium holds that it is outdated, if not even incorrect, because it would transmit an idea of Marriage as an outlet for base instincts. If this were the case, it is clear that it would be a reductive perspective, and perhaps that is why the mentioned texts avoid using it. But such an expression is present in the previous Magisterium, for example, in the Code of 1917[127] and (although not *ad litteram*) in the encycli-

---

[127] "*Matrimonii finis primarius est procreatio atque educatio prolis; secundarius mutuum adiutorium et remedium concupiscentiae*— The primary end of marriage is the procreation and

cal *Casti Connubii* of Pius XI. This beautiful Encyclical has often been overly criticized, to the point of raising suspicion that some of its critics have not truly read it, or they have not done so with serenity. Pius XI does not teach there that the *remedium concupiscentiae* would be the most qualifying aspect of Marriage. The Encyclical, on the contrary, underlines the beauty and grandeur of the Sacrament, understood as a means for growth in holiness, and it adds that among the secondary aspects there is also that of placing limits on moral disorder:

> For in Matrimony as well as in the use of matrimonial rights there are also secondary ends, such as mutual aid, the cultivating of mutual love, and the quieting of concupiscence [*concupiscentiae sedatio*] that husband and wife are not forbidden to consider so long as they are subordinated to the primary end and so long as the intrinsic nature of the act is preserved.[128]

We need to recall that the doctrine of *remedium concupiscentiae* has a rather explicit biblical basis:

> Now in regard to the matters about which you wrote: "It is a good thing for a man not to touch a woman," but because of cases of immorality every man should have his own wife, and every woman her own husband.... Now to the unmarried and to widows, I say: it is a good thing for them to remain as they are, as I do, but if they cannot exercise self-control they should marry, for it is better to marry than to be on fire. (1 Cor 7:1–2, 8–9)

This does not mean that the main reason God instituted Marriage is medicinal: in fact, it was instituted (at least as a natural reality) before original sin. But since original sin and its consequences are a reality, the fact that Marriage has as a secondary purpose a healthy remedy to disordered drives is also a reality.[129] It should not be forgotten that the word "remedy" still has a positive

---

education of children. Its secondary end is mutual help and the allaying of concupiscence" (*Codex Iuris Canonici* [1917], can. 1013 §1, in *The 1917 or Pio-Benedictine Code of Canon Law*, ed. Edward N. Peters [San Francisco: Ignatius Press, 2001], 351).

[128] Pius XI, *Casti Connubii* (DS 3718).

[129] "The notion of Sacrament entails its being a remedy [*remedium*] of holiness for the human being against his or her sins, a remedy shown through sensible signs. Given that this is recognized in Marriage, it must be counted among the Sacraments" (*ST*, "Supplement," q. 42, a. 1 [our translation]).

value. It is not necessary to choose: *either* Marriage is a reality of the exaltation of human love, *or* it serves as a cure for deviations. Marriage, in the concrete economy of salvation, is both things: *both* a means of elevation, *and* a means of purifying love and sexuality. Thanks to faithful and indissoluble Marriage, the wounded sexual impulse is healed, rescued from egoism, and placed in the service of the mutual self-giving between spouses and of the transmission of life, as well as the psychological and social stability of human beings.

5. *Christological Figuration*

From the standpoint of the positivity of sacramental Marriage, the primary text of the New Testament is clearly Ephesians 5:21–33, in which Saint Paul reveals the Christological-ecclesial figuration of Christian Marriage:

> Be subordinate to one another out of reverence for Christ. Wives should be subordinate to their husbands as to the Lord. For the husband is head of his wife just as Christ is head of the church, he himself the savior of the body. As the church is subordinate to Christ, so wives should be subordinate to their husbands in everything. Husbands, love your wives, even as Christ loved the church and handed himself over for her to sanctify her, cleansing her by the bath of water with the word, that he might present to himself the church in splendor, without spot or wrinkle or any such thing, that she might be holy and without blemish. So [also] husbands should love their wives as their own bodies. He who loves his wife loves himself. For no one hates his own flesh but rather nourishes and cherishes it, even as Christ does the church, because we are members of his body. "For this reason a man shall leave [his] father and [his] mother and be joined to his wife, and the two shall become one flesh." This is a great mystery, but I speak in reference to Christ and the church. In any case, each one of you should love his wife as himself, and the wife should respect her husband.

Saint John Paul II comments extensively on this text in eleven catechesis delivered in his *General Audiences*.[130] In order to understand the cited Pauline passage, we refer the reader to the Pope's teachings.

---

[130] See the *General Audiences* of the following dates: July 28, 1982, August 4, 1982, August 11, 1982, August 18, 1982, August 25, 1982, September 1, 1982, September 8, 1982, September 15, 1982, September 22, 1982, September 29, 1982, October 6, 1982.

The Sacraments in Particular

4.1.5. Ministry

Regarding the minister of this Sacrament, there is a difference in views between Catholics and Orthodox. For the latter, the minister of the Sacrament is the priest who performs the "coronation" of the bride and groom.[131] In fact, in the Eastern rites, it is believed that the moment in which the Marriage pact is sealed corresponds to this liturgical rite, in which the celebrant places the crowns on the head of the spouses. This rite is absent in the Latin liturgical Tradition, even if the Italian Episcopal Conference decided to include it as an optional rite in its recent Ritual of Marriage. Beyond the suitability (or not) of such a choice, its optionality indicates that it is not considered a constitutive part of the Sacrament. The Catholic Church teaches, in fact, that the ministers of the Sacrament are the bride and groom themselves, who exchange their consent.[132] The minister of the Church (who can also be a deacon in the Latin Rite) only assists the fiancées, but he does not celebrate the Sacrament. The fact that the ministers of the Sacrament are the spouses themselves implies that in this case too, as for the other Sacraments, the intention required of the minister, who makes the celebration valid, is that of wanting to "do what the Church does." This annotation is important primarily in our days, in which there is no shortage of proposals for declaring many sacramental Marriages void, for the reason that they would have been contracted without sufficient/formed faith on the part of the fiancées. Today, these proposals are justified almost to the point of finding a "Catholic way" to divorce. But it is theologically unsustainable. First of all, the Church recognizes Marriages between Catholics and non-Catholic Christians (who do not have the same faith at the time of marriage); moreover, the Church recognizes the Marriages of non-Catholic Christian couples as valid Sacraments, whether or not they later enter the Catholic Church, even if at the moment of their Marriage (for

---

[131] See the specifications made on this point in the previous chapter.

[132] This dogmatic truth should not, however, be invoked as the foundation of liturgical abuses, which are widespread today in Italy and elsewhere, such as, for example, that of the priest who invites the spouses to turn towards the assembly while they exchange their consent (remember that consent is exchanged before God and the Church as a whole, not simply before the community gathered at that time); or when the priest invites the spouses to stand beside him at the altar during the Eucharistic Liturgy (even in the consecration!) and let them self-communicate with him; or when he gives the consecrated Host and Chalice to the bride and groom to communicate each other (almost like at the reception in the banquet hall where the spouses often give each other drinks from the cup of the other); or when the spouses are told to distribute Holy Communion to those present; and so on. Contrary to all this, it should be recalled that the spouses are ministers of the Sacrament of Matrimony, not of the Holy Mass in which it is celebrated.

example, in the Protestant community), their faith did not recognize its sacramental nature.[133] To say that an imperfect subjective faith on the part of the contracting parties is cause for nullity implies declaring all of these marriages null. Above all, it means asking of the ministers of this Sacrament something that is not asked of the ministers of any other Sacrament: that is, that the personal faith of the minister determines its validity while the Church teaches that the Sacraments are valid *ex opere operato*, considering as a condition the minister's generic intention to do what the Church does when she carries out that Sacrament, even if the minister did not have personal faith, or was doctrinally ill-formed in it.[134] Therefore, despite the general climate of religious ignorance even among Catholics, it is prudent to believe that the vast majority of Marriages celebrated in the Church are valid. Benedict XVI confirmed all this by saying: "The indissoluble pact between a man and a woman does not, for the purposes of the Sacrament, require of those engaged to be married, their personal faith; what it does require, as a necessary minimal condition, is the intention to do what the Church does."[135]

4.1.6. Matter and Form

As for matter and form, this is the Sacrament in which it is most difficult to clearly identify them. It is sure that what constitutes Matrimony is the consent of the spouses: "*Verba quibus consensus matrimonialis exprimitur sunt*

---

[133] See Benedict XIV, *Matrimonia Quae in Locis* (1741), §2 (DS 2517).

[134] "It is worth clearly reiterating that the essential component of marital consent is not the quality of one's faith, which according to unchanging doctrine can be undermined only on the plane of the natural. Indeed, the *habitus fidei* is infused at the moment of Baptism and continues to have a mysterious influence in the soul, even when faith has not been developed and psychologically speaking seems to be absent. It is not uncommon that couples are led to true Marriage by the *instinctus naturae* and at the moment of its celebration they have a limited awareness of the fullness of God's plan. Only later in the life of the family do they come to discover all that God, the Creator and Redeemer, has established for them. A lack of formation in the faith and error with respect to the unity, indissolubility and sacramental dignity of Marriage invalidate marital consent only if they influence the person's will. It is for this reason that errors regarding the sacramentality of Marriage must be evaluated very attentively" (Francis, *Address to the Roman Rota*, January 22, 2016: we have omitted the references to the *Codex Iuris Canonici*).

[135] Benedict XVI, *Address to the Roman Rota*, January 26, 2013, §1. Obviously, as the Pope subsequently points out in the discourse, the theme of the subjective participation of the fiancées cannot be completely passed over in silence, and it requires sufficient analysis. It remains true, however, that the Church considers the fact that the engaged person accepts the natural goods of Marriage to be adequate formation to validly receive the Sacrament (see Saint John Paul II, *Address to the Roman Rota*, January 30, 2003, §8).

forma huius Sacramenti" ("The words with which marital consent is expressed constitute the form of this Sacrament").[136]

1. Form

The ordinary form of the Roman Rite provides three different forms for expressing this consent. A first form is said like so: "I, (*Name*), take you, (*Name*), to be my wife [husband]. I promise to be faithful to you, in good times and in bad, in sickness and in health, to love you and to honor you all the days of my life." Or, there is a second version of it: "I, (*Name*), take you, (*Name*), for my lawful wife [husband], to have and to hold, from this day forward, for better, for worse, for richer, for poorer, in sickness and in health, until death do us part." In a second form, the two spouses ask each other about their will for mutual and indissoluble union. Finally, in a third form, the priest questions the contracting parties one at a time, expressing the same contents of the first formula, and they express their consent publicly, assenting with "I do." In all these cases, the form of the Sacrament consists in the clear and public declaration of one's own will to unite oneself to the other in an indissoluble and faithful Marriage. The exchange of this consent between the spouses is believed by the Church to be the indispensable element that constitutes Marriage (see CCC §1626). Thus, for example, Pius XI:

> Yet although Matrimony is of its very nature of divine institution, the human will too enters into it and performs a most noble part. For each individual Marriage, inasmuch as it is a conjugal union of a particular man and woman, arises only from the free consent of each of the spouses; and this free act of the will, by which each party hands over and accepts those rights proper to the state of Marriage, is so necessary to constitute true Marriage that it cannot be supplied by any human power.[137]

"Consummation" follows matrimonial consent, that is, the corporeal union between the spouses. Consequently, the canonical formula considers

---

[136] *ST*, "Supplement," q. 42, a. 1 (our translation). In q. 45, a. 1, Saint Thomas drops the specification that it would be *the words* of consent that constitute the form and more correctly says only "*mutuum consensum*—mutual consent." However, immediately after (q. 45, a. 2) he reiterates his position that "it is necessary that marital consent be expressed orally [*verbis*]," because "this verbal expression is to Marriage as the external washing is to Baptism." We shall return to this point soon.

[137] Pius XI, *Casti Connubii* (DS 3701).

a Marriage that is "ratified" (by consent) and "consummated" to be indissoluble.[138] We need, however, to remember that from the dogmatic standpoint, consummation is not an essential part of Marriage: "Let the consent alone suffice for those whose union is in question; and if, by chance, this consent alone is lacking in the Marriage, everything else is vain, even if solemnized by intercourse itself, as attested to by the great Doctor John Chrysostom, who said: 'What makes a Marriage is not intercourse, but the will.'"[139] Hence, a Marriage that is not consummated can be canonically dissolved,[140] but if this does not happen, it remains a perfect Marriage (like the chaste marriage of Mary and Joseph).[141] The Council of Florence confirms with no ambiguity: "The efficient cause of Matrimony is, according to the rule,[142] the mutual consent expressed in words relating to the present [*per verba de praesenti expressus*]."[143]

2. Matter

What then is the matter of the Sacrament? It is not easy to determine. One

---

[138] It is known that the *Decretum Gratiani* (ca. 1140) declared "ratified and consummated" Marriage to be perfect; this statement is confirmed by Pope Alexander III (d. 1181) and from there goes on to all subsequent canonical legislation. We would need to propose here some specifications of a historical nature, but what is of interest to us is that for a long time now, the terms "ratified and consummated" are meant in the way that we indicated.

[139] Nicholas I, *Ad Consulta Vestra* (866), ch. 3 (DS 643). The Pope cites Pseudo-Chrysostom, *Opus imperfectum in Mattheum* 32.9. See also *ST*, "Supplement," q. 42, a. 4; q. 46, a. 2.

[140] See, for example, the letter to the archbishop of Salerno by Alexander III, *Verum Post* (DS 755–756).

[141] See *ST*, III, q. 29, a. 2; "Supplement," q. 48, a. 1. In the work of his youth *Scriptum super Sententiis* IV, d. 30, q. 2, a. 2, the Angelic Doctor approves the opinion of Peter Lombard, according to whom the opinion that holds that without the conjugal act the Marriage is null, is erroneous; if this were true, a consequence would follow that "between Mary and Joseph there was no Marriage, or that it was imperfect. But it is sinful to think this: because a holy Marriage is holier and more perfect, the more it is immune from carnal works" (our translation).

[142] This word (*regulariter*) does not mean that in exceptional cases a Marriage can be constituted without consent, but that it is possible to express consent not with words but with gestures. In fact, Innocent III, *Cum apud Sedem* (1198), had already ruled, in reply to Humbert of Arles: "You have asked us whether the mute and the deaf can be united to each other in Marriage.... It seems that, if such a one wishes to contract (a Marriage), it cannot and it ought not to be denied him, since what he cannot declare by words he can declare by signs" (DS 766).

[143] Council of Florence, *Exsultate Deo* (DS 1327). We have changed the English version provided by the DS, because it translates "*regulariter*" as "duly," relating it to "*expressus*" (DS: "duly expressed").

may be tempted to say that the matter is the spouses themselves who give themselves and receive each other: in fact, Marriage sanctions exactly this union. But it would be the only case in which the ministers and the matter of the Sacrament are the same. It would also be the only case in which the human persons themselves are the matter of the Sacrament, which does not seem possible. Perhaps we can respond by taking up what Saint Thomas says in a text that we have just quoted above. He states that the form of Marriage is consent and indicates that this consent must be expressed in words. Maybe he does not take into account the fact that there are different forms of language and that therefore consent can also be expressed in other ways: for example, in writing (Marriage by proxy) or through gestures, as in the case of a mute. But it is interesting what the Angelic Doctors says in *ST*, "Supplement," q. 45, a. 2: the words of consent are to Marriage what the external washing is to Baptism. It should be noted that consent is the form of Marriage, while in Baptism it is the formula pronounced by the celebrating minister. The external washing is the matter in Baptism (poured water). It seems then that Saint Thomas—more or less consciously—suggests that the "necessity" of the words of consent would be analogous to that of the matter of Baptism. Thus, a distinction could be made between the internal consent (intention of the spouses' wills to be bound in a matrimonial bond) and the external consent that is manifested: normally in words, in particular cases with other forms of language. The latter would act as a matter of the Sacrament. The internal consent (the form) obviously requires the matter (external consent), and only in this way is the (wanted and manifested) consent what produces the Marriage. This interpretation seems to be confirmed by a later text of the Common Doctor: "Just as those who receive external ablution are not baptized who do not have the intention of receiving the Sacrament, but for play or deception; thus Marriage does not occur for one who in expressing [assent] in words does not give inner consent."[144]

4.1.7. *Effects*

Now proceeding to the effects of the Sacrament, we note that the primary one is the very bond that is caused by Marriage. This bond, as the word itself suggests, indicates a bond that is created by God as an indissoluble union that entails a covenant for life. This concerns a new reality, which is called a family. Being that this union is sanctioned by God, no one can separate what He has joined. God enriches this new reality with a particular effusion of grace,

---

[144] *ST*, "Supplement," q. 45, a. 4 (our translation).

generated, as an instrumental cause, by the very Sacrament of Marriage. This grace is aimed at preserving and increasing the properties of Marriage, which Saint Augustine fixed in the following way: *fides, proles et sacramentum*, which in modern terms we translate as fidelity, fruitfulness, and indissolubility[145]:

> Now this good [of Marriage] is threefold: fidelity, offspring, and Sacrament. *Fidelity* means that there must be no relations with any other person outside the Marriage bond. *Offspring* means that children are to be lovingly received, brought up with tender care, and given a religious education. *Sacrament* means that the Marriage bond is not to be broken, and that if one partner in a marriage should be abandoned by the other, neither may enter a new Marriage even for the sake of having children. This is what may be called the rule of Marriage: by it the fertility of nature is made honorable and the disorder of concupiscence is regulated.[146]

For Augustine, the primary good of Marriage consists in offspring: even Roman law asserted that the *matrimonium iustum* was the one contracted *liberorum procreandorum causa* (to procreate children), so the will to generate distinguished the right and true Marriage from other types of union. Augustine also placed the education of offspring within the procreative task. The term *fides* refers here to the holy fidelity between the spouses and the love exchanged between them, while with *sacramentum*, Augustine makes reference to the sacred oath of the Roman soldiers, so the term takes on a sense of indissolubility—in fact, the military oath was indissoluble for the entire duration of service. However, he also puts the term in relation to Ephesians 5:32, from which, moreover, he borrows it. As we have seen, in that verse Saint Paul exclaims: "This is a great mystery, but I speak in reference to Christ and the Church." The indissolubility of Christian Marriage, therefore, is linked to the *mysterium/sacramentum* of the spousal relationship between Christ and the Church, marked by faithful indissolubility.

Saint Thomas accepts (through Peter Lombard) the Augustinian conception of the *tria bona*, which would later be adopted by the Council of

---

[145] See Saint John Paul II, *Familiaris Consortio* (1981), §§13–15.

[146] Saint Augustine of Hippo, *De Genesi ad litteram* 9.7.12, in *The Literal Meaning of Genesis*, vol. 2, trans. John Hammond Taylor (New York: Newman Press, 1982), 78. Other writings of Augustine on this topic are *De bono coniugali*, *De coniugiis adulterinis*, *De nuptiis et concupiscentia*, *De sancta virginitate*, and *De bono viduitatis*.

Florence,[147] but he transposes it into the Aristotelian categories. For Aristotle, the good consists in being appetible (*id quod omnia appetunt*—"what everyone desires"), and the purpose is nothing other than the final stage (or end) of an appetite, that is, of any tendency even if it were subconscious.[148] Hence, in Thomas, the Augustinian doctrine of the three goods experiences new emphases in a finalistic lens, even if the Angelic Doctor continues to use the terminology of the "goods." While in Augustine the primary good is the generation of offspring, in Thomas it is indissolubility:

> The indissolubility, which is implied in the Sacrament, belongs to Marriage in itself, since it is precisely from the fact that with the Marriage contract the spouses have granted themselves the mutual domain in perpetuity, and it follows that they cannot be separated. And this is why Marriage can never be distinct from inseparability: rather, it can be free of fidelity and offspring, because a thing's being or existence does not depend on its use. And on this side, the good of the Sacrament is more essential to Marriage than fidelity and offspring.[149]

Vatican II would seem to be more inclined toward the Thomistic doctrine:

> Marriage to be sure is not instituted solely for procreation; rather, its very nature as an unbreakable compact between persons, and the welfare of the children, both demand that the mutual love of the spouses be embodied in a rightly ordered manner, that it grow and ripen. Therefore, Marriage persists as a whole manner and communion of life, and maintains its value and indissolubility, even when despite the often intense desire of the couple, offspring are lacking.[150]

The stability of Marriage, therefore, cannot be considered secondary to the generation of offspring, and it is for this reason that Marriage remains indissoluble whether the couple voluntarily abstains from procreating, or the conjugal compact is unfruitful, or when the children become autonomous and leave the family home. However, Saint Thomas recovers the primacy of offspring (understood as the *intention* to procreate) over other goods/purposes

---

[147] See Council of Florence, *Exsultate Deo* (DS 1327).
[148] See Saint Thomas Aquinas, *Summa contra gentiles* I, ch. 37.
[149] *ST*, "Supplement," 49, 3 (our translation).
[150] Second Vatican Council, *Gaudium et Spes*, §50.

of Marriage, if it is viewed less as a Sacrament and more from the standpoint of natural law.[151] One can summarize his position by saying that the good of indissolubility is primary if one looks at what is most excellent; but that of procreation is primary if the standpoint assumed is the one that seeks what is most essential.

4.1.8. Pauline and Petrine Privileges

As strange as it may seem given the insistence of Scripture, the Fathers, the Doctors, and the Magisterium on indissolubility, there are still some cases in which the Church knows she has the power to dissolve Marriages. She recognizes this power as her own, in that she finds it taught directly or indirectly in Revelation. There are two main cases, and they are named after the two Apostles to which they refer: they are the "Pauline privilege" and the "Petrine privilege."

1. The Pauline Privilege

The Pauline privilege is expressed directly in 1 Corinthians 7:12–16:

> If any brother [any Christian] has a wife who is an unbeliever, and she is willing to go on living with him, he should not divorce her; and if any [Christian] woman has a husband who is an unbeliever, and he is willing to go on living with her, she should not divorce her husband. For the unbelieving husband is made holy through his wife, and the unbelieving wife is made holy through the brother [her husband]. Otherwise your children would be unclean, whereas in fact they are holy.
>
> If the unbeliever separates, however, let him separate. The brother or sister is not bound in such cases; God has called you to peace. For how do you know, wife, whether you will save your husband; or how do you know, husband, whether you will save your wife?

This is the case of two spouses who were married before becoming Christians. If only one of them believes and is baptized and the other does not accept this change, separation *in favorem fidei* ("in favor of the [Christian] faith") that was embraced by one of the two, is licit.[152] The underlying

---

[151] See *ST*, "Supplement," 49, 3.
[152] There is also the case of polygamous converts (see *Codex Iuris Canonici*, can. 1148) and

principle is that the faith has such a value as to trump even that of the indissolubility of natural Marriage.[153]

2. The Petrine Privilege

Unlike the Pauline privilege, the Petrine privilege does not have a direct biblical foundation, but rather an indirect foundation. It consists in the fact that the New Testament, as we saw in Chapter Eight, recognizes in Peter and his successors, the Roman Pontiffs, the power of the keys. This power, however, is not unlimited. The Pope is not omnipotent and therefore he cannot dissolve what God has united. No man can dissolve a ratified and consummated sacramental Marriage, not even the Pope.[154] Nevertheless, in very rare and very grave cases, he has the power to dissolve a ratified, but not consummated, sacramental Marriage. Pius XII mentions this:

> The ratified and consummated Marriage is indissoluble by divine law, it cannot be dissolved by any human power; while the other Marriages, though intrinsically indissoluble, do not however have an absolute extrinsic dissolubility, but, given certain necessary presuppositions, they can (these are, as is known, very rare cases) be dissolved, as well as by virtue of Pauline privilege, by the Roman Pontiff by virtue of his ministerial power.[155]

In reiterating the indissolubility of the ratified and consummated marriage, the Pope proposes a distinction between the intrinsic indissolubility, which is always absolute, and an extrinsic one that is not absolute in every single case. In the case of a Marriage that is ratified but not consummated, extrinsic indissolubility is not absolute, and thus it can be dissolved in rare cases by the Supreme Authority, using his "ministerial power" of the vicarious

---

the case of those who cannot reestablish marital cohabitation (can. 1149). See, moreover, the Congregation for the Doctrine of the Faith, *Potestas Ecclesiae* (2001) (rules for establishing the process for the dissolution of the Marriage bond *in favorem fidei*).

[153] The essential normativity is presented in the *Codex Iuris Canonici*, cann. 1143–1147. There are more details in the following: Congregation for the Doctrine of the Faith, *Instructio pro Solutione Matrimonii in Favorem Fidei* (1973); and *Normae Procedurales pro Conficiendo Processu Dissolutionis Vinculis Matrimonialis in Favorem Fidei* (1973), also known under the title *Potestas Ecclesiae*, the most recent version of which was published in 2001, as mentioned in the previous footnote.

[154] "A marriage that is *ratum et consummatum* can be dissolved by no human power and by no cause, except death" (*Codex Iuris Canonici*, can. 1141).

[155] Pius XII, *Address to the Roman Rota*, October 3, 1941 (our translation).

(with respect to Christ) type. Naturally, there is no right of the spouses who are in this situation to obtain dissolution. The papal intervention has a character of grace, which can be granted or not. The current *Code of Canon Law* regulates the Petrine privilege in the following terms: "For a just cause, the Roman Pontiff can dissolve a non-consummated marriage between baptized persons or between a baptized party and a non-baptized party at the request of both parties or of one of them, even if the other party is unwilling."[156]

4.2. Reconciliation

We shall conclude this chapter's discussion by presenting the last two Sacraments, known as the Sacraments of healing: Reconciliation and Anointing of the Sick. We have already discussed the first Sacrament that has a healing effect: Baptism. The Sacrament of Penance, as well as others, can be referred to in different ways, according to the perspective from which it is considered or the emphasis that one intends to place on the discussion. Here, we shall use the terms Penance, Confession, and Reconciliation. In fact, all these terms refer to cardinal elements of this Sacrament. (1) When Confession is used, it refers to the act of telling the priest what sins were committed.[157] To confess, in this sense, refers to revealing what has been done wrong, and so is used in a different sense than the confession of faith (e.g., confessing/professing the Creed). However, in the background, a link remains between the two senses of the term. Sins are confessed within a life of faith, in which the holiness of God and His work of salvation are confessed, and therefore one recognizes and indicts himself or herself as a sinner before the minister. (2) In using the word Penance, one refers to the Latin term *conversio* and to the Greek word *metanoia*, or conversion. This Sacrament is therapeutic because it favors and provokes penance as a change of thought and life. It is a painful process, which requires a "death" to the self, and thus the word Penance seems

---

[156] *Codex Iuris Canonici*, can. 1142.

[157] Although the following specification falls more into the sphere of moral theology and the pastoral care of the Sacrament, it is opportune to provide the indication, though without further analysis: "Since 'the faithful are obliged to confess, according to kind and number, all grave sins committed after Baptism of which they are conscious after careful examination and which have not yet been directly remitted by the Church's power of the keys, nor acknowledged in individual confession', any practice which restricts confession to a generic accusation of sin or of only one or two sins judged to be more important is to be reproved. Indeed, in view of the fact that all the faithful are called to holiness, it is recommended that they confess venial sins also" (Saint John Paul II, *Misericordia Dei* (2002), §3; the quote is a citation of *Codex Iuris Canonici*, can. 988 §1).

appropriate because it puts together the positive aspect of conversion with the onerous one of trial. (3) Finally, Reconciliation is used to refer primarily to the effect of the Sacrament that, as we shall say, is the return to communion with God and with the Church, as a consequence of the forgiveness of the sins that had interrupted this communion.

4.2.1. The Objectivity of Sin and Forgiveness

From what has been said about the nomenclature, we immediately realize that this Sacrament, in order to be understood, must be linked to the themes we have already encountered: of original sin, the concupiscence that remains even in the baptized, and of the reality of the effects both of original sin and of personal sins in the human being (see Chapter Three). If there is no clear vision of sin, there cannot be an adequate theology of the Sacrament of Penance either.[158] This also applies, in its own way, in the spiritual life of individuals and in the pastoral life of the Church. A more careful analysis of the theology of sin, which goes beyond what we have already said, concerns moral and spiritual theology, and thus we shall abstain from it. Nevertheless, we shall offer an overview of the concept of sin in the Bible a little later.

Another important element to keep in mind for developing a correct theology of Reconciliation is the real possibility of eternal damnation ("Hell"), of which we shall speak in the final chapter. Here, we can only say the following: if sin and the possibility of Hell are not realities, but chimeras and bogeys, then the Sacrament of Reconciliation cannot have a meaning that extends beyond that of (pseudo-) psychological support. From this perspective, we should talk more about counseling than a Sacrament. But in this regard, it will be useful to make a distinction between sin and a sense of guilt.

The (psychological) sense of guilt can (and in certain cases must) be dealt with through the help of a good psychologist, in order to prevent it from creating self-destructive processes. Sin as a theological reality, rather, is not a knot that human beings can untie, even if human beings themselves commit them. The lesson of Saint Anselm of Canterbury (d. 1109) should be recalled. He taught in *Cur Deus homo* that, although it is the human being who sinned, once the sin was committed, he or she is no longer able to repair it with human strength alone (see Chapter Four). In fact, sin, as an act of a limited being, which is the human being, is in itself a finite act, which produces a negative effect and is therefore solvable by human beings. But since sin repre-

---

[158] Not being able to spend time on it, we refer the reader to Saint John Paul II, *Reconciliatio et Paenitentia* (1984), §§14–18.

sents an offense to divine honor, which is infinite, the scope of this act actually escapes the possibility of resolution by a finite creature.[159] Although human beings are the ones who sin, only God can absolve them from the sins they have committed. Scripture affirms this human inability to overcome sin in various places; for example, in Psalm 51:5: "For I know my transgressions; / my sin is always before me." Even if the pious psalmist prays and participates in some form of divine Worship, he knows that his sins always remain before him. This certainly refers to the future redemption in Jesus Christ, but reflexively affirms—precisely because of this—that without a specific intervention of God, there is nothing that human beings can do that can purify them from their sins. The Sacrament of Confession is the ever-renewed implementation of this divine intervention of the purification of human beings from their sins. That is why a classic way of referring to this Sacrament is that of "Second Penance."[160] Just as Baptism is the divine intervention that purifies the human being from original sin, Reconciliation washes him or her from the sins committed after Baptism.

4.2.2. Biblical Revelation

1. Forgivable and Unforgivable Sins

Of course, not a word about the Sacrament of Confession is said in the Old Testament. However, we do encounter some elements that help it to be better understood. In particular, the distinction between two types of sin: one forgivable, the other not—for which the death penalty was imposed. The Book of Numbers speaks of it:

> If through inadvertence you fail to do any of these commandments which the LORD has given to Moses—anything the LORD commanded you through Moses from the time the LORD first gave the command down through your generations—if it was done inadvert-

---

[159] As is known, Saint Anselm's view was much criticized in the twentieth century for its excessive juridicism. Without returning to the question here, his argument on the specific point on which we are focusing now remains valid even if applied to other expressive registers, such as, for example, the personalistic and relational ones.

[160] See Tertullian of Carthage, *De Paenitentia* 7.10 ("*Paenitentia secunda*"). In 4.2 and 12.9, he speaks of "*secunda planca salutis*—second plank of salvation" (the image is that of a castaway who has lost the plank to which he clung in order to not drown and finds another). This expression was then cited by the Council of Trent, *Decretum de Iustificatione* (1547), ch. 14 (DS 1542).

ently without the community's knowledge, the whole community shall sacrifice one bull from the herd as a burnt offering of pleasing aroma to the Lord, along with its prescribed grain offering and libation, as well as one he-goat as a purification offering.... Not only the whole Israelite community but also the aliens residing among you shall be forgiven, since the inadvertent fault affects all the people.... But anyone who acts defiantly, whether a native or an alien, reviles the Lord, and shall be cut off from among the people. For having despised the word of the Lord and broken his commandment, he must be cut off entirely and bear the punishment (Num 15:22–24, 26, 30–31).

Even in the Old Testament, therefore, the possibility of obtaining forgiveness through a liturgical rite was provided. But this possibility was limited to sins committed inadvertently. In the New Testament, this scheme will be confirmed and specified. Beyond what is sometimes thought, in fact, even in the New Testament it is taught that there is a sin that cannot be forgiven, the "sin against the Holy Spirit." In line with the dynamic that is typical of the New Testament with respect to the Old, an elevation in understanding also occurs in regard to this sin: it is no longer a question of sending to death, but of recognizing the impossibility of salvation for those who remain in that unforgivable sin. Here are the main texts:

Therefore, I say to you, every sin and blasphemy will be forgiven people, but blasphemy against the Spirit will not be forgiven. (Matt 12:31)

I pray for them. I do not pray for the world ... (John 17:9)

If we sin deliberately after receiving knowledge of the truth, there no longer remains sacrifice for sins but a fearful prospect of judgment and a flaming fire that is going to consume the adversaries. Anyone who rejects the law of Moses is put to death without pity on the testimony of two or three witnesses. Do you not think that a much worse punishment is due the one who has contempt for the Son of God, considers unclean the covenant-blood by which he was consecrated, and insults the Spirit of grace? (Heb 10:26–29).

Sin against the Holy Spirit, in the past called "final impenitence," consists in willing not to recognize one's own error in order not to have to change one's life (see John 9:41). It is the voluntary refusal to be reached by the saving efficacy of Christ. Here, the human person cannot be forgiven for the simple reason that he or she does not intend to ask for forgiveness at all. In this, the person assimilates himself or herself to Satan (see John 8:44). But if he or she converts, then even this sin is forgivable.[161] The New Testament, then, broadens the teachings of the Old, because it admits two species of remissible sins: those which in the language of the catechesis and moral theology are called "venial sins" and "mortal sins." This distinction is based primarily on the following text:

> If anyone sees his brother sinning, if the sin is not deadly, he should pray to God and he will give him life. This is only for those whose sin is not deadly. There is such a thing as deadly sin, about which I do not say that you should pray. All wrongdoing is sin, but there is sin that is not deadly (1 John 5:16–17).

According to Saint John, there are light sins ("venial sins") that can be relieved through prayer. But there are also grave sins, which lead to death ("mortal sins"), and prayer is not sufficient for their purification.[162] It is here that the message of the New Testament is grafted onto the Sacrament of Reconciliation instituted by Christ. As a first step, it is good to remember that the forgiveness of sins played an important role in the ministry of Jesus, alongside preaching, healing, and exorcisms. On more than one occasion, Christ explicitly says that He forgives sins, an affirmation that caused scandal for the Jews (see Luke 7:49).[163] As with other aspects of His ministry, Jesus does not ask

---

[161] Thus, here we are not joining the Montanist line of Tertullian of Carthage, for whom there are some sins (idolatry, murder, adultery) that were irremissible (see *De pudicitia* 3.3; 9.20; 18.18; etc.). For Christ, there are no irremissible sins and, consequently, there are also none for the Church, which forgives them *in Persona Christi*. The sin against the Holy Spirit is irremissible not because Christ and the Church do not have power over it, but because this expression indicates precisely the obstinacy of those who do not ask for forgiveness and do not want to receive it. In this case the sin is irremissible because God does not force anyone to be saved. All of this is expressed with great clarity by Saint Gelasius I (d. 496), *Ne Forte* (DS 349).

[162] As it was written by Saint John II, *Reconciliatio et Paenitentia*, §17: "Venial sin does not deprive the sinner of sanctifying grace, friendship with God, charity and therefore eternal happiness, whereas just such a deprivation is precisely the consequence of mortal sin"; "mortal sin is sin whose object is grave matter and which is also committed with full knowledge and deliberate consent."

[163] Saint Augustine of Hippo offers a profound commentary on the pericope of Luke 7:36–50, with specific reference to the theme of the remission of sins and in polemic with the Donatists, in *Sermo* 99.

The Sacraments in Particular

that forgiveness be granted by God or pray so that God forgives the sinner: it is Christ Himself who forgives. In some cases, the forgiveness of sins is connected with being cured from an illness (see, e.g., John 5:14). This is to show that, as the Son of man has the power over the body to heal it from evils, so He has power over the soul, which He is able to free from sin:

> He entered a boat, made the crossing, and came into his own town. And there people brought to him a paralytic lying on a stretcher. When Jesus saw their faith, he said to the paralytic, "Courage, child, your sins are forgiven." At that, some of the scribes said to themselves, "This man is blaspheming." Jesus knew what they were thinking, and said, "Why do you harbor evil thoughts? Which is easier, to say, 'Your sins are forgiven,' or to say, 'Rise and walk'? But that you may know that the Son of Man has authority on earth to forgive sins"—he then said to the paralytic, "Rise, pick up your stretcher, and go home." He rose and went home. When the crowds saw this they were struck with awe and glorified God who had given such authority to human beings. (Matt 9:1–8)[164]

2. Conversion

A second general aspect concerns the very mission of Christ, marked as it is by the theme of conversion: "This is the time of fulfillment. The kingdom of God is at hand. Repent, and believe in the gospel" (Mark 1:15). Jesus affirms that His whole mission is in effect aimed at the recovery of the "sick," that is, sinners who need to convert: "Those who are well do not need a physician, but the sick do. I did not come to call the righteous but sinners" (Mark 2:17). Moreover, in the famous parable of the "prodigal son and the merciful father," Christ teaches that when the penitent sinner returns home to ask for forgiveness, his father (God) readmits him to communion and re-establishes him in the exact position he was in before (see Luke 15:11–32). This is possible specifically because Christ has shed His blood for many, for the forgiveness of sins (see Matt 26:28, and what was already said in Chapter Four).

---

[164] Contemporary commentators observe that from the final proposition, "He had given such power to men" (found only in Matthew), we can notice the original Christian community's awareness of having received from Christ the power to remit sins through their ministers.

3. The Institution of the Sacrament

From the perspective of these fundamental facts, we can understand why Christ wanted to institute the Sacrament of Reconciliation and entrust it to the Twelve: so that His mission of forgiveness and healing from sin could continue after His Death and Resurrection. In this sense too, the Eucharist and Reconciliation are closely linked, given that the Council of Trent teaches that the Eucharist was instituted precisely to leave a visible Sacrifice to the Church (Holy Mass) "by which the bloody (sacrifice) that He was once for all to accomplish on the cross would be represented, its memory perpetuated until the end of the world, and its salutary power applied for the forgiveness of the sins that we daily commit."[165] This concerns the extension into time of the work that Christ performed while He was on earth. The Sacraments are all an extension of the Incarnation (see the previous chapter), but these two Sacraments are one such extension in a special way. It is unsurprising then that they are also strictly linked to one another, with Penance being aimed at communion with God, which is carried out in the Holy Mass in the Eucharistic Communion. But the reason for this link is further strengthened by reversing the relationship, and noting that, from the Eucharist as the true sacramental Sacrifice of Christ, the merit of redemption flows, which comes to be applied through Confession for the expiation of sins (CCC §1436).

There are three fundamental texts concerning the Sacrament of Reconciliation in the New Testament:

> I will give you [Peter] the keys to the kingdom of heaven. Whatever you bind on earth shall be bound in heaven; and whatever you loose on earth shall be loosed in heaven. (Matt 16:19)

> Amen, I say to you, whatever you bind on earth shall be bound in heaven, and whatever you loose on earth shall be loosed in heaven. (Matt 18:18)

> And when he had said this, he breathed on them and said to them, "Receive the holy Spirit. Whose sins you forgive are forgiven them, and whose sins you retain are retained." (John 20:22–23)

The first text is part of the pericope of Matthew concerning the primacy of Saint Peter (see Chapter Eight). Peter appears as the plenipotentiary of

---

[165] Council of Trent, *Doctrina et Canones de ss. Missae Sacrificio*, ch. 1 (DS 1740).

The Sacraments in Particular

Christ on earth: what He decides on earth is ratified in Heaven. Binding and loosing are two Semitisms that mean prohibiting and allowing. The second text shows that the power to loose or bind, which Peter possesses in a personal capacity as an individual, is also given to the group of the Twelve as a whole. The third text is decisive: in it, Christ explicitly affirms that the power to loose and to bind is also exercised in regard to the sins of human beings.[166] Peter and the Twelve receive the power to bind people to their sins (i.e., not to absolve them) or to free people from them. Jesus transfers to His disciples that authority which He used several times during His earthly ministry: "Child, your sins are forgiven" (Mark 2:5). Now the Apostles can say the same, as representatives of Christ (see above, regarding Holy Orders). From the beginning, the Apostles have had the awareness that they possessed this faculty:

> And all this is from God, who has reconciled us to himself through Christ and given us the ministry of reconciliation, namely, God was reconciling the world to himself in Christ, not counting their trespasses against them and entrusting to us the message of reconciliation. So we are ambassadors for Christ, as if God were appealing through us. We implore you on behalf of Christ, be reconciled to God. For our sake he made him to be sin who did not know sin, so that we might become the righteousness of God in him (2 Cor 5:18–21).

Recent exegesis claims that these words are to be understood in the sense of a ministry of pacification of the community and of individuals with God, rather than with reference to the ministry of "hearing Confessions" from the faithful. If the first meaning certainly appears to be the most literal one, it does not change the fact that the text demonstrates the awareness of Saint Paul of possessing the capacity to reconcile human beings with God, in a context in which the Apostle speaks with an emphasis on sins and their remission. The text, therefore, certainly remains open to sacramental application, even if its first meaning is more general.

The apostolic awareness of the ministry received in regard to sins, and more generally, to loosing and binding, is manifested not only in the loosing, but also in the binding. The faculty of excommunication that they exercise is an example of it:

---

[166] Holy Office, *Lamentabili* (1907), §47 (DS 3447), condemns the modernist thesis that the text of John 20:22 does not refer to the Sacrament of Penance. See Council of Trent, *Canones de Sacramento Paenitentiae*, can. 3 (DS 1703).

We instruct you, brothers, in the name of [our] Lord Jesus Christ, to shun any brother who conducts himself in a disorderly way and not according to the tradition they received from us.... If anyone does not obey our word as expressed in this letter, take note of this person not to associate with him, that he may be put to shame. (2 Thess 3:6, 14)[167]

4.2.3. Historical Development

Recent studies on Reconciliation willingly focused on the history of the Sacrament, emphasizing in particular the intervention of the eighth-century Irish monks. They favored transitioning from the ancient use to the medieval and modern use. In the ancient use, it was possible to receive forgiveness for grave sins only once in life, while the Irish monks started the practice of the multifold repetition of the Sacrament. Here we would like to quickly reread the information that emerges from the historical analysis within the principle of *et-et*, showing that the historical change depends on progressively identifying the primary member in the binomial "gravity of sin—gratuitousness of forgiveness," or more simply, "justice—mercy," or again, if one prefers, "rigor—indulgence." Both aspects are involved in the understanding and pastoral care of this Sacrament and, as for any binomial, one of the two elements—without excluding the other—has greater value.

1. First Centuries

The Church in early times was formed above all by those who had received Baptism as adults, therefore with full consciousness, after a long preparation and often at the cost of considerable renunciations and dangers. The Community was then rather small in number and very cohesive. Thus, in the early Church, the spiritual tension was very high ("*marana tha!*": see 1 Cor 16:22 and perhaps Rev 22:20) and the practice of sin, at least grave sin, can be presumed to have been infrequent. The Church in the ancient era, even if it grew rapidly, had in the beginning, characteristics similar to those of the very first days. But, as time went on, the number of baptized children increased. Above

---

[167] In 1 Tim 1:20, Saint Paul speaks of "Hymenaeus and Alexander, whom I have handed over to Satan to be taught not to blaspheme." See 2 Tim 4:14–15 concerning Alexander the coppersmith. See again, as a general rule, the indication of Titus 3:10–11 and 2 John 10. The fact that excommunication has a medicinal value is noted clearly, in addition to the texts cited, in 2 Cor 2:5–11.

The Sacraments in Particular

all, the spiritual tension was decreasing, both on account of a more correct interpretation of New Testament eschatology, decline in persecution (and the possibility of martyrdom), and the growing social acceptance of Christianity.[168]

All this soon brought the Church before a new situation: it is not only pagans who are sinners, but some Christians seriously betray the Lord as well. This issue began to arise in the era of persecutions, which, though it stirred up holiness in many, also led to serious defections from the faith. There are a number of categories that developed to indicate various types of infidelities. The *"turificati"* were those who, under pressure, had agreed to burn incense before the statue of the emperor or an idol. The *"traditores"* were those who had delivered (in Latin *tradere*) the books of Scripture to the persecutors, so that they would be burned. The *"sacrificati"* had offered sacrifice to idols, out of fear of being condemned. Finally, the *"libellatici"* had obtained a false attestation stating that they had made a sacrifice to a pagan god. In this way, while not materially fulfilling this act of idolatrous worship, they officially presented themselves as apostates from Christianity in order to save their lives. All of these are traced back to the category of *"lapsi,"* or "fallen": they were in fact fallen from the true faith into sin, betraying Christ and the Church.

There was a great dispute about the problem of the *lapsi*, in which the Church—faced with a new problem—was able to affirm both justice and mercy, avoiding both laxity and rigorism. There was no shortage, in fact, of bishops and priests who thought that they no longer had to admit traitors in the Church (rigorism). Among them, Tertullian (who in the meantime switched to Montanism), Hippolytus, and Novatian. The Great Church, however, chose a different path: that of the *Paenitentia secunda*, that is, of the possibility of returning to the bosom of the community after a long and burdensome penitential period. This period could last from two to thirty years, and included a series of successive steps. In this sense, the Church did not espouse rigorism because, using the power of the keys, she opened the way for the return of the *lapsi*. But the very harsh demands of penitential practice, as well as the fact that Reconciliation was possible only once in a lifetime, clearly show that in that phase the emphasis in the binomial "justice—mercy" fell clearly on the first term. This is also because there is no sin graver than apostasy, since faith—for which the martyrs die—is the greatest good for the Christian in this life.

---

[168] As is known, in the fourth century Christianity would become initially *religio licita*, i.e., religion admitted in the Roman Empire (with the Edict of Serdica, or of Galerius, of 311, and with the Edict of Milan or of Constantine, of 313) and then even the official religion of the empire (Edict of Thessalonica or of Theodosius, 380).

Repeatable Sacraments

2. The Irish Monks

Over time, a change in circumstances and a broader reflection led naturally enough to the recognition that, in the theological and pastoral understanding of Confession, the theme of mercy and reconciliation should be emphasized more than that of justice. Therefore, the penitential needs also diminished, and Reconciliation came to be repeatable. As was mentioned, the practice began in Ireland, where the monks gradually extended to laypeople the practice of the *manifestatio conscientiae*, a custom among them. This was an opening of conscience that the monk did to the abbot or to another wise and authoritative monk, carried out primarily in cases in which he felt guilty of some shortcoming. The origins of the *manifestatio* date back to the sixth century, and at first the bishops did not view it favorably.[169]

3. Developments in the Middle Ages

Naturally, for many centuries, the penitential dimension would still remain an element taken very seriously even in the extra-sacramental sphere: emphasizing mercy more did not mean forgetting that there is also justice. Therefore, in the Middle Ages and in the modern age—even within a theology and a practice that allowed for frequent repetition of the Sacrament—the theme of just satisfaction for sins was nonetheless taken into account. Penance, compared to the first centuries, became something more personal and less public, but it was still required, and in many cases also quite demanding, although the rigor of the early days had been abandoned.

Another novelty in the sacramental practice was the fact that, starting from the ninth century, absolution (when granted by the priest[170]) immedi-

---

[169] For example, the Third Synod of Toledo (589): "We have known that in certain churches of Spain the faithful do penance of their sins not according to the canonical way, but in a scandalous way: each time they have sinned they ask to be reconciled by the priest" (our translation).

[170] The fact that it was the priest to absolve also took on a character of novelty: in ancient times, the remission of sins was usually reserved to the bishop, while the priests could only grant it in case of grave necessity or danger of death (this implies, however, that this faculty was also recognized for the priest). When the new penitential practice was spread, the practice of Reconciliation celebrated by the priest was also strengthened. In this area too, Penance and Eucharist have much in common: it is known, in fact, that—although the priests are ordinary ministers of the Eucharistic Celebration—the exercise of their ministry in this area has increased with the territorial expansion of the local Churches, which entailed the construction of "parochial" churches, which is one reason why not all Christians could manage to participate every day in the bishop's Mass in the cathedral

ately followed the confession of sins and was not delayed as it was in the early centuries of the Church, when people had to wait years before receiving it. This is also because the value of the reception of the Eucharist was better understood: therefore, the possibility of being immediately and many times absolved allowed the faithful to approach sacramental Communion, from which the ancient penitent had to abstain for years. As a consequence of these and other changes, it was also realized that the properly penitential element (*satisfactio*) became less central than in the first centuries, losing ground in favor of the confession of committed sins, which almost became the first penitential form, due to the natural shame felt by the faithful to tell their own sins to the priest. This also explains the progressive mitigation of the works of penitence required for forgiveness. In the twelfth century, the new practice was so extensive and universally accepted that the Fourth Lateran Council, at the beginning of the following century, would prescribe Confession at least once a year.[171]

4. Evaluation

This whole development should be understood in a positive way. It should not be viewed as a decline in the spiritual seriousness of Christian faithful; if anything, it represents a remedy to it. The historical overview on the Sacrament of Reconciliation shows that the Church has always been able to maintain the *et-et* of justice and mercy, evolving in the positive sense on her path and appropriately addressing different historical contexts. The lesson that is drawn is that of keeping, in every era, this healthy equilibrium, which knows how to hold both aspects together, remembering that mercy is more important, but that at the same time it does not eliminate, but rather implies, justice and truth. Moreover, coming to the reiteration of the Sacrament even an indefinite number of times is a consequence not only of circumstances, but also of a more in-depth reflection on the theology of Christian life. If it is in fact true that reconciliation with God occurs at the moment in which one believes and receives Baptism (justification), it is also true that the event of reconciliation with God is part of a process in which the Christian becomes progressively perfected: in this sense, one comes to be saved *both* at the beginning, *and* during the arc of one's whole life. Growth is proper to human nature.

---

and would assist in the rites celebrated by the priest in the church closer to their home.

[171] "All the faithful of either sex, after they have reached the age of discernment, should individually confess all their sins in a faithful manner to their own priest [i.e., their pastor] at least once a year" (Fourth Lateran Council, *Firmiter* [1215], ch. 21 [DS 812]).

This also applies in the supernatural sphere. Earlier, we cited the concept of "ordered growth in the good" of which Saint Irenaeus of Lyon spoke, which applied even in the case of the prelapsarian human being (see Chapters Three and Five, and especially Chapter Four). In short, grace is a reality given at a precise moment, but it is also a yeast that fosters a leavening throughout life. In the postlapsarian state, the dynamic of justification is not developed without the help of the Sacraments, the rewards and medicines of the soul and body. Repeating sacramental Confession many times in life is therefore understood in this clearly dogmatic perspective, and it is not only the result of disciplinary and pastoral decisions dictated by the contingent situation (though this has certainly supported the process of theological reflection).

4.2.4. The Minister

1. The Minister

The foregoing leads us to the question of the minister of the Sacrament. From the historical elements briefly summarized above, we realize that Penance has an original link with the bishop and, alternatively, with the priest. In the ancient Church, the bishops usually administered it and, in cases of necessity, priests as well—but never a deacon or layperson. From the beginning, it was understood that the power to forgive sins is linked to the priesthood, which is found in its fullness in the bishop and participated in by the presbyters. It is in fact the power of the keys that operates in sacramental Reconciliation. This Sacrament is celebrated *in Persona Christi* by the priests alone.[172]

2. Indicative Formula

Also significant in this regard is the evolution that the formula of absolution has undergone from the deprecatory to the indicative form, that is, from the original, "May Almighty God have mercy on you, forgive your sins," to, "I absolve you from your sins." The reason for this change is documented by Radulphus Ardens (d. ca. 1190), who discusses the theme of Confession quite extensively in one of his sermons. He first recalls that true sacramental Reconciliation is done by confessing the sins to a priest:

---

[172] "The priest, as the minister of Penance, acts '*in Persona Christi*'" (Saint John Paul II, *Reconciliatio et Paenitentia*, §29).

The Sacraments in Particular

> *Cui fieri debet Confessio? Confessio criminalium debet fieri sacerdoti et nominatim, qui solus habet potestatem ligandi atque solvendi, sicut et leprae iudicium solis sacerdotibus in lege erat commissum*—To whom should Confession be made? The Confession of our criminal acts must be made with precision to the priest, who only possesses the power to bind and loosen, just as in the Old Testament the judgment concerning leprosy was entrusted only to priests.[173]

He goes on to add that a confession of venial sins, since they do not separate the human being from God (*propter venialia non separatur homo a Deo*), may be done even to others who are not priests, because this confession is not sacramental, and it serves only as means of humility and to request that our brothers and sisters pray for us. Therefore, in these cases, says Radulphus, the indicative formula is not used but rather the deprecatory formula:

> *Unde et non dicimus: "Ego dimitto tibi peccata tua", sed dicimus orando: "Misereatur tui omnipotens Deus, etc."*—So we do not say: "I absolve you from your sins," but instead we say, praying: "May Almighty God have mercy on you, etc."[174]

Radulphus already takes the transition between the two formulas as a given, seeing in it a clear sign of the fact that mortal sins can be absolved by the priest alone, who does so *in Persona Christi*, and therefore the most correct formula is exactly, in this case, the indicative one, because it is Christ Himself who absolves through His minister. It is Christ who says to the penitent: "I absolve you from your sins," and He does this through the ecclesial-sacramental mediation. Therefore, the lay faithful and deacons cannot be ministers of this Sacrament, because they are not priests.

3. More Grave Sins

The fact that Penance—even in the practice of the second millennium, in which priests hearing Confessions is an ordinary fact—remains deeply linked

---

[173] Radulphus Ardens, *Homilia 64: In litania maiori* (our translation).

[174] This text, moreover, explains why in the Holy Mass mortal sins are ordinarily not remitted (Confession is there for absolving these), but only venial ones. The "absolutory" formula that the priest pronounces at the beginning of the Mass—as can be understood here, thanks to Radulphus—liberates from venial sins, in order to have the faithful better prepared to participate in the Liturgy. See *ST* III, q. 79, aa. 3–4: two articles answering the question of whether the Eucharist liberates from mortal and venial sins.

to the bishop, can also be seen from the ecclesiastical discipline that provides that the priests are generally authorized by their Ordinary to hear the Confessions of the faithful. For the more grave sins, there is the reservation to the Apostolic See (crimes against the faith and *delicta graviora*).[175]

4. The Sacramental Seal

Linked to the theme of the ministry of the Sacrament, there is the reality of the sacramental seal. Priests are bound to total secrecy regarding what they hear in the confessional:

> Given the delicacy and greatness of this ministry and the respect due to persons, the Church declares that every priest who hears confessions is bound under very severe penalties to keep absolute secrecy regarding the sins that his penitents have confessed to him. He can make no use of knowledge that confession gives him about penitents' lives (Cf. CIC, can. 1388 §1; CCEO, can. 1456). This secret, which admits of no exceptions, is called the "sacramental seal," because what the penitent has made known to the priest remains "sealed" by the sacrament. (CCC §1467)[176]

4.2.5. Matter and Form

In the thirteenth century, the understanding of Penance developed with regard to matter and form. Saint Thomas explains that the acts of the penitent, as the external manifestation of the desire and commitment of the faithful to convert, form an integral part of the Sacrament. He considers them the matter, or the "quasi-matter" of this Sacrament. The fundamental *et-et* is also manifested here, since this Sacrament is composed of two elements: "the acts of the penitent ... and the absolution of the priest."[177]

---

[175] See Congregation for the Doctrine of the Faith, *Normae de Delictis Congregationi pro Doctrina Fidei Reservatis seu Normae de Delictis contra Fidem necnon de Gravioribus Delictis* (2010). The crimes against the faith are heresy, apostasy, and schism (art. 2). The more grave (*graviora*) delicts are sins against the holiness of the Eucharistic Sacrifice and Sacrament (listed in art. 3), against the Sacrament of Penance (in art. 4), against the Sacrament of Orders (art. 5), and against morality (art. 6).

[176] See *Codex Iuris Canonici*, can. 1388, §1 (the penalty for the priest who violates the seal is automatic [*latae sententiae*] excommunication reserved to the Apostolic See. It is in fact one of the *delicta graviora* to which we referred in the previous note: see art. 4, no. 5).

[177] *Compendium of the Catechism of the Catholic Church*, §302.

The Sacraments in Particular

1. Acts of the Penitent (Matter)

The *Catechism*—repeating the teachings of the Florentine and Tridentine Councils—lists three acts of the penitent: contrition, confession of sins, and satisfaction (CCC §§1450–1460).

(1) Citing the Council of Trent, the *Catechism* explains that contrition is "the sorrow of the soul with the detestation of the sin committed, together with the resolve not to sin any more."[178] This sorrow of the soul is perfect when the suffering is due to the fact of having offended God with sin; it is imperfect, if it is due to the fear of the pains merited by the sins. In this case, it is called "attrition." Contrition can obtain from God the forgiveness of sins in certain cases, when it is impossible to receive absolution; this is on the condition, however, that one has the desire to receive the Sacrament as soon as possible. Even in those cases in which the penitent feels deep contrition over his or her sins, he or she can still not approach Eucharistic Communion without first making a sacramental Confession.[179] Attrition, on the other hand, does not merit divine forgiveness, but orients one toward Confession, with the grace of which it can become contrition. This is expressed by the classic saying: "*Impius ex attrito fit contritus*" ("From being attrite, the sinner becomes contrite").[180] Concretely, even those who approach the Sacrament with an insufficient disposition of soul receive from the grace and the experience of the Sacrament a help to change their sorrow from imperfect to perfect.

(2) The second act of the penitent is the accusation of sins: "All mortal sins of which penitents after a diligent self-examination are conscious must be recounted by them in Confession, though they may be most secret and may have been committed only against the last two precepts of the Decalogue,"[181] that is, even sins of intention. This specification sheds light on a double aspect of Confession: it is *both* judgment *and* medication. Inasmuch as it is this judg-

---

[178] Council of Trent, *Doctrina de Sacramento Paenitentiae* (1551), ch. 4 (DS 1676).

[179] "No one who is aware of personal mortal sin, however contrite he may feel, should approach the Holy Eucharist without first having made a sacramental Confession" (Council of Trent, *Decretum de ss. Eucharistia* (1551), ch. 7 [DS 1647]).

[180] The principle was also reprised by Saint John Paul II, *Reconciliatio et Paenitentia*, note 185: "Of course, in order to approach the Sacrament of Penance it is sufficient to have attrition, or imperfect repentance, due more to fear than to love. But in the sphere of the Sacrament, the penitent, under the action of the grace that he receives, '*ex attrito fit contritus*,' since Penance really operates in the person who is well disposed to conversion in love."

[181] Council of Trent, *Doctrina de Sacramento Paenitentiae*, ch. 5 (DS 1680).

ment in which the priest plays the role of a judge,[182] it is understandable why the penitents must also confess those circumstances that change the species of the sin, because without them not only would Confession be incomplete, but sins would also not be "made known to the judges," and thus it would be "impossible for the latter rightly to estimate the gravity of the faults and to impose on the penitents the penance appropriate to them."[183] For example, if a religious disobeyed a superior, he or she cannot generically confess having violated the fourth commandment, as would a child who disobeyed his parents: the religious must declare to the confessor his or her state of life, which will make it clear that one of the sacred vows has been violated.

(3) The third act of the penitent is satisfaction, today commonly called penance. Here we can recall how brilliantly Saint Anselm of Canterbury explains the concept of "*satisfacere*" ("to do enough") in *Cur Deus homo* (see Chapter Four). To every sin there corresponds a fault, but also a penalty. This principle also applies to the Sacrament of Reconciliation, which through absolution remits the fault of the sins, but not the penalty due to them.[184] This is why in the Church, from her beginnings, forgiveness is accompanied by penitential practice, which in ancient times preceded absolution, but today follows it. When the Confession occurs, the priest imposes a medicinal penalty, called exactly satisfaction or penance, which is not optional but required for the integrity of the Sacrament. In our days, this penance is purely symbolic, while for many centuries it was quite consistent and in certain cases also very burdensome, especially in the early centuries. The reduction of penance to a mere sign of good intention, as it is today, is due to various factors, both theological

---

[182] This is a classical doctrine (see Council of Trent, *Doctrina de Sacramento Paenitentiae* chs. 2 and 6 [DS 1671 and 1685]; can. 9 [DS 1709]), which was also confirmed by Saint John Paul II, *Reconciliatio et Paenitentia*, §31. In the letter *Misericordia Dei*, the same Pope speaks of "the judgement entrusted to the priest in the Sacrament." Clearly, the function of judge in the sacramental sphere is to be understood in an analogous and not univocal way with respect to the role of the judge in the civil courts.

[183] Council of Trent, *Doctrina de Sacramento Paenitentiae*, ch. 5 (DS 1681).

[184] A simple example: If someone breaks his or her neighbor's window by simple carelessness or even as a result of personal animosity, but afterwards, sincerely repentant, apologizes, he or she receives forgiveness for the mistake made. However, the damage still needs to be repaired and, to "do enough," he or she will need to replace the broken window at his or her expense. By means of an act of condescension, the injured party could, however, dispense the guilty person from having to complete the *satisfactio*, or commute the penalty. The injured party could therefore consider himself or herself "satisfied" even beyond the strict demands of justice; this depends, however, on the liberty of the one who has suffered damage, while justice requires that a commensurate satisfaction correspond to a penalty.

and of other types. Among the first is certainly the consideration of the fact that it is above all the grace of Christ that forgives the sinner and brings him or her back to friendship with the Father, rather than human work. But if the excessive penances are to be discouraged, an excessive "race to the bottom" could also reduce the penitents' perception of the gravity of the sins committed. The *Catechism* teaches that although the imposition of the satisfaction "must take into account the penitent's personal situation and must seek his spiritual good," nonetheless "it must correspond as far as possible with the gravity and nature of the sins committed" (CCC §1460).

2. Form

As for the form, it is clearly the absolution pronounced by the priest, which in the ordinary form of the Roman Rite is this: "I absolve you from your sins in the name of the Father, and of the Son, and of the Holy Spirit." It is no coincidence that it is a very similar formula to that of Baptism: in fact, Penance restores the sinner to the state of purity, thus restoring the cleanliness of the baptismal garment, freeing him or her from the blemishes of the committed sins.

4.2.6. *Indulgences*

The theme of indulgences is connected with the theme of *satisfactio*. The practice of indulgences, one of the points that was most criticized by Martin Luther partially because of objective exaggerations, arose to alleviate the difficulties of the penitents linked to the satisfaction for the punishment due to their sins. The underlying idea is that the Church, which uses the power of the keys to absolve from guilt and to demand a just penalty, can use the same power to reduce that penalty or commute it. In itself, once the theology of the power of the keys is accepted, that of indulgences is not at all a difficult subject to digest from the theological point of view, even if some historical manifestations of the practice of indulgences may be. But having purified the practice from some past excesses,[185] indulgences continue to have a meaning

---

[185] In confirming the practice of indulgences, the Council of Trent, *Decretum de Indulgentiis* (1563), also prescribes: "In granting [indulgences], however, it [the Council] desires that moderation be observed . . . lest too much relaxation should weaken the ecclesiastical discipline. Desiring, too, to correct and punish the abuses that have crept in and are the occasion for heretics to blaspheme this distinguished name of indulgences, it enacts in general by this present decree that all base gain for securing indulgences . . . should be abolished" (DS 1835).

and a value today, and in every era, because sins are always committed and there is always need for forgiveness. Moreover, the term appears very pleasing to contemporary sensibilities, which is more attracted to a spirituality of mercy than one of justice. "Indulge" means in theology "to benignly concede," "to benevolently judge, without severity," "to be compliant," and the like. The Church is indulgent in many ways, and her maternal mercy is also manifested with the benevolent concession of indulgences. Being so strictly bound to the power of the keys, it is clear that indulgences are *per se* the prerogative of the Roman Pontiff, the Successor of Peter.[186]

We can borrow a definition from the current *Code of Canon Law*: "An indulgence is the remission before God of temporal punishment for sins whose guilt is already forgiven, which a properly disposed member of the Christian faithful gains under certain and defined conditions by the assistance of the Church which as minister of redemption dispenses and applies authoritatively the treasury of the satisfactions of Christ and the saints."[187] The indulgence "is partial or plenary insofar as it partially or totally frees from the temporal punishment due to sins."[188]

Shortly after the Second Vatican Council, Saint Paul VI issued an apostolic constitution on the theme of indulgences, in which he recorded that, "The doctrine and practice of indulgences which have been in force for many centuries in the Catholic Church have a solid foundation in divine revelation"—namely—that "it is a divinely revealed truth that sins bring punishments inflicted by God's sanctity and justice. These must be expiated either on this earth through the sorrows, miseries and calamities of this life and above all through death, or else in the life beyond through fire and torments or 'purifying' punishments."[189] In summary, indulgences are bound to the theological consideration of the gravity both of the sin and its effects. The merit

---

[186] See Leo X, *Cum Postquam* (1518) (DS 1448). This decree was issued by the Pope following the publication of the 95 Thesis by Luther and was addressed to the famous commentator of Saint Thomas, Cardinal Thomas Cajetan (d. 1534). Some years later, in 1522, Cajetan would cite the most important part of the pontifical text in his commentary on *ST* III, q. 48, a. 5.

[187] *Codex Iuris Canonici*, can. 992. This canon corresponds, to the letter, to norm no. 1 issued by the constitution *Indulgentiarum Doctrina* (cit. *infra*). The same citation of Saint Paul VI is proposed as the definition of indulgences at CCC §1471, which cites Paul VI and not the *Codex*.

[188] *Codex Iuris Canonici*, can. 993. This corresponds to norm no. 2 of *Indulgentiarum Doctrina* (cit. *infra*).

[189] Saint Paul VI, *Indulgentiarum Doctrina* (1967), §§1–2. The general norms issued in this constitution were then applied in the new *Enchiridion Indulgentiarum*, published by the Apostolic Penitentiary (first edition, 1968, fourth edition, 1999).

of the text of Paul VI is also that of having highlighted the twofold value of indulgences, according to the principle of *et-et*. The indulgences, on the one hand, teach "how it is 'sad and bitter to have abandoned . . . the Lord God'"; and on the other, they renew "trust and hope in a full reconciliation with God the Father, but in such a way as will not justify any negligence nor in any way diminish the effort to acquire the dispositions required for full communion with God."[190] Finally, it should also be remembered that indulgences stimulate charity among one's brothers and sisters in faith, because Christians can obtain them (or "gain" them) not only for themselves, but also for the deceased.[191] Thus, they are a precious occasion for living the ecclesial communion and charity between brothers and sisters in the faith, and are a magnificent expression of the *communio sanctorum* (see Chapter Eight).

4.2.7. Effects

The effect of Confession is twofold: this Sacrament carries out *both* reconciliation with God, *and* reconciliation with the Church, with the first aspect clearly being the primary and the other derived, but not entirely secondary. As for the first, the Council of Trent teaches:

> As to the reality [*res*] and the effect of this Sacrament, so far as concerns its power and efficacy, it consists in reconciliation with God. In persons who are pious and receive this Sacrament with devotion, it is likely to be followed at times by peace and serenity of conscience with an overwhelming consolation of spirit.[192]

In pastoral language, it is customary to say that sacramental absolution restores our friendship with God, which was lost because of sin. This occurs because we are washed in the merits of the Blood of Christ, of which a single drop is sufficient to heal the sins of the whole world.[193]

As regards reconciliation with the Church, the text of the *Catechism* is very clear:

---

[190] Saint Paul VI, *Indulgentiarum Doctrina*, §§9–10.

[191] It is not possible, however, to gain them for other faithful who are still living: see Apostolic Penitentiary, *The Gift of the Indulgence* (2000), §7.

[192] Council of Trent, *Doctrina de Sacramento Paenitentiae*, ch. 3 (DS 1674).

[193] "*Cuius una stilla salvum facere / totum mundum quit ab omni scelere*" (Saint Thomas Aquinas, *Adoro Te Devote*, stanza 5; a variation substitutes "*quit ab*" with "*posset*").

This sacrament *reconciles us with the Church*. Sin damages or even breaks fraternal communion. The sacrament of Penance repairs or restores it. In this sense it does not simply heal the one restored to ecclesial communion, but has also a revitalizing effect on the life of the Church which suffered from the sin of one of her members (Cf. *1 Cor* 12:26). Re-established or strengthened in the communion of saints, the sinner is made stronger by the exchange of spiritual goods among all the living members of the Body of Christ, whether still on pilgrimage or already in the heavenly homeland (Cf. *LG* 48-50). (CCC §1469)

It is necessary to emphasize that reconciliation with the Church is the fruit of reconciliation with God, which is the primary effect of this Sacrament. "There reigns among men, by the hidden and benign mystery of the divine will, a supernatural solidarity whereby the sin of one harms the others just as the holiness of one also benefits the others."[194] This is why Confession also reconciles people with the Church, because it heals the wound that sin has caused to the ecclesial community. It is in healing the relationship with God, therefore, that this Sacrament also heals the relationship with one's brothers and sisters. This is why *"reconciliation with the Church is inseparable from reconciliation with God"* (CCC §1445).

4.3. Anointing of the Sick

4.3.1. "Extreme Unction" and "Anointing of the Sick"

This Sacrament underwent a development in the twentieth century that, in some ways, was similar to the development of Confession in the eighth century. We noted that there was then a shift of emphasis between the complementary aspects in the *et-et* of Confession: the aspect of merciful forgiveness was emphasized more, without denying the severity of the just judgment upon the sins committed. The shift of emphasis represented theological and pastoral progress that did not imply the negation of one of the two aspects but only the inversion of the axiological order between them.[195] Something

---

[194] Saint Paul VI, *Indulgentiarum Doctrina*, §4.

[195] A similar shift of emphasis corresponds to a better understanding of divine Revelation on the theme of sin and its remission, and it does not represent an arbitrary act of the Church. It should be remembered that the hierarchy between the elements of a bipolarity is constitutive, that is, established in the very nature of things, and not decided by human beings. Therefore, the evolution of the penitential practice does not only correspond to a disciplinary decision of ecclesiastic authority, nor is it due to purely circumstantial

similar happened for what we call today the Anointing of the Sick, previously referred to as Extreme Unction. It is actually still permissible today to call it by this name, because it corresponds to a true aspect of the Sacrament, that of being immediate preparation for death. However, the Second Vatican Council teaches that it is better to call it by the other name: "'Extreme Unction,' which may also and more fittingly be called 'Anointing of the Sick,' is not a Sacrament for those only who are at the point of death. Hence, as soon as any one of the faithful begins to be in danger of death from sickness or old age, the fitting time for him to receive this Sacrament has certainly already arrived."[196] As one can see, the text is very balanced: it does not deny that this Sacrament is intended for those who are in immediate danger of death, but it also points out that it is not intended only for these people. Therefore, the Council also maintains the traditional wording of Extreme Unction. But it prefers to emphasize the other aspect of the Sacrament more, that is, it can also heal.[197] In this sense it is not only the Sacrament of the dying but of those who are ill (with a certain gravity) and may recover.

It is important not to break the "synthetic" unity between the two aspects of the Sacrament: to affirm and highlight the therapeutic character of the Sacrament, it is not necessary to deny the other in order to do this. On the contrary, a denial of the value of Unction as a viaticum would imply an unacceptable concept for the Christian faith, that is, that the true good of the human person consists in corporeal health and in life in this world. Death would always be a bad thing to avoid.[198] We have said in its own place that death itself is an evil, being the result of sin (see Chapter Three). But it also implies something very positive for those who die in grace: entrance into

---

reasons, but rather, it represents a case of doctrinal development.

[196] Second Vatican Council, *Sacrosanctum Concilium* (1963), §73.

[197] Actually, the Council of Trent had prepared this pronouncement: "... this anointing is to be administered to the sick, especially to those who are so dangerously ill that they seem near to death; hence it is also called the Sacrament of the dying. If, however, the sick recover after receiving this anointing, they can again receive the help and assistance of this Sacrament if they fall into another similar critical condition" (*Doctrina de Sacramento Extremae Unctionis* (1551), ch. 3 [DS 1698]).

[198] The correct Christian view is instead expressed by the *Canticle of the Creatures* of Saint Francis of Assisi (d. 1226), who writes that death represents an evil only if it catches the human being in a state of sin, condemning him or her to Hell. In the contrary case, it is a blessing, because it rescues him or her from the "second death," that is, damnation. Therefore, the Saint calls it "Sister Death": "Praised be You, my Lord, through our Sister Bodily Death / from whom no one living can escape. / Woe to those who die in mortal sin. / Blessed are those whom death will / find in Your most holy will, / for the second death shall do them no harm" (translation: *custodia.org*).

eternal salvation. This is exactly what the Sacrament is ordered toward as Extreme Unction: to place or to confirm the faithful in a state of communion with God, who prepares for him or her a judgment of salvation and entry into heavenly life—life that for the Christian is the greatest good ever, much more important than health and terrestrial life (this is why martyrs prefer to lose the latter than to lose the former).[199]

4.3.2. Holy Scripture

1. James 5:14–15

The fundamental text of the New Testament regarding the Anointing of the Sick is James 5:14–15: "Is anyone among you sick? He should summon the presbyters of the church, and they should pray over him and anoint [him] with oil in the name of the Lord, and the prayer of faith will save the sick person, and the Lord will raise him up. If he has committed any sins, he will be forgiven." Although there is no lack of modern and contemporary exegetes who doubt the interpretation of this passage in the sacramental sense, this exegesis has officially been taught by the Church: "By these words [James 5:14–15], as the Church has learned from the Apostolic Tradition [!] handed down and received by her, he [James] teaches the matter, the form, the proper minister, and the effect of this salutary Sacrament."[200]

2. Other Texts

Immediately before this, the Council of Trent affirmed that Christ Himself instituted this Sacrament, citing Mark 6:13 as proof: the Twelve—says Saint Mark—"drove out many demons, and they anointed with oil many who were sick and cured them." This verse, although subordinate to the text of James, is therefore a second traditional biblical *locus* for the study of this Sacrament. Recent theologians broaden the circle of biblical quotations primarily

---

[199] The Council of Trent, *Doctrina de Sacramento Extremae Unctionis*, "Proemio," teaches that while with the other Sacraments Christ wants to provide the Christians with a remedy against the various spiritual evils during life, with Extreme Unction He wanted to "protect the end of life ... as with a very strong safeguard" (DS 1694).

[200] Council of Trent, *Doctrina de Sacramento Extremae Unctionis*, ch. 1 (DS 1695). In can. 1 (DS 1716), the Council excommunicates anyone who affirms that the Sacrament was not instituted by Christ and promulgated by the text of James. Benedict XVI has confirmed the traditional exegesis of the Church, writing: "The *Letter of James* attests to the presence of this sacramental sign in the early Christian community" (*Sacramentum Caritatis*, §22).

to frame this pastoral activity of anointing of the sick, commanded by Jesus and carried out by the Apostles, within Christ's overall message regarding sickness and death. Note, first of all, the change in perspective between the Old and New Testament regarding these two themes. In the Old, sickness is seen as punishment for sin, as a trial for the believer, or as expiation. In common Jewish religiosity, however, the first aspect prevailed, as can be seen from various statements by the crowd or adversaries in various passages of the Gospel (see, for example, John 9:2).

Jesus proposes a more complete teaching. In the Beatitudes (Matt 5), He first of all shows the value of suffering: pain, persecution, and suffering are not evil in all cases. If borne well, they can on the contrary provide remarkable goods.[201] In John 9 (healing of the man born blind and theological discussion about it), Christ definitively refutes the equivalence between sickness and fault: not everyone who suffers an illness is being punished for a sin of his or her own, or that of a family member.[202] This does not, however, imply that such a connection does not exist in any case: in John 5 (the healing at the pool of Bethesda), Christ stated the opposite. After healing the paralytic, He tells him: "Look, you are well; do not sin any more, so that nothing worse may happen to you" (v. 14). Even if these words were to be understood without the implication that the previous paralysis was caused by a sin of the sick person, the warning for the future would still remain. And this means that there may be cases where something bad happens because of sin. In summary, Christ declares wrong any theology that in every case connects disease to a personal sin of the sick person or one of his or her family members. But He does not say that this does not happen under any circumstances. Only God knows, case by case, how things are. Therefore, theology can only indicate what the possible cases of cause/effect are according to Revelation; but it is not able to rule on the individual case.

The Gospels, then, show Christ's compassion toward the sick, recounting different healings, which are also a sign of the fact that "God has visited his people" (Luke 7:16). This therapeutic activity of Christ comes to be defined

---

[201] Remember what we said in Chapter Four about the Christian value of suffering, with privileged reference to Saint John Paul II, *Salvifici Doloris* (1984).

[202] Thus, the concept of "innocent" pain was born. It must be understood in the sense of innocence with respect to an immediate evil, when it is not a consequence of personal guilt (see Luke 13:2–5). But from the theological standpoint, given original sin, there is no completely innocent person (aside from the immaculate Christ and Mary). Therefore, even the terminology of "innocent" pain, or of "innocent" victims of negative historical events or natural disasters, though not incorrect, should not be emphasized—in fact, "no one is good but God alone" (Mark 10:18).

by the *Catechism*—resuming a patristic theme[203]—as the work of "Christ the Physician" (*Christus Medicus*), who heals the whole person: soul and body (CCC §§1503–1505). This ministry is then communicated to the Twelve: "cure the sick" (Matt 10:8), Jesus commands His disciples.

Other texts that focus on the therapeutic activity of Christ and the Apostles are Mark 16:18—those who believe "will lay hands on the sick, and they will recover"; and John 12:7—Jesus then says: "Leave her alone. Let her keep this for the day of my burial." In the latter, Christ mentions and approves the practice of anointing a person with oil on the occasion of death. This cannot be used as a direct biblical proof of the Sacrament of Anointing, because the latter is administered before dying, but it approves the use of oil on the occasion of death.[204] Oil in the circumstances of death, and the laying of hands on the sick for healing, are the aspects that are then illustrated by Saint James as essential elements of the Anointing of the Sick.

4.3.3. Matter, Form, and Minister

Such essential elements, as we know, are the matter, form, and minister. Following the text giving commentary on James 5, cited above, the Council of Trent teaches that the Church "understood that the matter is oil blessed by the bishop, because the anointing very aptly represents the grace of the Holy Spirit with which the soul of the sick is invisibly anointed."[205]

The form—in the current English version of the ordinary form of the Roman Rite—is given by the words: "Through this holy Anointing may the Lord in His love and mercy help you with the grace of the Holy Spirit. May the Lord who frees you from sin save you and raise you up."[206]

---

[203] The theme is developed above all by Saint Augustine of Hippo, who makes multiple and frequent references to it, with different applications. Here are just a few texts among many: "The reason for the coming of Christ the Lord is none other than that of saving sinners. . . . If the great Physician came from Heaven, [it is because] throughout the whole great world lay a sick man. The sick is mankind" (*Sermo 175*.1.1 [our translation]); "The human race from Adam onwards lay sick. . . . It was to this mankind lying sick in the great bed of the world that the great Physician came to our help . . . : He is a good, loving, just, and merciful Physician who predicted the disease; He did not cause it. He came to console you and truly heal you" (*Sermo 346/A*.8 [our translation]); ". . . the Teacher and Healer of their minds and souls [*Medico mentium*]" (*De civitate Dei* 5.14, in *FCNT*, vol. 8, trans. Demetrius B. Zema and Gerald G. Walsh [Washington, DC: CUA Press, 2008], 275).

[204] We must not forget that oil, among its many effects and symbolisms, was believed in antiquity also to be medicinal, as we see in Isa 1:6 and Luke 10:34.

[205] Council of Trent, *Doctrina de Sacramento Extremae Unctionis*, ch. 1 (DS 1695).

[206] See Saint Paul VI, *Sacram Unctionem Infirmorum* (1972). The Latin formula goes like

As for the minister of the Sacrament, this is also specified in the text of James 5 with the term "presbyters of the Church." According to the official exegesis of the Council of Trent, with this expression "in this text, this word [refers] either to bishops or to priests duly ordained."[207] Regarding the ancient practice in which laypeople also anointed the sick, who at times were cured, the scholastics, especially Saint Thomas, teach that these anointings were not true Sacraments and that the effect of physical healing occurred at times by virtue of the merits of those who conferred them or received them (*ex opere operantis*), but not by a true sacramental grace (*ex opere operato*).[208]

4.3.4. Effects

The effects of the Sacrament are the following[209]: (1) A particular gift of the Holy Spirit that offers comfort, peace, and courage in the suffering of illness or in the frailty of old age. This gift helps in attaining final perseverance and in saving the soul (see Luke 21:19). But, in certain cases, the divine consolation can also postpone death, restoring physical health.[210] (2) Union with the Passion of Christ, by which human suffering is elevated to a level of participation in the saving work of Jesus (see Col 1:24). This also has an ecclesial implication because the Church intercedes for the sick, while the sick offer their sufferings for the Church in particular, and for the whole world. (3) The preparation for the final journey, supporting them in the fight against the ultimate temptations before passing to the other life.[211] That is why the

---

this: "*Per istam sanctam Unctionem et suam pissimam misericordiam adiuvet te Dominus gratia Spiritus Sancti, ut a peccatis liberatum te salvet atque propitius allevet.*"

[207] Council of Trent, *Doctrina de Sacramento Extremae Unctionis*, ch. 3 (DS 1697). Note well the expression "in this text" (*eo loco*), with which the Council specifies that in James 5, and not in all of the New Testament, the word "presbyters" also indicates bishops.

[208] See *ST*, "Supplement," q. 31, a. 1. As for the well-known reply of Saint Innocent I to Bishop Decentius of Gubbio (*Si Instituta Ecclesiastica* (416), ch. 8, §11 [DS 216]), in which he applies the basic text of James 5 both to anointings done by priests and by others, the careful analysis of the text, conducted by contemporary scholars, notes that the Pope intended to refer to two different realities: the Sacrament, on the one hand, and the private use of the chrism by the faithful, on the other.

[209] See Council of Trent, *Doctrina de Sacramento Extremae Unctionis*, ch. 2 (DS 1696).

[210] See *ST*, "Supplement," q. 30, a. 2.

[211] It is a common doctrine, with a certain foundation in Revelation, that Satan launches a final attack on the soul before death. Here we shall only recall the second reading of the Office of November 11, on the memorial of Saint Martin of Tours (d. 397), an eminent figure of holiness, who at the time of his death also had to face this last attack by the enemy: "He saw the devil standing near. 'Why do you stand there, you bloodthirsty brute?' he cried. 'Murderer, you will not have me for your prey. Abraham is welcoming me

Anointing also remits sins, mortal and venial, which had not already been absolved[212] (particularly in the case of the sick who are in an unconscious or diminished mental state).

4.3.5. Active Participation

The Second Vatican Council also has another reference, in addition to *Sacrosanctum Concilium* §73, concerning the Anointing of the Sick. It occurs in *Lumen Gentium* §11:

> By the sacred Anointing of the Sick and the prayer of her priests the whole Church commends the sick to the suffering and glorified Lord, asking that He may lighten their suffering and save them (see James 5:14–16); she exhorts them, moreover, to contribute to the welfare of the whole people of God by associating themselves freely with the Passion and death of Christ (see Rom 8:17; Col 1:24).

The passage is found in a paragraph in which the Second Vatican Council recalls the irreplaceable value of the seven Sacraments in the sanctification of all Christians. It confirms the traditional reading of James 5 and recalls the values and effects of the Sacrament. It is interesting that the Council also recalls that the Anointing must help the sick to unite their sufferings to those of Christ: in this way the concept of "active participation," which was seen in the previous chapter, also applies to this Sacrament—that is, uniting oneself with the offering that Christ made of Himself to the Father. Therefore, although Vatican II also wanted to re-evaluate the aspects of hope linked to the Sacrament (healing and consolation), it did not deny those that relate to physical and spiritual suffering. At the pastoral level, that means that this Sacrament, although it is not to be experienced as a tragedy or simply as the last act before expiring, also cannot be understood as a celebration to be enjoyed with euphoria. Therefore, it is not in conformity with the real teaching of the Council to implement the current and widespread practice that is present in different countries in which community celebrations are organized in the church, during which all those present (even people in good health and

---

into his embrace.' With these words, he gave up his spirit to Heaven" (Suplicius Severus [d. ca. 420], *Epistulae* 3 [*Ad Bassulam socrum suam*]).

[212] See *ST*, "Supplement," q. 30, a. 1. It should be noted, however, that such forgiveness is granted *per accidens*, in the case in which the one who receives the Sacrament is unable to Confess. In fact, the proper effect of the Anointing is not to forgive sins, as is the case with Confession.

children!) are invited to receive the Anointing of the Sick. Despite the more positive emphasis given by the Council, it remains a Sacrament linked to situations of serious illness (old age included) or imminent danger of death.

This was confirmed after the Council by Paul VI, who, in promulgating the renewed liturgical rite of this Sacrament, prescribed: "The Sacrament of the Anointing of the Sick is administered to those who are dangerously ill."[213] This also applies to elderly people "whose frailty becomes more pronounced" (CCC §1515), though they may not be suffering from a specific pathology. In these cases, it is appropriate to administer the Sacrament, given the classic maxim: "*senectus ipsa est morbus*" ("old age is an illness in itself").[214]

4.3.6. Relation with the Other Sacraments

Finally, the Anointing is also closely linked to the other Sacraments. In the first place, it is linked to Baptism because together they represent a sort of "frame" of one's whole existence. In fact, sacramental life accompanies the Christian "from the cradle to the grave." Secondly, the Anointing is related to Penance—being that both are Sacraments of healing. Finally, we also see a link with the Eucharist. It is connected to the latter due to its viatic character, that is to say, because it offers provisions for the final voyage. It is not by chance that the liturgical rite prescribes, when it is possible, that both Confession and sacramental Communion accompany the Anointing.

---

[213] Saint Paul VI, *Sacram Unctionem Infirmorum*.
[214] Terence [Publius Terentius Afer] (d. 159 BC), *Phormio* 4.1.9.

11

The Eucharist

We are discussing the Eucharist in its own chapter, not because it is separate from the other Sacraments, but, on the contrary, because it represents their apex. There is no doubt about the fact that the Eucharist is the greatest Sacrament and that the others are by their nature directed toward it. The reason is very simple. While the other Sacraments confer grace (see Chapter Nine), in this one there is really present the very Author of grace, Christ the Lord. Therefore, the Eucharist, as a Sacrament, is an efficacious sign of grace. On the other hand, it is much more than this, because it is not only a "thing," a reality—even if most noble and supernatural, as the sacramental realities are. The Eucharist is a Person: the Person of the incarnate Word, really present under the "veils" of consecrated bread and wine. From the Eucharist we not only receive the grace of Christ, but we receive *both* the grace of Christ *and* Christ Himself in Person. It is the Sacrament of the personal encounter with the incarnate Word. Thus, not only in classical theology, but also in our approach of Trinitarian Christocentrism, this Sacrament is recognized for its own dignity: we could speak of it as the "source and summit" of all the Sacraments of the Church, as well as of the spiritual life of the faithful.

Saint Thomas Aquinas—who is also called the Eucharistic Doctor[1] for the high level of his doctrine regarding the Sacrament of the altar—confirms this primacy of the Eucharist. For the Angelic Doctor, the Eucharist is the greatest of the Sacraments for three reasons[2]: (1) it contains Christ

---

[1] See Pius XI, *Studiorum Ducem* (1923).
[2] See *ST* III, q. 65, a. 3.

The Eucharist

substantially, while the other Sacraments possess only an instrumental power participated from Christ; (2) all the other Sacraments are directed to the Eucharist; and (3) the other Sacraments are generally celebrated within the Holy Mass or are directed to it and to Eucharistic Communion. Moreover, the Eucharist is so important because, uniting us to Christ, it also incorporates us into the Church.[3]

Therefore, the Eucharist represents the center and foundation of the spiritual life of Catholics, because it unites them to the "*Christus passus*" ("Christ who has suffered"[4]) and, consequently, transmits to them the merits of Jesus' Passion.[5] In this way, it is both Sacrament and Sacrifice. The Common Doctor defines it as "*praecipuum sacramentum*" ("the principal Sacrament").[6] The fundamental reason for this—it is good to repeat it again—is in the fact that, although the virtues of Christ's Passion operate in the other Sacraments, it is Christ in Person Who is present, as the One who has suffered (*Christus passus*), in the Eucharist.[7]

Another difference between the Eucharist and the other Sacraments that is not to be overlooked consists in the fact that the former is carried out through the consecration of matter, while the others are carried out only with the use of the matter (for example, in Baptism, water is poured out and this constitutes the Sacrament, along with the form; but in the Eucharist, the essence of the Sacrament is not Communion, the moment in which the matter is used, but before, the consecration of the Species). Moreover, in the other Sacraments, the matter is blessed; only in the Eucharist is it consecrated. Finally, only in the Eucharist is the matter ontologically transformed into something else.[8]

The Most Holy Eucharist, therefore, deserves its own chapter, and this will provide more space for the discussion of it—even if such a treatment will always be small in comparison to the matter being considered. Indeed, the Eucharist is "the sum and summary of our faith" (CCC §1327).

---

[3] See *ST* III, q. 73, a. 4.
[4] See *ST* III, q. 65, a. 5, ad 2.
[5] See *ST* III, q. 73, a. 5.
[6] *ST* II-II, q. 83, a. 9.
[7] See *ST* III, q. 73, a. 1, ad 3.
[8] See *ST* III, q. 78, a. 1. From this the consequences concerning the form of the Sacrament are derived, which we shall see further on.

1. Sacred Scripture

1.1. Old Testament

1.1.1. Orientation of History toward the Eucharist

The Old Testament contains a certain number of events and realities that, in light of the knowledge of the New Testament, represent prophecies, however obscure, of the future Eucharist. In fact, the Eucharist is a reality so great—it is the Son of God made flesh, sacramentally present among us—that it can be said that in a certain way all of salvation history is directed toward it, given that this history is undoubtedly directed toward Jesus Christ. Moreover, it can be said that not only salvation history, but the entire world religious history tends toward the celebration of the Eucharistic Sacrifice. All the sacrificial rites of the religions of every place and age—though in various cases they also present ambiguous or even monstrous aspects, such as human sacrifice—attest that sacrificial ritual is not only a religious rite, but also an anthropological need. Even when human beings create their own religions, the sacrificial element (or something corresponding to it) is virtually ubiquitous.

Although the sacrifices of the various religions do not have any direct relationship with the Eucharistic Sacrifice—which far surpasses all of them—the practice of such sacrifices can be considered a sort of anthropological "hook" onto which the Revelation of the Christian Eucharist, given from above, can be connected. We can note, in this regard, that the celebration of the Eucharist is linked to the apostolic activity of evangelization from the very beginning (see Acts 2:42; 20:7–12). Thus, the sacrificial rituals of all of human history are like an expression of a necessity of which human beings are aware, of being in relation with God (even when poorly worshipped through the cult of gods) through sacrificial offerings and immolation. This is why all of human history, and not only the biblical salvation history, tends toward the Sacrament of the Christian altar. We can read in this regard a beautiful text of Saint Augustine (d. 430):

> God, not demons, made incense, God made myrrh, God made gold. The magi, and magicians in general, sin by giving them to demons and thereby showing them honor, thus using creatures to wrong the Creator. Today, however, you must get used to the idea that these magi gave the same sort of things as they had been accustomed to give to their gods. Still, it wasn't to no purpose that Christ allowed them to give Him such things; they were signs rather more than

gifts. He accepted incense as God, gold as King, myrrh as One due to die, for His burial. At that time, though, it was not only incense but also animal victims that were offered both by pagans and by Jews, that is, by those who were worshipers of many false gods and by those who were worshipers of the one true God. These things, I repeat, used to be offered to God according to the old covenant, but He changed it under the new covenant.[9]

Classical theology interpreted a text of Malachi as a prophecy of the future Eucharist: "From the rising of the sun to its setting, / my name is great among the nations; / Incense offerings are made to my name everywhere, / and a pure offering; / For my name is great among the nations, / says the Lord of hosts" (Mal 1:11).[10]

The New Testament itself, revealing the Eucharistic Mystery, makes recourse many times to the themes and terms of the Old Testament, and at least on two occasions, as will be said, it explicitly re-reads the Old Testament as a prophecy of the future Eucharist. Both the Lord Jesus and Saint Paul offer us an exegesis of episodes and realities of the Old Testament through a Eucharistic lens, thus authorizing us—with due caution—to do the same.

1.1.2. The Covenant and the Passover Meal

This is a central theme of the Old Testament and the New: here we mention the covenant only for its relation with Eucharistic theology. Jesus, in the Upper Room, will speak of the "Blood of the covenant" (Mark 14:24; Matt 26:28) and of the chalice that "is the new covenant in my blood" Luke 22:20; 1 Cor 11:25). The adjective "new," reported by Luke and Paul, is very significant, because it connects the covenant stipulated in the Blood of Christ to a previous, or "old," covenant. The Old Testament itself (which, as was seen in the second chapter, means Old Covenant) predicts a new and definitive covenant in the future. The classical text is that of Jeremiah 31:31–34:

> See, days are coming—oracle of the Lord—when I will make a new covenant with the house of Israel and the house of Judah. It will

---

[9] Saint Augustine of Hippo, *Sermo 374 augm.*, 18, in *The Works of Saint Augustine: A Translation for the 21st Century*, vol. III/11: *Newly Discovered Sermons*, trans. Edmund Hill (Hyde Park, NY: New City Press, 1997), 403.

[10] As an example of the Christian use of this text through a Eucharistic lens, see the *Didache* (end of the first century) 14.3; Saint Irenaeus of Lyon (d. ca. 202), *Adversus haereses* 4.17.5.

not be like the covenant I made with their ancestors the day I took them by the hand to lead them out of the land of Egypt. They broke my covenant, though I was their Master—oracle of the Lord. But this is the covenant I will make with the house of Israel after those days—oracle of the Lord. I will place my law within them, and write it upon their hearts; I will be their God, and they shall be my people. They will no longer teach their friends and relatives, "Know the Lord!" Everyone, from least to greatest, shall know me—oracle of the Lord—for I will forgive their iniquity and no longer remember their sin.

The Fathers interpreted this passage both in a general sense, as an announcement of the coming of Christ, and with a specific application to the Sacraments, particularly—given the words of Christ over the chalice—to the Eucharist.[11]

With Jesus Himself having recalled the theme of the covenant in His Passover meal with the Apostles, naturally the Passover meal of the Jews is also included among the Eucharistic figures of the Old Testament. The central text is Exodus 12. God commands the Israelites who are about to leave Egypt to celebrate this domestic rite. They will have to slaughter a lamb "without blemish" (v. 5) and spread its blood over the doorposts and lintel of the door of the house, to avoid death (see v. 13). Moreover, at verse 14, we read the following words of God: "This day will be a day of remembrance for you, which your future generations will celebrate with pilgrimage to the Lord; you will celebrate it as a statute forever." This is a true and proper institution. God institutes a rite that will have to be repeated perennially and, notably, He defines it as a "memorial." The theology of memorial (*zikkaron*) was highly valued by the specialists of the twentieth century.

We shall now try to bring out the Eucharistic typology in Exodus 12: (1) The dinner commences the exodus from Egypt to the Promised Land—the Eucharist is the "bread for the journey," the *cibus viatorum*[12] while we Christians direct ourselves toward the true Promised Land of Heaven—"a land flowing with milk and honey" (Ex 3:8; etc.). (2) In the Jewish supper, a lamb is consumed—and Christ, who is received in the Eucharist, is the true Lamb

---

[11] Concerning the interpretation with respect to Christ and the New Testament in general, see Saint Augustine of Hippo, *De spiritu et littera* 19.33–20.35. For the exegesis through sacramental and Eucharistic lenses, see, Saint Augustine of Hippo, *De gestis Pelagii* 5.14; *Epistula 138*.1.7.

[12] "Food of wayfarers": this is what the Sacrament is called in the hymn composed by Saint Thomas Aquinas, *Ecce panis angelorum*.

The Eucharist

of God (see John 1:29). (3) The blood of the lamb spread over the house saves those who are within—the Blood of Christ, poured out for the Church, saves those who live within it.[13] (4) The lamb for the Passover meal had to be without blemish—Saint Peter, in the New Testament, says that Christ is "a spotless unblemished lamb."[14] (5) In Exodus 12:15ff, it is specified that the Passover meal gives rise to the Feast of Unleavened Bread, lasting seven days—Christians (at least in the Latin Rite) will make use of unleavened bread for the Eucharistic Celebration. (6) The Jewish supper is a "memorial"—so is the Christian Eucharist (in a sense that will be specified later).

1.1.3. The Quails and the Manna

Other figures (*typoi*) of the Eucharist, which we shall see in this and in the following sections, appear during the journey of the Israelites in the desert. First is the episode of the quails (Ex 16). The people complain about their hunger and God says to Moses: "I am going to rain down bread from heaven for you" (v. 4). The Lord then specifies further and says to all the people: "In the evening twilight you will eat meat, and in the morning you will have your fill of bread, then you will know that I, the LORD, am your God" (v. 12). It is worth quoting the biblical passage at length:

---

[13] So it is interpreted, among the many Fathers who share this view, by Saint Justin the Martyr (d. ca. 165), *Dialogus cum Tryphone iudaeo* 111.3: "And the blood of the Passover, which was smeared on the side posts and transoms of the doors, saved those fortunate ones in Egypt who escaped the death inflicted upon the first-born of the Egyptians. The Passover, indeed, was Christ, who was later sacrificed, as Isaias foretold when he said: 'He was led as a sheep to the slaughter' (Isa 53:7). It is also written that on the day of the Passover you [Jews] seized Him, and that during the Passover you crucified Him. Now, just as the blood of the Passover saved those who were in Egypt, so also shall the blood of Christ rescue from death all those who have believed in Him. Would God have been mistaken [killing also the Hebrews], then, if this sign had not been made over the doors? That is not what I say, but I do say that He thus foretold that salvation was to come to mankind through the blood of Christ" (*Writings of Saint Justin Martyr*, in *FCNT* [New York: Christian Heritage Inc., 1948], 319–320).

[14] 1 Pet 1:19. Among other things, the passage seems to allude precisely to Exodus 12, since in v. 18 it says: "[You realize] that you were ransomed from your futile conduct, handed on by your ancestors, not with perishable things like silver or gold." The reference to silver and gold could allude to Exodus 12:35: "The Israelites ... asked the Egyptians for articles of silver and gold and for clothing." However, just as it was not those goods that saved their ancestors, but rather the blood of the lamb spread over the doors of the houses, so now it is the "Blood of Christ" (1 Pet 1:19) that saves us.

In the evening, quail came up and covered the camp. In the morning there was a layer of dew all about the camp, and when the layer of dew evaporated, fine flakes were on the surface of the wilderness, fine flakes like hoarfrost on the ground. On seeing it, the Israelites asked one another, "[*man hu*] What is this?" for they did not know what it was. But Moses told them, "It is the bread which the Lord has given you to eat. / Now, this is what the Lord has commanded. Gather as much of it as each needs to eat, an omer for each person for as many of you as there are, each of you providing for those in your own tent." The Israelites did so. Some gathered a large and some a small amount. But when they measured it out by the omer, the one who had gathered a large amount did not have too much, and the one who had gathered a small amount did not have too little. They gathered as much as each needed to eat. Moses said to them, "Let no one leave any of it over until morning." But they did not listen to Moses, and some kept a part of it over until morning, and it became wormy and stank. Therefore Moses was angry with them. / Morning after morning they gathered it, as much as each needed to eat; but when the sun grew hot, it melted away. On the sixth day they gathered twice as much food, two omers for each person. When all the leaders of the community came and reported this to Moses, he told them, "That is what the Lord has prescribed. Tomorrow is a day of rest, a holy sabbath of the Lord. Whatever you want to bake, bake; whatever you want to boil, boil; but whatever is left put away and keep until the morning." When they put it away until the morning, as Moses commanded, it did not stink nor were there worms in it. Moses then said, "Eat it today, for today is the sabbath of the Lord. Today you will not find any in the field. Six days you will gather it, but on the seventh day, the sabbath, it will not be there." Still, on the seventh day some of the people went out to gather it, but they did not find any. . . . The house of Israel named this food manna. It was like coriander seed, white, and it tasted like wafers made with honey. . . . Moses then told Aaron, "Take a jar and put a full omer of manna in it. Then place it before the Lord to keep it for your future generations." As the Lord had commanded Moses, Aaron placed it in front of the covenant to keep it. / The Israelites ate the manna for forty years, until they came to settled land; they ate the manna until they came to the borders of Canaan (Ex 16:13–27, 31, 33–35).

The Eucharist

Let us now decipher the Eucharistic typology in the briefest way possible: (1) This food comes from Heaven—therefore, in John 6, Jesus will use the manna as a prefiguration of His descent from Heaven.[15] (2) As confirmation of the supernatural origin of this food, the Israelites confess that they do not know what it is: "*man hu?*" (Aramaic: "what is it?"), they ask themselves, and from here comes the word "manna"[16]—the Eucharist is also a supernatural gift, "unprethinkable" before it is given by Christ (for this reason, after His discourse in John 6, many were scandalized and abandoned Him). (3) The Israelites must gather the manna for those of their own tent: in this way, the food represents a sort of repetition of the Passover supper, which also was made in the home and eaten with the family. It is a way of repeating the original event each day—the Christian Eucharist, carried out among those who form a single Family in Christ, is likewise a way to relive each day the sacrifice of Golgotha, offered again in each Holy Mass (see further on). (4) The manna is given along with the quails: bread and meat (flesh)—the Christian Eucharist is a bread in which the Body of Christ is present. (5) The Israelites did not know the manna before, while they did know quails—we Christians did not know the Eucharist before it was given to us, while we knew how the human body was made and also knew the physical body of Christ in the years in which He lived before instituting the Sacrament. (6) Whoever consumed a little manna did not lack any and whoever took much of it did not have more: therefore, this food is nourishing in itself and not on the basis of the quantity of it that one eats—this is also the case with the Eucharist, where

---

[15] It should be emphasized that although—as we shall see—John 6 also presents a Eucharistic reading of Exodus 16, the primary significance of that passage refers to the Incarnation of the Word more than the Eucharist. Not by accident, in his *Super Ioannem*, Saint Thomas Aquinas develops this incarnational aspect much more than the other one, considering the theme of the Incarnation in sapiential terms: the eternal Wisdom descends from Heaven to earth.

[16] Historical-critical exegesis has shown that the manna does not, *per se*, seem to be a miraculous food. What is perhaps the most widespread opinion among specialists identifies the manna with a crystallized secretion of certain cochineal insects, which among other things is a great source of carbohydrates (for this reason, the Israelites of the story call it "bread"). This secretion dries rapidly, especially in desert environments, thus easily decaying—another detail that fits with the biblical text. Even if this were true, it would still not explain why on the seventh day such a deterioration did not occur (unless one denies the historicity of this detail). Thus, if one accepts a non-supernatural origin of the manna, then one would need to perhaps accept the supernaturality of at least two details of the story: (1) that the Israelites found it in great abundance for forty years; (2) that it did not perish on the Sabbath and, moreover, that on this day it did not form in the fields. It would thus remain a "bread" that has something extraordinary about it with respect to purely biological laws.

Christ "is entirely in the whole, as well as in the fragment,"[17] and thus it is the same whether one receives a large Host or a very small fragment of it. (7) The manna is not found on the day of the sabbath; moreover, it is eaten only until arrival in the Promised Land—the Eucharist as well, as "bread for the journey," accompanies us only in this life, toward the eternal goal. In Heaven, the Sacrament will no longer be celebrated.[18] (8) Moses ordered Aaron to place part of the manna before the Lord, in the Sanctuary—the Eucharist is also preserved in the tabernacle of the Christian churches, which are the Sanctuary of God on earth. (9) The manna had the taste of focaccia (bread with honey). "Milk and honey" indicate the Promised Land, as noted above; thus, here we have a bread that has the incomplete taste of the Promised Land; there is honey but not milk—the Eucharist is also a food that offers a foretaste of eternal goods; it is a "pledge" of the full joy that will only be had in Heaven.

All these similarities manifest the typological character of the manna in relation to the Eucharist. It will be the task of the following pages to show that the Eucharist is an infinitely greater reality than the miracle of the manna, which nonetheless points to it and prepares for it. Thus, the Old Testament could already guarantee that God "rained manna upon them for food; / grain from heaven he gave them. / Man ate the bread of the angels."[19]

1.1.4. *The Water from the Rock*

In chapter 17 of the Book of Exodus we find another Eucharistic figure: the episode of the waters of Massah and Meribah. It is considered in a negative light in the Old Testament, as an example of disobedience and distrust in God on the part of the Israelites (see Num 20:24; Deut 6:16; 9:22; 32:51; 33:8;

---

[17] "*Tantum esse sub fragmento / quantum totum tegitur*" (Saint Thomas Aquinas, *Lauda Sion*).

[18] In fact, in the City of God, there will no longer be a temple in which to celebrate the rites, "for its temple is the Lord God almighty and the Lamb" (Rev 21:22). The Sacraments (figures) disappear, to give way to the Reality, contemplated "face to face" (1 Cor 13:12). We read in this regard the beautiful text of Saint Augustine of Hippo, *Sermo 59*.3.6: "But when this life is over, we won't be requiring either the bread of the altar, because then we shall be with Christ whose body we receive, nor will these words have to be spoken which I am speaking to you, nor will a book have to be read, when we see Him who is the Word of God through Whom all things were made, on Whom the angels feed, by Whom the angels are enlightened, by Whom the angels are made wise. They don't require the words of a long-drawn-out speech, but they drink their fill of the single Word" (in *The Works of Saint Augustine*, part III: *Sermons*, trans. Edmund Hill, ed. John E. Rotelle [Brooklyn, NY: New City Press, 1991], 128).

[19] Ps 78:24–25. See also Ps 81:11; 105:40; 106:15; Wis 16:20–21.

The Eucharist

Ps 95:8; 106:32; etc.). While in the previous episode the people complained about the lack of food, now they complain about a lack of water. God, then, commands Moses to strike a rock with the same staff with which he had struck the Nile (see Ex 7), so that water may flow from it. And so it happens. Here the Eucharistic typology is less evident, but it is equally apparent when viewed from three perspectives.

1. Presence

The text of Exodus 17 affirms that the Lord carries out this miracle not so much to quench the thirst of the Hebrews, but to demonstrate that He truly accompanies them in the desert. In fact, the Israelites rebelled against Moses saying, "Is the LORD in our midst or not?" (v. 7). Here is a first Eucharistic typology: the Eucharist is given to us by Christ to ensure us that He is always with us, that He accompanies us along the journey of this life with His Real Presence.[20]

2. Saint Paul

A second reason that allows us to grasp the Eucharistic typology of Exodus 17 is the exegesis proposed by the Apostle Paul:

> I do not want you to be unaware, brothers, that our ancestors were all under the cloud and all passed through the sea, and all of them were baptized into Moses in the cloud and in the sea. All ate the same spiritual food, and all drank the same spiritual drink, for they drank from a spiritual rock that followed them, and the rock was the Christ. Yet God was not pleased with most of them, for they were struck down in the desert. These things happened as examples for us (1 Cor 10:1–6).

Here, Saint Paul provides a typological interpretation—with sacramental lenses—for several episodes from Exodus: the cloud (see Ex 13:21–22), the

---

[20] "I am with you always, until the end of the age" (Matt 28:20). Once again, we should cite that precious gem left to us by Saint Leo the Great (d. 461): "What was visible of our Redeemer has passed into the Sacraments" (Saint Leo the Great, *Sermones* 74.2, in *NPNF*, vol. 12, trans. Charles Lett Feltoe [Peabody, MA: Hendrickson Publishers, 1994], 188 [with our corrections]). By bringing the two texts together, we understand that Jesus—ascended to Heaven—truly remains with us through His Sacraments and especially in the Eucharist, which is He.

Red Sea (see Ex 14:21–31), and the manna from above. Finally, he refers to the episode of Massah and Meribah. The cloud and the sea are interpreted as figures of Christian Baptism, while the manna and water bursting out of the rock are taken as spiritual food and drink. They are spiritual because the first comes from Heaven (Saint Paul does not say it, but we noted it in the previous section) and the second gushes out of a "spiritual rock that followed them, and the rock was the Christ." He concludes by confirming again the typological character of those Old Testament episodes: "These things happened as examples [*typoi*] for us."

The Pauline passage is interesting for at least two reasons: (1) it allows us to read the episode of Massah and Meribah with Eucharistic lenses—and also, more generally, to do this for the rest of the Old Testament; and (2) it emphasizes that the spiritual drink came from Christ—how much more, then, does the chalice of the Eucharist! In this way, Saint Paul reveals the Christocentrism of the Sacraments, even in their prefigurations, and particularly the Christocentrism of the Eucharist. The Apostle invites us to reflect on the Christian Eucharist above all as a gift that springs forth from Christ. Other aspects are not excluded, but this is preeminent.

3. Saint John

There is an important detail of Jesus' Passion that only the Fourth Gospel reports. In John 19:33–37 we read:

> But when they came to Jesus and saw that he was already dead, they did not break his legs, but one soldier thrust his lance into his side, and immediately blood and water flowed out. An eyewitness has testified, and his testimony is true; he knows that he is speaking the truth, so that you also may (come to) believe. For this happened so that the scripture passage might be fulfilled: "Not a bone of it will be broken." And again another passage says: "They will look upon him whom they have pierced."

A few observations: (1) Jesus spoke in the same Gospel of water that flows out from His "body," as an image of grace (see John 7:37–38, which uses the Greek word *koilia*, meaning the belly, the womb, the heart, or any organ in the abdomen, and, more generally, the inner man). Jesus speaks of Himself as the One from Whose body flows living water that quenches for all eternity. At the well, He had spoken with the Samaritan woman of the living water (see John 4:10). In the Gospel of John, therefore, this symbol

The Eucharist

is taken up several times. The passage of chapter 19, however, has a particular resonance with Exodus 17, because just as the rock in the desert was struck by the staff of Moses, so "the rock [that] was the Christ" (1 Cor 10:4) is struck by the lance of the soldier. In both cases, water flows out. It is not surprising that since the earliest times, the theological and magisterial Tradition interprets the blood and water flowing from the side of Christ as a symbol of the Church's Sacraments. In fact, Saint Paul unveils the typology, and Saint John gives us the narration of the historical event. (2) The link between this Johannine passage and the Eucharist is also provided by another detail: Jesus' bones are not broken. The Evangelist cites Exodus 12:46: "You shall not break any of its bones" (see also Num 9:12), referring to the lamb of the Passover supper, which was mentioned above. John re-reads the death of Christ on the cross in light of the figure of that lamb whose blood saved the Israelites from extermination. And he does this in the same passage in which he speaks of the Sacraments flowing out from Jesus. Therefore, the Eucharist was foreshadowed in a hidden way in the water that flowed from the rock and the lamb that the Jews ate. (3) Saint John concludes with another citation from the Old Testament: "when they look on him whom they have thrust through" (Zech 12:10). Jesus is pierced, "thrust through," by the lance of the soldier. (4) Numbers 21:9 can also be recalled: "Accordingly Moses made a bronze serpent and mounted it on a pole, and whenever the serpent bit someone, the person looked at the bronze serpent and recovered." In fact, still in the same Gospel, Jesus recalls that episode and applies it to Himself: "And just as Moses lifted up the serpent in the desert, so must the Son of Man be lifted up, so that everyone who believes in him may have eternal life" (John 3:14–15).[21] Therefore, to look at the Crucified One means to look at the One who has been pierced and, looking at him, to be saved from the bite of the devil (the serpent: see Gen 3 and Rev 20:2) in order to obtain eternal life. In the Christian Eucharist, the possibility of looking with faith at the One who was pierced is offered in order to obtain redemption and life without end.

1.1.5. The Blood of the Covenant

Another Eucharistic theme in the book of Exodus is the blood of the covenant, which would later be connected to the cult of the Temple in Jerusalem. In Exodus 24, the ritual stipulation of the covenant with God is narrated.

---

[21] A comparison between the text of Numbers 21 and that of John 3 is also made by the Liturgy, which makes use of them respectively as the first reading and Gospel reading on the Feast of the Exaltation of the Holy Cross (September 14).

Moses erects an altar at the foot of the covenant mountain (Sinai), an altar with twelve pillars, representing the twelve tribes of Jacob (v. 4). Then he offers holocausts and peace offerings (v. 5). Half of the blood of the immolated animals is used to sprinkle the altar, and the other half is preserved to sprinkle the people (v. 6); then he reads the book of the covenant before the assembly of Israelites (v. 7). Finally, he sprinkles those present with the sacrificial blood, saying: "This is the blood of the covenant which the LORD has made with you according to all these words" (v. 8). Immediately afterwards, accompanied only by some representatives of the people, he climbs the mountain and there "they beheld the God of Israel.... They saw God, and they ate and drank" (vv. 10–11).

Here, too, there are several typological details: (1) A sacrificial liturgical celebration takes place—the Christian Mass is also a sacrificial liturgical celebration, but with an infinitely greater perfection, as we shall discuss later. (2) The covenant is signed with the blood of the victims—the new covenant is ratified in the Blood of Christ, offered in the Eucharist. (3) Moses says: "This is the blood of the covenant"—Jesus will say: "This is my Blood of the covenant" (Mark/Matt) or "This chalice is the new covenant in my Blood" (Luke/1 Cor). (4) The Mosaic rite takes place on an altar with twelve stones, which indicate the ancient People of God—the Christian rite of the Holy Mass also has an unalterable link with the Church, the new People of God, because it is a sacred banquet that gathers the Church in unity, as we shall see. (5) The Mosaic Liturgy has two fundamental moments: the reading of the Book and an immolation of victims—so it is with the Christian Mass, the two fundamental hinges of which are the Liturgy of the Word and the Liturgy of the Eucharist. (6) After the conclusion of the rite, some could see God and then eat and drink[22]—in the Christian Eucharist, one also "sees" God (hidden under the veils of the Species) and, after having worshipped Him, one receives spiritual food and drink.

1.1.6. From Ritual Sacrifices to the Sacrifice of Jesus

1. Sacrifices

The blood of the covenant is directly connected to the following sacrificial

---

[22] As can be deduced from other passages of the Old Testament, this does not mean that, after having seen God, they went down from the mountain to consume a meal, but rather that—despite having seen God—they did not die and continued earthly life (indicated concretely by the meal).

The Eucharist

practices that will be carried out in the Temple of Jerusalem when Israel reaches and conquers the Promised Land. The sacrificial Law is found above all in Leviticus 1–7. The first five chapters are concerned with the holocaust or burnt-offering (*olah*), oblation (*minhah*), peace offering or communion sacrifice (*zevah*), expiatory sacrifice (*hatta't*), and the reparation sacrifice or guilt offering (*asham*). Chapters 6 and 7 add some supplementary rules for the celebration of these sacrifices.

There are numerous other places in the Old Testament that speak of the sacrificial practice—in various eras of the history of the chosen People—which allow certain distinctive features to emerge: (1) The offered victim must be pure (see Gen 8:20; 15:9). (2) Property acquired illegally cannot be an object of sacrifice (see Deut 23:19), because the person must offer something of his own—better yet, something he has earned by the sweat of his brow. (3) Among things that the person possesses, he must reserve the best part for God, not the worst or even the mediocre parts (see Lev 1:3). Many texts emphasize that the animal must be "without blemish" (e.g., Deut 15:21). (4) Even though the Bible records certain contrary cases (see 2 Kings 21:6 and Judges 11:29ff), due to a certain influence of surrounding religions, in Israel human sacrifice is categorically forbidden. (5) In addition to animals, other goods were offered as well, such as incense (see Ex 30:7), oil (see Gen 28:18), grain (see Ex 40:29; Lev 2:1), or wine (see Num 28:7). (6) Without going into every detail about the ritual execution, we only recall the element that has the greatest connection with the blood of the covenant, referenced in the last section, namely, the fact that the priest took the blood of the victim, gathered it in a bowl, and sprinkled it on the corners of the altar (see Lev 1; 3; 7:2). (7) Several sacrifices, but not all, ended with the eating of what remained of the offered animal. Some parts of the animal were reserved for the priests and their families (see Lev 6:19; 10:14; etc.).

In the ritual sacrifices of Israel, unlike other ancient religions, there was no pretense of claiming to appease a wicked divinity, nor the intention of offering the god a pact or equal exchange (*do ut des*, "I give so that you will give"), much less the performance of an act of magic. Instead, sacrifice in Israel is the essential act of external Worship, commanded by God, but which requires much more than simple material execution—as is the case with acts of magic. True sacrifice requires the inner desire to praise and thank God, and the intention of re-establishing communion with Him. Sacrifice has as an end the union of the human being with God. It is an external sign that must lead to this effect. Thus, even if it could appear strange, Saint Thomas Aquinas spoke of the "sacraments" of the Old Testament, obviously in an analogical and not univocal sense with respect to the New Testament.[23] Because of human weakness, the believer can treat the rite more like an act of magic, executing it as a purely mechanical external act. This explains the preaching of the prophets. In appearance, it seems as if they reject ritual sacrifices, but in reality they want to bring them back to their integrity: an upright heart is necessary for true sacrifice (see Isa 1:11, 15–17; Mic 6:6–8; Jer 7:21–23; Am 5:21–24; etc.).

2. Jesus' Sacrifice

Jesus associates Himself with this prophetic tradition, citing Hosea 6:5–6: "Go and learn the meaning of the words, 'I desire mercy, not sacrifice'" (Matt 9:13; repeated in Matt 12:7 with respect to unjust condemnations). The Lord then approves the scribe who says to Him: "To love him [God] with all your heart, with all your understanding, with all your strength, and to love your neighbor as yourself is worth more than all burnt offerings and sacrifices" (Mark 12:33). But He did not reject sacrificial Worship altogether; He wished, rather, to bring it back to its deepest truth (see Matt 5:23: "If you bring your gift to the altar, and there recall that your brother . . ."; see also Matt 8:4). The Lord wants to purify Temple Worship not so that it will remain a place of Liturgy for the new People of God—in fact, it will disappear (see Mark 13:2 and parallel passages)—but because He wanted the people to live the sacrifices of the old law in their deepest inspiration—that of a pure heart, of an interior sacrifice, as the prophets recalled. In this way, the Jews could then recognize the true Sacrifice, His crucifixion, which put an end to the Worship of the Temple, when the veil of the Sanctuary was torn (see Mark 15:38 and parallels), decreeing the end of the figures (types) and the beginning of the sacramental economy of the Church.

Jesus articulated the most complete sacrificial theology when He instituted the Eucharist: His words, while not mentioning explicitly the word sacrifice, have a clear sacrificial appeal, as we will see later. Thus, in the Gospel of John, He says: "I consecrate myself for them" (17:19; see the discussion of these words in Chapter Four), which clearly has the value of a self-offering, of a self-sacrifice. In Jesus, the sacrifice is no longer an external act carried out from time to time in life. Jesus understood His entire life as a self-offering for us, thus all of

---

[23] "In the old law there was a sort of sacraments, that is, signs of a sacred thing, such as the paschal lamb and other sacraments in conformity with the law, which nonetheless signify the grace of Christ but do not cause it" (Saint Thomas Aquinas, *De articulis fidei et ecclesiae sacramentis* 2 [our translation]).

The Eucharist

Jesus' life is a sacrifice, and the whole of His life is salvific. The Letter to the Hebrews shows that the sacrifice of Jesus is the true existential sacrifice, the perfect sacrifice, which takes the place of the ritual sacrifices that point to it.

1.2. New Testament

Naturally, the New Testament is the true biblical *locus theologicus* of Christian sacramental theology and therefore of Eucharistic theology. It is in the writings of the new covenant that this mystery is revealed and, as has been noted, the Old Testament Eucharistic typology can only be grasped after the message of the New Testament has been accepted in faith. Let us proceed to learn the fundamental features of the Eucharist from the New Testament biblical texts.

1.2.1. The Names of the Eucharist

1. Eucharist

The substantive "Eucharist" is not found in the New Testament, but the verb "*eucharistein*" ("to thank") is found in the institution narratives of Paul and Luke, which we shall see later. It will be the Apostolic Fathers, such as Saints Ignatius of Antioch and Justin Martyr, who will be the first to coin the word *eucharistia*.

2. The Lord's Supper

According to current academic exegesis, the older account of the Eucharistic institution is the one contained in 1 Corinthians 11:23–25. In that passage, which we encounter again in the next section, Saint Paul speaks of the banquet/supper of the Lord (*kyriakon deipnon*: 1 Cor 11:20)[24] and of the Lord's chalice (*poterion Kyriou*: 1 Cor 11:27). The Apostle, in the same chapter of the letter, denounces the presence of divisions in the community of Corinth (see 11:18). Because of these, he declares that the gathering of the Corinthians "is not to eat the Lord's supper" (v. 20). The division generates

---

[24] The terminology of the "Lord's Supper" (*kyriakon deipnon*) and a good part of the expressions relating to table-fellowship, did not prevail in the early Church, perhaps because it evoked too directly the Hellenistic sacred meals of the era. In fact, as happened in Corinth, to consider the Eucharist principally as a "meal" entailed the risk that, like many banquets in the pagan cults, the Christian sacred supper would also degenerate into disorder of various sorts, or that it would be subjected to reductive interpretations.

selfishness and thus it happens that on the occasions of the gatherings there is no communion among the brethren. There was then the custom not only of receiving the Eucharistic Species, but also consuming a meal in common: "for in eating, each one goes ahead with his own supper, and one goes hungry while another gets drunk" (v. 21). Hence comes the strong admonition of the Apostle to receive the Eucharist with the awareness that it is not just any meal, but the Lord's Body (see vv. 23–32), and for this reason, "A person should examine himself, and so eat the bread and drink the cup. For anyone who eats and drinks without discerning the body, eats and drinks judgment on himself (vv. 28–29)." Based on the words of Saint Paul, the doctrine appears clear: the Eucharist is certainly the "Lord's supper," but it cannot for this reason be equated with a common fraternal meal.

3. Spiritual Food and Drink

In 1 Corinthians 10:3–4, Saint Paul speaks of spiritual food (*pneumatikon broma*) and spiritual drink (*pneumatikon poma*).

4. Communion

In 1 Corinthians 10:16, we find the expressions "cup of blessing" (*poterion tes eulogias*) and "bread that we break" (*arton hon klomen*). It says of the first that it is "participation [communion] in the Blood of Christ" and of the second that it is "participation [communion] in the Body of Christ." The Greek term for "participation" (or communion) is the well-known *koinonia*, which we have already encountered in our discussion of ecclesiology (see Chapter Eight). Here Paul adds what will be the foundation for what he says in 1 Corinthians 10:17 about the relationship between the Eucharist and the Church: "Because the loaf of bread is one, we, though many, are one body, for we all partake of the one loaf" (v. 17). An important characteristic stands out: the Christian Eucharist is not an empty external ritual. It is properly understood with deep terms such as "communion" and "participation." These are not simply words that indicate an external fact, the mere coming together in the same place to celebrate the Lord's supper and to participate *de facto* in the same consecrated bread (see v. 16). Here communion and participation take on connotations that go beyond the sociological aspect, to become a mystery, an ontological reality. Since we participate in the *coena dominica*, we enter in to effectively become part of the one Body of the Church, symbolized in the Eucharistic bread. The table-fellowship aspect of the supper does not then correspond to the fact of being a simple fraternal gathering where we meet to celebrate. The table-fellowship of this encounter really has a much deeper sense, which is expressed well by the term "communion," given its wide semantic reach.

5. The Lord's Table

Verse 18 adds a comparison between the Christian table and the altar of Old Testament sacrifices: "Look at Israel . . . ; are not those who eat the sacrifices participants in the altar?" Here too, the sense of communion cannot be understood in a purely external way. Whoever eats of the flesh sacrificed to God on the altar of the Temple of Jerusalem, enters into communion with what the altar signifies and produces. But this entering into communion is not merely an act of desire (extrinsic sense), nor is it an act of magic (esoteric sense). It is a communion intrinsic both to the intention of the offeror and to the sacrifice itself, because the sacrifice has real value, insofar as it is offered to God. For this reason, Saint Paul can argue against the pagan sacrifices made to idols (vv. 19–22). Such sacrifices are in vain, because "[they sacrifice] to demons, not to God" (v. 20). Regarding the subjective aspect, one cannot partake at the same time of Jewish or Christian sacrifices and those of the pagans (v. 21). But as regards the objectivity of the sacrifice, it comes from God and not from the one who offers it or participates in it. In participating at the Lord's table, we need both: the power of God and the holiness of the human being. Finally, the aforementioned verse 21 reports two other expressions for referring to the Eucharist: "cup of the Lord" (*poterion Kyriou*) and "table of the Lord" (*trapezes Kyriou*).

6. Bread of Life, Heavenly Bread

The terminology of food and feeding, but not of the table, is found in John 6:57, with a clear realistic emphasis: "Just as the living Father sent me and I have life because of the Father, so also the one who feeds on me will have life because of me." John 6:48–51 also speaks of the bread of life (*artos tes zoes*) and of the heavenly bread (*artos ho ek tou ouranou*). We shall analyze this passage shortly.

7. "Fractio Panis"

The Acts of the Apostles report the well-known expression "breaking of the bread" (*klasis tou artou*: Acts 2:42). Some scholars argue that this refers to the practice of *agape*, that is, to the communal meal that initially was held alongside the Eucharistic celebration.[25] Given the immediate context of the passage of Acts 2:42, however, it seems more probable that the "breaking of bread" was an archaic way of referring to the Eucharist.[26] This, evidently, also recalls the practice of fraternal communion, for which those who assist in the breaking and distribution of the Eucharistic Bread by the Apostles, must learn to share with their brethren material bread as well, namely, their own goods.

8. Altar

The Letter to the Hebrews makes explicit the reference to the theme of the Sacrifice of Christ, calling the Eucharistic table an "altar." In Hebrews 9, the author gives a summary of the ritual of Jewish sacrifice and then makes reference to Christ, Who enters into the Sanctuary not with the blood of animals, but with His own blood and thus ratifies the perfect and eternal covenant through His sacrificial death (see Heb 9–10). Hebrews 13:10 affirms: "We have an altar from which those who serve the tabernacle [the Temple of Jerusalem] have no right to eat." It is evident that the main direction of the text is not in reference to the Eucharist. It wants to show the difference, albeit in continuity, between Jewish Worship and Christian Worship, between belonging to the old People of God or to the new and, consequently between frequenting the Temple and participating in the Christian Liturgy. Nonetheless, in an indirect way, we are given a new term to indicate the Eucharistic Mystery, namely, "the altar." The Christian altar is an altar of Sacrifice (see again Chapters Nine and Ten), but of a Sacrifice far superior to the Jewish sacrifices. Here the Eucharist, even if not expressly named, can be understood in light of the Sacrifice of Christ, a theme that occupies a very relevant place within the Letter to the Hebrews. Saint Augustine may have been inspired by this when he introduced the expression "sacrament of the altar."[27]

1.2.2. The Institution Narratives

Four texts in the New Testament report the institution of the Eucharist:

---

[25] There is a mention of this custom also in an apocryphal writing, the *Epistula Apostolorum*, composed around 160, in which the following words are attributed to the Lord (ch. 15): "And when you complete my Agape and my remembrance [=the Eucharist] . . ." (*New Testament Apocrypha: Gospels and related writings*, vol. 1, ed. Wilhelm Schneemelcher [Westminster: John Knox Press, 1991], 258).

[26] John Paul II also made his own this Eucharistic interpretation of the expression "breaking of bread" in *Mane Nobiscum Domine* (2004), §3.

[27] See Saint Augustine of Hippo, *Sermo 59.3.6*.

The Eucharist

Mark 14:22–26	Matthew 26:26–30	Luke 22:14–20, 39	1 Cor 11:23–25
²²While they were eating,	²⁶While they were eating,	¹⁴When the hour came, he took his place at table with the apostles.	²³ The Lord Jesus, on the night he was handed over,
he took bread, said the blessing [*eulogesas*], broke it, and gave it to them, and said,	Jesus took bread, said the blessing [*eulogesas*], broke it, and giving it to his disciples said,	¹⁹Then he took the bread, said the blessing [*eucharistesas*], broke it, and gave it to them, saying,	took bread ²⁴and, after he had given thanks [*eucharistesas*], broke it and said,
"Take it; this is my body."	"Take and eat; this is my body."	"This is my body, which will be given for you [*hyper hymon*]; do this in memory of me."	"This is my body that is for you [*hyper hymon*]. Do this in remembrance of me."
²³Then he took a cup, gave thanks [*eucharistesas*], and gave it to them, and they all drank from it.	²⁷Then he took a cup, gave thanks [*eucharistesas*], and gave it to them, saying, "Drink from it, all of you,	²⁰And likewise [gave thanks, *eucharistesas*] the cup after they had eaten, saying,	²⁵In the same way also [gave thanks, *eucharistesas*] the cup, after supper, saying,
²⁴He said to them, "This is my blood of the covenant, which will be shed for many [*hyper pollon*].	²⁸for this is my blood of the covenant, which will be shed on behalf of many [*peri pollon*] for the forgiveness of sins.	"This cup is the new covenant in my blood, which will be shed for you [*hyper hymon*]."	"This cup is the new covenant in my blood. Do this, as often as you drink it, in remembrance of me."

²⁵Amen, I say to you, I shall not drink again the fruit of the vine until the day when I drink it new in the kingdom of God."	²⁹I tell you, from now on I shall not drink this fruit of the vine until the day when I drink it with you new in the kingdom of my Father."	¹⁸for I tell you [that] from this time on I shall not drink of the fruit of the vine until the kingdom of God comes."	
²⁶Then, after singing a hymn, they went out to the Mount of Olives.	³⁰Then, after singing a hymn, they went out to the Mount of Olives.	³⁹Then going out he went, as was his custom, to the Mount of Olives, and the disciples followed him.	

1. Context

Notice the placement of these narratives in the context of the Gospels. Mark places the Last Supper within the framework of (what we identify as) chapter 14 of his Gospel, which is dedicated to Jesus' Passion. Since the text of Mark is considered by the majority of exegetes to be the most ancient Gospel, it can be said that this text presents the story of the Eucharistic institution for the first time (which does not imply that the form used is the most ancient: see below), immediately placing it in the context that is proper to it. From the beginning of the Gospel Tradition, the account of the Last Supper is found in the context of the suffering and death of Christ. Christ's Passion does not begin after the institution of the Eucharist, but the Eucharist forms part of the mystery of Jesus' Sacrifice.

2. Redactional Threads

The synopsis of the four passages brings to light multiple convergences, which have allowed scholars to identify two main redactional threads characterized by common elements: on the one hand, the First Letter to the Corinthians and the Gospel according to Luke (the so-called "Pauline redactional thread") and, on the other hand, the Gospel according to Mark and the Gospel according to Matthew ("Petrine redactional thread"). However, there are other elements proper to each author. Let us look at certain elements that allow us

The Eucharist

to identify the two major redactional threads: (1) The mention of the blessing of the bread in Mark/Matt, rendered with *eulogesas* ("[Jesus] said the blessing"), is rendered in 1 Cor/Luke with the expression *eucharistesas* ("after He had given thanks") concerning the bread. In fact, they can be considered synonymous expressions. (2) In Mark/Matt, the narrative of the institution flows smoothly from the bread to the wine, while in Luke, the cup is postponed until the end of the supper ("after they had eaten"). Moreover, the first two say "will be shed on behalf of many"; Luke, instead, says "for you" both with respect to the Body and the cup. Paul only says it with respect to the Body. 1 Cor/Luke, moreover, also add "given for you" to the words pronounced by Jesus over the bread. (3) In 1 Cor/Luke there is the order to carry this out ("do this": two times in 1 Corinthians and once in Luke), while in Mark/Matt it is absent. (4) The words of institution are different in the two threads, although with important elements in common: "this is my Body" is identical in all four texts and the formula over the cup is very similar, especially because all four mention the covenant in the Blood.

3. Concordance

The four accounts, considered together, are identical. It is very difficult, if not impossible, to reconstruct with certainty the exact words that Jesus used in the Upper Room, in the act of instituting the Eucharist. On the other hand, there is no need, because the general sense of them is clear and common to all four narrations. The nuances do not change the general sense of the words, which, considered as a whole, beyond a shadow of a doubt, go back to Jesus Himself.[28]

4. The Words of Institution

One last consideration is dedicated to the essential meaning of the words of institution. We shall again present the version of each text:

---

[28] From the perspective of theology and sacramental practice, it is not strictly necessary to know the exact words used by Jesus: certainly only they consecrate, but this does not happen in a magical way, as if in Christian Liturgy the *ipsissima verba Jesu* (the exact same words of Christ) should be used. If this were so, the Canon of the Mass could not even be recited in Latin, Italian, and so forth, but the consecratory words would have to be repeated in the same language in which they were pronounced by the Nazarene (Hebrew or Aramaic?). To admit this is entirely different than saying that the consecratory words of Jesus can be omitted in the Eucharistic Liturgy (see below).

Mark: Take it; this is my Body.
This is my Blood of the covenant, which will be shed for many (*hyper pollon*).

Matthew: Take and eat; this is my Body.
Drink from it, all of you, for this is my Blood of the covenant, which will be shed on behalf of many (*peri pollon*) for the forgiveness of sins.

Luke: This is my Body, which will be given for you (*hyper hymon*); do this in memory of me.
This cup is the new covenant in my Blood, which will be shed for you (*hyper hymon*).

Paul: This is my Body that is for you (*hyper hymon*). Do this in remembrance of me.
This cup is the new covenant in my blood. Do this, as often as you drink it, in remembrance of me.

The Latin version of the traditional Roman Missal (extraordinary form) has put together the biblical versions in this way:

Accipite et manducate ex hoc omnes. Hoc est enim Corpus meum.

Accipite et bibite ex eo omnes. Hic est enim calix Sanguinis mei, novi et aeterni testamenti, mysterium fidei,[29] *qui pro vobis et pro multis effundetur in remissionem peccatorum. Haec quotiescumque feceritis, in mei memoriam facietis.*

The ordinary form of the Missal presents the consecratory words in the following way:

Accipite et manducate ex hoc omnes. Hoc est enim Corpus meum, quod pro vobis tradetur.

Accipite et bibite ex eo omnes. Hic est enim calix Sanguinis mei, novi et

---

[29] Note this insertion of a Pauline formula, which remained in the institutional words of the Holy Mass for many centuries and was removed in the Missal of Saint Paul VI, which moves it after the words over the chalice.

The Eucharist

aeterni testamenti, qui pro vobis et pro multis effundetur in remissionem peccatorum. Hoc facite in meam commemorationem.[30]

The current English version in the United States (2011) is translated as such:

Take this, all of you, and eat of it, for this is my Body, which will be given up for you.

Take this, all of you, and drink from it, for this is the chalice of my Blood, the Blood of the new and eternal covenant, which will be poured out for you and for many[31] for the forgiveness of sins.

---

[30] We could make several observations both concerning the words of the extraordinary form reproduced above, and concerning those, both Latin and English, of the ordinary form of the Missal, but here we must abstain from it. We leave to the reader the task of comparing, word for word, the different versions, possibly also consulting the Greek text of the New Testament.

[31] Surprisingly, the "for many" of Scripture, which has remained intact in the Missal of Paul VI (*pro multis*), is translated in many nations (even the United States before the new translation of 2010) as "for all." On October 17, 2006, the Congregation for Divine Worship and the Discipline of the Sacraments sent a letter (Prot. No. 467/05/L) to the presidents of all the national episcopal conferences, asking that in the next two years the bishops, through appropriate catechesis, prepare the faithful of their dioceses to review the expression "for all," which is found in various translations of the Missal in the national language. The Congregation writes that, in future translations into the vernacular of the *editio typica* of the Roman Missal, it will be necessary to introduce a more faithful translation of the *pro multis*. In Italian, for example, the current "*per tutti*" ("for all") must turn into "*per molti*" ("for many"). The text of the letter is published in several languages in *Notitiae* 43 (2006): 441–458. After six years, since almost nothing had happened, Pope Benedict XVI repeated this provision in a *Letter to the President of the German Episcopal Conference* (April 14, 2012), in which he provided a broad explanation of the theological-liturgical grounds for which it is necessary to translate the institutional words with the formula "for many" and not "for all." Among many remarkable things, the Pope notes that "it was decided by the Holy See that, in the new translation of the Missal, the expression '*pro multis*' should be translated as such and not together already interpreted. In place of the interpretative version 'for all' the simple translation 'for many' must go." He also recalls that "the Church has taken up this formulation from the accounts of the institution in the New Testament. It thus says out of respect for the Word of Jesus, to remain faithful to Him even within the Word. The reverential respect for the Word of Jesus is the reason for the formulation of the Eucharistic Prayer." On September 3, 2017, Pope Francis published the motu proprio *Magnum Principium*, which assigns to the episcopal conferences the major responsibility in translating, approving, and publishing the liturgical books for the regions for which they are responsible. Previously, new translations of the liturgical books needed to receive a *recognitio* (a deep, word-for-word examination) and approval by the Apostolic See. The new norms of *Magnum Principium* state that only a *confirmatio* is required from Rome, namely the ratification of the approval of the new translation. Such

Do this in memory of me.

We clearly find at the center of these words the Body and Blood of Jesus. It does not speak of bread and wine. The bread and wine—it can be said—do not exist for these words. Only the Body and Blood of Jesus exist, from the moment in which He identifies the preexisting elements with them. The terminology is especially marked by the sacrificial sphere. The Body is "given" and the Blood "shed" or "poured out." This happens for the remission of sins. This Sacrifice of Jesus is carried out "for you (pl.)" (namely, those present, or the disciples in general) and "for many."

The sacrificial aspect must be combined with that of participation in the Eucharistic supper. Theology defines it as the "communal aspect" of the Eucharist. Both aspects—communal and sacrificial—are present from the words of Jesus, although the sacrificial aspect is attested in all four versions of the institution narratives, while the communal aspect, certified by the imperatives "eat" and "drink," is clearly attested only in Matthew (Mark and Paul use the verb to drink, but not in the imperative). Thus, even on the basis of the words of the institution alone, it can be said that the sacrificial aspect is prioritized over the communal aspect, which, if understood in light of John 6 (see below), assumes its value only in dependence on the sacrificial aspect. In fact, our ability to partake of the Body and Blood of the Lord is a gift of the loving sacrifice of Jesus.

1.2.3. The Last Supper

The words of institution were pronounced in the context of the Last Supper of Jesus with His disciples. We shall thus outline the theology of this meal.

---

an approval is now made by the episcopal conference itself and ratification made by the Holy See does not entail a thorough examination of the texts. As a consequence of this new law, it is to be expected that some (or several) episcopal conferences will go back to the translation "for all," or will just keep it, if they never changed it. This is the case, for example, of the Italian Episcopal Conference: a new Italian translation of the Missal had been in preparation since 1983 (year of the second official translation, the first being from 1973). For reasons hard to understand, the new (third) translation was never submitted to the Holy See for the *recognitio*. After *Magnum Principium* was published, it took only a few months to the experts of the Italian Episcopal Conference to prepare and submit to the bishops the new version, which was approved. The new Italian Missal maintains "for all" in the translation of the words over the chalice.

The Eucharist

1. Chronological Questions

There are, above all, complex questions of chronology, since the Synoptic Gospels and the Gospel of John indicate different dates for the celebration of the supper. The Jewish paschal supper was always held on the same day—the fourteenth day of the month of Nisan, called the day of the "Parasceve" (Matt 27:62)—which was the day of preparation for the Passover, celebrated on the fifteenth of Nisan. In the Synoptics, the fourteenth of Nisan is a Thursday, so the Passover fell on a Friday that year, coinciding with the crucifixion and preceding the usual Saturday rest. In John, on the other hand, the fourteenth is a Friday, the day of Jesus' death on the cross. Consequently, as the Last Supper occurred the evening before the Lord's crucifixion, for the Fourth Gospel the institution of the Eucharist would have happened on the evening of the thirteenth of Nisan. This means that the Last Supper would not have been held at the same time as the Jewish Passover, as the Synoptics state. This raises the question of whether or not the Last Supper was also a Jewish Passover meal, celebrated according to the provisions of the ritual, and thus drawing on the theology of this rite.

We have dedicated more space elsewhere to settling the question. Here, we shall be very brief, indicating only the conclusion of our assessments: (1) The exact chronology, from the historical point of view, is given by John: various details of the Gospel narrations point toward this solution.[32] (2) Therefore, the Last Supper was held the evening before the Jewish commemoration of the Passover. (3) Nevertheless, the Last Supper presents elements that are typical of this celebration, even if other elements included in the Jewish meal are not there. It seems unquestionable that the theological setting of Jesus' supper with His disciples was that of a "*zikkaron*" ("memorial"). (4)

---

[32] Very recently, an excellent exegete who previously held that John's chronology is the more historical one, has proposed a new theory. He says that the synoptical and the Johannine chronology are not opposed to each other while affirming that the "solemn day" of which John speaks ("it was a solemn feast that Shabbat") is not the Jewish Pasch but another feast: the feast of the sheaves or the firstfruits (see Lev 23). Though the feast was celebrated on the day after the Shabbat, the priest would go at the end of the Shabbat [Saturday evening] to harvest the sheaf that was meant to be presented in the Temple on the next morning. John's "solemn day" would be, according to this view, not a feast in itself (Pasch) but the day to prepare the solemn feast of the sheaves. The author builds a very interesting hypothesis that has the advantage of considering the synoptical and Johannine chronologies not in contrast. He also maintains that Jesus celebrated the first Eucharist in the context of a real Jewish Passover meal. As brilliant as his treatment of the topic is, against it stands the fact that John 19:31 says that the day in which Jesus was crucified was the Parasceve, thus the preparation of the Passover and not of another feast.

Jesus substantially anticipates the commemoration of Passover by one day, but celebrates it with a ritual that He has modified: the bread and wine now become central instead of the lamb with bitter herbs. (5) Attentive study of the four Gospels reveals that the Eucharist was instituted in a supper of a Jewish Passover sort, we could say, in such a theological "setting."[33] This, on the one hand, means that the theology of that Jewish supper is useful for understanding the Christian Eucharist; on the other hand, such a theology is not sufficient for completely expressing the sense of the gesture instituted by Jesus.[34]

2. The Jewish Passover Meal

There are four main theological elements of the Jewish meal: (1) it is both a sacrifice of a victim, and a meal of the gathered family; (2) it celebrates the liberation from bondage in Egypt; (3) it is a commemoration or *anamnesis* (*zakar*, from which comes *zikkaron*, "memorial"): the memorial is the living and represented memory, which confers actuality to the event in salvation history; and (4) the meal is a memorial, specifically, of the liberation from the Egyptians and the passage through the Red Sea.

3. Jesus' Supper

There are several elements in the Last Supper that recall a Jewish Passover meal: (1) the community at table is formed, with the head of the family (in this case Jesus) leading the ritual; (2) it is celebrated in Jerusalem; (3) there are elements that seem to correspond to the Jewish ritual: the first cup (Luke 22:17?); the starter of bitter lettuce dipped in a sweet fruit preserve (Matt 26:23?, John 13:26?); the breaking of bread by the head of the family and passing it to others; the third cup (Luke 22:20?); the recital of the *Hallel* (Mark 14:26?; Matt 26:30?).

It can be hypothesized that "after supper" (1 Cor 11:25) indicates the order followed in carrying out the institution. That is, Christ would have

---

[33] "We should keep in mind that [the institutional words] were spoken in the context of the Paschal meal, which for the Jews was indeed a 'memorial'" (Saint John Paul II, *Letter to Priests for Holy Thursday* [2005], §5).

[34] "Jesus thus brings his own radical *novum* to the ancient Hebrew sacrificial meal. For us Christians, that meal no longer need be repeated. As the Church Fathers rightly say, *figura transit in veritatem*: the foreshadowing has given way to the truth itself. The ancient rite has been brought to fulfillment and definitively surpassed by the loving gift of the incarnate Son of God" (Benedict XVI, *Sacramentum Caritatis* [2007], §11).

The Eucharist

given His Body during the supper. For this reason Matthew 26:26 says: "While they were eating, Jesus took bread." By contrast, He would have consecrated the Blood after the supper. Thus in Luke 22:20: "And likewise the cup after they had eaten." Aquinas accepts the idea that the Eucharist was celebrated by carrying out a twofold consecration of the bread and wine, with a certain temporal separation interposed between the first and the second. He interprets it theologically in this way:

> The reason for this is that the Body of Christ represents the mystery of the Incarnation, which happens when the legal prescriptions still persisted, among which the most important was the supper of the paschal lamb. Whereas in the Sacrament the Blood of Christ directly represents the Passion through which it was poured out and with which all the legal prescriptions were concluded (see Heb 9:12: "He entered once for all into the sanctuary ... with his own blood, thus obtaining eternal redemption").[35]

However, there are several missing elements, or elements conflicting with the ritual of the Jewish supper: (1) the second cup is not mentioned and the fourth is entirely missing, because Jesus and the disciples leave after the *Hallel*, interrupting the rite; (2) Jesus does not distribute the lamb with the bread, but only the bread; (3) He declares that the bread is His Body and that the (third?) cup contains His Blood! (in practice, He is presented as the victim in the place of the lamb); and (4) the memorial is not of an event of the past, but of a Person: "Do this in memory of me" (Luke 22:19).

Consequently, Jesus celebrates a supper in a Jewish theological "setting," but at the same time detaches Himself from the ritual and interprets signs and gestures according to what He wishes to communicate to the Apostles. The Master actually institutes a new rite, starting from elements of the previous one (continuity), but also incorporating unpredictable novelty. The Christian Eucharist is not a Jewish Passover supper, even if it was instituted within that context. The Eucharistic Doctor expresses the novelty and continuity in a beautiful commentary on Matthew 26:26 where, among other things, there is a true gem of a statement: "*sicut ille erat vere cibus, ita et iste agnus,*" which emphasizes the union and hierarchy between the sacrificial aspect and the communal one:

---

[35] Saint Thomas Aquinas, *Super I ad Corinthios* XI, *lectio* 6 [*reportatio Reginaldi*] (our translation).

"Jesus took bread" (Matt 26:26): Here Christ touches the matter [of the Sacrament]. It should be noted that this Sacrament relates to the old sacraments as the truth relates to a figure. The old sacrament was taken as food, because it was commanded that the lamb be eaten: and this one, which is taken in its place, must be taken as food. And as the old lamb was truly food, so this food [the Eucharist] is true lamb [*et sicut ille erat vere cibus, ita et iste agnus*]. The opinion for which Christ is in the Host only in a symbolic way is also shown to be false: in fact, if the consecrated bread were only a figure, in what way would it be different from the figures of the Hebrews? Those were only figures, this is a figure and truth [*Illud erat signum tantum, hoc autem est figura et veritas*].[36]

Regarding the fact that Christ distributed the Eucharist after the conclusion of the Jewish supper and immediately before leaving toward the Mount of Olives, Saint Thomas writes:

The Lord did this in a reasonable manner for three reasons. (1) First, because, according to a fitting order, the figure precedes the truth. In fact, the paschal lamb was the figure, namely, the shadow of this Sacrament. Thus after the supper of the paschal lamb, Christ distributed this Sacrament.... (2) Secondly, because from this He passed immediately to the Passion, of which this Sacrament is the memorial.... (3) Thirdly, so that this Sacrament would more deeply be imprinted on the hearts of the disciples, to which He consigned Himself in His extreme departure. But out of reverence for such a great Sacrament, the Church established that it be taken only on fast; and from this only the sick are exempted...[37]

4. The Eucharist

The theological content of the Eucharist is that it is a memorial, but not only a memorial of past historical events, re-actualized in the ritual gesture, but rather the memorial of the Person of Christ and—in this Person—of the salvific work carried out by Him, in a special way with the Passion. Because it is a memorial of the Person, it can also be a memorial of the

---

[36] Saint Thomas Aquinas, *Super Matthaeum* XXVI, *lectio* 3 (our translation).
[37] Saint Thomas Aquinas, *Super I ad Corinthios* XI, *lectio* 4 [*reportatio Reginaldi*] (our translation). See *Super Matthaeum* XXVI, *lectio* 3.

events. The Christocentrism must be clearly affirmed here. The events of the life of Jesus—especially the holy Triduum of Passion, Death, and Resurrection—can be present in the Eucharist, and they can be represented, re-actualized, and commemorated only because the Eucharist is the memorial of Christ.[38]

Moreover, the sacrificial character clearly takes precedence over the communal character, though the latter is clearly attested. It is true that bread is eaten and wine drunk, but these nourishments are in reality Him: His Body "given" and His Blood "poured out" for many. The sacrificial character is very clear. Jesus applies the sacrificial and victimary terminology to Himself. He is the Lamb served at this supper; He is the Victim that is offered for the sins of many. If the Jewish supper provided for a previous immolation of the lamb in the Temple—but as such was primarily the consummation in a context of praise and thanksgiving—now, in the Eucharist of Jesus, the sacrificial theme is no longer prior to the supper, but is instead placed at its center. This bread and this wine were not already immolated; they are immolated now. This *is* right now my Body given/immolated; this *is* here and now my Blood poured out. The Sacrifice is the heart of the supper, it occupies its center, without denying the communal aspect (which is essential, but secondary). In the institution of the Eucharist, Christ wanted to give the Church the memorial of His immolated Body and Blood; that is, He wanted to give Himself to us as a Victim under the appearance of bread and wine. The Eucharist is the Sacrifice of Jesus to which a communal participation is granted. Let us read a passage by Pope Benedict:

> When, on the banks of the Jordan, John the Baptist saw Jesus coming towards him, he cried out: "Behold, the Lamb of God, who takes away the sin of the world" (John 1:29). It is significant that these same words are repeated at every celebration of Holy Mass, when the priest invites us to approach the altar: "This is *the Lamb of God* who takes away the sins of the world. Happy are those who are called to His supper." Jesus is the *true* paschal Lamb who freely gave Himself in sacrifice for us, and thus brought about the new and eternal cov-

---

[38] Perhaps, from this perspective, the mode in which the Missal of the extraordinary form translates it is better than that of the ordinary form (in Latin), because the latter presents the formula "*Hoc facite in meam commemorationem*," ("in my memory/commemoration"), whereas the other one says "*in mei memoriam*," ("in memory of me"). The current version of the Missal used in the United States translates it "in memory of me" instead of "in my memory." The former is more accurate theologically, while the latter would translate the *editio typica* more literally.

enant. The Eucharist contains this radical newness, which is offered to us again at every celebration.[39]

1.2.4. The Multiplication of Bread, and the Supper in Emmaus

Two other Gospel passages—if reread in light of the institution narratives—can be seen as also referring to the Eucharist.

1. Multiplication of Bread

This miracle is attested by all four Gospels. In Mark and Matthew, there are actually two accounts of multiplication (see Mark 6:30–44; 8:1–9; Matt 14:13–21; 15:32–38; Luke 9:10–17; John 6:1–15). The bread and fish are multiplied (we shall leave aside the comparison between the different narrations and the symbolism of the numbers reported in them). The elements that we wish to highlight are these: (1) The deeds that Jesus performs are very similar—but not equal—to those of the Eucharistic institution (He took, He blessed, He broke, He gave to be distributed). (2) Although the fish are also multiplied and distributed, some details of the narration make it so that the bread is especially prominent (for example, except for Mark 6:43, the pieces of bread are advanced and then collected, the fish are not; etc.). Based on these two elements, we understand that the account is a sort of prophetic anticipation of what Jesus will do in the Upper Room. (3) Elements of the content of these texts help in our study of the theology of the Eucharist: for example, the fact that Christ divides the crowd into small groups, or that He orders the Apostles to distribute it (without having—*sit venia verbis*—a sort of self-service directly from the baskets); (4) Also relevant is the Eucharistic typology of the many loaves that "come out of," but continue to be, one unique bread blessed by the hands of Christ.

In spite of these similarities, however, the differences between the multiplication of the loaves and the accounts of institution should not be neglected, otherwise we would lose sight of the radical *novum* carried out by Jesus during the Last Supper.

2. Supper at Emmaus

A second passage with Eucharistic symbolism is that of the supper that the

---

[39] Benedict XVI, *Sacramentum Caritatis*, §9. See also §10.

The Eucharist

risen Christ has with the two disciples in Emmaus (see Luke 24:30–35). It could be thought that, on this occasion, Christ has celebrated the Eucharist in a true and proper sense. We doubt this, both because there is no mention of a cup, and because Christ does not say the words, "This is my Body." Additionally, in instituting the Eucharist, He entrusted it to the Apostles to celebrate it. Although Jesus is the High Priest of our faith, it appears more correct to say that He does not celebrate the Liturgy of the Holy Mass, having commissioned the Apostles to do so.[40]

Despite these specifications, there is little doubt about the fact that the account of the supper in Emmaus presents a teaching regarding the Eucharist.[41] The connection with the institution of the Sacrament is again in the gestures: Jesus "took bread, said the blessing, broke it, and gave it to them" (Luke 24:30). The most significant element of the account for a theology of the Eucharist is verse 31: as soon as Jesus broke the bread and gave it to them, "their eyes were opened and they recognized him." Thus, the account helps us to focus our attention on the theme of the presence of Christ in the sign of broken and distributed bread—a clear reference to the Sacrament of the Eucharist.

There are then other useful elements from a Eucharistic perspective, if one considers the account as a whole (vv. 13–35): (1) the Eucharist is a response to the spiritual hunger of human beings (compare vv. 13–24 with 32–35); (2) the Eucharist is an experience of the centrality of Christ, crucified and risen; (3) it expresses the closeness of Jesus to those on the way (*viaticum*, see v. 15); (4) the Eucharist is the permanent presence of the risen crucified One "under" the sign of bread (see the "stay with us" of v. 29); and (5) the Sacrament foments ecclesial unity: the two disciples were moving away from Jerusalem, where Peter and the others are staying, but—immediately after supper with Jesus—they turn back, toward the Church, full of joy and zeal (see vv. 33–35).[42]

1.2.5. Chapter Six of John's Gospel

We will conclude our discussion of the New Testament by looking at one of

---

[40] In this regard, it is significant that in John 3:22, it is said that Jesus "baptized." Shortly after, however, the evangelist clarifies: "although Jesus himself was not baptizing, just his disciples" (John 4:2). Jesus baptized—He is the Author of the Sacraments—but Jesus does not baptize in Person—He does so through His ministers.

[41] In *Mane Nobiscum Domine*, Saint John Paul II offers deep points of reflection concerning the Eucharist, based on the account of the supper in Emmaus, without ever affirming that this was a true and proper celebration of the Holy Mass.

[42] See, for the last aspect, *Mane Nobiscum Domine*, §24–28.

the most significant passages: John 6. In a more or less direct way, the whole chapter has to do with the Eucharist—with it the Evangelist fills, so to speak, the gap of not having presented the institutional narrative of the Sacrament.

1. The Multiplication

The first part of the text (vv. 1–15) is dedicated to the Johannine version of the multiplication of the loaves. Having already discussed this theme, we shall only emphasize here a peculiarity of this version. In verse 12, Jesus commands the disciples to gather the leftover bread: "Gather the fragments left over, so that nothing will be wasted." "Wasted" is a translation of the Greek *apoletai*, a form of the verb *apollymi*, which means "to ruin, make perish, to send to ruin, to lose, to allow to corrupt," etc. At verse 39, Jesus says: "And this is the will of the one who sent me, that I should not lose anything of what he gave me, but that I should raise it [on] the last day." Here we find the same verb: that I should not "lose" (*apoleso*), says the Lord. Thus, the same term in the same chapter is used both in reference to the fragments of bread, and to the eternal salvation of human beings. The term highlights indirectly the relationship between the Eucharist and the Church: the fragments of multiplied bread (an image of the Eucharist) must be collected with great care and attention; and this is an image of the zeal with which the Shepherds of souls—imitating the Good Shepherd—must take care that no one is lost from among the sheep of Christ's flock.[43]

2. The Bread Come Down from Heaven

After a break—the narration of the miracle of Christ walking on the water (vv. 16–21)—we pass to the second part of the chapter, in which the Eucharistic discourse becomes progressively more explicit. The opening of the section is linked with the preceding one: Jesus recalls the miracle of the multiplication and notes that the crowd now seeks Him because it was satisfied by the loaves (see v. 26). But the tone of the discourse is immediately elevated: "Do not work for food that perishes but for the food that endures for eternal life" (v. 27). Exegetes link these words to another passage of John, namely 4:14:

---

[43] The Church instructs priests who celebrate the Holy Mass that they be attentive not to disperse the fragments of the consecrated Host because—as will be said—each fragment contains the Real Presence of Christ. The zeal of priests in carrying out this ritual deed, performed out of respect for Christ, could also foment their pastoral zeal in the *cura animarum* ("care of souls"). Gathering with great attention the Eucharistic fragments also becomes a symbol of the attention with which one pursues each individual soul, so that it does not get lost.

"whoever drinks the water I shall give will never thirst; the water I shall give will become in him a spring of water welling up to eternal life." The juxtaposition of the two passages is also made possible—in addition to the common reference to "eternal life"—by the words that Jesus Himself pronounces, shortly after the discourse, where He brings together the image of eating bread that satisfies, with that of quenching one's thirst: "I am the bread of life; whoever comes to me will never hunger, and whoever believes in me will never thirst" (John 6:35). Verse 29 clarifies the deep connection among these three Johannine passages: "This is the work of God, that you believe in the one he sent." In brief, at the center of this is the theme of faith in the One sent by God, a fundamental aspect of the entire Gospel according to John. In chapter 6, this theme is also applied to the bread of eternal life. If the discourse, at least in this passage, could originally be detached from a Eucharistic sense, there is no doubt that in the final redaction of the Johannine text we find this truth revealed by God: one must approach the Eucharistic bread with living faith in the One who is present in it.

At verse 30, the Jews ask, according to a mentality that can be recognized as their own (see 1 Cor 1:22), for a supernatural sign to prove that what Jesus says is true. Until now, Jesus had not yet provided a detailed explanation of the nature of this bread. He had simply affirmed that the Son of Man, the One consecrated by God, would give food that lasts for eternal life (see v. 27). The Jews understand that Jesus recognizes Himself in this image, and they also understand that He considers the food that He promises to be superior even to the food given from Heaven through Moses. The latter, in fact, perished and did not last for eternity, with its purpose being that of sustaining the people in the desert (see Ex 16:20; Josh 5:12). Therefore, Jesus implicitly claims a condition of superiority with respect to Moses, which must be proven—according to the biblical mentality—by miraculous signs. Evidently, Jesus was right when, at verse 26, He had said that the people had not followed Him because they had "seen the sign," but only because they had been satiated. If they had "seen" or believed in that sign, they would not now ask for another. Verses 30–31 recount the question of the people, which mentions the manna given by God long ago.

Jesus' response begins to reveal the "personal" nature of the new manna: it was not Moses who gave true bread from Heaven, because it is granted only by the Father of Jesus: "For the bread of God is that which comes down from heaven and gives life to the world" (v. 33). Then, in light of the request of those present ("give us this bread always" [v. 34], which also corresponds in this case to 4:15: "Sir, give me this water, so that I may not be thirsty or have to keep coming here to draw water"), Jesus repeats in an even more undoubtable way the identification between Himself and this food: "I am the bread of life" (v. 35). Thus we note the evolution that the expression has undergone in the span of a few verses: from the "bread from heaven" (vv. 31–32), to the "bread of God" (v. 33), and finally "bread of life" (v. 35). It is clear that in all cases, for John this bread is Jesus Himself, the Envoy of God.[44]

The Jews, however, react negatively to the self-revelation of Jesus as bread descended from Heaven, bread of God, and bread of life (see vv. 41–42). They call into question the family of Jesus, whom they all know. His father is Joseph and His mother is Mary; they also know His brothers and sisters (concerning them: see Chapter Seven): How can Jesus claim to be descended from Heaven? But Christ fully confirms His self-designation.

3. The Flesh that Gives Life

The words with which the Master repeats that He is heavenly bread introduce a further aspect:

> I am the bread of life. Your ancestors ate the manna in the desert, but they died; this is the bread that comes down from heaven so that one may eat it and not die. I am the living bread that came down from heaven; whoever eats this bread will live forever; and the bread that I will give is my flesh for the life of the world (vv. 48–51).

The term "flesh" (*sarx*) is introduced here, which clearly recalls the fundamental verse of John 1:14. The discourse steers in this last part towards a clear Eucharistic realism. Now Christ no longer speaks just of food and drink. He speaks of flesh and blood. Verses 52–58 are the properly Eucharistic part of the entire chapter. To receive the bread of Heaven means to eat "the flesh of the Son of Man" and—implicitly—to take the cup is the same as drinking "his blood" (v. 53). This flesh and this blood are "true food, and ... true drink" (v. 55), that is, truly nourishing and quenching, for eternity (see above, v. 35). And this is so because, "Whoever eats my flesh and drinks my blood has eternal life, and I will raise him on the last day" (v. 54). The Eucharistic elements, therefore, contain the divine power of eternal life; the flesh and the blood of Christ confer the seed of immortality and of the future bodily resurrection to those who receive them.[45] Given the context of the entire chapter,

---

[44] See the discourse on Jesus as Source of life in John 5:24–30.

[45] Let us also connect to this theme the passage of Matt 6:11, with its parallel in Luke 11:3. This concerns the prayer of the Our Father, at the point in which Christ speaks of

The Eucharist

it is implied that the effect is guaranteed to those who receive them while believing in the Envoy, that is, to those who receive them with faith. The personalistic aspect—of encountering Jesus in the Eucharist—is made explicit: "Whoever eats my flesh and drinks my blood remains in me and I in him" (v. 56). In conclusion, this is the reality of the bread of Heaven, which is why those who eat of it will live forever (see v. 58).

4. The Proof of Faith

The concluding part of the chapter concerns the reaction of the people to the revelation of the Eucharistic Mystery. Many of His disciples were scandalized: "This saying is hard; who can accept it?" (v. 60). They represent here all of the Christians who do not believe in the Eucharistic dogma: not just members of the Protestant communities, but even those Catholics who—while professing with their words the doctrine on the Eucharist—show, with their behavior, that they do not *truly* believe it. Jesus says: "But there are some of you who do not believe" (v. 64). Peter, on the contrary, represents in himself those who do believe: "Master, to whom shall we go?" (v. 68).

In this last pericope of the passage, Jesus reconfirms what He said earlier—which scandalized part of the audience (see v. 61)—and also adds something that further specifies the Eucharistic doctrine: "It is the spirit that gives life, while the flesh is of no avail. The words I have spoken to you are spirit and life" (v. 63).[46] This complex expression means, in short, that the

---

"daily" bread. In Greek, the term is *epiousion*. If one wants to translate literally, like Saint Jerome translated Matt 6:11 in his *Vulgate*, it would need to be translated as "supersubstantial—*supersubstantialis*." The meaning of the Greek word is at least dual: (1) a bread that exceeds the very essence of bread (and then the Eucharistic reference is explicit); and (2) a bread that, as food, sustains our essence, that is, it makes us stay alive, nourishing us. In this second acceptation, *epiousion* can be translated as "necessary" or "daily," because it indicates the food by which we are nurtured every day to gain energy (the reason why Saint Jerome translated *epiousion* in Luke 11:3 as *cotidianum*, "daily"). The two meanings may stand together: Jesus has taught us to ask God to give us *both* the Eucharist, the supernatural food that nourishes us spiritually, *and* natural bread, which we need to live on earth. But in the versions of the Our Father translated from Greek, the first meaning usually remains hidden, since the word is generally translated as "daily."

[46] On this verse, the commentary of Saint Augustine of Hippo, *In Ioannis Evangelium tractatus* 27.5 is famous: "What, then, does it mean, 'the flesh profits nothing'? It profits nothing, but as they understood it; for, of course, they so understood flesh as [something that] is torn to pieces in a carcass or sold in a meat market, not as [something that] is enlivened by a spirit. Accordingly, it was said, 'The flesh profits nothing,' just so as it was said, 'Knowledge puffs up.' Ought we, therefore, to hate knowledge? Far from it. And what does 'knowledge puffs up' mean? Alone, without love. Thus he added, 'but

teaching of Jesus must be grasped in its true sense, which is this: the Eucharist is truly His flesh and blood. But this does not mean that, taking that bread and cup, one eats the physical flesh and drinks the material blood of Christ: the Eucharist and anthropophagy have nothing to do with each other![47]

It can be said that the teaching of Christ on the Eucharist avoids the two extremes of pure symbolism and of rough physicalism. The Eucharist is not only a symbol that refers to something outside of itself—in the sign of the bread (and in the cup) is the real flesh and blood of Christ. At the same time, this does not mean that we eat the flesh and blood of the physical body of Jesus as it was two thousand years ago on earth. It is Eucharistic realism, not physicalism. Bread and wine surpass the mere symbolic value that refers to Christ and His Passion: they give us in a real presence Jesus and his Paschal Mystery. However, the Body and Blood of Christ are present with a different reality from that of the mere level of biological body and blood. This is what Christ clearly suggests and what theology must then elucidate, while always remaining faithful to Revelation.

2. Theological Reflection, and the Teachings of the Magisterium

We shall now present, according to a thematic subdivision, the main aspects of ecclesial Eucharistic theology, confirmed by the approval of the Magisterium of the Church, which throughout the centuries has collected and made its own the very best of the reflection of the Fathers and of the Doctors concerning the Sacrament of the altar.

That the Eucharist is a Sacrament is seen by the fact that the Sacra-

---

love edifies.' Therefore, add love to knowledge, and knowledge will be useful, not in itself but through love. So too, now, 'flesh profits nothing,' but flesh alone; let spirit be added to flesh, as love is added to knowledge, and it profits very much. For if flesh profited nothing, the Word would not have become flesh to dwell among us" (in *FCNT*, vol. 78, trans. John W. Rettig [Washington, DC: CUA Press, 1988], 280).

[47] Remember that the earliest Christians were persecuted because they were accused—among other things—of "Thyestean feasts." According to classical mythology, Atreus invited his brother Thyestes to dinner with the pretext of reconciliation with him, and fed him the meal of his own slaughtered children for dinner as revenge for the wrongs suffered. The term Thyestean feasts therefore refers to cannibalism, which was probably imputed to Christians because their accusers did not understand the meaning of their Eucharist, in which the pagans heard that Christians ate the flesh and drank the blood of Jesus.

ments have been instituted by Christ to provide for the spiritual needs of wayfarers (see Chapter Nine). Saint Thomas observed that spiritual life has analogies with physical life and thus—as we have seen—the seven Sacraments have similarities with the stages and activities of human life. In this sense, the Eucharist corresponds to nourishment. We need to eat food every day, and quench our thirst, in order to replenish the energy lost through various activities and to accumulate new strength for the future. The Eucharist is thus spiritual food and drink, which sustains us on the road toward the celestial Homeland.

Resuming, then, the famous scholastic distinction between *res* or *res tantum* (the thing meant, the effect of grace), *sacramentum* or *sacramentum tantum* (the visible sacramental sign) and *res et sacramentum* (the grace produced in a permanent way: the character or the "quasi-character"),[48] Saint Thomas adds that in the Eucharist—like in the other Sacraments—it is also possible to make a similar distinction, but with one difference, which is due to the fact (see further along) that while the other Sacraments coincide with the use of the matter, the Eucharist instead coincides with the consecration of matter. For this reason, the Eucharist is the only Sacrament that has *res et sacramentum* (which is Christ Himself)[49] in the matter; by contrast, the other six Sacraments produce the *res et sacramentum* in the one who receives them. The *res tantum*, however, for all seven Sacraments, is produced in those who receive.[50]

Being that the Eucharist is therefore a true Sacrament, let us first analyze the structural elements that it has in common with the other sacramental signs: matter, form, and minister. We shall then study the aspects that are specific to this Sacrament: transubstantiation and the Real Presence, the effects, the Sacrifice, and Communion.

2.1. Matter, Form, and Minister

2.1.1. Matter

1. Matter in Itself

The matter of the Eucharistic Sacrament are without a doubt, on the basis of the institution narratives, the bread and wine. Saint Thomas explains the

---

[48] This terminology is also used by Innocent III, *Cum Marthae circa* (1202) (DS 783).
[49] See *ST* III, q. 73, a. 4.
[50] See *ST* III, q. 73, a. 1.

reasons why it was fitting that the Lord chose to be contained in this Sacrament "*sub specie aliena*" ("under a different type"): "First, because it would be a horrible thing for the faithful if they took this Sacrament if they ate human flesh and drank blood in their proper manifestations; second, so that it was not a source of laughter for non-believers; third, so that the merit of faith may grow, which consists in the fact that things that are unseen are believed."[51]

The bread must be made of wheat (*triticum*) because Christ compared Himself to the grain of wheat that falls to the ground (see John 12:24–25).[52] The wine must be that of the grapevine, that is, fermented grape juice.[53] This is because Christ compares Himself to the vine in John 15. Moreover, in Luke 22:18, the Lord affirms that this was the drink consumed at the Last Supper: "from this time on I shall not drink of the fruit of the vine."[54] Consequently, a Eucharistic Celebration that makes use of other elements than those mentioned would be invalid. Bread and wine, in fact, are of "divine law," and no one can change them, since Christ in Person chose these elements.

---

[51] Saint Thomas Aquinas, *Super I ad Corinthios* XI, *lectio* 5 [*reportatio Reginaldi*] (our translation).

[52] *ST* III, q. 74, a. 3. Council of Florence, *Exsultate Deo* (1439): "The third Sacrament is the Eucharist. The matter of this Sacrament is wheat-bread [*panis triticeus*] and grape-wine [*vinum de vite*]" (DS 1320). The Latin Church uses unleavened bread. The Eastern Churches, on the contrary, use leavened bread. Saint Thomas says that both are valid matter, but that for the licitness of the celebration the sacred ministers must comply with the custom established by their own Church. The Angelic Doctor, however, affirms that the Latin custom is more fitting for various reasons, among which is the fact that in the Scripture leaven is often (but not always) a symbol of corruption, such as in Luke 12:1 (see *ST* III, q. 74, a. 4).

[53] Especially in recent times, there has been a great increase in the number of those who, on account of dietary intolerances, cannot receive the Species of bread or that of wine. For guidelines in this regard, see the *Circular Letter to all Presidents of the Episcopal Conferences concerning the Use of Low-Gluten Altar Breads and Mustum as Matter for the Celebration of the Eucharist*, sent on July 24, 2003, by the Congregation for the Doctrine of the Faith.

[54] See *ST* III, q. 74, a. 5. See the already cited passage of the Council of Florence. The liturgical rite requires that a small amount of water be mixed with the wine. The symbolism of this consists in highlighting the participation of the faithful in the Sacrament, because it indicates the union with Christ. For the Angelic Doctor, since sacramental Communion, which unites with Christ, is not absolutely indispensable (see *ST* III, q. 73, a. 1; however, see the specifications of q. 73, a. 3), it also follows that this rite of the infusion of water is not necessary for validity (*ST* III, q. 74, a. 7). This obviously does not imply that priests can ignore it, both because the Church establishes it, and for its important symbolic value (explained in q. 74, a. 6).

2. Symbolism

Bread and wine are the matter of the Sacrament for two reasons: (1) First and foremost, because Christ chose them. (2) Also, they possess a very expressive symbolism—a reason for which they were probably chosen by the Lord. The symbolism is explained by Saint Thomas: bread and wine are very fitting elements for establishing the matter of the Eucharist because the latter is consumed by eating it and because, as a Sacrifice, it is in relation to the Passion of Christ. Now, the Passion happened through the separation of the blood from the physical body of Jesus and the duality of the Eucharistic Species visibly reproduces this separation. Finally, bread and wine are a fitting choice, because they manifest well the principal effect of the Sacrament, which is the unity of the Church.[55]

2.1.2. Form

1. From Matter to Form

As we recalled at the beginning of the chapter, the Sacraments coincide with the use of the matter; things are different for the Eucharist alone, because this Sacrament is performed in the consecration, not at the moment of Communion. In general, then, in the Sacraments the matter is blessed, in the Eucharist it is instead consecrated. Moreover, in the other Sacraments the matter remains of its own essence, only a supernatural power (grace) is added to it, which makes it suitable to work as a sacramental element. By contrast, the Eucharistic matter is transformed into something else: the substance of the Body and Blood of Christ, as will be explained later. This also has consequences for the form of the Eucharist, which must express what happens in the Sacrament.

2. The Form

If in the other Sacraments the form indicates the use that one makes of the matter, in this Sacrament it must instead express the substantial change of the

---

[55] See *ST* III, q. 74, a. 1, where Saint Thomas also adds a fourth reason of suitability, to which he also makes recourse on various other occasions in his treatment of the Eucharist: because—he says—the Eucharist preserves the soul and body of the human being. The Body of Christ preserves the body of the human being and the Blood preserves the soul, considering the fact that blood is life (i.e., soul), as Scripture states (Lev 17:14).

bread and wine into the Body and Blood of Christ. Actually, in the form of the Eucharist there is also reference to the use of the Sacrament in Communion. This corresponds to the first part of the formula: "Take . . . and eat; take . . . and drink." But this is not the essential part of the consecratory words, which instead is:

Hoc est [*enim*] *Corpus meum* ("This is my Body").[56]

Hic est [*enim*] *calix Sanguinis mei novi et aeterni testamenti,* [*mysterium fidei*] *qui pro vobis et pro multis effundetur in remissionem peccatorum* ("This is the chalice of my Blood, the Blood of the new and eternal covenant, [the mystery of faith] which will be poured out for you and for many for the forgiveness of sins").[57]

The efficacy of these formulas consists in the fact that, while the forms of other Sacraments are pronounced by the minister "*ex persona Christi,*" the Eucharistic words are pronounced "*ex persona ipsius Christi loquentis.*" The difference is in the fact that the minister, for example, of Baptism, says: "I [minister of Christ, with His power and through His command] baptize you . . ." In the Eucharist, so to speak, the minister only makes his lips and his voice available to Christ because it is Christ in Person who pronounces, "This is my Body," and, "This is the chalice of my Blood."[58]

3. Differences in the Two Forms of the Roman Rite

If we compare the two formulas presented above—which are quoted from the Missal of the extraordinary form—with those currently in use in the ordinary form of the Roman Rite, it is clear that several variations are present. Where the traditional formula says only "*Hoc est enim corpus meum,*" the new formula of the Mass of Paul VI adds the words "*quod pro vobis tradetur*" ("which will be given up [in oblation/sacrifice] for you"). The words over the chalice have also undergone a variation, since the expression *mysterium fidei* has been removed from the center of the formula and placed instead after its end. It is true

---

[56] Council of Florence, *Cantate Domino* (1442): "In the consecration of [the] Body of the Lord, [the Church] uses this form of the words: *Hoc est enim Corpus meum*" (DS 1352).

[57] The formula "for the consecration of the Blood: *Hic est enim calix Sanguinis mei novi et aeterni testamenti, mysterium fidei qui pro vobis et pro multis effundetur in remissionem peccatorum*" (Council of Florence, *Cantate Domino*).

[58] See *ST* III, q. 78, a. 1.

The Eucharist

that none of the four New Testament accounts of the Eucharistic institution mentions such an expression; however, it is also true that the Church, in establishing the formula of consecration of the chalice, almost combining the various elements scattered throughout the four texts, decided from a very early time to also add the words *mysterium fidei*,[59] which is clearly biblical (see 1 Tim 3:9), and which means to indicate the supernatural character of transubstantiation.[60] The inclusion of these words may even come from the Apostolic Tradition, even if is not possible to demonstrate it.[61] Moreover, the Council of Florence, as noted, includes it as part of the form of the Sacrament.

This raises a question of greatest importance: What parts of the consecratory formulas are absolutely necessary "*ad validitatem*" ("for the validity") of the celebration, and which parts can be removed or moved? Concerning the addition of the words over the bread "*quod pro vobis tradetur*," it does not represent a problem, because in the Holy Mass the priest reads many formulas, both before and after the consecration, which are not part of the form of the Sacrament. Therefore, the addition of these words in the Missal of Paul VI can be considered more or less fitting, but it does not represent a danger for the validity of the celebration.

As for the expression *mysterium fidei*, we must note that it was not removed,[62] but rather moved: the priest pronounces it all the same, but at the end of the consecration. Thus, it seems that there are also no doubts concerning validity regarding this. A doubt can arise concerning the moment of transubstantiation. As we shall say in what follows, transubstantiation happens when the priest has finished pronouncing the form of the Sacrament.

---

[59] The words of consecration over the chalice present the expression from the earliest sacramentaries. The insertion of the formula must have a Roman origin, because it is attested in the seventh century in the *Expositio* of the Gallican Mass, which in turn derives from the more ancient Roman Mass.

[60] This character is linked to sacramentality, that is, to the fact that God intervenes supernaturally in the Sacraments. *Mysterium* is a Latin rendering of the Greek equivalent of *sacramentum* (*mysterion*). In this sense, *mysterium fidei* or *sacramentum fidei* are synonymous expressions.

[61] *Constitutiones apostolorum* 8.12.36, from the fourth century, presents the words over the bread in this way, attributing them to Christ Himself: "This is the *mystery* of the new covenant: take and eat, this is my Body" (our translation). For Saint Thomas (see *ST* III, q. 78, a. 3), the words "eternal" and "mystery of faith" are not found in the biblical formulations, but they are added because they derive from Apostolic Tradition (he cites 1 Cor 11:23).

[62] A pronouncement of the Holy Office was thus respected, which, in response to the proposal of eliminating the formula *mysterium fidei*, it responded (July 24, 1958): "*Nefas esse in rem tam sanctam immutationes inducere*" ("It is sacrilege to introduce changes into a matter so sacred" [our translation]).

If, therefore, *mysterium fidei* formed part of the essence of the formula, only when the celebrant pronounces these words would the consecration happen, not before. This would create a theological-ritual problem, since in the rubrics of the Missal of Paul VI it is prescribed that after the words "poured out for you and for many for the forgiveness of sins," the priest genuflects and only afterward pronounces "the mystery of faith." The genuflection is a sign of adoration. There is no genuflecting before wine, because this would be idolatry. One can genuflect only before the Blood of Christ. If therefore the Missal prescribes genuflection (and, even before, to elevate the chalice, in such a way that the faithful may adore), this means that, immediately after saying "for the forgiveness of sins,"[63] transubstantiation has occurred. From what has been observed, the Missal of the ordinary form considers that the words "*mysterium fidei*" are not essential, so much so that it makes the minister say them after he has already adored the consecrated wine.

4. The Essential Elements of the Form

The celebration of the Holy Mass is formed by a collection of parts, rites, and rather broad formulas, but the *conficere sacramentum*, the "producing" of the Sacrament, in a strict sense, happens at the moment in which the minister pronounces the right form over the right matter. We already spoke of the matter. The form was also indicated, but it is evident that in different editions of the Missal it is present with some variations, thus—since with regard to the essential elements of the Sacraments we need to be (in a good sense) scrupulous—we must identify the absolutely essential words of the form of the Eucharist, without which there is not a valid celebration.

Saint Thomas has already indicated the criterion to follow: the form must express the substantial conversion of the matter, that is, the fact that the substance of the bread becomes the substance of the Body of Christ and that of the wine becomes the substance of the Blood. Now this is clearly and sufficiently indicated respectively by the words "This is my Body" and "This is [the chalice of] my Blood." Thus, these are the absolutely essential words. Concerning the formula of the bread, Saint Thomas and the Council of Florence agree completely. The term *enim* is not necessary and is inserted by the Church to link these words to the previous ones.[64] Concerning the formula to consecrate the wine, we have already seen that the Florentine Council indi-

---

[63] As we shall say shortly, "do this in memory of me" is not relevant in this regard.
[64] See *ST* III, q. 78, a. 2. In this article, there are other interesting details about the theme we are discussing.

cates not only the first words, but the entire form provided by the Missal (of the extraordinary form). If the intention was that of defining that each individual word of that formula is necessary for validity, then the formula that is used by the Missal of Paul VI would entail an act of idolatry, because it would make the priest and the faithful adore the content of the chalice before having concluded with the "*mysterium fidei.*" The reason that the Florentine Council holds that the entire formula is the form of the Sacrament is simply because—following Saint Thomas—it cites the entire formula of the ancient Missal. And Saint Thomas had expressed the opinion that not only the first words spoken over the chalice, but the entire formula, so as it is determined by the Church, were essential. This is based on the motivation that the words that follow the first ones are determinations of the predicate, that is, of the Blood of Christ and thus pertain to the integrity of the formula.[65] On the contrary, the Angelic Doctor continues, the words "*haec quotiescumque feceritis*"—that were changed in the Missal of Paul VI to "*hoc facite in meam commemorationem*"—indicate the use of the Sacrament and thus are not essential.[66] Saint Thomas concludes by saying that the formula over the chalice should be kept in its entirety, even if the first words indicate the transubstantiation and the others indicate only the power (*virtus*) of the Blood of Christ poured out in the Passion.[67]

Now, concerning this position we must say that, by accurately studying the entire Eucharistic treatise of the *Summa Theologiae,* it is evident that the Angelic Doctor intends to comply completely with the liturgical form that the Church has established with her authority. This leads him to always hold the choices of the Latin Church in the celebratory sphere as perfect, or at least as the best possible. Catholic theology certainly has much to learn from this ecclesial spirit of the greatest of the Doctors. Nonetheless, it does not imply the denial of the authority of the Church and the overall correctness of her choices to point out, from time to time, ways to improve on what is good. Therefore, to comply entirely with the custom of the Church does not mean having to assume a completely apologetic position concerning the present state of the Liturgy. Otherwise, ritual change at some point would force one to deny everything said beforehand. Clearly, if we strive to follow Saint Thomas in everything, there may be a very rare case in which we can,

---

[65] In addition to fidelity to the Gospels (in specific, Luke), perhaps also for this reason Paul VI decided the addition of some words to the formula over the bread.

[66] But, oddly, in the ordinary form, the priest elevates the chalice and genuflects only after having said them. This is not so in the extraordinary form.

[67] See *ST* III, q. 78, a. 3.

for serious reasons, deviate slightly from his opinion, while remaining on the paths traced by him.

On this particular point, therefore, we do not find it necessary to defend each and every word that the Church has established for the formula of the Missal as essential (also because no one knows what exact words the Church of the first centuries used to consecrate—but the essential ones were certainly not missing!). What truly matters is that: (1) There are essential words that must be pronounced by the minister for the validity of the Sacrament. (2) They express—as the Common Doctor says—the essence of the Sacrament. Thomas himself distinguishes, in the formula over the chalice, the first words from the second ones and says expressly that the latter do not refer to transubstantiation. But since he himself has taught us that the essential words of the Mass are those that express the Eucharistic conversion we can—precisely by fidelity to his teaching—conclude by maintaining our opinion, expressed above, for which the essential form of the Eucharist are the words "This is my Body" and "This is [the chalice of] my Blood."

All of this implies that the formula of the Missal of Paul VI is not only valid, but also that the accessory ritual does not involve any act of idolatry, given that the words *mysterium fidei* are not strictly necessary. Our position does not entail, however, that the priests can add or remove other "nonessential" words on their own initiative.

2.1.3. Minister

1. The Minister

In treating of the form of the Sacrament, Saint Thomas also studied an aspect which we have momentarily skipped. He says that the words of consecration receive a created power (grace) from the Holy Spirit that is capable of transforming the consecrated elements. Such a power is instrumental, like that of the other Sacraments.[68] On the basis of this teaching, it could be thought that anyone, even a layperson, could consecrate the Eucharist, if the power of transubstantiation is found in the words and not in the minister. Moreover, if a layperson can baptize, why can he or she not celebrate the Holy Mass? These and other arguments were used by followers of Peter Waldo (d. 1217) to deny any real distinction between the ministerial and baptismal priesthood.

An opposite objection could be that the Eucharist should be reserved only to bishops and not presbyters. In fact, if it is reserved to bishops to con-

---

[68] See *ST* III, q. 62, a. 3–4; q. 78, a. 4.

secrate less important things, such as chrism oil, why would this not be the case with the consecration of the Sacrament that is greater than all the rest?

Saint Thomas responds to such questions first and foremost by posing a statement of principle: "*hoc sacramentum tantae est dignitatis quod non conficitur nisi in persona Christi*" ("This Sacrament is of such a dignity that it cannot be confected [or celebrated] except in the Person of Christ").[69] As we know, "*in persona Christi*" is a technical expression applied only to ordained priests.[70] The Angelic Doctor says that whoever does something in the place of another must have been delegated by that person. Christ delegated all power to baptize, while He reserved the faculty of consecrating the Eucharist to His Apostles alone, saying: "Do this in memory of me." Therefore, only one who has received Holy Orders in the priestly degree is a minister of this Sacrament, just as only those who are baptized can receive it.[71] It is true, Thomas says, that the words cause the consecration, but the power of the words must always be united to the *munus* given to the priest. It is true that a layperson can baptize, but this was arranged by God because Baptism is absolutely necessary for salvation; therefore, God intended to offer the possibility of being baptized even in the absence of a priest. On the other hand, to receive Eucharistic Communion in a sacramental way is not strictly necessary for going to Heaven and thus God did not will that anyone could celebrate the Eucharist. Finally, for what regards the objection concerning it being reserved to the bishop, the Common Doctor recalls that the bishops have exclusive authority only over what regards the governance of the Church and thus they alone consecrate the chrism and holy oils, since they are in charge of regulating

---

[69] *ST* III, q. 82, a. 1.

[70] The doctrine of "*in persona Christi*" is very ancient. We read, for example, in Saint Cyprian of Carthage (d. 258), *Epistula 63*, 14 and 17: "For if Christ Jesus, our Lord and God, is Himself the great High Priest of God the Father and if He offered Himself as a Sacrifice to the Father and directed that this should be done in remembrance of Him, then without a doubt that priest truly serves in Christ's place who imitates what Christ did and he offers up a true and complete Sacrifice to God the Father in the Church when he proceeds to offer it just as he sees Christ himself to have offered it." The "mimetic" and not merely "symbolic" character of the celebration is then repeated shortly after: "And because at every Sacrifice we offer we mention the Passion of our Lord (indeed, the Passion of our Lord is the Sacrifice we offer), then we should follow exactly what the Lord did" (in *The Letters of St. Cyprian of Carthage*, vol. 3: *Letters 55–66*, trans. Graeme W. Clarke [New York, NY—Mahwah, NJ: Newman Press, 1987], 106–107).

[71] "Matt 26:26: 'giving it to the disciples.' It says 'to the disciples' because this Sacrament must not be given to anyone who is not baptized. As an unordained priest does not consecrate the Eucharist validly, so this cannot be given to one who is not baptized [*sicut non conficeret sacerdos nisi consecratus, sic non debet alicui illud administrari nisi baptizato*]" (Saint Thomas Aquinas, *Super Matthaeum* XXVI, *lectio* 3 [our translation]).

the dispensation of the Sacraments from the disciplinary perspective. In this sense, it is the bishop who gives canonical faculty to celebrate Mass or hear Confessions. But the sacramental power to do so is not reserved to him and is thus also given to presbyters.

Even before Saint Thomas, the Fourth Lateran Council recalled, "No one can perform this Sacrament except the priest duly [*rite*] ordained."[72] And later on, the Council of Trent will teach that Christ "offered his Body and Blood under the Species of bread and wine to God the Father, and, under the same signs, gave them to partake of to the disciples (whom He then established as priests of the New Covenant) and ordered them and their successors in the priesthood to offer, saying: 'Do this in remembrance of me.'"[73] In more recent times, these teachings have been repeated again, given the opposition to which they have been subject on the part of some, even within the Catholic Church.[74]

2. The Sanctity of the Minister

As with the other Sacraments, the personal moral condition of the minister is irrelevant to the validity of the celebration.[75] This is because the Sacraments are the objective gift of the grace of Christ to the Church and cannot be linked to uncertainty and to the subjectivity of the personal conditions of the minister. On the other hand, for Catholic doctrine, nobody can have absolute certainty of being in God's grace.[76] If, therefore, the sanctity of life were a necessary element for the validity of the Mass, there could never be any certainty in this regard, with the consequence (among others) of not knowing whether or not to worship the Host (if it is not transubstantiated, it is bread, and one cannot adore a creature), or knowing whether the Host we receive is indeed Communion with the Body of Christ or if the Hosts preserved in the

---

[72] Fourth Lateran Council, *Firmiter* (1215) (DS 802).

[73] Council of Trent, *Decretum de ss. Missae Sacrificio* (1562), ch. 1 (DS 1740).

[74] See Congregation for the Doctrine of the Faith, *Sacerdotium Ministeriale* (1983).

[75] "For the evil life of a bishop or a priest has no harmful effect on either the Baptism of an infant or the consecration of the Eucharist or other ecclesiastical duties performed for the faithful" (Innocent III, *Eius Exemplo* [1208] [DS 793]).

[76] See Council of Trent, *Decretum de Iustificatione* (1547), ch. 9 (DS 1534). Consider the well-known episode that took place in the context of the trial of Saint Joan of Arc (d. 1431), to whom was posed a difficult question concerning her state of grace. If the Maid of Orleans had responded that she were not in the grace of God, the judges would have more easily condemned her. Likewise, however, if she had responded that she was in such a state, precisely because this would represent presumption. So she answered. "If I am not [in a state of grace], may God put me there; if I am, may God keep me there."

tabernacle really contain the actual presence of Christ, etc.

Saint Thomas supports this position with a brilliant exegesis of a Gospel passage: Matthew 24:48, in which—narrating a parable—Christ says: "... but if that wicked servant says to himself..." The Angelic Doctor notes that even though he is wicked, the Master still considers him His servant. Thus, even the sinful priest does not cease to be minister of Christ and validly celebrates the Holy Mass.[77] On the other hand, it is the power of Christ (as God) that brings about transubstantiation. With reference to 1 Kings 18, the Angelic Doctor comments: "If the word of Elijah had such power to make fire come down from heaven, much more could the Word of God change a body [the bread] into something else."[78]

The Magisterium has confirmed this teaching. The Council of Constance establishes this in the examination of those who were accused of following Wyclif or Hus. Among other things, the Council inquired as to "whether he believes that a bad priest [*malus sacerdos*], making use of the proper matter and form, who has the intention of doing what the Church does, truly confects."[79] The Council of Trent pronounced the following condemnation: "If anyone says that a minister in the state of mortal sin, though he observes all the essentials that belong to the effecting and conferring of the Sacrament, does not effect or confer the Sacrament, let him be anathema."[80]

2.2. The Eucharistic Conversion

2.2.1. Transubstantiation

1. Difference with the Orthodox and the Protestants

The doctrine of the conversion of bread and wine into the Body and Blood of Christ is a dogma of the Catholic faith, which distinguishes the one who professes this faith from all Christians who belong to the various Protestant denominations. As was said in the first chapter, in fact, Luther professed "con-

---

[77] See *ST* III, q. 82, a. 5. It is understood that the priest must try his best to be in the grace of God, because even if the celebration is valid, he commits sacrilege if he celebrates it in mortal sin. Saint Thomas also adds that—only from the standpoint of the effect of the prayers received based on the merit of those who recite it; therefore not from an objective point of view—the Mass celebrated by a good priest obtains more grace than that celebrated by a wicked one (see *ST* III, q. 82, a. 6).

[78] Saint Thomas Aquinas, *Super Matthaeum* XXVI, *lectio* 3 (our translation).

[79] Council of Constance, *Inter Cunctas* (1418), §22 (DS 1262).

[80] Council of Trent, *Decretum de Sacramentis* (1547), can. 12 (DS 1612).

substantiation," while other Protestants deny any form of the Real Presence of Christ in the Sacrament, preferring to express it in terms of a symbolic or spiritual presence. When we consider specifically the use of the word "transubstantiation" in speaking of this doctrine, Catholics are also distinguished from the Orthodox, who (see again Chapter One) profess the Real Presence but do not intend to investigate the ontological mode through which it comes about.

2. Ontological Character

The Catholic faith, however, has always made it a point of honor to profess and defend the Real Presence, seeking to understand—as much as humanly possible—the ontological character of this change. The Catholic Church has explained this through the theological doctrine—now a dogma—of transubstantiation (*transubstantiatio*). The term is obviously not biblical and is influenced by classical philosophy, in particular Aristotelian philosophy. It was coined by the theologians of the twelfth century. It is not certain whether the first to use it was the Englishman Robert Pullen (d. 1146) or the Italian Roland of Siena, who became Pope Alexander III (d. 1181). The fact is that the word spread very rapidly and encountered quick approval on the part of the Magisterium, given that it was accepted by the Fourth Lateran Council a few decades later, in 1215. The doctrine of transubstantiation teaches that the Eucharistic change is ontological.[81] It is not a mere symbolism, nor is it

---

[81] It is for this reason that certain proposals advanced in the twentieth century—whose proponents believe that they can overcome the theology of transubstantiation, proposing only a "transignification" or a "transfinalization"—are unsatisfactory. It is true that the Eucharistic consecration confers to the bread and the wine a new meaning and a new finality, but this occurs because it confers above all a new being. Saint Paul VI, *Mysterium Fidei* (1965), §47 (DS 4413), has thus taught that "as a result of transubstantiation, the Species of bread and wine undoubtedly take on a new signification and a new finality, for they are no longer ordinary bread and wine but instead a sign of something sacred and a sign of spiritual food; but they take on this new signification, this new finality, precisely because they contain a new 'reality' that we can rightly call *ontological*. For what now lies beneath the aforementioned Species is not what was there before, but something completely different; and not just in the estimation of Church belief, but in reality, since once the substance or nature of the bread and wine has been changed into the Body and Blood of Christ, nothing remains of the bread and the wine except the Species—beneath which Christ, whole and entire in his physical 'reality,' is even corporeally present." And in the *Credo of the People of God* (1968; reproduced by us at the beginning of this volume), speaking of transubstantiation, Pope Paul VI writes, "every theological explanation which seeks some understanding of this mystery must, in order to be in accord with Catholic faith, maintain that in the reality itself, independently of our mind, the bread and wine have ceased to exist after the Consecration, so that it is the adorable Body and Blood of

···817

The Eucharist

the addition of the presence of Christ in the bread and wine, which would remain as such. Bread and wine are transubstantiated, that is, their substance is transformed into another substance. Scholastic theologians, moreover, were dedicated to explaining why the bread and wine retained their appearance after the consecration. Several explanatory theses were proposed, some of them a little fanciful. In any case, everyone intended to oppose the Eucharistic symbolism of Berengar of Tours (d. 1088).[82]

3. Thomas Aquinas

There is no doubt that the most complete and consistent theology of transubstantiation is that of the Angelic Doctor. His proposal has great value not only for its internal consistency but also because—so to speak—it turns Berengar's logical weapons back on Berengar himself. The latter, in fact, denied the ontological presence of Christ by referencing the sayings of Aristotle. Saint Thomas defends transubstantiation by using the same philosophical instrument. Let us thus proceed to summarize the principal points, leaving aside several deeper developments proposed by Saint Thomas.

(1) The first question is, naturally, whether Christ is present in the Sacra-

---

the Lord Jesus that from then on are really before us under the sacramental Species of bread and wine."

[82] Despite using the terminology of the "real" Eucharistic presence, Berengar is considered the leader of all those who reject the ontological realism of the presence of Christ in the consecrated Species. This is because he is opposed to a ninth-century theologian, Saint Paschasius Radbertus (d. 865), author of *De Corpore et Sanguine Domini*, the first dogmatic monograph dedicated to the Sacrament of the altar. The realism of Paschasius is extreme: after the consecration, in the bread there is the physical/historical flesh of Christ, born of Mary. His contemporary Ratramnus (d. 868), who placed greater emphasis on the symbolism of bread and wine, was opposed to him. Berengar chose the line of Ratramnus, against that of Saint Paschasius, in his debate with Blessed Lanfranc of Canterbury (d. 1089), who wrote the *Libellus de sacramento corporis et sanguinis Christi contra Berengarium*. In the *Libellus*, Lanfranc argues that, after the consecration, bread and wine are transformed into the Body and Blood of Christ, even if they maintain their same appearance. Berengar responded with the *De sacra coena adversus Lanfrancum*, in which he argues that, for Aristotle, it is impossible that the substance is changed if the accidents remain identical. Consequently, the Body and Blood of Christ cannot be in the Eucharist in the ontological sense. Bread and wine are only a sacred sign whose symbolism refers to the Passion of Christ. The "memorial" of the Mass is rather a simple "memory." Saint Leo IX condemned the heresy of Berengar at the Synod of Rome in 1050 (see DS 690). After some ups and downs, Berengar finally withdrew his theory and submitted himself, signing a declaration of faith that had been prepared under instructions of Saint Gregory VII (d. 1085): see *Iusiurandum Berengarii Turonensis* (1079) (DS 700).

ment, or rather contained,[83] either only in a symbolic way (*secundum figuram vel sicut in signo*) or in a real way (*secundum veritatem*). He responds that Christ is really present with His Body and His Blood in the Eucharist, even if this presence of His is not perceivable to the eyes, but only by faith. The Angelic Doctor argues his position by recalling the commentary—cited previously in a footnote—that Saint Augustine made of John 6:63 ("the flesh is of no avail"). Far from meaning that the Body of Christ would not be in the Eucharistic bread, those words should be understood as Augustine understood them, that is, add the Spirit to the flesh and the flesh avails greatly! This is said not in a strictly Eucharistic sense, but it also applies to the theme of the Real Presence. This is why if there is no faith, the flesh of Christ offered in the Sacrament is of no avail.[84]

(2) Therefore, with the consecration, the appearances remain, but the substance changes. Almost three centuries before Luther, Saint Thomas already responds to the thesis of consubstantiation, noting that before the consecration, the Body and Blood of Christ are not in the Species. Now, he says, there are two ways in which something makes itself present where before it was not: either with local movement, or because something else is transformed into it. But Christ is not locally present in the Eucharist, since this would entail that He leave Heaven to descend into the Host; moreover He could be present in only one place and not in all the tabernacles of the earth at once.[85] Therefore, He is present because the bread and wine are transformed into Him. But what changes—he continues—after the change has happened does not remain (for example, if the wine becomes vinegar—when it is vinegar, there is no longer wine). Moreover, if there were consubstantiation, the Host could not be adored with a worship of *latria*, because the divinity of Christ would be joined

---

[83] Ordinarily, the Doctor does not speak of the "presence" of Christ in the Sacrament (he rarely uses the terms *praesens, praesentia, praesentialiter*), nor does he use the formula, "Christ is rendered present in the Sacrament" (he does not use the verb *praesentare*). This is because in his conception of the presence, common to medieval authors, being present implies not only being, but also being perceived by the senses in a concrete place. This is why Saint Thomas makes recourse to other expressions such as *esse sub, esse in, contineri sub*. In this way, he affirms the ontological, real presence of Christ in the Eucharist, highlighting at the same time the peculiarity of the Eucharistic presence ("under" the accidents).

[84] See *ST* III, q. 75, a. 1.

[85] "Thus we say that the Body of Christ is present in many altars not locally, but sacramentally. In saying this, we do not mean to say that Christ is present only under the form of a symbol . . . but that He is present according to the special mode of this Sacrament" (*ST* III, q. 75, a. 1, ad 3 [our translation]).

The Eucharist

together with a creature, bread or wine, which cannot be adored.[86]

Note that the teaching on the non-locality of the Eucharistic presence was confirmed in recent times by Pope Paul VI: "Once the substance or nature of the bread and wine has been changed into the Body and Blood of Christ, nothing remains of the bread and the wine except for the Species—beneath which Christ is present whole and entire in His physical 'reality,' corporeally present, although not in the manner in which bodies are in a place."[87]

(3) The very words of consecration represent the best argument against consubstantiation. In fact, Christ does not say "My Body is here," but rather "This is my Body"[88]: "If in this Sacrament the substance of the bread coexisted with the true Body of Christ, the Latter would have to say: 'My Body is here' and not 'This is my Body'. Since 'here' would indicate the substance that appears, namely of the bread, if in the Sacrament it remained together with the Body of Christ."[89]

Strengthened by these teachings, the Council of Trent was able to define the doctrine of transubstantiation as a dogma of faith, rejecting, as a consequence, Protestant consubstantiation:

> If anyone says that in the most holy Sacrament of the Eucharist the substance of bread and wine remains together with the Body and Blood of our Lord Jesus Christ and denies that wonderful and unique change of the whole substance of the bread into his Body and of the whole substance of the wine into his Blood while only the species of bread and wine remain, a change which the Catholic

---

[86] See *ST* III, q. 75, a. 2.

[87] Saint Paul VI, *Mysterium Fidei*, §47 (DS 4413).

[88] Saint Cyril of Jerusalem (d. 387), *Catecheses mystagogicae* 4, 1; 3; 6; 9, writes: "Since He himself [Jesus] said plainly about the bread, 'This is my Body,' who will dare to cast doubts from now on? And He, having also confirmed and said, 'This is my Blood,' who will ever doubt saying, 'It is not His Blood'? . . . For in the figure [*typos*] of bread is the Body given to you, and in the figure of wine the Blood is given to you. . . . Stop, therefore, considering the bread and wine to be ordinary; for they are Body and Blood according to the Lord who made the declaration. Do not judge by the taste, but be informed without doubt from faith that you have been made worthy of the Body and Blood of Christ . . . What appears to be bread is not bread—even if that is suggested by taste—but it is the Body of Christ, and that which appears to be wine is not wine—even if this is suggested by taste—but it is the Blood of Christ" (in *Lectures on the Christian Sacraments: The Procatecheses and the Five Mystagogical Catecheses ascribed to St Cyril of Jerusalem*, trans. Maxwell E. Johnson [Yonkers, NY: St. Vladimir's Seminary Press, 2017], 113–119).

[89] Saint Thomas Aquinas, *Summa contra gentiles* IV, ch. 63 (our translation). Therefore, when it is said that Christ is "contained under the bread and wine," what is always meant is "under the appearances," never "under the substance" of bread and wine.

Church very fittingly calls transubstantiation, let him be anathema.[90]

(4) For what regards the accidents, which remain, Saint Thomas explains in *ST* III, q. 75, a. 5, the reasons why it is fitting that they not change. A more speculative reflection on the accidents is the object of question 77.

(5) Transubstantiation, the Angelic Doctor continues, does not happen progressively, but immediately. He determines the precise moment of it, which is the moment in which the priest concludes the pronouncement of the form of the Sacrament, "in such a way that the last instant of the speaking of the [consecratory] words is the first instant of the presence of the Body of Christ in the Sacrament, while in the whole preceding time there was the substance of bread."[91] Saint Thomas explains that the meaning of the words is only complete when the sentence has ended. Since it is precisely the meaning that the form gives to matter that works effectively in the Sacraments, it is clear that it is necessary to pronounce to whole formula in order to have the desired effect. Thus, transubstantiation coincides with the moment itself in which the minister finishes pronouncing the last syllable of the sacramental form. In that moment, the words receive from the Holy Spirit the consecratory *virtus*, and in fact, they consecrate. Already Augustine instructed neophytes in this way:

> And from there [the Preface] we come now to what is done in the holy prayers which you are going to hear, that with the application of the word we may have the Body and Blood of Christ. Take away the word, I mean, it's just bread and wine; add the word, and it's now [*iam*] something else. And what is that something else? The Body of Christ, and the Blood of Christ. So take away the word, it's bread and wine; add the word and it will become the Sacrament.[92]

This teaching is important, particularly in the present theological context in which there is no shortage of authors, even among Catholics, who do not clearly affirm the consecratory efficacy of the institutional words. These authors, tending to an agreement with the Orthodox, believe it better to think that consecration happens throughout the entire Eucharistic Prayer, in such a way as to also place greater value on the epiclesis. Particularly for those Eucharistic Prayers in which the epiclesis is not before but rather after the

---

[90] Council of Trent, *Decretum de ss. Eucharistia* (1551), can. 2 (DS 1652).
[91] *ST* III, q. 75, a. 7.
[92] Saint Augustine of Hippo, *Sermo 229.3*, in *The Works of Saint Augustine*, vol. 6, trans. Edmund Hill, ed. John E. Rotelle (New Rochelle, NY: New City Press, 1993), 266.

The Eucharist

so-called "institution narrative," they cannot easily accept the idea that transubstantiation happens through the speaking of the words of Christ. But if *lex orandi, lex credendi*—a principle generally used by these authors—we must ask ourselves why the Church makes it so that the Host and chalice are elevated and a genuflection occurs immediately after the speaking of the words of institution and not at the end of the Eucharistic Prayer.

Furthermore, the Magisterium has solemnly taught that it is precisely the words of consecration that bring about transubstantiation.[93] The Council of Florence actually seems to approve the thesis of Saint Thomas, for which transubstantiation happens "*in instanti*" ("instantaneously"), when it teaches that "there should be no doubt whatsoever that [the bread] is immediately [*mox*] transubstantiated into the true Body of Christ after [*post*] the above-mentioned words of consecration."[94] The Council of Trent puts it in this way:

---

[93] Among the Eucharistic Prayers, there is one that does not contain the words of consecration completely and immediately, but rather spread throughout the text: it is the *Anaphora of Addai and Mari*. In 2001, a document by the Pontifical Council for Promoting Christian Unity stated that this Anaphora would validly consecrate the Eucharistic Species. Among the arguments adopted in support, we shall mention the third: "The words of Eucharistic Institution are indeed present in the Anaphora of Addai and Mari, not in a coherent narrative way and *ad litteram*, but rather in a dispersed euchological way, that is, integrated in successive prayers of thanksgiving, praise and intercession" (*Guidelines for Admission to the Eucharist between the Chaldean Church and the Assyrian Church of the East* [2001], §3). A sector of scholars of dogmatic theology and liturgists relies on this pronouncement to reduce the weight of the words of consecration within the Eucharistic Prayer in general. For them, these words would constitute a narration ("institution narrative") that no matter how important one considers them, the words are still not absolutely necessary for a valid consecration. Beyond what one may think about this non-definitive pronouncement of a Pontifical Council that does not have authority either in liturgical or dogmatic matter, the fact remains that the text does not speak of the absence of words, but of their presence, albeit in an anomalous form compared to the other Eucharistic Prayers (as if to say that the exception confirms the contrary rule). However, this is not enough, given that St. Thomas and, above all, the ecumenical councils teach that the words are necessary and do consecrate. A better solution is proposed by some contemporary scholars, who believe that the most ancient manuscripts that report the Anaphora do not reproduce the consecratory words only to better preserve the Mystery (*disciplina arcani* – discipline of the secrecy), but in reality these words were pronounced by celebrant ministers. In this case, there is no question of the validity of the consecration made using this Anaphora.

[94] Council of Florence, *Cantate Domino* (DS 1352). It is true, however, that *mox* and *in instanti* do not mean exactly the same thing, even if they are very close concepts. It is also certain that the Florentine Council would not have said "immediately," if it had wanted to teach that for there to be real presence we must wait for the end of the Eucharistic Prayer, or at least the epiclesis. The *Catechism* discusses the epiclesis and the "institution narrative" at §1353, teaching beyond a shadow of a doubt that it is not the epiclesis that consecrates the oblates, but rather the words of the Lord.

"immediately after the consecration [*statim post consecrationem*] the true Body and Blood of our Lord, together with His soul and divinity, exist under the Species of bread and wine."[95]

Finally, the theory proposed again in these days concerning the consecratory value of the epiclesis, and not of the institutional words, was already rejected by Benedict XII in 1341.[96]

(6) Saint Thomas also emphasizes the eminently supernatural character and origin of transubstantiation and does so in different ways, particularly when he explains the way in which the accidents of the bread and wine remain, despite the change of substance. Before this, however, he also allows us to understand it indirectly by addressing a question that may appear superfluous to our modern sensibility. Thomas wonders if the statement is correct that affirms "*ex pane fit corpus Christi*" ("from the bread comes the Body of Christ.").[97] It is an affirmation that is found in a work of the patristic era, which Saint Thomas believed to have been written by Saint Ambrose, the authority of which—therefore—he recognized. Here the explanation becomes slightly more complicated, but we shall seek to simplify it as much as possible.

Transubstantiation, in the first place, resembles creation *ex nihilo*, because in both cases there is no common *subiectum* at the ending point and the starting point.[98] Just like there is no common *subiectum* between nothing and

---

[95] Council of Trent, *Decretum de ss. Eucharistia*, ch. 3 (DS 1640).
[96] See Benedict XII, *Cum Dudum* (1341) (DS 1017).
[97] See *ST* III, q. 75, a. 8.
[98] Recall that in the third chapter we had mentioned the expression "*ex nihilo sui et subiecti*." The *subiectum* is "that-which-is-under": a term from Aristotelian philosophy. In the *Metaphysics*, Aristotle begins with the affirmation that the *ousia* (essence) is "*tode ti*" ("this here"), that is, the individual thing. Then he clarifies that *ousia* also has other meanings, two in particular: (1) subject or substrate, and (2) essence. In the first sense, *ousia* is synonymous with *hypostasis* ("that which is under"), that is, that which lies beneath the sensible appearances, which in Latin is called *sub-iectum* or *sub-positum*. In the second sense, *ousia* is synonymous with *hypokeimenon* ("substrate"), which can indicate matter, form, or even *synolon* (composed of both). This substrate is imperceptible to the senses, but it is knowable to the intellect (usually through abstraction, when it concerns corporeal beings). It is in this substrate (essence) that one finds the ultimate and permanent subject of the attribution of the properties of a being. In conclusion, the *subiectum* of Thomas is the essence of a concrete being (e.g., the essence of bread of/in this piece of bread that will be consecrated). In *ST* III, q. 75, a. 4, the Angelic Doctor explains that natural mutations presuppose a *subiectum* that is in potency to changing and passing into act precisely through the change that is a transition of the *subiectum* from potency to act (e.g., fresh bread becomes stale; the egg becomes a chick; the living die). He adds that things are not so in transubstantiation, because it is a change that does not occur in a *subiectum* but between two *substantiae* (essence). The natural mutations do not change the whole nature of a being, but only its form in the same *subiectum*. Rather, the Eucharistic conversion

being, there is none between the bread and the Body of Christ. Secondly, transubstantiation has similarities with the natural processes of mutation, because in both cases one of the two extremes is transformed into the other: the air into the fire and the bread into the Body of Christ. Moreover, in both the mutations there lies a permanent fact, something that does not change, despite the mutation (which is not the case with creation).

However, transubstantiation differs a great deal, despite the similarities, from the other types of mutation. Indeed, in creation it is not the case that one extreme is converted into another, because the first extreme is simply not there, it is nothing. Therefore, creation is not a conversion. As to the differences from natural mutations, there are two: (1) in natural mutations, the matter receives another form, because of the loss of the previous form, while in the Eucharist there is the conversion of the whole substance into another substance; and (2) in natural mutations, the matter remains identical (even if informed by the new form), while in the transubstantiation only the accidents remain.[99]

In conclusion, Saint Thomas says, the phrase attributed to Ambrose cannot be accepted literally,[100] because the substance of the bread does not have the natural capacity of being transformed into the substance of the Body of Christ (whereas, e.g., wine has the natural capacity to become vinegar). The bread is not in natural potency to be the Body of Christ. However, this phrase can be accepted if it is meant to indicate the two extremes of the succession of Eucharistic change, for which it means that the bread is the starting point and the Body of Christ the endpoint. This explanation, we said, emphasizes the supernaturality of the Eucharistic conversion, which cannot be explained in any respect as something natural. This should be noted because in contemporary theology at times there is too much focus on the symbolism—however correct—of the Eucharistic Species from the natural and social perspective, leaving the totally gratuitous and supernatural "miracle" of the transubstantiation in the shadow.

---

transforms the whole substance of the bread into the substance of the Body of Christ and likewise with wine into Blood. It is not a formal mutation, but a substantial one, which does not exist in nature and is therefore supernatural.

[99] As strange as it may seem to moderns, in the Eucharistic conversion everything in the bread and wine changes, both matter and form. After consecration, there are only accidents; there is no matter or form of the bread and wine. In fact, the whole substance (*synolon*) is transformed into the substance of the Body and Blood of Christ. For us it is difficult to understand this because we do not have a metaphysical mentality and therefore we make the concept of matter coincide with what falls under the senses.

[100] It is striking, therefore, that the new prayers of the Offertory of the Missal of the ordinary form are expressed precisely in such terms: "*ex quo nobis fiet panis vitae/potus spiritalis.*"

2.2.2. Real Presence

An effect of the transubstantiation is the Real Presence of Christ under the appearances of bread and wine. The Council of Trent emphasizes the terms, speaking of a true, real, and substantial presence of Christ.[101] Saint Thomas provided satisfying responses on this doctrinal point and concerning various doubts that could be raised against it. The objections that could be advanced, even by simple common sense, concern the possibility that an entire human being is truly contained in a little piece of bread and in a drop of wine. A response to this objection points out not only what was said above concerning the non-local character of the Eucharistic presence and the fact that the conversion is substantial, but three other explanations as well.

1. "Sub Specie Aliena"

Saint Thomas recalls that the presence of Christ at the local level is only in Heaven, at the right hand of the Father, where His body, glorified through the Resurrection, is found. The presence in the Eucharist is equally true and real, but of another sort; it is sacramental and substantial presence. Christ is in the Species because the substance of the bread and wine have been transformed into the substance of His Body and Blood. Here, the Angelic Doctor takes up and explores in-depth what was said about the non-local presence, because he observes that, before the consecration, the substance of the bread was also not locally but rather substantially present under its own (local) dimensions. After the consecration, the local/accidental dimensions remain, but the substance has changed: the substance of the Body of Christ is present with its essential dimensions under the accidental dimensions of the bread. The difference is that the substance of the bread was in that place under its own accidents: the accidental dimensions of the bread; while the substance of the Body of Christ is there under accidents that are not its own, being precisely those of bread.

---

[101] "If anyone denies that in the Sacrament of the most Holy Eucharist the Body and Blood, together with the soul and divinity, of our Lord Jesus Christ and, therefore, the whole Christ is truly, really, and substantially [*vere, realiter et substantialiter*] contained . . . let him be anathema" (Council of Trent, *Decretum de ss. Eucharistia*, can. 1 [DS 1651]). *Vere* means that the Eucharist is not only a symbol: Christ is truly contained in the Species. *Realiter* indicates the ontological and objective presence: a presence that is at the level of being and does not depend on us, on the subject. *Substantialiter* refers, on the one hand, to the passage that happened from the substance of the bread and wine to that of the Body and Blood; and, on the other hand, it refers to the fact that Christ is found and acts *under* the appearances of the Species.

The Eucharist

Thus, He is not localized in the Host, because the localization happens with the accidental dimensions that are a substance's own, that are proper to that substance.[102] In fact, the proper accidents of bread are not suitable to the Body of Christ, because the Host is too small with respect to a human body. *In propria specie* ("in His own species"), Christ is only in Heaven. But *sub specie sacramenti*, He is on many altars throughout the world.[103]

2. "Ex Vi Sacramenti" *and* "Ex Naturali Concomitantia"

Another important distinction that helps with understanding the Real Presence is that proposed in *ST* III, q. 76, a. 1: the components that make up Christ, Who is the incarnate Word—namely, body, blood, and a human soul, in addition to His divinity—can be present in two ways: "*ex vi sacramenti*" ("by virtue of the Sacrament"), or "*ex naturali concomitantia*" ("by natural concomitance"). By virtue of the Sacrament, the substance of the Body and that of the Blood of Christ is present, as the words of the Eucharistic form state, which accurately indicate the effect that is achieved.[104] Concomitance refers to the fact that "where two things are really united to one another, where there is really one, there must also be the other." Thus, where there is the Body and Blood of Christ, there must be His Person and thus His two integral natures. This means that there are also in the Sacrament His human soul and His divinity.[105] The whole Christ, then, is really contained in the Sacrament and

---

[102] When the Eucharistic procession is done, or the pyx is moved from one tabernacle to another, Christ does not move locally because He is in Heaven and there "*quietum residet*" (is at rest). However, the accidents move, the accidents under which is the substance of His Body, and thus, *per accidens*, Christ also moves: in fact, if you remove the pyx from a church, Christ is not moved from Heaven, but His Eucharistic presence is no longer *there*. See *ST* III, q. 76, a. 6.

[103] See *ST* III, q. 76, a. 5.

[104] Thus *per se* and directly the Eucharistic consecration produces this and only this: that the substance is transformed into another; the bread into the Body and the wine into the Blood. The other elements that make up the incarnate Person of Christ (human Soul and Divinity) are present through an unbreakable concomitance, not because it is an effect of the Sacrament in the strict sense. In other words, the Sacrament makes it so that the substance of the bread is transformed into the substance of the Body of Christ; nothing more. But the Body of Christ is never without His Blood, His Soul, and His Divinity, because—as we say—the Christological synthesis of the *Verbum caro* is indissoluble.

[105] William of Champeaux (d. 1122), founder of the school of Saint Victor, is the first to interpret the Augustinian formula of the *Christus totus* in a new way. For Augustine, the *Christus totus* is the Church, the Mystical Body in its entirety as Head and members. William applies the expression to the Eucharist, saying that in it there is the total Christ: Body, Blood, Soul and Divinity (see *De sacramento altaris: fragmentum*). The technical

this is explicable in a reasonable way, without having to imagine—pardon the expression—that Christ must "shrink to enter into the Host."

The doctrine of concomitance is accepted by the Council of Trent:

> The Body exists under the Species of bread and the Blood under the Species of wine by virtue of the words [*ex vi verborum* (corresponds to the sense of *ex vi sacramenti*)]. But the Body, too, exists under the Species of wine, the Blood under the Species of bread, and the soul under both Species in virtue of the natural connection and concomitance by which the parts of Christ the Lord, Who has already risen from the dead to die no more, are united together. Moreover, the divinity is present because of its admirable hypostatic union with the Body and the soul.[106]

This pronouncement also includes what Saint Thomas said in *ST* III, q. 76, a. 2—a direct consequence of the doctrine of concomitance—namely, that under each of the Species the entire Christ is contained, even if for different reasons. By virtue of the Sacrament, under the veils of bread there is only the substance of the Body and under those of the wine only the substance of Blood. But by reason of concomitance for which Christ cannot be divided, He is present with all the components of His Being as the Incarnate Word under each Species.[107]

2.2.3. Permanence of the Accidents

Aristotle calls that which, while pertaining to a being, does not essentially pertain to it, *sumbebekos*, "accident." In this way, the Stagirite could distinguish in every being what belongs to it as a changeable and not strictly necessary element, from that which always persists as identical to itself. The substance is stable, thus it guarantees the identity of the *subiectum* even amid the mutability of its qualities.

The substance is simple when it is a form without matter, as is the case

---

term "concomitance" appears however only with the Dominican theologian Richard Fishacre (d. 1248). Not many years later, Saint Thomas will already use it with ease.

[106] Council of Trent, *Decretum de ss. Eucharistia*, ch. 3 (DS 1640).

[107] "[Christ] is present under either of the two Species as He is present under both. For Christ, whole and entire [*totus et integer*], exists under the Species of bread and under any part of that Species, and similarly the whole Christ exists under the Species of wine and under its parts" (Council of Trent, *Decretum de ss. Eucharistia*, ch. 3 [DS 1641]; see can. 3 [DS 1653] and *ST* III, q. 76, a. 3).

with angels. By contrast, a material or corporeal substance is immersed in matter: its essence is a result of a composition (*synolon*) of prime matter and substantial form, with the latter being what gives being, and is thus the source of the activity and the specific properties of a determinate being.

This philosophical doctrine is at the base of Thomas's usage of the term "accidents," both in general, and in the treatise on the Eucharist. Thus, accidents of the bread and wine are visible, but not essential, elements, because they are neither the form nor the matter, but they manifest and "inhere" in it. In fact, an accident does not have its own being, like a substance, because its being is "being-in," in Latin *inesse*. It follows from this that accidents (e.g., the color white of hair, or the weight of a body) can subsist only in a *subiectum*. But if the substance goes away, and thus the *subiectum* goes away,[108] so will the accidents. By contrast, something happens in the Eucharist that never happens in nature: we have the accidents of the bread and wine remaining, despite their respective substances changing into something else.

Now, if the *esse* of the accidents is that of inherence, to-be-in, they must—so to speak—"lean" on a substantial subject in order to exist. But in the Eucharist, the accidents of the bread and wine do not lean on their own subject, because it changes into another. On the other hand, such accidents cannot lean on the *subiectum* of the substance of the Body and Blood of Christ because the substance of a human body is not manifested with the accidents of bread, but with its own accidents (it is indeed impossible to confuse a human being with a piece of bread). Medieval theologians, therefore, sought to find solutions to the dilemma. For example, we can recall the proposal of Peter Abelard (d. 1142) according to which the accidents of bread and wine would be supported by the surrounding air.[109]

Saint Thomas demonstrates the absurdity of this theory and teaches that in the Eucharist, by supernatural intervention, the accidents remain without a subject.[110] For Saint Thomas this miracle makes it so that the accidents main-

---

[108] Recall that for Aristotle, and for Thomas, substance subsists in itself, without a *subiectum*. Instead, the latter does not subsist without substance. For example, humanity exists in itself, but the human being subsists because he participates in the human substance, without the latter being (exhausted) in him. Applied to the Eucharist, this helps us understand why, the substance of the bread having changed, all the bread of the world is not changed into the Body of Christ; but only that bread which is consecrated.

[109] He is opposed by Saint Bernard of Clairvaux (d. 1153) in the Council of Sens (1141).

[110] See *ST* III, q. 77, a. 1. The Angelic Doctor is also opposed to the Abelardian theory in *Super I ad Corinthios* XI, *lectio* 4 [*reportatio vulgata*]. Among the errors of John Wyclif, which were condemned by the Council of Constance, is this: "The accidents of bread do not remain without a subject in the same Sacrament [of the altar]" (*Errores Iohannis Wyclif* (1415), §2 [DS 1152]).

tain all their natural characteristics; thus, even if it is no longer truly bread insofar as it is consecrated, it does nourish if it is eaten in sufficient quantities; and even though the content of the Eucharistic chalice is no longer wine, it likewise preserves the ability to quench thirst.[111]

Finally, the Eucharistic Doctor also specifies the way in which, in his opinion, the accidents are supported, given that they are not supported by a subject. Thomas holds that—by the power of God—something happens that never happens in nature, namely, that the accidents inhere in another accident. And for him this accident is the *quantitas dimensiva*, that is, the quantity of bread and wine that were consecrated. The Angelic Doctor recognizes that it seems impossible that the quantity of bread and wine serves as a subject for the other accidents of the Species, because there are no accidents of other accidents, but only accidents that inhere in substances. However, our senses show that the Species after consecration maintain their accidents in their prior dimensions, in the dimensions of the Species themselves. Therefore, the dimensions of bread and wine that were consecrated move to acting as *subiectum* of the accidents of bread and wine. The extended quantity of the consecrated bread and wine is the subject of the other accidents (color, taste, etc.). This generally is not possible, but in the case of the Eucharist it depends on the prior miracle, for which God granted quantity to subsist, though no longer in the subject of bread or wine. For this reason, it can act as a subject for the other accidents.[112]

2.3. Effects of the Sacrament

The effects of the Eucharistic Sacrament are multiple and can be subdivided according to a binary scheme, which we have already used for other Sacraments, in agreement with our soteriological discussion in Chapter Four. In fact, the Sacraments are salvific means that are ordered by God for the realization of His plan for human beings. Consequently, their end and the effects that express and realize it also follow the elements that are intrinsic to this plan. As we have seen, we can distinguish two concepts after the sin of Adam: the "positive" one of salvation—that is, of the elevation of the human being in grace (filial adoption, deification) leading to eternal glory—and the "negative" one of redemption (negative in the sense that it removes evil)—that

---

[111] See *ST* III, q. 77, a. 6. And this is valid for every other aspect: the Species continue to have the same characteristics they had when they inhered in their own subject (see III, q. 77, aa. 3–5)

[112] See *ST* III, q. 77, a. 2.

is, redemption from the condition of slavery in which human beings have placed themselves because of sin. The effects of the Sacraments are aimed at achieving the salvation and redemption of the human being.

We can gather the multiple effects produced by the Eucharist according to the scheme presented.

2.3.1. Salvific Effects

The Eucharist saves us. It does so by giving us grace and predisposing us to future glory. The grace of the Eucharist is, therefore, multifaceted.

1. Identification of the Effects

Saint Thomas[113] teaches that the effect of the Sacrament can be seen from: (1) what is contained in it (Christ); (2) what it represents (the Passion); (3) the mode in which it is offered (food and drink); and (4) the Species.

(1) That the Eucharist confers grace, that is, supernatural life, is drawn from the fact that it is Christ, the One who has come into the world to give us life (see John 6:52). That is why Jesus says: "Whoever eats this bread will live forever" (John 6:58). (2) The Eucharist, moreover, gives grace because it re-actualizes the Passion, through which the Lord has obtained for us the remission of sins (see Matt 26:28). (3) The sign of bread and wine is also a symbol of Eucharistic grace because natural bread and wine sustain the body and make it grow, restore energy that the body expends each day, and give enjoyment.[114] All of these effects, at the supernatural level, are communicated to us through the Eucharistic bread and wine. (4) Saint Thomas adds a fourth element regarding the Species, to which we shall dedicate the next subsection, given its importance.

2. Unity of the Church

The appearances of bread and wine, which are preserved in the Sacrament (i.e., that remain even after the substantial change), have a very important

---

[113] See *ST* III, q. 79, a. 1.

[114] The Council of Florence confirms the position of Saint Thomas: "The effect that this Sacrament produces in the souls of persons who receive it worthily is to unite them with Christ. For, since it is by grace that persons are incorporated into Christ and united to his members, it follows that those who receive this Sacrament worthily receive an increase of grace. And all the effects that material food and drink have on the life of the body—maintaining and increasing life, restoring health, and giving joy" (*Exultate Deo* [DS 1322]).

symbolism of grace: the ecclesial symbolism. The bread is the fruit of the union between many grains of wheat, which were previously scattered on the ears and then, through grinding, have become one. The same thing happens with the grapes that form the wine. This image, present in Christian writings since the era of the Fathers,[115] indicates the union of the individuals in the Mystical Body of Christ. The grace and effect of the Eucharist is to give the supernatural charity that establishes and keeps in unity the Mystical Body, the Church.

The main effect of the Eucharist, to which the other effects are also ordered, is that of supernaturally guaranteeing the unity of the Church. Among the Fathers, Saint Augustine is the one who perhaps more than all the rest emphasized the relationship between the Eucharist and the Church.

In the twentieth century, an expression that was formulated based on the theology of the Fathers became famous: "The Church makes the Eucharist and the Eucharist makes the Church." The Church makes the Eucharist because it celebrates it. In this sense, there would be no Eucharistic Celebration if there were no Church. But the inverse is also true (circularity of the *et-et*) for which the Church not only makes, but is also made by, the Eucharist. As with all the bipolarities, the internal hierarchy will also have to be indicated in this case. A request to this effect was made by the Fathers of the Synod of Bishops in 2005. They asked for clarification as to which of the two elements had greater weight. This request was answered by Benedict XVI:

> In the striking interplay between the Eucharist which builds up the Church, and the Church herself which "makes" the Eucharist, the primary causality is expressed in the first formula: the Church is able to celebrate and adore the mystery of Christ present in the Eucharist precisely because Christ first gave Himself to her in the Sacrifice of the cross. The Church's ability to "make" the Eucharist is completely rooted in Christ's self-gift to her. Here we can see more clearly the meaning of Saint John's words: "He first loved us" (1 John 4:19). We too, at every celebration of the Eucharist, confess the primacy of Christ's gift. The causal influence of the Eucharist at the Church's origins definitively discloses both the chronological and ontological priority of the fact that it was Christ who loved us "first." For all eternity He remains the One who loves us first.[116]

---

[115] See the *Didache* (composed between AD 100 and 150) 9.1–5; Saint Cyprian of Carthage, *Epistola 63.13*; Saint Augustine of Hippo, *Sermo 272*.1; etc.

[116] Benedict XVI, *Sacramentum Caritatis*, §14.

The Eucharist

3. The Pledge of Glory

Precisely by incorporating ourselves into the Church, the Eucharist also prepares us for glory[117] at the eschatological entrance into the heavenly Jerusalem, that is, in the Church that has reached the state of final triumph (see Chapter Eight).

4. The Applying of Benefits

It must not be forgotten, however, what was said at the ecclesiological level concerning the communion of saints or what has always been mentioned in that regard—and which we shall return to studying in the next chapter—concerning the souls of Purgatory, which constitute the Church in a state of purification. Grafting us to the *unitas Ecclesiae*, the Eucharist inserts us into the communion of saints, which goes beyond the strictly horizontal dimension of relationships between Christians here on earth. The Eucharist also puts us in supernatural communication with the dead. The Liturgy has always expressed this truth, because in its rites and in its texts it prays for the dead and not only the living, particularly in the Holy Mass. This supposes that the effects of the grace of the Sacrament do not only benefit living Christians, but others too. Saint Thomas points out that this implies the Eucharist is not only Communion but also, and even prior to that, a Sacrifice. In fact, only the person who communicates with the due dispositions receives grace through Communion. And clearly the dead do not communicate sacramentally; neither do the living who are absent from the celebration, for whom we also pray in the Mass. Since the Eucharist is a Sacrifice—that Sacrifice that Christ willed to suffer for the salvation of many—its grace and its effects can also be received by those who do not sacramentally communicate. Obviously, this happens on the condition that one is spiritually united to the Eucharist through faith and charity.[118]

The efficacy of the Holy Mass offered for others, living or dead, is not only a theological opinion. The Council of Trent stated: "If anyone says that the Sacrifice of the Mass ... benefits only those who communicate; and that it should not be offered for the living and the dead, for sins, punishments,[119]

---

[117] See *ST* III, q. 79, a. 2.

[118] See *ST* III, q. 79, a. 7. The Angelic Doctor adds that the Eucharistic effects can be efficacious even for the one who is outside the Church, but only according to the measure of his or her "devotion," the meaning of which we can render with "sincerity and honesty" toward God.

[119] This does not contradict what Saint Thomas says in *ST* III, q. 79, a. 5, concerning the remission of punishments as an effect of the Eucharist. In fact, Aquinas admitted this

2.3.2. Redemptive Effects

There are also effects of the Eucharist linked to the redemption of the human being and to the purification of his or her sins.

1. Remission of Mortal Sins

A first question is whether the Eucharist washes away mortal sins—we have already mentioned this before. To respond to this, Saint Thomas[121] makes a distinction: (1) One thing is the Eucharist in itself—which is Christ. From this perspective, given that Christ merited the remission of all sins, the Eucharist has the power of taking away all sins, even the most grave ones. (2) Another thing is the Eucharist considered on the part of the one who receives it. Scripture indeed says (see 1 Cor 11:29) that whoever is aware of having committed a mortal sin (and has not been reconciled) cannot receive Communion. If Saint Paul says this, it means that the Eucharist does not take away mortal sin; otherwise, anyone could receive it, because the Sacrament itself would wipe away the grave sins.[122]

Ante litteram, this response of the Eucharistic Doctor is also valid for the

---

effect, saying however that not all the punishment is taken away, but only according to the measure of the devotion of the one who must make satisfaction. Thus, the Mass can also be celebrated for the satisfaction of punishments in addition to the expiation of sins and for other needs.

[120] Council of Trent, *Decretum de ss. Missae Sacrificio*, can. 3 (DS 1753).

[121] See *ST* III, q. 79, a. 3.

[122] It is important to emphasize that the Eucharist is the "medicine of immortality" according to the expression of Saint Ignatius of Antioch that we already cited in Chapter Nine. But the same medicine is not suitable for all ailments. The Eucharist is not understood as a medicine for the healing of mortal sins. For this, there is Reconciliation (see the previous chapter). Moreover, the expression of Ignatius of Antioch designates the Eucharist as a reality that by eating of it one receives eternal life. Now, this was the characteristic, in Eden, of the tree of life: whoever ate of it, lived forever (like the bread of life of John 6). And it should be recalled that, after the sin, Adam and Eve were estranged from Eden precisely so they could not extend their hand toward the tree and eat of it (see Gen 3:22). God did this to stop the two sinners from worsening their situation, condemning themselves to a perpetual state of sinfulness. And should the Church not do the same, keeping sinners away from the Eucharist to avoid it damaging them instead of benefitting them? Saint Thomas, on the basis of 1 Corinthians 11:27–32, in the *Lauda Sion* writes: "*Sumunt boni, sumunt mali / sorte tamen inaequali / vitae vel interitus*" ("the good receive, the bad receive / but with unequal outcome / of life or of death").

The Eucharist

Protestant perspective, according to which the Eucharist had as its only effect the remission of sins (naturally, according to the Protestant concept of remission, see Chapter One). Consequently, according to this perspective, whoever approached the Eucharist was not in grace. The Council of Trent condemned the Protestant position, indirectly confirming the Thomistic one.[123]

2. Remission of Venial Sins

Second, it must be asked whether the Eucharist remits venial sins. Here the response is positive and corroborated by two motivations: (1) The Eucharist is food: just as natural food recuperates the resources consumed by the body, so supernatural food repairs the little daily spiritual losses due to concupiscence (venial sins). (2) An effect of the Eucharist (see above) is to infuse charity in us; but charity eliminates venial sins, and thus this is a Eucharistic effect.[124]

The Magisterium of the Church agrees with the position of Aquinas. It was written at the Council of Trent: "Our Savior . . . wished, however, that this Sacrament be received as the soul's spiritual food, which would nourish and strengthen . . . and that it be also a remedy to free us from our daily faults [venial sins] and to preserve us from mortal sin."[125]

Saint Pius X, in the decree in which he recommends daily Communion, notes: "The desire, in fact, of Jesus Christ and of the Church that all the faithful of Christ approach the sacred banquet daily consists above all in this, that the faithful of Christ being joined with God through the Sacrament may receive from it the strength to restrain passion, *to wash away the little faults that occur daily*, and to guard against more grievous sins to which human frailty is subject."[126]

3. Preservation from Future Sins

The two magisterial texts just presented also contain a reference to another effect of the Eucharist, which is that of preventing future sins. The Eucharist confers a special grace of strengthening, which makes the human spirit more

---

[123] "If anyone says that the principal fruit of the most Holy Eucharist is the forgiveness of sins or that no other effects come from it, let him be anathema" (Council of Trent, *Decretum de ss. Eucharistia*, can. 5 [DS 1655]).

[124] See *ST* III, q. 79, a. 4.

[125] Council of Trent, *Decretum de ss. Eucharistia*, ch. 2 (DS 1638)

[126] Saint Pius X, *Sacra Tridentina Synodus* (1905) (DS 3375; our emphasis).

ready to battle against the tendencies that lead it to sin, just as in the natural sphere nutritious food gives the human body strength that will help it to avoid failures and falls.

In speaking of this aspect, Saint Thomas cites in its support John 6:50: "this is the bread that comes down from heaven so that one may eat it and not die"; and he accompanies the Gospel verse with a splendid expression of Saint John Chrysostom: "Like lions that breathe fire, we return from that table, made terrifying to the devil."[127] The Christian that returns from the Eucharistic banquet and has communicated with the due dispositions, is so strengthened from the spiritual point of view that the devil sees him or her as a threatening lion, who breathes flames from the mouth! They are the flames of charity, hidden in the Eucharistic bread, which come out of the mouth that received the Host.

Naturally, the fact of receiving the Eucharist does not take free will away from the human being, thus even the one who communicates can always fall into sin if he or she turns toward evil. Therefore, the Sacrament "has in itself the strength to preserve from sin, nonetheless it does not take away from the human being the possibility of sinning."[128]

4. Remission of Punishments

A final redemptive effect of the Eucharist is that it also remits the punishments due to sins, even if not entirely. In fact, if the Eucharist took away all the punishment of sins, then the Church could not command sinners to do other penances, such as those after Confession (sacramental *satisfactio*), or in other circumstances.

This point, too, should be considered under a dual aspect: (1) As a Sacrament, the Eucharist was not instituted to satisfy the punishments of sin, but rather to spiritually nourish the faithful through union with Christ and with His Church. Since, however, this union comes about through charity, and charity remits both the fault and the punishment, by concomitance with the primary effect, the Eucharist also remits the punishments, though not all of them, but only according to the measure of the devotion and fervor of charity. (2) As a Sacrifice, the Eucharist has the effect of satisfaction, in which, however, the disposition of the offeror holds more weight than the greatness of the thing offered (on this, see the next section). Also in this case, therefore, not all the punishment is remitted, but only the part corresponding

---

[127] *ST* III, q. 79, a. 6; see Saint John Chrysostom, *Super Ioannis Evangelium* 46.
[128] *ST* III, q. 79, a. 6.

to the measure of the devotion and fervor of the one who offers.[129]

2.4. Sacrifice

That the Eucharist is a true Sacrifice is a revealed doctrine taught by the Church from her earliest times.[130] There can be no doubt about it. The *Catechism* summarizes the essential elements, recalling that the Eucharist is Sacrifice "because it *re-presents* (makes present) the sacrifice of the cross, because it is its *memorial* and because it *applies* its fruit" (CCC §1366). We shall focus now on the teachings on this matter of both the Eucharistic Doctor and the Magisterium.

2.4.1. Saint Thomas

Among the names by which the Eucharist is identified, in addition to Communion (or Synaxis) and *Viaticum*, Saint Thomas recalls that the Holy Mass is Sacrifice. This is because it commemorates the Passion of the Lord.[131] The Angelic Doctor proposes an important distinction, which is the basis of everything else he says concerning the sacrificial character of the Eucharist; the Mass is a Sacrifice for two reasons: First, as an image. In fact, the celebration is a representative image of the Passion of Christ, which was a true immolation. Second, because of the links that it has with the effects of the Passion, because through this Sacrament we become participants in it.[132]

---

[129] See *ST* III, q. 79, a. 5. As was already seen, the Council of Trent also contemplated the remission of the penalty as an effect of the Eucharist. The presence in the Missal of "votive Masses" is based on this doctrine, as is the habit of the faithful of having Holy Masses that have the effect, among several, of growing their own devotion toward Christ, Mary, or a Saint. With growth of devotion, the effect of partial remission of the penalties due to sins committed also increases.

[130] For example, Saint Cyprian of Carthage, *Epistula 63*.14, notes that the Eucharist is "*dominicae passionis et nostrae redemptionis sacramentum*" ("Sacrament of the Passion of the Lord and of our redemption"). It is an "*oblatio et sacrificium*" ("oblation and Sacrifice": *Epistula* 63.9).

[131] See *ST* III, q. 73, a. 4. It had already been expressed in this sense in the Christological part of the *Summa*: "The Sacrifice that is offered each day in the Church is not different from the Sacrifice that Christ Himself offered, but it is its commemoration" (*ST* III, q. 22, a. 3, ad 2 [our translation]).

[132] See *ST* III, q. 83, a. 1.

Theological Reflection, and the Teachings of the Magisterium

1. *Representative Image*

It needs to be recalled that the medievals interpreted the liturgical celebration in not only a theological way, but also a symbolic and even allegorical way.[133] That is, the unfolding of the celebration appears to their eyes as a representation of the prominent events of the life of Christ and above all His Passion. For example, when the priest moves from the center of the altar to the side to wash his hands and then returns to the center, some interpret this as a symbol of Jesus, who was sent by Pilate to Herod and then back again to the Roman procurator. Saint Thomas also presents a symbolic reading of the rites of the Mass in *ST* III, q. 83, aa. 4–5. Nonetheless, he does not exaggerate the allegory, even if some of his interpretations might prove difficult to accept for today's sensibilities. Such symbolic interpretations of ritual details are not of concern to us here, but rather the comprehensive interpretation of liturgical ritual as a reproduction of the Passion of Christ.

Saint Thomas says that the exact moment in which the sacramental Sacrifice occurs is the consecration of the Species.[134] This means that transubstantiation and Sacrifice, while distinct, happen at the same instant and from this perspective coincide. Where the Eucharistic change produces the Real Presence of Christ, there is also the Sacrifice of Christ.[135] We shall return to this in the next point. At a ritual level, the Angelic Doctor argues his position by noting that the Lord established that in this Sacrament there is a dual separated consecration of the Species. Bread and wine are not consecrated in one act, but first the bread and then the wine separately. Among other things, given what was said about the moment of transubstantiation, Saint Thomas also affirms that the bread is transubstantiated immediately, without—so to speak—"waiting" for the words over the chalice.[136] This marks a clear distinction between the two acts, even though they are related and comprise the one consecration of the Eucharist.

This ritual distinction of the dual consecration is an external and representative sign of the Passion and Death of Christ, in which the body was physically separated from the blood. In fact, the physical blood of Jesus flowed

---

[133] A classic of the genre is the work of William Durand (Durandus) (d. 1296), *Rationale divinorum officiorum*. The celebration of the Holy Mass is studied there in Book 4.

[134] See *ST* III, q. 82, a. 10, ad 1.

[135] The Council of Trent (cited below) teaches: "In this divine Sacrifice that is celebrated in the Mass, the same Christ who offered Himself once in a bloody manner on the altar of the Cross is *contained* [Real Presence] and is *offered* ["immolated": Sacrifice] in an unbloody manner" (emphasis added).

[136] See *ST* III, q. 78, a. 6.

out from the body through the wounds inflicted on it and was separated from it. This is reproduced in the sacramental separation of the Eucharistic Species. It is true that in the Eucharist there is the risen and living Christ—from this perspective, He does not die at all: from the historical point of view, the Sacrifice only happens once and is never again repeated (see Rom 6:10; Heb 7:27).[137] But the Mass is the repetition and renewal of this death in a way that is not physical, which is impossible, but rather sacramental (i.e., through signs). And through the signs that death is effectively reproduced each time with the separated consecration of the Body and Blood.[138] This is a first way in which the Holy Mass is a true Sacrifice: as a ritual image of Golgotha.

2. Paschal Mystery

In recent theology it is willingly emphasized—and not without reason—that the Eucharist is the memorial of the Paschal Triduum, or the Paschal Mystery as a whole: Passion, Death, and Resurrection. Saint Thomas does not deny this but, in agreement with a long-preceding Tradition that continued until recent times, he maintains that the Holy Mass is a memorial especially of the Passion. In fact, in the Mass, Christ is principally—though not exclusively—in the state of being Victim.[139]

---

[137] Saint Thomas knows this well: "This Sacrament is a sign of the Passion of Christ and not the Passion itself" ("*hoc sacramentum est signum passionis Christi, et non ipsa passio*": *Scriptum super Sententiis* IV, d. 12, q. 1, a. 3, qc. 1 ad 2 [our translation]).

[138] "For by the 'transubstantiation'... his Body and Blood are both really present: now the Eucharistic Species under which He is present symbolize the actual separation of his Body and Blood. Thus the commemorative representation [*memorialis demonstratio*] of His death, which actually took place on Calvary, is repeated in every Sacrifice of the altar, since Jesus Christ is symbolized and displayed [*significatur atque ostenditur*] by separate signs to be in a state of victimhood" (Pius XII, *Mediator Dei* [1947] [DS 3848]).

[139] In Chapter Nine—on the Liturgy—we saw that Pius XII, in *Mediator Dei*, teaches precisely this and puts this doctrine at the base of the right concept of "active participation" in Worship, where to participate means above all "that they [the faithful] must assume to some extent the character of a victim," i.e., unite themselves to the Sacrifice of the Redeemer. It is also noteworthy that the liturgical books—including the Missal of Saint Paul VI (see *Institutio Generalis Missalis Romani: editio typica tertia emendata* [2008], §308)—prescribe that, during the act of celebrating the Eucharist, the image of the crucified Christ *must* be located on the altar (currently it is also permitted that it be at the side of the altar, though it is much better if it is at the center—in either case, it is obligatory). N.B. Images of the crucifix that were located on the apse walls do not satisfy the obligation: the altar must have its own crucifix, even if there is a representation on the altarpiece or on the wall). Although it is true that Christ is risen and that as the living One he comes among us under the Species, the most important theological-liturgical element (which through the *et-et* does not deny the other element) is without a doubt that Christ comes

Theological Reflection, and the Teachings of the Magisterium

The Common Doctor proposes another teaching of great importance here, when he specifies that the Eucharist contains the "*Christus passus*" ("Christ who has suffered").[140] Here the connection with transubstantiation, mentioned above, is clarified. Transubstantiation produces the Real Presence: Christ is now present under the Species in His Body, Blood, Soul and Divinity, entirely under each Species. But in what state is He? In the state of the One who has suffered.[141] In the Eucharist, Christ comes in a state of Victim, He comes to offer His Body and His Blood in Sacrifice. This teaching of the Angelic Doctor was interpreted by scholars in at least two different ways: (1) Some proposed an "interiorist" interpretation, which says that Christ comes as Victim in the sense that He, when He is in the Eucharist, has in Himself, in His soul, always the same intention that drove Him to take on the Passion (i.e., to give His life for us). (2) Others instead stop at the symbolic explanation: the victim state of Christ corresponds to what we already said, that the liturgical rite symbolically represents what happened historically two thousand years ago.

As always, we prefer to hold together the two things, rather than oppose them. In this case, the reasons are as follows: (1) It is true that Christ always maintains the intention of saving us, but if this were absolutized we would not even need to celebrate an external rite such as the Mass (why then would Christ institute it? As a mere symbol?). If the Mass effectively produces the grace of our redemption—this is *de fide*—then something more than the pure inner intention of Christ is needed for a good explanation. (2) On the other hand, to focus only on the execution of the rite is equally insufficient. If the rite alone were enough, an ontological value—and not merely a symbolic one—would have to be given to it *as such*. This proposal was advanced in the twentieth century and has obtained much consent, to the point that today perhaps the majority of specialists hold that the rite renders mystically present the historical events of two thousand years ago! But Saint Thomas would not easily accept this perspective: he speaks of "*Christus passus*" ("Christ who has suffered"), not "*Christus patiens*" ("Christ who suffers"). This interpretation was also rejected by the Magisterium, practically in the same years in which it was proposed:

> The liturgical year ... is not a cold and lifeless representation of the events of the past, or a simple and bare record of a former age. It

---

on the altar as the immolated Lamb, that is, as Victim of expiation for our sins.

[140] See *ST* III, q. 65, a. 5, ad 2.

[141] See also Saint Thomas Aquinas, *Scriptum super Sententiis* IV, d. 8, q. 1, a. 2, qc. 3 co.

The Eucharist

is rather Christ himself Who is ever living in His Church . . . with the design of bringing men to know His mysteries and in a way live by them. These mysteries are ever present and active *not in a vague and uncertain way as some modern writers hold*, but in the way that Catholic doctrine teaches us. According to the Doctors of the Church, they are shining examples of Christian perfection, as well as sources of divine grace, due to the merit and prayers of Christ; they still influence us because each mystery brings its own special grace for our salvation.[142]

Therefore, (3) the rite cannot be understood on its own, nor is it sufficient to recall the saving intention of Christ. A complete theology of the Eucharistic Sacrifice is based on the Person of Christ (Christocentrism), who is always alive to intercede for sinners (see Heb 7:25). The salvific events, or Christological mysteries, are not made present "in a vague and uncertain way as some modern writers hold," but because the concreteness of the celebration ritual—willed by Christ—not only recalls but also efficaciously re-actualizes, by producing its proper effects, these events, *since Christ comes in Person to represent them in Himself*. In a few words, the greatest defect of these recent proposals consists in wanting to understand the rite in relation to the "mysteries," without considering the Protagonist of the mysteries: Jesus. The attitude is to look to the historical event, neglecting the One who lived it and Who, alone, has the power of re-presenting its salvific efficacy.[143] In conclusion,

---

[142] Pius XII, *Mediator Dei* (DS 3855; emphasis added).

[143] CCC §468 teaches that "everything in Christ's human nature is to be attributed to his divine person as its proper subject, not only his miracles but also his sufferings and even his death." The Subject of the actions and passions, carried out or undergone by the two natures of Christ, is always the one Person. In other words, both when He carries out a great miracle, and when He is scourged by soldiers, the One who says "I" is always the same: the divine Word. This implies that historical events—in themselves always unique and unrepeatable—being personalized by the eternal "I" of the Word, Who lives in the present of perpetuity, while as historical events remain in the past, they are in some sense "eternalized." Seen in themselves, they have happened and remain in the past. Seen on the part of the "I" who lived them historically, they are always present, because that Subject lives today in the same condition as, for us, He had two thousand years ago. For the "I" of Christ there is no variation, nor temporal succession. The Word is saying "I" in this moment, which coincides perfectly with His saying "I" while He suffered the Passion and died on the cross. All that is changeable and temporal is on our part, not on His. Consequently, He is saying "I" today; and this is the same act of saying "I" as a million years ago, or before; the same as two thousand years ago; and the same in a million years (if there will still be the world and time). This is the reason historical events can be made present in a supernatural way in the liturgical rites (which always speak of "today": today

we hold the two interpretations of Thomas's thought together, saying that in order to theologically explain the efficacy of the Eucharistic Sacrifice one needs to maintain *both* the salvific intention of Christ, *and* the efficacious ritual that He instituted, which has value because it contains and offers Him. If the main element is clearly the salvific will of Christ, the ritual element—well understood—cannot be absolutely ignored. The Mass is *both* internal *and* external Sacrifice.

2.4.2. The Magisterium

We will present here the teaching of the Magisterium on the Eucharistic Sacrifice in two points: on one side, there are pronouncements of a dogmatic nature—here, the Council of Trent is especially important. On the other, the recent Magisterium focuses many times on highlighting the sacred character of the Eucharistic Celebration in the face of numerous misrepresentations of the exact nature of the Holy Mass that have occurred in recent times.

1. The Council of Trent

The Council of Trent represents the endpoint of the synthesis of the Eucharistic reflection and practice of the Middle Ages, as well as the official and authoritative response of the Magisterium to the new Protestant doctrines.

(1) The Council was convened to respond to the Protestant Reformation. In the *Decree on the Sacrament of the Eucharist*, this is manifested in an undoubtable way:

> The most holy, ecumenical, and general Council of Trent ... from the beginning, it has had, in particular, the desire to uproot completely the cockle of damnable errors and schisms that, in these turbulent times of ours, the enemy has sown in the doctrine of the faith, use, and worship of the most Holy Eucharist.[144]

Three sessions were dedicated to the Eucharist: the thirteenth, which would produce the aforementioned *Decree on the Sacrament of the Eucharist*;

Christ is born, today Christ has died). This is so because we do not disconnect the salvific events from the Person who lived them in time. When this disconnection happens, such a theology of the mysteries remains "vague and uncertain," as Pius XII said, indeed it would even be impossible.

[144] Council of Trent, *Decretum de ss. Eucharistia*, "Prooemium" (DS 1635).

The Eucharist

the twenty-first, which would be concerned with Communion under the two Species and the Communion of children; and the twenty-second, which would focus on the Sacrifice of the Mass. This thematic tripartition (Sacrament—Communion—Sacrifice), due more to practical than theological reasons, would become classic in post-Tridentine Eucharistic theology. We have already discussed the Sacrament and the Real Presence—and later we shall look at the theme of Communion—so here we shall focus only on the Sacrifice.

This was probably the biggest area of contention in the field of Eucharistic doctrine between the Church and the reformers. Luther's thesis, as seen in Chapter One, consisted in the denial of the sacrificial character of the Mass, because affirming it would have implied, in his way of viewing it, the sacrilegious emptying or devaluation of the one and perfect Sacrifice accomplished by Christ on the cross. The Council dedicated nine chapters to this matter. The first two of them are certainly fundamental. Given the rather intricate literary form of the texts, in order to facilitate this for the reader, we have reduced them considerably and have made a few small modifications:

> *Ch. I*: He, then, our Lord and God [Jesus Christ . . .] because His priesthood was not to end with His death, at the last supper— . . . in order to leave to . . . the Church *a visible Sacrifice . . . by which the bloody (Sacrifice) that He was once for all to accomplish on the cross* would be re-presented, its memory perpetuated until the end of the world, and its salutary power applied for the forgiveness of the sins that we daily commit . . . He offered His Body and Blood under the Species of bread and wine to God the Father, and, under the same signs, gave them to partake of to the disciples (whom He then established as priests of the New Covenant) and ordered them and their successors in the priesthood to offer it. . . . For, after He celebrated the old Pasch . . . Christ instituted a new Pasch, namely, *Himself, to be offered by the Church through her priests* under visible signs.
>
> *Ch. II*: *In this divine Sacrifice that is celebrated in the Mass, the same Christ who offered Himself once in a bloody manner on the altar of the Cross is contained and is offered in an unbloody manner.* Therefore, the holy Council teaches that this Sacrifice is truly propitiatory. . . . For the Lord, appeased by this oblation . . . pardons wrongdoings and sins, even great ones. *For, the Victim is one and the same*: the same now offers Himself through the ministry of priests Who then offered Himself on the cross; *only the manner of offering is different*. The

fruits of this oblation (the bloody one, that is) are received in abundance through this unbloody (oblation). By no means, then, does the latter detract from the former.[145]

We have resumed and emphasized only the most meaningful parts of the first two chapters, with respect to the nine that comprise the text as a whole. There are also nine canons of which we have chosen the following to reproduce:

Can. 1: If anyone says that in the Mass a true and proper Sacrifice is not offered to God or that the offering consists merely in the fact that Christ is given to us to eat, let him be anathema.

Can. 3: If anyone says that the Sacrifice of the Mass is merely offering of praise and thanksgiving or that it is a simple commemoration of the Sacrifice accomplished on the cross, but not a propitiatory Sacrifice, or that it benefits only those who communicate; and that it should not be offered for the living and the dead, for sins, punishments, satisfaction, and other necessities, let him be anathema.

Can. 4: If anyone says that the Sacrifice of the Mass constitutes a blasphemy against the most holy Sacrifice that Christ accomplished on the cross or that it detracts from that Sacrifice, let him be anathema.[146]

The Holy Mass must be understood as the restatement or representation of the Sacrifice of Christ on the cross and not as a *"nuda commemoratio"* ("a simple commemoration": can. 3). The Council takes care to emphasize that the one and only Sacrifice of Christ is not repeated in the Mass, but that it is re-offered in a new way. On the cross, the Lord offered Himself once for all (see Heb 7:27), with the perfect bloody Sacrifice, that is, through the effective donation of Himself in His blood. In the Mass, the Victim that is offered to the Father for human beings is the same, but the way in which He is offered is very different, because now it occurs in a sacramental and bloodless way. Therefore, there is a unicity of the Victim, but multiplicity and differentiation

---

[145] Council of Trent, *Doctrina et Canones de ss. Missae Sacrificio*, chs. 1–2 (DS 1740–1743; our emphasis).

[146] Council of Trent, *Doctrina et Canones de ss. Missae Sacrificio*, chs. 1–2 (DS 1751, 1753–1754).

of His immolations. Christ is offered in a bloody way on the cross, once for all. There are, however, other innumerable times in which the same Christ is offered, in a sacramental and bloodless way, to the Father in our favor. This occurs in the Church, through the Eucharistic immolation done by the priests of the new and eternal covenant.[147]

It is interesting that the Council argues its own authoritative pronouncement on the basis of that Christocentrism we have noted when discussing the theme of Sacrifice in the theology of St. Thomas. Since the main Actor of the celebration is Christ in Person (through His ministers), the Holy Mass can be a true Sacrifice. In fact, the Victim is the same, and the Sacrifice—contrary to Luther who sees the idea of a "multiplication" of Golgotha in Catholic doctrine—is the same. What changes is only the mode of the offering: bloody and historical at Golgotha, bloodless and sacramental on the altar. The former occurs in "*specie propria*" (in the physical body and blood), and the second occurs in "*specie aliena*," that is, under the veil of the bread and wine.

(2) Inspired by the Tridentine doctrine, we shall also briefly discuss two questions that we could define as "post-Tridentine" theology.

(A) The first question deals with the very essence of the sacrificial rite of the Eucharist. There have been different opinions, but there are two that appear to be the most meaningful: that of those who believe that the "formal constituent" (the essential element) of the Sacrifice is the oblation, that is, the offering; and that of those who believe, rather, that it is the immolation, that is the destruction of the offering.

In the case of the oblative theory, the sacrifice in general is interpreted as a visible offering, which manifests the inner sentiments with which the man honors the divinity and offers himself to God as his principle and end. This text of St. Thomas is used as support:

> Natural reason dictates to man, following the inclination of nature, to lend submission and honor to those who are superior to him. . . . Therefore, it derives from natural reason that man uses some sensible things to offer them to God as a sign of the submission and honor owed to Him, like those who offer gifts to their masters in recognition of their dominion. Now the notion of sacrifice lies precisely in this.[148]

---

[147] Saint Cyril of Jerusalem, *Catecheses mystagogicae* 5.10: "We offer Christ slaughtered for our sins, propitiating God the Lover of humanity both for them [those for whom we pray] and for ourselves" (in *Lectures on the Christian Sacraments* 127).

[148] *ST* II-II, q. 85, a. 1 (our translation).

This concept is applicable to the sacrifices of all of the religions, thus also to Judaism and Christianity (in which the "oblates" are presented: bread and wine). Based on this concept of sacrifice, the French school of theology, active even in the twentieth century—whose origin can be traced back to the Cardinal Pierre de Bérulle (d. 1629)—affirmed that the oblation is the fundamental element (or "formal constituent") of the sacrifice, and therefore also of the Eucharistic Sacrifice.

On the other hand, those who hold the immolative thesis start from a famous phrase of St. Thomas: "*Omnis sacrificium est oblatio, sed non omnis oblatio est sacrificium*" ("every sacrifice is an oblation, but not every oblation is a sacrifice").[149] This specification impedes the identification *tout court* of oblation and sacrifice. The oblation is just offering something, not necessarily sacrificing it. Thus, we need an additional element to add to the oblation so that it is really a sacrifice: "One speaks properly of sacrifice when one does some [sacrificial] act upon the things offered to God: animals, for example, are killed; the bread is broken, eaten, and blessed.... Oblation, rather, directly indicates the offer made to God, even if no act is performed upon it.... Therefore, every sacrifice is an oblation, but not vice versa."[150]

We believe that the second theory is more correct: Christ, indeed, always had the will to offer Himself to the Father; but His Sacrifice was only accomplished when, on the cross, He was immolated for sinners. Moreover, the immolative theory corresponds to the principle of *et-et*, for which the sacrifice is given both by the offering and by the immolation of it. The main element between the two is the (internal, out-of-charity) offering because that which is sacrificed is offered, and if there were no oblation, there would be no immolation either. If it is indeed true that the offering alone is not yet sacrifice in the full sense, it is also true that if the offering is missing, the sacrifice is impossible. Moreover, what makes the external sacrifice worthy is the inner intention to offer oneself. The external sacrifice, that is, the public and visible rite, acquires its religious value from the internal or moral sacrifice. In this regard, Saint Thomas states: "The external sacrifice represents the internal one, which is the true one, in which the human mind offers itself to God."[151] And in the *Summa* he reiterates: "The sacrifice offered externally signifies the

---

[149] Saint Thomas Aquinas, *Super Psalmos* 39.4 (our translation). The passage continues: "This is because the sacrifice involves the realization of what is sacred. Therefore, since there is nothing in the oblation but that something comes to be used by the priest, it is none other than a mere offering; when instead another action is taken on something, for example, that it is burned, then it is called sacrifice."

[150] *ST* II-II, q. 85, a. 3, ad 3 (our translation).

[151] Saint Thomas Aquinas, *Summa contra gentiles* III, ch. 120 (our translation).

spiritual interior sacrifice with which the soul offers itself to God."¹⁵²

(B) The second question concerns the relationship between the unique Sacrifice and its ritual "multiplication." Having categorically excluded (following the teaching of the Council) that the historical event at Golgotha is multiplied in the Holy Mass, can we speak of multiplication in some other sense? In order to respond, we shall cite another Thomistic text. The Angelic Doctor affirms that, in the Holy Mass, "Communion regards the Sacrament, the oblation the Sacrifice. Therefore, from the Communion to the Body of Christ on the part of one or many does not come any benefit to others. Likewise, due to the fact that a priest consecrates many Hosts in one Mass, the effect of this sacrament is not increased, because it is only a matter of one Sacrifice." Therefore, nothing changes whether the priest only consecrates one Host or thousands: the Eucharistic Sacrifice is not multiplied. On the contrary, things change if we consider it from the second perspective reported in the *incipit* by Thomas: "Instead, in more Masses the oblation of the Sacrifice is multiplied. And then the effect of the Sacrifice and the Sacrament is multiplied."¹⁵³

The Eucharistic Doctor argues that if the Hosts consecrated in a Mass are multiplied, the Mass is always one; however, if Mass is celebrated many times, the celebrations are multiple because the sacrificial oblation is offered many times. We can deduce from this that the effect of grace is also multiplied. If, therefore, we must remember that the event of Calvary as such is never multiplied, then we also need to note that the effect of grace, which that event produces, is multiplied each time the Mass is celebrated. This means, in concrete terms, that when more Masses are celebrated, more grace is produced and offered. Indeed, this is especially relevant today given that, in the ordinary form of the Roman Rite, the ancient practice of concelebration, that is, the fact that more ministers celebrate the Mass together, has been reintroduced. In itself, there are no dogmatic problems with the validity of such concelebration. What, however, must be noted is that this is precisely *one* concelebration, not many simultaneous celebrations. It is, therefore, only one Mass and not many Masses (i.e., as many as the number of concelebrants).¹⁵⁴ Since the practice of concelebration is very widespread today, even beyond the original intentions of the post-conciliar liturgical reform, the consequence is that

---

[152] *ST* II-II, q. 85, a. 3, ad 3 (our translation).

[153] *ST* III, q. 79, a. 7, ad 3 (our translation).

[154] See *ST* III, q. 82, a. 2: in the case of concelebration, the same Host is not consecrated multiple times because, as Innocent III (d. 1216) said in *De sacrosancto altaris mysterio* 4.25, all the ministers must then have the intention to consecrate at the same instant.

every day, for several decades, the Church loses the fruit of the grace of the thousands of Masses that are no longer celebrated by priests. If, for example, ten priests concelebrate instead of celebrating individually, there will be a single Mass instead of ten, with the "loss" of nine Masses and therefore the Church will receive a tenth of the offer of grace that she would have received if each minister had personally celebrated the holy Sacrifice of the altar. This theological interpretation has been and is still contested by a considerable number of theologians, but it has the approval of Pius XII on its side.[155]

2. Recent Pronouncements

In the post-conciliar era, a certain forgetfulness of the primarily sacrificial dimension of the Eucharistic Celebration has occurred more than a few times. There has been, and still is, a very widespread attitude of wanting to overturn the hierarchy between the sacrificial and communal aspect (see further on) of the Holy Mass. The Celebration ran the risk of being understood, in the theological and practical sense, more in line with the Protestant view—that focuses on the *congregatio fidelium* ("the gathering of the faithful")—than with the Catholic one, which understands the Mass as participation in the sacramental Sacrifice of Christ, to which He also gives us a communal participation. Faced with all of this, the recent Magisterium has intervened many times. We have selected a few passages.

(1) Saint Paul VI recalls that the sacrificial aspect is *"summa et caput"* ("the synthesis and apex") of the Eucharistic doctrine:

---

[155] See Pius XII, *Address to Participants in the International Congress of Pastoral Liturgy*, September 22, 1956: "In the case of a concelebration in the true and proper sense of the word, Christ, instead of acting through one minister alone, acts through more." This implies that the concelebrant participates in a single action of Christ carried out by more priests, rather than by one alone. But the concelebration of more priests does not multiply the actions of Christ. Two years later, the Sacred Congregation of Rites published the *Instructio de Musica Sacra et Sacra Liturgia* (1958), in which §38 reads: "But when there are many priests gathered for a meeting, it is permissible 'for only one of their number to celebrate a Mass at which the others (whether all of them or many) are present, and receive Holy Communion from one priest celebrant.' However, 'this is to be done only for a justifiable reason, and provided the bishop has not forbidden it because of the danger that the faithful might think it strange'; also, the practice must not be motivated by the error, pointed out by the Supreme Pontiff Pius XII, that *'the celebration of one Mass at which a hundred priests devoutly assist is equal to a hundred Masses celebrated by a hundred priests'*" (translation: adoremus.org [with our corrections]). The text refers to both the aforementioned address as well as a previous one by Pius XII, i.e., the *Allocutio Cardinalibus atque Antistitibus*, November 2, 1954.

The Eucharist

> It is profitable to recall ... what may be termed the synthesis and apex of the [Eucharistic] doctrine, namely that, by means of the Mystery of the Eucharist, the Sacrifice of the cross which was once carried out on Calvary is re-enacted in wonderful fashion and is constantly recalled, and its salvific power is applied to the forgiving of the sins we commit each day.[156]

The value of the Eucharistic Celebration is not provided by the number of faithful that participate in it. Although Vatican II had recommended communal celebration, the so-called "private" Mass maintains all its value, precisely due to its sacrificial character. The Mass is in fact always the Sacrifice of Christ that saves the world, even if for some reason there is no attending assembly:

> It is also only fitting for us to recall the conclusion that can be drawn from this about 'the public and social nature of each and every Mass' (*Sacrosanctum Concilium*, §27). For each and every Mass is not something private, even if a priest celebrates it privately; instead, it is an act of Christ and of the Church. In offering this Sacrifice, the Church learns to offer herself as a sacrifice for all and she applies the unique and infinite redemptive power of the Sacrifice of the cross to the salvation of the whole world. For every Mass that is celebrated is being offered not just for the salvation of certain people, but also for the salvation of the whole world. The conclusion from this is that even though active participation by many faithful is of its very nature particularly fitting when Mass is celebrated, still there is no reason to criticize but rather only to approve a Mass that a priest celebrates privately in accordance with the regulations and legitimate traditions of the Church, even when only a server to make the responses is present. For such a Mass brings a rich and abundant treasure of special graces to help the priest himself, the faithful, the whole Church and the whole world toward salvation—and this same abundance of graces is not gained through mere reception of Holy Communion.[157]

---

[156] Saint Paul VI, *Mysterium Fidei*, §27 (our translation).

[157] Saint Paul VI, *Mysterium Fidei*, §33. It is therefore necessary to put an end to the widespread prejudice against the private celebration of the Holy Mass, as if in the absence of faithful attending, the Eucharist had no value. Today there is no shortage of those who argue that a Mass without people would not make sense. At §34, Paul VI responds: "We recommend from a paternal and solicitous heart that priests, who constitute Our greatest

(2) Saint John Paul repeatedly called priests to respect the sacred character of the Holy Mass, mainly due to its sacrificial character, as well as its sacramental character (Real Presence). If we forget that the Mass is above all the Sacrifice of Christ, we lose sight of its essence:

> If separated from its distinctive sacrificial and sacramental nature, the Eucharistic Mystery simply ceases to be. It admits of no "profane" imitation, an imitation that would very easily (indeed regularly) become a profanation. This must always be remembered, perhaps above all in our time, when we see a tendency to do away with the distinction between the 'sacred' and 'profane', given the widespread tendency, at least in some places, to desacralize everything.[158]

> The Eucharist is above all else a Sacrifice. It is the Sacrifice of the redemption and also the Sacrifice of the New Covenant.... All who participate with faith in the Eucharist become aware that it is a 'Sacrifice,' that is to say, a 'consecrated offering.'[159]

Once again, in his final encyclical, the Pontiff returned to reiterate the importance of the sacrificial character of the Eucharist. He notes that the current context is marked by many lights, but "there are also shadows," among which is "an extremely reductive understanding of the Eucharistic mystery. Stripped of its sacrificial meaning, it is celebrated as if it were simply a fraternal banquet." And he adds: "How can we not express profound grief at all this? The Eucharist is too great a gift to tolerate ambiguity and depreciation."[160] John

---

joy and Our crown in the Lord, be mindful of the power they have received from the bishop who ordained them—the power of offering Sacrifice to God and of celebrating Mass for the living and for the dead in the name of the Lord. We recommend that they celebrate Mass daily in a worthy and devout fashion, so that they themselves and the rest of the faithful may enjoy the benefits that flow in such abundance from the Sacrifice of the cross. In doing so, they will also be making a great contribution toward the salvation of mankind." The invitation to the daily celebration even in the absence of faithful was repeated three months after the publication of the encyclical, by the Second Vatican Council, in *Presbyterorum Ordinis* (1965), §13; as well as less than two years later by the Sacred Congregation of Rites, *Eucharisticum Mysterium* (1967), §44.

[158] Saint John Paul II, *Dominicae Cenae* (1980), §8.
[159] Saint John Paul II, *Dominicae Cenae*, §9.
[160] Saint John Paul II, *Ecclesia de Eucharistia* (2003), §10. The expression "profound grief" is unusual in such a high-level magisterial text. It reveals the wounded soul of the holy Pontiff for the abuses suffered today by the Eucharistic Sacrament in vast sections of the Church.

The Eucharist

Paul II repeats the doctrine on the primarily sacrificial nature of the Mass:

> "The Lord Jesus on the night he was betrayed" (1 Cor 11:23) instituted the Eucharistic Sacrifice of His Body and His Blood. The words of the Apostle Paul bring us back to the dramatic setting in which the Eucharist was born. The Eucharist is indelibly marked by the event of the Lord's Passion and death, of which it is not only a reminder but the sacramental re-presentation. It is the Sacrifice of the cross perpetuated down the ages. This truth is well expressed by the words with which the assembly in the Latin rite responds to the priest's proclamation of the "Mystery of Faith": "We proclaim your death, O Lord!"[161]

The Supreme Pontiff also recalls the intimate relationship between the sacrificial and communal aspects of the Holy Mass, highlighting the primacy of the Sacrifice, which causes the banquet to be a sacred Banquet. This understanding, both of faith and theology, must—he concludes—manifest itself, as happened in the past, in the visible way of honoring the Eucharist:

> Like the woman who anointed Jesus in Bethany, *the Church has feared no "extravagance,"* devoting the best of her resources to expressing her wonder and adoration before the *unsurpassable gift of the Eucharist*.... Though the idea of a "banquet" naturally suggests familiarity, the Church has never yielded to the temptation to trivialize this "intimacy" with her Spouse by forgetting that He is also her Lord and that the "banquet" always remains a sacrificial banquet marked by the blood shed on Golgotha. *The Eucharistic Banquet is truly a "sacred" banquet*, in which the simplicity of the signs conceals the unfathomable holiness of God.

> With this heightened sense of mystery, we understand how the faith of the Church in the mystery of the Eucharist has found historical expression not only in the demand for an interior disposition of devotion, *but also in outward forms* meant to evoke and emphasize the grandeur of the event being celebrated.[162]

---

[161] Saint John Paul II, *Ecclesia de Eucharistia*, §11. See §§12–14, in which the sacrificial doctrine is developed on the basis of the Tridentine decrees.

[162] Saint John Paul II, *Ecclesia de Eucharistia*, §§48–49.

(3) Benedict XVI dedicated the important apostolic exhortation *Sacramentum Caritatis* to the Eucharist. On the sacrificial character of the Mass we read: "Jesus is the *true* paschal lamb who freely gave Himself in Sacrifice for us, and thus brought about the new and eternal covenant. The Eucharist contains this radical newness, which is offered to us again at every celebration."[163] "In instituting the Sacrament of the Eucharist, Jesus anticipates and makes present the Sacrifice of the cross and the victory of the resurrection. At the same time, He reveals that He himself is the *true* sacrificial Lamb."[164]

2.5. Communion

In addition to being a true Sacrifice, the Eucharist is also a participation in it, participation that comes to be called "convivial," because the altar is also the sacred table (see CCC §§1382–1383), on which Christ, offering Himself as the Victim of atonement to the Father for us, is also offered to us as the Food and Drink of salvation. The Holy Mass is therefore *both* Sacrifice *and* Communion (or Sacred Banquet). In the current era, it is necessary to emphasize more accurately the hierarchy of this bipolarity: the sacrificial aspect is preeminent. Indeed, to recognize that the Eucharist is also a Banquet, implies maintaining the dipolar hierarchy even within this same category. Banquet actually refers to two aspects: sacred meal at which God convenes us and sacred dinner of brethren in faith. The Holy Mass is Banquet in both senses, but it should not be forgotten that—as the first commandment is to love God and the second one to love one's neighbor (see Mark 12:28–33)—the Mass is above all the Banquet of each one with Christ (see Rev 3:20: "[I will] dine with him, and he with me") and then also of each one with his or her brethren in the faith. We shall now briefly discuss some topics related to the Mass as a sacred Banquet of Communion.

2.5.1. Sacramental and Spiritual Communion

There are three ways of communicating the Eucharist,[165] related to the the-

---

[163] Benedict XVI, *Sacramentum Caritatis*, §9.

[164] Benedict XVI, *Sacramentum Caritatis*, §10.

[165] "As regards the use, our Fathers have correctly and appropriately distinguished three ways of receiving the holy Sacrament. They teach that some receive it only *sacramentally* because they are sinners. Others receive it only *spiritually*; they are the ones who, receiving in desire the heavenly bread put before them, with a living faith 'working through love': experience its fruit and benefit from it. The third group receive it *both sacramentally and spiritually*; they are the ones who examine and prepare themselves beforehand to

ological distinction between *res* and *sacramentum*, which we have already encountered. We speak of a "sacramental Communion" when the faithful receives the sacramental sign (the consecrated bread and/or wine). We speak of "spiritual Communion" when, without receiving this sign, the grace (*res*) of the Eucharistic Sacrament is obtained as a gift from God. Finally, there is the perfect way to receive Eucharistic Communion, which is both sacramental and spiritual, that is, when the consecrated bread and/or wine is received with the necessary personal dispositions (state of grace, fasting, etc.), in such a way that the grace of the Sacrament is effective. Otherwise, if the personal dispositions are not present, a purely sacramental Communion can happen where the sign is received, but not the grace contained in it. Under certain conditions, the opposite is also possible: to receive the Eucharistic grace without having received Communion in a visible, sacramental way. This occurs through "spiritual manducation" ("*spiritualis manducatio*"), which today is called "spiritual Communion." It has already been seen in the previous chapters that the effect of a Sacrament can also be obtained with the *votum*, the desire, under certain conditions. But sacramental Communion is not superfluous, because, "this produces the effect of the Sacrament more perfectly than the desire alone."[166]

2.5.2. Communion of Desire and Desire of Communion

The question of the Communion of desire has been widely discussed in recent times, on account of the fact that many Catholics today make life choices that place them in the permanent impossibility of receiving the Eucharist in a sacramental way. In these cases, it is commonly suggested that they make recourse to spiritual Communion. However, a certain confusion about this can arise, because spiritual Communion in a true and proper sense is a mode of receiving the fruit of grace of the Eucharist, even if—for some contingent reason (e.g., there is not a celebration available, or the Eucharistic fast was not observed)—it cannot be received sacramentally. But to obtain such a spiritual effect, the due dispositions are required, especially being in the state of grace.[167]

---

approach this divine table, clothed in the wedding garment" (Council of Trent, *Decretum de ss. Eucharistia*, ch. 8 [DS 1648]).

[166] *ST* III, q. 80, a. 1. From what is said in the "ad 2," it can be understood that spiritual Communion stands in relation to sacramental Communion as imperfect to perfect. See also Saint Thomas, *Super Ioannem* VI, *lectio* 6.

[167] "Anyone conscious of a grave sin must receive the sacrament of Reconciliation before coming to communion" (CCC §1385). Recalling this number of the *Catechism*, Saint John Paul II, *Ecclesia de Eucharistia*, §36, wrote: "I therefore desire to reaffirm that in the

Theological Reflection, and the Teachings of the Magisterium

It is difficult to think that an impenitent sinner could receive the fruit of the Eucharist through spiritual Communion.[168] In fact, in this case, he or she could certainly have the desire for the Sacrament, which, however, is not the same as a Sacrament received by desire.

Therefore, when the Magisterium invites the faithful who cannot approach Communion on account of a permanent impediment (for example, the remarried divorced[169]) to make spiritual Communion, it should be under-

---

Church there remains in force, now and in the future, the rule by which the Council of Trent gave concrete expression to the Apostle Paul's stern warning when it affirmed that, in order to receive the Eucharist in a worthy manner, 'one must first confess one's sins, when one is aware of mortal sin' [see Council of Trent (DS 1647; 1661)]."

[168] Indeed, whoever receives the Eucharist while in mortal sin, sins gravely because he or she commits a falsehood against the Eucharist by implicitly declaring—because he or she communicates—to be in communion with Christ, while in reality he or she is not. This falsity is a profanation or sacrilege (see *ST* III, q. 80, a. 4). In the *Super I ad Corinthos* XI, *lectio* 7 [*reportatio Reginaldi*], Saint Thomas stated: "It would seem that sinners do not unworthily approach this Sacrament. In fact, in this Sacrament, Christ is consumed, and He is the spiritual Physician, who says of Himself in Matt 9:12: 'It is not the healthy who are in need of a physician but the sick.' But it must be said that this Sacrament is spiritual nourishment, like Baptism is spiritual birth. Now, one is born to live, while one does not eat if he or she is not alive. Thus, this Sacrament is not for sinners who do not yet live by grace, while Baptism is. Moreover, the Eucharist is the 'Sacrament of charity and of ecclesial unity' as Augustine says in his *Commentary on John's Gospel*. Therefore, since the sinner is deprived of charity and is, with reason, separated from the unity of the Church, if he or she approaches this Sacrament then a falsehood is committed due to the pretense of having that charity that he or she does not actually possess" (our translation).

[169] "*The Church reaffirms her practice, which is based upon Sacred Scripture, of not admitting to Eucharistic Communion divorced persons who have remarried*. They are unable to be admitted thereto from the fact that their state and condition of life objectively contradict that union of love between Christ and the Church which is signified and effected by the Eucharist. Besides this, there is another special pastoral reason: if these people were admitted to the Eucharist, the faithful would be led into error and confusion regarding the Church's teaching about the indissolubility of Marriage. Reconciliation in the Sacrament of Penance which would open the way to the Eucharist, can only be granted to those who, repenting of having broken the sign of the covenant and of fidelity to Christ, are sincerely ready to undertake a way of life that is no longer in contradiction to the indissolubility of Marriage. This means, in practice, that when, for serious reasons, such as for example the children's upbringing, a man and a woman cannot satisfy the obligation to separate, they 'take on themselves the duty to live in complete continence, that is, by abstinence from the acts proper to married couples.'. . . *By acting in this way, the Church professes her own fidelity to Christ and to His truth. At the same time she shows motherly concern for these children of hers, especially those who, through no fault of their own, have been abandoned by their legitimate partner*" (Saint John Paul II, *Familiaris Consortio* [1981], §84 [emphasis added]). This teaching was reiterated by the Congregation for the Doctrine of the Faith, *Annus Internationalis Familiae* (1994).

stood in the sense that they, in participating in Sunday Liturgy—to which they are nonetheless duty-bound and accepted—can foment their desire for the Sacrament through this practice,[170] in such a way that this desire may cooperate in that conversion that pushes them to remove the obstacles that impede the worthy and licit sacramental reception of the Eucharist.

2.5.3. Efficacy

An adequate understanding of Holy Communion depends on sufficient attention being given to the doctrine of the Real Presence. Communion is efficacious and bears fruit in the one who receives it if—as was previously noted—it is received with the due dispositions. Among these is awareness of the One who is being received.[171] This is, in turn, based on the clear profession of faith in the Real Presence. If the Real Presence is denied, doubted, or softened, the attitude with which Communion is approached and its efficacy will also be compromised. On the contrary, to believe strongly in the fact that the Eucharist is truly Christ, involves positive consequences, both at the level of faith and liturgical practice.

Regarding the first aspect, what Saint Irenaeus says is instructive:

> How can they [the heretics] say that the flesh [of Christians], which is nourished with the Body of the Lord and with His Blood, goes to corruption and does not partake of life? ... For as the bread, which is produced from the earth, when it receives the invocation of God, is no longer common bread, but the Eucharist, consisting of two

---

[170] In fact, Saint John Paul II, *Ecclesia de Eucharistia*, §34, writes that "it is good *to cultivate in our hearts a constant desire for the Sacrament of the Eucharist.* This was the origin of the practice of 'spiritual Communion.'" Spiritual Communion is always directed at cultivating the desire, both in the case of a Communion of desire in which grace is received, and in the case of a desire for Communion, in which—through some impediment—grace is not received. Benedict XVI, *Sacramentum Caritatis*, §55, likewise speaks of cultivating "a desire for full union with Christ through the practice of spiritual Communion," "where it is not possible to receive sacramental Communion." Again, one thing is "a desire for full union," another is "union of desire (*votum*)."

[171] In the *Catechismus* of Saint Pius X, §628, it is taught that the due dispositions to "make a good Communion" are the following: (1) being in a state of grace; (2) fasting from midnight until the act of Communion [today the discipline is reduced to only one hour]; (3) knowing what you are receiving, and approaching Holy Communion with devotion. At §636, the expression "knowing what you are receiving" is explained: "[It] means to know and firmly believe what is taught in Christian doctrine concerning this Sacrament" (translation: *ewtn.com*).

realities, earthly and heavenly; so also our bodies, when they receive the Eucharist, are no longer corruptible, having the hope of the resurrection to eternity.[172]

In the Eucharist we communicate in the Real Presence of the One who is Life (John 14:6), Christ risen from the dead, and the Firstborn of those who will rise again (see Col 1:18). He gives life in abundance (see John 10:10) and does so especially through the bread of life (see John 6:35, 48). Holy Communion transmits divine life to us, the life of grace, which is the life of Jesus Christ Himself: "Just as the living Father sent me and I have life because of the Father, so also the one who feeds on me will have life because of me" (John 6:57). In the Christological dispute with Nestorius, Saint Cyril of Alexandria (d. 444) reminded his adversary precisely of the life-giving character of the Eucharist:

> We celebrate the unbloody Sacrifice in the Churches.... And we do this, not as men receiving common flesh, far from it, nor truly the flesh of a man sanctified and conjoined to the Word according to a unity of dignity, or as one having had a divine indwelling, but as the truly life-giving and very own flesh of the Word himself. For, being life according to nature as God, when He was made one with His own flesh, He proclaimed it life-giving. Wherefore even if He may say to us, "Amen, I say to you: Except you eat the flesh of the Son of Man, and drink His blood," we shall not conclude that His flesh is of someone as of a man who is one of us, (for how will the flesh of a man be life-giving according to its own nature?), but as being truly the very flesh of the Son who was both made man and named man for us.[173]

This is why the consecrated Host—if it is permissible to express it in these terms—is "indwelt" by the incarnate Word, Who is the God-man and

---

[172] Saint Irenaeus of Lyon, *Adversus haereses* 4.18.5 (see also 5.2.3), in *ANF*, trans. James Donaldson and Alexander Roberts (Peabody, MA: Hendrickson Publishers, Inc., 1994), 486.

[173] Saint Cyril of Alexandria, *Epistula III ad Nestorium*, in *FCNT*, vol. 76, trans John I. McEnerney (Washington, DC: CUA Press, 1987), 86–87. Several centuries later, Saint Thomas Aquinas, *Super Ioannem* VI, *lectio* 4, will say: "The Word of God himself is principally called the bread of life.... And since the flesh of Christ is united to the Word of God, it has also become life-giving, so much so that His Body received sacramentally gives life" (our translation).

the Deifier of man. It is thus truly incomprehensible how some theologians of the twentieth century could speak, with respect to truths such as the Real Presence or transubstantiation, of a "static vision" of the Sacrament. It is unthinkable that there could be anything static in the fact that in receiving Communion we are receiving the true presence of the Author of life. This is why Pope Benedict wrote:

> The Eucharist draws us into Jesus' act of self-oblation. More than just statically receiving the incarnate *Logos*, we enter into the very dynamic of His self-giving. The imagery of marriage between God and Israel is now realized in a way previously inconceivable: it had meant standing in God's presence, but now it becomes union with God through sharing in Jesus' self-gift, sharing in His Body and Blood. The sacramental "mysticism," grounded in God's condescension towards us, operates at a radically different level and lifts us to far greater heights than anything that any human mystical elevation could ever accomplish.[174]

The *Catechism* recalls that the fruits of a well-received Communion are as follows: (1) it produces growth in our union with Christ; (2) it separates us from sin; (3) it erases venial sins; (4) it preserves us in the future from mortal sins; (5) it strengthens the unity of the Mystical Body; and (6) it commits us to the poor (CCC §1391–1397).

2.5.4. Communion and Adoration

1. Spirit of Adoration

From this clear doctrinal understanding, we can derive the proper attitude for approaching the Blessed Sacrament. In conformity with the composite character (visible/invisible) of every liturgical act (as was said in Chapter Nine), this refers both to the spirit with which one approaches the altar, and to the external attitudes. The spirit with which the Catholic approaches Holy Communion is the spirit of adoration, because the faithful firmly believes that he or she is not receiving a simple piece of bread or a sip of wine, but Jesus Christ, God and man.

Saint Augustine offers a true pearl of wisdom: "He [the Word] walked here in very flesh, and gave that very flesh to us to eat for our salvation; and no

---

[174] Benedict XVI, *Deus Caritas est* (2005), §13.

one eats that flesh, unless he has first worshipped." The last phrase resounds in Latin: "*Nemo autem illam carnem manducat, nisi prius adoraverit.*" And Augustine concludes: "Not only do we commit no sin in worshipping it; we should sin if we did not" ("*Non solum non peccemus adorando, sed peccemus non adorando*").[175] The internal attitude that is necessary for worthily receiving Communion is therefore the spirit of adoration that recognizes the presence of Christ: "Approach participation of this altar with fear and trembling. Recognize in the bread that same [Body] that hung on the cross, and in the chalice that same [Blood] that gushed from His side."[176] Whoever approaches the Eucharist without worshipping it at the same time, sins.

2. External Signs of Adoration

Internal adoration is made visible through a series of signs (gestures and actions), according to the bipolarity of human nature (see Chapter Three), which is respected by the liturgical act (see Chapter Nine). This is why the Church surrounds the Eucharist with clear signs of the proper Worship of adoration, such as genuflection, and kneeling during the consecration. This Worship is offered both during the celebration and also outside the celebration, where it is given to the consecrated Hosts conserved in the tabernacle.[177] Among these signs of care are those to be attended to on the occasion of Holy Communion.[178] The Church has always given the utmost attention to the consecrated Species and to each tiny fraction of them. As early as the third century, Origen (d. 254) wrote:

> You who habitually attend to the divine mysteries know the respectful caution with which you keep the Body of the Lord when it is given to you, for fear that some crumbs will fall off and that a part of the consecrated treasure will be lost. For you would consider yourself

---

[175] Saint Augustine of Hippo, *Enarrationes in Psalmos* 98.9, in *The Works of Saint Augustine: A Translation for the 21st Century*, vol. III/18, trans. Maria Boulding (Hyde Park, NY: New City Press, 2002), 475. This text has been recently brought back to the attention of the Church by Benedict XVI, *Sacramentum Caritatis*, §66. The Pontiff adds: "Receiving the Eucharist means adoring Him whom we receive. Only in this way do we become one with Him, and are given, as it were, a foretaste of the beauty of the heavenly Liturgy."

[176] Saint Augustine of Hippo, *Sermo 228/B*.2 (our translation).

[177] See Saint Paul VI, *Mysterium Fidei*, §57; CCC §1378.

[178] Saint Paul X, *Catechismus*, §637: "What do the words: To receive Holy Communion with devotion mean? To receive Holy Communion with devotion means to approach Holy Communion with humility and modesty in person and dress; and to make a preparation before, and an act of thanksgiving after, Holy Communion" (translation: *ewtn.com*)

guilty—and in this you would be right—if by your negligence you lost something.[179]

A famous text on the necessity of taking care not to disperse fragments of the consecrated Host is the following:

> Receive [the Body of Christ . . .] paying close attention so you do not lose any of it. For if you lose this it is like losing one of the members of your own body. For, tell me, if someone gave gold dust to you, would you not hold onto it with every care, guarding it, lest it be lost from you, and you suffer under the loss? Should you not be more careful then, watching closely so as not to let a crumb of what is more precious than gold and precious stones fall from you?[180]

The Lord Jesus literally put Himself into our hands through the Eucharistic Sacrament. It is therefore up to us to take care of Him with the greatest attention, which springs forth from a living faith in the Real Presence. However, a daily habit with a Mystery so great makes even the most fervent and faithful Catholic run the risk of losing sight of the greatness of what is entrusted to us. Saint John Paul II, in *Ecclesia de Eucharistia*, called for an awakening in the Church of an adoring spirit that he calls "Eucharistic 'amazement.'"[181] Moreover, Benedict XVI recalled the necessity of always keeping watch, so that we do not lose our reverential awe toward the Most Holy Sacrament. He speaks of "ceaselessly struggling" against the recurring temptation of treating the consecrated Species with excessive familiarity, a spirit of sufficiency and superficiality:

> No one is closer to his master than the servant who has access to the most private dimensions of his life. In this sense "to serve" means closeness, it requires familiarity. This familiarity also bears a danger: when we continually encounter the sacred it risks becoming habitual for us. In this way, reverential fear is extinguished. Conditioned by all our habits we no longer perceive the great, new and surprising

---

[179] Origen of Alexandria, *Fragmenta ex commentariis in Exodum* (our translation).
[180] Saint Cyril of Jerusalem, *Catecheses mystagogicae* 5.21, in *Lectures on the Christian Sacraments*, 135. On the fact that even the individual fragments of the Host are the Body of Christ, to be guarded with great reverence, see Congregation for the Doctrine of the Faith, *Cum de Fragmentis* (1972).
[181] Saint John Paul II, *Ecclesia de Eucharistia*, §6.

fact that He himself is present, speaks to us, gives Himself to us. We must ceaselessly struggle against this becoming accustomed to the extraordinary reality, against the indifference of the heart, always recognizing our insufficiency anew and the grace that there is in the fact that He consigned Himself into our hands.[182]

2.5.5. The Rite of Communion

According to what was just explained, it is clear that the liturgical rite of Communion should express the dogmatic truths and favor a deep spiritual reverence and cares consequent to it. We shall mention two aspects about the latter point: Communion under the two Species and the mode of receiving Communion (in the hand or directly on the tongue).

1. Communion under the Two Species

From the dogmatic standpoint, as we have seen, under each consecrated Species there is the presence of the whole Christ: Body, Blood, Soul, and Divinity. For this reason, it is not at all necessary to receive both Species: whoever receives only the Host or only the cup, receives no less than one who receives both.[183] This is explained by the Council of Trent in a special decree.[184]

If communicating under the two Species is not necessary, this does not mean that it is always to be forbidden, or that it cannot also express important symbolic aspects. For this reason, the Second Vatican Council decided to prudently reopen the question, without determining the specific liturgical rules.[185]

---

[182] Benedict XVI, *Homily in the Chrism Mass*, March 20, 2008.

[183] "The people may receive the Body without the Blood, without that procuring any inconvenience, because the priest offers and consumes the Blood in the name of all; moreover because ... in each of the two Species Christ is contained in His entirety" (*ST* III, q. 80, a. 12, ad 3).

[184] See Council of Trent, *Doctrina et Canones de Communione sub Utraque Specie et Parvulorum* (1562) (DS 1725–1734). See also Council of Trent, *Decretum sub Petitione Concessionis Calicis* (1562) (DS 1760). More briefly, the Council of Constance had already expressed itself previously in *Cum in Nonnullis* (1415) (DS 1198–1200).

[185] See Second Vatican Council, *Sacrosanctum Concilium* (1963), §55. The general rules for the distribution of Communion under the two Species is found in the *Institutio Generalis Missalis Romani*, §§281–287. It is good to also keep in mind the specifications of the Congregation for Divine Worship and the Discipline of the Sacraments, *Redemptionis Sacramentum* (2004), §§100–107. In the extraordinary form of the Roman Rite, this form of distribution of the Sacrament remains excluded.

The Eucharist

2. The Mode of Receiving Holy Communion

Even if the Second Vatican Council did not say anything about it, the post-conciliar liturgical reform reintroduced the practice that the Church observed in the first centuries, of distributing the consecrated Host on the palm of the hand of communicants. This ancient way was, almost from time immemorial, even forbidden. It is not our intention here to explain in detail the way in which we have arrived at the present situation, in which almost *ubique, semper et ab omnibus*, Communion is distributed on the hand. Here we must limit ourselves to noting that the way of communicating should manifest the faith of the Church in the Real Presence and sustain the respect and the reverence that are a consequence of such faith.

According to Saint Thomas, distributing (and therefore also touching) the Body of Christ is a task of the priest alone and not of the layperson.[186] There are three reasons for this: (1) The priest consecrates in the Person of Christ: Christ consecrated His own Body and then distributed it; therefore, it is the priest's task both the consecration and the distribution of Communion. (2) The priest is mediator between God and the people, so it is his duty both to offer God the gifts of the people and to give God's gifts to the people. (3) Out of respect for the Eucharist, it is not to be touched by anything unconsecrated: for this reason—that is, because they enter into contact with the sacred Species—the corporal and the chalice (in the extraordinary form) are consecrated, as well as the hands of the priest (in both forms of the Roman rite). Others (non-priests) are permitted to touch the Eucharist only in cases of necessity, if for example the Host was about to fall to the ground, or in other exceptional situations.[187]

The Council of Trent, then, even sees in the Communion distributed only by the priests a custom that derives from the Apostolic Tradition:

> In the reception of the Sacrament, there has always been a custom [*mos*] in the Church of God that the laity receive Communion from priests, but that priests, when celebrating, administer Communion to themselves. This custom, as coming from Apostolic Tradition [*ex*

---

[186] For Saint Thomas, rather, this is not even the responsibility of the deacon, who in the ordinary form of the Roman Rite is an ordinary minister of Communion, but in the extraordinary form does not have the faculty of touching the Host and thus cannot even distribute Communion to the faithful.

[187] See *ST* III, q. 82, a. 3.

traditione apostolica], should rightly and deservedly be retained.[188]

The reasons for being in favor of distributing Communion directly on the tongue and not on the hand of the communicants are numerous and unfortunately cannot be explained here. We have to limit ourselves to say, without going into great detail, that reserving the distribution of the consecrated Host only to the priest is not in any way based on a sentiment of disrespect to the lay faithful, almost as if they were unworthy of touching the Eucharist. Instead, it rests entirely on a series of theological, symbolic, and spiritual elements that have great value for the benefit of Christian life of the faithful themselves. Withdrawing the current indult that allows for the reception of Communion on the palm of the hand would not then be a clerical coup, aimed at discrediting the role of the other baptized. On the contrary, it would be another one of many acts of love that Mother Church would develop in the liturgical field when she establishes signs and rites, which help the minds of the faithful to be elevated to God and to thus better attend to their sanctification.[189]

2.5.6. *Communion as Viaticum*

Communion is given to the dying in the form of Viaticum, that is, as accompaniment, consolation, and reinforcement for traveling the last stretch of road, which leads to eternity. This aspect also reveals the so-called eschatological character of the Eucharist, which being bread of eternal life, has an evident reference to the ultra-terrestrial and definitive dimension. The eschatological aspect of the Eucharist has been especially valued by contemporary theology, even in relation to the fact that this Sacrament has not only or not mainly been studied in relation to the *Christus passus*, but rather within the Paschal Mystery of the Passion, Death, and Resurrection, where—we must admit— oftentimes the emphasis has been more willingly placed on the risen Christ

---

[188] Council of Trent, *Decretum de ss. Eucharistia*, ch. 8 (DS 1648).

[189] Given its importance, we shall reiterate a citation that was already offered in Chapter Nine: "And as human nature is such that it cannot easily raise itself up to the meditation of divine realities without external aids, holy Mother Church has for that reason duly established certain rites, such as that some parts of the Mass should be said in quieter tones and others in louder; and she has provided ceremonial such as mystical blessings, lights, incense, vestments, and many other rituals of that kind from apostolic order and Tradition, by which the majesty of this great Sacrifice is enhanced and the minds of the faithful are aroused by those visible signs of religious devotion to contemplation of the high mysteries hidden in this Sacrifice" (Council of Trent, *Doctrina et Canones de ss. Missae Sacrificio*, ch. 5 [DS 1746]).

than on the immolated Christ. In this way, while not denying the sacrificial nature, the Eucharist was considered preferably according to other categories, which also influenced the widespread understanding of it, as well as the celebratory practice. To put it in simple terms: today not all priests and faithful who celebrate or participate in the Holy Mass believe that they are assisting in the sacramental form of the Sacrifice of Christ at Golgotha. The aspects of light, joy, and fraternity are highlighted much more. The Mass is more frequently considered as the joyous reunion of the local community with itself and with the *risen* Christ.

Of course, these aspects are not wrong; the problem is that of a shift in emphasis in the dipolar hierarchy, where now the primary aspect (the Sacrifice) is considered—when it is considered at all—secondary, and vice versa. Currently, the joyous Banquet trumps the Sacrifice. The Viatic aspect might also represent a corrective to all of that. This first of all reminds us that the Eucharist does not ever happen in the closed circle of the local community, in the narrow *hic et nunc*. The Eucharist—as has already been recalled in Chapter Eight—is always "the Worship of a wide open Heaven," "a glimpse of Heaven on earth."[190] Moreover, since the Eucharist is given as Viaticum at the approach of death, it inevitably brings with it a dimension that is not only of eternity and of passage, but of suffering and obscurity as well. This can represent a healthy counterweight to a view of the Eucharistic celebration that is sometimes too euphoric.

In its Viatic dimension, Communion orients us toward eternal life and reminds us that there is an "Elsewhere" for which we must prepare. It brings to our minds the eschatological orientation of the Liturgy: "The Church celebrates the mystery of her Lord 'until he comes', when God will be 'everything to everyone' [1 Cor 11:26; 15:28]" (CCC §1130). Aside from being a commemorative sign of the past and a demonstrative sign of the grace that is offered to us on earth, the Eucharist is a prognostic sign and a pledge of future glory.[191] These three dimensions of the Eucharist—toward the past, the present, and the future—are found again in the prayer *O sacrum convivium*:

> *O sacrum convivium / in quo Christus sumitur. / Recolitur memoria passionis eius; / mens impletur gratia / et futurae gloriae nobis pignus datur.*

> O sacred Banquet / in which Christ is received / We remember His

---

[190] These two expressions are found in Benedict XVI, *General Audience*, October 3, 2012, and *Sacramentum Caritatis*, §35, respectively.

[191] See *ST* III, q. 60, a. 3.

Passion [of the past] / the soul is filled with grace [at the present] / and a pledge of future glory is given to us.

In order to highlight the eschatological orientation of the celebration, the Missal of Paul VI added some words to the formula (called "embolism") that follows the Our Father: "*expectantes beatam spem et adventum Salvatoris nostri Jesu Christi*" ("as we await the blessed hope and the coming of our Savior, Jesus Christ"). The Church therefore celebrates the Eucharist both turning towards the past: to the adoration of the *Christus passus* really present under the Species; and towards the future: that is, to the return of Christ in His "*parousia*" (glorious return). It can be said that in each Holy Mass, while she thanks Christ for all the benefits that He has obtained for us through the Passion and that He unceasingly re-offers, the Church also shouts: "*Marana tha*" ("come, O Lord!": 1 Cor 16:22). It is therefore completely natural that, after having discussed the great Eucharistic Sacrament, which offers us both the fruit of the Redemption and orientation toward glory, we conclude the entire treatise with a chapter dedicated to the last things.

12

The Last Things

The concluding chapter of our presentation is focused on what is succinctly expressed by the Niceno-Constantinopolitan Creed, which professes that Christ "will come again in glory to judge the living and the dead; and His kingdom will have no end"; and, "I await the resurrection of the dead and the life of the world to come." The Apostles' Creed professes the same faith with similar expressions, saying that Christ sits at the right hand of God the Father and "from there He will come to judge the living and the dead"; and it concludes by saying: I believe in "the resurrection of the flesh [and] life everlasting." It is with these expressions that the two most famous Creeds of the faith refer to the "last things."

1. Introductory Observations

1.1. The Novissimi

The expression "last things" is a literal translation of the Latin *novissima*, a term traditional theology has used to describe the realities that belong to the great beyond. Recent theology often prefers to use the corresponding Greek word and speaks of the *eschata*, from which the word "eschatology" (and the adjective "eschatological") derives, which indicates the branch of theology that deals specifically with the last things.

What are these realities? The recent *Compendium of the Catechism of the*

Catholic Church lists them as four: Death, Judgment, Hell, Heaven.[1] These are the four definitive realities, which mark the beyond in a permanent way, even if the concept of "definitive" is applied to them in an analogical and not univocal way.[2] In the study of eschatology, a fifth reality can be added, which is not enumerated in the *Compendium* because it is not eternal but transitory: Purgatory. Thus, in this chapter we will focus on these five eschatological realities, and we shall add some further information on the theme of the two limbos.

1.2. Metaphors and Reality

If all theology, in each of its branches, must always take into account the limitation of human thought and language, as well as the mysterious nature of the doctrines revealed by God, the difficulty in this field is even greater (if that is possible). This is not because these doctrines are more mysterious in an absolute sense—indeed it can be said that the most incomprehensible mysteries are the unity and trinity of God and the Incarnation of the Word—but because Revelation tells us little about them, and often uses cryptic language; furthermore, because the realities of the afterlife are not yet, so to speak, "complete," they undergo a state of awaiting their own fulfillment.

Prior to the revelation and redemption carried out by Christ, human beings have always intuited that there must be an afterlife; however, they knew nothing about it. Jesus Christ was the first to reveal to human beings the hidden realities of the hereafter: "No one has gone up to heaven except the one who has come down from heaven, the Son of Man" (John 3:13). Since the Word has seen Heaven, from which He descended in the Incarnation, He can speak about what He knows. He has spoken to us of the positive aspects, but also of the negative realities of the beyond, which He alludes to when He refers to having seen, in an evidently[3] very remote time, the fall of Satan from Heaven to Hell: "I have observed Satan fall like lightning from the sky" (Luke

---

[1] *Compendium of the Catechism of the Catholic Church*, Appendix.
[2] We could speak of complete finality for Heaven and Hell and relative finality for Death and Judgment, since they forever remain not so much in themselves, but in their effects.
[3] We affirm this evidence based on the explicit and implicit information of scriptural Revelation: the first chapters of Genesis, in fact, go back to the act of the creation of the material universe, but they do not mention the fall of Satan and his angels, who are revealed elsewhere in Scripture but without temporal specifications. However, even in Genesis 3, one may notice the existence and activity of Satan, who is presented as a tempter serpent. Therefore, the fall of Satan must have even preceded the creation of the material cosmos and, as such, is very remote. Regarding all of this, see the part dedicated to the angels and demons (Chapter Three).

10:18). As can be seen from the two quotes, the Lord often uses the metaphor of high and low and therefore of a descent or fall from on high toward the bottom; indeed, ascending or lifting up is also mentioned in other passages:

> Luke 24:51: "As he blessed them he parted from them and was taken up to heaven."

> John 12:32: "And when I am lifted up from the earth, I will draw everyone to myself."

> John 20:17: "Stop holding on to me, for I have not yet ascended to the Father. But go to my brothers and tell them 'I am going to my Father and your Father, to my God and your God.'"

> Acts 1:9–11: "When he had said this, as they were looking on, he was lifted up, and a cloud took him from their sight. While they were looking intently at the sky as he was going, suddenly two men dressed in white garments stood beside them. They said, 'Men of Galilee, why are you standing there looking at the sky? This Jesus who has been taken up from you into heaven will return in the same way as you have seen him going into heaven.'"

Naturally, the modern sensibility has emphasized that Paradise or Heaven cannot really be above from an astronomical standpoint. Heaven, as has been emphasized, cannot be a place in a proper sense, but rather a state of life that surpasses all our categories and that Scripture, using—as they say—primitive or childish language, paints with comprehensible images. Of course, there is something true in these specifications, which nonetheless should not be exaggerated. After all, the Lord has revealed divine and mysterious things to us in a human language and through categories that, however obscure and enigmatic, are understandable on the part of created minds like those of human beings. Hence the need to decipher the so-called apocalyptic language, which often accompanies what Christ wanted to tell us about the great beyond. On the other hand, we must remember that if it is difficult (sometimes impossible) to specify details about the hereafter, there is no doubt about the real existence of the last things, therefore a first fundamental point is this: Hell, Purgatory, and Paradise, as well as Death, and the Last Judgment in the end times—which includes the resurrection of the flesh and the end of this world—are not myths or images to be interpreted exclusively as calls for the ethical responsibility of human beings in this life.

When dealing with man's situation after death, one must especially beware of arbitrary imaginative representations: excess of this kind is a major cause of the difficulties that Christian faith often encounters. Respect must however be given to the images employed in the Scriptures. Their profound meaning must be discerned, while avoiding the risk of over-attenuating them, since this often empties of substance the realities designated by the images.[4]

Of course, these realities certainly also solicit responsibility, but this does not express their entire meaning. The last things exist and will exist forever. The representative language through which they are revealed does not imply that they can be easily dismissed as myths or symbols.

1.3. "Hic et nunc" *but also* "alibi et tunc"

In the past fifty years or so, it has been pointed out that understanding the treatment of eschatology only in reference to the last things would be in itself reductive, almost a final appendix with which to conclude the presentation of dogmatic theology. Therefore, an extension of the eschatological vision to all theological treatments has been proposed, not forgetting to frame the whole within the history of God's interventions in the world, and above all its central event: Christ and His Paschal Mystery. If part of this critique is justified, because it is true that "the eschatological" is not only "at the end," we must not forget that the treatise on the *Novissimi* should not oscillate from one extreme to the other. If before—according to recent criticism—we ran the risk of understanding the eschatological treatise almost as a theological version of Dante's *Divine Comedy*, that is, as a "physical" description of the places of an afterlife that has little to do with earthly life; today the risk is the opposite, of immanentizing the scope of what is eschatological. Indeed, too often in our times, it is primarily understood as that which is "definitive and irreversible" among the things that God accomplishes *in salvific history*, that is, *here and now* (*hic et nunc*). This often leads to not having the courage to say much about the great beyond (an excess of apophatism). The consequence is that, while the classic treatise on the *Novissimi* studied the last things as realities to be found at the end of history, in the current formulation the events of (salvific) history are called "eschatological," no longer in the sense of "beyond time," but rather in the sense of being "definitive and irrevocable, in time."

---

[4] Congregation for the Doctrine of the Faith, *Epistola de Quibusdam Quaestionibus ad Eschatologiam Spectantibus* (1979), §7.

Introductory Observations

Facing such a situation, we must remember that the eschatological treatise, although it must certainly affect all theological treatises, must also remain a definite and consistent treatment, not only providing perspective, but also proposing a specific content. With this in mind, we propose to join—according to the *et-et*—with the most fortunate formula of the "*hic et nunc*" ("here and now"), this other: "*alibi et tunc*" ("elsewhere and then"). Eschatology (and really all of theology and its pastoral applications) cannot be grasped only in its relevance for the human being in the world, but also and especially for the human being beyond this world. Faith is not only a guiding lighthouse to better approach the storms and challenges of the *hic et nunc*; it is also a reference to, and a prognosis of, the *alibi et tunc*, whose contemplation, done in the dark certainty of faith, helps us to navigate the journey and provides us with hope.

Therefore, we dare to have the courage here to say something about the great beyond, naturally following the only walkable path, that of the Revelation authentically interpreted by the Magisterium and by trustworthy theologians, but also keeping in mind the constructive aspect of the most recent criticism, which will nonetheless remain in the background.[5] In order to do this within the confines of space and keeping with the character of this book, we shall frame the eschatological realities, once again faithful to the indispensable principle of *et-et*, within a dipolar structure whose fundamental pillars are divine predestination and human freedom. What will thus emerge is that the *Novissimi* are indeed last things, but they are also in deep continuity with historical-salvific development.[6]

---

[5] We shall not directly focus here on the various questions faced by the eschatology of the twentieth century, like the "resurrection at death," the "final option," eschatology that is "consistent," "realized," or "inaugurated." On the "eschatologism/incarnationism" relationship, some indications have been offered in several of the previous chapters (for example, Chapter Four). It is not our task here to enter into debates that are indeed interesting but do not seem to have been completely resolved as of yet. The goal of this book is to provide "secure" knowledge and criteria, especially to those who are beginning their study of dogmatic theology.

[6] The eschatological teaching of the Second Vatican Council—which will be referenced at various times throughout this chapter—likewise unfolds with a structure of bipolarity, given that it develops eschatology both through a Christocentric lens (see *Gaudium et Spes* [1965], §22) and through an ecclesiological lens (see *Lumen Gentium* [1964], §§48–51, dedicated to the eschatological character of the Church). We focused on these aspects in Chapters Four and Eight, which is why we shall not explicitly discuss them again here, even if we shall keep them present in the background.

2. Divine Predestination and Human Liberty

2.1. Predestination to Salvation by the Logos

"Predestination" is customarily used to mean the design that God has for each individual human being. This doctrine has some foundations in the Old Testament (which, however, never uses the term) and the New Testament, within which the two Pauline passages of Ephesians 1:3–12 and Romans 8:28–30 are especially noteworthy. The two texts shed light on each other: whereas Ephesians speaks of a predestination of believers in Christ (the Word incarnate), Romans speaks of a predestination in the Son, without necessarily referring to the Incarnation (it can be interpreted this way if it is understood with reference to the natural filiation of the Son from the Father and our adoptive filiation in grace, even aside from redemption). In light of what we have seen in the previous chapters, we interpret this doctrine in the sense of a predestination toward salvation carried out by the Word, which is concretely achieved through the redemptive and salvific work of the Word in the state of the Incarnation (in the hypothetical situation that original sin had not been committed, predestination would still be *ab aeterno* in the Word and therefore human beings could not be saved without the action of the *Logos*). Thus, we do not interpret Ephesians in the sense of a predestination that *ab aeterno* already necessarily involved the decree of the Incarnation as well (even if, obviously, God always *knows* that He will be incarnated in the Person of the Son; see Chapter Two).

2.2. Double Predestination?

Predestination concerns all human beings. Each human being, insofar as he or she is created, is also predestined. In this sense, although it certainly remains possible for God to create a human being without calling him or her to eternal salvation,[7] indeed—for the sole reason that God does not will it[8]—this never occurs. And while Calvin (d. 1564) sustained the theory of double predesti-

---

[7] Pius XII, *Humani Generis* (1950) (DS 3891): some theologians "destroy the gratuity of the supernatural order, since God, they say, cannot create intellectual beings without ordering and calling them to the beatific vision."

[8] God, in fact, "wills everyone to be saved" (1 Tim 2:4). If, therefore, He creates a human being, He also directs him or her toward the beatific vision in Heaven (supernatural end). But this occurs only because God so "wills" it. If He willed otherwise, He could create human beings without ordering them toward the supernatural end, because grace is never a right of the creature, but rather a free gift of the Creator.

nation,⁹ for which human beings are sent to Heaven or Hell by pure divine decree without any real involvement of human freedom, the Church has absolutely rejected this view from the most ancient times. The Synod of Arles imposed a Formula of Submission to the priest Lucidus, in which he declared that he no longer professed the doctrine "which states that some have been condemned to death, others have been predestined to life."¹⁰ In the year 529, the Second Synod of Orange was held. Its conclusion was written by the bishop Saint Caesarius of Arles (d. 543), in which we read:

> According to the Catholic faith we also believe that after grace has been received through Baptism, all the baptized, if they are willing to labor faithfully, can and ought to accomplish with Christ's help and cooperation what pertains to the salvation of their souls. Not only do we not believe that some are predestined to evil by the divine power, but if there are any who wish to believe such an enormity, we with great abhorrence anathemize them.¹¹

The Council of Trent has definitive pronouncements in direct opposition to the Protestants, especially the aforementioned Calvin:

> If anyone says that it is not in man's power to make his ways evil, but that God performs the evil works just as He performs the good, not only by allowing them, but properly and directly, so that Judas' betrayal no less than Paul's vocation was God's own work, let him be anathema.
>
> If anyone says that the grace of justification is given only to those who are predestined to life and that all the others who are called are

---

⁹ We have spoken of it in Chapter One, in which we mentioned Gottschalk of Orbais (d. 869) and other authors who, in different ways, have sustained the *"gemina praedestinatio"* ("double predestination") and have thus been condemned by various synods and councils. This expression derives from Saint Isidore of Seville (d. 636), who in *Sententiarum libri* 2.6 had written: *"gemina est praedestinatio."* Isidore, however, gave the expression a different meaning from what Gottschalk and Calvin would give, proposing that God, predicting the free response of human beings to grace, predestined some to salvation, while abandoning others to condemnation, in the sense that He allows them to be lost, without determining *a priori* their damnation.

¹⁰ Synod of Arles, *Lucidi presbyteri Libellus subiectionis* (473) (DS 335).

¹¹ Second Synod of Orange, *Conclusio a Caesario Episcopo Arelatensi Redacta* (529) (DS 397). CCC §1037 summarizes this teaching with the formula: "God predestines no one to go to hell (Cf. Council of Orange II [529]: DS 397' Council of Trent [1547]: 1567)."

called indeed but do not receive grace, as they are predestined to evil by the divine power, let him be anathema.[12]

From these teachings it is understood that the decree of God's predestination for human beings is not double (some destined infallibly, however they behave, to Heaven; others with equal infallibility to damnation), but rather single, since scriptural Revelation teaches that God "wills everyone to be saved" (1 Tim 2:4). The predestination is therefore always for Paradise, never for Hell. The same Scripture teaches, however, that the human person can also choose to reject God's predestination and damn himself or herself (see, for example, Mark 8:36; Luke 16:19–31). Though it is impossible for someone to be saved without God, the person can damn himself or herself by rejecting God. This concept was expressed efficaciously by the Synod of Quiercy in May 853, when it affirmed:

> The omnipotent God wishes "all men" without exception "to be saved" (1 Tim 2:4), although not all may be saved. That some, however, are saved is the gift of the One who saves; that some, however, perish is the fault of those who perish.[13]

2.3. Predestination and Divine Prescience

Divine predestination, therefore, is single and not double, though the destiny that follows this predestination is double: eternal salvation or eternal damnation. In the ecclesial Tradition, this seemingly problematic teaching has been explained through the connection between the doctrine of predestination and that of divine prescience. God knows everything from eternity, and therefore He also knows from eternity who will be saved and who will be damned. The human mind, however, bound to the scheme of temporal thought, expresses this doctrine using expressions such as: "Even *before* creating human beings, God already knows which ones will go to Hell." This mode of expression is ambiguous and may even scandalize: How can God create human beings and predestine them to glory while knowing infallibly that some will go to Hell? But the weak point here does not lie in the doctrine in itself, but rather in our minds and our language. On the theological level, we should strive, as far as possible, to understand that in God, "before" and "after" do not exist. The progression of salvation history is real for us, but to God, history is *already*

---

[12] Council of Trent, *Decretum de Iustificatione* (1547), cann. 6 and 17 (DS 1556 and 1567).
[13] Synod of Quiercy, *De Libero Arbitrio Hominis et de Praedestinatione* (853), ch. 3 (DS 623).

finished *before* it begins. God already knows everything that "has happened" even if for us (*quoad nos*) it has yet to happen. This is the great mystery of the divine prescience, due to the fact that God is eternal and eternity is the dimension in which the past and the future do not exist, but only the present. In the eternal present of His most perfect life, God knows by infallible knowledge everything that "is." Thus, He "already" knows now, "before" it happens, what the eternal destiny of every human being is. The fact that He knows does not imply that human beings do not choose freely, within a history, a life that for us really is—and not in an illusory way—the temporal sequence of moments that gives rise to the past, present, and future. In this sense, we speak of one single predestination for which God decides with His eternal and immutable decree to exercise gratuitous mercy for those who will be saved not without Him, and righteous judgment for those who will be damned because they chose to oppose Him. The link between divine prescience and predestination explains how it is possible for a single predestination to achieve a double result.

In this regard, let us read some illuminating passages taken from a synod of the year 855:

> We faithfully hold that "God foreknows and has foreknown eternally both the good deeds that good men will do and the evil that evil men will do" (Florus of Lyon, *Sermo de praedestinatione*). . . . Furthermore, God's foreknowledge has not placed a necessity on any wicked man, so that he could not be otherwise; but what this one would be by his own will, He foreknew as God, Who, from His omnipotent and immutable majesty, knows all things before they come to be. . . . Certainly, as God, Who foresees all things, He foreknew and predestined the punishment that follow their demerit, since He is just and before Him, as St. Augustine says (*De praedestinatione sanctorum*), there is for absolutely everything a fixed decree as well as certain foreknowledge. . . . Concerning this unchangeableness of the foreknowledge and of the predestination of God, through *which in Him future things have already taken place*, even in Ecclesiastes the saying is well understood: "I recognized that whatever God does will endure forever."[14]

Saint Thomas says it in a similar way when, while recognizing the infallibility of God's predestination, he specifies that "nevertheless the free will

---

[14] Synod of Valence, *De Praedestinatione* (855), cann. 2 and 3 (DS 626–629).

[of human beings] is not abolished, and thus the effect of predestination is achieved in a contingent way."[15] This means that what is established by God in the eternity of His knowledge is carried out historically as the effect of human liberty. It is in light of this clarification that biblical passages such as Rom 9:16–24 and some patristic statements, especially of Saint Augustine (d. 430), must be interpreted. In spite of what the Protestants argue, Augustine never affirmed predestination to Hell in the Calvinist sense.[16]

2.4. Human Liberty and Eschatological Consequences

It follows from all this, yet again, that it is necessary to keep in mind *both* the original plan of God for human beings *and* their free response. In the discussion of eschatology, we again see clearly that the divine plan is infallibly carried out, but its specific realizations vary based on human response. Additionally, studying the *Novissimi*, we are made aware that the unfaithful response of human beings to the will of God is the cause of superterrestrial realities that would not exist if humankind had not sinned. We are not referring here to Hell, because its existence depends not only on the sin of human beings, but also—and even before—to that of the rebellious angels. We refer, rather, to two transitory realities, which are the "Limbo of the Fathers" (*limbus patrum*) and Purgatory, of which we shall speak. While there is an open debate about the existence of the *limbus puerorum* (the Limbo of infants), which we shall also discuss, there is no doubt about the previous existence of the Limbo of the Fathers, which has already ended, and that of Purgatory, which still exists. Even if the Limbo of infants were proven to be only a theological hypothesis, the fact remains that at least two superterrestrial realities came to exist as a consequence of the sin of human beings. If humanity, in fact, had not sinned, these "places" would not have been necessary.

---

[15] *ST* I, q. 23, a. 6 (our translation).

[16] Augustine defines predestination as "the foreknowledge and the preparation of God's favors, by which those who are delivered are most certainly delivered" (*De dono perseverantiae* 14.35, in *FCNT*, vol. 86, trans. John A. Mourant and William J. Collinge [Washington, DC: CUA Press, 1992], 302–303). The expression in *De praedestinatione sanctorum* 8.14 is stronger: "Why, then, does not the Father teach all people, in order that they might come to Christ, unless it is that all those He teaches, He teaches because of mercy, but those whom He does not teach, because of judgment He does not teach?" (*FCNT*, vol. 86, 234–235)—but these words are to be understood in the sense that was already specified.

3. The Question of Souls Separated from Bodies

This theme presents different questions that can be summarized in two primary ones: (1) If the human being is by nature a unity of soul and body,[17] how can it be taught—as it is in Christian doctrine—that there is a state, though transitory, in which the souls are (in Limbo, Hell, Purgatory, or Paradise) separated from the body? (2) The separated souls do not have a *where* (*ubi*), since they are separated from the matter of the body. Thus they do not have any localization. Hence, how can the last things be places "where" the souls would be?

3.1. The Eschatological "Where" (Ubi)

We can begin with the second question and respond by saying that the eschatological realities, more than places, are states of existence or conditions: being-damned, being-in-purgation, being-beatified. But in a certain sense they are also "places,"[18] for a number of reasons: (1) Even if the immaterial souls do not occupy space, since they are creatures, they are in space in some sense. (2) One day, in the end times, the bodies will resurrect and re-compose the perfection of the human being with soul and body. There will therefore be bodies as well. It is true that this refers to resurrected bodies—the characteristics of which it is very difficult to speak about (see 1 Cor 15:35–50)—but they will still be bodies, which by definition occupy a space. (3) At least Christ and Mary are already in Heaven with their bodies as well. Their corporeality, therefore, is "situated" in Paradise.[19] Although we should carefully avoid any imaginative exaggeration when we dare to speak of the "other world,"

---

[17] "*Homo non est anima tantum*" ("the human being is not only a soul": *ST* I, q. 75, a. 4 [our translation]). "The integrity of human nature consists both in the soul and the body" (Saint Thomas Aquinas, *Summa contra gentiles* IV, ch. 41). Saint Augustine of Hippo, *De civitate Dei* 19.3, had already praised Marcus Terentius Varro (d. 27 BC) because he taught that man is "neither the soul alone nor the body alone but the combination of body and soul." About this Varronian *et-et*, Augustine emphasizes that the same author "has no doubt whatever that of these two the soul is the better and by far the nobler element" (in *FCNT*, vol. 24, trans. Gerald G. Walsh and Daniel J. Honan [Washington, DC: CUA Press, 1954], 191–192).

[18] See *ST*, "Supplement," q. 69, a. 1. The reasons that follow in our text, however, are not taken from this article of the *Summa*.

[19] "We believe that the multitude of those gathered around Jesus and Mary in Paradise forms the Church of Heaven where [*ubi*!] in eternal beatitude they see God as He is" (Saint Paul VI, *Credo of the People of God* [1968]).

we do need to leave the door open to the consideration of the last things as places. They are, therefore, *both* states of existence *and* localized "kingdoms," although it is difficult to explain in this case the concept of place, which comes to be understood in an analogous and not univocal way with respect to the common use of the word.

Saint Augustine deals with the problem in these terms:

> No hearing should be given to the advocates of the theory that Hell is found in this life and not after death. Let them devise their interpretations of the poets' fictions. We must not depart from the authority of Sacred Scripture; on this alone our faith in this matter rests. We may, however, be able to show that the wise men among the pagans had no doubt at all about the reality of the lower world, where the souls of the dead are received after this life. But why the lower world is said to be under the earth, if it is not a corporeal place, or why it is called the lower world (*inferi*), if it is not under the earth—these are questions that are discussed, and not without reason. But the soul is incorporeal, and this I proclaim confidently, not as my opinion but as certain knowledge. However, anyone who says that it is impossible for the soul to have a likeness of the body or of any members of the body ought also to deny that the soul in sleep sees itself walking or sitting or being borne away and returned, now this way, now that, on foot or through the air. None of this happens without some likeness of the body. Hence, if the soul in the lower world bears this likeness, which is not corporeal, but similar to a body, it seems also that it is in a place not corporeal but like the corporeal, whether at rest or in torment.[20]

---

[20] Saint Augustine of Hippo, *De Genesi ad litteram* 12.33.62, in *The Literal Meaning of Genesis*, vol. 2, trans. John Hammond Taylor (New York: Newman Press, 1982), 224–225). All of book 12 develops a dense interpretation of 2 Corinthians 12:2 in which Saint Paul claims to know a man (himself) who was elevated in a vision up to the third heaven and saw Paradise. While highlighting the eminently intellectual character of this vision and, reflexively, the primarily spiritual character of Paradise, Augustine remains suspended in an *et-et* that also makes him recognize a certain localization of the kingdom of the blessed. In the *Enarrationes in Psalmos* 85.17–18, the Doctor comments on the verse: "You have rescued me from the depths of Sheol—*Eruisti animam meam ex inferno inferiori*" (Ps 86:13) and he recognizes that there must be two hells, because Scripture would not speak of "*infernus inferior*" ("lower hell"), if not to distinguish a higher and lower one. Or, he continues, it refers to the lowest part of Hell, where the worst sinners are punished. However, here too we find a recourse to a "local" expressive register. The terminology of the "lower hell" is found in the epistle *Super Quibusdam ad Mekhithar Catholicon Armen-*

3.2. The Separate Souls

The problem of the "separate souls" may be even more difficult. It must be understood in the context of what we have already said, both on the anthropological level (creation and fall) and the Christological level (see Chapters Three and Four). Human beings are certainly not only souls. The Second Vatican Council teaches, "made of body and soul, man is one—*corpore et anima unus*."[21] In these terms, the Council translates the classical Scholastic teaching, which says that human beings are "composed of soul and body." The real distinction between soul and body and their ineliminable reciprocal relationship has not only been taught by classical philosophy, but also dogmatically defined by the Church:

> We reject as erroneous and contrary to the truth of the Catholic faith any doctrine or opinion that rashly asserts that the substance of the rational and intellectual soul is not truly and of itself the form of the human body [*corporis forma*] or that calls this into doubt. In order that the truth of the pure faith may be known to all and the path to error barred, we define [*definientes*] that from now on whoever presumes to assert, defend, or obstinately hold that the rational and intellectual soul is not of itself and essentially [*per se et essentialiter*] the form of the human body is to be censured as a heretic.[22]

The tone of the text clearly suggests—despite the differing opinions of some interpreters—that the Ecumenical Council of Vienne intends to dogmatically define that the soul is the "form" of the human body. The Council resorts to the philosophical terminology of form and matter, even if the origin of the dogma is not philosophical wisdom, but rather Scripture and the Apostolic Tradition. The form-matter binomial is used because it is believed that it effectively explains what God has revealed about the constitution of the human being, whose unity is given by the relationship between soul and body. The corporeal matter is the passive principle that is "informed" by the soul. The human form, in turn, tends toward matter to "inform it," because *per se* it

---

iorum (1351) of Pope Clement VI: "By descending into hell, Christ did not destroy the lower hell" (*Doctrinae Erroribus Armeniorum Speciatim Oppositae*, §13 [DS 1077]).

[21] Second Vatican Council, *Gaudium et Spes*, §14.

[22] Council of Vienne, *Fidei Catholicae (contra errores Petro Iohannis Olivio attribute*; 1312) (DS 902). See *ST* I, q. 75, a. 1 (the soul is not corporeal and is the act of the body); q. 75, a. 4 ("It is proper to the nature of the soul to be the form of a body" [our translation]); q. 76, a. 1.

always subsists with its informed matter. This is exactly what gives rise to the problem that we are dealing with: If the human being is a unity between soul and body and there is no human being without this unity, then is it truly possible that after death and for a very long time (millennia . . .), the soul subsists as separate from its body? In a dualistic view of anthropology, in which body and soul are not reciprocally matter and form, this problem is not present. But the great theological-ecclesial Tradition has never accepted (at least not officially) that dualism by which the Eastern Fathers have been tempted, at least regarding the themes of matrimonial and sexual morality. The Church sees human being as *"corpore et anima unus."* But then, when somebody dies, how can the human form be separated from human matter?

This question is further complicated by recalling the words of Saint Thomas: *"Anima separata est pars rationalis naturae, scilicet humanae, et non tota natura rationalis humana, et ideo non est persona"* ("The soul separated [from the body] is part of the rational nature, i.e., human nature, and not the whole rational human nature; and thus it is not a person").[23] It thus seems that the saints of Paradise and the other souls of the great beyond are not persons. We need, however, to read this teaching of the Angelic Doctor in its context, which is that of explaining and defending the famous definition—we have already encountered it in Chapter Six—of Saint Severinus Boethius (d. ca. 525), for whom the person is "an individual substance of a rational nature" (*"naturae rationalis individua substantia"*).[24] Saint Thomas, therefore, does not propose saying that the soul and body are inseparable, but rather that the concept of human person requires the composition of the two. Moreover, he respects the original context of the Boethian statement, which was Christological and not anthropological: in fact, he says that the person is *"substantia individua"* in the sense of *"quoddam completum per se existens"* ("something complete existing/ subsisting *per se*"). He concludes that the humanity in Christ, obviously composed of soul and body, is not a person; otherwise there would be two persons in Jesus, which would represent Nestorianism (as we saw in Chapter Four). In fact, humanity in Christ does not subsist *"per se"*; it subsists in the Person of the Word. In the chapter on the Redeemer, we have mentioned the mystery of His descent into hell after death: the soul and body of Christ separate from each other and yet remain assumed by the Person of the Word, who until then

---

[23] Saint Thomas Aquinas, *De potentia* 9.2 (our translation); see *ST* I, q. 29, a. 1: "The soul is only a part of the human being . . . thus neither the definition nor the name of person suits it."

[24] Saint Severinus Boethius, *Liber de persona et de duabus naturis contra Eutychen et Nestorium* 3 (our translation).

had assumed them in their natural conjunction, and after His death on the cross continued to assume them in their unnatural separation, until they were reunited by the Resurrection.

For the rest of humanity, in speaking of our existence as "persons," we can say that the soul and body *per se* still do not make the human person, but that the person exists only insofar as the union of a soul and body subsists *per se*. In death, the original union of our nature is separated in an unnatural way (against the plan of God). This, as we have seen in the chapter on God the Creator, is one of the most dramatic consequences of original sin: man, created as a unity of soul and body, now knows their separation. The spirit breathed by God into our nostrils abandons the body, and it decomposes in the earth. Even this dramatic separation is therefore revealed by God, as well as the fact that the dead are judged by God and sent to the "place" where they belong (see, for example, the parable of the poor Lazarus and the rich glutton: Luke 16:19–31, to which we shall return later). Theology is responsible for seeking to understand, as far as is possible, the mystery of this separation, which is unnatural, but nevertheless real.

Saint Thomas, in a long and very important article of the *Summa*—which we cannot explore in detail here—examines the union of the soul (form) with the body, especially highlighting the intellectual principle of the soul, which marks it not only as superior to the body, but also as principle of consciousness and of the distinction of the agent subject: "The principle by which a being immediately operates is the form of the subject to which the operation is attributed [*forma eius cui operatio attribuitur*]."[25] From this we deduce that, although the soul and the person do not coincide (either in the common man or in Christ as man), it is especially the soul—and subordinately the body—that carries out what is attributed to the subject, to the "who." In fact, the body performs its activities through the movement of the soul, which is therefore, in the composition of human nature, what primarily identifies the person who performs what is being done.[26] Applying this general observation to the eschatological sphere, we understand that in the "intermediate state," God can also reward or punish the souls alone—which for the moment are separated from their bodies—because, although they are not complete human persons in themselves, they are still responsible for the merit or demerit attributed to persons. Saint Thomas affirms in different places of his work that the

---

[25] *ST* I, q. 76, a. 1 (our translation).

[26] "The soul communicates to the matter of the body, which together with it forms one single entity, the being of its own subsistence, in such a way that the being of the composition is nothing but the being of the soul" (*ST* I, q. 76, a. 1 [our translation]).

The Last Things

souls can subsist even when separated from the body (the reverse affirmation, however, is not true).[27] This does not negate the fact that the condition of the soul separated from the body is and can only be transitory: the soul tends naturally toward being united with matter.[28] This is why the Christian faith speaks of two Judgments: a particular one immediately after death,[29] and a final one with which human beings occupy the "place" that is proper to them as complete human beings. The Church believes in the final resurrection of bodies and in the reunification of bodies with their souls,[30] which is why the Church respects bodies even when they are separated from their souls.[31] The eschatology of the intermediate state is clearly provisional, and salvation

---

[27] "The intellectual soul by virtue of its being is united to the body as its form; and nonetheless, when the body perishes, the soul continues in its being" (*ST* I, q. 76, a. 2 [our translation]). "The soul remains in its being, even when the body perishes: it is not so with the other forms" (q. 76, a. 1 [our translation]).

[28] "The soul is made naturally to be united to the body, like it belongs to a light body to be raised up. And as the latter always remains light even when removed from its proper place, and maintains the attitude and inclination towards its natural place; thus, the human soul remains in its being, when separated from the body, maintaining its disposition and natural inclination to be reunited with the body" (*ST* I, q. 76, a. 1, ad 6 [our translation]). "The soul is only one part of the human being and as such, even when it is separated it retains the capacity for reunion [to the body: *retinet naturam unibilitatis*]" (*ST* I, q. 29, a. 1 [our translation]). See Saint Thomas Aquinas, *Super I ad Corintios* 15, d. 2.

[29] See, further along, the teaching of Benedict XII.

[30] *Didache* (late first century) 16.6; Saint Clement I (d. ca. 100), *Ad Corinthios* 24–26; Saint Ignatius of Antioch (d. ca. 107), *Ad Smyrnenses* 2; Saint Polycarp of Smyrna (d. 155), *Epistula II ad Filippenses* 5.2; (Ps.-) Clement I, *Epistula II ad Corinthios* [between 140 and 160] 9.1–5; Saint Justin Martyr (d. 165), *I Apologia* 18.6; Tatian the Syrian (d. ca. 180), *Oratio ad graecos* 6; furthermore, the entire treatise of Athenagoras of Athens (d. ca. 190), *De resurrectione mortuorum*; etc. The Magisterium also abounds in references to the resurrection of the flesh: see, for example, the Second Council of Lyon, *Professio Fidei Michaëlis Palaelogi Imperatoris* (1274): "We believe also (in) the true resurrection of this body that we now bear.... The same most Holy Roman Church firmly believes and firmly asserts that nevertheless on the Day of Judgment all human persons will appear with their bodies before the judgment seat of Christ" (DS 854; 859).

[31] "Following the most ancient Christian Tradition, the Church insistently recommends that the bodies of the deceased be buried in cemeteries or other sacred places.... Burial is above all the most fitting way to express faith and hope in the resurrection of the body.... By burying the bodies of the faithful, the Church confirms her faith in the resurrection of the body, and intends to show the great dignity of the human body as an integral part of the human person whose body forms part of their identity" (Congregation for the Doctrine of the Faith, *Ad Resurgendum cum Christo* [2016], §3). For this reason, "the Church continues to prefer the practice of burying the bodies of the deceased, because this shows a greater esteem towards the deceased. Nevertheless, cremation is not prohibited, 'unless it was chosen for reasons contrary to Christian doctrine'" (Congregation for the Doctrine of the Faith, *Ad Resurgendum cum Christo*, §4).

is definitively accomplished with the Final Judgment only. Thus, even those who are already saints in Heaven are still in waiting.[32] This does not imply that the eschatological resurrection is a natural fact, already inscribed in the tendency of the created soul as form of the body.[33] This resurrection and glorification remain a gratuitous supernatural gift, which is not owed to us. But it is not something that goes against the nature of human beings; on the contrary, it elevates and confirms it.

4. The Limbo of the Fathers and the Limbo of Infants

4.1 Limbus Patrum

The Limbo of the Fathers (or "of the Patriarchs") is the state of life in which the souls of the righteous dead who came before Christ had to await the coming of Christ the Redeemer. As the reader may remember from Chapter Three, among the consequences of original sin was the closing of the door to Eden (see Gen 3:23–24): man could no longer recover friendship with God. This is why no one could reach their ultimate end, that is, cross the threshold of Heaven to enter Paradise. Nevertheless, even before the coming of the Redeemer, there were good and righteous people who did not despise God and therefore did not merit Hell. The theological tradition, based on Scripture,[34] has thus developed the concept of *limbus patrum*: all of the righteous who lived before Christ waited in Limbo—a state of waiting without the suffering of Hell or the joy of the vision of God—for the coming of Jesus, the Conqueror of sin and death.[35] The Gospel refers to this reality of the Limbo

---

[32] "[The soul] possesses a kind of natural appetite for managing the body. By reason of this appetite it is somehow hindered from going on with all its force to the highest Heaven, so long as it is not joined with the body, for it is in managing the body that this appetite is satisfied" (Saint Augustine, *De Genesi ad litteram* 12.35.68, in *The Literal Meaning of Genesis*, vol. 2, 229).

[33] "The principle or cause of the resurrection cannot be nature, although it ends with the restoration of natural life" (*ST*, "Supplement," q. 75, a. 3 [our translation]). Even more so, the resurrection cannot be explained on the basis of a supposed natural inclination of the "ashes" to reunite with the soul (see q. 78, a. 3).

[34] See Acts 2:27, 31; Luke 16:23, 26; 1 Pet 3:19; 2 Cor 5:8.

[35] In a letter to Archbishop Humbert of Arles (by the title *Maiores Ecclesiae Causas* [1201]), Pope Innocent III writes: "Even though original sin was remitted by the mystery of circumcision [in the Old Testament] and the danger of damnation avoided, nevertheless, one could not enter into the kingdom of Heaven, which remained closed

of the Fathers in three places in particular: (1) In the parable of Luke 16, known as the parable of the rich glutton. It is noteworthy that Christ tells it before His Death and Resurrection, therefore, when the Limbo of the Fathers still existed. The Lord tells of the poor and good Lazarus who, once dead, reached the "bosom of Abraham." Theological tradition sees an indication of the *limbus patrum* in that parable, where Abraham is found with Moses, David, Adam himself, the prophets up to Saint John the Baptist, along with all of those who had merited salvation. (2) In the difficult passage of Matthew 27, which speaks of the dead saints who leave their tombs—opened up at the time of Jesus' death—after His resurrection and were seen in Jerusalem. (3) In Jesus' words to the so-called "good thief," when He assures him: "Amen, I say to you, today you will be with me in Paradise" (Luke 23:43). As has been rightly noted, Christ Himself was not in Paradise on that "today" and, technically, He was not there three days later, that is, at the moment of His Resurrection. As we saw when we discussed it, Christ would go to Paradise a little more than forty days after the crucifixion, that is, on the day of His Ascension. How can Christ tell the good thief that he will be in Paradise with Him on the day he dies? The most credible opinion recognizes that in using the word "Paradise" here, Jesus is not referring to Heaven, to the dwelling of God, but rather to the so-called "bosom of Abraham," which indicates the dwelling of the righteous souls after death, to which the Lord Himself referred in the parable of Luke 16.[36] The real distinction between Hell, where the rich glutton is found, and this "place" that we call the *limbus patrum*, is clearly inferred from this parable.[37] In fact, Abraham says to the rich glutton: "between us and you a great chasm is established." Here too we should not imagine a chasm in the literal sense (à la Dante Alighieri). This term indicates, in a concrete and easily comprehensible way, that there is no communication between these two worlds: that the damned souls can never pass into the *limbus patrum*, and vice versa; that is, in the great beyond it is impossible to change one's state of life.

Finally, we must also recall what the Scripture says about the fact that Christ, after His death, went into the underworld to liberate the spirits that

---

to all until the death of Christ" (DS 780).

[36] In the Greek text of Luke 16:22 we find the word *kolpos*—breast or chest or bosom—referring to Abraham. To be "in the bosom of" means being very close and in intimate friendship with someone, like when the beloved disciple of Jesus rested his head on the bosom/chest of Jesus during the last supper (see John 13:25 where the word *stethos*—chest [also in the figurative sense as the center of the soul or of sentiments] or sternum—is used).

[37] See Saint Augustine of Hippo, *De Genesi ad litteram* 12.33.63; 12.34.66; *ST*, "Supplement," q. 69, a. 4.

were imprisoned there, as we have already seen earlier in Chapter Four. In the Symbol of the faith, this victorious entrance of Christ in the *limbus patrum* is called the "descent to the dead/to hell" (also theologically called the "harrowing of hell"). From that moment, the Limbo of the Fathers has ceased to exist, as Saint Gregory (d. 604) taught: "After the coming of the Mediator who has to come into this world, we are led to the kingdom immediately after we leave the body, and we obtain without delay what the ancient Fathers instead merited to perceive with great delay."[38]

4.2. Limbus Puerorum

Another eschatological reality is the *limbus puerorum*. This is not a reality that is revealed directly by the Scripture, but it is a very ancient, widespread, and traditional theological thesis, which derives from a revealed truth—that of the necessity of Baptism for eternal life.[39] Since Christ revealed that we need to be reborn from on high to enter into the kingdom of Heaven (see John 3), from the most ancient times the Fathers and Doctors wondered what becomes of the babies who died before receiving Baptism and without having committed any personal sin. The doctrine of the Limbo of Infants responds that they do not go to Hell because they have no personal sin, but they also do not go to Heaven because they are guilty of the original sin that has not been washed by Baptism.[40] The Limbo of infants would therefore be a state of life in the great beyond in which the souls do not suffer the pains of Hell but also do not enjoy the beatific vision of God. Depending on the author, then, they hypothesize either the suffering of small torments,[41] or the total absence of all torments

---

[38] "*Illud sine mora percipimus, quod antiqui patres cum magna percipere dilatione meruerunt*" (Saint Gregory the Great, *Homiliae in Evangelia* 1.19.4 [our translation]).

[39] See what was said about this in Chapter Ten (the section on Baptism).

[40] "It is quite foolish (to imagine) that little children can be given the rewards of eternal life even without the grace of Baptism.... Those who claim this (i.e., eternal life) for them without their being born again seem to me to wish to make Baptism itself null and void, since they proclaim that these (children) have that which, it is believed, cannot be conferred upon them except by Baptism. If, therefore, they wish (to maintain) that not being born again is not of any consequence, it is necessary that they also profess that the sacred cleansing of rebirth does no good" (Saint Innocent I, *Inter ceteras Ecclesiae Romanae* (417), ch. 5 [DS 219]. See the Fifteenth Synod of Carthage [DS 224] of the next year). According to Saint Thomas, Christ did not free these children when He descended into the *limbus patrum* (see *ST* III, q. 52, a. 7).

[41] For example, Saint Augustine of Hippo, *Enchiridion de fide, spe et charitate* 23.93, in *FCNT*, vol. 2, trans. Bernard M. Peebles (Washington, DC: CUA Press, 1947), 446: "Surely the lightest punishment will be for those who added no sin to that which they

and the experience of purely natural joy (which includes natural knowledge and love of God). It is certain, however, for most if not all of the authors, that babies who died without Baptism—and without personal sins—are certainly not punished like the souls damned to Hell.[42] This is because it would be unjust to punish original sin, which is received without personal consent, with the same severity as sins consciously committed. Innocent III therefore specifies that: "The penalty of original sin is the deprivation of the vision of God, but the punishment of actual sin is the torment of eternal Hell."[43] It follows that in Limbo, unbaptized babies live in a state of simple natural happiness, not achieving their supernatural end, but also being spared the infernal torments that they have not deserved.[44] What is ruled out, however, is that the Limbo of infants is a place in which the supernatural happiness of Paradise is enjoyed in an inferior way.[45] The *limbus puerorum* is not, in fact, an intermediate place between Heaven and Hell:

---

brought with them originally." Augustine does not speak of Limbo as an intermediate "place" between Heaven and Hell, thinking instead of a "region" of Hell in which very light punishments are applied (see *Sermo 294*.3). In a different way, his distant disciple Saint Fulgentius of Ruspe (d. 533), in *De Fide Trinitatis ad Petrum diaconum* 27, writes: "Believe most firmly and do not doubt in any way that not only adults gifted with reason, but also children . . . having died without the Sacrament of Baptism, administered in the name of the Father and of the Son and of the Holy Spirit, will be subject to torment without end in the eternal fire" (our translation). This rigor, however, does not represent the traditional position of the Church and is explained in the context of the sour polemic against the Pelagians, of whom we have already discussed when speaking of the theme of grace (Pelagius believed that children could be saved without Baptism because he doubted the universal transmission of the sin of Adam).

[42] See Second Council of Lyon, *Professio Fidei Michäelis Palaeologi Imperatoris* (1274): it is argued that both those who die in mortal sin and those who die with only original sin do not go to Paradise and descend "*in Infernum*," but that these two categories of dead are punished "*poenis disparibus*" ("with different punishments") (DS 858).

[43] Innocent III, *Maiores Ecclesiae Causas* (DS 780).

[44] Thus, for Saint Thomas, the only penalty for children in Limbo is the privation of glory (see *ST* "Supplement," q. 69, a. 6), that is, the so-called "pain of loss." According to Saint Thomas, there would be no "pain of sense," that is, no suffering (*ST* I-II, q. 89, a. 6; Saint Thomas Aquinas, *De malo* 5.2–3). A text may also be seen, which is an annex to the *Summa*, but whose authorship is uncertain: see *ST*, "Appendix II," q. 1–2.

[45] Whoever says "that it is understood that in the kingdom of Heaven there is some place in the middle or elsewhere where little children may live blessedly even if they have gone forth from this world without Baptism, without which they cannot enter into the kingdom of Heaven, which is everlasting life, let him be anathema" (Fifteenth Synod of Carthage, *De Peccato Originali* (418), can. 3 [DS 224]).

The doctrine that rejects as a Pelagian fable that place in the netherworld (which the faithful commonly designate by the name of the Limbo of Children) in which the souls of the dead with only original sin are punished with the punishment of damnation without the punishment of fire, as if those who remove the punishment of fire were thereby introducing some intermediate place and state exempt from guilt and punishment between the kingdom of God and eternal damnation, as the Pelagians have imagined, (is) false, rash, and injurious to Catholic schools.[46]

Since the "pain of loss" (that is, the lack of the vision of God) is present, Limbo is considered more as a "detached district" of Hell,[47] than an "antechamber" of Paradise.[48]

The theological doctrine on the Limbo of Infants, which boasts a solid (even magisterial) Tradition, has never been dogmatically defined by the Church; therefore, discussion about it remains open. It must also be said that this is a very ancient doctrine in its origin and that it has been handed down and developed throughout the course of the ecclesial Tradition even to our time. These elements cannot be easily overlooked. In the Liturgy, the Church has never prayed for babies who died without Baptism and even denied them ecclesiastical burial. Only with the Roman Missal of 1970 was a funeral Mass introduced for such babies, which allowed the *Catechism* to affirm—probably for the first time in a magisterial text—that "as regards children who have died without Baptism, the Church can only entrust them to the mercy of God, as she does in her funeral rites for them," and the *Catechism* adds that we are allowed "to hope that there is a way of salvation" for them (CCC §1261). Without wanting to defend the doctrine of the *limbus puerorum* to the bitter end, we still need to say that, unless it is *demonstrated* from the theological standpoint and it is taught *officially* by the Magisterium (not by

---

[46] Pius VI, *Auctorem Fidei* (1794), §26 (DS 2626).

[47] According to *ST*, "Supplement," q. 69, a. 6, the *limbus puerorum* is located in the higher part of Hell (and was underneath the Limbo of the Fathers, while it still existed).

[48] "The souls, however, of those who die in mortal sin or with original sin only descend immediately [*mox*] into Hell; to be punished, though with different pains and in different places [*locis*]" (John XXII, *Nequaquam sine Dolore* [1321] [DS 926]): a pronouncement confirmed by the Council of Florence, *Laetentur Caeli* [1439] [DS1306]). About ten years later, John XXII began to teach differently, that is, that the eternal reward or punishment did not happen immediately [*mox*] after death, but only after the Last Judgment. However, he recanted this position the day before he died (see *Ne Super His* [1334] [DS 990–991]).

para-magisterial commissions) that it is nothing more than a *theologoumenon* (theological opinion), the mere possibility that it exists is a sufficient reason not to delay the Baptism of newborns,[49] which is an unfortunately common occurrence today. It seems right to baptize babies as early as possible, without giving priority to theological-pastoral motivations which, upon a careful analysis, actually prove rather inconsistent, especially compared to what is at stake (eternal life).

5. Death

The first of the *Novissimi* mentioned by the *Compendium of the Catechism* is Death.

5.1. The Reality of Death

Like birth, death is a part of life. Everyone who is born must die.[50] A popular saying wisely recognizes that in our earthly life everything is uncertain and that 'the only certainty in life is death.'[51] However, the meaning of death and

---

[49] The document of the Congregation for the Doctrine of the Faith, *Pastoralis Actio* (1980), which deserves to be read carefully, notes (among many valuable observations) that: "The Church has thus shown by her teaching and practice [!] that she knows no other way apart from Baptism for ensuring children's entry into eternal happiness. Accordingly, she takes care not to neglect the mission that the Lord has given her of providing rebirth 'of water and the Spirit' for all those who can be baptized" (§13).

[50] See, in Chapter Three, the quote of *ST* II-II, q. 164, a. 1, ad 1, where Saint Thomas explains the sense in which death is, on the one hand, a natural fact, and on the other, the consequence of original sin.

[51] Similar wisdom is recounted in Saint Augustine of Hippo, *Enarrationes in Psalmos* 38.19: "What is certain on this earth? Only death. Consider all the vicissitudes of this life, both good and bad, all that befalls us in our righteousness or in our iniquity. What among all these is certain? Only death. You have made some progress, have you? You know what you are today, but you do not know what you will be tomorrow. A sinner, are you? You know what you are today, but not what you will be tomorrow. You hope to get money, but whether it will come your way is uncertain. You hope to find a wife, but it is uncertain whether you will find one, or what she will be like if you do. You hope to have children, but you cannot be certain that any will be born. If they are born, it is not certain that they will survive. If they do live, you cannot know whether they will grow up well or prove to be weaklings. Whichever way you turn, everything is uncertain except for one sole certainty: death [*incerta omnia, sola mors certa*]. If you are poor, there is no certainty that you will ever be rich; if you are uneducated, you cannot be certain of being taught; if you are in poor health, it is uncertain whether you can recover your strength. You have been born, and so you can at least be certain that you will die, but even in this certainty

the mode of death is different depending on whether or not the Gospel of Christ has reached the person, influencing his or her convictions and behavior.[52] Death has been a central element of the Christian faith from the beginning, along with (new) life. Jesus speaks of having come to suffer and to die (see Mark 10:45; Matt 16:21; etc.). As we saw in the part dedicated to redemption, it is precisely through Jesus' sacrificial death that we are liberated from the power of death. This is why Saint Paul could joyously exclaim: "Death is swallowed up in victory. / Where, O death, is your victory?" (1 Cor 15:54–55). That death that has reached all human beings because of the sin of Adam (see Rom 5) is defeated by the work of Christ. Nonetheless, all the baptized—even those who are saints—die. Therefore, a distinction is necessary here; a distinction that allows us to understand death in different senses: (1) Death as a natural fact: meaning the end of life on this earth. As we saw in Chapter Three, this would be part of the natural destiny of human beings, even if they did not sin, but it would not be marked by the drama that we experience as fallen creatures. (2) Death as a preternatural fact: this above all indicates the loss of the goods given by God to man in Eden—sin, in fact, involves the death of the soul through the loss of grace. (3) Death as an experiential fact: from Adam on, we humans have always experienced—and always will experience—death as tragedy, physical and moral pain, doubt, and anxiety. All of this is due to the state of human beings as fallen creatures, which can be renewed with the grace of Christ to rise again to new life, and yet remain bound to the damage caused by sin.[53] (4) Death as the personification of the devil who, inducing man to sin, has succeeded in condemning all humankind to sin's law of death.

5.2. Death as Mystery

From all this complexity, it emerges that death is a mystery, which man cannot comprehend with natural reason alone. Its meaning (as well as the way to

---

of death uncertainty lurks, because you do not know the day of your death" (in *The Works of Saint Augustine: A Translation for the 21st Century*, vol. III/16, trans. Maria Boulding [Hyde Park, NY: New City Press, 2002], 190).

[52] See the *excursus* on the Christian meaning of suffering in Chapter Four.

[53] "'It is called death because it is bitter, or it is called this way because of the bite taken by the first human being. In fact when the progenitor of the human kind, disobeying, touched the forbidden tree, through the bite he fell into death' [*per morsum mortem*]. Precisely for this reason, from the morsel death itself takes its name [*a morsu mors*]" (Saint Julian of Toledo [d. 690], *Prognosticum futuri saeculi* 1.4, trans. Tommaso Stancati [New York: The Newman Press, 2010], 380). This work represents the oldest systematic treatise of eschatology.

prepare for and deal with it) must be illuminated by the supernatural Revelation of God, without which one may grasp true aspects, but not the whole truth about the mystery of death:

> It is in the face of death that the [enigma of] human existence grows most acute. Not only is man tormented by pain and by the advancing deterioration of his body, but even more so by a dread of perpetual extinction. He rightly follows the intuition of his heart when he abhors and repudiates the utter ruin and total disappearance of his own person. He rebels against death because he bears in himself an eternal seed which cannot be reduced to sheer matter. . . . Although the mystery of death utterly [eludes] the imagination, the Church has been taught by divine Revelation and firmly teaches that man has been created by God for a blissful purpose beyond the reach of earthly misery. In addition, that bodily death from which man would have been immune had he not sinned will be vanquished, according to the Christian faith, when man who was ruined by his own doing is restored to wholeness by the almighty and merciful Savior. For God has called man and still calls him so that with his entire being he might be joined to Him in an endless sharing of a divine life beyond all corruption. Christ won this victory when He rose to life, for by His death He freed man from death.[54]

An example of the fact that the mystery of death can only be fully illuminated by the light of divine Revelation is found in the doctrine of the metempsychosis or transmigration of souls, which is present in different philosophies and religious systems. This doctrine imagines that death is repeatable, since, according to it, the earthly life of human beings would be repeatable, because they would be reincarnated in a cyclical way and, at least according to some systems of thought, could also be reincarnated in forms of life that are inferior to the human form, such as animals or plants. Christian Revelation, on the contrary, teaches that "it is appointed that human beings die once, and after this the judgment" (Heb 9:27), thus eliminating every possible reincarnationist doctrine at the root. Earthly life is unrepeatable: it is a passage through which human beings, created by God and redeemed by Him in Christ, can, by accepting the grace of Christ poured out by the Holy Spirit, be purified from their sins and merit eternal life. There is one death, just as there is one life, and human beings are judged immediately after it. On

---

[54] Second Vatican Council, *Gaudium et Spes*, §18.

the other hand, the unicity of death and the sudden destination of the human being in his or her deserved "place" is revealed with incontestable clarity in the event of the first Man who also rose from the dead: Jesus Christ.

5.3. The "Second Death"

Naturally, the fact that there is only one death refers to death in a physical sense, not a spiritual sense. From the spiritual standpoint, in fact, Scripture uses the expression "second death" (Rev 2:11) to indicate the eternal damnation that the "winners" escape, that is, those who have fought and won the good fight of faith (see 1 Tim 1:18; 6:12; 2 Tim 4:7; Eph 6:12; 2 Cor 10:3).

5.4. Christian Preparation for Death

Christian spirituality has always been very well-nourished by the theme of death and by preparing for it through a holy life. We can recall here the treatise of *De arte bene moriendi*, written by Saint Robert Bellarmine in 1620, or the better-known *Preparation for Death* (Italian original: *Apparecchio alla morte*) printed in 1758 by Saint Alphonsus de Liguori—both authors are Doctors of the Church. We can also go much further back in time to the succinct attestation of Saint Irenaeus (d. ca. 202), for whom, "The business of the Christian is nothing else than to be ever preparing for death."[55]

For those who live far from Christ, and for those who are little transformed by His Gospel even while professing it, death remains an agonizing and terrible moment. However, for those who are already transformed by the Lord in this life, death no longer assumes the characteristic of fear or doubt, but rather peace and joy. "Undoubtedly, death is the penalty of all who come to birth on earth as descendants of the first man; nevertheless, if the penalty is paid in the name of justice and piety, it becomes a new birth in Heaven. Although death is the punishment of sin, sometimes it secures for the soul a grace that is a security against all punishment for sin."[56] This is not because "death, which before was an evil, has now become something good. But it means that God has rewarded faith with so much grace that death, which

---

[55] Saint Irenaeus of Lyon, *Fragmentum* 11, in *ANF*, vol. 1, trans. James Donaldson and Alexander Roberts (Peabody, MA: Hendrickson Publishers, Inc., 1994), 570. See Chapter Four, note 8.

[56] Saint Augustine of Hippo, *De civitate Dei* 13.6, in *FCNT*, vol. 14, trans. Gerald G. Walsh and Grace Monahan (Washington, DC: CUA Press, 2008), 306–307.

seems to be the enemy of life, becomes an ally that helps man enter into life."[57] Thus, "the Christian who unites his own death to that of Jesus views it as a step towards him and an entrance into everlasting life" (CCC §1020).

The saints have always considered death as a blessing (not in its tragic side, but in its outcome: the unfolding of eternal life). Saint Francis of Assisi (d. 1226) even used to attribute the appellative of "sister" to it, and Saint Teresa of Ávila (d. 1582) sings in her poetry:[58]

> My God, how sad is
> Life without You!
> *Longing to see You,*
> *Death I desire.*
>
> This earth's journey
> How long it is;
> A painful dwelling,
> An exile drear.
> Oh, Master adored,
> Take me away!
> *Longing to see You,*
> *Death I desire.*
>
> [...]
>
> O kind death
> Free me from trials!
> Gentle are your blows,
> Freeing the soul.
> Oh, my Beloved, what joy
> To be joined to You!
> *Longing to see you*
> *Death I desire.*
>
> [...]

---

[57] *De civitate Dei* 13.4, in *FCNT*, vol. 14, 305.
[58] Saint Teresa of Ávila, *Poetry*, no. 7: "Lamentations of Exile," in *The Collected Works of St. Teresa of Avila*, vol. 3, trans. Kieran Kavanaugh and Otilio Rodriguez (Washington, DC: CUA Press, 1985, 382–383).

Who fears
The body's death
If one then gains
Pleasure so great?
Oh, yes, in loving You,
Forever, my God!
*Longing to see You,
Death I desire.*

[...]

As we can see from the text, the desire for death is not the same as the desire to die (which is and remains an evil), but rather it is the effect of death that is desired by those who love God: to be with Him forever. The Christian desire for death is not the desire of dying, a self-destructive tendency, a refusal of life, but rather a course toward the true and definitive life. Saint Paul has manifested in himself the sentiment of those who make of their own life a service to the Gospel. He neither desired to live nor to die, but to do the will of God in life and in death—although his heart would prefer death, in order to finally be with Christ:

> ... now as always, Christ will be magnified in my body, whether by life or by death. For to me life is Christ, and death is gain. If I go on living in the flesh, that means fruitful labor for me. And I do not know which I shall choose. I am caught between the two. I long to depart this life and be with Christ, [for] that is far better. Yet that I remain [in] the flesh is more necessary for your benefit. (Phil 1:20–24)

The way one dies is therefore indicative of the way in which one has lived: with or without Christ. Hence, even in the Old Testament we read: "Call none happy before death, / for how they end, they are known" (Sir 11:28). This, among other things, is why the Church never declares Christians blessed or saints while they are still alive, and also why, once they are dead, she provides for the recognition of their remains in view of such solemn proclamations.[59]

---

[59] See Prospero Lorenzo Lambertini (later Pope Benedict XIV), *De Servorum Dei beatificatione et Beatorum canonizatione*, 4 vols. (5 tomes), Bologna 1734–1738; *editio secunda locupletior* 1743; *editio typica* 1747–1751.

6. Judgment

The Christian image does not allow for an all-just God without mercy, nor does it allow for an all-merciful God without justice. God is always *both* just *and* merciful:

> God is justice and creates justice. This is our consolation and our hope. And in His justice there is also grace. This we know by turning our gaze to the crucified and risen Christ. Both these things—justice and grace—must be seen in their correct inner relationship. Grace does not cancel out justice. It does not make wrong into right. It is not a sponge which wipes everything away, so that whatever someone has done on earth ends up being of equal value.[60]

In this light, it is understood why the God who is Love (see 1 John 4) can also be the eschatological Judge, the Judge of the living and of the dead (see Acts 10:42; 1 Cor 4:4; 2 Tim 4:8; Heb 12:23; James 4:12; 5:9). We have to distinguish the particular Judgment from the Last Judgment in this eschatological reality.

6.1. Particular Judgment

Particular Judgment occurs at the time of death. This Judgment is already definitive, that is, it destines the human being to the condition that corresponds to him or her based on merit from this life: good people have merited salvation, the wicked have merited damnation. It is called particular Judgment because it concerns only the individual person who, right after dying, is judged by God.

> Each man receives his eternal retribution in his immortal soul at the very moment of his death, in a particular judgment that refers his life to Christ: either entrance into the blessedness of heaven—through a purification purification or immediately—or immediate and everlasting damnation. (CCC §1022)

It is a defined doctrine that the Judgment occurs immediately after death and that immediate retribution is likewise given to the soul for its faults or merits.[61]

---

[60] Benedict XVI, *Spe Salvi* (2007), §44.
[61] The Second Council of Lyon, *Professio Fidei Michaëlis Palaelogi Imperatoris*, teaches that

6.2. Last Judgment and the Resurrection of the Flesh

6.2.1. Universal Retribution

The Last Judgment, on the other hand, is the divine work that brings an end to the entire salvific economy. At the end of time, all the dead will rise corporally and will reach "the hour ... in which all who are in the tombs will hear his [Christ's] voice and will come out, those who have done good deeds to the resurrection of life, but those who have done wicked deeds to the resurrection of condemnation" (John 5:28–29). In chapter 25 of the Gospel of Matthew, Jesus also refers to the Final Judgment that He will conduct:

> When the Son of Man comes in his glory, and all the angels with him, he will sit upon his glorious throne, and all the nations will be assembled before him. And he will separate them one from another, as a shepherd separates the sheep from the goats. He will place the sheep on his right and the goats on his left. Then the king will say to those on his right, "Come, you who are blessed by my Father. Inherit the kingdom prepared for you from the foundation of the world ..." Then he will say to those on his left, "Depart from me, you accursed, into the eternal fire prepared for the devil and his angels" (Matt 25:31–34, 41).

6.2.2. Role of the Angels and the Apostles

The angels accompany Christ in this final separation of the good from the evil, and they also actively work in it as "harvesters":

> His disciples approached him and said, "Explain to us the parable of the weeds in the field." He said in reply, "He who sows good seed is the Son of Man, the field is the world, the good seed the children of the kingdom. The weeds are the children of the evil one, and the

---

the souls that die in grace are immediately (*mox*) welcomed into Heaven but those in sin go immediately (*mox* is used again) to Hell (see DS 857–858). The dogmatic definition of this doctrine, however, occurred with Benedict XII, *Benedictus Deus* (1336), who wanted to reiterate this teaching against what his predecessor John XXII had argued (see above, note 48). Benedict XII determines [*diffinimus*] that the souls "immediately after death [*mox post mortem*]" receive the reward due to their merits (DS 1000), in particular, the vision of God.

enemy who sows them is the devil. The harvest is the end of the age, and the harvesters are angels. Just as weeds are collected and burned [up] with fire, so will it be at the end of the age. The Son of Man will send his angels, and they will collect out of his kingdom all who cause others to sin and all evildoers. They will throw them into the fiery furnace, where there will be wailing and grinding of teeth. Then the righteous will shine like the sun in the kingdom of their Father. Whoever has ears ought to hear" (Matt 13:36–43).

In other texts, the angels are given the eschatological role of trumpet players[62] (see Matt 24:31; 1 Cor 15:52; 1 Thess 4:15; Rev 8–11) and that of organizing the various ranks of people under judgment.[63] The twelve Apostles too are presented as collaborators in the Judgment (see Matt 19:28–30), although this does not exclude others.[64] Saint Isidore of Seville believed that in the Judgment there will be two categories of protagonists: those who judge and those who are judged. These two categories are in turn further distinguished, for a total of four:

> There are two different kinds or classifications of human beings in the Judgment, that is, the elect and the wicked. These, however, will be divided into four categories. One classification of perfect ones is that which judges with the Lord and the other is the one that is judged. Both, however, will reign with Christ. Similarly the classification of the wicked is divided into two, whereby those who are evil within the Church need to be both judged and condemned. Those, on the other hand, who are found outside the Church are not judged but only condemned (cf. John 3:18).—For the first classification, composed of those who are judged and will perish, is opposed to that classification of the good ones in which are those who are

---

[62] According to Saint Gregory the Great, "to sound the trumpet means nothing but to show to the world the Son as Judge" (cited by Saint Albert the Great [d. 1280], *Commentarii in IV Sententiarum Librum* d. 43, a. 4 resp. [our translation]).

[63] See Saint Augustine of Hippo, *Enarrationes in Psalmos* 49.11–12; *De civitate Dei* 20.24.

[64] According to Saint Augustine of Hippo, *De civitate Dei* 20.5, the passage of Matt 19 does not mean that only the Apostles will judge, because the number twelve indicates the multitude of those who will judge. Saint Thomas Aquinas pointed out that human beings will judge in the sense that "they will make known to others the verdict of the justice of God" (*ST*, "Supplement," q. 89, a. 1 [our translation]). The angels have several tasks in the Judgment, but they do not judge, except insofar as they approve God's sentence (see q. 89, a. 3).

judged and reign. The second classification, composed of those who are not judged and perish, is opposed to that classification of the perfect ones in which are those who are not judged and reign. The third classification is composed of those who are judged and reign as opposed to that classification in which are those who are judged and perish. The fourth classification is composed of those who are not judged and reign as opposed to that contrary grouping in which are those who are not judged and perish.[65]

6.2.3. Mercy and Justice, Hope and Fear

The merciful acceptance into Heaven for the saved, and the implacable justice towards the wicked, both form part of the concept of the Last Judgment. We can add Matthew 11:20–24 and 12:41–42 (reproach and threats to certain corrupt cities) to the passages cited above. It is also interesting to read the passages in which Christ (or the Evangelist) puts together the prophecies concerning the future destruction of Jerusalem by the Romans with the announcements about the end of the world. A classic treatise on these passages (see Matt 24–25; Mark 12; Luke 16) is found in a famous letter of Saint Augustine to Hesychius.[66] Among the apocalyptic signs of the return (*parousia*[67]) of Christ, the following are foreseen in these texts: "the sun will be darkened, / and the moon will not give its light, / and the stars will fall from the sky, / and the powers of the heavens will be shaken" (Matt 24:29). Saint John Chrysostom (d. 407), in light of the following verse (v. 30)—"And then the sign of the Son of Man will appear in heaven, and all the tribes of the earth will mourn, and they will see the Son of Man coming upon the clouds of heaven with power and great glory"—provides an interesting interpretation of these apocalyptic signs:

---

[65] Saint Isidore of Seville, *Sententiarum libri* 1.27.10–11, trans. Thomas L. Knoebel (New York: The Newman Press, 2018), 80–81.
[66] See Saint Augustine of Hippo, *Epistula 199* (*De fine saeculi*).
[67] From the Greek verb *pareimi*, "to arrive, to be present." The *parousia* is the solemn coming of a great figure. It was also used in ancient times to signal the manifestation of a god. The final *parousia* of the Son of man in glory was already prophesied in Dan 7:13–20. As we have seen, Christ reprises this prophecy by applying it to Himself during His trial before the Sanhedrin (see Matt 26:64, Mark 14:62). There are numerous passages from the New Testament that allude to or explicitly speak about the final *parousia* of Christ Jesus.

The Last Things

The eminence of the splendor of Christ will be so great that even the brightest lights of the sky will be dimmed before the brightness of the divine light. Then "the stars will fall . . . when the sign of the Son of Man will appear in heaven." Have you considered how great is the force of the sign, that is, of the cross? "The sun will be darkened, and the moon will not give its light" (Matt 24:29–30). Instead, the cross will shine and, the heavenly bodies having dimmed and the stars fallen, it alone will radiate light, so that you learn that the cross is brighter than the moon and the sun, whose splendor it will overcome, illuminated by the divine brightness.[68]

The implacable aspect of the Judgment (accompanied, however, by a faithful trust in divine forgiveness[69]) stands out in the famous medieval hymn of *Dies Irae*, which also forms part of the Liturgy: in the extraordinary form of the Roman Rite, in the *Requiem* Mass; and in the ordinary form, in the Liturgy of the Hours, as an optional hymn for the last week of Ordinary Time.

The text of the hymn—often attributed in the past to Thomas of Celano (d. ca. 1265) and set to music by many composers (a very special mention goes to the masterpiece and final work of W.A. Mozart [d. 1791], *Requiem in Re Minore* [K 626])—reads as follows:

Dies Irae, dies illa,	The day of wrath, that day,
solvet saeclum in favilla:	will dissolve the world in ashes,
teste David cum Sybilla.	David having witnessed along with Sibyl.
Quantus tremor est futurus,	How great will be the tremor,
Quando judex est venturus,	when the Judge is to come,
Cuncta stricte discussurus.	investigating everything strictly.

---

[68] Saint John Chrysostom, *Homilia prima de cruce et latrine* 3–4, cited by Saint Julian of Toledo, *Prognosticum futuri saeculi* 3.5 (pp. 432–433).

[69] Christians await the return of Christ, and therefore even the Judgment, with hope and joy: "Come, Lord Jesus!" (Rev 22:20). They know, in fact, that He has shed His blood to redeem them and to prepare a place in Heaven for them (see John 14:1–3). But, as we mentioned in several previous chapters (see, for example, the reference to Saint Joan of Arc in Chapter Eleven), no one can be certain of being in a state of grace. For this reason, the dimension of Christian hope never completely nullifies a restrained, but necessary, fear of Judgment.

Judgment

Tuba, mirum spargens sonum,
per sepulcra regionum,
coget omnes ante thronum.

A trumpet, releasing a marvelous sound
through the tombs of the regions,
will summon all people before the throne.

Mors stupebit et natura,
cum resurget creatura,
judicanti responsura.

Death and nature will stand in wonder,
when all creatures rise again
to respond to the Judge.

Liber scriptus proferetur,
in quo totum continetur,
unde mundus judicetur.

The written book will be offered
in which all is contained
from which the world is to be judged.

Judex ergo cum sedebit,
quidquid latet, apparebit:
nil inultum remanebit.

When the Judge thus sits,
whatever is hidden, will come to light,
Nothing will remain unpunished.

Quid sum miser tunc dicturus?
quem patronum rogaturus,
cum vix justus sit securus?

What shall I, wretch that I am, have to say?
Which patron will I beseech?
When a righteous one is scarcely safe?

Rex tremendae majestatis,
qui salvandos salvas gratis,
salva me, fons pietatis.

King of tremendous majesty,
Who freely saves those who are saved,
save me, O source of mercy,

Recordare, Jesu pie,
quod sum causa tuae viae,
ne me perdas illa die.

Remember, merciful Jesus,
That I am the cause of your path,
lest you lose me on that day.

The Last Things

Quaerens me, sedisti lassus,
redemisti crucem passus:
tantus labor non sit cassus.

Seeking me, you sat down weary,
you redeemed having suffered the cross,
may so much labor not be in vain.

Juste judex ultionis,
donum fac remissionis,
ante diem rationis.

Just judge of wrath,
make a gift of remission,
before the day of rendering.

Ingemisco, tamquam reus,
culpa rubet vultus meus,
supplicanti parce, Deus.

I sigh, so guilty am I,
With guilt my face reddens,
Spare this supplicant one, O God.

Qui Mariam absolvisti,[70]
et latronem exaudisti,
mihi quoque spem dedisti.

You who absolved Mary,
and heard the robber,
and also gave me hope,

Preces meae non sunt dignae,
sed tu bonus fac benigne,
ne perenni cremer igne.

My prayers are not worthy,
but You who are so good, kindly make
it so,
that I am not burned in the eternal fire.

Inter oves locum praesta,
et ab haedis me sequestra,
statuens in parte dextra.

Afford [me] a place among your sheep,
and separate me from the goats,
placing [me] at your right.

Confutatis maledictis,
flammis acribus addictis,
voca me cum benedictis.

Once the cursed are silenced,
sentenced to searing flames,
call me with a blessing.

---

[70] In the most recent version, this verse was substituted with "*Peccatricem qui solvisti,*" which means "The sinner you forgave," probably to avoid the identification of Mary Magdalene with the sinner mentioned in Luke 7:36–50.

Judgment

Oro supplex et acclinis,	Kneeling and bowed down I pray,
cor contritum quasi cinis:	my heart crushed like ashes,
gere curam mei finis.	take care of my outcome.

Lacrimosa dies illa,	Tearful [will be] that day,
qua resurget ex favilla,	on which from the ashes will arise,

Judicandus homo reus,	the guilty one to be judged.
huic ergo parce, Deus.	Spare him, O God.

Pie Jesu Domine,	Merciful Lord Jesus,
dona eis requiem. Amen.	Grant them rest. Amen.

God revealed clearly that there will be such a Judgment, but He did not specify the moment at which it will take place:

> The Lord wanted the time or the day of Judgment to be unknown to us. We read, in fact, that to the disciples who questioned Him about the last day, asking Him, "what will be the sign of your coming and of the end of the age?" (Matt 24:3; Mark 13:4), the Lord himself answered: "But about that day or hour no one knows, neither the angels in heaven, nor the Son, but only the Father" (Mark 13:32; see Matt 24:36). Although He claims not to know the same thing, it cannot be judged that the Son himself knew not, but that, although knowing it, He did not want to say so to the others. "In fact, when the same Lord through the prophet says: 'For the day of vengeance was in my heart' (Isa 63:4), He thus indicates that He knows it, but that He does not intend to reveal it to all."[71]

---

[71] Saint Julian of Toledo, *Prognosticum futuri saeculi* 3.1 (p. 430). The last quotation of the passage is of Saint Isidore of Seville, *Sententiarum libri* 1.27.1. Later, the theologian-monk Rupert of Deutz (d. 1129) would comment on this same Gospel passage observing that when Jesus says that "only the Father knows" the day of Judgment, He means "only God," and so the whole Trinity—and consequently He, the Son, too. If in saying "Father," He had meant only that one Person, He would have used, "my Father." Therefore, the Son also knows that day, and even by experience, insofar as He is God; but He does not know it from experience as a man (because it has yet to take place), even

6.3. The Cosmic Dimension

The cosmic dimension also forms a part of the Last Judgment: the current world passes away, giving way to "new heavens and a new earth" (Isa 65:17; 2 Pet 3:13; Rev 21:1).[72]

6.3.1. Destruction and Renewal

The universal renewal of the cosmos implies both a destruction of the former, and a reconstruction of its splendor.[73] The basis for this is the text of Romans 8:18–23. This work of renewal will consist in a purification of the cosmos, which will be liberated from the consequences of original sin[74] and elevated to a perfect state. Augustine describes it with the formula: "For it will be by a transformation [*mutatione*], rather than by a wholesale destruction [*interitu*] that this world of ours will pass away."[75]

In our times, faith in the end of the cosmos encounters and inevitably clashes with the models developed by cosmologists about the end of the material universe. Among the theories proposed, probably the best-known are those of the *Big Crunch*, an eventual reversal of the *Big Bang*; and that of "thermal death," based on the principle of entropy. When we considered the creation of human beings (see Chapter Three), we had mentioned the problem of comparing it with the current, almost universal, acceptance of the theory of evolution, referring to the specifications of Pius XII in *Humani Generis*. We can apply the same criteria here: there is no contradiction between the universe ending in a Big Crunch or thermal death and faith in the Final Judgment of God that brings the cosmos to an end. God can indeed use secondary causes if He wants to. The Creator can therefore have predetermined in cosmic matter its end, as—provided that the theory of evolution is correct—He guided the process that led from animals to human beings (excluding the soul).

6.3.2. Millennialism

The heresy called Millennialism or Chiliasm should be accurately distin-

---

if He knows it theoretically—also as a man—because of infused science (see *De sancta Trinitate* 1.29).

[72] Second Vatican Council, *Lumen Gentium*, §48; *Gaudium et Spes*, §39.
[73] See *ST* "Supplement," q. 91, aa. 3–4. All of *quaestio* 91 contains different details about the renewed world.
[74] Saint Thomas Aquinas, *Scriptum Super Sententiis* IV, d. 47, q. 2, a. 1.
[75] Saint Augustine of Hippo, *De civitate Dei* 20.14, in *FCNT*, vol. 24, 287.

guished from what the faith holds about the renewal of the cosmos. Such a heresy is based on an erroneous interpretation of Revelation 20:1–10. The millennialists misinterpret the text not only because they take literally the indication of the thousand years contained in it, but above all because they immanentize the application of this prophecy. They believe that the Book of Revelation foretells a period of *terrestrial* peace for the elect, before the eschatological end. There would be, that is, an eschatology carried out on earth for a millennium: without injustices, lies, wars, or any other evil (in fact, Satan would be enchained).

In the first centuries, even some of the most commendable authors were deceived by this interpretation.[76] At least two versions of it were developed: a moderate one, which was generally given by classical authors, and a radical one, which theorized in the millennial reign even moral libertinism, or else the revival of Jewish practices. But several eschatological texts of the New Testament are incompatible with Millennialism. For example:

> Concerning times and seasons, brothers, you have no need for anything to be written to you. For you yourselves know very well that the day of the Lord will come like a thief at night. When people are saying, "Peace and security," then sudden disaster comes upon them, like labor pains upon a pregnant woman, and they will not escape (1 Thess 5:1–3).

Saint Paul did not actually foresee a long reign of peace and security, but rather a sudden and unforeseen arrival (like a thief in the night) of Christ. The apocalyptic texts of the Gospels do nothing but confirm all of this: the *parousia* does not reach the end of a millennium of the peaceful and prosperous earthly kingdom of Christ, because on the contrary, it is sudden and accompanied by frightening things (the falling of the stars or their darkening, earthquakes, the terror of peoples, fleeing, etc.)[77]

---

[76] See Saint Justin Martyr, *Dialogus cum Tryphone iudaeo* 81. A little earlier however (see 80.2) he warned that "many authentic and devout Christians think differently" (our translation).

[77] This is not meant to deny the doctrine on the social kingdom of Christ (that is discussed in Chapter Four), which has characteristics that distinguish it from the millennium kingdom of Christ. Suffice it to say here that the social kingdom of Christ is developed not in the absence of temptation (with Satan enchained), but rather on account of the generous martyrial dedication of those who belong to Christ, who, precisely by pursuing His social reign on earth, must fight against the attacks of the devil and carry their cross every day.

In the modern era, the Chiliast thesis has been exported from the Christian theological sphere into philosophical systems that believed themselves capable of theorizing (and then carrying out) a kingdom of earthly peace, founded no longer on the action of God, but that of human beings.[78] The Church, however, rejected Millennialism, even in its moderate variation, as incompatible with Christian eschatology.[79] Moreover, this pronouncement of the Magisterium is based on the best theological Tradition.[80]

6.4. Particular Aspects

The classical authors also pondered questions that today are often believed to be superfluous, and by some, even laughable.

6.4.1. Place, Date, and Duration

As for the place of the Final Judgment, some believed that an indication of it is found in Joel 4:1–2, which indicates the Valley of Josaphat. But Saint Jerome (d. 420) explains that the passage is to be understood in the figurative sense: "Josaphat must be understood as 'judgment of the Lord.'"[81] Others wondered about the duration of the Judgment. Augustine responds that it is not possible to determine the number of days.[82] The search for the exact date was also considered important, with some seeking to extract it from scriptural data. But Augustine was negative and categorical on this too, since Jesus had said to the Apostles, "It is not for you to know the times or seasons that the Father has established by his own authority" (Acts 1:7), and "the fingers of all such calculators were slackened [*digitos resolvit*] by Him who imposed silence."[83]

6.4.2. The Form of the Risen Body

More than a few have then wondered about the form that the body will

---

[78] For a recent criticism, see Benedict XVI, *Spe Salvi*, §42.
[79] See Holy Office, *Decretum de Millenarismo* (1944) (DS 3839).
[80] See Saint Augustine of Hippo, *De civitate Dei* 20.7–9.
[81] Saint Jerome of Stridon, *Commentarium in Ioelem*, ad locum (our translation).
[82] "By the last day or time of divine judgment I mean what the whole Church of the true God means when she believes and openly proclaims that Christ will come from heaven to judge the living and the dead. Just how many days this judgment will take we do not know, since even the most casual reader of Scripture knows that the word 'day' is often used for 'time'" (Saint Augustine of Hippo, *De civitate Dei*, 20.1, in *FCNT*, vol. 24, 250).
[83] Saint Augustine of Hippo, *De civitate Dei* 18.53, in *FCNT*, vol. 24, 177.

assume in the eschatological resurrection.[84] Augustine is less apophatic on this, affirming that everyone will have the corporeal form that he or she had in youth or—if they died younger—that they would have had in youth: at the age of about thirty years. That is how he interpreted Eph 4:13 ("to the extent of the full stature of Christ").[85] Since, however, the same Pauline texts speak of "mature manhood" or the "perfect man [*virum*]," Augustine also reassures the reader of the fact that women rise again as women and are not transformed into men.[86] He then argues in favor of the resurrection of various categories of human beings, about which some may hold doubts. He argues that neither aborted fetuses nor deformed individuals are excluded.[87] Predicting an easy objection, regarding the corporeal matter that dissolves after death, he writes:

> Now, God does not permit the perishing of the material from which the body of mortals is created. It matters not into what dust or ashes it is dissolved, into what exhalations or vapors it is dispersed, into the substance of what other bodies it is converted (or even into the elements themselves), into the food or the flesh of what animals (man included) it is changed, this material, in a moment of time, returns to that human soul which originally animated it, so that it could become man, live, and grow.[88]

Saint Julian of Toledo, referring primarily to texts of Julianus Pomerius (d. early sixth century) that are now lost, also specified that the risen in Heaven do not need food, drink, or material clothing.[89]

---

[84] For a sampling of very deep reflections on many aspects and particular characteristics of risen bodies, see *ST*, "Supplement," qq. 79–86.

[85] See Saint Augustine of Hippo, *De civitate Dei* 22.15. Thus, the same author writes: "The bodies of the saints, then, will rise free from any blemish or deformity, as they will be free from any corruption, burden, or impediment; their freedom of movement will be as complete as their happiness. It is for this reason that these bodies are called spiritual, since without doubt they are to be bodies and not spirits" (Saint Augustine of Hippo, *Enchiridion de fide, spe et charitate*, 23.91 [in *FCNT*, vol. 2, 445]; see *De civitate Dei* 22.19).

[86] See Saint Augustine of Hippo, *De civitate Dei* 22.17.

[87] See Saint Augustine of Hippo, *Enchiridion de fide, spe et charitate* 23.85–87.

[88] Saint Augustine of Hippo, *Enchiridion de fide, spe et charitate* 23.88, in *FCNT*, vol. 2, 443. According to Saint Thomas Aquinas, the angels, in addition to tasks already mentioned above, also have a role in the resurrection of human bodies: "In all of the works relating to the bodies, God uses the ministry of angels. Now, in the resurrection there is something that concerns the transmutation of the bodies, that is, the collection of ashes and their preparation for the reconstruction of the human body. Well, for this work God will use the ministry of angels" (*ST*, "Supplement," q. 76, a. 3 [our translation]).

[89] Saint Julian of Toledo, *Prognosticum futuri saeculi* 3.25–26. He cites Julianus Pomerius, *De*

6.4.3. The "Book of Life"

We must not forget the element of the "book of life" (Phil 4:3; Rev 3:5; 13:8; 17:8). This book contains the names of those who are predestined to eternal salvation. Those whose name is not written in the book are destined to Hell. So says the Book of Revelation:

> Next I saw a large white throne and the one who was sitting on it. The earth and the sky fled from his presence and there was no place for them. I saw the dead, the great and the lowly, standing before the throne, and scrolls were opened. Then another scroll was opened, the book of life. The dead were judged according to their deeds, by what was written in the scrolls. The sea gave up its dead; then Death and Hades gave up their dead. All the dead were judged according to their deeds. Then Death and Hades were thrown into the pool of fire. (This pool of fire is the second death.) Anyone whose name was not found written in the book of life was thrown into the pool of fire. (Rev 20:11–15)

Tradition teaches that the good and evil works we do are constantly registered in heavenly books. Whether or not our names are found in the book of life is based on what comes to be written in them. Saint Augustine writes: "All the evil done by the wicked is registered unbeknownst to them."[90] Since Revelation 20:12 speaks of "scrolls" in the plural, and of the "book of life" in the singular, Saint Julian interpreted these books as the consciences of the individuals, which will be opened wide before the Lord in judgment and, again with reference to Augustine, he adds that the book of life represents the omniscient power of God who knows the lives of individuals in detail.[91]

---

natura animae vel qualitate eius 8 (a text almost completely lost).
[90] Saint Augustine of Hippo, *Sermones* 18.4 (our translation).
[91] See Saint Julian of Toledo, *Prognosticum futuri saeculi* 3.36. He cites Saint Augustine of Hippo, *De civitate Dei* 20.14. In this same place, Augustine instead disagrees about "the books," which for him are those of the Old and New Testament that contain the dictates of the will of God.

7. Hell

7.1. The New Testament

7.1.1. The Darkness

Jesus referred many times to Satan and his action, which He Himself experienced in the desert and during His Passion (see Matt 4; Mark 1; Luke 4; 22:53; etc.). It is significant that the New Testament often uses the word "darkness" to refer to the devil and his dominion.[92] If Christ is the "light of the world" (John 8:12), it makes sense that His enemy represents the darkness, which human beings often prefer to light (see John 3:19). Many passages of the New Testament speak of the liberation accomplished by Christ exactly in terms of being removed from the darkness (see Matt 4:16; Luke 1:79; John 12:46; Acts 26:18; Rom 13:12; Col 1:13; 1 Pet 2:9; etc.). Thus, no *et-et* concerning the light-darkness binomial is possible. As we know, this fundamental principle is not, in fact, applied to keep good and evil (nor holiness and sin) together: "For what partnership do righteousness and lawlessness have? Or what fellowship does light have with darkness?" (2 Cor 6:14). Therefore, one is either in the light or in the darkness. Nobody who is in the darkness can claim to be in the light (see Eph 5:11; 1 Thess 5:4–5; 1 John 1:6; 2:9, 11; etc.), because this would imply an irresolvable contradiction.

"Darkness," however, is not only a moral condition, that of sin. It is also a "place." Revelation 16:10 explicitly says that the kingdom of the beast is wrapped in darkness. Jude 6 teaches that "the angels too, who did not keep to their own domain but deserted their proper dwelling, [God] has kept in eternal chains, in gloom, for the judgment of the great day." Jude 13 reiterates that "the gloom of darkness has been reserved forever" for the "ungodly" (v.

---

[92] We are limiting our discussion to the New Testament, but we shall at least mention the *sheol* (underworld) of the Old Testament, which is the background of what the writings of the new covenant say about Hell. Originally *sheol* was the place of the dead under the earth (see Wis 1:14), where both the good and the evil went. But the Old Testament message is later differentiated by recognizing that the wicked merit *sheol* (see Ps 9:18; 31:18; 49:14–15, 18–20; etc.) with its pains (see Jdt 16:17; Isa 50:11: 66:24; Wis 4:19; etc.), while resurrection and eternal life are for the just (see Ps 9:19; 16:10; 59:16; Dan 12:2; etc.). The New Testament cites *sheol*, translating it into Greek with *hades* (see Acts 2:27, which resumes Ps 16:10; see also Rev 1:18). A Hebrew term that the Old Testament uses with a similar meaning to *sheol* is *abaddon*, which means "place of ruin." Both terms recur in Job 26:6: "Naked before him is Sheol / and *abaddon* has no covering (emphasis added)." Other texts in which the two terms are used together are Ps 88:11; Prov 15:11; 27:20. In Rev 9:11, *abaddon* is used as the name belonging to the angel of the abyss.

The Last Things

4) men. 2 Peter is in full agreement. It likewise speaks of a prison for the fallen angels (see 2:4) and adds that "for them the gloom of darkness has been reserved" (2:17).

Furthermore, Christ Himself referred to a place of gloom and torments: "I say to you, many will come from the east and the west, and will recline with Abraham, Isaac, and Jacob at the banquet in the kingdom of heaven, but the children of the kingdom will be driven out into the outer darkness, where there will be wailing and grinding of teeth" (Matt 8:11–12); "Then the king said to his attendants, 'Bind his hands and feet, and cast him into the darkness outside, where there will be wailing and grinding of teeth'" (Matt 22:13).

7.1.2. The Fire of Gehenna

In addition to the wailing and grinding of teeth, Jesus uses the image of fire[93] to describe the place of torment, and calls it by the name Gehenna:

> But I say to you, whoever is angry with his brother will be liable to judgment, and whoever says to his brother, "Raqa," will be answerable to the Sanhedrin, and whoever says, "You fool," will be liable to fiery Gehenna. (Matt 5:22)

> If your right eye causes you to sin, tear it out and throw it away. It is better for you to lose one of your members than to have your whole body thrown into Gehenna. And if your right hand causes you to sin, cut it off and throw it away. It is better for you to lose one of your members than to have your whole body go into Gehenna. (Matt 5:29–30; see 18:9; Mark 9:43–47)

> And do not be afraid of those who kill the body but cannot kill the soul; rather, be afraid of the one who can destroy both soul and body in Gehenna. (Matt 10:28; see Luke 12:5)

---

[93] Indeed, fire is a recurring term both in the eschatological passages of the New Testament, and in the Christian literature that depends on them. For example, in the ancient story of the martyrdom of Saint Polycarp of Smyrna, the proconsul, after having uselessly threatened to send him to the wild beasts, says to the Martyr: "'If you scorn the wild beasts, I will have you burned by fire, unless you repent.' But Polycarp said: 'You threaten the fire that burns for an hour and in a little while is quenched; for you do not know the fire of the future Judgment and of eternal punishment, the fire reserved for the wicked'" (*Martyrium Polycarpi* 11.2, in *FCNT*, vol. 1, trans. Gerald G. Walsh [Washington, DC: CUA, 2008], 156).

Hell

> Woe to you, scribes and Pharisees, you hypocrites. You traverse sea and land to make one convert, and when that happens you make him a child of Gehenna twice as much as yourselves. (Matt 23:15)

> You serpents, you brood of vipers, how can you flee from the judgment of Gehenna? (Matt 23:33)

The modern exegetes note that *Gehenna* is a Hellenization of the Aramaic *gehinnam*, which is connected to the Hebrew *gehinnom*, that is, Valley of (Ben-)Hinnom (Josh 15:8; 18:16). This name referred to a valley to the south of Jerusalem (today *Wadi er-Rababi*) in which around the seventh century BC, sacrifices of children were made in honor of Moloch (see 2 Chron 28:3; 33:6; etc.). Josiah, as a result, would declare that place to be impure (see 2 Kings 23:10). According to the prophet Jeremiah, this valley would be the place of the future judgment, and Jeremiah re-named it the "Valley of Slaughter" (see 7:32; 19:6–7). Thus, in the non-canonical texts of Judaism, that place is identified as the place of fire and the Last Judgment. This does not mean that Jesus has learned what He reveals about Hell from the Jewish apocalyptic literature. Instead, it means that Christ used a term and conceptual category that was common to His time, so that His listeners could understand. About the definitive and irreversible nature of the condemnation to the fire of Gehenna, the Lord is very clear in Mark 9:48, where He affirms of the damned that "their worm does not die, and the fire is not quenched" (it is a citation of Isa 66:24[94]). And, in Matthew 25:41, He reveals that the "eternal fire" is found there.

The message of the New Testament, therefore, clearly reveals the existence not only of moral evil, but also of a "place" of punishment for evil committed, which we commonly call Hell. As regards this name:

> Hell is said or believed to be under the earth because of the way it is represented appropriately in the spirit by means of the likeness

---

[94] Some recent exegetes raise questions about the applicability of this quote to Hell, thus disputing the exegesis of Christ in Person! The text of Isaiah says: "They shall go out and see the corpses / of the people who rebelled against me; / for their worm shall not die, / their fire shall not be extinguished; / and they shall be an abhorrence to all flesh." It should be noted that Isaiah mentions corpses. Reading the above-cited passages from Jeremiah, in which he renames the valley of Hinnom the "Valley of Slaughter," note that in it God says that the bodies will be buried in that place and the bodies of the killed victims will be food for the birds. The link between the two places is quite evident, like the exegesis of Isaiah's text carried out by Jesus.

of corporeal things. Now the souls of the dead who are deserving of Hell have sinned through love of the flesh. They are affected, therefore, by the likeness of bodies and are subjected to the same experience as the dead flesh itself buried under the earth. Finally, Hell is called the lower world, or *inferi* in Latin, because it is beneath the earth. In the corporeal world all the heavier bodies occupy a lower place if the natural tendency of their weight is not interfered with; and so in the spiritual order the gloomier realm is in a lower position.[95]

7.2. Historical Freedom and Eternal Damnation

Hell is the eschatological condition of those who die separated from the love of God offered in Christ. It is therefore the unending continuation of life as one has decided to live it: "*etsi Deus non daretur*" ("as if God did not exist"). Whoever has chosen to live without God and against God will continue to do so forever, because the Lord respects the human being's self-determination, even when he or she goes against His salvific plan.[96] However unacceptable it may sound, even one mortal sin can be enough for condemnation to Hell.[97] Thus, the *Catechism* teaches: "To die in mortal sin without repenting and accepting God's merciful love means remaining separated from him forever by our own free choice. This state of definitive self-exclusion from communion with God and the blessed is called 'hell'" (CCC §1033). And Benedict XII writes: "We define that according to the general disposition of God, the souls of those who die in actual mortal sin go down

---

[95] Saint Augustine of Hippo, *De Genesi ad litteram* 12.34.66, in *The Literal Meaning of Genesis* vol. 2, 227.

[96] With reference to Purgatory, Saint Gregory the Great, *Dialogorum libri* 4.39, recalls certain biblical passages (John 12:35; Isa 49:8; 2 Cor 6:2; Eccles 9:10; Ps 97) to conclude that "*qualis hinc quisque egreditur, talis in judicio praesentatur*" ("in the state in which someone exits [from this life], so is this person presented at Judgment" [our translation]).

[97] However, Judgment is the prerogative of God alone. But the danger (for salvation) connected even to only one serious sin has been affirmed from the very earliest Christian literature. Leveraging his talent for metaphors, Hermas, in his work *The Shepherd* (in the first half of the second century), notes: "If you take a very little bit of absinthe and pour it into a jar of honey, is not all of the honey spoiled, and is not so much honey ruined by the very least amount of absinthe, and does it not destroy the sweetness of the honey, and it no longer has the same flavor with its owner because it has been made bitter and it has lost its usefulness?" (33.5, in *The Apostolic Fathers: A New Translation and Commentary*, vol. 6, trans. Graydon F. Snyder [Toronto: Thomas Nelson and Sons, 1968], 74 [with our corrections]).

into Hell immediately after death and there suffer the pain of Hell."[98]

7.3. "Apocatastasis"

The Church has clearly refuted the doctrine known as "apocatastasis," which affirms the temporality of the pains of Hell. She teaches instead that these pains are eternal: "If anyone says or holds that the punishment of the demons and of impious men is temporary and that it will have an end at some time, that is to say, there will be a complete restoration [*apokatastasis*] of the demons or of impious men, let him be anathema."[99] Some modern theologians have doubted whether human beings can truly be eternally punished for sins committed in time. According to their view, an unending penalty would be disproportionate to one or more sins of very limited duration. But this is answered by the principle posed by the Angelic Doctor, for whom "the duration of the penalty," even in human law, "refers to the disposition to those who sin." If, on earth, a human being merits a perpetual penalty (for example, exile), it lasts indefinitely, in reference to his or her finite earthly existence. But if that person lived for all time on earth, Thomas continues, he or she would remain in the state of punishment forever. "Well, even according to divine justice, one can, out of sin, make himself worthy of being completely separated from the city of God."[100]

7.4. The Pains of Hell

7.4.1. The Pain of Loss

"The chief punishment of hell is eternal separation from God" (CCC §1035). Specifically, this means that for the damned, the *visio Dei*[101] (of which we will speak later) is forever precluded: "The Church believes ... that there will be

---

[98] Benedict XII, *Benedictus Deus* (DS 1002).
[99] Synod of Constantinople, *Edictum Iustiniani Imperatoris ad Menam Patriarcham Constantinopolitanum* (543), can. 9 (DS 411). The canons are addressed explicitly against the eschatological doctrine of Origen of Alexandria, *De Principiis* 1.6.1, which had argued for the finitude of Hell. However, in the cited text, Origen claims to propose his opinions as questionable and revisable, without claiming definitive statements. Saint Pelagius I speaks of "eternal and inextinguishable flames" in *Humani Generis ad Chidebertum I Regem* (557) (DS 443).
[100] *ST*, "Supplement," q. 99, a. 1 (our translation).
[101] "When there is sin in a man, such a man cannot see God" (Saint Theophilus of Antioch, *Ad Autolicum* 1.2, trans. Robert M. Grant [Oxford: Clarendon Press, 1970], 5).

eternal punishment for the sinner, who will be deprived of the sight of God, and that this punishment will have a repercussion on the whole being of the sinner."[102] The latter expression means that a "pain of sense," that is, a series of torments suffered and perceived by the damned, also corresponds to the "pain of loss" (privation of the vision).

7.4.2. The Pain of Sense

The pain of sense corresponds, in biblical language, to the "fire" that burns, and the "worm" that devours the damned.[103] The question, thus, is reasonably posed: If the damned, for now, are in Hell only in soul and without their bodies, how can the fire burn them? Hence, the proposal of some to understand this teaching of Christ only in a metaphorical way: the fire would be the image of displeasure and remorse for having wasted one's own life and the despair at never being able to see God again. This aspect is certainly there, but it is already included in the meaning of "pain of loss." In the *Summa Theologiae*, Saint Thomas says that the fire of Hell is not only a metaphor, noting that Christ taught that the fire that torments the damned is the same that was "prepared for the devil and his angels" (Matt 25:41), who are incorporeal, like the soul. Therefore, in Hell, there is a fire capable of burning even spirits, although there are various opinions on how this occurs.[104] We shall consider one of these, offered by Tertullian, later, when we speak of the pains of Purgatory.

---

[102] Congregation for the Doctrine of Faith, *Epistola de Quibusdam Quaestionibus ad Eschatologiam Spectantibus*, §7.

[103] According to Saint Thomas Aquinas, since animals and plants will not be re-established in the eschatological renewal of the universe (see *ST* "Supplement," q. 91, a. 5), the worm that eats away at the damned cannot be understood in the literal sense: "This concerns the remorse of the conscience" (q. 97, a. 2 [our translation]). He thinks, however, that the fire is corporeal (see q. 97, a. 5).

[104] See *ST*, "Supplement," q. 70, a. 3. The opinions reported (drawing mainly on Saint Gregory the Great, Saint Julian of Toledo, and Peter Lombard) are these: (1) the soul suffers because it sees the fire; (2) the soul suffers because it considers it harmful and fear arises from this consideration; (3) the fire burns the soul by virtue of the principal agent (God) of which it is a punitive instrument of avenging justice (something analogous and opposed to the beneficial spiritual effect that the Sacraments produce in the soul); and (4) the material fire is given by God the capacity of preventing the soul from freedom of action, imprisoning it in Hell. The *Summa* prefers the last opinion; therefore, for Saint Thomas, the fire torments the souls by uniting itself to them in some way, that is, forcing them to remain prisoner in that "place" where they burn: Hell. And the soul is tormented by fire because it recognizes in it the cause of its imprisonment and its interminable torture.

7.5. Paraenetic Implications

The truths of faith that concern Hell are also proposed with paraenetic (i.e., hortatory) ends. We need to avoid the error of thinking that this is their sole purpose: if we thought that way, then we would have to believe that Hell is only a bogeyman to try to get people to behave well. But this is in conflict with the nature of Christian Revelation, since God does not lie. Since God revealed in Christ the existence of eternal penalties for sinners judged worthy of them, then there really is a Hell, which is not a myth composed simply for exhortative purpose—God does not deceive human beings.[105] Therefore, Hell is *both* a reality *and* it represents a positive stimulus for the moral life of the "wayfarers."

It is Christ in Person who has kept the two aspects together: "Enter through the narrow gate; for the gate is wide and the road broad that leads to destruction, and those who enter through it are many. How narrow the gate and constricted the road that leads to life. And those who find it are few" (Matt 7:13–14). The Lord urges us to take the path of righteousness, because at the end of the two ways there are actually two different eternal destinies. This lesson was immediately relayed in Christian preaching from the very first centuries. A very ancient anonymous treatise, the *Didache*, begins with this exact theme: "There are two ways, one of life and one of death; and great is the difference between the two ways."[106] Saint Ignatius of Antioch says it in this way: "Seeing, then, all things have an end, these two things are simultaneously set before us—death and life; and every one shall go unto his own place." Then he introduces a new metaphor, comparing it to the Gospel's metaphor of the two ways: "As there are two currencies, the one of God, and the other of the world, each stamped in its own way."[107] The paraenesis is even more explicit in another very ancient writing, traditionally called *The Letter of Barnabas*:

> The Lord will judge the world "without respect of persons." Each man will receive according to his deeds. If he be good, his goodness will lead him, if he be evil, the reward of injustice is before him. And so, since we are called, let us never slacken and slumber in our sins, lest the prince of evil gain power over us and cast us out from the kingdom of the Lord.[108]

---

[105] God "does not lie" (Titus 1:2) and, in revealing Himself, He "can neither err nor deceive" (First Vatican Council, *Dei Filius* [1870], ch. 3 [DS 3008]).
[106] *Didache* 1.1, in *FCNT*, vol. 1, 171.
[107] Saint Ignatius of Antioch, *Ad Magnesios* 5.1–2, in *FCNT*, vol. 1, 97.
[108] *Epistula Barnabae* 4.12–13, in *FCNT*, vol. 1, 196.

The Last Things

The *Epistle to Diognetus* applies this paraenesis to martyrdom, saying that those who pass through the fire and torments of persecutors will be spared the fires of the great beyond:

> You will love and admire men who suffer because they refuse to deny God; you will condemn the deceit and error of the world as soon as you realize that true life is in Heaven, and despise the seeming death in this world, and fear the real death which is reserved for those who are to be condemned to eternal fire which shall torment forever those who are committed to it. When you have faith, you will admire those who, for the sake of what is right, bear the temporal fire, and you will think them blessed when you come to know the fire.[109]

These are just a few of the many adducible examples, which allow us to illustrate what the *Catechism* expresses in these terms: "The affirmations of Sacred Scripture and the teachings of the Church on the subject of hell are a *call to the responsibility* incumbent upon man to make use of his freedom in view of his eternal destiny. They are at the same time an urgent *call to conversion*" (CCC §1036). The fact that many have lost sight of this is one of the reasons why the theme of Hell, along with those of Death and Judgment, have practically disappeared from preaching in recent times. When arguments that are so biblical and so solid are removed from homiletic and catechetical exhortation, it inevitably happens that, on the one hand, one slides into a certain vague eschatological "correctness" ('all are saved') and, on the other, that it diminishes the eschatological tension that is typical of biblical spirituality ("*marana tha!*").[110]

---

[109] *Ad Diognetum* 10.7–8, in *FCNT*, vol. 1, 366–367.

[110] It has been noted that the Second Vatican Council never uses the term Hell, and this information is used to argue for the practice of being silent about the theme in ecclesial pastoral work. But, in response to that claim: (1) not every council must speak on every theme; (2) Vatican II clearly confirms the doctrine of eternal damnation—without using the word Hell—in resorting to biblical images of darkness and fire (see *Lumen Gentium*, §48); and (3) the Council refers to the devil (see *Lumen Gentium*, §§17 and 48; *Gaudium et Spes*, §22). It is good to remember that referring to the theme of Hell and of the devil in preaching and in catechesis does not imply any sort of "psychological terrorism." There are, for example, numerous references of the post-conciliar popes to the devil: from the famous "smoke of Satan" of Saint Paul VI (*Homily of June 29, 1972*) to the frequent references by Pope Francis, especially during his first year as Pope.

8. Purgatory

In Catholic doctrine, this name refers to the "place" and the condition of purification after death of the souls who have neither forfeited salvation nor merited damnation, but who are also not ready for Paradise. The word Purgatory is not found in Sacred Scripture, but there are some passages in it that allude to it with a certain clarity, while from other biblical passages its existence can be deduced.[111]

8.1. Sacred Scripture

8.1.1. The Prayer for the Dead

Even the Old Testament speaks of a prayer of intercession for the dead. In this regard, we must mention 2 Maccabees 12:38–45. Judas Maccabeus sends his followers to collect the corpses of the fallen in battle and it turns out that they hid images of foreign cults under their clothes. This represented a grave sin, which is also interpreted as a cause of the death of those men. What is interesting to us here is that the people start to pray so that the sin committed may be forgiven and Judas "took up a collection," and sent it to the Temple "to provide for an expiatory sacrifice. In doing this he acted in a very excellent and noble way, inasmuch as he had the resurrection in mind" (v. 43). And the text concludes:

> For if he were not expecting the fallen to rise again, it would have been superfluous and foolish to pray for the dead. But if he did this with a view to the splendid reward that awaits those who had gone to rest in godliness, it was a holy and pious thought. Thus he made atonement for the dead that they might be absolved from their sin. (2 Maccabees 12:44–46)

The passage indirectly affirms that the dead may be found in the great beyond in a condition that is neither one of definitive salvation nor one of definitive condemnation. It is possible therefore to pray for them, so that they may be freed from the sin on the day of the resurrection. The Church always

---

[111] In *Exsurge Domine* (1520), among the many errors of Luther, Pope Leo X condemns the following: "Purgatory cannot be proved from any Sacred Scripture that is in the canon" (no. 37 [DS 1487]). Consequently, Catholic doctrine believes that Purgatory is revealed in Scripture.

The Last Things

prays in the Liturgy for the living and also for the dead (see below).

8.1.2. The Words of Jesus

1. Matthew 5:25–26

As for the words of Christ Himself, the clearest in regard to Purgatory are those reported in Matthew 5:25–26: "Settle with your opponent quickly while on the way to court with him. Otherwise your opponent will hand you over to the judge, and the judge will hand you over to the guard, and you will be thrown into prison. Amen, I say to you, you will not be released until you have paid the last penny" (see also Luke 12:58–59). Christ speaks of the "wayfarers," of those who are on the way of this life, and urges them to settle with their adversary before they go before the judge. For those who do not do so, there is condemnation and imprisonment. But in this case, He could not be referring to condemnation to Hell, because Jesus speaks of a penalty with a term, until every last penny is paid (condemnation to Hell, on the contrary, is unending). Here, therefore, Jesus alludes to a state of penal captivity, due to what is not accomplished while "on the way," and that is expiated only for a certain amount of time, after which the prisoner is free. It is difficult to interpret these words if not in reference to what the Christian Tradition would later call Purgatory: a state of temporary purification due to the sins committed in life.[112]

2. Matthew 12:32

Christ Himself, in a passage we have already seen above, indirectly teaches that there are forgivable sins in the afterlife: "And whoever speaks a word against the Son of Man will be forgiven; but whoever speaks against the holy Spirit will not be forgiven, either in this age or in the age to come" (Matt

---

[112] Why have some of those who have sinned in life been condemned to Hell and others to Purgatory? We can respond with two observations: The first is that not all sins have equal gravity, which is why it is right that mortal sins and venial sins are punished differently (for some biblical passages, see Chapter Ten, the section on Reconciliation). In the second place, even in the case of people who have committed mortal sins and do not go to Hell, we need to remember that God, with His inscrutable Judgment, evaluates everything appropriately and knows not only actions, but intentions and circumstances as well. He is capable of establishing those who, through their sins, are rendered irredeemable, and those instead, who while having sinned, are admissible into Heaven after a necessary purgation.

12:32). A brilliant exegesis of this teaching has been offered by Saint Gregory the Great:

> As for some light faults, one must believe that there is, before the Judgment, a purifying fire; indeed, He who is the Truth affirms that, if someone utters a blasphemy against the Holy Spirit, he will not be forgiven in this age or in the future. From this statement it can be deduced that certain faults can be remitted in this age, but others in the future age.[113]

8.1.3. Saint Paul

Another classic biblical passage on the theme of Purgatory is provided by Saint Paul, who makes recourse not to the image of those walking on the way (as Jesus does in Matt 5), but to the image of the construction of a building—with which, however, he intends to make reference to the same meaning, that is, to the way in which each person lives on earth:

> According to the grace of God given to me, like a wise master builder I laid a foundation, and another is building upon it. But each one must be careful how he builds upon it, for no one can lay a foundation other than the one that is there, namely, Jesus Christ. If anyone builds on this foundation with gold, silver, precious stones, wood, hay, or straw, the work of each will come to light, for the Day will disclose it. It will be revealed with fire, and the fire [itself] will test the quality of each one's work. If the work stands that someone built upon the foundation, that person will receive a wage. But if someone's work is burned up, that one will suffer loss; the person will be saved, but only as through fire (1 Cor 3:10–15).

To understand the meaning of the passage, we can refer to Benedict XVI:

> Saint Paul, in his First Letter to the Corinthians, gives us an idea of the differing impact of God's Judgment according to each person's particular circumstances.... Paul begins by saying that Christian life

---

[113] Saint Gregory the Great, *Dialogorum libri* 4.39 (our translation). The Pope limits himself to recognizing this possibility only for venial sins ("*de parvis minimisque peccatis*;" "*peccata minima atque levissima*"), of which he gives some examples in the rest of the passage: idle speeches, excessive laughter, etc.

is built upon a common foundation: Jesus Christ. This foundation endures. If we have stood firm on this foundation and built our life upon it, we know that it cannot be taken away from us even in death. Then Paul continues: "Now if any one builds on the foundation with gold, silver, precious stones, wood, hay, straw—each man's work will become manifest . . ." In this text, it is in any case evident that our salvation can take different forms, that some of what is built may be burned down, that in order to be saved we personally have to pass through "fire" so as to become fully open to receiving God and able to take our place at the table of the eternal marriage-feast.[114]

Pope Benedict therefore interprets the passage of Saint Paul in conformity with Tradition, as referring to Purgatory, that is, to the passing through purgative fires, before entering the beatific vision.

8.2. Teachings of the Magisterium

8.2.1. The Council of Florence

At the level of ecclesial pronouncements, the most important texts are found in the Ecumenical Councils of Florence and Trent. The Florentine Council teaches:

> (We define) that if those who are truly penitent die in the love of God before having satisfied by worthy fruits of penance for their sins of commission and omission, their souls are cleansed after death by purgatorial punishments. In order that they be relieved from such punishments, the acts of intercession of the living faithful benefit them, namely, the Sacrifices of the Mass, prayers, alms, and other works of piety that the faithful are wont to do for the other faithful according to the Church's practice.[115]

In this text we want to emphasize the reference to the theme of the *communio sanctorum*. In effect, the dogma of Purgatory speaks not only about divine justice carrying out a purification of sins committed in life, but also about the communal bond that binds the different states of life of the Christian, so that the wayfarers and the souls in Purgatory are, as members of the

---

[114] Benedict XVI, *Spe Salvi*, §§45–46.
[115] Council of Florence, *Laetentur Caeli* (1439) (DS 1304).

same Church in two different states (the militant/pilgrim Church and the suffering/purgative Church), in a deep communion of love and prayers, so that suffrages, works of charity, and those of penitence can benefit the souls in Purgatory, and the prayers of the latter can obtain graces from God for the wayfarers.[116]

8.2.2. The Council of Trent

The Council of Trent focuses on Purgatory on two separate occasions, in response to the erroneous conceptions of the Protestants on this topic.

1. The Decree on Justification

A first and very important reference is found in the *Decree on Justification*, in which the Council emphasizes the fact that the Sacrament of Confession remits the faults of sins and the penalty of damnation connected to them; but it does not remit the temporal penalty due to sins, which must therefore be paid for with prayers, almsgiving, fasting, and pious practices. The canon corresponding to this teaching therefore refers to Purgatory explicitly: "If anyone says that after the grace of justification has been received the guilt is so remitted and the debt of eternal punishment so blotted out for any repentant sinner that no debt of temporal punishment remains to be discharged, either in this world or in the future one, in Purgatory, before access can be opened to the kingdom of Heaven, let him be anathema."[117]

2. The Decree on Purgatory

The second text dedicated by the Council to the theme is a specific *Decree on Purgatory*, which, however, is an extremely brief text and distinctly pastoral by nature. It teaches the same doctrines already taught in Florence and elsewhere in Trent; the bishops are urged to be vigilant that the doctrine of Purgatory be maintained and believed entirely, "taught and preached everywhere"; it is ordered that, in preaching, the most difficult and subtle questions that do not edify or produce any increase in the piety of the faithful are to be avoided, while, at the same time, they should encourage the people to offer prayers and

---

[116] The same ecclesiological perspective is expressed in a beautiful text of Leo XIII, *Mirae Caritatis* (1902), §§11–12.

[117] Council of Trent, *Decretum et Canones de Iustificatione* (1547), ch. 15 and can. 30 (DS 1544; 1580).

penances for the dead and especially the Sacrifice of Mass as a suffrage.[118]

8.2.3. The Recent Magisterium

The Second Vatican Council has first of all confirmed the faith of the Church in the existence of Purgatory: "Until the Lord shall come in His majesty . . . some of His disciples are exiles on earth, some having died are purified, and others are in glory."[119] The Council has also reiterated the importance of prayer for the souls in Purgatory as a patrimony of ecclesial life of all time:

> Fully conscious of this communion of the whole Mystical Body of Jesus Christ, the pilgrim Church from the very first ages of the Christian religion has cultivated with great piety the memory of the dead, and "because it is a holy and wholesome thought to pray for the dead that they may be loosed from their sins," also offers suffrages for them.[120]

Consequently, the Magisterium's recommendation is to ensure that, in our days, such a charitable and precious practice does not fail: "I wish—writes Benedict XVI—to remind all the faithful of the importance of prayers for the dead, especially the offering of Mass for them, so that, once purified, they can come to the beatific vision of God."[121] As a matter of fact, all the Eucharistic Prayers of the Mass contain orations for the faithful departed.

8.2.4. Other Pronouncements

The aforementioned magisterial teachings were based on previous affirmations regarding this theme. For example, in 1254, Innocent IV had explained

---

[118] See Council of Trent, *Decretum de Purgatorio* (1563) (DS 1820).

[119] Second Vatican Council, *Lumen Gentium*, §49.

[120] Second Vatican Council, *Lumen Gentium*, §50. The quote cited is a frequent inscription in the Roman catacombs.

[121] Benedict XVI, *Sacramentum Caritatis* (2007), §32. And, in *Spe Salvi* §48, the Pope writes: "The souls of the departed can, however, receive 'solace and refreshment' through the Eucharist, prayer and almsgiving. The belief that love can reach into the afterlife, that reciprocal giving and receiving is possible, in which our affection for one another continues beyond the limits of death—this has been a fundamental conviction of Christianity throughout the ages and it remains a source of comfort today. Who would not feel the need to convey to their departed loved ones a sign of kindness, a gesture of gratitude or even a request for pardon?" (The terminology of "refreshment" is already found in Saint Irenaeus of Lyon, *Adversus haereses* 4.6 ("eternal refreshment").

the fundamental points on Purgatory and imposed on Catholics of the Eastern Rite to use this name to indicate the place of purification in the great beyond.[122] It is true, however, that on the magisterial level, the pronouncements on Purgatory increased after the thirteenth century. This is because the theological honing of Purgatory occurred precisely in the medieval era. Hence, some historians have formulated the thesis of the "birth of Purgatory," attributing it to circumstantial reasons (e.g., the rise of the first bourgeoisie), rather than theological ones. In order to respond to this thesis, in addition to the already-mentioned biblical foundation, we need to refer to the Fathers of the Church who lived before the Middle Ages and who testified to the ecclesial faith in the superterrestrial purification, well before this faith was better explored by the Scholastics.[123]

8.3. The Fathers of the Church

8.3.1. The "Prison" and the "Purgation"

The first author to ever use the terminology of the "purgation" of sins after death was Saint Cyprian (d. 258).[124] Therefore, the term Purgatory finds its foundation as early as the first half of the third century. But even several years earlier, Tertullian (d. 220) had spoken of a place where the faults of sins are expiated prior to the corporeal resurrection at the end of times: "If we understand the 'prison' [*carcerem*], of which the Gospel speaks, as the underworld [*inferos*], and 'the last penny' (Matt 5:26) as the smallest defect that has to be atoned for there before the resurrection, there will be no doubt that the soul suffers in the underworld some retributory penalty, without denying the complete resurrection, when the body also will pay or be paid in full."[125] The idea of *post mortem* purification from sins is also clearly implied, in another affirmation of Tertullian, according to whom only the martyrs go directly into Paradise: "No one who 'has journeyed away from the body,' dwells immediately with the Lord, unless he is to turn aside thither from the privilege

---

[122] See Innocent IV, *Sub Catholicae Professione* (1254), §23 (DS 838). Innocent refers, without citing him, to Gregory the Great's interpretation of Matt 12:32.

[123] Saint Pius X, *Ex Quo Nono* (1910), condemned as an error of the Eastern Christians their questioning that the dogma of Purgatory was admitted "by holy men of the first centuries" (DS 3554).

[124] See Saint Cyprian of Carthage, *Epistula 51*.20. It is no coincidence that he mentions Matt 5:26 in the text.

[125] Tertullian of Carthage, *De anima* 58, in *FCNT*, vol. 10, trans. Edwin A. Quain (Washington, DC: CUA Press, 1950), 308 (with our corrections).

The Last Things

of martyrdom, Paradise of course, not the lower world."[126] Consequently, for those who do not die as martyrs, there is a period of purification before entrance into Paradise.

8.3.2. Suffrage for the Departed

The ancient Christian custom (attested to from the very beginning) of praying for the deceased and celebrating the Holy Mass for them, as documented earlier, is even stronger evidence than these patristic attestations.[127] How can one explain this custom if not for the conviction of faith, held without a doubt, that the dead can receive a benefit from such prayers? Faith in the existence of temporary penalties due to sins and not yet paid in life—penalties that must be satisfied after death and can also be satisfied through the prayers of the living—is thus implicitly expressed in this custom. Julianus Pomerius interprets the custom of suffrage in this exact sense:

> Since the Church effectively pleads here [on earth] for those spirits that leave this world with not such perfect holiness as to be able to go immediately to Paradise after the deposition of their own bodies, and do not live so badly and reprehensibly or persevere in their own crimes so much as to deserve to be damned with the devil and his angels, once they are purified with healing punishments, when their bodies attain blessed immortality and they participate in the heavenly kingdom, they will remain there without anything to detract from their beatitude.[128]

This faith in the power of suffrage is present throughout all of Christian history up to this day.

8.3.3. Paraenetic Value

We should also add the theme of paraenesis to that of suffrage. It is not only the teaching on Hell that has a hortatory value, but the dogma of Purgatory as well. Purgatory is often viewed a little superficially, as if it were little more

---

[126] Tertullian, *De resurrectione carnis* 43, in *Concerning the Resurrection of the Flesh*, trans. A. Souter (New York: The Macmillan Company, 1922), 105.

[127] Another ancient testimony of it is found in Tertullian, *De corona* 3.

[128] Julian Pomerius, *De animae natura dialogus* 8, cited by Saint Julian of Toledo, *Prognosticum futuri saeculi* 2.10 (p. 404).

than a boring waiting room where we anticipate being received by an important person. Purgatory, on the contrary, is a place of great suffering. Saint Augustine, interpreting the fundamental passage of 1 Corinthians 3, states: "That fire will nevertheless be harder to bear than anything we can endure in this life."[129] The Purgatory paraenesis should be extended in a double direction: (1) to encourage wayfarers to have Masses of suffrage celebrated, and to offer prayers, penitence, and alms to God for the souls in Purgatory; and (2) to urge an unceasing conversion even regarding the lighter sins, as well as the making of reparation for penalties due to those already committed.[130]

8.4. The Pains of Purgatory

The question about the pains proper to Purgatory still needs to be addressed. The cited Pauline text speaks of fire, which is why one could hypothesize that Purgatory is some kind of temporary Hell: the same sufferings of the kingdom of darkness are suffered, mitigated only by the certainty that they will one day end. It would be a Hell without the despair of Hell. But the theological reality of Purgatory is better described as an "antechamber" of Paradise, rather than the "periphery" of Hell. Saint Paul actually says, "the person will be saved, but only as through fire" (1 Cor 3:15). Therefore, one could hypothesize that the fire of Purgatory and that of Hell do not represent the same kind of suffering.[131]

8.4.1. Suffering as Fire, Shame, and Love

As we have seen, the fire of Hell, according to an accredited theology, causes suffering because it keeps prisoners away from God forever. This certainly does not occur in Purgatory. Moreover, absolute hatred is experienced in Hell—for God, for oneself, and for others—while in Purgatory the love and gratitude of salvation are already lived, even if the *visio* is lacking. Therefore, while the fire of Hell is the fire of the hate that consumes, the fire of Purgatory is the fire of love that burns. This certainly implies suffering, but of

---

[129] Saint Augustine of Hippo, *Enarrationes in Psalmos* 37.3, in *The Works of Saint Augustine: A Translation for the 21st Century*, vol. III/16, 148.

[130] In the same text, Augustine concludes: "Earthly sufferings are therefore much more bearable: and you nevertheless see that human beings, in order to not suffer them, are ready to do anything you command them. Whereas it would be better if they did what God commands, so as not to endure those other much more serious pains!" (our translation).

[131] See Saint Augustine of Hippo, *De civitate Dei* 21.26.

another kind.[132] It is not the suffering of those who hate and know that they will eternally hate. It is the suffering of those who love and cannot wait to meet the One they love, and Who loves them. Even on earth we speak of "burning love," or of "the fire of love." The person brings this way of living love into Purgatory, and now addresses it primarily to the Creator, more than to creatures. Of course, there can also be the dimension of shame, as a consequence of the possibility of being laid bare in regard to one's own infidelities before the Love of our life, with the fear of being presented naked (see Gen 3:10) before the eyes of God, Who sees all. Even this healthy shame can be a source of suffering and purification. Only when the soul is liberated from it will it be able to present itself before the face of God. We can thus apply the words of Saint John to the purification process of Purgatory: "In this is love brought to perfection among us, that we have confidence on the day of judgment because as he is, so are we in this world. There is no fear in love, but perfect love drives out fear because fear has to do with punishment, and so one who fears is not yet perfect in love" (1 John 4:17–18). Purgatory, as the school for the love that did not reach perfection on earth, is the "place" and the "time" in which we learn perfect love, that which casts out the fear of appearing before God. After Purgatory, Adam can come out from behind his bush (Gen 3:8).

> Some recent theologians are of the opinion that the fire which both burns and saves is Christ himself, the Judge and Savior. The encounter with Him is the decisive act of Judgment. Before His gaze all falsehood melts away. This encounter with Him, as it burns us, transforms and frees us, allowing us to become truly ourselves. All that we build during our lives can prove to be mere straw, pure bluster, and it collapses. Yet in the pain of this encounter, when the impurity and sickness of our lives become evident to us, there lies salvation. His gaze, the touch of His heart heals us through an undeniably painful transformation "as through fire." But it is a blessed pain, in which the holy power of His love sears through us like a flame, enabling us to become totally ourselves and thus totally of God.... The pain of love becomes our salvation and our joy.[133]

8.4.2. Temporal Punishment

This interpretation of fire as love also explains the concept of a temporal

---

[132] Purgatory "is entirely different from the punishment of the damned (Cf. Council of Florence [1439]: DS 1304; Council of Trent [1563]: DS 1820; [1547]: 1580; see also Benedict XII, *Benedictus Deus* [1336]: DS 1000)" (CCC §1031).

[133] Benedict XVI, *Spe Salvi*, §47.

punishment. In dispensing partial indulgences, the Church for a long time used to specify a number of days. For example, for the recitation of a prayer it was possible to obtain "one hundred days" of indulgence. This means that one will have to spend one hundred fewer days in Purgatory . . . But what does that really mean? Can we imagine a "time" of Purgatory completely the same as ours? What seems more likely is that time in Purgatory is not a cosmic time, linked to the materiality of the seasons, months, years, or lunar and solar orbits. Since Purgatory is a state of souls without bodies, it is permissible to think that it is a subjectively perceived time, which for obvious reasons the pilgrim Church had to express through temporal categories (days, weeks, years). Time, however, may have various "durations" according to the internal state of the subject who is waiting: one minute is always formed by sixty seconds, but it can "last" less than one second or feel like an eternity, depending on the particular situation of the one who is waiting. Pope Benedict XVI has emphasized that "it is clear that we cannot calculate the 'duration' of this transforming burning in terms of the chronological measurements of this world. The transforming 'moment' of this encounter eludes earthly time-reckoning—it is the heart's time, it is the time of 'passage' to communion with God in the Body of Christ."[134]

In this sense, one can hypothesize that joy and suffering in Purgatory are always together and that together they gradually increase, little by little, as the day of entry into Paradise approaches. With our categories and our experience, we know that when we are waiting for someone we dearly love, joy grows as the days that separate us from him or her pass, as the inner thorn of anxiety also increases, which torments us until we meet him or her. Not only the joy, but also this pain of being "on pins and needles," increases more and more as the hour approaches. There is therefore a progression of purification in Purgatory, where love and suffering progressively increase; and also in this, its character as the school of perfect love is revealed.

Let us conclude by citing a text by Tertullian, which we anticipated when we were discussing the suffering of Hell. This text is useful because it supports what we are saying about Purgatory as a simultaneous experience of joy and pain. In fact, souls suffer from psychological and spiritual pain, as they enjoy psychological and spiritual joy:

> Does the soul always have to await the body that it may feel sorrow or joy? Can't the soul of itself experience these emotions? Often, in fact, with no pain of body the soul alone is tortured by indignation,

---

[134] Benedict XVI, *Spe Salvi*, §47.

anger, or boredom, sometimes without being conscious of it. And again, when the body ails, the soul seeks out some haven of joy all its own and scorns the irritating company of the body. If I mistake not, the soul even rejoices and glories in the sufferings of the body. Take the case of Mucius Scaevola, when the fire was melting his right hand, or of Zeno when the torments of Dionysius passed over him. The bites of wild animals are the pride of youth, as Cyrus who gloried in the scars left by the bear. So the soul can easily manage to rejoice or be sad without the body in the underworld; during life it can weep when it pleases, though the body is unhurt, and likewise it can rejoice even in the midst of bodily suffering. Now, if it can do this by its own power in life, much more so after death can it by divine decree.[135]

In Purgatory, the soul suffers and rejoices. It rejoices over the Judgment of God that has declared it eternally saved; it suffers for the Judgment of God that has declared it not yet ready for Paradise. It rejoices because it desires to be with God forever and knows that it will; it suffers because it desires to be there immediately and it cannot. In both cases, the root is the will, which is also the root of love, to-will-good.

9. Paradise

9.1. Darkness, Fire, and Light

In beginning the treatment on Hell, we recalled the irreconcilable light-darkness binomial. If Hell is the place of darkness, Paradise is that of light. Dante expressed it poetically referring to the Empyrean as the "Heaven which is itself pure light."[136] The kingdom of Paradise is characterized by two aspects: that of divine light and that of love, and both are omni-expansive. Paradise is describable poetically as "light intellectual, which is full of love,"[137] "whose only boundaries are light and love."[138] This makes sense, if one keeps in mind that Heaven is the dwelling of God the Trinity. When treating the

---

[135] Tertullian, *De anima* 58, in *FCNT*, vol. 10, 307–308).
[136] Dante Alighieri (d. 1321), *Paradiso* 30.39, trans. Courtney Langdon (Cambridge: Harvard University Press, 1921), 351.
[137] Dante Alighieri, *Paradiso* 30.40.
[138] Dante Alighieri, *Paradiso* 28.54.

theme, we saw that Intellect and Love coincide perfectly in God, and this corresponds personally to the *Logos*/Son and the Holy Spirit. The Christocentric reference, then, gives further foundation to the character of Paradise as supernatural light: Jesus Christ is the Word incarnate, He who—according to the Niceno-Constantinopolitan Creed—is in Person "light from light" ("*lumen de lumine*"). The *Catechism* emphasizes that "to live in heaven is 'to be with Christ'" (CCC §1025). Since Christ is the divine Light incarnate (see John 1:4–5, 9; 3:19; 8:12; 9:5; 12:35–36, 46), Christocentrism is the second reason—along with the Trinitarian one—why the best image that describes Paradise is that of light. The three "kingdoms" of the great beyond, therefore, making reference to the main images that describe their reality, could also be called: the kingdom of darkness, the kingdom of the fire of purification, and the kingdom of light.

9.2. The Biblical Revelation

The existence of Paradise is revealed by Sacred Scripture, making recourse to different expressive registers.

9.2.1. The Kingdom of Heaven

A first word is that of Heaven or the kingdom of the heavens, understood as the place of the divine dwelling: "Our God is in heaven" (Ps 115:3). The Lord Himself attests: "The heavens are my throne, / the earth, my footstool" (Isa 66:1). In the First Book of Maccabees, the word "Heaven" is used simply to refer to God (see 1 Macc 3:18–19, 50, 60; 4:24, 55), even if other passages specify that this is not to be understood in the literal sense, because "the heavens and the highest heavens cannot contain you [O God]" (1 Kgs 8:27). Moreover, although the Old Testament generally retains that the dead do not ascend to Heaven, but rather go into *sheol*/underworld (see above), at least one exception is made in the case of Elijah: "Elijah went up to heaven in a whirlwind" (2 Kgs 2:11).[139] In this way, the great prophet represented a prefiguration of the true ascension, that of Christ, Who after the Resurrection is seen ascending into Heaven (see Acts 1:9–11; Heb 4:14; 9:24; Col 3:1). Saint Matthew the Evangelist, moreover, when he reports the sayings of Jesus regarding the kingdom of God, uses the Semitic expression "kingdom of heaven."

---

[139] The disappearance of Enoch is also understood in this way (see Gen 5:24; Sir 44:16; 49:14; Heb 11:5).

9.2.2. Eternal Life

A second expressive register is that of life. In fact, Paradise is the place of eternal life, of the true life. In Matthew 7:14, Christ calls the way that leads to Paradise, "the road that leads to life." In Matthew 10:39 (see also 16:25), the Master promises to those who have lost their earthly life for His sake, that they will find life again (in Heaven). And in Matthew 18:8–9 (19:17), Christ says the passage into Paradise is to "enter into life," contrasting it with being trapped in Gehenna. Finally, Matthew 25:46 speaks of "eternal life." The other synoptic Gospels confirm all of this.

In Saint John, the theme of Heaven as life is further reinforced. Baptism already causes a spring within us to gush forth that gives water in view of everlasting life (John 4:14): in fact, we do not enter Heaven by natural ordering, but as a result of elevation to a supernatural end, usually as a consequence of the first Sacrament. Christ speaks of "eternal life" in various passages (see John 4:14, 36; 5:24; 6:27; etc.).

The gift of life is explicitly linked to the other eschatological theme of the resurrection of the dead in John 5:21. The final resurrection will be "of life" for the good and "condemnation" for the others (see 5:29). The magnificent chapter 6, then, links the theme of life to the reception of the Eucharist, the "bread of life" (see 6:51, 53–54, 57, studied in the previous chapter). Naturally, John adequately highlights the theme of belief: in order to have eternal life we need to have faith in God and in the One whom He has sent, Jesus Christ (see 5:40; 6:33, 40, 47; 8:12; 11:25; 17:3; 20:31). This theme is reprised several more times in the Acts of the Apostles. Saint Paul also uses the terminology of life to refer to Heaven: "Those who receive the abundance of grace and of the gift of justification [will] come to reign in life through the one person Jesus Christ" (Rom 5:17). "For the wages of sin is death, but the gift of God is eternal life in Christ Jesus our Lord" (Rom 6:23). Numerous other New Testament passages could be cited.

9.2.3. The Celestial Jerusalem

A third term that describes the nature of Paradise is that of a city, Jerusalem in particular. Paradise is the celestial Jerusalem. Saint Paul accurately distinguishes the terrestrial Jerusalem from the one "above," intending these also as images of the ancient covenant in the law and of the new covenant in Christ (see Gal 4:21–26). Hebrews 12:22–23 says to believers: "You have approached Mount Zion and the city of the living God, the heavenly Jerusalem, and countless angels in festal gathering, and the assembly of the firstborn enrolled in heaven, and God the judge of all, and the spirits of the just made perfect." But the more important text on this topic is that of Revelation, in which the Seer refers to having contemplated the celestial Jerusalem that descends from Heaven (see Rev 3:12; 21:2, 10). The link between the two cities lies in the fact that Jerusalem was considered a holy city and the place of election: a holy city because it is the place of the Temple, that is, of the presence of God himself on earth; and the place of election because those who dwell within it were members of the chosen People of God. Thus, the analogy with Heaven is evident: Paradise is the true and proper dwelling of God and it is the place where His elect dwell (see Rev 21:3, 22).

As regards the word "city," it is often used in the eschatological sense in the same writings (see, in addition to the already-cited passages, Heb 11:10, 16; 13:14; Rev 21:14–16, 18–19, 21, 23; 22:2–3, 14, 19). The passage that says that in the middle of the city there "grew the tree of life" (Rev 22:2) is especially interesting. In this way, Revelation—the last book of the Bible—is reconnected with the first, Genesis. In Chapter Three we considered the fall of man and his expulsion from Eden, ordered by God so that he could not reach out to the tree of life (see Gen 3:22–24). Now, this tree is definitively interpreted as the gift of eternal life in Heaven. Revelation thus exclaims: "Blessed are they who wash their robes so as to have the right to the tree of life and enter the city through its gates" (22:14). The phrase "wash their robes" refers to 7:14: to those who "have washed their robes and made them white in the blood of the Lamb." This primarily concerns martyrs, but also those who have been washed of their sins in the merits of the Passion of Christ (the baptized; see Chapters Five and Ten).

9.2.4. "Lux Perpetua"

Among the passages just cited, there is one that leads back to the theme of light, with which we began this section: "The city had no need of sun or moon to shine on it, for the glory of God gave it light, and its lamp was the Lamb" (Rev 21:23). The text continues at verses 24–25, affirming that this light is perennial: all nations walk in that light and the gates of the celestial city never close because there is never night (this is repeated in 22:5). The throne of God and of the Lamb not only sheds light, but is contemplated by those present, who can fix their gaze on the light: "The throne of God and of the Lamb will be in [the city], and his servants will worship him. They will look upon his face" (Rev 22:3–4). After these two verses, the Book of Revelation offers only annotations (though very important ones) about the way to treat the Sacred Scripture, together with some exhortations. Therefore, this book and, along with it, the whole Bible, ends with this grandiose vision of the heavenly light of Paradise, contemplated by the elect. Light is the last word about Heaven, and in some ways also the last word of Sacred Scripture. This happens because it is also the first one. Indeed, God introduced Himself at the beginning as He who brings light into the world: the world was dark, but God said "let there be light" and there was light (see Gen 1:1–5). The God who "is light" (1 John 1:5) and lives in His own light (see 1 Tim 6:16), creates starting from light: He is the "Father of lights" (James 1:17). Light is the primary dimension, the fundamental environment desired by God for His creatures, especially for human beings; and the whole work of creation can be compared with the diffusion of light.[140] Human beings are therefore also destined to live in a superior light beyond this world. Since grace is not owed to nature, but also does not overturn nature, God created the natural world in light, because then the undue and gratuitous gift of the call to eternal life could confirm the natural desire that human beings experience, to be in the light more than in the darkness (when a child is born, it is said in Italian that he or she is "*dato alla luce*" ["brought to light"]—for human beings it is natural to come to light, to live is to be in the light).

Sin has disrupted all of this: because of it, human beings often prefer darkness (see John 3:19; 13:30). But Christ has come to reorient people toward the light, and He has come to call them "out of darkness into his wonderful light" (1 Pet 2:9): He is thus the *Orientale Lumen*, the Sun of Justice (Mal 3:20) that rises from on high to shine on those who stand in the darkness (Luke 1:78–79). He says of Himself: "I came into the world as light, so that everyone who believes in me might not remain in darkness" (John 12:46). Whoever follows Him—the Light of the world (John 8:12; 9:5)—can in turn become a small light in the world (see Matt 5:14) that directs others toward the narrow door of the eternal city, and above all that will have access to the celestial Jerusalem, reach out to the tree of life, eat of it, and "shall always be with the Lord" (1 Thess 4:17).

9.3. The Vision of God in Heaven

9.3.1. From Terrestrial Light to Celestial Light

God is therefore light,[141] He "who alone has immortality, who dwells in unap-

---

[140] "Creation occurs instantly, in such a way that when something is being created it is in the same moment created, just like when something is being illuminated it is simultaneously illuminated" (Saint Thomas Aquinas, *Summa contra gentiles* II, ch. 19 [our translation]).

[141] "Being light is proper to God; there are other beings that are luminous, that is, which

proachable light" (1 Tim 6:16). And the divine Word is also light, Who came from Heaven to dwell among us (see John 1:5, 9). Just as Christ is the Son by nature—which makes those who accept Him adopted children by grace (see John 1:13)—so He who is the Light makes us lights (see Matt 5:14, 16) and children of light (Luke 16:8). This is why whoever does evil despises the light, while whoever "lives the truth" comes toward the light (John 3:20–21). Saint John the Baptist was a witness who spread light around him (see John 5:35). The angels of God present themselves with a strong light, which is that of God himself (see Luke 2:9; Acts 12:7). This light of the faithful creatures comes from God and His Christ. In many cases, Jesus presents Himself with light: at the Transfiguration, or when He disarms Saul of Tarsus (see Acts 9:3; 22:6; 26:13). The divine light of Christ is shared with us: thus, we were once in darkness, but now we are light in the Lord (Eph 5:8).[142] If we conduct ourselves like children of the light, doing works of light (Eph 5:8–9), then we can one day "share in the inheritance of the holy ones in light" (Col 1:12). In Paradise, therefore, for the saved, "night will be no more, nor will they need light from lamp or sun, for the Lord God shall give them light, and they shall reign forever and ever" (Rev 22:5).

9.3.2. "Visio Beatifica"

Paradise, therefore, consists for human beings in being in the light and in contemplating the luminous face of God. Heaven is, essentially, seeing God—*visio Dei*. This vision fills souls with unspeakable joy, so it is called the "vision that renders happy" ("*visio beatifica*"). The *visio* is different from the *fides*, the faith that is given to us in this world while "we await the blessed hope" (Titus 2:13). As long as we live in this life, we live in the faith of the Son of God, Who has loved us and has offered Himself for us (see Gal 2:20). Thus, as Saint Paul writes, "at present we see indistinctly, as in a mirror, but then face to face. At present I know partially; then I shall know fully, as I am fully known" (1 Cor 13:12). Heaven, therefore, is a cessation of faith that gives way to vision. It is no coincidence that the Apostle recalls the theme of

---

participate in light. But only God is light by essence [*Deus lux est per essentiam*]" (Saint Thomas Aquinas, *Super Ioannem* XII, *lectio* 8 [our translation]). "God is light in the most proper sense [*propriissime Deus est lux*] and those who come closer to Him, the more they receive from the nature of light" (Saint Bonaventure of Bagnoregio [d. 1275], *In II Sententiarum*, d. 13, q. 1, a. 1, ad 3 [our translation]).

[142] It is no coincidence that Baptism is called "illumination" by the Eastern Christians. See Heb 10:32, which speaks of the trials to be faced by Christians after having received the "light of Christ."

knowing and being known. In Heaven, there is a vision that here on earth is only confusedly anticipated in faith, and there is a knowledge of God that is finally clear and direct: it is no longer indirect—like through a mirror—but unmediated. And this knowledge is not only of the notional order (the truth about God, the world, and the others), but it is also relational: knowledge of persons.[143] In that "place," we will be able to see God "face to face," which was not even granted to Moses while he was on earth. In fact, Scripture says that the Lord spoke to him "face to face" (Ex 33:11), but really this only indicates an intimacy of relationship that was not granted to anyone else in Israel. In fact, the story goes on like so:

> Then Moses said, "Please let me see your glory!" The LORD answered: I will make all my goodness pass before you, and I will proclaim my name, "LORD," before you; I who show favor to whom I will, I who grant mercy to whom I will. But you cannot see my face, for no one can see me and live. Here, continued the LORD, is a place near me where you shall station yourself on the rock. When my glory passes I will set you in the cleft of the rock and will cover you with my hand until I have passed by. Then I will remove my hand, so that you may see my back; but my face may not be seen. (Ex 33:18–23)

The face of God cannot be seen in this life. This is the conviction of those Old Testament figures who are afraid of dying because, having witnessed a theophany or angelophany, they believe they have seen God himself (see Gen 32:31; Judg 6:22–23; 13:22; etc.). The New Testament confirms that "no one has ever seen God" (John 1:18), precisely because He dwells in an "unapproachable light" and thus "no human being has seen or can see [Him]" (1 Tim 6:16). On the other hand, the New Testament promises that the day will come in which believers can truly contemplate the divine face (see Rev 22:4). "We do know that when it is revealed we shall be like him, for we shall see him as he is" (1 John 3:2). Actually, prior to the Apostles, this promise was made by Christ himself: "Blessed are the clean of heart, / for they will see God" (Matt 5:8).

---

[143] "In the context of Revelation, we know that the 'heaven' or 'happiness' in which we will find ourselves is neither an abstraction nor a physical place in the clouds, but a living, personal relationship with the Holy Trinity. It is our meeting with the Father which takes place in the risen Christ through the communion of the Holy Spirit. It is always necessary to maintain a certain restraint in describing these 'ultimate realities' since their depiction is always unsatisfactory. Today, personalist language is better suited to describing the state of happiness and peace we will enjoy in our definitive communion with God" (Saint John Paul II, *General Audience*, July 21, 1999, §4).

9.3.3. John XXII and Benedict XII

There have also been some doctrinal incidents regarding the question of the *visio beatifica*. Pope John XXII, as has been mentioned, had a personal opinion that was out of step with the one that was common in his time, and he believed that the *visio beatifica* could only be possible after the resurrection of the flesh at the end of time. In the intermediate state, therefore, the souls of Paradise would only have the vision of Christ's glorified human nature, but not of the divine essence. He presented this opinion in some homilies, which clearly have no definitive value as magisterial pronouncements. However, the day before his death, the Pope retracted with the following words: "We therefore confess and believe that the purified souls separated from the body are gathered together in Heaven . . . and that they, according to the common precept [*de communi lege*] clearly see God and the divine essence face to face, insofar as the state and the condition of the separated soul allows."[144]

The bull of retraction of John XXII would be published by his successor, Benedict XII, who wanted to bring the issue back to normalcy by publishing a constitution with which he expressed once and for all the faith of the Church on the *visio beatifica*. As a matter of fact, he had previously dedicated himself to the problem as a private author when, still as Cardinal Jacques Fournier, he had written the work *De statu animarum sanctarum ante generale iudicium* at the request of John XXII himself, who had been attacked rather harshly for his opinions by theologians such as Michael of Cesena (d. 1342), William of Ockham (d. 1347), and Durandus of Saint-Pourçain (d. ca. 1334). Fournier, while in his writings maintaining the common opinion in which the holy souls enjoy the *visio Dei* even before the Last Judgment, also wrote that the Pope had the right to offer, as a private author and not in an official way, his own opinion on the matter, even if this were different from the consensus of theologians. Upon becoming Pope, however, Cardinal Fournier—after instructing a commission of theologians to examine the issue—would define the faith of the Church on this matter:

> By this Constitution, which is to remain in force forever, We, with apostolic authority define the following:
>
> • According to the general disposition of God [*secundum communem Dei ordinationem*], the souls of all the saints . . . already before they take up their bodies again and before the general Judgment,

---

[144] John XXII, *Ne Super His* (DS 991).

have been, are and will be with Christ in Heaven, in the heavenly kingdom and Paradise, joined to the company of the holy angels;

- Since the Passion and death of the Lord Jesus Christ, these souls have seen and see the divine essence with an intuitive vision and even face to face [*visione intuitiva et etiam faciali*], without the mediation of any creature by way of object of vision [*nulla mediante creatura in ratione obiecti visi*]: rather the divine essence immediately manifests itself to them, plainly, clearly, and openly;

- And in this vision they enjoy the divine essence. Moreover, by this vision and enjoyment the souls of those who have already died are truly blessed and have eternal life and rest. Also the souls of those who will die in the future will see the same divine essence and will enjoy it before the general Judgment;

- Such a vision and enjoyment of the divine essence do away with the acts of faith and hope in these souls . . . ;

- And after such intuitive and face-to-face vision and enjoyment have or will have begun for these souls, the same vision and enjoyment have continued and will continue without any interruption and without end until the Last Judgment and from then on forever.[145]

There is no doubt about the will of the Pope to define these dogmas, which therefore pertain to the patrimony of the Catholic faith. Benedict XII defines the *visio beatifica* as a dogma of faith: the Church believes that in Heaven the saints are rewarded immediately after death (concerning this point, see what was said before) with the vision of God qualified as "intuitive," "immediate," and "face to face." In reality, John XXII had not completely denied the *visio*, but held that it would be postponed until the Final Judgment and that in the "intermediate state" it would be substituted with a provisional vision of the glorified humanity of Christ. Contrary to this position, the Church professes that when the soul enters Paradise, even before the Final Judgment, it already receives the reward that lasts eternally. Such a reward consists in seeing in an intuitive and direct way the essence of God and not only the glorified humanity of Christ. The *visio* brings an end to faith and hope, theological virtues practiced on earth precisely in the absence of the vision of God and yearning

---

[145] Benedict XII, *Benedictus Deus* (DS 1000–1001).

for it. In fact, "faith is the realization of what is hoped for and evidence of things not seen" (Heb 11:1): thus, when the human being finally sees God, he or she no longer has faith, no longer sees "through a mirror," but directly. As regards hope, "now hope that sees for itself is not hope. For who hopes for what one sees?" (Rom 8:24). Even hope, therefore, ceases in Heaven, because this virtue aims confidently at a good; when this good is present and provided, it is not longer hoped for, but rather, enjoyed. The only theological virtue that remains even in Paradise is thus charity: "Love never fails" (1 Cor 13:8).

9.3.4. Intellective Vision

As was said, at the time of these pronouncements, western theology had for some time reached a consensus regarding the *visio Dei*. Saint Thomas, strongly sustaining that in Paradise human beings enjoy the vision of the divine essence, provided an argument that is difficult to gloss over:

> With it being the case that intellection is the most proper and specific operation of the human being, it is necessary that on the basis of it beatitude is determined, when, that is, the intellect reaches its perfection. Now, since the perfection of the one who intends is the intelligible object itself, if in its most perfect intellective operation the human being did not reach vision of the divine essence, but another object, it would have to be said that this object renders the person blessed and not God.[146]

It is clear that one could invalidate the argument by casting doubt on the idea that intellection is the most proper and specific act of the human being. But this affirmation of principle is based on the more classical philosophical consideration of the human being, who is understood as a "rational animal," that is, an animal whose specificity is rationality. To this, however, one could still counter with what was just recalled in Saint Paul: that the one virtue that remains in Heaven is charity—love—and not knowledge. Thus, in Heaven, there would be no knowledge or intellection, or at least it would not constitute what is essential to the eternal reward. But here too we clash with the basic conception that Christianity has of the human being: in fact, love, if it is genuine, must proceed from knowledge of the truth. It is the intellect that provides the will the desired object. First one knows, then one loves (these aspects were touched on in various places in the previous chapters). This fun-

---

[146] *ST* "Supplement," q. 92, a. 1 (our translation).

damental anthropological structure is preserved even in Paradise, where the beatific love is a direct consequence of intuitive knowledge of God. Augustine writes: "We shall rest and see, see and love, love and praise."[147]

Intuitive (from *intus-ire*, to go within) knowledge means that it will be a form of knowledge different from what we usually have on earth[148]: here we know through concepts and by forming judgments; in Paradise the divine essence is known in a different way. According to Peter Lombard and Saint Thomas, the divine essence is united to the human intellect in a similar (but not equal!) way to that of how form and matter are united, for example, the soul to the body.[149] One can see in this proposal of the two eminent theologians an exegesis of the Pauline saying, according to which in Heaven God will be "all in all" (1 Cor 15:28). The fact that the vision of God will not come about through the mediation of creatures implies, then, that the divine essence will be seen directly by the intellect, without the aid of corporeal eyes,[150] which is one reason why the saints immediately gain access to their final state with respect to *visio*, even before the resurrection of their bodies. The eyes, as corporeal, are not in fact capable of seeing the divine essence. But, after the resurrection of the body, the glorified eyes will be able to bear the vision of the divine glory that reflects off the glorious bodies, especially that of Christ.[151]

9.3.5. "Lumen Gloriae"

We must add that the human intellect is not in itself capable of seeing God, not even through incorporeal and intuitive vision. The vision of the divine essence surpasses the capacities of the human intellect,[152] which thus require a special grace to be able to stare in contemplation on the nature of God. This special grace has assumed in theology the name of "*lumen gloriae*" ("light

---

[147] Saint Augustine of Hippo, *De civitate Dei* 22.30, in *FCNT*, vol. 24, 510.

[148] Thus "it is impossible for the soul of man, as long as it is in this (earthly) life, to see the essence of God" (*ST* I, q. 12, a. 11 [our translation]).

[149] See *ST* "Supplement," q. 92, a. 1, which cites Peter Lombard (d. 1160), *Sententiarum Libri*, II, d. 1, 10. See also *ST* I, q. 12, aa. 1, 5, and 9.

[150] "It is impossible for God to be perceived with the sense of sight" (*ST* I, q. 12, a. 3 [our translation]).

[151] See *ST* "Supplement," q. 92, a. 2. Saint Augustine of Hippo, *De civitate Dei* 22.29, affirms that the blessed will see God "with the spirit" even after the resurrection of their bodies. The Doctor, then, proposes different reflections on the possibility that God is also seen with glorified corporeal eyes.

[152] "It is impossible for a created intellect to see by its own powers the essence of God" (*ST* I, q. 12, a. 4 [our translation]).

of glory"), and it consists precisely in the grace of intellectual illumination that only the saints in Paradise receive, which renders their created intellect capable of intuiting the divine essence:

> The [human] intellect is proportionate for this contact [with the divine essence] not by its nature, but by the *lumen gloriae* that descends therein, strengthening it beyond its natural possibilities: and this is [also] called theophany.[153]

> To see the essence of God a certain similitude [with this essence] of the visual power is necessary, namely, the *lumen gloriae*, which strengthens the intellect so that it can see God; of which [*lumen*] is said in Psalm [36:10]: "and in your light we see light." One cannot, in fact, see the essence of God through some created similitude, which would represent this divine essence as it is in itself.[154]

> Since the natural power of the created intellect is insufficient for seeing the essence of God . . . it is necessary that by divine grace its capacity for understanding is increased. And this growth of the intellective power we call the illumination of the intellect. . . . By virtue of this light [the blessed] become deiform, that is, similar to God, according to the saying of 1 John 3:2; "when [God] is revealed, we shall be similar to Him, for we shall see Him as He is."[155]

The doctrine of the *lumen gloriae* was confirmed by the Ecumenical Council of Vienne.[156] On the basis of it, it again becomes clear why Paradise should be understood especially as light: *both* divine light—the light that is God—*and* the light of grace that elevates intellects for contemplating God's nature. Moreover, the beatifying character of the *visio Dei* (which is therefore called *visio beatifica*: it gives joy without end) is better understood. It is absurd to affirm that Paradise would be something static: to be staring at the divine essence, which could not offer true joy but rather monotony, even boredom. God is Love and infinite Beauty, in whose contemplation the soul experiences

---

[153] Saint Albert the Great, *Super Dionysium de divinis nominibus* 13.27 (our translation).
[154] *ST* I, q. 12, a. 2 (our translation).
[155] *ST* I, q. 12, a. 5 (our translation).
[156] The Council of Vienne condemns, among other errors of the Beguines and the Beghards, the following: "Any intellectual nature in its own self is naturally blessed, and the soul does not need the light of glory raising it to see God and to enjoy Him beatifically" (*Ad Nostrum Qui* [1312], §5 [DS 895]).

endless, and therefore always new, delight, free from any possible monotony:

> What is more admirable than divine Beauty? What reflection is sweeter than the thought of the magnificence of God? What desire of the soul is so poignant and so intolerably keen as that desire implanted by God in a soul purified from all vice and affirming with sincerity, 'I languish with love' [Song 2:5]? Totally ineffable and indescribable are the lightning flashes of Divine Beauty. . . . The rays of the morning star, or the brightness of the moon, or the light of the sun—all are more unworthy to be mentioned in comparison with that splendor and these heavenly bodies are more inferior to the true light than is the deep darkness of light, gloomy and moonless, to brightest noonday. This Beauty, invisible to the eyes of the flesh, is apprehended by the mind and soul alone.[157]

No boredom is possible where the soul is made capable of fixing its gaze on the infinity of the divine Beauty, which it will discover in an incessantly new way forever. Saint Thomas explains that the vision of God cannot but generate immense joy[158] and that this joy will be proportionate to the degree of sanctity reached.[159] On the other hand, Saint Augustine had already taught that in Heaven, God "will be the consummation of all our desiring—the object of our unending vision, of our unlessening love, of our unwearying praise."[160]

9.4. The Communion of the Triumphant Church

The reward of Paradise is also differentiated according to the merits obtained on earth, but this distinction is not a reason for envy and jealousy, where nothing that is disordered is admitted:

---

[157] Saint Basil the Great (d. 379), *Regulae fusius tractatae*, "Responsio II," 1, in *FCNT*, vol. 9, trans. Sister M. Monica Wagner (Washington, DC: CUA Press, 1962), 234–235.

[158] "*Visio Dei non potest esse sine delectatione*" ("There cannot be a vision of God without delight": *ST* II-II, q. 175, a. 3); "*Ille qui Deum videt, delectatione indigere non potest*" ("Whoever sees God cannot be lacking in delight": *ST* I-II, q. 4, a. 1 [our translation]; see *ST* I-II, q. 5, a. 4).

[159] "*Qui plus habebit de caritate, perfectius Deum videbit, et beatior erit*" ("Whoever will have more charity, will see God more perfectly, and will be happier": *ST* I, q. 12, a. 6 [our translation]).

[160] Saint Augustine of Hippo, *De civitate Dei* 22.30, in *FCNT* vol. 24, 506.

Who can imagine, let alone describe, the ranks upon ranks of rewarded saints, to be graded, undoubtedly, according to their variously merited honor and glory. Yet, there will be no envy of angel for archangel—for this is one of the great blessednesses of this blessed City. The less rewarded will be linked in perfect peace with the more highly favored, but lower could not more long for higher than a finger, in the ordered integration of a body, could want to be an eye. The less endowed will have the high endowment of longing for nothing loftier than their lower gifts.[161]

The comparison between angelic choirs and the choirs of saints was taken up by the Doctor of the Church Saint Robert Bellarmine (d. 1621), in one of his works entitled *The Eternal Happiness of the Saints*, written in 1616: in Paradise, before the nine angelic choirs, there stand nine human choirs of saints: (1) Patriarchs; (2) Prophets; (3) Apostles; (4) Martyrs; (5) Confessors; (6) Shepherds and Doctors; (7) Priests and Levites; (8) Monks and Hermits; and (9) Holy Women (virgins, widows, and wives).[162] Further on, Bellarmine reinforces these teachings, speaking of the harmony that prevails among the citizens of the heavenly City and writes that human beings who are saved come—as is taught in Rev 5:9— from every tribe, tongue, people, and nation, and that to them are added the choirs of angels: angels who "are much more numerous than human beings and are distinguished not by race, peoples, and languages, but by the diversity of their nature, namely, the specific difference of each."[163] Despite the greater number of angels with respect to humans, and their individual specific difference between themselves, which human beings do not have, it is still the case that "all [angels and humans] are effectively citizens [of Heaven], concordant, unanimous, and they treat each other according to the one and only law of charity. Therefore, they are of one heart

---

[161] Saint Augustine of Hippo, *De civitate Dei* 22.30, in *FCNT*, vol. 24, 506–507.

[162] See Saint Robert Bellarmine, *De aeterna felicitate sanctorum* 1.2. The title of the work was probably chosen by Saint Robert making reference to *De civitate Dei* 22.30, which is entitled "*De aeterna felicitate civitatis Dei, sabbatoque perpetuo*" ("the eternal happiness of the city of God and the everlasting sabbath"). Saint Robert sustains an opinion different from that of Saint Gregory the Great, which had been largely accepted by the medieval theologians. According to Gregory, the saved human beings would have formed a tenth choir, after the nine angelic ones (see *Homiliae in Evangelia* 2.34.6: the opinion is based on an allegorical reading of Luke 15:8–10).

[163] Saint Robert Bellarmine, *De aeterna felicitate sanctorum* 2.2 (our translation). Concerning the specific difference of the angels, see Chapter Three. Implicit reference is made to *ST* I, q. 50, a. 4.

and mind."[164] As is well-known, these last words come from the Acts of the Apostles (4:32), where they describe the communion existing among Christians. The fact that Saint Robert used this verse in another context suggests that angels and human beings form a true celestial communion in Heaven, the communion of the triumphant Church.

9.5. Vision, Faith, and Theology

The reflection on the *lumen gloriae*, in addition to confirming the absolutely undue character, in Heaven too, of divine grace and the elevation of the human being to the supernatural level and end, is also connected to the theme of faith and theology. We have said above that faith subsists as long as one does not have the vision. It is also true, however, that faith is oriented toward the vision of God in Heaven and that it prepares one for it. Therefore, even if not seeing the divine essence is proper to faith, this virtue develops a way of seeing on the part of the soul, which will reach its fullness and end only in the *visio beatifica*. This is why Saint Augustine says "*habet fides oculos suos*" ("faith has its own eyes").[165] If, on the one hand, faith is obscurity—lack of vision—it develops, on the other hand, our spiritual eyes. "Faith comes from what is heard" (Rom 10:17), but faith also produces a vision. We receive faith

---

[164] Saint Robert Bellarmine, *De aeterna felicitate sanctorum* 2.2 (our translation). We can use this as a cue to mention a theme of scholastic theology, which passes under the name of "*Cur homo?*" ("Why [was] the human being [created]?"). For a time, the idea was held that the human being was created and ordered to heavenly glory in order to occupy the places left by the fallen angels. In fact, this was sustained by Saint Gregory the Great in the same homily mentioned two notes above: "The woman [mentioned in Luke 15] had ten drachmas because nine are the angelic orders and, so that the number of the elect was achieved, as the tenth, man was created" (our translation; Saint Anselm of Aosta, in *Cur Deus homo*—discussed in Chapter Four—is inclined toward this thesis). This, however, would render the human being only a means to an end: to make it so that the celestial city not be imperfect, with it presenting gaps. Honorius of Autun (d. 1154) took a stand against this idea in the *Liber XII quaestionum* and then again in the *Libellus VIII quaestionum*. Peter Lombard, *Sententiarum libri*, II, 1.5, would say that it should not be thought that man would not have been created if the angel had not sinned; but we can accept that, among other and more important causes, this one too may have been a reason for the divine decision to create humanity, that is, to complete the number of the elect in Heaven. In the *Scriptum super Sententiis* II, d. 1, q. 2, a. 3, Saint Thomas Aquinas would maintain a similar position, while highlighting better than Lombard the centrality and importance of the human being in the universe.

[165] Saint Augustine of Hippo, *Epistula* 120.2.8 (our translation). The link with eternal life becomes explicit in the same passage: "The faithful must therefore believe what they do not yet see in such a way as to hope and love to see in the future."

from on high: we believe by hearing and accepting the words of God. But then faith also teaches us to look at the world, the present and the future, with new and better eyes, in the light of the Word of God that we have accepted. It thus helps us to evaluate the world and our life in light of the Paradise that calls us and awaits us as our destiny. As Pope Francis has written, "hearing God's Word is accompanied by the desire to see His face."[166]

For theology too, being the science of faith, all of this cannot be irrelevant. If faith "sees" and prepares for the beatific vision in Heaven, the science of faith should also in its own way live in this contemplative dimension. Saint Thomas teaches that sacred doctrine, or theology, is a participation on earth in the science enjoyed by God and the blessed in Paradise.[167] In light of the last things, it is confirmed that theology cannot be an arid and self-satisfied science, separated from true spirituality, that is, separated from a sure faith and the devout prayer that cultivates and conserves it. Theologians, in light of their final destination in Heaven, must know that they are not superior Christians, but rather, humble servants of God called to be instruments of the salvific plan in their particular role as scholars or teachers. They are not scientists of the faith in the sense that they possess a superior level of faith—a purer and disenchanted level—which distances them from the despicable ignorance and the spirituality of the great mass of the baptized that borders on superstition. They are Christians like all the others, torn from the slavery of sin and death by the pure mercy of God, and called to serve their brothers and sisters in faith, that is, the Church, with a humble, zealous, and devout service. It is this service, free from worldly conditioning and the search for personal affirmation, that also gives simplicity and purity of heart, as well as joy, despite the toil of the work.

This is why we can conclude this brief discussion on Paradise, and with it the whole work, by referring to the criterion, which the Lord Jesus has shown us, for knowing whether we are on the right path to reach Paradise:

> Amen, I say to you, unless you turn and become like children, you will not enter the kingdom of heaven. Whoever humbles himself like this child is the greatest in the kingdom of heaven. . . . Let the children come to me, and do not prevent them; for the kingdom of heaven belongs to such as these. (Matt 18:3–4; 19:14)

---

[166] Pope Francis, *Lumen Fidei* (2013), §29 (most of the encyclical was delivered to the Pope already redacted by his predecessor Benedict XVI: see §7).

[167] See *ST* I, q. 1, a. 2.

Epilogue

I believe the whole revealed dogma as taught by the Apostles, as committed by the Apostles to the Church, and as declared by the Church to me. I receive it, as it is infallibly interpreted by the authority to whom it is thus committed, and (implicitly) as it shall be, in like manner, further interpreted by that same authority till the end of time.

I submit, moreover, to the universally received traditions of the Church, in which lies the matter of those new dogmatic definitions which are from time to time made, and which in all times are the clothing and the illustration of the Catholic dogma as already defined.

And I submit myself to those other decisions of the Holy See, theological or not, through the organs which it has itself appointed, which, waiving the question of their infallibility, on the lowest ground come to me with a claim to be accepted and obeyed.

Also, I consider that, gradually and in the course of ages, Catholic inquiry has taken certain definite shapes, and has thrown itself into the form of a science, with a method and a phraseology of its own, under the intellectual handling of great minds, such as St. Athanasius, St. Augustine, and St. Thomas; and I feel no temptation at all to break in pieces the great legacy of thought thus committed to us for these latter days.

Saint John Henry Newman, *Apologia pro Vita Sua* (1864), Ch. 5.

Biblical Index

Old Testament

Genesis (Gen)
1, 121, 220–221, 221n56, 229, 232
1:1, 401
1:1–2, 349
1:1–5, 928
1:3, 204, 404
1:26, 122n14, 401, 406, 433
1:26–28, 220
1:27, 224n64
1:28, 121, 554, 727
1:31, 142
1–3, 120n12
1–11, 295
2, 221n56, 225, 228, 230
2:7–9, 15–25, 229
2:18, 21–23, 726
2:22, 638n49
2:24, 727
2:25, 246n101
3, 232, 240–241, 246, 250, 254–255, 780, 866n3
3:1–7, 240
3:8, 922
3:10, 922
3:12, 729
3:14–19, 245
3:15, 488
3:16, 225, 246n101, 729
3:20, 250
3:22, 222n57, 406, 833n122
3:22–24, 927
3:23–24, 881
3:24, 218n52, 327
5:24, 925n139
6:17, 346
8:20, 782
11:1–9, 546n10
11:6–7, 406
12, 295
14:17–20, 295, 697
15:9, 782
17:7–8, 401
19:1, 407
28:18, 782
28:21, 401
32:31, 930

Exodus (Ex)
1, 206n16
3:5, 581

Biblical Index

3:8, 773
3:14, xxvii, 282, 286
4:11, 256n118
4:22–23, 402
7, 778
12, 773, 774, 774n14
12:5, 773
12:15, 774
12:35, 774n14
12:46, 780
13:21–22, 778
14:21–31, 779
16, 774
16:13–27, 31, 33–35, 775
16:20, 55, 802
17, 778, 780
19:6, 697
20:1, 403
20:23, 401
24:4–10, 780–781
29, 697
30:7, 782
32:10, 521
33:11, 930
33:18–23, 403, 930
34:28, 403

Leviticus (Lev)
1, 782
1:3, 782
1:4, 603
1–7, 782
3, 782
6:19, 782
7:2, 782
8, 697
10:14, 782
11:44, 581, 582
11:45, 401
16, 312

16:20–22, 603
16:21, 602
16:34, 297
17:11, 264, 312
17:14, 808n55
24:18, 312

Numbers (Num)
8:10–12, 603
8:23–26, 697
9:12, 780
15:22–24, 26, 30–31, 744
15:41, 401
16:3, 697
20:24, 777
21, 780n21
21:9, 780
27:18–23, 603
28:7, 782

Deuteronomy (Deut)
6:16, 777
8:5, 402
9:22, 777
15:21, 782
18:15, 302
19:21, 312
22:20–21, 531
23:19, 312
24:1–4, 727
32:8, 215n45
32:39, 256n118
32:51, 777
33:8, 777
34:9, 603
34:10, 403

Joshua (Josh)
5:12, 802
15:8, 907

18:16, 907

Judges (Judg)
6:22–23, 930
11:29, 782
13:22, 930

1 Samuel (1 Sam)
2:6, 256n118

2 Samuel (2 Sam)
7:12–16, 403

1 Kings (1 Kgs)
8:27, 925
18, 816

2 Kings (2 Kgs)
2:11, 925
21:6, 782
23:10, 907

2 Chronicles (2 Chron)
28:3, 907
33:6, 907

Judith (Jdt)
16:17, 905n92

1 Maccabees (1 Macc)
3:18–19, 50, 60, 925
4:24, 55, 925

2 Maccabees (2 Macc)
12:38–45, 913

Job (Job)
1:12, 241
2:6, 241
2:10, 256n118

26:6, 905n92

Psalms (Ps)
2:7, 296, 403
8:6, 210, 241
9:18, 905n92
16:10, 905n92
24:7-8, 10, 327
31:6, 345, 411
31:18, 905n92
32:8, 393
33:6, 204, 349, 404
39:10, 533
49:14–15, 18–20, 905n92
51:5, 743
51:7, 519n85
68:34, 658n85
78:24–25, 777n19
81:11, 777n19
86:13, 876n20
88:11, 905n92
89:27–28, 403
95:8, 778
97, 908n96
106:10, 328n109
106:32, 778
110:4, 296, 697
111:10, 394
115:3, 925
139:7. 404
147:15–18, 404

Proverbs (Prov)
8:35, 369
9:10, 394
15:11, 905n92
27:20, 905n92

Ecclesiastes (Eccles)
5:1, 28

Biblical Index

9:10, 908n96

Wisdom (Wis)
1:5–7, 405
1:7, 348, 404
1:14, 905n92
2:13, 402
2:23–24, 209, 247n104
2:24, 241
4:19, 905
7:25, 431
13:5, 128
16:20–21, 777n19
18:14–16, 404

Sirach (Sir)
11:14, 256n118
11:27–28, 127
11:28, 891
23:4, 402
44:16, 925n139
49:14, 925n139

Isaiah (Isa)
1:2, 401
1:6, 765n204
1:11, 15–17, 783
6:3, 407, 413
6:8, 406, 424n23
7:14, 494, 494n23, 532
9:6, 393
11:2, 348
11:2–3, 367
11:12, 566n43
22:22, 599
32:15, 405
40:3–5, 495
42, 299n57
42:1–4, 344
44:3, 405

45:7, 256n118
49, 299n57
49:8, 908n96
50, 299n57
50:11, 905n92
52:13–15, 300n58
52–53, 299n57
53:4, 312
53:5, 312
53:6–7, 299
53:7, 774n13
55:8–9, 93
59:21, 405
61:1–2, 344
63:4, 899
65:17, 900
66:1, 925
66:24, 905n92, 907

Jeremiah (Jer)
6:16, 102
7:21–23, 783
7:32, 907
19:6–7, 907
31:31–34, 235, 772
32:40, 235

Lamentations (Lam)
3:38, 256n118

Ezekiel (Ezek)
11:19, 405
16:60, 235
18:31, 405
33:11, 239, 930
36:26–27, 405
36:27, 366n45
37:26, 235

Daniel (Dan)
7:13–20, 895n67
10:12–14, 20–21, 215n45
12:1, 215n45
12:2, 905n92

Hosea (Hos)
6:5–6, 783
6:6, 295n54

Joel (Joel)
3:1, 374
3:1–2, 405
4:1–2, 622, 902

Amos (Am)
5:21–24, 783

Micah (Mic)
6:6–8, 783

Zechariah (Zech)
4:1–2, 85n103
12:10, 780

Malachi (Mal)
1:11, 772
3:20, 928

New Testament

Matthew (Matt)
1:18, 344, 494
1:18–19, 531
1:18, 20, 344
1:20, 283, 494
1:20–21, 533
1:21, 362, 501
1:23, 494

1:24, 534
1:24–25, 494
1:25, 501
2:2, 178
2:13–14, 534
2:16–18, 688
2:19–21, 534
3:1–3, 495
3:11, 344
3:16, 344
4, 270, 905
4:1, 344
4:4, 377
4:16, 905
4:18–19, 597
5, 325, 764, 915
5:8, 930
5:14, 928
5:14, 16, 929
5:21–48, 302
5:22, 906
5:23, 783
5:25–26, 914
5:26, 919, 919n124
5:29–30, 906
5:37, 94, 597
5:44–45, 414
5:48, xxviii, 582
6:9, 347, 361n33
6:10, 612
6:11, 803n45, 804n45
6:24, 93n116, 319
6:25–32, 414
6:30, 234n82
6:33, 190
7:6, 685
7:13–14, 911
7:14, 926
7:15, 613
8:4, 783

Biblical Index

8:11–12, 906
9:1–8, 746
9:12, 853n168
9:13, 295n54, 783
9:37–38, 357
10:8, 765
10:20, 345
10:28, 906
10:29–31, 414
10:38, 319
10:39, 926
10:40, 302, 561
11, 538n128
11:11, 538n128
11:20–24, 895
11:27, 416
12:7, 783
12:18–21, 344
12:28, 344, 347, 411, 851
12:31, 744
12:31–32, 346
12:32, 914–915, 919n122
12:38–40, 336
12:41–42, 302, 895
12:46–50, 535n117
12:47, 507
13:24–30, 621
13:36–43, 894
13:52, 2, 56
13:55, 535n116
14, 303
14:13–21, 799
14:31, 597
15:24, 302
15:32–38, 799
16:4, 336
16:13–19, 595, 598
16:15–16, 417
16:18, 549
16:19, 562, 747

16:21, 324, 887
16:25, 926
17:24–27, 597
18:3–4, 939
18:8–9, 926
18:9, 906
18:18, 562, 600, 747
19, 894n64
19:3–6, 727
19:8, 302
19:10, 728
19:10–12, 505n48
19:17, 926
19:27–30, 717
19:28, 119
19:28–30, 894
20:28, 266, 300n58
21:22, 333
21:33–44, 415
22:13, 906
23:15, 907
23:33, 907
24, 151n67
24:3, 899
24–25, 895
24:27, 658, 658n85
24:29, 895, 896
24:30, 895
24:31, 894
24:35, 165
24:36, 899
24:48, 816
25, 15
25:31–34, 41, 893
25:31–46, 549
25:41, 907, 910
25:46, 926
26, 772
26:23, 795
26:25, 159

948...

26:26, 796, 797, 814n71
26:26–30, 788
26:28, 266, 674n3, 830
26:30, 795
26:64, 895n67
27, 882
27:50, 345
27:52, 539n133
27:62, 794
28:18, 440
28:18–19, 426
28:18–20, 386
28:19, 257, 346, 375n65, 588, 623
28:19–20, 20, 161, 322, 375, 445, 683
28:20, 581, 603, 678, 778n20

Mark (Mark)
1, 270, 905
1:1, 417
1:1–4, 495
1:8, 344
1:9–11, 410
1:10, 344
1:11, 417
1:12, 344
1:15, 746
1:16–17, 597
2:5, 748
2:17, 746
3:13, 715
3:14, 322
3:28–29, 346
5:37, 597
6, 303
6:3, 507
6:13, 763
6:30–44, 799
6:43, 799
7:31–37, 347
8:1–9, 799

8:31, 324
8:32, 597
8:33, 597
8:34, 319
8:36, 547, 872
9:2, 597
9:7, 417
9:35, 702
9:37, 302
9:43–47, 906
9:48, 907
10:12, 728
10:17–22, 15
10:18, 764n202
10:43–44, 612
10:44, 612n122
10:45, 116, 612, 887
11:1–11, 305n65
12:26, 559
12:28–33, 851
12:33, 783
12:35–37, 305
13, 151
13:2, 783
13:4, 899
13:11, 345
13:32, 899
14, 772
14:22–26, 788
14:24, 309
14:26, 41, 795
14:33, 597
14:34, 512
14:36, 322, 411
14:37, 597
14:53–65, 409n9
14:61, 305
14:62, 895n67
15:38, 783
15:39, 417

Biblical Index

16:15, 375n65, 384n86
16:16, 360, 383n82, 683
16:18, 765

Luke (Luke)
1:7, 495
1:8–20, 59–66, 495
1:26–35, 410
1:28, 483, 502
1:31, 283
1:34, 496, 504
1:35, 343–344, 417, 486, 497, 582, 591
1:38, 485, 513n73
1:41, 344
1:43, 500
1:44, 538n128
1:46–55, 520n86
1:48, 526, 531n108
1:78–79, 928
1:79, 905
2:9, 929
2:22–38, 534
2:25–27, 344
2:35, 511
2:48–49, 535
2:49, 520n86
2:52, 270
3, 303
3:1–6, 495
3:16, 344
3:22, 344
4, 270, 905
4:1, 344
4:18, 43, 302
5:1–11, 597
5:3, 597
5:35, 323
6:13, 589
7:16, 764

7:36–50, 745n163, 898n70
7:49, 745
8:21, 520n86
9:10–17, 799
9:23, 319, 389
9:48, 302
10:9–10, xxxii
10:16, 302, 561, 611
10:18, 218, 866–867
10:21, 345
10:34, 765n204
10:38–42, 322
11:3, 803n45, 804n45
11:13, 345
11:20, 347–348, 411
12:1, 39n40, 807n52
12:5, 906
12:10, 346
12:12, 345
12:47–48, 384
12:48, 598
12:58–59, 914
13:2–5, 764
15, 938n164
15:8–10, 937n162
15:11–32, 414, 746
16, 327n107, 882, 895
16:8, 929
16:13, 42, 93n116
16:19–31, 872, 879
16:22, 882n36
16:23, 26, 881n34
18:1, 661
18:13, 52n59
19:44, 558
21, 151n67
21:19, 766
22, 772
22:8, 597
22:14–20, 39, 788

22:17, 795
22:19, 699, 796
22:20, 235, 795–796
22:31–32, 598
22:32, 171
22:53, 905
23:43, 882
23:46, 324, 345, 411
24:26, 324
24:30, 800
24:30–35, 800
24:39, 334
24:39–40, 300
24:47, 375n65
24:48, 376
24:49, 340, 570
24:50–53, 339
24:51, 867

John (John)
1, 282–283
1:1, 27, 33, 126, 144, 425, 429n36
1:1–3, 284n34, 403, 434
1:1, 18, 144
1:2–3, 142
1:4–5, 9, 925
1:5, 9, 929
1:9, 85n103
1:12, 418, 418n19, 446, 555, 677
1:12–13, 418
1:13, 929
1:14, 3, 27, 115, 144, 266, 273, 277, 803
1:14, 18, 144
1:17, 148, 302
1:18, 282n31, 591, 930
1:19–23, 495
1:29, 298, 300, 774, 798
1:32, 344
1:32–33, 410
1:33, 344
1:36, 298
1:40–42, 597
1:42, 597
2:1–11, 497
2:1–12, 69
2:4, 410
2:10, 56
3, 240, 780, 883
3:3, 418, 617
3:5, 383, 683
3:5–7, 542
3:8, 359
3:13, 866
3:14–15, 780
3:16, 418, 424, 555n25
3:16, 18, 418
3:17, 302, 424n25
3:19, 905, 925, 928
3:20–21, 929
3:22, 800n40
3:35, 416
4:1–2, 622
4:2, 800
4:10, 413n14, 454, 468, 779
4:14, 801, 926
4:14, 36, 926
4:15, 802
4:18, 728
4:23, 345
4:24, 345
4:34, 302
5, 416, 764
5:2, 151n67
5:14, 746
5:19–23, 410
5:21, 926
5:23–24, 416
5:24, 302, 926
5:24–30, 803n44
5:25, 418n19

...951

Biblical Index

5:28–29, 893
5:29, 926
5:30, 424n27, 612
5:35, 929
5:36, 410, 591
5:36–37, 417
5:40, 926
6, 802
6:1–15, 799, 801
6:12, 801
6:16–21, 801
6:20, 282
6:26, 801–802
6:27, 678, 801–802, 926
6:29, 802
6:30, 802
6:30–31, 801
6:31–32, 801
6:32, 302
6:33, 40, 47, 802–803, 926
6:34, 802
6:35, 48, 803, 855
6:39, 801
6:41–42, 803
6:48–51, 786, 803
6:50, 835
6:51, 53–54, 57, 926
6:52, 830
6:52–58, 803
6:53, 803
6:54, 803
6:55, 803
6:56, 804
6:57, 786, 855
6:58, 804, 830
6:60, 804
6:61, 804
6:63, 346, 804, 819
6:64, 804
6:68, 3, 804

7:16–17, 424n27
7:37–38, 779
7:37–39, 335
8:12, 905, 925–926, 928
8:24–29, 58, 282
8:31–32, 303
8:32, 378
8:34, 264
8:34, 36, 303
8:40, 283
8:42, 424n26
8:44, 217, 745
8:58, 302
9, 764
9:2, 764
9:5, 925, 928
9:41, 745
10:8, 613
10:10, 855
10:14–18, 266
10:15, 266, 324
10:17–18, 266, 311, 335, 511
10:28, 366
10:30, 284, 416, 436n55, 591
10:33, 712
10:36, 591
11, 330
11:25, 926
11:51, 324
11:52, 556n27
12:7, 765
12:20–36, 417n17
12:24, 333
12:24–25, 807
12:26, 513n73
12:32, 340, 867
12:35, 908, 925
12:35–36, 46, 925
12:45, 444
12:46, 905, 928

13:3, 424n26
13:6, 597
13:20, 561
13:23–24, 597
13:25, 882n36
13:26, 795
13:30, 928
14:1–3, 337, 896n69
14:2–3, 270
14:6, 140, 142, 303, 379n72, 394, 571, 663, 855
14:8–11, 416
14:10–11, 468
14:13, 333
14:15–17, 421
14:16, 521
14:16–17, 347
14:17, 348, 350, 359
14:18, 561
14:23, 364
14:26, 347, 422
14:28, 284, 436n55, 440
15, 676, 807
15:1–11, 562
15:5, 355, 367
15:14, 232n76
15:16, 333
15:20, 695
15:26, 347, 359, 422, 445
16:5–15, 570
16:7, 335, 347, 476
16:7, 13–15, 347
16:7–15, 423
16:13, 42, 100, 173, 350, 359, 381
16:23–24, 333
16:24, xxxii
17, 552
17:3, 380, 926
17:9, 744
17:19, 311, 311n76, 783

17:20–21, 577
18:1, 682
18:5–6, 282
18:33–37, 306
18:36, 377
18:37, 304, 307
19:11, 307
19:15–27, 598
19:25–27, 500
19:33–37, 779
19:34, 512, 638n49
20:17, 339, 361n33, 867
20:19, 331
20:22, 347, 748
20:22–23, 347, 628, 747
20:23, 562, 600n99
20:26, 339
20:27, 300
20:31, 418n19, 926
21, 603
21:15–19, 598
21:19, 23, 602
21:24–25, 150
21:25, 629n29

Acts of the Apostles (Acts)
1:1–3, 629
1:2, 345
1:3, 339
1:4–5, 340, 376, 925
1:6–11, 339
1:7, 902
1:8, 375, 695
1:9–11, 867, 925
1:13, 15, 598
1:15–26, 598
1:16, 419
1:24, 610
2:1, 588
2:1–13, 374

Biblical Index

2:3, 348
2:14–21, 405
2:14–36, 285, 374
2:14–41, 598
2:22, 410n10
2:24, 334, 412
2:27, 881n34, 905n92
2:27, 31, 881n34
2:32–33, 335, 412
2:33, 335, 347
2:36, 336
2:42, 395n115, 771, 786–787
2:42–46, 180
2:42–47, 579
3:6–7, 598
3:11–26, 285
3:14–15, 336
3:18, 324
3:22, 302
4:8, 285, 418, 598
4:8–12, 285
4:12, 255
4:32, 938
5:1–11, 598
5:29, 285, 598
5:29–32, 285
5:34–39, 305
6:6, 603
7:51, 419
7:59, 411n12
8:14–17, 691
8:20–23, 598
8:29–40, 299
9:3, 929
9:5, 561
9:32–42, 598
10:23–24, 598
10:34–43, 285
10:35, 554
10:38, 624

10:42, 301, 892
10:48, 598
11:24, 418
11:26, 28
12:5, 598
12:7, 765, 929
12:7–11, 598
13:2, 419, 646
13:2–3, 323, 603
13:9, 418
13:16–41, 285
14:23, 323
14:27, 682
15, 271
15:7–11, 598
15:28, 419
16:6–7, 419
17:22–31, 285
17:26, 231n73
17:28, 209
17:31, 336
17:34, 592
19:1–6, 691
20:7–12, 771
20:28, 309
22:6, 929
26:13, 929
26:18, 905
28:16, 604

Romans (Rom)
1:3–4, 345
1:5, 176, 176n123
1:7, 582
1:19–20, 128
1:20, 133n35, 139n41
2:14–15, 206
3:25, 116, 313
5, 249, 254, 255n117, 887
5:1, 292

New Testament

5:8–11, 291
5:10, 263
5:12–21, 249
5:15–17, 257
5:17, 926
5:20, xxix, 258
6:3–7, 686
6:4, 682n23
6:9, 330
6:10, 838
6:23, 247n104, 511, 926
8, 229, 245, 420
8:9, 348, 359, 476n134, 571
8:9–11, 420
8:10, 247, 247n105
8:14–16, 420
8:15, 345, 348
8:17, 767
8:18–23, 900
8:19–22, 219, 249
8:20–21, 237
8:24, 933
8:24–25, 91
8:27, 582
8:28–30, 870
8:29, 571
8:31–32, 337
8:32, 159, 266, 324
9:1–5, 559
9:16–24, 874
9:22–24, 558
10:7, 328
10:17, 178, 938
11:11, 558
11:28–29, 557
11:29, 696
11:30-32, 557
11:36, 391
12:2, 83, 101, 390, 552
12:4, 562

12:4–5, 562
12:5, 562–563
12:6, 111
12:13, 582
12:21, 238
13:12, 905
15:15–16, 646
15:25–26, 31, 582
15:26–27, 646
16:1, 713
16:2, 15, 582
16:26, 176, 176n123

1 Corinthians (1 Cor)

1:2, 582
1:13, 621
1:22, 802
1:24, 393
1:30, 362
2:10–11, 421, 457n99
2:11, 348, 350
2:13, 421, 577
2:16, 254, 348
3, 921
3:1–2, 685
3:10–15, 915
3:15, 921
3:16, 364
3:16–17, 420, 571
4:1, 611, 622
4:4, 301, 892
4:15, 256, 611, 802
6:19, 420, 571
6:20, 309
7:1–2, 8–9, 730
7:12–16, 739
7:23, 309
10:1–2, 686
10:1–6, 778
10:3–4, 785

Biblical Index

10:4, 780
10:16, 785
11, 772
11:1, 304
11:2, 159
11:18, 784
11:19–22, 786
11:20, 784
11:21, 785
11:23, 159, 589, 628, 810n61, 850
11:23–25, 784, 788
11:23–32, 785
11:24, 311n77, 699
11:25, 235, 795
11:26, 862
11:26–30, 674
11:27, 784
11:27–32, 833n122
11:28, 785
11:28–29, 617
11:29, 833
12, 562
12:4, 91
12:4–11, 421, 581
12:4–13, 420
12:7, 3, 187
12:12–21, 562
12:13, 577
12:27, 562
12:28, 187
13:8, 933
13:9, 303
13:12, 6, 147, 194, 777n18, 929
14:33, 582
15, 334
15:1–3, 589
15:3–8, 330
15:5, 598
15:12–14, 329
15:20–23, 270

15:20–24, 337, 549
15:20-28, 549
15:26, 247n104
15:28, 862, 934
15:35–50, 875
15:36, 333
15:45, 119n9, 256, 269, 335
15:47, 119n9, 255, 265, 269
15:52, 894
15:54–55, 887
16:22, 341, 749, 863, 882n36

2 Corinthians (2 Cor)

1:3, 192
1:17–19, 94
1:21–22, 421
1:22, 678
1:23–24, 613
2:5–11, 749n167
3:3, 351
3:5, 367
3:6, 235
3:7–18, 302
3:8–9, 611
3:9–10, 557n29
3:17, 348, 359, 406n4, 571
3:18, 571
4:6, 304
5:6–7, 147
5:8, 881
5:14–15, 17–21, 292
5:17, 119, 556n26, 687
5:18–21, 748
5:19, 292
5:21, 67
6:2, 908
6:14, 623, 905
9:11–12, 646
10:3, 889
11, 717

11:2, 717
12:2, 876n20
13:13, 426

Galatians (Gal)
1:19, 598
2:11–14, 83n100
2:20, 159, 311, 316n86, 591n91, 929
3:13, 66, 314n80
3:26–27, 360
3:27, 687
3:27–28, 563
4:4–6, 420
4:6, 345, 419, 476n134, 571
4:21–24, 156
4:21–26, 926
5:1, 358
5:7, 359
5:13, 358
5:22, 367
5:24–25, 351
6:15, 119

Ephesians (Eph)
1:3, 192
1:3–12, 870
1:3–14, 425
1:7, 309
1:13, 348, 678
1:17, 425
1:22–23, 562
2:3, 555n25
2:8, 175
2:14–18, 293, 567
2:18–22, 425
2:19–22, 589
2:20, 614
3:1–12, 618
4:4–5, 577
4:4–6, 426, 547n10

4:5, 178
4:9–10, 339
4:11–16, 614
4:12, 9, 562
4:13, 903
4:15, 562
4:23–24, 222n58
4:30, 678
5, 76–77, 717
5:1, 304
5:2, 311
5:8, 929
5:8–9, 929
5:11, 905
5:21–33, 731
5:22, 225
5:23, 225
5:25, 225
5:25–26, 581
5:27, 687
5:32, 737
5:33, 225
6:10–17, 676n7
6:12, 889
6:18, 661

Philippians (Phil)
1:6, 175
1:19, 571
1:20–24, 891
1:29, 175
2, 282
2:7–8, 328
2:13, 366n45, 369
2:17, 646
2:29–30, 646
3:8, 394
3:20, 543
4:3, 904

Biblical Index

Colossians (Col)
1:12, 929
1:13, 905
1:15, 29n24, 227n66, 571
1:17–18, 562
1:18, 270, 562, 855
1:20, 217
1:21–22, 292
1:24, 317, 320, 766–767
1:26, 618
2, 562
2:9, 483
2:9–10, 562
2:12, 686
2:15, 328
2:19, 562
3:1, 925
3:10, 223n58
3:12–13, 322

1 Thessalonians (1 Thess)
4:15, 894
4:17, 928
5:1–3, 901
5:4–5, 905
5:17, 661

2 Thessalonians (2 Thess)
2:13–14, 426
2:15, 150n65
3:6, 14, 749

1 Timothy (1 Tim)
1:18, 889
1:20, 749n167
2:4, 65, 149, 304, 870, 872
2:5, 663
2:5–6, 290, 591
3:2, 717n100
3:2–5, 717

3:2–5, 12, 49
3:9, 810
3:12, 717n100
4:14, 603n104, 703n72
5:9, 717n100
6:3, 161
6:12, 161, 889
6:16, xxvii, 928–930
6:20, 161

2 Timothy (2 Tim)
1:6, 603, 703n72
1:12, 24n14
1:14, 161
2:2, 161
3:14–17, 155
4:2, 20, 302
4:7, 889
4:8, 301, 892
4:14–15, 749

Titus (Titus)
1:2, 911n105
1:6, 717n100
2:13, 929
3:4–7, 426
3:10–11, 749n167

Hebrews (Heb)
1:3, 29n24, 677n10
1:7, 646
1:14, 646
2:7, 210, 241
2:16, 122
2:17, 313, 663
3:1, 663
4:13, 236n86
4:14, 925
4:15, 313, 582
5:8–14, 189n160

5:11–14, 685
6:1–2, 691
7, 295
7:7, 296
7:9–10, 298
7:24–25, 332
7:24–27, 311
7:25, 840
7:26, 582
7:27, 838, 843
8:1–2, 646
8:4, 298, 698
8:6, 646
8:13, 235
9–10, 787
9:7, 297
9:11–15, 24–28, 311
9:12, 297, 309, 313, 796
9:13–14, 309
9:14, 345, 411
9:15, 235
9:24, 925
9:27, 888
10:9–14, 311
10:26–29, 744
10:32, 929n142
11:1, 5, 177, 933
11:5, 925
11:6, 178, 380, 683
11:10, 16, 927
11:13–16, 543
12:2, 100
12:22–23, 926
12:23, 892
12:24, 235
13:8, 100, 289
13:9, 100
13:10, 787
13.14, 927
13:20, 235

James (James)
1:13, 241
1:17, 928
4:7–8, 241
4:12, 892
5, 765–766, 766n207, 766n207, 766n208, 767
5:9, 892
5:14–15, 628, 763
5:14–16, 767

1 Peter (1 Pet)
1:3, 192
1:11, 359
1:18–19, 116, 266, 299, 310
1:19, 774n14
1:20, 117n6
2:4–5, 9, 671
2:5, 9, 698
2:9, 9, 309, 905, 928
3:15, 4, 187
3:19, 327, 881
3:20–21, 686
4:6, 327
4:14, 348
5:1–3, 613
5:3, 171

2 Peter (2 Pet)
1:2–3, 5–6, 8, 304
1:3–4, 360
1:4, 555n25
1:16–21, 155
2:4, 217, 906
2:20, 304
3:13, 900
3:18, 304

1 John (1 John)
1:1–3, 403

Biblical Index

1:5, 928
1:6, 905
2:1, 521
2:2, 116, 277, 313, 591
2:9, 11, 905
2:20, 240n91
2:27, 240n91
2:29, 418
3:2, 471, 930, 935
4, 892
4:6, 359
4:9–10, 416
4:10, 116, 266, 313
4:17–18, 922
4:19, 831
5:16–17, 745

2 John (2 John)
10, 749

3 John (3 John)
8, 143

Jude (Jude)
6, 217, 905

Revelation (Rev)
1:5, 389
1:18, 328, 905n92
1:20, 215n45
2:10, 389
2:11, 889
3:5, 904
3:7, 599
3:12, 927
3:20, 304, 851
4:2–3, 5–6, 8, 412
4:5, 85n103
5, 301
5:5, 309

5:6, 84, 300, 412
5:9, 937
7:14, 301, 927
8–11, 894
9:11, 905n92
12:1, 502, 509
12:7–9, 218
12:9, 241
13:8, 904
16:10, 905
17:8, 904
20:1–10, 901
20:2, 780
20:11–15, 904
21:2, 10, 927
21:3, 22, 927
21:14, 589
21:14–16, 18–19, 21, 23, 927
22:1, 85, 412, 413n14
21:22, 626, 777
21:23, 85, 927
21:24–25, 927
22:2, 927
22:2–3, 14, 19, 927
22:3–4, 927
22:4, 930
22:5, 927, 929
22:14, 927
22:18–19, 55
22:20, 341, 749, 896n69

Index of Names

Abelard, Peter, 828
Adam of Saint Victor, 481
Adrian I, 369
Aëtius of Antioch, 443
Agatho (Pope), 469n125
Alacoque, Margaret Mary, 53, 373
Albert the Great (Albertus Magnus), 203n7, 894n62, 935n153
Alcuin of York, 474, 474n132
Alexander III, 735n138, 735n140, 817
Alexander VII, 374n61, 501n35
Alighieri, Dante, 93n116, 93n22, 523, 882, 924nn136–138
Ambrose of Milan, 94n118, 241n93, 248n106, 427n31, 464, 489n13, 551n18, 584n78, 591n91, 641n55, 658n84, 674n3
Andrew of Crete, 490, 490n15, 503, 503n41
Anselm of Canterbury, 5, 115, 130, 131n31, 185n151, 314n80, 315, 452n88, 456n, 461n112, 478, 484n5, 503, 742, 757
Apollinaris of Laodicea, 272, 273
Arius of Alexandria, x, 126, 271–273, 427n30, 441, 447
Aristotle of Stagira, 63, 94, 136, 140–141, 141nn47–48, 189, 219n53, 233n81, 457, 585, 738, 818, 818n82, 823n98, 827, 828n108
Arnauld, Maria Angélique, 373
Arnauld, Antoine, 373
Athanasius of Alexandria, x, 29n24, 124n17, 202n3, 362n34, 441, 441nn66–67, 442nn68–69, 443, 447–448, 464, 941
Athenagoras of Athens, 430–431, 880n30
Augustine of Dacia, 156n78

Augustine of Hippo, x, 5, 11, 43, 72, 101, 110, 120n11, 129, 139n43, 148, 148n60, 154n74, 156nn79, 158, 170, 175n119, 177, 178n131, 180n139, 185n150, 189n158, 208, 211, 214n41, 222, 222n57, 223nn58–59, 231n74, 234n82, 236n85, 238, 240n91, 244n97, 247n103, 247n105, 248n107, 253–254, 254n116, 261n1, 277n24, 285n34, 306nn66–67, 307n69, 318n90, 344n3, 353, 353n18, 354, 356, 356n24, 360n28, 362n34, 368, 372, 386n91, 391n101, 394, 407n6, 408, 415n15, 438, 440–441, 448–451, 451nn87–88, 452–457, 459, 461, 461n112, 462, 467, 468n123, 472, 475, 476n134, 477, 478n142, 495n24, 502n37, 506, 506n54, 517, 518, 556, 561, 586n82, 612n122, 619, 619nn3–4, 621–623, 630–631, 632n35, 639n53, 647n63, 654n79, 658, 658n86, 661n94, 662, 680n18, 684n27, 718, 737–738, 745n163, 765n203, 771, 772n9, 773n11, 777n18, 787, 804n46, 819, 821, 826n105, 831, 853n168, 856–857, 857nn175–176, 873–874, 874n16, 875n17, 876, 876n20, 881n32, 882n37, 883n41, 886n51, 889n56, 894nn63–64, 895, 900, 902, 902nn80–83, 903, 903nn85–88, 904, 904nn90–91, 908n95, 921, 921nn129–131, 934, 934n151, 936, 937n161, 938, 938n165, 941

Baius, Michael, 372–373
Balthasar, Hans Urs (von), 11, 187–188, 188nn155–156
Bandinelli (see Roland of Siena)
Báñez, Domingo, 370–371
Barnabas (*Letter of*), 122n14, 161n93, 222n57, 911
Basil the Great, 84n101, 151, 152n68, 214n44, 215n45, 392n107, 407n7, 442–443, 443n70, 444–446, 450, 475, 477n138, 936
Bay, Michel (de) (see Baius, Michael)
Bede the Venerable, 38, 355
Bellarmine, Robert, 172, 213, 543n4, 573, 574n59, 666n103, 889, 937, 937nn162–163, 938n164
Benedict of Norcia, 86
Benedict VIII, 475
Benedict XII, 44n45, 171, 823, 880n29, 893n61, 908, 909n98, 931–932
Benedict XIV, 36, 117, 481n1, 538n128, 679n15, 696n53, 733n133, 891n59
Benedict XV, 108, 535n119
Benedict XVI, 13–14, 17–18, 18n8, 19n9, 32n30, 53n61, 83n100, 91n113, 99n122, 105, 110, 111n151, 117, 127n22, 128, 129n27, 140, 143, 143n53, 145n57, 149, 149n63, 152–153, 153n70, 157n83, 158n86, 171n112, 177nn129–130, 180nn137–138, 181, 182n143, 188, 188n156, 191n163, 197, 199n170, 205n13, 205n15, 224n64, 230n69, 255n117, 262n2, 281n30, 296, 297n55, 300n58, 311n76, 316n84, 320n94, 321–323, 338, 360n29, 376n67, 379n71, 386n91, 387n94, 389, 520n86, 525, 537n127, 543, 550n17, 588,

588n87, 592n93, 609n117, 614n125, 635n44, 652n75, 655–656, 663n96, 665n102, 667n114, 682n23, 700n59, 703, 709n81, 722, 733, 733n135, 763n200, 792n31, 795n34, 799n39, 831, 851, 854n170, 856n174, 857n175, 858, 862n190, 892n60, 902n78, 915, 916n114, 918, 918n121, 922n133, 923, 939n166

Berengar of Tours, 818

Bernadette (see Soubirous, Marie-Bernarde)

Bernardine of Feltre, 539n132

Bernardino of Siena, 530n106, 531n107, 539n132

Bernard of Clairvaux, 2, 38, 213n40, 265n7, 497n28, 498–499, 502n38, 507n56, 512n69–70, 523, 526n95, 533n112, 828n109

Bérulle, Pierre (de), 845

Biel, Gabriel, 80

Bloy, Léon, 22

Boethius, Severinus, 455, 460, 878

Bonaventure, 116, 189, 189n159, 190, 191n165, 197, 264n5, 436, 456, 656, 710, 929n141

Boniface II, 175n121

Boniface VIII, 564n38, 583

Boniface IX, 710n89

Bossuet, Jacques-Bénigne, 236, 367n50

Bozius, Thomas, 574n59

Bridget of Sweden, 703

Bultmann, Rudolf, 198, 311n76

Buonarroti (see Michelangelo)

Cajetan, Thomas (see De Vio, Thomas)

Calixtus, Georg, 59

Calvin, John (Jehan Cauvin), 35, 65, 65n74, 68, 72–73, 76, 77n91, 78, 101, 327, 369, 372–373, 508, 870, 870–871, 871n9

Cano, Melchor, 195–196

Caravaggio (Michelangelo Merisi), 136

Cassian, John, 366n49

Catherine of Siena, 599

Celestine I, 95n119

Cerularius, Michael, 35, 475

Caesar, Gaius Julius, 206n17, 307, 428

Caesarius of Arles, 355n21, 871

Chardon, Louis, 682n22

Charlier de Gerson, Jean (see Jean Gerson)

Cicero, Marcus Tullius, 206n16, 324n100, 647, 648n66
Cyprian of Carthage, 382n79, 548, 577, 578nn66–67, 814n70, 831n115, 836n130, 919n124
Cyril of Alexandria, 31, 52, 52n60, 275n23, 276, 284n33, 311n76, 447, 448n81, 477, 855
Cyril of Jerusalem, 541n1, 587, 820n88, 844n147, 858n180
Clement of Alexandria, 129
Clement of Rome, 604
Clement I, 880n30
Clement VI, 78n94, 877n20
Clement VII, 654n79,
Clement XII, 107n134
Constitutiones apostolorum, 657n84, 810n61
Copernicus, Nicolaus, 203n7
Cornelius a Lapide, 538n128
Cornelius (Pope), 578
Constantine the Great, 750n168

Damasus I, 390
Decentius of Gubbio, 766n208
De Vio, Thomas, 108, 172n113, 759n186
Didascalia Addai, 657n84,
Didascalia apostolorum, 657n84
Didache, 544, 772n10, 831n115, 880n30, 911
Didymus the Blind, 443
Diognetus (Letter to), 912
Dionysius of Halicarnassus, 645n62
Dionysius (Pope), 468–469
Dominic of Guzmán (also known as Dominic of Osma), 614
Donatus of Casae Nigrae, 621
Duns Scotus, John, 116, 117nn5–6, 205, 205n13, 491, 503, 518n83
Durandus of Saint Pourçain, 931
Duvergier de Hauranne, Jean (called Saint-Cyran), 374

Eadmer of Canterbury, 503
Eck, Johann, 573, 573n58, 574n59
Elizabeth of Hungary, 248n108
Elizabeth of the Trinity, 360n30
Epiphanius of Salamis, 505n50, 515
Erasmus of Rotterdam, 24n15

Index of Names

Escollar, Juan, 535n118
Escrivá, Josémaria, 210
Eunomius of Cyzicus, 442
Eusebius of Caesarea, 381n76
Eutyches of Constantinople, 278, 280

Faà di Bruno, Francesco, 203n7
Ferreri di Guarda, Zaccaria, 654n79
Ficino, Marsilio, 93n115
Fishacre, Richard, 827n105
Flavian of Constantinople, 279
Florus of Lyon, 64n71, 873
Fournier, Jacques (see Benedict XII)
Francis of Assisi, 224n63, 486n7, 614, 703, 762n198, 890
Francis de Sales, 507, 534n115, 539, 539n133
Francis (Pope), 15–17, 21, 22n12, 25–26, 26n18, 28n22, 83, 99–100, 105n130, 149, 176n122, 177n127, 178n133, 179nn135–136, 187, 188n156, 203n4, 224nn62–64, 304n64, 537, 568n47, 676n7, 712, 733n134, 792n31, 912n110, 939
Francis Xavier, 373
Fulgentius of Ruspe, 277n24, 464, 469n124, 884n41

Galerius, Valerius Maximianus, 750n168
Galilei, Galileo, 203n7
Gaunilo of Marmoutiers, 131
Gelasius I, 745n161
Gennadius of Massilia, 283n32
Gerbert of Aurillac (see Sylvester II)
Germanus of Constantinople, 513, 513n73
Gottschalk of Orbais, 64n71, 871n9
Gregory of Nazianzus, 42, 273n22, 348, 348n7, 408n8, 425n28, 442, 445, 445nn75–77, 446–447, 447n120
Gregory of Nyssa, 214n44, 442, 444n73, 445–446, 446nn78–79, 447, 447n80, 450, 477n138
Gregory of Tours, 510, 511n65
Gregory the Great, 30, 213, 213n39, 214n42, 217n49, 278nn24–25, 561, 561n36, 612n122, 676n7, 883n38, 894n62, 908n96, 910n104, 915, 915n113, 937n162, 938n164
Gregory VII, 719, 818n82
Gregory XVI, 379n72

···965

Grignion de Montfort, Luigi Maria, 486n7, 499n33, 521, 522n88, 528
Grosseteste, Robert, 436
Guerric of Igny, 486n8

Hegel, Georg Wilhelm Friedrich, 88n109, 103n126, 119n10
Henry II, 475
Henry VIII, 705
Hermas, 202n1, 908n97
Hilary of Poitiers, 215n45, 308n72, 440, 441n65
Hildegard of Bingen, 203n7, 583n77
Hippolytus of Rome, 693n40
Hobbes, Thomas, 184n149, 216, 216n46
Honorius of Autun, 938n164
Honorius I (Pope), 171n113
Hormisdas (Pope), 468n121
Hosius, Stanislaus (Hozjusz, Stanisław), 574n59
Hugh of Saint Victor, 626n22
Humbert of Arles, 735n142, 881n35
Hume, David, 216, 216n46
Hus, Jan, 58, 64n71, 816

Iamblichus of Chalsis, 645n61
Ignatius of Antioch, 202n3, 317, 486n8, 578, 578n68, 582, 585n81, 604, 638n48, 676n7, 698, 702n67, 702nn69–70, 784, 833n122, 880n30, 911
Ignatius of Loyola, 51
Ildefonsus of Toledo, 506n53
Innocent I, 693n42, 766n208, 883n40
Innocent III, 218n50, 392n106, 620n8, 684n27, 694n45, 735n142, 806n48, 815n75, 846n154, 881n35, 884
Innocent IV, 918, 919n122
Innocent VI, 108n138
Innocent VIII, 710n89
Innocent X, 374
Irenaeus of Lyon, 23n13, 29n25, 78n93, 119n9, 163, 163n95, 179n134, 211n33, 222n57, 246n100, 261, 261n1, 263n3, 266n8, 327n108, 349n11, 351n13, 433, 434nn49–50, 435n52, 489, 489n14, 497n27, 503n42, 505n49, 507n56, 571n53, 590, 604, 604n105, 604n108, 680n17, 753, 772n10, 855n172, 889n55, 918n121
Isaac Israeli ben Solomon, 142n49
Isaac of Stella, 523

Isidore of Seville, 871n9, 894, 895n65, 899n71
Isidore of Isolanis, 539n132

Jacopone da Todi, 511n66
Jansen, Cornelius, 373
Jean Gerson, 539n132
Joachim of Fiore, 466
Joan of Arc, 815n76, 896n69
John of Antioch, 485n6
John of Ávila, 362, 496n26
John of the Cross, 14n2, 51n58, 165
John Chrysostom, 551, 659n88, 735, 835, 895, 896n68
John Damascene, 38, 64n72, 122n15, 210n29, 215n45, 227n67, 268n12, 326n106, 492, 506n53, 510, 658n84
John IV of Constantinople (Nesteutes), 612n122
John XXII, 107, 108n137, 171n113, 885n48, 893n61, 931–932
John XXIII, 13, 108, 168n105, 207nn20–21, 537, 537n126, 540n133, 652n74, 720
John Paul II, 13, 50n56, 109, 109n146, 110n147, 126, 126n20, 127nn23–24, 129n27, 140n44, 168n106, 169n107, 170n108, 183, 199, 216, 216n47, 223n60, 230n69, 230n71, 244n97, 246n101, 247n102, 270n17, 291n46, 308n72, 318, 319nn91–93, 320n95, 345n5, 349n10, 361n32, 374n63, 375nn64–65, 376n67, 376n69, 377, 378n70, 384n86, 387, 387n93, 418n21, 479, 482n2, 486n7, 487n9, 488n10, 491n16, 494n23, 496nn25–26, 500n34, 514n74, 527–528, 528nn102–103, 534n115, 536, 536n121, 537n125, 538n130, 546n9, 550n17, 559n31, 568n47, 584, 592n93, 609n117, 659n88, 709, 709n82, 715–716, 716nn98–99, 721, 721n113, 725n120, 727nn124–126, 731, 733n135, 737n145, 741n157, 742n158, 753n172, 756n180, 757n182, 764n201, 787n26, 795n33, 800n41, 849nn158–160, 850nn161–162, 852n167, 853n169, 854n170, 858, 858n181, 930n143
Jovinian of Rome, 505n52
Jerome of Stridon, 215n44, 604n105, 902n81
Julian of Toledo, 887n53, 896n68, 899n71, 903, 904n91, 910n104, 920n128
Justin Martyr (of Nablus), 222n57, 263n3, 328n112, 489n12, 774n13, 784, 880n30, 901n76

Kant, Immanuel, 130
Kepler, Johannes (von), 203n7
Kolbe, Maximillian Maria, 528, 613n123
Konrad von Marburg, 248n108,

···967

Kopernik, Mikołaj (see Copernicus, Nicolaus)

Lambertini, Prospero Lorenzo (see Benedict XIV)
Lanfranc of Canterbury, 818n82
Lactantius, Lucius Caecilius Firmianus Leibniz, Gottfried Wilhelm (von), 129, 604n105
Leo the Great, 47n50, 239n90, 258, 275n23, 277n24, 279, 331n116, 341, 341n132, 436n55, 468n121, 560–561, 561n33, 584, 584n79, 604, 605n109, 625, 625n19, 719, 778n20
Leo II, 171n113
Leo III, 474–475
Leo IX, 391n100, 818n82
Leo X, 606, 606n112, 654n79, 759n186, 913n111
Leo XIII, 106n133, 108, 108n138, 109n146, 192n167, 207n19, 238n89, 307n70, 322, 322n97, 345n6, 353n18, 391, 391n102, 392, 392n105, 392n107, 394, 394nn113–114, 395n117, 396n123, 468n123, 470n128, 527, 536nn121–122, 564, 565n39, 571, 631n34, 705, 705n78, 917n116
Leontius of Byzantium, 455
Leontius of Jerusalem, 32n31
Lessing, Gotthold Ephraim, 267, 267n10
Liguori, Alfonsus, 353n18, 512nn67–69, 514n77, 528, 889
Livy (Titus Livius Patavinus), 647
Longo, Bartolo, 514
Lucidus of Gaul, 871
Luther, Martin, 7, 9, 11, 24n15, 35n33, 58–61, 61n68, 62, 62n69, 63, 64, 64n72, 66, 66n75, 67, 68, 69, 69n78–79, 70, 70n82, 71, 71n83, 72–75, 75n87–88, 76–78, 78n95, 79–80, 101, 147, 148, 150, 182, 287, 314n80–81, 369, 532n109, 573, 606, 627, 665n102, 758, 759n186, 816, 819, 844, 913n111

Macedonius of Constantinople, 444
Majella, Gerard, 320
Marcellus of Ancyra, 268n13, 238n59
Marcion of Sinope, 147, 433, 468, 623
Martin of Braga, 464
Martin of Tours, 766n211
Martin V, 620n8, 710n89
Maximus of Turin, 682n21
Maximus the Confessor, 85n103, 280
Melanchthon, Philip (Philipp Schwarzerdt), 69n80

Melito of Sardis, 512n68
Michael of Cesena, 931
Michelangelo, 136, 332n118
Molina, Luis (de), 369–370, 370n54, 371, 371n55
Montfort (see Grignion de Montfort)
Montini, Giovanni Battista (see Paul VI)
Moscati, Giuseppe, 203n7
Mozart, Wolfgang Amadeus, 896
Muhammad, 154

Nestorius of Constantinople, x, 31–32, 52, 52n60, 275, 275n23, 276–279, 284n33, 369n52, 447, 485, 500, 855
Newman, John Henry, 11, 104n130, 156n79, 174n117, 223n58, 389n96, 737n146, 941
Nicholas of Cusa, 93n115
Nicholas I, 735n139
Nicetas of Remesiana, 582
Nicodemus the Hagiorite, 50n55
Novatian of Rome, 437, 437n58, 438n60

Oresme, Nicolas (d'), 203n7
Origen of Alexandria, 29n24, 202n3, 215n45, 308n72, 328n109, 438, 439n61, 638n49, 658n84, 684n26, 858n179, 909n99
Ottaviani, Alfredo, 544n5

Pacelli, Eugenio (see Pius XII)
Pacian of Barcelona, 254, 256, 256n119, 676, 677n8
Paulinus of Aquileia, 474
Paul III, 654
Paul IV, 509, 509n62, 654
Paul V, 371, 371n56, 372n57
Paul VI, xxvii, 13, 19, 82, 95, 106, 109, 217n48, 231n72, 251n110, 256n118, 338, 349, 376n66, 385n88, 386n89, 387n92, 426, 483n3, 514, 524n92, 526, 544n5, 545n7, 594, 615, 625, 634n40, 652n74, 663, 691–693, 705n77, 713, 715, 720, 759, 759n187, 759n189, 760, 761n194, 765n206, 768, 791n29, 792n31, 809–813, 817n81, 820, 838n139, 847, 848nn156–157, 857n177, 863, 875n19, 912n110
Parmenides of Elea, 142n49
Pascal, Blaise, 374
Paschasius Radbertus, 818n82

Pelagius (Britannicus), x, 356, 368, 372, 884
Pelagius I, 469n125, 909n99
Philip III, 371
Photios of Constantinople, 35, 37, 475, 479
Pico della Mirandola, Giovanni, 93n115
Peter Damian, 673n1
Peter Chrysologus, 506n54
Peter Lombard, 619n5, 673, 735n141, 737, 910n104, 934, 934n149, 938n164
Peter Waldo, 813
Pius II, 239n90
Pius IV, 606n112, 679n14
Pius V, 104, 104n129, 372, 372n58, 488n11, 634n40, 654n79
Pius VI, 885n46
Pius IX, 45, 208n23, 209n27, 379n72, 382n81, 501, 501nn35–36, 536n120, 537n126, 538n129
Pius X, 107n134, 108, 108nn139–140, 139n41, 160n90, 165, 186n152, 667, 667n105, 692n39, 696n51, 834, 834n126, 854n171, 919n123
Pius XI, 108–109, 667, 718, 730, 734
Pius XII, 46, 89n110, 103n125, 108, 108n143, 120n12, 230, 231nn72–73, 251, 316n86, 367, 367n51, 382n81, 383n83, 393n109, 394nn113–114, 396n125, 491, 491n18, 492n20, 503, 503n44, 504n45, 509, 509n63, 512n71, 517, 518n83, 527n98, 537n126, 538n130, 545nn7–8, 554n23, 555n25, 565, 565n40, 570n52, 571n54, 584, 585n80, 586n83, 643–644, 644n58, 645, 645n59, 651, 651nn73–74, 652, 654n78, 658n86, 659n87, 660, 660nn91–93, 662, 664, 664n99, 665, 665nn100–102, 667n104, 668, 668nn107–108, 669n109, 671, 704, 704nn75–76, 706n79, 719n105, 726n122, 740, 740n155, 838nn138–139, 840n142, 841n143, 847, 847n155, 870n7, 900
Pius of Pietrelcina, 323, 528
Polycarp of Smyrna, 880n30, 906n93
Pomerius, Julianus, 903, 903n89
Praxeas, 435
Proclus of Constantinople, 681n20
Prosper of Aquitaine, 95n119, 369, 641n54, 643, 920, 920n128
Prudentius of Troyes, 64n71
Pseudo–Celestine, 369, 641n54
Pseudo–Chrysostom, 735n139
Pseudo–Dionysius the Areopagite, 213, 592
Pullen, Robert, 817

Index of Names

Quiñones, Francisco, 654n79
Quodvultdeus of Carthage, 688, 688n33

Rabanus Maurus, 381n75
Ratramnus of Corbie, 818n82
Ratzinger, Joseph (see Benedict XVI)
Remigius of Auxerre, 533n114
Remigius of Lyon, 64n71
Rhetius, Lorenz, 245n99
Richard of Saint Victor, 184, 184n148, 456, 460n108, 478
Radulphus Ardens, 753–754, 754n173–174
Roland of Siena (see Alexander III)
Roncalli, Angelo Giuseppe (see John XXIII)
Rosmini, Antonio, 42n44
Rupert of Deutz, 478, 483n4, 899n71

Scaevola, Gaius Mucius, 924
Schmidtner, Johann Georg Melchior, 489n14
Scotus Eriugena, John, 64n71
Sicard of Cremona, 673
Sylvester II, 593n94
Symeon the New Theologian, 42
Siricius (Pope), 396n126, 719, 719n106
Sixtus V, 527
Sophocles of Colonus, 207n18
Soubirous, Marie–Bernardette, 501n36
Steensen, Niels (see Steno, Nicolas)
Stephen I, 56
Stein, Edith, 559n31
Steno, Nicolas, 203n7
Sulpicius Severus, 767n211

Tacitus, Publius Cornelius, 648n65
Tatian the Syrian, 327n108, 429, 429n36, 880n30
Theodosius I, 750n168
Theophilus of Antioch, 211n33, 222n57, 431, 431n44, 432, 432n45–46, 909n101
Terence (Publius Terentius Afer), 768n214
Teresa Benedicta of the Cross (see Stein, Edith)
Teresa of Ávila, 11, 370, 536, 536n123, 890, 890n58

Teresa of Calcutta, 11, 378
Thérèse of Lisieux, 320
Tertullian of Carthage, 17, 17n6, 116n2, 118, 118n7, 183n147, 254n116, 264n5, 308n72, 362n34, 388, 389n95, 406n5, 435, 435n51, 436, 436n55, 437, 437n56, 438–439, 449, 505n52, 578, 579n69, 590, 590n88, 604n105, 618, 618n1, 619n2, 685, 685n28, 743n160, 745n161, 750, 910, 919, 919n125, 919n127, 923, 924n135
Thomas Aquinas | Summa Theologiae (ST), x, 5, 10–11, 26n17, 27n20, 29, 29n26, 39n40, 106, 107n135, 108–110, 116, 130, 142n49, 155n74, 156n78, 157n82, 189, 219, 243n95, 244n97, 251, 258, 268n12, 269n15, 280n28, 310n74–75, 316n85, 415n16, 427n30, 448, 456, 459n102–103, 460n109, 462, 478, 481, 481n1, 492, 532n110, 538n128 539n133, 550n15, 563n37, 573n57, 582n75, 588n86, 591n92, 602n103, 619, 624n17, 626n22, 636, 673, 738n148, 760n193, 769, 773n12, 776n15, 777n17, 782, 783n23, 796n35, 797n36–37, 807n51, 814n71, 816n78, 818, 820n89, 839n141, 845n149, 845n151, 855n173, 875n17, 878n23, 880n28, 884n44, 894n64, 900n74, 903n88, 910n103, 928n140, 929n141, 938n164
Thomas of Celano, 896
Tournély, Honoré, 574n59

Urban VIII, 374, 374n60

Valdes of Lyon (see Waldo, Peter)
Varro, Marcus Terentius, 875n17
Vianney, Jean-Baptiste-Marie (the Curé d'Ars), 665
Vigilius (Pope), 279, 469, 469n125
Vincent of Lerins, xixn1, 102, 102n124, 103, 111n150, 163, 163n94, 165, 165n99, 167n105, 172–173, 173n114, 174n117, 464
Virgil (Publius Vergilius Maro), 493, 493n22
Voltaire (François–Marie Arouet), 130

Waldo, Peter, 57n65, 813
Walfrid Strabo, 474n132
William Durand (Durandus), 837n133
William of Champeaux, 826n105
William of Ockham, 931
Wyclif, John, 58, 64n71, 239n90, 816, 828n110

Zeno of Verona, 506n54
Zeno of Elea, 134n37, 924

Zeno (emperor), 31
Zosimus (Pope), 369
Zwingli, Huldrych, 35n33, 65, 65n73, 72–73, 76

Index of Magisterial Documents

1. Popes

Clement I (88–97), 880n30
Ad Corinthios (95), 880n30

Cornelius (251–253), 578
Epistola ad Cyprianum (256), 56n62

Dionysius (259–268), 468, 468n22, 469n124
De Trinitate et Incarnatione (262), 468n122, 469n124

Damasus I (366–384), 390
De Trinitate divina (382), 390n98, 467n120, 468n121, 469n126, 474.129

Siricius (384–399), 396n126, 719, 719n106
Directa ad Decessorem (February 10, 385), 396n126, 719n104
Cum in Unum (386), 719n104
Dominus Inter (386), 719n104

Innocent I (401–417), 693n42, 766n208, 883n40
Si Instituta Ecclesiastica (March 19, 416), 693n42, 766n208
Inter Ceteras Ecclesiae Romanae (January 27, 417), 883n40

Zosimus (417–418), 396
Epistula Tractoria (418), 253n115, 369

Leo the Great (440–461), 47n50, 239n90, 258, 275n23, 277n24, 279, 331n116, 341, 341n132, 436n55, 468n121, 560–561, 561n33, 584, 584n79, 604, 605n109, 625, 625n19, 719, 778n20
Lectis Dilectionis Tuae (*Tomus ad Flavianum* or *Tomus Leonis*) (June 13, 449), 275n23, 279, 331n116, 436n55
Licet per Nostros (June 13, 449), 277n24
Quam Laudabiliter (July 21, 447), 239n90, 468n121
Sermo III, 605n109
Sermo XXI, 584n79
Sermo LIV, 561n33
Sermo LXXIV, 341n132, 625n19, 778n20

Gelasius I (492–496), 745n161
Ne Forte (495), 745n161

Hormisdas (514–523), 468n121
Inter Ea Quae (March 26, 521), 468n121

Boniface II (530–532), 175n121
Per Filium Nostrum (January 25, 531), 175n121

Vigilius (537–555), 279, 469, 469n125
Professio Fidei (February 5, 552), 169n106, 469n125, 693n40, 880n30, 884n42, 892n61

Gregory the Great (590–604), 30, 213, 213n39, 214n42, 217n49, 278nn24–25, 561, 561n36, 612n122, 676n7, 883n38, 894n62, 908n96, 910n104, 915, 915n113, 937n162, 938n164
Consideranti Mihi (591), 278n25
Quia Caritati Nihil (June 22, 601), 278n24
Homiliae in Evangelia (590–592), 214n42, 883n38, 937n162
Dialogorum Libri (593–594), 908n96, 915n113

Agatho (678–681), 469n125
Consideranti Mihi (March 27, 681), 469n125

Index of Magisterial Documents

Adrian I (772–795), 369
Institutio Universalis (785–791), 369

Nicholas I (820–867), 735n139
Ad Consulta Vestra (November 13, 866)

Leo IX (1049–1054), 391, 391n100, 818n82
Congratulamur Vehementer (April 13, 1053), 391n100

Gregory VII (1073–1085)
Iusiurandum Berengarii Turonensis (February 11, 1079)

Alexander III (1159–1181), 735n138, 735n140, 817
Verum Post (date uncertain), 735n140

Innocent III (1198–1216)
Cum apud Sedem (July 15, 1198)
Maiores Ecclesiae Causas (1201)
Cum Marthae circa (November 29, 1202)
Cum Venisset (February 25, 1204)
Eius Exemplo (December 18, 1208)

Innocent IV (1243–1254), 218n50, 392n106, 620n8, 684n27, 694n45, 735n142, 806n48, 815n75, 846n154, 881n35, 884, 884n43
Sub Catholicae Professione (March 6, 1254), 919n122

Boniface VIII (1294–1303), 564n38, 583, 583n76
Unam Sanctam (November 18, 1302), 564n38, 583n76

John XXII (1316–1334), 107, 108n137, 171n113, 885n48, 893n61, 931, 931n144, 932
Consistory Speech (1318), 108n137
Nequaquam sine Dolore (November 21, 1321), 885n48
Ne super His (December 3, 1334), 885n48, 931n144

Benedict XII (1334–1342), 44n45, 171n113, 823, 823n96, 880n29, 893n61, 908, 909n98, 931–932, 932n145
Benedictus Deus (January 29, 1336), 44n45, 893n61, 909n98, 932n145
Cum Dudum (August 1341), 823n96

Truth Is a Synthesis

Clement VI (1342–1352), 78n94, 877n20
Unigenitus Dei Filius (January 27, 1343), 78n94
Super Quibusdam ad Mekhithar Catholicon Armeniorum (September 29, 1351), 876n20

Boniface IX (1389–1404), 710n89
Sacrae Religionis (February 1, 1400), 710n89

Martin V (1417–1431), 620n8, 710n89
Inter Cunctas (February 22, 1418), 620n8, 816n79
Gerentes ad Vos (November 16, 1427), 710n89

Pius II (1458–1464), 239n90
Cum sicut Accepimus [*errores Zanini de Solcia*] (November 14, 1459), 239n90

Innocent VIII (1484–1492), 710n89
Exposcit Tuae Devotionis (April 9, 1489), 710n89

Leo X (1513–1521), 606, 606n112, 654n79, 759n186, 913n111
Cum Postquam (November 9, 1518), 759n186
Exsurge Domine (June 15, 1520), 606, 606n112, 913n111

Paul IV (1555–1559), 509, 509n62, 654
Cum Quorumdam Hominum (August 7, 1555), 509n62

Pius IV (1559–1565), 606n112, 679n14
Iniunctum Nobis (November 13, 1564), 606n112, 679n14

Pius V (1566–1572), 104, 104n129, 372, 372n58, 488n11, 634n40, 654n79
Ex Omnibus Afflictionibus (October 1, 1567), 372n58
Quo Primum Tempore (July 19, 1570), 104, 104n129

Paul V (1605–1621), 371, 371n56, 372n57
Formula pro Finiendis Disputationibus de Auxiliis (September 5, 1607), 371n56

Urban VIII (1623–1644), 374, 374n60
In Eminenti Ecclesiae (March 6, 1642), 374n60

Innocent X (1644–1655), 374, 374n61
Cum Occasione (May 31, 1653), 374n61

Index of Magisterial Documents

Alexander VII (1655–1667), 374n61, 501n35
Ad Sanctam Beati Petri Sedem (May 22, 1656), 374n61
Sollicitudo Omnium Ecclesiarum (December 8, 1661), 501n35

Clement XII (1730–1740), 107n134
Apostolicae Providentiae Officio (October 2, 1733), 107n134

Pius VI (1775–1799), 885n46
Auctorem Fidei (August 28, 1794)

Gregory XVI (1831–1846), 379n72
Mirari Vos (August 15, 1832), 379n72

Pius IX (1846–1878), 45, 208n23, 209n27, 379n72, 382n81, 501, 501nn35–36, 536n120, 537n126, 538n129
Apostolic Constitutions
Ineffabilis Deus (December 8, 1854), 501n35, 538n129
Encyclicals
Quanto Conficiamur Moerore (August 10, 1863), 379n72
Syllabus [Quanta Cura] (December 8, 1864), 209n27, 379n72
Decrees
Quemadmodum Deus Iosephum (December 8, 1870), 536n120
Allocutions
Singulari Quadam (December 9, 1854), 382n81

Leo XIII (1878–1903), 106n133, 108, 108n138, 109n146, 192n167, 207n19, 238n89, 307n70, 322, 322n97, 345n6, 353n18, 391, 391n102, 392, 392n105, 392n107, 394, 394nn113–114, 395n117, 396n123, 468n123, 470n128, 527, 536nn121–122, 564, 565n39, 571, 631n34, 705, 705n78, 917n116
Briefs
Cum Hoc Sit (August 4, 1880), 106n133
Encyclicals
Aeterni Patris (August 4, 1879), 108n138, 192n167
Libertas Praestantissimum (June 20, 1888), 207n19, 238n89
Quamquam Pluries (August 15, 1889), 536nn121–122
Sapientiae Christianae (January 10, 1890), 571
Satis Cognitum (June 29, 1896), 565n39, 571
Divinum Illud Munus (May 9, 1897), 345n6, 391n102, 392n105, 392n107, 394n113, 396n123, 468n123, 470n128
Annum Sacrum (May 25, 1899), 307n70

•••979

Mirae Caritatis (May 28, 1902), 917n116
Apostolic Letters
Apostolicae Curae (September 13, 1896), 631n34, 705n78
Letters
Testem Benevolentiae (January 22, 1899), 322n97, 353n18, 395n117

Pius X (1903–1914), 107n134, 108, 108nn139–140, 139n41, 160n90, 165, 186n152, 667, 667n105, 692n39, 696n51, 834, 834n126, 854n171, 919n123
Catechismus (June 14, 1905), 160n90, 692n39, 696n51, 706n80, 854n171, 857n178
Briefs
Ex Quo Nono (December 26, 1910), 919n123
Encyclicals
Pascendi Dominici Gregis (September 8, 1907), 108, 108n140
Motu Proprio
Tra Le Sollecitudini (November 22, 1903), 667n105
Sacrorum Antistitum (September 1, 1910), 139n41, 186n152
Doctoris Angelici (June 29, 1914), 107n134, 108n139
Decrees
Sacra Tridentina Synodus (December 17, 1905), 834n126

Benedict XV (1914–1922), 108, 108n141, 535n119
Bonum Sane (July 25, 1920)
Fausto Appetente Die (June 29, 1921)

Pius XI (1922–1939) 108–109, 667, 718, 730, 734
Bulls
Divini Cultus (December 20, 1928), 667n106
Encyclicals
Studiorum Ducem (June 29, 1923), 107n136, 108n142, 109n145, 769n1
Quas Primas (December 11, 1925), 307n68, 308n70
Casti connubii (December 31, 1930), 251n110, 725n119, 730, 730n128, 734n137
Ad Catholici Sacerdotii (December 20, 1935), 718n103
Divini Redemptoris (March 19, 1937), 536n124

Pius XII (1939–1958), 46, 89n110, 103n125, 108, 108n143, 120n12, 230, 231nn72–73, 251, 316n86, 367, 367n51, 382n81, 383n83, 393n109, 394nn113–114, 396n125, 491, 491n18, 492n20, 503, 503n44, 504n45, 509,

Index of Magisterial Documents

509n63, 512n71, 517, 518n83, 527n98, 537n126, 538n130, 545nn7–8, 554n23, 555n25, 565, 565n40, 570n52, 571n54, 584, 585n80, 586n83, 643–644, 644n58, 645, 645n59, 651, 651nn73–74, 652, 654n78, 658n86, 659n87, 660, 660nn91–93, 662, 664, 664n99, 665, 665nn100–102, 667n104, 668, 668nn107–108, 669n109, 671, 704, 704nn75–76, 706n79, 719n105, 726n122, 740, 740n155, 838nn138–139, 840n142, 841n143, 847, 847n155, 870n7, 900
Apostolic Constitutions
Sacramentum Ordinis (November 30, 1947), 704, 704nn75–76
Munificentissimus Deus (November 1, 1950), 509n63, 512n71, 645n59
Encyclicals
Mystici Corporis (June 29, 1943), 367n51, 383n83, 394n113, 396n125, 545nn7–8, 554n23, 555n25, 565, 565n40, 570n52, 571n54, 585n80, 586n83, 658n86, 667n104
Mediator Dei (November 20, 1947), 643, 644n58, 651, 651n74, 654n78, 659n87, 660nn91–93, 664–665, 665nn100–102, 668nn107–108, 669n109, 838nn138–139, 840n142
Humani Generis (August 12, 1950), 89n110, 120n12, 231nn72–73, 469n125, 870n7, 900, 909n99
Fulgens Corona (September 8, 1953), 503, 503n44, 504n45, 518n83
Sacra Virginitas (March 25, 1954), 719n105
Ad Caeli Reginam (October 11, 1954), 491n18, 492n20
Haurietis Aquas (May 15, 1956), 316n86, 393n109
Apostolic Exhortations
Menti Nostrae (September 23, 1950), 103n125, 719n105
Letters
Philippinas Insulas (July 31, 1946), 527n98
Allocutions
Discourse to the Roman Rota (October 3, 1941)
Allocutio Cardinalibus atque antistibus (November 2, 1954), 726n122
Inaugural Discourse of the Fourth International Congress of Thomist Philosophy (September 14, 1955), 108n143
Address to the International Congress on Pastoral Liturgy (September 22, 1956), 847n155

John XXIII (1958–1963), 13, 108, 109n144, 168n105, 207nn20–21, 537, 537n126, 540n133, 652n74, 720, 720n111
Encyclicals
Pacem in Terris (April 11, 1963), 207nn20–21
Apostolic Letters
Le Voci (March 19, 1961), 537n126

Truth Is a Synthesis

Motu proprio
Dominicianus Ordo (March 7, 1963), 109n144
Allocutions
To the participants in the Second Session of the Diocesan Synod of Rome (January 26, 1960), 720n111
Discourse to the Fifth International Thomistic Congress (September 16, 1960), 109n144
Gaudet Mater Ecclesia (October 11, 1962), 168n105
Moonlight Speech (October 11, 1962), 13
Homilies
Canonization of Saint Gregory Barbarigo (May 26, 1960), 540n133

Paul VI (1963–1978) xxvii, 13, 19, 82, 95, 106, 109, 217n48, 231n72, 251n110, 256n118, 338, 349, 376n66, 385n88, 386n89, 387n92, 426, 483n3, 514, 524n92, 526, 544n5, 545n7, 594, 615, 625, 634n40, 652n74, 663, 691–693, 705n77, 713, 715, 720, 759, 759n187, 759n189, 760, 761n194, 765n206, 768, 791n29, 792n31, 809–813, 817n81, 820, 838n139, 847, 848nn156–157, 857n177, 863, 875n19, 912n110
Credo of the People of God, see also *Homily for the Conclusion of the "Year of Faith"* (June 30, 1968), xxvii, 217n48, 817n81, 875n19
Apostolic Constitutions
Indulgentiarum Doctrina (January 1, 1967), 256n118, 759nn187–189, 760n190, 761n194
Pontificalis Romani (June 18, 1968), 705n77
Missale Romanum (April 3, 1969), 332n119, 524n92
Divinae Consortium Naturae (August 15, 1971), 691n37, 693n41
Sacram Unctionem Infirmorum (November 30, 1972), 765n206, 768n213
Encyclicals
Ecclesiam Suam (August 6, 1964), 82n99, 385n88, 386n89, 387n92
Mysterium Fidei (September 3, 1965), 1, 338n128, 625n20, 817n81, 820n87, 848nn156–157, 857n177
Sacerdotalis Caelibatus (June 24, 1967), 720
Humanae Vitae (July 25, 1968), 615
Apostolic Exhortations
Marialis Cultus (February 2, 1974), 526n96
Evangelii Nuntiandi (December 8, 1975), 19n11, 376n66
Apostolic Letters
Lumen Ecclesiae (November 20, 1974), 109n145
Allocutions
At the Conclusion of the Third Session of the Second Vatican Council (November

21, 1964), 483n3
Address to the Members of the "Consilium de Laicis" (October 2, 1974), 19n11
Homilies
Conclusion of the "Year of Faith" (June 30, 1968), xxvii–xxxii, 217n48, 817n81, 875n19
Mass on the 9th Anniversary of his Crowning (June 29, 1972), 912n110
Audiences
General Audience (May 25, 1966), 544n5, 545n7

John Paul II (1978–2005), 13, 50n56, 109, 109n146, 110n147, 126, 126n20, 127nn23–24, 129n27, 140n44, 168n106, 169n107, 170n108, 183, 199, 216, 216n47, 223n60, 230n69, 230n71, 244n97, 246n101, 247n102, 270n17, 291n46, 308n72, 318, 319nn91–93, 320n95, 345n5, 349n10, 361n32, 374n63, 375nn64–65, 376n67, 376n69, 377, 378n70, 384n86, 387, 387n93, 418n21, 479, 482n2, 486n7, 487n9, 488n10, 491n16, 494n23, 496nn25–26, 500n34, 514n74, 527–528, 528nn102–103, 534n115, 536, 536n121, 537n125, 538n130, 546n9, 550n17, 559n31, 568n47, 584, 592n93, 609n117, 659n88, 709, 709n82, 715–716, 716nn98–99, 721, 721n113, 725n120, 727nn124–126, 731, 733n135, 737n145, 741n157, 742n158, 753n172, 756n180, 757n182, 764n201, 787n26, 795n33, 800n41, 849nn158–160, 850nn161–162, 852n167, 853n169, 854n170, 858, 858n181, 930n143
Angelus
Angelus (December 31, 1995), 514n74
Apostolic Constitutions
Universi Dominici Gregis (February 22, 1996), 609n117
Encyclicals
Redemptor Hominis (March 4, 1979), 270n17
Dominum et Vivificantem (May 18, 1986), 345n5, 349n10
Redemptoris Mater (March 25, 1987), 482n2, 486n7
Redemptoris Missio (December 7, 1990), 291n46, 308n72, 320n95, 374n63, 375nn64–65, 378n70, 384n86
Ut Unum Sint (May 25, 1995), 387n93
Fides et Ratio (September 14, 1998), 387n93
Ecclesia de Eucharistia (April 17, 2003), 488n10, 849n160, 850nn161–162, 852n167, 854n170, 858, 858n181
Apostolic Exhortations
Catechesi Tradendae (October 16, 1979), 140n44
Familiaris Consortio (November 22, 1981), 247n102, 737n145, 853n169
Reconciliatio et Paenitentia (December 2, 1984), 742n158, 745n161, 753n172, 756n180, 757n182

Christifideles Laici (December 30, 1988), 376n67, 592n93
Redemptoris Custos (August 15, 1989), 534n115, 536n121, 537n125
Pastores Dabo Vobis (March 25, 1992), 709n82, 721n113
Apostolic Letters
Salvifici Doloris (February 11, 1984), 319nn91–93, 764n201
Ordinatio Sacerdotalis (May 22, 1994), 169n107, 715, 716n98
Orientale Lumen (May 2, 1995), 50n56, 550n17, 658, 659n88, 928
Ad Tuendam Fidem (May 18, 1998), 168n106, 170n108
Novo Millennio Ineunte (January 6, 2001), 546n9
Misericordia Dei (March 7, 2002), 741n157, 757n182
Rosarium Virginis Mariae (October 16, 2002), 527, 528n102
Mane Nobiscum Domine (October 7, 2004), 787n26, 800nn41–42
Letters
Dominicae cenae (February 24, 1980), 849nn158–159
Letter to the Families of Rome (December 8, 1997), 418n21
Letter to Priests for Holy Thursday, 2005 (March 13, 2005), 795n33
Allocutions
Address to the Roman Rota (January 30, 2003), 733n135
Messages
Message delivered to the Pontifical Academy of Sciences (October 22, 1996), 230n69
Homilies
Homily for the Beatification of Sr. Teresa of the Cross (May 1, 1987), 559n31
Homily for the Canonization of Blessed Teresa of the Cross (October 11, 1998), 559n31
Audiences
General Audience (September 19, 1979), 727n126
General Audience (September 26, 1979), 727n126
General Audience (November 7, 1979), 727n124
General Audience (November 21, 1979), 727n125
General Audience (April 2, 1980), 727n126
General Audience (May 14, 1980), 244n97
General Audience (June 4, 1980), 246n101
General Audience (June 18, 1980), 246n101
General Audience (October 8, 1980), 725n120
General Audience (July 28, 1982), 731n130
General Audience (August 4, 1982), 731n130
General Audience (August 11, 1982), 731n130
General Audience (August 18, 1982), 731n130
General Audience (August 25, 1982), 731n130

Index of Magisterial Documents

General Audience (September 1, 1982), 731n130
General Audience (September 8, 1982), 731n130
General Audience (September 15, 1982), 731n130
General Audience (September 22, 1982), 731n130
General Audience (September 29, 1982), 731n130
General Audience (October 6, 1982), 731n130
General Audience (January 29, 1986), 216n47
General Audience (April 16, 1986), 223n60, 230n71
General Audience (January 13, 1988), 528n103
General Audience (January 10, 1996), 487n9
General Audience (January 31, 1996), 494n23
General Audience (May 15, 1996), 496n25
General Audience (June 12, 1996), 538n130
General Audience (July 24, 1996), 496n26
General Audience (April 2, 1997), 500n34
General Audience (August 6, 1997), 491n16
General Audience (July 21, 1999), 930n143

Benedict XVI (2005–2013), 13–14, 14n1, 17, 17n7, 18, 18n8, 19n9, 53n61, 83n100, 91n113, 99n121, 105, 105nn130–131, 110, 110n148, 111n151, 112n152, 117, 127n22, 128, 128n26, 129n27, 140, 140n45, 143, 143nn52–54, 145n57, 149, 149n63, 152–153, 153n70, 157n83, 158n86, 171n112, 177nn129–130, 180nn137–138, 181, 181n141, 182n143, 188, 188n156, 191n163, 197, 199n170, 205n13, 205n15, 206n15, 224n64, 230n69, 255n117, 262n2, 281n30, 296, 297n55, 300n58, 311n76, 316n84, 320n94, 321, 321n96, 322–323, 336n126, 338n127, 360n29, 376n67, 379n71, 386n91, 387n94, 389, 389n96, 520n86, 525, 525n94, 537n127, 543, 543n3, 550n17, 588, 588n87, 592n93, 609n117, 614n125, 635n44, 652n75, 655, 656n81, 663n96, 665n102, 671n114, 682n23, 700n59, 703, 703n73, 709n81, 722, 722n114, 733, 733n135, 763n200, 792n31, 795n34, 799n39, 831, 831n116, 851, 851nn163–164, 854n170, 856n174, 857n175, 858, 859n182, 862n190, 892n60, 902n78, 915, 916n114, 918, 918n121, 922n133, 923, 923n134, 939n166
Apostolic Constitutions
Anglicanorum Coetibus (November 4, 2009), 387, 387n94
Encyclicals
Deus Caritas est (December 25, 2005), 128n26, 143, 143n52, 262n2, 520n86, 856n174
Spe Salvi (November 30, 2007), 91n113, 112n152, 177n129, 321n96, 336n126, 525n94, 543n3, 892n60, 902n78, 916n114, 918n121, 922n133, 923n134
Caritas in Veritate (June 29, 2009), 83n100, 143, 143n54, 316n84, 360n29, 592n93

Apostolic Exhortations

Sacramentum Caritatis (February 22, 2007), 550n17, 656n81, 671n114, 722n114, 763n200, 795n34, 799n39, 831n116, 851, 851nn163–164, 854n170, 857n175, 862n190, 918n121

Verbum Domini (September 30, 2010), 153n70, 157nn83–84, 158n86

Apostolic Letters

De Aliquibus Mutationibus in Normis de Electione Romani Pontificis (June 11, 2007), 609n117

Summorum Pontificum (July 7, 2007), 663n96

Omnium in Mentem (October 26, 2009), 635n44, 700n59

Ubicumque et Semper (September 21, 2010), 376n67

Porta Fidei (October 11, 2011), 140n45, 379n71, 682n23

Normas Nonnullas (February 22, 2013), 609n117

Letters

Letter Proclaiming a Year for Priests (June 16, 2009), 665n102

Letter to Seminarians (October 18, 2010), 19n9

Letter to the President of the German Episcopal Conference (April 14, 2012), 792n31

Allocutions

To the Members of the International Theological Commission (December 1, 2005), 100n122

Christmas Greetings to the Members of the Roman Curia (December 22, 2005), 32n30, 112n151, 652n75

To the participants of the Plenary Assembly of the Congregation for the Doctrine of the Faith (February 10, 2006), 182n143

To the University of Regensburg (September 12, 2006), 205n13

Meeting with the Clergy of the Rome Diocese (February 22, 2007), 281n29

Meeting with the Clergy of the Dioceses of Belluno–Feltre and Treviso (July 24, 2007), 281n30

Address to Heiligenkreuz Abbey (September 9, 2007), 99n122, 188n156

Meeting with the Clergy of the Diocese of Bolzano–Bressanone (August 6, 2008), 389n96

To Participants in the Plenary Assembly of the Congregation for the Doctrine of the Faith (January 15, 2010), 180n137

Meeting with the Parish Priests of the Diocese of Rome: Lectio Divina (February 18, 2010), 297n55

Vigil on the Occasion of the International Meeting of Priests (June 10, 2010), 199n170

Address to Members of the International Theological Commission (December 3, 2010), 191n163

Index of Magisterial Documents

Awarding of the "Ratzinger Prize" (June 30, 2011), 127n22
Visit to the Federal Parliament in the Reichstag Building (September 22, 2011), 206n15
Meeting with the Parish Priests of the Diocese of Rome: Lectio Divina (February 23, 2012), 614n125
Benediction Bestowed upon Participants in the Candlelight Procession Organized by Italian Catholic Action for the Opening of the Year of Faith (October 11, 2012), 14n1, 180n138
Ordinary Public Consistory for the Creation of New Cardinals (November 24, 2012), 588n87
Address to the Roman Curia (December 21, 2012), 224n64
Address to the Roman Rota (January 26, 2013), 733n135

Messages
"Urbi et Orbi" Message (April 8, 2007), 177n130
Message for the Centenary of the Birth of Fr. Hans Urs von Balthasar (October 6, 2005), 188n156

Homilies
Homily at the Mass for the Beginning of the Petrine Ministry (April 24, 2005), 171n112, 230n69
Homily at the Mass with the Members of the International Theological Commission (October 6, 2006), 18n8, 191n163
Homily in the Chrism Mass (March 20, 2008), 859n182
Homily at the Mass in St. Patrick's Cathedral, New York (April 19, 2008), 54n61
Homily at the Mass on the Solemnity of Pentecost (May 11, 2008), 588n87
Homily in the Chrism Mass (April 9, 2009), 311n76
Celebration of Vespers with the Benedictine Abbots and the Community of Benedictine Monks and Nuns gathered in the Archabbey of Monte Cassino (May 24, 2009), 338n127
Homily at the Mass with the Members of the International Theological Commission (December 1, 2009), 105n131
Homily at the Mass Concluding the Year for Priests (June 11, 2010), 665n102
Homily in the Chrism Mass (April 5, 2012), 320n94
Homily at the Mass for the Opening of the Year of Faith (October 11, 2012), 14n1, 180n138

Audiences
General Audience (May 31, 2006), 182n143
General Audience (April 18, 2007), 129n27
General Audience (December 3, 2008), 255n117
General Audience (June 24, 2009), 709n81
General Audience (January 27, 2010), 703n73

General Audience (June 2, 2010), 110n148
General Audience (June 23, 2010), 481n1
General Audience (July 7, 2010), 117n6, 205n13
General Audience (August 11, 2010), 300n58
General Audience (October 3, 2012), 550n17, 862n190
General Audience (October 17, 2012), 145n57, 181n141
General Audience (November 14, 2012), 149n63, 386n91
General Audience (November 21, 2012), 17n7

Francis (2013–), 15, 15n3, 16, 16n4, 21, 22n12, 25, 25n16, 26, 26n18, 28n22, 83, 90, 100, 105n130, 149, 176n122, 177n127, 178n133, 179nn135–136, 187, 187n154, 188n156, 203n4, 224nn62–64, 304n64, 357n26, 537, 537n127, 568n47, 676n7, 712, 733n134, 792n31, 912n110, 939, 939n166

Encyclicals
Lumen Fidei (June 29, 2013), 24n14, 176n122, 177n127, 178n133, 179nn135–136, 187n154, 939n166
Laudato Si' (May 24, 2015), 203n4, 224n62

Apostolic Exhortations
Evangelii Gaudium (November 24, 2013), 15n3, 16, 25n16, 26n18, 179n136, 304n64, 357n26, 676n7

Apostolic Letters
Magnum Principium (September 3, 2017), 792n31, 793n31

Allocutions
Address to the Community of the Pontifical Gregorian University (April 10, 2014), 16n4
Address to the Roman Rota (January 22, 2016), 733n134
Meeting with the Polish Bishops (July 27, 2016), 224n64
Address to Participants at the 20th Plenary Assembly Of The International Union Of Superiors General (August 2, 2016), 712
Address to Participants at the 21st Plenary Assembly Of The International Union Of Superiors General (May 10, 2019), 712

Homilies
Holy Mass with the Cardinal Electors (March 14, 2013), 22n12
Holy Mass in Saint Francis of Assisi Square (October 4, 2013), 224n63

2. Ecumenical Councils

First Council of Nicaea (325), 84n101, 126n19, 217n48, 271, 274–275, 439, 442, 447

First Council of Constantinople (381), 217n48, 264n4, 268n13, 272–275, 308n71, 393n109, 443, 446, 575, 575n60

Council of Ephesus (431), 31, 269, 275–278, 369, 485, 485n6, 500

Council of Chalcedon (451), 31–32, 34, 47n50, 275n23, 278, 278n26
Symbolum Fidei (October 22, 451), 278n26

Second Council of Constantinople (553), 30–32, 32n31, 33, 33n32, 34, 37n38, 279, 281n29, 340n130, 390, 390n99, 391, 504n46, 505n50
Anathematismi de Tribus Capitulis (June 2, 553), 33n32, 281n29, 340n130, 390n99, 504n46

Third Council of Constantinople (680–681), 30, 42, 171n113, 266, 279

Second Council Nicaea (787), 142n51, 279n27, 394n112
Definitio de Sacris Imaginibus (October 13, 787), 394

Fourth Council of Constantinople (869–870), 37

First Lateran Council (1123), 37

Second Lateran Council (1139), 719, 719n107
Canones (April 4, 1139)

Third Lateran Council (1179), 37

Fourth Lateran Council (1215), 194n168, 211n36, 382n80, 393n109, 466, 466n118, 467n120, 549n14, 752, 752n171, 815, 815n72, 817
Firmiter (November 30, 1215), 194n168, 211n36, 382n80, 393n109, 466, 466n118, 549n14, 752n171, 815n72

First Council of Lyon (1245), 37

Second Council of Lyon (1274), 37, 476, 478n140, 504n46, 693n40, 880n30,

884n42
De Processione Spiritus Sancti (May 18, 1274), 452n88, 478, 478n140
Professio Fidei Michaëlis Palaeologi Imperatoris (July 6, 1274), 693n40, 880n30, 884n42, 892n61

Council of Vienne (1311–1312), 219n54, 223n61, 877, 877n22, 935, 935n156
Ad Nostrum Qui (May 6, 1312), 935n156
Fidei Catholicae (May 6, 1312), 219n54, 877n22

Council of Constance (1414–1418), 64n71, 239n90, 539n132, 816, 816n79, 828n110, 859n184
Errores Iohannis Wyclif (May 4, 1415), 239n90, 828n110
Cum in Nonnullis (June 15, 1415), 859n184
Errores Ioannis Hus (February 22, 1418), 64n71
Inter Cunctas (February 22, 1418), 620n8, 816n79

Council of Basel, Ferrara, and Florence (1431–1445), 37
Laetentur Caeli (July 6, 1439), 478nn141–142, 606n111, 885n48, 919n115
Moyses Vir Dei (September 4, 1439), 606n110
Exsultate Deo (November 22, 1439), 619n6, 633n39, 639, 639n53, 675n5, 679n11, 687n30, 692n39, 693n42, 694n44, 695n48, 704n74, 735n143, 738n147, 807n52
Cantate Domino (February 4, 1442), 154n74, 211n37, 452n88, 467n119, 469n124, 478n142, 809nn56–57, 822n94

Fifth Lateran Council (1512–1517), 11, 37

Council of Trent (1545–1563), xxviii, 37, 39–40, 62n69, 72n84, 75n88, 107, 112n152, 148, 148n62, 150n65, 152n69, 153, 153n71, 158n87, 159, 159n89, 160, 176n124, 181n142, 244n97, 247n104, 250n109, 251, 251n110, 252, 254, 363n36, 366n47, 369, 372n57, 395, 395n122, 396n124, 396n136, 606n112, 620n7, 627, 627n24, 628n25, 629n28, 652, 652n76, 666n103, 673, 678, 679nn12–13, 684n26, 688n34, 693, 693n42, 696, 696n54, 699, 699n57–58, 705n78, 706n80, 719, 719n106, 719n108, 723n118, 743n160, 747, 747n165, 748n166, 756, 756nn178–179, 756n181, 757n182–183, 758n185, 760, 760n192, 762n197, 763, 763nn199–200, 765, 765n205, 766, 766n207, 766n209, 815, 815n73, 815n76, 816, 816n80, 820, 821n90, 822, 823n95, 825, 825n101, 827, 827n106–107, 832, 833n120, 834, 834n123, 834n125, 836n129, 837n135, 841, 841n144, 843nn145–146, 852n165, 853n167, 859, 869n184, 860, 861nn188–189, 871, 872n12, 917, 917n117, 918n118

Decretum de Libris Sacris et Traditionibus Recipiendis (April 8, 1546), 148n62, 150n65, 153n71, 154n74, 159n89

Decretum de Vulgata Editione Bibliorum et de Modo Interpretandi Sacram Scripturam (April 8, 1546), 158n87

Decretum de Peccato Originali (June 17, 1546), 244n97, 250n109, 251n110, 684n26

Decretum de Iustificatione (January 13, 1547), 62n69, 176n124, 251n110, 363n36, 369, 395n122, 396n124, 688n34, 743n160, 815n76, 872n12

Canones de Iustificatione (January 13, 1547), 181n142, 917n117

Decretum de Sacramentis (March 3, 1547), 72n84, 366n47, 620n7, 627n24, 679n12, 723n118, 816n80

Canones de Sacramento Confirmationis (March 3, 1547), 693n42

Canones de ss. Eucharistiae Sacramento (October 11, 1551), 75n88

Decretum de ss. Eucharistia (October 11, 1551), 756n179, 821n90, 823n95, 825n101, 827nn106–107, 834n123, 834n125, 841n144, 852n165, 861n188

Doctrina de Sacramento Extremae Unctionis (November 25, 1551), 628n25, 762n197, 763n199–200, 765n205, 766n207, 766n209

Doctrina de Sacramento Paenitentiae (November 25, 1551), 396n124, 756n178, 796n181, 757nn182–183, 760n192

Canones de Sacramento Paenitentiae (November 25, 1551), 748n166

Doctrina et Canones de Communione sub Utraque Specie et Parvulorum (July 16, 1562), 396n126, 629n28, 859n184

Doctrina et Canones de ss. Missae Sacrificio (September 17, 1562), 652n76, 699n57, 747n165, 843nn145–146, 861n189

Doctrina et Canones de Sacramento Ordinis (July 15, 1563), 679n13, 696n54, 699n58, 719n108, 723n118

Doctrina et Canones de Sacramento Matrimonii (November 11, 1563), 719n108, 723n118

Decretum de Purgatorio (December 3, 1563), 918n118

Decretum de Indulgentiis (December 4, 1563), 758n185

First Vatican Council (1869–1960), 47, 111n149, 126n21, 128n25, 133n35, 147, 147n59, 148n61, 149n64, 150n66, 170, 170n111, 171, 175n119, 175n121, 176n123, 177n128, 178n132, 182n144, 183nn145–146, 192n166, 203n6, 208n23, 216, 217n48, 236n86, 395n116, 396n124, 435n53, 566, 566n43, 574n59, 607, 607n114, 608, 608n115, 911n105

Dei Filius (April 24, 1870), 78n94, 111n149, 126n21, 128n25, 133n35, 147n59, 148n60, 149n64, 150n66, 154n74, 175n119, 176n123, 177n128, 178n132, 182n144, 183nn145–147, 192n166, 203n6, 236n86, 277n24, 396n124, 435n53, 566n43, 574n59, 911n105

Pastor Æternus (July 18, 1870), 170n111, 395n116, 607n114, 608n115

Truth Is a Synthesis

Second Vatican Council (1962–1965), 13, 22, 26, 81, 101, 112, 140, 153, 160, 240, 288–289, 338, 381, 383, 385, 394, 487, 514, 517, 524, 537, 541–542, 548, 549, 554, 566, 568, 572, 575, 578, 581, 586–587, 608–612, 649, 663–664, 689, 693, 695, 701–702, 710, 720, 738, 759, 762, 767, 859, 860, 877, 888, 912, 918
Constitutions
Sacrosanctum Concilium (December 4, 1963), 174n118, 542n2, 567n46, 638n50, 649, 649n67, 650, 650nn71–72, 651n74, 653n77, 654n78, 655, 655n80, 660nn89–91, 661n93, 661n95, 667, 668n107, 669n111, 670, 670nn112–113, 672n115, 762n196, 767, 848, 859n185
Lumen Gentium (November 21, 1964), 2, 37, 69n79, 166n103, 170, 170nn109–110, 237n87, 240n91, 290nn44–45, 292n49, 293n51, 357n25, 376n68, 379n71, 380n73, 381n77, 383n82, 383n86, 394n111, 394n114, 395nn115–120, 396n127, 482n2, 487n9, 498n30, 507n57, 515n78, 516nn79–81, 519n84, 522n89, 524n92, 544n6, 548, 548n12, 549n13, 554n21, 554n24, 556, 556n27, 566, 566n42, 567, 567n45, 569nn49–50, 570n51, 571n55, 573, 575n59, 578n66, 580n72, 581n73, 586n83, 587, 592n93, 594n96, 596n97, 600n100, 609n116, 609n118, 610n119, 611n120, 612n121, 649, 649n68, 652n74, 663n98, 664, 664n99, 683, 687n31, 693n43, 695n49, 700n60, 700n62, 701n64, 701n66, 702nn68–69, 710n88, 767, 869n6, 900n72, 912n110, 918nn119–120
Dei Verbum (November 18, 1965), 120n12, 139n42, 146n58, 148nn60–61, 149, 149n64, 153, 153n70, 153n72, 154n73, 155, 155nn74–76, 156n80, 157–158, 158n85, 158n87, 160, 160n90, 164n96, 164n98, 166n102, 175n119, 176n123, 195n169, 652n74
Gaudium et Spes (December 7, 1965), 204n8, 209n28, 210nn30–31, 227n68, 235n83, 247n104, 253n113, 270n17, 316n86, 323n99, 383n84, 392nn103–104, 395n119, 395n121, 396n128, 633n37, 652n74, 683n25, 726n123, 729, 738n150, 869n6, 877n21, 888n54, 900n72, 912n110
Decrees
Unitatis Redintegratio (November 21, 1964), 82n98, 385n87, 576n63, 577n64, 687n32
Optatam Totius (October 28, 1965), 107n135, 720n112
Perfectae Caritatis (October 28, 1965), 357n25
Apostolicam Actuositatem (November 18, 1965), 591n90, 687n31
Ad Gentes (December 7, 1965), 375–376, 683n24
Presbyterorum Ordinis (December 7, 1965), 649, 649n69, 701n63, 702n68, 706n79, 709, 720n112, 849n157
Declarations
Gravissimum Educationis (October 28, 1965), 107n135
Nostra Ætate (October 28, 1965), 379n72, 385n87, 558n30

Index of Magisterial Documents

3. Catechism of the Catholic Church

§§27–30	352n15
§67	166n101
§114	111
§§115–119	156n78
§118	155n78
§150	177n126
§291	204n12
§306	235
§319	209n26
§328	217n48
§365	223n61
§366	231n72
§389	254
§393	122n15
§404	251n110, 252
§405	252
§§410–411	245n99
§412	258
§§441–445	417n18
§§446	286
§§447–451	286n35
§461	116n1
§468	840n143
§478	316n86
§487	499n32, 529n105
§633	328n110
§645	331n117
§664	339
§687	350
§689	572n56
§690	343n1
§§694–701	348n8
§698	678
§702	350n12
§720	351n13
§727	343n1
§730	345n4
§737	349n9

Truth Is a Synthesis

§811	576n62
§§857–865	590
§863	591
§§897–933	592n93
§1008	247n104
§1020	890
§1022	14n2, 892
§1025	925
§1031	922n132
§1033	908
§1035	909
§1036	912
§1037	871n11
§1074	650n71
§1076	629
§1115	624n18
§§1115–1116	561n34
§1121	678
§1128	620
§1130	862
§1131	618
§1137	397n129, 413n14
§1257	683
§§1259–1260	689n35
§1261	885
§1327	770
§1353	822n94
§1366	836
§1378	857n177
§§1382–1383	851
§1385	852n167
§§1391–1397	856
§1436	747
§1445	761
§§1450–1460	756
§1460	758
§1467	755
§1469	761
§1471	759n187
§§1503–1505	765

§1515	768
§1547	700n61
§1582	696
§1585	707
§1602	723
§1623	635, 635n42
§1626	734
§2207	726
§2566	227n68

4. Codex Iuris Canonici (CIC)

can. 331	47n51
can. 338	37n37
can. 341	37n37
can. 517 §2	701n65
can. 732 §1 (CIC 1917)	680n16
cann. 747–755	164n97
can. 841	629n28
can. 844 §2	36n34
can. 845 §1	680n16
can. 890	160n90, 696n52
can. 988 §1	741n157
can. 992	759n187
can. 993	759n188
can. 1009	700n59
can. 1013 §1 (CIC 1917)	730n127
can. 1141	740n154
can. 1142	741n156
cann. 1143–1147	740n153
can. 1148	739n152
can. 1388 §1	755n176
can. 1404	172n113, 601n102
can. 1752	547n11

5. Dicasteries of the Holy See

Congregations

Congregation for the Clergy
General Catechetical Directory (April 11, 1971), 26n17

Congregation for Divine Worship and the Discipline of the Sacraments
Responsa ad Quaestiones de Nova Institutione Generali Missalis Romani (September 25, 2000), 667n82
Redemptionis Sacramentum (March 25, 2004), 836n130, 859n185
Letter to the Presidents of the National Episcopal Conferences (October 17, 2006), 792n31
Decretum ut Nomen Sancti Ioseph Precibus Eucharisticis II, III et IV, posthac adiciatur, post nomen Beatae Virginis Mariae Additis Verbis (May 1, 2013), 537n127
Homiletic Directory (June 29, 2014), 16, 16n5

(Sacred) Congregation for the Doctrine of the Faith
Epistula ad Venerabiles Praesules Conferentiarum Episcopalium (July 24, 1966), 288n38
Mysterium Filii Dei (February 21, 1972), 288n39, 400n2
Cum de Fragmentis (May 2, 1972), 858
Mysterium Ecclesiae (June 24, 1973), 395n116
Instructio pro Solutione Matrimonii in Favorem Fidei (December 6, 1973), 740n153
Normae Procedurales pro Conficiendo Processu Dissolutionis Vinculis Matrimonialis in Favorem Fidei (December 6, 1973), 740n53
Inter Insigniores (October 15, 1976), 713, 714nn93–95, 715n96
Declaratio circa Librum R.P. Iacobi Pohier:"Quand je dis Dieu" (April 3, 1979), 288n40
Epistula de Quibusdam Quaestionibus ad Eschatologiam Spectantibus (May 17, 1979), 868n4, 910n102
Pastoralis Actio (October 20, 1980), 886n49
Letter to Rev. Fr. Edward Schillebeeckx, O.P., Regarding His Christological Positions (November 20, 1980), 288n40
Sacerdotium Ministeriale (August 6, 1983), 815n74
Libertatis Nuntius (August 6, 1984), 292n48
Libertatis Conscientia (March 22, 1986), 208n22, 292n48
Donum Veritatis (May 24, 1990), 99n121, 186, 188n157
Communionis Notio (May 28, 1992), 568n48

Index of Magisterial Documents

Annus Internationalis Familiae (September 14, 1994), 853n169

Responsum ad Propositum Dubium circa Doctrinam in Epist. ap. "Ordinatio Sacerdotalis" Traditam (October 28, 1995), 716n99

Notification concerning the Text "Mary and Human Liberation" by Fr. Tissa Balasuriya, O.M.I. (January 2, 1997), 288n40

Notification concerning the Writings of Fr. Anthony De Mello, S.J. (June 24, 1998), 288n40

Illustrative Doctrinal Note of the Conclusive Formula of "Professio Fidei" (June 29, 1998), 169n106

Note on the Expression "Sister Churches" (June 30, 2000), 57n63

Dominus Iesus (August 6, 2000), 175n121, 269n16, 288, 289n41, 291n46, 308n72, 361n31, 382, 554n22

Notification on the Book Toward a Christian Theology of Religious Pluralism *by Fr. Jacques Dupuis, S.J.* (January 24, 2001), 299n40

Potestas Ecclesiae (April 30, 2001), 740nn152–153

Doctrinal Note on Some Questions Regarding the Participation of Catholics in Political Life (November 24, 2002), 205n15, 592n93

Circular Letter to All Presidents of the Episcopal Conferences concerning the Use of Low–Gluten Altar Breads and Mustum as Matter for the Celebration of the Eucharist (July 24, 2003), 807n53

Notification Regarding the Book "Jesus Symbol of God" of Fr. Roger Haight, S.J. (December 13, 2004), 289n40

*Notification on the works of Father Jon Sobrino, S.J.:*Jesucristo liberador. Lectura histórico–teológica de Jesús de Nazaret *and* La fe en Jesucristo. Ensayo desde las víctimas (November 26, 2006), 289n40

Responsa ad Quaestiones de Aliquibus Sententiis ad Doctrinam de Ecclesia Pertinentibus (June 29, 2007), 554n22, 576n61, 580n70, 587n83, 657n82

Nota Doctrinalis de Quibusdam Rationibus Evangelizationis (October 6, 2007), 386n90

Responsa ad Proposita Dubia de Validitate Baptismatis (February 1, 2008), 685n29

Normae de Delictis Congregationi pro Doctrina Fidei Reservatis seu Normae de Delictis contra Fidem necnon de Gravioribus Delictis (May 21, 2010), 755n175

Iuvenescit Ecclesia (May 15, 2016), 187n153, 364n41, 395n117, 613n124, 703n71

Ad Resurgendum cum Christo (June 15, 2016), 880n31

Response of the Catholic Church to the Joint Declaration of the Catholic Church and the Lutheran World Federation on the Doctrine of Justification (June 25, 1998) [with the Pontifical Council for Promoting Christian Unity], 80, 80n96, 81, 81n97

Sacred Congregation for Studies
Decretum (July 27, 1914), 133n135

Sacred Congregation of Rites
Inclytus Patriarcha Joseph (September 10, 1847), 536n120
Instructio de Musica Sacra et Sacra Liturgia (September 3, 1958), 668n107, 669n110, 847n155
Novis Hisce Temporibus (November 13, 1962), 537n126
Eucharisticum Mysterium (May 25, 1967), 849n157

Supreme Sacred Congregation of the Holy Office
Errores Iansenistarum (August 24, 1690), 374n62
Lamentabili (July 3, 1907), 165, 165n100, 748n166
Decretum de Millenarismo (July 19, 1944), 902n79
Letter to the Archbishop of Boston (August 8, 1949), 382n81
Monitum (July 24, 1958), 810n62

Pontifical Councils

Pontifical Council for Interreligious Dialogue
Dialogue and Proclamation (May 19, 1991), 385, 386n89

Pontifical Council for Promoting Christian Unity
Response of the Catholic Church to the Joint Declaration of the Catholic Church and the Lutheran World Federation on the Doctrine of Justification (June 25, 1998) [with the Congregation for the Doctrine of the Faith], 81n97

Pontifical Council for Promoting Christian Unity – Lutheran World Federation
Common declaration on the Doctrine of Justification Issued by the Catholic Church and the Lutheran World Federation (October 31, 1999), 80n96

Pontifical Council for Promoting Christian Unity
Guidelines for Admission to the Eucharist between the Chaldean Church and the Assyrian Church of the East (July 20, 2001), 822n93

Pontifical Council for Justice and Peace
Compendium of the Social Doctrine of the Church (April 2, 2004), 592n93

6. Synods

Synod of Rome (382)
Decretum Damasi, 394n110, 396n126

Second Synod of Carthage (June 16, 390), 719n106

First Synod of Toledo (400)
Regula Fidei contra Errores Priscillianorum, 468n121

Synod of Seleucia–Ctesiphon (410), 473

Fifteenth Synod of Carthage (May 1, 418), 369
De Peccato Originali, 244n97, 247n104, 250n109, 251n110, 253n115, 684n26, 884n45

Synod of Arles (473), 871
Lucidi Presbyteri Libellus Subiectionis, 871n10

Synod of Orléans (692), 511n38

Second Synod of Orange (July 3, 529), 175, 369, 871
Conclusio a Caesario Episcopo Arelatensi Redacta, 871n11
Canones de Gratia, 175n121

Synod of Constantinople (543)
Edictum Iustiniani Imperatoris ad Menam Patriarcham Constantinopolitanum, 909n99

First Synod of Braga (561), 214n43
Anathematismi contra Priscillanistas, 239n90

Third Synod of Toledo (May 8, 589)
De Trinitate Divina, 390n98, 468n121, 469n126, 474n129

Fourth Synod of Toledo (633), 474
Symbolum Triado–Christologicum, 474n130

Sixth Synod of Toledo (638), 474, 469–470
De Trinitate et de Filio Dei Redemptore Incarnato, 470n127, 474n131

Truth Is a Synthesis

Lateran Synod (October 31, 649)
Can. 3, 505n47

Eighth Synod of Toledo (653), 474

Eleventh Synod of Toledo (675), 393n108, 467, 469, 468n121, 469, 470n127
De Trinitate Divina, 468n121

Synod of Rome (March 27, 680)
Omnium Bonorum Spes, 464n115

Sixteenth Synod of Toledo (693), 470n127
Symbolum, 394n112
De Trinitate Divina, 467n120

Synod of Cividale (796–797)
De Trinitate Divina, 469n126

Synod of Quiercy (853)
De Libero Arbitrio Hominis et de Praedestinatione, 872n13

Synod of Valence (January 8, 855), 873
De Praedestinatione, 873n14

Synod of Sens (1140–1141)
Propositio 2, 392n104

Synod of Bishops (1985), 567, 567n47, 568, 568n47
Relatio Finalis

Synod of Bishops (2005), 831

Synod of Bishops (2012), 376n67

Pan–Orthodox Synod (June 17–26, 2016)
The Importance of Fasting and Its Observance Today, 49n54

General Index

TABLE OF CONTENTS, xiii

Foreword To The English Edition, xv

Preface, xix

Abbreviations, xxiii

Niceno-Constantinopolitan Creed, xxv

Credo Of The People Of God, xxvii

Introduction, 1

I. The "Synthetic" Principle, 13

1. A Glance at the Faith, Preaching, and Theology of Today, 13
1.1. After the Council, 13
1.2. Fideism and Pragmatism, 17
1.3. "Synthetic" Theology, 20

2. Jesus Christ: "Synthetic" Principle of the Faith and of Theology, 27

2.1. *The Particular Importance of the Second Council of Constantinople*, 30

3. The Missing Synthesis: The Orthodox and the Protestants, 34

3.1. *The Orthodox*, 35
    3.1.1. *Ecumenical Councils*, 37
    3.1.2. *Sacramental and Liturgical Aspects*, 38
    1. *Sacramental Character*, 39
    2. *Eucharistic Consecration*, 39
    3. *Eucharistic Communion and Adoration*, 40
    4. *Matrimony*, 40
    5. *Confirmation*, 41
    6. *Chants and Sacred Music*, 41
    3.1.3. *Dogmatic and Theological Development*, 41
    3.1.4. *Dogmas*, 43
    1. *The Trinity and the Beatific Vision*, 43
    2. *Salvation and Purgatory*, 44
    3. *Transubstantiation*, 45
    4. *Mary*, 45
    5. *The Pope*, 46
    3.1.5. *Ecclesiastic Discipline*, 48
    1. *Clerical Celibacy*, 48
    2. *Fasting and Abstinence*, 49
    3. *Religious Orders and Monasticism*, 50
    3.1.6. *Spiritual Life and Devotion*, 51
    1. *Meditation*, 51
    2. *Devotion*, 52
    3. *Sacred Images*, 53
    4. *New Spiritual Movements*, 54
3.1.7. *Concluding Reflections*, 54
3.2. *Protestants*, 57
    3.2.1. *Fundamental Principles*, 58
    1. *Biblicism*, 58
    2. *Justification*, 60
    3.2.2. *Dogmas*, 63
    1. *Predestination*, 63
    2. *Redemption*, 65
    3. *Mary*, 68
    4. *Church*, 70
    5. *Purgatory*, 70

3.2.3. The Sacraments, 71
1. General Sacramental Theology, 71
2. Baptism, 73
3. Eucharist, 73
4. Holy Orders, 75
5. Matrimony, 75
3.2.4. Spirituality and Discipline, 77
1. Eucharistic Spirituality, 77
2. Cult of Saints, Relics, and Images, 77
3. Indulgences, 78
4. Clerical Celibacy, 79
3.2.5. Concluding Reflections, 79
3.2.6. Brief Considerations on Ecumenism, 80

4. The "Synthetic" Principle of *Et-Et* (Both/And), 83
4.1. Other Approaches, 83
4.2. The Concept of "Synthesis", 86
   1. What does "Synthesis" Mean?, 86
   2. How Does the Synthesis Happen?, 87
   3. What Does the Synthesis Imply for the Spirit and for Matter?, 88
   4. Is It a Synthesis in a Hegelian Sense?, 88
   5. Is the Synthesis Necessary?, 89
   6. Is the Synthesis Foreseen from the Beginning of Creation?, 89
   7. Are There More Ways of Carrying Out the Synthesis, or Only One Way?, 90
4.3. The Dipolar Nature of the Christian Faith, 90
   1. Limit of et-et, 92
   2. Axiological Difference, 92
   3. Logical Consistency, 93
4.4. Confirmation from the Liturgy, 95

5. Method of Treatment, 98
5.1. Alethic Approach, 98
5.2. Ecclesiality, 99
5.3. Ecclesial and Ecumenical Parrhesia, 100
5.4. Criteria to Identify the Truth of the Faith, 101
5.5. A Choice against the Current, 103
   1. Why is No Theologian of the Last Two Hundred Years Cited?, 103
   2. Why Two Hundred Years?, 104
   3. What about the Magisterium?, 105

5.6. *The Importance of Saint Thomas Aquinas*, 106
5.7. *"Nexus Mysteriorum"*, 111

2. REVELATION, FAITH, THEOLOGY, 115

1. The Reason for the Incarnation of the Word, 115
1.1. *New Creation*, 118
1.2. *The Salvation of the Angels*, 122
1.3. *Response to an Objection*, 124

2. *Verbum* (Word), 126
2.1. *The Word as Reason*, 126
2.2. *Natural Theology*, 127
    2.2.1. *Certain but Limited Knowledge*, 128
    2.2.2. *Christian Faith and Philosophy*, 128
    2.2.3. *Proofs of God's Existence*, 129
    1. Leibniz, 130
    2. Saint Anselm, 131
    3. Saint Thomas, 132
    4. Divine Attributes, 137
2.3. *The Word Precisely as Word*, 139
2.4. *The Word as Truth*, 140
2.5. *The Word as Love*, 143
2.6. *The Word as Son*, 144

3. *Caro* (Flesh), 145
3.1. *Divine Revelation*, 146
    3.1.1. *"Re-velatio"*, 146
    3.1.2. *Old and New Testament*, 147
    3.1.3. *Object*, 148
    3.1.4. *Channels*, 150
    3.1.5. *Sacred Scripture*, 154
        1. *A Book both Human and Divine*, 154
        2. *Inspiration and Inerrancy*, 154
        3. *Literal and Spiritual Sense*, 155
        4. *Correct Hermeneutic*, 157
        5. *Canon*, 158
    3.1.6. *Sacred Tradition*, 159
        1. Traditio/Paradosis, 159
        2. *Act and Content*, 160

   3. *Subject*, 161
   4. *Tradition and Traditions*, 162
   5. *Plurality and Pluralism*, 163
3.2. The Magisterium of the Church, 163
  3.2.1. In Service of the Word, 163
  3.2.2. The Completeness of Revelation, 164
  3.2.3. The Tasks of the Magisterium, 166
  3.2.4. The Living and Faithful Magisterium, 167
  3.2.5. Forms of Exercise, 168
   1. *Ordinary*, 168
   2. *Extraordinary*, 168
  3.2.6. Object, Infallibility, and Possibility of Error, 169
   1. *Object*, 169
   2. *Infallibility*, 170
   3. *Extrincism and Historicism*, 172
  3.2.7. Doctrinal Development, 173
  3.2.8. Hermeneutic of Continuity, 174
3.3. Faith, 174
  3.3.1. Grace and Freedom, 174
  3.3.2. Love and Duty: The Obedience of Faith, 176
  3.3.3. Intellect and Will: Hearing and Vision, 177
  3.3.4. Salvific Necessity and Meritorious Will, 178
  3.3.5. Unity and Plurality, 178
  3.3.6. Person and Community, 179
  3.3.7. "Credere Deo, Credere Deum, Credere in Deum", 180
3.4. Supernatural Theology, 182
  3.4.1. Philosophy and Theology, 182
  3.4.2. The Superiority of Sacred Theology, 184
  3.4.3. "Fides Quarens Intellectum", 185
  3.4.4. The Necessity of Faith, 186
  3.4.5. Ecclesial Horizon, 186
  3.4.6. "Theology on Bent Knee", 187
  3.4.7. The Ends of Theology, 188
  3.4.8. The Object, 190
   1. *Subject*, 190
   2. *Object*, 191
   3. *Theocentrism and Christocentrism*, 192
  3.4.9. Limits, 193
   1. *Reason*, 193
   2. *Original Sin*, 193

Truth Is a Synthesis

    3. Language, 193
    4. Provisionality and Certainty, 193
  3.4.10. Analogous Language, 194
    1. Univocal and Equivocal Language, 194
    2. Analogy, 194
  3.4.11. "Loci Theologici", 195
    1. Primary Sources, 195
    2. Secondary Sources, 195
  3.4.12. Internal Subdivision and Fundamental Unity of Theology, 197
3.5. Appendix: A Text of Pope Benedict XVI Concerning Theology, 197

3. The Creator, 201

1. Creation and the Attributes of the Creator, 201
1.1. The Creator, 201
1.2. "Denumification" and Secularization, 202
1.3. "Creatio ex Nihilo", 204
1.4. The Natural Law, 204
1.5. Other Specifications Concerning Creation, 208
  1. A Doctrine of Faith, 208
  2. Time, 208
  3. A Work of Love, 209
  4. "Continuous Creation", 209
  5. Autonomy, 210
  6. Work, 210
  7. Work of the Trinity, 210

2. The Heavenly Spirits, 211
2.1. Invisible Creation, 211
2.2. Celestial Hierarchy, 213
2.3. Angelic Missions, 214
2.4. Materialism and Pantheism, 215
2.5. Reconciliation between Heaven and Earth, 217
2.6. Good and Evil Angels, 217

3. The Human Being, 219
3.1. Angels and Humans: Genera and Species, 219
3.2. Genesis I, 220
  3.2.1. The Summit of Visible Creation, 221
  3.2.2. A Creature Willed in Advance, 221

3.2.3. *"Let Us Make"*, 221
  3.2.4. *Biblical Anthropology*, 222
  3.2.5. *God's Representative in the World*, 223
  3.2.6. *Differentiation between Man and Woman*, 224
    1. *Differentiation*, 224
    2. *Equal Dignity*, 225
    3. *Nuptiality*, 225
  3.2.7. *"In the Image and Likeness"*, 226
3.3. *Genesis 2*, 228
  3.3.1. *The Man–Material Cosmos Relationship*, 229
    1. *"Adam"*, 229
    2. *Evolutionism*, 229
  3.3.2. *Eden*, 231
  3.3.3. *The Edenic Commandment*, 232
  3.3.4. *The "Preternatural" Gifts and Immortality*, 233

4. Divine Providence, 234

4.1. *Providence as "Continuous Creation" ("creatio continua")*, 234
4.2. *Providence in the History of Salvation*, 235
  4.2.1. *Toward the Elect People*, 235
  4.2.2. *Toward Individuals*, 236
  4.2.3. *The Infallibility of Providence, and Human Freedom*, 236
4.3. *Providence and the Evils Present in the Cosmos*, 237
  4.3.1. *The Origin of the Evil in the World*, 237
  4.3.2. *Why God Allows Evil*, 238
  4.3.3. *Providence and Fatalism*, 239

5. Original Sin, 239

5.1. *Genesis 3*, 240
  5.1.1. *The Serpent*, 241
  5.1.2. *The Temptation*, 241
  5.1.3. *The Historical Character of Original Sin*, 242
  5.1.4. *Disobedience*, 242
  5.1.5. *Pride*, 243
  5.1.6. *Loss of Innocence, Beginning of Concupiscence*, 243
  5.1.7. *"Natura Lapsa"*, 244
    1. *Trial and Judgments*, 244
    2. *Etiology*, 245
    3. *"Protoevangelium"*, 245
  5.1.8. *The Effects of Original Sin on Human Relationships*, 246

5.1.9. *The Effects of Original Sin on Human Nature*, 247
    1. *Childbirth and Work*, 247
    2. *Diseases and Death*, 247
5.1.10. *The Effects of Original Sin on the Cosmos*, 249

5.2. *Romans 5*, 249
    5.2.1. *In Light of Christ*, 250
    5.2.2. *The Spreading of Original Sin*, 250
    5.2.3. *Originating and Originated Sin*, 251
    5.2.4. *In the Face of Death*, 252
    5.2.5. *"In Quo Omnes Peccaverunt"*, 253
    5.2.6. *Adam and Christ*, 255
    5.2.7. *The Universality of both the Condemnation and the Redemption*, 255
    5.2.8. *Abundance of Sin, Overabundance of Grace*, 257
    5.2.9. *Consequences regarding Baptism*, 257
    5.2.10. *"Felix Culpa"*, 258

6. The Bipolarity of the Doctrine of Creation, 258

4. THE REDEEMER, 261

1. Jesus Christ, True God and True Man, 262

1.1. *Salvation and Redemption*, 262
    1.1.1. *Salvation*, 262
    1.1.2. *Redemption*, 264

1.2. *The Value of Christ's Life*, 265
    1.2.1. *The Will of the Father, the Will of Jesus*, 265
    1.2.2. *One Man Alone Saves All*, 267
    1.2.3. *Jesus' Humanity as an Instrument of the Divinity*, 268
    1.2.4. *"The Last Adam"*, 269
    1.2.5. *Jesus "Grew in Grace"*, 270

1.3. *The Person and Natures of Christ*, 271
    1.3.1. *Like the Father, Jesus is True God (First Council of Nicaea)*, 271
    1.3.2. *Like His Mother, Jesus Is a True Human Being (First Council of Constantinople)*, 272
    1.3.3. *Christ Is One (Council of Ephesus)*, 275
        1. *"Unio Hypostatica"*, 275
        2. *"Theotokos"*, 276
        3. *"Communicatio Idiomatum"*, 277
    1.3.4. *Christ Is Twofold (Council of Chalcedon)*, 278

1.3.5. The Unity in Christ Is Due to the Person (Second Council of Constantinople), 279
1.3.6. In Christ There Are Two Wills and Two Natural Operations (Third Council of Constantinople), 279
1.3.7. "One Person—Two Natures", 280
1.3.8. "Unus de Trinitate", 281
1.4. Elements of Christology in the New Testament, 281
    1.4.1. Divine Nature, 282
        1. Christology "From Above", 282
        2. "I Am", 282
        3. "Abba", 283
    1.4.2. Human Nature, 283
    1.4.3. One Person, 283
    1.4.4. Christological Titles in the Acts of the Apostles, 285
1.5. Open Christological Questions, 286

2. Jesus Christ, the Only Savior of the World, 289

2.1. Unique Mediation and Participated Mediations, 290
2.2. Reconciliation and Liberation, 291
2.3. Jesus the Priest, 293
    2.3.1. The (High) Priest and Priests, 293
    2.3.2. Mediation, 294
    2.3.3. The Letter to the Hebrews, 294
        1. Levitical Priesthood, 294
        2. Priesthood of Melchizedek, 295
        3. Priesthood of Jesus, 296
        4. Priest and Victim, 298
2.4. Lamb of God (Victim), 298
    2.4.1. The Fourth Song of the Servant of YHWH, 299
    2.4.2. The "Corpus Ioanneum", 300
2.5. Prophet, 301
    2.5.1. The Prophets and Christ, 301
    2.5.2. The Essence of Propheticism, 302
    2.5.3. Christ the Prophet, 303
2.6. King, 304
    2.6.1. The Messiah in the Old Testament, 304
    2.6.2. Jesus' Messianicity, 305
        1. Facing Pontius Pilate, 305
        2. Characteristics of Jesus' Kingship, 307
        3. "The" Christ, 308

3. The Value of Jesus' Sacrifice: Soteriological Categories, 309

3.1. Battle, Ransom Price, and Victory (Redemption), 309
3.2. Sacrifice, 309
3.3. Atonement (Expiation) and Propitiation, 312
    3.3.1. The Old Testament, 312
    3.3.2. The New Testament, 313
    3.3.3. Vicarious Atonement, Not Penal Substitution, 313
    3.3.4. Atonement and Propitiation, 314
3.4. Satisfaction, 315
3.5. Excursus: The Value of Suffering in Christianity, 317
    3.5.1. Difference between Evil and Suffering, 318
    3.5.2. Redemption in, and of Suffering, 318
    3.5.3. To Suffer with Joy, 319
    3.5.4. Oblative Spirituality, 321
    3.5.5. Active and Passive Virtues, 321
    3.5.6. Penitential Spirituality, 322
    3.5.7. Consoling the Afflicted, 323
3.6. The Death and Descent into Hell of Jesus, 323
    3.6.1. The Gravity of Sin, and the Cruelty of Crucifixion, 324
    3.6.2. A Sign of God's Love, 324
    3.6.3. The Cause of Our Redemption, 325
    3.6.4. The Exemplar Cause of Christian Life, 325
    3.6.5. Jesus' Death: Christological Perspective, 326
    3.6.6. Descent into Hell, 326
3.7. The Resurrection and Ascension of Christ, 328
    3.7.1. The Historical and Physical Character of Jesus' Resurrection, 329
    3.7.2. Transcendent and Mysterious Character, 330
    3.7.3. Characteristics of the Resurrected Body, 330
    3.7.4. The Heavenly High Priest, 332
    3.7.5. The Resurrected Crucified One, 333
        1. Cross and Resurrection, 333
        2. "Animal Body" and "Spiritual Body", 334
    3.7.6. Resurrection as a Work of the Trinity, 334
    3.7.7. The Apologetic Value of the Resurrection, 336
    3.7.8. Catholic Optimism, 337
    3.7.9. Presence of the Risen Christ, 338
    3.7.10. Ascension into Heaven, 339
    3.7.11. The Ascension and the Effusion of the Holy Spirit, 340
    3.7.12. The Ascension of Christ and the Attraction of Believers, 340

5. The Sanctifier, 343

1. Jesus and the Spirit, 343

1.1. The Presence and Action of the Holy Spirit in the Life of Jesus, 343
    1.1.1. The Holy Spirit in the Earthly Life of Christ, 343
    1.1.2. The Holy Spirit and Jesus' Disciples (Election, Mission, Prayer), 344
    1.1.3. The Holy Spirit in the Death and Resurrection of Jesus, 345
1.2. Jesus' Teaching Concerning the Holy Spirit, 346
    1.2.1. "Ruah" in the Old Testament, 346
    1.2.2. "Pneuma" in the New Testament, 346
    1.2.3. The Cooperation of the Holy Spirit and the Sending on the Part of Jesus, 346
    1.2.4. The Trinitarian Dynamic of Christ's Works, 347
1.3. The Names of the Holy Spirit in the New Testament, 348

2. The Spirit's Action in the Church and in the World, 348

2.1. The Spirit, the Giver of Life: Grace, 351
    2.1.1. The Gratuitousness of the Divine Gift, 351
    2.1.2. "Potentia Oboedientialis", 352
    2.1.3. The Cooperation of Nature with Grace, 353
    2.1.4. Prevenient Grace, 354
    2.1.5. Pelagianism and the Life of the Church, 356
    2.1.6. Pelagianism and the Liturgy, 358
    2.1.7. Grace and Freedom, 358
        1. Freedom as Absolute Autonomy, 359
        2. The Freedom of the Children of God, 359
    2.1.8. Filial Adoption, 360
    2.1.9. The Justification of the Sinner, 362
    2.1.10. Grace and the Moral Life, 363
    2.1.11. The Theological Classification of Grace, 363
        1. Created and Uncreated Grace, 363
        2. Habitual and Actual Grace, the Charisms, 364
        3. Operant and Cooperant Grace, 365
        4. Prevenient and Subsequent Grace, 365
        5. Sufficient and Efficacious Grace, 366
    2.1.12. Gifts and Fruits of the Holy Spirit, 367
2.2. Doctrinal Errors and Theological Discussions about Grace, 368
    2.2.1. Pelagianism and Semipelagianism, 368

          1. Pelagianism, 368
          2. Semipelagianism, 368
          3. Response of the Magisterium, 369
    2.2.2. The "Quaestio de Auxiliis", 369
          1. Molina and "Middle Knowledge", 369
          2. Báñez and "Physical Predetermination", 370
          3. Evaluation, 371
          4. The Intervention of the Magisterium, 371
    2.2.3. Jansenism, 372
          1. Michael Baius, 372
          2. Cornelius Jansen, 373
          3. Famous Jansenists, 373
          4. The Intervention of the Magisterium, 374
2.3. The Universal Expansion of the Kingdom of Christ, 374
    2.3.1. "Missio ad Gentes", 375
    2.3.2. The Salvation of Non-Christians, 378
    2.3.3. Religious Pluralism and the Need for the Church, 381
    2.3.4. The Universal Attraction of the Spirit toward Christ, and Missionary Zeal, 383
    2.3.5. Ecumenical and Interreligious Dialogue, 385
          1. The Importance and Risk of Dialogue, 385
          2. Dialogue and Proclamation, 385
          3. Specifications about Dialogue, 386
    2.3.6. Testimony of Charity, 388
    2.3.7. The Fruit of Holiness and Martyrdom, 388

3. Magisterial Pronouncements, 390
3.1. The Holy Spirit in Creation, 390
3.2. The Holy Spirit in the History of Salvation, 392
3.3. The Holy Spirit in the Church, 394
3.4. The Holy Spirit in the Life of the Baptized, 395

6. THE TRINITY, 399

1. Entering into the Divine Sanctuary, 399

2. The Old Testament Pedagogy, 400
2.1. The Hebrew Name 'Elohim', 401
2.2. The Paternity of God, 401
    1. God Is Father of the Chosen People, 402

    2. *God Is the Father of the Righteous*, 402
    3. *God Is Father of the Messiah-King*, 402
2.3. Dabar, 403
2.4. Ruah, 404
2.5. Divine Plural, 406
2.6. Theophanies, 407

3. The New Testament Fullness, 408
3.1. The Trinity in the Life of Jesus, 409
    3.1.1. The Annunciation, 409
    3.1.2. The Baptism in the Jordan, 410
    3.1.3. The Miracles Carried Out by Jesus, 410
    3.1.4. The Exorcisms, 411
    3.1.5. Passion and Death, 411
    3.1.6. Resurrection, 412
    3.1.7. The Ascension and Seating at the Right Hand of God, 412
3.2. The Teaching of the New Testament on the Holy Trinity, 413
    3.2.1. God as Father of Believers, 414
    3.2.2. God as the Father of Jesus, 415
        1. *The Parable of the Murderous Vineyard Tenants*, 415
        2. *The Sending of the Son into the World on the Part of the Father*, 416
    3.2.3. The Sending of the Spirit of the Son into the World on the Part of the Father, 418
        1. *The Spirit Dwells*, 420
        2. *The Spirit Makes Us Children of God*, 420
        3. *The Spirit Freely Chooses to Those Who Give Charisms*, 421
    3.2.4. The Paraclete, 421
        1. *John 14:15–17*, 421
        2. *John 14:26*, 422
        3. *John 15:26*, 422
        4. *John 16:7–15*, 423
        5. *In Summary*, 423
3.3. Other Trinitarian Texts of St. Paul, 425

4. The Mystery of the Trinity, as Treated by Christian Thinkers, 427
4.1. Fathers of the Church and Ecclesiastical Writers, 427
    4.1.1. Saint Justin of Nablus (d. ca 165), 427
    4.1.2. Tatian the Syrian (d. ca. 180), 429

Truth Is a Synthesis

    4.1.3. Athenagoras of Athens (d. ca. 190), 430
    4.1.4. Saint Theophilus of Antioch (d. ca. 185), 431
    4.1.5. St. Irenaeus of Lyon (d. ca. 202), 433
    4.1.6. Tertullian of Carthage (d. ca. 230), 435
    4.1.7. Novatian of Rome (d. 258), 437
    4.1.8. Origen of Alexandria (d. 254), 438
    4.1.9. Saint Hilary of Poitiers (d. 368), 440
    4.1.10. Saint Athanasius of Alexandria (d. 373), 441
    4.1.11. The Cappadocian Fathers, 442
        1. *St. Basil the Great (d. 379)*, 443
        2. *St. Gregory of Nazianzus (d. 390)*, 445
        3. *Saint Gregory of Nyssa (d. 394)*, 446
    4.1.12. Saint Cyril of Alexandria (d. 444), 447

5. The Best Trinitarian Theologies of the West, 448

5.1. St. Augustine of Hippo, 449
    5.1.1. Exposition of Dogma (Books 1–4), 449
        1. *Method*, 449
        2. *Divine Simplicity and Relations*, 450
        3. *Works "ad extra"*, 451
    5.1.2. Defense of Dogma (Doctrine of Relations: Books 5–7), 451
        1. *Relations and "Circuminsessio"*, 451
        2. *Identification of the Three*, 452
        3. *"Filioque"*, 453
        4. *Personal Names*, 453
        5. *The Spirit as Love*, 454
        6. *The Spirit as Gift*, 454
        7. *The Concept of Person*, 455
    5.1.3. Illustration of Dogma (Books 9–15), 455
        1. *"Capax Dei"*, 455
        2. *"Vestigia Trinitatis"*, 455
        3. *Psychological Analogy*, 456
5.2. Saint Thomas Aquinas, 456
    5.2.1. Processions, 457
        1. *Psychological Analogy*, 457
        2. *Divine Processions*, 458
    5.2.2. Relations, 458
        1. *Divine Substance and Relations*, 458
        2. *Real Relations*, 459
    5.2.3. Persons, 459

1. "Naturae Rationalis Individua Substantia", 459
2. "Subsistens in Rationali Natura", 460
3. "Relatio Subsistens", 461
4. Relations of Opposition, 461
5.2.4. Missions and Notions, 462

6. Magisterial Pronouncements, 464
6.1. The One and Triune God, 464
6.2. The Persons and Relations, 467
6.3. Mutual Indwelling, 468
6.4. The Works "Ad Extra", 469

7. The Trinity and the Principle of *Et-Et*, 470
7.1. Relativization of the Et-Et, 470
7.2. The Et-Et Found Again, 471
7.3. Hierarchy between Unity and Trinity, 472

8. Excursus: The *Filioque*, 473
8.1. Historical Data, 473
    8.1.1. Ctesiphon, 473
    8.1.2. Synods of Toledo, 473
    8.1.3. The Carolingians, 474
    8.1.4. Pope Leo III, 474
    8.1.5. Benedict VIII and Michael Cerularius, 475
8.2. Theological Elements, 476
    8.2.1. Biblical Elements, 476
    8.2.2. Saint Augustine, 477
    8.2.3. The Eastern Fathers, 477
    8.2.4. The Middle Ages and the Ecumenical Councils, 478
    8.2.5. Distinction between Liturgical Custom and Dogmatic Assent, 479

7. THE MOTHER OF GOD, 481

1. The Placement of the Treatise on Mary, 481
1. Link with the Trinity, 481
2. Christocentrism, 482
3. Full of Grace, 482
4. Mother of the Church, 483

2. Mary and the Trinity, 483
2.1. *Mary and the Individual Divine Persons*, 483
    2.1.1. *Appropriations*, 483
    2.1.2. *Daughter of the Father*, 485
    2.1.3. *Mother of the Son*, 485
    2.1.4. *Bride of the Holy Spirit*, 486
    2.1.5. *Temple of the Holy Spirit*, 487
    2.1.6. *Handmaid of the Trinity*, 487
    2.1.7. *Guardian of the Mystery*, 487
2.2. *The New Eve*, 488
    2.2.1. *Christological Value*, 489
    2.2.2. *Anthropological Value*, 490
    2.2.3. *Pneumatological Value*, 490
2.3. *The Privileges of Mary Most Holy*, 491
    2.3.1. *Predestination*, 491
    2.3.2. *Regality*, 492

3. Mary and Christ, 493
3.1. *The "Infancy Narratives"*, 493
    3.1.1. *Natural Link*, 493
    3.1.2. *Supernatural Conception*, 494
        1. *Matthew*, 494
        2. *Luke: Birth of the Baptist*, 495
        3. *Luke: The Annunciation*, 496
        4. *The Importance of Mary's "Fiat"*, 497
3.2. *The Marian Dogmas*, 499
    3.2.1. *"Per Mariam ad Jesum" and Vice Versa*, 499
    3.2.2. *Mother of God*, 500
        1. *The Dogma*, 500
        2. *Explanation*, 501
    3.2.3. *Immaculate*, 501
        1. *The Dogma*, 501
        2. *Explanation*, 502
    3.2.4. *Ever-Virgin*, 504
        1. *The Dogma*, 504
        2. *Explanation*, 505
    3.2.5. *Excursus: Other Children of Mary and Joseph?*, 507
    3.2.6. *Assumption into Heaven*, 509
        1. *The Dogma*, 509
        2. *Explanation*, 510

3.3. Other Marian Titles, 513
    3.3.1. Queen, 513
    3.3.2. Mediatrix, 514
    3.3.3. Co-Redemptrix, 515
        1. Doctrinal Content, 515
        2. Terminological Expression, 516

4. Mary and the Church, 517
4.1. Daughter and Mother, 517
4.2. First of the Redeemed, 518
4.3. Mother of the Redeemed, 519
4.4. Advocate, 520
4.5. Image and Model of the Church, 522
4.6. Sign of Hope, 523
4.7. Marian Devotion, 526

5. Mariology and the "Synthetic" Principle, 528
5.1. Virgin and Mother, 528
5.2. Christotypical and Ecclesiotypical Interpretations, 529
5.3. Other Binomials, 529

6. Excursus: Saint Joseph of Nazareth, 530
6.1. Humility and Justice, 531
6.2. The Obedient Silence, 533
6.3. His Death, 535
6.4. Care of Christ and of the Church, 535
6.5. Hypothesis to Examine, 537
    1. Immaculate Conception, 537
    2. Assumption in Soul and Body, 538

8. THE CHURCH, 541

1. The Church in the Salvific Plan of God, 541
1.1. The Church: Society and Mystery, 541
    1.1.1. Baptismal Adoption, 542
    1.1.2. Social Character, 543
    1.1.3. Society for Sinners, 545
    1.1.4. Mysterious Character, 546
    1.1.5. Primacy of the Mystery, 547
    1.1.6. Relation with the Trinity, 548

   1.1.7. Founder, 548
   1.1.8. Three States, 550
   1.1.9. Eschatological Nature, 552
   1.1.10. Communion of Saints, 552
1.2. The People of God in the Old and New Testaments, 553
   1.2.1. From the Origins, 553
   1.2.2. Analogy between Christ and the Church, 555
   1.2.3. "Ecclesia ab Abel", 556
   1.2.4. Old and New People of God, 557

2. What Is the Church?, 559

2.1. Extension of the Incarnation, 560
   2.1.1. Ecclesial Synthesis of Spirit and Matter, 560
   2.1.2. The Sacraments, 560
   2.1.3. "Christus Totus", 561
2.2. Mystical Body of Christ, 562
   2.2.1. The Pauline Image, 562
   2.2.2. The Adjective "Mystical", 563
   2.2.3. Mystical Body and the Christological Principle, 564
2.3. Sacrament, 566
   2.3.1. Sign and Instrument, 566
   2.3.2. The Analogical Use of the Term, 567
2.4. Communion, 567
   2.4.1. "Communio", 567
   2.4.2. Hierarchical Communion and Communion in Charity, 568
   2.4.3. Gift and Task, 569
2.5. Creature of the Holy Spirit, 570
   2.5.1. Once Again on the Relationship between Christ and Spirit, 570
   2.5.2. Ecclesiological Application, 571
2.6. Other Images of the Church, 572

3. How Is the Church Composed?, 573

3.1. The Notes and Properties of the Church, 573
   3.1.1. "Notae" or "Proprietates", 573
   3.1.2. The Original Character and the Order of Listing, 575
   3.1.3. Organic Unity, 576
   3.1.4. One, 576
     1. Christ the Principle, the Spirit the Guarantor of Unity, 577
     2. The Apostles, Sign and Instrument of Unity, 577
     3. The Successors of the Apostles, 578

    4. *Objective Elements of Unity*, 579

    5. *One Church, Divided Christians*, 579

    6. *Unity and Plurality in the Church*, 580

  3.1.5. *Holy*, 581

    1. *Holiness in the Bible*, 581

    2. *The Communion of "Saints"*, 582

    3. *A Holy Church or a Sinful One?*, 583

  3.1.6. *Catholic*, 585

    1. *"Kath'holon"*, 585

    2. *Quantitative and Qualitative Sense*, 586

    3. *Catholic Church and Particular Churches*, 588

  3.1.7. *Apostolic*, 589

    1. *Apostolic Succession*, 589

    2. *The Indissoluble Link with the Origin*, 590

    3. *Apostolicity and Apostolate*, 590

  3.1.8. *"Mysterium Lunae"*, 591

3.2. *The Sacred Hierarchy*, 592

  3.2.1. *Heavenly and Earthly Hierarchies*, 592

    1. *Heavenly Hierarchy*, 592

    2. *Ecclesiastical Hierarchy*, 593

  3.2.2. *Sacramental and Juridical Distinction*, 593

    1. *Sacramental Distinction*, 593

    2. *Juridical Distinction*, 594

  3.2.3. *The Slant of the Treatment*, 595

  3.2.4. *The Apostle Peter*, 596

  3.2.5. *The Role of Saint Peter and His Successor*, 598

    1. *The Power of the Keys (Opening and Closing)*, 599

    2. *Loosing and Binding*, 600

    3. *The College of the Apostles and Its Head*, 600

  3.2.6. *From the Apostolic College to the Episcopal College*, 601

    1. *The "Tria Munera"*, 601

    2. *The Transmission of the "Tria Munera"*, 602

    3. *The Laying On of Hands*, 602

  3.2.7. *The Petrine Primacy*, 603

    1. *The New Testament*, 603

    2. *Exercise of the Primacy Since the Beginning*, 604

    3. *Primacy of Honor and Jurisdiction*, 605

    4. *The First Vatican Council*, 607

  3.2.8. *The College of Bishops*, 608

    1. *Truly Collegial Power*, 608

2. *Ecumenical Council*, 608
  3. *The* Sede Vacante, 609
  4. *Visible Signs of the Distinction between the College and Its Head*, 610
  5. *Authority of the Episcopal College over the Entire Church*, 610
  6. *Authority for Service*, 612
  7. *The Obedience Owed to the Shepherds*, 613
  8. *Authority and Charisms*, 613

9. The Sacraments In General And The Liturgy, 617

1. The Notion of Sacrament in General, 618
1.1. Sign and Instrument, 618
    1.1.1. Meaning of "Sacrament", 618
    1.1.2. The Objective Efficacy of the Sacraments, 620
    1.1.3. The Validity of the Sacraments, 621
1.2. The Sacraments: Works of Christ, 624
    1.2.1. Extension of the Incarnation, 624
    1.2.2. Elements of the History of Salvation, 625
    1.2.3. Number and Institution, 627
1.3. Bipolarity, Causality, Ends, and Effects of the Sacraments, 629
    1.3.1. Dipolar Structure, 630
    1.3.2. Matter and Form, 631
    1.3.3. Intention of the Minister, 633
    1.3.4. Minister, 634
    1.3.5. Causality, 636
    1.3.6. Purpose and Effects, 638
    1.3.7. Moral and Catechetical Implications, 640
        1. *Moral*, 640
        2. *Catechesis*, 640

2. The Liturgy, 642
2.1. A Question of Method, 642
2.2. The Nature of the Sacred Liturgy, 645
    2.2.1. "Liturgy," "Worship," and Annexed Terms, 645
        1. *Classical Greek*, 645
        2. *The Septuagint*, 645
        3. *The New Testament*, 646

    4. *The Word "Worship"*, 646
    5. *Other Terms*, 647
  2.2.2. *Definition*, 648
    1. *Description*, 649
    2. *Definition*, 650
  2.2.3. *Sacramental Character*, 653
    1. *Mutability of Signs*, 653
    2. *Different Types of Signs*, 655
    3. *Signs of Christian Worship*, 655
2.3. *The Participation of the Faithful in Divine Worship*, 656
  2.3.1. *Purpose of the Liturgy*, 656
    1. *The Liturgical Orientation*, 656
    2. *Sanctification of Time and Space*, 659
  2.3.2. *Liturgy and Priesthood*, 661
    1. *Theological Description of the Activity of Worship*, 662
    2. *The Liturgical Priesthood*, 663
  2.3.3. *Active Participation*, 667
    1. *Prior to the Second Vatican Council*, 667
    2. *In the Liturgical Constitution of the Council*, 669
    3. *After the Second Vatican Council*, 671

10. The Sacraments In Particular, 673

1. Subdivision of the Sacraments, 673

2. The Sacramental Character, 667

3. Unrepeatable Sacraments, 681

3.1. *Baptism*, 681
  3.1.1. *The Baptism of Christ in the Jordan*, 681
  3.1.2. *The Necessity of Baptism*, 682
  3.1.3. *Sacrament of Faith*, 684
  3.1.4. *Rite*, 685
  3.1.5. *Effects*, 686
  3.1.6. *Baptism of Blood and of Desire*, 687
    1. *Baptism of Blood*, 688
    2. *Baptism of Desire*, 688
  3.1.7. *The Fate of Children who Die without Baptism*, 689
3.2. *Confirmation*, 690
  3.2.1. *The Link with Baptism*, 690

3.2.2. *Confirmation in the New Testament*, 691

3.2.3. *Rite*, 692

3.2.4. *The Minister*, 693

3.2.5. *Effects*, 694

3.2.6. *Necessity*, 696

3.3. *Holy Orders*, 696

3.3.1. *The Old Testament*, 697

3.3.2. *The New Testament*, 698

3.3.3. *The Relationship between Orders and the Priesthood*, 699

3.3.4. *Hierarchical Authority and Charisms*, 703

3.3.5. *Matter*, 704

3.3.6. *Form*, 704

3.3.7. *Essence of Priestly Ministry*, 706

1. *Christotypical/Cultic Model*, 706

2. *Ecclesiotypical/Pastoral Model*, 707

3. *"Synthetic"/Representative Model*, 708

3.3.8. *Episcopate-Presbyterate Distinction*, 709

3.3.9. *Ordination of Women?*, 711

1. *Arguments in Support*, 711

2. *Responses to the Arguments*, 712

3. *Magisterial Interventions*, 713

3.3.10. *Clerical Celibacy*, 716

1. *The New Testament*, 717

2. *"Unius Uxoris Vir"*, 717

3. *Ecclesiastical Discipline*, 718

4. *Recent Magisterium*, 720

4. Repeatable Sacraments, 722

4.1. *Marriage*, 723

4.1.1. *Natural Reality and Sacrament*, 723

4.1.2. *In Salvation History*, 723

4.1.3. *Essential Natural Elements*, 724

1. *Sexual Complementarity*, 724

2. *Fecundity*, 724

3. *Indissolubility*, 724

4.1.4. *Sacred Scripture*, 726

1. *Confirmation and Elevation of the Natural Values*, 726

2. *Jesus and the Indissolubility of Marriage*, 727

3. *The Weight of Original Sin*, 729

4. *Medicinal Value*, 729

        5. *Christological Figuration*, 731
    4.1.5. Ministry, 732
    4.1.6. Matter and Form, 733
        1. *Form*, 734
        2. *Matter*, 735
    4.1.7. Effects, 736
    4.1.8. Pauline and Petrine Privileges, 739
        1. *The Pauline Privilege*, 739
        2. *The Petrine Privilege*, 740
4.2. Reconciliation, 741
    4.2.1. The Objectivity of Sin and Forgiveness, 742
    4.2.2. Biblical Revelation, 743
        1. *Forgivable and Unforgivable Sins*, 743
        2. *Conversion*, 746
        3. *The Institution of the Sacrament*, 747
    4.2.3. Historical Development, 749
        1. *First Centuries*, 749
        2. *The Irish Monks*, 751
        3. *Developments in the Middle Ages*, 751
        4. *Evaluation*, 752
    4.2.4. The Minister, 753
        1. *The Minister*, 753
        2. *Indicative Formula*, 753
        3. *More Grave Sins*, 754
        4. *The Sacramental Seal*, 755
    4.2.5. Matter and Form, 755
        1. *Acts of the Penitent (Matter)*, 756
        2. *Form*, 758
    4.2.6. Indulgences, 758
    4.2.7. Effects, 760
4.3. Anointing of the Sick, 761
    4.3.1. "Extreme Unction" and "Anointing of the Sick", 761
    4.3.2. Holy Scripture, 763
        1. *James 5:14–15*, 763
        2. *Other Texts*, 763
    4.3.3. Matter, Form, and Minister, 765
    4.3.4. Effects, 766
    4.3.5. Active Participation, 767
    4.3.6. Relation with the Other Sacraments, 768

11. The Eucharist, 769

1. Sacred Scripture, 771
1.1. Old Testament, 771
  1.1.1. Orientation of History toward the Eucharist, 771
  1.1.2. The Covenant and the Passover Meal, 772
  1.1.3. The Quails and the Manna, 774
  1.1.4. The Water from the Rock, 777
    1. Presence, 778
    2. Saint Paul, 778
    3. Saint John, 779
  1.1.5. The Blood of the Covenant, 780
  1.1.6. From Ritual Sacrifices to the Sacrifice of Jesus, 781
    1. Sacrifices, 781
    2. Jesus' Sacrifice, 783
1.2. New Testament, 784
  1.2.1. The Names of the Eucharist, 784
    1. Eucharist, 784
    2. The Lord's Supper, 784
    3. Spiritual Food and Drink, 785
    4. Communion, 785
    5. The Lord's Table, 786
    6. Bread of Life, Heavenly Bread, 786
    7. "Fractio Panis", 786
    8. Altar, 787
  1.2.2. The Institution Narratives, 787
    1. Context, 789
    2. Redactional Threads, 789
    3. Concordance, 790
    4. The Words of Institution, 790
  1.2.3. The Last Supper, 793
    1. Chronological Questions, 794
    2. The Jewish Passover Meal, 795
    3. Jesus' Supper, 795
    4. The Eucharist, 797
  1.2.4. The Multiplication of Bread, and the Supper in Emmaus, 799
    1. Multiplication of Bread, 799
    2. Supper at Emmaus, 799
  1.2.5. Chapter Six of John's Gospel, 800
    1. The Multiplication, 801

  2. *The Bread Come Down from Heaven*, 801
  3. *The Flesh that Gives Life*, 803
  4. *The Proof of Faith*, 804

2. Theological Reflection, and the Teachings of the Magisterium, 805

2.1. Matter, Form, and Minister, 806
 2.1.1. Matter, 806
  1. *Matter in Itself*, 806
  2. *Symbolism*, 808
 2.1.2. Form, 808
  1. *From Matter to Form*, 808
  2. *The Form*, 808
  3. *Differences in the Two Forms of the Roman Rite*, 809
  4. *The Essential Elements of the Form*, 811
 2.1.3. Minister, 813
  1. *The Minister*, 813
  2. *The Sanctity of the Ministry*, 815

2.2. The Eucharistic Conversion, 816
 2.2.1. Transubstantiation, 816
  1. *Difference with the Orthodox and the Protestants*, 816
  2. *Ontological Character*, 817
  3. *Thomas Aquinas*, 818
 2.2.2. Real Presence, 825
  1. *"Sub Specie Aliena"*, 825
  2. *"Ex Vi Sacramenti" and "Ex Naturali Concomitantia"*, 826
 2.2.3. Permanence of the Accidents, 827

2.3. Effects of the Sacrament, 829
 2.3.1. Salvific Effects, 830
  1. *Identification of the Effects*, 830
  2. *Unity of the Church*, 830
  3. *The Pledge of Glory*, 832
  4. *The Applying of Benefits*, 832
 2.3.2. Redemptive Effects, 833
  1. *Remission of Mortal Sins*, 833
  2. *Remission of Venial Sins*, 834
  3. *Preservation from Future Sins*, 834
  4. *Remission of Punishments*, 835

2.4. Sacrifice, 836

　　　　2.4.1. *Saint Thomas*, 836
　　　　　　1. *Representative Image*, 837
　　　　　　2. *Paschal Mystery*, 838
　　　　2.4.2. *The Magisterium*, 841
　　　　　　1. *The Council of Trent*, 841
　　　　　　2. *Recent Pronouncements*, 847
2.5. *Communion*, 851
　　　2.5.1. *Sacramental and Spiritual Communion*, 851
　　　2.5.2. *Communion of Desire and Desire of Communion*, 852
　　　2.5.3. *Efficacy*, 854
　　　2.5.4. *Communion and Adoration*, 856
　　　　　1. *Spirit of Adoration*, 856
　　　　　2. *External Signs of Adoration*, 857
　　　2.5.5. *The Rite of Communion*, 859
　　　　　1. *Communion under the Two Species*, 859
　　　　　2. *The Mode of Receiving Holy Communion*, 860
　　　2.5.6. *Communion as Viaticum*, 861

12. The Last Things, 865

1. Introductory Observations, 865
1.1. The Novissimi, 865
1.2. Metaphors and Reality, 866
1.3. "Hic et nunc" but also "alibi et tunc", 868

2. Divine Predestination and Human Liberty, 870
2.1. Predestination to Salvation by the Logos, 870
2.2. Double Predestination?, 870
2.3. Predestination and Divine Prescience, 872
2.4. Human Liberty and Eschatological Consequences, 874

3. The Question of Souls Separated from Bodies, 875
3.1. The Eschatological "Where" (Ubi), 875
3.2. The Separate Souls, 877

4. The Limbo of the Fathers and the Limbo of Infants, 881
4.1. Limbus Patrum, 881
4.2. Limbus Puerorum, 883

5. Death, 886
5.1. The Reality of Death, 886
5.2. Death as Mystery, 887
5.3. The "Second Death", 889
5.4. Christian Preparation for Death, 889

6. Judgment, 892
6.1. Particular Judgment, 892
6.2. Last Judgment and the Resurrection of the Flesh, 893
    6.2.1. Universal Retribution, 893
    6.2.2. Role of the Angels and the Apostles, 893
    6.2.3. Mercy and Justice, Hope and Fear, 895
6.3. The Cosmic Dimension, 900
    6.3.1. Destruction and Renewal, 900
    6.3.2. Millennialism, 900
6.4. Particular Aspects, 902
    6.4.1. Place, Date, and Duration, 902
    6.4.2. The Form of the Risen Body, 902
    6.4.3. The "Book of Life", 904

7. Hell, 905
7.1. The New Testament, 905
    7.1.1. The Darkness, 905
    7.1.2. The Fire of Gehenna, 906
7.2. Historical Freedom and Eternal Damnation, 908
7.3. "Apocatastasis", 909
7.4. The Pains of Hell, 909
    7.4.1. The Pain of Loss, 909
    7.4.2. The Pain of Sense, 910
7.5. Paraenetic Implications, 911

8. Purgatory, 913
8.1. Sacred Scripture, 913
    8.1.1. The Prayer for the Dead, 913
    8.1.2. The Words of Jesus, 914
        1. Matthew 5:25–26, 914
        2. Matthew 12:32, 914

    8.1.3. Saint Paul, 915
8.2. Teachings of the Magisterium, 916

    8.2.1. The Council of Florence, 916
    8.2.2. The Council of Trent, 917
        1. *The Decree on Justification*, 917
        2. *The Decree on Purgatory*, 917
    8.2.3. The Recent Magisterium, 918
    8.2.4. Other Pronouncements, 918
8.3. The Fathers of the Church, 919
    8.3.1. The "Prison" and the "Purgation", 919
    8.3.2. Suffrage for the Departed, 920
    8.3.3. Paraenetic Value, 920
8.4. The Pains of Purgatory, 921
    8.4.1. Suffering as Fire, Shame, and Love, 921
    8.4.2. Temporal Punishment, 922

9. Paradise, 924
9.1. Darkness, Fire, and Light, 924
9.2. The Biblical Revelation, 925
    9.2.1. The Kingdom of Heaven, 925
    9.2.2. Eternal Life, 926
    9.2.3. The Celestial Jerusalem, 926
    9.2.4. "Lux Perpetua", 927
9.3. The Vision of God in Heaven, 928
    9.3.1. From Terrestrial Light to Celestial Light, 928
    9.3.2. "Visio Beatifica", 929
    9.3.3. John XXII and Benedict XII, 931
    9.3.4. Intellective Vision, 933
    9.3.5. "Lumen Gloriae", 934
9.4. The Communion of the Triumphant Church, 936
9.5. Vision, Faith, and Theology, 938

EPILOGUE, 941

BIBLICAL INDEX, 943

INDEX OF NAMES, 961

INDEX OF MAGISTERIAL DOCUMENTS, 975

1. Popes, 975
2. Ecumenical Councils, 989

3. Catechism of the Catholic Church, 993
4. Codex Iuris Canonici (CIC), 995
5. Dicasteries of the Holy See, 996
    Congregations, 996
    Pontifical Councils, 998
6. Synods, 999

GENERAL INDEX, 1001